St. David's St. Paul's

Trinity St. Barnabas'
St. Bartholomew's
St. Matthew's

St. John's Christ
Ascension
Christ Advent
Holy Cross
St. Augustine's St. Paul's
Holy Comforter
Good Shepherd Trinity
St. Mark's

Prince Frederick
St. Alban's All Saints
St. Matthias' Holy Cross & Faith Mem.
Redeemer Messiah

St. Stephen's
Epiphany St. Luke's
Trinity Prince George
St. John's St. Cyprian's
Guild Hall
Pompion Hill St. James' Santee

Epiphany St. Thomas & St. Denis'
St. Paul's Holy Cross
Christ St. Andrew's Chapel

Christ St. James'
St. John's
Trinity
St. Helena's CHARLESTON

Diocese of
South Carolina

CHARLESTON & VICINITY

Calvary   St. John's
Grace   St. Luke's and St. Paul's
Good Shepherd (No. Chas.)   St. Mark's
Holy Communion   St. Michael's
Redeemer   St. Peter's
St. Andrew's, King St.   St. Peter's -by-the- Sea
St. Andrew's, (Col.)   St. Philip's
St. Andrew's (Parish)   St. Stephen's

ST. PHILIP'S, CHARLESTON
The Mother Parish of the Church in South Carolina

A HISTORICAL ACCOUNT

OF THE

Protestant Episcopal Church
in South Carolina

1820-1957

Being a Continuation of Dalcho's Account

1670-1820

ALBERT SIDNEY THOMAS, LL.D., D.D., S.T.D.

Copyright, 1957

ALBERT SIDNEY THOMAS

PRINTED BY

THE R. L. BRYAN COMPANY, COLUMBIA, S. C.

To my fellow Churchmen
in the State of South Carolina

Preface

This book, in intention at least, is a Volume II to the Rev. Dr. Frederick Dalcho's *Historical Account of the Protestant Episcopal Church in South Carolina.* This invaluable work covered the period from the settlement of the Province to A. D. 1820. The first suggestion of the preparation of a work in continuation of Dr. Dalcho's *Account* is to be found in a resolution introduced in the Convention of the diocese nearly one hundred years ago. It was the Rev. Alexander Gregg, then rector of St. David's Church, Cheraw, who proposed to the Convention of 1859 the preparation of such a work as would be both an "enlargement" and a "continuation" of Dr. Dalcho's *Account.* Probably due to the disturbed condition of the country, the resolution was indefinitely postponed. The same year, the Rev. Mr. Gregg went to Texas to be its first Bishop. This, however, did not prevent his valuable contribution to the history of his native state and Church in 1867 when he published *The Old Cheraws.* In subsequent years, the suggestion was from time to time renewed. Mr. J. Pringle Smith, while Registrar gathered valuable material used here and now in the archives of the diocese. However, it was not until 1915 that official action was taken by the Church in the Convention of the diocese which constitutes authority for the preparation of the work herewith given to the Church. Bishop Guerry then recommended the creation of the office of Historiographer, distinct from and in addition to that of Registrar. This was duly effected by a constitutional amendment. The Bishop defined the duties of the new officer,—"to revise and edit" the material gathered by the registrar, "with a view to writing a history of the diocese," to bring Dr. Dalcho's record up to date and to fill in the gaps in the account. The Rev. Percival H. Whaley, D.D., was appointed by Bishop Guerry the first Historiographer of the diocese. Very soon, however, Dr. Whaley was called away (September 2, 1915) to higher service and the Rev. John Kershaw, D.D., was appointed to the office. Dr. Kershaw devoted a great deal of time and labor to the task until his death April 6, 1921. His work consisted chiefly in reviewing the Episcopates of the succeeding Bishops and is incorporated as far as seemed practicable in this volume, his authorship being always carefully indicated.

The present author was appointed to the office of historiographer immediately after Dr. Kershaw's death. He has held the office continuously since then. The part of his work looking to the publication of the history was for many years that of collecting and preparing. Since his retirement in 1944, he has labored on the undertaking more or less continuously. Some three or four years ago, the thought occurred that since this volume was planned and authorized during the years of the undivided diocese and so intended to include both the old and new diocese, it would be proper to find in it a voice from the new diocese. It was on the suggestion of Mr. James R. Cain, Historiographer of the diocese of Upper South Carolina, that Augustus T. Graydon, Esq., of Columbia, was induced to prepare the accounts of the three Episcopates of Bishops Finlay, Gravatt, and Cole, with biographical sketches of these Bishops. Thus the book owes not a little of whatever value it may have to Dr. Kershaw and to Mr. Graydon. There are others also to whom the author is indebted. First, I must mention my wife, Emily Jordan Carrison Thomas, who through many years assisted me constantly and in manifold ways. I owe much to the patient care of two ladies who converted my oft-amended manuscripts into clear typed copy—Miss Hallie E. Coffin, and Mrs. John M. (Lillie) Jenkins. I am indebted especially to Commander Charles E. Thomas, my cousin, for a most valuable revision of the paged proof and for the preparation of the splendid index. We are indebted to the artistic ability of Mr. C. R. Banks for the pictures. He went over the whole state to secure them.

Nor shall I omit to mention my indebtedness to the Rev. Dr. Henry DeSaussure Bull for his encouragement in this undertaking through many years and for his reading the manuscript and making many helpful suggestions. Just as this book goes to press, he has passed on to higher services. And not least am I grateful to the Bishop of South Carolina, the Rt. Rev. T. N. Carruthers, for his valuable cooperation in bringing the work to fruition.

So much for the history of this book. A word should be added concerning its character. In the "advertisement" in the front of his book, Dr. Dalcho, after enumerating its purposes, makes this statement: "The work, however, must rather be considered as a chronological arrangement of facts, connected with the Church in Carolina, than as an ecclesiastical history; as a record of events, rather than of principles and opinions." Doubtless this humble statement is correct, and yet his work has proven invaluable. Likewise the present work is rather an *account* than a *history*. We can only hope in all humility that it will nevertheless also prove of value in years to come as has Dr. Dalcho's.

There yet remains the inviting task for someone to publish a new addition of Dalcho's *Account* to 1820, enlarged from new material now available and with its remarkably few errors corrected. This is now a much needed work.

There is another feature of this undertaking in which, less desirably, we have followed the former work—there are no footnotes giving authority for the statements. It is fully realized that this is a serious omission. However, such notes would have involved too much enlargement of the book, and a prohibitive task for the years of the author. In lieu there will be found a list of authorities in the Addenda. It has been a joy by the grace of God to spend my entire long ministry laboring for our beloved Church in our beloved State, whether in the past or in the present —there is much to be forgiven, but I know in Whom I have believed.

ALBERT S. THOMAS.

Note: In the winter of 1956-57, the preparation of the *Account* being near completion, Bishop Carruthers appointed as members of a Committee on Publication for the diocese of South Carolina the Revs. H. D. Bull, D.D. and R. J. Hobart, and Messrs. John L. Frierson, H. S. Reeves, and C. R. Banks. Bishop Cole appointed on the committee for the diocese of Upper South Carolina Messrs. James R. Cain, A. T. Graydon, and Commander Charles E. Thomas, completing the committee, the Bishops being *ex officio* members. The committee met first at the headquarters of the diocese of South Carolina on March 13, 1957. Commander Thomas was appointed chairman and the work considered at length. A second meeting was held in the office of Mr. Graydon in Columbia on April 8, 1957, when plans for the publication were practically completed, including the important matter of the illustrations. Mr. Banks consented to prepare these. We are thus indebted to this committee for the publication of the *Account*.

A. S. T.

Table of Contents

PART ONE

DIOCESE OF SOUTH CAROLINA

SECTION I

DIOCESAN HISTORY

SECTION II

PART TWO

DIOCESE OF UPPER SOUTH CAROLINA

SECTION I

DIOCESAN HISTORY

SECTION II

Table of Contents

APPENDICES

PART ONE

DIOCESE OF SOUTH CAROLINA

SECTION I

DIOCESAN HISTORY

Introduction
1663-1820

The plan of this book is to continue the *Account* from the end of Dalcho's *Historical Account of the Protestant Episcopal Church in South Carolina*, i. e., from 1820. However, here in this Introduction, we depart from this plan in order to supply a background for this work—or to connect it in some measure with Dalcho's valuable history.

Carolina was settled under the auspices of a group of eight "Lords Proprietors" who obtained a grant from Charles II in 1663, including a part of North Carolina, and all of South Carolina and Georgia. Nothing was done immediately. The Lords Proprietors received a second charter in 1665 including a grant to all territory between 29 degrees and 36 degrees and 30 minutes north latitude. Under this charter the colony, specifically now called "Carolina", was founded. It granted to the Lords Proprietors "the patronage and advowsons of all the churches and chappels which as the Christian religion shall increase within the Province, territory, islets and limits aforesaid, shall happen hereafter to be erected, together with license and power to build and found churches, chappels, and oratories in convenient and fit places within the said bounds and limits, and to cause them to be dedicated and consecrated according to the ecclesiastical laws of our Kingdom of England."

The Proprietors engaged the celebrated philosopher, John Locke, to draw up a model form of government for the Province. This he did in what was known as the "Fundamental Constitutions." The limits of this Introduction permit us to say little about this remarkable instrument. It provided for an aristocratic form of government with an hereditary nobility. The eldest Lord Proprietor was called Palatine—"a sort of king of the Province"; a deputy Palatine was called Governor who took the place of the Palatine in his absence. In addition there were three other orders, Land-

[3]

graves, Cassiques, and Barons. Nearly all the governors under the Proprietors were Landgraves. The nobility were given two-fifths of the land and the people at large three-fifths. The "Fundamental Constitutions" were never accepted by the colonists. However, they continued to be nominally in effect for fifty years and had a distinct influence until the Revolution of 1719, when Carolina became a royal province.

Following the provision of the Charter, the Fundamental Constitutions contained the following clause: "As the country comes to be sufficiently planted, and distributed into fit divisions, it shall belong to the Parliament to take care for the buildings of churches and the public maintenance of divines, to be employed in the exercise of religion, according to the Church of England; which being the only true and orthodox, and the national religion of all the King's dominions, is also of Carolina; and therefore it alone shall be allowed to receive public maintenance by grant of Parliament." Although the Constitutions were never assented to by the people and never constitutionally in force, yet under the Charter, the Church of England was considered in a general way as established. However, the second charter provided "that no dissenter from the Established Church shall be in any way molested for any difference of opinion, so long as he behaves himself peacefully, any law or statute of England to the contrary notwithstanding." The Constitutions provided that "no man could become a freeman, or have any estates or habitation in Carolina, who did not believe in a God, and that He was to be publicly worshipped; but that Jews, Heathen and other dissenters from the purity of the Christian religion, were to be tolerated. Any seven or more persons agreeing in any religion might constitute a church, and should be protected in their worship. No person, however, over seventeen years of age not a member of some church or religious profession, could claim the protection of law or hold any place of honor or profit." Provision for such liberty in religion was perhaps unequaled among the American colonies save probably in Rhode Island. In the actual history that followed there were indeed not a few lapses from the ideal provided, but these were always temporary—they were quite promptly and successfully resisted, and liberty of opinion did generally prevail.

It must be admitted that this liberty in religion may in the beginning have been somewhat at the expense of intensity of conviction. None could claim that the religious motive predominated in the settlement of Carolina; it was secondary doubtless to economic and political motives, but nevertheless the religious motive was conspicuous as would appear from the provisions cited and from facts which we must now recount.

Under direction of the Lords Proprietors the first permanent settlement in South Carolina was made in 1670 at Charles Town, on the west bank of the Ashley River, with William Sayle as Governor and colonists from England. The site chosen never seems to have been considered permanent. Very soon the present site of Charleston, between the Ashley and Cooper rivers, was chosen as a permanent location, and a town laid out. It was occupied in 1680. A prominent location was reserved for a Church in the new town and here the first church was built with the name of St. Philip, about 1681. The same site is now occupied by St. Michael's Church, built in 1751-1762, when a second parish became necessary in the city. St. Philip's had been moved to Church Street, its present location, in 1723, when the first building of "black cypress" began to decay. This second structure was greatly admired. Dalcho says, "The celebrated Edmund Burke, speaking of this Church, says, it 'is spacious and executed in a very handsome taste, exceeding everything of that kind which we have in America,' and the biographer of Whitefield calls it 'a grand Church resembling one of the new churches in London.'" It was destroyed by fire in 1835 and succeeded by the even more beautiful present St. Philip's Church.

Notwithstanding the fact that apparently no Church building was erected in the colony for some ten or fifteen years after the first settlement (though very soon after the permanent site was occupied), yet the religious motive was active in the colony from the first. Within three months after the first landing we find Governor Sayle importuning the Proprietors to send to them a clergyman, asking for "one Mr. Sampson Bond," then in Bermuda. He did not come, although the Proprietors made him a generous offer. Another effort was made a few months later backed by the leading men of the colony; the need of an able minister was urged, by which youth might be reclaimed and the people instructed. "The Israelities' prosperity decayed when their prophets were wanting, for where the ark of God is," said the Governor, "there is peace and tranquilty." It was not until about 1680 that the desire for a clergyman was attained by the coming of Rev. Atkin Williamson, who exercised his ministry in the colony for thirty years and was given a pension by the Assembly in his old age (1710). Rev. Samuel Marshall, A.M., was appointed to the cure of St. Philip's in 1696. This "sober, worthy, able and learned devine" died of yellow fever in 1699—his successful ministry was all too short. In 1698, the Assembly established a living for the rector of St. Philip's. In the same year Mrs. Afra Coming left a valuable glebe for the Church. Both St. Philip's and St. Michael's churches still enjoy an income from this donation. Marshall was succeeded as rector by Rev. Edward Marston, A.M., a Jacobite, who caused great contention. Toward the end of the century Rev. William Corbin ministered to the settlers about Goose Creek, where a Church had been erected. This was the first Episcopal Church erected outside of Charles Town. Thus by the end of the century, four clergymen of the Church of England had ministered in the colony. In Charles Town there had also been erected a Congregational Church (about 1690), a French Protestant Church (about 1693), a Quaker Meeting House (about 1696), and a Baptist Church (about 1700).

Meanwhile there was taking place a movement destined to have great effect upon the life of the colony. A few Huguenots settled in Carolina within the first decade after the original settlement, but after the Revocation of the Edict of Nantes they came in large numbers, establishing themselves principally in Charles Town and at three or four other points where churches were established. The gospel was first preached outside of the city by the Huguenots. The coming of these moral and religious people with their industrial habits added greatly to the social and economic life of the province. They met with difficulties—there was a disposition among the English to withhold both political and religious liberty from them, notwithstanding the liberal provisions of both the Charter and the Constitution. However, the Lords Proprietors espoused their cause very warmly and in a few years the differences were adjusted. Within about twenty-five years, practically all the Huguenots and their churches were absorbed into the Establishment, the only exceptions being the Church in Charles Town, which to this day maintains its identity in its beautiful house of worship, and a later settlement at New Bordeaux in the upper country which turned to the Presbyterians.

In view especially of the untrue and almost absurd representation of the early settlers of Carolina in a popular American Church history, McConnell's, based on a prejudiced witness, as a band of "bankrupt pirates" and desperadoes, it may be said that while they were not a company of saints (though there were saints among them), they have been correctly described in these words:

"They were not adventurers imbued with the spirit of conquest, but they were earnest men from every walk in life who came to seek new homes in a new country. They brought with them the customs and traditions of an older civilization. Some were colonists prepared to work in field and forest and some were men of means who came with their retinue of slaves to seek new fortunes in a new land. The settlement grew slowly. A spirit of self-reliance was necessarily engendered. What made this feeling of independence all the more prevalent was the distance that separated the colony from the other English settlements to the north of Carolina. The settlements in Carolina from the very beginning were isolated and the colonists realized that their safety depended upon themselves alone. This cultivated in them the practice of taking care of themselves and of not looking for help from the outside." (*Address*: John P. Thomas, Jr. *General Society of Colonial Wars*, 1934). It is not difficult to trace this independence of spirit in the subsequent history of South Carolina. As early as 1682 we find the Assembly passing an Act for "the better observation" of the Lord's Day, and for the suppression of idleness, drunkenness, and profanity. Similar Acts were promulgated later from time to time.

The year 1702 is notable in this period. The Society for the Propagation of the Gospel in Foreign Parts had been incorporated in England in June, 1701. Their first missionary to South Carolina was the third sent by the Society to America. This was the Rev. Samuel Thomas, who arrived on Christmas Day, 1702. Not until the arrival of this missionary, who labored zealously for four years, had any systematic work been done by the Church of England outside of Charles Town. It was designed that Thomas should work among the Indians, but these being at war, Governor Johnson assigned him to work at Goose Creek and on the Cooper and Wando Rivers. He died of a "pestilential fever" October, 1706, having made one visit back to England, submitting to the Society a very full report of conditions in Carolina at that time and pleading for the sending of more missionaries to Carolina. The Governor and Council in reporting Mr. Thomas's death applied to the Society for four more ministers. This was the beginning of the very great work done by the Society in South Carolina. In all 54 missionaries were sent to this colony—more than to any other American Colony except New York, to which 58 were supplied. One hundred and twenty-nine clergymen are listed as laboring in South Carolina during the colonial period. Thus approximately two-fifths of the whole number were missionaries of the Society. In 1771, however, the Church had become so strong in the colony that the Society had only one missionary here. Not only did the Society send missionaries but they established a school in Charles Town, distributed books, and established parish libraries.

Although it was intended that the Church of England should be established in the colony, and this was nominally conceded, yet if we except the voting by the Assembly of a maintenance for the rector of St. Philip's Church in 1698, this establishment did not take definite form until the famous "Church Act" of 1706. Indeed it was in 1704 that the first Church act was passed for establishing the Church, but some of the provisions of this act caused so much irritation to both dissenters and churchmen that it was repealed. One provision was the appointment of a Lay Commission for the trial of ecclesiastical causes. The S. P. G. resolved not to send any more missionaries until the law was repealed. The provision, it may be said, was intended as a means of getting rid of a pestilent rector (Marston) of St. Philip's.

By the act of 1706 the Church was legally established. This Church act is a very elaborate instrument. Beginning with directions for worship by the use of the Book of Common Prayer, it goes on with detailed provision for every element of parish life. By the act the colony was divided into nine parishes in addition to St. Philip's in Charles Town, as follows: Christ Church Parish; St. Thomas'; St. John's; St. James's, Goose Creek; St. Andrew's; St. Dennis; St. Paul's; St. Bartholomew's; St. James', Santee. The names of these parishes reveal the influence of the Barbadoes in early Carolina. Many of the settlers came from there. As in the Barbadoes, by this act the Church Wardens and Vestrymen were invested with many civil as well as ecclesiastical duties. Especially were they entrusted with the duty of caring for the poor. Thus a Church organization was set up covering practically the whole colony. Provision was made for the immediate erection of churches in six of the parishes as also for rectories and glebes. These provisions of the act were soon executed. Some of the Church buildings which were erected under the act were succeeded by other and larger buildings—some fell into ruin. However, three still stand and are in use—St. James', Goose Creek; St. Andrew's, and Christ Church. Other parishes were soon established. At the time of the Revolution the number had increased to 21. Governor Glen, writing in 1710, states that the population was at this time about ten thousand. One-half were Episcopalians. There were three thousand Negroes. Of the total number, three thousand lived in Charles Town. The results of the Church act were highly successful. Ramsay says, "Endowing the Episcopal Church was the means of introducing about one hundred Episcopal clergymen into the country, who were men of regular education and useful in their profession."

From an early date the missionaries gave attention to a matter otherwise much neglected in the colony, education—both Thomas and LeJau spent much time in instructing white and black. In 1711 the S. P. G. established a school in Charles Town. Its success being demonstrated, the next year the Assembly passed an act establishing free schools in all the parishes—that in Charles Town was immediately combined with the S. P. G. school. Education received an impetus through the influence of the first royal Governor in 1721. Bequests for the education of the poor were made by Richard Beresford of St. Thomas's parish, and by Richard Ludlam, missionary at St. James', Goose Creek, who was indefatigable in his efforts for the instruction of both whites and Negroes. It is interesting that both of these legacies, though much depleted, are still contributing to the cause of education in these old parishes. Commissary Garden established a school for Negroes in Charles Town in 1742. In 1719, South Carolina revolted from the Lords Proprietors and became a royal province.

The Church in Carolina suffered much from the many disasters that befell the colony—the repeated scourges of yellow fever, the terrific hurricanes, and especially in the terrible Indian massacre of 1715 and the ensuing war with the Yemassees. Ruin and the ashes of churches and dwellings marked the progress of the enemy. In spite of all its difficulties, the Church grew steadily. Hewatt, the historian, testifies soon after 1730, "The Episcopalian form of Divine worship had gained ground in Carolina and was more countenanced by the people than any other. That zeal for the right of private judgment had much abated, and those prejudices against the hierarchy which the first emigrants carried from England with them, were now almost entirely worn off from the succeeding generation. . . . At this time the S. P. G. had no less than twelve missionaries in South Carolina. . . . Spacious churches had been erected, which were pretty well supplied with clergymen." However, all did not move smoothly. There was no little religious dissension in the colony and opposition to the Church. A letter from the clergy to the Bishop of London in 1724 represents the Church as in "a very prosperous and flourishing condition . . . so neither can we but testifie that it is without the least infringement of any of the rights or liberties of dissenters. . . . We have now a flourishing school in

Charles Town. . . . Dissention from the Church is chiefly supported by means of dissenting teachers from New England, and that part of Great Britian called Scotland, who transplant hither their dissenting principles."

The jurisdiction of the Bishop of London was acknowledged in Carolina practically from the first. He was fortunate in the three men who served successively as his commissaries here, all being men of integrity and ability—the Rev. Gideon Johnson, 1701-1716; the Rev. W. T. Bull, 1723; and the Rev. Alexander Garden, 1726-1756. The last named as rector of St. Philip's and commissary became the leading figure for a generation in the life of the Church. He was both firm and gentle, a leader and a disciplinarian, not hesitating to arraign the clergy for misconduct. The clergy early formed the habit of meeting in Convocation or "Visitation". LeJau in 1712 says, "The clergy met and conferred together in a most loving and unanimous manner." The commissaries held regular visitations. On the 13th Visitation of Commissary Garden it was agreed that thereafter assize sermons should be preached by the clergy in order of seniority. While Carolina had a share in that worthless class of men from which all the colonies suffered, it is remarkable that they were as a rule a high class of men, as the best historians all testify. Concerning his visit in 1737, John Wesley says that he had "such a conversation on Christian Righteousness" as he had not heard at any visitation, or hardly on any other occasion. In 1762, the clergy formed themselves into a Society for the Relief of the Widows and Orphans of the Clergy. Later laymen were included as members. This society still continues its beneficent work.

The churchmanship of a leading missionary just before the Revolution is described as "of that steady character which is not easily shaken by alarms"; for while he mentions without comment that surplices were worn only in the three towns, he also tells us equally without comment, that "St. Philip's was built after the model of the Jesuits' Church at Antwerp, and has rich cloths and coverings not only for the pulpit, but also for the altar."

The Church in Carolina just before the Revolution, with its twenty-two parishes nearly all filled with clergymen, was in a flourishing condition—a large work was being done among both whites and Negroes, but dark days were ahead.

The Revolution delivered a crushing blow to the Church in South Carolina. No other state was so completely overrun by the invader from mountain to seaboard; in no other state were the citizens so divided upon the issues, and in no other did they so generously participate personally in the struggle. With the war had come disestablishment (1778) of the Episcopal Church and loss of all ministerial supply and support, followed by disintegration and destruction. After the war, there were only a few churches outside of Charleston which were not practically in ruins, either burned, dilapidated, or abandoned, and mostly without clergymen. However, God at the critical juncture raised up men of faith and vision to lead the "remnant" to a better day.

First we must mention Robert Smith who in 1757 had come from England to be, first, briefly assistant, then rector of St. Philip's Church, continuing until his death in 1801. During this entire period he was the leading figure in the life of the Church in South Carolina. Acquiring by marriage a comfortable estate, he was enabled to fulfill a natural tendency to become the active and efficient friend of his professional brethren in less favorable circumstances. He was probably the chief founder of the Society for the Relief of the Widows and Orphans of the Clergy in 1762. The fact that the Bishop of London had no commissary in South Carolina, in the years before the Revolution, doubtless added to his responsibilities as rector of the "mother parish." He was active in supplying and filling vacant cures in this state. Possessed of just those attributes of character, attractive in personality, broad in sympathy, wise, and of outstanding ability, he was the man qualified to guide the Church through the tempestuous period ahead. Though at first in the troubles which arose with the mother country he was loyal to the Crown, he soon threw his whole influence on the side of his adopted home. He volunteered as a common soldier at the beginning of the Revolution and later preached a noted sermon before the Common House of Assembly advocating the American cause. He was chaplain to the Continental Hospital in South Carolina. When Charleston fell to the British in 1780, with other leading citizens he was banished to the North where he took temporary work in Maryland. In 1783, he was welcomed home with acclaim, both in the Church and in the community. After his return from the North, in addition to his ecclesiastical duties, he opened, to supply a great need, an excellent academy which afterwards became incorporated as the College of Charleston of which he was principal until 1798. Thus was he re-established in his work in time to guide the Church through those organizing Conventions beginning in 1785. But for his influence it is likely that South Carolina would not at this time have acceded to the proposed union of the Episcopal churches throughout the United States. He returned also in time to be elected to represent South Carolina in the first General Convention. He did not attend the first, but took a leading part in several Conventions. It was only natural, then, when South Carolina at last decided to elect a Bishop, that he should have been chosen unanimously as the first Bishop of South Carolina. This was February 10, 1795. His Consecration took place at the next following General Convention in Philadelphia, September 13, 1795, by presiding Bishop White with Bishops Provost, Madison, and Claggett. He was the sixth Bishop in the American succession.

It was, as Dalcho relates, "through the unwearied exertions of the sound and judicious zeal" of this man that the churches in South Carolina were led to associate in a State Convention, from which delegates were sent to the earliest General Conventions held for the organization of the Protestant Episcopal Church in the United States. On May 12, 1785, in the State House in Charleston, the first Convention of the diocese was held. Another meeting was held in the same year, July 12, when deputies were elected to the first General Convention. So does this diocese reckon its beginning in 1785. In the same year were founded the six other oldest dioceses in America—New York, New Jersey, Pennsylvania, Delaware, Maryland, and Virginia. Deputies to the first General Convention elected on July 12, 1785, were the Rev. Robert Smith, Hon. Jacob Read, Hon. Charles Pinckney, John Bull, and John Kean. Mr. Smith could not attend; Rev. Henry Purcell was elected in his place.

It was not, however, as we have seen, until 1795 that the vital need of a Bishop, which had been lacking to the Church in South Carolina for over a hundred years, was supplied by the Consecration of the Rev. Robert Smith, D.D. It has been contended that South Carolina acceded to the plans of General Convention on condition that "no bishop would be sent to South Carolina." It is also said that South Carolina has always resented this. Doubtless both of these statements are correct, but they are not difficult of explanation. When the first is understood the second is thereby explained. I need not recall that background of opinion prevalent in all the colonies that Episcopacy was a sort of appendage of monarchy with pomp and powers temporal as well as spiritual. This did tend to caution, perhaps overcaution. It might well be conceded also that through long deprivation some had learned to undervalue the office. However, this is what really happened. The sixth section of the Constitution proposed by the General Convention was in part as follows: "The bishop or bishops, in every state shall be chosen agreeably to such rules as shall be fixed by the respective Conventions, and every bishop, etc." Now, when the Convention of the diocese in April 1786 came to consider this section, the action was, "Rule 6. Objected to; so far as relates to the establishment of a bishop in South Carolina. But recommend that the word State be inserted between the words respective and Conventions." Whether the Convention had reason or not to think "respective conventions" might refer to the General Convention, it was evidently so construed by them. What the diocese objected to therefore was not to the establishment of a Bishop in South Carolina, but the mode of such establishment. What they feared was something similar to our present method of electing missionary Bishops. That this position did not indicate any weakness concerning the necessity of the Episcopal Order but only caution as to its "establishing" is made perfectly clear by the fact that another Convention meeting five weeks later adopted as Article IV of its own Constitution this, "That the succession of the Ministry be agreeable to the usage which requireth the three Orders of Bishops, Priests and Deacons (with the exception, however, to the establishing of Bishops in this State), that the rights and powers of the same be respectively ascertained, and that they be exercised according to reasonable laws to be duly made." The most that can be said is that South Carolina was possibly over-jealous of its ancient right as a diocese to choose its own Bishop. This it did after some delay.

These were difficult times. The vestries were jealous of their rights; it was with the greatest difficulty that agreement could be reached as to a diocesan Constitution and by-laws. In contrast with what we find before the Revolution, for a generation after the Church's light burned low in South Carolina.

During the ensuing period, the attendance at the Conventions (twenty-four were held in the first thirty years) did not average over eight parishes, although most of the twenty-two parishes had delegates present from time to time. We have seen how difficult were the problems with which the first Bishop had to deal. It is probably incorrect to refer, as has been done, to Bishop Smith's short Episcopate as "inactive," after his leadership of the diocese for more than a generation. There is no evidence that he made regular visitations, but he assisted the vestries in their problems. He held no confirmations, indeed, but there is evidence that the time had not perhaps become ripe to inaugurate a practice, however important, which had necessarily been in abeyance for a hundred years in the province. He held eleven ordinations for South Carolina and two for Georgia. As to the latter, having had his attention invited to the condition of the congregations in Georgia, he "sought to cherish and preserve them in soundness and stability." Certainly he did not do less for his own diocese. Doubtless he had had much to do in removing prejudices against the office of Bishop. The Bishop's death seems to have stunned the diocese. No effort was at once made to replace him. There was a difference of opinion about the expediency for the time. Bishop Gadsden thus describes the situation: "In 1804 the Diocese was reduced we may say, to its original elements. The Bishop was gone to his rest, no Convention had been held for five years, and there was no Standing Committee in existence."

However, there were appearing at this time signs of light: a reorganizing Convention was held in 1804 when rules were adopted and when an effort was made to secure a Bishop. The Rev. Edward Jenkins, D.D., was elected but declined on account of age. It was Rev. Nathaniel Bowen, future Bishop of the diocese, the youngest minister in the Convention, then rector of St. Michael's, who was a principal leader in this preliminary revival in the diocese. He was secretary of the Convention and also of the Standing Committee. But the movement dragged. Before the Rev. Mr. Bowen left the diocese in 1809, he had suggested significantly a society, after the style of the S. P. G. Theodore Dehon, after becoming rector of St. Michael's, put into effect Bowen's suggestion. The Society for the Advancement of Christianity in South Carolina was established on July 2, 1810. This event and the Consecration of Theodore Dehon to be Bishop of the diocese on October 15, 1812, constituted a mountain top from which the new day could be seen to dawn—the 40 years of wandering in the wilderness was over.

The Advancement Society immediately began its great work— the promotion of Christian knowledge, encouragement of candidates for the ministry and, above all, missionary work. Few new churches in the diocese for the next century were established without the fostering care of this Society. Its first missionary was Andrew Fowler who founded the Church in Columbia and refounded it in Camden while many other missionaries under the auspices of the Society began the great work of re-establishing the Church in the old depleted churches in the low country. One would be blind indeed if he could not recognize the hand of Providence in the coming of Theodore Dehon to South Carolina from Newport,

R. I., in 1810 to be rector of St. Michael's Church and then to be Bishop of South Carolina (elected February 20, 1812). He was Consecrated by Bishop White, assisted by Bishops Hobart and Jarvis, in Philadelphia, October 15, 1812. Now began in earnest a forward movement in the Church in South Carolina. The Convention of 1813 was attended by 12 clergymen and 18 lay delegates representing 13 churches. These represented 612 white and 256 colored communicants, of which 715 were in the three Charleston churches—all told probably 1,000 in the diocese. None of these communicants, as we have seen, were confirmed. Bishop Dehon in his first annual address only a few months after his Consecration emphasized the importance of confirmation and explained why there had been none to that time. Early in his Episcopate, Bishop Dehon delivered sermons and lectures on confirmation, and on March 30, 1813, the rite was established in the diocese by confirmation on Edisto Island. During the year, 516 persons were confirmed, but it was many years before anything like a necessity for the rite, when it could be had, was fully established.

Bishop Dehon's first Episcopal act after his return to the diocese, however, was the Consecration of St. Paul's Church, Stono, on January 10, 1813. Thus was this rite also established in the diocese. Possessed of talents of the first order, he at once devoted himself to the administering of his office in an intensive way—visiting, preaching, and teaching. As did Bishop Smith, he lent his aid to the Church in Georgia. It was through him that the General Theological Seminary in New York was established. He at once increased the importance of the anual Convention by complying with the canonical requirement of an Annual Address. Bishop Dehon died of yellow fever on August 6, 1817, greatly lamented for his deep learning, pure and exalted virtue, sincere Christian character, and devotion to his high office. A tribute by St. Michael's Church said, "He fertilized the soil which was barren and unproductive, and gave life and activity to the waste places in Zion."

With this Introduction, we are now prepared to go on from where Dalcho's history left off (approximately 1820).

Chapter I

EPISCOPATE OF BISHOP BOWEN

1818-1839

JOHN KERSHAW, D.D.

(With additions by the author in brackets)

At the Convention of 1818, the Rev. Nathaniel Bowen, D.D., was unanimously elected Bishop of the diocese. Dr. Bowen had been the rector of St. Michael's from 1802 to 1809. When Bishop Dehon died, he was invited again to become its rector, but a few days before he entered upon the rectorship, he was elected Bishop. Consecrated Oct. 8, 1818, by Bishop White of Pennsylvania, Hobart of New York, Kemp of Maryland, and Croes of New Jersey, he entered at once upon the duties of his office, while continuing to be rector of St. Michael's. From his first annual address, it is evident that the Advancement Society had begun to function vigorously. He speaks of the Society as tendering assistance to several of the destitute parishes, mentioning Christ Church Parish, St. Andrew's and St. George's, Dorchester, St. Mark's, Camden, and Trinity Church, Columbia. He mentions a Sunday School as having been instituted in Charleston "for the benefit of the poor of our Church in this City and others," under the superintendence of the Rev. Andrew Fowler, which "thus far is flourishing and useful." He laments the scarcity of clergymen and the consequent vacancies in the parishes. He notes that the number of candidates for Holy Orders does not keep pace with the needs of the Church, and attributes the fact to the "want of means of a regular ecclesiastical education." He calls attention to the efforts being made throughout the Church to create a general seminary of theological education, and urges its claims upon his diocese. He commends to their support also the Advancement Society which even at that early date was assisting generously a number of parishes to support their ministers.

We learn from a report on the subject of defraying the expenses of the Convention that there were at that time "about thirty Episcopal congregations in the Diocese," of which perhaps ten were unable to contribute anything for that purpose (Journal 1819, p.

33). The clergy seemed to number thirteen, but by the next Convention the number had increased to twenty-one, while lay delegates were present from seventeen churches. Thus we obtain a fair notion of what Bishop Bowen had in the way of Church strength with which to begin his Episcopate. Thirty churches, ten of them very weak, twenty-one clergy, about 1,400 communicants, the Society for the Advancement of Christianity in South Carolina already functioning, the beginnings of the permanent fund for the support of the Episcopate, and the hope of seeing the General Theological Seminary founded.

[The support of the Bishop was a serious problem during the early and weak years of the diocese. There being no diocesan funds, the Bishop was obliged in South Carolina, as in other dioceses, to find his support as rector of a parish. Bishop Smith was dependent upon his rectorship of St. Philip's and Bishop Dehon of St. Michael's. In the latter case, the problem became more acute as Episcopal duties greatly increased. Some effort to supply a measure of diocesan support was begun near the end of Bishop Dehon's Episcopate, a collection having been made by the Rev. Albert A. Miller. However, it was at the same Convention, 1818, at which Bishop Bowen was elected that definite steps were first taken to provide a permanent fund for the support of the Episcopate, and to relieve in part of least the Bishop's parish, St. Michael's, of the burden. There were to be collectors appointed in every parish, not more than three-fourths of the annual income was to be applicable to the support of the Bishop (called the *Common Fund*), the remainder to go toward the accumulation of the *Permanent Fund*. It was required that when the annual income shall amount to more than $4,000.00, the excess shall be at the disposal of the Convention, and the Bishop shall then immediately cease to be the rector of any particular parish unless this condition be removed by the Convention. This was not to be for many years. The Advancement Society was to hold and administer the fund. St. Michael's was to regularly receive reimbursement from this fund for its expenses in providing an assistant minister. In 1823, the permanent fund amounted to $8,655.00. The plan did not produce adequate funds; in 1824 it was found that the diocese was in debt to St. Michael's Church (causing it "embarrassment") in the amount of $1,190.82. More active measures were now taken and a plan adopted by which the arrears with interest would be paid in the course of some time, and the amount for the current years paid promptly in full. This was done. The obligation henceforth was fully met; after 1826, St.

Michael's was paid annually $1,200.00 for its assistant. The arrears due St. Michael's were also paid with interest but not fully until 1835. Latterly, the annual payments were made directly to the Bishop who was to relinquish that much of his stipend as rector. The diocese continued to appropriate annually for an assistant to the Bishop $1,200.00 through Bishop Bowen's Episcopate. The amount was increased to $1,500.00 during Bishop Gadsden's Episcopate and then called "salary".]

It is easy to see also that the Church was emerging from its period of depression into a brighter and more hopeful condition which increased with the passage of the years. At this time the Church, so long almost wholly confined to the coast counties, had been carried over into the middle country, and promising missions established in Columbia, Camden, Stateburg and Cheraw. As the means of communication increased, so did the intercourse between the upper and lower country, and wherever churchmen from the low-country settled they sought to have the ministrations of their Mother. Churches began to be built, also, and we read in the Bishop's address to the Convention of 1820, of the Consecration of three churches and of the administering of the rite of confirmation at a number of points in the diocese. The Bishop, in concluding his address, says: "Permit me to congratulate you on the progressive improvement of the state of our Church in this diocese. There is a larger number of ministers usefully employed in it than any other period since the revolution. Its laity evince a disposition to maintain its offices respectably and to profit by the services of a pious and faithful ministry." The proceedings of the Convention included the trial of a clergyman for immoral conduct—one of the very few that have ever taken place in the history of the diocese—and the record of his unanimous acquittal on both specifications. In the face of such unanimity it is difficult to avoid the conclusion that the charges were the outcome of vicious spitefulness and of that alone.

In his address before the Convention of 1821, the Bishop alludes to his being present at the General Convention of 1820. He speaks of Consecrating Edmundsbury Chapel on the Ashepoo, of ordaining three persons, and of having supplied services to some "remoter parts of the State where members of our Church had settled," mentioning particularly Chatham, now Cheraw, Pendleton, Greenville and the South Carolina Armory, and Abbeville. The Revs. Andrew Fowler, Patrick H. Folker and Rodolphus Dickinson were the men who did this work of Church extension, while the funds were supplied by the "generous aid of the Advancement Society." The Bishop refers to the institution of the General Theological Seminary in New York City in 1817. Instruction began May 1, 1819. By the general Convention of 1820, it was removed to New Haven, Conn., but it remained there not quite two years when it was returned to New York, where it has been ever since.

[This diocese, as the originator of the General Theological Seminary, continued its great interest in this school. Carefully prepared reports were regularly made by the trustees from this diocese to the Convention, and subscriptions for its support kept up and constantly the Bishop commended it to the diocese. In the first period of the life of this school, South Carolina had contributed by far the largest share, $4,560.00 out of a total of $6,246.00. While this ratio was not kept up by any means, yet in 1835 the diocese had given to the Seminary $11,494.54—entitling it by rule to 11 trustees.

[During the Episcopate of Bishop Bowen, three scholarships for theological education were established. Soon after his death in 1817, the "Bishop Dehon Scholarship" was founded by the ladies of the diocese in testimony of their attachment to a revered name. At first, it was under the charge of the rectors of the three Episcopal churches in Charleston, but soon committed to the trusteeship of the Advancement Society. In reporting to the Convention of 1825 that this scholarship was ready to be immediately useful, Dr. Gadsden moved the founding by the Convention of another to be called the "Bishop Bowen Scholarship" in tribute to the Bishop of the diocese. This was done and a committee of one person from each parish, to raise the necessary funds, was appointed. This was done and the trusteeship placed with the Advancement Society. It was only a few years later, 1833, that Rev. Thomas Gates, D.D., left to the Society $2,000.00, establishing the "Gates Scholarship" for a student from this diocese at the general Theological Seminary. When the diocese was divided in 1922, the first two of these scholarships was assigned to the diocese of Upper South Carolina, the last to this diocese. All three scholarships still serve their purpose. In 1835, the corpus of the Dehon Scholarship amounted to $4,335-.00; Bowen, $2,207.00; Gates, $2,014.00. The Advancement Societies in the respective dioceses are still the trustees.]

At the Convention of 1821 the revised Constitution of the Church in South Carolina was adopted. Many of its provisions may be found today surviving in the Constitution and canons of the diocese, an evidence of the care with which the work had been done by the able committee in charge. The journals of the next several years disclose a condition of "progressive improvement" in the diocese. Churches were Consecrated in St. Mark's, Clarendon, Pendleton, St. Luke's Parish; a new Church "erected near (the site of) the original Parish Church," confirmation was administered at many points, but the Bishop's opportunities for visitation were evidently seriously hampered by his obligation to St. Michael's as its rector, while the strenuous efforts of the Convention to increase the Bishop's Permanent Fund indicated the desire generally felt to provide for the proper support of the Bishop so that he might cease to be the rector of a Church and be thereby enabled to devote his entire time to diocesan duties.

The Bishop devotes a considerable portion of his address to the Convention of 1823 to the subject of Christian Education and to the indifference manifested by churchmen in it, in marked contrast to the zeal evinced by others in their own denominational schools. The disastrous result of this policy of indifference towards our Church schools is indicated by the facts recently published whereby it appears that of the 21 colleges and universities once owned by our Church in this country, only three are left. Eleven of them have been "starved to death"; seven of them, including the University of Pennsylvania, Columbia University and Lehigh, taking warning from the fate of these others, "got out of the lap of their Mother and went out into the world at large, and the Church that once owned and controlled them has lost them from her family." The three that the Church still owns are the University of the South, Kenyon College and St. Stephen's College, and with two of the three it is a serious question, at this writing (1920) whether or no they will continue to live. A more terrible indictment of our policy towards our Church's institutions of learning it would be impossible to frame.

Speaking of the clerical changes in the diocese, in this address in 1823, the Bishop refers to the word of the Rev. Mr. Phillips as serving the "Charleston Protestant Episcopal Domestic Missionary Society, which consisting of respectable pious female members of the Church, is characterized by a zeal of Christian Charity as prudent as it is unostentatious, and adorned with the meek and quiet spirit which is of so great a price in the sight of God." The work of this Society resulted in the erection of St. Stephen's Church on Anson Street "for the accommodation of such members of our communion as may not be able to defray the expense of seats in other places of worship." It was Consecrated in 1824 and over its portals is inscribed the sentence: "My house shall be called a house of prayer for all people." But what a reflection upon the practice of rented pews in churches, and how painful to realize that to this day the separation of the "poor" from the "rich" in many of our churches still persists. [See St. Stephen's Church *in loco*.]

[During this Episcopate, the first periodicals to be published in this diocese appeared. On January 3, 1818, the first number of *The Sunday Visitant, or Weekly Repository of Christian Knowledge* was issued. It was published in Charleston by that versatile and active clergyman, Andrew Fowler, A.M. This four-page weekly (issued and delivered in the city every Saturday) was, chiefly, less to give news and more to supply religious instruction—especially for young persons—Scriptural, biographical, and obituary notices "proper to be read on the Lord's Day". This paper continued for two years. It contained especially valuable biographies, ancient and modern.

[In his address to the Convention in 1822, Bishop Bowen strongly recommended that the Convention undertake the publication of a diocesan periodical. The Convention refused to do so. However, the Bishop had his work gratified when on January 1, 1824, there appeared the first number of *The Gospel Messenger and Southern Christian Register*. It was published by "A Society of Gentlemen". The leaders and editors in the enterprise were Rev. Frederick Dalcho, assistant at St. Michael's, and the Rev. C. E. Gadsden, then rector of St. Philip's. They had the warm support of the Bishop. This monthly church magazine continued with marked success for over thirty years until 1853. Its file constitutes a storehouse of historical information. Another literary event in this Episcopate was the publication of our valuable "Historical Account of the Protestant Episcopal Church in South Carolina" in 1820 by the Rev. Frederick Dalcho, M.D. At the time, this important work was thus well described. "It is a collection of facts and documents, variously interesting, rather than a regular history of the Church; and as a book of reference, is greatly useful." Dr. Dalcho, as secretary of the Convention, librarian of the Advancement Society, one of the editors of *The Gospel Messenger,* and author of this valuable book, rendered the Church an outstanding service. Bishop Bowen took the lead in 1826 in the organization of the Charleston Anti-Duelling Association in a strong protest against a custom common at that time.]

The rule of voting by orders was adopted in 1824. A note appended to the list of those who attended the Convention of 1828, gives the information that "the Church in this Diocese consists of the Bishop, 26 Priests, 5 Deacons, and 42 Congregations." From the reports made to this Convention the secretary (p. 17), summarizes the following chief items: Communicants, white 1,443, colored 440; families, whites 1,276, colored 21; non-communicants, white 2,387; children under 14, 635.; making a total number of 5,465. He notes that the reports are incomplete and that no reports were received from some of the parishes, as is the case even to this day.

In his annual address to the Convention of 1829 the Bishop brought before it, not for action but for consideration the subject of the "material difference existing betwen the relation which the clergy of our Church in this diocese hold to the churches in which they pastorally minister, considered in the light of legally created corporations, and that which in this respect is almost everywhere else sustained by them." The reference is to the exclusion of the rector from membership in the vestry. He notes that prior to the Revolution the Acts of Assembly provided that the rector should be one of the vestry. In the Acts of incorporation subsequent to the peace of 1783, there was no provision to that effect. He attributes this to the apprehension, on the part of the laity, of the exercise, or the attempt to exercise ecclesiastical power and prerogative by the clergy. He shows the baselessness of such apprehension, and advocates that the rector should be made a member of his vestry. What effect the Bishop's views had is not easy to estimate, but even now [1920] there are churches in the diocese whose rectors are not recognized as members of their vestries.

In his Convention address of 1830 the Bishop adverts with great force to the subject of the deficiency of clergy throughout the Church. "What is chiefly wanting, is not, I sincerely believe, the ready means of gratification to a worldly ambition, or sensibility to personal interest or distinction, but the evidence, merely, of a more generally prevalent, liberal and friendly temper towards the ministry, sufficient to justify the confidence of any willing to pursue it, that at least they should not in doing so, enter on a life of too absolute privation. The moral interest of society makes this a subject worthy the attention of the citizen and the patriot, since nothing can be plainer than the dependence of the whole welfare of a civil community on the general religious virtue of its people. Philosophy without the religious instruction that shall give the fear of God to be the Companion of its pursuit, will soon be found the philosophy that had been most delusively so called; and letters separated from the Christian discipline of the youthful mind and affections, but the weapon or the vehicle of infidel ingenuity." The scarcity of clergy still remains, but the effort to give them adequate financial support has gone far towards success in recent years. Yet the fact that in entering the ministry men must expect more or less of privation should not be suppressed; it is part of the following of Him who being rich yet for our sakes became poor. "Thy couch was the sod, O Thou Son of God, in the desert of Galilee."

The Bishop refers also to the formation of the Domestic and Foreign Missionary Society by the General Convention and commends it as deserving "a principal place in your esteem." He regards the recently formed Sunday School Union of the Protestant Episcopal Church as "eminently entitled to our patronage", much preferring it to "union charities of various denominations" seemingly then in vogue.

He speaks of the deep anxiety which has always been in his mind in reference to the religious and moral instruction of the slaves, suggesting that the clergy might arrange with the proprietors of plantations to visit them at stated intervals and "hold divine service, accompanied by pastoral counsel and instruction." In this way he believes that the white residents on plantations as well as the slaves may be reached and receive the benefits of "the sober, sound and practical character of the worship and doctrine of the Church. In the annual addresses of this period (1830-35) the Bishop refers to the detrimental effect of the political excitement attending the Nullification era upon the life of the Church in the withdrawal of the interest of the laity in the Church and its means of grace, deploring the fact and urging upon his people not to overlook eternal realities in the presence of pending political issues that are transitory in their character. He animadverts upon the "protracted or revival meetings, where our Ministry and others have been commingled in religious services, and where canonical obligations have, I fear, been somewhat overlooked by our Clergy," referring, no doubt, to the movement in Beaufort and elsewhere in the diocese, in which the eminent Presbyterian evangelist, the Rev. Daniel Baker, took a leading part, as has elsewhere been told in this volume, and which led to large accessions to the number of candidates for holy orders and to the number of communicants of the Church.

[In his annual address for 1832, the Bishop expresses strongly his fears of "revivalism" but he "will not refuse to acknowledge any satisfactory evidence" of resulting good. Dr. Kershaw gives us this fine account of the remarkable "revival" in Beaufort.]

During the years 1831-32, there passed through several Southern states, South Carolina included, a Presbyterian evangelist, the Rev. Daniel Baker. It was his custom to stop at a town and conduct a series of services through which he sought to revive the spiritual life of such as had previously confessed the Christian faith, and to bring into the fold of Christ those who had not made such confession. It is said of him that in his preaching, he was earnest and impressive rather than oratorical, and proclaimed a gospel of love rather than of fear. It is also said that when he visited a community in which there was no Presbyterian Church, he did not seek to organize one but confined his efforts to the winning of souls to Christ, to the upbuilding of such as had lapsed, and the strengthening of those who were upstanding. He visited a number of places in South Carolina, and in all of them his work was blest of God, while in some of them remarkable results followed. Notably was this the case in the town of Beaufort to which Dr. Baker was invited by the Rev. Joseph R. Walker, rector of St. Helena Church. Dr. Walker was of the Evangelical school. He had, through his life and doctrine, impressed himself strongly upon the community during the years of his ministry antedating this period. It was a community small in numbers, but more than commonly cultured and refined. Probably at that time, it had a white population of not more than six hundred, nor did this population increase to any considerable extent during the years following, up to the period of the War between the States in 1861. There were in 1831, only the two churches, the Episcopal and the Baptist, in the town. When Dr. Baker received and accepted the invitation to go to Beaufort, it was arranged by the resident pastors to hold services alternately in the two churches. There were those who while unaccustomed to such services as were contemplated, trusted their pastors and were prepared to give their interest and encouragement to them. There were others who looked askance at the innovation and viewed it with rather critical if not hostile eyes. When the time came, the entire community was in a state of eager expectation. A notice was sent out daily to every house, giving the place and the hour at which services were to be held. From the first it was apparent that the time was ripe for the ingathering of the harvest of souls. As the services continued, the interest extended and deepened until the entire community, almost without exception, was profoundly affected. The churches were crowded at every service, and the manifestations of religious feeling were frequent and marked. Young men as well as their elders experienced emotions previously unknown—the conviction of sin was strong upon them and the desire for pardon so wrought in them that they were drawn in numbers to confess their sins and seek forgiveness. Young women also were drawn into the current of the movement and gave themselves to God in Christ. Of nine members of a whist club, eight confessed the faith of Christ crucified, and seven of the eight, in due course, entered the ministry. Out of a certain law office in the town, six men successively left the law for the Gospel. Among these were: Richard Fuller, Stephen Elliott, afterwards first Bishop of Georgia; the Rev. Doctors Charles Cotesworth Pinckney and James H. Elliott. The first Bishop of our Church in China, the Rt. Rev. William Jones Boone, was also a product of this revival. When in 1882, on the occasion of the unveiling of a mural tablet in St. Helena Church, a memorial to Dr. Walker, the Rev. Dr. C. C. Pinckney delivered the address from which the facts stated herein have been taken; he counted up the men he knew who, under the influence of this movement had entered the Church's ministry; they numbered thirty-nine. The late Rev. Lucius Cuthbert, a Baptist divine, who himself was a product of this revival, told the writer of eleven men who to his knowledge had entered the ministry of the Baptist Church within the period 1832-1882, so that out of that one small community, in the course of fifty years, fifty men had given themselves to the ministry, one for each year, which is probably a record unmatched in either ancient or modern times. Dr. Pinckney testifies that every morning from nearly every home in the town, the notes of prayer and praise were heard, as a result of this remarkable movement, while on "Communion Sunday"—the first Sunday in each month—he says that after the prayer for the church militant, when those withdrew who did not expect to receive, he has seen what he never saw anywhere else in the course of his long ministry, viz., every adult in the congregation remain, and only the children go out, and this not once, but often. What a contrast to what may be observed today in our churches, where it is not uncommon to see a third to a half of the congregation withdraw, many, if not most of them, communicants. So markedly is this the case that on one occasion when the Bishop of the diocese was present in a certain Church where he had just confirmed a class, and seeing a large part of the congregation withdrawing, he whispered to the rector: "Are they *all* going out?"

The movement at Beaufort had the effect of bringing into the ministry a number of men who were tinctured, some of them strongly, with Calvinism. It was, perhaps, natural that it should be

so, influenced as they were by the theology of Dr. Baker, a Presbyterian, but for a generation at least, there was among our clergy a
distinct school of Calvinistic thought which may be traced in the
public sermons of the men of that period, and that has left its mark
upon many of the aged Church people even to the present day.
There were some too who set no particularly high value upon the
Episcopate as the form of Church government coming down from
the apostles' time, and therefore, to be adhered to, and who held
to the doctrine of "the parity of orders" in the ministry. Others of
them, however, were strong advocates of the doctrine of the Apos-
tolical Succession, but were equally strongly opposed to ornateness
in worship or in ritual, and especially were they careful to avoid
acts and postures that to them seemed to be expressive of "high"
views of the Holy Communion. It was almost coincident in point
of time with the origin of the Oxford or Tractarian movement in
the Church of England, echoes of which had come across the sea
and found lodgment in the hearts and minds of some of the clergy
of this Church, a circumstance that caused party feeling to run
high in this country as in England for many years, and that even
to this day exists, though not characterized by the bitterness which
prevailed in the earlier days, when the upholders of the movement
were opprobriously termed "Puseyites" and were accused of endeavoring to corrupt the Church by the advocacy of doctrines and
practices essentially Romish. It was an age of controversy aggravated by the defection to Rome of Bishop Ives of North Carolina,
who, among other things, had founded at Valle Crucis a school of
the prophets, or seminary for the training of candidates for holy
orders, which has survived in the form of a school for young men
and women of the mountain region of North Carolina included in
the missionary district of Asheville.

One noteworthy effect of the Beaufort revival was to increase
very largely the interest of some of our churches in foreign missions. The Consecration of Bishop Boone as the Church's first missionary Bishop to China gave great impetus to this interest, and
for some years, St. Helena, Beaufort, was one of the largest contributors to foreign missions in the American Church, though its
membership was small compared with that of many others. Bishop
Boone's son, William Jones Boone, became the fourth Bishop of
China, in 1884. He could hardly have been reckoned as a South
Carolinian, because he was born in China. The Rev. James Warley
Miles became a missionary in Mesopotamia and Constantinople in
1843, and for several years served in that field. He died in 1875.

This diocese has not since sent to the foreign field a clerical representative. [But see Appendix VI.] Bishop Ferguson of Liberia, though a native of this State, was not a clergyman of this diocese at the time of his Consecration in 1885. For nearly seventy years, in relation to service in the foreign field, the Church in South Carolina, to use the striking figure of Hosea, seems to have been afflicted with "a miscarrying womb and dry breasts."

At this time also the Bishop again refers (Journal 1834, p. 17) to the importance of having the Bishop's support provided for in some manner other than as rector of a parish, citing the fact that "the burden of the Episcopate has undergone at least a threefold increase since I assumed it", and saying that while he continues in the dual capacity of Bishop and rector, the interests of the Church in the diocese must suffer in some degree, but it was not until many years later that this condition was relieved and the Bishop independently supported. We find in the Journal of 1835, p. 13, a rather obscure reference to certain "differences of sentiment" as the Bishop calls them, among candidates for the ministry in the diocese, arising out of "circumstances of preparation, differing according to prepossessions existing among us." These tend to induce contrarieties and jealousies of feeling and opinion, he says, which should not be permitted to disturb "our perfect peace and fellowship in Christ." It is probable that he refers to the differences of opinion developed in regard to the protracted or revival services conducted in Beaufort and elsewhere in which ministers of other religious bodies took part, as has been stated. It will thus appear that the same question that of late has agitated the Church, viz.: of the right of persons not ministers in this Church officiating in any congregation thereof, was raised in South Carolina ninety years ago, and such right has been specifically denied by the cannon law of the Church, although it is provided that the Bishop may give permission "to Christian men, who are not Ministers of this Church, to make addresses in the Church, on special occasions."

[The parochial situation in Charleston saw several changes in Bishop Bowen's time: first, as we have seen in the opening of a "free church", St. Stephen's, in 1824 (See in loco). Ten years later, St. Peter's Church was established on Logan Street (See in loco) where an exceedingly active parochial work was conducted under Rev. W. H. Barnwell and his successors until the Church was destroyed in the great fire of 1861. Another parochial event of an outstanding character was the burning of the grand St. Philip's Church in 1835. Bishop Bowen lived to Consecrate the new St.

Philip's Church—grander than the former (See *in loco*). This Episcopate saw also the beginning of the sixth Church in the city, 1839 —St. John's, Hampstead (See *in loco*). After Bishop Bowen's death, there was found among his papers an unfinished sermon adapted for the occasion of the Consecration of St. John's, which was held after his death on July 14, 1840, by Bishop Gadsden.]

In his annual address 1836, the Bishop refers to a pastoral letter which, at the request of the previous Convention he was asked to prepare, treating of the importance of promoting among the Negroes moral and religious instruction. When it was about to be sent out "the public mind was thrown into a state which it was supposed would render it worse than useless to offer its contents to any, by the discovery of an utterly unwarranted, and reckless interference with this description of our population, by the systematic measures of an ill-advised, abused and malignant philanthopy of abolitionism." It appears that on July 30, 1835, there came to the post office through the mail a bag containing a great number of incendiary documents addressed to the colored people of the city. That night certain "turbulent spirits" broke into the post office and seized this bag. The contents becoming known, great excitement prevailed and at a public meeting of all political parties there was an effort made to induce the taking over of the post office by the citizens, which would have resulted in a very serious breach between the general Government and the city. At the instigation of the Hon. Robert Y. Hayne, cooler counsels prevailed, and no such attempt was made. The postmaster, the Hon. Alfred Huger, reported the occurrence to the Postmaster General in Washington, and agreed to withhold the delivery of the seditious pamphlets and newspapers, until that official should be heard from. These documents bore the titles of "Emancipator" and "Human Rights." (Jervey's "Robert Y. Hayne and His Times," pp. 379-380.) The Bishop says "Nor can it easily be seen how the measures referred to can be made possibly conducive to the moral benefit or indeed any other benefit, of these people; unless savageism and outlawry be a preferable state of human existence to that of domestic servitude under the benign influence of Christian principles and institutions." Thus already became visible and audible the forerunners and mutterings of that irrepressible conflict which, twenty-five years later, culminated in an appeal to arms, and resulted in the emancipation of the former slaves, with all the far-reaching consequences that have resulted.

An item of much interest is found in the proceedings of the Convention of 1837. It concerns the Rev. William J. Boone who is spoken of as having "destined himself to the work of foreign missions" and who afterwards was Consecrated as the first Bishop of China (Journal, p. 15). Another item of interest should also be named, *viz.*, a plan of systematic giving for the missions of the Church, which of recent years has received with some modifications widespread adoption to both missions and local Church support. The plan was to persuade the people to lay up in store, on the first day of every week as God may have prospered them, the amount they were willing to give for the purpose, and one Lord's Day of each month these amounts were to be collected in the Church and in the Sunday School, notice having been previously given. The lack of clergy is again alluded to (Journal 1838, p. 10) and the comment made that what hinders young men from entering the ministry is "the character of the day. The ambition of wealth and secular influence is the prevailing and predominant principle of action." Hence the difficulty of turning the thoughts of the young "to a pursuit whose lot in general is poverty and at best is little else." It might have been written by a Bishop of the present day, only perhaps the character of the day is manifoldly more marked by the power of material considerations than it was then, and nearer by far does the day seem when it shall come to pass that

"Religion veils her sacred fires,
And, unawares, morality expires."

We now approach the end of Bishop Bowen's career, and it is pathetic to note how, in his last Convention address, he speaks his mind on a subject always dear to his heart, *i. e.*, the religious education of the youth of the Church. After referring to the attention which the subject had received in the General Convention of 1838, the Bishop goes on to say: "There is still, however, a very prevailing objection among members of our communion, and among them almost alone, to what is termed sectarian education. I freely confess that I think the sentiment erroneous. You cannot now be detained with the argument which might show it to be so. All the denominations into which the Christian world has become divided, it must suffice me at present to remark, have long since practically evinced their sense of the necessity of conforming the minds of their young, by education, to their peculiar principles, in order that their instruction in religion might be of permanent avail; and it is time perhaps that Protestant Episcopalians should cease to be afraid, where no fear reasonably is, of being reproached with the bigotry of being in some degree consistent. It is time for all to countenance no more the liberalizing away of all the moral influences of education. There is surely no bigotry in desiring to transmit to others who are in their generations to follow us, the principles which we hold ourselves; and I see not how this can be without elementary and academic education that at least is not at enmity with those principles." (Journal 1839, pp. 13, 14.)

It is hardly necessary to add that the Bishop's plea did not materially, if in any degree whatsoever, avail to overcome the existing prejudice against so-called "sectarian education." Nor have subsequent like appeals availed. It has not been given to our people to realize the vital importance of the subject, and dearly have they paid for their lack of vision in this respect. For whereas in 1760 our Church people constituted forty per cent. of the white population of South Carolina, they now constitute only a fraction more than one per cent. of the same, and that this reduction is due in large part to their opposition to Church schools, is as self-evident as that the large increase in membership of several other bodies of Christians in the state is due to their enthusiastic support of their denominational schools and colleges. The absurdity of the invalidity of their alleged objection to sectarian education is intensified by the well-established fact that a considerable percentage of our boys and girls are sent to these denominational schools in preference to our own, in which sectarianism is emphasized, defended and, in some instances, regarded as the very reason of the being of the institution.

Bishop Bowen died August 25, 1839. His remains were interred by the side of those of his predecessor, Bishop Dehon, "under the altar" of St. Michael's Church. It is noteworthy that both of these eminent divines were born in Boston, Mass. In its appropriate place will be given a sketch of the life of our third Bishop, under whom the Church prospered, and by whose example the cause of Christ was advanced in this diocese. As nearly as can be ascertained from the reports made to the Convention of 1818, at which Dr. Bowen was elected Bishop, there were in the diocese twenty clergymen, twenty-one churches, and about 1,400 communicants. In 1840, the year after he died, there were 50 clergymen, serving 40 Churches, and communicants about 2,900. Bishop Bowen Consecrated many Churches during his Episcopate.

[Bishop Bowen rendered much Episcopal service beyond the confines of his diocese, as did his predecessors. By canonical arrangement, the Churches in Georgia were placed under the superintendency of the Bishop of South Carolina. In 1821, he Consecrated St. Paul's, Augusta, the Rev. Hugh Smith, rector. He presided at the Convention in Macon in 1826, and often held confirmations in Augusta and Savannah and elsewhere. In 1834, he Consecrated the Church in St. Augustine, Florida, and held confirmation, the Rev. Mr. Brown, missionary. This Church came from the mission of Rev. Andrew Fowler from this diocese, 1821, under the Young Men's Missionary Society. In 1838 Bishop Bowen felt obliged to decline all Episcopal duty in Georgia, except Savannah and Augusta— more not being consistent with other duty and his strength. Also, there was then a prospect that the Bishop of Tennessee would assist in Georgia.]

Bishop Bowen's passing was lamented throughout the dioceses of South Carolina and Georgia as well as through the country at large. He left behind him a strong and vigorous diocese and clergy, healthy and growing.

Chapter II

EPISCOPATE OF BISHOP GADSDEN

1840-1852

John Kershaw, D.D.

(With additions by the author in brackets)

[Bishop Bowen died on August 25, 1839. The following Fifty-first Convention of the diocese held its sessions in the different churches in Charleston. It was in St. Michael's Church on Friday, February 14, 1840, that the Rev. Christopher Edwards Gadsden, D.D., was elected on the first ballot as the fourth Bishop of South Carolina. His election was by a large majority of the laity but a small majority of the clergy. The division among the clergy of the diocese had lately developed on the question of revivalism in the Church. Gadsden, along with some of the other clergy, stood with Bishop Bowen in opposition to it; while others, including Stephen Elliott, afterwards first Bishop of Georgia, were sympathetic. A doubt arose in Gadsden's mind because of this and perhaps other reasons, as to whether he should accept his election. He delayed decision overnight, held a consultation with the clergy, and pleaded with them "to unite on some other person; but the sincerity and magnanimity of his appeal had the effect of removing all opposition." The next day, he gave his conditional acceptance to the Convention. At this Convention, serious consideration was given to the importance of separating the office of Bishop from that of rector-ship of a parish, which dual responsibility had been the custom in South Carolina as in many other dioceses. Steps had already been taken as we have seen to raise an endowment for the support of the Episcopate as early as 1818; further steps were now taken, and while the purpose was not accomplished until later in the next suc-ceeding Episcopate of Bishop Thomas F. Davis, the Convention now fixed a "salary" of $1,500.00 for the Bishop. This was continued until Bishop Gadsden's death, bringing an increase over the $1,-200.00 paid during Bishop Bowen's Episcopate.

[After due announcement, the Consecration took place on the first Sunday after Trinity, June 21, 1840, in Trinity Church, Boston. In addition to the presiding Bishop as Consecrator, the following

Bishops took part: G. W. Doane, of New Jersey, and S. A. Mc-
Coskry, of Michigan. Bishop Doane preached the sermon. The
Banner of the Cross remarked:

"A happier illustration of the true doctrine of the one, holy,
Catholic, and Apostolic Church, need not be desired than in the
consecration, in the remotest northern seat of our Episcopacy, of
the diocesan from the fartherest South, by the Bishop of the Eastern Diocese, assisted by the Bishop of one of the most central, and
one of the most western sees. Bishop Gadsden is the thirty-fifth who
has been consecrated for the Church, of whom eighteen are now
living. We rejoice that the mantle of Dehon and Bowen has fallen
on him who for thirty years was their bosom friend, and counsellor;
and we beseech Almighty God to shower his choicest blessings on
the bishop and Diocese."

[A first act of the new Bishop on his return to the diocese was to
confirm 126 persons at a service in St Michael's Church. In those
days, a single confirmation for all candidates in the churches in
Charleston was held in rotation in the different churches. This class
was from six congregations.

[Bishop Gadsden's first annual address to the diocesan Convention was characteristic of his entire Episcopate, a key to it both in
the matters considered as well as in the spirit and the motives
which acuated it. In all his annual addresses, he consistently refers
and defers to the purposes and the wisdom that characterized the
Episcopates of his predecessors. Bishop Smith was his pastor in
his boyhood, and he had undoubtedly been the chief confidant of
both Dehon and Bowen. He not only admired but loved them all.
Notably in his first address, he defined the purpose of Church
Conventions in general after the example of the very first, described
in Acts XV, as the "harmony and advancement of the Church—its
stability, its increase, its prosperity." He appealed, "May we come
to a happy agreement, or at least maintain a unity of heart even
if we cannot have a like judgment in all things?"

[First of all, revealing his missionary spirit, he deplores the fact
that in only 13 of the 29 districts (now counties) in South Carolina
were there congregations of the Episcopal Church. That this was
in some measure accounted for by the fact that the up-country of
the state was almost entirely settled by Scotch-Irish and other non-
conformists from Pennsylvania and Virginia, and not by members
of the Church of England, as was the seaboard, was no sufficient
excuse in Gadsden's mind for the condition. He said earnestly that

the advice of the Convention on this matter would be thankfully received.

[At great length, he considered the urgent call for the evangelization of the vast numbers of the Negroes in the diocese, both slaves and free, dwelling upon the best methods to be followed. He had himself been chairman of the committee under his predecessor that had prepared a suitable catechism to be used in what he calls "baptismal education." "To make these fellow creatures, who share with us the precious redemption which is by Jesus Christ, good Christians, is a purpose of which the Church is not, and never has been, regardless." He calls upon the clergy to take the lead, saying, referring to the Negroes, "If the people will not come to the Church, and to the minister's house, let him go to them (and free consent of their masters being of course indispensable), to their cabins, and give those individually, in family, or in the congregation, some suitable place being provided, the word of truth, and the prayer of faith." However, the Negroes did come to the churches in large numbers, usually occupying a gallery provided for them, or else occupying the entire parish Church in services specially for them. In 1847, he stated, "In our diocese, the master and the servant, the descendants whether of Shem, Ham, or Japheth, have been encouraged to unite in public worship and receiving Christian instruction." Oftentimes chapels were provided for them on the different plantations. It was during Gadsden's Episcopate that the outstanding and notable work among the Negroes, in All Saints' Parish, was begun by the Rev. Alexander Glennie. (See All Saints' *in loco.*) So successful was Dr. Glennie in this work that he was elected to be the missionary Bishop of Cape Palmas or Western Africa (afterwards Liberia). For good reasons, Dr. Glennie declined the election and continued his labors in the diocese.]

In a report made on the subject [of instructing the colored population] in 1843, it was stated that "the Church Service is used, at least in part"; the prayers were taught orally and memorized by many who could not read; the hymns were given out by two lines at a time; the sermons were chiefly directed to the inculcation of good morals, the commandments were often explained and enforced; sometimes during the sermon the people stood, at other times a hymn was sung, experience having taught that it was "impossible for this class of people to sit long without drowsiness"; the catechising was conducted by causing all to repeat the answers in union. Before admitting them to confirmation a probation is required of periods varying from one month to a year. This gives us a comprehensive glance at the methods employed by the instructors of the slave population of that day, in so far as they came under the influence of our Church in this diocese. Doubtless similar methods were used in other dioceses having large slave populations. It should be understood that while these methods prevailed on occasions of instructing the colored people alone, in many if not in most places of worship they were free to attend the services conducted for the whites, a part of the Church, particularly the galleries, being set aside for their accommodation.

In his address to the Convention of 1847, the Bishop adverts to the subject of the worshiping together of all Church people, whatever be their creed or station or their mutual relations. The question arose in connection with the Consecration of a Church in Prince William's parish, built "for the special benefit of the colored population" at the expense of the assistant minister. The Bishop doubted the expediency of having a Church for the exclusive use of only one class of persons, and in the Sentence of Consecration of this particular chapel, it was stated that although erected for the special benefit of the colored people, it was in general for all persons in the said parish. He goes on to say that the experiment of separating the rich and the poor whites in churches had not been a success, and instead of "churches for the poor" had been substituted "free churches, such as are open to all human creatures". Thus in our diocese the master and the servant, the descendants whether of Shem, or Ham, or Japheth, have been encouraged to unite in public worship and receiving Christian instruction". (Jour. 1847, p. 25.) But in this same year resolutions were adopted by the Convention providing for the establishing and maintaining of a congregation of black and colored persons in Charleston, which finally resulted in the organization of Calvary Church, not wholly, however, as a congregation of colored persons, but to be composed in part of whites. In connection with the establishment of Calvary Church, there occurred certain incidents that well illustrate the sensitiveness of racial conditions at that period. When the Church was nearly finished in the summer of 1849, as we learn from the committee's report, (Jour. 1850, pp. 31, 32) "Great excitement pervaded our city by reason of a very painful occurence at the workhouse (a penal institution of the city), a large number of persons assembled near the spot at night, some of whom threatened its destruction". The "painful occurence" was a revolt of a portion of the inmates, led by one Nicholas, in the course of which thirty-odd of them overcame the guard and took to flight. In time they were all brought or came back, but Nicholas and two or three others were tried, condemned and executed. The committee go on to say that the number of those threatening to destroy the Church was small, the great majority of those present being drawn there for the purpose of preventing lawless violence. No damage was done, but the matter was regarded as serious enough to warrant the calling of a general meeting of citizens at the City Hall, when the subject of the design of the organization of the Church was discussed, and finally submitted to a committee of fifty, to report to a subsequent meeting. This committee was a very representative one, "so constituted as to embody every variety of opinion on the various topics that were to come under discussion". They divided themselves into three sub-committees, one on Calvary Church, one on the whole subject of the religious instruction of the Negroes, and one on the law governing such matters. The report was not made until November of 1849—the city being in a fever of anxiety concerning the prevention of cholera, then prevalent in other coast cities to the northward, and also in the throes of a hot municipal contest. In their report, after describing that "the plan of the Church provides accommodations for fifty white members, by seats set apart and raised, and by a distinct entrance; keeping before the eyes of the congregation at all times a sensible image of the subordination that is due to those to whom, by the course of Providence, they are to look up to as their rulers" the committee say that nothing could be further from the intention of the founders than to weaken the safeguards of public peace and order; that it is evident that Calvary Church is erected for a lawful purpose; that the safeguards against disorder and unlawful combination in that Church are much greater than the jealousy of the law has hitherto imposed, and that so far from a bad example, it may be deserving of attention as a model for others engaged in the same laudable work. One of the resolutions appended to the report and unanimously adopted by another large meeting of the citizens, was this, viz.: "Rosolved, That the establishment of religious worship in Calvary Church, on the plans adopted by the authors of that undertaking, contravenes no law of the State and furnishes no ground of alarm". So the storm blew over and Calvary Church was Consecrated December 23 of that year.

One curious occurrence of this period was the "employment of a minister not of our persuasion" by the vestry and wardens of

St. James', Santee. In offering a defense of their conduct the vestry explained that it was a choice between having the person they secured to conduct services, and closing the Church. The irregularity was remedied and the matter dropped. It seems that at this time (1843) an arrangement was entered into by the rectors of the churches in Charleston, whereby "a daily morning public service was held and 'the Holy Communion' to be celebrated each Lord's day". The Bishop says (Jour., p. 17) "It is true the number of attendants at the daily services has been few, but we trust they have, the grace of God assisting, both received and imparted a blessing." The matter of postures during worship also received attention. The custom of kneeling for prayer, standing for praise, and sitting for instruction, was cited as expressing the mind of the Church on this subject. While it may be said that these postures are recognized everywhere now as proper, yet as to kneeling in prayer it is evident that by a majority of worshipers in this day, a new conception of kneeling has been introduced and bending of the body forward while still sitting, has become the substitute for that "kneeling upon the knees" that was intended by the rubrics on this subject.

[In 1845, we find Bishop Gadsden with eight other clergymen of Charleston resolving unanimously not to officiate at any funeral when a subsequent religious service was contemplated, upon the ground that "the Burial Service prescribed by our Church is in our judgment a full and complete committal of the body of the deceased to the dust out of which it was formed". The Bishop's strict administration of the discipline of the Church was never without the quality of mercy as well as justice. In a case of discipline referred to him by the rector of St. Peter's Church in Charleston in August, 1852, shortly before his death, he restored the party suspended by the rector. The vestry evidently interfering, he records in his journal that he informed the vestry "that in a case of discipline, there was no third party between the Bishop and those parties, viz., the rector and the member suspended. A letter was also addressed to the rector to inform him, the party was 'restored by me'." The vestries of this diocese have been slow to learn the limitations to their authority.]

Perhaps it will be news to some that at this time there was a considerable excitement concerning the vestments of the clergy during divine service. We learn that "one of these vestments is now adopted by many of those communities who once strenuously objected to it. And, to the other, what reasonable objection can be made—the most significant—the one sanctioned by holy Scripture—the proper ecclesiastical dress, whereas the black gown is of scholastic origin? It is not necessary to dwell on this subject, even were I inclined to do so, but believing that the surplice must be generally approved, its use by our missionaries as by other ministers is recommended." (Journal 1843, p. 22.) This excited the query: What, if any, vestments were worn by our clergy at and before this period? The oldest representation of the clerical dress known to the writer is that of the gown and bands and wig worn by one of our rectors at the close of the Revolutionary War. The portrait of our first Bishop represents him in the same Episcopal robes with which we are familiar today. But at the time when the scholastic gown was strenuously objected to, and the day of the surplice had apparently not dawned, it becomes an interesting speculation as to what, actually, did the parson wear when he officiated in the Church? It was the custom seventy years ago that the minister should wear the surplice and a black stole, commonly called "the scarf" while conducting the service. Then, when about to preach, during the singing of a hymn, he would disappear into the vesting room or sacristy, divest himself of his surplice and stole, invest himself with the black gown and bands, and reappear ready to ascend the pulpit steps and deliver his sermon. After the War, 1861-65, these black gowns and accompanying bands began to disappear altogether, partly, it is probable, because they were expensive, but chiefly because custom had removed the prejudices that existed against the surplice, which has itself undergone considerable modifications since the clergy have used the cassock, now in universal use, though the writer remembers more than one of the "old guard" who could not be induced to wear a cassock, and to whom any stole that was not jet-black was an abomination. He also remembers that when the first colored stole was seen in one of the old churches of the diocese, worn by a graduate of a seminary under suspicion as being "high church", the comment of one of the outraged observers was "just like one of those S.... asses!" and when more recently a rector appeared at a service in his Church wearing a D.D. hood, he felt it necessary to explain that it had no ecclesiastical or ritual significance, but was merely the symbol of an academic degree that his alma mater has seen fit to confer upon him.

The attention of the Church was also at this time (1844) drawn to "the duty devolving upon the Christian Church to adopt the most efficient measures for supplying the Indians with the Gospel.

The Government had adopted the policy of removing the Indian tribes to the remote regions of the West, away from the immediate neighborhood of Christian Communities" and it was felt that measures should be taken for their evangelization. It was proposed therefore to bring before the General Convention the expediency of sending out a Bishop for the express purpose of organizing and extending the Church among the Indians. It is evident from these facts that the missionary spirit had been enkindled in the diocese, and that it had begun to take an interest in matters beyond the scope of immediate parochial and diocesan affairs. This opinion is strengthened by the fact that about the same time on the occasion of a visit to Charleston by Bishop Southgate, missionary Bishop of our Church sent to Constantinople to get into touch with the authorities of the Orthodox Eastern Church and aid in its rehabilitation in that vicinity, the Rev. James Warley Miles, a presbyter of this diocese, volunteered to go and did go with the Bishop on this important mission, which later paved the way for the entente that prevails between that Church and the Anglican Communion, and aided still more recently in securing the cooperation of a number of the authorities of the Greek Church with the proposed World Conference on Faith and Order soon to be held (1920).

[The spirit of evangelism and the motive of missions, especially diocesan missions, dominated Bishop Gadsden's heart. He constantly thought of the quarter of a million slaves in those districts in the state where there were no congregations at all. His spirit must have entered into the diocese in regard to missions in general, for it was during his Episcopate that South Carolina supplied many laborers for fields beyond its limits: Boone for China, Elliott for Georgia, Rutledge for Florida, and just a little later, Gregg for Texas; then James Warley Miles to Constaninople. St. Peter's, Charleston, contributed $1,000.00 a year for the support of Bishop Boone in China. Mr. Miles received from the diocese of South Carolina his entire support while a missionary in the East, and we cannot mention the name of this remarkable scholar, preacher, and priest without noticing another instance of his missionary zeal. While a student at the General Theological Seminary, he advanced among his colleagues a plan for erecting a house of meditation, study, and work in the West. The plan matured in the Nashotah House Seminary, and the Rev. James Warley Miles is credited with being its originator.

[Thus was revealed the Bishop's concern for a great evangelistic effort by the Church in the state. He made also a strong appeal in behalf of the Domestic and Foreign Missionary Society of the Church. He was one of the first trustees of this society when it was organized in 1821. While admitting that contributions from the diocese had been large in proportion to members and to contributions from other dioceses, they had been "small, very small, in comparison to our debt to God and His Church and the standard set forth in the example and precepts of our Divine Redeemer." In view of the hundreds of thousands of unconverted and unchurched Negroes and the many unoccupied districts in the state, he gave diocesan missions the priority, saying, "that there are stronger claims on our religious benevolences than those presented by this society (the Domestic and Foreign Missionary Society) is freely admitted. I allude particularly to the claims of our own diocese and State, but that the spiritual destitution of our own large country has not yet sufficiently awakened our liberality, cannot reasonably be questioned."

[In this connection, he dwelt in his first address and others upon the important threefold work of the Society for the Advancement of Christianity in South Carolina: to distribute the Bible, Prayer Book, and tracts; to educate candidates for the ministry; and, above all, to send out missionaries, to build and support churches. He had himself, with Bishops Dehon and Bowen, been a co-founder of this society, which was practically the Board of Missions of the diocese and did a very important work for some two or three generations. This society, succeeded in its larger responsibilities in the latter part of the century (1877) by the diocesan Board of Missions, now the Department of Missions, is still active in advance work in the diocese. He commended also the Society for the Relief of Widows and Orphans of the Clergy, founded in 1762, and the more lately organized Association for the Relief of Aged and Infirm Clergy, as not only having the effect of checking "emigration", and encouraging "immigation", but as removing any excuse among the clergy to lay up treasures on earth, and furnishing a motive to their giving undivided "solicitude and energies to the service of the Church."

[Another topic dwelt upon at length in his first address, and of ever-recurring emphasis throughout his Episcopate, was Christian education. He was here again following in the footsteps of his predecessors. We may see how much attention he gave this matter in his own parish. The Bishop's efforts in this line were not without some practical results, though not commensurate with his efforts. By action of the Convention, a diocesan school (planned under Bishop Bowen) was opened in Charleston in 1842. However, notwithstanding constant appeals, the school received but scant support and was suspended in 1850. This school occupied the old rectory of St. Philip's Church on Glebe Street, where Bishop Smith had conducted his academy fifty years before. Immediately after the close of the diocesan school, Bishop Gadsden as rector opened a parochial school in St. Philip's Parish. In his last address in 1852, he did have the satisfaction of reporting nine schools in the diocese under Church influence. It is a great misfortune that the Bishop was not more loyally supported in his plans for Christian education in the diocese, including not only academies but a contemplated college. We may say that the Bishop himself, by word and example, constantly illustrated the teaching office of the ministry. He recommended very highly Dr. Jarvis' *History of the Church,* just being published. He made himself personally responsible for the sale of 100 copies in South Carolina.

[With all his constant emphasis on the value of parochial schools and Sunday schools, he was extremely emphatic on the importance of the "School of the Pastor." No clergyman should ever allow the former to supplant the latter. Nor did he hesitate himself on any occasion, even in his addresses to the Convention, to seize the opportunity to dwell on the above matters, on postures in worship, appropriate vestments (he advocated the surplice which was just then coming into use as more churchly than the common black collegiate gown), and observance of the Church year. It was his strong protest which on one occasion in Charleston stopped a great ball, planned to be held on Maundy Thursday night. He was seconded by a stern appeal from the Rev. Paul Trapier of St. Michael's. The leader of the diocese at this time plainly was a high churchman, but not of the type of the Oxford Movement, which had little effect on him, but of the Anglican divines of the seventeenth century—Hooker, Andrews, and Thorndyke. He himself called his predecessor, Bishop Bowen, a "Protestant Catholic"; it would apply also to Bishop Dehon and to himself. So it was that practically the first half of the nineteenth century, this diocese was under the leadership of "Protestant Catholic" Bishops.]

Echoes of controversies are audible in the annual addresses of the Bishop at this period; "the doctrine of the three orders of the ministry", "the extent of redemption," whether to all mankind as in our catechism, or to the "elect" only, the meaning of "regeneration" as related to holy baptism. "The elements" says the Bishop, "of alienation, contention and strife, which we all deprecate, are insubordination, meddling, and uncharitableness," and he urges that these be avoided for the peace of the Church (Jour. 1844, pp. 33, 34). The Bishop notes (Jour. 1844, p. 37) that "we live in an age of insubordination. There is too little deference to the authority of experience and intelligence—of character and station, and scarcely more to that of law. The right of private judgment is ultraized." What would he have said if he had been speaking of the age in which we are living? It is very evident also that the Church in America and in this diocese was experiencing the influences of the controversies that for a decade had been agitating the Church of England, having their source in what was called "Tractarianism" or "the Oxford Movement", because it originated in the University of Oxford and was carried on chiefly through the instrumentality of certain tracts composed by the leaders of the movement and circulated throughout the Mother Church.

While this diocese was not seriously affected by the Oxford Movement as regards its peace and harmony, there were some of our clergy who sympathized with many of the objects of the movement, and whose opinions conflicted with those held by a majority of their brethren, and who therefore were made to feel themselves distrusted and suspected as men holding Romanizing tendencies. There were those who held "high" views as regards the ministry and the sacraments, maintaining that the government of the Church by Bishops, in succession to the apostles, is essential not only to the well-being but to the being of the Church; that in holy baptism, duly ministered, there occurred that spiritual change in the recipient, called in the Scripture and the Prayer Book "regeneration" and that in the sacrament of Holy Communion our Lord was really though spiritually present, not alone in the heart of the worthy recipient but in the sacrament itself, this being known as the doctrine of the Real Presence. There were those, on the other hand, who held that Episcopacy was neither divinely appointed nor necessary to the being of the Church; that of baptism it could not certainly be said that the recipient of it was therein and thereby regenerated; that the Presence of our Lord in the Holy Communion was purely subjective, in the heart of the worthy recipient, and certainly not more or more really than He was whenever and wherever two or three were gathered together in His Name, and that the Holy Communion was merely a memorial act, like the Jewish Passover. There were those also who regarded all these things as of secondary importance, who stressed "preaching and living" more than doctrine or ritual, whose conception of religion was well expressed in the familiar lines:

A charge to keep I have,
A God to glorify;
A never-dying soul to save
And fit it for the sky.

And, later, there were those who found truth in all great religions; who laid stress upon the importance of the intellectual and the rational in religion, as a check to mysticism and emotionalism, who cared but little for the refinements of doctrine or the use of the symbolic in worship, and were "liberal" in their views of the Church, the ministry and the sacraments as "means of grace". Thus, imperfectly and perhaps open to criticism as being not altogether fair, though not intentionally unfair, may be sketched the tenets of the schools of thought known in the Church as the "high", the "low", and the "broad". Following in the line of the development of the Oxford Movement, there came to be in due time a school in the Church known as the "ritualists", whose designation sufficiently describes them, and who, it may be said, are a recognized power in the Church, somewhat suspected and feared as being consciously or unconsciously in sympathy with Romanism and seeking to influence their people in that direction. The Bishop speaks of the recent agitation in the Mother Church and in our own, brought about by the Tractarian Movement, and prays that churchmen may be roused to contend yet more earnestly "for the faith once delivered to the Saints". These recent developments, he adds, ought to persuade the clergy to adhere strictly to the teachings of the Church, and the laity to remonstrate if these teachings are set aside or curtailed. "The teaching of the pulpit, even in our own Church; and of the press, although guided by those who call themselves churchmen, is discrepant in such a degree, if not contradictory, as to embarrass the many. Let us be faithful in the use of the Cathechism, the Articles, the Liturgy and the Prayer Book in general and all will be well". In all this we recognize the prevalence of a certain uneasiness as to the trend of events in the Church, although it did not seriously affect its progress in this diocese.

Whether or no the foregoing remarks are of importance, the mention of the subjects to which they allude is pertinent to this history, at this juncture, because the Convention of 1844, alleging by resolution that rumors affecting the reputation of the General

Theological Seminary had been brought to their ears, had appointed a committee to investigate and report upon the same. A report was made in 1845 (Jour., p. 17). From it we glean that an investigation had been conducted by the Bishops of the Church as visitors of the seminary. "Questions, many and minute, were propounded to the professors and answered in like manner. These all, with sundry resolutions or recommendations resulting therefrom" were published and placed within reach of any who desired to know what had transpired. Among these resolutions are two, in the first of which the Bishops state that having visited the seminary and inspected the same they do not find in any of its interior arrangements any evidence that superstitions or Romish practices are allowed or encouraged in the institution. Also that as regarded the doctrinal teaching of the seminary, the published questions of the Bishops and the answers of the professors were the best refutation of the rumors unfavorable to the institution. It must have been quite a thorough investigation, since the "Court of Bishops" as it was called, sat for twenty-two days. (Jour. 1845, p. 27.)

The Bishop comments upon the work of the General Theological Seminary in training so many of the clergy of the Church, about one-fifth of the whole number and about one-third of our diocesan clergy. He says: "The professors are perhaps of almost every shade of Theology tolerated in the Church. Of the students, some may have had a too great leaning in one direction (Romanism), and others in the contrary direction (Genevaism). To either tendency no countenance should be given. But wherefore is the one danger so much talked of and the other scarcely if at all noticed?"

[Always interested in the General Theological Seminary and the relation of his diocese to it, Bishop Gadsden became very much concerned in the matter of the $100,000.00 legacy of Mr. Frederick Kohne to the seminary, practically in view of the bylaw which stipulated that the number of trustees of this institution was to be determined by the amount of the contributions from the respective dioceses. At a meeting of the trustees of the seminary in New York in September, 1850, at which he presided as senior Bishop present, a committee of three, with himself as chairman, was appointed to report on the subject. At a following meeting, he made a careful report, but the two other members of the committee did not concur. His statement of the case was as follows:

["The late Mr. Kohne, it is understood, (and the legal proof can be adduced if deemed necessary,) passed, by far the greater part of his life, and acquired his property by industrious pursuits in South-Carolina. In that diocese, he was an attendant on the worship of our branch of the Church, and there was made acquainted with the necessities of our 'General Theological Seminary,' and it is believed directly or indirectly invited to contribute to it by his Pastor, the late Bishop Dehon. In advanced life, Mr. Kohne procured a residence in Pennsylvania, but he retained his residence in South Carolina, and his pew in St. Michael's Church, Charleston; and in those Dioceses passed the year, the summer in the former and the winter in the latter, continuing while in South Carolina to attend the services of St. Michael's Church, Charleston, and it is understood, was recognized by the rector as one of his charges."

[He then recommended that Mr. Kohne should be considered as resident in both dioceses, and that the dioceses of South Carolina and Pennsylvania were entitled to additional trustees in equal proportion. The trustees concluded that it was a matter for the General Convention to decide. After due reference, the General Convention deferred action, as a civil case involving the same issue of citizenship was pending in the Supreme Court of the United States. This Court later declared that Mr. Kohne "had so lived in the two States of Pennsylvania and South-Carolina, and amassed property in both, that his domicile might be claimed in either." Thereupon the next General Convention (1856), but only after much argument, decided practically in agreement with Bishop Gadsden's decision, and Pennsylvania was allotted five new trustees and South Carolina four, but the Bishop did not live to know that his judgment had been confirmed.]

At the Convention of 1851 a memorial was presented from Christ Church, Greenville, citing the fact that in "the back country districts, which contain about two hundred thousand inhabitants, chiefly white", there were but three clergyman and five Church buildings, and that there were fifteen villages of some importance where the Church should be established, and many densely populated neighborhoods which would justify the expense of a mission, and praying that means should be devised whereby the Church might be established in this important missionary field. A committee was appointed to report to the next Convention. In their report, after setting forth quite fully the religious conditions existing in the territory referred to in the memorial, being virtually all that part of the State generally termed "the up-country", the committee suggested the sending out of eight missionaries, their salary to be

$250.00 each and a horse, one each to the section east of the great Pee Dee, to that between the Pee Dee and Lynch's Creek, that between Lynch's Creek and Broad River, that between the Broad River and the Enoree, that between the Enoree and the Saluda, that between the headwaters of the Saluda and the Savannah, and the eighth in Edgefield, Lexington and Barnwell. The committee further recommended this plan as having been proved successful by the Methodists. They say that under the plan pursued up to that time, only seventeen parishes had been organized since 1812, a period of forty years, and of these but six have become self-supporting, and they ask if this can be regarded as satisfactory progress. They advocate as an aid and support to this active missionary scheme, the establishment of two high schools, one for each of the sexes. The consideration of the subject was postponed to the next Convention. Before the Convention of 1853 met, Bishop Gadsden had died, and much time having been occupied in choosing his successor, the matter was referred to the Convention of 1854. It is melancholy to have to narrate that after so considerable a flurry, the whole matter, so far as the Convention was concerned, lapsed into a state of "innocuous desuetude." Nevertheless the progress of the Church in the diocese of South Carolina during Gadsden's Episcopate is striking. The Bishop reviews this progress in his last annual address, February 12, 1852. While he was sad to note the fact that there were still twelve districts (counties) in the state without churches, the statistics were encouraging. We count twenty-two churches which he Consecrated, some of these being very handsome buildings, such as Trinty Church, Edisto Island; St. Thaddaeus', Aiken; Trinity, Abbeville; All Saints', Waccamaw; Trinity, Columbia; Grace, Charleston; and St. Helena, Beaufort. Holy Cross, Stateburg, the most nearly perfect example of Gothic in South Carolina, was Consecrated by Bishop Rutledge, a few weeks after Bishop Gadsden's death. But there were many other churches established in Bishop Gadsden's Episcopate. Christ Church, Mars Bluff, was established about 1843; Zion Church, Richland, in 1844; St. Luke's, Newberry, and Epiphany Church, Laurens, in 1846; Church of the Advent, Spartanburg, 1847; Church of the Holy Communion, Charleston, Church of the Holy Apostles, Barnwell, Church of the Ascension, Gillisonville, all in 1848; Calvary Church, Glenn Springs in 1849; Redeemer, Orangeburg, and Grace Church, Anderson, in 1851; and the Church of the Good Shepherd, Yorkville, and St. Jude's, Walterborough, in 1852. This is truly an impressive list; no decade before or since has seen such rapid growth. The Church strengthened its position in Charleston, Columbia, and Beaufort, developed hitherto vacant rural areas, and pushed farther into the up-country—almost to the borders of Georgia and North Carolina. The accomplishment which this number of new churches, rebuilt churches, and consecrations of churches evidences is perhaps the greatest and most memorable achievement of the Episcopate. Bishop Gadsden held also 54 ordinations, and it is remarkable that of these a large number was from St. Helena, Beaufort. Barnwells, Pickneys, and Elliotts led the roster, and one of this number became presiding Bishop of the Church in the Confederate States.

[Bishop W. S. Perry states that Gadsden's Episcopate was "marked by growth and spiritual development, and made noteworthy by his untiring labors and marked success." The statistics of the first ten years of his Episcopate bear this out. The clergy of South Carolina numbered 46 in 1840; 71 in 1850; an increase of 54 per cent. The number of parishes and congregations rose from 37 to 53, an increase of 43 per cent. Communicants increased 67 per cent. in the decade—from 2,936 in 1840 to 4,916 in 1850. But what is particularly notable about this latter record is the remarkable increase in the number of Negro communicants, indicating that the Church in South Carolina was doing a splendid work among the colored people; whereas the white communicants increased from 1,936 in 1840 to 2,659 in 1850, or 35 per cent., the colored communicants increased from 973 in 1840 to 2,247 in 1850, or 130 per cent.

[There were other things in the diocese that must have cheered the Bishop in his latter years. The year before his death saw the beginning of a new institution in the diocese, the Church Home, which recently celebrated its centennial, doing splendid service in its two branches: the Home for Women in Charleston and the Home for Children in York. Not long before the Bishop's death, Mrs. Eliza Kohne bequeathed $25,000.00 to the Society for the Advancement of Christianity in South Carolina, $10,000.00 to St. Michael's Church, $9,000.00 to the Bishop's Permanent Fund, and other smaller donations. Also about this time, there was a bequest by Francis Withers, Esq., of $20,000.00 for the Association for the Relief of Aged and Infirm Clergy, and $5,000.00 for the Society for the Relief of the Widows and Orphans of the Clergy. Both of these institutions of the diocese had been close to his heart. About the same time, there was organized in the upper part of the diocese "The Mountain Convocation", with a view to the expansion of the

Church in that section, which today is the diocese of Upper South Carolina. These events must have cheered him as the end of his Episcopate approached.

[There was another event also which must have been a great satisfaction to the Bishop. Always South Carolina had been interested in the planting of the Church in Florida. The indefatigible missionary, Andrew Fowler, had gone in 1821 under the auspices of the Men's Missionary Society of Charleston to St. Augustine to help organize the Church there. Bishop Gadsden had often held confirmations in that state, and now on October 15, 1851, he had the honor of acting as Consecrator and preaching the sermon when Francis Huger Rutledge was Consecrated to be the first Bishop of Florida. It was in the beginning of his Episcopate that he had assisted in the Consecration of Stephen Elliott to be the first Bishop of Georgia, and in each case it was a brother South Carolinian who was Consecrated. Both Bishops Elliott and Rutledge, especially the latter, officiated on request of the standing committee during the interregnum following the death of Bishop Gadsden. Bishop Gadsden died June 24, 1852. His mortal remains were deposited under the altar of St. Philip's Church, in which he had served for forty-two years. The spacious building could not contain the large company who gathered to pay their last tribute of esteem. The services were conducted by the Rt. Rev. F. H. Rutledge, Bishop of Florida, assisted by the Rev. J. B. Campbell, assistant minister of St. Philip's.]

Chapter III

EPISCOPATE OF BISHOP DAVIS
1853-1871
JOHN KERSHAW, D.D.
(With additions by the author in brackets)

I. ANTE BELLUM—1853-1865

On the twelfth ballot in the Convention of 1853, sitting in St. Michael's Church, Friday, May 6, the Rev. Thomas F. Davis, rector of Grace Church, Camden, was elected Bishop of the diocese in succession to Bishop Gadsden. He was Consecrated in New York, together with the Rev. Thomas Atkinson, Bishop-elect of North Carolina, October 17, 1853. At that time, including the Bishop, there were 69 clergymen in the diocese and 56 organized congregations. Churches for whites continued to be erected during the years following the Bishop's Consecration. [Among these in the decade before the war were: St. Stephen's, Ridgeway, 1854; Christ Church, Charleston (now St. Peter's), 1854; St. Jude's, Walterboro, 1855; Trinity, Black Oak, 1855; Ascension, Combahee; 1857; St. Mark's, Chester, 1857; St. Luke's, Charleston, 1858; Christ, Columbia, 1858; Holy Comforter, Sumter, 1858; St. John's, Richland, 1858; Nativity, Union, 1858.] The work among the colored people was largely developed, the Bishop stating in his annual address to the Convention of 1857 that there were 45 places of worship for the slaves, about 150 laymen and women engaged in giving them catechical instruction, and 150 congregations of slaves while of the 873 persons confirmed during the year previous, 628 were colored. [In 1853, Miss Harriott Pinckney donated the corner of her garden to be held in trust until there should accrue from the rental a fund sufficient to finance the erection of a Church for the free use of seamen in the port. A corporation, the Church of the Redeemer, was organized which administered the funds. In time the Charleston Port Society and the Church of the Redeemer joined forces, and, in 1916, the Church of the Redeemer was Consecrated, being associated with the Harriott Pinckney Home for Seamen. It was at this time that the *Southern Episcopalian* succeeded the *Gospel Messenger* as the diocesan periodical.]

The first movement to establish a diocesan theological seminary was made at the Convention of 1857. Having been referred to a committee, a report was made the year following recommending the proposal, but it was not until 1859 that the seminary was opened in Camden. Since there will appear elsewhere in this volume a sketch of the history of the seminary, the subject will not be pursued further here, except to say that the former distrust of the teaching given, and the practices permitted, in the General Theological Seminary, had not ceased to prevail among our people, and this, coupled with the growing agitation for the abolition of slavery, led to the desire to have our candidates for Holy Orders trained among the people whom they were to serve in the ministry. The defection to the Roman Church of Bishop Ives of North Carolina doubtless had its influence also in suggesting the establishment of the diocesan seminary. (See Theological Seminary, Appendix V.)

Among other interesting matters relating to the history of this period is one involving the marriage of slaves by clergymen of our Church. An able and exhaustive report was presented on the subject to the Convention of 1859, in which the position is taken that the relation of husband and wife is of divine institution, and the duties which appertain to it are of universal obligation and bind with the same force the master and the slave; that our Lord's injunction forbidding men to separate those whom God has joined together, is obligatory upon the conscience of every Christian master, and prohibits the separation of those who have been united in marriage; that the power over the slave conferred upon the master by the law of the land should be exercised by every Christian in conformity with the law of God; and therefore every Christian master should so regulate the sale or disposal of a married slave as not to infringe the divine injunction forbidding the separation of husband and wife; that in cases of separation where neither party is in fault and the separation appears to be final and permanent, a second marriage is recommended (Jour. 1859, pp. 30-35).

The resolutions thus reported were never adopted, but that they were introduced into the Convention at such a time of crisis in our national history, and that many were prepared to support them, should effectually dispose of the slander that Southern men were all oblivious to considerations of Christian duty and to the dictates of mercy in dealing with their slaves. Such separations of married slaves had been for years of increasing infrequency, while not a few Southerners were in favor of a gradual manumission of the slaves.

In the Bishop's annual address to the Convention of 1857 he calls attention to the action of the Bishops of the dioceses of Tennessee, Louisiana, Georgia, Alabama, Mississippi, Florida, South Carolina, North Carolina, and the diocese of the South West, meaning Texas, taken during the session of the General Convention of 1856, to establish a Southern University, which finally resulted in the incorporation of the University of the South at Sewanee, Tenn. The action of the Bishops was endorsed by the Convention and trustees were appointed to attend the next meeting of the Board of Trustees. At that meeting measures were taken to procure funds for the nascent enterprise, and in 1859 the Bishop states that the effort to raise these funds had been crowned with much success. The cornerstone of the University was laid with becoming ceremonies and only the near approach of the War between the States prevented the opening of the institution to students. Of course, the war upset all plans for the development of Sewanee, and it was not until 1868 that Bishop Quintard of Tennessee, attended by a little handful of students, planted a rude cross on the ground afterwards occupied by St. Luke's Hall, recited the Apostles' Creed, and with sublime faith declared the University opened, the service ending with the Gloria in Excelsis and the Apostolic benediction. The subsequent history of the University does not belong here, but briefly it may be said that hundreds of South Carolina's boys have received their higher education at Sewanee, and a very large proportion of our candidates for Holy Orders, for the past forty-five years, have received their theological training there.

[As we have seen, the Convention in 1818 formed both a permanent and a common fund for the purpose of a salary for the Bishop that he might be eventually relieved of any rectorship. During Bishop Bowen's Episcopate, the funds yielded only enough to pay $1,200.00 a year, which relieved St. Michael's Church of the burden of assistance in view of the Episcopal duties of its rector, Bishop Bowen. Immediately after Bishop Gadsden succeeded him (he being rector of St. Philip's), this amount now called "salary" was increased to $1,500.00. This continued in force until immediately after the Rev. Mr. Davis, rector of Grace Church, Camden, was made Bishop in 1853, the "salary" was increased to $3,500.00. It was then considered an entire support by the diocese of its Bishop but it was not until 1858 that the goal of $4,000.00 was reached. Bishop Davis, however, continued rector of Grace Church, Camden, the Convention having revoked the formerly proposed requirement that the Bishop "cease to be the rector of a particular

Church" when the diocese should pay his salary. Bishop Davis always had an assistant and did not allow any parochial duties to interfere with his Episcopal duties. It is interesting to note that the old custom of the Bishop continuing the rectorship of a parish lingered on into Bishop Howe's Episcopate. He continued nominally as rector of St. Philip's for a year and a half. Bishop Davis's ill health and absence from the country had prevented his attendance on meetings of the trustees of the University of the South.]

The abstract of parochial reports from May, 1859, to May, 1860, shows that there were at that time 6,126 communicants of whom 2,960 were colored; baptisms 1,644, of which 1,156 were of colored persons; marriages 314, of which 209 were of colored persons; burials 683, of which 118 were of colored persons; confirmed 389, of whom 173 were colored. The clergy numbered 72, the congregations 70.

[At the beginning of the war, Bishop Davis addressed a letter of admonition to the diocese because of the "threatening and critical condition of the country at the present." The Bishop sent with this letter a prayer and collect to be used twice daily "on all occasions during the ensuing session or sessions of our legislature." It is of especial interest that the Episcopal Church in the United States was one of the few that did not divide into separate churches, North and South, during the Confederate war.

Bishop Davis' letter and prayer and collect were as follows:

"Beloved Brethren: In every time of public anxiety and trial it becomes us as a people to humble ourselves before God and seek unto Him in prayer. The threatening and critical condition of the country at present calls upon us for such humiliation and supplication before God. I have felt it my duty, therefore, to set forth the ensuing prayer and collect to be used before the two final prayers of morning and evening services on all occasions during the ensuing session or sessions of our legislature. Let me request that it shall be so used by you and let us all come before God continually in prayer that we may find grace and help in our time of need.

"Very affectionately, your brother in Christ, Thomas F. Davis, Bishop of the Diocese of South Carolina. Camden. November 1, 1860.

PRAYER

"O, Almighty and eternal God, who dwelling in the heavens, rulest over all and governest the nations upon earth, dispensing to all their destinies according to Thy holy and righteous will, we acknowledge our entire dependence upon Thee. We humble ourselves before Thee, under a deep sense of our unworthiness and awful apprehension of Thy divine majesty. Be merciful to us, O God of our salvation, in this our day of trial and necessity. Hear our prayer and let our cry come unto Thee. Look down from heaven, we beseech Thee, upon the people of these United States; visit and enlighten their hearts; order their will and affections and overrule all their purposes to the ends of truth and justice, of righteousness and peace. We beseech Thee especially to bless the people of this state. Thou, O God, sittest upon the throne judging right. Our hearts are open unto Thee. To Thee we make our prayer. Pardon the sins of Thy people and direct all their ways. Make them obedient to Thy blessed will and acceptable in Thy sight, that so we may be Thy people and Thou may'st be our God. Endue the general assembly of this state, now in session, with the spirit of wisdom, of courage and of a sound mind. Sanctify and rule their hearts by the mighty power of the Holy Ghost. Save them from all error and inspire and guide their counsels that so their decisions may be righteous in Thy sight and such as Thou wilt bless, prosper and establish. Bless our governor and all others in authority. Give unto them wisdom and strength that all their acts may tend only to the promotion of Thy glory and the happiness of Thy people. And, O God, Father of our Lord Jesus Christ and Redeemer of all mankind, pour Thy spirit upon all orders and degrees of men among us and subdue their will to the blessed Gospel of the Son of God; so that Thy people may be adorned with that righteousness which becometh a nation and blessed by Thee forever more. Through Jesus Christ our Lord to whom with Thee and the Holy Ghost be glory and dominion world without end. Amen.

THE COLLECT

"O, Almighty God, the supreme governor of all things, whose power no creature is able to resist, to whom it belongeth justly to punish sinners and to be merciful to those who truly repent; save and deliver us, we humbly beseech Thee, in this, the day of our great need and peril; that we, secure in Thy defense, may be preserved ever more to glorify Thee, who are the only giver of peace, prosperity and safety, through Jesus Christ our Lord. Amen."]

Thus our Church affairs stood when came the call to arms. The Convention of 1861 met in Trinity Church, Abbeville. The Bishop in his address spoke of the War. He said; "Our hearth-stones are upturned. Our brothers and our children are in the field. Our youths with whom hitherto we have only sported have sprung up into armed men. We are filled with deep emotions and trying expectations. But this is no time for weakness or fear. A country was never so saved. We are called upon for manly resolution and for Christian hope and trust. Our cause is right and our God is true. Let us show the world that we can trust both. Let us show them, too, that we are Southern men, and claim independent opinions and a sustaining individuality. We are not dependent upon circumstances or combinations or numbers for our inward strength, but can stand erect in personal character, in the sense of integrity and in the fear of God."

Speaking of the condition "in which we are now placed as a Church" he argues that "we are a free and independent diocese. We are so, too, without sin or schism, and our way is open before us to do what we deem best for ourselves and promoting the glory of God. Our best interests, our actual necessities, require of us an independent Southern organization as a Church." This part of his address was referred to a committee which, in their report, say that they sympathized deeply with the feeling with regard to the conditions of our country expressed by the Bishop in his address; that the dangers surrounding our state and country demand our most earnest prayer to God for His aid, and our most earnest cooperation with the authorities of the Commonwealth in their endeavor to defend our rights, our homes and our lives; that we regard the present controversy as forced upon us by the action of others and while we earnestly desire and pray for peace, yet we feel bound, not less by our obligations as Christians than as citizens, to continue the struggle until aggression and invasion of our enemies shall cease; that while we mean to cultivate a spirit of charity towards all men, and especially towards all Christians, yet we cannot but express our great surprise and mortification, that none of those who have been united with us in the household of faith, have raised their voice against the measures now in progress for our subjugation—all having with one consent united in the endeavor to throw the sanctions of religion around a government which has violated the most fundamental principles of its own Constitution and of civil liberty, and around a war which can be successful only by the extermination of one of the races inhabiting these states and the total ruin of the other, or the final demoralization and degradation of both.

The committee on that part of the Bishop's address as concerns the relations of the Church in this diocese to that in the United Sates and in the Confederate states, reported concurrence with the Bishop's views; states that the Church in this diocese, adhering to the faith it has held hitherto, and yet being at liberty through its constituted authorities to adapt its worship to changes of civil relations, that this Convention do approve of the alterations set forh by the Bishop in the prayers for the President and for Congress, but hereby declares its intention to adhere to the Prayer Book and other formularies of the Church, and to the Constitution and canons of the Church in the United States, so far as circumstances may allow, and until departures are properly authorized.

The Bishop referred also to his attendance upon the general provisional Convention of the Southern Church held in Montgomery, Ala., and the adjourned meeting of the same body sitting in Columbia, S. C. in October of 1861. Both of these bodies were able, earnest, thorough in discussion and generally united in council. Although provisional, their acts are real and authoritative; as much so as those of any future general Convention that must be founded upon them, and the sources which authorized them. Concluding his address, he said: The times that try men's souls are upon us. We are visited with a war, cruel and unnatural. Those who were our brethren are invading our soil and desolating our homes. Every day brings with it increased intelligence of their encroachments, ravages and bloodshed. But let none of these things move us. Let us "not be afraid of their terror, neither be troubled, but sanctify the Lord God in our hearts". All things work together for good to them that love Him. He is chastening us for our sins, and proving our faith, that it may be found in His sight "laudable, glorious and honorable."

This sufficiently indicates the Bishop's principles and motives in the face of the trials that were besetting the South. It may be of interest to know that four out of five of his sons entered the Confederate Army and served honorably until the war ended.

We begin to read now of the services to the soldiers stationed along the coast, rendered by our clergy. The Revs. J. R. Fell of Christ Church Parish, Christopher P. Gadsden of St. Luke's, Charleston, who as chaplain of the Palmetto Guard Artillery, stationed near Pocotaligo, preached to them frequently, the Rev. C. E. Leverett, driven from his work on Beaufort Island by a raid in Nov. 1861, visiting the "five hospitals in the neighborhood" of Aiken and preaching to the sick soldiers, the Rev. Stiles Mellichamp of St. James', James Island, holding services either for the soldiers or "the Negroes on some plantation", John D. McCollough who as "Chaplain of the Holcombe Legion," officiated regularly in camp, twice on Sundays, and generally conducting prayers with the men when the labors of the day were over; A. Toomer Porter, who "has spent much of his time with our Army in camp"; Edward Reed of Sheldon Church, who has held "services for the soldiers encamped in the neighborhood" and has given up the chapel at McPersonville for a hospital for soldiers; Stephen Elliott of St. Bartholomew's, who "accepted the position of Chaplain to the Ninth Regiment of South Carolina Volunteers in June 1861 and continued to perform the duties of his office at the two forts at Port Royal, until their abandonment." Before the meeting of the Convention in 1863 all the students of the seminary had entered "the military service of their country," [Among these William Porcher Du Bose] all which speaks well for the patriotism of the clergy.

[Through the interest of Mr. Jacob K. Sass the Female Bible, Prayer-Book, and Tract Society of the diocese had published a soldiers' manual of prayers, Scriptural passages, meditations and hymns, *The Confederate Soldier's Packet Manual of Devotions*. It was compiled by the Rev. Charles Todd Quintard, chaplain and surgeon to the First Tennessee Regiment, later Bishop, and dedicated to the benefactor, Mr. Sass. The *Church Intelligencer* said, "We have seen nothing yet that we had rather put into the hands of our soldiers. . . ." The second little work, prepared by the same chaplain, *Balm for the Weary and Wounded*, was for the use of those who were hospitalized. It was dedicated to a comrade, killed at Chickamauga, whose body Quintard had carried from the field. The first four copies of this book to come from the press were forwarded directly to Lt. General Leonidas Polk, sometime Bishop of Louisiana, in the field. Three of these copies were found in his breast pocket shortly thereafter, stained with his blood. Dated two days before his death and assigned to three of his fellow generals whom he had baptized in the field, they were forwarded to the officers for whom he had intended them. This society began distributing as early as the latter part of 1861 thousands of its religious tracts and pamphlets to local military hospitals, sending them also as far as Virginia and the Army of Tennessee. In addition to circulating its own tracts, the society imported through the blockade many favorite English items for free distribution. It was forced by private suffering and public calamities to inactivity before the end of the war, "but not before it had done immense service." The publications of these ladies were praised by the *Church Intelligencer* as "decidedly the most to our judgment and taste of anything we have seen in that line—plain, practical, full of good sense, reasonable, and to the point."]

In his address to the Convention of 1863, the Bishop (Jour., p. 27) speaks of having taken his seat in November preceding "in the House of Bishops of the First General Council of our Church" in the Confederate States. In the Council "there was no prejudice, no party, no passion, no local divisions, no selfish ends; it was all one great issue for our Country and our Church. There were some minor divisions of opinion—there were some human infirmities; but seldom has there been more concentrated purpose and effort. The result has been happy." Even in that dark hour the Bishop looked forward to the time when "it shall please God to hear our prayer, and when our liberties and independence shall be acknowledged". "If Southern men", he says, "have free spirits, bold resolves and high appreciations, let them show it in their religion and towards their God. If they be true men, let it be known in a true and living faith in Him who died for them. Let this be the inscription of their spiritual standard, 'He died for all, that they which live should not henceforth live unto themselves, but unto Him who died for them and rose again.'"

As the war progressed, there was an increasing exodus of refugees from the coast country into the interior, and particularly so after the capture of Morris Island by the Federals in the fall of 1863, when the bombardment of Charleston began. The influx of the refugees often doubled the size of congregations in the middle and upper sections of the diocese, which gave them a sort of fictitious prosperity during the remaining period of the war, followed by a depressing reaction when the war ended and the exiles returned to their homes.

The Convention of 1864 met in Spartanburg, twenty of the clergy and representatives from twenty parishes answering the roll call. There was little except matters of routine to engage their attention and in the address of the Bishop and the reports of the clergy one feels the presence and pressure of impending disaster and of hope chilling into despair. Nevertheless one notes the action of the Convention in taking steps to establish a school for boys, on Christian principles and of a high classical character, and of an effort to place additional chaplains in the field. At the date of the meeting, May 11, services were being held in St. John's, Hampstead, the Holy Communion, and St. Paul's, where the congregations of St.

Philip's and St. Michael's unitedly worshiped. Services were held also, intermittently, in Christ Church [now St. Peter's], Charleston. The other Charleston churches, being within the range of the shells sent into the city, were closed. The steeples of St. Philip's Church and of St. Michael's were the objects at which the shells were directed for many months, and while these two churches and Grace Church were struck, the first two several times, yet the damage sustained by them was much less than that which resulted from the earthquake of Aug. 31, 1886.

A pamphlet of 26 pages contains the "diocesan records of the year A. D. 1865." The meeting of the Convention was appointed for Grace Church, Camden, May 24. There were present of the clergy sixteen, and lay representatives from six parishes. There being no quorum in the lay order, the meeting took the shape of an informal conference, at which the Bishop's address was read, from which it appears that so late as January 22, 1865, the Bishop was in Charleston and on the islands adjacent, administering confirmation. Later, April 9, while on his visitation at Sumter, Potter's Raid approached that town during the hour of service. What few men were in the town—soldiers on furlough and convalescents, members of the militia, even the rector of the Church—were summoned to resist the approach of the enemy. But the Bishop, assisted by the Rev. Mr. Glennie, continued to hold the service, afterwards barely escaping capture as he was driven towards Camden in haste, while the enemy occupied the town and turned the Church into a temporary hospital. In his address the Bishop commented on "the events of momentous and evil character that had passed over the country, the State, and the Church. Calamities and sadness press upon us. We feel that we are suffering under the mighty hand of God but let us look up with continued and unwavering trust to Him who is our God and reconciled Father in Christ Jesus." He notes also the destruction "by the act of an incendiary" of the diocesan seminary buildings, with about two-thirds of the books contained in it. This sums up the brief record of the Church's history during the last year of the great war. The sun of the Confederacy was setting in a blackness of darkness that held no ray of hope except that which streamed from the courage and faith of its people, a courage that had dared everything during the four years of war, and a faith that looked beyond the darkness to the dawn that was sure to come.

In 1865-6 there came before the standing committee an application for "consent" to the Consecration of Bishop-elect Kerfoot of the diocese of Pittsburgh, and the committee after stating that they realize "that we are One Body, and rejoice in the Catholic Communion of Christ's faithful people, together with the essential unity of the Protestant Episcopal Church in America", declined to give its consent on the ground that this diocese not being in legislative union with the diocese of Pittsburgh, the committee was not competent either to give or withhold its consent to the proposed Consecration. This brought up the relation of this and other Southern dioceses to the Church in the United States, which was touched upon by the Bishop in his address to the Convention of 1866, in which he advised the immediate return of the diocese into union with the Church of the United States.

This seems an appropriate place to insert a short sketch of the "Church in the Confederate States," since there are probably comparatively few who know much about it, though the subject has been well and fully treated by the Bishop of North Carolina in a volume that bears this title.

So soon as the Confederacy had been organized, steps began to be taken to determine what should be done in regard to the Church in the dioceses, then all coterminous with the states that had seceded. A meeting was held in Montgomery, Ala., July 3, 1861, attended by Bishops Elliott of Georgia, Green of Mississippi, Rutledge of Florida and Davis of South Carolina, and by fourteen clergymen and eleven laymen, representing the dioceses of South Carolina, Georgia, Florida, Alabama, Mississippi, and Louisiana. It was more of a conference than a Convention, wherein developed a variety of opinions, but marked by a spirit of harmony and mutual respect. The meeting adjourned to reassemble in Trinity Church, Columbia, S. C., Oct. 16, following. By that time matters had so developed that every Southern diocese felt free to cooperate. Of the Southern Bishops, the Bishop of Louisiana, Polk (being in the Army), was alone absent. Bishop Meade of Virginia presided. A Constitution was adopted similar in most respects to that of the Church in the United States, but introducing the principle of the provincial system, which, with some modifications, now prevails in the American Church. The subject of a change of the name of the Church was discussed—the title proposed being that of "Reformed Catholic". It was however rejected. The Constitution as adopted also changed "Convention" to "Council" to designate the legislative bodies both of the diocese and the general body. After a session of nine days, the meeting adjourned. The Constitution was adopted by all of the Southern dioceses except Tennessee and

Louisiana, in which, owing to the partial occupation of their territory by the Federal Army, no Conventions could be held. Upon this, Bishop Elliott, in virtue of his seniority, notified, through what was termed a "Declaration and Summons," the Bishops, the clergy and the laity in the Confederate states, of the ratification of the Constitution, and summoning the first (and last) General Council of the Church to a meeting to be held in Augusta, Ga., in November 1862. Meantime the Rt. Rev. Richard Hooker Wilmer had been Consecrated as Bishop of Alabama. The Council met in St. Paul's Church on the day appointed, Bishops Elliott, Johns, Davis, Atkinson, Lay and Wilmer, present, together with thirty clerical and lay deputies representing seven dioceses. The Council enacted a body of canons, said by competent judges to have been an improvement upon those from which they were taken, the canons of the General Convention of the Church in the United States.

It pledged itself to the duty of engaging "in missionary labor coextensive with the limits of fallen humanity", with a special recognition to provide for the spiritual needs of "that class of our brethren, who in the providence of God have been committed to our sympathy and care in the national institution of slavery." The Council devolved upon the Bishops "as the natural leaders of the Church" the work of promoting foreign and domestic missions. The Bishops' Pastoral issued at the close of the Council, contained "one of the noblest utterances ever put forth by the Church of Christ in modern times" on the subject of missions. It called attention to the camps and hospitals throughout the South full of the men of the South, and urging upon the clergy who had been exiled from their parishes by the war, to minister to them as their present duty. The eminent Dr. John Fulton speaks of this Pastoral as follows: "The Pastoral letter of the House of Bishops at the Council in Augusta will never cease to be precious to the Church of God. It is the noblest epitaph of the dead, and, if they needed such, it is the noblest vindication of the living, that their dearest friends could wish". It is understood to have been written by that eminent son of South Carolina, Stephen Elliott, the first Bishop of Georgia.

In due time the war came to its end, and with it ceased the separation of the Church, North and South, caused by it. The then presiding Bishop, John Henry Hopkins of Vermont, wrote to each of the Southern Bishops urging them to attend the general Convention to meet in Philadelphia, Oct. 4, 1865, and promising them a cordial welcome. Unfortunately the organization of the Church in the Confederate states had been regarded and spoken of by many

Northern Churchmen as schismatical. This was bitterly resented by Southern Bishops and churchmen. The Bishop of Virginia defended the action of his Southern brethren in organizing their Church and repudiated the charge of schism. Bishop Wilmer, in a letter in reply to Bishop Hopkins, urged delay, that time might heal the wounds of war, and lead to the offer of such terms of reconciliation as Southerners could accept. He called attention to the fact that with few exceptions the class of men chosen in the South as lay deputies to General Convention, had been excluded from the general amnesty extended at the close of the war, and that the President had but recently declared them to be "unpardoned rebels and traitors". The matter was much discussed in the meantime by churchmen both North and South. North Carolina's Bishop (Atkinson) decided to attend the Convention. Bishop Lay also attended. These two consulted the Bishop of New York (Alonzo Potter) as to their taking their seats in the House of Bishops, and especially desired to be assured of the course likely to be taken in the case of Bishop Wilmer, who had been Consecrated during the war and whose Consecration had been pronounced as schismatical by some of the churchmen of the North. Bishops Atkinson and Lay would do nothing that might seem to be an acquiescence on their part in any attempt to repudiate the validity and regularity of Bishop Wilmer's Consecration.

Bishop Potter, after consulting with other influential members of the House of Bishops, carried back an invitation to the two Southern Bishops to take their seats and "to trust to the honor and love of their brethren." They did so and were received with most cordial expressions of joy and affection. Lay delegates from North Carolina, Texas and Tennessee were also present at this Convention. Bishop Davis, in his Pastoral of 1865, appears to have clung to the hope that "the Southern Church may be enabled to maintain her present independent and Catholic position," but, as we have seen, in his Convention address of 1866, he advocated an immediate return of the diocese into union with the Church in the United States. Thus, in part, was the desired reunion effected. But there was in the mind of more than one Southern Bishop the feeling that not until the civil status of the several states composing the Confederacy had been restored would the Church in those states be in position to reunite with the Church in the United States, and there was a disposition on the part of some to await more concerted action by the Southern dioceses before taking any further step toward reunion. The General Council of the Southern Church, in accordance with the provisions of its Constitution, was to meet in November, 1865. Mobile had been chosen as the place of meeting, but it was changed to Augusta, Ga., because of a military order closing the Alabama churches. On the day appointed, the Bishops of Georgia, Virginia, Mississippi and Alabama met in St. Paul's Church, and meeting with them were deputies clerical and lay from Virginia, Georgia and Alabama, clerical deputies alone from South Carolina and Mississippi, and after the first day, one lay deputy from South Carolina, eighteen in all. The Rev. Dr. Pinckney of Charleston was elected president of the House of Deputies. The deliberations extended over a period of three days and the most significant action of the Council is set forth in certain resolutions adopted by both houses, among which were these:

"Resolved, 1, That in the judgment of this Council it is perfectly consistent with the good faith which she owes to the Bishops and Dioceses with which she has been in union since 1862, for any Diocese to decide for herself whether she shall any longer be in union with this Council.

"That whenever any Diocese shall determine to withdraw from this Ecclesiastical Confederation, such withdrawal shall be considered as duly accomplished when an official notice, signed by the Bishop and Secretary of such Diocese shall have been given to the Bishops of the Dioceses remaining in connection with this Council."

Virtually and in fact from this time the Church in the Confederate states ceased to be. The dioceses not represented at the General Convention of 1865, during the year following one by one in their diocesan Conventions met and adopted resolutions renewing their connection with the Church in the United States. "And Southern churchmen still recall with pride, and with humble gratitude to God, the history of that brief episode. As their fathers repelled the name and thought of schism, in connection with that Southern Church, so we believe that the true story of their conduct does abundantly show that they were fully justified in their claim to have preserved throughout its brief existence the Catholic Faith and the Catholic Spirit. And we believe that the page which records the history of the 'Church in the Confederate States' is one of the fairest and brightest pages in the history of our American Church, and of our American Christianity". (Bishop Cheshire in "The Church in the Confederate States," p. 252, from which, in greatly condensed form, this account has been taken.)

[Union operations to surround Charleston began on Morris Island in the harbor July 10, 1863, and continued about two months.

August 21, 1863, was appointed by President Jefferson Davis as a day of fasting, humiliation, and prayer. It was celebrated throughout the armies of the South by Church services and the cessation of all but the most essential military duties. It was celebrated by the Union forces surrounding Charleston as the first day of the siege of the city and of an unprecedented artillery bombardment of 586 days, lasting until February, 1865. After November 19, 1863, St. Michael's and St. Philip's were closed because of the shelling, but services were held in St. Paul's Church farther removed from the target area. On February 17, 1865, Sherman's forces set fire to Columbia; on February 18, 1865, Charleston capitulated. The Convention of 1865 was of necessity postponed, and, when it was recalled, in May of the year, only a few clergymen could be present and only six churches were represented. The tragedy of defeat was revealed in confused and harried reports. The Rev. Mr. Shand reported from Trinity Church, Columbia: "Gen. W. T. Sherman, U. S. A., on the surrender of Columbia to him, by the city authorities, on the 17th of February, 1865, having occupied it with a large part portion of his army, the greater part of the town was, on the night of that day, set on fire by his troops and reduced to ashes. The rectory having perished in the general conflagration, the Parochial Register, containing a record of all my official acts during the thirty-one years of my connection with the parish as its Rector, and those of the past year, was destroyed with the dwelling."

[The Rev. Paul Trapier and the Rev. Stiles Mellichamp reported from Redeemer, Orangeburg: "The statistics of this parish are postponed, as they cannot be given now with any approach to accuracy; the army of Gen. Sherman, which passed through Orangeburg in February last, having thrown everything into confusion, and hindered one of the ministers from going thither since January 28th. He knows only that most of the few who were well off among his parishioners are now poor; that widows and orphans, who had saved a little from the wreck of their property in the low country, are stripped of that little, and that defenceless families are living on the scraps left by those who had taken from them their supplies for domestic use. The other Missionary, though obliged, for many weeks, to walk, in his 64th year, five miles to and from the Church, his horse having been carried off with most of his food and clothing, has been holding service regularly. He writes on the 1st of May: 'I do not now walk, as my sister-in-law, who has lost all else, is here with a broken down mule and a carry-all, so that I am able to officiate every Sunday morning. Our dear flock is bearing up bravely in tribulation. Faith, patience and fortitude seem immeasurably extended to them from the treasure-house of grace above. Our congregations are still respectable. The Sunday-school is going on reasonably well.' "]

II. POST BELLUM, 1865-1871

The Annual Convention of 1866 met in Charleston, February 14. It was well attended, considering the poverty of the people and the difficulties of transportation. Twenty-eight laymen, representing twenty parishes, were present. The Bishop's address, with his record of official acts, covered the period from May 13, 1864 to Feb. 11, 1866. Referring to matters within the diocese, he speaks of the prostration of its physical resources, the loss of diocesan funds, the poverty of the parishes, and the privations and sufferings of the clergy, saying: "Your Ministers have stood by you in the days of your trial and calamity; let them not want nor suffer any more. I ask that you will use your strongest efforts to support your clergy, and let their just claims be next to those of your own family". He adds: "I have said that our physical forces are prostrated. But what then. The arm of the Lord is not shortened, and His Word is not bound. There is spiritual life left with us, and faith, and hope, and purpose. Suffering is the mark of God's people and their strength. Christians have been taught much when they have been instructed how to bear and to improve sufferings; they have learnt more when, by the grace of God they have been enabled to step upon disappointment and to mount over it. To this we are called—let us come up to our position. I feel a cheerful confidence that the Church will rise and shine and be glorified." Brave words these to be spoken at such a time!

Referring to the "diocese in her Confederate relations", the Bishop said: "I had hoped that it might be the will of our God that we should have an independent, united and self-sustaining Southern Church. To such a hope my sympathies and affections strongly clung; I thought I could see, too, a purer atmosphere for faith. There is now no longer hope; the Providence of God has otherwise determined; we will follow the Divine determination. Let us rise to our new responsibility, not sluggishly, reluctantly or opposingly, but with clear judgments, the spirit of alacrity, and Christian confidence. I advise the immediate return of the diocese into union with the Church of the United States."

He refers to the establishment of the Freedmen's Aid Commission as a department of domestic missions of the Church in the

United States, and of offers to aid the diocese in its work among the colored people. He said he had not accepted such offers because official relations had not been reestablished between "this diocese and the Northern Church", but he commends to the earnest consideration of the Convention the whole subject of "our Christian responsibilities to the colored population of the State."

This portion of the Bishop's address was referred to a special committee of three clergymen and three laymen. They brought in a comprehensive report and resolutions, in substance as follows: After reciting the fact that the subject being beset with difficulties, they hoped only to make suggestions, the committee reviewed the history of the Church's relations to persons of color, showing that from colonial days they had been commended by the S. P. G. to its missionaries; that our Bishops in their annual addresses had done all in their power to keep alive the interest of the diocese in their spiritual welfare; that the parochial clergy and missionaries had cooperated with the Bishops, and that the laity had generously contributed of their means, to this end; that the results were evident in the fact that in 1861, nearly three thousand of the colored people were reported as communicants—one half of the entire number reported; that owing to the war and its results, this work had been almost entirely suspended; that though released from the duties of ownership, yet as partakers with them of a common redemption and as fellow members of the same household of faith, we cheerfully acknowledge ourselves as debtors both to bond and free, wise and unwise, being all one in Christ Jesus. The committee recalls the faithful services of the late slaves during the war period, and how, with rare exceptions, they resisted all instigation to revolt and insurrection, and remained true to their former owners and their families; that it is not surprising that they have been carried away by their freedom and the vague and extravagant expectations they had been led to indulge in; that the only cause for wonder is that they have not run to greater excesses; attributing the fact that they have not to the religion of Christ that had been faithfully preached to them, alleging that, in the committee's opinion, unless their spiritual welfare can be cared for by the Church a relapse into flagrant heathenism must ensue; that as those whose destiny is most closely identified with them, we have the deepest interest in their moral and spiritual elevation; if the Gospel fails, all other agencies must be regarded as powerless; we, as longest associated with them and understanding them best, must undertake this or they will be left to the invidious instruction of others or to their own ignorant and blind guides; duty, self-interest, religion, humanity, all urge us to keep or retain them to the wholesome teachings of the Church. The committee say they recognize that our capacity for usefulness has been greatly curtailed by our poverty, but feel that in their disinterested Christian charity, our people will give out of their poverty and that others, who have not suffered so much will come to their aid. They refer to the Freedmen's Aid Commission organized by action of the General Convention of 1865, as offering material aid of which we may gladly avail ourselves, especially as the diocese of South Carolina has never in time past received any aid from the Domestic Missionary Society of the Church. The moral difficulty arises from the mistaken and prejudiced teaching the colored people have received, since freedom, engendering distrust of their former guides. This is not as general nor so strong, however, that it cannot be removed. They, the freedmen, will soon discover who are their true, tried and abiding, because judicious, friends. In any event the Church should do all in its power to revive their confidence. Appreciating the entire change in social status of the colored people, with a view to fitting them for their new duties and enable them to meet as Christians should; their responsibilities to society and the Church, the committee recommended:

1. The formation of a diocesan Board of Missions for this special work.

2. The duty of this board to revive and sustain the missions existing before freedom; to consider the expediency of organizing congregations of colored persons under such regulations as may seem advisable and consistent with the Constitution and canons of the diocese; to establish parochial schools, industrial features being engrafted, wherever practicable; to search out and take by the hand such colored men as they may find desirous of entering the ministry of the Church and to provide for their education and training, with the sanction and approval of the Bishop; to seek to have such Church property as is no longer used or needed by whites turned over to the board for Church and Sunday School purposes among the colored people, to receive and disburse funds whether received within the diocese or without; to decide on the expediency of appointing a missionary agent to visit the colored people and ascertain their general condition, needs and wishes, to collect all information pertaining to the work and to solicit aid beyond the diocese.

When we consider the circumstances in which this action was taken by the Church in South Carolina we cannot but commend the enlightened and Christian spirit that inspired it. The civil conditions of that period were almost chaotic. It had not been determined whether South Carolina and the other commonwealths composing the Southern Confederacy were in the Union or out of it. The people had not begun to recover from the prostration and poverty that were the results of the war and of the freeing of the late slave population which at one stroke wiped out hundreds of millions of personal property. The fermentation among the freedmen emerging from the state of slavery into the state of freedom, aggravated by the teachings of persons sent among them by individuals and societies that assuredly had no love for our white people, who were regarded generally by these emissaries and those who sent them out as desirous of oppressing the freedmen and even of re-enslaving them, if that were possible, added greatly to the difficulties of the problem. Our towns were garrisoned by soldiers of the U. S. Army who often usurped the functions of the civil authorities, virtually placing us under martial law and engendering much unnecessary friction between the races, because in any controversy in which the two races became engaged, the position taken by the military was invariably against the whites, no matter how great the resulting injustice might be. It was in these circumstances that the Church adopted the liberal and enlightened policy outlined above, not refusing to acknowledge its obligations to the colored people but rather emphasizing them and placing itself in the way of meeting and discharging them in our exalted Christian spirit, when it might well have decided to leave them to their fate and concentrate its efforts upon the conservation of what was left of the white element in its composition. No one who did not live here at that time can possibly appreciate the adverse conditions confronting the Church or the height to which it rose in meeting them in the form and spirit that it did. The Church might well have decided to leave to those who had brought about these conditions the full responsibility of dealing with them, but instead it showed its disposition at least to share that responsibility and do what lay in its power to follow the dictates of "duty, interest, religion and humanity" towards the colored people. The Church in South Carolina has no cause to blush for the stand it took on this subject in 1866 and continued to hold until later developments rendered it necessary to modify its policy as will appear in the sequel.

To follow up the results of the Church's action in the year last mentioned, we learn from the report of the Board of Missions appointed for the purpose, made to the Convention of 1867, by which it appears that with the assistance of brethren in the North, the cooperation of the General (Howard) commanding this department and a donation of a thousand dollars from the President of the United States, a building had been secured for a school and was being furnished at the time of the writing of the report. By the next year, aided also by the Church's Freedmen's Commission, this school, situated in Charleston, had a corps of twelve teachers and a student body of eight hundred. One other was opened in Winnsboro and in the Bishop's address (p. 47, Jour. 1867), it is stated that under the Freedmen's Aid Commission there were four schools in active operation in this diocese.

In his address to the Convention of 1868 (p. 50, Journal), he speaks of the large proportion of colored people who have been lost to the Church; those who remain are chiefly in the congregations of St. Mark's and Calvary, Charleston, in the missions in vigorous operation in St. John's and St. Stephen's parishes, under the Rev. P. F. Stevens, and the congregations remaining in Upper St. John's. We hear in the address for the first time of the school established in 1867 by the Rev. Dr. A. Toomer Porter, afterwards known as the Holy Communion Church Institute and later still as the Porter Military Academy, a sketch of which appears elsewhere. The Bishop alludes to the prostrate condition of the Church in this diocese, "greater even than it is understood to be." The clergy were, many of them, in great uncertainty, and in straits as to how to obtain a living. Some of them had felt obliged to go to other dioceses while others had resorted to teaching as a means of supplementing their meager salaries, so as to remain with their people, altogether a sorry and depressing situation. Twenty-two parishes were without a rector, while from seven parishes there was "no report". To the Bishop, blind and growing old, on whom devolved "the care of all the churches," it was a time of deep distress. The general state of the Church and the public mind also disturbed him. His analytical mind described an unusual restlessness in politics and religion, "In the Church," he said, "there seems to be an increasing disposition in favor of visible constitutions, and a more ornate culture of external administration and worship. You understand me as referring to the subject sufficiently indicated under the general designation of Ritualism." Believing that the system called Ritualism impairs the soul's direct access to the throne of God, and the sources of life and strength, by misdirecting the attention of the worshippers by acts and ceremonies, external or sensuous, that gratify the taste or captivate the imagination, he declares himself "the inflexible advocate of simplicity of worship." Probably the Bishop was influenced, in some measure, in making this declaration by an occurrence that was very painful to him. He had been appointed by the presiding Bishop as one of the Consecrators of the Bishop-elect of Georgia—Beckwith. Reaching Savannah he learned that it was proposed to have the service choral at the Consecration. As he deemed this "wholly unauthorized" and as he himself was "entirely opposed to the system", he declined to take part in the Consecration and at once returned to his own diocese.

[One very significant advance was the establishment by the Rev. A. Toomer Porter at Holy Communion, Charleston, of a parochial school, December 9, 1867. It was designed primarily to accommodate "the children of our fellow citizens who have been reduced by the war from wealth to poverty." It soon outgrew its parochial status and in 1869 had 300 children and three male and seven female teachers.]

The Bishop mentions in his address a peculiar incident that occurred on Waccamaw the same year (1867). He and the Rev. Alex Glennie who had spent many years in fruitful labors among the colored people there, on invitation to meet the people and preach to them, as they were in a great state of excitement. A female prophet had arisen among them and was betraying many into error. So serious had the matter become that the military had interfered and arrested the woman. They were withdrawing her from the plantation in the midst of much excitement when the Bishop and Mr. Glennie arrived. They had some conversation with the Negroes, inviting them into the Church. Only a few followed and they were in no mental condition to listen "to the old truths of the Decalogue", but "some of them spoke kindly to us, and Mr. Glennie was asked to baptize some children". The year following, in the report of the Committee on the State of the Church, are found a number of interesting items, such as the reduction of the funds of the Advancement Society from $89,108.00 to $33,485.00; of the Bishop's Fund from $70,186.00 to $59,995.00; the entire loss of the Theological Seminary Fund; of the great reduction in the salaries of the clergy, five of them receiving from $1,000.00 to $2,500.00 and thirty others an average of $340.00 each; of the decrease of colored communicants from 2,960 in 1860 to fewer than 300 reported in 1868. "Political and other influences combine to alienate them from their former pastors. Their physical, mental and moral condition, in many sections of the diocese are becoming worse daily. In some places belief in false prophets, priests, confessors, sorcerers and other forms of African superstitution has revived. Reports from some of our clergy, however, forbid us to abandon hope or relax our efforts on their behalf. We appeal to every member of our household of faith, as they prize the redemption that is in Christ Jesus and their own interests therein, to suffer no political agitation, no railing accusation however unjust, no alienation or distrust infused into their minds by others, or resulting from their own ignorance, prejudice or passion, to abate one iota in the patience and long-suffering with which we await a return of confidence, or the readiness with which we embrace every opportunity to regain that confidence, which their (the colored people's) own hearts may testify they have always merited at their hands." The committee adds this striking appeal: "The way must be found through self-denial to keep our clergy in the diocese and our Churches open. Let clergy and laity arise each in their peoples' sphere, and suffer, and do their utmost for the house of our God and the ordinances thereof. The tempest of civil and religious discord is howling around us; let us possess our souls in patience and have peace and love one with another. The ship may be suddenly dismantled, her bulwarks rent, her seams opening, but she bears the God of the tempest and storm." The committee advocates that the parishes on the seaboard, outside of the cities and towns, be grouped and an itinerant missionary sent to minister to each group.

In 1869 at the Convention that met in St. Philip's Church, the managers of the Advancement Society were constituted a Board of Missions for the diocese. The special Board of Missions to the colored people reported the school in Charleston as in full vigor, supported by the Freedmen's Convention of the Church; that they had received encouraging reports from many of the clergy who were ministering to the colored people. The Bishop, in his address, thinks he sees dawning the light of a better day. There is, he says, a more settled state of affairs in the state; financial resources are more secure; there is greater confidence in the future; men's minds are more relieved. The signs of religious life are more apparent, and the heart of the Church is beating more hopefully. Many old parishes are however minus the ministrations of the clergy, but by earnest cooperation of sincere efforts and willing hearts the waste places of the Church will, in time, be restored. We hear of churches, chapels and rectories being restored, or erected, showing a slow recovery from the effects of the war. How greatly the Church had suffered during the war period, especially along the coast, appears very clearly in the report made in the Convention of 1868 by the committee previously appointed for that purpose. This report is presented just as it was made and is as follows:

DESTRUCTION OF CHURCHES AND CHURCH PROPERTY

The Committee to whom was referred the duty of gathering information with regard to the destruction of Churches and loss of Church Property during the war, beg leave to Report:

That they have discharged the trust committed to them as accurately as they could. It has required much patience and perseverance to obtain definite information as to the condition of many of the Churches which lay in the track of the invader.

That fierce tornado which swept over our State from its south-western to its north-eastern borders, leaving the ashes of cities, and villages, and Churches, and homesteads to mark its desolating track, so uprooted the foundations of our social and domestic life, as sometimes to leave few survivors to tell the tale. The destruction of railroads, the absence of postoffices, the loss of Church Records, and the removal of those members of the congregation who were familiar with their parochial history, have often rendered it exceedingly difficult to obtain information authentic enough to embody in this report.

But the Committee believe that they have at last succeeded in their efforts to present a true and accurate statement.

They begin with the Churches in the southwestern portion of the diocese, and will trace their history geographically in the order of Sherman's march.

St. Peter's Church, Robertsville.—Was the only Episcopal Church in that parish. It was a new Church, built in 1859, of wood. It was burnt by the Federal army in January, 1865, together with the residences of every member of the congregation. The small congregation has been entirely dispersed. There is neither building, nor minister, nor people. The Church may be considered dead.

St. Luke's Parish.—The Church of the Holy Trinity, Grahamville, escaped with the destruction of its organ and furniture, and some injury to chancel and pews. Its parsonage was burnt with the greater portion of the town. Only five dwelling houses escaped the torch. A portion of the congregation have returned, but almost every member is in a state of bankruptcy. The systematic destruction of houses, barns, buildings, and fences around the rich man's estate, and the poor man's cabin, forbid any prospect of speedy restoration to this portion of the country.

The recent death of their long-esteemed Pastor has added to their calamities. By the action of our Diocesan Missionary Society, the remnant of this Church is supplied with missionary services monthly.

The Church at Bluffton has a similar history to its sister Church in this parish. It was not involved in the destruction of the town, being protected from the flames by its beautiful grove of oaks. But the dispersion of the population, with the poverty of the few remaining families, has caused a suspension of religious services. The Rector, the Rev. James Stoney, after trying in vain to revive the parish, has been compelled to leave the diocese for want of support. The Church is, therefore, suspended.

THE CHURCH ON HILTON HEAD, a chapel of ease to St. Luke's Parish, has entirely disappeared. It was a wooden structure, not of much value. The materials, it is believed, were removed by the negroes in order to build houses for themselves on that island.

This appears to have been the fate with many of the chapels built by the planters all around Beaufort, for the religious benefit of their people. Chapels and materials have both disappeared, probably with the same destination.

ST. HELENA CHURCH, BEAUFORT.—Established in 1712, one of the oldest Churches in the State, has had a varied experience of the changes through which we have passed. Upon the capture of Port Royal in November, 1861, the entire population of Beaufort fled from their homes, including every family connected with the Church. The Federal forces converted the building into a hospital, removed the pews and galleries, and floored it across so as to form a second story.

Dr. Walker, for forty years the venerated Rector of the Church, has returned to his home, and officiates in the lecture room to a small remnant of his former flock. The confiscation of the property of St. Helena Parish, by acts of Congress, has reduced this congregation to more than ordinary destitution. They can neither repair their Church nor support their Rector. The Domestic Board of Missions has placed Dr. Walker upon their lists of missionaries, and thus enabled him to resume his ministry; and the aid of friends has partially restored the Church, so that it can now be used for worship. The Rector and remnant of this parish must needs recall the years when St. Helena Church, in proportion to numbers, stood *first* among the donors to the cause of missions in the United States. It has contributed more than wealth to God's house. The late beloved bishop of Georgia, STEPHEN ELLIOTT, went out from this devoted altar, to consecrate his lofty intellect and capacious heart to Christ. And ten or twelve other ministers of our Church claim this Church as their spiritual home.

THE CHURCH ON ST. HELENA ISLAND, also one of the old Churches of the diocese, was completely stripped of pews and furniture, and is now in the hands of the Methodists. It is used by the freedmen, who constitute the sole population of the island, as a place for their meetings. It may be considered dead.

SHELDON CHURCH, PRINCE WILLIAMS' PARISH.—It has been the fate of this venerable Church to pass through two revolutions, and to experience the same fortune in each. It was burnt "by the British in 1780, on their march from Savannah to Charleston,:" and it was burnt again by the United States army on their march from Savannah to Charleston in 1865. It had previously been stripped of pews and furniture by the negroes. All that was combustible was consumed, except the roof, which was above the reach of fire; and its massive walls survive the last as they did the former conflagration.

From 1780 to 1830 it remained desolate. The writer can remember how an oak tree which grew in the centre of the venerable pile filled the interior, and threw its ample branches over the lofty walls, while a cedar sprang from the chancel recess, and hyssop and ivy coated the ruin with green. It was rebult about 1830, and has been a living parish up to the early part of the war. Its services were suspended by the death of its valued Rector, Rev. Edward Reed. May it rise once more from its ruins to become a temple of the living God.

THE MISSION CHAPEL, in the same parish, built by Rev. S. Elliott for the negroes on the Combahee, was taken down by Sherman's troops in order to build a bridge over that river. The materials were visible last year in the bridge.

It was Mr. Elliott's design to revive his Church among the colored population, to whom he had been preaching the gospel for thirty years. Our Diocesan Board of Missions had encouraged him to resume his work among the members of his former charge; but his unexpected death deprived the diocese of the labors of one of the most experienced African missionaries known to our Church. He had built this Chapel, and given his gratuitous services for many years for the benefit of the African race. For this work he had a peculiar adaptation; but his work has ceased, his congregation is scattered, and his Church destroyed. What fruit he will find garnered up in another world, we know not. But when "Ethiopia shall stretch out her hands unto God," some of her sable sons, we doubt not, will be given him for his hire.

ASCENSION CHURCH, Combahee, which Mr. Elliott served in connection with his chapel, is in good repair, but not used for religious service. Very few of the congregation remain, and those who are attempting to plant in that vicinity, are not attached to the Episcopal Church.

THE ASHEPOO CHURCH, St. Bartholomew's Parish, partially survives—the frame is standing, but its weather-boarding and flooring are entirely gone. Foster's troops used them to build a bridge over the river. Every planter's house has been burnt for miles around, and the population generally dispersed. A few men are trying to plant the rice lands, but no families have returned, nor have they the means of rebuilding Church or homes.

CHRIST CHURCH, WILTON.—This beautiful building is standing, embowered as of old in its venerable oaks, but its doors are closed, and its congregation scattered. The pews were in part removed by the Confederates, and the building used as a commissary depot. The pleasant homes of the planters on the Edisto River were generally burnt in the march of the Federal troops. No white family lives near the Church; freedmen occupy the country, and inhabit the only surviving mansion. A remnant of this congregation have settled ten miles below, where educated, and once wealthy men, may be seen ploughing their lands, and grinding their corn, while their wives and daughters cook and wash. A missionary service once a month constitutes the extent of their religious privileges.

CHURCH FLATS.—This was a new building erected by the planters on the Stono, for the use of that portion of St. Paul's Parish extending along the banks of the river. It was burnt by the Federal army on the 22d February, 1865, accidentally rather than intentionally. The troops set fire to a neighboring house; the fire extended to the Church and destroyed it. The Rector, Rev. Joseph Seabrook, and family, were at the same time driven from their home to seek shelter in Charleston. The Church may be considered extinct.

ST. PAUL'S, Stono, was repaired thoroughly in 1863; was converted into a commissary store by Confederate troops in 1864, being not then used for divine service; the pews and Church furniture torn out and destroyed; its funds, of some three thousand dollars, were invested in Confederate scrip, and are valueless. Its plate is in possession of the Vestry of St. Paul's, Summerville.

THE CHURCH ON JOHN'S ISLAND was entirely destroyed by a disastrous fire which swept over the Island in the spring of 1864, consuming many other buildings in its course. The fire is believed to have been accidental. It is not known whether it originated in some of the Federal camps, or in the carelessness of negroes.

This Church had also a considerable fund, about $30,000, invested in stocks and bonds. The stocks are worthless, and it is estimated by its treasurer that $3,000 only can be realized from its bonds. Few of the former residents have returned to their homes, and there is no present prospect of reorganizing the congregation. The pecuniary losses of this parish, including Church, parsonage and funds, exceed those of any other congregation in the diocese but one.

THE CHURCH AT LEGAREVILLE, a summer resort of the planters on this Island, was also burnt during the war. The village was deserted when the Island was abandoned by the Confederate forces. On the return of peace the Church had disappeared. The mode of its destruction is not known. It adds another item to the losses of the Parish.

ST. ANDREW'S PARISH.—This venerable Church, built in 1706, survives—but in the midst of a desert. Every residence but one, on the west bank of Ashley River, was burnt simultaneously with the evacuation of Charleston, by the besieging forces from James Island. Many of these were historical homes in South Carolina; the abodes of refinement and hospitality for more than a century past. The residence of the Rector was embowered in one of the most beautiful gardens which nature and art can create—more than two hundred varieties of camelia, combined with stately avenues of magnolia, to delight the eye even of European visitors. But not a vestige remains, save the ruins of his ancestral home.

The demon of civil war was let loose in this Parish. But three residences exist in the whole space between the Ashley and Stono rivers. Fire and sword were not enough. Family vaults were rifled, and the coffins of the dead forced open in pursuit of plunder.

It must be many years before the congregation can return in sufficient numbers to rebuild their homes and restore the worship of God.

(NOTE.—A delegate to this Convention informs us that he attended the recent election at this Church, and found three freedmen holding the poll in the chancel, while a door of the Church, laid across the chancel rail, formed the table for the reception of votes. This needless desecration, it is hoped, will not be continued.)

James Island.—The Church on James Island was accidentally destroyed during the siege of Charleston. It was between the Confederate lines. Some of our troops, amusing themselves in rabbit hunting, set fire to the grass in an old field. The fire communicated with the Church and destroyed it. It was a wooden building, and not a costly one, but quite sufficient for the wants of the congregation. The Parish has neither Church, congregation, nor Rector.

The Churches in Charleston have suffered their share of the calamities of war, in proportion to their proximity to the enemy's batteries on Morris Island.

St. Michael's Church, the most Southern Episcopal Church in the city, was exposed to peculiar danger. For a year and a half its beautiful spire was a target for their artillery. The public buildings around were torn by shells aimed at it. The grave yard was ploughed, and its monuments scarred by the balls so remorselessly rained upon it. But the lofty spire still lifts up its head, a beacon to the homeward bound mariner. Several shells penetrated the Church, destroying portions of the interior. The roof, pews and floor suffered from the dangerous missiles. One struck the centre of the chancel wall and burst just within, tearing in pieces the carved panels of English oak, with its exquisite paintings, and massive rails. Its fine organ, the gift of our English ancestors more than a century since, was removed to a place of safety, and has been restored to the Church. But its chime of bells, one of the best in the country, was not so fortunate. They were sent to Columbia, and placed under a shed in the State House yard. The Federal soldiers set fire to the shed, and the heat cracked and destroyed the bells. They were shipped to England, and recast by the same firm by whom they were manufactured a hundred years since. They have recently been restored to their place, and now invite our people to the house of God with their familiar sound, and break the otherwise painful silence of the Sabbath morn. These bells have known the vicissitudes of war. In the Revolution they were taken away and exposed for sale in England. They were purchased by a Mr. Ryhineu, an English gentleman, and generously restored to the Church. After calling our population to public worship for one hundred years, and giving utterance to the public joy or the public grief through that eventful period, they perished in the second and more calamitous Revolution through which our country has just passed. Their restoration to the old spire was hailed with joy by our citizens, and the preservation of that graceful spire, as well as the venerable church itself, now the historic church of the diocese, is a subject of devout gratitude to our city and our State.

St. Philip's Church suffered more than St. Michael's, or any other in the city. The marks of twelve shells were visible, which had penetrated the roof and walls. The costly organ was irreparably damaged. Its lofty spire escaped injury. It has been repaired, and is now regularly open for divine service. The injury to the church and organ will cost the congregation eight thousand dollars.

The financial condition of our diocese is illustrated by a fact in the history of these two churches, the largest and wealthiest in the State. St. Philip's could not raise the amount necessary to make their church habitable, until the sum was advanced by an individual whose means had escaped the ravages of war.

Nor could St. Michael's pay the customhouse dues upon their bells, without the aid of public subscriptions, and voluntary concerts.

GRACE CHURCH was struck by a single shell, but that proved a destructive one. It crushed one of the central columns and cracked the superincumbent walls up to the roof, tore away twelve pews, and cut the interior in many places. The injury was temporarily repaired by a wooden pillar.

Soon after the evacuation of the city, this church was re-opened for service, and for a year it afforded to the Episcopalians of Charleston a place of worship while our other sanctuaries lay desolate.

ST. LUKE AND ST. STEPHEN's also received damage from shells in roof and walls. But they have been repaired, and restored to their holy uses.

ST. PETER'S, CHARLESTON.—This church was destroyed during the war, though not directly by it. It perished in the great conflagration which swept over our city on December 12th, 1861. It was founded in 1830, and formed the scene of the zealous ministry of Rev. W. H. Barnwell. In zeal and good works this church was, for thirty years, a burning and shining light to our diocese, and its influence lives though its light has perished.

The congregation has been divided among other churches, and there seems to be little prospect of its revival in the diminished population of our city. It was insured for $20,000 in Georgia; but the failure of the companies in which they have vested their funds, render the policy useless.

St. Michael's, St. Paul's, St. Peter's and Grace Church, lost their communion plate in whole or in part. It was sent to Columbia during the siege of Charleston, and was either stolen or destroyed in the burning of that city. One piece of ante-revolutionary date, was purchased in New York and restored to St. Michael's. Their Parish Records generally shared the same fate.

GRACE CHURCH, SULLIVAN'S ISLAND.—This was a brick building, originally erected for a lazaretto. It was purchased in 1816, and formed into a Parish Church for the Episcopalians who made the island their home during the summer. When the houses on the island were removed to give place to those formidable batteries which, for four years, protected the harbor from hostile fleets, the Church was exposed to the chances of war. When the United States forces established their batteries on Morris Island, the Church then came in reach of their shells, which riddled roof and floor, and consumed the wood work.

Its roofless walls still lift up their solemun sides in the silence of the scene. Houses and population have both disappeared The green earth-works with their frowning guns, cover the site of the once populous village—but you may walk along their entire length without meeting soldier or citizen, or hearing any sound save the ceaseless roll of the sea.

There is a strange and painful solitude reigning around those shores, where once our citizens flocked to stroll along the crowded beach; and a more solemn silence reigning over those massive works, whose thunders shook our city by day and night. Is this desolation the sure wages of war?

The few families who inhabit the Island are chiefly Irish Romanists. No members of our Church remain, nor is there any prospect of its revival.

CHRIST CHURCH PARISH.—The old Church, six miles from Charleston, lay just within the lines on the east of the city, and was occupied by the Confederate troops. It received some damage from them. But after the evacuation of the city, its ruin was completed by the Federal soldiers; pews, pulpit, floors, doors and windows were destroyed, and the brick walls cut through in many places.

History has reproduced itself in this old Church. It was desecrated by the British in the Revolution, and their cavalry stabled within it. The Federal troops put it to the same use when stationed in the vicinity. It stills lies desolate, its open doors affording shelter to the stray cattle and to the birds of the air. Its fund of $6000 is nearly worthless.

ST. JOHN'S, BERKELEY.—Previous to the war no Parish in the Diocese was better prepared to take care of its clergyman. It owned a rice plantation which rented for twelve hundred, sometimes for fifteen hundred dollars per annum, and about ten thousand dollars in stocks. It owned a winter parsonage and a summer residence for its minister, in a healthy position. But almost all this has gone. Biggin Church was much injured and its walls defaced; all the pews, the desk and chancel rails were torn down and burnt. The congregation is not revived, except by a monthly service.

The Churches on the seaboard north of Charleston fared better than those which bore the brunt of the invasion.

THE TWO CHURCHES ON NORTH AND SOUTH SANTEE escaped, though they were stripped of furniture, organ and all movables. The Church plate was stolen, but the set belonging to St. James' was recovered by application to a Federal officer commanding a gunboat on the river. The Bible and prayer book (the gift of Rebecca Motte, of revolutionary fame,) were saved. The Bible was stolen by British soldiers, at the close of the Revolution, and carried to London for sale. It was exposed in a bookseller's stall, where the owner's name attracted the notice of WILLIAM BULL, former Lieutenant Governor of the Province of South Carolina, by whom it was purchased and restored to the Church. No service has been resumed in either Parish, nor do their means afford any present prospect of supporting a clergyman.

THE FIVE CHURCHES AT GEORGETOWN AND WACCAMAW suffered less, only two of them losing their carpets and furniture. But the prostration of the once flourishing Churches on Waccamaw is complete. They contained more wealth than any other rural Parish in South Carolina, or perhaps in the South. There were the homes of the largest rice planters on this continent. Their provision for the temporal and spiritual welfare of their slaves was a standard to other planters. Numerous chapels, built by the proprietors for the use of their people, adorned the estates, where the services of our Church were as well performed as in any other congregation in the land. The faithful labors of their revered Pastor, Rev. A. Glennie, for thirty years, had wrought blessed results, aided by the systematic teachings of the planters and their families. Hundreds of the colored race were communicants of our Church—thousands of colored children recited the catechism, and answered as intelligently as any of their age in Europe or America; and the Lord's work seemed prospering and sure. Alas, for the change in five or six years! Poverty has overtaken these desolated homes; the rice fields, rich as any land between the Mississippi and the Nile, lie desolate; their former laborers can scarcely be induced to work.

Their religious deterioration is painful. They have forsaken the way which they had learned, and taken to themselves teachers of their own color. Fanaticism and extravagance rule in their religious assemblies to such an extent as to require the aid of the military to keep order and repress violence. There are indications of a return to African barbarism. There is no religious services re-established in the three Churches on Waccamaw. The planters are bankrupt; their houses despoiled; their costly libraries torn to pieces or shipped to Northern ports. What good the Lord may work out of the present confusion we know not; but to human eyes the present state of things is only evil to both races which inhabit these beautiful shores.

(NOTE.—Arrangements have just been made with the Rector of Prince Frederick's Parish, to hold a monthly service in one of the Churches on Waccamaw.)

The other Churches between the seabord and Columbia, at Barnwell, Pineville, Sumter, Richland and Orangeburg escaped destruction, but received more or less damage.

CHRIST CHURCH, COLUMBIA, shared the fate of that beautiful city when burnt by General Sherman's army in February, 1865. With the exception of its elder sister in that city, it was the largest and handsomest Church in the diocese, outside of Charleston. It was consecrated in 1859, and was in the height of its prosperity. The Church with its organ, carpets, books and all that it contained, was destroyed in that fearful night. The loss to the congregation amounted to $30,000. A disputed title to the lot on which the original Church stood has involved them in additional losses, and the removal of many of their members in the depopulation of Columbia has reduced to the lowest ebb this once flourishing congregation. The few survivors find themselves quite unable to support a minister. Their services are maintained by the aid of the Domestic Board of Missions. The destruction of this Church may be considered the heaviest blow to the welfare of our diocese.

TRINITY CHURCH, COLUMBIA, suffered the loss of its picturesque parsonage, which was burnt, as well as the Sunday School house, with their contents, including the records of the Parish from its organization. The loss to the Church amounts to $9,000 or $10,000.

The communion plate, a valuable set, was forcibly taken from the Rector, by a band of soldiers, as he was endeavoring to carry it from his burning house to a place of safety. It has never been recovered.

ST. JOHN'S CHURCH, WINNSBORO'.—This Church was wantonly burnt by Sherman's troops, on their march through Winnsboro'. The public square was destroyed, but the Church was not touched by that fire. It was on the outskirts of the town in a large lot, and was deliberately set on fire by the soldiers, after the central square was consumed. The organ, furniture, books, and all the Church property perished. It has involved a small congregation in a loss of $5,000. Their services are maintained, and there is some prospect of rebuilding the Church—*the only instance* in the diocese of any such proposal. Its bell has an interesting history. It was the survivor of the chime once belonging to the old Church at Dorchester. When that Church was deserted, the bells were loaned to St. Paul's, Charleston. This one at length found its way to Winnsboro', and perished with so many records of the past in our disastrous conflict.

GRACE CHURCH, CAMDEN.—The Church escaped (but has, unfortunately, been burnt in the last year); the Bishop's residence was respected; but the brick building owned by the Church, and loaned to the Theological Seminary, was burnt by incendiaries after the troops passed through. The greater part of the library belonging to the Society for the advancement of Christianity in South Carolina was thus destroyed. The loss to the seminary and the diocese is heavy, for this library was the accumulation of fifty years, and contained many rare and costly books, whose money value it is impossible to estimate.

ST. DAVID'S CHURCH, CHERAW.—Was the last Church in the eastern part of the State in the line of the Federal invasion. It was seriously damaged by an explosion of ammunition near it, and doors, windows, and part of the wall shattered. The Church plate was stolen, with books and furniture, and its enclosure torn down. But the Church is habitable, and its worship continues.

To sum up the losses of the diocese it appears:

That ten Churches have been burnt;

That three have disappeared;

That twenty-two Parishes are suspended;

That eleven parsonages have been burnt; that every Church between the Savannah River and Charleston has been injured, some stripped even of weather-boarding and flooring; that almost every minister in that region of the State has lost home and library; that along the entire seaboard, from North Carolina to Georgia, where our Church had flourished for more than a century, there are but four Parishes which maintain religious services; that not one, outside the city of Charleston, can be called a living, self-sustaining Parish; that their Clergy live by fishing, farming, and mechanic arts; and that almost every Church, whose history appears on this record, has lost its communion plate, often a massive and venerable set, the donation of an English or Colonial ancestor.

Our Diocesan funds have shared the fate of all Southern investments.

The Society for relief of the widows and orphans of the Clergy has lost $100,000.

The Society for advancement of Christianity in South Carolina has lost $56,000.

The Bishop's fund, $18,000.

The three Scholarships in the General Seminary (maintained by this Diocese,) $10,000; making the total loss of vested Diocesan funds $184,000.

Many of the older Churches also owned Bonds and Stocks, which have been sadly reduced or rendered worthless. From partial returns these losses amount to $98,000.

The pecuniary losses might be repaired if the diocese was as in days gone by. But in its present impoverished condition, no hope remains of speedy restoration. This generation can scarcely behold it.

May the God of all grace grant us, in faith and patience, to try and build again the waste places of Zion. "O Lord of Hosts, look down from Heaven, behold and visit this vine, which thy right hand hath planted." "It hath been burnt with fire, and the wild boar out of the wood doth root it up." "Comfort us again after the time that thou has plagued us and for the years wherein we have suffered adversity." "Show thy servants thy work, and their children thy glory." Prosper thou the work of our hands, "O, prosper thou our handy work!"

C. C. PINCKNEY,
PETER J. SHAND,
PAUL TRAPIER.

In 1870 the death of the Rev. Christian Hanckel, D.D., was reported by the standing committee and by the Bishop in his annual address. The standing committee says of him: "The oldest of our clergy, he connects us with the Episcopate of Bishop Dehon, by whom, in 1813, as his first official act, he was ordained to the diaconate. As the friend and counsellor of both Bishops Bowen and Gadsden, he took an active part in the affairs of the diocese." His active ministry extended over a period of fifty-seven years, a record of service seldom attained and more seldom exceeded.

Two important reports were made to this Convention, one relating to the duties of vestrymen and the history of the origin and development of vestries, a matter of interest and information to which but little attention is paid by those of today who are elected to serve their respective congregations in this capacity, a circumstance greatly to be regretted. The other report contained a suggested method of organization of new parishes, which has since been in large part adopted as the basis of such organizations in the diocese. The Bishop reported that on July 25, 1869, he had Consecrated the new St. John's Church at Winnsboro, "this being the first Church in the diocese which has been built since the war." He notes the service held at South Santee Nov. 28 of the same year, as participated in by "several of our fellow Christians of both sexes from North Santee, who had labored hard to cross the river to be able once more to go to Church." The Bishop in closing his address, said: "Before I close this address, permit a few remarks from one who has closely observed the condition of the Church in all parts of the Diocese. That there is a crisis upon us cannot be doubted; we are compelled to feel it at every point. The old Church of South Carolina is gone—in those particulars, I mean, that gave especial character to its visibility; but with this there was embodied also, be it remembered, its spiritual and eternal influences. In its old forms and realizations it is more than probable that it can never be established. Its history is fulfilled, its record is on high, and what is written is written;

the reflection carries sadness to many a loving heart, and many a tear has been shed over the desolations of Zion. We are entering then, upon a new era. Shall Zion arise? your hearts reply, she shall! I ask, by whom? Brethren, you who are in the midst of health and life, you who are young and vigorous—clergymen and laymen— this work is yours. Buckle on your armor in the name of Christ and His Church. Trials prove our manhood and sufferings lead to glory. Up, then, to this great work, and rebuild the temple of the Lord. The old men, who are yet lingering upon the walls, stretch out their hands to you and bid you Godspeed". The Bishop gave notice that at the next Convention he would request the election of an assistant Bishop, on the ground of his conviction that his health and strength were not equal to the necessities of the diocese. The next Convention (1871) adopted a scheme for the division of the diocese into five missionary districts, being the first step towards the system of Convocations which subsequently came into operation and still exists, the number of such districts having been reduced from five to three.

The Convention also adopted a scheme for the government of the board of managers of the Advancement Society as the diocesan Board of Missions, providing for three meetings of the board each year to be held at points designated by the Convention, during which a public missionary meeting shall also be held, under the direction of the Bishop or the presiding officer of the board, and providing for the receipt and disbursement of all contributions for diocesan missions, for all annual reports of the same to the Convention, and specifying what churches or missions have been aided by the board during the year and to what extent. Out of this has developed the annual missionary meeting of the Convention on the second evening of its session, a custom that still prevails. On May 13, 1871, on the thirty-fourth ballot, the Rev. William Bell White Howe, rector of St. Philip's Church, Charleston, was elected assistant Bishop of the diocese, his election being, on motion, declared unanimous, and his salary fixed at $3,000.00, the same as that of the Bishop.

In his annual address Bishop Davis mentions a number of matters of interest, such as his visit to St. Andrew's parish, then under the charge of the Rev. John Grimke Drayton, where he confirmed forty colored persons; his visit to Edisto Island where he confirmed seventy-two of them; the remarkable service at St. Stephen's where he confirmed eleven whites and nineteen colored, presented by the Rev. P. F. Stevens and the Rev. J. V. Welch, his assistant.

Several hundred persons were present. He notes that the Church, a colonial one, had not been opened regularly for divine service since 1804, the reason being that the original population, largely churchmen, had removed to other places. He mentions the establishment of the "Monthly Record", a diocesan paper, intended chiefly to disseminate diocesan intelligence, which, through many vicissitudes and several suspensions, has been revived and is now published under the name of "The Diocese".

[Bishop Davis took part in Dr. Howe's Consecration. His last official act was the holding Nov. 19, 1871, of the first service in the new Church building in Camden, preaching the sermon.

[On December 2, 1871, he died at his home in Camden (being succeeded by Bishop Howe, the sixth Bishop of South Carolina). The funeral service was held the next day; Bishop Howe noted in his journal: "December 3d. By special train over the South Carolina Railroad, I attended and officiated at the funeral of the late Bishop, which took place, with every mark of respect on the part of the citizens of Camden, on the 4th of December. There accompanied me of the Clergy from Charleston, Rev. Dr. Marshall, Rev. Messrs. Elliott, Prentiss, Hanckel, and J. Johnson. The Rev. Mr. Babbitt, of Columbia, we found awaiting us, and others of the Clergy would have been with us, but did not reach Camden in time. These clergymen, assisted by the Vestry of Grace Church, Camden, carried your Bishop to his burial in hopes of a joyful resurrection." In 1873, an imposing monument was erected to his memory in Camden by his brethren of the diocese.]

Chapter IV

EPISCOPATE OF BISHOP HOWE
1871-1894

JOHN KERSHAW, D.D.

(With additions by the author in brackets)

[With the death of Bishop Davis on December 2, 1871, began
the tempestuous Episcopate of William Bell White Howe. He has
well been called the "Puritan-Cavalier"—not only in a geographical sense, born in New England and serving in South Carolina, but
because both the character of the Puritan and that of the Cavalier
was illustrated in his strong personality. Elected on May 13, 1871,
he had been Consecrated in St. Paul's Church, Baltimore, on October 8, 1871. The presenters were the Bishops of South Carolina and
Texas; the preacher was the Lord Bishop of Litchfield, England.
The Consecrators were, besides the presiding Bishop and those
mentioned, the Bishops of Nassau, Maryland, and North Carolina.
Thus were united the succession in the two lines, England and
America. Bishop Howe was Consecrated "to assist the Bishop of
South Carolina and to succeed him in case of survivorship."

[The Convention of 1873 met in Grace Church, Camden. The
matter of the purchase of an Episcopal residence in Charleston was
brought before the body, but no action was taken upon it. It was
decided to elect a Registrar to collect and take charge of all publications relating to the history of the Church in the diocese, and
to collect and keep for reference a set of the journals of the general Convention. The Rev. John Johnson was elected to the office.
The canon of vestries was first enacted in 1875. It stipulated that
wardens must be communicants, a qualification not required of
vestrymen until 1925. Bishop Howe did not resign the rectorship
of St. Philip's Church until January 1, 1873.]

The Bishop mentions the formation of a Brotherhood in the diocese, the main purpose of which was to relieve the family of a
deceased clergyman by the members contributing to a fund to be
used for the immediate relief of the family, the members paying
in one dollar each on being notified of a death. The Brotherhood
idea was at first popular and the membership ran into the hun-

dreds, perhaps a thousand, and one can hardly estimate the relief it was to the family of a deceased clergyman to receive within a month or so, such substantial sums as were at first contributed. The Brotherhood's good work covered several years, but by degrees the membership decreased until it became very small and it finally, like so many other good things, passed into oblivion.

Referring to the work of the Church among the colored people, the Bishop said "If our Church is to do any work of moment among this people, it must be done by the Church at large. Let a missionary jurisdiction be erected by the general Convention with express reference to these people and let a missionary Bishop be Consecrated who shall give his whole time and thought to this. He shall organize congregations, provide them with Church schools and pastors, and, in due time, raise up from among the colored people themselves, and to minister to themselves, deacons and priests who shall be educated men, and competent to the work of the ministry". From this position Bishop Howe never varied. The legislation of the General Convention bearing on this subject has fluctuated between the creation of missionary jurisdictions such as he suggested, and the election of Bishops-Suffragan in the dioceses, of their own race, under the diocesan, to minister to them. The latter policy is now being carried out in several of the Southern dioceses, among them South Carolina, North Carolina and East Carolina, which between them support a colored Bishop-Suffragan, who ministers to the colored congregations within these dioceses [1920]. Though fifty years have elapsed since Bishop Howe first enunciated his position on this subject, it cannot be said that the Church at large has definitely committed itself to any one policy. Both schemes as suggested have had and still have their advocates. The present plan of Bishops-Suffragan of their own race is admittedly an experiment as yet. But that Bishop Howe, thus early in his Episcopate, advocated the setting up of a special jurisdiction for the colored people, should disabuse the minds of those who in the heat of controversy subsequently charged him with the desire to ignore racial lines in the Church and break down social barriers.

The Bishop advocates the use of the offertory as a stated part of our public worship, "as much as prayer and praise". "Let us," he said, "attend to it conscientiously, and see to it that our alms and oblations, as well as our prayers, go up as a memorial before God". It is in the records of some of our older parishes that on certain Sundays it was the custom for the wardens to stand at the doors and receive in their hats the alms of the congregation as they passed out. Later on there was an improvement in this respect. The wardens and vestrymen were accustomed to move along the aisles, having a staff with a velvet or silk bag at one end, which they passed to the occupants of the pews to receive their offerings. The staves were then placed in the chancel, but the offerings were never presented as the rubric directs: "whilst these (the offertory sentences are in reading) the Deacons, Church-wardens, or other fit persons appointed for that purpose, shall receive the alms for the poor, and other Devotions of the people in a decent Basin to be provided by the Parish for that purpose; and reverently bring it to the Priest, who shall humbly present and place it upon the Holy Table." This was the rubric for several hundreds of years, but it is only quite recently that its directions have been generally followed in our American Church, and this lost "act of worship" restored to its rightful place in the public services of the Church. A summary of statistics for the year ending May 1, 1873, will be of interest, although they are not complete. Baptisms 696; confirmed 343; communicants, white 3,133, colored 657, total 3,770; clergy 48; contributions $87,438.65, an increase of $35,000.00 over previous year. (But see last paragraph of the report of the committee on the State of the Church, p. 62, Journal 1873.)

The Convention of 1874 met in St. Paul's Church, Charleston. In his address the Bishop spoke of attending the Whitsun celebration of the united Sunday Schools of our Church in Charleston, and adds a word of exhortation to the clergy advocating the catechising of the children in the Church, a custom once quite common but that has now passed generally into a state of noxious desuetude. He mentions his attendance upon the occasion of the celebration of the fiftieth anniversary of the diocese of Georgia, which at one time long prior to its organization as a diocese had been placed under the jurisdiction of Bishops [Smith], Dehon, and Bowen, his venerated predecessors. He speaks also of the formation in St. Philip's, Charleston, and Trinity Church, Columbia, of associations to provide for the support of students preparing for Holy Orders, commending their example to other "principal parishes of the diocese". He alludes with strong words of commendation to the fact that "at most if not all our public institutions for the sick and poor and the guilty of Charleston, we are represented by Christian men and women, who supplement the work of the clergy" in ministering to the souls and bodies of these unfortunates. He speaks also of the character of the times and how necessarily the Church now reflects the condition of things in the State, "broken fortunes, disastrous seasons, mal-administration in civil affairs, will be reflected in impoverished churches, a clergy meagerly supported, and parishes vacant of ministry, or, to put the matter in the words of old Fuller (Church History, A. D. 501), (writing of the British Church in the day of the Saxon inroad): "Needs, then, must religion now in Britian be in doleful condition; for he who expects a flourishing Church in a failing Commonwealth, let him try whether one side of his face can smile when the other is pinched". Yet, as he proceeds to say, "The Church's inner light and life have never burned more brightly than when adverse circumstances passed upon her." Would that it might be so with us. He sees signs of hopefulness in the diocese in the increased number of candidates for Holy Orders, in the evident desire to secure clergymen for vacant parishes, in the disposition, all over the diocese, shown by the laity to engage in Church work, in the increased reverence shown by those who attend public worship.

The Bishop refers with sadness to the withdrawal of the assistant Bishop of Kentucky from the communion of the Church, Bishop George David Cummins, who left the Church to organize the "Reformed Episcopal Church." A more causeless schism never was made. There were those in the Church who believed that they saw tendencies towards Rome in the doctrine and the ritual, as some practiced it, of the Church and the Prayer Book. In their alarms they forsook the Church and set up another schismatical communion. Instead of remaining in the Church and fighting their battle of reform there, they fled from her, forgetting that reformation never has been or can be effected from without, but must take place within the body that is sought to be reformed. To have taken the reforming element out of the Church was like taking the leaven out of bread. . . . "What" asks the Bishop, "is the standing reproach of Christendom at this moment? Are not the divisions and subdivisions of the flock of Christ throughout the world? Why are not Mohammedans and heathens given to the heritage of God and of His Christ? Is it not to a very great extent because there are strifes and contentions in the household of faith? There are the Oriental Churches, and the Churches of the Roman obedience, and the Anglican Churches, and the almost countless names of divided Protestantism, and how, until we are one, and have communion one with another, upon a common basis—the ancient Creeds and the ancient general Council—can we expect an unbelieving world to receive the Gospel of Jesus Christ to the glory of God the Father?"

[On February 8, 1876, the Rev. P. F. Stevens, having defected to the newly organized Reformed Episcopal Church, was deposed from the ministry of this Church. The stories of our parishes reveal the devoted work of this clergyman through many years. He became a Bishop of this Reformed Church. His work in the diocese had included much work among our colored members and many of these followed him into the Reformed Episcopal Church. It has its branch now (1955) in South Carolina with many churches presided over by a white Bishop.]

The Convention of 1875 met in St. Philip's, Charleston. There was an unusually large attendance on the part of the laity, it having been understood that St. Mark's, Charleston, a Church composed of persons of color, would apply for admission into union with the Convention, the first application of that sort coming from such a source in the history of the diocese, and to the granting of which it was generally understood many were strongly opposed.

The Convention adopted the report of the general committee "On times for special Offerings" appointed previously. The days and objects fixed were, for Foreign Missions the first Sunday after the Epiphany; Domestic Missions, second Sunday in Lent; Home Commission (work among the colored people), second Sunday after Trinity; Advancement Society, first Sunday after Easter; Candidates for Orders, Bishop's Visitation; University of the South, third Sunday in Advent; Society for Relief of Widows and Orphans of the Clergy, Whitsunday. With a few modifications there continued to be the objects for which special offerings were taken until the nationwide campaign of 1919, when these and other diocesan and extra-diocesan purposes were otherwise provided for. Reference is made in the Bishop's address to the establishment of a "House of Rest" for convalescents and incurables in the City of Charleston, under Church supervision. . . . He refers also to the recent celebration in St. Philip's Church of the first planting of the Church of England on these shores, "nearly if not quite two hundred years ago." It was an occasion of great interest. By request of the Convention the Bishop's sermon and the historical address of Mr. J. J. Pringle Smith, accompanied by an account of the preparatory proceedings and of the arrangements for the service held at the commemoration, with other pertinent matter, were published in book form, to perpetuate a substantial record of the occasion.

In the memorable Convention of 1876, which met in Trinity Church, Columbia, the matter of chief interest coming before it was the application of St. Mark's Church, Charleston, to be admitted into union with the Convention. This, therefore, is the proper place for the insertion of the account hereinbefore referred to, taken from the journals of the Convention, covering the period 1876-88, in which, in one form or another, came up the question of the relations of the colored members of the Church in the diocese to the Convention thereof, and other questions arising out of these relations.

COLORED CHURCHMEN AND THE CONVENTION

In order to understand clearly the profound feeling disclosed by many members of the Convention when St. Mark's Church applied [May 13, 1875] to be admitted into union therewith, which if consented to would have led to the admission of colored lay delegates to the enjoyment of "all the privileges of the Convention", it must be remembered that South Carolina, in common with all the other States composing the Southern Confederacy, had been for seven years subjected to the intolerable experience of the Reconstruction era. Indignities had been heaped upon the white people of the State such as could not but exasperate and inflame them against those who had come into power through the votes of the recently enfranchised "persons of color" who outnumbered the whites in the proportion of nine to six. These State officials were for the most part not natives but men who had come into the State after the war for purposes of plunder, and who used the colored vote to further their ends. There were others, natives indeed, but, with few exceptions, selfish and self-seeking also, who united with the "carpetbaggers" to plunder and oppress the whites, who owned practically all the property and paid all the taxes. The orgy of misrule, oppression and plunder had been going on with cumulative energy and thoroughness for seven years when St. Mark's applied for admission into union with the Convention. It is not surprising that an application unprecedented in this diocese, presented at such a time, should have been met by opposition. It was felt by many that the occasion called for unusual caution and careful inquiry, and the entire subject-matter was referred to a special commission to report to the next Convention. By the time that Convention met, the spirit of the white people of the State had been aroused to the pitch of stern resolution to overthrow the political party then in power, and redeem the State from the tyranny and degradation it had suffered at the hands of those who had so long misgoverned and laid it waste. No more unpropitious time could have been selected for a calm and dispassionate consideration of such a question. Comparatively few are now living [1920] who went through the war 1861-65 and the period of so-called reconstruction that followed it, and who, therefore, can adequately conceive of the intensity and the universality of the wave of passionate desire and determination that swept over the State for its political redemption, in 1876. Those who can remember all that occurred during that momentous year, will agree that it was no time for quiet consideration of, and cool judgment upon, any subject that involved the discussion of questions of the relations of the two races that made up the body politic. But, as in duty bound, the special commission reported to the Convention, three of them uniting in a report recommending that St. Mark's application be not granted while the other two made separate reports favoring its admission. Of the seven members of the commission originally appointed, one had removed from the diocese in the interim and one had become incapacitated through illness, leaving five to act. It was conceded that as originally composed a majority of the commission favored the proposed measure, but for the reason stated the minority became the majority. The majority report in recommending that St. Mark's application be not granted, gave the following as their reasons:

1. Because the admission of all other colored congregations must follow that of St. Mark's, as there is no sound reason for making it an exception; and in the opinion of the undersigned the Church is bound to recognize, in all its relations to the world, and its offices to mankind, that distinction between the races of men which God has been pleased to ordain, and to conform its polity and ecclesiastical organisms to His divine ordinance.

2. Because our colored population are, at this time, and must, for a long time to come, be a missionary field, and our Right Reverend Fathers in God have already taken the matter in hand, and will, probably, make ample provision for them and other races within our territorial limits.

3. Because, in the opinion of the undersigned, St. Mark's congregation cannot now send delegates competent to act as legislators for our diocese.

4. Because their admission may drive away some of the Churches now in our union, and make others indifferent to preserving their connection with this Convention.

5. Because the members of St. Mark's congregation can, without their admission to this body, enjoy every catholic Christian right: and their introduction to our representative legislative body involves their participation in powers they are not prepared to exercise advantageously to the Church in the diocese.

The Rev. James H. Elliott, D.D., a member of the commission, made a separate report. While favoring the application for the admission of St. Mark's, he offered no resolution to that effect, nor did he sum up his reasons as the majority had. It is therefore necessary to resort to the report itself for the reasons influencing him in favoring the application.

1. Because, in asking to be admitted into union with this Convention, St. Mark's is only asking for what would be granted, as a matter of course, to a white congregation possessing the same constitutional and canonical qualifications.

2. Because, since the Convention itself has the power to grant or deny such applications as this, if it should be threatened at any time by the apprehended danger of a large number of like applications, "we can shut our doors" against them.

3. Because, in such bodies as this, social considerations should not enter. If the members of a congregation are fit to be in the Church of Christ, their delegates are fit to be here.

4. Because in several Southern dioceses colored clergymen and delegates from colored congregations had been admitted to the privileges of diocesan Conventions, and no such ill results as were apprehended had followed their admission. To refuse St. Mark's application would be to raise a barrier against the Church work among persons of color, and to yield to prejudices of class and education.

Dr. Elliott also gave a brief statement of the history of St. Mark's Church. It was founded in May, 1865. It first worshipped, by permission in the Orphan House Chapel, the orphan children being then in Orangeburg. It then purchased the wooden chapel in which St. Luke's congregation had formerly worshipped, and called the Rev. J. B. Seabrook, a white clergyman, as its rector. The first motion towards applying for union with the Convention was in 1866. Bishop Davis counselled delay. In 1872 they approached Bishop Howe on the subject. He also advised delay. In 1875, with the Bishop's sanction, they made application, after waiting for ten years since the organization of the congregation.

The Rev. C. C. Pinckney, D.D., another member of the commission, also made a separate report. Its main points may be thus summed up. He began with a review of "our former relations to the colored race", referring to the missionary system in operation among the Negroes, by which the Gospel was preached to them either by our parochial clergy or by others especially devoted to their service. He refers to the fact that under this system nearly one-half of our 5,000 communicants were colored. He favored the admission of St. Mark's on the ground that they had complied with the canonical requirements. He thought their admission would bind them more firmly to our Church, while to repel them would weaken our hold upon them and upon the colored race in South Carolina. He suggested that in view of the wide range of the question under consideration, the Church at large should advise some measure that would best enable us to fulfill our mission to the colored race. He found this in the proposed action of the general Convention to ordain missionary Bishops or Suffragans "for different tongues and races in the United States". Meanwhile he does not see our right to reject St. Mark's application either legally or morally, nor does he see the "imminence of any such dangers as some anticipate" from its admission. He submitted the following resolutions, viz.:

Resolved, That the application of St. Mark's Church for admission to union with this Convention be granted.

Resolved, That this Convention memorialize the general Convention to provide missionary or Suffragan Bishops, for the spiritual oversight of the colored race.

It was, after these reports had been read, agreed that the Bishop, at his request, be heard on the question and the vote be then taken without further debate. Bishop Howe stated that in his opinion if "we reject the application of St. Mark's, we shall, as a Convention, make a serious mistake, not only in reference to Church principles, but likewise in regard to the lower ground of expediency." He cited the canon of the diocese which declared "that any Church so organized and recognized (i. e., organized according to the canon and recognized by the ecclesiastical authority) shall be an integral part of the Church in this diocese, whether admitted into union with the Convention or not." He argued that, according to this principle, to deny admission into union with the Convention, on the ground of race, a congregation complying with all the requirements of the Constitution and canons of the diocese, would be "to do a most uncatholic act, and register the Church in this diocese as the Church of a caste." He asked, "Why refuse such a congregation admission? Are they not a part of the Church? Is it not a foundation principle of this Church that the laity shall have a voice in its councils? And do you not go counter to this conceded principle, if you refuse it to laymen because of African descent?" At the conclusion of the Bishop's address, a vote was taken by orders on the first resolution offered by Dr. Pinckney. It resulted as follows: Of the Clergy, ayes 17; nays 9; Of the Laity, ayes 12; nays 17; divided 2. So the resolution was not adopted.

It will be observed that the issue at this time was whether lay delegates from a congregation composed of colored persons should be admitted to the privileges of the Convention (which would be the result of the admission of St. Mark's into union with the Convention) if that congregation had complied with all the requirements of the Constitution and canons of the Church in this diocese. But it was inevitable that the decided differences of opinion as expressed in the vote as given, should lead to subsequent discussion which aroused much antagonism and feeling in the diocese, and although there never was any renewal by St. Mark's of their application to be admitted into union with the Convention, even down to this day [1920], yet the agitation of the questions involved continued. It had a depressing effect upon diocesan life and activity, as the records of that period show, and the strained relations between pastors and people induced by their being on opposite sides of the question, not seldom resulted in a severance of those relations. Altogether it may be characterized as a period of distrust and suspicion, of severed friendships and divisions among these who had been united.

The matter, so far as the Convention was concerned, slumbered and slept until 1885, when two colored clergymen having come into the diocese and taken work at St. Mark's, Charleston, and St. Luke's, Columbia (another colored congregation organized in the meantime), were reported on the roll of the clergy by the Bishop. The Committee on the Roll of the Clergy reported the accuracy of the list and recommended concurrence. A motion was made to amend the report by striking out the names of the two colored clergymen and referring the question of their eligibility to membership in the Convention to a committee of five—two clergymen and three laymen—to report to the next Convention. This was sought to be amended later so as to read that the committee should report "whether or no any other than white delegates have a legal and constitutional right to be admitted to membership of the Convention of the diocese of South Carolina." On a motion to amend by striking out all after the names of the two colored clergymen, a discussion ensued, pending which a motion was made to lay the whole subject on the table. A vote by orders was called for and taken, resulting in nonconcurrence. A similar vote was then taken on the motion to amend the original resolution, resulting also in non-concurrence of orders. These votes revealed the same divergence of opinion between the clergy and the laity as existed when the question of the admission of St. Mark's into union with the Convention came up nine years before. Notice was given of a protest against the seating of colored clergymen in the Convention. It was presented the next day. The first ground of protest was against the action of the Convention in refusing to consider a motion to adopt the report of the Committee on the Credentials of the Clergy, as being unparliamentary and illegal, and as drawing into question the very organization of the Convention itself. The second ground of protest was against the position announced by the President and acted upon practically by the Convention, *viz.*: that by virtue of their names being on the Bishop's list and reported upon by the Committee on Credentials, the two colored clergymen were entitled to occupy seats in the Convention. The third ground of protest was against the action of the Convention in affirming that under our Constitution and laws persons of color and not belonging to the white race are entitled to seats upon the floor of this Convention and participation in the government of the Church in this diocese; whereas it is respectfully submitted by these protestants that such an innovation in the government of the Church can and should be effected only by the consent of the Church, expressed unequivocally at a Convention, after a full, fair, calm and deliberate discussion of the question on its merits.

The protest was signed by three clergymen and thirty laymen, members of the Convention, some representing entire delegations from parishes, others delegations in part, and others individually.

One layman presented his individual protest, first against the failure of the Convention to adjudicate the question whether the two colored clergymen "are constitutionally entitled to seats in this Convention", second against "the declaration, by their votes, of the majority of the clerical delegates to this Convention" that the two colored clergymen "are so entitled, as being based upon an unfair and erroneous interpretation of the language of the Constitution and the canons."

No action was taken on these protests. The next year, after the roll of the clergy and the roll of deputies had been called and it appeared that a quorum of both orders was present, the president as directed by canon, declared the Convention to be duly organized, and the committees on the list of the clergy and on the credentials of deputies, were appointed. He then appointed the regular standing committees, after which, according to the rules of order, he announced that the next business in order was the election of a secretary. At this juncture a lay delegate asked if the chair ruled that the Convention was so organized as to proceed to all its business. The chair announced that he so ruled. An appeal was taken from the decision of the chair. Pending the discussion of the appeal, the Committee on the List of Clergy reported the correctness of the list. According to the Journal (1886) no action was taken on this report. The next day the committee on the list of lay delegates presented their report:

First, That they find the lay deputies, whose names appear on the list furnished by the secretary, to be duly elected.

Second, That in addition to these, certificates from deputies from four other parishes had been received by the committee, and they recommended that the names of these deputies be added to the secretary's list as being duly elected.

On a motion to adopt the report, the chair held the motion out of order except as to the recommendations of the report. Appeal was made from this decision. On motion to that effect, the report of the Committee on the List of the Clergy was read again, and it was then moved to adopt the report. The chair ruled the motion out of order on the ground that the Convention having been declared duly organized, the clergy were seated under the provisions of the Constitution and canons, and not by a direct vote of the Convention. An appeal was taken from this decision. The chair stated that he held the same principle to apply to the roll of deputies as to the list of the clergy, viz.: that they were entitled to seats upon their credentials, and not upon the vote of the body. Pending the discussion of the two appeals, the Convention adjourned. The next morning, after further discussion, a vote by orders was taken on the question of sustaining the decision of the chair as to the list of the clergy, resulting as follows: Of the Clergy, Aye, 24; Nay, 4; Of the Laity, Aye, 9, casting the vote of five parishes; Nay, 46, casting the vote of twenty-six parishes; Divided, 1. So the decision of the chair was not sustained. The question recurred upon the motion to confirm (instead of adopt) the report of the Committee on Credentials of the Clergy. On a vote by orders, there was a non-concurrence and the motion was declared lost. On a vote to reconsider there was the same non-concurrence. It was then moved that "the clergymen whose names were referred to the Committee on the Clergy list be declared entitled to all the privileges of this Convention, according to the classification of the report of the committee". A vote by orders was taken resulting as follows, *viz.*: Clergy, Aye 11; Nay 8; declining to vote 8; Laity, Aye 43, representing 27 parishes; Nay 1.

On motion to declare the laymen whose names were referred to the Committee on Credentials of Lay Delegates, entitled to the privileges of the Convention, according to the report of said committee, the same was adopted without division. Several amendments to the Constitution and Canons, bearing on the organization of the Convention, were proposed and referred to the appropriate committees.

This ended the matter for that year, but it was well understood that in the Convention to follow, the whole question would again be revived. Since the previous Convention the two colored clergymen, whose rights in Convention had been questioned, had removed from the diocese, and the subject-matter of discussion now related to the organization of the Convention itself. On the one hand it was contended that until the reports of the committees on the clergy list and the credentials of the lay deputies had been accepted and confirmed, the Convention was not fully organized. On the other hand it was contended that the clergy took their places in Convention not as delegates or deputies but by virtue of their being clergymen and conforming to the requirements of the Constitution and Canons; that in Convention they represent their order but not their congregations, and hence are not delegates or deputies as the laymen are; that the only questions which may rightly be asked in regard to their title to the privileges of the Convention are these, *viz.*: Are they recognized and listed by the ecclesiastical authority as clergymen of the diocese? Has that authority reported them correctly as having conformed to constitutional and canonical requirements as to their being entitled to both seats and votes, or to seats only? If these questions are answered affirmatively, the rights of the clergy in Convention cannot lawfully be denied them. And, as regards the rights of the laity in Convention, it was contended that after the roll of the clergy as handed in by the Bishop and the list of lay deputies in the secretary's hands had been called, and a quorum of both orders ascertained to be present, and the Convention declared to be duly organized, the clergy and the lay deputies were seated on the strength of their credentials and not by direct vote of the Convention. It was conceded also that had it not been for the presence of the two colored clergymen in Convention the year before, and the apprehension that there would be more of them coming in, no question would have been made involving the organization of the Convention, nor of the right and title of either clergymen or laymen (as deputies), to the privileges of the Convention, if they had complied with the requirements of the Constitution and Canons.

Thus matters stood when the Convention of 1887 met in St. Philip's Church, Charleston. Meantime one colored clergyman had come into the diocese. His name appeared on the roll of the clergy as entitled to a seat but not a vote in Convention, the reason being that he had not then resided for twelve calendar months in the diocese—a constitutional provision. When the Committee on the Roll of the Clergy reported, it was moved to accept their report. An amendment was offered to strike out the name of the colored clergyman. On this amendment, three of the clergy voted aye, 25 nay. The lay vote stood—aye 38, casting the vote of 23 parishes; nay 12, voting for eight parishes. It was then moved to divide the question on the adoption of the report, so as to take the vote first upon those reported as entitled to all the privileges of the Convention. On a vote by orders, there was a non-concurrence, and the motion was lost. The question was then taken by orders on the motion to accept the report. The same result followed as before. On a motion to refer a part of the Bishop's address to a committee, the mover was called to order on the ground that the Convention was not properly organized. The chair ruled that the motion to refer was in order, the Convention having been declared "duly organized". An appeal was taken from this ruling. On the question, "Shall the decision of the chair stand?," 22 clergy voted "aye" and two "nay". Of the laity, 14 "aye", representing eight parishes, 31 "nay", representing 19 parishes. The chair directed the secretary to proceed with the reading of the rules of order. Objection was made that the Convention was not fully organized. The chair overruled the objection. An appeal was taken from this decision. The chair refused to entertain the appeal, the Convention, according to canon, having been declared "duly organized", and the reading of the rules of order having been, on motion, dispensed with, the election of a secretary, being the next business in order, was proceeded with. No one who was present can fail to remember the tenseness of the atmosphere at this moment. It was felt by all that a crisis had come. The silence that prevailed was broken by the secretary's reading of the following notice: "The lay delegates from St. Paul's Church, Charleston (Radcliffeboro), to the Diocesan Convention, finding it impracticable to organize the Convention according to the directions of the Constitution and Canons of the Church, deem it wise to withdraw from the said Convention, and hereby notify their colleagues of their intention." After the reading of this notice, the lay deputies from St. Paul's withdrew. They were followed by their colleagues from twelve parishes. One clergyman also withdrew. When all had withdrawn who desired to do so, the roll of parishes was called to ascertain if a quorum was still present. It being ascertained that there was a quorum present, the Convention proceeded with its business. The next day, the rolls of both the clergy and the parishes were called and a quorum being present in both orders, the business went on according to the rules of order. During the day the Convention unanimously adopted a resolution offered by one of the clergy, as follows, viz.: "Resolved, That this Convention profoundly regrets the action of the deputies from certain parishes in withdrawing from the Convention yesterday evening, and affectionately and most earnestly requests their brethren to reconsider their action and resume their seats in the Convention."

This was conveyed to the brethren who had withdrawn by a committee appointed for that purpose. They returned bearing the following communication, viz.: "Resolved, That we accede to the request submitted to us by the committee: provided, that when we return and resume our seats in the Convention the President of the Convention shall entertain the appeal taken yesterday, and shall forthwith put the question to the Convention."

The following resolution was then adopted by the Convention: "Resolved, That the Convention, having heard the report of the committee appointed to wait on our brethren who withdrew yesterday evening, regrets that it finds itself unable to accede to the proviso contained in their response to our appeal."

This ended negotiations between the Convention and those who had withdrawn for that year. In 1888 the Convention met in Anderson. A resolution was offered for the appointment of a commission to prepare a constitutional amendment providing for the separation of the colored people (members of this church) into a distinct organization, under the Bishop. A more extended preamble and resolutions, bearing on the same subject, offered by another member of the Convention and accepted by the mover of the first resolution referred to, was unanimously adopted.

After reciting the fact that the great problem was yet unsolved, which had been agitating the diocese for thirteen years, resulting in the alienation of the clergy and laity, and the withdrawal of several parishes from the Convention, and that the interests of Christ and His Church, among both races, are placed thereby in great jeopardy, so that we have been forced to the conclusion that the absolute necessity has arisen for the separate organization of the two races in this diocese, therefore,

Resolved (a) That in the judgment of this Convention such a separation, entire and complete, is now essential;

(b) That a committee of three clergymen and three laymen, with the Bishop as chairman, be appointed to "effect the separation", to report to the next Convention;

(c) That this committee be requested to confer with the vestries of the four organized colored congregations in the diocese, and with the clergy, for the purpose of effecting the complete separation, into two complete organizations, under the Bishop of the diocese.

The relief felt by the Convention as a consequence of this action which promised to pave the way for a reconciliation between brethren so long estranged, and for the peace of the diocese, was expressed by uniting in singing "Gloria in Excelsis".

The next year several of the parishes whose delegates had withdrawn from the Convention of 1887, were represented in the Convention. They united in a statement to the effect that in view of the resolutions contemplating a separate organization for the colored people, they would waive the question of the legality of the Convention of 1888 "and take their seats in this body".

It is noteworthy that in 1888 the reports of the committees on the clergy list and the credentials of deputies, were, on motion, "received", and that in 1889 they were "accepted", thus removing all objections previously made relating to the organization of the Convention. The commission, raised the year previous to provide for a separate organization for the colored people under the Bishop, made their report. It provided for the foundation of a "missionary district" to be composed of "all congregations and missions of colored persons within the limits of this diocese"; for a "Convocation of such district" to be composed of delegates from such congregations and missions as shall come into the organization thus provided for. In the conference that took place between the members of the commission and the colored clergy and laity, they failed to come to an agreement, but the proposed legislation was strongly disapproved by the colored clergy and laity present, with the exception of the laymen from one congregation [St. Luke's, Columbia]. The commission also reported certain amendments to the Constitution which provided that only such clergymen as were in charge of congregations in union with the Convention, and had been resident in the diocese for one year next before the meeting of Convention, and had complied with other ordinary requirements of the Constitutions and canons, should be entitled to all the privileges of the Convention, but it provided also that no clergyman who was entitled to a seat and a vote or a seat only in the Convention of 1889, should be deprived of those rights "by reason of anything in this section contained". This protected the rights and privileges of the one colored clergyman who was then in the Convention. No application for admission into union with the Convention by congregations of colored persons has since been made. The separation provided for has continued to the present time [1920]. The Convocation meets annually under the presidency of the Bishop. All the colored clergy with the exception of the rector of St. Mark's; and representatives of all the colored congregations in the diocese, with the exception of St. Mark's, attend it. The work has gone forward notably under the scheme as outlined in 1889. All the congregations whose representatives withdrew from the Convention of 1887 are now 1920 and for many years have been, represented in our annual Conventions, although several of them continued to send no deputies for some time after this compromise had been effected.

Thus ended a controversy which greatly affected the life of the Church in South Carolina for more than a decade, threatening it with disaster. That both parties to it were actuated by strong and sincere convictions cannot be doubted. That either party always or even often understood the other is equally apparent from the history as given. That all concerned breathed a sigh of relief when it was over is the testimony of the survivors of that trying time, when brethren certainly did not dwell together in unity. That the agitation extended far beyond the borders of this diocese and had its decided influence upon the Church at large, is evinced by the fact that ever since that time the question has been before the General Convention in one form or another, and that even now

[1920] the policy of the Church with regard to it is not settled. (See below "In the Convention of 1889 held at Aiken" p. 109.)

The Bishop in his address [1876] referring to the impoverished condition of many of the parishes in the coastal region of the diocese, and of the necessity of taking some action whereby the ministrations of the Church might be maintained in them, advocated that "some of our Lay Readers (in this section) take Deacon's orders and serve the Church in this higher capacity, still continuing their secular calling so as to secure a support". To this suggestion there was but one response (speaking subject to correction). This was made by Mr. Benjamin Allston of Georgetown County, whose secular business was rice-planting. After a service of some length as deacon, he was advanced to the priesthood in which he served until his death. The Bishop refers also to the canon on missions passed in 1875, in which it was provided that instead of making the Advancement Society through its Board of Managers, the missionary agency and arm of the diocese, which, since 1869, it had been, there should be a Board of Missions to be composed of the Bishop and eight members, four clergymen and four laymen, two from the diocese at large and two each from the three Convocational districts into which the diocese is divided; providing also for a missionary meeting of the Convention, to be held on one evening during the annual session thereof—substantially the same as is now held at each annual meeting.

In this address, in advocating more frequent celebrations of the Holy Communion, the Bishop delivered a most illuminating interpretation of those holy mysteries. In part he said (Sec. pp. 78 et seq., Journal 1876). 'We have . . . in the Eucharist both an altar and a table—the altar looks toward God, because on it are the duly authenticated representatives and memorials of our Lord's most blessed Body and Blood; and we have a table, because on it is the Lord's Supper, whereof we partake to the refreshing of our souls, as our bodies are refreshed by the bread and wine. Now we are apt to dwell most on the Holy Eucharist as a *supper*, because it may be that under this aspect it comes more home to us and our needs, or because we fear lest in any way we may obscure the One Sacrifice of the Cross. But the Godward aspect of the Eucharist, wherein is a true memorial-sacrifice, because it points back to the Cross and its Death, and represents on earth what is ever going on within the veil, where our Lord continually offers Himself to the Father—surely this most soul-touching aspect of the great Sacrament must not be slighted, if we would rightly divide the

Word of God. Every true prayer pleads the merits of Jesus—how much more, then, the great act which he has bequeathed to His Church. This is that pure offering which the Church delights to offer continually. No taint attaches to it, as to our alms, deeds, prayers, and other services, through the evil that is within us, because God himself sanctifies the elements of bread and wine, and when the Church offers them back to Him, they are what He Himself has made them—meet memorials of His Son's Body and Blood. . . . As we stand before the altar, so will we think of Him before the throne; and as we break the bread and bless the cup, we will do it in honor of, and by way of memorial of, that precious Body, bruised upon the Cross, but now in Heaven, as a pledge and earnest of our reconciliation; and when we afterwards eat and drink of the Supper of the Lord, we will do it, not asking *how* but content with knowing that we eat His Flesh and drink His Blood, whereby He dwells in us and we in Him."

The year 1877 found the country in a very depressed financial condition, which was reflected in the current contributions to Church purposes. The Bishop stated in his annual address that the general Board of Missions had not been able to make an appropriation for work in this diocese. Two churches, however, were Consecrated, Prince Frederick's Chapel, Pee Dee, and All Saints', Prince William's parish. The Bishop said this fact had "refreshed his soul". He refers to the erection of St. Luke's Theological Hall at Sewanee by Mrs. Manigault, a former member of this diocese then resident in England. [Mrs. Manigault also endowed a theological scholarship for S. C. students at Sewanee.] He stresses Sunday observance. Sure as he was that God cannot be pleased with such an observance of the day as to make its weekly return a burden and grief to our children, yet he discerned the dangers that arose out of indifference and laxity, more than of austerity. Let the social part, the reception, the public promenade, the drive, be given to other days of the week. Neglect or misuse of the Lord's day will tell with disastrous effect upon our spiritual life and character. Purity in public life grows out of purity in family life and spiritual instruction. We rob our own souls if we secularize our Sundays.

In the little more than four decades that have elapsed since those words were penned the secularizing of Sunday has proceeded apace. In the minds of very many the day possesses no sanctity whatever, but is reckoned as a day entirely to be given to physical rest, recreation and dissipation. It is a general condition that promises to become worse before a reaction sets in that shall re-establish the day in the place where it belongs in the religious life of Christian people.

The Bishop "in that spirit of self-abnegation that has character-ized all his acts since he has assumed the Episcopate," mindful of the stringency of the times, desired his salary to be reduced one-fourth, "so as to relieve the parishes from any contributions towards the payment" thereof (Jour. 1877, p. 50). Very properly the request was not complied with.

The working of the recently organized diocesan Board of Mis-sions is dwelt upon at some length by the Bishop. He showed that up to the time of the meeting of the Convention of 1878, the board had been but the "almoner of the Advancement Society", which for twenty-five years had been the missionary agency of the dio-cese, and he suggested that if this was to continue to be the sole function of the board, it would be better to restore the society to its former place and abolish the board. But this would be to cease to stress "the broad and fundamental principle that every member of the Church is a member of a missionary organization" and under obligation to contribute thereto—a principle asserted by the General Convention of 1835, by which our General Board of Missions was created. He therefore advocates the making of more than one annual offering for diocesan missions, and urges upon the parochial clergy the duty of bringing the subject earnestly before their con-gregation. This appeal of the Bishop met its response in the action of the Convention whereby collections for diocesan missions were, for many years on "fifth Sundays", whenever the same occurred.

Notice is taken of the action of the General Convention of 1877 in regard to the proposal to change the name of the Church in this country so as better to express the fact of its Apostolic and Catholic lineage, showing that the proposal was emphatically refused. So with the proposal to authorize "shortened services", which all seemed to regard as desirable but nevertheless declined to authorize them. The canon on Marriage and Divorce was considered by the Bishop in his address. He said: "The sanctity of the marriage-tie, and its indissolubility, save for the one cause named (adultery), lies at the very basis of Christian society, and one of the most startling signs of the times, foreboding the destruction of the family is the levity with which, in many parts of the country, it is dis-solved, and that, too, under the sanction of law. . . . It may be that we in this diocese do not need the remonstrance of the canon as much as do others, owing to the healthier traditions of the past, which in this State, to its high honor be it said, forbade divorce for any cause. But let us remember that one generation does not live forever. Those who made the laws and those who grew up under them, are fast passing away, and what shall prevent the rising generation in this State from learning their lessons at the lips of those who teach that marriage, so far from making a man and a woman 'one flesh', is nothing better than a partnership, which may be dissolved with ease and without sin".

He refers also to the fact of the repeal by the Legislature of the law permitting divorce. By way of explanation it should be said that during the Reconstruction period, while the control of the State was in the hands of carpetbaggers and Negroes, a law permitting divorce in certain cases had been passed, but almost as soon as possible after that control had been wrested from those who had debauched it, this stigma upon our unbroken tradition in this particular was removed. Of those who availed themselves of the law permitting divorce, while it remained of force, very few availed themselves—a striking tribute to the prevailing sentiment of the people of the State. [But alas! within a generation (1949) South Carolina was to surrender to the spirit of the age.] This year there was also inaugurated the assuming of the support, by the several dioceses of the South, of the theological department of the University of the South.

[In 1878 Bishop Howe in his annual address emphasized the importance of an incorporated body with whom would be entrusted the possessions of the diocese. Committees were appointed by the Conventions, but it was not until February 20, 1880, that the movement culminated in the incorporation by the Legislature of the "Bishop and Standing Committee" as such holding body. This plan continued until 1899, when a separate body known as the "Trustees of the Diocese" was constituted by the Convention of 1899. The controlling canon was adopted in 1902, and on February 20, 1902, the Legislature amended the Act of 1880 transferring the incorporation of the "Bishop and Standing Committee" to the new body of trustees as it exists today. Its first meeting was held October 5, 1899.]

The Rev. J. D. McCollough, as chairman of a committee appointed to report upon the parishes and Churches of the diocese, submitted their report, which was ordered to be published. From it we learn that there were of parishes and Churches in union with the Convention at that date, 56; of congregations and Churches not in union with the Convention, 4; of dormant parishes and

Churches, 13; of extinct parishes and Churches, 4. (Jour. 1879, pp. 31-33.) Mention is made of the death of the Rev. Joseph R. Walker, rector of St. Helena, Beaufort, for fifty-five years—a long and fruitful ministry. Under his ministry very many were led to the Saviour, and as many as twenty-five or more, from that single parish, have entered Holy Orders.

The importance of making provisions for the holding of property deeded to the Church, is brought to the Convention's attention. It seems that there were instances in which property, intended to inure to the benefit of the diocese, had been conveyed to "the Bishop and his successors in office." From an eminent lawyer the Bishop had received the opinion that, in this country, such a conveyance did not convey the entire legal estate, and therefore that the intention of the donors of such property might sometimes be defeated. Hence the need for a holding body of *trustees*—a need that has since been filled in the manner suggested, authorized by the State legislature and regulated by canon law of the diocese.

At the close of this decade, there were 44 clergy at work in the diocese; number of families reported, 2,006; whole number of souls, 7,395; communicants, 4,455; total contributions, $65,474.19. Offerings for diocesan Board of Missions, $1,835.02.

In 1880 there came before the Convention a memorial from Sewanee in reference to the proposed provincial system then pending in the House of Bishops, whereby the ten dioceses at that time united in the support of the University of the South would be separated and divided among three of the four provinces proposed, a step that it was feared would work to the prejudice of the institution. The committee on the memorial made an elaborate report, reviewing the history of provinces from the beginning. Their conclusions are presented in the resolutions accompanying the report. The first resolution was to the effect that the provincial plan, as proposed, was unwise and calculated more to aggravate difficulties than to meet them, in reference to the welfare and advancement of the Church in the United States. The second resolution requested our deputies to General Convention to present this protest and give it their support. A third resolution was adopted to the effect that this Convention is not now prepared to admit that the General Convention has the power to divide the territory of the United States by arbitrary lines into separate provinces, an assertion of diocesan rights as against those of the whole Church, altogether in keeping with the principles that South Carolina as a State had always maintained in regard to the powers of the general government.

An interesting detail of the Bishop's address (Jour. 1880, pp. 54, 55) was that relating to the condition of the diocese in regard to clerical supply and the maintenance of public worship. It was shown that of Churches in union with the Convention there were six that were vacant, fifteen that had a monthly service "by a non-resident clergyman", and twelve of them had service on other Sundays conducted by lay readers, that in dormant Churches not in union with the Convention, numbering five, similar services were held, and that in five others no services of any sort were held. It must be remembered that during this period the controversy was still in progress, arising out of the application in 1875 of St. Mark's Church, Charleston, for admission into union with the Convention, and that conditions in the diocese were such as to offer no attractions to clergy from without to accept work in South Carolina, but rather tended to deplete the ranks of those then canonically connected with the diocese. This would account in part for the spiritual destitution then prevailing.

Reference is made by the Bishop to his having been in charge of the Church of the Holy Communion, Charleston, while its rector, the Rev. Dr. Porter, was absent in England soliciting aid for the Holy Communion Church Institute. Another matter of interest touched upon by the Bishop in his address related to the manner of conducting the services in St. Luke's Chapel and St. Augustine's Chapel at Sewanee. St. Luke's was the chapel attached to the hall of the Theological Department, while St. Augustine's was the university chapel. It appears that rumors had been circulated to the effect that the ritual observances in these chapels were rather advanced in character, and considerable uneasiness had been excited thereby in the minds of some of Sewanee's trustees and patrons. The Bishops present investigated the reports and united in giving the assurance that the services in the two chapels were in strict accordance with the Book of Common Prayer, and in no way countenanced the charge of ritualism made against the University. At the same meeting of the Bishops it was decided that the practice of turning to the East in singing the "Gloria" and in saying the Creed had better be omitted, as furnishing a possible ground of offense to some who ought to be enlisted in behalf of the University.

The death of the Rev. Alexander Glennie in 1880 called forth this remark by the Bishop: "The good Minister is not, for God takes him, and as his body is borne to its burial, what touches me most are not the bells of Georgetown and the flags at half-mast, but the many colored people on the Waccamaw, who come from the neighboring plantations, to honor their old pastor in his burial, and in memory of faithful labors of other years, when he sought their spiritual good in heat and cold, in sunshine and in storm."

He notes the opening of the Caroline Wilkinson Home in connection with the Church of the Holy Communion, for ladies in reduced circumstances, and mentions the other institutions of like character in the City, viz.: The Church Home on Laurens street; the St. Philip's Church Home; and the House of Rest on Ashley Avenue, as evidence that "we are not unmindful of our brethren". He mentions that there were "in building some nine or ten Churches and Chapels". He wishes the diocese would relieve the general Board of Missions of the small appropriation it was making to "aid clergymen serving white congregations." [This goal was not reached until 1930.] He alludes to the formation of the American Church Building Fund Commission, an organization that has done much for the erection of churches and rectories in most if not all of the dioceses and missionary jurisdictions of the American Church. This diocese, it may be said, has profited very largely by the generosity of the commission. He speaks at length upon the subject of *duelling*, the matter having been brought conspicuously before the Church and the State by the recent death in a duel of a prominent citizen of South Carolina. He shows how inconsistent with the Christian man's profession the practice of duelling is and urges with great force and earnestness the abstention by churchmen from it. It may be added that the "catastrophe which rocked the State from end to end", resulted in the formation of such public sentiment and consequent legislative enactment, that there has never been another duel fought on South Carolina soil.

[In 1882 the Committee on the State of the Church sees progress in the diocese, but much ground unoccupied—low salaries being again the cause—28 out of 48 clergymen in the diocese received less than $500.00 salary, lack of candidates for orders, but more lay readers, more building of churches, organs, and parsonages. Resolutions were adopted at this Convention, advocating the Christian education of the colored people of the South, saying that to make "this Church effective among them, it is essential that they should have a ministry from their own race near them in habits and feelings," and requesting the Bishop and Standing Committee to devise such canonical measures as will make this practicable, and report to the next Convention.

[The Convention of 1883 met in St. Philip's, Charleston. The first fact that arrests attention is the resolution requesting each adult to give at least $2.00 to diocesan missions, and asking the young children of the Church to aid in this matter. It is evident that the missionary spirit was developing in the diocese, and while sixteen cents per month cannot be considered as a very large request for a work of such paramount importance, yet the fact that it was asked for shows that the board was endeavoring to bring to the members of the Church personal and individual responsibility in the matter.]

The Bishop [in 1883] referred to the meeting in Richmond, Va., of the Church Congress, where was considered the "Relations of the Church to the Colored Race." He read, by invitation, a paper on the subject. He suggested the Consecration of Suffragan Bishops, under the direction of the diocesan, to have charge of the work for and among the colored people in the several dioceses of the South. The difficulty in the way of this proposal was a canon of the Church forbidding the election and Consecration of Suffragans. It had been sought to repeal this canon, but the effort had failed. There was much diversity of opinion among the churchmen of the South, whom the question particularly affected, and it had been repeatedly said by the General Convention to their Southern brethren, "Agree among yourselves as to how this work ought to be done, and the whole Church will come to your assistance". An effort to effect this result was made at Sewanee, Tenn., in the summer of 1883, at a conference attended by twelve Bishops, seventeen presbyters and eleven laymen, representing fifteen dioceses extending from Virginia to Western Texas. With great unanimity the conference adopted a scheme, to be presented to the general Convention then approaching, in the form of a proposed canon, providing that in any diocese containing a large number of persons of color, it should be lawful to constitute such population into a special missionary organization under the charge of the Bishop; providing also for an advisory council to the Bishop, composed of clergymen and laymen, to aid him in the establishment of mission schools, by seeking out suitable candidates for the ministry and for their support during candidateship; authorizing the appointment of archdeacons over the work who, by the Bishop's consent, might call the colored clergy and laity to meet in Convocation for the furthering of the work; asking for such an amendment to the canon relating to candidates for Holy Orders as would allow men to enter the ministry who, while not able to comply with all the educational requirements of the existing canon on the subject, were certified by at least two presbyters of the Church, to possess sound understanding and judgment, aptitude to teach and a large share of prudence. The measure was not adopted by the General Convention, though a way out was suggested in the assertion contained in the report of the Committee on Canons of the House of Deputies, to the effect that in their opinion it was competent for any diocese, through its Convention, to provide every suitable agency for carrying on the work contemplated, so that no legislation by the General Convention was necessary. It may be added that this suggestion was acted on, somewhat later, by this diocese, and it should be remembered that the Bishop of South Carolina was the only man at the Sewanee Conference who went there with a constructive plan to present, and that it received the support of the conference "with singular unanimity. (Jour. 1883, p. 20.) The committee appointed to report on the subject to the Convention of 1883, after reviewing the matter in the light of the action of the General Convention, recommended the adoption of a resolution embodying the substance of the proposed Sewanee Conference Canon, pledging the liberal support of the diocese to the measures recommended and appealing to the general church, through its Board of Missions, to come to our aid. In order to anticipate any question that might arise as to the right of membership in Convention of such persons as might enter the ministry under the proposed separate organization, such right by amendment, was vested only in presbyters possessing the other canonical requirements.

The committee previously appointed on woman's work in the diocese made an interesting report, setting forth how greatly indebted the Church is to women for the valuable work done by them in the parishes, but stating that there was no really organized diocesan work done by them, a fact much to be regretted. They submitted a resolution declaring the sympathy of the diocese with the Church of England and certain dioceses in the American Church, in the organization of Sisterhoods and the revival of the ancient order of Deaconesses, and that the Church in this diocese would welcome the formation of such agencies and rejoice in the day when such opportunities for service should be offered to our women. This resolution, somewhat modified, was adopted. (Jour. 1884, pp. 55 and 56.)

The Bishop called attention in his address to the organization in 1885 of a branch of the Woman's Auxiliary in the diocese. He reported that there were sixteen parochial branches in the diocese with a membership of about six hundred. During the year past the auxiliary had furnished boxes to missionaries in various parts of the country valued at $1,200.00 and contributed in cash $1,300.00 to the missionary work of the Church. It was the day of comparatively small beginnings. How it has expanded since then is a story of the deepest interest that has been told elsewhere.

The year was signalized by the occurrence of a destructive tropical hurricane along the coast, Aug. 25, 1885, which did great damage to a number of our Churches, besides inflicting serious losses upon other city property and upon the planters near the coast. In the Bishop's address mention is made of the great earthquake of August 31, 1886, and of its disastrous effects. He reported that he had received and distributed $40,588.07 sent him chiefly through Church offerings. This in response to "a simple statement of the disaster" published in the Associated Press and our principal Church papers. "The House of Bishops in a Pastoral kindly seconded my statement". It appears by the detailed statement accompanying the Bishop's address that contributions were received from forty-eight dioceses, twelve missionary districts of the Church in the United States, from England and Japan, of which distribution was made in compliance with the directions of the donors. About one-tenth went to "personal relief", the balance to the repairing of churches and institutions that had suffered by the earthquake. The Bishop notes that upon some of the Churches will rest for a long time to come the burden of debt, due to damages inflicted by this destructive agency.

In the Convention of 1889 held at Aiken, a number of delegates who had withdrawn from the Convention of 1887, returned and took their seats, prefacing the act by a statement that in view of the express declaration of the clergy and laity who met in Anderson last year of intention to provide for a separate organization of the two races, they would waive objection to the legality of that Convention. The seventeen men signing this paper, represented in whole or in part thirteen parishes. In the second place the commission appointed to carry into effect the resolutions providing for a separate organization for the colored people in the diocese, submitted their report. It provided for the creation of a missionary district under the Bishop, to be composed of all congregations and missions of colored persons in the diocese. Its legislative body, called a Convocation, "to be composed of representatives elected by the respective congregations and missions, with authority to elect its own officers, and in the absence of the Bishop, to be presided over by an officer of their own choice. Coupled with this was a carefully prepared amendment to Article III of the Constitution relating to membership in the diocesan Convention, whereby it was provided that no clergyman who was entitled to membership in the Convention of 1889 should lose his rights in Convention by reason of anything contained in section ii of this Article but that such rights and privileges should be determined by the terms of the Article as it was of force May 1, 1889. This was adopted. The effect of it was to save to the Rev. J. H. M. Pollard, rector of St. Mark's, Charleston, his rights and privileges in this and subsequent Conventions.

An important step was taken at this Convention by the adoption of a resolution to sell the property given to the diocese by Mr. James Thomas Welsman of Charleston in December, 1866, in consideration of his "wish and desire to contribute to and promote the cause of theological education". The property was situated in the city of Spartanburg and consisted of more than thirty acres of land with buildings thereon, the main building being unfinished, but the wings being habitable, in which, after the destruction of the seminary buildings in Camden, in March, 1865, for a year or two the theological students were instructed. The report of the trustees, asking for authority to sell, gave as a reason that for years the property had been of no use or benefit to the diocese. They stated that they had received an offer from the trustees of Converse College of $10,000.00 for the property, and advised that it be accepted. The Convention authorized the sale at that price on bond and mortgage, the annual income to go to theological education, according to the wish and intent of the donor. It may be remarked that it was a great pity the trustees and the Convention could not have seen into the future some few years, since the property at this date, even without the buildings since completed or added, is probably worth half a million dollars, being in the heart of the best residential portion of the thriving city of Spartanburg.

The Bishop in his address referred to the approaching General Convention and the proposed change of the Church's name in the title page of the Prayer Book, announcing his opposition thereto, but adding that if we had to begin over again we might choose a name more in accord with our claim to a true historic connection, through the unbroken succession of the Episcopate, with the Church established at Jerusalem under the Apostles. He also called attention to the matter of using only the fermented juice of the grape in the celebration of Holy Communion. He said that he did so because at a certain Church grape juice had been brought to him for use in the celebration, He said: "My advice to the clergy is not to Consecrate where only substitutes for the proper elements are present. There can be no substitutes by us for what our Lord appointed on the night in which He was betrayed". (Jour. 1889, p. 39.)

Reference is made by the Rev. John Johnson, rector of St. Philip's, to the establishment of a night school at the Charleston Cotton Mill, through funds provided by the young men of St. Philip's, with some assistance from St. Michael's, St. Paul's and the Church of the Holy Communion—an early instance of "social service".

The Centennial meeting of the Convention was held in the Church of the Holy Communion, Charleston. The Bishop delivered the sermon. The Convention adopted the new Article III of the Constitution, which, among other things, provided that in order to enjoy all the privileges of the Convention, a clergyman must have been in charge of a congregation in union with the Convention, but providing also that no clergymen who was entitled to a seat and vote, or to a seat only, in the Convention of 1889, should be deprived of his rights by the adoption of this Article. A paper was read signed by two of the clergy and one hundred and two of the laity, as a protest against the adoption of the Article on the ground that in their opinion it impaired safeguards already existing in the Constitution, without affording in their stead any sufficient fulfillment of the pledges given in Anderson to effect a separate organization of the races in the Church. By request the protest was ordered published in the Journal. Note was made in the Bishop's address of the Consecration to the Episcopate of Bishop Ferguson, a colored man, and of the presence at the general Convention of 1889 of a colored clergyman, and a clergyman from the diocese of Texas, as a member of that body. He referred to the losses sustained by the Church of persons confirmed who often remove to places where we have no place of worship and for that reason join other Christian bodies. He advocated the employment of three missionaries, one for each Convocation, whose duty it should be to look up these dispersed brethren and minister to them, so that they might see and feel that they were neither overlooked nor forgotten. Efforts have been made from time to time to carry the Bishop's suggestion into effect, but it cannot be said that it has been adopted even yet as the fixed policy of the diocese. The Bishop referred at some length to the question of what sort of a vote there must be, in voting by orders, to sustain or overrule the decision of the chair, when appeal from that decision is made, and, upon the authority of recognized parliamentarians, whom he quotes, said he would be governed hereafter in such cases by this rule, *viz.*: that "when there is a non-concurrence (of orders) there is no decision by Convention, and where there is no decision by Convention the President's decision continues to stand, . . . a concurrent majority in both orders will be necessary to overrule the chair in questions of appeal." During the years in which the controversy had continued, beginning with the application of St. Mark's, Charleston, to be admitted into union with the Convention and involving at the last the organization of the Convention itself, in the many instances of appeals from the ruling of the President, it had been held that where there was a non-concurrence of orders his decision had been overruled. It is strange that among the parliamentarians who were deputies to those Conventions, no one had raised the question, during all those years, or advised the President that unless there was a concurrence of the majority in both orders, there was no decision and that his ruling stood. "Could I have seen this", says the Bishop, in the Convention of 1887, "probably the retirement of deputies might have been avoided"—a remote probability in view of the intense feeling that existed. A somewhat unusual situation is referred to in the minutes. The rector of St. Philip's, with the consent of its delegates to the Convention of 1889, had invited the Convention of 1890 to meet at St. Philip's—it being the Mother-Church of the diocese, and the Convention being the Centennial Convention, St. Philip's seemed to be the logical and appropriate place for it to meet. It was so felt by the Convention of 1889, and St. Philip's invitation was accepted. Subsequently, certain members of the congregation objected to the holding of the Convention in St. Philip's. In consequence, a congregational meeting was held, and by a majority vote of those present, the action of the rector and delegates, in extending the invitation to the Convention to meet at St. Philip's, was approved. "But inasmuch as many of the members of the Congregation are nevertheless concerned and disturbed at the expected attendance at the said Convention of a colored clergyman, whose seat in the same they question, and the propriety of his being received they do not admit; but on the contrary, object to his admission as one of the clergy of the diocese," the Bishop was requested to change the place of meeting of the Centennial Convention, "in the exercise of his constitutional power in such case provided." The Bishop thereupon designated the Church of the Holy Communion instead of St. Philip's for the holding of the Convention. (Jour. 1890, pp. 55, 59.) Statistics at this date show 47 clergy in the diocese, 57 churches in union with the Convention

4 not in union, 14 dormant, 24 missions organized and unorganized, 4,844 communicants, contributions $66,485.40—eight churches and missions not reporting.

The Convention of 1891 met in Christ Church, Greenville. The missionary work of the diocese claimed and received a large share of attention. The board was enabled to report receipts amounting to $5,130.43; when the board was organized in 1877, there were twenty-six parishes and missions receiving aid, in 1891, there were forty-nine. During these fourteen years, notwithstanding the controversy that had agitated the diocese, missions had been established at Seneca, Walhalla, White House, Welford, Gaffney, Blacksburg, Lancaster, Darlington, Marion, Graniteville, Trenton, Ridge Spring, Blackville, Hardeeville, Hampton, Ellenton, Ochitie, Pee Dee, and one near Camden. Churches or chapels had been built at fifteen places. Of the ninety-five parishes and missions of the diocese, only sixteen were self-supporting, and only thirty-six clergy to minister to all the ninety-five. This condition of lack of clergy was due, in good measure, to the fact that during the prevalance of the distressing controversy alluded to, a number of our clergy had received and accepted calls elsewhere. Before the next Convention met Bishop Howe's health had failed to some extent. The strain of those years wherein, owing to conscientious differences of opinion, friendships had been severed and alienations had occurred between clergy and laity, and between the Bishop and some of his flock, both clergymen and laymen, had proved too much for him and when the tension of years had been relaxed by the compromise adopted at the Convention of 1889, the Bishop's health gave way. The Standing Committee, through Dr. C. C. Pinckney, its president, addressed a communication to the Bishop, suggesting and requesting that he turn over to the committee the administration of the diocese for a time and seek recovery in resting from his labors. This was in the spring of 1892. The Bishop acceded to the committee's suggestion, and hence, when the Convention met in Sumter that year, he was absent and Dr. Pinckney presided over its deliberations. Amongst the first things that were done after organization was the unanimous adoption by a standing vote of a series of resolutions offered by Mr. E. McCrady, Jr., a deputy from St. Philip's Church, in which the Bishop was assured of "our deepest sympathy in his affliction" and of "our most anxious concern for his recovery"; tendering him "the assurance of the most affectionate and reverential esteem of the diocese and the sincerest desire and hope that in God's providence he may be spared to his flock";

commending him "to the prayers of his people" for a complete recovery. These resolutions were communicated to the Bishop by the
president of the Convention. In his journal the Bishop speaks of
his visitation in St. John's, Berkeley, in July, 1891, referring to
"Biggin" Church where in 1847 he had preached his first sermon—
an interesting reference. The development of missionary interest in
the diocese is apparent in the report of the Board of Missions and
in that of Archdeacon Joyner, in charge of the work among the
colored people. The offerings for this purpose were larger and more
churches were giving to missions than before. To the Convention
of 1893 the Bishop communicated his consent to the election of a
Coadjutor, assigning to him when elected and Consecrated "all
such duties as properly belong to the office of a Bishop in the
Church of God, within the Diocese of South Carolina." The Bishop
had previously tendered his resignation to the House of Bishops,
but that body had declined to accept it, and it is proper to add
that this action met with the entire approval of the diocese, while it
appreciated the sensitive delicacy of the Bishop's feeling that being
unable to administer the affairs of the diocese he should relieve it
of any embarrassment in relation to himself by resigning.

In lieu of his address the Bishop sent a communication to the
Convention, in which he spoke of his resignation to the House of
Bishops and their decision not to accept it, expressing his appreciation of the energy and zeal of the Standing Committee in their
administration of the affairs of the diocese, and extending his thanks
to the Bishops of East Carolina, North Carolina, Georgia and Maine,
for services rendered in making visitations in the diocese and administering the rite of confirmation. "For the future" he adds, "with
regard to myself, I am in God's hands".

[After the reading of Bishop Howe's communications, an election of a Coadjutor was ordered and the Rev. Ellison Capers, D.D.,
was elected on the first ballot, May 4, 1893. The Bishop-Coadjutor-
elect was presented to the Convention. He accepted the wish of the
diocese and expressed and declared his purpose to devote his best
energies to the furtherance of the Master's work. As soon as the
election had been declared, a committee was appointed to wait on
Bishop Howe and inform him of the action taken. The committee
returned with a communication from the Bishop in which he expressed his great satisfaction with the election and his belief that
it would redound "to the glory of God, the good of souls, and the
welfare of the State and the Church". It was at this Convention
that the Rev. A. R. Mitchell secured the passage of a resolution to

interest the children of the Church in this diocese in raising funds
for diocesan missions. Thus came into being what was known as
the "Sunday School Advent Offering", through which most of the
Sunday Schools contributed to this object, substantial aid to the
diocesan board from that time until in 1919 the entire system of
Church finances was changed by the adoption of the nationwide
campaign project.

[Bishop Howe died on November 25, 1894. His Episcopate,
though tempestuous as we have seen, marked a great recovery from
the effects of the war. A most devout and earnest Christian, he
was a preacher and theologian of distinguished ability and a true
chief pastor. His remains lie in the cemetery of St. Philip's Church,
Charleston.]

Chapter V

EPISCOPATE OF BISHOP CAPERS

1894-1908

JOHN KERSHAW, D.D.

(With additions by the author in brackets)

[Dr. Ellison Capers was elected Coadjutor Bishop of South Carolina on May 4, 1893. He was Consecrated on July 20, 1893 in Trinity Church, Columbia—being the seventh Bishop of South Carolina and the first to be Consecrated in this State. His Consecrators were the Bishops of North Carolina, Florida, and the Assistant Bishop of Alabama (H. M. Jackson) who preached the sermon. He seemed indeed to have been the logical man for the leadership of the Church in South Carolina at this time, a distinguished Confederate soldier, state officer, and then clergyman, beloved over the entire State, having been known chiefly as General Capers.]

During the negotiations that went on between the Convention and those who had withdrawn from it in 1888, he had acted as the mediator at Anderson, where the Convention decided to organize separately the work among the colored people, thus winning the good will of all concerned, and their appreciation of his services in that capacity was expressed in their choice of him as their Bishop-Coadjutor—it was a happy choice. A list of the properties held by the trustees of the diocese at this time will be found in the Journal of 1894.

The Convention of 1894 met in Trinity Church, Columbia. Bishop Capers presided over the Convention. Almost its first action was to send greeting to Bishop Howe, wishing him grace, mercy, and peace from our Lord Jesus Christ. In the new Bishop's address, he states that he first administered Confirmation in St. John's, Winnsboro, August 6, following his Consecration. He referred also to the disastrous storms that swept our coast in the fall of 1893 and to the contributions made by churches within and without the diocese for the relief of the sufferers. The Bishop praised the work of the diocesan Board of Missions as of prime importance and the increasing interest of our people in it, as shown by the fact that in spite of financial depression the Board had been able to meet all its obligations. He feels that "we have gone forward in this diocese—wherever I have gone I have felt the throb of spiritual life beating in the hearts of my brethren". He calls attention to the Porter Military Academy and the great work it has been and is doing for the young men of our State, commending it to the support and patronage of our people. In response to a letter from the president of the Clergy Society stating the desire of the society to revive the interest of both clergy and laity in its objects, the Bishop gives his warmest sanction to the appeal "of this most sacred charity" and hopes to see its work promoted in the measure it so eminently deserves. As a matter of most interesting diocesan history, the Bishop records the fact that his was the first Consecration to the Episcopate to be held in this diocese, his six predecessors having all been Consecrated elsewhere. Bishops Smith, Dehon and Bowen in Christ Church, Philadelphia; Gadsden in Trinity Church, Boston; Davis in St. John's Chapel, New York; Howe in St. Paul's Church, Baltimore. Thus Bishop Capers' Episcopate began with much to encourage him—a reunited diocese, with whom he was in full accord, and an outlook free from the clouds that for many years had hung upon the horizon of the Church in South Carolina. Before the Convention of 1895 which met in Camden, Bishop Howe had entered upon the rest that remaineth for the people of God. His successor delivered the sermon at the opening of the Convention—a memorial tribute to his predecessor—in response to a request from the Convention.

At this meeting the matter of the purchase of an Episcopal residence in the city of Columbia was broached. A number of churchmen residing in that city had met and organized themselves into a committee for this purpose and had secured some $1,500.00 in pledges after a partial canvass. The Bishop had decided to establish his residence in Columbia as being most central and accessible to all portions of the diocese; this committee, through its chairman, Mr. Robert W. Shand, reported their action to the Convention and asked for its approval and sanction, which was given and a committee appointed to further the project. The Convention also decided to change its name to Council, and authorize the secretary to make the necessary changes in the Constitution and Canons. [The name "Convention" was restored in 1922.] Action was taken to secure and preserve, through the trustees of the diocese all Church property in places where for years the offices of the Church had been suspended because of the removal of parishioners and the lapse of parochial organization. The Bishop reported that there were 106 separate places requiring his visitations, necessitating his use of many week days in order to reach them all during the year. He notes his presence at Grace Church, Charleston, Feb. 17, 1895, at a service commemorative of the sixtieth anniversary of the Rev. Dr. Pinckney's ordination to the ministry. In this connection it may be added that Dr. Pinckney's service at Grace Church, first as assistant minister and afterwards as rector began in 1851 and continued until his death in 1898—a period of forty-seven years.

The Council of 1896 met in St. Philip's Church, Charleston. The Committee on the Episcopal residence made a report, with resolutions appended, which were adopted "without a dissenting voice", authorizing a committee to purchase the property then occupied by Bishop Capers, requesting the trustees of the Bishop's Permanent Fund to lend for this purpose so much money as might be necessary, and making provision for the interest on the loan. The endowing of the Porter Academy occupied the attention of Council. In the report of the Special Committee appointed by the previous Council, the scheme devised by the founder, the Rev. Dr. Porter, for endowment was warmly commended and the hope expressed that churchmen would cooperate. The scheme was, in brief, to secure subscriptions to bonds of the Academy in sums running from fifty dollars upwards, payable in ten annual installments or at the pleasure of those taking the bonds. It may be added here that the scheme met with only a very partial success, but with what was received, Dr. Porter was enabled to build several dwellings on the property and make a number of needed additions to the equipment of the Academy.

A report was made by Mr. Edward McCrady on the funds, held and administered by the Advancement Society, belonging to the Bishop's Permanent Fund, how the same originated, and under what terms the trust was held. A sketch was given of the origin of the fund in 1818 and of its subsequent history, relating the transfer of the fund to the Advancement Society as trustee, and the nursing care given it by that society. There was also a report made at this meeting which sought to provide a budget system for diocesan supplies and appropriations, the consideration thereof being postponed to the next Council. The matter of ministering to the vacant parishes of the diocese particularly those along the seacost, occupied a considerable part of the Bishop's address. His appeal to the laity ended thus: "As well might a general expect to win victories without the active cooperation and efforts of his army, as a clergyman set over a parish or ministering to missions, expect to succeed without the active cooperation of his people. His work is their work, and for their sakes he is their minister'. He speaks words of praise in commending the Woman's Auxiliary and the Brotherhood of St. Andrew, to the interest and support of the Church— [chapters of the latter were then being organized in many parishes.]

The Council of 1897 met in Grace Church, Anderson. The Rev. John D. McCollough, D.D. who for thirty-four years had been the very efficient secretary of the body asked to be retired and the duties of secretary placed upon younger shoulders. After complimentary words had been spoken by the Bishop and the Rev. Dr. Porter, relative to Dr. McCollough's long service and his eminent qualifications for the office, the Rev. James G. Glass was elected secretary. A petition was read from St. Helena, Beaufort, reciting the serious damage sustained by the Church in the storm of Sept. 29, 1896 and the exhaustion of their funds in making the necessary repairs, asking for the remittal of their diocesan assessments, was granted. The presence was noted of the Rev. William P. DuBose, S. T. D., Dean of the Theological Department of the University of the South, and a warm greeting was extended to him. The Council adopted a resolution requesting the Advancement Society as trustee to reinvest the corpus of the Bishop's Permanent Fund so as to realize a larger income therefrom. The Committee on the Episcopal Residence reported a fund in hand of $1,150.00, deposited in Bank and drawing interest. In the report of the Committee on the State of the Church, recommending and urging the more general use of the practical system of offerings for Diocesan Missions now in force, and commenting on the fact that it was not carried out in many of the parishes, quoted this observation: "We have a Church with the greatest of Constitutions—the Holy Bible; but it has the poorest of governments, because its penalties are all inflicted in another world". The subject of aid for the thirteen candidates for holy orders in the diocese was discussed, and it was resolved to place Theological Education among the objects for which regular annual offerings should be taken. A resolution was also adopted requesting the Bishop to call upon the clergy to preach on a Sunday to be appointed by him on the subject of the crime of homicide and the growing disregard of human life evinced by the people of this state and country. The Bishop, in his address, briefly reviewed the condition of the Church in the Piedmont section of the State about the year 1850. From families numbering 120 and communicants numbering 158, in the same territory there were in 1897, 418 families and more than 1,000 communicants. Of the 65

clergy in 1852, 40 were on the sea-coast and only four in the Piedmont. In 1897, on the coast there were 16, in the middle country,
14, and in the Piedmont, 10. These clergy in 1897 served 76 parishes
and missions, while of the ten others only three together were strong
enough to support a minister. On this showing he makes an earnest
plea for more generous contributions to the Board of Diocesan
Missions. He refers to the Church's work among the colored people
under the charge of Archdeacon Joyner, showing that he and
twelve others of the clergy were engaged in this work, and twenty-
seven teachers and cathechists. Attention was drawn to the work
and the needs of the Clergy Society, the origin of which dates back
to 1762, and a resolution was adopted asking the clergy to revive
the ancient custom of preaching on Whitsunday a sermon on the
aims and needs of the society and take an offering for it.

At the Council of 1898, which met in the Church of the Holy
Communion, Charleston, resolutions were adopted remitting the
diocesan dues of a number of churches and admitting their delegates to the Council. Some, if not all, of these were churches whose
delegates had withdrawn from the Convention of 1887, accompanied by several of the clergy, as has been related. The way of
return was thus made easy and they took advantage of it, to the
gratification of the Bishop and brethren.

The Rev. Dr. Pinckney asked that after a service of forty years
on the Standing Committee he be excused from further duty thereon. It was brought out that Dr. Pinckney was absent from the Council by reason of protracted illness and that he was the senior presbyter of the diocese. The Council adopted resolutions expressive of
their love and esteem for him and their sympathy in his illness. Reference was made to the imminence of the Spanish-American War,
and the departure of many of the Church's sons for the front. The
claims of the Porter Academy for the support of the clergy and laity
of the diocese were stressed by the trustees representing the Council. Likewise the development of the University of the South was
brought before Council by the trustees from this diocese. The
matter of the Episcopal residence was reported upon by its committee. It was evident that no earnest or concerted effort had been
made to interest the diocese as a whole in the project, but the fund
continued slowly to increase nevertheless. The fact was noted in the
Bishop's address that the Church in which the Council was assembled was celebrating its semi-centennial, and that Dr. Porter,
its rector-emeritus had been identified with it from its founding in
1848. This was an era of long pastorates, especially in Charleston,

the aggregate number of years served by the rectors of St. Michael's, St. Philip's, Grace, Holy Communion and St. Paul's being not quite two hundred.

At the meeting of Council in 1899 at Cheraw, St. Mary's School at Raleigh, N. C. was adopted as the diocesan school for girls, making it such for the three dioceses and the missionary district of Asheville, in the two Carolinas. Efforts were continued to get the control of the fund known as the Bishop's Permanent Fund vested in the Council, it being held in the trust by the Advancement Society, with a view of reinvesting it at a higher rate of interest, and constituting the trustees of the diocese the trustees instead of the Advancement Society. A motion to amend Canon VI. by striking out the word "male", so that it should read: "Provided, That at such meetings and elections, none shall vote except members of the age of twenty-one years." This canon related to parish meetings to be held annually on Easter Monday for the election of wardens and vestrymen and deputies to Convention or Council. The striking out of the word "male" would have the effect of admitting women of the age of twenty-one years to take part in such elections, provided the by-laws of parishes did not prohibit them from participating. When the matter came to a vote, the amendment was adopted by a majority of both orders, awaiting final action at the next meeting of the Council. The amendment then failed of passage. The Bishop in his address briefly sketched the history of St. David's Church in which the Council was meeting. The Bishop, by the advice of the diocesan Board of Missions, erected an "Emergency Fund", the object of which was to meet deficiencies in the receipts of that board, and thus enable its treasurer to pay the stipends of the missionaries as they became due. The plan adopted by the Bishop was to send a request to a certain number of persons in the diocese asking them each to subscribe ten dollars annually to a fund for the purpose indicated, to be paid quarterly if needed. The plan worked very well for a number of years and until the methods of raising funds for this purpose was altered and assessments levied, for which the parish, Church or mission was made responsible, thus placing diocesan mission dues on a similar basis as assessments for the support of the Episcopate and of the expenses of the Council. A resolution adopted by the Convocation of the third missionary district, on the subject of "Church entertainments," was forwarded to the Bishop with a request from the Convocation that he should comment upon the subject in his address. The essay that caused this action of Convocation was also sent to the Bishop.

His comments were as following, *viz.*: "Since receiving the essay, I have not had time to do more than glance through it, but with its general statement of the evil effects, and even destructive influence of many of Satan's devices to raise money for the Church, I am in entire accord. I agree with the essay that raffling is a form of gambling, and however mild a form it may be, should never be allowed at a Church entertainment. The support of the Church of Christ is both the duty, the high duty, and sacred privilege of its members. The man who neglects the support of his own family, and leaves its maintenance to the general public, could not command the respect of the public which feeds and clothes his children. And we, to whom our Risen Lord has entrusted the maintenance of His Body, the Church, are under no less an obligation to maintain the family and household of Christ, and vindicate its character. . . . For us in South Carolina, let one rule govern us, and let that be the apostolic rule: "Every man according as he purposeth in his heart, so let him give; not grudgingly or of necessity, for God loveth a cheerful giver.""

At this, [1899] which by some was designated as a Revolutionary Council, there came up at the instance of the Convocation of the second missionary district the subject of the expediency of dividing the diocese. (See following chapter.)

The Bishop alludes to the death, Aug. 12, 1898, of the Rev. Dr. C. C. Pinckney, in his 86th year, for more than sixty years a presbyter of the diocese, the last of Bishop Bowen's clergy. His life touched the beginning of Bishop Dehon's Episcopate and his ministry connected him with five of his successors. When he was born there were but ten active clergy in the diocese, and with the exception of St. David's, Cheraw, there was not a Church or mission outside the bounds of what is now Charleston Convocation, *i. e.*, chiefly the tide-water section of the diocese. He lived to see our churches and missions in every quarter of the State. The Council of 1900 met in St. Thaddeus' Church, Aiken. Among the matters of interest engaging the attention of the Council was that of a history of the Church in this diocese. This appears to have been the initial step in a process that has taken [over a half-century] to reach the point at which such a history has become an accomplished fact. Steps were taken to incorporate the trustees of the diocese through an Act of the Legislature. For some years the Bishop and Standing Committee had been made, by the same authority, the board of trustees, but it was felt that it would be more expedient to substitute for these a board, the personnel of which should be annually elected by Council. The necessary action was taken to carry this into effect, and it may be added that the plan has worked very satisfactorily in the promotion and conservation of the interests of the diocese.

The Committee on the State of the Church found encouragement in many evidences of zealous, earnest work, and of spiritual life and progress. In his address the Bishop notes that since July 1893 he had "ordained fourteen of our young men to Ministry". Speaking of the work of the Board of Diocesan Missions, he says that the Church had generously sustained the board during the past year, giving as much as $6,000.00 to it,—"and nothing is more cheering to me, as we come together to deliberate concerning the affairs of our beloved diocese, than to have such an expression of loyalty and love."

The Council of 1901 met in Christ Church, Greenville. At the opening service, instead of a sermon the Bishop read his annual address. He commented on the rise and progress of the Church in Greenville. The Bishop deferred to the action of the Council in Cheraw whereby it was sought to take the custody of the Bishop's Permanent Fund out of the hands of the Advancement Society and place it in the hands of the trustees of the diocese. The Advancement Society was unwilling to surrender the custody of the fund, and until they should be willing, there was no way by which the resolution of the Council could be carried out. The Bishop sees no bright future for certain of the old colonial parishes along the seaboard, but urges that the ministrations of the Church shall be maintained in these so far as is possible, through the aid of the Board of Diocesan Missions. Elsewhere in the diocese he sees signs and token of growth on every side, in the erection of churches, the founding of missions and the interest of the people as shown by the large congregations that meet him at his visitations, for which he thanks God and takes courage.

The Registrar, Mr. Joseph I. Waring, reported the recovery of certain old parish registers, among them those of Prince Frederick, Pee Dee, and St. Thomas and St. Denis, which Dalcho in 1819 said were lost.

It was learned that the congregation of St. Philip's Church intended to erect a mural tablet in the Church to the memory of Bishop Howe, who for many years had been their rector, prior to his elevation to the Episcopate. Bishop Capers himself offered a series of resolutions, which were adopted, requesting the privilege on behalf of the Council of uniting with the members of St. Phillip's in contributing to the erection of the tablet. The request was granted and through a committee appointed for the purpose a respectable sum was contributed by the people of the diocese towards the tablet, which occupies a conspicuous place on the south wall of St. Philip's near the door that opens into the church-yard.

In 1902 the Council met in the Church of Prince George, Winyah, Georgetown. There were no "burning questions" to disturb the serenity of the meeting which busied itself in matters of routine. The Bishop opened his address with a brief review of the history of Prince George, Winyah. The Bishop referred to the considerable number of vacancies in the diocese, and the difficulties he was experiencing in supplying them, deploring in this connection the growing frequency of clerical changes, and exhorting the clergy to adhere to their parishes despite disappointment and discouragement. He spoke of the recent action of the General Convention in adopting the Apportionment Plan for raising funds for the general missionary work of the Church. By this plan each diocese was apportioned a certain amount by the board of managers of the general Board of Missions. This amount was to be subdivided by a committee to be appointed by each diocesan council among the parishes. If the parishes accepted the apportionment thus asked of them, it became an assessment for which the parish was liable. The method of raising the amount asked for was left to the parishes. This was a great forward step, since it served to impress and impose upon every parish its responsibility to support the general missions of the Church. When it was instituted in 1902, South Carolina was apportioned $2,683.00 only. When the nationwide Campaign was put into force, the apportionment had been tripled. The Bishop alluded to the decision of the House of Bishops of the American Church to give the Episcopate to the Church in Mexico, as a step towards the organization of a national Church in that country. Events have operated to delay such an organization indefinitely, and our ecclesiastical interests there are still entrusted to a missionary Bishop of this Church and Mexico is regarded as belonging to the foreign missionary field. [1920] The Bishop alludes to the deaths of the Rev. Dr. Porter and the Rev. John D. McCollough. Of the former he said: "The remarkable energy of his active nature; the force of his will; the school he has founded and the great good it has done; the untiring zeal and purpose with which he supported it up to the last; the final break-up of a strong mind, then a brief rally, and then a pathetic ending on Easter night." Of the latter he says: "He was a true evangelist. For more than half a century he was the leading spirit in Church work in upper South Carolina, and has left behind, in the beautiful walls of Zion, and in the lasting creations of his own handiwork in Chapel and Church, memorials of his love for the worship of Zion—his zeal for the truth—his devotion to God. I could wish for myself—I could wish nothing better for my brethren than that we might have to rest upon us—to abide within our spirits— the mantle of his zeal, his faith, his self-sacrifice, his endurance, his uncomplaining cheerfulness, and his cheerful devotion to his ministry."

This year, by virtue of an Act of the General Assembly approved Feb. 20, 1902, the trustees of the diocese were made a body politic and corporate.

The Council of 1903 met in the Church of the Good Shepherd, Columbia. In his address the Bishop devoted considerable space to the subject of the change of name of the Church referred by the General Convention of 1901 to the several dioceses and missionary districts, with the view of ascertaining the mind of the people of the Church concerning the matter. The name proposed was, "The American Catholic Church in the United States". The subject was referred to a committee which reported that they fully concurred in the Bishop's views and adopted them as their views. The resolution reported by the committee was to the effect that "this council declares its unalterable opposition to any change in the name of the Church". It was unanimously adopted. (Journ. 1903, p. 32.) The Bishop commended the Church Home and Orphange to the diocese. At that date fifty children were sheltered in it, well cared for by the Church. The representative of the Church Building Fund Commission directed the attention of the Council to the fact that while in the last twenty years this diocese had received grants from the commission—loans and gifts—to the amount of more than $10,000.00, the diocese had contributed to the commission only $820.61. . . . The report of the Archdeacon in charge of work among the colored people, showed that there were 36 places at which missions were established, served by nineteen clergymen and nine other workers. The summary of statistics, made up from parochial reports, discloses the following, viz.: Clergy, 60, Candidates and Postulants, 8, Ordinations, 3, Churches Consecrated, 2, Parishes, Churches and Missions (not including those composed of colored persons) 117, Families, 3,087, whole number of souls, 12,888, Communicants, 7,557. Offerings for all purposes, $94,626.05.

The 114th Council met in St. John's, Florence, May 3, 1904. Among the matters of interest before the Council, was the notification of the election of the Rev. Theodore D. Bratton to the Episcopate of Mississippi and his acceptance of the same, whereby the rectorship of St. Mary's School was made vacant. The Council commended his work at St. Mary's and wished him Godspeed in his work as Bishop. A committee was appointed to consider the project of a diocesan preparatory school for girls. Action was taken favorable to the use of the Revised Version of Holy Scripture in the churches. A committee was appointed to consider and report upon the subject of a training school for Deaconnesses in this diocese, and for the establishment of a diocesan Sunday School Institute.

In his address the Bishop referred to the foundation of the town of Florence and the parish of St. John's. He related that in 1853, when the question was under discussion as to where the Cheraw and Darlington Railway should intersect the Wilmington and Manchester Railway, two members of the Council there in session, the Rev. Dr. John Johnson of St. Philip's, Charleston, and Dr. James Evans of Florence, then civil engineers, met others of their colleagues in a pine forest, and after making their decision, drove the stakes that located Florence. The parish made its first appearance in Convention in 1868. Since then its growth has been almost uninterrupted. The Bishop referred to the death, since the last council, of General Edward McCrady, and to his long and valued services to the diocese. He referred to the exercises in Trinity Church, Columbia, held in commemoration of the tenth anniversary of his elevation to the Episcopate, July 22, 1903. He also referred in fitting terms to the deaths, during the year, of the Rev. Barnwell Bonum Sams and Churchill Satterlee. The board of diocesan missions reported all their obligations as paid in full, with a small balance in bank. Most of the parishes and missions had met their apportionments, substantial aid had come through specials and the Sunday School advent offerings, and altogether the missionary condition of the diocese was most encouraging. A hopeful feeling prevailed throughout this meeting of the Council.

The Council of 1905 met in Grace Church, Camden. The honor conferred upon Bishop Capers in being elected Chancellor of the University of the South was communicated to Council by the trustees of that institution. A service of thanksgiving for the restoration to health of the Bishop, was held. The Bishop briefly sketched the history of the Church in Camden.

The Bishop pays to the Rev. E. N. Joyner Archdeacon in charge of the work among colored people this tribute, on the occasion of his resignation; "The organization of this work is due to his energy, wisdom and zeal. In laying it down he will enjoy a sense of having done a good work, and having done it well. We will part with the Archdeacon with sincere regret, and assure him of the grateful love of his Bishop and brethren". Owing to the recent illness of the Bishop and the feeling that the extent of diocesan work was becoming too great for any one man, there was some talk of giving him relief by the election of a coadjutor. The Bishop mentions the matter and stated that while he considered himself equal to the work of the diocese, yet if the Council thought otherwise he would give the subject his earnest consideration. The subject of the expansion of the Church Home Orphange was referred to by the Bishop. The point had been reached in its history where, in order that it should live, the whole diocese must come to its support. He himself was of the opinion that it should be removed to some more central place, more accessible than Charleston to all parts of the diocese and in more direct contact with a larger number of its friends. The subject was referred to a committee with power to act.

[The serious illness of Mrs. Capers prevented the Bishop's presence at the Convention in Grace Church, Anderson, in 1906. A special committee reported that it was inexpedient to move the orphanage in Charleston but being now a diocesan institution, it was resolved that four of its trustees be elected by the existing corporation known as "The Church Home" and eight by the Council, and the canon changed to conform. The Bishop reported that he had secured the services of Rev. T. Tracy Walsh as general missionary in accordance with the action of the last Council and that he was actively engaged in the duties of the office. This was regarded as a step forward in fulfillment of the desire to minister to the scattered families of Church people, temporarily caring for vacant parishes, and assisting the Bishop to secure rectors and missionaries. The Bishop saw cause for encouragement in the diocese in the prevailing peace in the devotion of the clergy and the loyalty of the laity but cause for searchings of heart because of the lack of a more general interest in the institutions of the diocese. He deplored the parochialism that concerns itself with its own immediate affairs and less with the larger interest of the diocese and the Church at large. Above all else, we need more love for the Master, a deeper personal religious life as the result of love for Him and of living near to Him. This note which the Bishop strikes so clearly in his address is expressive of the character of his own life, especially as it drew near to its earthly close. Sanctified in the furnace of affliction in unusual degree, it was nevertheless with serene patience he awaited the Master's will concerning himself, and asking with the Psalmist: "And now Lord what is my hope?" made answer: "Truly my hope is even in Thee."

The diocesan board of missions in their report (1906) state that they feel encouraged in reviewing this year's work. Handsome churches built in Darlington and Greenville, one purchased from the Baptists also in Greenville (St. James') buildings projected in other places, two rectories completed and one other contemplated, made for encouragement and progress. The board urges greater attention to work in rural districts, in view of growing influx of population in cities and towns. It also stresses the necessity for a more generous support of the Clergy in view of the increased cost of living. "Give us the men and the means and it would not be long before the influence of the Church would be felt more potently in the diocese."

Before the meeting of the Council in 1907, the Bishop had given notice that owing to failing health he would ask for a coadjutor. At the meeting the Rev. William Alexander Guerry was elected. As in the case of Bishop Howe, in view of the additional tax upon the diocese for the support of the Coadjutor, Bishop Capers relinquished one-fourth of his salary. This offer was respectfully and affectionately declined. The committee on the state of the Church at this time found cause for encouragement in that the Church was not only holding its own but progressing. It cited the healthy conditions of the several Church institutions: the Church Home Orphanage, the Porter Academy, St. Mary's School, the University of the South, the benefit to the Church of the work of the general missionary, and the fact that debts on several new churches had been paid off, and provision made for the erection of rectories. The Bishop, in his address, commented with much feeling upon the deaths of Rev. John Johnson, D.D., for many years rector of St. Philip's Church, and the Rev. E. Edmund Bellinger, the senior presbyter of the diocese and one of its most zealous and devoted missionaries. Speaking of vacancies in the diocese and the difficulty of finding men to fill them, owing chiefly to the fact of insufficiency of support offered, the Bishop prays for a "band of devoted and unmarried men, who for Christ's sake and the people's sake, will undertake to give at least five years of their ministry to building up the waste places of Zion." Bewailing the lack of such a body of men, he goes on to say: "With the vast majority of our young men, a call to Holy Matrimony comes very soon after a call to the Holy Ministry, and as our people love to have it so, they must increase the salaries of the clergy, or parishes and missions must suffer from the want of efficient clerical ministration." He advocates the organizing of the Negroes in the South into missionary jurisdictions under Bishops of their own race, as the best solution of the question of how to deal with that class of our Church membership. It may be incidentally remarked that this policy has since been rejected by the general Convention, and the election of Suffragans of the colored race, under the diocese, for work among the colored people of the Church favored. The abundant labors of the general missionary, Rev. T. T. Walsh, were reported; they, however, had become less of a strictly missionary character and more as assisting in weak or vacant existing parishes and missions, and searching for isolated Church members lest they be forgotten. He states that to one who travels over the State, it is a revelation to learn how little hostility there is toward the Episcopal Church. "What prejudice exists is due mostly to ignorance. Everywhere the attitude is that of curiosity, toleration, and kindliness."

Bishop Capers passed from the Church militant into paradise, April 22, 1908. All that was said of him in the religious and secular press, by his successor in office and by the venerable presbyter and president of the Standing Committee, the Rev. W. B. Gordon, who by appointment of the deceased Bishop preached the sermon before Council—illustrated the fact that a remarkable, almost an unique character, had passed away, not however to be forgotten, but cherished and honored as comparatively few have been. It was resolved that the most appropriate memorial to the Bishop should take the form of a building "which would bind his name forever with the Church home and orphanage at York." The building was soon erected—it is duplex, one part a memorial of "Bishop Capers," and one of "General Capers."]

Chapter VI

EPISCOPATE OF BISHOP GUERRY
1908-1928

On Wednesday, May 15, 1907, in Trinity Church, Columbia, the Rev. William Alexander Guerry, then Chaplain of the University of the South and professor in the Theological department, was elected on the third ballot to be Bishop-Coadjutor of the diocese of South Carolina. He was Consecrated in the same Church on September 15, 1907, Right Rev. Daniel S. Tuttle, presiding Bishop of the Church, conducting the service. The Bishop of Tennessee, Right Rev. Thomas F. Gailor, preached the sermon. Bishop Capers was too ill to be present. Other Bishops in attendance represented the dioceses of Missouri, Florida, North Carolina, Mississippi, East Carolina, and the District of Asheville. Deputy Registrar, the Rev. A. S. Thomas.

When the Council met in St. Philip's Church in May 1908, Bishop Guerry paid tribute to Bishop Capers, who had died on April 22. His address was a masterly review of the condition of the diocese, and illustrated the fact that it had developed into a great and complicated organism, exacting from its head unceasing attention and strenuous and varied labors such as, to a like extent, had not been required of his predecessors, but nevertheless represented under God the fruits of their devotion and wisdom for more than a century. In 1908 the diocese formally adopted a seal (see appendix). This year the long-standing issue of amending the canon by striking out the word "male", to allow women to vote in parochial elections was acted on favorably and confirmed the next year. In 1908 there were in the diocese: 60 clergymen; 101 parishes and missions; 3,519 families, 8,747 communicants; total expended $121,-643.55; 7 postulants and 8 candidates for Holy Orders. A notable event in diocesan history in this year 1909 was the removal of the Church Home Orphanage from Charleston to York (See Appendix IV, 7). At this time, the matter of the division of the diocese was raised with a considerable amount of urgency. As the question continually recurred for ten years, we defer further comment for a consolidated story a few pages further on.

The need for an Episcopal residence in the diocese had been recognized as early as 1871, as we have seen by a resolution introduced in Convention in 1871, but nothing practical resulted. It is true the trustees of the Bishop's permanent fund had invested of its capital $10,000.00 in 45 East Bay, Charleston, which was thereafter called "The Episcopal residence", but no Bishop ever lived there. It continued for many years simply as a part of the fund as it really was. Previous to the Council of 1895, $1,500.00 had been raised privately for a residence in Columbia in Trinity and Good Shepherd churches in that city. This was reported to this Council by Rev. A. R. Mitchell, the leader of the movement which was endorsed but little was done. Mr. Mitchell reported to the Convention of 1909 that $2,238.31 was in hand for the purpose. The move was again endorsed but the fund grew slowly. It was at this Council that the plan to organize a colored Council was adopted (see Archdeaconry). There was at this time acquired a burial lot in Magnolia Cemetery for use of the diocese on order of the Bishop.

For the first time in 1910, Columbia had a city missionary in the person of the Rev. W. S. Poynor. Included in his work especially were St. Timothy and Trinity missions. New missions were established at Rion, Manning, and Conway. The Church in Hartsville was completed. In his address the Bishop emphasized the importance of the unity of the Church.

At the Convention of 1915, Bishop Guerry recommended the creation of the office of Historiographer. This was done by a constitutional amendment (1915-16). The Rev. Percival H. Whaley, D.D., was appointed. His duties were defined to revise and edit the material of the Registrar with a view to bringing Dalcho's History down to date. Dr. Whaley died a few months later and the Rev. John Kershaw, D.D., was appointed to succeed him. Dr. Kershaw labored on the task until his death in 1921. The greater parts of the preceeding chapters of this book are from his pen. The Rev. Albert S. Thomas was appointed to succeed Dr. Kershaw and continues in the office.

COLORED SUFFRAGAN

In the Council of 1911, the Bishop spoke at length upon the subject of the Episcopal supervision of the Church among the Negroes. He was opposed to the missionary jurisdiction plan and favored the Suffragan plan. A committee was appointed to consider the latter plan and to report to the next Council. There was much agitation in the diocese over this question. Many views pro and con were published in *The Diocese*. The Bishop again in the Council of 1912 set forth in strong terms his approval of the Suffragan plan. The majority of the committee on the subject appointed in 1911 made a favorable report, a minority one unfavorable. After warm discussion, the following resolution offered by Rev. W. H. Barnwell was adopted: "Resolved, That this Council is not in favor of the election of a Negro Suffragan Bishop *at this time.*" Thus was the colored question set aside once more for a time. Council appropriated $500.00 toward the salary of an Archdeacon to have charge of the work. In 1915 the Bishop withdrew his request for a Negro Suffragan, the Negroes themselves no longer favoring the plan. The Bishop never favored the alternate Racial Missionary District plan as leading ultimately to the un-Catholic principle of two Bishops over the same territory. In 1918, the diocese of North Carolina adopted the plan of a colored Suffragan. The Rev. H. B. Delany was elected and consecrated. By agreement, he assisted Bishop Guerry in the work of the Archdeaconry in this diocese until his death, April 14, 1928.

In these years the diocese was stirred also by another vital matter—the division of the diocese the history of which follows later. Notwithstanding the sometimes heated consideration of these matters, this was a period of growth in the diocese. The report of the Committee on the State of the Church in 1912 reflects this: The Committee reported a favorable financial status in the diocese and in its institutions generally, including especially the Church Home in York and the Porter Military Academy. The finance committee of the Council had been able to assist weaker churches in forward movements; the diocesan Board of Missions had a balance on hand. The Church had a part in the interdenominational Sunday School movement of the time and its Social Service Commission was active. The Church Congress met in Charleston, April 1-4, 1913.

In 1916 the Council approved and formally entered into the newly proposed clergy pension fund, and plans were made accordingly. The next year under Mr. J. C. Bissell, $25,000.00 was raised in the diocese for the $5,000,000.00 Reserve Fund necessary before the plan could be put into effect. As a matter of fact, over $8,000,000.00 was raised. The Convention decided to make the paying of the required pension premiums on each clergyman in the diocese a diocesan project rather than to have each Church make direct payments to the fund. In pursuance, an assessment of 7½% of current expenses was levied on each Church payable to the diocesan treasurer. This diocesan plan of paying pension premiums continued until 1951 when the obligations were assumed by the respective churches.

In 1917, Mr. Powell Evans, a native of Florence, established a scholarship ($5,000.00) at Hobart College, the income primarily for a boy or girl from South Carolina. It was in honor of his parents and is known as the "James and Marie Antoinette Evans Fund". In these years, there was a regular assessment on the churches for an Education Fund used for Sewanee, Porter's, and St. Mary's. The Duplex Envelope System was very generally being adopted in the diocese at this time. A large share of the energies of the diocese and in many parishes was now given to ministrations, religious and social, to soldiers of World War I encamped in the State. In 1917, the Church of the Redeemer and the Harriet Pinckney Home for Seamen were organized (see Appendix IV). In the summer of 1918, Bishop Guerry went overseas and served among the troups there as special preacher under the auspices of the Y. M. C. A. Before his departure, the diocese presented him with a set of communion vessels. He preached in many churches in England, as well as among the troops. He was overseas from August 31, 1918, until February 23, 1919.

The year 1919 was a great one in the history of the Church in our country and not less in this diocese. Following the almost revolutionary plan of a presiding Bishop and executive Council, adopted at the general Convention of October, 1919, the Council of the diocese in May, 1920, by canon adopted a parallel plan (which was to become universal in the dioceses of the Church) of an executive Council with its departments to carry on the work of the Church including missions, religious education, Christian social service, finance, publicity, and for a time a department of the nation-wide campaign. The other notable movement which signalized this year 1919 was the launching of the great Nation-wide Campaign for the purpose of reviving the spiritual life of the Church and its missionary activity—to sweep the Church along to a broader appreciation of her mission, with an immediate purpose of raising $20,000,000.00 as a forward movement fund. Headquarters for the campaign in the diocese were opened in Trinity Parish House in Columbia (July 30, 1919) with Hon. R. I. Manning as chairman, when Mrs. W. P. Cornell, executive secretary and Miss Henrietta P. Jervey, assistant, moved to Columbia from Charleston and the campaign was carried on with great enthusiasm. At the end of a year, May, 1920, Mr. Manning reported "an almost unqualified success": the total budget for the diocese was $160,-

535.00, and the total returns $158,045.66, but the returns were not only financial; over 1,000 persons in the diocese had pledged themselves to "special service" in the Church, and its work in the diocese as in the general Church and world had received a great impetus.

Another organization destined to a short life arose at the time and place of the General Convention of 1919. It was the Church Service League, formed and fostered by the Woman's Auxiliary but distinct from it. It was designed to coordinate all the women's work of the Church. However, it practically passed out of existence at the time of the next general Convention in Portland, Oregon. In the meantime, it was very active in the diocese of South Carolina. With the approval of the Bishop and the executive Council of the diocese, the Church Service League of South Carolina was organized at a meeting of 300 women at Grace Church in Charleston on May 27, 1920; by-laws were adopted and Mrs. W. P. Cornell of Columbia was elected president of the league with a full set of officers. The second annual Convention of the league was held at Christ Church, Greenville, May 31, 1921, when Mrs. James R. Cain was elected president. Many units of the league in the meantime had been established in the diocese, and through institutes, lectures, and printed matter, the work was advanced. In some cases, units of men's parochial organizations were enrolled. While much had been accomplished by the league during the three years of its existence it was decided at the General Convention of 1922 that a reorganization was needed to perhaps include definitely men's organizations, and that, therefore, the further development of the league be turned over to the presiding Bishop and Council. The League soon ceased in the diocese. A memorial of the league in this diocese is a gavel given to it by the Woman's Auxiliary, now in possession of the diocese of South Carolina.

It was now that the question of "division" arose again with great emphasis. Here is related the story of the movement from the beginning to its accomplishment:

DIVISION OF THE DIOCESE

This question which agitated the diocese for about two decades began with a memorial from the Convocation of the second missionary district of the diocese (*i. e.*, the Columbia Convocation), presented to the Council of 1899 meeting in St. David's, Cheraw. In behalf of the Convocation, Rev. W. B. Gordon offered the following resolution:

"Resolved, That a committee of two clergymen and two laymen from each Missionary District be appointed to consider the advisability and feasibility of dividing the diocese, and, if they deem best, to bring in a scheme for such division: and this committee shall report to the Council of 1900, A. D." Bishop Capers who had previously been consulted concerning the question said that he regarded the movement as premature: "The diocese is growing, and the time is past when the Bishop can visit every parish and mission once a year, unless he spends his entire time in travel. But if the brethren will be patient, the Bishop will not neglect any congregation of his charge, and he feels assured that he is doing his best to be the Chief Shepherd of his flock." Meanwhile, he freely gave his consent to the appointment of the committee and promised to cooperate with any decision made by the Council as best to be done.

The committee on division of the diocese submitted a majority and a minority report. The majority report did not favor division, submitting a resolution to that effect, which, after a long discussion, was adopted. The reasons for not dividing at that time were, first, that a single Bishop, with the considerate cooperation of his clergy and the use of a judicious itinerary, can give to each Church and mission a reasonable portion of his time and service; second, that grave legal issues involved in the matter of the vested funds of the diocese and their divisions, should give us pause; third, that financial difficulties were such that a heavier burden should not now be imposed upon the diocese, such as would attend division. The minority report, signed by Dr. McCollough and Mr. Gordon, contended that division was not only advisable but highly important to the welfare and progress of the diocese, that the work is too great for one man to do, that division in every instance has made for Church expansion, that the rapid increase of population in portions of the State where the Church is least known calls loudly for Apostolic work; and that now that division is possible, if the Church wills it. Those who favored division decided by common consent to let the question rest for the lifetime of Bishop Capers out of love for him and regard for his opinion. It is interesting to note that in considering the question, Bishop Capers favored, if it should ever come, a division line northwest to southeast along the line of rivers in order that both elements of the population of the State (up-country and low-country) would be represented in each diocese to complement each other—the idea did not prevail.

In the year succeeding the death of Bishop Capers, the question was revived and a committee of five clergymen and six laymen appointed to study the division in every aspect and to report to the next Council. The committee was as follows: the Revs. W. B. Gordon, John Kershaw, D.D., A. R. Mitchell, L. G. Wood, H. H. Covington, and Messrs. A. M. Lee, P. T. Hayne, H. P. Duvall, John P. Thomas, Jr., Walter Hazard, and R. I. Manning. Before making a report to the Council of 1910, the committee secured the opinion of the Bishop, who stated that while he was in favor of the general policy of small dioceses, in this case he must be satisfied that division would be for the best interest of the diocese, and in order to do this we should have for the support of the Episcopate an additional endowment of $40,000.00. After submitting the report of the committee, a motion that "it is desirable and advisable to divide the diocese" was lost—the clergy voted 23 to 11 in favor, the churches 21 to 25 against. The Bishop expressed the hope that the matter would be considered settled for some years at least. He thought the renewed agitation was doing the diocese harm. The question did now remain dormant for a time. The diocese was agitated by the question of a Negro Suffragan in 1911-14. The question of division came up again in 1914 in connection with the question of the use to be made of the Edmund's property in Aiken, recently given to the diocese. It was resolved by the Convention that the proceeds of the sale of the property be added to the Episcopal fund looking to the division of the diocese, the idea being that the balance needed to complete the required $40,000.00 ($18,000.00) could easily be raised and would be done before the next Council. However, the question came up in a new form in the Council of 1915 when the Charleston Convocation proposed that the need for increased Episcopal supervision in the diocese be supplied by the election of a Suffragan Bishop, but as the requisite initiative by the Bishop was lacking the proposition was only received as information. Later a motion to elect a Coadjutor was also dropped. The policy of not dividing until proper endowment could be secured remained in force.

In 1916, the Bishop informed the Council that in view of the desire in the diocese for increased Episcopal supervision, he believed the time had come for either division or an assistant Bishop. A committee appointed to consider the question reported to the next Convention (1917) that in view of the increased financial burdens at the time resting on the diocese (*viz.*, Sewanee debt, $5,000,000.00 Reserve Pension Fund, and especially 7½% annual pension obligation) it was entirely "inexpedient if not practically impossible to assume such a new burden." The Convention agreed to this conclusion, the Bishop also assenting. So again action was postponed. But only for a time. The Bishop had asked for an increase in Episcopal supervision and the need was generally felt and admitted in the diocese.

The question came to the front in the fall of 1919 and was warmly discussed in the pages of *The Diocese*. Then at last at the Council in Spartanburg in May, 1920, after about two decades of consideration, the question came up for final action on request of the Bishop. Asserting the need for increased Episcopal supervision in the diocese, he left it to the Council as to whether it would take the form of a Suffragan Bishop, a Coadjutor, or the division of the diocese. In case of a Coadjutor, the Bishop thought a plan of territorial jurisdiction which had been suggested would not be canonical. The Council then decided in favor of division. However, as this could not be effected until the meeting of the general Convention in 1922, it was decided that steps be taken immediately to elect a Coadjutor Bishop. It was decided that a special Council be called to meet in Trinity Church, Columbia, October 12 next for this purpose, and to receive reports of two committees to be appointed, one on increasing the Episcopal endowment and another on the necessary steps to perfect the division. The plans for the division were somewhat delayed by a suggestion based on the revised consent to the election of the Coadjutor, which had been issued by the Bishop by which it was thought by some that the division might wisely be postponed for a time. However, this plan was disapproved at the Convention held in Sumter in 1921 and arrangements for division then proceeded. Largely it was felt that such delay would not be fair to the Rev. Mr. Finlay, who had accepted his election with the understanding that he would immediately become Bishop of a new diocese, but he himself offered no objection. It should be said that the division was adopted not without much sadness of heart in all parts of the State because of the partings involved.

At the next Council held in St. Philip's Church in Charleston, Mr. A. W. Smith, for increase of the Bishop's Permanent Fund, reported that $41,411.33 had been subscribed—all except $305.00 in the proposed new diocese in the upper part of the State, it having been understood that Bishop Guerry would retain the old diocese. Here now follows in essence the report on plans submitted by its chairman, Rev. W. H. K. Pendleton, with the resolutions adopted:

1. *Resolved,* That the consent of the Council of the diocese of South Carolina be and is hereby given to the erection and establishment within the limits of this diocese of a new diocese to be composed of the territory embraced within the following Counties; to-wit: Abbeville, Aiken, Anderson, Cherokee, Chester, Edgefield, Fairfield, Greenville, Greenwood, Kershaw, Lancaster, Laurens, Lexington, McCormick, Newberry, Oconee, Pickens, Richland, Saluda, Spartanburg, Union, and York; and that this Council requests the Bishop of the diocese and its duly elected deputies to present to the general Convention, at its next ensuing session, a Memorial setting forth all necessary canonical information accompanied by the proper documents and evidence, and praying that the said division of the diocese be sanctioned and confirmed.

This division gives to the old diocese and to the proposed new diocese the following items in accordance with the latest figures available from the diocese and from the United States Census:

	Population		Churches		Clergy		Bapt. Pers.	Com.
Diocese	W.	C.	W.	C.	W.	C.	W.	W.
Lower	305,597	470,332	75	14	34	4	10,185	6,427
Upper	513,841	394,387	46	14	24	4	5,945	3,801

CONTRIBUTIONS

Diocese	Self Support	Church Extension	Total
Lower	$182,993.45	$76,502.88	$259,584.33
Upper	$173,543.26	$66,239.83	$239,773.09

Separate statistics for colored communicants for different Counties were not available. The total number for the whole diocese is 1,302. The total number of communicants, white and colored, for the whole diocese is 11,616.

CHURCH HOME ORPHANAGE AND LADIES' HOME

With regard to these institutions, the committee makes the following recommendations:

2. *Resolved,* That the Church Home Orphanage, at York, and the Church Home, in Charleston, shall be and become the joint property of the two dioceses, and that the affairs of the said institutions shall be managed by a Board of Trustees composed of an equal number of members elected by the Council of each diocese,

and that the Senior Bishop in term of service shall be *ex-officio* president for the time being and the Junior Bishop *ex-officio* vice-president of the board.

RELATIONS OF THE NEW DIOCESES TO SEWANEE, PORTER ACADEMY, AND ST. MARY'S

The committee anticipates that the relations of the new diocese to the University of the South, at Sewanee, Tenn., to Porter Academy, Charleston, and to St. Mary's School, Raleigh, N. C., shall be of the same nature as those already enjoyed by the present diocese of South Carolina, and that no special resolution by this Council is necessary to effect these relations.

DIVISION OF FUNDS

With regard to the division of funds, the report of the sub-committee appointed to investigate this subject was adopted with certain amendments by the full committee, which recommends the following:

3. *Resolved,* That since the committee appointed to investigate has found no legal objection to a division of the following funds:

1. The Theological Education Fund .... $ 10,100.00
2. The Shuler Fund 2,300.00
3. The Pringle Frost Memorial Fund 3,600.00
4. The Bishop's Permanent Fund 80,000.00

This Council adopts this principle in dealing with these funds, Mr. Hazard dissenting.

4. *Resolved,* That the Theological Education Fund, the Shuler Fund, and the Pringle Frost Memorial Fund be divided equally between the two dioceses, and that in the division of the Pringle Frost Memorial Fund and the Shuler Fund, each diocese shall preserve and continue the names and purposes of the funds.

5. *Resolved,* That the Bishop's Permanent Fund of $80,000.00 be divided between the old and the new dioceses, $55,000.00 being allowed to the old diocese, and $25,000.00 to the new diocese. That the subscriptions toward this fund reported to this Council be allocated to the new diocese.

6. *Resolved,* That all other funds to whose division the Committee on Division has found no legal objection be equally divided between the two dioceses, namely:

1. The Weston School Fund .... $ 10,350.16

2. Elizabeth LaBorde Fund (for Diocesan Missions)   460.63
3. The Protestant Episcopal Prayer Book and Tract Society Fund 4,257.29
4. And any other funds which may be discovered to which the same conditions are applicable.

These funds are in the hands of the Bishop of the diocese, as trustee, and the committee assumes that every consideration will be given to his judgment in the disposition of these funds.

7. *Resolved,* That the fund heretofore collected for the purpose of securing an Episcopal residence in Columbia, now amounting to $4,860.27, be allotted to the new diocese, such action being most consistent with the purposes for which this fund was created.

8. *Resolved,* That all funds which in their nature and by the terms of the trusts are local, be allotted to the diocese to whose territory the use of these funds is restricted, or be placed in the hands of the proper authorities of the churches or institutions for whose benefit they were devised or created, namely:

1. City Missionary Fund (for the City of Charleston) $ 1,000.00
2. North Augusta Church Fund 1,039.18
3. Fund for Church of Good Shepherd, Greer 392.25
4. Fund for All Saints, Calhoun Falls 1,500.00
5. Fund for St. Paul's, Batesburg 1,637.60
6. Fund for the Church of the Messiah, North Santee 975.37
7. Mary Zimmerman Legacy (for Salary of Rector at Glenn Springs) 1,000.00
8. Nora Zimmerman Legacy (for Diocesan Missions in up-country) 1,000.00
9. Fund for Parish House of Prince George, Winyah . 2,114.30
10. For colored Church on Edisto Isld. 339.22
11. Anna Stille Legacy (for colored Church and school at Columbia) 6,344.50
12. Julia Bachman Legacy (for indigent members of the Episcopal Church in the City of Columbia) .. 14,000.00
13. Elizabeth Martin Legacy (Hampton) 3,000.00
14. Martin Memorial Fund (for the Orphanage) 150.00
15. Pauline S. Thompson Legacy (for Ladies' Home in Charleston) 3,750.00

(The amount of this fund is given as $5,000.00, but only $3,750.00 has been paid to the Bishop of the diocese as trustee.)

16. Any other funds which may exist subject to the
same conditions as stated above.

9. *Resolved*, That since the funds held by the "Society for the Relief of the Widows and Orphans of the Clergy of the Protestant Episcopal Church in the State of South Carolina," are the property of a separate and distinct corporation over which the Council has no control, this Society be, and hereby are, requested to divide the income of the funds held by them equitably between the two dioceses.

10. *Resolved*, That the trustees or officers of the Society for the Advancement of Christianity in South Carolina, being a corporation over which the diocesan Council has no control, but with which it is intimately associated, be requested to divide its income equally between the two dioceses.

11. *Resolved*, That until such time as the new diocese desires to establish its own diocesan organ, *The Diocese* shall be the organ of the two dioceses, and that the expense of conducting this paper, including the Editor's salary, shall be shared equally by both dioceses.

At the next General Convention the petition of the dioceses of South Carolina to divide and to erect a new diocese was approved by both houses and ratified on September 11, 1922.

The special Council of the dioceses appointed by the Annual Council in Spartanburg May 11-13, 1920, met in Trinity Church, Columbia, S. C. The Bishop read a revised "consent" making the up-country the chief scene of the Coadjutor's work. The Rev. Kirkman George Finlay was elected on the third ballot. The Rev. Mr. Finlay was Consecrated in this same Church, of which he had been rector for 14 years, on January 20, 1921. The Right Rev. Henry J. Mikell, D.D., Bishop of Atlanta, formerly of this diocese, preached the sermon. Bishop Guerry was the chief Consecrator. Bishop Finlay immediately entered upon his duties. The trustees of the diocese were authorized to use the funds for an Episcopal residence (now about $4,500.00) to provide the new Bishop with a residence in Columbia.

After the division of the diocese was confirmed (September 11, 1922), a special Council was held in Grace Church, Charleston, October 19, 1922, to reorganize the diocese. The comparative strength of the diocese before and after the division is represented as follows:

	1922	1924
Clergy canonically resident	68	46
Lay readers	45	32
Parishes in union	67	41
(not in union)	2	1
(dormant, extinct)	19	16
Organized Missions	28	18
Unorganized Missions	12	6
Colored	24	11
Communicants, white	10,863	6,762
colored	1,370	1,120
	12,233	7,882
Sunday School Pupils	5,777	3,774
Rectories	39	28

EXPENDITURES

	1922	1924
Parochial	$258,541.48	$ 98,252.85
Diocesan	76,371.78	41,807.50
General	40,600.79	15,119.33
Total	$375,514.05	$155,179.68

On request in his address of 1922, Bishop Guerry, after consultation with the Chancellor, made an important ruling stating that by the passage of Canon 7, Section 3, in 1875, the rector of a parish should preside at all meetings and in his absence one of the wardens, including vestry meetings, but that the rule does not apply when it conflicts with the laws and usages which existed in established churches in 1875.

The succeeding years of the Episcopate of Bishop Guerry were marked with many important events in the history of the diocese. Most of these are related more fully elsewhere in this account. We should mention among these: The Council of 1922 decided to resume the old title of the annual meeting in the diocese to "Convention" (called "Council" since 1895); the organization of the Young People's Service League in 1923 (see *in loco*); the Charleston Vacation Bible School at P. M. A. in Charleston, 1923 and after; the relinquishing of an appropriation for white mission work in the diocese by the general Church in 1924, notwithstanding the "boll-weevil depression" from which the diocese suffered at this time; the taking over of Voorhees School in 1925 (see *in loco*); the canonical requirement that vestrymen must be communicants was enacted in 1925; the gift of the Mercy Hospital by Mr. W. King McDowell for the diocesan Home for Women (see Church Homes). The sole condition was that the old home at the southwest corner of Spring Street and Ashley Avenue be sold and the proceeds used for the Home. Another subject that received attention was a proposition advocated by the Bishop to establish St. Paul's Church, Charleston, as the Cathedral of the diocese, with the use of the funds of old St. Peter's Church. However, when in 1928 it was decided to give these funds to Christ Church forming a new St. Peter's, Charleston, the plan of the Cathedral was then abandoned (see St. Peter's, Charleston). Bishop Guerry constantly emphasized the cause of Church unity. Among his last acts in this cause was the proposal of a League of Church Unity. The Bishop's untimely death halted his steps in this behalf. A notable event of 1927 was the great Bishop's crusade, held in this diocese at St. Paul's in Charleston by Bishop Penick of North Carolina. It was then that Rev. R. H. Jackson volunteered for missions and went to Japan.

In his last annual Address in May, 1928, the Bishop gave a review of the twenty years of his Episcopate in which, with great modesty, he reported many events indicating the progress of the Church. At this time, the total number of communicants in the diocese was practically the same as in 1907, notwithstanding the loss of some 4,500 by the division of 1922—the total number in both dioceses being approximately twice the number in 1907. Of the division, he gave this witness: "The experience of these past six years has also proved conclusively the wisdom and necessity for dividing the diocese. The work, as I can testify, was more than one man could properly do; and while it has been hard to part from our friends and clergy of the upper diocese, yet I feel sure that it was for the best interest of the Church that the division should have taken place when it did and the results have more than justified our action." He considered, however, that the greatest forward step in the twenty years was the reorganization of the diocese with an executive Council after the plan put forth by the General Convention of 1919 for a national Council with its five departments. This review by Bishop Guerry was actually to become, alas, his final report to the diocese.

On June 9, 1928, the Right Rev. William A. Guerry fell asleep, his death resulting after five days from wounds inflicted by an apparently demented non-parochial clergyman of the diocese, Rev. James Herbert Woodward, who at the same time took his own life.

The Bishop was apparently in the act of proferring aid to his assailant. The tragedy, full of inexpressible pathos, brought sorrow to the hearts not only of the members of his diocese, but to many others both within and beyond its borders, to whom his remarkable personality, his brilliant intellectual attainments and his ardent and liberal churchmanship had made him an object of admiration and respect.

Rev. Albert S. Thomas, Editor of *The Diocese*, and upon whom, as president of the Standing Committee, fell much responsibility in the crisis, had this to say in *The Diocese*: "Suddenly, without any semblance of warning, the diocese had its Bishop taken from it. In the full career of his usefulness, his life is ended, his work is stopped. We must accept the situation with the grace God gives His children, believing he can make the wrath of man to praise Him. But it is only human nature to bewail the great loss we have suffered." At the time of Bishop Guerry's death the author as Editor of *The Diocese* at that time wrote: "This Bishop, after a brave fight through some years with disease, had apparently won the victory and had seemed so restored, especially during the last few months, as to give promise of many years of vigorous service to the Church. Never were his interests in the larger problems of Church life greater than in recent months. His vigor of intellect and energy of will were unabated. And these we may say were characteristic with him, for never in his career did he fail, when called upon for any important work, to put into it the best he had out of his well-stored mind and experience. The training of his early ministry had been of such a character as to supply that culture and learning which was an ideal preparation for his office as preacher for which he possessed talents of a high order. He ranked among the few great preachers in our American Church.

"He was loyally devoted to the Church in which he was Bishop. He believed in the greatness of her mission, not alone to gather in souls to Christ, but as a keeper and witness to the faith and as a rallying ground for the unity of Christendom. He was a devout student of the Holy Scripture and deeply versed in theology. While always loyal to the faith of the Church, his mind was open and he looked to modern developments of thought, not only without fear, but with hope that through them would come a deepening understanding of revealed religion.

"One thought comes prominently to mind—he always stood for progress. When once he was convinced that any proposition gave promise of some betterment or development in the life of the

Church or society, he could be counted upon to espouse it with all his strength. We shall indeed miss his zeal, his energy, his rigor of mind and will in his high calling. But the impress of his character upon the diocese is permanent, and though passed to the higher life of service in the Church Expectant, his spirit still abides with those who labor on in the Church Militant."

A large concourse of bereaved people, including many Bishops and the clergy of the diocese, attended the funeral held in St. Michael's Church on June 12, 1928, conducted by the president of the Standing Committee. The interment was in St. Philip's Churchyard. A tablet erected to his memory in St. Michael's bears on it the tribute of his diocese.

Chapter VII

EPISCOPATE OF BISHOP THOMAS
1928-1944

After the tragic death of Bishop Guerry there arose in both dioceses in South Carolina quite a discussion concerning the advisability of a reunion of the two dioceses in this State. This was notwithstanding the recent utterance by Bishop Guerry in his annual address that the experience of six years had "proved conclusively the wisdom and the necessity for dividing the diocese". The question was argued during the summer of 1928 in *The Diocese* and at several conferences. The Standing Committee, on request, revised its call for a special Convention to elect a Bishop to permit the consideration of this question at the meeting. Finally, Mr. Walter Hazard, a distinguished churchman of Georgetown, on request, prepared a pamphlet giving a thorough examination of the question from many angles. The publication of this pamphlet had the effect of settling the question in both dioceses. When the Convention met in Florence, the advocates of reunion stated that the question would not be brought before the Convention.

This special Convention met in St. John's Church, Florence, on September 18, 1928, "while the wind and rain of a West Indian hurricane romped over the whole coastal plain" and prevented many deputies from attending. The Holy Communion was celebrated by Right Rev. T. F. Gailor, D.D., of Tennessee, who preached a sermon commemorating the life and work of Bishop Guerry. At three o'clock the Convention assembled, the president of the Standing Committee presiding. The storm had not abated. The Rev. Albert Sidney Thomas was elected on the fifth ballot by candlelight—two-thirds majority being required by the Constitution in view of the reduced attendance. Mr. Thomas was then rector of St. Michael's Church and president of the Standing Committee. His election was confirmed by the general Convention meeting soon after in Washington. The newly elected Bishop was Consecrated by the presiding Bishop John Gardner Murray and six other Bishops in St. Michael's Church on St. Andrew's Day, 1928. The Right Rev. T. D. Bratton preached the sermon. This was the first Consecration of a Bishop to be held in Charleston. While some of the deputies were detained in Florence by impassable roads and rivers, time was not lost. They conferred informally and reached the conclusion that a residence for the Bishop was badly needed. This discussion, as we shall see, culminated in 1933 in the erection of the residence of the Bishop.

During Bishop Thomas' Episcopate, the nation passed through a severe economic depression. In fact, this depression almost became, it perhaps may be said, the determining factor in diocesan life in those times, as was the case in the national Church. It was scarcely two weeks after his election when Mr. Thomas, as Bishop-elect and president then of the Standing Committee, was called upon to face a serious crisis—the failure of the bank in which were deposited the current funds of the diocese. Very soon after his Consecration, one of the largest banks in South Carolina with branches throughout the State also failed, and funds of the Church in many parishes were similarly lost. These losses were rendered more acute by comparable losses of individuals, who found themselves no longer able to contribute to the Church with their accustomed liberality. Practically all incomes were reduced and in jeopardy. Naturally in consequence of the general depression, which was more or less world-wide, diocesan activities depending on funds were for some years curtailed: stipends of nearly all diocesan missionaries were reduced ten percent, including the Bishop's salary at his own request. In one year (1933) the best the diocese could do on its apportionment for general missions was $1,717.22. However, through a special Whitsunday Offering, which continued for some years, this amount was kept generally above $5,000.00. In 1928 the Executive Council was forced to reduce the diocesan budget from $46,000.00 to $40,000.00, including $8,000.00 on an apportionment of $11,600.00 for general missions—but sometimes more was actually paid. During the period of the depression, the expenditures in the entire Church fell from $46,000,000.00 to $30,000,000.00, the budget of the national Church from $4,000,000.00 to $2,300,000.00. In the diocese, total expenditures dropped steadily from $187,000.00 in 1928 to a low of $106,000.00 in 1936. Not until toward the end of this Episcopate was the lost ground recovered—in 1943 the amount ($188,000.00) had risen slightly above the pre-depression level. These were difficult days: the appropriation by the national Council for the Seaman's Home was cut off, that for the archdeaconry for colored people was cut in half. However, owing to the activity of Archdeacon Baskervill this latter work suffered little during this period. It must be said at least that the diocese nevertheless was kept out of debt and much of the credit for this was due to the chairman of the Field Department, Mr. O. T. Waring, and the treasurer, Judge F. K. Myers. There actually were nevertheless bright spots of accomplishment even in the realm of finances: in 1932 the diocese surrendered at last a small appropriation by the national Church for white mission work; at one Convention $2,000.00 was raised spontaneously to pay a deficit to the Church Home on account of bank failures; Porter Military Academy was fully maintained and so was Voorhees, but with a struggle. The wonderful help of the Woman's Auxiliary in these days under the leadership of the president, Mrs. L. D. Simonds, should not be overlooked. *The Diocese* remarked on the depression that the effect of its heavy blows was "to bring our people to a more solemn realization of the value of the Church". A review of the many activities in the diocese during these years, which we must soon relate, would seem to have justified this saying, but first some details of diocesan history.

The gift of Mr. W. King McDowell of the Mercy Hospital for a Home for Women of the two dioceses of South Carolina became effective when the old Home at the southwest corner of Ashley Avenue and Spring Street was sold, and, with the proceeds, the hospital was renovated and remodelled for the different purpose. The ladies moved into their new home in the fall of 1929. At the 139th Convention of the diocese, May 14-15, 1929, the first for Bishop Thomas, steps were immediately taken to set up a memorial to Bishop Guerry. This came to effect with the dedication of a handsome mural tablet on the wall of St. Michael's Church on October 31, 1937. Judge William H. Grimball made the presentation in behalf of the diocese. It was received by Bishop Thomas and an address was made by Bishop E. A. Penick of North Carolina. Acknowledging the need of a home for the Bishop of the diocese (following the lead of the laymen in Florence during the storm with Dr. R. S. Cathcart at their head), a committee was appointed at the Convention of 1929 to take steps either to buy or to build. The depression led to some delay, but in 1933 a plan was suggested by the Bishop that the trustees of the diocese make a loan to the diocese, the interest to be paid by the Bishop himself in lieu of the rent he was accustomed to pay for his residence. This was done, plans being made for the amortization of the loan. A committee consisting of Messrs F. G. Davies, chairman, David Huguenin, and H. L. Tilghman, was appointed to secure a residence. Being unable to purchase a suitable building, the committee bought the lot at 129 South Battery in Charleston and erected the present residence after plans of Simons and Lapham, architects, with Ralph Simmons, contractor. The entire cost, including the lot, was $17,943.12. The residence was occupied by Bishop Thomas in the spring of 1934. Soon after, a reception was given in it by the Bishop to the people of the diocese.

The seal of the diocese was revised in 1933 (See Appendix VI.1).

Following the nation-wide campaign, the method of financing all diocesan obligations was by an apportionment of a single sum to each church. In 1933-34 this plan was abandoned and a return was made to the old system of an *assessment* for diocesan support (including pension premiums) and an *apportionment* for missions and benevolent purposes. This system is still in force, except that in 1952, the payment of pension premiums of the churches was turned over to them individually. Beginning in 1930, it became the custom of the Bishop to deliver a Lenten message to the diocese on the night of Ash Wednesday from the pulpit of Grace Church, Charleston, this being followed yearly by a series of community services every Thursday evening with visiting preachers, usually Bishops. This continued to the end of the Episcopate. In 1933, the Bishop inaugurated a pre-Lenten Quiet Day for the clergy of the diocese, conducted either by the Bishop or a visiting clergyman. For many years these exercises were held at old St. Stephen's Church, the clergy bringing box lunches. Another custom of this Episcopate was a yearly text or motto given the classes by the Bishop at confirmation. At Christmas time he sent letters to all the young people of the diocese away from home at school. In April, 1930, Miss Henrietta P. Jervey resigned as Headquarters secretary, having served in this office since it was created in 1923 just after the division of the diocese. After a short interregnum filled by Miss L. E. Heins and Miss Minnie T. Hazard who declined the position permanently on account of condition of health, Miss Hallie E. Coffin was appointed and served until 1944. In 1931, John P. Thomas, Jr., Esq., of Columbia, resigned as secretary and treasurer of the Trustees of the diocese, having served 32 years without the loss of a penny of interest or capital. Though a resident of Columbia, he had continued in this office for nine years after the division of the diocese.

Two meetings of general interest in the diocese in these years were, first, the celebration at St. Michael's Church on April 13, 1930, of the 250th anniversary of the founding of the Church of England in South Carolina on the identical spot of this Church.

Then again on the 29th day of the same month, the Church Congress met for the second time in Charleston (the first April 1-4, 1913). At the Convention of 1932, a canon (numbered XXIV) was adopted creating a diocesan court in marital relations under a canon of the general Convention recently adopted. During these years several movements in the Church of a national character had a very marked reflex influence in the diocese. The first of these was the "Teaching Missions on the Great Commission". In consequence, in the fall of 1931, a diocesan-wide mission was held under the leadership of Rev. C. H. Goodwyn, Chairman of the' Diocesan Commission on Evangelism. In connection with this emphasis on evangelism, there was quite a revival of the Brotherhood of St. Andrew in the diocese—in one week ten chapters were organized or reorganized. In connection at this time the observance of the annual men and boys' Corporate Communion became more general, having been inaugurated in the Church by the Brotherhood in 1916. At this time, too, the diocese assumed its part in a proposed nation-wide endeavor called the Advance Work Program. Each diocese was requested to adopt a project for the advancement of the work of the Church. This diocese undertook two buildings in Arizona, the diocese of Bishop Walter Mitchell, the former head of Porter Military Academy—Holbrook Church and Salome Parish House. Though this movement was arrested very generally by the depression, this diocese finally fully accomplished its objective, but practically entirely by the efforts of the Woman's Auxiliary which merged its corporate gift with this cause. The undertaking of the diocese of Pittsburgh was $10,000.00 with which to erect a chapel at State College in Orangeburg. This diocese suspended its effort because of the depression but its Woman's Auxiliary contributed $2,250.00. This chapel was finally built in 1952.

Steps were taken in the General Convention of 1931 to a better organization of the men of the Church in the form of a Laymen's League. Already there had been men's clubs in different parishes, but in his address in 1935, Bishop Thomas called attention to the need of some diocesan organization. A committee was appointed to study and report. In the fall of this year, the special activity of the Men's Club of St. John's Church, Florence, encouraged by the rector, Rev. W. S. Poynor, led to the calling of a meeting of the men of the Pee Dee Convocation at the Church of the Advent, Marion, November 19, 1935. Mr. H. L. Tilghman was made temporary chairman. There were present 75 or 80 laymen. The meeting was addressed by Dr. L. W. Glazebrook and also by Dr. H. K. Jenkins, telling of the missionary work in the Philippines. Marion W. Seabrook of Sumter was elected the first president, Pee Dee Branch of the Laymen's League of the diocese of South Carolina; W. E. Duvall of Cheraw was elected vice-president; S. Hughes Schoolfield of Marion, secretary; Preston Manning of Florence, treasurer. At a later meeting when 120 men were present on February 27, 1936, there were addresses by Bishop Penick of North Carolina and Bishop Thomas. The League now expanded in the Pee Dee Convocation. In connection with its other interests, the League decided to adopt some concrete objects of endeavor of a practical kind—the first two being to further the building of a needed Church at Myrtle Beach, and, secondly, to assist the work of the associate mission centering at Eutawville. Judge R. W. Sharkey succeeded Mr. Seabrook as president. At the Convention in Georgetown in 1939, a supper meeting was held with the purpose of extending the League to include the Charleston Convocation. This came only by degrees. It was at the meeting of the Pee Dee Laymen's League on Friday, November 3, 1939, that a notable action was taken, proposed by Mr. W. E. Duvall of Cheraw, when a plan of an annual Men's Thank Offering was adopted. This action came to fruition during the meeting of the 151st Convention in St. David's Cheraw, 1941, when at an evening service the first Laymen's Thank Offering in the diocese was presented. It amounted to $300.00 and was from the men of the Pee Dee Convocation but this offering was destined to include the whole diocese as a regular institution. The fourth offering presented at the Convention in Sumter in 1944 amounted to $463.00. Again the Church was stirred by a ringing call to deeper devotion and wider work called "The Church-Wide Endeavor". However, the national movement which proved of greatest significance in these years, having much effect on the life of the Church in the diocese, was the "Forward Movement". This was inaugurated by a commission appointed by the general Convention of 1934. Approximately $100,000.00 was appropriated to carry on the movement to re-invigorate the Church in respect to prayer, meditation, church attendance, and monetary contributions,—an effort to bring the Church back to the fundamentals of discipleship. Bishop H. W. Hobson of Southern Ohio was president of the commission. The diocese entered heartily into this movement, a diocesan commission with the Rev. H. D. Bull as chairman was raised by the Convention of 1938 to further this movement in the diocese. The "Forward Movement" was largely educational and devotional through the publication of tracts, more especially "Forward Day by Day", the influence of which has been great.

In the fall of 1935 when the "Forward Movement" was being emphasized and when missions of prayer were being held in the diocese under the Commission on Evangelism, with the Rev. Harold Thomas as its chairman, Bishop Thomas founded the "Prayer Guild of the Diocese of South Carolina". The single rule was to pray daily for the work of the Church in the diocese. An invitation to membership was published monthly in *The Diocese*. It met with a ready response and enrolled 417 members in the Church. The League continued until the end of Bishop Thomas' Episcopate, and it is hoped its purpose is still fulfilled. One event of particular interest in this Episcopate was the establishment in 1936 of the associate mission in the area between the Santee and Cooper Rivers. Three young priests, the Rev. Messrs. David N. Peeples, Lincoln A Taylor, and Duncan M. Hobart, took charge of the missionary area in St. Mark's, St. John's, Berkeley, St. Thomas' and St. Denis', and St. Stephen's parishes, and in Williamsburg County, opening or re-opening much beneficial church work in these rural areas. Under the Rev. E. B. Guerry, the old mission work at the Barrows had been reopened. The associate mission especially developed this work (See *in loco*). However, probably the most outstanding feature in the life of the diocese in these years was the expansion of the youth movement: Young People's Service League, Camps and Conferences (including St. Christopher's), Canterbury Clubs, annual gatherings of Church Schools from all over the diocese at St. Philip's Church with the presentation of the Lenten offering, the employment of a field worker (Miss Alice Hartley), then the first all-time youth worker, first for both dioceses (Miss Gertrude Bull), a student worker at Winthrop College (Miss Agnes Dibble). The greath youth convention at the time of the General Convention of 1940, with the organization of the "United Movement of the Church's Youth" reacted on this diocese, and in the fall of 1943 the permanent "Youth Commission" of this diocese was organized (See *in loco*).

In connection with the youth movement, in 1935 the Church work among the cadets at The Citadel was better organized when Rev. A. R. Stuart, rector of St. Michael's, celebrated the Holy Communion every Sunday morning at 6:50 in Summerall Chapel. As early as 1918 there had been organized by Rev. Harold Thomas a Chapter of the Brotherhood of St. Andrew. Other meetings were also now held. There were at this time 180 Episcopalians among the cadets. Encouraged by the president of The Citadel, Gen. C. P. Summerall, this work has continued. In 1940, the Rev. W. W. Lumpkin, having succeeded Dr. Stuart as chaplain, organized at The Citadel a "college parish" of a unique character named St. Alban's with its wardens and vestry. Cadets K. R. Nelson and R. L. Oliveros were the first wardens. The Rev. C. R. Campbell assisted Mr. Lumpkin. The latter entering the Navy was succeeded as chaplain by Rev. F. R. Harding. Then in 1942, the Rev. A. R. Willis (*locum tenens* at Church of the Holy Communion) became chaplain. Two laymen, Major Lewis Simons and Major John Anderson, nurtured and sponsored this work at The Citadel for years. Many gifts have been received by this "parish" for its use in the chapel.

The sesquicentennial of the diocese was celebrated with a great diocesan service in St. Philip's Church on October 27, 1935, when Right Rev. H. J. Mikell gave a survey of the long history of the Church in South Carolina. Beginning in 1938, a new method of balloting for elective offices called the "Single Transferable Ballot" was adopted. After some years it was abandoned as too complicated.

The news of the sudden death on August 27, 1938, of Bishop Kirkman G. Finlay of the diocese of Upper South Carolina was received with great sorrow. Not only had he for a short time been Coadjutor Bishop of this diocese before the division, but his presence and leadership at Kanuga had endeared him to large numbers of our people, young and old. Quite a discussion arose now (as also after the death of Bishop Guerry) in both of the dioceses concerning the advisability of a reunion of the two dioceses of South Carolina. The question was decided negatively at a joint meeting of the Standing Committees of the two dioceses with Bishop Thomas. In these years *The Diocese* was constantly used as a forum for the discussion of church policies by subscribers and the Editor. This matter had been freely discussed in its pages. Again in 1944, following the resignation of Bishop Thomas, the question was raised in the lower diocese, but as before, no action was taken. Tribute was paid to Bishop Thomas in a diocesan service on St. Andrew's Day, 1938, the tenth anniversary of his consecration. He was presented a pastoral staff carved with the seal of the diocese for the use of the Bishop of the diocese, and a personal gift of a silver bowl and platter, and also a check and a "Book of Remembrace" with signatures from over the diocese. Bishop Darst of East Carolina preached the sermon.

The Convention of 1940 was the 150th in the history of the diocese (although 155th year). This anniversary was duly celebrated at the meeting. In the evening of April 16th, a historical sermon was preached by the Rev. Oliver J. Hart, then rector of Trinity Church, Boston, now Bishop of Pennsylvania. At the opening service in the morning, Mrs. Henry Jervey, on behalf of the Woman's Auxiliary and others, presented a very handsome private communion set, inscribed with the seal of the diocese, for the use of the Bishop of the diocese. In the late afternoon, the delegates attended a showing of a moving picture of the activities of the diocese (also shown in many places in the diocese). The great hurricane of August 11, 1940, brought near tragedy at Camp St. Christopher. Some sixty-odd young people there barely escaped. Damage to the buildings being slight was all repaired promptly and camp was held the next year. However, on account of the war, the exposed position rendered the site unsafe, and therefore, the camps were held at Burnt Gin in Sumter County for some years after this time. In the summer of 1941, a campaign was launched in both dioceses to raise $75,000.00 for the renovation of the Home in York. Mr. W. M. Manning, then of Stateburg, was chairman for this diocese. The whole amount was not secured, but a considerable sum. For years it had become the custom to have pilgrimages to the Home every spring; as also pilgrimages were held to Voorhees. A new development in diocesan life was an annual Religious Conference of the women of the diocese, at first held at Poinsett Park, the first September 15-20, 1941. This movement called *The Pilgrims Conference*, at the suggestion of Mrs. H. D. Bull, was launched by the Woman's Auxiliary under the leadership of Mrs. W. H. Grimball, educational secretary. The Synod of the Province met in St. Michael's Church, November 4-6, 1941, the preacher at the opening service being Right Rev. H. St.G. Tucker, presiding Bishop of the Church.

The year 1942 was a very sad one for a large section of the diocese, especially old St. John's, Berkeley. The Santee-Cooper development involved the taking down of old Black Oak Church with all its sacred memories, with the removal of some of the surrounding graves; the abandonment of Rocks Church left on an island and later de-consecrated and removed; to say nothing of the many old plantations with historic homes that were flooded with the diverted waters of old Santee. The whole face of this site of a veritably unique civilization was now a body of water. In the Convention of 1939, on motion of Rev. A. R. Stuart, this resolution was adopted: *"Whereas,* the need for more adequate diocesan headquarters is apparent, *Be it resolved* that the Bishop be requested to appoint a committee of three to investigate this matter with a view to procuring more adequate and dignified headquarters for the diocese of South Carolina." The Rev. A. R. Stuart, Gen. C. P. Summerall, and F. P. Prettyman were appointed. Investigations and efforts were made by this and succeeding committees in this behalf until finally plans for raising funds were made in Bishop Thomas' last year and a house actually bought. However, the succeeding administration reversed this action, the house was returned to its owner and the plan as abandoned for the time. It would seem in the light of subsequent events that God had a better plan for the purpose, which in due time as will be seen was realized.

In 1942, Messrs. Percy R. Porcher and Mr. Richard Dwight gave the diocese a valuable property on Lake Moultrie for a diocesan conference center but later it was decided to return to St. Christopher's at Seabrook Island for the center. During the years of World War II, there was much activity in churches near camps and air fields. The clergymen entering the service as chaplains were the Revs. W. W. Lumpkin, A. R. Stuart, St. J. A. Simpkins, Jr., and H. L. Hoover.

Of material advance worthy of mention in this period, notwithstanding the depression, we list: The Episcopal residence; the new Calvary Church with parish house and St. Peter's Church, both in Charleston; parish house, St. John's, Charleston; school house at Pawley's, and later here buildings for Camp Baskervill; Mediator, Edisto; Church at Myrtle Beach; steeple added to St. Helena's, Beaufort; parish houses at Advent, Marion, and Christ Church, Adams Run; parish house at Plantersville, several buildings with chapel at Camp St. Christopher; two buildings at Redeemer, Pineville; Guild Hall in the Barrows. Also jointly with the diocese of Upper South Carolina: renovation of the Home for Women; chapels at Children's Home in York, at Kanuga, and at Voorhees with other building here. The number of communicants increased from 8,425 to 10,050.

Bishop Thomas submitted his resignation (his age for compulsory retirement being near) to the House of Bishops at its meeting in 1943. It was accepted to take effect December 31, 1943. At the request of the Standing Committee, Bishop Thomas continued to officiate until May, 1944. A farewell service was held as a tribute to Bishop Thomas in St. Philip's Church on the evening of January 16 when Bishop E. A. Penick of North Carolina spoke and Bishop Thomas delivered his last message to the diocese in a discourse concerning its future called "A Vision".

In *The Diocese* for January, the retiring Bishop issued to the diocese "A Bidding Prayer", appropriate to the war time and to the impending change in the life of the diocese, with these words: "The above prayer constitutes my last 'official message' to the diocese. I trust it will be used by our people. Especially do I ask that my 'Prayer Guild' take it as my last suggestion to them. This Guild I now leave to the 413 members individually. I hope that each one will continue 'instant in prayer'. May the New Year be full of blessing for the diocese, and for each one in the family of the diocese, no matter what may happen, and this is my prayer for you, not only for A. D. 1944, but on and on. Affectionately, Albert Sidney Thomas, Bishop."

Chapter VIII

EPISCOPATE OF BISHOP CARRUTHERS
1944- . . . .

On January 18, 1944, a special Convention met at St. John's, Florence, for the purpose of electing a new Bishop. The Rev. F. W. Ambler, president of the Standing Committee, presided. For the first time in the history of the diocese, it is believed, there were nominating speeches. On the third ballot, the Rev. Thomas Neely Carruthers, D.D., rector of Christ Church, Nashville, Tennessee, was elected. Bishop Carruthers was Consecrated in St. Philip's Church, Charleston, May 4, 1944, by the presiding Bishop, the Right Rev. Henry St. George Tucker with Bishop Thomas and Bishop Maxon of Tennessee; assisting were the Right Rev. Bishops of Florida, Georgia, South Western Virginia, Delaware, Upper South Carolina, Louisiana, West Texas, and the Coadjutor of Tennessee. Bishop Quin of Texas preached the sermon. Among the gifts received by the new Bishop was an Episcopal ring from the congregation of Christ Church, Nashville, and a pectoral cross from Trinity Church, Houston—both former charges of the Bishop.

The two succeeding days, Bishop Carruthers was in attendance upon the Young People's Convention in Marion. He made an address to the Convention, celebrated the Holy Communion, and held his first confirmation of two people. On the 9th and 10th of this month, at the Holy Comforter in Sumter, he presided over his first Convention. Then followed a busy month: trustees of the diocese, trustees of Voorhees School, district meetings of the Auxiliary, trustees of the Church Home, meditation at the Pilgrims' Conference, ordination to the diaconate of Victor Bland Stanley. The Church of the Messiah, Myrtle Beach (now Trinity), was Consecrated on July 23. The diocese by July 1st had paid $6,500.00 on its quota for general missions, overpaying the expectation of $4,167.00, indicating the beginning of a new era in the finances of the diocese. A clergy conference was held by the Bishop September 26-28 on Pawley's Island. The total budget of the diocese adopted in the fall of this year was $51,647.54—a large increase over the previous year.

The Council of Colored Churchmen met in Calvary Church September 14, presided over by the Bishop who, at this time, appointed the Rev. Stephen B. Mackey to be Archdeacon. Renewed plans were made for self-support in this work. The national Council had agreed to assist in the improvement of the Archdeaconry property. About 1948 the designation of the annual meeting in the Archdeaconry was changed from Council to Convocation. The archives of the diocese were, at this time, removed from St. Philip's Home to the Fireproof Building, the Historical Society having kindly agreed to have them kept there. Later, at the time of its occupation by the diocese, the archives were removed to 138 Wentworth Street. Miss Ida Dwight now succeeded Miss Hallie E. Coffin as headquarters secretary. On January 24th, 1945, another step forward took place in the better organization of the laymen of the diocese in Church work. It was now called the Episcopal Churchmen's Association with the object to encourage local clubs and leagues in the Advent Corporate Communion, the Thank Offering, lay reading, and ministry to servicemen. J. Arthur Tuten was elected president; W. E. Duvall, Cheraw, vice-president; and John Gibbs, secretary and treasurer. Later, under the leadership of Mr. Harold S. Reeves, the laymen's work in the diocese was largely developed. Mr. Reeves was succeeded by Mr. Francis Marion Kirk, and he in 1955 by Mr. H. Quentin Foster. The Pre-Lenten Clergy Conference was this year held in St. Andrew's, Mount Pleasant.

At the Convention of 1945, a very extensive advance work program for the diocese was adopted. It was carried forward in connection with and in cooperation with the fund for reconstruction and advance work proposed by the national Council. The objective of this fund as adopted was $63,000.00 in this diocese, half to go to the national Church. T. W. Thornhill was chairman of the committee to raise this amount (R. W. Sharkey, vice-chairman, and L. W. Barrett, treasurer). In less than a year, over the total amount was subscribed, and finally the total amounted to nearly $70,000.00—perhaps the largest amount ever raised in the diocese by any similar effort. Among the larger appropriations made from this fund, besides the $37,464.30 which went to the national Church, were $3,000.00 for the Home for Children, $1,500.00 for the Home for Women, and $2,500.00 for the renovation of the Church on Sullivan's Island.

Notable in the missionary work in the diocese in 1945 was the organization of a new mission at Denmark, to be called Christ Church, and the renovation of St. Andrew's mission in St. Andrew's parish at a cost of $5,000.00–$4,000.00 from the national Council, $400.00 from the Men's Thank Offering, and $600.00 by the mission. At this time the status of the official organ of the diocese, *"The Diocese"* was changed. Previously it had been sent only to paid subscribers. Now it was decided that it be sent free to every family in the diocese, and this has since been done, issues being reduced from 12 to 8 yearly.

At the Convention of 1945, a committee had been appointed to study the question of colored representation. The next year, on presentation of this committee, a motion was adopted revising Article III of the Constitution to provide for the representation of any groups of churchmen not otherwise represented. This amendment, as proposed, was adopted, but when it came up for final passage the year following (1946), it failed of adoption in a vote by orders, the laity not concurring. The question was presented again in 1949 in the same form, and after rather heated debate, as before, again received preliminary adoption by *viva voce* vote. The next year, the proposed amendment, on motion, was slightly amended, deferring final action until 1951 when once again the plan was rejected by a failure of the laity to concur in its adoption. The question, however, was not easily set aside and continued to be agitated in the diocese. At the Convention in Cheraw (1953), the Committee on Constitution and Canons presented the question once more in the same form of a revision of Article III of the Constitution. A motion for adoption was duly made and seconded, but thereupon the Rev Louis A. Haskell offered a substitute to the simple effect that the Negro churches be invited to apply for admission to the Convention in accordance with the Constitution and Canons of the diocese. This substitute was adopted by a vote of 85 to 31. Under this action in 1954, St. Mark's Church, Charleston, was admitted into Convention as a parish; and Calvary Church, Charleston, and St. Paul's, Orangeburg, as organized missions, all three colored congregations. Thus for the first time in its history colored congregations were admitted to regular representation in the Convention of the diocese. In 1945 the old Berresford Bounty Fund of the parish of Sts. Thomas and Dennis amounting to $37,-336.21 was turned over to the trustees of the diocese (see Journal of the Convention, 1945, p. 83).

In 1947, the diocese was the recipient of the munificent gift by Miss Margaret C. Miller of 138 Wentworth Street for a headquarters of the diocese, thus supplying a long-felt need. It is a very imposing building of Greek revival architecture, with handsome columns in front. A considerable sum of money was soon raised and the building put into form for its purposes. The house was Dedicated by the Bishop on December 5, 1948, having already been adapted and in use since the spring. In it is contained not only the Bishop's office, but a chapel (called The Chapel of the Holy Spirit), reception room and library, office for the registrar and historiographer, for the executive secretary, and for the youth worker with work rooms, and also bedroom for transient visitors. Some of these rooms were renovated, decorated, and furnished as memorials. The next year the diocese was the recipient of another very handsome gift—a trust fund of $275,000.00, to be called the "William H. Schaefer Fund," from the estate in turn of his first wife, Florence Moulton of Boston, his own estate, and finally, by the legacy of Mr. Schaefer's second wife, Lena Warren. The income from this largest gift the diocese has ever received was to be the means of much development in the diocese.

In the fall of 1948, Bishop Carruthers attended the Lambeth Conference in London. He directed the Adult Conference at Kanuga from 1949 to 1953. He was president of the Synod of Sewanee from 1953 to 1956. Beginning from the first, this Episcopate witnessed a very great building development of churches, and especially of parish houses and other buildings, as will be seen in pages following. Not least in the advance work of the diocese was that among the young people with camps and conferences. In 1945, Miss Gertrude Bull resigned as youth worker for both Upper S. C. and this diocese. She was replaced in the diocese alone in 1946 by Miss Mary Harper, who has served until now, except for less than one year, 1950-51. During the years of and following World War II, Camp St. Christopher, being driven from the coast, had been conducted for some years first at Burnt Gin in Sumter County, and then at Camp Juniper near Cheraw. In 1949, it was decided not to develop the site given by the Porchers on Lake Marion but to return to the former site on Seabrook Island. Extensive improvements were made at the old site of Camp St. Christopher. It was developed with many new buildings as the Conference Center of the diocese, including an attractive chapel. A regular Board of Managers was now organized. The entire island was given to the diocese by Mrs. Morawitz December 10, 1951. (See Appendix—Camps and Conferences.) Parallel with these developments, and before, many improvements were made at Camp Baskervill near Pawley's Island, several new buildings being erected. (See Chapter on Archdeaconry and Appendix.) The work of the Archdeaconry for colored work consumed a great deal of the energies of Bishop Carruthers as it did in the case of the former Bishops. Its story is found elsewhere in this volume in the chapter on the Archdeaconry. In this connection, Bishop Carruthers said in his address of 1952: "I am very happy to announce that the diocese also has reached the status of full self-support. For a number of years we have received assistance from the national Council for our Negro work, the figure varying from year to year and for a considerable period being around five or six thousand dollars a year. During the Second World War years, we received a small amount for work in industrial areas. Three years ago the Executive Council voted in a three-year program to relinquish this aid from the general Church and to carry all our work through our own missionary funds. I have already advised the Director of the Home Department of the national Council that beginning with January, 1953, we shall expect no assistance from the national Council. I am sure that it will be a source of satisfaction to the members of this convention to know that South Carolina will no longer be listed among the 'Aided Dioceses' of the Episcopal Church."

In 1949-50, the Woman's Auxiliary raised approximately $6,000.00 for the renovation of the Pinckney Cottage at the Home in York and about the same time, under the leadership of Mr. W. T. C. Bates, the diocese raised and contributed over $14,000.00 toward the building of the new Gadsden Cottage (to cost $50,000.00) at the Home. After the death in 1946 of Rev. Wallace Martin, for twenty-five years chaplain of the Seaman's Home, the work there was continued under the Rev. E. A. LeMoine and then by the Rev. E. M. Claytor. Following the example of the national Church, in 1951, the Convention established *The Church Foundation of the Diocese of South Carolina.* Its purpose is to receive funds by gift, devise, and bequest and administer the same for evangelical, educational, and charitable purposes in the diocese. This purpose was accomplished without the creation of a new corporate body by adopting, with certain conditions guaranteeing diocesan control, of *The Society for the Advancement of Christianity in the Diocese of South Carolina.* This old society thus has acquired this additional character. At the Convention of 1952, $15,000.00 was appropriated to assist the expansion of the Church's work in the "Atomic area" near Barnwell and North Augusta. Results will be noted in the parishes and missions in that area.

In 1952, the diocese cooperated with the trustees of the Porter Military Academy in a campaign to raise funds to clear the school of debt and advance its work. At the same time the Academy revised its Constitution and by-laws, by which the diocese now has more control of the school by the power of nominating trustees (see Appendix).

In 1952 the office of the executive secretary was authorized to assist the Bishop in the work of the diocese. The Rev. Roderick J. Hobart was appointed to this office and continued until 1957 when he was succeeded by the Rev. Waties R. Haynsworth. In 1953 quite a change in the procedure of the Convention of the diocese was inaugurated by the adoption of the system of dividing the Convention into "Workshops" for the study and recommendation of action to be taken by the Convention. A very notable event in diocesan history in 1954 was a great evangelistic mission conducted by the noted evangelist, Canon Bryan Green of England, and his assistant, the Rev. Harold Frankham, in the County Hall in Charleston. It continued from February 21 until March 2. The congregations numbered as many as 3,000. The evangelist spoke also in many other parts of the state and people came from all over the diocese. In the spring of 1954 the national campaign called "Builders for Christ" was organized in the diocese. The diocesan objective, under the leadership of Mr. Ervin E. Dargan with Mr. L. W. Barrett as treasurer, was $65,000.00. Of this, $24,000.00 was for the national fund, chiefly for overseas mission work and theological seminaries— the balance to be used ($21,000.00) for a revolving building fund and for improvements in the diocese. The final result of the campaign was about $45,000.00.

The diocese was well represented at the Anglican Congress held in 1954 in Minneapolis—Bishop Carruthers having served as chairman of the program committee of this great gathering. The diocese has enjoyed quite an expansion in the years of this Episcopate, as will be seen from statistics as well as from the above account and the parish sketches:

	1944	1955
Clergymen	42	56
Parishes and Missions	76	75
Communicants	9,907	12,353
Church Schools	3,018	5,682
Budget	$ 46,519.46	$114,428.88
Total Expended	$188,976.35	$650,978.83

The progress in building with the economic revival has been outstanding; new churches have been built: St. Paul's, Meggett; St. Paul's, Orangeburg; St. Peter's-by-the-Sea, Naval Base; Christ, Denmark; Holy Cross and Faith Memorial, Waccamaw Neck; Messiah, Maryville (removed from North Santee and rebuilt); St. John's, John's Island. New rectories have been built or purchased as follows (14): Charleston, Grace, St. Luke and St. Paul, Holy Communion; Cheraw, James Island and John's Island, Marion, Naval Base, North Charleston, Pinopolis, Sumter, Dillon, Grahamville, Florence. New Parish House: St. Andrew's, Allendale, Barnwell, Bennettsville, Charleston, St. Mark's, St. Luke and St. Paul, Holy Communion; Cheraw, Conway, James Island, John's Island, Mount Pleasant, Myrtle Beach, Naval Base, North Charleston, Orangeburg, Pinopolis, Plantersville, Walterboro, Denmark, Mullins, Kingstree, Sullivan's Island, Fort Motte, Edisto. Also, several buildings at Camp St. Christopher and at Camp Baskervill (see *in loco*). Perhaps the most striking advance has been the number of churches which have attained a status of self-support.

Bishop Carruthers' tenth anniversary was celebrated at the Convention of 1954, held at St. Luke and St. Paul Church. The sermon was preached by Bishop Quin of Texas. Bishop Carruthers was presented a silver bowl and a purse by the people of the diocese, and gifts by the young people. Later, at its Convention, the Woman's Auxiliary presented him with 2,919 dimes. The Bishop expressed his gratitude. The large expansion in the work of the diocese in this Episcopate still continues. The Bishop reported 589 confirmations in 1955—the largest number ever confirmed in one year in the history of the diocese. The diocesan Convention, meeting in the Church of the Holy Communion, Charleston, April 17 and 18, 1956, recommended the raising of a diocesan advance fund, mainly for Church extension, and set up a goal of $25,000.00 for next year, this fund to be entirely separate from assessment and apportionment. It is to be promoted by a special committee and funds handled by a special treasurer.

The Convention voted 94 to 43 for a resolution asserting "there is nothing morally wrong in voluntary recognition of racial differences" and that "voluntary alignments can be both natural and Christian."

The Convention amended the Constitution and canons of the diocese as recommended by a special committee which had been working on this matter for the past two years. The Constitution, among other changes, was amended to admit all active clergy to the diocesan Convention. This was the final step in the needed legislation in the diocese to give regular representation in the diocesan Convention to its Negro churchmen.

SECTION II

LIST OF PARISHES, MISSIONS, AND ARCHDEACONRY, WITH SKETCHES

Adam's Run, Christ Church
Allendale, Holy Communion
Andrews, St. Luke's
Barnwell, Holy Apostles
Beaufort, St. Helena's
  St. Helena's, St. Helena's Island
Bennettsville, St. Paul's
Berkeley County, St. John's
Blackville, St. Alban's
Bluffton, The Cross (St. Luke's Parish)
Bradford Springs, St. Philip's
Charleston, Calvary, Line Street
  Grace, Wentworth at Glebe
  Holy Communion, Ashley at Cannon
  Redeemer (Seamen), Market and East Bay
  St. Andrew's, King St.
  St. John's, Hanover and Amherst
  St. Luke's, Charlotte St.
  St. Luke and St. Paul, Coming St.
  St. Mark's, Thomas and Warren
  St. Michael's, Meeting at Broad
  St. Paul's, Coming
  St. Peter's, Rutledge Ave. at Sumter
  St. Philip's, Church St.
  St. Stephen's, Anson St.
Charleston Heights (Navy Yard), St. Peter's-by-the-Sea
Charleston County
  St. Andrew's Parish
  Old St. Andrew's
  St. Andrew's Mission
  Holy Trinity, Windermere
Cheraw, St. David's
Combahee, Ascension
Conway, St. Paul's
Darlington, St. Matthew's
Denmark, Christ Church
  St. Philip's, Voorhees
Dillon, St. Barnabas'
Dorchester, St. George's (See Mission, St. George's)
Edisto Island, Trinity
Estill, Heavenly Rest

[164]

Eutawville, Epiphany
Florence, St. John's
Florence County, Christ Church, Mars Bluff
Fort Motte, St. Matthew's
Georgetown, Prince George's, Winyah
    St. Cyprian Mission
Gillisonville, Ascension
Goose Creek, Charleston County, St. James'
Grahamville, Holy Trinity
Hagood, Ascension
Hampton, All Saints'
Hartsville, St. Bartholomew's
Huger, Good Shepherd (See Wando)
James Island, St. James'
John's Island, St. John's; Grace, Wadmalaw Island
Kingstree, St. Alban's
Lake City, Mission
Manning, All Saints'
Marion, Advent
Marion County, Britton's Neck and Sandy Bluff
Maryville, Messiah; and Messiah, North Santee
McClellanville, St. James'
McPhersonville, Sheldon
Meggett, St. Paul's
Moncks Corner, Guild Hall, The Barrows
Mount Pleasant, Christ Church and St. Andrew's
Mullins, Christ Church
Myrtle Beach, Trinity
North Charleston, Good Shepherd
Oketee, Grace
Orangeburg, Redeemer
    St. Paul's, State College
Pawley's Island, All Saints', Waccamaw
    Holy Cross and Faith Memorial
Pee Dee, St. Peter's
Pineville, Redeemer
Pinewood, St. Mark's
Pinopolis, Trinity (and Black Oak)
Plantersville, Prince Frederick's
Purysburg, St. Peter's
St. Stephen's, St. Stephen's
St. George's, Mission
Society Hill, Trinity
Stono, St. Paul's
Sullivan's Island, Grace
    Holy Cross
Summerton, St. Matthias'
Summerville, Epiphany
    St. Barnabas'
    St. Paul's

Sumter, Good Shepherd
  Holy Comforter
  Holy Cross, Claremont, Stateburg
Varnville, All Saints'
Walterboro, Atonement
  St. Bartholomew's Parish
  St. Jude's
Wando, St. Thomas' and St. Dennis' (Pompion Hill Chapel)
Wedgefield, St. Augustine's
Yemassee, All Saints'
Work among Colored (Archdeaconry)

CHRIST CHURCH, WILTON, ADAM'S RUN
Established 1834

Wiltown, on the South Edisto River, was one of the earliest settlements in South Carolina—elections were ordered to be held there in 1683. In early days, it was called New London. There were eighty houses in the town in 1740. The Presbyterian Church was established at Wiltown at a very early date, apparently before 1710. It was served by the famous Presbyterian minister and missionary, the Rev. Archibald Stobo, until his death in 1741. The site of the first Presbyterian Church is described by Howe in his history of the Presbyterian Church in South Carolina, as a beautiful and picturesque spot in St. Paul's Parish, Colleton District, on the east bank of the Edisto River. "Standing on the Bluff, one is surrounded by widespreading live-oaks, and looks over the beautiful stream below him, an extensive reach of country covered by rice fields which in spring-time or at harvest is one of the loveliest prospects in the low country of the State." The Presbyterian Church on this site was moved in 1767 to a more convenient location for the congregation four miles distant.

This region was located in St. Paul's Parish and under the charge of its rectors. There was no Episcopal Church here until "Christ Church, Wilton" was organized here in 1835 on account of the great distance from St. Paul's. Services had been begun the year before by the Rev. Stephen Elliott, later Bishop of Georgia. The first regular minister was the Rev. James H. Fowles, who had been converted in the great Beaufort revival in 1831 and was an ardent evangelical. Bishop Bowen reports in 1836 a new Church being erected in Wilton, and later, "The building was rapidly and neatly finished and both it and its site have been highly and generally admired." The site of this building was the same as that of the first Presbyterian Church at Wiltown, which had evidently fallen into ruins. This new Church was described as ". . . a beautiful specimen of chaste and simple Grecian architecture." It was Consecrated by Bishop Bowen April 27, 1836, assisted by Mr. Fowles and the Rev. Messrs. Gadsden, Leverett, and Dalcho. The Bishop commented "Besides the Church, which is of singular beauty and completeness, the same liberal temper has led to the provision of a residence near it, for the minister, with every circumstance consulted, necessary to his comfort. We are rejoined in the example thus set." Among laymen prominent in the Church when it was established were Colonel Morris, John LaRoche, Henry Seabrook, John H. Wilson, first lay delegate to the diocesan Convention, William Brisbane, and Joseph W. Faber.

Mr. Fowles, in his first report in 1837, gives the number of families as 24; communicants, 25; services twice every Sunday in the season (six months) and as many on the plantations, great attention being given to the spiritual needs of the Negroes. On account of malaria thereabouts, the Church was not kept open all summer as a rule, but in 1840 we are told it was—chiefly for the Negroes—half as many whites attending as in the winter and 200 or 300 Negroes. Mr. Fowles resigned in November, 1840. Rev. J. B. Gallagher took charge a year later but only for about a year, going to Georgia. Then from this state in 1844 came the Rev. Edward T. Walker, who continued as rector for nine years. In 1848, a chapel was erected in Adamsville that services might be held the year round. A bell was given and a very comfortable parsonage was also built at this time, costing $1,000.00, through the generosity of Joseph W. Faber. Mr. R. I. Middleton gave an organ. The rector at this time took charge of a large congregation of Negroes, who had been under the care of Methodist missionaries.

Rev. Richardson Graham became rector January, 1853, continuing until January, 1855. The services were held regularly at the parish Church, and at the chapel in summer. In 1853, a gallery was added to the chapel at Adamsville. When the Rev. W. O. Prentiss assumed charge in 1855, he reports that most of the Negro communicants had left for other denominations. He resigned August, 1857, but returned in November, 1868, the Rev. J. B. Seabrook becoming assistant minister. Mr. Prentiss left November, 1860; Mr. Seabrook continued some services in 1861, the Rev. John H. Elliott (deacon) having taken charge the end of 1860, continuing until 1863.

Being in the very path of the Union Army, the Church and its members suffered dreadfully in the War between the States. Such, however, was the loyal devotion of the membership of the Church that services seem never to have been entirely suspended in those trying days. The chapel at Adamsville disappeared at the end of the war. This is the report concerning the parish Church made in 1868: "This beautiful building is standing, embowered as of old in its venerable oaks, but its doors are closed and its congregation scattered. The pews were in part removed by the Confederates and the building used as a commissary depot. The pleasant homes of the planters on the Edisto River were generally burnt in the march of the Federal troops. No white families live near the Church— freedmen occupy the country and inhabit the only surviving mansion. A remnant of this congregation have settled ten miles below, were educated and once wealthy men, may be seen plowing their lands and grinding their corn, while their wives and daughters cook and wash. A missionary service once a month constitutes the extent of their religious privileges." But many services were held by lay readers in private homes.

The white population had nearly all left the neighborhood of the Church. The Rev. Mr. Bellinger, who was now missionary in charge, in 1869 reports holding services in the Presbyterian Church in Adam's Run, loaned for the purpose, at the residence of Mr. Edward LaRoche on Toogoodoo, and at Maj. Hawkins King's. For the succeeding years services were held at many different places, at those places mentioned and also at Mr. R. J. LaRoche's and Mr. J. C. Whaley's. In 1877, at Lewis Bluff at the head of North Edisto Inlet, a cotton house was "fitted with seats and garnished for public worship—twenty to forty persons attended the services." Rev. J. H. Cornish, having succeeded Mr. Bellinger in 1876 in charge, reported, "The responses were given with a voice and heartiness which is cheering." During this period of a depression such as our generation knows not of, the parish could not support a rector. Mr. Cornish reports amount paid to the rector in money nothing, and yet he received, he says, "no inconsiderable sum being the time and labor expended in conveying the minister from the railroad and between the stations, of at least two days of a man and horse or mule, or ox and cart and a dug-out, and a man to paddle, on every occasion of the rector's visit, besides providing for his sustenance while among them."

In 1880, the Rev. W. O. Prentiss became rector and in this year he reports the parish now dilapidated and inconvenient of access to the majority of the congregation, and so plans began to be formulated to build a Church in Adam's Run. Conditions in the parish now steadily improved. In 1881, a communion service was purchased and other properties added. At last the congregation, so long practically homeless because transportation to the old Church under the conditions existing was impossible, now was able to take active steps toward the building of a Church at Adam's Run. This was actually accomplished in the year following the earthquake (1886) when the present building was completed. That must have been a joyful day for the veterans of that long and hard depression, when they gathered here on Sunday, November 13, 1887, to Consecrate the Church. The Rev. W. O. Prentiss, the rector, said Morning Prayer; Rev. John Johnson of St. Philip's said the Ante-Communion; Mr. Bellinger preached the sermon. Bishop Howe Consecrated the Church and afterwards confirmed three persons and celebrated the Holy Communion. At this time, there were 15 families connected with the parish and 24 communicants. Mr. Prentiss continued in charge until 1893. The Rev. W. F. Bellinger began to officiate December, 1893, continuing until 1895. After a period of vacancy, the Rev. J. M. Pringle became rector in 1897. The wardens now were D. McK. Allston and J. O. McCants, and the secretary-treasurer, John C. Wilson. Mr. Pringle was rector until 1905. Rev. L. F. Guerry became rector March, 1905, serving until ill health compelled him to resign in 1907 when Rev. Thomas Perry Baker became rector.

In 1910-11, a recessed chancel with a triple window was built and soon after a Sunday School and robing room. Mr. Baker resigned in January, 1915. At this time, the wardens were: M. W. Simmons and John C. Wilson, also Mr. Wilson was secretary and treasurer; the lay reader, H. K. Jenkins. Rev. Herbert Frederick Schroeter served from 1915 until December, 1917, being succeeded then by the Rev. W. B. Guion for 1918. The Rev. Alexander M. Rich became rector September, 1919, serving until 1922. The Rev. Paul Duè was rector for a time in 1923. The Rev. Capers Satterlee, after his ordination as a deacon in June, 1923, became, first, minister-in-charge and the next year rector. Mr. Satterlee's short ministry was marked especially by an increase of work among young people. He resigned Easter 1926, being succeeded by the Rev. Richard E. Page, the Rev. E. S. Middleton, D.D., having had the services for a short time. Mr. Page left the end of 1928, the Rev. Alvin W. Skardon becoming rector soon after. In 1930, the wardens were Thomas C. Legare and W. M. Barnwell; Gordon S. Taylor, secretary and treasurer. In 1930, the parish house was built opposite the Church on the south side of the highway. Mr. Skardon resigned April, 1935, when the Rev. Sumner Guerry became rector.

The parish celebrated its Centennial on November 29, 1936, with a service by Mr. Guerry when Bishop Thomas preached a historical sermon. Mr. Guerry resigned January, 1944. Rev. F. W. Ambler then supplied services until Rev. E. A. Le Moine became rector in 1946. The Rev. Lawton Riley succeeded Mr. LeMoine the next year, continuing until 1951 when the Rev. Thomas L. Crum became rector in conjunction with St. Paul's, Meggett, the two Churches being united again. In the summer of 1951, the Church was re-painted and a brick walk laid to the Church. Also, the parish house was improved with better equipment added. In 1956 a brick porch was added to the Church and extensive other improvements made to it and to the parish house. Mr. Crum resigned at the end of 1955. The Rev. George La Bruce is now in charge, haven taken charge in the fall of 1956.

HOLY COMMUNION, ALLENDALE
Established 1875

In July of 1875, the Rev. E. E. Bellinger inaugurated services in Allendale. For the following year he reports five families and 29 services, nine on Sundays, held at the residence of Mr. Gibbes about five miles from the depot. In 1877 the Church members united with other denominations in erecting a Union Church where the services were then held. The Convocation met in Allendale April, 1882 (and also in December, 1883). Besides Mr. Bellinger the following clergymen were present, Messrs. Allston, Barnwell, Guerry, Kershaw, La Roche, Johnson, Sams, Scott, and Tillinghast. In 1886 Mr. Bellinger reports 13 families in the mission, now making efforts to build a Church. Services still held in the Union Church.

A site for a Church was purchased in 1892. The Rev. S. E. Prentiss succeeded Mr. Bellinger in the charge of Allendale in 1894. He resigned in 1901, being succeeded by Rev. J. B. Walker who served until May, 1902. For a time beginning about 1899 this mission was called "Advent, Allendale". The Rev. J. C. Waring followed Mr. Walker in 1903.

Under Mr. Waring the Church lot was sold, a new one bought, and a Church building was soon begun. It was completed and furnished at a cost of about $1,900.00, and Consecrated by Bishop Capers on November 12, 1903, during a meeting there of the Charleston Convocation. The Bishop described the new building as "a very becoming and churchly edifice of brick." The old "Union Church" and its furniture was sold and the proceeds given to the Episcopalians to assist in the building. It has been said that the Church is a monument to Mr. Waring and to Mr. Tudor Farmer. The name of the mission was now changed from "Advent" to "Holy Communion". The warden was then H. T. Farmer, the treasurer H. W. Montague. Among the first gifts to the Church was a silver chalice presented by Mrs. S. L. Clarkson in memory of her son, Richard S. Clarkson, a brother of Dr. C. D. Clarkson of Allendale. Mr. Waring resigned April, 1905, being succeeded by the Rev. S. C. Beckwith. Mr. Waring resumed charge May 1, 1906, for a short time. Rev. A. E. Evison assumed charge June, 1908, and until 1918 when Rev. A. Rufus Morgan succeeded until 1920. The Rev. C. W. Boyd was the next minister, October, 1921, for a short time. In 1923 the mission was organized into a parish and admitted as such into Convention. The Rev. I. deL. Brayshaw was in charge in 1924.

In 1925, the Rev. Frank M. Brunton coming from St. George's, Bermuda, became rector and the first resident minister of the Church in Allendale. Vesper lights of exquisite design were installed at this time. At this time the wardens were C. B. Farmer, Jr., and Dr. A. A. Patterson; treasurer, Mrs. C. W. Wilson; deputies to Convention, A. A. Patterson, C. R. Wilson, J. R. Boyleston, and C. B. Farmer, Jr. Rev. Joseph Burton was appointed Archdeacon of the Beaufort District of the Charleston Convocation and took charge in 1927. In 1928 he assumed charge of Holy Apostles, Barnwell, and moved to the rectory there but resigned the next year. Rev. S. R. Guignard of Upper South Carolina and the Rev. L. G. Wood, retired, supplied services until Rev. John Adams Pinckney took charge June 28, 1931, just after his ordination to the diaconate. Soon after this, steps were taken to build a rectory. An attractive frame building adjoining the Church was completed and occupied by the Rev. and Mrs. J. A. Pinckney soon after Mr. Pinckney's ordination to the priesthood by Bishop Thomas. This service was held in the Holy Communion on May 18, 1932. Mr. Pinckney was presented by the Rev. W. B. Sams, the Rev. R. M. Marshall preached the sermon, Messrs. Bull and Burnz also assisting. After seven years of devoted service in this field Mr. Pinckney resigned, going to Tryon, N. C. His leaving was a great loss to the young people's work in the diocese. The Rev. Theodore Porter Ball took charge the summer after his ordination on June 30, 1938, serving for two years. At this time the wardens were C. B. Farmer and Dr. Alfred A. Patterson; Mr. Stoney Sanders, secretary; and Miss Eunice Keel, treasurer. The Church suffered a great loss January 24, 1944 in the death of Dr. Alfred Patterson. He had served as a warden for many years. There were some supplies but no regular rector until the Rev. W. L. Martin took charge on his ordination in 1944. Mr. Martin resigned January 15, 1947. He was soon succeeded by the Rev. Gordon D. Bennett. At this time a Church school building was erected.

In 1950 the wardens were C. B. Farmer and J. Reid Boyleston who was also secretary, and treasurer Mrs. J. M. Riley, Jr. Mr. Bennett resigned in 1950. A lot was given the Church for a parish house by Mrs. J. Sims Spigenor in 1951. In this summer Rev. George Milton Crum became rector. The parish house was built the next year being completed and Dedicated on June 22, 1952, quite a spacious building with 1,500 square feet of floor space. The parish was now better prepared for the increasing population in that section due to the atomic plant on the Savannah River. Recently lights of exquisite design were installed by the Guild. Mr. Crum was succeeded temporarily by the Rev. John Rivers in the fall of 1956. He had gone to England for a year's study at St. Augustine's College, Canterbury, having been selected for this by the general Church. He resumed charge in the spring of 1957.

ST. LUKE'S, ANDREWS
Established 1916

It was while the Rev. A. R. Mitchell was Archdeacon of the Charleston Convocation and by him that this Church was established. It would be impossible to tell better of the beginnings of St. Luke's than Mr. Mitchell himself does in *The Diocese* (February, 1924).

"The growth of the town of Andrews was phenomenal, starting with a few families, it rapidly grew and now has about 2,000 inhabitants. It was named in honor of Mr. Walter H. Andrews, to whom it owes its origin and great development. So much impressed was Bishop Guerry with the bright promise of the place, and learning that a few communicants of our Church resided there, that he requested Archdeacon A. R. Mitchell to visit the place and see what was the outlook for a mission. After communicating with some of our Church people, the Archdeacon visited the town on March 15, 1916, for the purpose of holding a service. On arriving there, he learned that there was to be a union service that night in the Baptist Church, and he was requested to preach, which he did, to a large and interesting congregation. He stated the object of his visit and was most cordially welcomed by all the people of the town. Arrangements were made to have the Holy Communion service the next morning in the Methodist Church, which was kindly offered to him. So on March 16, 1916, the first Episcopal Service was held in the town."

The Archdeacon found about ten communicants. On June 8, he again preached in the Methodist Church; and in the home of Mrs. Ettie Payne, the mission was organized as St. Luke's with the appointment of Messrs. A. A. May and Reese Ford as wardens, and Mr. LeRoy Payne as secretary and treasurer on November 4, 1916. A committee of three, A. A. May, W. Fred Ebert, and George M. Tuten, were appointed to see Mr. Andrews and secure a suitable lot. June 9, service was held in the school house, and that afternoon, the Archdeacon baptized two children of Mr. and Mrs. W. F. Ebert. On December 3, service was held again in the school house and a fine vested choir, trained by Miss Marie Rivers, one of the teachers in the graded school, rendered the whole Church service beautifully. The evening of the same day, Bishop Guerry preached and held confirmation for the first time, that of Marion Louise Wheeler. A guild was formed with Mrs. Etta Payne as president. It was decided that the proposed Church be erected in memory of Bishop Ellison Capers. The Charleston Convocation met in the Presbyterian Church, April 18, 1918. A "large upper room" was secured on Main Street as a place of worship and a Sunday School was begun. Among the gifts to the mission was an altar from Christ Church, Greenville; the guild presented a brass cross and vases in memory of Bishop Capers; the altar service book was given by Mrs. Payne; the Archdeacon presented the Communion Service with glass cruets given to him for his work. The mission was regularly incorporated with the following trustees: Walter H. Andrews, A. A. May, Reese Ford, G. M. Tuten, Thomas Ford, D. O. DuBose, M.D., and S. Eugene Jenkins. A lot was given for a Church building but changed for a better location and a Church built. A handsome brick Church was planned, but the "boll-weevil depression" led to adoption of a simpler style Church, which was built in 1923.

Archdeacon Mitchell resigned on account of sickness February 1, 1921. He was succeeded by the Rev. J. S. Lightbourn, then in 1923 by Rev. John Ridout, for a year. The Rev. C. W. Boyd took charge in 1925, then the Rev. William Way supplied in 1926, until the Rev. J. M. Dick of Kingstree succeeded in 1927. The Church was Consecrated on May 20, 1928, as St. Luke's Memorial Church. The Rev. A. R. Mitchell, the founder, preached the sermon. As the Bishop wrote "the joy of the congregation was not unmixed with sorrow." The senior warden, Mr. A. A. May, one of the founders of the Church, though unwell, was able to take a part in the service. During the Communion service, he became ill and in a few moments passed away, having first seen this culmination in the establishment of the Church in Andrews, a wish of his heart.

Mr. Dick left the diocese the same month, being followed by Rev. H. D. Bull of Georgetown, who served until Rev. H. L. Hoover of Hartsville took charge January 1, 1931. On January 20, 1935, the mission suffered a great loss in the death of Mr. W. H. Andrews, founder of the town and one of the founders of this Church, and for 20 years a devoted and generous member. For many years, he taught a class of boys in the Church school. The Rev. D. M. Hobart succeeded Mr. Hoover in 1937; the warden at this time was S. E. Jenkins; secretary and treasurer, Mrs. Raymond Andrews. Mr. Hobart resigned as minister-in-charge early in 1940. During Mr. Hobart's time and after, the Church was connected with the associate mission. After his ordination June 5, 1940, the Rev. William Moultrie Moore was in charge. He resigned July, 1942, when the Rev. W. R. Haynsworth of the associate mission held the services, until the Rev. William Henry Hanckel, Jr., took charge after his ordination on St. Paul's Day, 1943. Mr. Hanckel resigned in the fall of 1944, when the Rev. R. C. Patton of Darlington began to supply services until succeeded by the Rev. Allen Webster Joslin, who was in turn succeeded in 1947 by the Rev. deSaussure P. Moore of Kingstree. In 1949, the wardens were S. E. Jenkins and R. M. Andrews; treasurer, Miss Sara D. Childress. The Rev. James Stoney had the charge in 1950 in connection with St. Paul's, Conway. The Rev. R. C. Patton conducted a helpful mission in 1950. Mr. Stoney resigned this year. Mr. Samuel Harper was now treasurer. After Mr. Stoney left, the Rev. Frank V. D. Fortune of Sumter supplied services until the Rev. Edward T. Small of Conway took charge, serving until the summer of 1956. At this time the charge was assumed by the Rev. Luther Parker. The Church in Andrews in 1956 was removed to a more eligible and larger site in the town and steps taken to build a parish house. The communicant membership had now increased to 32.

CHURCH OF THE HOLY APOSTLES, BARNWELL
Established 1848

This Church had its origin at a meeting of interested persons held in the Masonic Hall in Barnwell on Saturday, November 18, 1848. The Rev. T. J. Young, assistant minister of St. Michael's, Charleston, being present on invitation, presided. Resolutions to organize, providing other necessary steps, presented by A. P. Aldrich were unanimously adopted, the Church to be designated, "The Church of the Holy Apostles", the Bishop to be notified, charter to be applied for, as also admission to the Convention of the diocese, the Advancement Society to be asked for help in securing a minister. A committee was appointed to draft a Constitution and the following were elected as a vestry: wardens, D. D. Hallonquist, and A. P. Aldrich; vestrymen, B. F. Brown, James T. Aldrich, J. C. Buckingham. The Church was admitted to Convention February 20, 1850. Services in Barnwell were only occasional by missionaries for several years. These services were held in the Masonic Hall as was the case on April 14th, 1850, when a clergyman visited the Church, and on June 27th following reported that he had held services for three successsive days, having Communion and baptizing ten infants. At this time a subscription was opened for the building of a Church, reaching about $1,500.00 toward $3,000.00 needed. An appeal to the diocese was determined. There were then seven families connected with the Church, with eight white and two colored communicants.

The Rev. Edward Phillips resigned St. Thomas and St. Dennis and became the first rector of the Holy Apostles, July, 1852. For the year following he held service on alternate Sundays, having baptized six children. He reports a lot having been given for a Church, with prospects of building the Church without debt. After about a year Mr. Phillips was succeeded for a time by the Rev. Charles T. Bland but his tenure was short, the Bishop reporting in October, 1854, that the field was vacant. So the work was delayed again. The first sustained work of a minister was that of the Rev. E. A. Wagner who became rector December, 1855. He reports $600-.00 needed to build a Church. In 1856 Mr. Wagner bought a plantation on the edge of the town and set aside one and one-eighth acres for a Church and yard. Work soon began at last after eight years. The responsibility for the completion of the work was thus expressed: "Rector and one of the vestry for a part; and for the rest the rector alone". The Church is thus described in the *South-*

ern Episcopalian (Vol. IV, p. 44), we quote in part: "At the intersection of four streets and directly fronting the main street which leads out from the Court House . . . is the new edifice of the Church of the Holy Apostles as planned by Messrs. Barbot and Seyle of Charleston. It is a Gothic structure of wood, and combines in its exterior appearance and interior arrangements, a simplicity of plan and an architectural and ecclesiastical propriety, not often seen in our rural districts. It consists of nave, 25 x 50; chancel, 12 x 15; vestry, 8 x 9; and tower, 8 x 8, at its base which forms the northern extrance. . . . The steeple consists of tower, square 8 x 8, which is 40 feet high . . . finished with a plain cross. This symbol of Jesus crucified for many, may be seen in almost every part of the village." There was a gallery, stained glass, a chancel arch. The altar was the gift of the Rev. T. J. Young of St. Michael's, Charleston, and the service books were given by a layman in remembrance of benefits received from Mr. Young. The Church was Consecrated by Bishop Davis on Wednesday, March 11, 1857, with the name of "The Church of the Holy Apostles". It was a red letter day. On the night before a service was held in the Masonic Hall, the old place of worship of the congregation, the Rev. T. F. Davis, Jr. preaching. The Rev. J. H. Cornish preached at the Consecration service. That night the Rev. C. P. Gadsden preached, and the Bishop lectured on confirmation, confirming one. The next morning the Bishop preached, in the afternoon the Rev. Cranmore Wallace, at night the Rev. J. H. Elliott. Other clergymen taking part were the Rev. Messrs. E. A. Wagner, the rector, A. T. Porter, and J. D. McCollough. Barbot and Seyle of Charleston were the architects. The total cost of the building was $3,500.00.

Mr. Wagner resigned in 1860 going to Texas, and was succeeded by the Rev. Barnwell B. Sams, in May, 1862. The Church was badly damaged in the war. Mr. Sams continued in charge until 1871 doing in addition a large missionary work. The Rev. J. H. Cornish succeeded in 1874. Serious defects in the Church building rendered it unsafe in 1866, but this was corrected the next year, and the following year a new organ was installed and a chimney built. Mr. Cornish's rectorship ended with his death May 24, 1878. In 1876 the Church had so lost strength that it became dormant as a "parish," falling to the status of a "mission". After a period when the Church was vacant in March, 1883, the Rev. R. W. Barnwell took charge first as a deacon and then as rector, the parish being reorganized by the election of wardens and vestrymen. He was succeeded by the Rev. J. B. Williams who served until he went to

Georgetown in 1892. The Rev. S. E. Prentiss then served from 1895 until 1903, being succeeded by the Rev. Charles E. Cabaniss in 1904, then followed the Rev. S. C. Beckwith in 1905 to September, 1906. After a short vacancy the Rev. A. E. Evison had charge for eight years. Largely through his efforts a commodious rectory was built at a cost of $4,000.00. The Rev. A. Rufus Morgan followed (1918-1920) then the Rev. Charles W. Boyd, 1922, and the Rev. I. deL. Brayshaw, 1924. The Rev. Howard Cady was rector from 1924 to November, 1926.

Easter Day, 1925, was a great one in the history of this Church: a handsome pipe organ had just been installed largely through the generosity of Mr. Cady, in memory of Schuyler Merritt Cady, his brother; on the altar were new brass eucharistic candlesticks given by Mrs. L. M. Calhoun in memory of her daughter, Annie Elizabeth, all this and a large congregation. The Rev. Joseph Burton, being appointed Archdeacon of the Savannah River district, served as rector from 1928 until November, 1929, living in the rectory. In 1929 fine brass vases were placed in the Church in memory of Miss M. N. Brunson. The Rev. S. R. Guignard and the Rev. L. G. Wood supplied services until the coming of the Rev. John A. Pinckney in June, 1931, serving until 1936, living in Allendale. The Rev. R. H. Jackson supplied during an interregnum until the Rev. T. P. Ball took charge in the summer of 1938 serving for about two years. Mr. W. H. Hanckel held the services for a time. The Rev. W. L. Martin took charge in February, 1945, first as deacon then as rector, until 1947. At this time a vested choir was installed, Mrs. W. L. Molair, directress. In 1946 a new altar was given by Mrs. Edgar Brown and Miss Emily Jeffries and a new heating plant was installed; other gifts were a processional cross by Mrs. Louise Lightsey and her sister, and a Church flag by the Woman's Auxiliary. Mr. Martin resigned in January, 1947 and the Very Rev. S. Alston Wragg acted as rector until 1950. The Church was completely renovated and improved in 1948. The centennial of the Church was celebrated in February, 1949. The Rev. Roderick J. Hobart took charge in August, 1949.

Barnwell was now experiencing an unprecedented increase in population owing to the nearby atomic plant of the government. In 1952 a parish house was erected in the Church yard to meet the new demands. At this time Mr. C. F. Molair, senior warden for a great many years, retired and was made senior warden emeritus. The Rev. H. D. Bull, D.D., became rector July 1, 1953. After a useful and happy ministry Dr. Bull died suddenly April 27, 1957, a great loss not only to this parish but to the diocese, being president of the Standing Committee.

SAINT HELENA'S, BEAUFORT
Established 1712
(See Dalcho, p. 375)

Dalcho tells us that in 1817 the Church in Beaufort underwent considerable repairs and enlargement, being now 80½ by 37½ feet with a steeple 118 feet high. The Rev. John Barnwell Campbell had been rector since 1812. He left the diocese in 1821 and was succeeded in 1824 by the Rev. Joseph Rogers Walker, who then began one of the longest rectorships in the history of the diocese, especially famous for the number of men sent into the ministry. Dr. Thomas Fuller was the deputy to the Convention this year. In 1827 progress is noted in the parish—services on "Feasts and Fasts", on Wednesday mornings and Friday nights, lectures to children with "magic lantern", and Communion on first Sundays in each month. In 1829 both parish and Sunday School libraries were established, and at this time the galleries in the Church were reconstructed in a more seemly way; a year later a gallery was built "over the organ." Aside from their attendance in these galleries, services were provided for colored people in a house, fitted up for the purpose, on Wednesday and Sunday nights. A remarkable revival in this part of the diocese began in July, 1831, in Grahamville under the rector, the Rev. T. J. Young, who called in the Rev. Mr. Walker and the Rev. C. P. Elliott to assist. The movement culminated in this parish with the preaching of the Rev. Dan Miller, a Presbyterian minister. As a result of this revival the membership of the parish was doubled; 75 were confirmed at one time and some ten or eleven men became ministers. There were now 98 white and 234 colored, respectively, in two Sunday Schools with 51 teachers (Cf. Part One, Chapter I.) In 1834 Mr. Walker significantly reported eight scholarships for the education of pious young men for the ministry, $1,500.00 having been contributed the year previous for this purpose. Lacking the securing of a missionary, assistance was given to the Methodists in their work among the Negroes. Reporting in 1835 the loss of communicants, he states, ". . . six of them to serve in the ministry of the Church." In 1835 a rectory was bought. In 1838, $2,100.00 was expended for non-parochial purposes: $1,050.00 for general missions, $400.00 for missions among slaves, $200.00 for theological education, $130.00 for cause of Sunday Schools, etc., besides $800.00 to put the Church in becoming order. The parish was represented in the Convention of 1838 by John M. Verdier and B. B. Sams. Other deputies in this period were Henry McKee, Middleton Stuart, and Thomas Fuller, M.D. The Rev. Stephen Elliott, Jr., professor of S. C. College, assisted in the parish in the summer for some years previous to his Consecration as Bishop of Georgia in 1841.

The congregation had now so increased that it became necessary to enlarge the Church. This work of rebuilding and enlarging was completed in May, 1842; and the Church Consecrated with the name "St. Helena's" July 25, 1842. The Bishop remarked that the Church was so enlarged and altered as to be called *new*. It now measured 60 feet square with extreme length of 75 feet, the galleries 60 x 14 feet for increased accommodations for Negroes. Mr. Walker had strong ideas to the effect that work among these people had been too much restricted to education and that there should be more effort toward sustained religious influence to deepen and render permanent the teaching. "While separate schools and separate lectures cannot be dispensed with yet, there should be association with the whites in pastoral and sacramental privileges." He stated that the chief motive in the rebuilding of the Church was "to make suitable and sufficient accommodation for their slaves." In 1843 a new and superior organ was installed in the Church.

The Rev. Richardson Graham became assistant minister and missionary in 1847 for work especially among the slaves—"rides 25 to 30 miles on Sundays, preaches, catechises, and visits the sick during the week." In 1849 he had work on seventeen plantations. Rev. Stiles Mellichamp succeeded Mr. Graham as assistant in 1851. Because of overflowing congregations in 1852 the floor of the tower was opened into the Church thus gaining six large pews. Mr. Mellichamp resigned December 1, 1853, going to James Island. Proportionately, this parish was reputed to be the largest contributor to missions and education of any in the country. At this time the Rev. W. H. Barnwell, residing in Beaufort, often assisted in the parish. In 1854 the Rev. Edward T. Walker assisted in the colored work becoming regular assistant in 1856. In 1858 two chapels were erected for the Negroes, one in the town called Grace Chapel and one in the country called St. Stephen's. The latter, on the plantation of Mr. A. Seabrook, was Consecrated by Bishop Davis on February 28, 1858 when he also confirmed 24 colored persons. The Rev. Charles E. Leverett followed the Rev. E. T. Walker in charge of this work among the Negroes.

The original steeple, 118 feet high with a clock, was removed before the war, probably because it had become unsafe. The raid of the enemy on Beaufort on November 6, 1861, brought parish life to a sudden standstill. Mr. Walker went to St. Matthew's and Mr. Leverett ministered principally about Columbia; members scattered far and near. Mr. Walker returned to the parish in 1866 to find deep prostration. He recommenced services for a slowly returning congregation. On his visit May 20, 1866, the Bishop found the "contrast with other days strong and painful." The Church was a wreck of its former self and could not be used. The Federal forces had converted it into a hospital, removed the pews and galleries and floored it across to form a second story. The confiscation of all property in Beaufort had reduced the people to destitution. However, missionary funds and a self-sacrificing minister led to gradual improvement. Northern people settled in Beaufort helped, and so a partial restoration was effected and services again were held in the Church the Sunday after Easter, 1867. In 1869 by the kindness of friends in Virginia and Maryland the parsonage was so repaired as again to be occupied. There had been no restoration of property. The people were very poor and the rector received no fixed salary. At this time there were reported 35 families. Elected delegates to the Convention were, in 1870, Allard Barnwell, A. S. Gibbes, F. F. Sams and H. M. Stuart. A new roof was put on the Church in 1874, one-half of the expense being borne by friends in St. Peter's, Perth Amboy, N. J. A new organ to replace, on a smaller scale, that lost in the war was installed in 1876, officers of the U. S. Fleet assisting. The next year considerable repairs were again made, largely by help of the legacy of Mr. T. C. Moore of Plainfield, N. J., left to assist churches damaged in the war. Several churches in the diocese were benefitted by this legacy. This same Mr. Moore had given Mr. Walker $1,200.00 soon after the war for the poor in the parish. Mr. Walker died April 2, 1879, having served as a much beloved rector for 55 years, being absent only from the invasion of November, 1861, until peace was restored after four years. Mr. Walker was said to have been descended from the Rogers who was burned at the stake with Bishop Cranmer. (Three other clergymen of like descent who served in this diocese were his son, Albert R. Walker, Edward T. Walker, and his grandson, Joseph R. Walker.) Mr. Walker's was a profitable service, distinguished not least by the number of men who entered the ministry under his rectorship. In his semi-centennial sermon, he himself stated that during his rectorship here twenty-six had entered the ministry.

Mr. Walker was immediately succeeded by Rev. John Kershaw. He often also held services at Port Royal. He resigned to go to Georgia in 1884, and the Rev. P. D. Hay succeeded in 1885. A parochial guild was organized in 1887 with 50 members and seven branches. The following year a Sunday School building was completed, the plans being furnished gratuitously by the Bishop's son, W. B. W. Howe, Jr., architect. In 1891 the parish branch of the Woman's Auxiliary was organized. The Church and churchyard suffered great damage in the great storm of August, 1893, but restoration was soon effected. Mr. Hay resigned Easter, 1894. Rev. S. B. Rathbun served from 1895 until 1897, then followed William Louis Githens in 1898. He was made rector emeritus in 1906. The next rectors were Joseph W. Sparks (1907-09), and Theodore Wood Clift (1910-14). Mr. Clift died October 14, 1914, greatly beloved. Rev. C. W. Boyd came next (1915-17). The Rev. Ambler M. Blackford (1918-20) was also pastor at Marine Camp on Parris Island. Rev. Maynard Marshall became rector March 1, 1920. The officers of the Church in 1921 were: wardens, H. M. Stuart, H. M. Bristol; secretary, E. E. Lengnick; treasurer, W. H. Hull.

In 1930 the entire interior of the Church was renewed and beautified. At this time the old Hastings organ, through a friend's generosity, was rebuilt and additions made. In 1941 the handsome steeple on St. Helena's was built. It replaces the original one taken down before the war and is the same height—118 feet. It was designed by Albert Simons of Charleston after the style of both St. Michael's and St. Philip's in Charleston. It was the gift of Mr. and Mrs. John S. Williams and was Dedicated on June 1, 1941, by Bishop Thomas assisted by the rector. Mr. Marshall resigned in January, 1944, and was succeeded in the following April by the Rev. Malcolm W. Lockhart, who had served as chaplain of the Marine Corps on Parris Island and who served until his death early in 1946. He was followed by Rev. Henry Powers until the coming of the Rev. John W. Hardy in August, 1951.

ST. HELENA'S, ST. HELENA'S ISLAND
Beaufort County
Founded 1812
(See Dalcho, p. 395)

This Church existed long before 1812, as Dalcho tells us, as a chapel of ease to the parish Church in Beaufort. It was at this time, however, that its life as an independent parish began, the Rev. Philip Mathews becoming its first rector as Dalcho states.

(Diocesan records indicate 1814.) The old walls, of tabby, or as this historian says, "Tapia and brick," still stand on the island, an interesting reminder of a long history. Benjamin Jenkins represented the parish in Convention in 1813. There were 20 families connected with the Church in 1824. Mr. Matthews continued rector until his death in 1827, being succeeded December 11, 1827, by the Rev. John S. Field, deacon. He reported the Church very much depleted, the population of the island decreasing. Mr. Field was followed in 1831 by Rev. David McElheran, who continued until 1856. He found 21 families. During 1832 he held 72 services in the parish Church and at Helenaville (the summer residence), 42 services in private homes, mostly in the parsonage, there being no chapel at this time. The next year the parish Church was repaired and a gallery put in, and also a chapel built at Helenaville. It was Consecrated by Bishop Bowen in 1835. Thomas A. Coffin was the delegate to Convention in 1834.

In 1841 the Church lost many by an epidemic disease on the island. Mrs. McElheran taught the white Sunday School and also superintended the instruction of the Negroes. On his visit May 13, 1844, the Bishop described the summer chapel as "convenient, unadorned, yet neat and designated by an appropriate cupola, and it was built and finished *principally* by the hands of the worthy, humble minister, as was also his study apartment." In 1846 a cathechist was employed for work among the Negroes. The next year the parish Church and the vestry house adjoining were repaired and re-shingled. In 1850-1851 a new chancel, pulpit, desks, and vestry room were erected and the interior of the Church painted; an organ had been given a few years before. Thomas A. Coffin and Dr. N. H. Gibbes represented the parish in Convention in the year 1855. His health failing, Mr. McElheran resigned in July, 1856, and removed to Mt. Pleasant. Rev. William Johnson became rector the following December. He resigned June, 1858, after which the Rev. Charles E. Leverett often officiated, and then the Rev. J. Theodore Hutcheson until 1861. A new chapel at Helenaville was built and Consecrated July 20, 1859 by Bishop Davis, called St. Helenaville Chapel; Mr. Hutcheson and Rev. J. J. Sams assisted. The Rev. E. T. Walker became rector in May, 1860. He officiated for a short time. The Federal invasion of this region in November, 1861, brought the work of this parish to a sudden end. In fact, it was the death-knell of the Church. The white people left the island, most of them never to return. Mr. Walker went to serve in St. John's, Berkeley.

The Committee on Destruction of Churches in 1868 reported that this Church, stripped of pews and furniture, was in the hands of the Methodists, being used by the freedmen who constituted the sole population of the island. In 1879, with its several acres of land, it was still in the hands of the Methodists, the building in good condition. Whether or not the Methodists paid rent in these years we have not been able to discover, but in 1881 the trustees of the diocese agreed to lease the Church to them for five years. The Communion silver had been loaned, part to the Church in Anderson and part to St. John's, Charleston. Only the walls of the old Church stand today.

ST. PAUL'S CHURCH, BENNETTSVILLE
Established 1896

The first Church invasion of Marlboro County naturally was from St. David's, Cheraw. Unless a pre-Revolution missionary had visited this region, the first Episcopal services in Marlborough County were two held by the Rev. A. W. Marshall in 1830 at the Court House. Mr. Marshall also had a school for the poor in Marlborough, eight miles from Cheraw, where there was much ignorance. Two out of twenty knew the Lord's Prayer and most never heard of the Ten Commandments. In 1862 again we find the Rev. A. T. Brown, rector of St. David's, holding two services in Bennettsville where he found a "favorable opening" for building a congregation. These services were held in Temperance Hall. The Rev. J. M. Green, assisting in Cheraw during the war, also held some services in Bennettsville. Bishop Davis made a visitation there and preached, June 11, 1863, Mr. Brown assisting in the service. The Rev. J. H. Quinby next had missionary charge, preaching every other Sunday. The mission did not continue long—the war probably brought the effort to an end. Again now in December, 1870 the Rev. Mr. Motte of St. David's began monthly services, but in 1872 the visits to Bennettsville were found impracticable and the services were discontinued. Mr. Motte began again though before he left Cheraw to hold some services in Bennettsville. Bishop Howe, after evening service read by Mr. Motte, preached there December 4, 1888. In 1892 the work here was resumed by the Rev. W. A. Guerry, then rector of St. John's, Florence, being assisted the next year by Rev. Edward McCrady. At this time (1893) Mr. Guerry reports the congregation preparing to build a chapel costing $1,-100.00. Bishop Capers held services in Bennettsville on May 29 and 30, 1894. A lot had then been secured.

The Rev. T. P. Baker, when he became rector of St. David's and Trinity, Society Hill, in 1895 was placed in charge of Bennettsville. He began regular services in what was then called "The Bennetsville Mission," January 1, 1896. The next year the mission was given its name, St. Paul's, with officers reported for the first time: warden, H. H. Covington; secretary, William P. Breeden. The first lot purchased on Broad Street was sold and the present location on Fayetteville Avenue acquired for $350.00, February 15, 1897. There were now twelve members of St. Paul's mission, eleven of whom signed themselves as follows: "H. H. Covington, Thomas P. Baker, B. D. McLeod, B. F. Breeden, B. W. Jackson, J. M. Brown, S. E. Webster, M. F. Cannon, E. M. Munson, L. Rogers, Maggie Cobb." These, we believe, were all women except the first two, the minister-in-charge, Mr. Baker, and Mr. Covington, who soon after entered the ministry. The Church was now promptly built after plans made and donated by Rutledge Holmes, architect of Charleston. The total cost, including lot, was $1,173.50. The balance on hand the day the Church was completed was $00.46. As Rev. Roderick H. Jackson, who went from this Church into the ministry, expressed it in his valuable sketch of St. Paul's, "There was joy and thanksgiving in the hearts of the people over the successful completion of the Church." At the first service in the Church on Christmas Day, 1897, Jessie Breeden was baptized, the daughter of Mrs. W. P. Breeden who with Mrs. B. W. Jackson had done so much, with the help of their husbands, in the building of the Church. It was Consecrated on June 1, 1898 by Bishop Capers assisted by Mr. Baker when the Rev. W. E. Evans of Trinity, Columbia, preached. Eight persons were confirmed on this day. The font was given by Dr. C. Kollock of Cheraw, the Bishop's chair by a former member, and the Communion service by a lady in Baltimore. In 1900 the Church, up to this time ranking as an "unorganized mission" now became an "organized mission" with Dr. J. A. Faison as warden and W. P. Breeden, secretary and treasurer. Dr. Faison soon became treasurer also and held these offices most efficiently for fifteen years.

Mr. Baker resigned in 1900. The Rev. C. W. Boyd took charge August 1, 1900, continuing until Easter, 1908. The communicants numbered 23 at this time. The Rev. Albert S. Thomas then had the charge from September, 1908, until December, 1910, when the Rev. H. H. Lumpkin supplied a few services. The Rev. Robert W. Barnwell took charge January, 1911, continuing until January, 1912. In the summer of 1912, the Rev. E. A. Penick, Jr., assumed charge. He was the first resident minister. In 1914 the Church went up from "mission" status to become a "parish." The officers now were: wardens, Dr. J. A. Faison, H. W. Palmer; secretary, L. K. Breeden; treasurer and lay reader, Dr. Faison. The communicants now numbered 55. The rectory was built at this time. Mr. Penick resigned to go to the Good Shepherd, Columbia, in 1915 and was succeeded by the Rev. T. P. Baker (having had charge before, 1896-1900) on St. Paul's Day, January 25, 1915. He took charge also of the Church in Dillon. Mr. Baker continued as rector until early in 1918. Rev. Octavius T. Porcher became rector September 1, 1918, having supplied the Church with services for some months before. The wardens at this time were L. K. Breeden, who was also treasurer, and F. R. Crosland. Mr. H. W. Palmer was lay reader. In 1920 a Möller pipe organ was installed. Active organizations in the parish now included St. Paul's Guild, the Social Service Committee, Altar Guild, and two branches of the Woman's Auxiliary. Mr. Porcher did a great deal of mission work conducting a Sunday School in the country. He retired February 1, 1939, after 49 years of active service in the diocese and 22 years in this parish and at Dillon, priest and prophet indeed—scholar, teacher, friend, pastor—beloved by young and old. After retiring he still found work to do for his Master. A little more than two years later, after a long illness borne with characteristic fortitude, he died June 14, 1941. He published a valuable book, "Some Thoughts on Heaven and Hell and Other Essays."

The Rev. George H. Harris had succeeded Mr. Porcher in the spring of 1939. The officers at this time were: wardens, F. A. Rogers and F. R. Crosland; secretary, F. T. Hollis; treasurer, Walter W. Gregg. Notwithstanding the strain of war the parish work went steadily on under Mr. Harris. He resigned December 1, 1947. Stimulated by a legacy of $1,000.00 from Mr. Porcher for a parish house, funds for this purpose were gathered through some years until finally the parish house was built and occupied in the early fall of 1948. On Sunday, November 21 of this same year, the Semi-Centennial of the Church was celebrated, though, as we have seen, its roots go back much further. On this occasion a sermon was preached in commemoration by Bishop Thomas, a former minister, and a historical address was given by Rev. Roderick H. Jackson of St. John's, Portsmouth, Va., a former member of the parish. The Rev. H. L. Hoover served temporarily for some months after Mr. Harris left. The Rev. Robert Carlton Baird, coming from Sanford, N. C., succeeded as rector on January 1, 1949. A debt of nearly

$4,000.00 was fully discharged in 1951 and the next year the Church became entirely self-supporting, employing the entire time of Mr. Baird, Dillon having also a resident minister. On May 11, 1952, Bishop Carruthers Dedicated the new parish house to the Glory of God and in memory of a beloved rector, the "O. T. Porcher Memorial."

The vestry in 1948 was: wardens, J. M. Jackson and R. C. Charles, M.D.; vestrymen, J. J. Baldwin, W. W. Gregg (also treasurer), Dr. C. R. May, F. T. Hollis, W. A. Rogers, S. C. Breeden, H. B. Gregorie, F. A. Rogers, Jr., C. E. Lynch, and two life members, F. A. Rogers, Sr. and L. K. Breeden.

ST. JOHN'S PARISH, BERKELEY
Established 1706
(See Dalcho, p. 264)

St. John's, Berkeley, was the largest of the ten original parishes in South Carolina—forty or fifty miles from one end to the other, comprising the greater part of Berkeley County—someone said about half the size of Rhode Island. Accordingly it was divided into Lower, Middle and Upper St. John's and many chapels-of-ease were built. The parish Church known as Biggin Church being near Biggin Creek, was in Lower St. John's as also Strawberry Chapel, ten miles south. Trinity, Black Oak (now Trinity, Pinopolis) was in Middle St. John's and Epiphany (the Rocks Church) in Upper St. John's. The parish Church already had twice been almost destroyed by fire in 1755 and again by the British in 1781. But it had been repaired and the Rev. John Jacob Tschudy became rector in 1811 and served until his death in 1834. Mr. Tschudy's jurisdiction was confined to Lower St. John's. The valuable parsonage of the parish was the gift of Elias Ball, brother of John Ball, and uncle of Isaac Ball who died in 1925. Soon after the turn of the century, the Churches in Middle and Upper St. John's became separated from the parish Church and were united under one rector with St. Stephen's Church, but not entirely so at once, it appears. A plantation on Cooper River had been given to the parish by Sir John Colleton, the income being used to pay the rector's salary. Many of the congregation of Black Oak attended Biggin in earlier days, some individuals were vestrymen of both churches. After the churches in the upper part of the parish were opened, it was at first supposed that the income from the Colleton gift would be divided between all the churches. For a time this was done but contention arose and the Court decided the income belonged exclusively to the parish Church. This decision marked the definite separation of Middle and Upper St. John's from Lower St. John's. Mr. Tschudy reported 50 families in 1823. He held services alternately between the parish Church and Strawberry as also at Cordesville in summer. He died in 1834.

The Rev. James H. Fowles had temporary charge in 1835. The Rev. Edward Thomas was the next rector. Under date of February 4, 1836, he records, "I arrived in St. John's Parish, Berkeley, and reported myself to Sims White and Thomas Ashby, two of the vestry, as ready to enter upon my duties as Rector of the parish, gave notice of service to be held at Biggin Church the following Sunday." Mr. Thomas held services at four places regularly: Biggin Church, Strawberry, Cordesville, and Whiteville, the latter two in summer; as also for the Negroes on several plantations. It is reorded that about this time a class of 44 Negroes were taught regularly by members of the rector's family. His health began to fail in 1838 and in 1840 he died, and was buried under Strawberry Chapel. The mural tablet in his memory on the wall at Strawberry was first in Biggin Church, having been removed to Strawberry when Biggin fell into ruin. This rector was a direct descendant of the Rev. Samuel Thomas, first S.P.G. missionary to South Carolina. The Rev. C. P. Elliott had officiated in the parish from June to October, 1840. Rev. Cranmore Wallace became rector in 1842. He held services in the same four places and also on four plantations. There were estimated to be 2,000 slaves in the parish. In the year 1843, he baptized 50 Negroes. Mr. W. B. W. Howe resided in the parish at this time, studying for the ministry under Mr. Wallace. He assisted in the services. Being ordained deacon in 1848 he became assistant minister, continuing in charge after Mr. Wallace's resignation November 1, 1848. Mr. Howe, now ordained priest, became rector in 1850 and continued until June 1, 1860. The deputies to the Convention were this year, Sandford W. Barker, K. S. Ball, J. Harleston, and Benjamin Huger; the wardens were K. S. Ball and J. S. White. The Rev. J. J. Sams held services during the summer. The Rev. A. F. Olmsted became rector January 1, 1861. Services were first reported at the Barrows in 1863 by the rector of this parish together with those at Biggin, Strawberry, and Cordesville. Before the war St. John's was a prosperous parish having a summer and a winter parsonage, a rice plantation (which yielded $1,200.00 or $1,500.00 yearly) and $10,000.00 in stocks. The war depleted the parish. Biggin was badly damaged, the furniture being torn out and burnt. Mr. Olmsted died in 1866. There was no regular rector until the Rev. P. D. Hay took charge in 1873, the parish having had only monthly services for eight years. By the war the parish lost its Parish Register, Prayer Book, Bible, and Communion Service. The Prayer Book and Bible were soon recovered. Much later in 1947 the Communion Service (six pieces) was found buried in an old barn on Combahee Plantation, formerly owned by John C. Ball. After Mr. Hay came, the glebe was put in order, an income being restored. Old Biggin had become only a refuge for the wayfarer in storms. Strawberry Chapel about this time was repaired and a new organ installed. It practically now had taken the place of Biggin as the parish Church. Also the chapel at the Barrows, called St. John's Chapel, incompletely built during the war was now finished and furnished. In 1875 friends at the North gave Strawberry a handsomely bound Bible and Prayer Book. In 1876 this chapel was embellished with a new altar of chestnut, a credence shelf, and a brass cross. Also a handsome Communion Service was purchased about this time for $300.00 of Joseph Rogers and Son of Sheffield, England, which has been in use since.

In 1882 the old one being too small, a new chapel was built in Cordesville. The parsonage in this village burned down in March of this year; Mr. Hay's furniture was saved. He resigned in 1884, going to St. Helena's, Beaufort. The parish being vacant in 1885, Messrs. K. S. and Isaac Ball, wardens, reported the glebe yielded $500.00 for the year, other investments $100.00, lay services being regularly held. The Rev. H. H. Phelps became rector July 15, 1886. Strawberry Chapel was severely injured by the earthquake, but soon after was repaired by means of the Bishop's "Earthquake Funds". A parochial school was conducted in the parish at this time, a lot, with glebe was given, and building for the school erected. In 1890 pews were put in the chapel in Cordesville by the Ladies' Church Aid Society, and a marble font installed. Also at this time through the generosity of Mrs. F. W. Heyward, a new organ was installed in Strawberry Chapel, also a new rectory was built in Cordesville. Mr. Phelps left for East Carolina in 1890. The Rev. James Simonds became rector November, 1892 (with Trinity Church, Black Oak) but left after a few months. The Rev. J. S. Hartzell took charge in October, 1894, and was succeeded by the Rev. Andrew Ernest Cornish in 1897, continuing until Rev. John H. Brown became rector in 1900. At this time the wardens were St. Clair White and Elias Ball, secretary, Henry L. Barker, and treasurer, Frank W. Heyward. There were only nine families at this time with fifty individuals.

On July 6, 1902, the chapel in Cordesville, built years before but only recently finished, was Consecrated by Bishop Capers, assisted by the rector and Dr. Robert Wilson. Mr. Brown resigned March 22, 1903. The Rev. C. H. Jordan took charge in the spring of 1904 and served until September, 1906. The wardens at this time were J. St. Clair White and Charles Stevens; secretary, H. L. Barker; treasurer, John C. Porcher. The Rev. Dwight Cameron took charge in 1910 and the next year the Rev. G. H. Johnston, D.D., then in 1912 the Rev. J. W. Sparks. Strawberry Chapel was extensively repaired in 1913. Besides nearly $400.00 for this purpose from Church funds, Mr. Isaac Ball gave $175.00 and Mr. H. H. Ficken $50.00. In 1915 the Rev. A. S. H. Winsor (*locum tenens*) succeeded Mr. Sparks in charge, then in 1916 the Rev. A. R. Mitchell, Archdeacon, took charge. He reports renewed interest and increased congregations, holding services at Strawberry, Cordesville, the Barrows, and Moncks Corner. The churchyard at Strawberry was at this time enclosed with a wire fence and concrete posts. Other improvements were a new altar, and an altar service book with brass rest. The wardens in 1920 were Messrs. J. St. Clair White and Joseph Heyward. The Rev. Wallace Martin became rector in 1922 and continued in charge until his death on Good Friday, 1946. When Mr. Martin assumed charge the congregation for the most part had removed their residences. He continued the Sunday morning service during the winters for all these years at Strawberry Chapel, the congregation attending being mostly from the city. Services were discontinued at Cordesville. The pews, altar rail, and altar of this chapel were given to Epiphany, Upper St. John's. For the greater part of the year it is true of historic Strawberry, as Mr. Isaac Ball expresses it in his lovely poem—

"In sylvan silence stands our Shrine."

ST. ALBAN'S, BLACKVILLE
Established 1890
(Including missions at Bamberg, Midway, and Branchville)

St. Alban's Church dates from 1890, but services of the Church were held in Blackville many years earlier. In 1862, the Rev. Barnwell Bonum Sams began labors in this part of the diocese. Mr. Sams' title was "Rector of Holy Apostles', Barnwell, and Missionary to Blackville". He reports that through the courtesy of the Rev. Mr. Wilson, who loaned the Methodist Church for the purpose, he held services in Blackville on the first Sunday in every month—the congregations being quite as large as those in Barnwell. (The Rev.

John H. Cornish had held services in Branchville in 1857). The attendance was swelled by the presence of many war refugees from the low country. Bishop Davis reports his first visit to Blackville on July 17, 1862, when he preached and confirmed one person "the first confirmation ever held there". The service was in the Methodist Church conducted by Mr. Sams. These services were continued through 1863 and 1864; the Methodist Church was still used. Bishop Davis made a visitation on December 15, 1864. After the war, the services in Blackville were very irregular. In 1870, Mr. Sams was holding services in Bamberg, and the next year also at Brier Creek Church, Midway, which was loaned for the purpose. Midway was on the same road as Bamberg. After Mr. Sams left Barnwell in 1871, his principal work was at Midway, but this was difficult because there was no Church building at Midway—the services generally were held in a room loaned for the purpose. Mr. Sams took charge of St. Matthew's parish in 1873, so he had then less time for work in this field. His services were now confined to Midway. In 1875, Mr. Sams moved the services from Midway to Bamberg, the prospects there being better, as well as because the Methodist lady who had loaned her parlor for the services found that it was no longer convenient to do so. In 1876, Mr. Sams reported 40 services at Bamberg and four at Blackville. He also held services at Ridge Spring in 1877. Services in Bamberg were 30 in 1878 with none in Blackville. In 1879, he was missionary to Graniteville, but still held services in Bamberg where the people could do little, but he stated, "as long as I am not otherwise engaged, I propose to hold services for them." In 1880, Mr. Sams left this part of the diocese to take charge of the seacoast missions. The Rev. R. W. Barnwell had charge in 1884, reporting eight communicants and eight week-day services. In 1906 services were held in Bamberg by Rev. S. C. Beckwith. At a still later time from 1912 to 1916, a mission, called St. Paul's, Bamberg, was conducted by the Rev. J. W. Sparks and later by the Rev. A. E. Evison. It was discontinued in 1916.

Beginning in 1887, the Rev. A. E. Cornish did extensive missionary work in this section of the State. Among the many places he visited was the town of Blackville. In 1890, Blackville is first listed as an unorganized mission of the diocese. In May, 1891, Mr. Cornish reported 16 communicants; eight services; Sunday School, teachers and pupils, 28; salary paid $25.00. So began St. Alban's. In 1892, he reports that a neat little chapel, costing upward of $500.00, had been built—"the generous work of the few Church folks in that town" (near Hutto's gin). The lot was given by Mrs.

A. R. Carroll. Mr. Cornish removed to Charleston in 1894 and was succeeded by the Rev. S. E. Prentiss. In 1895, this mission was reported for the first time under the name of St. Alban's. The removal of the Turner family was quite a loss this year, but there was a gain in the coming of the Hammond family. Mr. William Morrison was the first reported officer of this Church. He was for many years both warden and treasurer. St. Alban's Chapel was Consecrated by Bishop Capers on February 4, 1898. The Rev. Mr. Kershaw preached, Mr. Prentiss read the request, and the Rev. Dr. Porter the sentence. In 1902, the Rev. T. T. Walsh succeeded Mr. Prentiss as minister. There were now nine families and 17 communicants. St. Alban's next minister was the Rev. Charles E. Cabaniss, who came in December, 1904. Then in 1905, the Rev. S. C. Beckwith had charge for about one year. After a vacancy for a year or so, the Rev. J. C. Waring had charge. After his brief charge, the Rev. T. T. Walsh, now general missionary of the diocese, held services.

The Rev. A. E. Evison became the minister in 1909. In 1914, Mr. Evison relates that the little chapel "in a cotton field on the very edge of town" had become unsafe. It would shake and rattle when the wind blew and was finally demolished by a storm. A movement for a new Church had resulted in the raising of $600.00, a new lot was bought, and in about 1918 the present pleasing Gothic Church was built. The old lot reverted to the Carroll family. After nine years of devoted service, Mr. Evison was succeeded by the Rev. A. Rufus Morgan. In 1919, St. Alban's stepped up to the position of an "organized mission", Mr. Morrison was still the warden and treasurer. The next year Mr. Thomas L. Wragg became warden, Mr. Morrison still treasurer. Mr. Morgan continued until April, 1920. In October of this year, the Rev. C. W. Boyd took charge but only for a few months. In 1922, Miss Mary B. Thompson gave to St. Alban's the sum of $1,500.00, as a memorial to her mother, a faithful member of the Church, to be known as the "Addie Thompson Memorial", in trust with the Bishop of the diocese, the income to be used for the "upkeep and furnishing of St. Alban's Church." If St. Alban's should be "discontinued or abandoned", the income is to be used for the education of a candidate for Holy Orders in South Carolina. The Rev. Howard Cady succeeded in 1925 and until November, 1926, when the Church was vacant for a period. In 1929, the Rev. Joseph Burton had oversight but gave only one Sunday a year, the congregation now worshipping in Barnwell.

When the Rev. John A. Pinckney took charge of Allendale and Barnwell in 1931, regular worship was resumed in St. Alban's and greatly renewed interest was manifested. Mr. Pinckney left in 1937, going to Tryon, N. C. The next year, the Rev. Theodore Porter Ball took charge, the Church now becoming very active. St. Alban's was admitted into union with Convention as an organized mission in 1940. Later in the year, Mr. Ball was transferred to the diocese of Upper S. C. Dr. O. D. Hammond was then, as for many years, the warden, and Mr. Nick V. Martin, secretary-treasurer. W. H. Hanckel, a candidate for orders, officiated in the summer of 1941. Mr. Martin now kept up the services by lay reading, with occasional services by visiting ministers. For many years, the women of the Church were organized as a guild; but in April, 1940, it was made into a branch of the Woman's Auxiliary which became very active in promoting the work of the Church.

The Church had remained vacant for some years until the Rev. William L. Martin took charge in 1945. Mr. Martin resigned February, 1947. The Rev. Gordon D. Bennett took charge in 1948. The Church was Consecrated by Bishop Carruthers on May 2, 1948. Mr. Bennett left November, 1950; Rev. R. J. Hobart then took charge for a year, followed by the Rev. George Milton Crum. Mr. N. V. Martin continued to serve for years as lay reader and superintendent of the Church school. Mr. L. L. Pearson was lay reader also, and Miss Ruth Hoffman, organist. The Rev. Gordon Mann took the charge in March, 1954, but left the latter part of the year when the Rev. H. D. Bull succeeded, serving until September, 1955, when the Rev. Walter D. Roberts took charge. The officers of St. Alban's at this time (1955) are: warden, N. V. Martin; secretary-treasurer, Miss Pearle Hoffman. In 1944, a large lot was purchased, adjoining the Church, with a view to the erection of a parish house.

THE CROSS, BLUFFTON
ST. LUKE'S PARISH (Zion, Hilton Head)
Established 1767
(See Dalcho, p. 387)

As we are informed by Dalcho this parish in old Granville County was cut off from St. Helena by Act of May 23, 1767. Plans were made but no Church was built until 1786 and the parish was incorporated February 29, 1788. The Church was vacant when Dalcho ended his history in 1820. The Rev. Samuel Sitgreaves officiated in 1821. William Heyward was deputy to the Convention of 1822 when the Rev. Peter Van Pelt, deacon, was officiating. The Rev. Philip

Mathews was the minister at Hilton Head. Van Pelt, rector the next year, reports two new churches contemplated, one in the vicinity of May River and one near Coosawhatchie. In 1824 the rector reports services at three points; at the parish Church of St. Luke's, at Coosawhatchie in the Court House and in a Union chapel at Grahamville. In 1825 a new Church near May River about one half mile from the parish Church, (the old Church now was said to be in a "ruinous condition") was built. This must have been on a part of the Bull Barony (later Verdier estate). Bishop Bowen reported to the Convention in 1825 that he had Consecrated this Church "near the original parish Church on ground given for the purpose by John Guerard, Esq." For this year the rector held 52 services at the new Church and at Grahamville. Van Pelt's rectorship ended in 1827 when he was succeeded by the Rev. Thomas J. Young. The cornerstone of the Church of the Holy Trinity, Grahamville, was laid on October 28, 1829, and was Consecrated in 1830, $1,800.00 being subscribed in the parish and $150.00 from "brethren of St. Helena's, Beaufort." Zion, Hilton Head, which had been "thrown out of use as to the worship for which it had been originally erected" was recovered and the Church Consecrated in 1833.

In 1833, services were held in four places in the parish: at St. Luke's (the old Church being still in use); at May River; at Zion, Hilton Head; and at Grahamville, as well as a great many services held for colored people on the plantations. A chapel for them was built in 1838. The Rev. B. C. Webb succeeded Mr. Young as rector (1836-1838) followed by the Rev. Alsop Woodward until 1853 when the Rev. James Stoney became rector. Services had been held at "the Bluff" after 1839, and in 1842 a chapel was built here and Consecrated with the name "The Cross, Bluffton" on a lot given by William Pope, Sr., Esq. It was described as a "neat little edifice 36 x 22 with gallery for colored people." This chapel was enlarged and plastered in 1848, and about the same time the Church on May River was materially altered. In this year also one mile from Bluffton a chapel for colored people was erected by a candidate for holy orders. In 1851, $1,500.00 was raised for a new Church in Bluffton, the Rev. James Stoney, rector, and the Rev. J. B. Seabrook, assistant. During the middle period of the century a large work was done among the Negroes involving an assistant minister; in this position besides Mr. Seabrook were, successively, the Revs. Thomas C. DuPont and P. G. Jenkins, and also at Hilton Head the Rev. J. W. Taylor, and a lay worker, Mr. C. R. Cross. Later the Rev. J. V. Welch did a large work among the slaves in the neighborhood of

Grahamville. He reports an offering for African missions by the slaves who were "glad of the privilege of contributing their mite to impart to their brethren the saving truths of the Gospel of Christ"—the amount was $9.27.

July 18, 19, and 20, 1857, were red letter days in the history of this parish: on Saturday the 18th forenoon, the Rev. C. C. Pinckney preached and nine white persons and one colored were confirmed by Bishop Davis. The Rev. Stephen Elliott preached in the evening; present also at the services were Revs. James Stoney, rector, J. B. Seabrook, J. W. Taylor, M.D. The new Church of the Cross was Consecrated on Sunday, July 19th, the same clergymen taking part and Mr. Pinckney preaching; the Bishop preached in the afternoon and Mr. Elliott at night. On the 20th in the forenoon, the Bishop preached and ordained Mr. J. Mercer Green to be deacon. The fine toned bell of the new Church of the Cross "a handsome cruciform Gothic building capable of holding five to six hundred persons" summoned the worshippers on each of these occasions. The Church cost $5,000.00, the architect was the noted Mr. E. B. White of Charleston who also planned Trinity, Columbia; Grace, Charleston, and St. Philip's steeple. In 1856 the rector reports winter services at St. Luke's Church and Zion, Hilton Head; in summer twice a Sunday for white and once for colored congregations at The Cross, Bluffton, and once every other Sunday at Hilton Head. The "St. Luke's Church" here referred to is the second St. Luke's Church. The original St. Luke's, built in 1786, fell into ruin and finally burned years before this date. Its site is now marked by one Bull grave. The second St. Luke's, built in 1824, was a half mile from the first and near May River, later called "Bull Hill Church" as it was on "Bull Hill Plantation" later Verdier property. After the Consecration of The Cross in Bluffton, Episcopal services in this second St. Luke's were discontinued—none are reported after 1856. This Church was sold to the Methodists in 1875. It still stands three miles from Prichardville P. O.,—a sign on its front reads, "St. Luke's Methodist Church Est. 1875". The north side of the Church was for a while reserved for Episcopalians. Here is the grave of a faithful slave "Mom Delia" buried at her request at the foot of Dr. Verdier. After the war began in 1861, Mr. Stoney went to Yorkville. Only occasional services were held in the parish during the war. The Bluffton Church was not involved in the destruction of the town, being protected from the flames by its beautiful grove of oaks. Mr. Stoney returned to the rectorship in 1867 and sought to revive the parish, serving at Bluffton and Hilton Head, but the families were dispersed; this, with the poverty of those remaining, led to a suspension of services in 1868. On a visit by the Bishop in this year the people rejoiced to see their Bishop for the first time since the war. Mr. Stoney was compelled to leave the diocese at this time for want of support. The Church at Hilton Head which was a wooden structure entirely disappeared soon after the war. It is surmised that the materials were taken away to build houses on the island. Two silver chalices (dated 1834) of Zion Church were recently restored.

Services were resumed at The Cross, Bluffton, by the Rev. E. E. Bellinger, missionary in 1870. Some of the badly needed repairs were made in 1873 by sale of some property. About this time through the efforts of the Rev. A. T. Porter, the bell formerly belonging to the Church was restored by the United States authorities. Repairs were made in 1876, and in 1878 a belfry was added to the Church and the recovered bell hung in it. "Its sweet and familiar tones again summon the congregation to the sanctuary of God." Mr. Bellinger ended his ten years of faithful service in the parish in 1880 and was succeeded by the Rev. Barnwell Bonum Sams. Mr. Sams at this time relieved Mr. Bellinger of the care of the "coast missions" including Bluffton, Ochitie, Hardeeville, Grahamville, and St. Peter's. There was at this time a renewal of interest with increase in the number of services and organization of a Sunday School, the Church also being refitted. In 1885 the churchyard was enclosed with a fence. In 1886 the number of families was 15 with 59 souls. St. Luke's was then represented in Convention by Messrs. Paul Prichard, M.D., T. R. Heyward, W. G. Allen, J. G. Verdier. The church was reroofed in 1892 when also the chancel was remodeled, and a walnut Communion table, lectern, and prayer desk, made out of the old pulpit and desk, were added. Mr. Sams resigned this Church May 1, 1895. He was succeeded by the Rev. J. M. Pringle in 1897. On account of a cyclone in August, 1898, services in the Church were suspended until after repairs, being resumed in the April following. Mr. Pringle resigned at the beginning of 1900, and was succeeded in the charge November 1st by the Rev. J. B. Walker until May, 1902. He in turn was succeeded by the Rev. J. C. Waring who served until April, 1905. The chapel in the vestibule of the Church was erected about 1900 chiefly for convenience of heating.

From this date St. Luke's is no longer listed as a "parish", it is now a "mission," The Cross, St. Luke's Parish. Dr. Paul Prichard was warden at this time and Alfred Fripp, treasurer. After an interval Rev. P. D. Hay assumed charge August, 1907, then the Rev. J. Herbert Woodward in 1912, coming into the diocese from Georgia. He continued in charge until 1926 when he resigned to accept work in the diocese of Georgia and the Rev. F. M. Brunton followed but only for a very short time, being succeeded in 1927 by the Rev. Joseph Burton who was appointed Archdeacon of the Beaufort District of the Charleston Convocation, having also in his charge Allendale, Heavenly Rest, Estill; and missions of Varnville, Hardeeville, and Okatee. Mr. D. N. Peeples held service in the summer of 1929, and later as a candidate for Holy Orders assisted in the Church in the summer of 1932, and at Hardeeville. At this time Mr. James Verdier was warden and Mrs. Alfred Fripp, secretary and treasurer. Mr. Fripp later succeeded as warden. In 1938 the Church having fallen into serious disrepair a fund was begun for its restoration. David Nathaniel Peeples was ordained deacon in the Church in 1934 by Bishop Thomas. Mr. Peeples held a camp for boys in Bluffton in 1935. This was the beginning of Camps and Conferences in this diocese. Mr. Burton resigned as Archdeacon November, 1929, going to St. Michael's, Savannah, but he retained charge of The Cross until he resigned his charge in Savannah, March, 1939, and was succeeded temporarily by the Rev. A. W. Skardon. The Rev. Howard McC. Mueller of St. Michael's Church, Savannah, took charge in October, 1940, continuing until he left Savannah in 1945. Already at this time the funds for repairs had grown to $2,100.00, members of the congregation, Mrs. Susie V. Allston, and others working for the fund.

The Church had only occasional services until the Rev. Robert E. Withers, Jr., came to the charge in November, 1946, and until 1948. Under Mr. Withers the congregation became quite active. The large task of putting a new roof on the Church was completed and under Mr. Withers a rectory was built in Grahamville. The Rev. Henry Powers had temporary charge until the coming of the Rev. G. Edward Haynsworth July, 1949, who resided in the new rectory in Grahamville. The warden in 1950 was B. J. Verdier; secretary, Percy Huger; treasurer, Mrs. Alfred Fripp. In this year the restoration of the Church was continued with the restoring of the colored windows and the repair of the walls and ceiling. All this work was completed and on June 27, 1954, a great service of thanksgiving and in commemoration of the One Hundredth Anniversary of The Cross was held. Bishop Albert S. Thomas had prepared a history of The Cross and St. Luke's Parish which was printed by the vestry and distributed on this occasion. Many clergymen were present and a large congregation, including Bishop Carruthers. Bishop Thomas who preached the sermon, said in conclusion: "It is a joy to me to be here and congratulate the congregation on such a wonderful accomplishment, more than we thought possible sixteen years ago. But 'with God, all things are possible'."

The Rev. Malcolm Prouty has only recently taken charge of this Church. Under his zeal and with the help of Mr. H. E. McCracken, warden and lay reader; Mrs. Augustin P. Wright, secretary and treasurer; and Church school superintendent, R. E. Gahagan; and also with the cooperation of the whole devoted congregation, we, today, not only look back with a spirit of thanksgiving, but also forward with hope and with confidence that our loving Father above, who is yet ever near, will lead His flock onward to even better things.

ST. PHILIP'S, BRADFORD SPRINGS
Established 1841

The salubrious climate of the neighborhood of Bradford Springs attracted large numbers of people from the malarial districts in the lower parts of the State in the ante-bellum days. Many homes were built in the vicinity. Among the names of those who came, as Mrs. W. B. Colclough tells us in her valuable sketch of St. Philip's, were Gaillard, Porcher, Stoney, Boyd, Colclough, Burrows, Bossard, Fraser, Tate, Davis, Capers—these were Episcopalians. The land was owned first by Nathaniel Bradford, then Gen. Thomas Sumter, William Colclough, John A. Colclough, and then Henry Britton. A demand arose for a Church, the nearest at Stateburg being 16 miles away. Henry Britton made deed of 3¼ acres (statement of "3¼ acres" by J. Porcher Gaillard, who had the deed in his possession in 1879) on September 15, 1840, to Peter W. Fraser, John A. Colclough, Alexander I. Tate, and James Gaillard for a Church. The site was on the old Stage Road from Charleston to Camden. The Church, 26 x 42, was built the next year, frame and simple but of fine material, solid today after more than a century; fine wainscoting, pews, and chancel rail. The windows were of Gothic style, there was a gallery for slaves over the front door. The font was of white marble. A Bible, printed in 1806, was given by Mrs. Elinor McBride in 1840. The vestry room was added later.

The Church was Consecrated by Bishop Gadsden, assisted by the Rev. Edward Phillips of Camden, on June 9, 1841, with the name St. Philip's Church, Bradford Springs. The Bishop stated that the diocese is indebted for the rearing of this Church chiefly to a lady who only occasionally resided in the place. This was Mrs. Esther Holbrook, *nee* Gourdin, of Charleston. Services were occasionally held; the Bishop reports a visitation in 1843. The first report of regular services were for seven Sundays in 1845 by the Rev. Charles P. Elliott, who stated the congregation was chiefly from the low country, here for the summer. On the occasion of his visit on July 23, 1846, the Rev. T. F. Davis of Camden preached; nine were confirmed, "the church in good repair, lately plastered, and completely glazed." The Rev. Charles Pinckney Elliott was called and became the first rector in August, 1846. He reported large congregations. After his resignation of St. Mark's parish in 1841 until his death in 1851, Mr. Elliott did a large missionary work in the entire region covering St. Mark's and Claremont, as well as Bradford Springs. He records baptizing on one occasion of public worship in Col. J. J. Moore's Church at Claremont 58 Negro children. He would hold services at Gum Swamp Church in Clarendon. In 1847, he received a formal invitation of a part of the Methodist Congregation in Hebron Church to be received into the Episcopal Church. Tentatively taking them over, he held services at Hebron for some years. He also held services at Manchester, working with the catechist, Mr. Jacob Welch. In 1849, he records having travelled 1,681 miles to meet his engagements. Mr. Elliott often served without "any pecuniary compensation," entirely gratuitously. The services he held in Sumter in 1851 were probably the first of our Church there.

St. Philip's was received into the Convention February 4, 1847. In his last report to the Convention in 1851, there were 19 families connected with the Church with 40 communicants. The extremely useful ministry of the Rev. C. P. Elliott came to a tragic end in 1851. In the words of Bishop Gadsden to his last Convention in 1852, he, who was to follow him in a few months, said: "It was on his way, on the Lord's Day, to the 'House of Prayer' that he was overtaken by a tornado, which, by the fall of a tree, instantly caused his translation, as we humbly trust, to the Church in Paradise, the blessed region which enjoys a continual Sabbath. The lesson inculcated by this providence is too obvious to need repetition." The Rev. C. P. Gadsden officiated for four Sundays in the fall of 1851 soon after Mr. Elliott's death.

There was no regular minister until the Rev. Thomas N. Lucas took charge in 1854. He officiated also in Col. J. J. Moore's Church near Stateburg and also on the plantation of Maj. James S. Moore. Mr. Lucas resigned St. Philip's August 1856. While Mr. Lucas was rector, services were begun at Providence, sponsored by himself chiefly and Mr. Roberts of Stateburg. Here Bishop Davis Consecrated a chapel named St. Matthew's on Saturday, September 20, 1856. He was assisted by Rev. Messrs. Lucas, Roberts, and T. F. Davis, Jr. Mr. Lucas continued to minister in this chapel to the end of 1858. (See Holy Cross, Claremont.) The Rev. Ezra Jones followed Mr. Lucas as rector in 1859 and then, in 1862, the Rev. Albert R. Walker, deacon, had the charge. Mr. Walker continued his widespread ministrations during the war, here and at Sumter, and at Providence, Mrs. John A. Colclough's plantation, etc. The Church itself suffered little in the war. However, the rector had his horse, harness, and conveyance stolen; and bereft of any means of travel from Sumter, he was forced to close the Church. The Rev. LeGrand F. Guerry became rector in May, 1866. In August of 1867, the Rev. Walter Guerry, a most promising minister, recently ordained, was buried in St. Philip's churchyard. Mr. Guerry was succeeded in rectorship by the Rev. John Johnson of Camden January, 1868. He held services also at St. Matthew's, Providence, until his resignation, the end of 1870, when he went to St. Philip's, Charleston. The Rev. J. S. Kidney officiated in 1871 and the Rev. F. Bruce Davis took charge the first of January, 1872. He reports at that time that St. Matthew's, Providence, was closed. However, the services at St. Matthew's were later resumed by Mr. Lucas of Stateburg. The Rev. L. F. Guerry again took charge January 1, 1873. The death of Mr. William Burrows in 1875 was a great loss to this Church. The Rev. W. H. Johnson became rector this year, but only for a short time. The devastating effects of the war were felt. The yearly pilgrimages from the low country ceased. There were few residents. At times, the Church was closed and there was no minister. Mrs. Eliza Macdonald Colclough, widow of John A. Colclough, did much during these trying times to keep the Church and churchyard in order.

In 1884, after an intermission of three years, the Rev. L. F. Guerry, then rector of St. Paul's, Summerville, at the request of the Bishop held services in St. Philip's. He reported six families, nine communicants, the people hungry for services. Soon after this, Rev. John Kershaw, rector in Sumter, assumed charge of St. Philip's. Later, he was assisted by the Rev. J. S. Hartzell (1891-94) and then by the Rev. W. T. Capers. Mr. Kershaw left this field of work for St. Michael's, Charleston, December, 1895. The Rev. S. B. Hillock now took charge in connection with Sumter, but only for a short time, the Rev. Benjamin M. Braden succeeding in 1898, but only until March, 1899. In 1900, there was no rector. Mr. W. Burrows was warden, secretary, and treasurer. The Church records were lost in 1901 when Pineville, the old Colclough home, burned. The Rev. H. H. Covington took charge the next year but only for fifth Sundays, continuing until the Rev. R. M. Marshall became rector in 1904. A new organ was installed in 1905. Rev. John Kershaw, Jr., then took charge in October, 1905, until October, 1908, followed briefly by Rev. Wallace Carnahan. The Rev. Mr. Covington had charge again in 1910. At this time, W. B. Colclough was senior warden; Stanyarne Burrows was junior warden, and secretary and treasurer. Rev. W. B. Gordon was next in charge from November, 1912, when Mr. Covington resigned, until 1917. The wardens in 1915 were W. B. Colclough and Stanyarne Burrows, the latter being also secretary and treasurer. The Rev. C. W. Boyd was rector from 1918 until 1921; Rev. W. S. Stoney from 1923 until 1926; and the Rev. Moultrie Guerry from 1926 until January 1, 1928.

The Rev. George H. Harris, after a short vacancy, became rector. In 1936, Col. Clark Williams, who had a home in the parish, had the Church painted and later had the graveyard enclosed with a substantial fence. After ten years, Mr. Harris resigned, May, 1939, and was succeeded the following summer by the Rev. Alfred Parker Chambliss. The wardens at this time were Stanyarne and William Burrows, the former being also secretary and treasurer. During the vacancy after Mr. Chambliss left, the Rev. J. B. Walker of Sumter supplied services. Though nearly all of the old members of St. Philip's have either died or moved away, Mr. Walker continues to maintain services (1955).

CALVARY CHURCH, CHARLESTON
Established 1847

We find its conception and the beginning of Calvary Church in a set of resolutions introduced on Saturday, February 6, 1847, in the Fifty-eighth Convention of the diocese of South Carolina meeting in St. Michael's Church, Charleston. It is worth remarking that the motion was made by a layman, Mr. Henry D. Lesesne, representing St. Philip's Church. The resolutions, deploring the lack of adequate Church provision for the colored people of the city, called for the election of six laymen to be a standing committee for the establishing and maintaining of a congregation of colored people in Charleston, the Bishop in conjunction with the committee to appoint a minister. In April following, the Rev. Paul

Trapier was appointed minister, having shortly before (November 25, 1846) resigned the rectorship of St. Michael's Church. Services were first begun by this noble clergyman in March, 1848, and were for some four months held in the basement of St. Philip's parsonage. It is interesting to note that Mr. Trapier's first annual report shows that both white and colored attended these services—in the morning 25 white and 30 colored, in the afternoon 40 white and 250 colored, including Sunday School scholars. The Sunday School numbered from 80 to 175. The name of the congregation was given as "Calvary Church" from its very first beginning. After the first four months, the place of assembage was moved from St. Philip's parsonage to "Temperance Hall". During the following year (1849) there developed some opposition to the founding of Calvary Church, which led to the owner's disallowing the services in "Temperance Hall". However, the opposition soon receded, and favor took its place through the influence of Bishop Gadsden and Mr. Trapier, "whence we can pray", writes Mr. Trapier, "that it may shine to the glory of God and the good of souls." (See, further, Bishop Gadsden's Episcopate.)

After the interruption in the services in "Temperance Hall", there was some dispersion of the congregation; however, the new Church building on Beaufain Street was nearing completion, so the congregation was not for long to be deprived of a place of worship. This Church was Consecrated on the Fourth Sunday in Advent, December 23, 1849, and services henceforth were held there regularly. Bishop Gadsden preached the sermon. We are told that on this occasion, "the congregation was large and the chanting and singing (though not aided by an organ) were cordial and animating." In the Sentence of Consecration, the Church is described as having been "erected and furnished (as a place) wherein the rich and the poor, the bond and the free, may meet together to worship their one Father, Redeemer and Sanctifier, three persons but one God, to partake of His holy sacraments and ordinances; and to receive the teachings and exhortations of His holy word, His holy Church, and His duly commissioned ministry." There was still at this time a debt of $600.00, but kind friends had given Communion plate, a font, carpet, and hangings for the chancel, desk and pulpit, so the Church was well furnished. In 1857 the congregation is reported as 40 in the morning and 300 in the afternoon, and upwards of 200 in the Sunday School. These figures are cited to show how large a work it was in those days—there were 24 teachers in the school. Mr. Trapier reports in 1856 that since the beginning of Calvary's services in March, 1848, 2,485 colored persons of all ages from 60 to 6 had been admitted into the Sunday School, and 78 to Communion.

The Rev. Paul Trapier, after eight years of unselfish service as first minister in charge of Calvary, resigned because of ill health in 1856. As we have seen, Calvary owed its origin to the action of the diocesan Convention of 1847, but it was this godly clergyman, Paul Trapier, who was the real founder of the congregation—he gathered it and organized it. He wrote a Church Catechism which was used in the Sunday School for years. Mr. Trapier was succeeded for two years by the Rev. W. H. Hanckel, lately of Trinity, Edisto, in the Episcopate of Right Rev. Thomas F. Davis; then again for two years the Rev. Lucian C. Lance was in charge, coming from All Saints', Waccamaw. Like so many other Churches in the diocese, Calvary's light burned low during the War between the States, 1861-1865. In 1866 we find the Church, after four years, however, again with a regular minister, Rev. W. O. Prentiss. In 1868 he reports Calvary as "slowly improving", the migrating character of the population in that troublous day being a great hindrance to its prosperity. But in 1870, he reported that the Church had so increased that a chapel of ease with a Sunday School of 28 was forming in the upper part of the city. In 1872 the Rev. J. V. Welch, deacon, became assistant minister under Mr. Prentiss and the hope was expressed that "with this addition to the clerical force of the parish its progress would be marked and rapid." In 1873 the Church was repaired and painted with the help of donations, Mr. Welch reporting that while the people were poor, there were "some willing to do all they can for the glory of God, and the good of His Church"—they were "kind and ready to assist in a good cause." In 1875 the congregation was increasing. Mr. P. J. Lindau was superintendent of the Sunday School in 1878, the rector testifying that he had been of great assistance to him in his work. This marks the beginning of this man's great career in Calvary Church, as Church school superintendent, and for very many years, faithful lay reader.

The year 1883 was a great one in the life of the parish. The Church was repaired, improved, and beautified—a new chancel, and a new vestry room were added and the large and beautiful window was placed in the chancel (memorial of Mr. Trapier); large reflector lights were placed in the ceiling instead of side lights, and the chancel was newly carpeted. Thanks were due especially to Mr. McBurney and Mr. P. J. Lindau for these improvements. The long and faithful ministry of Rev. Jacob V. Welch came to an end with his death in January, 1890. He had dedicated his life's work chiefly to colored people and served with unflagging devotion and with a sympathetic heart as Calvary's minister for eighteen years. There is a tablet in his memory brought from old Calvary on the wall of this Church. He was a rare man for sincerity of purpose and unselfish service. It was said of him that he would deny himself a ride in the street cars of a hot summer day, sometimes, in order to give the fare to some poor person.

Under the decision of the Right Rev. W. B. W. Howe, sixth Bishop of South Carolina, a change of policy came into the life of Calvary Church at this time. It was decided then that henceforth the rector of Calvary should be a colored minister, and thus it has been since 1890. The Rev. J. H. M. Pollard then became rector, while also rector of St. Mark's. He was assisted in the care of Calvary first by the Rev. E. N. Hollings and then by the Rev. G. F. Miller, who afterwards became rector of St. Augustine, Brooklyn, N. Y. The Rev. Mr. Pollard was also missionary in charge of all the colored churches in the Charleston district, as also the Rev. E. N. Joyner was made missionary to those in the vicinity of Columbia. In February, 1892, all the colored missions of the diocese were constituted an Archdeaconry, and the Rev. E. N. Joyner was appointed Archdeacon. This certainly was a step forward in the colored work to be organized and have one to represent the cause. This was the beginning of the final consolidation of the colored missions into the Council of Colored Churchmen, inaugurated by Bishop Guerry. Mr. Pollard's ministry at Calvary was followed by two short pastorates; from 1894 to 1898 by the Rev. E. N. Hollings, and the Rev. I. F. A. Bennett from 1898-1900. The Rev. A. E. Cornish assisted after Mr. Bennett left. The Rev. W. M. Jackson became rector in 1903 and served most acceptably for four years until 1907. Mr. Jackson assisted Bishop Capers in the affairs of the Archdeaconry after the resignation of Archdeacon Joyner in 1906. His family has been prominent in the life of the Church.

During all these checkered years, Mr. P. J. Lindau was the faithful lay reader of the Church, supplying services when there was no clergyman or when they were, as was often the case, away on other duties. His equally faithful successor was Mr. H. J. Chisholm, whose unflagging zeal for a great number of years was remarkable. In 1907 the Church was fortunate in securing the services of Rev. Jesse David Lykes. He was not long for this world—dying in 1912 after only five years of a devoted ministry. The Church flourished under him. It was said of him that he was "one of the most lovable ministers Calvary has had." In his annual address to the Convention of the diocese, Bishop Guerry said of Jesse David Lykes: "He did a splendid work at Calvary, and was greatly beloved by his congregation."

It must be mentioned that it was in 1909 that the Convention of the diocese granted the petition of the colored Convocation, which had been in existence for many years, that the Convocation be allowed to organize a separate *Council* to be known as the *Council of Colored Churchmen* of the diocese of South Carolina. Calvary has always taken a leading part in the Council, which was duly organized in September, 1910. The Rev. A. E. Cornish, who had served as Archdeacon for some time previous to this, resigned. Rev. Joseph Silas Quarles was appointed Archdeacon by Bishop Guerry in 1913. A great event in this history was the coming of Rev. Erasmus L. Baskervill to be rector and to have charge of adjacent missions in 1913. On the death of Archdeacon Quarles in November of this same year, Mr. Baskervill was made Archdeacon by Bishop Guerry. Thus began his great services to Calvary and to all the colored work in the diocese, continuing without letup for about 24 years until his death in 1937. His rectorship of 24 years in itself constituted an era in the history of Calvary Church. Under him Calvary, as has been said, became the "See Church" of the Archdeaconry. It was from here under the Bishop, but through the Archdeacon, that nearly all of the colored work of the diocese was controlled and in large measure assisted and encouraged.

It would take too long to tell in detail of all the advance movements in the parish during this rectorate. A rectory was purchased for $4,000.00, this was on Bogard Street; and the parish house known as Calvary Annex, next to the old Church on Beaufain Street, was erected at a cost of $8,550.00. This building at once became the center of a great social and religious work. Here, for the first time, was properly housed that noted institution, Calvary Kindergarten. This rector was unfailing in arranging year after year special Lenten Services and classes of various sorts for the people of the neighborhood. In 1929, a splendid pipe organ was installed. These services came to an end with the death of the Archdeacon and rector on June 12, 1937. After a brief illness, he received the Communion on his deathbed from the hands of his Bishop and passed to his reward. The Rev. Louis A. Baskervill succeeded his father as rector of Calvary and served very actively for three years, then accepted a call to Pittsburgh. He had been immediately appointed to be executive secretary of the Archdeaconry. An illustration of his active spirit was the operation of a bus for Calvary Kindergarten. The Rev. Stephen B. Mackey succeeded the Rev. Louis A. Baskervill immediately. No sooner had he begun his ministry than rumblings of some important happening were heard on Beaufain Street. Could it be possible that the sacred spot, consecrated by ninety-odd years of the worship of our Triune God, was to be abandoned? However, a government espoused housing development for white people practically surrounded the Church, and in large measure preempted that section of the city of the constituency of Calvary Church, its congregation moving to other parts of the city. The authority offered to buy the property. After a long struggle, including an appeal to Washington, a price of $25,000.00 was agreed upon and the property sold. At six o'clock in the afternoon of November 25, 1940, with sorrowful hearts, a small band of the faithful gathered at old Calvary, and Bishop Thomas, with appropriate ceremonies, removed the Consecration of the Church and services were formally ended there. Calvary already owned a lot with a graveyard on Line Street. N. B. Barnwell, chancellor of the diocese, secured a deed of an adjoining lot owned by the city and here a new Calvary Church was erected. The new Church was built after plans furnished by the architectural firm of Simons and Lapham; the contractor was Mr. T. W. Worthy; and the superintendent of construction was Mr. John R. Clayton, who became one of the first to be confirmed in the Church. The story would be incomplete without the mention of the name of Mr. Wallace Bonaparte of blessed memory, warden and chairman of the Building Committee, whose ability and zeal in such large measure brought the work to successful conclusion. N. B. Barnwell, Esq., chancellor of the diocese, freely rendered much service in all legal matters connected with the work, including the acquiring from the city of an adjoining lot. The new Church was opened for services on July 5, 1942. It was Consecrated on September 27 following by Bishop Thomas. The editor of the *Diocese* said of the building. "It stands today as one of the best looking Churches for its size in the diocese." With the adjoining parish house also completed, Calvary was now fully equipped once more. With the sale of the old rectory on Bogard Street, and the erection of the new one on the site of the Church, the equipment is complete. Under the zealous leadership of Archdeacon Stephen B. Mackey, the work of Calvary has prospered. The removal of the Church from Beaufain to Line Street may have been providential, for the Church's field of work is now larger than before. The vestry in 1942 was: Wallace A. Bonaparte, senior warden; Henry E. Thompson, junior warden; Francis C. Jackson, secretary; John W. Bonaparte, asst. secretary; Samuel Lee, treasurer; Augustus Gray, E. L. Briggs, H. W. Thompson, A. N. Bonaparte.

In looking back over this history, it is our regret that further mention could not be made of others of the loyal members of the Church—laymen like Mr. S. W. Clarke, senior warden, and laywomen like Mrs. E. L. Baskervill, whose name brings up the great work of the Woman's Auxiliary in this parish and in the Archdeaconry also. Not least should we mention the honored names of Mrs. Mary Rollins and Mrs. Eliza Lewis, among the oldest members who are present there today with many others.

GRACE CHURCH, CHARLESTON
Established 1846

Already early in the summer of 1845, a chapel at the corner of Wentworth and Glebe Streets was in contemplation in Charleston for the use of the school at St. Philip's Rectory on Glebe Street, for sojourners in the city, for residents in western part of the city between St. Paul's and St. Peter's, and for persons of color. They who favored the idea were to leave their names at Mr. A. E. Miller's, No. 4 Broad Street. A draft of the proposed chapel had already been prepared by E. B. White, Esq. The seats were to be free; Communion was to be celebrated every Sunday morning. This particular movement seems not at all to have materialized.

Grace Church properly traces its beginning to the action apparently unrelated to this movement, of the Rev. W. H. Barnwell in calling a meeting June 24, 1845, in the lecture room of St. Peter's Church, the enterprise being "first suggested" by him. At a meeting in the following February, this group organized itself into a Church by the name of "Grace Church, Charleston." A vestry was elected consisting of H. Sidney Hayden and T. Drayton Grimke, wardens; and vestrymen, F. P. Ford, David Jennings, F. A. Ford, and, added later, John Clarkson, Isaac M. Wilson, B. S. Rhett, and W. R. Taber. Subscriptions were taken for the building of a Church. As was the case with St. Peter's itself, a leading motive in the organization of Grace Church was to erect a Church for a particular minister; in this case, the Rev. James H. Fowles, who like Mr. Barnwell had been drawn into the ministry of the Church by the Beaufort revival. He found it impossible to leave his work in Philadelphia and declined a call. This was a great discouragement; however, a year later, the movement was renewed. Grace Church was admitted into union with the Convention February 16, 1846. It was incorporated December 18, 1846.

The Rev. William W. Spear of Philadelphia, who had lately been assistant and then rector of St. Michael's, accepted a call and services were promptly begun January 31, 1847, in the chapel of the Charleston College, loaned for the purpose. A Constitution was adopted on February 6, 1847. A lot for the Church was first purchased from the city at the corner of Meeting and Wentworth. It was returned to the city and the present one on Wentworth Street, a part of St. Philip's glebe, was secured by glebe rent from St. Philip's Church. There was some opposition to the building of another Church in the city, but as it would seem under the direction of Providence, the work proceeded. The architect of the Church was E. B. White, the building was by E. B. Brown at a cost of $16,000.00 for the Church and $3,000.00 additional for the spire. The work was begun in June, 1847. The cornerstone was laid on July 7th by the chairman of the Building Committee, Benjamin S. Rhett, Esq. The other members of the committee were F. A. Ford and William Gregg. Both the congregation and the Church made good progress the first year.

In February, 1848, the rector reported 40 families, a year later 110, of which 10 were colored. The Church was completed November 1, 1848. The total cost was $23,835.00. It was a handsome Gothic building, one of the first churches in Charleston to be built in this style. It would appear that the architect of Grace Church, Mr. White, inaugurated this style in South Carolina. He designed besides Grace, The Cross, Bluffton; Trinity, Columbia; etc. The Church was Consecrated by Bishop Gadsden on November 9, 1848. Clergymen participating were, besides the rector, the Revs. P. T. Keith, W. H. Barnwell, and E. Phillips. The pews were after the plan of those of St. Paul's, Richmond, Virginia. An excellent organ was provided, placed in the center of the chancel. Mr. J. D. Speissegger was the first organist. Rev. C. C. Pinckney became assistant in 1850. At this time, a beautiful font was given by Mrs. Eliza Kohne. The chancel of the Church was an evolution; at first it was not recessed. The organ, with the Lord's Table, behind the pulpit were all crammed into a narrow space against the north wall. In 1852, 20 feet were added at the north end of the Church, the upper part being occupied by the organ and the lower by the library and vestry room. Also at this time, a gallery was built over the entrance for the organ and choir, though the organ was not moved at this time. Additional pews were added near the chancel. This work was completed in a year under E. T. Jones, architect, and H. D. Walker, builder, for $2,000.00, the congregation again worshipping in the college chapel. In 1853, the budget of Grace Church was $4,565.00. The Church had its struggles in these years but continued to grow; by 1854 the number of communicants was 210, having almost doubled in five years.

The religious zeal which led to the founding of Grace Church was reproduced in that this Church was the scene of many great missionary meetings. The great missionary leaders, Bishops Boone, Payne, and Williams, preached in Grace. In 1856, responding to the appeal of Bishop Scott of Oregon, a great diocesan-wide missionary meeting was held here and the Sellwoods of Grahamville speeded on their way to Oregon. Mr. Spear resigned in 1855 on account of ill health. He received many tributes on his departure. Mr. Pinckney succeeded as rector. The Rev. R. P. Johnson served briefly as assistant in 1856 then after him in this office the Rev. Julius W. Stuart, who died after three months from effects of fever. The Rev. B. B. Sams was assistant from 1857 to 1863. The Church was closed on account of a yellow fever epidemic in 1858. It was in this year reported entirely out of debt. The Church was closed from August 15, 1859, to Christmas Day for a renovation which cost was $5,500.00. The organ was now removed to the gallery built for it in 1852, and the chancel entirely remodeled and redecorated with the addition of a new communion rail and new pulpit. Again the congregation, in this period of repairs, worshipped in the chapel of the Charleston College.

Regular services were held in Grace Church during the earlier part of the war. The organ was taken down and stored for safekeeping. The Rev. J. B. Seabrook was elected assistant minister at Easter, 1863, to ensure continuation of regular services. However, they became more occasional later and were entirely suspended January 1, 1864, the congregation, with St. Philip's and St. Michael's, uniting in services held at St. Paul's conducted by Mr. Howe, rector of St. Philip's and continued here until soon after the occupation of Charleston. The commander of the Federal forces then closed the Church, Mr. Howe refusing to use the prayer for the President of the United States, the war not being ended. Grace Church escaped injury in the war until towards the end when it was struck by one shell which did considerable damage. Temporary repairs were made and services were resumed in March, 1865, being held alternately by the Rev. J. B. Seabrook and Rev. J. Mercer Green. For a time now, this was the only Episcopal Church in the city open for worship. The organ of the Huguenot Church was used for a time until 1866, when it was returned and the Grace Church organ replaced. The next year, a new organ was purchased for $3,650.00.

During the difficult post-bellum days, this parish suffered as all other institutions of the State. It could not even pay the rector's salary in full. However, there was much Christian activity—an organization of District Visitors helped the destitute in all parts of the city. In 1869, $1,021.00 was contributed for the "relief of the Bishop." By 1873, the evidences of recovery were marked. There were now 137 families in the parish with 222 communicants, total offerings $4,509.70. At this time, the arrears for glebe rent were all settled and the parish received fee-simple titles to the three glebe lots occupied by the parish for $2,000.00 paid to St. Philip's Church. Now it was that the foundations under the chancel walls had begun to sink, involving repairs amounting to $5,000.00. Thus was the Church again thrown into debt. In 1874, the debts were all reported paid. The Rev. H. O. Judd became assistant minister July 1, 1877. At this time, a handsome Communion service made from silver contributed by the congregation replaced that lost in the Sherman fire in Columbia in 1865. A Sunday School building was erected in 1879 at a cost of $3,750.41. This was the result of efforts by the ladies of the congregation which had begun in the early seventies. The Sunday School at this time numbered 142 with 19 teachers. Mr. Judd resigned in this year. In 1883-84 a general renovation of the Church took place, especially as to lighting, windows, re-arrangement of chancel, and a new one built through the generosity of a warden. Four handsome alms plates were given as memorials in 1885.

Grace Church suffered severely from the earthquake of 1886; the north wall had to be rebuilt and likewise the pillars in the interior (where iron was substituted); the tower had to be massively buttressed; the great arch was cracked and had to be rebuilt; the organ was removed to the side of the chancel and a new vestry room built on the opposite side. The cost of the repairs was $21,500.00, of which $7,000.00 was supplied from the Bishop's Earthquake Fund. The congregation worshipped in the German

Artillery Hall on Wentworth Street while repairs were made. By 1891, all remaining debts were liquidated.

In 1888, the Church was flourishing with every pew rented. The wardens in 1887 were William Johnson and E. L. Kerrison, and vestrymen, William McBurney, S. B. Pickens, John D. Kelly, C. G. Matthews, Glen E. Davis, W. B. Ravenel, and E. K. Marshall. After the Rev. W. J. Page had served as assistant in 1889-90, the Rev. John Gass became assistant in 1890 serving until 1894. A notable mission was held in the parish in 1892, conducted by the Rev. Walpole Warren. In 1892, a new organ was installed at a cost of $4,000.00. This organ was placed on the Gospel side of the chancel. This year was marked by several important gifts: a brass pulpit, brass and walnut prayer desk, a brass altar rail, and a silver flagon. After Mr. Gass' departure there were several to serve as assistants, but only briefly: Revs. A. E. Beeman, 1895; J. L. Egbert, 1895; R. W. Barnwell, 1895-96; H. L. Shubert, 1897. Dr. Pinckney resigned in 1897 but at the earnest request of the vestry withdrew his resignation and served until his death August 12, 1898—after five years as assistant minister of Grace Church and forty-three as rector. Full of years and many honors in the Church he passed to his reward.

The Rev. Edward Lewis Goodwin, D.D., who had become assistant in 1897 now became rector and served for a year. The Sunday School building was enlarged in 1898 at a cost of $3,453-.11. At this time there were 170 families connected with this Church and 380 communicants. The total receipts were $10,036.20. The Rev. J. Wilmer Gresham became rector April 29, 1900, coming from St. James' Church, Baton Rouge, La. His ministry began with great promise, but his health failed, he serving less than two years. Grace Church's first rectory, 36 Rutledge Avenue, was bought in 1901 for $3,306.75. It was never so used and was sold in 1902 for $3,200.00.

The Rev. William Way was received into the diocese by letter dimissory from the District of Asheville in the fall of 1901, becoming assistant of Grace Church but at once having charge. He had served for some months in Grace Church, N. Y. Mr. Way was ordained priest by Bishop Capers November 13, 1901, and on call of the vestry, became rector of Grace Church May 1, 1902. He was rector for over forty-four years. In 1905, 138 Rutledge Avenue was purchased for a rectory, called the McBurney Memorial. A legacy of $5,000.00 had been given by William McBurney for a rectory. It was used until 1916 and then sold for $9,000.00. At this time, 98 Wentworth Street, next to the Church, was bought as a permanent rectory for the sum of $13,000.00—part payment being made with the restored McBurney legacy given for a rectory in 1894. In 1906, with the approval of the vestry and congregation, the rector established the Memorial Endowment Fund. In 1914, it was decided by the congregation to include all legacies not otherwise designated in this fund. It amounted to $50,000.00 in 1946 In 1907, the Church received a thorough renovation.

The Rev. R. E. Gribbin became assistant in 1912, serving until 1915. Grace Church at this time had a trained nurse on its staff of workers. It was one of the first Churches in the South to introduce the duplex-envelope system. The parish house was rebuilt and modernized at a cost of $25,000.00 in 1919 as a thank offering for the safe return of more than 100 men and women after World War 1 and as a memorial to three members who made the supreme sacrifice. In 1907-08, the chancel of the Church was remodeled and a choir building built adjoining the vestry room, all to accommodate a vested choir, which was installed Easter Day, 1908. For 62 years, the music had been rendered by a quartette.

The Roosevelt organ in use since 1892 was in 1924 rebuilt into a practically new three-manual organ. Among other events of importance in this period should be mentioned the construction of a Boy Scout Building on the northwest corner of the property, the reorganization of the Woman's Auxiliary into ten chapters, and the forming of the Men's Club of Grace Church which was in effect an outstanding event. In 1918, the charter of the Church was amended and a new Constitution and by-laws adopted, making the rector chairman of the vestry. The giving of the altar in 1917 in memory of Robert Cathcart and the reredos in 1929 in memory of Dr. A. Robert Taft and Mary W. Taft climaxed, we may say, the beautifying of the interior of the Church. We cannot here mention the long list of memorial gifts which have completed the beauty and usefulness of Grace Church. Dr. Way published a sketch of Grace Church in 1923. The Rev. C. A. Cole was assistant 1937-38 and the Rev. Edward M. Dart 1938-40. A great service was held in Grace Church on February 17, 1946, commemorating its Centennial. The Governor of South Carolina and many other distinguished men in Church and State were present or sent felicitations to Dr. Way and the congregation. In July of this year, Dr. Way resigned after his rectorship of 44 years, and was elected rector emeritus. At this time, the wardens were J. R. Hanahan and J. B. Hyde, vestrymen, R. F. Fraser, E. H. Poulnot,

E. T. Heyward, R. C. Barkley, E. L. Wilcox, W. B. Metts, H. W. Simmons, T. W. Thornhill, G. S. McDowell, and A. E. Geer; honorary, S. G. Snelgrove. Bishop Thomas supplied services from October until January. In 1948 the vestry published a complete history of the Church by Dr. Way.

The Rev. Ralph Sadler Meadowcraft becoming rector January 1, 1947, was instituted by the Bishop on the 26th of the month. Grace Church now entered upon another period of development. The Rev. Eugene J. West was assistant minister from 1948 to 1950. We can only list some points in this growth: a new heating plant, new flexible lighting system with handsome new lanterns in keeping with the church's architecture (1848), renovation of the fabric, roof, and interior of the Church, new Reuter three-manual organ, in 1952 (gift of Edwin R. Croft) new altar window, handsome new hangings (gift of Mrs. J. Freeman Williams); Mrs. Williams also gave a window placed in the rear of the Church typifying the offices of worship in the nave of the Church, with other improvements. In 1950, a department of Christian Education was organized with a director added to the parish staff.

CHURCH OF THE HOLY COMMUNION, CHARLESTON
Established 1851

For many years, a Church in the section of Charleston known as Cannonsborough had been contemplated by Bishop Bowen, and also later by Bishop Gadsden who availed himself of the proffered services of the Rev. Edward Phillips, rector of St. Thomas and St. Dennis. Mr. Phillips was appointed missionary-in-charge by the Bishop and gathered a group of those interested. On November 7, 1848, a meeting was convened, the Bishop presiding, and Mr. William C. Courtney acting as secretary. It was decided to proceed with the purpose and a tentative vestry was elected: wardens, St. John Phillips, M.D. and Col. A. O. Andrews; and vestrymen, George A. Trenholm, J. J. Pringle Smith, J. K. Sass, William C. Courtney, B. G. Heriot, William T. Sanders, and Capt J. Williamson, U.S.A. These all belonged to other Churches. The first service was held on November 12, 1848, the Twenty-first Sunday after Trinity, at the residence of the late Bishop Bowen. The week following, through the agency of the officer-in-charge of the United States Arsenal, an apartment was secured there for the services, where they were continued by Mr. Phillips, replaced for a time by the Rev. J. Ward Simmons. These clergymen were succeeded in the fall of 1849 by Mr. Edwin A. Wagner, a candidate for Holy Orders, who served as lay reader, and continued his ministrations when ordained deacon November 17, 1850; a salary of $200.00 was then voted him. The parish was incorporated in 1850, and was admitted to the Convention February, 1851. In 1850, the attendance of whites was 50 to 100, and in the afternoon 70 to 80 Negroes, about 20 families showed intention of regular membership. The Sunday School numbered 20 white and 100 colored.

On March 21, 1851, the vestry bought from Mr. Webb a lot at the corner of Ashley and Cannon Streets, 80 feet on Ashley and 120 on Cannon, at $20.00 per foot. In June, the rector was offered a salary of $130.00 with what could be "collected at the door." The Advancement Society for several years assisted with the rector's salary. Thanks were formally accorded Captain Bradford, U. S. A., for the fitting up and use of the commodious and comfortable room at the Arsenal. In December, 1852, it was resolved to erect a wooden building, but this action was almost immediately abandoned; Mr. Courtney had at first voted against it. After an urgent appeal by Mr. Wagner in March, 1853, on motion of Col. Andrews, it was resolved to build a Church of Brick 40 x 70 feet. On November 19, 1853, the cornerstone of a small Gothic cruciform building was laid by Bishop Davis, assisted by Mr. Wagner and the city clergy. Jones and Lee were the architects. This Church was never finished.

The Rev. Mr. Wagner resigned January 1, 1854, going to Spartanburg. Nanmes connected with this move to build another church in Charleston besides those mentioned were J. D. Alexander, A. V. Dawson, Dr. E. G. White, H. L. Toomer, A. R. Haig, W. T. Sanders. Mr. Wagner's departure led to considerable discouragement. However, a call was, on January 1, 1854, extended to Mr. Anthony Toomer Porter, then a candidate for Holy Orders, to come to Charleston and undertake the building of the Church. When he assumed this responsibility, the future of the Church was assured. The lot had been paid for and now many generous offers of help in kind were received, but no action was taken immediately. On May 16, Rev. Mr. Porter, having been ordained deacon, was made minister-in-charge at a salary of $180.00. By this time, $1,698.00 had been collected. At Easter, the gentlemen belonging to other Churches withdrew and now was elected the first real vestry of the Holy Communion: wardens, A. R. Haig and John Bryan; vestrymen, Dr. St. John Phillips, A. V. Dawson, J. D. Alexander, H. L. Toomer, W. S. Sanders, John H. Holmes and W. B. Williams.

The plan of the building not meeting the views of the minister or vestry as too small, another was adopted on July 2, 1854. This was done without the minister's knowledge. He was disappointed; but, being anxious to have a Church, decided to go on with it. A contract was made with L. Rebb for $15,000.00 and the work proceeded, $9,000.00 being borrowed. In the midst of all this, the rector had yellow fever; after recovery in October, he was given a leave to recuperate. The Advancement Society, which helped with the salary of the minister for six years, contributed $250.00 toward the building. There were many other gifts of furnishings: St. Paul's Church in the city gave its old organ (rebuilt at a cost of $1,000.00); the Sewing Society gave the four chancel tablets; St. Paul's Sewing Society, a handsome chancel carpet; St. Michael's, two chancel chairs; Mrs. H. W. Conner of St. Michael's, a beautiful font; also, there were many other gifts. The old Bible and Prayer Book were given to the Church in Laurens and the old font to Christ Church, Charleston (now St. Peter's). The Church was Consecrated by Bishop Davis on October 27, 1855; twelve clergymen besides the rector assisted. Rev. Paul Trapier preached.

In 1856, the rector purchased a lot adjoining the Church, giving his personal bond for $1,400.00. In three years, with the help of the Sewing Society, it was paid for. In June, 1859, a contract to build a school house for $6,400.00 was made with Walter Cade. Mrs. G. A. Trenholm gave $1,000.00 and $5,000.00 was borrowed. In 1859 Mrs. Andrew Milne gave $2,000.00 on the Church debt, leaving $4,800.00 due. The Church Building Society, which had been organized by Mr. John Bryan, warden, and the rector on July 8, 1859, gave $700.00 on the Church debt. From May to October, 1858, the rector was granted a leave of absence, and by generosity of a member of the congregation, he was enabled to travel in Europe with an invalid member of his family. In 1858, there were 108 white communicants and 34 colored, and 58 white families in the parish. In this year, the total raised was $5,071.50. The parish suffered a great blow in the death of Mr. John Bryan. This new parish under God owed much to his strong will and unfailing devotion. In January, 1863, Mrs. G. A. Trenholm gave a large lot on Rutledge Avenue (cost, $6,150.00) and $50,000.00 for a new Church after the war should be over, nearly all the money was lost having been put in 8% Confederate Bonds. The rector was absent on service in the Army much of the time of war. There was no vestry meeting from April, 1863 to March, 1866. On October 25, 1864, Mr. T. D. Wagner gave Dr. Porter a check, paying all indebtedness on the Church, and school house. This occurred while Dr. Porter was standing by the deathbed of his eldest child, born on the very day exactly ten years before when he had held his first service as lay reader at the Arsenal. Regular services were resumed in 1866. Dr. Porter went North in 1867 at the Bishop's request and succeeded in securing funds for the diocesan Seminary and the Freedman's School at the old Marine Hospital in Franklin Street. The Ladies' Sewing Society assisted in the current expenses of the Church in these years. On December 9, 1867, a large parish day school was opened, and the next year in March, a Home for Boys was opened in the house belonging to the rector north of the Sunday School, and soon after, the Rev. Dr. Porter again went North to procure funds for this work. The story of Dr. Porter's school work from this time will be given in a separate sketch of the Porter Military Academy. (See Appendix XI.)

Contributions in this parish in Confederate money in 1863 were $68,717.65; the next year, $641.00; in 1870, $5,631.83—the vicissitude of war. In 1868-69, Rev. E. C. Edgerton was engaged as assistant by the rector and served eight months. In 1868, the building east of the Church was acquired by the rector ($5,100.00) and repaired ($6,000.00) as an extension of the Home and later conveyed to the parish. In 1869, through the generosity of an unknown friend, extensive alterations were made in the Church building by the addition of the recessed chancel. Then also, by means of the sale of the lot on Rutledge Avenue, the north and south galleries were removed, that at the west end remaining for the colored; the ceiling of plaster was knocked down and the pine open-work roof construction substituted, the vestibule being removed; also, an organ chamber north of the chancel was added. The pews were now rearranged to give a middle aisle. At this time, a new charter was obtained and new parish constitution adopted (April 7, 1870), by which the rector became chairman of the vestry. Further additions were: a marble altar; a pulpit and lectern; a stone font, given by the rector's wife; a handsome stained-glass chancel window, and two side windows in the chancel by the children of the Sunday School; an organ at a cost of $3,000.00; also, a furnace. In 1870, the Sunday School was enlarged 17 feet. The Bluffton Church bell which had been kept at the Arsenal since the war was, with the permission of the vestry of The Cross, Bluffton, used for a time before being sent to Bluffton. Besides those already mentioned, vestrymen to 1871 had been G. A. Trenholm, A. M. Middleton, Louis Jervey, B. G. Pinckney, R. H. McDowell, H. S.

Peake, B. C. Wilkins, T. D. Wagner, John Hanckel, W. M. Lawton, M. S. Bartlett, Hutson Lee, William Crovatt, Edward Sebring, T. R. Waring, Alexander Macbeth, F. R. Mitchell, and J. M. Thompson. Communicants in 1870 were 170 whites, 6 colored. On May 9, 1875, the rector had a hemorrhage of the lungs and was off duty and away until Advent Sunday. The repairs to the Church going on for some time were completed in 1876, with the installation of stained-glass windows. The Rev. J. B. Perry became assistant October, 1875. He entered the ministry from his parish and at the time, there were three other candidates and four postulants. Next to the Rev. Mr. Walker of Beaufort, Dr. Porter influenced a greater number for the ministry than any other clergyman in South Carolina. The services at the Church of the Holy Communion were of a more ritualistic character than had been the custom in this diocese. Here was the first vested choir, and also many other points of ritual were observed including Eucharistic vestments, worn here alone in the diocese for many years. A porch and vestry room were added to the Church in 1876-77. The Rev. H. T. Gregory acted as assistant briefly after Mr. Perry from November, 1876. In 1879, the Holy Communion was celebrated every Sunday and on Saints' Days. There were at this time 169 communicants, including 4 colored. In this year, Dr. Porter went to Europe a second time, the Bishop taking the services. When the Arsenal was leased to Dr. Porter on January 8, 1880, and the school moved to it on 2nd of February,, the Home on Cannon Street was made a Home for needy ladies, called the Carolina Wilkinson Home in memory of the wife of the Rev. G. H. Wilkinson, vicar of St. Peter's Church, Eaton Square, London. In 1882, there were 17 inmates. About this time, a new eagle lectern, a gift of the children, was installed. The $50,000.00 of Confederate Bonds were now finally sold, the meager proceeds being used for the repair of the organ and the carpeting of the chancel and choir. The rector was the head of the House of Rest where he had the Communion on Saints' Days. The Rev. J. H. LaRoche became assistant in 1883 serving for two years. The Rev. T. A. Porter, son of the rector, became assistant in 1885. Holy Communion did not withdraw from Convention in the secession of 1887.

The earthquake of August, 1886, damaged the Church to the extent of $2,000.00, paid by friends in the North. Services were interrupted for only one Sunday when they were held on the Arsenal grounds. However, the large, three-story Sunday School building erected in 1856 had to be taken down. In 1888, the women of the parish were effectively organized into Tens, as King's Daughters. The Church was rough-cast at this time. In 1897, the wardens were F. A. Mitchell and Dr. A. Fitch; the secretary, H. M. Walker; the treasurer, C. C. Fuller. The year following, Dr. Porter became rector emeritus and the assistant previously, the Rev. T. A. Porter, became rector, and the next year the Rev. Henry J. Mikell, deacon, became assistant. He was made rector succeeding the Rev. T. A. Porter in 1900—subsequently Bishop of Atlanta.

Dr. Porter's notable services to this church and the Porter Military Academy ended with his death Easter Day, March 30, 1902. He was born in Georgetown, January 31, 1828. He was rector from 1854 until 1898 and rector emeritus until death. He founded the Holy Communion Church Institute (afterwards P. M. A.), in 1867, and was rector of St. Mark's, Charleston, from 1879 until 1888. In 1895, the Church had 303 communicants and the total current expenditures were $3,602.32. The Rev. Henry Hope Lumpkin became assistant in 1908. Both Mr. Mikell and Mr. Lumpkin resigned in 1909, the Rev. F. Harriman Harding becoming rector. He served until 1913 when the Rev. Frederick A. DeRossett became rector. At this time, the wardens were Julius M. Cater and Joseph Ioor Waring; the secretary, J. Waring Witsell; the treasurer, J. M. Cater. Mr. DeRosset was succeeded in the rectorship in 1916 by the Rev. Homer Worthington Starr, Ph.D. In 1917 the Church was redecorated and the organ rebuilt. Dr. Starr for years was the leader in educational and young people's work in the diocese and at Kanuga. The first branch of the Y. P. S. L. to be founded in the diocese was in this parish in October, 1921. Boy Scouts were active, also. Bird Hall was erected in 1920, named for the donor, Mr. W. M. Bird, long a faithful member of the parish. In 1926, a mural tablet was erected in memory of the second rector, Theodore Atkinson Porter. In the same year, the handsome sounding board was placed in memory of Joseph Ioor Waring, for many years vestryman and then senior warden. A new chapter of the Brotherhood of St. Andrew was formed about this time. In 1935, the wardens were: L. A. Prouty and C. B. Prentiss; secretary, William H. Cluverius; treasurer, F. W. Holmes; lay reader, L. A. Prouty. Dr. Starr, who was then president of the Standing Committee and chairman of the Board of Examining Chaplains of the diocese and Chaplain of the Porter Military Academy, died July 5, 1936. He was succeeded in October by the Rev. William Wallace Lumpkin. Under Mr. Lumpkin, "St. Alban's parish" was established at The Citadel. At this time music of the Church was given special attention, and in 1940, a fine Kimball organ replaced the Steere and Turner in use since 1869. The Rev. Colin R. Campbell served as assistant rector in 1941-42. Mr. Lumpkin in 1942 left the parish, on leave, to serve as a chaplain in the Navy until the fall of 1945 when he returned to the parish. During the period of his absence, the parish had the services as *locum tenens* first of the Rev. Arthur R. Willis until February, 1944, and then of the Very Rev. S. Alston Wragg until after the rector's return. St. Mary's Guild was organized in 1946, especially to conduct a nursery at 11:15 on Sundays. The Rev. Mr. Lumpkin was transferred to the diocese of Pittsburgh in 1949. He was succeeded by the Rev. William L. Hargrave, who continued as rector until 1954.

Two chapters of the Brotherhood of St. Andrew were still active in 1951. New windows were installed in the Church in 1951. In 1952-53, members of the congregation completed the large task of repainting Bird Hall and then the entire interior of the Church. Mr. Hargrave resigned in 1953. The old rectory on Ashley Avenue was now sold and a handsome new building purchased in Windermere. In January, 1954, Mr. Hargrave was succeeded by the Rev. Edwin Ballenger Clippard, coming from St. Luke's, Newberry. In this year, an extensive addition was made to Bird Hall at a cost of $35,000.00, making a very complete parish house with 15 classrooms and kitchen.

CHURCH OF THE REDEEMER
SEAMAN'S HOME, CHARLESTON
(See Appendix, Part One, IV, 2)

ST. ANDREW'S MISSION
KING STREET, CHARLESTON
Established 1900

The beginning of this mission is related by one of the early workers in the mission (*News and Courier,* July 30, 1951) as follows:

"A little more than half a century ago two Brotherhood of St. Andrew men, Clarence D. Schirmer and Thomas Hazelhurst of Grace Protestant Episcopal Church, with the assistance of Mrs. Jesse E. DeVeaux and Miss Margaret Smith, began weekly cottage meetings in the mill village of the Royal Bagging and Yarn Manufacturing Co. The mill and village occupied the area including Bertha and Poinsett Streets and portions of Grove and King Streets. Rivers High School occupies most of the village site and the mill building has been converted into County Hall.

"These four carried out the work until about 1902 or 1903, when Mrs. DeVeaux married the Rev. Mr. West, a Methodist minister, and moved to Spartanburg. Business took Mr. Schirmer and Mr. Hazelhurst away and Elias Ball was placed in charge, with assistance of Miss Caroline Lee (later Mrs. Middleton), Miss Julia Ball, Miss Caroline Whaley and others.

"They conducted afternoon Sunday School and evening services in a building erected by the mill authorities to be used for Church services, recreation and school. Mr. Ball and his workers assisted also with a night school, the teacher being paid by the mill owners. Children and adults attended, but mostly adults."

Bishop Capers placed the mission under the charge of the rector of the Church of the Holy Communion, the Rev. H. J. Mikell, with Mr. Thomas Hazelhurst, lay reader and superintendent, on May 1, 1904. On July 10 of this year was the first recorded Confirmation of seven persons. Mr. Elias Ball succeeded Mr. Hazelhurst as lay reader and superintendent. At this time, the Sunday School numbered 47. Offerings $70,00. For the year 1908, the Rev. H. H. Lumpkin, assistant, was associated with Mr. Mikell in charge. The Rev. F. H. Harding succeeded Mr. Mikell in 1909. There was a night school at the mission at this time. Services were held every Sunday night. Mr. Ernest H. Federwitz of St. Philip's assisted Mr. Ball and then Mr. E. H. Mellichamp of St. Luke's Church. In 1913, the charge of the mission passed to the new rector of the Holy Communion, Rev. F. A. DeRossett, and then in 1916 to his successor, Dr. Starr.

Until 1919 this work was a parochial mission. It now became a mission of the diocese. Mr. E. H. Mellichamp was treasurer and lay reader, Mr. R. Buford Sanders, secretary. The mission was still using the school room belonging to the factory for all gatherings. Shortly after this, Mrs. Jesse E. West returned to Charleston and entered the mission work again and worked with it until her death in March, 1921. She left her estate to St. Andrew's Mission to buy a lot and build a small chapel to be known as St. Andrew's Chapel.

The present building at the southeast corner of King and Poinsett Streets was built under the management of Robert Sanders, using the bequest of Mrs. West and funds solicited from Episcopalians of Charleston. The new chapel was opened for service on the evening of July 9, 1922. Dr. Starr read the service, the sermon was preached by the Rev. A. S. Thomas, then rector of St. Michael's Church, who had just been placed in charge of the mission by

Bishop Guerry. The Rev. H. D. Bull then paid a tribute to Mrs. West, who labored for many years in the mission and whose legacy made possible the building of the chapel. Mr. Thomas continued in charge preaching Sunday evening, baptizing, and having Communion services for four years. The self-sacrificing lay workers during these and after years were E. H. Mellichamp, warden, lay reader and treasurer; R. B. Sanders, C. D. Schirmer, Miss Edith M. Phin, Miss Addie Smith, with many faithful members of the congregation—not least the Barrineau family and especially Mrs. John Barrineau. It was toward the end of this period that the property to the south of the Church, including the barber shop and dwelling, was purchased chiefly with the loan of $1,000.00 of diocesan funds by Bishop Guerry, this was repaid during Bishop Thomas's Episcopate.

The Rev. John H. Morgan took charge in 1927 and '28 and then the Rev. G. F. Cameron for a short time. Mr. C. D. Schirmer now became warden, and secretary and treasurer. Mrs. Annie Leseman, daughter of Mr. Mellichamp, was for many years the faithful organist. In 1931 the Bishop appointed Miss Fannie B. Duvall of Cheraw, an experienced Church worker, to be the religious and social worker for the mission. Thus for the first time the mission was supplied with a full-time paid worker. Miss Duvall reorganized the Woman's Auxiliary (first formed years before) and developed its membership and labors. The many religious and social activities for all ages, male and female, cannot here be fully described. Her labors extended to the girls of the cigar factory. Miss Duvall enlisted the assistance of members of several Churches in the City. Among the leaders were Miss Mary Schirmer, Miss Addie Smith, Miss Caroline Williams, Mrs. A. S. Thomas, and Mr. Elias Ball, who now became secretary and treasurer, and lay reader. The Rev. C. S. Smith of St. Paul's Church had charge for a time in 1931, then different clergymen assisted. During the depression period, through the generosity of neighboring farmers many needy people were supplied with food. It was at this time that Mr. Horace L. Tilghman of Marion gave a carload of lumber with which by W. P. A. workers the parish house was built. Miss Duvall's resignation was regretfully received the end of summer, 1933. She went to be director of Appleton Home in Macon, Ga. The workers above mentioned with Mrs. C. J. Shuler and Miss Virginia Prouty resolved to continue the work of the mission. The Rev. E. G. Coe took charge in 1935, having already assisted for some time. In 1936, Mrs. Elias Ball gave the mission a pair of altar vases, and Miss Fannie Duvall a pair of cndlesticks, completing the beauty of the altar. It was at this time the chancel of the chapel was remodelled and beautified, the Church and hall repaired and repainted—chiefly by a free-will offering of members under the leadership of Mr. W. Moultrie Moore, a candidate for Holy Orders, who now was acting as lay reader and worker. Miss Caroline T. Williams was secretary and treasurer for a time, then Miss Mary Schirmer held this position with her other manifold duties in the mission. Mr. G. C. Pundt and Miss Clelia Missroon were among the many helpers. In 1937, a font was given the mission by the Advent Guild of St. Michael's in memory of Miss Caroline T. Williams who had done much for the mission.

In 1939, Mr. Floyd Harding was warden and lay reader. In 1941, the Rev. C. R. Campbell was in charge; later Mr. Coe resumed charge. In 1943, Rev. Lawton Riley was in charge briefly, then the Rev Harold Thomas in 1944. Mr. Thomas was succeeded by Rev. J. Q. Beckwith, who had followed him as rector of St. Luke's Church in 1948; the warden was now, T. W. Daniel; treasurer, A. B. Burnham; Church School superintendent and lay reader, Elias Ball. The Rev. A. C. Tucker, assistant of St. Philip's, had charge in 1950. Later other ministers assisted. The Rev. Harold Thomas resumed charge of the mission on his return to the diocese from Chester in 1951. In 1954, Mr. J. E. Stelling was warden and treasurer, and Mr. LeRoy F. Barrineau, Church School superintendent. This mission for over fifty years has gathered many souls into God's family. Its good work continues unabated. Mr. Thomas preaches every Sunday evening and ministers pastorally to young and old. On May 6, 1956, nine stained glass windows in the chapel were Dedicated by Bishop Albert S. Thomas.

Eight of the windows were the gift of Mrs. R. B. Smiley of Ludewici, Ga., the daughter of Mrs. Elizabeth Robinson of Charleston. One was the gift of the Women's Auxiliary of the mission. Windows installed in memory of past members of the mission were dedicated to Jessie E. Devoe West, a founder of the chapel; Edward H. Mellichamp; Clarence D. Schirmer and Thomas H. Hazelhurst; Adelaide H. Smith; James O. Bruce and Elias Ball. Present members of the mission honored by dedication of a window in honor of their services were Robert B. Sanders and Miss Edith M. Phin.

Bishop Thomas gave a sketch of the history of the mission and the Rev. Harold Thomas, minister in charge, read the Evening Prayer.

ST. JOHN'S CHURCH, CHARLESTON
Established 1839

The Rev. Paul Trapier, missionary, with his assistant, the Rev. R. T. Howard, in connection with their labors centering at St. Stephen's on Anson Street, began holding services in Hampstead in February, 1839, in a school room rented for the purpose. Very soon again, as in case of St. Stephen's, under the patronage of the Female Domestic Missionary Society, it was decided to build a chapel of wood. The Society had, in 1831, acquired a lot in Hampstead Village, then beyond the city limits, used in part as a burial ground for the city mission. This lot was selected as an appropriate place for the chapel together with a contiguous lot now added. The cornerstone was laid by Bishop Bowen on April 9, 1839. The chapel was completed at a cost of $4,000.00—only $300.00 remaining unpaid. It was opened for services October 13. At first, the attendance was small, but the prospects considered good. From the first, the mission was called St. John's. The Rev. Mr. Howard withdrew from the mission in May, 1840.

St. John's was Consecrated on July 14, 1840, by Bishop Gadsden —the first Episcopal act of the new Bishop of the diocese. He was assisted by the missionary, Mr. Trapier, and the rectors of St. Michael's and St. Paul's. The rectors of the four Charleston parishes constituted an Executive Committee who appointed the minister on nomination by the Bishop. Three days later, the chapel became a separate charge under Rev. Cranmore Wallace. He reported in February, 1841, 13 white and 10 colored communicants; Sunday School, 41 white and 39 colored. The Rev. Alexander W. Marshall succeeded Mr. Wallace after a few months, beginning his long and faithful services in this chapel and among the poor of the city, ministering, too, at the city almshouse. In 1852, the Church was repaired and the fences rebuilt. Mr. Marshall, at this time, was honored with the degree of Doctor of Divinity. Rev. Paul Trapier's "Cathechism" was used in the Sunday School. It was in 1857 that the fence on two sides (south and west) of the chapel yard was replaced by brick walls and iron costing $1,185.00. The rector was active not only in the chapel, but also in the city hospitals (especially the Marine Hospital), jail, and almshouse. The death of Mrs. Sarah Dehon, one of the founders of the city Female Missionary Society, marked the fall of a "Mother in Israel" for St. John's—a great loss to the Church. In 1859, there were 79 white communicants and 44 colored; whole number of services, including almshouse, 222.

While many members of the congregation had left the city on account of the bombardment, the work and workship of the chapel was otherwise normal in May, 1864. During and after the war, the chapel fell into considerable disrepair. It was reshingled at a cost of $362.00. Communicants reported in 1869, 114; Sunday School, 105; services, 204, including those at the almshouse. The colored communicants in the city had now largely gone to Calvary and St. Mark's churches. In 1870, through an appeal to the city churches and a contribution of $120.00 (total $657.00) by the city clergy, the chapel was put in thorough repair. In 1874, 121 communicants were reported. Part of the silver of St. Helena's, St. Helena Island, was loaned to St. John's. After 35 years of self-sacrificing labor in St. John's and among the poor of Charleston, having "the reverence of all who knew him", Rev. Alexander W. Marshall, D.D., died November 7, 1876. The Rev. J. M. Green was appointed to succeed Dr. Marshall in February, 1878. However, he and the Rev. W. H. Hanckel had assisted in the parish since almost a year before Mr. Marshall died. Mr. Green resigned January 31, 1880, becoming superintendent of public schools in Charleston. The Rev. R. W. Memminger had charge in 1881 and then in March, 1882, the Rev. J. H. Tillinghast succeeded. The old Ladies' Missionary Society was still assisting this missionary Church, as well as were other Church societies in the city.

In 1883, a neat vestibule costing $40.00 was added to the Church. Mr. Tillinghast resigned in 1884, when Dr. Robert Wilson took charge in June of this year, having charge until 1892, in connection with his rectorship of St. Luke's. Dr. John Johnson assisted in the work in the summer of 1884. Beginning at this time, Mr. J. J. Pringle Smith (who was Registrar of the diocese) began his long and efficient services as lay reader in St. John's, serving for many years. He was in sole charge from 1892-94. He carried a large share of the burden of the work in this chapel in these years. He was succeeded by Mr. A. F. deJersey, who was also treasurer. Organizations in St. Philip's and in St. Michael's rendered much assistance. The Rev. A. E. Cornish, city missionary, took charge in 1893. There were 166 communicants at this time. The property of St. John's was conveyed to the trustees of the diocese by the missionary society on April 6, 1894. In 1897, the active organizations of St. John's included St. John's Friendly Society, Brotherhood of St. Andrew, Woman's Auxiliary, Industrial School, and Relief Society. In 1899, the Rev. John Henry Brown assisted Mr. Cornish; the Rev. James Joyner did so in 1901 and 1902. Under the Rev. A. E. Cornish, who took charge in connection with his position as city missionary in 1893, the work in St. John's was enlarged. In 1906, 111 families were reported with 798 individuals; 44 baptisms; 262 communicants; 125 in Sunday School, with 16 teachers; services Sundays 156, other days 190; Holy Communion, 79, including private, 4 J. J. Horres was warden and H. C. Gill, treasurer. On April 1, 1907, the Rev. Joseph Jenkins Cornish succeeded the Rev. A. E. Cornish in charge.

The Rev. R. Maynard Marshall assumed charge in March, 1909. Soon after was effected the purchase for $3,000.00 of a building on Amherst Street, adapted for a parish house. This was to be influential indeed in the future work of St. John's. This parish house soon became the center of much activity in this Church. Several clubs were organized. Miss Caroline Preston, a trained Christian social worker, was a leader in these clubs, especially the Girls' Friendly. The Rev. Henry Hope Lumpkin had succeeded Mr. Marshall in 1912. In 1914, J. J. Horres was warden; L. M. Salvo, treasurer; and J. L. Stroeker and C. C. Pundt, lay readers. The total offerings in St. John's in this year were $1,936.00 The Rev. G. Croft Williams succeeded Mr. Lumpkin in 1915, continuing in charge until November, 1918. Then the Rev. A. R. Mitchell, Archdeacon, had charge for a short time, assisted by the Rev. W. B. Guion and the Rev. A. E. Cornish. The Rev. Willis P. Gerhart took charge May 1, 1919, but only for a very short time, being succeded by the Rev. A. E. Cornish. St. John's was now organized as a parish and admitted into union with the Convention on May 11, 1920. The Rev. Cameron Gregg Richardson became the first rector July 15, 1920. J. J. Horres and H. M. Bunch were wardens; Cecil R. Bold, treasurer; and Richard Williams, lay reader.

The Rev. Alexander M. Rich became rector in 1922, James W. Almeida becoming junior warden and also treasurer. A handsome pulpit was given in 1926 in memory of Andrew Earnest Cornish, twice rector, by the Junior League. A handsome new Möhler organ (two manual with 398 pipes) was installed in 1929 at a cost of $3,000.00. Mr. Rich, reaching the retiring age, resigned January 31, 1931, after nine years of active ministry in this Church. St. John's now numbered 420 communicants with a Sunday School of 145, total Church members 787. Mr. Rich was immediately followed in the rectorship by the Rev. John Creighton Seagle. The wardens now were J. J. Horres and S. B. Jones; secretary, Harry Mitchell; and treasurer, Thomas Lewis. During these years, the parish had to meet heavy assessments by the city for street paving. In 1931, memorials were given by Mr. and Mrs. E. A. Bissonette, a fan and a chandelier. The old parish house on Amherst Street was sold and a new one erected in the yard of the Church in 1939 after plans given by Albert S. Thomas, Jr., architect. Thus was a great need supplied. The building was Dedicated on October 15, 1939, by Bishop Thomas in connection with the celebration of the 100th anniversary of the Church. Mr. Seagle retired on April 15, 1940, going to live in his old home near Hendersonville, N. C. Mr. Seagle was succeeded by the Rev. Floyd R. Harding, first deacon in charge for some months, then priest and rector. At this time, 1941, the wardens were J. W. Almeida and S. B. Jones (also mission treasurer); Alvyn Meyer, secretary; S. F. Burbage, parish treasurer; M. A. Todd, lay reader and Sunday School superintendent. Mr. Harding served as rector until his retirement and resignation April 30, 1953. He died less than a month later, May 1, 1953. He was succeeded May 1, 1953, by the Rev. Waties R. Haynsworth who held the charge until he resigned to become Headquarters Secretary in the summer of 1957.

ST. LUKE'S CHURCH, CHARLESTON
Established 1857

There had long been a desire on the part of some residents of the Wraggboro section of the city for a more accessible place of worship than the existing churches. A meeting of those interested was held on December 1, 1857; Bishop Davis presided, and the Rev. A. T. Porter acted as secretary. A new parish was organized under the title, "St. Luke's Church." The following wardens were elected: Edward R. Miles and B. R. Stuart; and vestrymen, I. S. K. Bennett, M. P. Matheson, H. M. Howard, T. P. Green, M.D., John Mitchell, M.D., and F. Peyre Porcher, M.D. At its first regular meeting, the Rev. Christopher P. Gadsden, assistant of St. Philip's, was called and accepted the rectorship. A temporary building was at once erected at the intersection of Elizabeth and Chapel Streets.

The first services were held in this building on May 2, 1858, in the morning and afternoon with sermons by the rector; and in the evening again by the rector when addresses were made by him and by the Rev. Messrs. Elliott and Pinckney. The Rev. Messrs. Wallace, Porter, Hanckel, and Green also were present at this service. The Bishop visited the Church on Thursday, May 6, confirming two candidates—"a large congregation of both white and colored completely filled the building." From this time, regular services were held on Sundays at 10:30 A. M. and 4.30 and 8:00 P. M., and on Wednesday nights. Two Sunday Schools were organized for white and colored children respectively. The Church was admitted into union with the Convention on June 10, 1858. It was incorporated at this time. In May, 1859, a lot on the corner of Charlotte and Elizabeth Streets was purchased and on the 12th of the same month, the cornerstone of the Church here was laid by Bishop Davis, assisted by Bishop Boone of China. The stone was placed at the northeast corner of the chancel and contains the usual articles, including a Bible and a Prayer Book, given by Christ Church, Columbia. From July to December of this year, the rector was absent on leave in Europe for the benefit of a member of his family. While away, he wrote several interesting and instructive letters to the children of the Sunday School.

In 1861, the Church had a membership of 83 families, including 18 colored, with 109 white and 37 colored communicants; Sunday School, 90 white and 35 colored. The completion of the Church was delayed on account of war conditions. Though still incomplete, being ready for occupancy, it was Consecrated by Bishop Davis, February 15, 1862, the day after the meeting of the Convention in Grace Church in the city. The rector preached the sermon. Other clergymen taking part or present were: the Rev. Messrs. Philip Gadsden, Hanckel, Elliott, Drayton, Pringle, Marshall, Phillips, and Howe. The architect of the Church was Francis D. Lee, the contractor Patrick O'Donnell. The Church is an elegant Gothic edifice to seat about 1,200. It is in the shape of a Greek cross, 100 by 80 feet, with 100 pews on the floor and thirty others in the galleries. Each side of the edifice presents a single Gothic window 37 feet high. The center of the ceiling uniting the Tudor arches which spring from the columns is 55 feet from the floor. The chancel is provided with the usual tablets. It was the second largest Episcopal Church in the city, next to St. Paul's. A handsome white marble font, designed and executed by W. T. White of Charleston, was installed in 1862. At this time, part of the time of the rector was given to the chaplaincy of the Palmetto Guards. He held a prayer meeting for the colored on Monday nights. Though many members were refugeeing in the upper part of the State, the Church was regularly used until October 7, 1864, when it was struck by a shell in its southeast corner, exploding in the cistern below. The Church furniture was removed to a farm four miles from the city. Most of it was later destroyed but the font was recovered. The Church silver used for the first time April 3, 1859, was made in London of silver contributed by members of the Church, consisting of a flagon, two chalices, a paten and two plates. It was used for a time in Kingstree when St. Luke's was closed. After the evacuation of Charleston, the Church was stripped by Federal troops and desecrated by use for political purposes. It was also used by a colored female school.

The Church was restored to the vestry in October, 1865, and services were resumed and continued without interruption. These were years of anxiety and struggle for rector and congregation on account of the remaining debt and the hard times. Mr. Gadsden's self-sacrificing labors were sometimes without any salary. In 1870, the Church was still unfinished—window glass, organ and steeple were still only hoped for. A parochial library had been established. The Rev. W. O. Prentiss supplied the services during the rector's absence on sick leave April to November, 1870. Mr. Gadsden died July 24, 1871. Bishop Howe bemoaned his death and spoke of his "devotion to his Master, love of souls, intense missionary zeal, practical judgment, usefulness in the Convention." He was the first choice of many for Bishop just the year before. The handsome St. Luke's Church is a monument to his self-sacrificing zeal. He was succeeded by the Rev. W. O. Prentiss, who resigned May 14, 1874. The Church was still handicapped by a heavy building debt. The Rev. W. H. Campbell became rector February 1, 1875. The communicant membership at this time was about 100. The Church now was repaired and improved to the extent of $1,000.00. Mr. Campbell left and became rector of St. Paul's, Charleston, November 1, 1877. The Rev. J. E. Jackson became rector January 25, 1878. In 1879, a mission for colored people with a Sunday School was begun in the old chapel at the corner of Elizabeth and Chapel Streets which had formerly been occupied by St. Mark's Church. Mr. Jackson resigned July 30, 1880, being succeeded by the Rev. Edward R. Miles on December 7, 1880. At this time, St. Stephen's Church, of which he had charge, received the resignation of Mr. Miles, the doors of St. Stephen's were closed, its congregation uniting with St. Luke's. The membership (communicants) was now 138, and prospects of the parish encouraging. Mr. Miles resigned because of ill health November, 1883, and died January 7, 1885. Mr. J. R. Pringle Smith was the valued lay reader in these years. The wardens were F. P. Porcher and W. L. Daggett.

The Rev. Robert Wilson, D.D., succeeded as rector June 15, 1884. During the next year, the congregation nearly doubled in strength, communicants numbering 196. The Church building was badly damaged in the storm of August, 1885, but no sooner had repairs been made partially than the earthquake of a year later did more damage. This damage, however, was not so great as that suffered by other Churches in the city. After three weeks when Dr. Wilson held services in the open air on Wragg Mall, the Church was found not to be in a dangerous condition and services in it were resumed. By means of a quota from the Bishop's Earthquake Fund and the generosity of friends in the North, the Church was the next year fully restored. In completion of this renovation, a handsome carpet was laid, a beautiful altar of carved walnut (in memory of a member) and a handsome pulpit of brass and walnut were installed, the last as a thank offering for the preservation of the Church through the earthquake. In 1892, there were several gifts, among them a super-altar, brass vases, and altar cross, the last given by the congregation in memory of Mr. Christopher I. Whaley.

The large bonded debt of the parish was extinguished in 1893, leaving, however, still a debt of $3,000.00. Dr. Wilson's health retarded the work in 1892 and '93, especially with loss of voice. There were 119 communicants reported in 1897; the wardens at this time were M. W. Wilson and S. G. Stoney, the secretary, Joseph I. Waring, the treasurer, M. L. Hummel. In 1899, the remaining burdensome debt on the parish was at last removed. But it was not long after (December 31, 1900) that Dr. Wilson resigned on account of disability. In reality, this date ended the life of this parish, according to its original organization. Occasional missionary services were held in the Church by the Rev. A. E. Cornish, city missionary, until May, 1904.

St. Luke's was revived as a mission on May 5, 1904, by the Rev. Louis G. Wood with members of the Church who had recently withdrawn with him from St. Paul's Church, permission having been obtained from diocesan authorities to occupy St. Luke's Church which, having become dormant, had reverted to the ownership of the diocese. The congregation was then, with the Bishop's approval, on December 28, 1904, organized as a parish with Mr. Wood as rector; Walter Williman and John B. Reeves were the wardens; secretary, James G. Simmons; treasurer, William King McDowell; and lay reader, William C. Bissell. The number of communicants reported was 255, total raised for all purposes $4,217.00. This new St. Luke's was admitted into Convention on May 3, 1905, with the following deputies: John B. Reeves, J. P. Thomas, H. B. Bolger, and W. C. Bissell. In 1906, there were 112 families with 304 communicants, and 168 pupils in the Sunday School with 21 officers and teachers; total receipts, $7,109.21. A new organ was installed in 1905, and very soon a rectory was secured at a cost of $3,108.75 and then a parish house for $2,232.43, in which a chapel was provided. The interior of the Church was painted in 1910. The sounding board over the pulpit came from St. Paul's Church, Stono, 1908. The Rev. H. D. Bull assisted Mr. Wood in 1915. At the end of 1916, Mr. Wood resigned to become assistant secretary of the Board of Missions for the Fourth Province (later field secretary of the National Council). At this time, St. Luke's had grown to a communicant membership of 365. The Rev. H. D. Bull for a time after Mr. Wood left acted as rector.

The Rev. Harold Thomas succeeded as rector June 1, 1917. The wardens at this time were Walter Williman (also treasurer) and James G. Simmons; secretary, Thomas M. McCarrel; lay reader, E. H. Mellichamp. Mr. John B. Reeves was organist for sixteen years from 1904. The year 1919 was noted for a great mission held in Holy Week by Archdeacon P. C. Webber. Soon after Mr. Thomas came, the parish house with its chapel was remodeled into a more modernly equipped building to supply a place for the manifold activities of the organizations of the parish—the large Sunday School, the women's and men's Bible Classes, the Woman's Auxiliary, the Brotherhood of St. Andrew, the Men's Club, the Daughters of the King, the Scouts, the Y. P. S. L. and others. Perhaps the most outstanding feature of the life of the parish was the developed organization of the group system with the systematic tasks and careful reports of the different divisions. Mrs. W. L. Miller was for many years the organist.

A side altar was set up in 1928 in the north aisle of the Church and a chapel arranged for many smaller services. The Church was newly tiled in 1934 and in the year following thoroughly repaired inside and out at a cost of $3,000.00. Under Mr. Thomas, the parish grew to a communicant membership of nearly 900, the largest Church in the diocese up to this time. On his death April 20, 1934, Rev. Louis George Wood, late rector, was buried under the chancel of St. Luke's. When the Church was sold in 1950, his remains were removed to St. Philip's churchyard.

We cannot here list the large number of memorials placed in the Church. Nor can we in this sketch tell fully of the rector's services in the parish and beyond its limits, which were not less than the city; his work among Citadel cadets, frequently at St. Andrew's Mission on King Street, at the diocesan Home for Ladies on Bee Street where he was chaplain for many years, in the city hospitals, and in cooperation with interdenominational religious movements in connection with the Ministerial Association and the Y. M. C. A. His thirty years as rector of St. Luke's ended with his resignation September 30, 1947. During these years, he held 1,279 baptisms (of whom 221 were adults); 390 marriages; 476 funerals; 1,455 presented for confirmation. He accepted a call to St. Mark's, Chester.

The Rev. John Q. Beckwith succeeded as rector November 1, 1947. In the summer of 1949, negotiations were opened with St. Paul's Church, Radcliffeboro, which resulted in the union of the two churches July 10, 1949. St. Paul's was selected as the site of the new Church. St. Luke's Church edifice was sold to a colored Baptist organization in 1950; the proceeds went to the building of a new parish house for St. Luke and St. Paul. (See sketch of St. Luke and St. Paul *in loco*.)

CHURCH OF ST. LUKE AND ST. PAUL, CHARLESTON
Established 1949

This Church resulted from the merging of St. Paul's, Radcliffeboro, and St. Luke's Church, completed by the separate action of each congregation on July 10, 1949. The Rev. John Q. Beckwith of St. Luke's was elected rector. St. Paul's was selected as the site of the new Church. Its first service was here on July 17, 1949. Very soon plans were developed for a new parish house for the new Church. Old St. Luke's Church was sold to a colored Baptist Church organization for $55,000.00 (the rectory and another dwelling included). With this sum and the proceeds of a canvass, work on the new parish house was immediately begun. The cornerstone was laid on Sunday, January 28, 1951, by Bishop Carruthers, assisted by the rector, the building to cost approximately $105,-000.00. The building was completed and in use by the early fall of the year, and probably the largest and most complete parish house in the diocese. The work of the two former parishes is now proceeding with their combined strength. Mr. Beckwith resigned to become a professor in the Seminary in Alexandria, Va., in 1955. The Church underwent extensive repairs and redecoration in the summer of 1955. In 1956 the basement of the Church was developed into a sort of "Youth Center" with Boy Scout and other rooms. A Junior Young People's Service League has recently been organized. Chimes have been added to the organ in memory of Celestine Mowry Tucker and also in her memory a baptismal bowl and a silver alms basin.

After Mr. Beckwith's resignation there was no regular rector until the Rev. Earle C. Page succeeded in January, 1956. In the interregnum the regular Sunday morning services were supplied by the Right Rev. A. S. Thomas and many other services by the Rev. Harold Thomas, former rector of St. Luke's.

SAINT MARK'S CHURCH, CHARLESTON
Established 1865

The critical situation of the Church in Charleston after the city's evacuation and the occupation by the Union army (when many places of worship were closed) led a group of colored people to a decision to organize a Church (Easter, April 16, 1865). The use of the Orphan's Chapel on Vanderhorst Street was secured and services begun by the Revs. J. B. Seabrook and J. Mercer Green, both then of Grace Church. A committee on arrangement had been appointed at a meeting held at the same time as the first service, consisting of S. L. Bennett, chairman; J. N. Gregg, secretary; R. E. DeReef, treasurer; B. K. Kinlock, J. Wheaten, R. Holloway, S. O'Hear, and J. B. Mussington. This last member suggested the name of the Church "Saint Mark's" which was adopted by the congregation June 25, 1865. Later the committee was enlarged by the addition of W. E. Marshall and J. M. F. DeReef. There were 95 subscribers to the support of the Church.

The Rev. J. B. Seabrook was unanimously elected first rector September 24, 1865. The organization of the parish was soon after confirmed by the Bishop. After leaving the Orphan's Chapel, services were held for a time in the public school house on Meeting Street near Mary's, when the chapel, previously used by St. Luke's Church at the corner of Chapel and Elizabeth Streets, was secured for the services early in January, 1866. The first confirmation was held here by Bishop Davis. The Church was incorporated in this year. The chapel proving both inadequate and unsafe, a lot was secured in 1870 at the corner of Thomas and Warren Streets at a cost of about $5,000.00. Mr. Seabrook died October 8, 1877. He once used these terms to describe this congregation: "Earnest, active, kind, polite, and worthy." He was succeeded as rector by the Rev. A. T. Porter, D.D., of the Church of the Holy Communion, May 26, 1878, under whose guidance the Church, on which work had been suspended for about two years, was completed in five months. The congregation had given $15,-000.00 for the building. It was Consecrated on November 7, 1878. Mr. William H. Burney of the vestry read the Instrument of Donation, Dr. Porter the Sentence, and the Rev. Ellison Capers preached. There were also other clergymen attending. Thaddaeus Saltus was a candidate from the parish, the Rev. C. I. LaRoche was assistant rector. Mr. Saltus was ordained deacon by Bishop Howe in 1881 (the first colored man to be ordained in the diocese of S. C.)—he succeeded Mr. LaRoche as assistant.

An organ was purchased in 1882 at a cost of $1,675.00. A vested choir was introduced in February of this year. The purposes of his acceptance of the rectorship being accomplished, Dr. Porter was now leaving the work largely to Mr. Saltus, who had been ordained priest. In 1883, the communicants numbered 200, $3,-320.00 had been raised for Church work during the year. Mr. Saltus's health failed at this time. The Rev. H. C. Bishop came from Maryland to be assistant rector in 1885 until January 1, 1886, when he went to be rector of St. Philip's, New York. The Church was wrecked by the cyclone of August 25, 1885, but was at once repaired, chancel extended, and robing room added at a cost of $4,500.00. After Mr. Bishop left, the Rev. Theodore A. Porter conducted the services, E. H. Hollings assisting as lay reader. Mr. Porter turned over his salary to the cyclone debt. No sooner than the severe damages of the cyclone were repaired, than the Church only one year later was damaged again by the earthquake involving more expense which in time was met. During the period of the repairs from the earthquake, the congregation worshipped in St. Timothy's Chapel at Porter Military Academy. The Rev. J. H. M. Pollard became assistant in the spring of 1887, Dr. Porter was still rector serving until Mr. Pollard became rector in 1888. Mr. Pollard also did missionary work in St. Andrew's and in Summerville. He resigned January 31, 1898, to become Archdeacon in North Carolina. The Rev. F. I. A. Bennett acted for a brief time. The Rev. E. N. Hollings became rector November 1, 1898. The wardens at this time were E. F. Elfe and J. B. Dacoster; secretary, William Ingliss, Jr.; the treasurer, John Stokien. Bishop Capers preached on the occasion of the celebration of the 25th anniversary of the Consecration of the Church, November 1, 1903. Mr. Hollings left in March, 1906, being succeeded the following month by the Rev. Charles Irwin Smith. It was reported in 1907 that the women's "Sewing Society" had raised $20,000.00 for Church work since its beginning in 1866. In 1908, St. Mark's gave a font to the Liberian Mission and also supported a pupil in a mission school in Santiago under the Rev. Mr. Mancebo. Mr. Smith resigned in 1909 and then for a time the Rev. Walter Mitchell of P. M. A. and the Rev. J. D.

Lykes supplied services. The Rev. H. A. St. Aubyn Parris became rector in 1910. At this time, the Church received a bequest from the estate of C. C. Leslie, junior warden.

The Rev. F. A. Garrett was rector from 1912 until 1915, when he resigned to join the Roman Church. Under Mr. Garrett, the present altar was installed and dedicated to the memory of Bishop Howe. In 1916, the officers of this Church were: wardens, Norman Montgomery and S. H. Holloway; secretary and lay reader, Gustavus Sinkler; treasurer, John White. The Rev. Charles S. Sedgewick was rector 1917-18. The Rev. Charles A. Harrison became rector in the fall of 1918. Mr. Harrison retired June 15, 1934, but continued his services until the coming of the next rector, the Rev. Kenneth Hughes. On December 27, 1931, Bishop Thomas assisted by the rector, consecrated the new, rebuilt porch of the Church, dedicated to the memory of Augustus Sinkler and Adolphus de-Reef, two faithful members of this Church. After his retirement, Mr. Harrison became acting Archdeacon of the churches of the Council of Colored Churchmen. Mr. Hughes served from 1936 until December, 1940, going then to Cambridge, Mass. The next priest was the Rev. Matthew Wesley Davis, who served as *locum tenens* (not canonically resident), 1940-42. Then as *locum tenens* again the Rev. John R. Lewis, D.D., 1943-45, and then as rector until his death in February, 1947. He was succeeded by the Rev. Turner W. Morris, who served until 1951. The Rev. St. Julian A. Simpkins became rector in 1952.

ST. MICHAEL'S CHURCH, CHARLESTON
Established 1751
(See Dalcho, p. 211)

In 1820 the rector of St. Michael's was the Right Rev. Nathaniel Bowen, D.D. (1818-'39), third Bishop of South Carolina. St. Michael's supplied the diocese with its Bishop for two Episcopates. Our second and third Bishops, Dehon and Bowen, were rectors of St. Michael's as the first, fourth, and sixth—Smith, Gadsden, and Howe—were rectors of St. Philip's (the last continuing as rector only briefly). The Bishop's Common Fund begun in 1818 could only supply the Bishop's expenses, the income was not sufficient for the support of the Bishop until soon after the beginning of the fifth Episcopate, that of Davis. Bishop Davis, indeed, continued as rector of Grace Church, Camden, but was supported by the diocese. However, during the Episcopate of Bishop Bowen, St. Michael's was compensated for an assistant.

The Rev. Nathaniel Bowen had been assistant rector of St. Michael's early in the century (1802) and rector from 1804-09. The Rev. Frederick Dalcho, M.D., the historian, was assistant to Bishop Bowen (1819-35). When the Bishop's health began to fail, Rev. W. W. Spear was also an assistant in 1835 and also after Dalcho's death the next year, until 1839; then he served as rector for one year.

At the beginning of Bowen's rectorship St. Michael's had 480 communicants, 130 of whom were colored; at its end there were 330, a falling off mostly of colored (80) but also of white, due largely to the establishing of two new churches in the city, St. Stephen's (free Church) and St. Peter's on Logan Street. The rector of St. Michael's welcomed the new churches as St. Michael's did not have enough pews to supply the demand. The rector gave as a reason why St. Michael's had fewer colored members the fewness of sittings—less than St. Philip's and St. Paul's. The rectory (39 Meeting Street) was sold in 1825 and none after was acquired for 75 years.

When the fiftieth Convention of the diocese met in 1839 it was the 39th to meet in St. Michael's. It continued to be the regular place of meeting for twelve more years. In Bishop Bowen's rectorship many old features of parish life were abandoned or changed—the custom of decorating the Church for Whitsunday (which change was unfortunate), many semi-civic ceremonies—reading of Citations of the Ordinary, the once ceremonious Sessions Sermon, fallen now to a formality, the use of a clerk in the service, many annual celebrations of various societies—Masons, the Cincinnatis, Palmetto, etc. In 1834 extensive repairs were made on the Church and the old original Snetzler organ was rebuilt with the addition of an octave of pedals. There were men's and women's Bible classes at this time and regular public catechising of children in Advent and Lent. In 1832 the cross aisle and north door were closed, ten much needed pews being gained. A missionary association was formed in 1835 to assist the Domestic and Foreign Missionary Society of the Church.

In 1837 a convenient building near the Church was purchased, a part being used for the Sunday School. In 1838 two of the smaller bells were sent to England to be recast, having been cracked in 1832, it is thought, by the violent ringing for fires. The steeple was for a hundred years a watch tower for the city and the bells rang for fires. For a long time there was a regularly rung "evening bell." In 1833 heavy stone gutters were placed around the Church within the parapet which had been built previously. However, these were later removed as were the parapets, not proving satisfactory. Some of the stones therefrom are used today as stepping stones in front of the Church and some in the pavement. The long rectorship of Bishop Bowen came to an end with his death on August 25, 1839. He was loved for his own sake and for the Church he had proven himself so well fitted to benefit. The orderly services and appropriate music of St. Michael's was due in large measure to his attitude. He was succeeded by his assistant, the Rev. W. W. Spear, but only for about a year.

In 1840 the Rev. Paul Trapier became rector and Rev. Paul Trapier Keith assistant. In 1846 Mr. Trapier resigned and Mr. Keith succeeded as rector; the year following the Rev. T. J. Young became assistant serving until his death on October 11, 1852, when the Rev. James W. Miles became assistant but for only about a year, being succeeded by the Rev. James H. Elliott. About this time the steeple was painted brown. The great missionary activity which had developed in the Church at large was reflected in these years in this parish in its contributions to foreign and domestic missions and to the cause of diocesan missions. Mr. Trapier's rectorship marked an active period in the life of the parish in these prosperous years in the state. The yearly program of services was Sundays, all Saint's Days, Wednesdays, festivals and principal fasts, twice a week in Lent and a monthly service of preparation for the communion. This rector was equally zealous of Church order (possibly, by his own confession, over-zealous), especially in restoring confirmation to its legitimate place in Church life. The friction created led to his resignation but he smoothed the road in this important matter for his successors, not only in St. Michael's but in the diocese. Mr. Trapier's successor, Mr. Keith, carried on his active policies, though perhaps with more moderation. It is interesting to note the wide extent of Church aid extended beyond the walls of the parish—e. g., in 1850: Holy Apostle's, Barnwell, $247.50; Church in Alexandria, La., $194.00; Greenville, Tenn., $118.32; Asheville, $27.50; and blinds for Calvary Church, $94.50.

When the 62nd Convention of the diocese met in St. Michael's Church in 1851 it was the 48th meeting in this Church; only after this time were the meetings generally in other churches. This was a year of extensive repairs, the Church being closed for three months when the congregation worshipped either in Hibernian Hall or St. Philip's. Soon came war with its confusion and destruction. Services were continued for over two years, but in the fall of

1863 shells began to fall in the vicinity of the Church, its steeple being a target for the Federal batteries on Morris Island four miles away. The congregation (with those of St. Philip's and Grace) now retreated to St. Paul's Church where Mr. Howe held services until the spring of 1865 when he was banished (like Smith in the Revolution) having refused, since the Confederacy still existed, to use the prayer for the President of the United States. For a time Messrs. Keith and Elliott of St. Michael's assisted Mr. Howe in these services and later the Rev. J. Mercier Green. The Church was seriously damaged, several shells having entered the roof, one especially damaging the chancel revealing the place of an original chancel window which had been bricked up. This window was restored in the repairs with stained glass which, after the earthquake, was replaced by the present "St. Michael casting out the Dragon." The bells, carried to Columbia, were badly damaged in the burning of that city. Much of the Church silver was lost there, also, some being recovered after the war. The organ was taken down during the war and stored in a safer place. The repairs to the Church were completed and it was reopened for worship on November 26, 1865. The ministers (Keith and Elliott) had difficulty in getting transportation to the city after the war, the Rev. James Worley Miles holding the services in the meantime. Unable to support two ministers the vestry regretfully accepted Mr. Elliott's resignation in January, 1866. Probably suffering under the strain of the post-war period, Mr. Keith died August 23, 1868, after about twenty-eight years of faithful service; on his tablet in the Church are the words, "A man in whom was no guile." The bells were sent to England and recast in their original molds and later restored to the steeple.

The Rev. Richard S. Trapier was elected assistant before Mr. Keith's death but did not come to the Church until the fall. He was made rector January, 1869, and served until July, 1894, when, because of a disabling accident, he accepted the position of *rector emeritus* until his death in October, 1895. This period of reconstruction proved a sad one for both Church and state. Issues concerning Negro representation divided the Church in a sad way. St. Michael's and its rector were in the midst of all this and bore a heavy share. On Friday, May 13, 1887, the delegation of St. Michael's withdrew from the Convention of the diocese to remain out of union until 1899. These years, including the physical damage of the storm of '85 and the earthquake of '86 have been called "the saddest page in St. Michael's history." The vestry room was built in 1883; previously the robing was done in the south vestibule. The minister gained the chancel via the south aisle.

On August 25, 1885, a terrific hurricane visited Charleston, the upper part of the spire of the steeple with the ball was blown away and half the slates ripped off the roof of the Church. Scarcely were the repairs completed when there befell a greater disaster—the earthquake of August 31, 1886. The Church was terribly shattered with cracks in the walls here and there, the steeple settling nine inches. The building was expected to fall at any moment. It was called "the saddest wreck of all," but it did not fall and by expert engineering the imposing building was brought back to its original condition at a cost of $15,000.00 to $20,000.00. Considerable sums of money were contributed by churches and individuals all over the country, but it was chiefly through its own resources the vestry was able to complete the repairs and reopen the Church on June 19, 1887. The congregation, during the period of repairs, worshipped in the Sunday School room of St. John's Lutheran Church. As a token of appreciation St. Michael's presented this Church with two beautiful chalices. A rector of St. Michael's, Bishop Dehon, had once ministered to the pastoral needs of this Church when it was without a minister, hence the friendship between the churches.

The Rev. John Drayton Grimke was assistant from January, 1893 until February, 1894. Some confusion ensued as to the rectorship, and then through an accident Mr. Trapier was incapacitated and became *rector emeritus* July, 1894. Mr. Grimke was made rector in August following, the Rev. Thomas P. Baker becoming assistant in December. Mr. Grimke died March 27, 1895. The mural tablet near the vestry room door reveals the affection in which he was held by the congregation. Mr. Baker continued the services until the ensuing December. Mr. Trapier's career, marked by stern adherence to conscience, ended near Highlands, N. C. on October 22, 1895. Just at this time Rev. John Kershaw accepted the rectorship and began services in December, 1895, continuing until his death April 6, 1921. He was a prominent clergyman of the diocese all these years, often deputy to the general Convention and for many years president of the Standing Committee. Soon after his rectorship began the Sunday School building was renovated and enlarged providing a study for the rector. Many notable occasions marked Dr. Kershaw's rectorship. Among these was the placing of the new south door of stained glass designed by Silas Mc-Ree in 1897. Then the unveiling of the Confederate Memorial in the central vestibule, June 12, 1902, when Bishop Capers delivered the address. St. Michael's, under the rector and especially the advent guild, was instrumental in establishing St. Peter's-by-the-Sea at the Navy Yard. In 1905, under the supervision of Tiffany of New York, the chancel was exquisitely redecorated. After the storm of 1911, necessitating extensive repairs, the main vestibule of the Church was restored through the generosity of Mr. Edwin P. Frost, At this time a new organ was installed at a cost of $16,840.00. Some pipes of the old organ were retained. The electric lighting was now made to harmonize throughout the Church, including a chandelier in the vestibule hung by the old chain with which the large chandelier of the Church was formerly lowered for lighting when it held wax candles. On Sunday, January 29, 1911, the sesqui-centennial of the Church was duly celebrated, marked by an historical address by the rector and a sermon by Bishop Guerry at a great community service in the evening. With the cooperation of the city clergy noonday Lenten services were inaugurated in the Church continuing for about eight years. They were later resumed in the rectorship of Dr. Stuart. There were many gifts about this time, among them the Greenland legacy of $4,500.00, the Holy Table and credence, the reading desk, the great St. Michael's chancel window, the "Easter Morning" window, the litany desk, a silver christening bowl, the Annunciation window and many memorials. The duplex envelope system was introduced in 1915. The Social Service Committee did a city-wide work. The Rev. Oliver J. Hart became assistant in 1916 but soon went on leave to serve as chaplain in the Army. When he returned in 1919 he carried through the nation-wide campaign to victory in the parish. He resigned in 1920, much beloved. After a quarter century of faithful service Dr. Kershaw died April 6, 1921. His body lies at his original home in Camden. Later a mural tablet was placed in his memory, December 12, 1926, betokening the high regard in which he was held by the congregation.

At this time St. Philip's Church was undergoing repairs and modification following a fire of the previous year. Its rector, the Rev. S. C. Beckwith, on invitation assumed the pulpit of St. Michael's and served both congregations until the coming on October 1, 1921, of the Rev. Albert S. Thomas, who had been elected rector. The rectory, 22 Lamboll Street, underwent extensive repairs to the extent of $2,491.23 this summer. Mr. Thomas served for seven years and two months, until he was Consecrated Bishop of the diocese on

St. Andrew's Day, 1928. The officers of St. Michael's in 1921 were: wardens, Charles R. Valk and Edwin P. Frost; secretary and treasurer, E. P. Ravenel. Perhaps the chief characteristic of parish life at this time was the expansion of the young people's work with the growth of the Church school which, with Bible classes, reached the number of 225. A junior vested choir was organized by Mrs. Henry (Henrietta) Jervey. Mr. and Mrs. C. F. Middleton gave a processional cross for this choir. A branch of the Y. P. S. L. was organized under the leadership of Mrs. J. S. Townsend, Miss Leila Barnwell, Mrs. J. K. Heyward and others. The demand arose for a modern parish house. The Brotherhood of St. Andrew under Mr. C. Deas Gadsden, active at this time, especially espoused the movement. Additional space for the building on St. Michael's Alley was acquired, a plan was adopted and a decision made to build a parish house to include the old Sunday School building. The architects were Simons and Lapham and the builders Cheves-Oliver Construction Company. The cost was $33,414.82. On its being opened for use on April 16, 1925, on motion of the congregation it was Dedicated by the rector, Mr. Thomas, to the memory of Dr. Kershaw. This was one of the first modernly equipped parish houses built in the diocese. The old Sunday School building forms a wing of the new building. About this time the rector was given a part-time secretary, the first regular office of this kind in the city. In 1925 the old quartette, in use for some hundred years, was discontinued and succeeded by a vested choir trained by Prof. Bernard Hirous, who became the organist. During his time, and later under Mrs. Martha Laurens Patterson, the music was greatly improved and often oratorios were given; succeeding organists were Donald George and Mrs. Paul Davis. The rector held the charge and services (evening) at St. Andrew's Mission, King Street, for four years. Mr. Thomas' Consecration as Bishop of South Carolina in St. Michael's Church on November 30, 1928, was the first ever held in Charleston. The parish presented Mr. Thomas with a handsome Episcopal ring and his robes of office. He was also given a dinner in the parish house.

For several months the Church was then supplied by visiting clergymen until the Rev. Conrad Goodwin became rector (1929-35). The rectory at 22 Lamboll Street was sold at this time and a new one purchased, 32 Murray Boulevard. Mr. Goodwin's forceful sermons were enjoyed by the congregation. The "Men of St. Michael's" was organized at this time. Mr. Goodwin gave great attention to Bible instruction, conducting a Men's class, Young Woman's and Y. P. S. L. classes. On April 13, 1930, a service was held in commemoration of the first founding of the Anglican Church in the province on the spot where this Church stands. Addresses were made by the rector, Mr. Beckwith and Bishop Thomas. After Mr. Goodwin left in the summer of 1935 there was an interregnum of a year when services were supplied by the Rev. A. M. Rich, the Rev. Albert New and the Rev. C. A. Jessup of Buffalo, New York.

The Rev. Albert R. Stuart became rector July 1, 1937. He reorganized the Woman's Auxiliary and other activities of the parish, including the "Men of St. Michael's." The noonday services in Lent, which had been held in Dr. Kershaw's time, were now resumed. A tablet, erected by the diocese in memory of Bishop Guerry, was unveiled in December, 1937. The Church suffered great damage from the cyclone of September 29, 1938, a large part of the roof being torn off. Services were then held in the parish house. Free pews were established in the fall of 1941. Mr. Stuart served as chaplain in the Navy (1943-46) during the war. The Rev. William T. Capers had temporary charge during this period. Mr. Stuart resigned (1947) going as dean to Christ Church Cathedral, New Orleans, continuing there until elected Bishop of Georgia in 1954. The Rev. DeWolf Perry became rector the Advent of 1947. In 1951-52 the parish celebrated its Bi-centennial. A great community and historical service was held on June 14, 1951, when dignitaries of Church and state were present, the Rev. Edward Legare Pennington delivering a historical address. In the fall a mission was held and on February 17, 1952 a parish service was held when the Right Rev. Oliver Hart of Pennsylvania, once assistant rector, preached. The celebration was marked by the publication by the vestry of a complete history of the parish by George W. Williams, M.A., and by the establishment of a Bi-centennial Fund (for missions in or about the city) entrusted to the Society for the Advancement of Christianity in the diocese.

In 1952 the Church received two bequests of $10,000.00 and $5,-000.00 from, respectively, Mrs. W. H. Brawley and Miss Constance Frost, sisters. In 1952-53 the interior of the Church was completely renovated and in 1956 the exterior was cleaned, repaired, waterproofed, and repainted—a great work taking several months to finish.

ST. PAUL'S CHURCH, RADCLIFFEBOROUGH, CHARLESTON
Established 1810
(See Dalcho, pp. 212, 236)

Dalcho says that the motive for the building of St. Paul's was "the increasing popularity of the Episcopal Communion in Charleston." However, other motives have been suggested after investigation, *viz.*, the convenience of those residing at a distance from the existing churches, and again to provide a Church for the Rev. Dr. William Percy, who was favored by a group in St. Philip's Church, and perhaps St. Michael's. A committee of St. Paul's vestry later concludes that all three motives were involved, but none of these motives explains why such a large Church was built; maybe the hand of Providence was also operative. The congregation was first gathered and organized in the Huguenot Church in 1810. It worshipped here under Dr. Percy until 1815.

The building committee appointed on the 9th of October, 1810, was Charles Linning, chairman; Peter Smith, John Ball, Sr., William Brisbane, Thomas Parker, Jonathan Lucas, and Solomon Legare. These names engraved on a silver plate were placed under the cornerstone. This cornerstone of what was first called "The Third Church" was laid on November 19, 1811. "The brick work was executed by James and John Gordon, their plan for the Church being accepted, the carpenters work by Robert Jackson and Robert Galbraith." The spacious and elegant edifice was erected in what was then the suburbs of Charleston, of brick and rough-cast, the style of architecture was called "modern with a Gothic Tower." It is 164 feet long and 70 feet wide. At first the pulpit, reading and clerk's desks stood in the middle aisle. The beautiful white marble font was in the chancel. This was given by William Brisbane. The organ cost $2,600.00. The Church was incorporated December 21, 1814. The first vestry, elected April 5, 1815, was William Brisbane, chairman; John Ball, Sr., Jonathan Lucas, Jr., Peter Smith, Thomas Parker, Thomas Winstanley, and Solomon Legare; and Thomas S. Grimke, and Andrew Hasell, wardens. After Mr. Linning's death in 1814 Mr. Brisbane became chairman of the Building Committee and Thomas Winstanley a member of it. The Church was consecrated as "St. Paul's Church, Radcliffeborough" by Bishop Dehon on March 28, 1816. The next day Rev. William Percy, D.D. was re-elected rector and, at the same time, Rev. J. B. Campbell, assistant. The Rev. Frederick Dalcho followed Mr. Campbell as assistant, and then the Rev. Seymore Symmes, who also continued in charge for some time after Dr. Percy's resignation in 1819. The

Rev. J. S. Hanckel testified, "The congregation was quite a small one, and were lost in 'vasto gurgete nantes' when they moved into their new and spacious place of worship."

In January, 1821, Rev. Christian Hanckel, coming from Trinity, Columbia, and his duties at the S. C. College there, entered upon his rectorship to last 45 years. The parish was represented in Convention this year by William Brisbane and Major Andrew Hasell. The cost of the Church had been much larger than had been anticipated. There had been difficulties; the foundation of the proposed steeple proved insufficient. Cracks appeared, so the tower was substituted for the steeple. Assessments on pew holders led to much dissatisfaction, some even leaving the Church. However, in his address to the Convention in 1824 Bishop Bowen commended the congregation for its liquidation of a debt of about $30,000.00 remaining from the building of the Church—the task successfully completed in 1825 was accomplished largely by the zeal and ability of that prominent churchman of that day, Mr. William Clarkson. In 1825 the number of communicants was 285 (of whom 14 were colored), only a few less than the number in either St. Philip's or St. Michael's, and there were 120 in the Sunday School.

A society composed of ladies of St. Paul's was organized in 1826 and rendered much service both within and without the parish. In 1827 a much-needed Sunday School for the free colored was organized; later it was reorganized with colored teachers; opening and closing exercises were with the white on opposite sides of the Church. The parish now had a flourishing library. The parish clerk was Mr. Bonnetheau, the last but one (Smith at St. Philip's) to officiate in the diocese. He had abandoned the clerk's desk for the organ loft because of the sharp rap the rector would administer when he made a mistake, it is said. At about this time the troops of the Municipal Guard at The Citadel worshiped in St. Paul's, usually seated in the south gallery; the north gallery was often filled with the Negroes. In 1834 Mr. Thomas S. Deas was superintendent of a flourishing Sunday School numbering 262; it varied, however, up and down in the following years. Mr. Samuel Wagg was deputy to Convention the same year.

Reflecting the common revival of interest in missions in the Church in general, a society was formed in the parish in 1835 to aid foreign, domestic and diocesan missions, the last through the Advancement Society. At this time Mr. Francis Withers, always a liberal contributor, offered to give $1,000.00 a year for the purposes of the society if others would give $3,000.00—result is not known.

For a short period (1835-36) Rev. William Elliott served as assistant. Voluntary contributions in 1838, chiefly for elaborate repairs to the Church, amounted to $5,453.78, but the next year we find the rector complaining that the contributions were not in proportion to the size and wealth of the congregation. Repairs on the Church were burdensome, e. g., the plaster cornices fell and were replaced with stone. In 1838 the Church underwent extensive repairs within and without. By this time repairs on the Church had amounted, it was estimated, to $120,000.00—as much as the original cost, making the total cost of the church nearly a quarter million. At this time a cross was placed on the pediment of the great portico. In 1838 the Rev. J. Stewart Hanckel, eldest son of the rector, became assistant and served until 1851 (but in the winter at St. Andrew's). During these years the Sunday School building was erected, used not only for the school but as a lecture room. Here for a time a Sunday night service was held in it for the members of color who, however, also occupied the north gallery at the regular services. The north vestry room was used for an infant class for whites and rooms in the tower for colored.

During his long rectorship Dr. Hanckel was highly esteemed not only in the parish but in the diocese, being for many years president of the Standing Committee and deputy of the General Convention. Later he had a summer home at Flat Rock especially on account of failing strength. After Mr. J. S. Hanckel's resignation as assistant in 1851 the following served temporarily: The Rev. Augustus Moore (1853), the Rev. E. C. Logan (1856), the Rev. W. H. Hanckel, the rector's fourth son (1858), and also the Rev. T. J. Girardeau (1859-62). Shortly before the war the finances of the Church improved and the whole interior of the Church was renovated and repainted, and the organ gallery changed. At this time the fine pipe organ was purchased of the Messrs. Bates Organ Builders of London for $5,000.00. Mr. Reeves, the organist, and Mr. Speissegar specified the combination of stops of the organ. The communicants then numbered 326, of whom 57 were colored.

Soon after the beginning of the war of 1861-65 the congregation was dispersed and the Church closed. Later, however, the congregations in the lower part of the city, on account of the bombardment, were driven away and, led by Rev. W. B. W. Howe of St. Philip's with his congregation and those of St. Michael's and Grace, reopened St. Paul's. Mr. Howe at first was assisted by the ministers of St. Michael's, Rev. Messrs. Keith and Elliott, and later by the Rev. J. Mercer Green. Mr. Howe continued the services until March, 1865, when he (like Smith at the time of the Revolution) was banished for refusing to pray for the President of the United States, the war not then being ended. The Federal authorities first agreed to a plan to keep the Church open, omitting all prayers having a political reference, but later they insisted on the prayer for the President of the United States, whereupon Mr. Howe relinquished the Church.

The fine bell and the lead weights of the windows had been given to the Confederate government for ordnance purposes. The Church records and plate were sent to Columbia for safekeeping and lost, notwithstanding Dr. Shand's heroic efforts to save them. However, the plate was later all recovered except one cup. Mr. Hanckel gave one of his own to supply this loss. The Rev. Father Merriweather, a Roman priest, recovered some of the plate and returned it to Mr. Hanckel. After the war the vestry faced a heavy task of repairs. In the fall of 1865 an attempt was made to have Dr. Hanckel resume the service with the Rev. W. W. Lord, D.D. as assistant. However, his strength proving insufficient, he resigned February 21, 1866, after 45 years as rector; Dr. Lord was elected rector with Dr. Hanckel as "honorary rector." He served until January, 1870, going to Mississippi. He had successfully conducted a school for young ladies. At this time the Ladies' Aid Association was organized and did much auxiliary work. It was first called the Christian Hanckel Association, the name being changed at the request of his family.

The vestry sought to unite the Church with St. Luke's, its rector the Rev. C. P. Gadsden to have joint charge. Mr. Gadsden, feeling that St. Luke's demanded his entire strength, declined. Another vain effort was made to re-enlist Dr. Hanckel. This greatly beloved and respected clergyman died almost immediately after this. A tablet on the wall of the Church tells of the regard of the congregation for him. The eloquent Rev. J. W. Miles now served as *locum tenens* for a time. Rev. J. H. Elliott, then officiating in Masschusetts, accepted a call and entered upon his duties in October, 1870. In 1871 a beautiful chandelier was placed in the chancel through the efforts of J. Reid Boyleston, a member. The Church's pewing was changed in 1872, modern pews taking the place of the old, high boxed pews, cross aisles being eliminated. Also at this time the pulpit was moved from the middle aisle and placed on the north side of the chancel with the reading and prayer desks on the south side. The Sunday School was relocated in 1873. The next year the Sunday School itself installed a cabinet organ. In

1876 a carved walnut Communion table was installed. Mr. Elliott's ministry was eminently successful. He built up a large and flourishing congregation. Like Dr. Hanckel, he was a leader in diocesan life, one on whom the Bishop leaned. He died June 11, 1877, and was succeeded by Rev. William H. Campbell on August 1, 1877, who was at the time rector of St. Luke's Church. He served for 24 years and was greatly beloved. St. Paul's led in the withdrawal of the churches from the Convention in 1887 on the racial issue and continued unconnected for twelve years. The deputies in 1887 were C. G. Memminger, T. M. Hanckel, L. T. Jervey and T. G. Simons, M.D. Dr. Campbell died November 16, 1901. The officers of St. Paul's at this time were: wardens, G. L. Buist and Walter Williman; secretary, C. O. Dué; treasurer, Walter Williman.

The Rev. Louis G. Wood became rector early in 1902 and resigned in the spring of 1904, occasioned by a controversy with the vestry and congregation on questions of authority in the government of the parish. A large part of the congregation withdrew from membership with Mr. Wood. Mr. Wood at once began a mission at St. Luke's Church which had been closed and also served St. John's, Johns Island, and Trinity, Edisto. The Rev. William Henry Bowers of Rochester, England, succeeded as rector in September, 1904. Disagreements having arisen, he resigned the rectorship in 1907 when the Rev. William Wilkinson Memminger, deacon, was appointed minister by the Bishop, and in the fall when ordained priest (November 3, 1907) he became rector. Early in 1910 he left, going to All Saints in Atlanta. Rev. Walter Mitchell of Porter Military Academy then served as *locum tenens*. The Rev. Walter Raleigh Noe served as rector for a few months, 1910-11. In 1910 a beautiful stained glass angel window was given in memory of Hulde Witte Mazyck, wife of Pierre de St. Julian Mazyck, placed on the south side of the Church next to the vestry room. The Rev. Arthur Temple Cornwell became rector in 1912. The wardens now were R. P. Evans and A. L. Burton; secretary, O. J. Bond; and treasurer, J. Hume Lucas. Mr. Cornwell resigned February, 1915. No sooner had the Church been generally renovated in 1911 than by the great storm of August 27 it suffered much damage. However, all was soon restored. At this time a handsome memorial transom was placed over the door on the south aisle.

The Rev. Mercer P. Logan, D.D., took charge as rector in November, 1915. Dr. Logan removed the choir from the loft to the chancel, installing a vested choir. He stimulated the life of the parish in many ways. He resigned in 1922 going to DuBose Training School, Monteagle, Tenn. Rev. Carl S. Smith succeeded as rector in 1922. At this time the wardens were Dr. T. G. Simons and Walter A. Moore; the secretary, Dr. E. A. Kerrison; and treasurer, T. Russell Page. In 1930 the Sunday School was entirely renovated so that the church property (the church itself having been done over not long since) was in excellent condition. Mr. Smith resigned December 1, 1937. Rev. P. G. Linawever then served as *locum tenens.* Rev. John Pinckney became rector September, 1938, coming from Tryon, N. C. The parish now took on new life, especially in the Sunday School and among the young people; a Y. P. S. L. was organized with 30 members. Also, the Woman's Auxiliary was reorganized. In the spring of 1940 Mr. Pinckney installed a side altar in the southeast corner of the Church. The Church suffered great damage in the hurricane of August 11, 1940, a part of the roof being torn off and much consequent damage to the walls, as also to the windows. However the damage was repaired and often by the handiwork of the rector as well as by his leadership. At this time modern, indirect electric lighting was installed, a contribution almost entirely of two electrician friends of the rector who did the work. In the fall the console of the organ was removed to the east, back of the lectern. On Sunday, November 17, 1940, the congregation returned to worship in the Church, having a great service of thanksgiving for the restoration of the building. The work was done chiefly through the efforts of the rector, Mr. Pinckney, and Mr. Rene Ravenel, chairman of the vestry. Mr. Pinckney resigned February 1, 1941. The Church was then supplied with services by the Rev. F. W. Ambler until the Rev. Lawton Riley became rector, 1943-45. The officers in 1944 were: wardens, Rene Ravenel and Dr. Buist Kerrison; secretary, Charles C. Bolger; treasurer, Miss Mildred Bolger. The Rev. L. Stanley Jeffery was the next rector, September, 1945 until 1949. In the fall of 1948 a new rectory was purchased at 18 Hester Street. It was at once occupied by the rector. Early in 1949 Mr. Jeffery resigned. The wardens this year were Y. W. Scarborough and S. M. Colclough; secretary, J. Edward Coleman, Jr.; treasurer, Y. W. Scarborough, Jr. During the summer of this year the vestry entered into conference with St. Luke's Church, Charleston, the result of which was the merger of the two churches with the name, Church of St. Luke and St. Paul. The two congregations met separately on July 10, 1949, and each confirmed the merger, the new Church to occupy St. Paul's Church.

ST. PETER'S CHURCH, CHARLESTON
(Including Old St. Peter's, Logan Street [1833-61] and Christ Church [1854-1930])

Old St. Peter's Church on Logan Street had an unusual beginning. Uniquely, it was built with a view to the calling to its rectorship the Rev. William Hazzard Barnwell of Beaufort. However, this was not the sole motive—the Bishop testifies that there was a real demand for another Episcopal Church in Charleston at this time. On April 26, 1833, a group of Mr. Barnwell's friends in Charleston addressed a letter to the Bishop, requesting his consent and cooperation. This the Bishop gave after being assured of certain canonical requirements, including the consent of the existing parishes of the city and calling attention to the fact that Mr. Barnwell, being then only in deacon's orders, was not subject to a call. The letter was signed by C. J. Colcock, B. R. Smith, George Cleveland, W. R. Peronneau, and William Michel. In his Annual Address, the Bishop expresses his regret that his advice, apparently accepted at first, had not been followed in the by-laws of this Church by the making of the rector *ex officio*, chairman of the vestry. Not until recent years was this rule followed in this diocese.

St. Peter's was admitted into union with the Convention February 6, 1834, and Dr. William Michel took his seat as its first deputy. So it was that this Church in six months sprang full-fledged like "Minerva from the head of Jove" and was launched on its short but brilliant history. The Church was fully organized, but it had no place to worship. The Huguenot Church, always closely associated with the Episcopal Church, proved again to be the cradle in which (as in case of St. Paul's) was nurtured a newborn Episcopal Church. Here the worship was held for some months. Promptly in March, 1834, a lot was secured on the east side of Logan Street, between Broad and Tradd Streets, supplying a site for the correct orientation of the building to be. Funds were raised by an issue of stock at $100.00 per share, and soon a brick structure 82 x 57 feet, to contain 114 pews and two galleries for persons of color, was built.

A Sunday School was organized with Mr. Barnwell himself as superintendent. He gave great attention to this work, training his teachers carefully. The ladies provided a Communion service, and a library begun both for the school and for the parish. There were sixty-one families connected with the Church before leaving the Huguenot Church. The launching of this new Episcopal Church in the city did not seem to have involved any appreciable diminution in the already existing congregations in the city—St. Philip's, St. Michael's, St. Paul's, and St. Stephen's. There was then at the time a real demand for the new parish. The new Church was opened for worship and Consecrated by Bishop Bowen on December 31, 1836, the congregation having now moved over from the French Church. A fine organ was installed in 1837 and about the same time a vestry room was added and a marble font given. St. Peter's Day, 1837, was a notable one indeed, when the annual occasion for the joint Confirmation service, as was the custom at the time, for the entire city was held here. Fifteen persons were presented from St. Peter's.

Mr. Barnwell, although a young man, soon took a position of leadership in the diocese, being placed on the standing committee and in other important positions. In the parish, his attention to the spiritual growth of his people was marked. He rejoiced in the increase in the number of communicants. In February, 1839, all the pews on the ground floor were taken, and half in the galleries. The rector succeeded in stamping very deeply the missionary motive upon the congregation. In 1839, we find this congregation paying single-handed $1,000.00 for the salary of Rev. William J. Boone of Walterboro, missionary and later first Bishop of China, as well as about as much more for other missionary purposes. In 1838, the parish suffered a great loss by the death of Mr. C. J. Colcock, warden and chairman of the vestry, a great force in the establishment of this parish.

A significant event in the history of the Church occurred in 1839 when St. Peter's Education Society was organized. It accomplished a good work in aiding in the education of candidates for the ministry. The directors of the society were Thomas H. Jervey, Dr. William Michel, B. R. Smith, A. H. Belin, C. A. deSaussure, and William C. Bee, who was the secretary and treasurer. At one time, its capital was $2,838.00. However, the complaint was that there were "lamentably few" men offering for the ministry. The society seemed to have passed out of existence when Mr. Barnwell resigned in 1853.

In 1841, the rector was encouraged that as a body, his people refrain from worldly amusements and enjoy the peace which Jesus gives. The families had now increased to 132 white and 46 colored. At this time, a Sunday School and lecture room was erected at a cost of $4,000.00. On the lower floor of the building was begun a parochial school under Mr. Stiles Mellichamp, who was soon ordained and had charge also of St. James' Church, James Island. The school was discontinued in 1845, Mr. Mellichamp having resigned. A school for colored children, with 40 or 50, was conducted in the summer of 1844.

Mr. Barnwell's health began to fail about this time; Rev. E. T. Walker of Christ Church supplied services in the rector's enforced absence. Rev. W. O. Prentiss, to render distinguished services in the diocese in the years to come, was assistant in 1845, giving much attention to the work among the Negroes. The great event of 1845 was the springing up under Mr. Barnwell's leadership of the movement which led to the establishment of Grace Church—another illustration of the missionary zeal of the rector and congregation. (See *in loco* Grace Church.)

His health failing, Mr. Barnwell resigned the rectorship in 1853. He retired to his old home in Beaufort County, rendering much further occasional service to the Church until his death March 21, 1863. After Mr. Barnwell's retirement, Mrs. Emma C. Gadsden (*nee* Thayer) bequeathed to Hon. Robert W. Barnwell, brother of the rector, in trust, a fund to be known as "The James W. Gadsden Fund" for the benefit of the former rector and family during lifetime. After his death, it was to be conveyed to St. Peter's as a permanent fund, "The income thereof to be used for the disabled ministers of the said Church, and of the poor and destitute widows and orphans of the ministers of the said Church at the discretion of vestry of the said Church." She also left a "Mission Fund" of $1,000.00, the income to be used for the cause of missions. Both of these funds were always carefully administered by the vestry of St. Peter's, according to the trust, and were intact when the settlement was made combining St. Peter's and Christ Church in 1827—the former amounting then to $11,000.00 and the latter to $1,000.00, with certain amounts of cash in each case, a remarkable example of the faithful and efficient fulfilling of a trust.

The Rev. Stephen Elliott supplied services for five months in 1853. Then the Rev. J. A. Shanklin succeeded as St. Peter's second rector. This much-beloved servant of the Lord was stricken by yellow fever after only two years of service. He was an associate editor of the *Southern Episcopalian*. The next rector, after some interim, was Rev. Henry M. Denison (October, 1857), a man of unusual talents who attracted many of an intellectual turn to the Church, but also again, the dread yellow fever took him away. He died September 27, 1858. Those were tragic days. Now a year elapsed with no regular rector. The Rev. J. Grimke Drayton also served for some months and then became fourth rector of the Church December 11, 1859, for a brief time. The Rev. W. O. Prentiss returned and assisted Mr. Drayton and then became rector, the fifth and last, November 1, 1860. In a little more than a year, another tragedy—a fatal blow. The Church was totally destroyed in the great conflagration that swept across Charleston on December 12, 1861. The fire began at the eastern end of Hasell Street. In its southwestward course, it destroyed many important buildings, among them, the Circular Church, St. Finbar's Cathedral, Institute Hall, St. Andrew's Society Hall, and the Charleston Theatre. The fire burnt out in the neighborhood of St. Peter's, but not until the Church was entirely destroyed. After this, Mr. Prentiss reports 30 services in the Hall of the South Carolina Society on Meeting Street and then this, the end: "On the 10th of June [1862] the work of the Lord ceased, the Vestry judging it expedient to suspend my service, there being no attendance at the Hall."

The Vestry continued to function, although the congregation had disappeared. Its composition at the end of the war, 1865, was: Wardens, R. A. Pringle, Thomas Y. Simons; and Vestrymen, E. L. Kerrison, E. W. Edgerton, C. A. deSaussure, B. S. Rhett, J. L. Dawson, M.D., J. F. Green, F. E. Fraser. They continued to administer the Gadsden Fund and the Missionary Fund. The insurance of $20,000.00 on the Church proved worthless. However, the walls of the ruined Church were taken down and the bricks sold. In 1876, the fund, thus begun, amounted to $4,763.48. It was never found to be desirable to re-erect the Church, but this fund, ever-increasing by careful management, served a good purpose in the work of the Diocese through the loans made to the churches. In 1927, the general or "Brick Fund" amounted to $41,303.00; the Gadsden Fund, $11,000.00; and the Missionary Fund, $1,000.00; a total of $53,303.15. In fifty years, not a cent had been lost, and not an expense incurred, except for the care of the Church Yard on Logan Street—no commissions or lawyers' fees. Especial credit should be given to Mr. Edwin L. Kerrison and E. H. Pringle, but last and not least, especially for so many years to Hon. Joseph W. Barnwell.

In 1927, it was decided that the time had come for some fresh disposition of the funds. An act of the Legislature was secured by which a synthetic congregation of some sixty members of the churches in Charleston was formed, a new vestry elected, and a final decision made to turn over the funds to Christ Church, Charleston, on condition that its name be changed to St. Peter's.

Especial mention should be made in this connection of the wise judgment of Hon. Joseph W. Barnwell, N. B. Barnwell, Esq., warden of the new vestry, and Mr. G. L. B. Rivers, secretary of the vestry, who carried out the necessary legal transaction to effect the combination of the two churches. We turn back now the pages of history to the story of the Church with which St. Peter's decided to merge.

CHRIST CHURCH, CHARLESTON
Established 1854

The origin of the Church really goes back further than 1854. It was in 1823 that Mrs. Sophia Frances Shepheard gave a lot of land in the northwestern suburb of the city for a Church. The rectors of the three parishes in Charleston were made trustees of the property. No action was taken for many years, the site was remote and the population scarce. Some thirty years later, Rev. Edward Phillips was commissioned to carry out the design of the pious donor. At a meeting of those interested on July 6, 1854, it was decided to build a Church on the lot which had been given. The wardens elected were: T. Alexander Broughton and Edwin Heriot; vestrymen, Fred A. Ford, Charles D. Carr, Joseph Provost, Dr. L. A. Frampton, John Phillips, Octavious Faulkner, James R. Pringle, and the Rev. Edward Phillips. The building committee consisted of the missionary, the Rev. Mr. Phillips, with Messrs. Ford, Phillips, Heriot, and Col. E. B. White, the well-known architect, who furnished the plans. Very soon, a contract was entered into to build the Church. Rev. Mr. Phillips raised $1,000.00 for the purpose, but this was not sufficient, so the Church was long in building. The Church of the Holy Communion gave a font in 1855.

In the meantime, the energetic missionary was busy building up a congregation. The first services were in a dilapidated building on Nunan's Lane. The missionary was assisted by two candidates for the ministry, J. H. Quinby and J. M. Green. The Rev. Mr. Phillips died in September, 1855, and the work lagged.

Finally, the Church was completed by Col. John Phillips in memory of his brother, the minister, and services begun under Rev. J. M. Green, now a deacon. Bishop Davis consecrated the Church on January 5, 1858. The generosity of Col. Phillips was further illustrated by his gifts of a Communion service, organ, carpet, and books.

The Advancement Society, which had all the time largely supported the work, was compelled to withdraw its aid, and so Mr.

Green was obliged to leave. Mr. Green had reported 14 adults and 54 children baptized, 75 burials, 11 marriages, and 26 confirmed. He had erected on the grounds at a cost of $500.00 a building for a lecture room, industrial school, and Sunday School. The Church suffered another great loss at this time in the death of Mr. Edwin Heriot. He had done great service for both the temporal and spiritual welfare of the mission.

Ten years later, 1872, the Rev. J. Mercier Green returned to his old charge. He was now also city missionary. Mr. Henry P. Archer, a great educational leader and later superintendent of the city schools of Charleston, was senior warden. He was destined to be a veritable father of the Church—warden, lay reader, superintendent of Sunday School. Others of the vestry were: junior warden, J. Moultrie Lee; vestrymen, A. H. Hayden, A. C. Kaufman, A. P. Otis, A. Doty, Jr., H. E. Vincent, W. W. Sale, and E. J. White.

The Church was thoroughly renovated in 1874. There was now an industrial school conducted by "Grace Church Society". The Sunday School built up rapidly to 224 pupils, and 25 teachers mostly from other churches in the city. This large enrollment was not sustained for long. Mr. Green resigned in 1877, but Mr. Archer kept the work and worship going. In 1882, the Church was repaired and a handsome cross added. Mr. Samuel Sanders and Mr. John Birkley now in succession were junior wardens. The Rev. J. V. Welch, city missionary, gave communion services, later the Rev. A. E. Cornish did so; then the Rev. J. Maxwell Pringle from 1882, followed by the Rev. R. J. Walker.

In 1902, the responsibility for the conduct of the Sunday School was assumed by the Grace Church chapter of the Brotherhood of St. Andrew, under Mr. Clarence D. Schirmer as superintendent, and Mr. Thomas Hazelhurst as assistant. This was the beginning of many years of service to this Church by Mr. Schirmer as warden also, and lay reader. Here should be mentioned the fifteen years of devoted service to the church of Mrs. Mary R. Sinkler. Miss Florence C. Milligan was for years the faithful organist, and Mr. E. P. Milligan secretary of the vestry. Rev. R. J. Walker in these years held once a month an evening service and also a communion service. It was the Society for the Advancement that supplied the funds to maintain these clerical services. In 1909, the Rev. Percival Whaley became rector. Mr. Archer and later Mr. Schirmer supplied continuously regular lay reading in addition to the few clerical services. The former died in 1911. Mr. Schirmer now became senior warden, J. T. Salvo was junior warden and V. R. Salvo, secretary There were now 40 families, 79 communicants, and 80 Sunday School scholars connected with the Church. The great storm of 1911 involved extensive repairs on the Church.

The regular rectors for the following years were, after Mr. Whaley, the Rev. J. M. Stoney, 1913; the Rev. C. H. Bascom, 1916; the Rev. H. D. Bull, 1917; the Rev. A. W. Arundel, D.D. (*locum tenens*); the Rev. R. H. Jackson, 1924, who served until 1927 when he went as missionary to Japan. During Mr. Bull's rectorship, the communicant membership of the Church increased from 108 to 180; during Mr. Jackson's, from 180 to 227; the Church was increasing in strength. Both these rectors were much beloved by the congregation. Next came Rev. G. F. Cameron serving 1928-30. The Rev. C. Baird Mitchell supplied services in the interim until the Rev. John H. Morgan became rector February, 1930, until April, 1931. In the year 1930, we reach the climax of the history of Christ Church, when the building was torn down and the Church merged with old St. Peter's, changing its name to St. Peter's.

THE NEW ST. PETER'S CHURCH, CHARLESTON
Established 1930

The Convention of the diocese, by motion on May 7, 1930, gave its confirmation to the change of name of Christ Church to St. Peter's. The cornerstone of the new Church was laid on October 21, 1930, at 5 P. M., the Bishop of the diocese officiating. In his address on this occasion, Bishop Thomas used these words, which we may take as the epilogue of the story which has now been told: "We stand today at the confluence of two streams—two streams of spiritual endeavor which have been flowing separately in this city for over three-quarters of a century. As these streams are now coalescing into one, we wish to ask for God's blessing upon the union, that more good be done for the upbuilding of His Kingdom than they could now do separately. We witness today not the stopping of either stream but the flowing on of both. It is wonderful to think that old St. Peter's is rising again after all these years—sixty-eight—'Phoenix-like, from her ashes'—ready to begin again her active life of good work, 'to give light to them that sit in darkness and in the shadow of death; and to guide our feet into the way of peace.' As the streams mingle, old Christ Church is called upon to make a sacrifice—to give up its name. This was no easy matter, but sacrifice is the law of Christian life and we trust that this act will be taken by the members of the new named, combined Church, as a type of that self-abnegation which is essential in doing God's work. The laying of this cornerstone is an event in the ecclesiastical history of the church in this city and this diocese. We hold this service in the confidence that in response to our prayers now offered, God will bless this work. Our supreme prayer today is that, as these two churches are merged, so the hearts of all the members of the new St. Peter's will be merged in love, and they will go forward into the new period with the spirit of Christ in their hearts. It seems to me I can hear a voice now saying to us all, 'This have I done for you, what wilt thou do for Me?' "

The new Church was Consecrated on St. Andrew's Day, 1931. The Rev. H. D. Bull preached the sermon and the clergy of the city participated in the service. The wardens and vestrymen, who met the Bishop at the door of the church, were: C. D. Schirmer and C. S. Alston, wardens, and W. E. Douglas, W. E. Huxford, H. R. Jacobs, William Milligan, J. H. Nelson, C. R. C. Thompson, and T. P. Stoney, vestrymen. The Rev. Edwin Gwynn Coe, who had been ordained deacon the evening before in the Church of the Holy Communion, assumed charge of the Church on this day. With the handsome new Church, the complete parish house with an adjoining rectory, the plant was complete; the gift of old St. Peter's. The Church went forward now with manifold activities. When Mr. Coe took charge in 1931, there were 191 communicants; when he resigned in 1951, there were 489. He was succeeded in 1951 by the Rev. Henry Powers, coming from St. Helena's, Beaufort, and he was succeeded in 1954 by the Rev. L. Bartine Sherman.

ST. PHILIP'S CHURCH, CHARLESTON
Established 1670-80
(See Dalcho, p. 209)

When Dalcho leaves off his history of St. Philip's, the Mother Church of the diocese, the Rev. Christopher Edwards Gadsden is rector. He had become assistant to the Rev. James D. Simons in 1809, and then rector in 1814. The Rev. Allston Gibbes had just become assistant, succeeding the Rev. Thomas Frost. Dalcho testifies that at this time St. Philip's and St. Michael's were thronged with worshippers. Notwithstanding the recent addition of St. Paul's, another Church was now needed in the city. The deputies to Convention in 1821 were Thomas Lowndes, Thomas W. Bacot, and Thomas Corbet.

The Sunday Schools were now being organized, that of St. Philip's in May, 1821, numbering 200. There were 530 communicants, 340 white and 190 colored. The Sunday Schools for the white and colored met at different hours. In 1823 there were 240 families of whites. There were 148 pews in the church, soon increased to 163. In 1825 changes were made in the staircases and galleries; the reading desk was moved from the cross aisle standing with the pulpit on the north side of the middle aisle. The communicants in 1824 were 39 males and 263 females, whites, and 220 colored. It was estimated that there were at this time 1,000 whites and 400 colored persons in the parish, 1,400 souls. Public catechizings were held on about one-third of the Sundays in the year. The "Gregorie Society", which did fancy work for missionary causes, was active at this time. In these years services were held twice on every Lord's Day, morning of each Friday, on all fasts and festivals and on "most of the days in Passion Week," now called Holy Week. The rector, Dr. Gadsden, the future Bishop, was a leader in the diocese. It was he who, at the instigation of Bishop Dehon and the Convention, introduced in the General Convention the resolution which resulted in the founding of the General Theological Seminary. For many years he was the president of the Standing Committee. In 1836 the "Sunday School Society" of the parish was incorporated and purchased a four-story house with eight rooms to the east of the Church on Philadelphia Street for the use of the schools of the Church. At this time an infant department was opened leading to an increase of 100 pupils, now numbering 193 white, 174 colored with 27 teachers for white and 12 for colored—all teachers white. In 1834 a "Classical and English" school was conducted in the Sunday School house, continuing until 1837.

After a service of fifteen years as assistant, the Rev. Allston Gibbes resigned in 1834 and went to reside in Philadelphia. He later (1874) "renounced" the ministry and was deposed by Bishop Gadsden. He was succeeded by an unusually promising young minister, the Rev. Daniel Cobia. After a short time (1834-36) Mr. Cobia was stricken fatally by disease—"his name a praise in all our Zion." He was succeeded as assistant by the Rev. Abraham Kaufman. Cobia and Kaufman were both buried under the chancel of the Church.

Now was another crushing blow—the noble building called a "grand church" was totally destroyed. "The steeple first took fire between 2 and 3 o'clock, A. M., on the Lord's Day, February 15th

(1835) and before sun-rise the destruction was complete." Only parts of the organ and some furniture were saved. The "weeping flock" worshipped the same day in the Sunday School. The next day it met and resolved to rebuild, that services in the meantime be held in the most convenient place, and that the Friday following be observed as "a day of religious reflection, humiliation and prayer." This last was done and a general appeal was issued. Services were continued, either in the school house, the Methodist Church or St. Stephen's Church, but, after May, in the "temporary church" (sometimes called The Tabernacle) which had been erected in the west churchyard. Nothing is known as to the architect of the burned church. There are drawings of it by Mills, however, made shortly before the fire.

The cornerstone of the new Church was laid by Bishop Bowen on November 12, 1835. The Church was completed at a cost exceeding $75,000.00. The first service in it was held on May 3, 1838. Dr. Gadsden said, "We left this spot in tears for our Church. We return to it in tears for our city"—the latter reference being to the great fire at this time which destroyed a large part of Charleston, the new St. Philip's barely escaping. The Church was occupied before it was finished in order to turn over the "temporary church" to the Methodists, who had loaned their Church to St. Philip's three years before and who now lost one of their own in this great fire. The new Church, on the foundation of the old, did not differ very much in external appearance from the original save for its imposing steeple. It was Consecrated by Bishop Bowen on November 9, 1838. The cost, including the steeple, was nearly $100,000.00. The architect of the Church was Mr. Joseph Hyde.

An organ, made in London at a cost of $3,500.00, was installed in 1838. The Rev. Abraham Kaufman's death was greatly lamented in 1839. The Rev. John Barnwell Campbell succeeded him as assistant in April, 1840. The Holy Communion at this time was celebrated 18 times yearly in the Church, on great festivals and on the first Sunday in each month. Also morning prayer was said on Mondays and Fridays under a plan whereby it was said every morning in one of the churches in Charleston. Scholars in the Sunday School now were 64 white and 150 colored. Many children who formerly attended had now gone to one of the recently opened chapels, St. Stephen's or St. John's.

Both the rector and assistant minister assisted at the diocesan school begun in 1841. This school lasted for only a few years. The parish school of St. Philip's was reopened as its successor in 1849, being conducted by Mr. R. H. Mason in a room at the school house of St. Stephen's parish.

In 1847 a chime of bells and a musical clock were presented to the Church by Colin Campbell, Esq., of Beaufort. It was immediately determined to build the steeple in order to make this gift available. The handsome steeple, a landmark of the city was designed by E. B. White and built by a Mr. Brown. The ingenious mechanism of the clock was the work of Mr. F. Stein of Charleston. There were eleven bells, the largest weighing 5,000 pounds. The clock chimed the hours and quarters and at three different intervals in 24 hours played, "Welcome Sweet Day of Rest"; "Greenland's Icy Mount", and "Home, Sweet Home".

A new "Sunday School House" was built in the rear of the Church in 1850, 55 feet by 25 and 30 feet high, designed by Mr. Jones, architect, and opened August 11, 1850. It had over the door the inscription, "Feed My Lambs." The old school house after being sold was regained and used for the parochial school. A piece of land north of the western cemetery was purchased in this year as a site for a parochial school. Bishop Gadsden's last appeal was for funds for a building "on yon neighboring site." The Church was closed for four months in 1851 for extensive repairs. At this time the pulpit and desk were so changed as to render the chancel more conspicuous and to enlarge the space about it. Venerating the 84th Canon of the Church of England, an alms chest was placed in the vestibule of the Church in 1851. It was made in England and the expense met largely by Mr. Plowden Weston, Esq. It was designed by Charles Giles, Esq., of Taunton, England, and cost $70.00.

The body of John C. Calhoun, who died March 31, 1850, was interred in the western cemetery on April 26, his classmate at Yale, Bishop (and rector) C. E. Gadsden officiating. By action of the Legislature in 1880 the massive sarcophagus in the west cemetery, which now holds the mortal remains of the great statesman, was erected by the State of South Carolina. The coffin was removed to the east cemetery during the Confederate war for safekeeping.

After months of suffering the tolling of the bells in the city announced the end of the earthly career in the Church of Christopher Edwards Gadsden, Bishop and rector, in the sixty-sixth year of his life, June 24, 1852. He was buried under the chancel of the Church. The Rev. J. Barnwell Campbell succeeded as rector and the Rev. Christopher P. Gadsden became assistant minister. Mr. Campbell resigned February 17, 1858, and Mr. Gadsden the following March 1. The Rev. William Dehon succeeded as rector in January of 1859 and the Rev. W. B. W. Howe as assistant a year later. Mr. Dehon died in 1862 when Mr. Howe became the tenth rector of St. Philip's. John Smith, for 60 years clerk and sexton of the Church, died August 1, 1859 and was buried in the western cemetery. He was the last Church "clerk" in this diocese, having previously been a choir boy in St. Philip's.

At the beginning of the war the Church bells were given to the Confederate government to be cast into cannon, and about the same time the clock was taken down. During the bombardment of the city the Church was struck ten times—"the chancel destroyed, the roof pierced, the organ demolished." After the bursting of a shell near the Church, November 19, 1863, while the sermon was being delivered, the congregation retreated to the safer location of St. Paul's Church. Here the Rev. Mr. Howe continued services for St. Paul's, St. Philip's, St. Michael's, and Grace Church congregations until March, 1865. He was assisted at first by the Rev. Messrs. Keith and Elliott and later by the Rev. J. Mercier Green. He was (like his predecessor, Bishop Smith, during the Revolution) banished from the city for refusing to pray for the President of the United States while the war still continued. Services were resumed on March 6, 1866, in the Church which had been repaired with a loan from Mr. James T. Welsman. The rector and future Bishop greatly endeared himself to the congregation and city by his unfailing and courageous services during the war.

In 1868 a generous parishioner gave the chancel window and an organ. In these years after the war in this parish, as well as in other parishes in the city, a great charity work was carried on among those impoverished by the war. Rev. John Johnson became assistant in 1870, becoming rector January 1, 1873, when Bishop Howe resigned the rectorship; thus at last ended in the diocese the custom of the Bishop holding also a rectorship. At this time there were 389 white communicants and four colored; just before the war 80 colored were reported. In June, 1870, St. Philip's Home, on the south side of the Church, was dedicated, having been purchased for $11,000.00; so began this wonderful beneficence. Many societies were active at this time: the Bishop's Aid Association, the Young Gleaners (female), the Young Brotherhood (male).

On August 9, 1874, the parish commemorated the one hundred and fiftieth anniversary of the occupation of the present site of the parish. There was a notable sermon by the rector, the gift of a window on the east wall, south of the chancel, and also two handsome cups and an alms basin by John W. Mitchell. The next year, May 12-13, 1875, in connection with the meeting of the diocesan Convention, the two hundredth anniversary of the planting of the Church in South Carolina was commemorated in the Church. The proceedings on these occasions are preserved in a pamphlet with valuable sermons and addresses. As was the case in the whole diocese, the parish was entering upon the disturbing contention concerning racial representation in the Convention. St. Philip's withdrew from the Convention, but only for a year. The story is recounted elsewhere in this history. (See Section I, Chapter IV.)

The repairs after the war having been partial, in 1877 the Church was closed from August to November (congregation worshipping at St. Michael's, whose rector was away) when extensive repairs were made to the Church. Great improvements were made in the Home in 1882, reception room, library and reading room being developed. Further improvements were made with payment of a debt on the Home in 1889 by a legacy of $5,000.00 by Mr. J. W. Mitchell. On the afternoon of August 31, 1886, at a meeting of the vestry, all debts (save one secured debt on an original building) incurred by all these improvements were reported paid. In a few hours after, the Church was in ruins from the great earthquake. The large task of repairing again was completed at a cost of $20,000.00.

In 1890 many organizations were zealous in good works in the parish: the Home Aid, the City Mission, Young Men of St. Philip's (maintaining night school uptown) and the Woman's Auxiliary. New gas fixtures were installed in the Church in 1893, and in 1897 the marble pillar for the font was given by the Chancel Guild in memory of Bishop Howe. By arrangement with the Federal government the steeple with a beacon served to guide ships into the harbor from 1893 to 1915, and again for a short time in 1921. In 1901 the communicants in the parish numbered 312. In 1901 a tablet in memory of Bishop Howe, sometime rector, was placed on the south wall, the diocese uniting with the congregation in the placing of this memorial.

After a faithful service of 36 years Dr. Johnson became *rector emeritus* in 1906, being succeeded as rector by the Rev. S. Cary

Beckwith in April of that year. In 1909 repairs on the organ and church to the extent of $4,000.00 were made, and at this time a bequest of $10,000.00 was received. The present rectory at 92 Church Street succeeding the old rectory on Glebe Street (which had not been used as such for many years) was purchased in 1908 and soon occupied by Mr. Beckwith. In 1886, just before the earthquake, the Church acquired a lot of land to the north of the churchyard, and in 1914, by another purchase, the extension of this lot to Philadelphia Street. In 1920 by a munificent gift of Mr. W. Gordon McCabe the Church's holdings were extended to Cumberland Street.

The present vested choir of St. Philip's was instituted on Christmas Day, 1916. On April 27, 1927, the Church was seriously damaged by fire in the east end. The congregation took advantage of this situation to do more than make repairs. The Church was enlarged eastward with a choir and organ chamber in which a new organ was installed. An altar and raredos of wood was installed in place of the old "Communion Table", saved from the previous Church. There were many other changes and improvements, also. The congregation worshipped in the Seaman's Church of the Redeemer during part of the period of renovation until February, 1921, when under Mr. Beckwith, rector, and acting as rector of St. Michael's at St. Michael's Church services for both congregations were held. Services were resumed at St. Philip's in October, 1921. Officers of the parish at this time were: wardens, Henry C. Cheves and F. G. Davies; secretary and treasurer, W. G. Mazyck.

In November, 1926, the All Saints window (by Clement Heaton) was installed, and soon after the handsome marble altar and raredos, and during this same year the tablet to Dr. Johnson was erected. Following in June, 1927, a tablet was unveiled to Captain Edward Lawrence Wells, killed in France in 1918. The cornerstone of the parish house was laid on December 11, 1927. It was completed and Dedicated with the adjoining playground on October 7, 1928, by Mr. Beckwith. Simons and Lapham were the architects (as also of the Church renovation in 1921) and Mr. F. G. Davies was chairman of the building committee. Health failing, Mr. Beckwith resigned March 5, 1935, after 29 years of devoted service as rector. He then became and continued as *rector emeritus* until his death in Aiken, January 3, 1939. The Rev. Merritt F. Williams succeeded as rector October 1, 1935.

By a terrific tornado on September 29, 1938, the Church suffered much damage, as did the old Church school building in the rear, which was wrecked. The damage to the Church was promptly repaired. The charges of over $20,000.00, with a former debt of $24,000.00, were all retired by 1945. The old Sunday School was rebuilt as a chapel by Miss Eugenia C. Frost in memory of her parents, Thomas and Martha Calhoun Frost. In it is placed the old "Communion Table", saved from the fire of 1835 and used in the present Church for many years. The restored building was Consecrated by Bishop Thomas as The Chapel of the Good Shepherd. Rev. Mr. Williams resigned as rector September 1, 1941. Rev. W. H. Mayers supplied for some time, the Rev. Marshall E. Travers becoming rector December 1, 1942. The Rev. A. Campbell Tucker became assistant rector (August, 1947-August, 1950) followed by the Rev. James Stoney (1951-August, 1952) who in turn was followed by the Rev. Waddell Robey (March 1, 1953-57).

On May 4, 1944, in this Church the Right Rev. Thomas Neely Carruthers, D.D., was Consecrated to be Bishop of South Carolina. This was the second Consecration of a Bishop to be held in Charleston and the first in St. Philip's.

After a rectorship of 14 years Mr. Travers resigned October, 1956, to enter mission work in the diocese. During his active rectorship St. Philip's had grown from a communicant membership of 720 to 1,200. An extensive renovation of the parish house had just been completed at a cost of $65,000.00.

ST. STEPHEN'S CHURCH, CHARLESTON
Established 1822

About 1819, a group of devout Christian churchwomen in connection with visiting the sick as members of the Ladies' Benevolent Association became convinced of the need of some place of worship for Church people who could not afford to rent seats in the existing churches. As a consequence, in 1821 there was organized the Charleston Female Domestic Missionary Society. Its chief purpose was to supply the poor of the city with the ministrations of the Church. A room was rented and services begun. The Rev. Edward Phillips was ordained in March, 1822, and began work as city missionary under the patronage of this Society, which was described as a group of "respectable, pious female members of the Church in Charleston—prudent and unostentatious." Mrs. Sarah Russell was the leading benefactress. After nearly two years, en-

couraged by the success of Mr. Phillips' labors, it was decided by
the Society to erect a Church "for the gratuitous use of such members of our Communion, as may not be able to defray the expense of seats, in other places of worship." It was said that this
was the first undertaking of a purely "free church" in our Communion in the United States. A lot in Guignard Street was given
by Mrs. Sarah Russell, a committee of gentlemen appointed for
the purpose, and a Church built in 1824, smaller, the Bishop remarked, than could be desired. It was Consecrated by Bishop
Bowen March 18, 1824. Thus was this Church, named St. Stephen's,
launched on its long and useful career. The Rev. Mr. Phillips continued his earnest labors as missionary-in-charge until 1830, when
he went to Camden. He was assisted by the Rev. Philip Gadsden
in the summer of 1827. The Church's patron, the Female Domestic
Missionary Society, in 1829 received a bequest of $10,000.00 by the
will of the generous Mr. Frederick Kohne. At this time, Mr. Phillips reported that in his seven years of service, there had been 255
baptisms, 102 burials, 89 marriages, 56 confirmations, 100 communicants, 300 had been pupils of catechetical and Sunday School
instruction. The debt had been reduced to $300.00 and the library
had 400 volumes. His "painful instructions in the school of human
nature" make up a vivid story of Christian service.

For the year 1831, the Church was under the care of the Rev.
David M'Elheran. It was constantly emphasized that in this Church,
the seats are free. At this time a burial ground for this Church was
secured.

The Rev. W. H. Mitchell took temporary charge in March, 1832.
Then in August, 1833, the Rev. Daniel Cobia took regular charge,
holding services twice every Sunday, and in the summer and fall,
a service Thursday afternoons by the clergy of the city. In November, 1834, the Rev. Paul Trapier and the Rev. P. H. Folker
took charge, the latter assisting for one year. The Church was destroyed June 6, 1835, in the great fire that swept over part of the
city. The organ, furniture, and a monument to Mrs. Russell were
saved. Many members also lost their homes in the fire, this entail-
ing much charity work. A temporary place was secured and services continued.

A lot on Anson Street was purchased and the cornerstone of the
new Church was laid here on St. Stephen's Day, 1835, by Bishop
Bowen, the minister-in-charge, the Rev. Paul Trapier, making the
address. The whole cost was $11,285.00. As before, the Charleston

Female Domestic Missionary Society was the chief agency in the rebuilding, but help came from many quarters including especially Columbia and Beaufort. The Bishop consecrated the Church on November 24, 1836. The Rev. Paul Trapier, the missionary-in-charge, preached the sermon. The Board of Directors of the Society were Mrs. Alicia Middleton, Mrs. Sarah Dehon, Miss Sarah Rutledge, Mrs. Eliza R. Deas, Mrs. Mary W. Johnson, Mrs. Elizabeth Ryan, and Mrs. Ann Guerard. The trustees of St. Stephen's were the rectors of the three city churches. The missionary reports increase in membership in the new Church in 1838. In this year, the Rev. Robert T. Howard became assistant to Mr. Trapier, continuing until May, 1840. Mr. Trapier became rector of St. Michael's September, 1840, but continued in charge of St. Stephen's until the end of the year when the Rev. T. C. Dupont succeeded. In his first report, he enumerates 97 white and 11 colored communicants, average attendance of Sunday School, 136. He continued in the discharge of the manifold work of this mission until his death in 1849. On January 1, 1845, the mission school house being completed, a parochial school was opened in it with 32 boys and 34 girls. The male teacher resigned and Mr. Dupont undertook to fill this position, which he could only do by securing the services for a year of the Rev. J. R. Fell as assistant. Mr. Dupont felt the need of a home for orphans. He raised a fund for this purpose and made a beginning, two little orphan girls, whom he placed in the care of a pious lady and who were taught in the parochial school. This was the very beginning of our present two homes, the one for ladies in Charleston and the other for children in York. Mr. Dupont died in the spring of 1848. During the following summer, the Rev. Edward Phillips had charge. Then in November, 1848, the Rev. Cranmore Wallace took the charge, assisted by the Rev. James Ward Simmons. In 1849, the Church was repaired and gas lights installed. At this time on a Sunday, the entire lower floor of the Church was filled with worshippers. Mr. Dupont's policies as to the school and orphans, now two boys and two girls, were continued. The current expenses of the chapel were met by a collection taken at the door of the Church. The salary of the missionary was paid by the missionary society; that of the assistant by the earnings of Mr. Wallace as teacher in Mrs. DuPre's seminary for young ladies. The Rev. Mr. Simmons left in May, 1853. Soon after, he died of yellow fever. He was succeeded by the Rev. P. G. Jenkins, M.D., January 1, 1854, who assisted for a short time. The regular communicants about this time numbered 120 white and nine colored. Showing the extent of the work the number of parochial visits by the missionary was in 1854 2,215, increased probably by the yellow fever epidemic. In 1856, we find Mr. Wallace making an earnest appeal to a "charitable" and "wealthy" community for funds (fallen away) to pursue his labors in the midst of great poverty in the city—he bids them remember "the poor are the representatives of Christ." The parochial school was efficiently conducted at this time by Mrs. A. P. Whitson. The missionary constantly visited in Roper Hospital. He distributed Bibles not only in English, but German, Spanish, French, Italian, Danish, Welsh, and Norwegian. The Charleston Bible Society often supplied his needs in this line.

November 25, 1856, was an interesting day in St. Stephen's when Bishop Davis ordained Mr. H. L. Phillips deacon and the Rev. Lucien C. Lance to the priesthood. He was assisted by the Rev. Messrs. Wallace, Trapier, Porter, and Gadsden. In the evening, confirmation was administered. The parochial school was discontinued in 1856 owing to the difficulty of securing a competent teacher on the salary of $200.00 provided; the opening of the new and popular "Public School"; the removal of the girls to the Church Home, whom it was thought best to teach in the Home. Though a great sufferer himself in 1857, Mr. Wallace kept up his manifold duties, 293 services in St. Stephen's chapel, 312 at the Church Home. The Rev. Henry L. Phillips became assistant February 1, 1859. The long and laborious services of Rev. Cranmore Wallace ended with his death in 1860. He was succeeded by the assistant, the Rev. H. L. Phillips. In 1861, the Shoe Society of St. Stephen's contributed $78.00 to furnish children of the Sunday School with shoes. A collection of $17.37 was for supplying soldiers with Bibles and Prayer Books. Regular services were held during the war until May, 1864. The Church was damaged by shells in the war but soon repaired.

St. Stephen's became an independent Church in 1866 with the Rev. J. Mercier Green as rector. In 1869 only 28 communicants were reported; Sunday School, 33; services, 98. Mr. Green was succeeded by the Rev. W. H. Hanckel in 1871, serving until 1879. By the generosity of a churchman of another parish, the Church was put in thorough repair at this time, the Church of the Holy Communion giving new pews. The year 1874 was marked by the organization of a parish lay association and a Ladies' Working Society; 51 communicants were reported. The Rev. Edward R.

Miles assumed the charge in 1880. The end of this year, St. Stephen's closed its doors for the time, the resignation of Mr. Miles being accepted. The congregation, with the exception of two families, united with St. Luke's. Mr. Miles had become rector of that Church.

A second brief phase in the history of St. Stephen's Church occurred in 1892-93 when the Rev. G. F. Degan was city missionary. He reopened the Church under the Bishop and held regular services for a few months only, leaving the diocese March 16, 1893, going to the Church of the Advent, Nashville, Tenn. A considerable congregation was attracted by his ministrations. The Society conveyed the property of St. Stephen's (also St. John's) to the trustees of the diocese, April 6, 1894.

A third phase in the history of this Church began in 1911. In 1911, a mission with a parochial school was opened in the buildings on Anson Street. It continued for about 12 years. It was in 1923 that a congregation of Mount Moriah Union Methodist Church (colored) with its minister, the Rev. William M. Morgan, applied to Bishop Guerry to be admitted into union with the Church in this diocese. Obtaining the advice of the Standing Committee in April of the same year, the Bishop agreed to do so under certain conditions, among these, that the members be confirmed when prepared. St. Stephen's Church edifice on Anson Street was assigned to the congregation as its place of worship. On May 30, the Bishop confirmed Mr. Morgan and five of the Church officers; the class had been prepared by Archdeacon Baskervill. Mr. Morgan was appointed lay reader to officiate in the congregation and licensed by the Bishop to preach. After a course of training, he was ordained deacon May 22, 1926. Officers were duly appointed for the mission; wardens, Alexander Nelson and Edwin D. Rainey, with Mayer Powell, treasurer. In 1926, 103 communicants were reported. Mr. Morgan continued in the faithful discharge of his duties as deacon-in-charge of the mission until his death November 9, 1930. The Rev. Osmond Jonathan McLeod was placed in charge March 1, 1931, being also in charge of Mediator, Edisto, assistant to the Archdeacon, continuing in charge until 1939. Temporary arrangements obtained under the Archdeacon until 1940 when the Rev. St. Julian A. Simpkins took charge. A useful feature of the work in St. Stephen's for many years is a kindergarten conducted by Mrs. St. J. A. Simpkins.

SAINT PETER'S-BY-THE-SEA
CHARLESTON HEIGHTS, NAVY YARD
Established 1909

Under the leadership of the Rev. John Kershaw, dean of the Charleston Convocation and rector of St. Michael's Church, and principally with help from this Church, three lots were acquired in 1909 near the Charleston Navy Yard in recognition of the importance of opening Church work at and near the Navy Yard where a town was building up. The funds for the purchase of these lots were given Dr. Kershaw by members of St. Michael's Church in part, but in greater part by the Advent Guild of that Church. This guild later gave $500.00 toward the building. The work was organized soon after under the Rev. J. W. Sparks as missionary-in-charge, a room was fitted up and services begun in January, 1910. The Commandant of the Navy Yard soon after gave the use of a hall in the Marine Barracks where services were then held. Members of St. Michael's Church helped in the furnishings; the Episcopal Bible, Prayer Book, and Tract Society gave prayer books and hymnals, the men of the barracks built an altar. In the Journal of the Convention of May, 1911, the mission is, for the first time, reported as a regular "unorganized mission" with the name "St. Peter's-by-the-Sea" under Mr. Sparks; with a regularly organized Sunday School, a Bible class ,and also a parish school. Services were held twice a month on Sundays and twice a month on Fridays. There was a large attendance of Marines. The Rev. R. E. Gribbin, assistant of Grace Church, succeeded Mr. Sparks in the charge at the end of 1912. At this time, the Bishop reported $400.00 given by St. Michael's, the diocese $200.00, and raised by subscription $500.00 for a chapel, but $1,000.00 more was needed to erect the Church building in Chicora, the community adjoining the Navy Yard.

The undertaking was not long in being accomplished. It was opened for service April 19, 1914. The cost was near $4,000.00. Bishop Guerry preached and addresses were made by Mr. Gribbin and by Dr. Kershaw, the father of the mission. The Rev. Messrs. Way and Cornwell assisted. There were two floors—the upper was the chapel, the lower the parish house. Eighteen pews, the lectern, and credence table were donated by the extinct All Saints' Church, Yemassee. Grace Church gave the font and a Bishop's chair. The funds came through the Bishop by his efforts, largely from St. Michael's Church. At this time, the communicant membership was only seven, the Sunday School just reorganized 21, confirmations three. The mission was now equipped for services to the people in Chicora and for the Marines and others in the Navy Yard. This was the first Church in the community. The Rev. James M. Stoney, rector of Christ Church in the city, succeeded Mr. Gribbin in charge in 1915, but only for a short time when Dr. Kershaw took charge, being assisted by Mr. L. A. Prouty and Mr. W. G. Mazyck as lay readers. The Rev. Oliver J. Hart, assistant of St. Michael's, was in charge for some months from June, 1917, until he entered the Army; then Mr. H. P. Boggs of the faculty of P. M. A. had the charge. In the spring of 1919, St. Peter's-by-the-Sea became an "organized mission" under the Rev. W. B. Guion; the secretary and treasurer was Mr. Joseph F. Walker, who was also warden. After a few months, Mr. Guion was succeeded by the Rev. Andrew P. Magwood, who served also only for a short time.

The Rev. Randolph F. Blackford was appointed to the charge in 1920 with "a field of opportunity" at North Charleston and the Charleston Port Terminals and began a vigorous work. The wardens now were Joseph F. Walker and J. J. McMahon; secretary, Joseph Baumel; treasurer, W. H. Barnwell. Steps toward self-support were now made really for the first time, $800.00 being raised in Mr. Blackford's first year. The Sunday School went from 20 to 100, a vested choir was organized ,and a men's club formed. Also, a civic organization called the "Neighborly Club" operated at this time, formed by some ladies of St. Michael's Church. There was begun also a Girls' Friendly, and a Boy Scouts' organization. Gifts from the city churches, including a bicycle, made the missionary's work eaiesr. Such was the advance with this first resident minister of the Church.

In 1925, the Rev. John H. Morgan succeeded Mr. Blackford. After three years of faithful service, he went, May, 1928, to the diocese of New Jersey. The Rev. Sumner Guerry took charge December 1, 1928; for a while temporarily, then permanently. The officers were J. F. Walker and J. J. McMahon, wardens; Joseph Ahlsweh, secretary; and D. L. Spaulding, treasurer. The communicants now numbered 81, the Church school 51. A notable mission was held in February, 1930, conducted by the Rev. Oliver J. Hart of Chattanooga, Tenn. (afterwards Bishop of Pennsylvania.)

In 1933, the Church was much improved, being painted within and without. The work was done by members. A Bishop's chair with a mitre carved by Bishop Thomas was installed and dedicated by the Bishop on April 26, 1942, in memory of David L. Spaulding. The Rev. Mr. Guerry resigned in January, 1944. Mr. John J. Mc-Mahon was then warden; secretary-treasurer, F. C. Tillman. The Rev. Emanuel A. LeMoine took charge in March following, coming from Bel Air, Maryland. The communicants now numbered 118.

In 1944, the congregation began an earnest effort to build a new Church. Within two years, $15,000.00 was raised and work was begun under the leadership of Mr. LeMoine. The cost was much reduced by the contribution of labor by members, who were experienced craftsmen. The Woman's Auxiliary in one year contributed $2,000.00. Notwithstanding these efforts, the old chapel was much improved. The Church was so near completion that services were begun in it, the first being a celebration of the Holy Communion on Christmas Eve, December 24, 1946. In 1946, the name of the mission was changed from "St. Peter's-by-the-Sea" to "St. Peter's, Navy Yard"—this proved to hold only for a brief time. On April 3, 1947, two beautiful brass vases in memory of Mr. Reinhart Carl Hanold, and candlesticks and candelabra in memory of Mr. George Arthur Carpenter were blessed in the Church. On this occasion, three persons were confirmed and one received from the Russian Orthodox Church, making a total of 27 for the year. The Rev. Lawton Riley succeeded Mr. LeMoine June, 1947, officers now were: wardens, John J. McMahon and Joseph S. Leary; secretary, W. E. Spaulding; treasurer, David C. Spaulding.

In July of 1947, a new altar, reredos, pulpit, eagle lectern, and altar rail were installed; the altar and reredos given by the parish branch of the Woman's Auxiliary, the lectern by the Y. P. S. L., the altar rail by St. Michael's Church in memory of the Rev. John Kershaw. A credence table also had been dedicated in memory of Mrs. Anna Eliza Kolb by Mr. Riley. Mr. Riley left in 1948. Mr. Roderick Hobart, then a candidate for the ministry, had charge during the summer of this year. In September, Mr. LeMoine returned and continued in charge until August 1, 1950. The Rev. Edward M. Claytor became priest-in-charge February 1, 1951. Several memorials were given in this year: silver cruets in memory of her husband by Mrs. Helen Brock; silver lavabo in memory of her father, David L. Spaulding, by Mrs. Joe Stewart; a silver ciborium in memory of John Onorato by his family; the Altar Guild gave the minister a stole, and the auxiliary put down a carpet in the chancel. In 1951, St. Peter's-by-the-Sea had grown to a communicant membership of 272, with a Church school of 140.

St. Peter's was admitted to the Convention in 1951 as no longer a "mission" but a "parish." The Church became independent of missionary assistance January 1, 1952. Much of the interior finish on this Church has been accomplished by the labor of members. The Church for the first time acquired a rectory in April, 1952, where Mr. Claytor now resides (1955). In 1954, the original name of the church was restored—"St. Peter's-by-the-Sea." On Easter, 1954, the new pews were first used. The Church also has been tiled.

October 14, 1956, was a gala day for this Church—its day of Consecration by Bishop Carruthers. The Bishop preached. He was assisted in the service by the rector, Mr. Claytor, and by the Rev. E. A. LeMoine, former rector.

ST. ANDREW'S PARISH
CHARLESTON COUNTY
Established 1706
(See Dalcho, p. 344)

Old St. Andrew's
Established 1948

The last rector of St. Andrew's recorded by Dalcho was the Rev. Thomas Mills on whom the South Carolina College conferred the degree of Doctor of Divinity. He served from 1787 to 1816 when he moved to the upper part of the State, living to a great age, having married again at 80. At the beginning of our period (1820), this parish was at a low ebb, the Church was in disrepair. The Rev. Joseph M. Gilbert, who was also rector of Grace Church, Sullivan's Island, and professor of mathematics at the Charleston College, became rector in 1824. He reported then 15 families with about 60 persons, most of whom belonged to other congregations. Mr. Gilbert died the next year, "victim of pestilence," highly esteemed. Edward Pringle was lay delegate to the Convention this year. In 1825, the Rev. C. P. Elliott, deacon, was missionary-in-charge. In 1828, the Rev. Philip Gadsden, as visitor, reported 15 families, most of whom belonged to city churches, and that the Church was badly in need of repairs. Col. Simon Magwood was deputy at this time and, later, William Cattell. The Rev. Paul Trapier, deacon, was in charge in November, 1829. The Church from being "nearly in ruins" was now put into complete repair. Congregations at the weekly services were good, including about 75 Negroes.

In 1833, a working society was organized among the ladies; besides its chief charity work, it organized a library. In 1834, the parsonage, after lying in disrepair, was at last made habitable; however, Mr. Trapier resigned the rectorship in 1835. He was succeeded by the Rev. Jasper Adams, D.D., principal of Charleston College. The Church in these years was closed in the summer. The rector resided in the parish a part of the winter. Nearly all the pews were now occupied—apparently a wave of prosperity. Dr. Adams went to New York in 1838, being succeeded by the Rev. J. S. Hanckel, deacon. He was, on ordination to the priesthood the next year, made rector, continuing until 1849. When Mr. Hanckel became rector, there were 30 families. The colored members of the congregation received further instruction after service on every Lord's Day; the rector also ministered to them on three estates. In 1840, the Church was thoroughly repaired. All the white part of the congregation belonged to city churches. Services were from November to May. A baptismal font was secured in 1842. In 1845, two chapels were erected in the parish for Negroes. Services were held in them every alternate Sunday by the rector and the intervening Sundays by a candidate for orders or the owner. Mr. Hanckel resigned in 1849 resuming, however, the next year. A third chapel for Negroes was now erected at this time so that all the Negroes were now in reach of Church services every Sunday. These chapels were named Middleton (or Barker), Magwood, and Magnolia. Mr. Hanckel finally resigned in 1851. In all of these years of his rectorship, he was also assistant to his father at St. Paul's, Charleston, where he officiated in the summer.

The Rev. J. Grimke Drayton became rector in 1851. A. Mr. Shokes assisted as catechist in the chapels where services were held the year round. Regardless of what seems certainly to have been an upstanding work, at least among the Negroes, at this time, Mr. Grimke in a sermon preached on the occasion of the "reopening" of St. Andrew (December 16, 1855), after extensive repairs, expressed joy in the prospect, he said, of better days, but also tells of the depletion of the parish since Revolutionary times; he writes of the parish, "now so stript—so denuded of inhabitants, once swarmed with a thickly settled and increasing population"—the walks once beautiful now "matted with the pine and the oak and the myrtle"—"the fallen arches and the solitary chimney tops"— the seams in the walls of the church, the moth-eaten register. Contrary to the testimony of Col. William Izard Bull (a vestryman for many years) in a leter dated June 10, 1889, that the Church was not destroyed by fire, he supports Dalcho that it was—"This temple was consumed with fire, of which its walls bear witness." Mr. Drayton's description of the depletion of the Church extends to the spiritual matters as well—the loss of the true faith of the Church. But now he sees recovery ahead, symbolized by the actual restoration of the Church building. Col. William Izard Bull, who was warden from 1833 to 1865, was in charge of the extensive renovation. He left a letter describing the work. The extent of the enlargement of 1723 was revealed at this time by the different sort of brick used in the new part when the Church was then completed in the form of a cross. Recently (1952) on the wall under plastering that had to be removed was found a drawing of Col. Bull's plans. Mr. Drayton's hopes seem not to have been realized. St. Andrew's did not share the growth and prosperity of the years previous to the War Between the States common in most of the diocese. The rector spent about half of the year in Flat Rock, and the services were desultory. The most important work was that among the colored people centering about the three chapels, Barker, Magwood, and Magnolia. In 1856, there were 26 white communicants and 107 colored. In 1860, one of the chapels was closed (Barker) for a time, the congregation having removed. The rector reports falling off in the white congregation and all this was before the war.

Services continued during the war. The rector reports large congregations in the winter and spring of 1864, consisting mostly of troops quartered in the parish, also refugees from the islands, the regular parishioners away. In the last years of the war, the parish was reduced to ruin. The dwellings, with few exceptions, were in ashes. Both bridges across the Ashley had been burned. In 1867, few white residents had returned to the parish. People had no means of attending services at the parish Church and there were none. In the spring of this year, Mr. Drayton preached to a large congregation at Barker's Chapel; the Negroes appeared desirous of having their religious privileges restored. By the next year, the Church was appropriated for political purposes, registering and voting. "Where the Gospel was once preached, the voice of blasphemy and profanity is now heard." The next year (1869), the rector reports services at all three of the Negro chapels (Barker, Magwood, and Magnolia), but no services in the parish Church. In these years, Mr. Drayton was rector at the Church in Flat Rock where he officiated from May until November. In 1871, the Church was reported as "still desecrated," used as a polling place. The work at the chapels continued encouraging. On his visit in 1873, the Bishop confirmed 18 colored adults. He found these people still devoted to the Church. He baptized 24 in 1875 and 30 were confirmed. In March of 1876, the chapels were reduced to two by the burning of the Barker Chapel. This year saw the reopening of the parish Church after 13 years of disuse as either a place of worship or of desecration.

For all this time although Mr. Drayton continued his work among the Negroes, his work was free gratis, the rectorship was dormant. In 1876, he was recalled to the rectorship and regular services in the parish Church were resumed. The Church now received a new roof, new plastering, and new glazing. To this time, Mr. Drayton reports there had been no defections of the Negroes from the Church. Some whites worshipped with them at Magnolia Chapel. Repairs went on in 1878 at the Church and chapels. At this time there were reported 15 white communicants and 156 colored. In 1880, while Mr. Drayton was away, Magwood Chapel was seized and sold, the deed to the land having been found defective. On his return, Mr. Drayton raised $421.00 and recovered the chapel.

In 1884, the rector's health began to fail. The services soon ceased at the Church, the people going to the city by the railroad on Sundays. The Church was badly wrecked by the earthquake but soon repaired. The chapels were damaged, and Mr. Drayton's home rendered uninhabitable. His health failing, services were few. In 1889, the rector reported no services at the parish Church, the few members mostly going to the city on Sundays by railroad, and services only at Magnolia Chapel. Mr. Drayton died April 2, 1891, having served in the parish since 1851, sometimes almost entirely to the Negroes and seldom receiving any stipend; he not only planted seed in the earth to form what has been called the most beautiful garden in the world (Magnolia) but he planted many a seed of the Word which we doubt not will flower to all eternity. In 1893, the parish was classified as "dormant" and remained so for more than half a century, though services as we shall see were sometimes held. The colored work now became a part of the Archdeaconry for Colored People. The history will be found included therewith. On March 1, 1916, W. M. Wallace and C. N. Drayton, sole surviving members and vestrymen of the old Church, offered to turn over to the diocese the Church and its possessions on condition that the funds on hand be used for repair and improvements. The offer was accepted, the trustees of the diocese taking over the property. The condition was fulfilled, the Church being put in good condition at a cost of $1,400.00. Bishop Guerry raised about half of this sum. The glebe was rented to J. M. Harrison for $100.00 and the church insured for $2,500.00. The Society of Colonial Dames cooperated in this work. On November 17, 1916, the Rev. John Kershaw, D.D., rector of St. Michael's, held a service and made a historical address, reopening the Church for occasional services at least. In 1918, the glebe lands were rented to Porter Academy for $150.00. On the 4th Sunday in Lent in 1917 Dr. and Mrs. William Izard Bull presented to the Church a beautiful silver alms basin in memory of William Izard Bull.

In 1924, the Church was organized as a mission with Rev. Wallace Martin in charge; C. S. Dwight, warden; C. C. Pinckney, secretary; C. J. Ravenel, treasurer. At this time, a caretaker's cottage was provided. Mr. Martin held a monthly service in the old Church until his death in 1946. During his charge, the Church had repeatedly undergone repairs—once in 1928 at a cost of $375.00. After Mr. Martin's death on Good Friday, 1946, no regular services were held for some time, and St. Andrew's ceased to exist as an "organized mission." The last officer reported in this year was C. S. Dwight, warden-secretary-treasurer.

In the meantime, in view of the increasing population, efforts had been made to begin Church work within the boundary of old St. Andrew's Parish. This resulted in the beginning in 1945 of a mission called All Saints' Mission, St. Andrew's Parish, under the charge of the Rev. Eugene J. West. Mrs. Frank Chamberlain was secretary and Mr. S. M. Colclough, treasurer. Mr. West was succeeded in the charge the next year by the Rev. L. S. Jeffery, rector of St. Paul's Church in Charleston, and Mr. Arthur Ravenel became secretary-treasurer. Services were held every Sunday at 9 a. m. in the Exchange Club Building. Mr. Jeffery was succeeded in 1948 by the Rev. Lawton Riley. Under him, old St. Andrew's Church was reopened and organized as a mission; All Saints' was absorbed into this new mission. Seventy-six Church members were reported in 1949 and six confirmations. It was admitted into union with the Convention in 1949 under the name of "Old St. Andrew's Parish" but as a mission. The keeper's cottage was renovated for school purposes. The first officers reported of this "Old St. Andrew's Church" in 1950 were Joseph E. Dunham, warden; George E. Lancer, treasurer; Church school superintendent and lay reader, Samuel E. Dunham. Mr. Thomas Hannaford was warden for a time.

On the Bishop's visitation December 10, 1950, assisted by Mr. Riley, he dedicated two memorial tablets to a former rector, John Grimke Drayton, and a former member, Drayton Franklin Hastie. The Church now underwent extensive renovation, including replastering and installation of electric lights. There were many gifts for refurnishing the Church, including the restoration of the Church's old Bible (given it by Bishop Bowen in 1828) by C. Norwood Hastie. Mr. Riley resigned as rector in March, 1952. Mr. Alfred W. Butt had become warden, and C. Norwood Hastie, secretary.

The Rev. Lynwood Magee, after his ordination on June 24, 1952, became minister-in-charge. In the summer of 1950, a splendid parish house was built and enlarged in 1956. The old parish had now been completely revived; there were, in 1954, 139 communicants, and 150 officers and pupils connected with the Church school.

Mr. Magee was ordained to the priesthood in St. Andrew's on May 6, 1953. The Church was admitted into union with the Convention "as a newly organized parish" named "Old St. Andrew's Church", April 26, 1955. The parish has recently acquired a rectory.

ST. ANDREW'S MISSION
ST. ANDREW'S PARISH, CHARLESTON COUNTY
(See Archdeaconry, end this Section)

HOLY TRINITY, WINDERMERE,
CHARLESTON COUNTY
Established 1956

The Rev. Marshall E. Travers resigned the rectorship of St. Philip's Church, Charleston, in October, 1956, with a view to establishing a mission in the Windermere section across the Ashley River at Charleston—under the authority of the Bishop. A beautiful site had been rendered available at a greatly reduced price, through the generosity of Mr. and Mrs. Charles Dwight, at the corner of Folly Road and Yeaman's Street. Another lot, also located in the Crescent section of Windermere was given to Mr. Travers for a home. It was decided that the name of the mission should be Holy Trinity. The first service was held in the theatre in the Avondale section on the afternoon of October 21, 1956, and almost immediately a Church school was begun. Since this time, services are held in the theatre every Sunday at 11:15 a. m. with Church school at 10:00 a. m. The mission is under the auspices of Old St. Andrew's Church.

A little later a branch of the Young People's Service League was organized. Captain P. C. Corning has been appointed treasurer. Some memorials have already been given.

ST. DAVID'S, CHERAW
Established 1768
(See Dalcho, p. 326)

This was the last colonial parish of South Carolina. The Rev. Charles Woodmason, "itinerant missionary" for St. Mark's, tells in his Journal of preaching to a congregation of 500 at the Cheraws January 25, 1867, and baptizing 60 children. Back again (from Pine Top, or Camden) a few months later, he found Thompson's Creek swollen and had a terrible time getting across. On this occasion he prepared a petition to the Legislature to raise a new parish. While history shows the civic motive for this action, Woodmason shows it was also religious. This seems to have been the very beginning of St. David's. The petition was granted the next year and a new parish was raised on April 12, 1768, named St. David's, after the patron saint of Wales from whence many of the Cheraw settlers had come.

As Dalcho relates, the Church was built, but failing to secure a regular minister it fell into disuse. Its very ownership was forgotten during the generation following the Revolution. It was used by all denominations, the Baptists and Presbyterians especially contending for its possession. The Revolution had cut off the supply of Episcopal ministers from England, the only source of supply since there were no Bishops in America—commentary on the sad lack of foresight in the Church of England. The lost Church, however, was now soon to be recovered.

The Society for the Advancement of Christianity in South Carolina, when it "ascertained that a parish of the name of St. David's had been organized before the Revolution near the North Carolina line," employed the Rev. Andrew Fowler to visit the parish. He first went there, briefly, in December, 1819, and then later in 1820 when, under the society, he held services in Chatham, as Cheraw was then called, for a year. He reported an election of wardens and vestrymen at Easter in 1820, there being a hopeful prospect. It was at the service on this day that the Holy Communion was administered in St. David's Church for the first time. While in Cheraw Mr. Fowler founded the Church in Walterborough, N. C. It was he who discovered the old parish book at the residence of

Mrs. Sarah Pegues, which resulted in the re-establishment of the Episcopal ownership of St. David's. Mr. Fowler was one of the greatest missionaries of the diocese. He later, for many years, was rector of Christ Church, Mt. Pleasant, living to be over ninety years of age and was buried in 1850 in St. Michael's churchyard. The Rev. Thomas Wright of Wadesboro succeeded to the charge in 1822. He received support from both the Advancement Society and the Young Men's Missionary Society of Charleston.

St. David's now had the use of the Church only every other Sunday, the Episcopal ownership not yet being fully established. However, at a meeting of the members of the Church, February 3, 1823, this ownership was proclaimed by resolution, adjustment being planned with the Presbyterian minister, Rev. Mr. Morgan. At this meeting the following were elected as vestrymen: James A. Harrington, D. K. Dodge, Oliver Kollock, George Andrews, Joseph Pritchard; and wardens, Walter Mebane and John P. Tampled. Joseph Pritchard was elected deputy to the Convention of 1823.

Mr. Wright, who was highly commended for his work in re-establishing the Church in Cheraw, resigned in 1824 through "want of compensation" on account of a "numerous family." He was never canonically of this diocese. The Rev. George W. Hathaway, a deacon, took charge in 1824 for two years. At this time there was an influx of population and the Church increased in strength. The bell was secured from the North in 1825, a tree between the Church and the gate being adapted for a belfry. Mr. Hathway taught a school in Cheraw. The Rev. Charles P. Elliott followed him in 1827. At this time the interior of the Church was "re-accommodated to the manner of the Church's worship," and a fence was built about the churchyard. There were then thirteen families. Mr. Elliott went to North Carolina after only about a year.

The Rev. Alexander W. Marshall took charge in 1829, having been ordained deacon the preceding October 15. He was St. David's first rector of any degree of permanence and the Church now gained strength. The Bishop's comment was, "The Church . . . advanced . . . a small but respectable congregation . . . justifies the hope of its increasing prosperity." Mr. Marshall was a great worker with missionary zeal. In 1830 we find him preaching at Marlborough Court House (said to have been the first Episcopal service there), at Marvin and at Wadesborough, N. C.; and also at Society Hill, where he founded Trinity Church. In 1830 a vestry room was added to the Church. There was a Sunday school now of fifty-two, of whom twenty were colored. In 1833-34 a beautifully proportioned steeple, modeled after St. Martin-in-the-Fields, London, was added to the Church with a vestibule, arrangements had been under way for the addition since 1825. The plans were furnished by Dr. Maynard (father-in-law of the Rev. Mr. Marshall). A Mr. Steinmetz made the estimates and Major Laxarus was the builder. The bell (being removed from its tree) now found a more appropriate place from which to ring out its calls. A number of pews were also added at this time.

Two great losses to St. David's now were the deaths of Gen. Erasmus Powe and Mr. James A. Harrington, devoted Churchmen. The services of the rector were (1834) divided between St. David's and Trinity, Society Hill. The rector devoted much time to the pastoral care of the Negroes, including those on two plantations, later three. A Bible, Prayer Book and Tract Society was organized, auxiliary to that of the diocese in Charleston, also a parish library had been established. The Church was painted by the efforts of the ladies in 1836. The Communion was celebrated on the first Sunday in each month. The parish lost quite a number of members in these years through emigration to the West. Lay reading was held when the rector was absent. In 1839 Bishop Bowen described St. David's as "one of the most flourishing, devout and happy congregations of the diocese." In 1841 Mr. Marshall left to be rector of St. John's in Charleston. A stained glass window in the chancel of St. David's removed now from old to new Church) testifies to the high regard of the congregation to this servant of God.

The Rev. J. W. Miles served from 1841 to 1843. This eloquent and learned divine is commemorated by one of the chancel windows. At this time Rev. F. M. Hubbard, a deacon, conducted an academy in Cheraw. After Mr. Miles' departure in 1843 to be a missionary to the "Holy Catholic and Apostolic Church" in Mesopotamia, he was succeeded briefly by the Rev. A. Ford of Florida as *locum tenens*. Then the Rev. Henry Elwell, also of Florida, became rector in January, 1844. At this time a lady of the congregation conducted a day school for poor white children in the parish. Also at this time a Sunday school for colored children was conducted after the evening service. The rector was assisted in this school by Alexander Gregg, a candidate for Holy Orders, who practiced law in Cheraw. Mr. Elwell resigned in October, 1845. Mr. Gregg, being ordained deacon, took charge in 1846. There were now twenty communicants (two of these colored).

In 1848 the vestry room was rebuilt and enlarged. An organ was bought in 1850 at a cost of $1,200.00 and a solid silver communion service was purchased—a tankard and paten, two chalices and two plates. At this time the Church was extensively repaired, the gallery now being devoted entirely to the Negroes; also a new fence was built. From time to time Mr. Gregg conducted Sunday Schools in the surrounding country, being always active in ministering to the poor. He held services at the Chesterfield Court House in hope of establishing a Church there, a hope never realized. In 1858 there was a very extensive remodeling of the interior of the Church: chancel was enlarged, new pulpit, desk and altar, inside blinds, and two doors into vestibule with organ located between. Mr. Gregg being elected first Bishop of Texas resigned the rectorship October 2, 1859. After his notable work in Texas (died July 11, 1893) his body was laid to rest in St. David's churchyard. His wife was Charlotte Wilson Kollock of Cheraw. Rev. R. B. Croes of the diocese of New York was minister *pro tem* for four months in 1860.

Grace Chapel.—Though located in St. David's parish this mission was established jointly with the rector of Trinity, Society Hill, shortly before the war. It was located in the sandhills midway between these churches (near Cash's Depot) and was called Grace Chapel. Mr. Kidney of Society Hill and Mr. Brown of Cheraw ministered alternately. On appointment of Bishop Davis, the Rev. J. M. Green had charge for a time during the war, the two rectors soon resuming charge. Services continued after the war. Mr. Motte in 1871 reported a regular monthly service and a well-attended Sunday School, and the next year services were increased to twice a month. The Bishop held confirmation here on June 25, 1873. After a time the services became less frequent. Julia M. Howes on February 9, 1880 made deed of one acre of land in Chesterfield to the trustees of the diocese. This doubtless was the location of the chapel, but soon after this time the activities of Grace Chapel came to an end. The last service of this mission, we believe, was the funeral of Mrs. Atkinson in 1911, conducted by Mr. Thomas. The chapel had long since disappeared.

The Rev. R. Templeton Brown became rector October 20, 1861. The Rev. J. H. Quinby and the Rev. J. M. Green assisted the rector in 1862 when there were many refugees from the lower country in Cheraw. While Cheraw was in the line with Sherman's march, the Church though injured by a nearby explosion suffered no serious damage and there was no cessation of services in St. David's to any extent. Half of the communion silver was stolen and, of course, the parish reduced to poverty. Mr. Brown went to Virginia in 1866, when the Rev. P. D. Hay officiated. The Rev. John W. Motte, just ordained deacon, came in June, 1867. In 1870 he reports the parish recovering from its "desolate condition." At this time Mr. Motte began services in Bennettsville but soon abandoned them, for the time, as impractical. The year 1871 was marked by the securing of a parsonage, "the result of woman's work for the Church." In 1873 a handsome flagon was bought, completing the restoration of the communion silver taken in the war. In 1875 there were 77 communicants. The Church was reshingled in 1876. At this time Mr. Motte became rector also of St. John's, Florence, for a time. In 1877, through the kindness of the Bishop, a handsome white marble font was installed. Formerly it belonged to St. John's Church in All Saint's Parish, Waccamaw. The parish now acquired a beautiful portable communion service of silver.

In 1883 the Church underwent some changes—there were added recessed chancel, new vestry room, organ chamber, and a cross on top of the steeple in memory of Mrs. Claudia Godfrey McLean. A committee consisting of Dr. F. A. Waddill and Messrs. S. G. and W. R. Godfrey directed these changes. The Church was Consecrated on December 16, 1883 by Bishop Howe, but it had already become *consecrated* by many services. Dr. Kollock read the Request, Mr. Motte said the Sentence, Mr. Hay preached and Messrs. Steele and Brouse assisted. Mr. Motte resumed services in Bennettsville about this time. The stained glass chancel window was installed in 1885, also a new altar given by Mr. Motte in memory of two children; the pew doors were taken off in 1888. In the same year Mr. Motte resigned, going to Lake City, Fla. His personality and teaching left a strong impression upon the parish.

The Rev. A. A. McDonnough was the next rector (1890-95). In 1891 a movement developed to build a chapel in the center of the town, going so far that a group under the rector but without the consent of the vestry, bought a lot for its purpose. The object was to supply a chapel of ease for the Sunday School and evening services, continuing the Sunday morning service at the old Church. Opposition developed and the movement failed. In ill health, Mr. McDonnough resigned in May, 1895, dying January 22, 1896. The Rev. Thomas P. Baker succeeded (1895-1900) having charge also of Society Hill and Bennettsville. At this time a new Möller organ was installed, the old one being sent to the Good Shepherd, Columbia. In 1899 the wardens were C. Kollock, M.D. and S. G. Godfrey;

secretary, H. P. Duvall; treasurer, W. Allen Benton. The parish suffered a great loss later in this year through the deaths of both these wardens—the one a distinguished physician, the other a prominent business man—both devoted churchmen. A children's memorial window was placed in the Church in 1889. In 1899 a steel ceiling was put in the Church and the gallery removed. Mr. Baker gave way to the Rev. Charles W. Boyd who came August 1, 1900. The communicants now numbered 101; one was colored. Mr. Boyd, a deep thinker, was noted for his fine sermons. He married Marion Godfrey of St. David's. Mr. Boyd resigned after Easter, 1908.

The next rector was the Rev. Albert Sidney Thomas, September 1, 1908. As did Mr. Baker and Mr. Boyd, he also had charge of St. Paul's, Bennettsville. At this time the wardens were W. R. Godfrey and H. P. Duvall; secretary, E. W. Duvall; treasurer, William Godfrey; superintendent of Sunday School, H. L. Powe. Miss Elize Duvall at this time became assistant to Mrs. S. G. Godfrey, organist. In 1908 the old rectory was sold and a new one built facing Market Street at the corner of High and Market Streets for $3,700.00. It was occupied by the rector early in 1909 on its completion. At the call of St. David's, Mr. Thomas at the beginning of 1911 resigned St. Paul's, Bennettsville, in order to devote his whole time to this parish. He was allowed the fifth Sundays for missionary work, given mostly to the McBee Mission. About this time a lot was bought at the corner of Market and Huger Streets for a new Church, contemplated from the time of Mr. Thomas' coming. By the summer of 1912, $12,000.00 had been subscribed for the proposed Church.

McBee Mission.—In December, 1911, to supply services for a small group of Church people in McBee, 30 miles south of Cheraw on the Seaboard Railroad, and because the town showed signs of development, Mr. Thomas began services there. These were held once a month on Monday evenings and on fifth Sunday mornings with a celebration. Mr. Askew, a recent citizen of the town, gave an acre lot for a Church. (The deed is now held by the trustees of the diocese.) The services were held in the Presbyterian Church, kindly loaned. Names connected with the Mission were Wiliamson, Vetoe, Edgeworth, Robertson and J. E. Powe. All those interested moved away about 1918 and the mission was discontinued. The guild left $100.00, still accumulating in trust with trustees of the diocese ($468.76 in 1953).

A chapter of the Brotherhood of St. Andrew was organized in St. David's in 1914. In this year a contract was let for erection of a new Church and Sunday School on the lot at the corner of Market and Huger Streets. The cornerstone was laid with Masonic ceremonies conducted by Grand Master J. L. Michie of Darlington on September 1, 1914. The customary memorial articles were placed in the stone. Bishop Guerry made an address. The new Church, which was designed by the rector, is Gothic in style and includes a Sunday School building with robing room and organ chamber, built of brick with brownstone trimming. The handsome tower is a faint copy of the tower of the Chapel of the General Theological Seminary in New York. The building was completed and services held in it for the first time June 4, 1916; the rector celebrated, the Rev. A. R. Mitchell preached at this service, and the Rev. C. W. Boyd, former rector, at the evening service. The Rev. E. A. Penick assisted in the services. The Möller organ from the old Church had been rebuilt and installed in the new Church, with additions to the case by Mr. W. H. Monson, also the chancel windows were brought from the old Church. Mrs. S. G. Godfrey, in her 59th year as organist, presided and played, assisted by Miss Elize Duvall. (Mrs. Godfrey died February 8, 1921 in her 79th year, her 63rd as organist.) A newly organized, vested choir officiated. The bell from the old Church, nearly 100 years old, this day rang from its new tower. The total cost of the new Church and furniture was approximately $20,000.00.

At this time the duplex envelope system was introduced. April 1, 1918, Mr. Thomas accepted a call to the Church of the Good Shepherd, Columbia, especially to assist that Church to meet the demands for service among the soldiers there and at Camp Jackson. After the Armistice he was recalled and resumed the rectorship January 1, 1919. Mr. Thomas resigned October 1, 1921, going to St. Michael's, Charleston. All indebtedness being paid, the new St. David's was Consecrated on April 8, 1923 by Bishop Guerry. Mr. G. W. Duval read the Request and presented the instruments of Donation; the Rev. M. W. Glover read the Sentence; the Rev. A. S. Thomas, late rector, who had charge of the service, preached; the Revs. C. W. Boyd, J. S. Hartzell and O. T. Porcher assisted. Mr. Thomas read a list of memorials given since the erection of the Church: altar, altar cross, altar book rest and book, credence, chancel rail, paten, service books, baptismal ewer and processional cross. The Bishop preached at the evening service and confirmed eight at this service (and one in the afternoon) presented by Mr. Thomas. The Rev. Norvin C. Duncan succeeded in the spring of 1923. Both the parish and the diocese suffered a great loss in the death of Henry Powe Duvall on August 10, 1923. In 1924, through the efforts of the ladies, the property adjoining the Church was acquired.

A chapter of the Y. P. S. L. was organized this year. In the spring of this year, the Cheraw Chapter of the D. A. R. placed a bronze marker on old St. David's. In September, 1926, a window in memory of William Robbins Godfrey (the Resurrection) was unveiled, given by his wife. Mr. Duncan's health failing, he resigned in this year, being succeeded by the Rev. Claude M. Hobart in 1927. In December of this year, a window in memory of Henry Powe Duvall was dedicated, opposite that of Mr. Godfrey, with whom he served as warden for many years. On All Saints' Day, 1931, a window in the chancel was dedicated to the memory of Martha Eliza Duvall, Church and civic leader, member of choir for over 50 years.

On October 15, 1933, two windows were Dedicated by Bishop Thomas, assisted by the rector—one in memory of Mrs. H. P. Duvall, and the large transept window in memory of James H. and Josephine Elizabeth Powe, and the side panels of two daughters, Charlotte and Henrietta. In 1943, the wardens were William E. Duvall (also treasurer) and F. Turner Waddill; secretary, W. H. Thrower; the organist, Miss Elize Duvall; lay reader, E. W. Duvall; presidents of Chapter "A" of the Auxiliary, Miss F. B. Duvall, Chapter "B", Mrs. Louis Hill; chairman, altar guild, Miss Lulu Harrington (succeeding Mrs. W. R. Godfrey, who for many years held this office); Y. P. S. L. director, Robert W. Duvall.

In March, 1946, the congregation was organized into ten committees to further Church work; also, a men's club was organized.

Mr. Hobart resigned November 1, 1948. He contributed two sons to the ministry, D. M. and R. J. Hobart. The Rev. Robert L. Oliveros followed in July, 1949. For a year (1950-51) he was on leave, a student at Oxford, England. On April 13, 1952, Easter, a new parish house (added to old) was opened, making a very complete plant. At the annual parish meeting in 1953, W. E. Duvall resigned as treasurer after 40 years and H. P. Duvall after 20 years as superintendent of the Sunday School—one was given a watch and the other a silver bowl. Wardens this year were J. E. Powe and E. H. Duvall.

In 1953, old St. David's Church was thoroughly restored. Services are still held in it on some Saint's Days especially.

Mr. Oliveros left at the end of 1953 to go to Holy Trinity, Clemson. On April 21, 1954, the Rev. John M. Barr became rector.

The Rev. C. M. Hobart after serving Ascension, Hagood, and Holy Cross Stateburg, from 1949 to 1953, retired from the active ministry. He died on April 17, 1956, rector of this parish for 21 years. Another large addition was made to the parish house in 1956-57.

ASCENSION, COMBAHEE
Established 1856

This parish was formed of the portion of St. Bartholomew's lying along the Combahee river. It was admitted into union with the convention on May 7, 1857. A neat brick Church was built and services begun July 22, 1857. Rev. Stephen Elliott was the first rector serving from 1856 to 1865. The Church was Consecrated February, 1859. Not far off was Christ Church where Mr. Elliott ministered to the Negroes. In 1861 the war stopped services most of the people having moved. Mr. Elliott died in 1867. Mr. Bellinger held some services in 1868, and in 1870 the Rev. J. G. Drayton became rector. Conditions in the parish now greatly improved, the congregation being quite fully restored and the Church repaired. The nearby Christ Chapel for Negroes had been appropriated by Sherman to build a bridge over the Combahee. Mr. Drayton was succeeded as rector by Rev. W. O. Prentiss in 1875 for a couple of years. The Church was still vacant in 1880 when a report was made by W. E. Haskell, secretary. There is no record of further services in this church. In 1884 it was classified as *dormant*. James B. Heyward, Esq., of Charleston, nephew of Mr. W. E. Haskell, recalls visiting the Church when a boy, a carpet being still on the floor. It was still standing in 1915, but soon after entirely disappeared, the bricks being carried off. The silver of the Ascension was turned over to the diocese in 1953, having been in keeping of the S. C. National Bank.

ST. PAUL'S, CONWAY
Established 1910

The earliest certain records we have of the services of the Episcopal Church in this region was in a report of the Rev. John Fordyce, rector of Prince Frederick's, where he tells of a "fatigueing journey to the distant settlements in this parish, on Pee Dee River about 140 miles from Prince Frederick-town; that he had preached at four different places, and had baptized 29 children of his own Parish, besides 19 who were brought to him from the adjacent parts of North Carolina". This journey most likely reached into Kingston precinct. We well know that a colony of Church of England immigrants settled between the Great Pee Dee and Little Pee Dee Rivers at the place which came to be known as Britton's Neck. About the middle of the eighteenth century they built a Church described by Bishop Gregg as of "black cypress on a brick foundation". It was still standing in 1867 and its ruins much later. Mr. Fordyce constantly officiated among these people. Their leader was John Godbold whose family with others of the settlement united with the Methodists after the Revolution when no Episcopal ministers could be had. Kingston precinct came to be known as Conwayboro and the town of Kingston to be called Conway. Coming now directly to this town we have evidence that the Episcopal Church was here at an early date, some time in the eighteenth century. In 1908, the Rev. Thomas Tracy Walsh who was a native of Conway and then general missionary of the diocese of South Carolina held a service here on February 4th in the Presbyterian Church. He stated that this Church in which he preached stood within a few feet of the site of an Episcopal Church erected in Colonial days. He further states that his great-grandmother, who was born in 1791, remembered the old Church and had one of its pews on her front porch. Mr. Walsh's father stated that it "stood on the Lakeside, fronting the street leading to the Lake from the Court House." It was, he says, used by the Presbyterians as early as 1785, after which time it gradually decayed and disappeared.

We must now take a long leap in our history, indeed across an entire century and more. There is no record of an Episcopal service in Conway in the eighteenth century and not until that held by Mr. Walsh on February 4, 1908. There were only a few Episcopalians living in Conway at that time. It would seem, however, that a seed had been sown; and during a couple of years was germinating, for in 1910 the small group arranged to have occasional services and the Rev. J. E. H. Galbraith, rector of All Sants, Waccamaw, responded to the cry from this Macedonia and services were held from time to time by their gracious hospitality in the Presbyterian Church, and also in the Methodist Church sometimes. The first item we find in the docesan records concerning this Church in Conway is the statement of Bishop Guerry in his Journal of April 6, 1910 that he had paid his first official visit to Conway. He held service the night of that day in the Presbyterian Church. He preached, being assisted in the service by Mr. Galbraith and the Rev. Mr. Doak, the Presbyterian minister, who read the lesson. He states that Mr. Galbraith had been put in charge of the mission and reaffirms the starting of the mission in his address to the Convention in May of this year. The Bishop reports his second visit when Mr. Galbraith was still in charge on December 31, 1911. He preached twice in the Methodist Church through the hospitality of its pastor, Rev. Mr. Betts. After the morning service he met with the congregation and appointed a building committee consisting of Mr. J. E. Coles and Mr. J. J. Sanders. At this time $1,000.00 was subscribed and a lot bought and paid for. The Bishop found the prospects bright for an Episcopal Church in Conway. The next year the finance committee of the diocese appropriated $100.00 to assist.

The first report of the "Conway Mission" as it was then called was that in the diocesan Journal of May 1912 as follows: The Rev. J. E. H. Galbraith, minister-in-charge; and J. E. Coles, warden and treasurer. There were reported four families, ten baptized persons, and only one communicant. In those days practically the whole burden of the Church rested on one man's shoulders, Mr. J. E. Coles, who might well be called the founder of St. Paul's. So indeed it is that as we look back now we realize the truth of the adage that the day of small things is not to be despised. The building of the Church was begun early in 1913, over forty years ago, and went forward during the year. The mission now was under the charge of the Rev. Percy J. Robottom, rector of Prince George's, Georgetown. In September of this year when still not finished, the Church was totally destroyed by a hurricane. However, we find the Bishop in January, 1914, encouraging the people to rebuild. The response was prompt and soon a new fund was in hand for this purpose. The Church was reported as an "organized mission" for the first time in May, 1914, and the next year, 1915, for the first time it was called "St. Paul's, Conway." This name was given by the founders, having belonged to churches of this name. At this time the Rev. Wilmot S. Holmes, then rector of the Church of the Advent, Marion, succeeded Mr. Robottom as minister-in-charge. Mr. J. E. Coles was still warden and Mrs. Arthur M. Burroughs was treasurer. As has been said, "By the faith, persistence, and pluck of a very small band of church people" the Church was rebuilt. Mr. Robottom held the first service in it in October, 1914, though the building was not then completed. Mr. Holmes' first service was on the fifth Sunday in the next month, November. The pastor of the Methodist Church being away that Sunday, his congregation filled the Church to the door, occupying temporary seats. The congregation now had a place of worship but furnishings were lacking. Mr. Holmes leaving this field for Newberry in 1917 was succeeded by the Rev. Richard L. Merryman who continued in charge for two years, the Rev. Edgar Van W. Edwards came next, serving from September, 1920, until 1923. At this time Mr. P. C. Quattlebaum was treasurer of the mission and Mr. P. W. Williams, the lay reader. Mr. Williams deserves great credit for his services as lay reader, keeping the Church open many years from Sunday to Sunday when a minister was not available. The Sunday School was conducted by Miss M. Coles. Among the wardens that followed Mr. Coles were Mr. B. St. L. Summerlyn and later Mr. Richard Winstead, and still later Mr. Perry Quattlebaum. The Rev. W. Herbert Mayers was the next minister from 1925 until March, 1928. The Rev. Harold J. Lewis assumed charge September 1, 1929, serving a short period until his tragic death in Marion, March 12 following. At this time Mr. Paul Wooten was the warden; Mr. Jack Burroughs, secretary; and Mr. William Moore, treasurer.

For some years the mission suffered greatly through lack of ministerial leadership and some removals of members, but on the occasion of his visit on December 14, 1931, Bishop Thomas reported "new interest in the Church in Conway, and new people, inspired with the desire to go ahead with the work." There was still no minister in charge, but the Bishop announced then the appointment of Dr. Walter Green as another lay reader and that services would be held twice a month, and later every Sunday. Shortly after this, occasional services were conducted also by the Rev. Wallace Martin of the Seaman's Home in Charleston. In November, 1932, we have this report, "The Church at Conway has been greatly improved by the installation of a new altar with hangings, a new lectern, prayer desk and priests' chair." This altar had been used before in churches in Fairfield County. That which this replaced had been previously used in old St. David's Church, Cheraw. It was now restored to St. David's Church where it was placed in the parish house chapel. On Easter Day, April 16, 1933, the Bishop visited St. Paul's, reporting "a splendid congregation and a splendid service"—two were confirmed. In the summer of 1933 the Rev. Thomas Sumter Tisdale took charge of St. Paul's in connection with his rectorship of Advent, Marion. The wardens at this time were Mr. John Burroughs and Mr. Paul Wooten; secretary and treasurer, Mr. William Moore; lay readers, Dr. Walter Green and Mr. P. W. Williams. The year 1935 in this history is marked by an event of great importance, the organization in St. Paul's of a chapter of the Woman's Auxiliary, with the following officers, Mrs. A. M. Burroughs, president; Mrs. S. W. Green, vice-president; Miss Emma Pinckney, secretary; Mrs. Perry Quattlebaum, educational secretary; and secretary of supply, Mrs. Gillespie Godfrey. The Rev. Colin Campbell became minister-in-charge on February 1, 1942, Mr. Tisdale having moved from Marion to Orangeburg the year before. It was at this time that the parish house was built, the realization of a dream of some years.

Mr. Campbell was followed by the Rev. Allen Webster Joslin in January, 1945, coming as a deacon from Rhode Island. Mr. Joslin was the first minister-in-charge to reside in Conway. He was ordained to the priesthood by Bishop Carruthers in this Church on May 24, 1945. Twelve clergymen were present, the Rev. Edward M. Dart preached the sermon. After the service there was a reception at Mrs. A. M. Burroughs. Due to the generosity of Mr. and Mrs. S. G. Godfrey a rectory was supplied for the use of the Church. In 1946 the interior of the Church was renovated and redecorated. At this time a new altar, the third to be used in the Church, was installed in memory of John Edmunds Coles who had been fundamentally responsible for the building of the Church forty years ago. April 15, 1947, is a date of importance in the history of the Church; St. Paul's having now been duly organized as a "parish" was on this date admitted into union with the Convention of the diocese as a regular parish, thus ending its life as a "mission" which had thus lasted for thirty-seven years from 1910. In this year also a new heating plant was installed in the Church mainly by those two organizations of women which did so much for the Church through many years, the Altar Guild and the Woman's Auxiliary. Also on October 19 of this year, 1947, Bishop Carruthers formally instituted Mr. Joslin as rector. At the same service he dedicated a new pulpit given by Mr. and Mrs. Paul D. Wooten in memory of their mother, Mrs. Laura Pugh Wooten.

The officers of St. Paul's in 1947, which may be called a turning point in the history of the Church, were: wardens, Ervin E. Dargan and J. C. Burroughs; secretary, F. G. Burroughs; treasurer, S. G. Godfrey; Church school superintendent and lay reader, P. W. Williams. Mr. Joslin resigned in 1949, being succeeded by the Rev. James M. Stoney in August, who after less than two years went to be assistant at St. Philip's in Charleston. The wardens at this time were Dr. R. C. Smith and L. L. Rogers; secretary, F. G. Burroughs; treasurer, D. W. Green; lay reader, John H. S. Fowler. Mr.

Fowler rendered great service when for many months the Church was without a minister. The latest phase of this history begins with the coming of the Rev. Edward T. Small to be rector in January, 1953. He began his labors from a redecorated rectory and in a Church with beautified premises. This new phase in the life of the Church, signalized by fresh interest, has already given promise by its works—a confirmation class of nine and 16 added by transfer. This auspicious beginning of his services here under the wardens, Mr. F. G. Burroughs and Mr. Hoyt Hendrick, indicated prospects for growth, materially and spiritually enough indeed to inspire all with fresh zeal and happiness, and determination to go forward in the work and worship of the Father, the Son, and the Holy Spirit. After a ministry of over three years, Mr. Small resigned going to Wilmington, N. C.

ST. MATTHEW'S, DARLINGTON
Established 1886

Services of the Episcopal Church were held for some years in Darlington District at the Court House about the middle of the last century in connection with Mars Bluff. The first services seem to have been those of the Rev. Isaac Swarts beginning December, 1844, until 1849. He also officiated at Mars Bluff. Next was the Rev. Henry Elwell who reports holding twenty-six services in Darlington in 1849. In 1860 the Rev. T. F. Davis, Jr., held services in Darlington and organized a congregation under the name of Emmanuel Church. The Rev. J. H. Quinby held services in 1864. The war seems to have dissipated this work. It did not become permanent as that at Mars Bluff.

In November, 1886, the Rev. John Kershaw, then rector of Holy Comforter, Sumter, in response to an invitation from several ladies, held two services in the Methodist Church in Darlington, administering the Holy Communion to about twenty persons. During Christmas week, he held another service in the Baptist Church. The ladies referred to were Mrs. W. E. Snowden, Mrs. Hannah McIver, Mrs. Henry T. Thompson, Mrs. Frank Norment, and Mrs. W. B. Brunson. They formed themselves into a sewing society looking to the building of a Church. Mrs. Snowden was president and Mrs. Thompson, treasurer. The Columbia Convocation met in Darlington, April 13-15, holding a number of services in the Presbyterian Church. On its recommendation, Bishop Howe organized St. Matthew's mission, appointing Mr. Henry T. Thompson, son of the late Governor, warden and lay reader, and Mr. John McIver, treasurer.

A lot for a Church was immediately secured on Grove Street and a fund begun for building. The Bishop's first visit to the mission was on December 6, 1887, the service being held in the Presbyterian Church; and by the time of his next visit a year later a neat chapel had been erected at a cost of $625.00. The Rev. W. A. Guerry assisted Mr. Kershaw in the services, and Mr. Thompson regularly held lay services. Mr. Guerry succeeded Mr. Kershaw and continued in charge until he was called to be chaplain of the University of the South in 1894. He was assisted by the Rev. Edward McCrady, deacon, from the fall of 1892 until September, 1893. He was the first resident clergyman.

The Church was consecrated on January 17, 1892; Mr. Thompson read the request. From the first St. Matthew's Guild (the old sewing society) played an important part in the life of the Church. Its presidents for over half a century were, Mrs. W. E. Snowden, Mrs. W. B. Brunson, Mrs. H. T. Thompson, Mrs. Robert Hairston, and Mrs. W. C. Wilson. Much of the furnishing in the Church besides its building is due to the ceaseless work of this organization. In the very beginning it gave a handsome Bishop's chair, a neat altar, and a font. The credence table was at this time given by Mrs. W. J. Early. Mrs. E. C. Baker left the Church $500.00. Later the Guild gave other things: the beautiful chancel window in memory of Mrs. Henry (Fannie) Thompson, the new altar in memory of Adaline Adelia and Elihu Church Baker, the organ, lectern, and carpet.

The Rev. R. W. Barnwell (1894-1896) succeeded Mr. Guerry. Then followed the Rev. J. M. Magruder (1896-1899) under whom a new location for the Church on Florence Street was secured, the Baker legacy helping. Two buildings on this site were united to make a very comfortable rectory. The Rev. Albert Sidney Thomas took charge August 1, 1900. The Church was strengthened at this period by the coming of several families of men in the recently developed tobacco business—Sydnor, Hairston, Patton, Coleman and others. St. Matthew's was duly organized as a parish and admitted into union with the Convention May 14, 1902; E. M. Price and Abram Sydnor, wardens, G. T. Patton, secretary, and J. Witherspoon Evans, treasurer; the loyalty of these and many others led to the growth of the parish. Mr. Price was also superintendent of the Sunday School for many years. The cross on the altar is in his memory given by the school. Under Mr. Thomas the movement for a new Church went forward; and its cornerstone was laid May 31, 1905, the Rev. A. R. Mitchell officiating with the rector, the address by Rev. H. H. Covington. An offering of $1,000.00 for the new Church marked this event.

In the meantime the old Church had been moved from Grove Street to a position in the rear of the new Church to serve in future as a parish house. Services were held for the first time in the new Church on Easter Day, 1906, Bishop Capers presiding and confirming a class of 10, a newly organized vested choir taking part. The Church is Gothic, cruciform, built of brick, cement trimming with slate roof, total cost $7,000.00, plans by Shand and Lafaye of Columbia. Shortly after this service when new pews were installed, they were designated as a memorial to Mr. and Mrs. E. C. Baker. (The new altar was later given by the guild as also a memorial to them.) Under the following rector, Rev. H. Hope Lumpkin (1908-1912) the Church was Consecrated, on January 23, 1912. During the time of the next rector, the Rev. Octavius Theodore Porcher, a new altar and organ were installed. Mr. Porcher was very active in mission work at the cotton mill where he had a night school and with services at Auburn. He conducted a mission in Timmonsville 1918-19. The succeeding rectors were William Preston Peyton (1919-1920), William Brayshaw (1921-1923), Paul Dué (1924-1925), Mortimer W. Glover (acting 1925-1926), C. R. Cody (1927 until his death in 1939), the Rev. Richard C. Patton (1939-1949). For many preceding years Mr. George T. Patton and Mr. Pervis Jenkins Boatwright were wardens and loyal supporters of St. Matthew's as was also Mr. W. B. Brunson. They were all commemorated by windows in the Church as also Mrs. Patton and Mrs. Brunson. This Church contains many memorials; besides those mentioned are the processional cross to John McLean Wilson, a window to Mrs. Abram (Kate Ruffin) Sydnor, the rose window to the Peyton children, the pulpit to Edna and William Brunson, the lectern to Mr. and Mrs. Witherspoon Evans, communion silver to Eli Simon.

The Rev. Robert Tomlinson succeeded Mr. Patton as rector. On March 14, 1956, a great step forward was taken by this parish when its handsome new parish house was dedicated. It was built at a cost of $50,000.00. It adjoins the Church on the north built on a lot recently acquired.

CHRIST CHURCH, DENMARK
Established 1945

Early in 1945, there being a nucleus of Church members in Denmark, steps were taken to organize a mission. On his ordination in February, 1945, the Rev. William L. Martin was placed by Bishop Carruthers in charge of the mission which he then organized. The wardens appointed were C. D. Palmer and E. F. Ramsey, the latter being also secretary-treasurer. The first report in the Journal of the Convention (1947) was seven families and 11 communicants. Mr. Martin resigned January 15, 1947. He was followed by the Rev. Gorden D. Bennett who held charge until in the summer of 1949, when the Rev. Roderick J. Hobart succeeded as priest-in-charge. In 1950-51 under Mr. Hobart's leadership, the Church was built. The Church, being completed and fully paid for, was consecrated by Bishop Carruthers on the afternoon of September 9, 1951. he Rev. Gordan H. Mann succeeded Mr. Hobart in 1954. Many memorials and gifts have been bestowed upon this Church, among them: a paten given by Mrs. J. V. Bishop in memory of her father; Mrs. E. F. Ramsey with the help of the Auxiliary supplied hangings; Mrs. C. P. Guess supplied hymnals; Mrs. J. D. Copeland gave cruets; the Auxiliary an organ. In 1955 the original 11 communicants had increased to 39. The Rev. Walter D. Roberts succeeded to the charge in 1955. A study was added to the Church at this time. New doors to the vestibule of the Church were installed early in 1956. Recently Mrs. Ann Humphreys donated to Christ Church a lot for a rectory.

ST. PHILIP'S CHAPEL
VOORHEES SCHOOL, DENMARK
(See Archdeaconry, end this Section)

SAINT BARNABAS', DILLON
Established 1908

The first recorded service of the Episcopal Church in Dillon was that held by the Rev. T. T. Walsh, general missionary of the diocese, in January, 1908. Two weeks later, on January 22, Bishop Guerry visited Dillon. He held service with a large gathering in the school auditorium. After this, he met with our few Church members and took steps toward the organization of a mission, appointing a warden and a secretary and treasurer. A committee was appointed to raise funds to purchase a lot. The Archdeacon continued to hold occasional services.

In 1909, the Rev. Henry Cook Salmond was appointed to the charge of the mission. J. Cabell Davis was appointed warden, and Charles G. Dwight, treasurer. Mr. Salmond reported in May, 1910, that a lot in a fine location had been bought. This purchase seems not to have been completed at this time. He then reported nine communicants. The work in Dillon seemed now to lag, but Mr. Salmond continued to hold occasional services. The Rev. E. A. Penick took charge in 1913. He reported five communicants; Dr. J. C. Davis, warden and lay reader; treasurer, F. M. Niernsee. Also, he reported that a lot for a Church had been bought and paid for; an addition to the lot was secured the next year. Mr. Penick removing in 1915, the Rev. T. P. Baker succeeded him, serving until early in 1918. The Rev. O. T. Porcher took charge in November, 1919, beginning with two services a month in the Presbyterian Church, kindly loaned.

In 1920, a Church belonging to the Presbyterians was purchased for $2,000.00, moved to the lot owned by the Church, and set up in order there at a cost of another $2,000.00. The nation-wide campaign supplied $1,000.00 and $1,000.00 was borrowed from the Church Building Fund; the little congregation raised the balance. The next year, St. Barnabas' became an "organized mission." At this time, Dr. J. C. Davis was warden, and Sandford Stoney, secretary and treasurer. They continued the officers for many years. In 1933, Edward D. McCutchen succeeded Mr. Stoney, and in 1938, A. D. Barnes became treasurer. Dr. Davis was the only warden this Church had from its beginning until 1940.

After Mr. Porcher's retirement in February, 1939, the Rev. George H. Harris assumed charge June 1, 1941. In 1941, St. Barnabas' Church was completely remodeled as to its interior at a cost of $500.00, to effect a very churchly and pleasing appearance; the changes amounted to the building of a chapel inside the old Church. Mr. A. P. Salley conducted the reconstruction. The wardens now succeeding Dr. Davis were A. P. Salley and E. D. McCutchen, A. D. Barnes, treasurer. In the fall of 1947, a new communion service and a font were dedicated in memory of the late beloved rector, the Rev. O. T. Porcher. Mr. Harris resigned December 1, 1947. The Rev. W. S. Poynor (retired) conducted services in 1948. The Rev. Robert C. Baird became priest-in-charge January 1, 1949. The wardens now were W. L. Bethea and Edward D. McCutchen; the treasurer, Mrs. J. A. Steck; Church school superintendent, Mrs. Rudolph Jones; lay readers, Dr. J. O. Warren and W. L. Bethea. The Rev. Earle C. Page succeeded Mr. Baird

July 15, 1952. He was the first resident minister. On November 21, 1954, ground was broken for the erection of a parish house, located in the rear of the Church. The Rev. John B. Morris succeeded Mr. Page in 1955. Mr. Morris has recently opened a mission in the neighboring town of Latta.

ST. GEORGE'S, DORCHESTER
(See Dalcho, p. 345 and St. George's, Mission)

TRINITY CHURCH, EDISTO ISLAND
Established 1788
(See Dalcho, p. 390)

Beginning now with the last part of Dr. Dalcho's account of the Church on Edisto, the Rev. Edmund Matthews, we note, was one of the first clergymen ever to be ordained in South Carolina, being one of the seven ordained by our first Bishop, Robert Smith. His resignation, because of a severe "domestic affliction" September, 1799, was accepted by the vestry with sympathy and regret. He went to St. Simon's Island, Ga., in 1811 where he died in 1827. It is most interesting to note that eighty years after Mr. Matthew's resignation, his widow, still living in New Haven, Connecticut, gave $100.00 for the rebuilding of the present Church in 1881, as also a beautiful prayer book and lectern Bible. The gifts were through that zealous mother in Israel of Edisto, Mrs. R. J. LaRoche in 1879. The rectorship was vacant for ten years after Mr. Matthews' resignation. These were the dark days of the Church in the diocese when there was no Bishop. It was during the rectorship of the Rev. Joseph Warren (1809-1811) in 1811, that Mr. Edward Bailey presented the Church with a set of silver plate.

The next rector the Rev. Andrew Fowler after a ministry in the North following graduation from Yale University, came South and first to St. Bartholomew's parish; then later he was the first missionary of our Society for the Advancemtnt of Christianity in South Carolina and was instrumental in founding Trinity Church Columbia; Grace, Camden, and the Church in Wadesboro, when he was serving St. David's, Cheraw, also the Church in St. Augustine, Florida. He was often deputy to the General Convention. His ministry here was from 1813 to 1817 and is especially marked by the fact that he presented on Edisto the first class for confirmation in South Carolina. The short-sighted policy of the Church of England during colonial times in not sending Bishops to America had deprived members of the Church here of the sacrament of Confirmation. In his short Episcopate for some good reason no doubt our first Bishop, Robert Smith, never confirmed anyone. The Confirmation administered here in Trinity, Edisto, by Bishop Theodore Dehon on Tuesday, March 20, 1813, was the first in the diocese. It is an interesting story of how Mr. Fowler went to Charleston and finally prevailed on the Bishop to come for a Confirmation the next week. He at last agreed to give Edisto the preference because, he said, Mr. Fowler had written a tract on Confirmation. Mr. Fowler has left a story of difficulty in getting back from Charleston in time to prepare his candidates for confirmation. He relates, "When I was taking my breakfast (in Charleston) it began to rain. and continued to do so the greater part of the day, which prevented my returning to Edisto Island before Sunday morning; for the next day, that is Saturday, I had forty miles or nearly to ride, and when I came to the river between Slan's Island and Edisto, I could not pass over for want of an opportunity. As there was no house near, which was inhabited, I was obliged to take my lodging for the night upon the floor in an unoccupied building, and without anything to eat. I had missed of my dinner, and a good supper would not have been unacceptable. Having engaged two boys at one dollar each, to set me and my horse across the water the next morning, I left Slan's Island before the sun was up, and arrived at my house soon enough to attend church." From Slan's Island, he says, "to Edisto was three miles, then seven miles to his home, then three back to the Church." He made it; and gave notice of the confirmation on Tuesday, when he presented a class of twenty persons. These were as follows: "Joseph Seabrook and Martha, his wife; Joseph Jenkins and Elizabeth his wife; Benjamin Bailey and Sarah his wife; William C. Meggett and Elizabeth his wife; Benjamin Seabrook; Ann Seabrook; Edward Bailey; Edward Mitchell; Martha L'Roche; Sarah Patterson; Louisa Devaux; Charles Bailey; Isaac Jenkins; and Thomas Bailey." The second and third Confirmations in the diocese were in St. Michael's, Wednesday, August 4, 1813, and in St. Philip's the Friday following. A second Confirmation was held in Trinity, Edisto, on January 12, 1814, when thirteen white and six Negroes were confirmed. The old rite now new was evidently received joyfully in the diocese, for on February 15 the following, less than a year, Bishop Dehon reported 516 confirmations. About the time of Mr. Fowler's call it was resolved by the vestry that hereafter ministers would hold office "during good behavior" and not as before for a limited time. However, we note that the very next rector, Reverend Thomas Osborne, was elected for two years, so the vestry at once failed to abide by its own resolution and the rule of the Church, that a rector is elected for life or until dissolution of pastoral relations by mutual consent or if that fails by final decision by the Bishop. Again we see the outcome when an Episcopal Church has no Episcopate. Mr. Osborne soon resigned to become a professor in the University of Cincinnati. He was elected again in 1822 and returned. A rectory was secured in 1818 including thirty acres of land.

From an early time, the Presbyterian and Episcopal congregations worshipped together in the summer in an academy at Eddingsville, the ministers alternating, until, in 1824, the congregations joined forces and erected a chapel there at a cost of $1,200.00 for use in common. However, after some disagreement concerning furniture had arisen, by mutual and friendly agreement, the Episcopalians bought out the Presbyterians. Soon after the building was Consecrated (March 14, 1826) as St. Stephen's Chapel. A summer parsonage had already been built there in 1822. After Mr. Osborne's death, greatly deplored, he was succeeded in 1827 by the Rev. Edward Thomas, descendant in the fourth generation of the Rev. Samuel Thomas, the first missionary of the Society for the Propagation of the Gospel in Foreign Parts to South Carolina. Failure of health caused him to resign after eight years, Mr. Seabrook says, "to the great grief of his attached congregation." There are two graves in the churchyard, reminders of Mr. Thomas's sojourn as rector, those of a sister and an infant son. Another son, with the same name, Dr. Theodore Gaillard Thomas, gained great eminence in the medical profession in New York. He was author of an epoch making work on "Women's Diseases." After Mr. Thomas's death, when rector of St. John's, Berkeley, where he is buried under Strawberry Chapel, a volume of his sermons was published. A unique institution in the parish about this time was a parish library. There was also a Ladies' Working Society.

The Rev. Charles E. Leverette was the next rector. These must have been prosperous days on the island. In 1835 steps were taken looking to the building of a new Church; the cornerstone was laid December 28, 1840; it was completed in 1841. In his Sentence of Consecration of the Church November 14, 1841, significantly Bishop Gadsden said "Whereas the church built in 1774, which lately stood near this spot, was without proper sittings for the colored people, and was in other respects inconvenient, and it became desirable to erect a new one, not only larger with better accommodations, but also in correspondence with the increased prosperity of the congregation, and, from its form and appendages, more expressive of reverence for the Divine Being, of charity for mankind and of concern for their own spiritual welfare on the part of those by whom it was to be provided" and with other whereases, the Bishop then set apart and Consecrated the new, as he said, "beautiful edifice sufficiently furnished." The cost of the new Church was about $7,000.00, a large sum in those days when money was worth more. The old Church which stood near the site of the new was torn down and sold at auction. As stated before, the congregation worshipped in the Baptist Church during the construction of this new Church which the rector describes as follows: "This building . . . is a structure of 75 feet long, by 45 feet wide, including a portico, with brick columns, a vestibule, and robing room. It has a steeple 100 feet high, and galleries built for the accommodation of the colored people, a large body of whom, we are happy to say, are constant and interested worshippers. The semicircular wall of the chancel has the decalogue inscribed upon it (the Creed and Lord's Prayer are yet to be added), above which are the Bible and the symbol of our faith, the Cross, with the words, in large gold capitals, 'Jesus said, I am the Way, and the Truth and the Life.' Over this, in the arched part of the ceiling are clouds and the descending dove. The Church handsomely furnished, is well equipped to inspire the worshippers with suitable feelings of solemnity." The wardens at the time of the erection of this handsome Church were William C. Meggett and James B. Seabrook with Dr. Edward Mitchell, Joseph B. Seabrook, and Jabez J. R. Westcoat, vestrymen. Mr. Joseph E. Jenkins was chairman of the building committee. A new large organ was installed in 1845.

The parsonage and glebe of the Church was sold in 1843 to Miss E. Seabrook and Mr. Leverett's own house bought from him for a rectory. Mr. Leverett resigned in 1846 to accept a call to Sheldon Church, McPhersonville, and was succeeded by the Rev. W. H. Hanckel who continued in charge until 1858. This seems to have been a happy if uneventful period; a large work was conducted among the colored people, they exceeded the whites in the number of members; services and catechisings were conducted on the plantations, the gallery in the Church for the colored people, seating two hundred, was often filled. The vested funds of the Church amounted to upwards of $30,000.00. But also, this happy period was soon to come to an end; Rev. William Johnson succeeded Mr. Hanckel in 1858. Edisto being an exposed island, received the shock of war at a very early date. The white people in large measure fled from the island at its first outbreak. For several years the history of the Church is practically a blank. From 1861 until 1869, the Church had no lay representation in the annual Conventions of the diocese. In 1869, Mr. William Whaley took his seat in Convention—the Church once more was represented. The rector, Mr. Johnson, left the island in November, 1861, in company, he says with "all my congregation." He went to Yorkville accompanied there by a part of the congregation, others refugeed elsewhere. Mr. Johnson afterwards served in the vicinity of Columbia preaching and teaching. He did not return to Edisto until March, 1866. At first he did not have any congregation of whites, and very few colored who seemed indifferent. He found it best to hold the services at Eddingsville. Gradually some white families returned and the colored people began again to manifest interest. The chancel books were lost in the war but soon a lady of the congregation replaced them. The Church was used as a Confederate cavalry headquarters during the war; and, after, it was used as a U. S. Coast Survey observatory, i. e., I suppose that it was the steeple that was so used. In Mr. Johnson's last report of 1869, we find conditions greatly improved; numbers of both white and colored pretty well restored to pre-war level. The Rev. Mr. Johnson resigned in 1871 and was succeeded by the Rev. W. O. Prentiss who reports inhabitants so migratory that it was difficult to secure accurate statistics. In 1875, the Rev. George W. Stickney became rector, in connection with John's Island. He reports the Church in a much revived condition, plans being under way to abandon St. Stephen's, Eddingsville, on account of the encroachment of the "great waters", as well as "difficulty in passing the defiant river"; Negroes in large numbers occupying the galleries worshipping with the whites. Plans were now making, with the concentrating of the worship at the parish Church, to restore and beautify the dilapidated sanctuary.

But alas, changes sometimes come rapidly—on Friday, February 28, 1876, caught by sparks from Dr. Pope's field nearby, the splendid Church was burned to practically complete destruction. The loss of this beautiful and cherished landmark, for both the sea and the regions roundabout, was a great calamity. This happened at a time when the parish, impoverished by the war, could ill stand such a loss. Unfortunately also the vestry was just now at odds with the rector on the mode of the annual parish elections. Furthermore, just now a change in the parish began, accelerated by this loss of the Church, in the beginning of the withdrawal of the colored members. The promises of the so so called Reformed Episcopal Church further accelerated this movement. After the fire with some remodelling the rectory was used as a place of worship for several years. In 1879, determined efforts began looking to the building of a new Church. In 1881, this was completed at a cost of $2,000.00 and was Consecrated by Bishop Howe on December the sixteenth, 1881. Mr. J. R. LaRoche read the Request for Consecration, and Rev. Mr. Prentiss the Sentence. The Rev. John Kershaw preached the sermon. Present also in the service were the Rev. John Johnson, the Rev. Theodore A. Porter, the Rev. P. G. Jenkins of Arkansas, and the Rev. P. H. Whaley, then of Connecticut. The cornerstone which was under the second Church destroyed by fire, marks this Church, presumably on the same spot. Mr. Prentiss resigned in 1892 after fourteen years service. The Rev. Barnwell B. Sams succeeded Mr. Prentiss in 1895. The year 1896 was one of revival in the parish; the Church building was repaired and improved to the extent of $782.00, making it, it was said, "one of the neatest churches in the diocese."

It was in this same eventful year that Trinity Church Branch of the Woman's Auxiliary was organized. Mr. Sams died in 1903, his last service was in this Church when he was taken ill dying a week later. Since then the following rectors have served: the Rev. A. E. Evison, 1905-1908; the Rev. Percival H. Whaley, 1908-1912; the Rev. Christopher I. LaRoche, 1913-1918; the Rev. F. N. Skinner, 1919-1926; the Rev. R. E. Page, 1927-1928 and the Rev. Alvin W. Skardon until 1951. The Church was struck by lightning in the summer of 1905. The chancel and side entrance were damaged.

The beautiful stained glass window in the chancel is in memory of three former rectors: the Rev. William O. Prentiss, 1871-1874 and 1878-1892; the Rev. Barnwell B. Sams, 1875-1903; and the Rev. Percival H. Whaley, 1908-1912. In 1928 an altar cross was given in memory of the Rev. Frederick Nash Skinner by his wife. A Men's club was organized in the summer of 1933. On May 10, 1935, the handsome altar was dedicated by Bishop Thomas, and at the same time the cross on the Church, to the glory of God and in memory of two members of the Church. The sturdy and attractive fence with brick pillars is one of the improvements of these years. A great anniversary service was held on October 10, 1948 when Bishop Thomas delivered a historical sermon. Mr. Skardon was the nineteenth rector and served longest of all, twenty-two years, until 1951, when he resigned. The Rev. Mr. Skardon was followed in 1951 by the Rev. Harold Thomas. In these years many new gifts were dedicated: in 1952, the candelabra in memory of Frances Marion Whaley and Edward Mitchell Whaley; in 1953 the pulpit in memory of Arthur Murray Whaley, Richard Townsend LaRoche, Frances Allston Wilkinson, and William Charles Bailey; a litany desk given by Augustus P. Allen of Chester; hangings by the Woman's Auxiliary; in 1955 a processional cross in memory of Thomas Green Young; and in 1956 a Church flag in memory of Augustus P. S. Stoney by his wife. In 1952 the Church school was reopened. The parish hall was built in 1953, and in about two years an addition was made to it providing an assembly hall for the parish.

CHURCH OF THE HEAVENLY REST, ESTILL
Established 1891
(Originally St. Peter's Parish)
(See Dalcho, p. 385)

The mission in old St. Peter's parish in Hampton County called St. Peter's mission continued for many years under the Rev. E. E. Bellinger and the Rev. B. B. Sams, the services being held monthly in a Methodist Church. This privilege was withdrawn in 1891. It was then determined to build, a lot was donated, and a collection taken.

CHURCH OF THE HEAVENLY REST

St. Peter's mission was now (1891) replaced by the Church of the Heavenly Rest near Scotia in Hampton County. The donation of $1,000.00 by one member made the erection of a Church possible—a "neat and churchly building", the Rev. B. B. Sams, minister. The Church was Consecrated by Bishop Howe November 29, 1891, Mr. Sams reading the Sentence, and the Rev. E. E. Bellinger preaching. The Rev. T. T. Walsh succeeded Mr. Sams October, 1896, and the Rev. W. Norwood Tillinghast in turn in 1898, A. M. Mattin, warden, and Benjamin Rhodes, secretary and treasurer. In 1900 Mr. Tillinghast held some services in the school house in Estill. He resigned November 1, 1901, being succeeded by the Rev. A. E. Evison until 1906. The Rev. P. D. Hay took charge in 1907. He was succeeded by the Rev. J. H. Woodward in 1912. In 1920, Mr. Thomas Rhodes was warden and Mrs. E. S. Ramsey, treasurer. The Church in Hampton County has been greatly benefited by the generosity of the Martin family. It was Gen. W. E. Martin who in 1847 gave the lot for the Church at Gillesonville (Ascension). Mr. Edward Evans of Society Hill, Darlington County, a connection of the family, gave a handsome altar for the St. Peter's Church at Robertsville (burnt by the Federal Army in 1865). In 1914 the Heavenly Rest received the Elizabeth Martin Legacy, in 1922 the Augustus Jones Legacy, and in 1938 the Bessie Evans Martin Cozart

Legacy—all in trust of the Bishop of the diocese for the salary of the rector of the Heavenly Rest. Also by the will of Elize M. Jones the Church owns a domain of fifty acres adjoining the Church to be kept perpetually in forest. The storm of 1928 blew down many of the trees yielding about $2,000.00. It was used to put a new roof on the Church, secure a communion service, add a heating plant, and add $1,000.00 to the Jones Legacy.

The Rev. F. M. Brunton succeeded Mr. Woodward in 1925 and then Rev. Joseph Burton in 1927. Mr. Burton resigned November, 1929. First the Rev. S. R. Guignard of Upper South Carolina, then the Rev. L. G. Wood supplied services until the Rev. John Adams Pinckney took charge on his ordination June 28, 1931. This mission was admitted into union with the Convention April, 1932. The Messrs Thomas S. Rhodes and C. W. Ellis were the first deputies the next year. Mr. Pinckney resigned in the fall of 1936, and the Rev. T. P. Ball took charge in the summer of 1938, resigning two years later. The warden at this time was Mr. Carlton Ellis. The Church had only occasional services until the Rev. R. E. Withers took charge the end of 1946, leaving two years later; then in July, 1949 the Rev. G. Edward Haynsworth followed in charge. In 1950 the warden and treasurer was Carlton W. Ellis; secretary, A. M. Marshall.

FAITH, ESTILL

On account of the distance of the Church of the Heavenly Rest from Estill, in and near which lived a number of Church members a movement was begun in 1922 to raise funds to build a chapel in Estill. Mr. Brunton's work gave an impetus to this movement. Mr. T. R. Rhodes, warden, and Mrs. E. S. Ramsey were leaders. The chapel was completed in June, 1926. St. Jude's, Walterboro, gave an altar. Brass cross, vases, offertory plate, and altar book rest were given by the congregation. Prayer and hymn books came from St. Bartholomew's, Hartsville. The building was finally paid for and consecrated as Holy Faith, Estill, by Bishop Thomas on March 3, 1929. The services now alternated between this chapel and Heavenly Rest. In 1953 this chapel was moved to Hampton Court House.

EPIPHANY, EUTAWVILLE
(Upper St. John's)
Established 1864

There is no record of any Church or chapel in Upper St. John's until about 1760 when in the rectorate of the Rev. Levi Durand a log chapel was built at a place afterwards called Chapel Hill.

Here Mr. Durand officiated to overflowing congregations. Probably as successor to this chapel, by Act of the Assembly in 1770, a Chapel of Ease was directed to be built near Forty-five Mile House. The first Rocks Church, built in 1804, was the outcome of these chapels. As related in the sketch of St. Stephen's, Pineville, this Church was served by the same minister as that until 1864 when it became an independent parish. The first Rocks Church was two miles to the westward of the site of the later permanent Church, being at the entrance to the Rock's Plantation, hence the name. It was about eight miles east of Eutawville. In 1808 this Church was moved to the east on land belonging to Springfield Plantation. This Church was taken down, and, on the same site was erected in 1814 the third and permanent Rocks Church, the building being under supervision of John Palmer. The congregation was composed mostly of the people who had migrated from St. Stephen's parish. Thus, in reality, it was more a Chapel of Ease of St. Stephen's than of St. John's, though located geographically in this latter parish. (Cf. Sketch of St. Stephen's.) Rock's Church was consecrated under the name of "The Church of the Epiphany" on March 4, 1844. In 1855, services were held at Rocks, on several plantations, as well as at a chapel which had been built about 1849 in the village of Eutawville—not to be consecrated, so ministers of any denomination might hold services in it.

After its separation from St. Stephen's in 1864, the Rev. R. P. Johnson became the first rector of Epiphany as an independent parish. About 1868 a colored parochial school was conducted in Eutawville, as also a Sunday School with 80 pupils. The Eutawville chapel was enlarged and improved about this time. Mr. Johnson served until 1868 when his health failed. The Rev. F. M. Hall, a deacon, held charge for a few months in 1869 followed by the Rev. P. F. Stevens as missionary in 1869 and 1870. The Rev. N. B. Fuller succeeded as rector in 1870. When this rector lost his horse (no small matter for him) it was replaced chiefly by the Ladies' Sewing Society. In Eutawville a chapel for colored people, called St. Paul's, was completed in 1874, and services held in it for the first time on the occasion of the Bishop's visitation in February. The chapel and school for the colored people secured the services at this time of Lawrence Dawson, catechist and candidate for Holy Orders, a colored man. Mr. Fuller having gone to Spartanburg in 1876, the Church was vacant until the Rev. W. O. Prentiss took charge in 1877 continuing only until January 1, 1878. The Rev. F. G. Scott succeeded December 20, 1879. The Church and the rector's residence underwent extensive repairs in 1880 through the agency of the famous Ladies' Sewing Society. The chapel in Eutawville for a long time had remained unfinished. At this time a chancel and vestry room were added and the building reshingled. A rectory was bought in 1882 through the efforts of the same society. A handsome carved oak communion table was installed in the parish Church in 1884. Mr. Scott resigned this year and the Rev. J. H. Tillinghast succeeded, remaining until January 1, 1886. During a period of vacancy the Ladies' Society remodeled, enlarged, and beautified the village church. The Rev. B. M. Bradon was in charge for part of this time.

After several years, the Rev. John W. Motte began a long and useful ministry in this parish in 1891. The next year the parish Church was repaired. At this time on two plantations there were two Sunday Schools for Negroes, 150 to 200, old and young, conducted by members of the parish, and a new chapel for them was built. In 1893 an organ was placed in the Rocks and a new prayer desk and hymn tablet. The wardens in 1897 were W. H. Sinkler and A. P. Gaillard.

After twenty-three years of loyal and most valuable service in the parish and nearly fifty in the diocese, owing to bodily infirmity in 1914 Mr. Motte retired, going to live with his son in Savannah. The wardens of Epiphany at this time were W. H. Sinkler and E. F. Couturier. The Rev. John London succeeded Mr. Motte in 1914 but only for about a year, the Rev. Henry C. Mazyck becoming rector in 1915 and continuing until 1921 when the Rev. A. W. Taylor succeeded him. He was followed by the Rev. Walter Mitchell as acting rector in 1923 and until 1925. the Rev. A. W. Skardon became rector in this year.

Rock's Church burned down in 1926. Through contributions of members and friends it was promptly rebuilt, and on December 11, 1927, simultaneously the cornerstone was laid and the Church consecrated by Bishop Guerry, the Revs. A. W. Skardon and J. E. H. Gailbraith assisting. Mr. Skardon consecrated at this Church a Bishop's chair (on February 10, 1929) in memory of Mrs. William Henry Sinkler by her children and later a pair of brass candlesticks, a gift to the chapel by Mrs. Frank McLeod. Later in this year, a chair was given Rock's Church in memory of Mr. and Mrs. Frank K. Simons by their children. The wardens now were C. St. G. Sinkler and E. F. Couturier; secretary-treasurer, J. J. Simons.

The Rev. J. E. H. Galbraith became rector in March, 1929, continuing until November, 1933. In 1934, the Rev. David Nathaniel

Peeples succeeded. A parish house was now acquired and work among young people increased. On New Year's Eve the parish party given annually by Mrs. Caroline Sinkler of Philadelphia was held on Numertia Plantation. Mr. Peeples was ordained priest in Epiphany Chapel on May 28, 1935. In 1935, Mr. Peeples, with the assistance of the Rev. W. Moultrie Moore, took 25 boys to Bluffton on a camp for an outing and for Church training. This was the beginning of camps and conferences in this diocese. The next year under Mr. Peeples, the associate mission was organized with the Revs. D. M. Hobart and L. A. Taylor as associates. Under this association, a wide mission work was developed, covering a considerable part of the diocese, including old St. Mark's, Summerton, Pinopolis, the Barrows, Pompion Hill, St. Stephen's, Kingstree, Andrews, and adjacent territory. The Rev. D. M. Hobart removed his residence to Kingstree January 1, 1937. Mr. Peeples resigned March 1, 1938. After this, the Rev. L. A. Taylor had charge in connection with the associate mission until July, 1946.

A great change now came in the history of this parish through the "Santee-Cooper" development. Rock's Church and its graveyard were to be left an island in Lake Marion. The vestry was compelled to consent to the conveyance of the property to the South Carolina Public Service Authority. This was done by deed dated May 22, 1941, after obtaining canonical consent. The last service held in the Rock's Church was on May 17, 1942, Sunday after Ascension—Morning Prayer and Holy Communion, the Rev. Lincoln Taylor officiating.

The Rev. W. R. Haynsworth succeeded late in the year 1946 for a short time. After him came the Rev. deSaussure P. Moore for a brief time, then the Rev. Frank Levy (1947-48). The Rev. Joseph N. Bynum became rector in 1948. Epiphany Church, Eutawville, was consecrated by Bishop Carruthers on January 30, 1949. Mr. Bynum resigned April, 1952, when Mr. William States Belser, candidate for holy orders, acted first as lay reader then as deacon until February, 1954. The Rev. Kenneth Donald became rector March 1, 1954. The Consecration was removed from the Rock's Church on the 12th Sunday after Trinity, September, 1954 by Bishop Thomas (retired), acting for the Bishop of the diocese, assisted by the rector, the Rev. Mr. Donald. The Church was taken down soon after this. A monument has been erected marking the site of the old Church and the graveyard. In this is placed the cornerstone of the Church in which is contained the original contents of the stone and a copy of this sketch written by Bishop A. S. Thomas, 1955. A memorial slab is placed on top of the monument as well as is re-placed the white brick (on north side) which forms a cross as it did on the old Church building.

ST. JOHN'S, FLORENCE
Established 1866

We begin this sketch with two questions—the first from Miss Bessie Gregg's sketch of Christ Church, Mars Bluff: "In 1860 Mrs. Frances Church came as a refugee from Charleston to the (rail-road) junction which afterwards became the town of Florence. In her room at the hotel she had Episcopal Service every Sunday morning getting whomsoever she could to conduct it. Mr. Howe [later Bishop] . . . living in Christ Church neighborhood came to her aid and gave a service whenever he could. This little band became our St. John's Church." Later the services were held in the Masonic Temple on Front Street, then in a one-room dwelling west of the hotel on Coit Street.

We now let Mr. J. J. Pringle Smith, registrar of the diocese, take up the story, writing in 1878: "The first movement for a church in Florence was in the summer of 1866. During the next year the project took more definite shape and more than $600.00 were sub-scribed beside engagements to furnish building materials. (Mr. James A. Pettigrew gave a lot on the south west corner of Coit and Darlington Streets.) In July, 1867, Bishop Davis visited Florence and appointed to the work the Rev. Walter C. Guerry. This gentle-man began his labors in this field immediately, that is about the middle of the above month. After only some four or five weeks, he was called away from earth. This sad event deprived for a time the infant congregation of regular services and filled their hearts with sorrow. The window in the chancel of the Church was placed in memory of Mr. Guerry. His first sermon was from St. John's Gospel on St. John's Day and this Church received its name as well to commemorate his short ministry and to do honor to the Apostle of Love. The people felt called on to exert themselves in this work of the Lord and a meeting was held at which the congregation organized, elected a vestry, and after about two months invited the Rev. L. F. Guerry, a brother of their lamented pastor. [The Rev. J. W. Motte was present at this meeting and proposed the name St. John as stated above.] About the 20th of November Mr. Guerry began his labors. He found 15 or 16 communicants and Divine worship was held in the Masonic Hall which had been kindly lent for the purpose. After several months another building was fitted up and used until April, 1868. At the last-mentioned date the Church building was begun with something more than $600.00 in cash and some subscriptions of lumber, etc. In a short time the building was enclosed but without seats or window sashes. Gradually and by dint of persistent efforts (chiefly among the ladies) pews were added and here and there a sash to give light while most of the windows were boarded. [The first vestry, elected Easter Monday, 1868, was— wardens, S. A. Robertson and J. H. Johnson; vestrymen, Theo. Gaillard, S. P. Gause, C. E. Jarrot, Horace Mellichamp, and E. H. Lucas.] In May, 1868, the parish was admitted into union with the Convention. In December, 1868, the Bishop made a visitation and service was held in the building though little more than a shell. We extract the following from an account by the rector, Mr. Guerry: 'I remember the day well. It was very cold—the wind from the east, and we had no doors. It swept freshly up the wide center aisle chilling me at the desk, and our venerable Bishop just behind in the chancel, with many, I fear, of the congregation, but not affecting, I hope, our hearts. We worshipped God in earnest, and went home chilled perhaps in body but warm and grateful at heart. To add to the interest of the day, a class of seven persons was presented for confirmation, two of whom were young men.'"

Doors and window sashes were added in the summer with new subscriptions including one from St. Philip's, Charleston. A parsonage on the same lot as the Church was begun in 1870. The Church was completed and consecrated November 12, 1871, both Bishops Davis and Howe officiating. The Atlantic Coast Line Railroad gave the Church an engine bell that called the people to worship. It was subsequently given to the town for a fire bell. Mr. Guerry resigned April 1, 1873. The Rev. H. T. Lee supplied services for six months from July, 1873. At this time Mr. S. A. Robertson, warden, secretary and treasurer, reports that lay services were regularly held by the lay readers: Messrs. T. S. Gaillard, and Simons Lucas. The next year 1874-1875 Mr. Guerry was in charge again as missionary. Then followed the Rev. H. T. Lee again as rector for a year, 1875-76. The Rev. John W. Motte having already officiated in St. John's for several months became rector February, 1877, for a short time. The Rev. E. C. Steele was rector 1879-81, resuming charge for a while in 1882. At this time there were 15 families: 32 white communicants, two colored; offerings, $132.00. The Rev. J. Mercier Green was minister in charge 1882-1883. The Church has from the first made use of lay readers. Among the earlier ones were Messrs. Simons Lucas and E. H. Mellichamp.

In 1882 a committee of four ladies was appointed to raise funds to purchase a lot for a Church in a more suitable location. This resulted in the organization of the Ladies' Aid of St. John's Church with Miss Sally Schouboe as president. Eventually the lot was purchased of Mr. James Allen on the east side of Dargan Street for $250.00, and the adjoining lot for a rectory at the same price. Mrs. Church succeeded in a personal interview in securing a contribution of £ 5 for the Church from Queen Victoria. The Rev. George Waldo Stickney became rector April, 1883 until 1884. He reports considerable repairs on the old Church, also the placing of a Bishop's chair in memory of Bishop Davis whose last official act was to consecrate this Church. A paten and a plate was also given at this time. The Rev. John Kershaw gave the Church services once a month, coming from Sumter. Mr. Motte resumed charge of the Church in 1886 until 1888. The Mason and Hamlin Organ used in these years was the gift of Mrs. Church. The organist was Miss Sarah Schouboe. In 1882 a committee of ladies was appointed to raise funds for a new Church—Mesdames E. L. Hunter, James Evans, C. E. Jarrot, and Sarah Schouboe.

The old Church was badly damaged by the earthquake in 1886. The lot was sold for $700.00. For a time services were held in a hall over the James Allen store at the corner of Evans and Dargan Streets. In the fall of 1888, the Rev. W. A. Guerry, deacon, took charge being shortly joined by his bride, Miss Anne McBee, of Lincolnton, N. C. The cornerstone of a new Church on the lot on Dargan Street was laid June 11, 1889. The Church was designed by the distinguished churchman, Silas McBee (Mrs. Guerry's brother) modelled after St. Luke's, Lincolnton, N. C., built of stone from the Anson Quarries at Wadesboro, N. C. The Church was completed and paid for the following year and was consecrated by Bishop Howe on February 15, 1891, Mr. Guerry being ordained priest at the same time. The Rev. Ellison Capers, then rector of Trinity, Columbia, preached the sermon. At the same time the altar cross, vases, font, lectern, Bishop's chair, credence table (carved by Mr. McBee) and the altar were dedicated. In 1892-93 the school house next the Church was converted into a rectory at the cost of $600.00. A new organ was now soon secured.

In 1893 Mr. Guerry became chaplain of the University of the South, and professor, and was succeeded by the Rev. R. W. Barnwell. Before his arrival a great fire destroyed much of Florence including the rectory which was soon rebuilt. Messrs. J. W. Howard and H. M. Ayer served at different times as superintendent of the

Sunday School at this time. Mr. Barnwell resigned in 1895 and was succeeded by the Rev. W. S. Holmes. An altar guild was organized at this time. There were now 40 families in St. John's with 92 communicants. In 1897 the Rev. R. W. Barnwell resumed the rectorship when a new organ was installed and a vested choir organized by Miss Nettie Evans. On the much lamented death of Mrs. Barnwell in 1899, a new communion service, the movement for the securing of which she had inaugurated, was given in her memory. Mr. Barnwell resigned May, 1901, being succeeded by the Rev. Harold Thomas the following fall until 1905. Among his activities was a ten-minute address during lunch hour every Monday at the A.C.L. shops, a mission called St. Timothy's for white people was formed in East Florence, and also a school for Negro children. At this time the wardens were E. H. Lucas, and James Evans, M.D., secretary H. M. Ayer, treasurer E. H. Lucas, lay reader C. E. Johnson. Following Miss Nettie Evans, as organist, was Mrs. Penny, and then later Mrs. J. A. Grimsley (nee Miss Anne Darby). Mr. Thomas, going to Wilmington in 1905 was succeeded by the Rev. W. E. Callender for two years. A processional cross was now secured and the pulpit to be in memory of Mrs. Church planned. Mr. Thomas was then called back. After his return in 1907 St. John's Chapel was built at the corner of Evans and Gaillard Streets. Husband's Chapel, previously used for St. Timothy's mission, was now used as St. Titus, a school for colored children. The addresses at the A.C.L. shops were resumed by Mr. Thomas and continued for 11 years. St. Agnes' Altar Guild, a junior auxiliary, and the Brotherhood of St. Andrew, senior and junior, were organized about this time. In 1910 a brass lectern was installed in memory of Edward Henry Lucas, many years senior warden, and a chancel chair in memory of Mrs. James Evans, also a brass processional cross and an altar cross in the chapel in East Florence where also at this time Frances Hall was erected. The altar cross is now used in the chapel at Camp St. Christopher. In 1911 the candelabra and Eucharistic candlesticks were given, and also a new organ was installed. At this time the rector, in addition to the services at the Church and the chapel in East Florence also acted as chaplain at the State Industrial School and held services at Unity Chapel and at Black Creek Chapel, and at Christ Church, and also St. James, Mars Bluff. The Church is full of memorials. We cannot enumerate them all.

In 1914 the present brick rectory was built, the old one then for a time served as a parish house. The Rev. H. D. Bull was assistant rector 1915-1916, serving also Kingstree. Mr. Thomas resigned June

1, 1917. At this time the parish had increased to 761 baptized persons and 482 communicants. The Rev. Wilmer S. Poynor succeeded as rector March, 1918, and the parish continued to grow. A beautiful new parish house costing $25,000.00 was formally occupied with an address by Bishop Finlay on June 30, 1922. The building is dedicated to "The Glory of God and to the Memory of Mrs. Frances Church." At this time the Church school with R. W. Sharkey, Esq., as superintendent numbered 200. The officers of the Church were: P. J. Maxwell, R. W. Sharkey, wardens; secretary, R. W. Sharkey; treasurer, E. H. Lucas; lay readers, R. J. Kirk, R. W. Sharkey, S. J. Royal, J. W. Howard. During these years also the Woman's Auxiliary expanded, under its recent new constitution, in its activities, and the Men's Club was formed and became very active. When Mr. Poyner resigned July 1, 1946, the communicants of St. John's numbered 573. Mr. Poynor generally known as the "Parson" was greatly beloved in the congregation and in the community, as he still is in his retirement in Florence. The Rev. Louis A. Haskell became rector December 1, 1946. Officers now were wardens, R. W. Sharkey, Hugh L. Willcox; secretary, S. F. Arthur; treasurer, Miss Lucile Hook; Church school superintendent, E. D. Sallenger, Jr.; lay readers, Jack Wright, J. W. Howard, Hugh Willcox, R. W. Sharkey.

In 1947 began the publication of a weekly bulletin. In this year property in the rear of the Church, reaching to Railroad Avenue, was purchased for $4,000.00. Also this year was marked by a serious fire which damaged the parish house to the extent of $5,000.00. It was soon restored and redecorated. More recently about five and a half acres of land was purchased in West Florence in contemplation of a second Church. The parish possesses a portrait of Bishop Guerry first executed by Miss Jane Evans and finished by Eugene Kaufman. New communion silver was secured in 1950-51, partly by sale of old silver given by the congregation. In 1951 the women of St. John's gave a cottage to Camp St. Christopher named in honor of the late rector, "Wilmer Poynor Cottage." A new parish library was now begun. Among the many recent activities of the Men's Club has been its generous help in the building of the Gadsden Cottage at the Home in York. In 1949 the Wilmer Poynor Trust Fund was established to aid scholars at Sewanee and as a tribute to the former rector. A St. John's development fund was begun at this time. It has resulted in the erection in 1953 of a very handsome rectory. The sacristy was thoroughly renovated in 1951.

Both Bishop Thomas and Bishop Carruthers were elected in St. John's.

CHRIST CHURCH, MARS BLUFF
Florence County
Established 1856

Though the above date has been given as that of the founding of Christ Church when the Church was consecrated, its beginnings go much further back. The Rev. N. P. Tillinghast held some services while he was rector of Trinity Church, Society Hill (1843-45). This seems to have been the beginning. In 1844 came the Rev. Isaac Swarts from western New York, serving in the capacity of minister and school teacher. The Bishop reports in February, 1846, that Mr. Swarts had resigned Mars Bluff, continuing preaching and teaching in Darlington. He labored a great deal among the Negroes. He was followed by the Rev. Henry Elwell both as minister and teacher. At this time there was a chapel at Mars Bluff. Familiar names in the early membership were Ashbys, Bacots, Rogers, Harllees, Porchers, and Greggs. In 1849 Mr. Elwell held services 25 times at Mars Bluff and 26 times at Darlington Court House. He left in 1850 to become rector of St. Philip's school in Charleston and missionary, reporting that his former field no longer afforded a support for a missionary.

In February, 1853, the Rev. Alexander Gregg, rector of St. David's, Cheraw, reported that he had held services once a month from April, 1852, to the close of the year and that means were in hand to build a Church, also unavailing efforts to secure a rector. The services of Mr. Gregg continued through 1853, the Rev. Augustus Moore taking charge in 1854. He was a deacon and had served in Charleston the year previous. Plans were now made for building a Church. As so frequently was the case in that day the plans were made by the Rev. J. D. McCollough. In 1856 the Church was organized as Christ Church, Mars Bluff. On Sunday, May 17, 1857, after services in the Baptist Church (Rev. Mr. Napier, pastor) Mr. McCollough preaching, the cornerstone of the new Church was laid by Bishop Davis, the Rev. Alexander Gregg making the address. It was soon after admitted to Convention as a parish. The Church was consecrated on June 5, 1859 when Mr. Gregg preached; present besides the Bishop and preacher were the Revs. Messrs. Roberts, Howe, Phillips, Quinby and the rector Mr. Moore. Miss Bessie A. Gregg thus elegantly describes the Church: "The building is the shape of a cross, orginally painted white. The outside walls are 'boarded and battened'; in this case the boards are about ten inches wide running up and down, every seam covered with a beveled board about four inches wide and two inches in the center.

Inside walls are hard-finished plaster; the woodwork of all sorts is pine and the pews heavy heart pine. A door of Gothic design opens into each transept and the rear of the nave. Many beautiful Gothic windows, originally glazed in ground glass, but replaced with clear glass, give ample light. The vestry is placed separately at the back. The furniture is handmade, I think of walnut except the font, which is particularly beautiful of white marble. Instead of the altar there is the Communion Table. The first instrument was a melodian placed midway the nave; the white congregation sitting above it, and the Negroes behind it." As was the custom of the time there was no chimney or any general heating of the Church. Not until near 1880 was a stove installed. The vestry at the time of the building of the Church was as follows: Robert Rogers, warden; and vestrymen, J. A. Rogers, M. S. McCall, Peter S. Bacot, T. E. Gregg, F. M. Rogers, and W. W. Harllee. Mrs. Mandeville Rogers was the first organist, succeeded later by John Parker Gregg.

The congregation was swelled during the war by refugees from the low country—among these were the Fords, Lucas', Shackelfords, and Goodwyns, including Henry Timrod the poet—a number of who after the war moved into Florence and helped to build St. John's. After a faithful ministry of 24 years, spent wholly at Christ Church, except the first two in Charleston, his health, never good, failing, Rev. Augustus Moore resigned June 26, 1875. However, he continued to hold services in the Church until the following January and then he held services in his own home, saying in his last report: "With God's help I shall continue to do so until the Church is reopened for public worship." He died on the 4th of September, 1876, and was buried in the churchyard, Bishop Davis officiating. The Rev. Mr. Motte, coming over from Cheraw, succeeded Mr. Moore in 1877, holding services on fifth Sundays. Next followed a young minister, Rev. Edwin Carel Steele, who married Miss Mary Ashly of the parish. He accepted a call to Orangeburg in June, 1884, and after a very brief ministry there, he died in this parish on March 5, 1855 and was buried at Christ Church. Mr. Motte resumed charge and served until 1888 when the Rev. W. A. Guerry (later Bishop) assumed charge, serving until he went in 1893 to be chaplain of the University of the South, Sewanee. Then came another brilliant clergyman, the Rev. Robert W. Barnwell, for two years. Next in succession services were supplied by the Rev. W. H. Barnwell and the Rev. J. M. Magruder. The Rev. R. W. Barnwell returned to serve the Church again from 1897 to 1901. The Rev. Harold Thomas assumed charge in 1901, holding services once a month until 1905 when the Rev. Edward Callender succeeded for two years; under him was established Christ Church Guild which for many years rendered much service for the community and especially for the Children's Home in York. The officers of the guild were Mrs. Eli Gregg, president, Mrs. J. W. Wallace, vice-president, and Mrs. Robert Rogers, secretary and treasurer. The Rev. Harold Thomas returning to the diocese from Wilmington reassumed charge in 1907. The Rev. Henry Cooke Salmond was Mr. Thomas' assistant in this Church and held the services from 1909 to 1913. Mr. Thomas thereafter held services once a month. At this time he also conducted St. James' mission, Union Chapel, Back Swamp. The Rev. H. D. Bull assisted 1915-16. Mr. Thomas resigned June 1 1917, going to St. Luke's, Charleston. The Rev. Albert S. Thomas from time to time supplied services for Christ Church.

The Rev. W. S. Poynor took charge March 1, 1918, holding a monthly service, having returned to the diocese from Alabama. Soon, however, some of the families of Christ Church moving into Florence, services were discontinued. In 1927 a yearly homecoming service was inaugurated. In 1931 a mission Sunday School was established by Mr. Poynor continuing three years until the need no longer existed. In the winter of 1933 the Church was repaired and reopened for service. In 1934 the old Christ Church Guild reorganized itself as the Alice Gregg Chapter of the Woman's Auxiliary of St. John's Church, Florence. Thus did the parish honor the noted missionary who for so many years rendered brilliant and sacrificial service to our Lord in China, of whom not only her parish but her diocese is very proud. Under the leadership of Mr. Poynor with the help of Messrs. James Clark, Charles Edward Gregg, J. W. Howard and Chisolm Gregg a new roof was put on the Church and other repairs made. During the time when the Church was closed, the Bible was stolen and the communion silver lost. A beautiful chalice and paten were given in 1946 by Misses Mary and Emma Bacot and the three brothers of Macon Rogers, in his memory. He was lost on the ship *Juno*. This silver with several other gifts were consecrated by Mr. Poynor just before he left for Alabama at a service June 15, 1946. Mr. and Mrs. Poynor at the time were presented with a plate by Christ Church. In November, 1948, largely through the efforts of Miss Bessie Gregg, a meeting of those interested was held with Bishop Carruthers and it was planned that services be held twice a month by the Rev. L. A. Haskell. In January, 1950, the Bishop reorganized Christ Church into a mission as it is today: the Rev. L. A. Haskell, priest-in-charge, Thomas Ashley Gregg, warden, and R. M. Rogers, treasurer.

ST. MATTHEW'S PARISH, FORT MOTTE
Established 1768
(See Dalcho, p. 332)

Following Dalcho's account we note that the parish Church, built in 1767 at Half-way Swamp on the road to McCord's Ferry, had been twice moved; once in 1800 six miles, and again in 1815 when it was reerected in reduced size. This was a time of revival in the parish. In the absence of a rector lay reading was provided, and then in 1819 after a long vacancy, a rector was secured, and the parsonage repaired. Col. Edward Richardson was sent to the Convention, and Convention dues were paid. Bishop Bowen in his annual address referring to the new Church (Journal, 1820), says, "The Parish Church of St. Matthew's Parish recently erected on land given by Col. Heatly for that purpose in lieu of the original Parish Church, which had become inconvenient on account of its remoteness from them, for most of the present inhabitants to attend, was consecrated by request of the vestry, by the designation of St. Matthew's Church, St. Matthew's Parish." This was November 21, 1819. The vestry was reduced from seven to five with the two wardens in 1820. These for this year were W. S. Thomson and J. M. Caldwell; the vestrymen, A. Heatly, William Caldwell, James Stuart, W. J. Myddleton, E. Richardson. The Rev. Francis P. Delevaux was rector from 1819 to 1824; the Rev. M. I. Motte briefly in 1827; then the Rev. W. S. Wilson, 1830 until 1834. On June 13, 1830, the vestry met at Totness and took a collection to build a place of worship in that village. It was agreed with Col. Edward Richardson to build the house for the $300.00 raised at that time. The vestry accepted the building from Col. Richardson on July 7, "finished according to contract." They proceeded immediately to "number the benches & draw for seats." Some seats were set apart for the public. Four days later the vestry walked in procession to the new building which was then "dedicated by the rector, the Rev. W. S. Wilson, and on October 4th following it was consecrated as 'Totness Chapel, St. Matthew's Parish.'" It was quick work. In 1831, a parsonage was built at the summer residence and a bell given for the chapel by Mrs. Ann Lovell in 1833. Mr. Wilson died in 1834, and was succeeded by Rev. Richard Johnson, a deacon, in 1835. He became priest in 1837, the Rev. P. J. Shand came for communion services from the time of Mr. Wilson's death until Mr.

Johnson's ordination to the priesthood, as also the Rev. N. B. Screven from Wateree. On one of his trips from Columbia Mr. Shand lost his horse. A subscription was immediately taken to replace it. The amount $111.00 being tendered to Mr. Shand, he refused it "in a very feeling manner." However, "said amount was vested for the good of Mr. Shand." Mr. Johnson who became rector in 1836 endeavored to re-establish services at the old parish chapel. In 1837 he reports services at St. Matthew's Church 14 Sundays, at the old chapel three Sundays, and at Totness Chapel 20 Sundays. At this time the rector had an organized work among the Negroes. The death of Col. Edward Richardson in 1841 was a great loss to the parish because of his interest and generous benefactions. The rector reports that deaths and removals had reduced the membership—in 1834 he reports "numbers few but wealth great." Mr. Johnson was succeeded by the Rev. R. D. Shindler in 1846. In this year the chapel at Totness was enlarged to accommodate more Negroes. Mr. Shindler resigned December 31, 1847, and there was no rector until Rev. Benjamin Johnson succeeded in 1850. In 1852-53 a new winter Church was built in Gothic style 42 by 26 feet. At this time a large work was done among the Negroes in the parish, notwithstanding a strong "Baptist influence." There was a place of worship called Hampden Chapel five miles from the parish Church—at one time Bishop Davis confirmed 92 Negroes. Thus, he remarked, was shown what could be done by the Church for this race. Mr. Johnson's successful work ended with his resignation at the end of the year 1853. He was succeeded for five months by the Rev. J. J. Sams. Then followed a long period of stagnation without a rector when the large colored work mostly evaporated. The Rev. J. S. Hanckel, professor at the seminary in Camden came in 1861 and supplied for a couple of years, and then Rev. Joseph R. Walker, rector of St. Helena's, Beaufort, until the end of the war. He regretted that there was not enough room for the Negroes in the church. Rev. Stiles Mellichamp became rector in October, 1866. He refers to the poverty of the people who had been so opulent as due not only to the war but to an unprecedented drought. He came to live in the parish in 1870, having lived previously in Orangeburg. He was the last rector to live within the limits of the parish until 1953. He died in the parsonage October 23, 1872, and was succeeded on the following Easter Day by the Rev. B. B. Sams, who continued until 1875 when the Rev. William H. Johnson became rector, for part of 1875 and 1876, holding services mostly only once a month but lay reading was continued regularly. In 1875, the wardens were W. C. Hane and A. D. Goodwyn, and the vestrymen, J. K. Hane, W. H. Bryan, C. T. Goodwyn, A. E. Darby, C. A. Darby, and D. Zimmerman.

The Church was vacant for about two years and then the Rev. J. H. Tillinghast, residing at Eastover, took charge, giving one service a month from January 1, 1879. The next year the Church was repaired, and then from August, 1882, until May, 1885, the Rev. Thomas B. Clarkson had charge. Again there was a long period without a rector when clergymen of the Columbia Convocation supplied services from time to time. The Rev. A. R. Mitchell, one of these, reports a Sunday School in operation and the organization of St. Agnes' Guild. The Rev. J. B. Williams was then in charge briefly in 1892. At this time the chancel was recessed and a robing room added, and a new altar and lectern were installed, and the Church repainted. Then another discouraging vacancy occurred until the Rev. H. T. Gregory came in 1894 for two years.

In 1897, the Rev. W. N. Tillinghast, son of the former rector, assumed charge. He recounts a flourishing revival in the Church with the installation of a new organ and painting of the Church. A branch of the Woman's Auxiliary was organized in 1901 and a new carpet put down. The Rev. John Carl Jagar succeeded in 1903 for only about a year, and then the Rev. Tracy T. Walsh had charge for two years, then the Rev. Harold Thomas for about two years until 1906. The Rev. Wilmot S. Holmes was rector from August, 1907, until November, 1914. Mr. Holmes often held services in the village of Fort Motte. Then for two years the Rev. F. N. Skinner was rector, followed by Rev. John London in 1916 until September, 1918. The Rev. Richard L. Merryman had charge from 1920 to 1922. These "two years" rectorships often with intervening vacancies were not calculated to encourage growth and development, but the faithful would never say die. Another short rectorate followed, the Rev. Ilbert de Lacy Brayshaw, 1923 to August, 1924, and then Rev. Albert S. Cooper from 1926 until 1927. He was succeeded on February 1st, 1928, by the Rev. Edgar C. Burnz who resigned February, 1933, when he was at once succeeded by the Rev. Roderick H. Jackson who continued in charge until the fall of 1940 when he was succeeded by the Rev. Thomas S. Tisdale. The faithful officers of the Church for these years were, wardens, A. S. Trezevant and G. W. Willard, and treasurer, Mrs. S. F. Reid.

The Rev. Kenneth Donald took charge of this Church in 1954. A parish house has just been built. In 1955 St. Matthew's was pronounced "Rural Church of the Year in S. C." with award of $300.00, Sears-Roebuck Foundation; and "runner up" for "Rural Church of the South", with award of $200.00, Emory University. After two and a half years Mr. Donald resigned going to Black Mountain, N. C. During this period the budget of this parish increased from $1,200.00 to $4,200.00.

PRINCE GEORGE, WINYAH, GEORGETOWN
Established 1721
(See Dalcho, p. 303)

After being badly burned in the Revolution, this Church had been repaired and used, but not until about 1820 was it fully restored with galleries and steeple. Dalcho states at this time Prince George was "flourishing both in its spiritual and temporal concerns." An evidence of this was the adoption of an ambitious plan to endow the Church. A considerable fund was raised and the Convention of the diocese recommended the plan for all parishes in the diocese. This prosperity was due largely, no doubt, to the able line of rectors the parish had enjoyed; e. g., the eloquent Thomas Jones in 1787, and his successors, not the least of whom was the Rev. Maurice Harvey Lance (1815-27). Mr. Lance was the first minister prepared under the tutelage of the Society for the Advancement of Christianity in South Carolina. While studying at the South Carolina College, he had assisted in the founding of Trinity Church, Columbia, acting as lay reader. Many prominent members of Prince George's have been numbered among his descendants.

In this Church on May 9, 1823, Bishop Bowen ordained deacon him who was to be the first Bishop of Florida, Francis Huger Rutledge. The rector reported about this time 70 communicants. The handsome steeple and chancel were added to the Church in 1824, the architect being Major Warren. The vestry at this time was composed of Meredith Hughes and John Bell, wardens, with James Brown, John Hayes, Anthony White, and R. Smith as vestrymen. The Rev. P. T. Keith became assistant minister in 1826. For five months in the year (May-October), the services were held on North Island. Services were performed on all "fasts and festivals." A notable event on November 16, 1828, was the baptism of Anthony Toomer Porter, who was to become a distinguished priest and great benefactor of many young people in the state through the founding of the Porter Military Academy. His remains lie in the churchyard of Prince George's. There is a mural tablet in memory of his father, John Porter, in the Church.

Mr. Keith became rector in 1829, continuing until 1840. A falling off of the population in this section about 1834 led to a marked decrease in the congregation and to some financial embarrassment, leading even to a report by the rector "that the building may be sold." In 1840, Mr. Keith went as assistant to St. Michael's and the Rev. Robert Theus Howard became rector December 10 of this year. He was active in ministering to the Negroes, but states that many had gone to the Methodist and Baptist. The rector held services also at this time in the "pineland" near the Pee Dee in a temporary building built for the purpose, probably at Plantersville. In 1848 the parish suffered the loss of a great benefactor, Francis Withers. There is a tablet to his memory in the Church. The vestry for this years was: wardens, E. B. Rothmahler, J. J. Dickinson; vestrymen, J. G. Henning, M. H. Lance, J. Harleston Read, D. L. McKay, Dr. W. R. T. Prior, Edward Thomas, and B. H. Wilson. A new Mohler organ was installed in the Church in 1850 at a cost of $1,500.00. The next year the rector rejoiced in a "pineland rectory" built by the vestry, enabling him to have services in the parish Church the year round.

All through these years the sickliness of Georgetown was a great handicap to the work of the Church. Nevertheless, Mr. Howard's ministry at this time seems to have been quite an active one —there were gifts for the American Bible Society, and for the yellow fever sufferers in Charleston and in Virginia; $200.00 for the "Church Home"; services for the slaves on Mrs. S. C. Ward's and the adjoining plantations, as well as in the parish Church on Wednesday evening; also, services on Wednesday afternoons, and on fasts and feasts as well as on Sundays. In 1858 a parsonage was bought for $2,900.00, and in 1860 the Church was elaborately "improved." The vestry of 1863 was: wardens, J. R. Ford and A. J. Shaw; vestrymen, J. G. Henning, Dr. F. S. Parker, J. F. Pyatt, Dr. A. F. Forster, Dr. W. R. T. Prior, Rev. H. M. Lance. In February, 1863, Mr. Howard made this report: "Owing to the disturbed state of the country, the congregation has been scattered for more than a year. I have no report to make on account of the Church books having been removed to a place of safety [Cheraw] at a distance from the parish." However, he reports the next year, May, 1864, that services had been held regularly the preceding year. Mr. Howard ended his useful ministry of a quarter-century in 1865, with the congregation depleted by the war. The Rev. R. S. Trapier supplied services during the war. Rev. Alexander Glennie, resigning All Saints', accepted the rectorship in May, 1866. The Bishop, on confirming twenty-three persons on May 2, 1866, remarked that the parish then exhibited an "unusual appearance of animation and ability . . . having recovered from their recent trials," in contrast, we may say, to the prostration of the next neighbor, All Saints'.

In 1871 furnishings taken from the chancel in the war were replaced, the altar being enlarged. In 1874, through the agency of Mr. William St. Julian Mazyck, the Church was given the bell and clock, and later stained glass for the chancel from St. Mary's Chapel at Hagley on the Waccamaw. This probably was the bell later given to Grace Church, Ridge Spring, an inscription on which connects it with All Saints' parish. Also to this parish was given from St. Mary's a "gold" chalice (really gilt).

By the will of Miss Hannah Trapier, $300.00 was left for the usual chancel tablets. Proving insufficient for this, the money was later used to build the north wall of the churchyard. In 1879, a handsome rosewood communion table was installed in the Church, the gift of one of the families of the congregation. The year following, the vestry placed a window in memory of A. M. Forster, beloved chairman of the vestry. The Rev. Alexander Glennie died on All Saints' Day, 1880, and was buried in All Saints' churchyard on the Waccamaw. His entire ministry of forty-eight years was spent in the two parishes—1832-1866 in All Saints' and 1866-1880 in Prince George. He was distinguished especially for his great success in ministering to the Negroes on the Waccamaw (see All Saints'). He preferred to continue this work there rather than go as Bishop of Cape Palmas (Liberia) to which he was called. The Rev. Benjamin Allston took temporary charge January 1, 1881, serving until Rev. James Walter Keeble became rector later in the year. He went to West Virginia the next year and Mr. Allston became rector, 1883. While rector, he opened a mission the next year at a place twenty miles from Georgetown called Harper's Cross Roads. He resigned the rectorship January 1, 1886. Mr. L. F. Walker, lay reader, officiated until the coming of the Rev. Stewart McQueen from Alabama to be rector in 1887. As of July 1, 1891, at the suggestion of the rector, this parish abandoned the old pew rent system adopting, and that successfully, a voluntary subscription plan. This had been proposed by Dr. T. P. Bailey in 1877. Four stained glass windows of geometric design were installed at this time. Windows also were placed in memory of Mrs. Anne Elizabeth Read, Mrs. Anna Jane Munnerlyn, and Mrs. Sarah Hazzard Waldo—this last given by Col. Alexander Chisolm of New York, who also gave the brass cross on the altar.

Mr. McQueen left in 1892, going to North Carolina, being succeeded by Rev. John B. Williams (1892-98). In 1894 the parish received a legacy of $1,000.00 from Miss S. E. Carr and $3,000.00 from Mrs. Sarah Laura Lance, both for parish support. Mr. Williams resigned in 1898. He was succeeded in February, 1899, by Rev. George Harbough Johnston, D.D., who came from the diocese of Washington. The composition of the vestry at this time was: wardens, B. A. Munnerlyn and S. M. Ward; vestrymen, J. H. Reed, W. P. Smith, J. S. Pyatt, W. A. James, W. E. Sparkman, T. W. Allston, and T. P. Bailey. The deputies to the Convention were C. P. Allston, Walter Hazard, M. H. Tilghman, and F. B. Gardner. Under Dr. Johnson, a plan was inaugurated to build a parish house and a fund of $2,000.00 was raised, largely by the activity of Mrs. H. H. Gardner, and set aside for this purpose—realized some twenty-odd years later. Dr. Johnston resigned October, 1910, becoming *rector emeritus*. He was succeeded by the Rev. Percy J. Robottom in February, 1911, whose active ministry continued until 1916. Suffrage of women communicants was adopted in 1913. In 1914 the Church received a complete renovation. In the preceding twenty-five years, the parish had shown a marked increase in membership. In 1894 it was 103; in 1916, 227. The location of a large sawmill at Georgetown had caused a large increase in the population. Later the mill closed and the trend was reversed, but a few years later the great paper mill brought a still larger increase.

The Rev. John S. Lightbourn of Richmond became rector in June, 1916. Dr. Johnston continued as *rector emeritus* until his death, September, 1918. In 1917 the flag which had flown over the armory of the Headquarters Company of the Second S. C. Regiment in Georgetown was presented to the Church through Col. Holmes B. Springs.

December 1-4, 1921, the parish celebrated its bi-centennial under the leadership of Mr. Lightbourn. This great occasion was marked by a historical address by Walter Hazard, Esq., on Friday evening the 1st; a Quiet Hour by Bishop Guerry Saturday evening; a great service on the Lord's Day, with a sermon by the Bishop; an address to the young people by the Rev. A. R. Mitchell; a sermon by a former rector, the Rev. Stewart McQueen in the evening. The Rev. J. E. H. Galbraith also assisted in the services. Memorials Consecrated on the occasion were two brass Eucharistic candlesticks, given by the Altar Guild in memory of the late rector and *rector emeritus*, Dr. Johnson; a brass ewer by the D. A. R. in memory of the soldiers of the Revolution. Also, the Ladies' Aid Association restored the clock in the tower of the Church, which had been silent for thirty years. The wardens at this time were S. M. Ward and J. I. Hazard; the secretary and treasurer, H. W. Frazer; and the lay reader, Walter Hazard. The Prince George branch of the Woman's Auxiliary became a very active organization in the parish at this time, and has since continued to be so. Mr. Lightbourn died April 3, 1924, after eight years of valuable service, much beloved by the congregation. On Easter Day, 1930, a handsome lectern was dedicated to the memory of Mr. Lightbourn, given by the ladies of the Altar Guild. The Rev. Henry DeSaussure Bull, returning to the diocese after a period in Western North Carolina, became rector in 1924, beginning an active ministry of twenty-nine years.

Early in 1926, there was placed in the vestibule of the Church a greatly valued memorial gift from the Society for the Propagation of the Gospel in Foreign Ports, which fostered Prince George in colonial days—an alms box with a pelican on it, symbol of the Atonement. A fine parish house was built in 1926. Steps had been taken to this end some time before, and a lot purchased in the rear of the Church. Under a building committee headed by Mr. J. I. Hazard and with a plan by Simons and Lapham, the building was constructed by Cheves and Oliver of Charleston. Being of Georgian-Colonial architecture, it is in keeping in style with the Church.

Mr. Bull, in 1930, organized a Social Service Commission in the parish composed of representatives of the various parish organizations. The coming of the Southern Kraft Corporation about 1936 caused now a large increase in population and increased Church work, especially in the Church school. A Layman's League was formed. The rector's work extended much beyond the town including All Saints, Prince Frederick's, and St. Peter's-in-the-Pineland. For many years, Mr. Bull employed candidates for holy orders to assist him in his large field of work. Among these were W. L. Hargrave, A. B. Mitchell, Jr., T. S. Tisdale, D. N. Peeples, D. M. Hobart, W. R. Haynsworth, W. M. Moore, Jr., etc. After a rectorship of twenty-nine years, Dr. Bull resigned July 1, 1953, to become rector of Holy Apostles, Barnwell. His departure was greatly lamented in this parish and the neighboring parishes to which he had given long and faithful service. He had received the degree of D.D. from the University of the South. He was succeeded in November by the Rev. A. Nelson Daunt. The vestry now was: wardens, J. R. Parker and W. L. Foster; vestrymen, H. C. Miller, J. T. Maynard, C. Provost, R. L. Walker, E. H. Dean, J. B. Morrison and G. P. Lachicotte.

The Convention of the diocese has met in this parish five times (1902, 1910, 1928, 1939 and 1950) to date. The recent installation (1955) of two chandelier lights by the Woman's Auxiliary has enhanced the beauty of the Church.

ST. CYPRIAN'S MISSION, GEORGETOWN
(See Archdeaconry, end this Section)

ASCENSION CHURCH, GILLISONVILLE
Established 1840

The first record we have of Episcopal services at Gillisonville is in 1830 when the Rev. Thomas J. Young reports five services there. He held such services for several years and probably they were held occasionally in after years. But it was not until August, 1847, that a Church with the name, Ascension Church, was organized at this time at Colleton "Court House Village", about 14 miles northward from Grahamville. It was with the consent of the Church of the Holy Trinity as it was located within the confines of that parish. The wardens and vestrymen were: W. E. Martin, J. H. Gregorie, Jos. V. Morrison, Samuel Laurence, and J. E. Moore Mitchell. The Rev. Mr. Benjamin was elected rector. Having only a dilapidated building known as the "Free Church", steps were taken immediately for the building of a Church. An appeal to the diocese secured assistance especially from St. Peter's, Charleston, Bluffton, Grahamville, Beaufort, and Edisto, and a Church was promptly built. It was Consecrated by Bishop Gadsden June 11, 1848, this being Whitsunday and the feast of St. Barnabas. The *Gospel Messenger*, July, 1848, thus describes: "The church presents to the eye a remarkably agreeable object, being well proportioned, with gothic-resembling doors, sashes, and blinds, a modest steeple with a fine-toned bell, an open fence enclosure. The pews are sufficiently wide for kneeling; the chancel separation is neatly carved work; the desk and pulpit of uniform height, and quite suitable for the speaker and the hearer. The site, deeded by William E. Martin, Esq., is elevated, gently sloping from a lake in which the Church grounds and surrounding forest and shrubs are reflected. It is 45 feet long, 25 wide, 18 high, and understood to have cost $1,800.00. A gallery at one end will seat about fifty colored persons for whose accommodation it was put up. The lower floor would contain about 150 persons." Much attention was given to the work among colored people. Many of the leading families leaving the parish, Mr. Johnson resigned in May, 1849. There was no regular minister until Rev. John Sellwood, employed chiefly to minister to the poor near Grahamville, held services in 1853 but found almost no congregation. There seems to have been a suspension of all Church work here for many years. The Church was sold to the Baptists in 1872. However this event was coeval with renewal of services here by the Rev. E. E. Bellinger in connection with his charge of Grahamville. He continued occasional services in Gillisonville at least until 1878; one among the manifold places he served.

ST. JAMES' PARISH, GOOSE CREEK
Established 1706
(See Dalcho, p. 263)

Although this old parish, one of the original ten, has been practically dormant for nearly 150 years through the removal of population, its most dignified and interesting Church stands today in its original form bearing a steadfast witness to Jesus Christ, "the same, yesterday, today, and forever". It was built 1714-19, and is the oldest Church building in South Carolina. Perhaps we should add that it is possible that a portion of the walls of St. Andrew's on the west side of the Ashley is older. But not only is this our oldest Church, but on or near its site was its forerunner, a chapel built several years earlier than this permanent Church. Judge Smith, a reliable historian, thinks it was built as early as 1680, about as old as the first St. Philip's—years older than the first Pompion Hill chapel which Dalcho erroneously calls the oldest Anglican Church outside of Charleston. Dalcho tells us that St. James', Goose Creek, was the only country Church not profaned by the British in the Revolutionary War, attributed to the fact that the Royal Arms were suffered to remain over the altar. Rev. Milwood Pogson, one of

Bishop Smith's ordinands, was rector from 1796 to 1806, succeeded by the Rev. John Thomson (also ordained by Bishop Smith). He resigned and went to England in 1808.

Because of the unhealthiness of the parish, services were held only from November to June. Peter Smith was for many years deputy to the diocesan Convention; Barnard E. Bee was in 1824. The Rev. C. E. Gadsden held services during the vacancy of the rectorship. This was reassumed in 1821 by Rev. Milwood Pogson for two years. He was followed by the Rev. C. P. Elliott in 1826, who served for about one year. There was a school house located about a mile from the Church, built, it is supposed, in 1802. It was sold in 1828 and later used as a dwelling. From this time to the present day, St. James' has been practically a dormant Church with no regular rector, although a vestry has continued to function in the care of the old Church and its funds, and in the provision for occasional services. In 1825, the Rev. C. P. Elliott, deacon, was missionary and the next year rector. He reported only four or five communicants, seven or eight families. However, though officially the numbers were small, Mr. Elliott held services at first every other Sunday and then in 1826 every Sunday until he resigned in March of this year, going to Cheraw. Maj. Edward H. Edwards was deputy in 1832. In 1828, the vestry, by means of the Ludlam Fund, established two schools, one at Wassamasaw Chapel in the upper part of the parish and one at Groomsville in the lower part, the two masters each to receive $300.00 per year. The Church, in 1844, had fallen into almost a ruin, the roof had spread and the walls were cracked; the vestry, with a gift from St. Michael's Church, had the Church fully restored, including the Royal Arms over the pulpit and other decorations. The Church was replastered, the flooring relaid, the pews were cut down, the lower parts having rotted away. The forest which had encroached upon the Church was cut back. The completion of these repairs was celebrated by the Consecration of the Church, which had not been done, of course, in colonial days; except as far as a vestry could by very solemn and appropriate resolution adopted on the completion of the Church in 1719. But now the Church on April 17, 1845, received its first formal Consecration by Bishop Gadsden. Wardens at this time were Thomas Dixon and W. W. Ancrum; vestrymen, Thomas Gadsden, M. I. Keith, G. W. Egleston, Samuel Burger, John Parker, Dr. H. R. Frost, and Dr. Eli Geddings.

Now in December, 1845, after a long period of suspension, regular services of a missionary character were begun in St. James', conducted by the Rev. Philip Gadsden, rector of St. Paul's, Stono and Summerville, and later by the Rev. J. W. Taylor. These services continued, more or less regularly, for many years. Prof. Francis L. Holmes, who lived at Ingleside in the neighborhood of the Church, took great interest in its care. In 1860, the school fund amounted to $14,531.00. An interesting episode in this history occurred in 1864. Being shelled out of St. Stephen's, Anson Street, on January 17, 1864, at the suggestion of a member of St. James' and with the Bishop's approval, the Rev. Henry L. Phillips held services in the parish from March 13 to May 1st of this year—seven services in the Church, seven on the plantations for Negroes, baptized 23 colored, and celebrated the Holy Communion twice. He thought the field ripe for work, but his services, as the end of the war came on, did not last long. The Church now remained closed for many years. Large numbers of people visited the Church every year, being of great historic interest, as they do today.

Mr. F. S. Holmes, chairman of the vestry, in 1876 reported repairs on the Church and plans to begin services. The Church was reopened for services January 2, 1876, by the Rev. J. G. Drayton, rector of St. Andrew's Parish, every other Sunday during this and the following winter. Then again there were no regular services. In 1882, some of the fund ($3,379.00) which seemingly had been lost through a loan was recovered through the acquiring and sale of lands in Texas to the amount of $5,000.00. The vestry at this time was as follows: wardens, F. L. Parker, M.D. and James S. Mitchell; vestrymen, James S. Gantt, R. Rivers Lawton, Samuel G. Stoney, and J. T. Pendarvis. The Church was badly damaged by the earthquake of August 31, 1886. The west gable and part of the east gable fell out and the walls were cracked; ornaments and the Royal Arms over the altar were injured. The vestry at once raised funds and a complete recovery was effected in due time. The window shutters and doors were now sheathed with iron, and a slate roof, the gift of two English gentlemen residing in Charleston were added, rendering the Church fireproof. The vestry were always zealous in striving to keep the old Church in repair and to administer according to the trust the Ludlam school fund for the benefit of residents of the parish. The vestry in 1909 was composed of Dr. F. L. Parker and S. Porcher Stoney, wardens; vestrymen, Samuel Gaillard Stoney, Edwin Parsons, Joseph Ioor Waring, and Francis William Holmes. A custom was now adopted by the vestry to hold an annual service in the old Church on the first Sunday after Easter; some of those occasions were made notable by special events. Often in the earlier days, a special train would be run out to Otranto to accommodate people from the city. An interesting service took place on April 12, 1896, when the Rev. Robert Wilson, D.D., made a historical address and a tablet was dedicated, placed by the vestry on the north wall of the Church, with this inscription:

St. James', Goose Creek
Established by Act of the Assembly
November 30, 1706
Organized April 14, 1707
Present Church Built About 1713
Church Consecrated April 17, 1845

On the occasion of the annual service on April 17, 1904, a tablet was unveiled commemorating the coming of the Rev. Samuel Thomas, the first S. P. G. missionary to South Carolina, who labored at Goose Creek, when an address was delivered by Col. John Peyre Thomas, a descendant. Another notable service was conducted on April 22, 1906, by Bishop Capers commemorating the 200th anniversary of the Act establishing this and others of the first parishes in South Carolina. A tablet was then unveiled in memory of the Rev. Richard Ludlam, second rector and founder of the Ludlam Fund. After this service, Judge H. A. M. Smith made a valuable address on the early history of the parish. At the service in April, 1913, when Bishop Guerry preached, an offering was taken for a piece of silver for the chapel to be built at the Navy Yard, it being within the confines of this old parish. These annual services are still held on the Sunday after Easter. The old Church is carefully preserved, being repaired from time to time. A record of memorials (including the Ralph Izard Hatchment, said to be one of only two in America) in the Church, with a full description of it, will be found in "St. James' Church", Joseph Ioor Waring, Daggett Printing Company, Charleston, S. C., 1909.

Note: The Rev. Robert Wilson writing in 1922 derives the word "Goose Creek" from "Goes Creek", which he found in the records of the Probate Court, a transfer of land on a creek called "Goes Creek"—goes in Holland would be pronounced goose.

St. James' Goose Creek Chapel: Only a few gravestones are all that is left of Goose Creek Chapel, three or four miles north of the parish Church, 200 yards east of the highway. Some of the inscriptions on these stones will be found transcribed in the S. C. Historical and Genealogical Magazine, January 1912, page 67, but not all; another is Elizabeth (*nee* Thomas) Broun, wife of Dr. Broun and granddaughter of the Rev. Samuel Thomas, the S. P. G. Missionary.

HOLY TRINITY, GRAHAMVILLE
Established 1835

In 1835 the congregation of the "Church of the Holy Trinity" being a part of St. Luke's parish, on its application, was separated and organized as itself a congregation under this title. (See St. Luke's Parish *in loco.*) It was in Grahamville in this Church that the great Beaufort Revival really began under Mr. Young. On its invitation the Rev. Thomas John Young became its first rector, resigning, however, the next year, being succeeded by Rev. Thomas C. Dupont, November, 1836, until 1839. At this time a large work was done among the Negroes. The Rev. E. B. Kellogg took charge May, 1841, but for only about one year, the Rev. Edward Reed becoming rector in May, 1843. Dr. Thomas E. Scriven represented the parish in Convention this year, the year before Albert Rhett and F. J. McCarthey. In 1846 the Church was enlarged to nearly twice its capacity. After this a new parsonage was erected. The rector being absent in the summer at St. John's-in-the-Wilderness, N. C., the Rev. E. T. Walker held the services. Rev. B. Johnson also supplied in 1847—the rector's health was bad. He resigned December, 1847. The Rev. J. Howard Smith followed, August 1, 1848, coming from Virginia. He resigned in 1850, going to Connecticut. Through the liberality of Mr. James Bolan the Church was painted at this time. This great benefactor of Holy Trinity is buried at Holy Apostles, Barnwell. The Rev. J. H. Elliott became rector the next year and until 1853. The Rev. John Sellwood succeeded, coming from Illinois to do missionary work in St. Luke's parish and supply the new Church in Gillisonville. He supplied Holy Trinity in 1853 and on January 1, 1854 became rector, being assisted by his younger brother, J. R. W. Sellwood, candidate for deacon's orders.

In 1856 there came an appeal from Bishop Scott of Oregon for missionaries. Both Sellwoods volunteered. Much interest was stirred in the diocese. A great missionary service was held in Grace Church, Charleston. After ordination to the diaconate of the younger Sellwood, on April 3, 1856, the two set out on their long journey to Oregon, speeded by the prayers and some funds of the Church, not knowing what to befall them. En route at Aspinwall, Panama, they were set upon by brigands who stole all their money. The elder brother, a single man and one of his brother's children were badly beaten and bruised. Later they went on their way and labored in Oregon. The Church saw to the restoration of the pecuniary losses. The Rev. Arthur Wigfall was the next rector with the Rev. J. V. Welch, missionary to the colored people. The colored mission under the Rev. J. V. Welch was called St. Luke's, Grahamville. During the rectorship of Mr. Wigfall the Church was taken down and a new and more commodious one of Gothic design built on the same lot. It was in a grove of oaks set out by the ladies of the congregation. The Church was consecrated by Bishop Davis on July 10, 1859. In 1860 two chapels for Negroes were built near Grahamville, one named Bethel by Mr. James Bolan and one by Mr. John E. Fripp on the Oketee. Mr. Welch in 1861 reported 249 services in the various chapels and plantations. Bethel Chapel near Grahamville was consecrated on the afternoon of July 24, 1861. During the war there was a hospital for soldiers at Grahamville, also at McPhersonville.

Mr. Wigfall reported in 1864 that the war had broken up his Sunday School and Bible class. Bishop Davis deplores his death in 1867. The Church escaped destruction in the war but with the loss of the organ, some furniture, and the parsonage. Most of the town was burned. The Rev. E. E. Bellinger took charge in 1868 together with other destitute churches on the coast. Mr. W. C. Howard acted as lay reader and often officiated at funerals in the absence of the rector with his numerous flocks. Mr. Bellinger in 1875 reports travelling 6,766 miles at an expense of $144.00, in Barnwell, Colleton, and Beaufort counties. He reported varying conditions, both warmth and coldness. In 1876 Mr. Bellinger received a total of $1,189.29 for his services in the whole field and of this the Advancement Society paid $600.00. The congregation was greatly afflicted in 1876 by the murder of Gen. J. W. Howard, for many years chairman of the vestry and deputy to the Convention of the diocese. These years witness the loss of large numbers of Negro members. The rector in 1871 reported that a large number had left for the Methodist Church following a leader of their own color who had been made a preacher. The building formerly occupied by the colored people was sold and the services held in the residence of Robert Ford. In 1879 with 14 families and 25 communicants, the parish paid $125.00 for the rector's salary. The Rev. B. B. Sams became rector in 1880. In this year Mrs. John H. Screven of Prince William's parish presented the Church with an organ. The chancel was remodeled in 1883.

Holy Trinity was represented in Convention by the following deputies in 1890: H. D. Burnet, Charles E. Bell, Joseph Glover, and B. W. Seabrook. A branch of the Woman's Auxiliary was organized in 1893. Mr. Sams resigned this charge April 1, 1894. The people suffered greatly by the storm of August, 1893. The Rev. J. M. Pringle was the next minister, 1896 until October, 1899, the Rev. J. B. Walker succeeding in 1901 until May, 1902. Then Rev. J. C. Waring took charge in 1903, serving until April, 1905. The Rev. J. S. Hartzell from April to August, 1905, then the Rev. Paul Trapier Prentiss in 1909. At this time Mr. H. D. Burnett was warden, D. H. Wall, secretary, and Joseph Glover, treasurer. The Rev. Dwight Cameron had charge in 1910 for a short time. The Rev. J. H. Woodward took charge in 1912 until 1915. The Rev. A. R. Mitchell, Archdeacon, became rector in 1916. He held some services in Ridgeland. These were rather uneventful years in the life of the Church. The Rev. R. M. Marshall became rector in 1921. In 1923, Holy Trinity receded from status of "parish" to that of "organized mission." The Rev. J. H. Woodward was again in charge in 1924-25, Mr. Marshall resuming charge in 1926 and continuing until January, 1944. The Rev. M. W. Lockhart, D.D., took charge April, 1944. The wardens at this time were J. C. Tison and E. S. Horry; secretary, H. H. Horry; treasurer, N. B. Bass. Dr. Lockhart died on February 20, 1946. The Rev. Robert E. Withers became rector in December, 1946. Electric lights were now installed in the Church, and in May following work was begun on a rectory. Mr. Withers resigned after two years, being the first resident rector in many years. The Rev. Edward Haynsworth followed in July, 1949. His coming was signalized by the acquiring of a new organ and the putting of a new roof on the Church. In 1950 the wardens of Holy Trinity were James C. Tison and Edward S. Horry; treasurer, Wiley McTeer. Improvements at this time were a new heating plant and the partitioning off of two rooms under the gallery at the entrance to the Church providing better for the Church school. In 1954 a new organ was dedicated to the memory of Mrs. J. C. (Mattie J.) Tison, for many years organist and devoted church worker.

CHURCH OF THE ASCENSION, HAGOOD
Established 1895

This Church possesses a valuable history prepared by Mr. N. G. and Miss Sarah Ellen Ellerbe. It is here used extensively.

In 1807, two and a half acres of land were acquired from William Sanders by Stock Hunter, James Bates, and Ashberry Silvester, in Sumter district on the road from Camden to Stateburg. These men called themselves *The Shiloh Burying Association.* They built on it a school house and a blacksmith shop, and later it became a burying ground, the oldest grave probably being that marked 1802, of Mrs. William E. Ellerbe. There are also the remains of an old brick mausoleum. The plot of ground for many years was known as *Shiloh.* Some four score years after this, Mr. William C. S. Ellerbe moving with his family from Camden to this vicinity, chose this as the site for the Church, and, with the help of others, began work on the building of a Church, the means being supplied mostly by himself. One of his sons, N. C. Ellerbe, sawed the logs. The plan of the Church, as well as the construction, was by an ex-slave, Kennedy Lewis. In the midst of the work of building, Mr. Ellerbe died. The Rev. James M. Stoney said at his funeral service, "Mr. Ellerbe will need no monument but this Church." His wife followed in two months. There was further discouragement; the Church, while being built, was seriously damaged by lightning and wind. Three years later, it caught fire and was saved by young Marius Sanders who climbed to the roof and put out the fire. By much sacrifice and effort, chiefly by the women, the Church was built. Among these women were Mesdames R. M. James, Theresa Scarborough, Emma Alston, T. P. Sanders, Mary Haile, C. W. Sanders, W. E. Ellerbe, W. M. Lenoir, F. O. Sanders, Jr., and the Misses Ellerbe. The appeals of Miss Ellen Ellerbe brought considerable help from the outside. Mrs. W. E. Young of Brooklyn, N. C. (*nee* Miss Gibbes of Charleston) gave generous assistance. John Reid of Camden made the Bishop's chair of an old pulpit given by Grace Church, Charleston, which also gave the altar rail. Mr. W. M. Byrd of Charleston sent a colored glass window from the Holy Cross, Sullivan's Island.

The first service in the Church was conducted by the Rev. James M. Stoney of Grace Church, Camden, on June 30, 1895. He continued to hold occasional services. The Church was consecrated with the name, the Church of the Ascension, by Bishop Capers, assisted by Mr. Stoney, on March 8, 1896. The Ascension was reported as a mission of the diocese, first as *unorganized,* then in 1900 as *organized,* with W. M. Lenoir as secretary and Miss Ellen Ellerbe, treasurer. A new organ was installed at this time. In 1901, T. P. Sanders was warden and Miss Florence Ellerbe, treasurer. Serving as lay readers in these early days were S. I. Gaillard, A. P. Gaillard, and I. L. Sanders. The first regular minister was the Rev. W. H. Barnwell, rector of Holy Cross, Stateburg, and St. Mark's. His first service was in May, 1896. The Sunday School was active from the beginning, Mr. S. I. Gaillard being the first superintendent. Matt Floyd was the sexton for some twenty years. The young men of the Church built an enclosing fence two years after the Church was erected. The organ was bought by the congregation in 1900. John Reid made the prayer desk, the lectern, and other furniture. Miss Florence Ellerbe gave the Eucharistic candlesticks. The altar was given by St. Luke's Hall, Sewanee, at the suggestion of the Rev. W. S. Stoney. Among the memorials in the Church are seven-branched candlesticks given by Miss Ellen Ellerbe in memory of her brothers, Robert and William Elliott Ellerbe. She gave also a silver communion service in memory of her sisters, Florence and Allan Ellerbe. The cross was given by the congregation in memory of Mr. and Mrs. William C. S. Ellerbe. Miss Helen Rembert gave the vases in memory of her parents. Mr. Barnwell, with failing health, retired after 21 years of service in 1917, leaving behind memories of "unfailing friendliness and love". The Rev. C. W. Boyd took charge in 1918. He organized the guild and strengthened the Woman's Auxiliary. The Church was admitted into union with the Convention on May 14, 1919, as a parish. At this time, the wardens were Dr. M. S. Kirk and W. A. Alston; and vestrymen, R. M. Hildebrand, T. C. Haile, W. A. Boykin, H. D. Boykin, and A. H. Sanders. The communicants now numbered 60. Mr. Boyd left after four years, being succeeded in 1922 by the Rev. William Shannon Stoney, son of him who held the first service. He was the first resident rector. Under his very active ministry, the Church was repaired, a Sunday School room was erected in the churchyard, and a handsome brick rectory built near the Church, on land recently purchased, at a cost of $7,638.60, of which over $6,000.00 was raised in the parish. Mr. Stoney left in May, 1925. There were now 75 communicants. The Rev. Moultrie Guerry took charge in September, 1925. The Church prospered under him. He engaged in much interdenominational work; especially noted was a men's club for the entire neighborhood. He served also as chaplain of the state prison farms near Hagood. At this time, the old neighborhood school house was bought and moved and rebuilt as a parish house at the Church. He left to be chaplain at Sewanee, December 31, 1928.

After an interim of several months, the Rev. George H. Harris became rector, having charge also of Stateburg and Bradford Springs. He continued as rector for ten years until May, 1939. During this period, the Church prospered; the Sunday School, the Y. P. S. L., the Woman's Auxiliary, and the Men's Club were active agencies. Of the last, Mr. Willis Cantey was president, Dr. M. S. Kirk, vice-president, and Mr. Charles Sanders, Jr., secretary-treasurer. Mr. Kennedy Dwight gave a processional cross made by himself. Rev. and Mrs. Moultrie Guerry gave (1932) candelabra to replace those lately stolen from the Church. In 1935, the interior of the Church was remodeled and redecorated, the walls being panelled in pine. In 1937, the C. C. Camp in the neighborhood planted 1,000 trees on the Church grounds. After an interregnum of some months, the Rev. Alfred Parker Chambliss became rector. At this time, W. A. Boykin and P. B. Brown were the wardens; secretary, Walter Sanders; treasurer, I. L. Sanders; and lay reader, R. H. Atkinson. Mr. Chambliss was succeeded by the Rev. C. M. Hobart in 1949. After several happy years, Mr. Hobart resigned October 1, 1952, on account of failing health. After 33 years the Rev. William Shannon Stoney returned to become rector again (1955) much to the satisfaction of the congregation. A new pulpit designed by Bishop Thomas was dedicated on February 12, 1956. It is in memory of Charles Wesson Sanders and his wife, Ida Lenoir Sanders, communicants of the Church.

ALL SAINTS' CHURCH, HAMPTON
Established 1951

The Rev. E. E. Bellinger held services here in 1880 but they were soon discontinued, the members having removed. Services were resumed in 1885 by Mr. Bellinger. The services at this time were held partly in the academy and private residences and partly in the Methodist Church, and continued until 1891 when, because of another exodus, services were again abandoned. In 1889 services were begun at Varnville by Mr. Bellinger, also at Coosaw. In 1894 this great missionary had to abandon all his missions except Allendale and Ellenton on account of blindness. The Rev. Milton Crum, recently having taken charge of Holy Communion, Allendale, finding prospects for a Church in Hampton, began services on December 9, 1951—twice a month in the Methodist Church. After a time Faith Chapel in Estill not being in use, and all parties consenting, it was decided to move this chapel to Hampton. In the early part of 1953 it was moved bodily without being taken down from Estill 15 miles to Hampton by the use of large trucks. By the first of April it was located on Jackson Street in Hampton. The newly organized mission was given the name of "All Saints." This was the name of the Episcopal Church at Blountsville near Yemassee and also the name of the Episcopal mission in Varnville some years ago. Mr. Crum planned at this time to have services in Hampton at 9 a. m. every Sunday. There are some 20 members of this Church. The move was made possible by the raising of $1,000.00 by the congregation, some help from others, and a loan from the diocese. A parish house was built in 1956. At this time the wardens were Messrs. Heyward Sauls and Earl F. Peeples.

ST. BARTHOLOMEW'S CHURCH, HARTSVILLE
Established 1902

In 1902, in response to the desires of a group of Episcopalians (Harts, Gillespies, Eglestons, Stewarts, Dargans) residing in this town, and after several parochial visits, the Rev. Albert S. Thomas, missionary in charge of St. Matthew's Church, Darlington, and residing there, began services. The first was held in the Knights of Pythias Hall, loaned for the purpose, on Friday night, June 27, 1902. Miss Sophie Aldrich of Columbia played the organ and Mrs. William Egleston led the singing. Mr. Thomas preached on the text, "I am not ashamed of the Gospel of Christ, for it is the power of God unto salvation to every one that believeth." The next service was held on the following Sunday morning, being St. Peter's Day, when the Communion was celebrated. This, and the future services until the Church was built seven years later, was held in the Methodist Church, whose kind hospitality the mission enjoyed for all these years.

A temporary mission organization was at once effected with the object of a permanent planting of the Church in the town with William Egleston, M.D. as warden and Robert Stewart, Jr., secretary and treasurer. St. Bartholomew was adopted as the name of the Church, to perpetuate the name of one of the old parishes of the diocese at the suggestion of J. I. Waring, registrar of the diocese. This organization was later made permanent by the appointment of the Bishop of the same officers. Very soon a Ladies' Guild was formed to raise funds to build a Church, notably $1,000-.00 in shares were subscribed by members in the local Building and Loan Association. The year following Major J. L. Coker "the father of Hartsville" donated the lot upon which the Church was subsequently built. In July, 1905, the Society for the Advancement of Christianity in South Carolina contributed $100.00, and in 1908 $500.00 was appropriated from the men's thank offering made at the General Convention of 1907, whereupon it was decided to proceed with the building of a Church. Mr. Thomas was succeeded by the Rev. H. H. Lumpkin in October, 1908. A year later the erection of the Church was begun after plans originally drawn by Mr. W. B. W. Howe of Spartanburg, son of the late Bishop, for Darlington but not used there. They were somewhat modified by Mr. Thomas.

The services which for many years were held only once a month on Monday nights were now held twice a month. St. Bartholomew's was admitted into union with the Convention as an organized mission in 1909. R. P. Gillespie and William Egleston, M.D., were the first deputies in 1910. The first service in the Church was on Monday night, June 6, 1910, the Rev. H. H. Lumpkin officiating with an address by the Rev. A. S. Thomas. The Church was Consecrated by Bishop Guerry on January 24, 1912. Many beautiful gifts had been installed in the Church by the time of the Consecration—a silver chalice and paten, an eagle lectern, Bishop's and priest's chairs, hymn board, and font, and then about the same time a pulpit. It is worthy of note that the wardens, Dr. William Egleston and R. P. Gillespie each continued to serve as such until their death, respectively in 1935 and 1950. Mr. Lumpkin was succeeded by the Rev. O. T. Porcher, June, 1912. A pipe organ was now installed symptomatic of the reputation for fine music acquired from the first by this Church. The mission was organized as a parish and admitted into union with the Convention as such on May 13, 1914. The year 1916 was notable: the chancel and vestry were extended, the Church being enlarged and beautified; a chancel window was installed as also a handsome altar and raredos, a credence shelf, a chancel rail, and choir stalls. Also there was added to the building a very unique and massive tower and vestibule. The Church had become now suggestive of an old English chapel. About this time Mr. Porcher conducted services at Auburn. He resigned in 1918; and then for a period the Rev. J. B. Walker of Sumter supplied services. The Rev. Randolph F. Blackford succeeded as rector in 1919, being the first resident rector. The Church was incorporated February 8, 1922. Rev. Mortimer Glover followed as rector, 1921-25. A rectory was built in 1921-22, and about the same time a Church school building was erected in the rear of the Church connected with the Church by a passageway to the vestry room. The Rev. H. L. Hoover succeeded Mr. Glover January 1, 1926, and continued as rector until his retirement, April, 1947. The Church doubled in membership during Mr. Hoover's rectorship. A pipe organ was installed in 1942. He was absent for fifteen months, 1940-43, as chaplain of the 30th Division.

The Church suffered a great loss through the death on March 23, 1935, of William Egleston, M.D., one of the founders of the Church and warden since the beginning as also benefactor in manifold ways. His services are commemorated in a tablet on the walls of the Church, placed in 1946. The Church is rich in memorial windows: Margaret S. Merritt (chancel), William Egleston, M.D., Craig C. Twitty, Lilian Singleton Coker, Mary Evans Twitty, Robert Stewart and his wife, Etta Howle Stewart, and Elizabeth W. Moore. There are many other memorials, including a clergy chair in memory of Mrs. William (Bonnie Aldrich) Egleston, who for fifty years loyally served this Church. The lot to the west of the Church was acquired in 1942 with a view to erecting a parish house. Mr. Hoover was succeeded by Rev. Edmund T. Small in 1947. The Church became self-supporting in 1950. Rev. Moultrie McIntosh became rector October, 1953, soon after the Church celebrated its fiftieth anniversary. At this time the wardens were F. E. Fitchett and J. E. Copenhaver, M.D.; secretary, E. M. Floyd; treasurer, J. L. Coker; lay reader, E. M. Gunn; Church school superintendent, B. D. Clarkson. On January 29, 1956, a handsome new parish house costing about $60,000.00 was dedicated by Bishop Carruthers. Mr. McIntosh resigned in the fall of this year, going to Oak Ridge, Tennessee.

GOOD SHEPHERD, HUGER
(See Wando)

ST. JAMES', JAMES ISLAND
Established 1730
(See Dalcho, p. 339)

The first Church, built at a very early date, was destroyed by a hurricane in 1730 but immediately rebuilt. In 1756, already unofficially so, the Church now was made a chapel of ease of St. Andrew's parish by Act of the Assembly. The second Church was destroyed in the Revolution. Another chapel, the third, was built soon after this war, but the Church about 1800 became dormant and remained so for some thirty years. In 1831, there was a revival of interest. The Church on the island was reorganized in March of this year. By an arrangement with the vestry of St. Andrew's parish, the Church terminated its status as a chapel of ease of that parish and itself became a distinct parish, taking the name of St. James' Church, James Island. The chapel, after repair, was consecrated on April 22, 1831, by Bishop Bowen, Messrs. Gadsden and Trapier assisting. The parish was incorporated and also admitted into Convention February 15, 1832, conformity being promised to the Constitution and canons of the diocese. Mr. T. H. S. Thayer was seated as delegate. The St. Andrew's vestry transferred by deed the chapel and the glebe belonging to it to St. James'. In 1884, St. Andrew's made a claim for the glebe lands which, after much correspondence, was settled by the payment by St. James' of $708.60. The first vestry elected consisted of Winborn Lawton, J. B. Hinson, J. R. Rogers, J. B. F. Minott, J. R. Jervey, John Rogers, and Abram Wilson. Rev. Paul Trapier was elected rector.

There were 13 pews in the chapel accommodating 90 persons, two pews for Negroes. There were 17 families connected with the Church. Some of the services at this time were held at the summer residences of the people near Fort Johnson, 17 of a total of 50 in 1833. Communion plate for the Church was made of silver given by a "female communicant". A plain but commodious chapel of wood was completed at Johnsonville in 1836 on Government land, so, St. James' now had its own chapel of ease. Mr. Trapier having assumed city missionary duty in Charleston, his services were now reduced, but the Rev. Cranmore Wallace became first, assistant, then rector in 1837. He was also principal of the South Carolina Society's academy in the city. It is recorded in 1839 that a beginning was made toward a permanent fund for the Church, secured by bonds of the donors and a piece of land left by the will of J. B. Harby. This is the land known as Parrott's Point. Rev. Mr. Wallace resigned in 1839, and services were held by temporary arrangements by the Rev. Josiah Obear, by the Bishop, and by a lay reader. This lay reader was none other than Mr. Stiles Mellichamp, who was studying for orders. On his ordination as deacon on Trinity Sunday, 1842 (with J. H. Cornish at the same time) by Bishop Gadsden, he became minister-in-charge, then rector on his ordination to the priesthood the next year. The Sunday School in 1844 had 15 white and 20 colored children. A parsonage was purchased in 1845. Much attention was given to the "nurture and admonition" of the Negroes in the parish. In 1851, Mr. Mellichamp went to be assistant in St. Helena's, Beaufort. However, he still gave some services to St. James'. He removed from Beaufort in 1853 and soon after again became rector of this Church.

In 1853, the Church which had been built after the Revolution was taken down and a new (and fourth) Church erected, thus described by Robert E. Mellichamp, the rector's son: "It was wooden, tastefully built in Gothic style", surrounded by a splendid grove of live oaks. It was a few yards south of the Church taken down. He stated that the graveyard dated back to 1769. Mr. Mellichamp did an extensive work among the Negroes during these years in the parish Church and on the plantations. He reported in 1855, 147 services to Negroes, his ministrations reaching 250 Negroes. He preached three or four times each Sunday in what he called "the glorious cause". Nearly all the white people and several plantations of Negroes had left James Island by 1862—the battle drawing near. Mr. Mellichamp arranged with the Presbyterian minister to have services on alternate Sundays. On his off-Sunday, he held services either for the soldiers or the Negroes. There is no report of services at Johnsonville after the war. This chapel, like the parish Church, was destroyed during the war. The Church built in 1853 was accidentally burned in 1864. It was between the Confederate lines. The Rev. W. H. Campbell, who had command on the island, had given orders for its protection. The Presbyterian Church on the island was also destroyed at this time, rebuilt in 1867-68.

In 1863, services became impracticable. Mr. Mellichamp went to Orangeburg. The old records of the Church were all destroyed when Winnsboro was burned by Sherman's troops—Mr. Constant H. Rivers, the former treasurer, residing there at the time. The only property of the Church after the war was the glebe land adjoining the chapel and fifty acres of land known as "Parrotts Point", given by J. R. Harvey for the support of the clergyman officiating at the Church. In 1868-69, services were held in the Presbyterian Church by the Rev. W. O. Prentiss. At this time the vestry consisted of W. B. Seabrook, J. T. Dill, W. W. Lawton, E. L. Rivers, and W. G. Hinson who was secretary and treasurer. Mr. Mellichamp returned to the rectorship January 1, 1870, serving as such until May 12. The death of Mr. W. B. Seabrook who at one time was the "only male communicant" of the Church on the island was mourned. There was no Church and no parsonage, Mr. Mellichamp living in the city. There were the two glebes. These glebes have played an important part in the history of this parish, often supplying the means for advance work when funds were otherwise scarce. Mr. Mellichamp returned to the rectorship in Orangeburg, but gave St. James' some services. He was again called to the rectorship in 1872, a parsonage having been built on Parrott's Point. He was not to occupy it, dying in the parsonage in St.

Matthew's Parish on October 23, 1872, "warmly loved and esteemed by all who knew him". Among those who had returned to the island were W. G. Hinson, E. L. Rivers, W. W. and J. P. Lawton. St. James' received as a gift from the famous Plowden Weston St. Mary's Chapel, Hagley, in All Saints' Parish, the gift of a Bible, prayer book, altar service book, and oak book-rest. The first was used until a lay reader stumbled on the long "s's" when a more modernly printed Bible was secured and given as a memorial to Mr. Cornish.

For many years now, St. James' was listed as a "suspended parish". Mr. Prentiss again held services for some months in 1887-88. Then, after another intermission, the Rev. John L. Egbert and the Rev. A. E. Cornish held some services on the island in 1896-97. It was principally through the efforts of W. G. Hinson and E. L. Rivers and the leadership of Mr. Cornish that the present St. James' Church (the fifth) was built in 1898-99 by means of voluntary contributions and with money which had accumulated in the hands of the vestry. Services began in the Church in May, 1898, conducted by the Rev. A. E. Cornish. He was assisted for a short time by the Rev. J. H. Brown. St. James' was now an "organized mission". The Church was consecrated by Bishop Capers on June 30, 1902. Among the gifts and memorials in the Church should be mentioned the chancel window and that in the gable over the entrance by Mr. W. G. Hinson, as also the vases and font; the altar-rail by Dr. D. W. Ellis; prayer desk by Mrs. E. S. Thayer; alms basins by Miss Mattie Howe and Miss Annie Waring; choir stalls by Elias Rivers; silver alms basins in memory of Mr. W. G. Hinson and Capt. E. L. Rivers by the Woman's Auxiliary.

Mr. Cornish conducted a mission farm on the island at this time called Sheltering Arms. It was directly connected with his city missionary work. In May, 1907, his last year, Mr. Cornish reported six families and 13 communicants. The Church had never recovered from the effects of the war. The Rev. H. C. Mazyck now became minister-in-charge in connection with his rectorship of St. John's, John's Island. Mr. W. G. Hinson was warden and treasurer. The Rev. P. H. Whaley succeeded Mr. Mazyck May 1, 1913. On the sixth of this month, St. James' was admitted into union with the Convention as a parish—thus at last regaining its pre-war status. W. G. Hinson and St. J. Allison Lawton were the wardens, and John Rivers, treasurer and secretary. Mr. Whaley died on September 2, 1915. The Rev. A. E. Cornish in 1917 returned to become rector (in connection with the charge of the Seaman's Home), serving until his long and valued services to St. James' came to an end by his death on October 20, 1920. He is buried in the shadow of this Church he served so well.

In 1922, the Rev. Wallace Martin coming from Montrose, Pennsylvania, became rector in connection with his duties as chaplain and superintendent of the Seaman's Home. He continued in charge until his resignation, January, 1945. In 1922, the wardens were John Rivers and St. J. A. Lawton; the secretary and treasurer, John Rivers. During this period, the membership of the Church only increased slightly, from 37 to 41, but the Sunday School went from 16 to 55. The music was much improved by the introduction of a vested choir, Miss Martha Rivers being the efficient organist. On September 9, 1930, the Church celebrated its bi-centennial; Mr. Martin conducted the services, Bishop Thomas preached a historical sermon. A sketch of the Church by Capt. E. L. Rivers, revised and completed by Daniel W. Ellis, was published. The Bishop consecrated two seven-branched candelabra, memorials to Miss Anna Keim Stauffer and Mrs. Rose Perry Posey, on June 25, 1938. In 1942, an altar cross was given by the McLeod family in memory of their parents, William W. and Mollie E. McLeod. Mr. Martin died a year and a few months after his resignation on Good Friday, 1946. The Rt. Rev. Albert S. Thomas, retired Bishop of the diocese, acted as *locum tenens* from January, 1945, until April, 1946.

At this time, the Rev. Edward Brailsford Guerry assumed the rectorship in connection with St. John's, John's Island. He had just been released from chaplaincy in the Army. The officers of the Church in 1947 were St. J. A. Lawton (who died early in the year) and W. H. Mikell; secretary and treasurer, W. E. McLeod; school superintendent, W. G. Meggett; lay reader, J. F. Heyward. In 1947, the associated parishes erected a rectory on a lot given by the McLeod family. The commodious parish house was erected in 1948 at a cost exceeding $12,000.00, well-timed to meet the increasing work of the parish, especially among the young people. It was dedicated, when free from debt, October 30, 1949. The wardens in 1954 were W. E. McLeod and W. H. Mikell, the former being also secretary and treasurer; Church school superintendent, W. G. Meggett; lay readers, F. I. Dovell, Jr., John Rivers, and W. E. McLeod. The communicant membership of St. James' had increased to 157.

ST. JOHN'S, COLLETON, JOHN'S ISLAND
GRACE CHAPEL, WADMALAW
(See Dalcho, p. 360)

At the time we take up the story of St. John's (1820), Dalcho tells us it was a "flourishing and respectable Cure. It has a glebe and parsonage, and its funds are large and increasing." The old Church for some years had been a ruin. Now a new one of wood was built on the site of the old and consecrated by Bishop Bowen, April 10, 1817. The first rector of the new Church was the Rev. Paul Trapier Gervais (1817-19). This distinguished clergyman lived on the Island until his death in 1856, except 1840-41 when he resided in Charleston. He served on the Standing Committee, was elected deputy to the General Convention, and held many other posts of honor and leadership in the Church, including that of president of the Convention after Bishop Dehon's death. Though never regularly rector of St. John's after the three years, he often assisted or supplied vacancies to the last, and served on the vestry, acting as secretary and treasurer. His ministry was handicapped by a pulmonic disease. The Rev. William Stanyarn Wilson took charge after his ordination in Philadelphia March 14, 1819. John Holmes was deputy to the Convention in 1822. Thus, St. John's, having participated in the ruin of the Revolution which came over the diocese, now participated in the renaissance that came in the first two decades of the nineteenth century.

The fruitful ministry of the Rev. Thomas H. Taylor, D.D., followed (1824-34), the communicants increasing from 24 to 84. There were also many colored communicants; in fact, in 1831, there were 26 white and 41 colored. It was said that as many attended worship as the galleries would hold. In 1834, a plan was inaugurated to have the rector in the parish the year round. Because of this, in 1836 a house in Rockville, formerly owned by John Wilson, was purchased for $1,000.00 for a rectory. The Rev. J. A. McKenney followed Dr. Taylor as rector (1835-36); the Rev. Thomas J. Young was the next rector (1836-47). This was a period of growth: a Sunday School was begun; a chapel was built at Rockville at a cost of $1,500.00; a library was established. Mr. Young was the first minister to live in the rectory at Rockville. The side galleries for Negroes in the Church were completed at this time "making the number of eats between three and four hundred, the present average attendance." Mr. Young developed a most careful plan for the training of these people. He reported in 1838 worship in St. John's Church 32 Sundays, 3 other days; at Rockville, 16

Sundays, 20 other days. This year, 57 colored communicants were added. At the end of Mr. Young's rectorship in 1847, the number of colored communicants had increased from one in 1818 to 347. This great work among the Negroes continued until it was stopped by the War Between the States. The Rev. John Foster was missionary to the Negroes in the parish in 1854, and, after 1858, the Rev. Paul Gervais Jenkins ministered to them in Zion Chapel on Wadmalaw Island, built at this time for them.

In 1841, with the consent of the vestry of St. John's, the chapel at Rockville was organized with two wardens and three vestrymen, but this was a temporary arrangement, and it was never admitted to the Convention as a separate Church—it was St. John's chapel of ease as it is today. In 1846, the Church and the rectory were thoroughly repaired. This was a time of prosperity on the islands and the Church shared in this, endowments being increased. After Mr. Young left in 1847, the Rev. James W. Miles supplied for a few months, when the Rev. C. H. Hall became rector in 1848, serving until 1856. On Sunday, November 27, 1853, Bishop Davis confirmed 121 colored persons. During these years St. John's sent two men into the ministry, Paul Gervais Jenkins and Augustus Moore, who both acted as catechists in St. John's when candidates. The village of Legareville was the summer resort for the inhabitants of John's Island; a chapel was built there in 1856 and services held. Mr. Hall left the parish in December, 1856. In 1858, the Rev. R. S. Trapier became rector with the Rev. P. G. Jenkins missionary to the Negroes. The whites often attended Zion Chapel in which Mr. Jenkins ministered. Through the generosity of a gentlemen of the parish a cupola was added to Zion Church in 1860. He complained in 1861 that he had a large congregation of Negroes, but there would be more if the whites would not take the best seats. This faithful clergyman lost by fire his library and records on John's Island in 1861, and soon after lost his congregation. He spent three months as a private soldier in the Army in 1862, when he held services in his tent. He later ministered to the soldiers in the Confederate Hospital in Columbia, besides often holding other services. The people in 1862 were ordered off the islands; they refugeed in the up-country. Mr. Trapier was forced to leave in December, 1862, never returning to the parish. He was nominally rector of St. John's until he went to St. Michael's in 1869.

When the war ended, the people of John's Island faced ruin and want. The Church was entirely destroyed by a fire (origin unknown) which swept across the island in the spring of 1864. The beautiful chapel at Legareville, riddled with shells, was afterwards burned. The vested funds of the Church were reduced from $30,-000.00 to $3,000.00. Its loss by the war exceeded that of every other parish in the diocese, save one. The Bishop made a visitation of the parish January 27, 1865, holding services and confirming six soldiers at the parsonage on John's Island. Zion Church, built for the slaves, now became the principal place of worship on Wadmalaw; and on John's Island, the Presbyterians loaned their Church from 1868 to 1873. Zion Church was lost through some legal complication, and finally fell into the hands of the Negro Methodists. It was, however, used certainly as late as November 22, 1874, when Bishop Howe held a wedding in it. The parish having been without services for two years, in 1868 the Rev. E. E. Bellinger gave notice of service at the site of the old Church. There under the shade of the oaks to the south of the Church, "kneeling on the grass, they received the Holy Sacrament for the first time as a congregation after the war." (Account by Edward B. Bryan.) Mr. Bellinger continued in charge until 1873. He thought that the Negroes might be reclaimed if "men and means" could be procured. With Mr. Bellinger assisting, the Bishop held confirmations at Rockville (six), and at residence of W. S. Mathews at Legareville (two) in May, 1869. Deputies to the Convention in 1871 were Paul Gervais, D. J. LaRoche, R. B. Hanahan, and B. S. Whaley, Jr. A Church was now built on the site of the old Church, third on the spot; Mr. Richard J. LaRoche was the leader. It was consecrated by Bishop Howe April 27, 1873; Mr. Paul Gervais read the "donation," Mr. Bellinger the "sentence," Mr. Hanckel preached, and Mr. Cornish said the litany.

The Rev. J. H. Cornish became rector after Mr. Bellinger (1873-74); then Mr. Stickney, who resigned in a year after a dispute with the vestry as to the annual meeting of the congregation. The Rockville chapel at this time was first called Grace Chapel. The parish Church had been described as a "small frame building unfinished in the interior." Gifts in 1875 were $300.00 through a former rector, the Rev. C. H. Hall of Trinity, N. Y., used in completion of the Church, and an altar from Mr. R. J. LaRoche, made by himself. An organ was now installed, and communion silver given by Mrs. R. J. LaRoche. Then followed as rectors the Revs. W. O. Prentiss (1877-80), P. G. Jenkins (1881), J. Mercier Green (1882-90). In 1885, a question having risen concerning the title to the lot on which Grace chapel stood, it was rolled to a new one, its present location, given by Mrs. Elizabeth F. Jenkins. In

1888, the parish Church was enlarged, the chancel recessed, and new pews installed. Mr. Green had an apoplectic stroke in the pulpit, dying that day, March 15, 1891. Mr. Prentiss then returned for about a year (1891-92). Rev. Barnwell Bonum Sams took charge in 1894. Improvements now were the reclaiming of the rectory in Rockville (1896), the Church badly damaged (unroofed) in the storm of '93, more fully repaired (1897), and Grace Chapel renovated by young men of the parish and the rector, working with his own hands. Grace Chapel was consecrated by Bishop Capers, Epiphany, 1898. Among the wardens after the war were: Dr. W. S. Stevens, R. J. and later D. J. LaRoche, T. P. and later J. P. Grimball, then P. C. Grimball; deputies in 1900 were T. J. Grimball, B. H. Warner, E. B. Bryan, and M. W. Jenkins. Mr. Sams' son, William Bee Sams, was ordained deacon by Bishop Capers July 18, 1901 in Grace Chapel. Mr. Sams died November 19, 1903. After a vacancy for more than a year, the Rev. W. E. Callender served in 1905 until September 1, when Rev. Henry C. Mazyck became rector. There were many improvements now: Memorial windows and new paten in the parish Church; at Garce, new altar with cross, vases, book rest, new porch with belfry and bell given by Mr. J. S. Hart. Mr. Mazyck resigned November 1, 1912, and in 1914, Rev. Charles Innes LaRoche followed, serving until the summer of 1918. Rev. Frederick N. Skinner served from June 1, 1919, to 1926, then the Rev. E. S. Middleton was in temporary charge in 1927. In August, 1929, Grace Chapel was struck by lightning, the cupola and cross being badly damaged. In this year on the occasion of the Bishop's visitation, a ciborium was dedicated in memory of Mrs. Elizabeth T. Jenkins. The Rev. Wallace Martin now held services, but there was no regular rector until the coming of the Rev. Robert N. MacCallum May 1, 1930. At this time the wardens were: H. S. Whaley and T. P. Grimball, and J. S. Hart was secretary and treasurer. During most of this post-bellum period, the parish was associated with Edisto in the rectorship, but Mr. MacCallum had St. Paul's, Meggett, as his additional charge. A notable event of this rectorship was the commemoration of the 200th anniversary of the establishment of the parish on June 17, 1934. Bishop Thomas preached a historical sermon, a granite marker was Dedicated, and a very valuable history of the parish was presented, prepared by Mr. MacCallum with the aid of Sophia Seabrook Jenkins.

The Rev. Wallace Martin succeeded as rector in connection with his work at the Seaman's Home in Charleston when Mr. MacCallum left July 1, 1934. The latter was the last minister to live in the rectory at Rockville. It was bought by Bishop and Mrs. Thomas in 1946, and made their home. The Rev. Mr. Wallace Martin resigned January, 1945. He died suddenly on Good Friday the next year. Then for fourteen months, Bishop Thomas, now retired, supplied monthly services alternating between the parish Church and Grace Chapel. The Rev. Edward B. Guerry became rector May, 1946. Under him the parish was much more completely organized than ever, a rectory built (in conjunction with St. James', James Island) and a parish house erected to the south of the Church. A fund, now nearly $30,000.00, is being raised with a view to building a new Church; the communicants have increased from 158 in 1946 to 233 in 1953. In 1947, the wardens were T. P. Grimball and John F. Sosnowski; the secretary and treasurer, H. F. Rivers; and the Church school superintendent and lay reader, R. R. Bryan. On December 6, 1955 an altar book rest was given by Dr. G. Fraser Wilson in memory of Mrs. E. Bates Wilson. The Church built after the War between the States was removed and a new Church erected, the fourth on the same spot in 1955. Simons, Lapham, and Mitchell were the architects and G. W. Blanchard the builder. A marble tablet was placed in the south wall of the Church to mark the place of the burial under the Church of the Rev. Penuel Bowen, sometime rector. On July 1, 1956, the steeple according to the original plan of the Church, given by Bishop Thomas in memory of his wife, Emily Jordan Carrison Thomas, was dedicated. The firm of the Bishop's son, Albert S. Thomas, Jr. built the steeple. New pews and new furniture were installed in the Church also in 1956.

SAINT ALBAN'S, KINGSTREE
Established 1879

It was in the year 1879 that regular services first began in Kingtree, the minister being the Rev. Edwin C. Steele, then rector of St. John's, Florence. In May 1880, he reports having held services ten times in Kingstree. There were two communicants. The next year, he reports 35 services, the number of communicants four. After three years, there were ten communicants. The progress of the mission was, Mr. Steele thought, "extraordinary" with the town growing. This Church was indeed a child of faith. A lot for a Church was soon bought—the deed to the trustees of the diocese from William J. Lee bears date, June 29, 1882, one-half acre lot. Mr. Steele died in 1884.

There was now a long interregnum in the life of this Church. It was not until July, 1889, that the Rev. H. H. Phelps began holding services on the Fourth Sundays and steps were taken to build a Church. He states that there were five families and nine communicants. Really for the first time, the mission was listed among those of the diocese. Mr. Phelps left the diocese in 1891. Some time later, the Rev. W. A. Guerry, rector of St. John's, Florence, had charge. He was assisted by Rev. Edward McCrady and reports in 1893 that the "chapel here is soon to be completed." In March, 1894, the Rev. H. M. Jarvis took charge and by May had held here 26 services. The chapel was now partially completed and for the first time, the Kingstree mission assumes the name, Saint Alban's. The chapel seats about 80; it has Gothic windows of colored glass. There is a handsome octagonal font and a Bishop's chair, but most of the furniture and seats were of a temporary nature. In the spring of 1895, the Church was almost completed. An altar was installed, made by Mr. L. L. Simons of wood given by Mr. Thorne, and later other improvements were made. In 1897, the number of communicants had increased to 20. Rev. R. W. Barnwell became minister-in-charge in 1898. St. Alban's became an "organized mission" on May 8, 1898. Mr. P. Boone Thorne, warden, and secretary and treasurer, Mr. Lyons at first and then, Mr. Emille Arrowsmith.

The Rev. Robert Wilson, D.D., succeeded Mr. Barnwell April, 1902. Mrs. M. F. Heller was now treasurer. St. Alban's suffered a severe blow on April 11, 1905, when the Church was partically destroyed by fire—the roof was badly damaged, the wall scorched, the windows damaged, the pews destroyed. A handsome altar rail, recently installed, was almost ruined. The resources of the mission were severely taxed to make repairs. Mr. R. J. Kirk became treasurer in 1906, Mr. Thorne still warden. A Sunday School was organized in 1907, but continued only for a while. For some years after 1908, Dr. Wilson acted as treasurer. In 1914, Mr. O. P. Barton was treasurer, and Mr. R. J. Kirk, lay reader. The Rev. Dr. Wilson, after about twelve years of devoted service, resigned this work in 1914 and was succeeded in July by the Rev. Henry DeSaussure Bull. With the coming of the first resident minister, St. Alban's began to take on new life. Improvements now were painting of the Church, new windows, and a handsome altar cross. The Church had increased to 40 communicants. Mr. Bull left for Christ Church, Charleston, in 1917. The next year, the Rev. Walter Mitchell, rector of Porter Military Academy, began supplying the services and continued to do so until 1923 when the Rev. John Ridout became minister-in-charge, but only for about a year when the Rev. J. E. H. Galbraith took charge, supplying one service a month. W. F. Tolley was now warden, and W. L. Payne, secretary and treasurer.

The Rev. J. McDowell Dick became minister-in-charge in June, 1926, with Dr. G. W. Gamble, warden; secretary, Miss Marie L. Nelson; and J. E. Porter, treasurer. Mr. Dick left in 1928, when Rev. Mr. Galbraith resumed charge briefly. The Rev. C. R. Cody of Darlington succeeded in 1929. The long and faithful services as warden of Dr. G. W. Gamble came to an end with his death in 1933. Mr. Joseph Alsbrook was appointed by the Bishop to succeed him. The Rev. Duncan M. Hobart took charge in residence January 1, 1937. This connected this Church with the associate mission, including in this section St. Luke's, Andrews, St. Stephen's, and the new mission at Rhems, which continued two or three years where Rev. L. A. Taylor also labored. The use of old Black Mingo Baptist Church was obtained for the services of the Rhems mission. The Church suffered a great loss in the death on January 29, 1938 of Mrs. Caroline Simons Heller—St. Alban's "Mother-in-Israel". Mr. Hobart resigned early in 1940. During his period, St. Alban's Church was extensively remodelled and improved. The Rev. William Moultrie Moore took charge after his ordination in the summer of 1940, continuing in charge for two years. Rev. William H. Hanckel, Jr., succeeded after several months' vacancy in March, 1943. He resigned in September, 1944, when the Church was again vacant for quite a while. The Rev. R. C. Patton held services most of 1946. The Rev. deSaussure P. Moore entered upon the duties of priest-in-charge early in 1947, serving for two years. During this time, a parish house was built. The Rev. John Q. Crumly came in 1950. Mr. Crumbly left in 1951. The Rev. W. S. Poynor, retired clergyman of Florence, then took temporary charge. The Rev. Hallie D. Warren, Jr., assumed permanent charge in 1953, serving until the spring of 1956 when he went to Chattanooga.

MISSION, LAKE CITY
Established 1915

While in charge of St. Alban's, Kingstree, the Rev. H. D. Bull began services in Lake City, holding the first on Ash Wednesday, 1915, in the Baptist Church. There were eight communicants. On a later occasion, Bishop Guerry made a visitation, holding services in the Presbyterian Church. A mission was tentatively organized, with Mr. F. H. Arrowsmith as warden. A lot was given and $200.00 raised, but nothing permanent resulted although for many years services were held at least occasionally, the last by the Rev. C. R. Cody of Darlington and Kingstree. Services were finally discontinued in 1931.

ALL SAINTS', MANNING
Established 1909

On the 19th day of April, 1909, Bishop Guerry, in company with the Rev. Wallace Carnahan of Summerton, visited the town of Manning. They held service in the Presbyterian Church, kindly loaned for the purpose. The Rev. Mr. McDowell, the pastor, read the lessons. After this service, a meeting was held to organize a mission and purchase a lot. One member made himself responsible for $100.00 of the missionary's salary. The Bishop placed the mission under the charge of the Rev. Mr. Carnahan. Mr. Carnahan's charge lasted only a short time, until he resigned his work in Summerton, November, 1909. In November of the same year, the Rev. John Kershaw, Jr., having returned to the charge in Summerton, assumed charge. The work, however, was not actively resumed until the mission was reorganized at a service October 30, 1910, with the name All Saints'. The warden was R. B. Lyons and the treasurer F. P. Burgess. Neat quarters were obtained in a former private school building, and properly furnished. A sum of over $500.00 was in hand. Mr. Kershaw's health failed soon after this. Rev. H. C. Mazyck took charge December 1, 1912. Mr. A. H. Breeden became warden in 1914. At this time, there were eight families in the mission and 15 communicants, services held on 25 Sundays. For the year 1916-17, the Church was vacant part of the time; the Rev. T. A. Porter supplied for three months; the Rev. W. M. Walton took charge April 1, 1917. Mr. F. P. Burgess was now warden and B. B. Breeden, secretary and treasurer.

A lot was secured and a Church built in 1917, largely by the gift of $1,000.00 by the Church building fund. It was a Gothic building in imitation stone. The Rev. J. B. Walker became minister-in-charge in 1921. At this time, there were 21 communicants. Mr. Walker continued his charge of this Church for ten years until he resigned January, 1931. Mr. Burgess was still warden and Mr. Glennie Heriot, secretary and treasurer. After Mr. Walker gave up this work, the Rev. Edward B. Guerry assumed pastoral charge in October, 1932, but for a time services were not resumed. The Church was now classified as unorganized. There were reported in

1933 two families and 11 communicants. Mr. Guerry left his field of work in February, 1935. The Rev. D. N. Peeples then took over the charge. Services were resumed in 1936, being included in the work of the associate mission, the headquarters being at Eutawville. The Rev. L. A. Taylor succeeded in direct charge and then (1939) the Rev. W. R. Haynsworth. Mr. A. G. Heriot filled the offices of warden-secretary-treasurer. In 1944, 18 communicants were reported, with regular services. Mr. Haynsworth continued his faithful work here until 1947; Miss Harriott Burgess was then secretary-treasurer. The Rev. R. C. Patton took charge in 1948, and then the Rev. John Q. Crumbly in 1950. Mrs. Harry L. Harvin was treasurer at this time. Mr. Crumbly left in 1952.

Soon after this time, the Church was sold. The mission for the time is closed, the members worshipping in Summerton. The proceeds of the sale of the Church, some $4,000.00, is being held with the view of building a Church in the future.

ADVENT, MARION
Established 1868

While there were always some Episcopalians in what is now Marion County at least from before the founding of the Britton's Neck and Sandy Bluff churches in about 1735, there was no organized Church until late in the next century. Evidence of this is seen in such prominent Marion County names as Davis, Keene, Godbold, Evans, Ellerbe—all originally Episcopalians. From 1845 to 1848 the Rev. Messrs. Richard S. Seely and Henry Elwell officiated in Marion. Mr. Hugh Godbold who died in 1859 left a legacy to build a Church but it was lost in litigation. Services were held in Marion by the Rev. T. F. Davis, Jr., assistant Rector of Grace Church, Camden, in 1860. It was on July 31, 1867, that the Church of the Advent was organized by Bishop Davis who appointed the Rev. Walter C. Guerry minister-in-charge. The leading spirits in the movement were General and especially Mrs. W. W. Harllee, William S. Mullins, Dr. James C. Mullins, and Dr. D. S. Price. The Church was admitted into union with Convention on May 14, 1868, when Dr. Price and Mr. W. S. Mullins took their seats as deputies. After having organized not only the Advent but also a mission in Florence, both under the Rev. Walter C. Guerry, the Bishop parted company with the young missionary on Wednesday, August 7, who said to him, "Bishop, I must bid you good-bye, I feel very sick". When the Bishop went to Bradford Springs on the 17th, he found that the mortal remains of the young minister had just been deposited in the churchyard at that place. He was succeeded by his brother the Rev. Le Grande F. Guerry, who retained charge until January, 1869. After a long interregnum during which the Church was held together by the faithful lay reader, Dr. D. S. Price, the Rev. H. T. Lee, rector of Trinity, Society Hill, took charge, October, 1877, and continued until 1879. The first confirmation had been held by Bishop Davis on December 9, 1868. Soon after a Sunday School was organized. During these years the services were held in the Masonic Hall, the Court House, or the Presbyterian Church. Mr. Lee was succeeded by the Rev. Geo. W. Stickney and then by the Rev. Edwin C. Steele in 1880. Largely under the leadership of Mrs. W. W. Harllee, active steps were taken in 1877 to erect a Church building. A lot was bought for $200.00 from Cornerlius Graham (said to have been once the property of John Godbold of the Britton's Neck Church). After long and persistent efforts the Cornerstone of the Church was laid by Rev. Mr. Steele, April 29, 1880. It was built after plans made by W. B. W. Howe, Jr., son of the Bishop. The first service in it was held by the Rev. H. K. Brouse (1881-1887) on Trinity Sunday, 1881, he having taken charge in connection with Society Hill the year before. The Church was Consecrated by Bishop Howe on December 7, 1883. Dr. D. S. Price, faithful lay reader and warden, read the Request. Clergymen who participated in this service besides the Bishop were Revs. C. C. Pinckney who preached, Stickney, Johnson, Motte, Steele, Brouse who read the Sentence, and Memminger who preached at night. Leading families in these days were Mullins, Harllee, Price, Shaffer, and that of Major J. B. White, late Superintendent of The Citadel. Dr. Brouse reported: "The Church building is very neat and churchly, Gothic in style, with beautiful stained glass chancel window, handsomely painted within and without, and furnished with everything needed, excepting a font. It will seat between 250 and 300 and the entire cost was a little over $2,000.00." The building committee consisted of J. B. Price, J. C. Mullins, Frederick Shaffer, W. W. Harllee, and C. H. Penn.

The Rev. W. A. Guerry took charge 1889 and continued until 1893 when he became chaplain at University of the South and later Bishop of the diocese—the third Guerry to serve the Church. He was succeeded the next year by the Rev. R. W. Barnwell, for one year, and then the Rev. J. M. Magruder from October, 1897, for three years. The Rev. Albert S. Thomas followed for eight years from August, 1900. Henry Mullins was warden and treasurer of the church for many years. During this period, electric lights were installed in the Church given by Mrs. Archibald McIntyre (*nee* Elizabeth Mullins) and a lot for a rectory was purchased by the St. Agnes Guild and a fund of $200.00 in addition was raised for this purpose. From the fall of 1904 Mr. Thomas held services once a month, Monday evenings in Mullins in the Presbyterian Church. In 1904, the Sunday School presented the Church with a brass book rest for the altar in memory of Mrs. Martha S. Harllee who had been the leader in building the Church. The Church having gained in strength both before and after Mr. Thomas' resignation, August, 1908, the parish for the first time in its history had a resident rector, the Rev. H. C. Salmond, and more frequent services. Soon after his coming the rectory was built. Mr. Salmond left in December, 1913. The Rev. E. A. Penick, rector of St. Paul's, Bennettsville, acted as minister-in-charge. In 1915 the Rev. W. S. Holmes became rector, until 1917, followed by the Rev. R. L. Merryman and then the Rev. Edgar Van W. Edwards until 1922. In 1924 the Rev. W. H. Mayers became rector, serving until March, 1928. A new organ was installed in January, 1925. The Rev. Harrell J. Lewis served from September, 1929, until his tragic death March 12, 1930. The Rev. O. T. Porcher of Bennettsville held services once a month from early in 1932 until the Rev. Thomas S. Tisdale took charge immediately after his ordination to the diaconate, July 9, 1933, becoming rector on his ordination to the priesthood in the Church of the Advent June 14 the year following. Mr. Tisdale resigned to accept Redeemer, Orangeburg, October 1, 1940, after a fruitful ministry of seven years. During his rectorship the Church was entirely renovated and covered with brick veneer. In 1932 the lot adjoining the Church on the south was bought with a view to building a parish house. The Woman's Auxiliary was very active in this movement. On May 26, 1936, a handsome parish house was dedicated by Bishop Thomas who drew the plans. It is of Gothic style in keeping with the Church building. To the entire congregation's loyal cooperation with the rector are these improvements due. We should mention more especially the lay leadership and generosity of Horace L. Tilghman, warden, and lay reader for many years, and also Howard McCandlish, warden, lay reader and Bible Class teacher, and not least Mr. Thomas J. Moore, warden and loyal supporter of the Church. Mr. Tisdale among his many activities as rector instituted a Church school meeting on Saturday chiefly for the benefit of children in the community having no Church connections. The Rev. Colin R. Campbell (Feb. 1942-1944) succeeded Mr. Tisdale, and then Rev. Lawton Riley (1946-1947); the Rev. Waties R.

Haynsworth from June 8, 1947 until 1954, followed by the Rev. Ralph E. Cousins, Jr.

MARION DISTRICT
BRITTON'S NECK AND SANDY BLUFF

Bishop Gregg relates the founding of settlements about 1755 at these two points on the Great Pee Dee (*Old Cheraws*). John Godbold was the leading churchman of the region. He died in 1765 in the faith of the Church, leaving many descendants in this section. The colony at Britton's Neck between the two Pee Dee rivers was composed of Church of England families coming directly from England, a leading one giving its name to the settlement, called Britton's Neck. The area was partly in Prince George's Parish and partly in Prince Frederick's. Not much is known of this Church beyond what Bishop Gregg (p. 69) records as follows: "This building was of black cypress, with brick foundation, and is still to be seen (1867), or was a few years since, in a good state of preservation, on the road leading from Port's Ferry to Potatoe Ferry, on Little Pee Dee. About the year 1780, the congregation having been long without a minister, and doubtless very much broken up by the troublous times of the Revolution, united with the Methodists, and the building passed into the hands of the latter, by whom it has since been retained. Charles Wesley is said to have preached in it." Two early ministers were Dr. Robert Hunter and later the Rev. Mr. Allison; both later were found in lists of Presbyterian ministers and are not found in lists of Episcopal clergymen so it may be concluded that their officiating in the Church was by courtesy. The Rev. John Fordyce, rector of Prince Frederick's (1734-1751) did officiate in the Church and extensively up the Great Pee Dee into the Cheraws. He deplores the lack of a missionary in his ltter to the Bishop of London (November 4, 1745). Many of the names of the old settlers, some of these still extant, in Marion County may be found in Victor B. Stanley's "Marion Churches and Churchmen".

The Sandy Bluff colony was further up the Pee Dee opposite Mars Bluff. The settlers were English and Irish who came by way of Charles Town. Here a Church was soon built. The settlers are said to have brought with them the brick for the foundation of the Church. The Rev. William Turbeville came as minister with the colony, well educated and noted as a preacher, he was also sought after for his power to prevail in prayer. The growing unhealthfulness of the site, though the land was rich, led to the settlement being broken up at an early date. Bishop Gregg in company with the famous antiquarian, Hugh Godbold, visited the site in 1867 finding only some traces of it.

The final futility of these two efforts to plant the Church in Marion District well exemplifies the unwisdom of the Church of England in not sending Bishops to ordain ministers in America.

CHURCH OF THE MESSIAH, MARYVILLE
Established 1955

NORTH SANTEE CHURCH
Established 1812

CHURCH OF THE MESSIAH, NORTH SANTEE
Established 1842

When Prince George's Parish was taken off from St. James' Santee in 1721, North Santee was included in Prince George. Apparently no separate Church life of an organized character developed on North Santee until a Church was built there in 1804 as mentioned by Dalcho. It petitioned the legislature for incorporation about 1804, the petitioners being from both Prince George and St. James' parishes, however Dalcho seems to associate this Church for the "Worship of God" (no other name uesd) with the latter parish. A story of the building of this Church is interestingly told by S. G. Stoney (with names of incorporators) in Leaflet 21 of the Charleston Museum. It was described as near North Santee Ferry.

Lay reading and occasional services by clergymen were held here more or less regularly for many years. Bishop Bowen states in February, 1822, that the Rev. Thomas H. Taylor who had been appointed to officiate at the chapel near North Santee Ferry, "has been engaged by the proprietors of the Chapel to serve them until the first Sunday in June." The Church was represented in the Convention of February 1823 by Elias Horry. In a later Journal, North Santee was listed as admitted to representation "about 1817." Mr. Taylor was still officiating in 1823 but went next year to St. John's, Colleton. Rev. William H. Mitchell, rector of St. James' Santee, took charge in 1826 (continuing for about three years). This is the last year in which is found in the Journals delegates accredited to North Santee, Joseph Manigault and Elias Horry. Not again do we find a minister named as officiating regularly on

North Santee until the coming of the Rev. C. C. Pinckney in February, 1835, six or seven years after Mr. Mitchell left. He continued in charge until 1838, serving also latterly Christ Church, Greenville, to which he devoted his entire time after 1838.

North Santee was now to be succeeded by "The Church of the Messiah, North Santee".

The Church was, in 1842, reorganized under this name as the minutes show: "Pursuant to notice previously given a meeting of the inhabitants of North Santee, Prince George Winyah, was held at Millbrook House immediately after Divine Service by Rev. Robert D. Shindler on the 4th Day of December, 1842, for the purpose of organizing a Congregation in conformity with the Canon of the Protestant Episcopal Church in the diocese of South Carolina.

"The result of an election here held for Church officers was as follows:

James H. Ladson, Warden; William R. Maxwell, Robert Hume, Rawlins Lowndes, Andrew Johnson, Vestrymen.

John R. Pringle, Delegate to the Convention February 8, 1843.

The salary of the rector was fixed at $500.00. Two apartments at Millbrook House were to be prepared for his residence. By resolution the Rev. John H. Cornish was called. He accepted and entered upon his duties December 18, 1842.

The Church, built in 1804, had now apparently been destroyed or fallen into ruin in the latter years when Church life was at a low ebb. Mr. Cornish relates that "he had held service in a room very comfortably fitted up for the purpose." There were, at this time, 22 families, services well attended, the afternoon devoted to the Negroes, "great anxiety among them for the teaching of the word, and the outpouring of the Holy Spirit." On the 19th of June in 1843, Bishop Gadsden visited the Church and held services "in the temporary Chapel", i. e., the "room". The Messiah was admitted into union with the Convention in February, 1843. James R. Pringle was the first deputy to the Convention in the following year. Mr. Cornish resigned May 10, 1846. After about eighteen months, the Rev. C. C. Pinckney returned to the charge. Then in 1849, the Rev. E. C. Logan became his assistant, being in charge of the large work among the Negroes of the parish; this was on ten plantations among 1,000 slaves. Mr. Pinckney held services at Flat Rock in the summer, then also at one time acting as assistant of Grace Church, Charleston, becoming rector thereof in

1850. Mr. Logan succeeded him as rector of the Messiah in December, 1850.

In 1853, under Mr. Logan, a new Church was begun. During these years, the Church was closed in the summer. Mr. Logan resigned May, 1954. In April, 1855, the Rev. Thomas J. Girardeau became rector. The new Church was now completed. It was Consecrated by Bishop Davis April 13, 1856, assisted by the rector and Rev. Nathaniel Hyatt of St. James', South Santee. At this time the congregation built a summer chapel on South Island and also a parsonage. In 1862 the rector reported 37 white communicants and 200 colored; services at Messiah 14, 37 S. Island, 29 on plantations, total 80. Mr. Girardeau's ministry ended on July 30, 1862.

In 1868 the Committee on the State of the Church reported the Messiah as "one of the churches on the roll of the Convention then without any ecclesiastical organization." This, of course, doubtless was a consequence of the war. Thus by 1869 the Church on North Santee was almost extinct, but the spark of religion burned still in the hearts of some members of the Church, small in number and impoverished in condition, but not lacking in zeal. On November 20, 1869, several members of both sexes crossed the river to attend services in South Santee where Bishop Davis was making a visitation. They begged him and the rector, the Rev. T. F. Gadsden, to "come over and help us". The Bishop could not but Mr. Gadsden did, and held service on the Tuesday following, and immediately began reorganization, electing wardens and vestrymen, and taking steps to repair the Church which was badly in need of it, having been stripped of pulpit, desk and organ, and some pews. Messrs. S. E. Barnwell, A. G. Trenholm, and F. L. Frost, as delegates to the Convention in 1872, reported the efforts made; the Church had been repaired, a summer chapel built, and a summer parsonage given by three members. Lay reading having been begun by Simons Lucas, also an organ secured. They had $600.00 subscribed for a minister, with the promise of the services of Mr. William H. Johnson who was soon to be ordained. In due time, the plan succeeded, the Rev. W. H. Johnson taking charge July, 1872. Thus was the Church fully revived; $1,657.50 had been expended on Church, chapel, and two parsonages, one on the river and one on the island. Mr. Johnson's tenure was short, only until April, 1874. The Rev. W. O. Prentiss became rector January 1, 1875. The wardens at this time were F. L. Frost, M.D., A. G. Trenholm, and the vestrymen, S. E. Barnwell, A. W. Cordes, W. M.

Hazzard, E. S. Horry, W. C. Johnstone, R. I'On Lowndes, and A. Middleton. The Church elected as delegates to the Convention of 1877, A. M. Manigault, W. C. Johnstone, R. I'On Lowndes, and T. S. Ford. The Church underwent extensive repairs in 1880. Mr. Prentiss resigned in 1881 and the Rev. James Walter Keeble became rector December, 1881. For the first time in its history, North Santee was associated with Prince George in that Mr. Keeble was rector of both, giving Messiah first and fifth Sundays, but only briefly—he left the field in 1883. At this time a beautiful tankard was given by the Sunday School and Mrs. I'On Lowndes. The Rev. Benjamin Allston assumed charge June 1, 1885. The Church burned in December, 1886. After this, services were held at Annandale, the residence of Captain Hazzard. Mr. Allston continued until May, 1887; the Church was then vacant for many years. In 1892 (See Journal of Convention 1892, pg. 42) on application of the vestry, (based on the assumption of possible loss of title by the Church to the trustees of the diocese under the canon concerning dormant parishes) received from the trustees its consent to sell three acres of land, including the parsonage, with a view to rebuilding the Church.

There are no reports in the Journal from Messiah from 1887 to 1898. In this latter year no rector is reported but warden, Miles W. Hazzard; secretary and treasurer, William Lucas; number of families 12, and communicants 25. A revival was now beginning. In 1899, the Rev. J. C. Waring (also rector of St. James', Santee) became rector. Under his and Bishop Capers' encouragement, a society was formed to further the rebuilding of the Church, and soon the Bishop laid the cornerstone, on March 18, 1900. Mr. Waring left the charge for a few months, but returned January 1, 1901. The Bishop held the first service in the new Church December 4, 1900 and Consecrated it on April 17, 1901. He was assisted by the Revs. L. F. Guerry, John Kershaw, G. H. Johnston, D.D., and H. J. Mikell, the last preaching the sermon. The Rev. Dr. Robert Wilson uscceeded to the charge of the Church February 2, 1902. On December 9, 1902, the winter parsonage was destroyed by fire—$1,000.00 insurance. By 1907, the parish through decline in rice planting and many removals was much weakened. The following words in Dr. Wilson's report in May, 1909, may be regarded as Messiah's valedictory because from henceforth the parish is listed as dormant: "The disintegration of the parish by removals was completed in November when three strong families were lost besides several occasional attendants. This left an available congregation of six individuals, one of whom was the warden [Williams Lowndes who with Fred W. Ford, secretary and treasurer, were the last officers of the parish]. No services have been attempted since October. The parish has a vested fund of $1,000.00, and besides the church owns a chapel and summer rectory on South Island. Owing to the abandonment of the rice interest, there appears no prospect of revival."

After a suit at law in about 1920, the Church having been long "dormant", under the relative Canon V. of the diocese, the trustees of the diocese received $975..37, and a beach lot, which was later sold and the corpus of the fund thus increased to $2.074.98 in 1929. (See Annual Reports Trustees, Journals of the Convention 1921 and 1929.) The vestry of Prince George undertook the care of the Church building. In 1955 began a movement to resusitate this Church. South of the Sampit River near Georgetown at a place called Maryville, there had developed quite a center of population. The Rev. A. Nelson Daunt, rector of Prince George, began plans to organize a mission here to be called the Church of the Messiah, Maryville, being not very far from the old Church of the Messiah, North Santee. With the help of funds of the old Messiah in the hands of the diocese, the old Church on North Santee about fourteen miles from Georgetown was taken down and rebuilt at Maryville. The Bishop visited the mission on April 24 and confirmed eight persons. This mission was admitted into union with the Convention on April 26, 1955, Mr. A. Leon Roberts taking his seat as lay deputy. The officers of the mission are W. H. Shirer, warden, and A. Leon Roberts, secretary and treasurer. Mrs. W. H. Shirer is president of the Woman's Auxiliary and Mrs. Leroy Roberts, superintendent of the Sunday School. A mission council was formed with the following members: Roy Roberts, T. J. Forbes, J. Greenleaf, J. F. Alford, Leroy Roberts, Earl Wilson, Mrs. W. H. Shirer, Mrs. Leroy Roberts, and Mrs. A. A. Milligan. Rev. A. Nelson Daunt is priest-in-charge. A bell (the old St. Peter's, Carvers Bay bell) was hung in 1956. The Rev. Luther Parker took charge in June, 1956. A building has been purchased, removed and adapted as a parish house.

ST. JAMES' PARISH, SANTEE
Established 1706
(See Dalcho, p. 295)

St. James', one of the original ten parishes, had no rector after the Rev. Philip Mathews left in it 1811, and for a long period there

were only occasional services at Wambaw and Echaw churches.
The Rev. Albert Arney Muller supplied services in 1819. In 1821
Bishop Bowen with means provided by the Advancement Society,
appointed the Rev. William H. Mitchell, a deacon, to the charge
of this parish, resulting in his being called, when ordained priest,
to be rector in 1823. James J. P. White represented the parish in
the Convention of 1822. Mr. Mitchell also held services in a remote
part of the parish, and in the afternoon he held special services for
colored persons. In 1826 he reported 18 families. Mr. Mitchell resigned in 1831 on account of insufficient support and went to teach
in Charleston. In 1835 the Rev. Charles C. Pinckney, deacon, took
charge. He officiated on both North and South Santee and among
the colored population, and in the summer in Greenville. He resigned to go to Greenville as rector in 1839. In 1942 during an
interregnum, the vestry was called upon to explain the violation
of a canon in employing a non-Episcopal minister. The vestry made
out a pretty good case for itself. The matter was peacefully adjusted. The parish remained without a regular rector until the coming of the Rev. Nathaniel Hyatt January, 1845. The reopening of
the Church on his coming stimulated interest, and at a considerable expense the Church was repaired extensively. On his visit
Bishop Gadsden thus describes the interior of the Church: "Some
though not all the pews in the venerable and appropriate building are arranged for the seats to face the desk and the pulpit
(which is placed overhanging the desk), so that while seated to
hear the word, the worshipper looks toward the places whence
come the reading of Holy Scripture and the Sermon; but when he
is on his knees in prayer, his back is turned toward the desk and
his face toward the Chancel which is at one end of the church,
having the desk and pulpit on its right, in the middle of the
Church, against the western wall." So, he says, the congregation
is instructed, "in prayer to look towards the altar, when receiving
instruction to look towards the reader, and the preacher."

In 1847 a rectory was built, four acres of land having been given
by a parishioner for a glebe at a cost of about $1,500.00. A vestry
room was added to the Church in 1850-51. At this time there
were chapels on the plantations, one at Hampton, where Mr.
Hyatt officiated, also about this time there was a seashore chapel.
During the war a large part of the Church membership refugeed
away. The Church was closed after Mr. Hyatt's death in 1865
until Rev. C. C. Pinckney held some services in 1867. The Rev.
T. F. Gadsden became rector in 1869. He held services in the

winter in what first was called the Board Church. When this was given to the Negroes in 1871, the services were held in private homes. In summer the services were all held in McClellanville. In 1873 Wambaw Church was repaired and reopened after eight years. In McClellanville Mr. Gadsden reports in 1874 he had held the services there for five years in the school house. He visited the parish once a month. Lay reading was begun in the parish at this time. The people suffered greatly from a great freshet in June, 1876. The Rev. W. O. Prentiss succeeded Mr. Gadsden January 1, 1878. At this time there were 13 families. Mr. Prentiss resigned January 1, 1889, however, he continued in charge for two years more. In 1890 "a very handsome and commodious Church" was built and consecrated by Bishop Howe under the name, St. James', McClellanville, on November 2, 1890. Mr. Lucas read the "Request" Mr. Prentiss the "Sentence", the Rev. C. C. Pinckney preached the sermon.

The Rev. Phineas Duryea became rector in December, 1891, but only for a very short time, the Rev. H. M. Jarvis succeeding, December, 1892. Mr. Jarvis relates baptizing "a son of David Doar in the chapel in the midst of the great storm of August, 1893, while the rain was beating heavily upon the windows, several feet of salt water capped by the roaring waves surrounding the Church, and the fierce tempest unceasingly thundering its threatenings." The Church being vacant in 1894, the Rev. J. S. Hartzell supplied services in the summer. Dr. S. D. Doar, warden, reported in 1895 the death of Mr. A. H. Seabrook for 25 years the lay reader. Mr. A. H. Lucas was appointed to succeed him. Rev. J. Cash Waring became rector December 1, 1898. He left to study in 1900 but returned January 1, 1901, serving until November 1, 1901. S. D. Doar, M.D., and A. H. Lucas were the wardens. The Rev. Dr. Robert Wilson began his long and faithful charge of this parish in 1903, living in Charleston in days when transportation was difficult, he yet met his appointments with great regularity. The Colonial Dames of South Carolina in 1915 enclosed the Wambaw churchyard with a neat fence and later made repairs to the Church, including a new asbestos roof in 1932. Rev. Sanders R. Guignard succeeded Dr. Wilson January 1, 1918, serving until Rev. W. B. Sams took charge August 1, 1921, and continued in charge for 16 years. In 1932 Mrs. William Lucas gave an altar cross for the chapel in McClellanville and the Lucas family a window in memory of Mr. A. H. Lucas for many years warden and lay reader. In 1938 a small parish house was built in rear of the chapel especially for the use of the

Y. P. S. L. and the vested choir, which was installed at this time, and also a processional cross was given in memory of S. C. Doar, for many years warden of the parish. When Mr. Sams retired August 1, 1947, he was succeeded by Rev. C. Raymond Allington. The wardens in 1953 were A. H. Lucas and William Toomer; secretary Harrington Morrison; treasurer A. H. Lucas. Mr. Allington resigned in 1955. After about 1870, the life of the parish has centered at the chapel in McClellanville though for many years an annual service has been held at Wambaw Church during the Easter season. For nearly two and a half centuries this Church has never ceased to bear its witness to the faith.

PRINCE WILLIAM'S PARISH
(Sheldon Church)
McPHERSONVILLE
Established 1745
(See Dalcho, p. 382)

The British commander, General Augustine Prevost, on his march from Savannah to Charleston in May, 1779, devastated the parish and burned the beautiful Sheldon Church, with all its handsome adornments. Thus ended the first and perhaps greatest period in the history of this Church. It was three or four decades before prosperity began to return to the people of this region. Sheldon Church for this period remained the ruin left by the British—trees grew up within its walls, a large oak in the center spread out its braches above the walls and a cedar sprang from the chancel recess. There was no regular rector during these years after the Revolution but occasional services were held. The Rev. Christian Hanckel, subsequently a most distinguished clergyman of this diocese, held the first service on this spot after the Revolution in 1815, as related by Dr. La Borde in his history of the South Carolina College. "It was an occasion of rare interest. The building was in ruins; the walls and columns of the portico alone were standing—sad monument of the violence and lawlessness of those times. The forest had resumed its sway, and the interior was filled with a large growth of trees, which had to be cut down by one of the parishioners. Boards were placed on the stumps for seats, and with no covering but the clear blue sky of a balmy spring day, the man of God once more proclaimed, to a large and respectable audience the glad tidings of salvation." (His text was taken from the 84th Psalm, 1st, 2nd and 3rd verses.) A subscription was taken up in 1817, looking at last to the rebuilding of the Church. The vestry was reorganized in

1825, and the rebuilding begun. It was soon completed under the leadership of the Rev. Edward Neufville, and reconsecrated on April 11, 1826. Taking part in this service besides Bishop Bowen were the Rev. Messrs. Walker, Delavaux, and also Mr. Neufville. This rebuilt Church served its purpose but was not so "sumptuous" as the first, wealth was not so great.

"At the time of this rebuilding, the wardens of the Church received a letter from an old English lady living in Beaufort in which she stated that she had in her possession a package which was left with her for safe keeping by an English officer during the Revolution, which she desired to restore to the Church, it never having been called for. The package was turned over to the church warden and upon being opened was found to contain the handsome Communion Silver Service of Prince William, wrapped in the rector's gown. This silver is still in possession of the parish." (J. I. Waring in the *Diocese* February, 1917.)

At this time services were held every Sunday during the winter. Frederick Fraser represented the parish in Convention. The Rev. Thomas J. Young followed Mr. Neufville in the charge in 1827. He was ordained to the priesthood in Sheldon Church by Bishop Bowen, the Rev. Mr. Walker of Beaufort assisting. The Rev. Charles P. Elliott became rector in April, 1831. In July, 1831, a chapel was erected in McPhersonville where many members resided. Deputies to the Convention in 1834 were F. D. Fraser, and Dr. Edward Brailsford. The Rev. C. P. Elliott resigned in this year, being succeeded in April, 1835, by the Rev. Stephen Elliott, Sr., who was ordained priest in May, 1836. In 1837, Sheldon Chapel was improved and a gallery added to accommodate colored people, also a parsonage was purchased. At this time the Rev. Benjamin C. Webb took charge of the extensive work among the Negroes in the parish. The following year the parish Church was extensively repaired in its interior at a cost of $1,700.00. In 1845 Mr. Elliott resigned the rectorship and devoted himself to the colored work in the parish. The Rev. W. T. Potter of Pendleton officiated from January to May, 1846. The Rev. Charles E. Leverett became rector in May, 1846, with Mr. Elliott as assistant, and Mr. Webb continuing his work among the Negroes.

Rev. Stephen Elliott after serving ten years as rector of this parish voluntarily then became assistant and built a large Church, seating 600, at his own expense for the Negroes and ministered in it himself. It was consecrated as Christ Chapel, April 19, 1846. Mr. Elliott although he later became rector of St. Bartholomew's Church, continued to serve this chapel until driven off by the war. He had a flourishing congregation of colored people. "For this work he had a peculiar adaptation". The Committee on the Destruction of Churches reported the end of this chapel on the Combahee. "It was taken down by Sherman's troops in order to build a bridge over that river. The materials were visible last year in the bridge"—1868. In 1849 an organ loft was added to Sheldon Church, the gift of James C. Cuthbert, Esq., and a year later the Bishop speaks of a sweet-toned organ acquired since his last visit. There were generous laymen in the Church in those days and prosperity at last was returning. Mr. Cuthbert not only gave liberally to the Church but by himself established a day school for the poor of the parish. He died in 1852, leaving $5,000.00 to the Church. In 1852 a fund of $10,000.00 was raised to restore the Church to its pre-Revolutionary grandeur, and a contract was let for this purpose but for various causes the work was delayed. The Church was deeply afflicted by the death of Mr. F. G. Fraser, for many years a foremost loyal member, and by that also of Mr. Cuthbert who bequeathed $10,000.00 for various church purposes.

In 1855 it was discovered, "That fifty (50) acres of land given, in addition to the glebe (about the same time) by Gov. William Bull (1750-60?) has been recently discovered", used by a neighbor by mistake and readily restored. At this time in the parish services were at Sheldon Church, 25; Chapel, 27; for Negroes, 20; with others, total 100. However, this year saw the loss of the Rev. Stephen Elliott to St. Bartholomew's Parish but he retained "his" Christ Chapel; Mr. Webb removed to the up-country, dying shortly after. Also removals from McPhersonville Chapel greatly reduced that work. The parish was this year represented in the Convention by Messrs. L. M. deSaussure, Thomas M. Hanckel, and G. C. Mackey. The proposed work on Sheldon Church and a new parsonage there were still delayed. Mr. Leverett, 12 years as rector, resigned in 1858 and resided in Beaufort. The Rev. Edward Reed became rector in 1860 but there were clouds in the offing. He reports in 1862 only three services at Sheldon and these chiefly for soldiers encamped in the neighborhood; the congregation was now dispersed because of the proximity of the enemy. The chapel at McPhersonville had been converted into a hospital, services being held at private homes or at the Presbyterian Church until that also was taken over for a hospital. Mr. Reed died before the year was out. Exactly as it happened nearly a hundred years before in 1779 when Prevost, marching from Savannah into South Carolina burned the Church, so now in February, 1865, Sherman, marching from Savannah into South Carolina, burned it for the second time. The Church had already been stripped of its pews and other furniture by the Negroes before the Federal Army arrived.

After its second destruction in 1865, Sheldon Church was never rebuilt. This may be explained in several ways: the poverty of the people after the war, with the radical change in economic life and the consequent movement of population. However, while Prince William's Parish has never regained its former glory and this Church never rebuilt, it has never ceased to bear its witness to the gospel of Jesus Christ—"the same yesterday, today, and forever". The chapel in McPhersonville was finally torn down to build bridges for the army in 1865 and the parish remained dormant for some years. Later the faithful missionary of those days in the region, the Rev. Edmund E. Bellinger, continued services not only in McPhersonville but in Blountville, at Pocotaligo, and at the residence of J. W. Gregorie. The parish was reorganized in 1873. In 1877 through the generosity of a single layman, Major John H. Screven, All Saints' Church was built near Yemassee (as was also a rectory) and until toward 1908 this Church, organized as a separate parish in 1883, was the center of worship of the Episcopal Church in the confines of Prince William's Parish which became dormant when All Saints' was organized as a separate parish. In 1908 All Saints' was sold to the Methodists, a new chapel having been built in McPhersonville in 1898 and the parish was again reorganized in 1906. The wardens were W. F. Colcock and O. M. Reed. The Rev. P. T. Prentiss became rector in 1909; Rev. Dwight Cameron in 1910; the Rev. George H. Johnston, in 1911; and the Rev. J. Herbert Woodward in 1912, continuing until 1925. Mr. O. M. Reed had been warden for many years. The Rev. R. M. Marshall now became rector with Mr. Isaac McP. Gregorie, warden, and Louis Gregorie, secretary and treasurer. The Rev. A. W. Skardon succeeded Mr. Marshall in 1929. Mr. Alec Gregorie succeeded Mr. Louis Gregorie as warden—secretary-treasurer in 1937. Mr. Skardon retired in 1952 being succeeded by the Rev. James O. Bodley. In 1925 Mr. Marshall inaugurated a series of services in the ruins of old Sheldon Church, held on the second Sunday after Easter annually. On one of these occasions in 1937 Bishop Thomas dedicated a bronze tablet (giving the history of the Church) presented by the Columbia Chapter of the Colonial Dames. The services were suspended for the period of World War II. They were resumed in 1952 by the Rev. John W. Hardy of Beaufort.

On October 27, 1956, a handsome stone was dedicated to the memory of William Bull and to mark the place of his burial under the chancel of old Sheldon Church, now a ruin. Lieut. Gov. Bull was for a half century a civic, military, and church leader in South Carolina, becoming Lieutenant Governor. He was the chief commissioner for the building of this Church in 1745. The stone was placed by four brothers, his descendants: James Holmes, Francis Kinloch, Charles Mayrant, and the Rev. Henry deSaussure Bull, D.D.

Note: Inscriptions transcribed from tombstones at old Sheldon will be found in the S. C. Historical and Genealogical Magazine, Vol. 17, p. 181.

ST. PAUL'S CHURCH, MEGGETT
Established 1906

This Church takes its name from the old parish of St. Paul's, Stono, of which its territory is a part. It was in origin, however, a chapel of ease of Christ Church, Wilton, Adam's Run, which was also in the territory of old St. Paul's Parish. While the Rev. L. F. Guerry was rector of Christ Church in 1906, services were begun on Yonge's Island. Serveral hundred dollars were subscribed for a chapel on a beautiful lot given for the purpose. Soon after this, the chapel was built. In the meantime, Mr. Guerry's health failed, but lay readers continued services. For March 17, 1907, Bishop Capers relates: "After dinner in the village, Dr. Theodore Kershaw took me down to Yonge's Island in his automobile, and at 5 P. M., we had a Consecration service in the new chapel just completed. The chapel is to be a chapel of ease to Christ Church, Adam's Run, and will be a great convenience to the community of Yonge's Island. It will be placed under the pastoral charge of the rector of Christ Church, who will give them services as often as convenient. I was assisted in the Consecration service by the Rev. Dr. Kershaw, who came up especially for the service. The little chapel was crowded and the service very impressive, friends from Charleston furnishing the full musical part of the service. Only a year ago, I met the friends of this enterprise at Dr. Theodore Kershaw's home on Yonge's Island, and his energy and purpose have carried it to a successful issue."

Associated with Dr. Kershaw on the building committee were Messrs. C. H. Anderson, L. C. Behling, and H. H. Butler. The organization of the Woman's Auxiliary of the chapel antedated its buildings and has been active to this day. Immediately after the Consecration, the Rev. Thomas P. Baker, becoming rector of St.

Jude's, Walterboro, and Christ Church, Adam's Run, took charge of this work. It prospered and two years later plans were made to remodel and enlarge the Church at least a third. Mr. Baker reports this work completed in 1914, with further improvements at a cost of $500.00. Mr. Baker was succeeded after eight years (1907-June, 1915) by the Rev. H. F. Schroeter (July, 1915-Dec., 1917), who in turn was succeeded by the Rev. W. B. Guion, 1918; then by the Rev. A. M. Rich, 1919-22; and the Rev. Paul Dué in 1923. After his ordination as deacon in June, 1923, the Rev. Charles Capers Satterlee took charge of this work.

In February, 1925, the Meggett chapel ceased to be a part of Christ Church, Adam's Run. It was now organized as a separate parish to be known as St. Paul's Church, Meggett, taking its name from the old Parish of St. Paul's, Stono, which covered this area. Mr. Satterlee, after unanimous call, became the first rector of St. Paul's after Easter of this year. The first officers of the parish were: wardens, C. H. Anderson, and G. C. Parish, and J. E. Anderson, secretary-treasurer. Mr. Palmer Smith was lay reader and for many years superintendent of the Sunday School. St. Paul's was admitted into union with the Convention of the diocese in February, 1926, represented by the following deputies: F. L. Parks, G. C. Parish, B. K. Sanders, and J. E. Anderson. The organization was incorporated as St. Paul's Church, Meggett, August 18, 1926. During Mr. Satterlee's rectorship, a chapter of the Y.P.S.L. was organized with eight members, which soon grew to forty. The activity of the parish at this time is further indicated by the erection of a parish house, which was located across the highway from the Church, completed in the spring of 1926. At this time, a beautiful pair of candlesticks were given by Mrs. H. B. Sanders in memory of her son, Hal. Two cruits and a paten were given by the Y. P. S. L. and a chalice by the League's president, Miss Lucille Martin, her family, and friends, in memory of her father. After Easter, 1926, Mr. Satterlee departed to work at Clemson College, greatly beloved by all for his good works.

The Rev. E. S. Middleton of the diocese of Maine held the services for a short time. The Rev. Richard E. Page became rector in the fall of 1926 and left the end of 1928. After an interim, the Rev. R. N. MacCallum was rector from May, 1930 until July, 1934. With the assistance of some funds from old St. Paul's, Stono, about this time a rectory was built, located in Hollywood. At this time, James Whaley and J. P. Smith were the wardens, and Joe Anderson, treasurer. There were now 113 communicants. The Rev. A. W.

Skardon became rector April, 1935, and served until June, 1948. During this rectorship, the Woman's Auxiliary, which had always been an active organization, was especially so at this time, and for a while there were two branches—the junior branch being named after Mrs. Skardon. Eucharistic candlesticks were given in 1935 in memory of Mrs. Sue Anderson.

Bishop Thomas, in his journal, records his last official visit to St. Paul's on March 26, 1944, when four persons were confirmed, presented by Mr. J. E. Jenkins: "After the service, I attended a parish dinner in the Parish House. I was presented with a token by the vestry and congregation at this time, my farewell visit to St. Paul's. It was a happy occasion for me."

On the 10th of November, 1946, Bishop Carruthers dedicated the three chancel windows placed by members; the central window in memory of John Calder Wilson, one side window in memory of Dr. Theodore Gourdine Kershaw, and the other in memory of Richard Jenkins LaRoche and Abigail Jenkins LaRoche. At the same time, the credence was dedicated by the Bishop. At this time, electric lights were provided, chiefly through the efforts of Mrs. Isaac Jenkins. The handsome altar was given by Mr. James W. Whaley, for many years senior warden of the Church. It is in memory of Constantia Olivia Bailey LaRoche.

In the fall of 1944 in the parish house, a reception was given to Bishop and Mrs. Carruthers. This parish house was destroyed by fire in March, 1945. The congregation, undaunted, immediately raised $4,000.00 for a reconstruction fund. Later, the rectory was sold and finally after a few months, it was decided to merge all funds and build a new Church, converting the old Church into a parish house, after plans prepared by Right Rev. Albert S. Thomas, retired Bishop of the diocese, who was in temporary charge of the Church from June, 1948, for three years. The officers of the Church at this time were: wardens, Frank J. Towles and Clarke Sanders; secretary-treasurer, J. M. Butler; superintendent of the Sunday School, James W. Whaley. The cornerstone of the new St. Paul's, Meggett, was laid on the 29th of July, A.D., 1949, by James F. Risher, Grand Master of the Grand Lodge of South Carolina, Ancient Free Masons, and members of the Grand Lodge. Addresses were made by the Grand Master and by Bishop Thomas. The first service in the new Church, conducted by Bishop Thomas, was held on October 9, 1949. The old Church was now renovated to a limited extent for the use of the Sunday School, it having been placed to the north of the chancel of the new Church.

The new Church was Consecrated by Bishop Carruthers on June 4, 1950. He was assisted by Bishop Thomas, the Rev. E. B. Guerry, and Mr. Harold Barrett, who took charge of the Church for the summer, being a candidate for orders. On September 10 of this year, an altar cross was dedicated to the memory of Lieutenant Marion Innis Jenkins, son of Mr. and Mrs. John E. Jenkins—St. Paul's gold star soldier in World War II. Mr. Barrett trained four lay readers to carry on the services when he departed at the end of the season. In the spring of 1951, the Rev. Thomas L. Crum assumed the rectorship. Soon after his coming, the parish house was greatly improved, with the addition of a kitchen, robing room, and other equipment. In 1954, a new organ was installed. Mr. Crum resigned December 31, 1956 and was succeeded by the Rev. George La Bruce the following fall.

THE BARROW'S MISSION, MONCKS CORNER
ST. JOHN'S CHAPEL
ST. STEPHEN'S-IN-THE PINES,
CHAPEL OF THE HOLY FAMILY
Established 1862

The services of the Church were first held in this neighborhood called The Barrows beginning about 1862. Planters had summer homes in this pineland region. The Rev. A. F. Olmsted the next year reported a Sunday School and services. He was rector of St. John's Parish, the work being therefore connected with Biggin Church. A chapel which had been partially erected during the war was completed in 1873, and much improved with many new furnishings, including a new chancel rail, altar, credence, litany desk, lectern, and a richly bound Bible and prayer book. It was a summer place of worship called St. John's Chapel. It fell into disuse early in the century and was taken down. (It was, however, still standing as late as 1910.) However, concerning the mission work in The Barrows, there is another story. It was in the fall of 1887 that a devoted churchwoman of St. John's, Mrs. Frances W. Heyward, was touched in her heart by her observation of the natives of The Barrows neighborhood, who were as sheep without a shepherd, and decided that something should be done for them. She had the support of the Rev. H. H. Phelps, the rector, and a parochial school for "white children" was opened. For the purpose of the mission work, a piece of land was given by Major Theodore Barker a mile or so from St. John's Chapel. The patrons of the school themselves built the schoolhouse. Church services were also held. The success of the work was largely due to the faithful labors of Mr. Stephen L. DeVaux, who taught the school with some 30 pupils. This man's devoted work supplied the name of the mission; it was called St. Stephen's-in-the-Pines. The work continued off and on for years.

The Rev. H. T. Gregory, rector of Trinity, Black Oak, in 1896 reported four baptisms and a Sunday School. Later after an interregnum, the Rev. J. C. Johnes, rector of both St. John's and Trinity, Black Oak, reported that the work at St. Stephen's-in-the-Pines had been revived, reporting 11 baptisms, 20 services, and a parochial school of 33 running for three months. In 1910, the Rev. Dwight Cameron reported eight services and 100 baptized persons. Mrs. H. H. Cantwell at this time worked in the mission, teaching both the parochial and public schools. The services were continued by the Rev. A. R. Mitchell while he was Archdeacon of the Charleston District from 1916-1920. After him for a time, the Rev. A. P. Magwood held the services. Mr. J. L. Strohecker rendered valuable service as lay reader, and faithful women assisted. In 1917, Mr. Mitchell baptized five children, reporting "large congregations" on his visits. After Mr. Mitchell left the field in 1921, the work in The Barrows lagged and finally was abandoned for about ten or twelve years. The chapel fell into ruins and disappeared. After his ordination on October 5, 1932, the Rev. E. B. Guerry was placed in charge of The Barrows in connection with his wide field of work, including St. Stephen's, St. Stephen's; Trinity, Pinopolis; and All Saints', Manning. He was adopted as the missionary of the Society for the Advancement of Christianity in S. C., and it was the help given by this society that enabled the reopening of The Barrows' mission. Mr. Guerry held the services in the school house there and sometimes in private homes. He resigned his work in the diocese in February, 1935.

In July, 1936, The Barrows work was included in the then established associate mission, consisting of the Revs. David Nathaniel Peeples, Duncan M. Hobart, and Lincoln A. Taylor. The newly built highway from Moncks Corner to Summerville split the old mission property in two, but the State Highway Commission generously made amends by deeding a new lot to the south of the highway. The work was intensively carried on by the associate mission. Miss Magdalin Ball was the regular lay worker and many volunteers from Pinopolis assisted, especially Mr. S. R. Crick, lay reader and superintendent of the Sunday School. The work was more particularly under the Rev. L. A. Taylor. On the new lot in August, 1938, a Guild Hall, being a combined chapel and community house, was completed. There were reported in 1940 twenty confirmed persons and thirty-four baptized members. Miss Ball resigned as lay worker in June 1940, and was succeeded by Miss Josephine F. Marion, the very soul of the work for some 15 years. The center at The Barrows was now called the Guild Hall of the Holy Family. The Rev. Mr. Taylor resigned this work when he left Pinopolis, July, 1946. He was greatly beloved. Shortly before he left, the font which belonged to the chapel that had disappeared years before was recovered. On the suggestion of Miss Florence LeNoble Lucas, one of volunteer workers in the mission, Bishop Thomas made a pedestal for it and it was restored to its sacred use in the Guild Hall of the Holy Family. The Rev. S. L. Skardon succeeded in charge until 1952 when the Rev. Harold E. Barrett took charge, then the Rev. Loren B. Mead in 1955. Bishop Carruthers, assisted by the Rev. Mr. Barrett, set aside and dedicated a portion of the Church lot for a burial ground on November 17, 1952. A large addition to the Guild Hall was built in 1956.

CHRIST CHURCH PARISH
ST. ANDREW'S CHURCH
MT. PLEASANT
Established 1706
(See Dalcho, p. 275)

Old Christ Church, six miles from Mt. Pleasant, is the third on the same site, but probably with some part of the second Church begun in 1724. The first building of wood was destroyed by fire in 1724, rebuilt of brick and destroyed by fire again by the British in 1782, then rebuilt again about 1794. Dalcho records that the parish had been without a regular minister for many years when the Rev. Albert Arney Muller, A.M., was elected rector, November 1, 1819. The white communicants were only 12, the colored 40. The Church shared thus in the depletion of Church life in the diocese after the Revolution. William Hart and Col. Jacob B. I'On were the delegates to the Convention in 1821.

The Rev. Mr. Muller left the parish in 1823, going to Pennsylvania. The Rev. Francis H. Rutledge, taking charge as deacon, became rector in 1826. He reports the Church now in a "more flattering" condition than for many years, with an attendance at service of 30 or 40 whites and as many colored; a second service had been instituted for these latter; and a third service occasionally in Mt. Pleasant—so here already was the beginning of St. Andrew's Chapel, Mt. Pleasant. There was a parish library and a parish society organized as auxiliary to the Advancement Society. The Rev. Philip Gadsden followed in charge for one year (1827), and then, next year, the Rev. Andrew Fowler, the famous missionary, who gives a very discouraging account of the parish—it "had degenerated from its pristine love," having no glebe and no parsonage, but its funds were well managed by one man; the vestry had not met in three years. He is soon encouraged, however, especially in mode of worship of men, women and children: "As it had pleased God to bestow on them the faculty of speech, so they were not ashamed to use that inestimable gift in His service, and to His glory." From January to June, service was held in the parish Church; from June to Advent in the minister's house in Mt. Pleasant. Although in 1830 Mr. Fowler could say, "A love to my Church, and a desire not to be idle, are the only inducements that have fixed me here," he evidently learned to so love and admire the old parish that he served it for 14 years. The Bishop thus characterized this Church then, "A small congregation of pious people."

It was the help of the Advancement Society and his private means that enabled Mr. Fowler to remain. Mr. Fowler reported in 1834, "we have raised money sufficient to build a small chapel of ease, in the village of Mount Pleasant, in this parish, which we shall begin to erect as soon as I can raise $250.00, to purchase a proper site for it, having already collected $100.00 towards it." Plans were now made (1834) to erect a chapel of ease in Mt. Pleasant. In 1836 he states that the Mother Church had been repaired, her appearance rendered "agreeable," and in Mount Pleasant a chapel had been built 50 x 30 feet. With the name "St. Andrew's Chapel" it was consecrated by the Bishop, assisted by five presbyters and one deacon on September 29, 1835. In 1837, he reports 16 white communicants and 20 colored, services eight Sundays at Christ Church and 19 at St. Andrew's, with active Sunday School. There were two confirmations this year; twelve confirmed. In his 78th year, the rector is greatly helped by the good responses of the congregation whom he 'loved and respected.' He thanks Bailey John Hamlin and E. W. Hart for assisting in catechising; Thomas Barksdale, Esq., for his efficient care of the temporalities of the Church; and Col. J. B. I'On for the refurnishing of the parish Church. Mr. Hart was lay reader at this time.

Mr. Fowler resigned the rectorship June, 1842, having served the Church as lay reader and clergyman for 60 years. This great servant of the Lord died in Charleston eight years later, the Sunday after Christmas, December 29, 1850, age 90 years and 7 months, buried in St. Michael's Churchyard. Besides services in the North, before coming South, he labored with effect in Columbia, Camden, Cheraw, St. Augustine, Fla. (when a S. C. mission), Wadesboro, Trinity, Edisto, St. Bartholomew's and Christ Church. The parish was now without regular ministrations for a long time. The Rev. P. T. Babbitt supplied some services for a short time and the Rev. J. R. Fell became rector in 1847. Under Mr. Fell, work among the Negroes was encouraged—certain pews in the Church were assigned to them; he finds, however, two drawbacks in this work; their strong attachments to other denominations and no chapels for them.

The interior of the parish Church was improved in 1852. At this time, Mr. Fell was often assisted by Rev. David McElheran, lately of St. Helena's Island, residing in Mt. Pleasant. Mr. Fell was ill for nearly six months in 1858. The first St. Andrew's Chapel consecrated in 1835 becoming too small, it was now replaced by a new chapel consecrated by Bishop Davis May 11, 1858. It is of simple Gothic style with recessed chancel, having tablets with Creed, Lord's Prayer, and Ten Commandments. The rector was absent on account of ill health. The following assisted: the Revs. C. C. Pinckney, C. P. Gadsden, A. W. Marshall, David McElheran, J. G. Drayton, and B. B. Sams. The architect was Col. E. B. White.

Mr. Fell resigned in July, 1860, in consequence of continued ill health. He, however, resumed services at the Six Mile Church in January, 1861, ministering especially to the Negroes and later to a company of soldiers from Sumter encamped nearby. In the meantime, the Rev. David McElheran held services every Sunday in the chapel in Mt. Pleasant, continuing through 1862. Mr. Fell discontinued his services the winter of 1862-63 at the parish Church for lack of transportation. In his address in 1869, the Bishop commemorated his long and faithful service hampered by ill health. In 1867, the Rev. Thomas F. Gadsden was in charge and J. E. Dawson, P. P. Bonneau, and Elias Venning were deputies to the Convention. The parish Church was for the time being a ruin. It had been used as a hospital by the Confederate Army. Mr. Gadsden relates that at the evacuation of Charleston, he saw this himself, as he then a soldier marched by. It had been twice used as a stable, by the British in the Revolution, and by Federal Cavalry after the evacuation of Charleston—pews, pulpit, floors, doors—all were gone, open to cattle and the birds of the air.

On his visit to St. Andrew's, Mt. Pleasant, February 2, 1871, Bishop Davis called the congregation "large and attentive." The rector, at this time, held a monthly service for colored people about eight miles from Mt. Pleasant; an effort to minister to these fast departing members of the Church. In 1873, the Sunday School of St. Andrew's Chapel received the gift of an organ from the Church of the Memorial, Baltimore. The warm interest of the rector and some members led to a meeting of the congregation, held in St. Andrew's Chapel on March 8, 1874, to plan for the restoration of old Christ Church and its reopening for worship. At this time, the graveyard was neglected and the Church a ruin, having only four brick walls and a roof, no floor, no windows or doors. About $500.00, mostly contributed by friends in Charleston, was expended and the Church put in fair condition. Mr. L. A. McCants superintended the restoration. Also, he gave sixteen acres around the Church for a graveyard and other purposes. The lumber for the pews was given by Mr. A. Knox. The old Church for the first time was now consecrated by Bishop Howe on December 27, 1874. Some gifts at this time were a lectern and Bible from St. Andrew's Chapel, prayer book by Mrs. D. O. Clark. Communion silver on the altar that day was a large tankard (1850), paten (given by Jacob Motte, 1763), paten (given by Mrs. Mary Guyer, 1820), old chalice (no inscription). Regular services were begun by Mr. Gadsden on the second Sunday in the month, meeting a real need especially for about ten families living in that area. On other Sundays, lay reading was conducted.

The Rev. David McElheran died in July, 1875, age 82, and was buried at Christ Church. He had been living in Mt. Pleasant since his resignation of St. Helena's, St. Helena Island, in 1856, and almost instantly assisted gratuitously in Christ Church Parish for all these years. The parish, with others in the diocese, was benefited by the legacy of Thomas C. Moore of New Jersey left for churches in the diocese damaged by the war. The parish was devastated by a malignant fever in 1877. Mr. Gadsden resigned as rector at the end of 1877 and was succeeded by the Rev. George Waldo Stickney. T. H. Broughton, superintendent of the Sunday School, also served for many years as lay reader in the parish. In 1880, a new fence was built about the rectory. In 1882, the Rev. Robert F. Clute was rector, succeeded by the Rev. Mercier Green in 1883. Mrs. P. E. Porcher at this time gave for the parish Church a handsome white marble font. The Church chapel and rectory were damaged by the earthquake of August, 1886. With the help of $500.00 from the "Earthquake Fund," repairs were effected. Mr. Green resigned October 13, 1890. The Rev. W. O. Prentiss and the Rev. John Gass supplied services now for a time. The Rev. H. M. Jarvis was rector from December, 1892, to December, 1893.

The Rev. J. S. Hartzell was rector to 1903 when he went to reside in Cheraw. Mr. Hartzell was the editor of a widely used series of Sunday School leaflets published in Richmond, also he was the author of a treatise on the Eucharist, and a book of sermons (*Sin and Our Saviour*). The rectorship was vacant for some time; services were supplied mostly by Rev. L. G. Wood. The rectory was destroyed by five in 1907, but was immediately rebuilt and occupied by Rev. C. W. Boyd, who became rector May 1, 1908. Rev. J. W. Sparks succeeded him December 1, 1909. A new organ was placed in Christ Church at this time. W. J. Edmonston and John M. Mitchell, also treasurer, were now the wardens; Willington E. Freeman, secretary. Rev. Percival H. Whaley became rector April 15, 1912. A new altar was placed in St. Andrew's in 1914, the old being taken to the old Church which was reopened, having been closed for some time. Rev. Sanders R. Guignard became rector in 1915, and William B. Sams in 1921. In 1924, old Christ Church was restored and beautified, as well as the surrounding burial ground which was enclosed with a lasting fence by Mr. John F. Maybank, whose ancestors belonged to this parish. He also established a trust fund to provide perpetual care of the grounds. St. Andrews was presented with handsome seven-branched candlesticks in 1931 in memory of Capt. and Mrs. Frank D. Pinckney.

Miss Harriett A. Pearce left the Church a valuable legacy about this time. In 1942, a fine Wick organ was installed at a cost of $2,450.00. It was given by many as a memorial to many. The year 1945 was marked by the installation of a new heating plant in the chapel, by the raising of $5,000.00 for a parish house in Mount Pleasant, and by Mr. Sams' resignation on August 1 after a quarter-century of faithful service. The Rev. Llewellen B. Catlin became rector September 1, 1946. The parish house was completed in 1948. The two churches, Christ and St. Andrew's, which was originally the chapel of ease of the former, were separated into two Church organizations in 1954. St. Andrew's in Mount Pleasant was admitted into Union with the Convention as itself a parish and old Christ Church as an organized mission. Mr. Catlin became rector of St. Andrew's and the Rev. R. J. Hobart took charge of Christ Church with Ferdinand Gregorie, Jr., as warden, and Mr. I. D. Auld, treasurer. The wardens of St. Andrew's were then D. M. White, Jr., and Allan Sloan; treasurer, W. D. Freeman. In 1955, old Christ Church was given a bell by Mr. Floyd Edward Bliven of Erie, Pa., a visitor

at Porcher's Bluff. It was salvaged from the first all-electric loco-
motive which began operating in Erie in 1929. It is mounted in a
tasteful iron tower at the side of the Church, given by Julius W.
Nichols and made by Richard Millar of Charleston. The Rev. M.
John Bywater assumed charge of Christ Church March, 1956.

CHRIST CHURCH, MULLINS
Established 1904

In October, 1904, there being a group of a dozen or so Episcopalians in the immediate neighborhood of Mullins, desiring services there and there bring a prospect for establishing the Episcopal
Church in this town, the Rev. Albert S. Thomas inaugurated services there, the Presbyterian Church being kindly loaned for the
purpose. A tentative organization was effected with Dr. A. M.
Brailsford as warden and Mr. William McIntyre, treasurer. These
officers continued for many years, the latter until 1913 when Mrs.
S. B. Crawford became treasurer. Dr. Brailsford was warden until
1917 when he was succeeded by Mr. William McIntyre. The members of the mission were largely of the family of Mrs. J. J. McIntyre, a devoted Church member. Five shares of Building and Loan
Stock was subscribed by members with a view to building in the
future. Mrs. McIntyre gave a lot for a Church. This lot was exchanged for another in 1910. Mr. Thomas continued these services
in the Presbyterian Church, until he resigned the Advent, Marion,
September, 1908. The services were held on either the first Monday
or Friday of each month. He was succeeded by the Rev. H. C. Salmond in August, 1909. In 1910 the statistics of the mission were for
the first time reported separately from the Advent, Marion, being
now ranked as an unorganized diocesan mission. In 1911, the mission was given the name Christ Church, plans being inaugurated to
build a chapel, $600.00 being in hand. The Church was built in
1913-14 when the Rev. E. A. Penick, afterwards Bishop of North
Carolina, was in charge. The first service held in Christ Church was
Evensong on November 23rd, 1913. The Rev. Mr. Penick conducted
the service. Bishop W. A. Guerry and the Rev. A. S. Thomas, who
had founded the Church in Mullins, took part. From then on, services were held on the second and fourth Sunday nights. The Rev.
W. S. Holmes succeeded Mr. Penick in 1915. Then followed the
Rev. R. L. Merryman.

There are a number of beautiful memorials in the Church. A
stained glass window placed in the chancel directly back of the
altar was given by Mrs. S. H. Schoolfield in memory of her parents,

Mr. and Mrs. William Davis Cleveland. The altar cross was given by Dr. and Mrs. A. M. Brailsford in memory of their infant son, A. M. Brailsford, Jr. Two handsome seven-branched candlelabra were given by Miss Mayo Simpson, in memory of her parents. The marble baptismal font is a memorial to Curtis Bethea, Jr., given by his parents. On December 5, 1920, the Church was consecrated by the Rt. Rev. William Alexander Guerry, Bishop, assisted by the Rev. Edgar V. W. Edwards, who had taken charge in this year. Soon after the Church was built, chiefly under the leadership of Mr. and Mrs. S. B. Crawford, the mission had a remarkable Sunday School, numbering at one time eighty-four pupils.

The Rev. Edgar Edwards was succeeded after two years by the Rev. Herbert Mayers (1925). Next came the Rev. Harold J. Lewis in 1929. His tragic death came March 12, 1930. While the Rev. Thomas S. Tisdale was rector of the Church of the Advent in Marion, Christ Church was dormant, the people mostly worshipping in Marion. A revival of interest began when the Rev. Colin R. Campbell took charge of the Church in Marion. It was on Whitsunday, May 24, 1942, that Christ Church mission was formally reopened and has continued so ever since. Mr. L. R. Daniel was appointed warden and treasurer, and Mr. A. S. Reeder, lay reader. The Rev. Lawton Riley was in charge of the mission from 1945-47.

In May of 1947 the Rev. W. S. Poynor took over the care of the mission. He was the first Episcopal minister to live in Mullins, and under his leadership the mission identified itself with the community and made a definite contribution to the spiritual life of Mullins. The wardens now were L. R. Daniel and J. P. Cain; Miss Mayo Simpson, secretary and treasurer; and Mr. Arthur Reeder, lay reader. It is interesting to note that two of the ministers who have served this little mission have become Bishops. The Rev. Earl C. Page was in charge of this Church for about two years from 1953. The Rev. John B. Morris succeeded in 1954.

TRINITY CHURCH, MYRTLE BEACH
FORMERLY CHURCH OF THE MESSIAH
Established 1939

About the year 1936, Myrtle Beach was increasing in importance both as a resort and as a year-round place of residence, and in consequence the Bishop of the diocese, perceiving the importance of providing Church privileges there took steps for the erection of a Church. The Laymen's League of the Pee Dee Convocation agreed to sponsor the movement. The greatest encouragement was a gift of $1,000.00 by Mr. Horace L. Tilghman of Marion and the gift of a lot by Myrtle Beach Farms Company whose president was Mr. S. B. Chapin. Mr. N. C. Hughes of Myrtle Beach contributed valuable services from the beginning. The neighboring priests, the Rev. H. D. Bull who had pastoral charge and the Rev. T. S. Tisdale, rendered assistance in holding some services and in raising funds.

It was found necessary in order to finance the building of a Church to organize a corporation. This was done on June 13, 1939, with the following membership—Messrs. N. C. Hughes, Jr., S. H. Schoolfield, W. B. Moore, E. W. Duvall, and Bishop Thomas, chairman. A deed to the lot was received from Myrtle Beach Farms on July 19, 1939, and with over $3,000.00 in hand the corporation proceeded with the building of the Church according to plans prepared by Albert S. Thomas, Jr., architect, of Columbia. The plan of the corporation was to deed the property to the diocese as soon as the Church was completed and fully paid for. The cornerstone was laid with Masonic ceremonies on August 13, 1939, Grand Master S. Maner Martin presiding. Mr. Bull read a history of the beginnings of the Church by Bishop Thomas, and the Rev. T. S. Tisdale made an address. A granite tablet placed in the front wall of the Church by Major W. B. Moore bore the inscription: "Church of the Messiah, Myrtle Beach. My house shall be called a House of Prayer for all people." The rectory was the gift of Mr. W. B. Moore of York, also a generous benefactor of the Church. In this building on October 13, 1939, the Church was organized by the Bishop as a "mission" of the diocese with the name, "Church of the Messiah", perpetuating the old parish of this name on the North Santee River. The following officers were appointed by the Bishop: warden, N. C. Hughes; treasurer, Frank Orr; secretary, Mrs. L. P. LaBruce. On the advice of the Bishop the following were nominated and elected to act in advisory way as a vestry (but not a regular vestry as this is not canonical for a mission): Messrs. Albert A. Springs, Raymond Reinhart, St. Julian L. Springs, and L. P. LaBruce. Mr. Bull was appointed officially in charge of the mission. About 40 persons were present at this meeting and 28 signed the application for organization. At this meeting Mr. N. C. Hughes, Jr., who had superintended the building of the Church, reported that cost was $5,200.00, in addition the lot was valued at $1,500.00, and the rectory $2,750.00, furniture $412.30. Total value $9,862.30 with an outstanding debt of $1,900.00. The first service in the new Church was held on the afternoon of Thanksgiving Day, November 23, 1939. The Bishop of the diocese, after a regular Thanksgiving Day service conducted by the Rev. H. D. Bull, assisted by the Rev. T. S. Tisdale, offered prayers appropriate to the occasion. The Rt. Rev. John J. Gravatt of the diocese of Upper South Carolina preached the sermon. It was planned to have visiting ministers to occupy the rectory in the summer months and supply services every Sunday. It was the understanding with Mr. W. B. Moore of York when he gave the rectory that this privilege would be open to the clergy of both dioceses in South Carolina. The Rev. R. C. Patton of St. Matthew's Church succeeded Mr. Bull in the charge of the Church in 1941. A Church school was begun.

In 1943 chiefly through the efforts of Mr. St. Julian L. Springs and the generosity of Mr. Chapin the debt of the Church was entirely liquidated and the corporation in the fall deeded the property to the trustees of the diocese. The Church was consecrated the following summer, July 23, 1944, by the Rt. Rev. T. N. Carruthers, Bishop. In 1951, the congregation decided to change the name of the Church from the Church of the Messiah to Trinity Episcopal Church. The Convention of the diocese confirmed this action April, 1951. The Rev. Allen W. Joslin succeeded Mr. Patton in charge in 1946 and Mr. Hughes became warden again succeeding Mr. Springs. In 1949 this mission was organized as a parish and the same year admitted into union with the Convention as such, the deputies being, N. C. Hughes, Jr., James S. Thompson, W. P. Frier, and Walter Y. Hasien. In 1950, the Church had gained such strength to justify its call of the Rev. Eugene J. West as its first resident rector. The Rev. Manney C. Reid became rector in 1954.

THE GOOD SHEPHERD, NORTH CHARLESTON
Established 1922

As early as 1913 Dr. John Kershaw, dean of the Charleston Convocation, had pointed out North Charleston as a prospective field of work for the Church; however, it was not until the latter part of 1921 that the Rev. R. F. Blackford was appointed as missionary to North Charleston merely as to a "field of opportunity". He began work at once. The first service was held in an army tent in February 1922; home-made furniture was supplied and other necessities were given, including a Bible. The mission was "organized" with the following officers: warden, R. R. Bryan; secretary, Fenn Riddle; treasurer and lay reader, R. R. Bryan. Services were held regularly. There were twenty-seven communicants reported; a Church school was at once organized. The mission was incorporated with the name, Church of the Good Shepherd, and the lot on which the tent stood was bought. The tent soon proving inadequate, through the courtesy of the Seaboard Railroad the services for several months were held in its baggage room—not ideal with room half full of baggage and trains passing near! Nevertheless, Mr. Blackford could say, "Our baggage room is decidedly churchly in atmosphere."

A building fund was started by a contribution from the Nation-wide Campaign. By a sale of government barracks at the port terminals, a building was secured and re-erected into a Church building on the lot; on each side of the entrance passage were rooms for parish purposes. This chapel was opened for services on May 14, 1922, when Bishop Guerry celebrated the Holy Communion, assisted by Mr. Blackford, and confirmed two persons. The large congregation was augmented by the presence of members of neighboring congregations and their ministers, who had closed their own doors for the occasion.

In 1925, the Rev. John H. Morgan succeeded Mr. Blackford. He served for three years. The Rev. Sumner Guerry, recently returned from his work in China, took charge first temporarily December 1, 1928, and then permanently. The officers at this time were: wardens, R. R. Bryan and L. D. Eure; secretary, L. M. Rivers; treasurer and lay reader, R. R. Bryan. The communicants now numbered 39, the Church school 36. In 1933, new pews were installed and the Church improved, being painted within and without. The work was done by members. In 1933, the experiment of Church school on Saturday instead of Sunday was tried with some success at first, but was later abandoned. At this time a lot north of the Church was acquired. Mr. Guerry resigned the Church in January, 1944. At this time the warden was William E. Sparkman; treasurer, Mrs. Michael Onufer. The Rev. Emanuel A. LeMoine assumed charge in March following. The communicants now numbered 65. Mr. LeMoine was succeeded by the Rev. C. Raymond Allington in 1946, coming from central New York. Progress was now indicated by a greatly increased budget for 1947 which was fully subscribed. A new altar guild was formed at this time. On Whitsunday of this year, a notable class of 14, infants, children, and adults, were baptized. On Easter Day, 1948, an altar cross was dedicated in memory of Emery Blake Woodward, the gift of his aunt and grandmother. During this year, the congregation built a rectory adjoining the Church, into which Mr. Allington moved. In 1951, the

Good Shepherd was admitted to the Convention as a parish. It had now grown to a communicant membership of 144, with a Church school of 74. The activities of this Church under Mr. Allington had greatly expanded. Quite notable in the recent life of this Church has been the presentation of Christmas pageants, written by the rector—that of 1952 was called "The Birth of Charity". In 1954 the wardens were L. D. Eure and George Gladden; secretary, Frederick Hughes; treasurer, Mrs. Helen Brock.

GRACE CHAPEL, OKETEE
Established 1860

The first mention we have of Church work on the "Ocaty" (about 15 miles from Grahamville) is in 1860 when Mr. James E. Fripp built there a chapel for the Negroes; the Rev. J. V. Welch was the missionary. After the interruption of war the Rev. E. E. Bellinger in 1870, taking charge of this whole part of the diocese, held services on the Okatee (spelt in various ways, Ocaty, Ochitie, Ochetee, Okatee, Oketee) often in Mr. Fripp's house. They had services four times a year. Bishop Howe recounts services at Mr. John Fripp's on November 25, 1874. On observing the determination of the people to have services, he relates, "the wind and water being boisterous, I felt my heart go out towards these people, and was glad I could minister to them". In 1879 the services for four families were at Mr. John E. Fripp's.

A chapel was built at Oketee in 1880. Mr. Bellinger was at this time succeeded by the Rev. B. B. Sams. The chapel was blown down in the great storm of August 27, 1893. Due chiefly to a gift of $300.00, with other contributions, the chapel was rebuilt by the spring of 1894. It was consecrated by Bishop Capers on December 5, 1894. The Rev. J. M. Pringle took charge in 1897. The Rev. J. B. Walker succeeded him in 1901 and then the Rev. J. C. Waring from July, 1902, until April, 1907. Only occasional services were held here for years. The Rev. J. H. Woodward reported three families in 1917 and three services—Horry Fripp was treasurer, succeeded by Joseph Fripp. The mission in 1920 was called Grace, Oketee. Mr. Woodward resigned in 1926 and the mission passed to the charge of the Rev. R. M. Marshall in connection with Grahamville. In 1928 this mission was combined with Holy Trinity, Grahamville.

CHURCH OF THE REDEEMER, ORANGEBURG
Established 1851

This Church is located in old St. Matthew's Parish and its earlier interesting history is connected with that parish (see Dalcho). The Rev. Francis Padmore Delavaux became rector of St. Matthew's in 1819, but there is no mention of his holding services in Orangeburg. It would seem that the Episcopal Church pretty well died out in the town for the succeeding years. The Rev. R. D. Shindler became rector of St. Matthew's in 1846 but resigned the next year. He took up his residence in Orangeburg and reports services there in what he called the "Church of the Holy Trinity" which was organized on October 21, 1848. A vestry was elected consisting of: chairman, Dr. S. B. Dwight; wardens, Thomas S. Mood and John Marchant; vestrymen, Hon. John Felder, Capt. John C. Row, John H. Felder, and T. B. Whaley; treasurer, Henry Ellis; secretary, Addison Beach. The services were held in the Court House. A lot had been contracted for and a fund was proposed to build a Church. This attempt to establish an Episcopal Church in Orangeburg proved futile. Mr. Shindler's main purpose in the town was to teach a school but the effort to start an Episcopal Church produced opposition to his school and efforts were made to break it down. He was mainly dependent upon the school for support, so he says there was nothing left but for him to leave.

However, there was no intention of abandoning the plan to re-establish an Episcopal Church in Orangeburg; Rev. Benjamin Johnson had become rector of St. Matthew's and reports for 1851, the organization of a Church in Orangeburg called the Redeemer. It was admitted into Convention on February 12, 1851. He had held public worship 40 times and steps were taken to build a Church, plans had been agreed upon and a contract accepted. In 1852 a contribution of $125.00 was made by old St. Peter's Church, Charleston, and the ladies of that Church gave a communion service, a Bible, and prayer book; St. Philip's, Charleston, contributed $37.50. In February, 1854, it is stated that "a very energetic and zealous lady who spends her summers in this village has assumed the responsibility of erecting the Church here and the work is progressing." Mr. Johnson was succeeded very briefly by the Rev. J. J. Sams (1854-55). Still there was no Church building when the Rev. E. A. Wagner next took charge in 1856, but one was completed the next year (located near the depot) and was consecrated on Saturday, March 14, 1857, a great storm ushering in the day. Bishop Davis was assisted in the service by the Rev. Messrs. Wagner,

Cranmore Wallace, and J. H. Cornish; Mr. Wallace preached the sermon. Services were held again at night and three times on the next day, Sunday, when seven were confirmed. Mr. Wagner went to Texas in 1860 and the Church fell to the charge of the Rev. Paul Trapier. At this time the Church was in a flourishing condition, services twice every Sunday, a belfry built, and a bell for it being cast in Columbia to cost $250.00. In 1863 there were many refugees from the low-country to swell the congregation but it was "sad to miss so many males away in the war, and so many in mourning." In this year, the Rev. Stiles Mellichamp came to assist Mr. Trapier who was also a professor in the Theological Seminary in Camden. Mr. Mellichamp was rector of St. James, James Island, so neither minister lived in Orangeburg. The refugees had crowded the colored people out of the Church where formerly they had also worshipped. Sherman passed through the town in February and left the people impoverished. In 1866, Mr. Mellichamp became rector of St. Matthew's and of Redeemer, Orangeburg. He lost his horse and for a time had to walk five miles to hold services in Orangeburg. Later he lived in the town. In 1867, the report is that each Church, St. Matthew's and Redeemer, were to pay the minister $225.00. He received $75.00 from Orangeburg and $60.00 from St. Matthews. The unselfish soul attributed this to an "unprecedented drought," but more likely to be attributed to the poverty of the people after the war. In 1869, he notes "lack of zeal and interest" by some but numbers holding up. Mr. W. R. Treadwell was the deputy to the Convention at this time. Losing his place of residence in Orangeburg by the sale of a building belonging to the diocesan seminary, given to it by Hon. G. A. Trenholm, Mr. Mellichamp resigned in 1870, but he continued holding services once a month. He died in 1872, as did also the late rector Dr. Paul Trapier.

The Rev. William H. Johnson was in charge for a short time in 1874, followed briefly by the Rev. N. B. Fuller. The Rev. L. F. Guerry then took charge in 1877. At this time the ladies of the sewing society were working for a parsonage. In 1882 the Church was repaired and repainted and a silver tankard was purchased and also an organ. Mr. Guerry was succeeded by Rev. Edwin C. Steele in 1884 who died the next year, and was succeeded by the Rev. H. J. Broadwell, M.D., who continued only until December 15, 1886. The Church was vacant until the coming of the Rev. J. B. Williams in 1890, who served until 1893. A movement to build a new Church was inaugurated in 1891. The Rev. J. H. Tillinghast became rector in 1894 and under him the new Church became a reality. This second Church of the Redeemer was consecrated by Bishop Capers assisted by Mr. Tillinghast on December 15, 1895. The first Church was near the depot. The town had grown away from it. The new Church was built in a more central location. Bishop Capers called it "a more comfortable and more suitable Church." A memorial font was presented to the Church on Easter Day, 1897. The wardens this year were James F. Izlar and James H. Towles. Mr. Tillinghast resigned in January, 1901, and was succeeded the following summer by Rev. Thomas Tracy Walsh who served until November, 1905. Under Mr. Walsh's direction a pipe organ was installed in the Church. The Rev. Harold Thomas served as rector for about a year (1906-1907) installing a vested choir. He was followed by the Rev. W. S. Holmes, August 10, 1907, who served until October 1, 1914. The wardens in 1912 were Asbury Coward and T. O. S. Dibble. In 1914 a parish house was built on the Church lot made possible by a legacy of Mr. David Weston Shuler. Mr. Holmes was succeeded by the Rev. John London until 1918. At this time the rectory was enlarged and greatly improved and the next year, 1917, many improvements were made on the Church: painting, new pews, brick foundation, furnace, new glass in windows, new electric fixtures, prayer desk and choir stalls, eagle lectern, and memorial window. The Church was much improved by being brick-veneered.

The Rev. Richard L. Merryman became rector in 1920, serving about one year, being succeeded in 1923 by the Rev. Ilbert deLacy Brayshaw until August, 1924. The Rev. Albert S. Cooper, lately missionary in China, then followed in 1925 and until 1928. The wardens in 1925 were John Cantey and L. S. C. Barton, the deputies to Convention, John Cantey, F. A. Schiffley, W. L. Glover, and L. R. Van Orsdell. The Rev. Edgar C. Burns became rector February 1, 1928. He resigned February, 1933, being succeeded almost immediately by the Rev. R. H. Jackson, late missionary to Japan, under whom the Church prospered. He was succeeded by the Rev. Thomas S. Tisdale in 1940. In this year the wardens were W. H. Richardson and W. T. C. Bates, and there were 204 communicants. In 1945 Mrs. Lida C. Washington left the Redeemer an estate of about $45,000.00. In 1950 the vestry purchased the property of Mrs. W. R. Lowman adjoining the Church for $25,000.00. In 1954 a new parish hall was completed at a cost of around $35,000.00. In 1949 a new pipe organ was installed at an approximate cost of $9,000.00. The old rectory was sold in 1954.

In 1954 a lot was purchased in Scoville Woods for $2,875.00 as a site for a new rectory. It was completed the year following at a cost of $22,000.00. A kindergarten was begun in the summer of 1956. Recent memorials are: a chalice and paten in memory of Mrs. A. E. (Ellen) McCoy; silver alms basins in memory of William Preston Davis; silver cruets in memory of departed members of the Scoville family; a new altar and dossal in memory of Clem Buchanan Jennings (Mrs. R. H., Jr.). The number of communicants in this parish had increased to 345 in 1955.

ST. PAUL'S MISSION
STATE COLLEGE, ORANGEBURG
(See Archdeaconry, end this Section)

ALL SAINTS', WACCAMAW, PAWLEY'S ISLAND
Established 1767
(See Dalcho, p. 322)

It is thought that All Saints' received its name from this circumstance: On September 20, 1745, Lord Carteret and his heirs received a grant of one-eighth part of the Province of Carolina, yielding to His Majesty one-fourth part of all gold and silver ore found there and an annual rent of £1, 13s., 4d. "payable on the feast of All Saints' forever." This parish, like nearly all in the rural sections of the state after the Revolution, was largely dormant for many years. It was re-established by the distinguished priest and scholar, Hugh Fraser, rector from 1812 until 1817. The Rev. Andrew Fowler was then visitor for a short time. In 1793 Captain John Allston had the old Church taken down and a new one erected in its place at a cost of £100 sterling. This one was repaired and fitted with pews in 1813. On the 19th of November, 1816, it was consecrated by Bishop Dehon. All Saints' was represented in the Convention for the first time in 1813 by Dr. J. O. Watson. In 1819 a neatly furnished building was erected in the lower part of the parish on a site given by Joseph P. LaBruce, and was consecrated by Bishop Bowen in January, 1820. The Rev. Henry Gibbes, who had been lay reader in 1817 and 1818, now in 1819 became rector. He rendered a fine service and was highly esteemed until he resigned in 1829.

In 1817 a Church was erected in the southern part of the parish at Oak Hill, on a site given by Joseph P. LaBruce. It became known as "The Lower Church", having no other name. It was consecrated by Bishop Bowen in January, 1860. This was a chapel of ease—

the distance to the parish Church, seven miles, was great in that day—in fact, it was at least thirty miles from north to south in the parish. In the summer the people largely resorted to North Island where also was a chapel. Thus, Mr. Gibbes ministered at three places. The Rev. Hugh Fraser supplied services in the interim until Rev. Alexander Glennie took charge in 1832. Mr. Bull, in his admirable history of the parish, calls the following period until the war "Expansion and Collapse." It was coeval with the ministry of the Rev. Alexander Glennie, and was a period of great prosperity among the rice planters of the entire section. Wealth was probably greater here on these great plantations than in any other rural section of the state. Mr. Glennie had been brought from England by Francis Marion Weston to be tutor for his son, the distinguished Plowden C. J. Weston, who was destined to be a co-worker in the parish with Mr. Glennie who was soon ordained (1832) and put in charge of the parish.

Mr. Glennie was not content to do the ordinary work of the parish, holding services at the upper and lower churches and at the beach in summer, but at once started out in his great missionary work among the Negroes. There were something like five thousand slaves in the parish. He developed great aptitude in his ministry to these people, teaching them the catechism and training them in the worship of the Church. Bishop Philander Chase, on visiting Mr. Glennie's work, wrote "The black children of a South Carolina planter know more of Christianity than thousands of white children in Illinois." Up to the time of the war, he had built no less than thirteen chapels for those people on Waccamaw Neck. The most famous of these was that on Mr. Plowden's plantation at Hagley named St. Mary's—much more elegant and well furnished than many other churches in the diocese. Mr. Glennie's work among the Negroes received wide recognition. He was elected missionary Bishop of Cape Palmas (now Liberia) by the General Convention in 1844, but he declined. As Mr. Bull remarks, "He had Africa at his very doorstep." Towards the latter part of his rectorship he reported that in 1832 he found 10 colored communicants in the parish. Since then there had been added 519.

Mr. Glennie thus described his thirty years of mission work in All Saints', Waccamaw, in a letter to the Bishop of North Carolina written in 1862:

"When I commenced this work nearly 30 years ago I used only a portion of the daily Service, omitting the Psalter, the Psalms & the New Testament. But after a few years I abandoned this practice, & have habitually gone through the entire morning or evening Service with my Negro congregation, having taught them the versicles after the Lord's prayer & Creed, & directing them to repeat with me every alternate verse in one of the selections of the Psalms.

In congregations which have been for many years under my charge the responding is good, & the chanting & singing are conducted with much spirit.

Of late years when I have taken charge of a Congregation which have not been accustomed to the Services of our Church, I have invariably introduced the entire Service, & in a very short time the people have become interested in our mode of worship & have learned to respond correctly. As with few exceptions my services for the Negroes are in the afternoon and evening, the order of daily Evening Prayer is that which is most frequently used.

From the first I saw the necessity of carrying the Adults through a course of Catechetical instruction. This I gave them immediately after my Sermon. The Sermon is sometimes extemporaneous, upon a portion of one of the lessons, or it is a short written discourse; most frequently the latter. In this case I divide the sermon into three or four portions, after each of which I question the congregation upon what I have said. This keeps up their attention & gives me an opportunity of explaining to them more fully the subject in hand: its beneficial effects have been manifest: & some of the more intelligent among them have acknowledged to me with expressions of thankfulness that they have learned so much under this system of instructions. Before concluding I have from time to time gone through portions of the Church Cathechism, & of the Liturgy, explaining & asking questions.

The Plantations in this Parish extend for about 30 miles along the river. The Negroes therefore cannot be brought together from several plantations, & divine service is conducted in routine upon each of them under my charge. When I have two assistants with me, there is divine service on eight different plantations every Sunday, & on others at night during the week. On many of the Plantations very neat Chapels have been erected; some of these are superior to the ordinary country parish Churches.

The children are catechized during the week, I teach them the Church Cathechism, questioning them upon each answer after the manner of the Rev'd Paul Trapier's questions upon portions of the Book of Common Prayer written by myself. This exercise enlivened from time to time by singing hymns and chanting, occupies me and my assistants from one hour to one hour & a half on each plantation once a fortnight: on a few once a week.

When the Planter, or some member of his family engages in this work, conducting divine Service on Sunday, Cathechizing the younger Children frequently during the week, and the elder ones, who have been put to work, on Sunday, the improvement of the people in the knowledge of the divine truth is very perceptible. On one plantation I received most efficient aid in this way for many years. It was truly delightful to conduct divine Service in the crowded Chapel, to hear the loud and accurate responding and the hearty singing and chanting, and also to examine the children, sometimes for two hours, upon the Church Cathechism and portions of the Liturgy. They whose labour of love was thus blessed are now at rest, but their people are still cared for; their present owner having a resident Cathechist, so that the week-day catechizing and the services on the Lord's day are continued un-interruptedly.

On many of the Plantations the Master, and the Mistress stand as the Sponsors at the baptism of the children. On others, the Parents, or some of their friends undertake this duty.

At every visitation of the Bishop many of the colored population are confirmed.

The communicants who reside near the Church partake of the Lord's Supper along with the white communicants of the Parish. To those who reside at a distance from the Church the Holy Sacrament is administered from time to time in the plantation Chapel.

A most important regulation, connected with the moral improvement of the Negroes, is that which requires them to be joined together in matrimony according to God's ordinance. Many of the Planters of this Parish have for many years insisted upon this, and the benefit of such a rule, according so entirely with their obligations as Christians, has been very manifest. It is easier to carry out this practice on large plantations in the country, where the parties in almost all cases belong to the same owner, than in towns and villages: but the hope may be indulged that the time is approaching when provision shall be made by our Legislature to prevent the separation of married slaves.

When I was ordained in 1832 there were 10 colored Communicants attached to the Church in this Parish. Since that date there have been added 519. Of these, many have died, many have been moved away, and a few have been suspended: the number reported at the last convention was 289.

The sick and the aged are visited frequently. The discharge of the duties produces very happy effects. Human beings love sympathy and kind attentions, and the affections & confidence of the Negroes are thus gained, while we converse with them, listen patiently to them, and minister to their spiritual wants.

Along with the punctual and patient discharge of the duties required of a Missionary to our Negroes, what continued prayer is needed, that our convenant Gad may fully qualify us for this work, and that He may open the hearts of this portion of our flock, so that they may receive and love and follow the truth as it is in Jesus."

We find a foreshadowing of our great Woman's Auxiliary in this parish—in 1835, there was then formed in it a "Female Missionary Society, auxiliary to the Domestic and Foreign Missionary Society of the Protestant Episcopal Church." In 1841 the Lower Church was enlarged to provide 120 sittings for Negroes. In 1851 it received further alterations with the addition of a porch. A catechist was employed in this year to assist the rector. In 1838 Mrs. Mary Huger, daughter of Captain John Allston, gave by will to All Saints' $5,441.81. It was then determined to build a new Church of brick. A building committee was appointed, consisting of Edward T. Heriot, Frances M. Weston, Joshua J. Ward, T. Pinckney Alston, John H. Tucker. The old Church was removed and a cornerstone was laid on December 27, 1843. The Church was completed and consecrated April 8, 1845, but had been used since October, 1844. This building of colonial design, with massive columns on the front porch, having galleries on each side, was the third Church on the same site. There were several gifts for the new Church: an organ by Col. Joshua J. Ward; Bible, Prayer Book, chancel chair and font by Mrs. F. M. Weston, and furniture by Mr. Plowden C. J. Weston. The old Church was re-erected on Litchfield plantation (for the Negroes). For thirty years two schools were conducted in the parish in Mr. Glennie's time.

In 1849 Mr. Glennie was assisted for a time by Rev. C. T. Bland, and this year a new chapel was opened for the Negroes to seat 200.

A report at this time showed 39 services at the parish Church, 21 at the Southern Church, six at summer residence, and 184 for the Negroes especially; total 250. Mr. A. T. Porter, then a candidate for Holy Orders, assisted in 1853-54. In 1845 Col. Peter W. Fraser gave a large lot on Pawley's Island for a summer rectory. It was built in 1854 and has been in use ever since. In 1855 another Church was built eight miles north of the parish Church at a place called Wachesaw, two miles north of Laurel Hill, on a bluff on the river. Dr. Allard B. Flagg gave the site. The cornerstone was laid by Bishop Davis on April 2, 1855. It was opened on May 24, 1855, for services and consecrated April 15, 1859, under the name of Saint John the Evangelist. This Church was largely for the benefit of church members who lived on the west side of the river, having to come by boat. During the succeeding years, Mr. Glennie had some help: Rev. Lucien C. Lance, assistant minister (1855-60); the Rev. Henry L. Phillips, missionary (1857-58); the Rev. J. H. Quinby (1859-60); catechists, B. H. Carter, D. D. Rosa. Another chapel for Negroes was built in 1858 and two more in 1860.

But alas! Ominously in 1862 Mr. Glennie reported the work "interrupted"; in 1863 he states that he had left the parish the end of May before. He was now residing in Prince Frederick's at Plantersville serving there and from whence he visited the "few" people still in All Saints'; the Negroes had moved inland. Mr. Rosa ministered there to a few that were left. The war had done its work. On May 5, 1866, on his visitation, Mr. Glennie being with him, Bishop Davis found the Negroes in a great state of excitement, a female prophetess having arisen among them. She was being removed by the military authorities. The next day he and Mr. Glennie held services in the parish Church where he confirmed two persons. There were but few of the old parishioners present, but a few Negroes had returned, and were in attendance. "I preached as well as I could," he wrote, "upon the duties of submission to the will of God, and of fighting out bravely the battles of life under the only real power left—faith." The colored population seemed lost to the Church. Mr. Glennie, after thirty-four years of faithful service, resigned for want of means to sustain him, June, 1866. He accepted a call to Prince George which could promise no definite salary. The Rev. Lucien C. Lance became rector and served until 1867, when he went to Maryland. The parish was now vacant until 1877, with only occasional services. The Rev. W. H. Johnson acted as rector for about a year, leaving March, 1874.

Soon after the war the Church of St. John the Evangelist began to fall into ruins and was taken down. The pews were taken to Prince Frederick's in Plantersville. Its communion silver is now used at All Saints'. The Lower Church was preserved for some time after the war, until it was accidentally burned January, 1871; its bell was taken to All Saints'. "The prostration of the once flourishing churches on Waccamaw was complete." St. Mary's, the beautiful chapel for the Negroes built at Hagley, survived for some years after much abuse being used by the Negroes. Mr. W. St. Julian Mazyck, having in charge the Weston estate, gave most of the furnishing of this chapel to different churches, realizing they otherwise would be lost: to Prince George's, stained glass, clock and bell, and gold (gilt) cup with cover, and paten; to Grace, Camden, an English granite font; to Prince Frederick's, carved oak choir stalls; to James Island, Bible, Prayer Book, altar book, oak book rest. St. Mary's burned in July, 1931. (See Bishop Davis's Annual address, 1873, when he tells of the last of St. Mary's, and when he advocated a missionary Bishop for work among the Negroes.)

The Rev. W. H. Barnwell began to officiate in the winter of 1876, becoming rector in 1878. He was offered a salary of $700.00, not bad for that day. This was an indication of a rebirth in the parish, both spiritual and material. Rice had become profitable again, for a time at least. Work among the Negroes was not allowed to die. Bishop Howe tells of a service he held for them in St. Mary's Chapel in 1873. Mr. Barnwell resigned April 5, 1885. He was succeeded by the Rev. Curtis P. Jones almost immediately, who remained for just two years, and then came Rev. G. T. Wilmer, D.D., from 1888 to 1891. More organized work among the Negroes began again at this time with a mission at Brook Green having a hospital sponsored by the Willett family especially, and a mission and school at St. Mary's, Annieville, in 1892. The story of this work will hereafter be connected with that of the Archdeaconry for Colored Work. The Rev. L. F. Guerry became rector in 1892. Much of his time was devoted to ministering to the Negroes. The hurricane of 1893 did much damage in the parish. Dr. Arthur B. Flagg, devoted churchman, and his entire family lost their lives on Magnolia Beach with many others. The vestry book was found in the wet sand. In 1898 Francis W. and St. Julian Lachicotte conveyed to the parish an acre of land near the road leading to the causeway to Pawley's Island and there, out of the materials from one of the old chapels, built a summer chapel which was used for this purpose until 1934, when it was converted into a community center, automobiles and good roads having restored the parish Church to summer use. In 1901 the wardens were Ralph Nesbit and St. J. M. Lachicotte, the latter also treasurer, and B. P. Fraser, lay reader here and in Prince Frederick's, following in the footsteps of his grandfather of the same name.

In the spring of 1905, Mr. Guerry was succeeded as rector by the Rev. Charles E. Cabaniss (1905-07), then the Rev. J. E. H. Galbraith (1908-22). In 1915 both the Church and the rectory were repaired at considerable expense. Then suddenly on Sunday, December 12, 1915, the handsome old Church burned down. The destruction was complete—only the altar cross and vases, memorials to Col. Ralph Nesbit of Caledonia, a Bishop's chair and some books were saved. Undeterred, the congregation immediately raised a considerable sum for rebuilding. The new Church was completed at a cost of over $5,000.00 and consecrated by Bishop Guerry on December 9, 1917, almost exactly two years after the burning. The new Church, the fourth on the same spot, was architecturally very similar to the old Church of Colonial style, having porch with massive columns in front. The Rev. C. W. Boyd succeeded Mr. Galbraith as rector in 1923, serving for two years. In July, 1925, the Rev. H. D. Bull became rector, residing in Georgetown. In 1931 many improvements were made in All Saints'—electric lights, new organ, marble font, credence, hymn board. The year following, through the generosity of Dr. and Mrs. Henry Norris, the churchyard was enclosed with a brick wall with iron gates. In 1935 the old summer chapel was remodelled into a community house. Besides being used as a social center, here was held a Sunday School, week-day service, and adult Bible class. It assists in ministering to the summer residents of Pawley's Island, being much nearer than the parish Church. In 1949 Dr. Bull published a very valuable and complete history of All Saints with its records. After a devoted and useful ministry of twenty-eight years he resigned in July, 1953. He was succeeded by Rev. A. Nelson Daunt. Many improvements were made in the furnishings of the Church in the winter of 1955-56.

HOLY CROSS AND FAITH MEMORIAL MISSION, PAWLEY'S ISLAND

(See Archdeaconry, end this Section)

ST. PETER'S MISSION, PEE DEE
Established 1883

In 1883, the Rev. Benjamin Allston, rector of Prince Frederick's, began ministering to a neighborhood in the western part of Georgetown County in an area variously called Snow Mill, Chapel Creek, and Carver's Bay. He reported some fifty souls here living in "ignorance and sin." The diocesan Board of Missions at once appropriated $50.00 toward a chapel, an acre of land was given by a lady and a combination schoolhouse and chapel was erected at a cost of $238.00, Prince Frederick's and Prince George's assisting. Services were held regularly and a parochial school supported part of the year by the county was conducted for the much-neglected people of the neighborhood. It was the Rev. W. H. Barnwell's assistance of Mr. Allston which enabled him to carry on this work. When Mr. Allston left the parish in 1890, the work was in a healthy state, with its parochial school taught by A. E. Sparkman. Mr. Allston said, "One of the sorest spots in my heart in leaving the parish was the parting with this work." Mr. B. P. Fraser, at this time, started his many years as lay reader. After a brief charge by Rev. Stewart McQueen, the work fell to the care of Rev. L. F. Guerry when he became rector of Prince Frederick's. There was now no parochial or regular Sunday School. Then followed the Rev. C. E. Cabaniss (1905-1907) and then the Rev. J. E. H. Galbraith under whom the work was continued until 1922. The Rev. C. W. Boyd (1924-25) followed, and then the Rev. H. D. Bull carried on this work unfailingly from 1926 until its end in 1942. Under Mr. Bull, though he had three other regular charges, the work was actively prosecuted with Sunday School every Lord's Day. A legacy in 1926 from Mrs. J. J. Pringle provided for repair and repainting of the building.

In 1930, Miss Julia Gantt of Winnsboro became United Thank Offering worker in Prince Frederick's parish supported by the U. T. O., the diocese, and the Diocesan Woman's Auxiliary. She did both evangelistic and health work. On June 22, 1932, a large annex to the chapel was dedicated by Bishop Thomas, assisted by Mr. Bull. This work was accomplished, notwithstanding the loss of funds which had been accumulated for the work, by many donations and especially by labor contributed by nearly all members under the leadership of Mr. and Mrs. G. T. Skinner. Nearly all the people of this mission were on relief (Emergency Relief Administration) during the depression. In 1937, Mr. W. R. Haynsworth assisted Mr. Bull here and in Prince Frederick's. The next year the

Rev. Homer P. Starr assisted; Mr. W. L. Martin later assisted. For many years, Miss E. A. Gaillard was a vital force in the mission, in the Sunday School and as organist. She was assisted by Mrs. Sellers; Mrs. G. T. Skinner was also an active worker. With its seventy-five members, the mission, as it had since its beginning, ministered usefully to a section which had no other Church. Electric lights were installed in 1941.

However, this useful life was destined to come to a rather sudden end. The United States Army in 1941 took over a large area in the upper part of Georgetown County, 37,000 acres, for a bombing field. It included the territory of St. Peter's. Over one hundred families were moved out of the region. Mr. Bull pastorally followed many of the people to other parts of the county; some 30 or 40 were transferred to Prince Frederick's, Plantersville. St. Peter's never even reached the status of "organized mission", always called "unorganized", and yet for fifty-nine years it ministered the gospel of love to many souls otherwise neglected. So concludes the epic of St. Peter's, conceived and inaugurated through the love for souls of the Rev. Benjamin Allston, nurtured through years by other faithful priests and devoted lay workers, and brought to a climax of Christian service by Dr. Bull. It was unceremoniously ended by the demon of war. The old bell is hanging at the Church of the Messiah, Maryville.

REDEEMER MISSION, PINEVILLE
(See Archdeaconry, end this Section)

ST. MARK'S CHURCH, PINEWOOD
Established 1757
(See Dalcho, p. 323)

The original Church of this parish, set off in 1757, from Prince Frederick's, was built near the Santee River, on the north side, on a creek called Halfway Swamp, about ten miles from Wrights Bluff. The Assembly appropriated £ 700. Dr. Burgess in his *Chronicles* states that the ruins showed that it was built of "brick and stone" and not of wood as asserted by Dalcho. After the destruction of this Church in the Revolution (1781), there was no Church in the parish for over 25 years except Stateburg where there was a chapel of ease as early as 1770. Statesburg was cut off from St. Mark's in 1788 and a Church built in 1789. However, the parish was not entirely dormant, the Rev. Matthew Tate was the rector in 1790. He and Mr. Guignard were delegates to the diocesan

Convention of that year. The Rev. Mr. Tate doubtless had services in homes or in some sort of building in the parish at that time. In 1807 St. Mark's was represented by William Doughty, who also was lay reader. This invasion into Dalcho's period seems necessary here. He describes fully the first Church in the parish since the Revolution, built in 1809-16; this was called "Lower St. Mark's", or "St. Mark's, Williamsburg". It was built on land given by Charles Frederick Lesesne and was consecrated in 1816. The congregation was admitted into union with the Convention as a new Church separate from old St. Mark's, Clarendon, having its own vestry. The Rev. John J. Tschudy was visiting minister, 1815-1818. John White Chandler was ordained deacon at the opening of the Convention (1819) and took charge of this Church with St. Mark's, Clarendon. He resigned in 1822 and the Rev. B. H. Fleming served a short time in 1823, dying the year after his ordination. The Rev. David I. Campbell was visitor for some years but soon this Church went down, being reported not able to support a minister. There was a school house nearby where Gov. John P. Richardson received a portion of his education. It is related that when Gov. Richard I. Manning, father of John L. Manning, would pass this Church, he would stop in for private devotions. The Church was finally sold to the Methodists.

The original or Upper St. Mark's was without a Church building for many years after the Revolution until 1819 when one was built near the site of the pre-Revolutionary Church in the neighborhood of Remini. It was of wood consecrated by Bishop Bowen in 1822 at which time Rev. J. W. Chandler, who had served as deacon in charge since 1819, was advanced to the priesthood. The founders of this Church were James B. Richardson, Charles Richardson, Matthew James, Richard I. Manning, and Joseph Dyson. The Church was not far from the Great Highway (said to have been an Indian trail) laid out by Gen. Richardson from Nelson's Ferry to Manchester, Stateburg, Camden, and Lancaster—a great commercial line of communication. Here is the site of the old Richardson burying ground.

In 1822 Mr. Chandler organized a congregation at Manchester, fourteen miles from the parish Church. It was admitted into union with the Convention in 1822 but after nearly three years Mr. Chandler sadly reported that the work had been abandoned through non-support. "St. Mark's, Clarendon", "St. Mark's, Williamsburg", and "St. Mark's, Manchester" as well as Stateburg were all represented in the Convention of 1822—all three within the confines of old St. Mark's Parish. The deputies from Upper St. Mark's were James B. Richardson, Charles Richardson, and John P. Richardson (the year before Robert Brailsford was a deputy); from Lower St. Mark's, Theodore Gourdin (the year before William Alexander Colclough); St. Mark's, Manchester, John Spann, John Moore. In 1823, in St. Mark's, Clarendon, a Sunday School was organized, and a residence provided for the rector, and the next year the full time of the rector was engaged. In 1828 the rectory burned. In this year a communion service was presented by Charles Richardson, Esq. But this fell far short of exhausting the generosity of this man for in 1830, the old site of the Church at Remini proving unhealthy, he himself built for the congregation, a new Church or chapel in the Sand Hills, located in front of "Hyde Park" about one-fourth of a mile from the site of the present Church. The plan to rebuild the rectory failed and consequently Mr. Chandler resigned the rectorship in 1832 after about fourteen years of faithful service.

The Rev. C. P. Elliott succeeded to the rectorship in 1836. The new Church in the Sand Hills was consecrated in 1837. In this year for the first time since the organization of the diocese a rector, by *by-law*, became chairman of the vestry of his parish, when Mr. Elliott assumed this position in St. Mark's. At this time also a new parsonage was secured. The next year services were abandoned at the old Church at Remini by resolution of the vestry as "unworthy of repair". About three miles from this Church is a burying ground containing the remains of many distinguished people. At this time the rector was giving much time to church work among the Negroes laying foundations of work that has survived in the St. Augustine's Church of today. In 1839, the chapel in the Sand Hills was enlarged and improved, and the year following through the efforts of the "Ladies' Working Society" a new organ was installed. In the same year a mural tablet to the memory of the donor of the chapel, Charles Richardson, was erected. Mr. Elliott continued a wide missionary work in the entire region including St. Mark's Parish, Claremont, and Bradford Springs. He resigned in 1841 and was succeeded by Rev. Arthur Wigfall. Mr. Jacob Welch was employed as lay catechist in 1845 for colored work, his salary being paid half by the vestry and half by the "Society for Evangelizing Slaves" organized in February, 1844. Mr. Welch continued this work for about six years having 500 Negroes under his instruction. During these years baptisms in the parish were frequently by immersion. The Rev. Mr. Wigfall resigned in October, 1853 and was succeeded the following month by Rev. Edward Reed.

The chapel in the Sand Hills was destroyed in a forest fire. Then it was that the present Church was built on two acres of land given by Col. R. C. Richardson and Gov. R. I. Manning who also gave fifteen acres for a parsonage and glebe. The Church was built largely by these two gentlemen, with some contributions from other members of the congregation. The cornerstone was laid by Bishop Davis on February 25, 1854. The day after, he consecrated St. James' Chapel located ten miles below the new Church. This was a chapel of ease to the parish Church on the dividing line between the plantations of R. C. and J. B. Richardson, a plain wooden building but with spiral steps leading up to the pulpit with sounding board. It passed out of use after the war in 1865. The new St. Mark's was completed and consecrated on March 10, 1855. Mr. Reed preached the sermon. This is one of the handsomest rural churches in South Carolina. It is built in Gothic style of brick, beautifully adorned with stained glass windows. The architects were Messrs. Jones and Lee. The construction was supervised by Gov. R. I. Manning who had the brick burnt on "Hawthorne Hill". In the cornerstone among other things there is a Bible and prayer book which belonged to Col. Manning's mother. The day after the Consecration on Sunday, March 11, 1855, the catechist, J. V. Welch, was ordained deacon. In the parish this year services were held in St. Mark's 83 times, in St. James' Chapel 50; plantations and other places 173. During the absence of the rector in 1857 services were held by Rev. Mr. Hanckel. In 1857 Mr. Welch reported his work among nine or ten hundred slaves, preaching 343 times. During parts of 1856 and 1857, the Rev. W. T. Potter was assistant minister. The Rev. Mr. Reed resigned in 1857, and Mr. Welch left also, going to Grahamville early in 1858.

The Rev. J. W. Taylor, M.D., deacon, had charge from 1858 to 1860, then the Rev. B. E. Habersham was rector from 1860 until 1865. Mr. X. Y. Anderson was ordained deacon in St. Mark's Church on November 3, 1861, and became missionary to the Negroes in the parish, the mission being called St. Luke's. This work was carried on throughout the period of the war; fifteen colored persons were confirmed on March 6, 1864. During this period Divine services were regularly sustained with extra ministrations to the blacks "excepting a short interruption during a destructive visitation from the enemy." After Mr. Habersham's departure in 1865, there was no rector until the Rev. F. Bruce Davis, son of the Bishop, was ordered deacon July 12, 1868, and took charge. The Church after

a lapse of several years was represented in Convention in 1870 by
E. D. Brailsford and S. J. Gaillard. Mr. Davis held services at Manchester for the Negroes. He left the parish January 1, 1873, for
Union, and three weeks later was violently thrown from his horse
and died January 21, 1873, having spent with the exception of these
three weeks his entire ministry in St. Mark's with Sumter and
Bradford Springs. He was succeeded by the Rev. C. Bruce Walker.
In 1875 the Church and the parsonage were fully repaired and a
new roof put on the Church. Mr. Walker was much beloved. After
long ill health he died in his sleep in September, 1875. The Rev.
Zenophon Y. Anderson, deacon, who for some time served in the
parish as a catechist died in 1876 after many years of ill health,
living in retirement. The next rector was the Rev. Robert F. Clute,
1876-1880. On retiring from the rectorship in 1880, Mr. Clute stated,
"It is an immemorial custom of this parish to invite the rector to
officiate by the years." The cemetery was consecrated by Bishop
Howe July 8, 1876. The Rev. Theodore A. Porter was rector from
1882 to 1885 being succeeded by the Rev. John Kershaw who began
a new phase of the colored work in the parish, resulting in the
organization of St. Augustine's mission. We find it called by this
name in 1890. The Rev. J. S. Hartzell was Mr. Kershaw's assistant
from 1891 until 1894 when Rev. W. T. Capers took his place briefly,
until December, 1895, when Mr. Kershaw left. The Rev. William H.
Barnwell succeeded in 1896 and was rector for twenty-one years.
A new roof on the Church, repainting, and a neat iron fence around
the churchyard marked 1906. Mr. Barnwell resigned in 1917. During his latter years and later, services were sometimes held in the
Presbyterian and Methodist Churches in Pinewood. The Rev. William M. Walton took charge in 1918. In 1919 steps were taken to
build a chapel in Pinewood, a lot being secured, and shortly afterwards a modest building was erected. Mr. Walton retired in 1922.
The Rev. J. E. H. Galbraith held charge from 1923 to 1933. After
an interim of occasional services the Rev. D. N. Peeples assumed
charge in 1935. For several years the work in St. Mark's was conducted in connection with the associate mission with headquarters
at Eutawville. The Rev. W. R. Haynsworth, residing in Summerton, was in charge from 1939 to 1948. After the lapse of a few
months in 1948, the Rev. Joseph N. Bynum became rector. In 1955
Rev. Richard C. Patton was rector, wardens Lucien Richardson
and James Richardson; W. D. Epperson, secretary and treasurer.
Mr. Patton resigned in 1956.

TRINITY, PINOPOLIS
(Trinity, Black Oak)
Established 1856

The Church people in the Black Oak neighborhood (now submerged in Lake Moultrie) for a time continued to attend the parish Church (Biggin)—some of them being vestrymen. However, on account of the distance there was a demand for services locally. About 1800 the Rev. P. M. Parker officiated in a house on Southampton Plantation, then the property of Gen. William Moultrie, one mile from Black Oak. In Mr. Rene Ravenel's diary it is related that the gentlemen of the neighborhood met on January 19, 1808, and raised the Church. It was on land given by Mr. Ravenel himself. "Black Oak" was a warehouse near one of the Santee Canal locks. The Rev. C. E. Gadsden first officiated in this Church. It was soon detached from St. John's and also associated with St. Stephen's, Pineville. This association continued until 1855. (See sketch of St. Stephen's.) In 1846 a chapel was erected at Pinopolis and opened for services in October. Almost at the same time a new Church was built at Black Oak. The old building was given to the Methodists and moved to Macbeth. This new Church was consecrated by Bishop Gadsden as "Trinity Church, Black Oak" on the Feast of the Circumcision, 1847. When Trinity was detached from St. Stephen's and the Rocks in 1855, the Rev. J. J. Sams became its rector, serving until 1860. It was admitted into the Convention as an independent parish February, 1856. The Rev. P. F. Stevens succeeded Mr. Sams in 1861 but he had scarcely taken charge when he, being a trained soldier, was called away to the war. He returned after a year and continued in charge until 1873.

As noted in the sketch of St. Stephen's, Church life was very active in this section during the two decades before the war; also services were maintained without a break during the war. In 1864 Mr. Stevens reports: Confirmed, 13 white and 57 colored; services Pinopolis, 95; Black Oak, 21; Cedar Chapel, 21; Porcher Chapel, 25; Cain Chapel, 23; Morefield, 11; Total 196. Trinity was again associated with St. Stephen's in 1867, resources being so curtailed that it could not alone pay the salary of $600.00. In 1869 Mr. Stevens reports two chapels for colored people completed "Nazareth" and "Emmanuel" and two colored candidates for the ministry, studying under the Rev. O. T. Porcher, Frank C. Ferguson and Laurens Dawson. Mr. Stevens resigned January 12, 1873, going to Anderson and Newberry. The Rev. P. D. Hay then became rector. After a short ministry in the up-country Mr. Stevens was lost to the Church, by his defection to the Reformed Episcopal Church. In 1873 the chapel in Pinopolis was improved in its furniture, the "cumbrous and useless pulpit" being "somewhat retired". Mr. Hay resigned the next year. Now began a great loss of Negro members in the terrible Reconstruction times.

The Rev. W. O. Prentiss had the charge of Trinity for ten years, holding monthly services from 1876. In 1886 the chapel and rectory in Pinopolis were repaired. Mr. Prentiss resigned and the Rev. H. L. Phillips became rector July 1, 1886. The Church once more now had a resident rector and more frequent services. Mr. Philips resigned 1888. An oak altar in memory of Mrs. H. G. Macbeth and a font in memory of Miss H. M. Ravenel were installed at this time. Lay readers were active in the Church during an extended vacancy. Rev. James Simonds became rector in 1893 for a short time. In 1895 the Rev. H. T. Gregory became missionary in charge for a year. The Rev. A. E. Cornish took charge in 1898. The wardens now were Thomas P. Ravenel and John H. Porcher. The Rev. John H. Brown assisted Mr. Cornish in 1899 and became rector the next year. At this time the wardens were William Henry Cain and John Henry Porcher; secretary and treasurer, Henry F. Porcher; lay reader, H. K. Jenkins. The Rev. C. H. Jordan succeeded Mr. Brown in 1905 continuing until October, 1906; the Rev. Robert Wilson, D.D., from August, 1907, gave a monthly service, lay services were held on other Sundays. In 1911 Dr. Wilson reports heavy losses to the parish in deaths, including the senior warden, Mr. John H. Porcher. The junior warden and lay reader, Mr. Hawkins K. Jenkins and family who left the parish. Mr. H. R. Dwight was secretary and treasurer in 1911—the only officer reported this year and for several years. In 1913 Mr. J. L. Stroehecker was lay reader and in 1915 W. M. Manning. In June, 1915 a mission was held in pinopolis by the Revs. O. T. Porcher and W. S. Holmes. Dr. Wilson retired in 1918, the Rev. A. E. Cornish taking charge. Mr. H. R. Dwight was now warden and secretary and treasurer, and Mr. Stroehecker, lay reader. The Rev. A. W. Taylor (associated with Epiphany, Eutawville) succeeded Mr. Cornish in 1921. The Rev. Walter Mitchell assumed charge in 1923 as acting rector, then the Rev. Wallace Martin in 1925 until 1931. The Rev. E. B. Guerry became rector in residence in Pinopolis, October, 1932. After serving here and at St. Stephen's and reopening the Barrows Mission he resigned February, 1935. The Rev. D. N. Peeples and Rev. T. F. Walsh had charge for brief periods. The Rev. L. A. Taylor then took charge in connection with the associate mission in 1937 continuing until July, 1946. The old Church at Black Oak was condemned by the South Carolina Public Service Authority in 1941 and sold to it for about $7,000.00, being in the flooded area of Lake Moultrie. This Church had long since been abandoned except for annual "Memorial Service", and funerals. A parish house was built in 1944 in Pinopolis, made possible by a legacy of Mr. Behrmann and part of the proceeds of the sale of Black Oak. Bodies in the graveyard at Black Oak were removed, some to St. Stephen's, St. Stephens, and some to a spot set apart. A sad blow was all this to those who loved every foot of this land. In 1947 the wardens were H. R. Dwight and J. H. Massalon; secreary, L. W. Boykin, III; J. H. Massalon, treasurer; Church school superintendent, Miss Caroline P. Cain; lay reader, James Vardell, Jr. Rev. Stephen L. Skardon became rector in 1948. A rectory was built in Pinopolis in 1949. Two beautiful vases in memory of a former rector, the Rev. A. E. Cornish, were presented in this year. The Church received formal Consecration by Bishop Carruthers on May 23, 1948, when Bishop Thomas preached a historical sermon. Mr. Skardon was followed in the spring of 1952 by the Rev. Harold E. Barrett, and he in turn by the Rev. Loren B. Mead in 1955.

The Church has recently received a gift of land in rear of the parish house by Dr. and Mrs. W. K. Fishburne.

PRINCE FREDERICK'S, PLANTERSVILLE

Established 1734

(See Dalcho, p. 319)

When this parish was "taken off" from Prince George in 1734, for a time it included practically all of the State northward and westward—from the Santee River basin to the North Carolina line, and westward as far as His Majesty's subjects were settled. From this section, before the Revolution, was taken off St. Mark's, St. Matthew's, and St. David's parishes. In the division of 1734, Prince George's Church, built in 1726, fell within the limits of and to the heritage of the new parish of Prince Frederick's, and henceforth assumed this name. It was in honor of the eldest son of George II. It was located on a bluff on Black River, near Brown's Ferry, about fifteen miles from Georgetown. Rev. Hugh Fraser served from 1793 to 1810 when he went to All Saints', but he kept some oversight of the parish. There was no rector after him for many years; in fact, no regular rector until 1846. This is explained as follows: The cultivation of indigo was abandoned at about the beginning of the century. This led to the removal of the settlers to the lower banks of the Pee Dee to cultivate rice, so the Church on the bluff on the Black River was left without a congregation. This Church (which was a frame structure—not brick as Dalcho states) soon fell into ruin. There is no vestige of this old Church (first Prince George's then Prince Frederick's) left, only a few graves. In 1942, the Society of Colonial Wars of South Carolina placed there, and dedicated a stone with inscription to mark the spot. (Transcriptions of inscriptions on the old graves will be found in the S. C. Historical Magazine 1917, p. 91.)

A temporary revival of interest marked the year 1827 when an effort was made to build a Church between Black River Ferry and Dr. William Allston's plantation. A meeting was held at the Universal Church (inter-denominational) on Pee Dee on April 9, 1827. Those attending were Rev. Hugh Fraser, Dr. William Allston, Davison McDowell, and R. O. Anderson—mostly residents of Pee Dee. Committees were appointed, but plans could not be agreed upon and nothing was done. Not until January 28, 1835, was another meeting held at the same place. Davison McDowell, Robert F. W. Allston, and Francis Weston were appointed a building committee to erect a chapel on land given by Rev. Hugh Fraser, after a plan by one of the committee. The desk, pulpit, communion table, etc., of cedar, and the usual tablets for the chancel were given by Francis H. Weston of All Saints' Parish. Services were held in the chapel in the spring of 1837 by the Rev. Hugh Fraser, who continued to officiate until his death in December, 1838. He had given not only the lot for the chapel, but also a right-of-way fifteen feet wide along his north line to the river, surveyed by Robert F. W. Allston. On April 19, 1837, under the name of Prince Frederick's Chapel, Pee Dee, this building was consecrated by Bishop Bowen, Rev. Messrs. Hugh Fraser, M. H. Lance, P. Trapier, and Alexander Glennie assisting. The cost was $1,196.93. The wardens were D. McDowell, and R. F. W. Allston; the treasurer, Alexander Robertson. The Rev. Mr. Lance, who had already held services, continued to officiate until 1840; then followed the Rev. J. B. Gallagher for some months in this and the following year. From February until May, 1842, the Rev. R. D. Shindler officiated. In 1842-43, land was bought for a glebe, and a parsonage built on it. Mr. Lance officiated again for a time. Rev. John R. Fell was rector for the calendar year 1846; the Rev. Joseph Hunter of Brooklyn, N. Y., officiated first temporarily in May, then permanently in November, 1847, and continued as rector until 1862. He often also officiated on the plantations for the Negroes.

In 1848, a summer parsonage was built in Plantersville on land given by Dr. J. R. Sparkman who also gave a fence about the chapel. About this time, a paten was given by Mrs. R. S. Izard; a silver cup to match one in use by Mrs. J. Harleston Read; and a silver alms plate and a Bible by Mr. and Mrs. Poinsett. On Easter Monday, 1857, it was determined to build a new brick Church. A committee consisting of S. T. Gaillard, S. R. Sparkman, and F. Weston was appointed to raise funds and build the Church. The plans proceeded, Louis J. Barbot being employed as architect. The work was begun on November 10, 1859, and on the 17th of the same month, the cornerstone was laid by the rector, the Rev. Joseph Hunter, and an address was delivered by ex-Governor R. F. W. Allston. This splendid address is given in full in the *Southern Episcopalian,* Vol. VI, p. 561. It gives forcibly the full program of the Church, ending in a strong appeal for the University of the South. The work on the Church was stopped by the war, but the building had been "erected and covered in." The materials necessary for the completion were on the spot. It was planned that the building was to cost about $12,000.00, Philip and Edward Green, contractors. Just before the war of 1861 the parish was very much alive. Mr. Hunter, to whom Governor Allston attributed the "flourishing condition" of the parish, held 37 services in Prince Frederick's; 38 in Plantersville; and 54 on the plantations in 1860. He left in 1862 and Rev. Alexander Glennie officiated until 1865, who while residing in Plantersville was still rector of All Saints'. The congregation was augmented during the war by many from that parish. In these days in Plantersville, an "open pole building" served as a chapel in the summer, and in the winter, services were held in the parsonage.

The Rev. R. S. Trapier officiated for a while in 1866 and 1867; he was then rector of St. John's, John's Island. Then followed that devastating effect of war, from which the Church in this state has suffered so intensely on two occasions—lack of clergymen. The Church was vacant from 1867 until 1876. During a large part of the time after 1872, lay services were conducted by Benjamin Allston (yet to be ordained), who was junior warden, J. R. Sparkman being senior warden. In the meantime, the new brick Church had remained unfinished. The contractor died in the midst of the work. There was much delay. Materials which had been gathered were stolen or destroyed, furnishings and finishings ordered from abroad were lost in the blockade, and the building was so damaged as to require refinishing of the entire interior. After the war was over the people were too poor to undertake the repairing and completion of the building. It remained as it was until 1876, when through the generous gift of $1,700.00 by John Earle Allston of Brooklyn, N. Y., the building was repaired and completed. It was consecrated by Bishop Howe, assisted by the Rev. Mr. Glennie, of Prince George, and the Rev. Mr. Barnwell, of All Saints', on Palm Sunday, March 25, 1877. The "Request for Consecration" was read by Dr. J. R. Sparkman. F. W. Macusker was the contractor in the completion of the building. Mr. G. B. Mosman executed the rail and the furniture of the chancel. The exquisitely chaste and pure white marble baptismal font now in the chapel in Plantersville was presented in 1860 by Mr. J. D. Sparkman, of New York. The choir stalls came from the St. Mary's Chapel at Hagley and also a lock, bolt and hinges. All Saints', Waccamaw, gave the pews. So the dream of the parish was realized in this beautiful building completed and furnished. Rev. Benjamin Allston took charge June 1, 1877. Mr. Allston was the eldest son of Gov. Allston. He was a graduate of West Point and served gallantly in the War Between the States. For some years, he served as junior warden and lay reader for All Saints'. He was ordered deacon May 27, 1877, in St. Michael's, Charleston, by Bishop Howe.

Immediately after the completion of the handsome brick Church on the Pee Dee, the urgent need of a chapel of ease in Plantersville presented itself to the vestry. There had been indeed since 1848 a chapel erected for the use of summer residents mostly from Prince George's parish. This building had become very dilapidated and actually unsafe; so the need of a new place of worship in Plantersville was urgent. The old chapel on the Pee Dee, which had been replaced by the brick building, was taken down and removed to Plantersville. The Plantersville Company gave the lot. The form was slightly altered by recessing the chancel, adding a small wing on each side and surmounting it with a belfry and cross. The chapel now became the chief place of worship in the parish. It was consecrated by Bishop Howe on the 23rd of July, 1879, the service being conducted by the Rev. Benjamin Allston. For some years, the Rev. W. H. Barnwell assisted Mr. Allston in the work of the parish, the latter giving much attention to St. Peter's Mission, founded in 1883. He also held services at Harper's on the edge of Williamsburg County. Mr. Allston left to go to Union in 1889. Through the secretary of the General Board of Missions, the chapel at this time received the gift of an organ. The Church was left vacant until Rev. L. F. Guerry took charge in 1894. In the meantime, Mr. McQueen, rector of Prince George, had held some services and Mr. B. P. Fraser, with great regularity, lay read. In 1897 the wardens were B. P. Fraser and William Ford, and the treasurer, John Richardson. In May, 1905, the Rev. Charles E. Cabaniss succeeded Mr. Guerry. Mr. Cabaniss died August 28, 1907, and the Church was vacant until May, 1908, when the Rev. J. E. H. Galbraith took charge. In 1911, the wardens were B. P. Fraser, who was also lay reader, and John Richardson, and A. B. Flagg was secretary and treasurer.

The Church received a legacy of $5,000.00 from Mrs. Hunter, widow of the Rev. Joseph Hunter, former rector, income for the upkeep of the Church and rectory. Mr. Galbraith, after twelve years, resigned in 1922, going to St. Mark's parish. The Rev. C. W. Boyd had charge in 1924 and 1925 when his health failed. The Rev. H. D. Bull began in 1926 a ministry of twenty-seven years in this field, including the charge of Prince George and All Saints' as well as Prince Frederick's and St. Peter's, Pee Dee at Carver's Bay. The parish, on September 28, 1930, mourned the death of its senior warden Benjamin Porter Fraser, in his 89th year. He had served as lay reader for forty-five years, as also for St. Peter's, Dee Dee. In 1943, Mr. Fraser's grandchildren gave to the Church a handsome altar, dedicated by Bishop Thomas on his visit on January 31, 1943, to his memory. B. P. Fraser, Jr. succeeded as senior warden, with S. T. Harper as junior warden, and Mr. G. T. Skinner, secretary. Miss Julia Gantt, U. T. O. worker, assisted at this time in the parish. The Young Peoples Service League was active. The Men's Club installed electric lights in the chapel and parish house in 1932. On April 9, 1934, the parish celebrated its Bi-Centennial with a great service in the large handsome brick Church on the Pee Dee. The service was conducted by Mr. Bull and Rev. T. S. Tisdale. Bishop Thomas was prevented by illness from attending. His address on the history of the parish was read by B. Allston Moore, Esq., grandson of Rev. Benjamin Allston, sometime rector of the parish. The Church, in 1942, received accession of some 30-odd new members by transfer from the closed St. Peter's Mission. With an adult Bible Class conducted by Mr. Bull on Wednesday evenings, the Sunday School, the Y. P. S. L., and the Woman's Auxiliary, the parish, though not large in numbers, did an extensive work. The facilities for this work were greatly increased in 1947 by the erection of a modest but adequate and useful new parish house, which adjoins the Church. It was enlarged in 1951. Mr. Bull, after twenty-seven years in Georgetown County, ministering to Prince George, Prince Frederick,

All Saints', and until 1942 St. Peter's, Pee Dee, went to Barnwell July 1, 1953. Rev. Edward T. Small, living in Conway, had charge from 1953 until 1956.

The graveyard of old Prince Frederick's has recently been fenced.

ST. PETER'S PARISH, PURYSBURG

Established 1747

(See Dalcho, p. 385)

This old parish, now extinct as such, has from time to time included territorily the following Churches: St. Peter's, Robertsville (extinct, see herewith); St. Edmund's, Hardeeville (extinct, see herewith); Church of the Heavenly Rest, originally St. Peter's Mission (see *in loco*); All Saints', Hampton C. H. (see *in loco*); All Saints', Varnville (see herewith); Holy Communion, Allendale (see *in loco*).

ST. PETER'S, ROBERTSVILLE

This parish to the west of St. Luke's on the Savannah River became dormant and remained so for many years after the Revolution. Within its confines in 1859 a Church named St. Peter's was organized at Robertsville. Bishop Davis held service here on July 13, 1859. in a room. Rev. Richard Johnson of the diocese of Georgia was the first minister and continued in charge for three or four years. The Church was admitted into Convention May 12, 1859. Delegates the next year were Isadore Lartigue, A. M. Martin, E. B. Bostick, and J. Tison. In 1861, a chapel was built to hold 50 people and services were held twice every Sunday. Mr. Edward Evans of Darlington presented a beautiful walnut lectern and Mr. W. T. Robert two beautiful walnut chairs. The year before died Mrs. W. D. (Maria) Martin, a veritable "mother-in-Israel", widow of Hon. W. D. Martin. As late as January 30, 1864, Bishop Davis visited this chapel and confirmed eight persons. He was assisted by the Rev. J. B. Seabrook. The Church "was burnt by the Federal Army in January, 1865, together with the residences of every member of the congregation. There is neither building nor minister or people", as reported in 1868. Beginning soon after, he took charge of the coast missions in 1870; Mr. Bellinger and later the Rev. B. B. Sams for some years held services in the confines of old St. Peter's parish at various places—Lawtonville, Brighton, Brunson, "Mr. Morrison's residence", Union Church—this was called St. Peter's Mission; also, at Allendale and at Ellenton in Aiken County where the Baptist Church was loaned. However, the principal place was at Hardeeville, the mission here at first called St. Peter's but later St. Edmund's.

ST. EDMUND'S, HARDEEVILLE

The first report of services at Hardeeville is by Mr. Bellinger, May, 1871, for the preceding year. Efforts were made at once to build a Church, a lot being given by Mr. William Heyward. There were seven families in 1878. The progress was slow but in 1879, the Church was "raised and weatherboarded", and services held in it—completed in 1882. The mission in 1885 was designated "St. Peter's Church, Hardeeville". At this time Mr. G. M. Blake of Savannah presented the Church a bell, and a porch with belfry above was added to the building and a chancel carpet given by Mr. James B. Heyward. Mr. Sams resigned this work in 1888. The Rev. W. F. Bellinger took charge December, 1893. The Church was consecrated by Bishop Capers September 20, 1894, with the name "St. Edmund's Chapel" (previously St. Peter's) in honor of the Rev. Edward Edmund Bellinger who had organized the mission. The Rev. J. Maxwell Pringle took charge December, 1895, coming from the diocese of Kentucky. The failure of the culture of rice in that section at this time led to the removal of many church members, weakening the mission. The Rev. J. B. Walker assumed charge 1901 and then Rev. J. C. Waring in 1903 who reports 'no warden, no secretary, no treasurer' but the next year Mr. William Heyward was warden, and Mr. G. M. Blake, treasurer. Mr. Waring resigned April, 1905. The Rev. P. D. Hay succeeded in 1908 continuing until the Rev. J. H. Woodward came in 1912. Robert Blake was treasurer for many years until 1916. In 1917, he reported only two families. He served this mission for 14 years resigning in 1926, when the Rev. F. M. Brunton succeeded, and then the Rev. Joseph Burton in 1927. Mr. Burton went to Savannah November, 1929. Services were discontinued at St. Edmund's except for a brief time in the summer of 1932 when D. N. Peeples, a candidate for Holy Orders reopened the Church for a short time. The Church was taken down and sold about 1950.

ALL SAINTS', VARNVILLE

The Rev. E. E. Bellinger held services in Varnville in 1891 and 1892, in the academy and in the Methodist Church. These services were soon abandoned. When the Rev. A. R. Mitchell served as Archdeacon of the Charleston Convocation (1916-1921), he found a group of Church people in Varnville, and held services for them in the Methodist Church kindly loaned. In 1917 the group was formed into a mission with Charles Kerrison as warden and E. C. Glenn, treasurer. In 1921, it was formally organized and admitted into Convention as All Saints', Varnville—warden, E. C. Glenn; secretary, Charles Kerrison; treasurer, W. W. Simmons. In 1922 the Rev. A. M. Rich, rector of St. Jude's, took charge. The Rev. Capers Satterlee was in charge for a short time, and then succeeded the Rev. Frank M. Brunton in 1924, then in 1927 Rev. Joseph Burton. The mission was now abandoned, the people going elsewhere.

ST. STEPHEN'S PARISH, SAINT STEPHENS
Established 1754
(See Dalcho, p. 328)

After the resignation of the Rev. James Connor in 1802, services were almost entirely discontinued at the parish Church. In fact, the people having largely moved away from the neighborhood, it fell into disrepair. A chapel was erected about ten miles west of the Church where services were held. Soon after the beginning of the century the people from a sense of loyalty put the old Church into thorough repair. Efforts were made from time to time, notably in 1828 and in 1833, to reopen the Church but with success only occasionally until the Rev. P. F. Stevens opened it for regular services in 1870 as we shall see. In the meantime since 1794 Pineville had become a popular summer resort for the people of St. Stephen's and of Upper St. John's—an academy and a library were built there. The beginning of Church life in Pineville came soon after the turn of the century when Mr. Baker from New Hampshire, the head of the academy, conducted lay services at the old chapel two miles to the northwest of the village. Later the chapel in the village was built, being completed in 1810. The Rev. Charles Blair Snowden after having succeeded Mr. Baker as lay reader for a time, and having been ordained, took charge. He also ministered at Black Oak Church (Middle St. John's) and at the Rocks Church (Upper St. John's). All three of these churches were originally chapels of ease, the first of St. Stephen's parish, the two latter of St. John's, Berkeley. All three continued united under the care of the same minister until 1855 when Trinity, Black Oak, became an independent parish. In 1819 Mr. Snowden was succeeded by the Rev. David Irving Campbell who also had previously acted as a lay reader while a candidate for Holy Orders. He served until 1840. The Rev. J. W. Miles officiated from November, 1841, until the following January. The Rev. Cranmore Wallace held some services in 1842, then in December of this year Rev. William Dehon, son of the second Bishop of the diocese, began a notable ministry in this field, serving all three churches, besides five or six chapels erected by planters on their plantations for 1,800 Negroes to whom Mr. Dehon ministered; 300 of these were communicants. The religious tone of the parish rose at this time. St. Stephen's, Pineville, was consecrated by Bishop Gadsden in 1845, when it was admitted into union with the Church in the diocese, having previously resisted cooperation with the diocese.

Mr. Dehon had for his assistant first the Rev. C. P. Gadsden (1848-1853), then Rev. R. P. Johnson (1853-1854). Occasional services were held in old St. Stephen's. Trinity, Black Oak, in 1855 after about a half century destroyed the trinity of churches, becoming an independent parish with the Rev. J. J. Sams as its rector. The Rev. J. Hamilton was then assisting Mr. Dehon among the Negroes at this time in St. Stephen's. Mr. Dehon resigned in 1859, being succeeded by Mr. Johnson, who was assisted first by the Rev. LeGrande Guerry and then by the Rev. W. W. Patrick. In 1864, the original trinity of churches was further broken when St. Stephen's and Epiphany were separately admitted into union with the Convention after an association of sixty-odd years. Mr. Johnson retained Epiphany and for some time St. Stephen's had no rector though Mr. Johnson continued to supply services. In December, 1867, St. Stephen's again became associated with Trinity, Black Oak, with the Rev. P. F. Stevens as rector. On assuming charge he found the Church very reduced as to whites, the effect of the war: casualties, destruction of the village of Pineville by U. S. troops, and consequent dispersion of the people. There was still a large field of work open among the Negroes. Mr. Stevens resigned both churches in 1870 in order to give himself to the work of reopening old St. Stephen's. He removed his residence to that vicinity and single handed had the Church repaired at a cost of $874.28, and opened a school. The elaborate repairs are described in the *Monthly Record* of September, 1871, with the thanks of the vestry which he called on for only $10.00. However he did not entirely desert Pineville and Black Oak, continuing to supply all three churches. The services in the old parish Church were begun in the summer of this year, 1870. The Bishop in 1872 reported 99 presented for confirmation by Mr. Stevens—95 of these "persons of color". The Rev. J. V. Welch was Mr. Stevens' assistant at this time. Mr. Stevens resigned in 1873. He carried with him the sincere thanks of the congregation for his great service. The parish became "dormant" now as a parish through the war's depletion of its strength. However, it now passed under the care of the rector of the Epiphany, the Rev. Nathaniel B. Fuller, who also had the charge of Redeemer mission for Negroes near Pineville. Thus was the old association of the two churches renewed. The Rev. W. O. Prentiss had the charge in 1876. Mr. Welch continued as missionary in the parish. Services now were held in the old parish Church, at Pineville, and at Redeemer. For some years until he left the parish in 1884, Mr. J. S. Walton rendered a fine service as superintendent of the Sunday School. At this time there were 34 communicants.

After serving the parish as missionary for many years, Mr. Welsh was succeeded by the Rev. H. H. Phelps, rector of St. John's, Berkeley, in 1889, giving a monthly service at the parish Church, and also at Redeemer in the afternoon. A lay reader also served here. Mr. Phelps went to East Carolina in 1891, leaving the parish vacant. The Rev. H. M. Jarvis had charge in 1893-94. In 1894 Mr. L. G. Harmon was appointed lay reader for the parish, holding many services during the vacancy for many years, both at St. Stephen's and at Redeemer. The parish Church was reshingled in this year. In 1899 the wardens were: W. Mazyck Porcher and L. G. Harmon, and the treasurer, Edward B. Marion. In 1901 Rev. Andrew E. Cornish was missionary to this parish. Then followed the Rev. J. H. Brown from Pinopolis, for two or three years. Mr. J. K. Gourdin was treasurer at this time. The Rev. A. E. Cornish had charge again in 1907 for a short time. At this time Mr. F. M. Shipman began his services as warden which lasted for many years. The Rev. R. W. Barnwell held monthly services in the chapel in Pineville for a time.

In this year, the Rev. Harold Thomas took charge of St. Stephen's, St. Stephens, reorganizing it as a mission. In 1912 he reported ten families and twenty-five communicants, including Pineville; repairs and improvements $176.90; Sunday School 35. In the meantime in the fall of 1912, the Rev. Henry C. Mazyck took charge of the chapel in Pineville. When Mr. Thomas resigned St. Stephen's, St. Stephens, in 1916 he was succeeded for a year by the Rev. H. D. Bull. The next year Mr. Mazyck took charge of this Church with Pineville, continuing in charge of both churches until he left the diocese in May, 1920. In 1921 the Rev. A. P. Magwood held services in the parish church for a time. There was no regular minister in this field now until the Rev. J. E. H. Galbraith began services in 1929, and the next year by the Rev. F. W. Ambler. There were no services during these years at the parish Church.

In October, 1832, the Rev. E. B. Guerry as missionary reopened the old Church at St. Stephens, the congregation of Pineville uniting. The present altar was then installed, made of walnut from the Cain's Somerset Plantation. Mr. E. B. Marion was secretary and treasurer, and the warden was Mr. W. H. Shipman. Mr. Guerry continued his charge until February, 1935. During this period through Mr. Guerry's activity repairs to the amount of about $600.00 were made on the old parish Church. Simons and Lapham of Charleston generously superintended the redecoration of the interior. In 1935 St. Stephen's was placed under the care of the associate mission for a while, under the Rev. D. N. Peeples. The Rev. T. F. Walsh had charge for six months, 1936, then Rev. D. M. Hobart. Work was conducted actively at the old Church until Mr. Hobart resigned early in 1940; the Rev. William Moultrie Moore succeeded in June following and continued until July, 1942. Under Mr. Moore the chapel in Pineville which had fallen into disrepair was put into good condition, a new sanctuary being constructed and services resumed there as well as at the parish Church. The Rev. William H. Hanckel was next in charge. At this time, 1943, the warden and treasurer was Edward St. J. Marion. Mr. Hanckel resigned in the fall of 1944. The Rev. L. A. Taylor followed in charge for a while, then the Rev. DeSaussure P. Moore (1947-1949). The Rev. J. Q. Crumbly officiated 1950-52. Mr. E. St. J. Marion after years of service as warden and treasurer died in May, 1947. The old Church was again repaired in 1949. Extensive renovations of the parish Church have taken place in the following years as this sketch shows: 1808, 1870, 1934 and the last. More recently begun under the Rev. Hallie D. Warren, an even more complete restoration has been accomplished.

ST. GEORGE'S MISSION, ST. GEORGE
1910

ST. GEORGE'S, DORCHESTER (EXTINCT)
(See Dalcho, p. 345)

This mission was opened by the Rev. W. S. Holmes in 1910. Bishop Guerry held service for his first time in the Masonic Lodge on November 30, 1910, assisted by Mr. Holmes. He appointed a committee to secure a lot. The next year, Mr. Holmes reported two families, seven communicants, and the year following, 13 services. Soon after, a lot was bought with a view to building a chapel. This was never done. Mrs. J. Otey Reed was the treasurer at first, then

Mr. Reed. In 1915, the Rev. John London succeeded Mr. Holmes and continued the services for about two years, when they were suspended for several years. The Rev. Roderick H. Jackson, under appointment by Bishop Thomas, endeavored to renew the services in 1940. Since that time, the mission had been suspended. The original lot in St. George's was sold and another bought in a more eligible location in about 1940. The name of this mission was derived from that of old St. George's, Dorchester (see Dalcho). Concerning old St. George's, Dorchester, it is important to note that on May 31, 1893, the property of this Church was deeded to the trustees of the diocese (See Journal 1894, p. 77).

TRINITY CHURCH, SOCIETY HILL
Established 1834

Notwithstanding the village of Society Hill on the northeastward edge of Darlington County was long noted for its social atmosphere it received its name not from this but from the famous Welch Neck Society whose headquarters were at Greenville across the Pee Dee River. This society owned the elevated land which was known as the "Society's Hill" and then "Society Hill." It was settled about the end of the eighteenth century by inhabitants removing from the plantations on the river to this salubrious spot. Here the Welch Neck Baptists built a church. So it was about 1830 that at least seven families of Episcopalians, or would-be Episcopalians, who had long been deprived of the services of their Church sought to have this want supplied. St. David's some fifteen miles up the river at Cheraw had been reestablished about ten years before and here ministered at this time the Rev. Alexander W. Marshall. He extended his labors to Society Hill and with the assistance of the Rev. C. P. Gadsden and the Rev. G. W. Hathaway supplied the group with services. The Church was organized in January, 1833, and incorporated by Act of the General Assembly December 19, 1833. Before the building of a Church, services were held in St. David's Academy. The seven families that founded the Church were Judge Josiah J. Evans, United States Senator; Col. Nicholas Williams; John D. Witherspoon; Major John Dewitt; Enoch Hanford (professor of the South Carolina College); Edward Edwards; John McCollough, and also Miss Julia Hawes.

The Church was built at once, $1,150.00 being promptly subscribed. The cornerstone was laid with Masonic ceremony. John D. McCollough as a boy was present and placed, it is said, a prayer book in the stone. Also he contributed $5.00. He it was who became the well-known missionary. Mr. Elias Gregg gave the lot. The Church was consecrated by Bishop Bowen April 25, 1834. The design of the Church was suggested by Bishop Bowen. He calls it "large and commodious and in its style and appearance affords evidence of more than ordinary liberality of expenditure in proportion to the number concerned". The first vestry were: wardens, William F. De Witt and William Henry Snipes; vestrymen, Maj. John De Witt, Judge J. J. Evans, John D. Witherspoon, John N. Williams, and John J. Marshall. The Church plate was given by ladies, members of the congregation. The Church was admitted into Convention May 5, 1834, John De Witt being deputy. The Rev. U. M. Wheeler became rector in 1836. He held services for the colored people on Sunday afternoons. Mr. Wheeler died in 1841 and was buried in the churchyard as also his wife and daughter, near the chancel. After Mr. Wheeler the following ministers succeeded until the War between the States: the Revs. John Burke, 1839; Charles P. Elliott, 1841; F. M. Hubbard, 1842; N. P. Tillinghast, 1843; L. C. Johnson, deacon, 1845, rector, 1846; M. A. Curtis, 1847; A. F. Olmsted, 1856-1858; J. S. Kidney, 1858-1865. In 1861, the chancel was added to the Church and the building generally repaired to the extent of $2,000.00. The Rev. P. D. Hay came as a deacon in 1867, becoming rector the next year.

This Church has received several memorials: a considerable sum of money to establish a perpetual churchyard fund, given by Captain Edward McIntosh in memory of his wife, Dora Evans. We understand this endowment was lost through bad investment; a hymn board by Mrs. M. W. H. Ames in memory of her parents, Colonel and Mrs. Nicholas Williams; two brass altar vases by N. W. Kirkpatrick in memory of his mother, Mrs. J. D. Kirkpatrick; a handsome brass cross by the congregation in memory of Maj. J. J. Lucas, warden and lay reader for many years. This Church was consistent in the use of lay readers when the services of a minister was not available—this to the end of its active life. Before Maj. Lucas were Col. William H. Evans and John Witherspoon. The Rev. Henry Tucker Lee became rector in 1873, serving until 1880, having resigned and was re-elected in 1876. During his incumbency a very fine pipe organ was installed in the Church; "fourteen stops purchased from Messrs. W. B. D. Simons and Co. of Boston", cost $1,250.00. With some unusually fine voices in the congregation, the Church was famous for its music at this time. The Rev. H. K. Brouse succeeded Mr. Lee continuing until 1886. In

1882 a walnut font, gift of the children of the Sunday School, was presented to the Church. After a vacancy, the Rev. A. A. Mc-Donough took charge, serving until 1894. The Rev. T. P. Baker was in charge from 1896 until the Rev. Albert S. Thomas became rector in 1900, serving then until 1908. The Rev. H. H. Lumpkin was in charge from 1909 until 1912 being succeeded by the Rev. O. T. Porcher until 1914, when Mr. Thomas resumed charge until 1921, except for a short time in 1920 when the Rev. R. F. Blackford had charge. Then followed the Rev. M. W. Glover (1922-1925) and the Rev. H. L. Hoover (1926-1930). By this time there was scarcely any congregation and regular services were abandoned. The parish records were destroyed by fire about 1934. Bishop Thomas yearly until his retirement held a "Homecoming Day Service" largely attended by friends and descendants of the members of the old congregation living in neighboring towns. By means of the offerings at these services and other contributions the Church was repaired and a new roof put on it in 1948. Maj. Thomas S. Lucas closed a historical address in 1934 with these words:

"Dear to the hearts of every member is the building, within whose portals the first sacred rite of Baptism was administered to them; at whose altar rail, two hearts beating in unison, plighted their troth; at that same altar rail, earthly saints and sinners knelt side by side to partake of the Holy Communion; and in which the Church's last offices were given to those who have passed to That Farther Shore. And within the quiet, hallowed precincts of whose 'God's Half Acre', rest the ashes of four generations of our forebears, sleeping their last long sleep, awaiting the reveille trumpet. LOVE IT? OF COURSE, we love it! How could we do otherwise?"

ST. PAUL'S PARISH, STONO
Established 1706
(See Dalcho, p. 331)

Dalcho's last record concerning St. Paul's (1820) was that he himself was rector since about 1814 and the first since 1784. He reported in 1815 only eight communicants. The parish was incorporated in 1805. A new Church of wood had been built in 1810-12 (the old Church on this spot had fallen down in 1778) the glebe having been sold to Benjamin Jenkins in 1809 for "940 Pounds sterling". The contract price of the new Church was $5,000.00. The Rev. Dr. Dehon and the Rev. C. E. Gadsden held the first service in the new Church on April 7, 1812. It was consecrated by Bishop Dehon, January 10, 1813—"the first Episcopal act performed by that Prelate, and this was the first church consecrated in South Carolina." The Rev. Messrs. Gadsden, Muller, and Lance assisted, the first preaching. The Church was "at or near the foundation of the old church." This refers however not to the original Church of 1708 on the South branch of the Stono River where Church Creek joins it (Church Flats) but to the Church built in 1736 at the junction of Parker's Ferry Road and Dorchester Road. This second Church in the parish was at first a chapel of ease but later it took the place of the original parish Church when the latter fell into ruins. Dr. Dalcho resigned in 1817 and there was no regular minister until the Rev. William S. Wilson, a deacon, came from John's Island and took charge in 1823 and until 1825. The parish was represented in the Convention at this time by H. L. Alison, M.D., and John S. Peake. The Rev. M. A. Perry of New York officiated in the winter and spring of 1826. Immediately on Mr. Wilson's resignation, Bishop Bowen was requested "to send up such young men as may wish the situation, upon trial, every Sabbath alternately until a choice is made." We do not know how far this plan was pursued but in December of 1826 began the long rectorship of the Rev. Philip Gadsden, lasting until 1864. He was a deacon at this time and as there was no rectory he lived in Charleston, having charge also of Christ Church Parish. He thought highly of the prospects of the Church at this time, but in 1820 we note a change already, the Church is "languishing", numbers decreasing. In 1829 the vestry voted to pay Mr. Clark $35.00 "as a compliment for his attention in the services of the church in Psalmody, etc.". The Church was painted this year. In 1833 the plantation of Dr. H. L. Alison was bought for a rectory for $600.00. Two years later it was sold to Joseph Allen Smith for $1,000.00. Apparently they could not resist the profit. In 1829 the vestrymen were Charles Boyd, John Miles, John S. Peake, Hugh L. Alison, Edward D. Perry, Joseph Ioor Waring, Thomas W. Boone, and wardens, Thomas Gelzer and Benjamin Perry. Mr. Gadsden was ordained to the priesthood by Bishop Bowen in St. Paul's on April 14, 1830. Summerville was the summer resort of the inhabitants of St. Paul's and in 1829, the rector, Mr. Gadsden, began holding services there at first only from May until November. Later (1836) in winter also he alternated the services between the two places. In 1835 some effort to secure a rectory failing, Mr. Gadsden was requested to remain in Summerville. His salary was $650.00.

The parish lost a large part of its funds in the burning of the Union Insurance office in Charleston in 1838. In their consequent need, the vestry appealed for help to the Advancement Society. The Society responded with an appropriation of $150.00 on condition the vestry made up the balance of the salary. In 1841 Mr. Gadsden reports a congregation of 70 in Summerville, but few at the parish Church in winter. The two churches were sixteen miles apart. Unlike some other parts of the state there seems not to have been much prosperity in St. Paul's Parish at this time. In 1854 the vestry could not, on request, repair Mr. Gadsden's house in Summerville for lack of means. Mr. Gadsden often ministered to the Negroes on the plantations. The vestry that met on November 7, 1858, consisted of E. B. Scott, chairman, James Perry, C. R. Boyle, Thomas B. Miles, and also I. M. Dwight and Charles Dwight, elected at this meeting. In February, with a view to sale, it was ordered to have the Church lands resurveyed. This was done by A. L. Campbell, showing 443 acres. Mr. C. S. Dwight later measured off 28 acres in the eastern corner of the tract (the old Church site in the center of it) to be reserved for the use of the Church. This land (less the reserved portion) was sold in May, 1859, to Edward Callen for $800.00. It was resolved to spend $500.00 of this to repair the Church and reserve $300.00. The Church was thoroughly repaired in 1863.

In the meantime another Church was built on this reserved part of the Church land. Bishop Davis (January 6, 1861) says in his journal. "The Church Flats, St. Paul's—here were some remains of one of the oldest churches in the diocese." He states "chiefly through zeal and activity of Rev. Joseph Seabrook, a new church has been built in sight of where the old one stood, etc." Mr. Seabrook reports regular services at Church Flats in 1862, preaching largely to soldiers. But the congregation being "broken up and dispersed by the war" he left May 1, 1862, going to Anderson. The chapel was burnt by the Federal army on February 22, 1865. After the parish Church had been repaired it was, alas, soon devoted to a new use, a commissary store by the Confederate troops. The parish funds amounting to $3,000.00 were invested in Confederate scrip and so lost. The communion silver went to St. Paul's, Summerville. The last record in the old minute book of the parish (covering the period 1786-1864) is a resolution expressing its regret in accepting the resignation of the Rev. Philip Gadsden as rector. This seems to record about the last activity in this old parish though the Church was still standing in 1879. The sounding board of the pulpit was installed in St. Luke's Church in Charleston.

In 1923 the trustees of the diocese, acting under the canon of dormant parishes sold for $1,000.00 timber off the St. Paul's, Stono, land. This amount later was given St. Paul's, Meggett, being within the confines of old St. Paul's, to assist in building a rectory. In 1932 the land was sold, except a graveyard of 4.25 acres, for $500.00. In 1951 the balance in the hands of the trustees of the Stono fund, amounting to $1,100.77 was again given to St. Paul's, Meggett, to assist in building a new Church.

GRACE CHURCH, SULLIVAN'S ISLAND
Established 1817 (Extinct)
(See Dalcho, p. 396)

In his last Annual Address to the 29th Convention of the diocese in February, 1817, Bishop Dehon said: "A building has been purchased by subscription, to be converted in the ensuing season into a place of public worship, on Sullivan's Island, whither so many of our community resort in summer for comfort and health." Previously, public worship had been celebrated on the island for many years, but the room where these services were held was small and inconvenient. It was mainly through the Bishop's efforts that the more commodious place was secured and converted into a neat place of worship. It was a brick building intended for a lazaretto. On its wall was placed a memorial tablet to the Bishop —'the last days of whose pious and devoted life were devoted to the religious edification of this island and the establishment of this church.' While geographically in the confines of Christ Church, it had no special relation to that parish and so was in no proper sense a chapel of ease. In the records of the Convention of 1818, Rev. Albert Arney Muller, then a deacon, was listed as in charge of the Protestant Episcopal Church on Sullivan's Island and Gen. Daniel Elliot Huger, the accredited delegate (a leader in the Convention, later from All Saints'). The next year, Hon. Joel R. Poinsett was also delegate. The Rev. Mr. Muller having been ordered priest became "rector", this title showing the Church had no connection with Christ Church on the mainland. However, Mr. Muller became rector also of Christ Church at the same time. It was consecrated by the name of Grace Church by Bishop Bowen June 10, 1819. Services were held only in the summer season from June until October. After Mr. Muller, Rev. William H. Mitchell officiated (1821). The Rev. Joseph M. Gilbert became rector in 1823. The next year, he reported 30 families and 150 persons in the congregation who generally belonged to other congregations, except the officers and soldiers of Fort Moultrie who regularly attended the services. The Church nevertheless was usually represented in the Convention of the diocese; among the delegates in these early years besides those mentioned were: Daniel E. Huger, Edward Brailsford, M.D., William Blamyer, Charles C. Pinckney, Jr.

The Rev. F. H. Rutledge was the rector in 1826-32. The prospects of this Church now became more "flattering", it being "happily relieved from all pecuniary difficulty," but not for long. The Rev. Thomas H. Taylor becoming rector in 1833 reported that it was desirable that the pews should be made free—some sort of pew rents seemingly existed although the pews were not the property of individuals. Mr. Taylor left for the North the next year and Mr. Rutledge returned to the charge, but finding the financial condition of the church not so "happy", an effort was made to establish a permanent fund; $2,000.00 was raised, but the end was not reached. In 1839, Mr. Rutledge officiated not only also in St. Thomas and St. Dennis but also in St. Augustine, Florida, where he was soon after entirely engaged—prophetic of his Episcopate there! The Rev. Robert Theus Howard became rector in 1840, succeeded by the Rev. Thomas John Young, the next year holding service every Sunday morning, June through September: 30 to 35 white children were catechised before service, and 12 to 15 colored after service. The Bishop this year confirmed five colored. The Rev. C. P. Elliott came in 1842 to the rectorship, removing from Society Hill. During the year, he held 36 services on the island, and 58 at other points in the diocese rendered without "temporal compensation". Mr. Elliott went the next year to the Spartanburg district. The Rev. John H. Cornish officiated as missionary of the Advancement Society in 1843 and until 1846. The Rev. Nathaniel Hyatt had the charge in 1847 and 1848. He complained that Bishop Dehon's original purpose that this should be a "free church" had never been accomplished. The Rev. Mr. Benjamin held the services in 1849; then Mr. Hyatt again from 1850 to 1854. The deputy this year was Col. J. Bond I'On.

In 1854, improvements were made on the building, including the erection of a vestry room. The Rev. R. P. Johnson officiated in 1855, then Mr. Hyatt again in 1856. The Rev. E. T. Walker had

the Church for the summer of 1858. His ministry was quite active
—having service morning and afternoon, children were taught
after the afternoon service; at night Mr. Walker preached to the
Negroes. The Rev. Samuel J. Pinckerton of the diocese of Georgia officiated in the summer of 1860. Thus have we arrived very
near the termination of the history of Grace Church, Sullivan's
Island. Before another summer came around, the first battle of
the war was within cannon range of the Church. "When the United
States Forces established their batteries on Morris Island, the
church then came in reach of their shells, which riddled roof and
floor, and consumed the wood work." The roofless walls stood for
years. So ended the history of "Grace Church, Sullivan's Island".
It was reported in the Journal of the Convention after the war of
1861 as "suspended", then as "extinct." In the *Monthly Record*
of July, 1879, it is stated, quoting a report, "The site has been
sold and the proceeds are in the care of some of the former
vestry." These proceeds later passed into the custody of the
trustees of the diocese.

CHAPEL OF THE HOLY CROSS, SULLIVAN'S ISLAND
Established 1891

No regular services of the Church were held on Sullivan's Island after the war until Mr. W. G. Mazyck as lay reader began
services in 1886, the services being held in the Presbyterian Church
for nearly six years. Three or four years later, we find the trustees
of the diocese which held some funds of the suspended Grace
Church looking into the feasibility and necessity of a Chapel on
Sullivan's Island. In May, 1891, the trustees reported that they
had purchased a suitable lot for a Church with the funds belonging
to the old Church on the island, and had appropriated the balance with some addition from other sources for the purpose of
erecting a Church on the lot purchased. The trustees appointed
a committee consisting of Messrs. A. M. Lee, W. M. Bird, and
W. G. Mazyck to superintend the erection of the Church. They
paid over to the committee $2,385.76. In May, 1892, the lay reader,
Mr. Mazyck, who had been holding the services for nearly six
years, could report that the services had been held on the island
every Sunday morning with but three omissions, during the preceding year—all by himself, except two services by clergymen,
Mr. Gass and Mr. Kershaw. Plans for the Church by W. W. Deveaux of New York, formerly of Charleston, were adopted and a

contract for the construction made with Robert McCarrel on August 1, 1891. The cornerstone was laid with appropriate ceremonies on September 12 following, by the Rev. Robert Wilson, D.D., Dean of the Charleston Convocation, assisted by the Rev. Messrs. John Gass, James M. Stoney, Theodore A. Porter, and John Kershaw who made the address. The design was "Medieval Gothic", the material rubble granite. The first service in the new Church was the Holy Communion on July 10, 1892, celebrated by the Rev. George F. Degan, then Charleston city missionary, under whose care the Holy Cross remained for a short time, Mr. Mazyck resuming charge in September. Many handsome furnishings were placed in the Church, including a handsome stained-glass window in memory of Miss Ella M. Benjamin, and a silver communion service in memory of the "Faithful Departed." The Church was completed by a loan of $1,000.00 from the Church building fund. The total cost of the very beautiful granite Church was something over $6,000.00. In his report of 1893, Mr. Mazyck, who was the leading spirit in this work for many years, expressed appreciation for the loan of the Presbyterian Church for nearly six years. In 1895, a bell was given through the efforts of Miss Susan Gunnell, and cement walks were laid to the entrances of the Church.

The entire debt on the Church being extinguished, it was consecrated as the Chapel of the Holy Cross, Sullivan's Island, by Bishop Capers on September 12, 1895, this being the fourth anniversary of the laying of the cornerstone. He was assisted by six clergymen. Mr. Mazyck, the faithful lay reader, continued in charge, holding services with few exceptions on Sundays the year round, but with various clergymen officiating in the summer. The lay reader also had sunset services on Tuesdays and Holy Days in the summer. A. Markley Lee was the warden, William M. Bird, secretary, and Mr. Mazyck, treasurer. These three gentlemen were the founders of the mission. The members of the congrgation mostly belonged to other churches. The roof of the chapel was badly damaged in a storm in September, 1896, but friends of many faiths came forward and the damage was promptly repaired. The chapel was well supplied with beautiful hangings. In 1900, the mission was ranked as "organized", previously "unorganized". The condemnation of a large tract of land by the Federal Government near the center of the island in 1902 leading to the removal of many residents to the upper end of the island reduced the congregation at this time. This did not augur well for the future of this beautiful Church.

In 1905, the trustees agreed to sell it to the Government for $9,000.00. In August, the sale was completed and a committee appointed consisting of Messrs. W. M. Bird, W. G. Mazyck, and Henry O. Strohecker to act as agents of the trustees for the purchase of a lot and the erection of a suitable chapel and rectory on it. The Rev. W. E. Callender was minister-in-charge for a brief period in 1905. The lot was purchased for $1,063.50, and soon after, the erection of the new Church on the lower end of the island began. It was after the style of the Church sold, but of cement block instead of granite. The former chapel keys were surrendered to the Government on November 1, 1907, whereupon as the new Church was not yet completed, services were discontinued for the winter months for the first time since the mission was begun in 1886. The total amount turned over to the building committee by the trustees, including interest, was $9,581.94. The new chapel was opened for worship on Whitsunday, June 7, 1908, services being held every Sunday morning during the summer, mostly by Mr. Mazyck, with an occasional celebration of the Holy Communion by a priest. In 1910, electric lights were installed in the rectory, which had been acquired in connection with the new Church, and also, the chancel was carpeted and the organ repaired. In 1911, for the first time since the beginning in 1886, except for the brief charge by Rev. Mr. Callender in 1905, the mission was in charge of an ordained minister, the Rev. J. W. Sparks. Mr. Mazyck, however, was still warden and lay reader, and Mr. Bird, treasurer. Services were now held most of the year. In the hurricane of August 27, 1911, the chapel was badly damaged and services discontinued for the remainder of the year. In 1913, Mr. Mazyck was again in charge. In 1917, the Rev. S. R. Guignard, rector of Christ Church, assumed charge. The services reported at this time were on 41 Sundays, mostly by the lay reader. In 1920, the mission fell to the "unorganized" status.

The Rev. W. B. Sams succeeded Mr. Guignard in 1922. Mr. W. G. Mazyck was reported warden for the last time in 1923. He had practically founded the mission in 1886 himself, and for all these years, he was its leader, usually both as warden and lay reader. Mr. Sams continued in the charge for many years, mostly with some services only in the summer. Mr. J. J. Smith became warden in 1932, and with his wife conducted a Sunday School, Mr. Sams having a monthly service in winter. The work suffered a severe loss in the death in December of 1937 of Mrs. Smith. Mr. Smith continued warden until 1942. After the beginning of World

War II, services became impractical. The Church was turned over temporarily to be used as a first aid center for the duration. Mr. Sams continued to minister to the few communicants on the island. He retired August 1, 1946, ending his connection with this mission, being succeeded in this field by the Rev. Llewellyn B. Catlin.

The mission was reopened by Mr. Catlin in 1947. Services for some months were held in the chapel at Fort Moultrie. The Church had fallen into bad disrepair. In 1947, with an appropriation of $2,500.00 by the diocese, it was fully restored. The committee in charge of the restoration consisted of Messrs. S. A. Guilds, P. P. Porcher, and L. S. Damewood. This was celebrated by a service in the Church on July 20, 1947, conducted by Mr. Catlin. For 1948, Mr. Catlin reported 49 services, 20 communicants, and a Church school of 17. The mission resumed its status as an "organized mission" in 1949. The wardens were William Mazyck (son of the founder) and Leslie G. Damewood, who was also secretary-treasurer, and superintendent of the Church school. In February, 1950, 17 adults and children were baptized at one service.

ST. MATTHIAS', SUMMERTON
Established 1899

Toward the close of the last century, there were quite a number of old St. Mark's people living in the neighborhood of Summerton who found it difficult because of the distance to attend services at the parish church in the sandhills, and so arose a demand for a nearer place of worship. Some frequently attended services at the Presbyterian Church. At the request of the author some years ago, Mrs. L. E. Brailsford (*nee* E. Norvelle Richardson) prepared an invaluable sketch of the history of St. Matthias' Church. Much of this sketch is from hers. We must quote in full what she relates of the very beginning in which she played a leading part. "On one of these Sundays at the Presbyterian Church, after the service, when about all of the congregation had left, leaving Maj. and Mrs. Briggs, Mrs. R. H. Belser, Sr., Mr. John Dingle and my parents, I think Col. David Brailsford was there, too, but I am not sure of this, however, he took an active part and was much interested in the building of our little chapel. So the few that were left in the Churchyard were all Episcopalians except Maj. and Mrs. Briggs. While talking about things in general, as people do after service, Maj. Briggs said to Mrs. Belser, 'I am going to get Tourie [my Father's nickname, Mr. James Manning

Richardson] interested in church work. I am going to take him with me to Cuddo's this afternoon to our mission church.' Mrs. Belser answered, 'Well, if Tourie wants to get interested in church work, there is a plenty in his own Church to do.' Mr. Richardson replied, 'Yes, Mrs. Belser, you are right, there is plenty in our church for me to do.' He called to John Dingle, who was just about to leave and was unhitching his horse to drive off, to come back, and right there in the old or first Presbyterian Churchyard is where St. Matthias' was started."

Mrs. James Frierson had accumulated a fund to build a Church in her neighborhood. She agreed to apply this fund to a Church in Summerton. Mrs. Belser gave the lot for Church and rectory. On the appeal of Mrs. Richardson, Mrs. E. A. Coxe of Philadelphia and her family assisted generously (Mrs. Coxe continued to contribute to the Church for many years until her death). With this start and other contributions by the members and others, the Church was built. The Church being completed and paid for, it was consecrated by Bishop Capers on St. Matthias' Day, February 24, 1899. The congregation asked the Bishop to name the new Church; characteristically he in turn passed this privilege to Mrs. Capers who gave it the name of the day, St. Matthias. The Request was read by Mr. J. M. Richardson; the Sentence by the Rev. John Kershaw; Morning Prayer by the Rev. W. H. Barnwell. The sermon was preached by the Rev. Dr. W. E. Evans of Trinity Church, Columbia. Five persons were confirmed. W. G. Frierson was the first warden and John R. Dingle, secretary and treasurer. During the summer, services were held by H. H. Covington, a candidate for Holy Orders, then the Rev. P. D. Hay took temporary charge until Mr. Covington's ordination in the summer of 1900 when he succeeded. There were 16 communicants in the mission at this time. Mrs. Lucien E. Brailsford was the organist from the first and for many years.

The Rev. R. Maynard Marshall succeeded Mr. Covington December, 1903. He was the first resident minister. The rectory adjoining the Church was built at this time at a cost of $1,223.38. The warden now was J. M. Richardson; the treasurer, R. C. Richardson. Rev. John Kershaw, Jr., followed Mr. Marshall in 1906. Mr. Kershaw left in 1908 on account of ill health when Rev. Wallace Carnahan served until November, 1909, when Mr. Kershaw returned and served until his health failed and he resigned in 1911. There were many improvements in 1910; the Church was improved inside and outside; a handsome pulpit was installed, given by Mr.

H. B. Richardson in memory of his wife; a new chancel rail given by Mrs. John Ashley Colclough in memory of her daughter, Miss Screven Burrows Colclough. John R. Dingle was warden at this time and Lucien E. Brailsford, treasurer. The chancel of the Church was recessed. After a period of vacancy, Rev. H. C. Mazyck took charge November, 1912. A new organ was installed in 1914 at a cost of $225.00. The Rev. William M. Walton assumed charge in the spring of 1917. He had come from Little Rock, Arkansas. He remained until Easter, 1922. During his incumbency, the Church was remodeled and rebuilt of concrete blocks. It was furnished with stained-glass windows and some memorials, and also a valuable pipe organ was installed—the cost for all these improvements was estimated at about $14,000.00. The warden now was L. E. Brailsford; the secretary, Hugh Belser; the treasurer, H. E. Davis. The Rev. J. E. H. Galbraith became minister in the fall of 1922. Up to 1927, there had been 59 baptisms in the mission, 74 confirmations, and 102 communicants during the life of the mission. After about eleven years of faithful service, struggling with a debt left by his predecessor, bravely assisted by his wife in this, Mr. Galbraith resigned in the fall of 1933. The Rev. Sumner Guerry was appointed temporarily to hold one Sunday morning service a month. The following summer, the Rev. D. N. Peeples became priest-in-charge of St. Matthias'. The wardens now were L. E. Brailsford and R. H. Belser; secretary, H. E. Davis; and treasurer, J. P. Richardson. The next year this Church was connected with the Associate Mission with headquarters at Eutawville. The Rev. Mr. Peeples' associates were the Revs. Duncan M. Hobart and Lincoln A. Taylor. Mr. Peeples left the diocese March 1938 when the Rev. Mr. Taylor assumed charge, followed the next year by the Rev. W. R. Haynsworth, who also was connected with the associate mission. The organization conducted a mission at Remini named St. Mary's. When the mill located at that place moved down the river, this mission followed to the neighborhood of Greelyville.

Mr. Haynsworth's helpful ministry in this parish was climaxed by the burning of the mortgage on this Church after twenty-odd years, the debt having occurred in the existence remodelling of the Church Mr. Haynsworth had set the goal to eliminate the debt in five years. It was done in a little less time than this, and during a service of thanksgiving, participated in by Bishop Thomas on December 10, 1943, the warden, L. E. Brailsford, and the treasurer, J. P. Richardson, came forward and burned the mortgage papers in a metal urn in the chancel. Mr. Haynsworth resigned in June, 1946. The Rev. Frank L. Levy served for a few months. The Rev. Joseph N. Bynum succeeded in 1949. Mr. Bynum resigned April, 1952. Mr. William States Belser, a candidate for orders, then acted as lay reader. The Rev. Richard C. Patton became rector in 1954. The wardens now were L. E. Brailsford and J. W. Sconyers, the latter also secretary; H. B. Rickenbaker, treasurer. Among the founders of this Church, these names should not be forgotten: Mrs. G. M. Belser, Mr. and Mrs. J. M. Richardson, Mrs. James Frierson, Mr. and Mrs. J. J. Dingle, Mr. D. W. Brailsford, and Mr. and Mrs. Lucien Edward Brailsford. On June 3, 1956 a processional cross was given by Miss Sallie B. Anderson in memory of her sisters. A bronze tablet given by members of the Congregation, inscribed with the names of the Church's founders was dedicated on September 9 by the rector, Mr. Patton.

EPIPHANY MISSION, SUMMERVILLE
(See Archdeaconry, end this Section)

ST. BARNABAS' MISSION, SUMMERVILLE
Established 1885 (Extinct)

The Rev. L. F. Guerry in December, 1884, founded a Sunday School among the poor white people within two miles of the town of Summerville eastward. He planned a day school also. In December, 1885, a school house was erected just beyond the town limits and in January, 1886, a day school was begun, taught by a lady of the congregation. The next year the missionary reported that the accommodations were inadequate and $200.00 had been raised for a chapel. The minister was ably assisted by a layman, Mr. W. R. Dehon, who continued the zealous sponsor of this work for some thirty years. Eleven children were baptized on one occasion in the spring of 1886. The Rev. P. H. Whaley, rector of St. Paul's for the time, was in charge in 1889-90. At this time the Rev. A. R. Stuart of Georgetown, D. C., gave an organ and from the same place one gave a font, and Mr. Tylee of Summerville gave an altar and an altar desk. Thus did St. Barnabas' begin. In his first report in May 1891, the Rev. J. G. Glass, who took charge of this work with vigor, when becoming rector of St. Paul's, reports that a chapel was nearly completed—pews to seat 200 had been installed and a fence built around the lot. In 1893 there were 100 souls connected, 45 in the Sunday School. By uniting with the public school authorities the day school was continued for eight months each year. The mission received help for the first time from the diocese in 1892. The chapel was consecrated by Bishop Capers April 15, 1895, present besides Mr. Glass, were the Rev. Messrs. John Johnson, A. E. Cornish, and Dr. Porter; the request for Consecration being read by Mr. Dehon. The recessed chancel was added the next year largely by the help of Dr. Porter. The St. Barnabas' land which had been deeded to St. Paul's Church, June 26, 1896, was in turn deeded to the trustees of the diocese September 20, 1898. In 1897 Mr. Glass reported a year of "unprecedented prosperity". It had seen added to the mission the Samuel Prioleau Infirmary. For some years the work of the mission was of a threefold character centering in the chapel, the school, and the infirmary; so did it minister to soul, mind, and body. The work was largely sustained and maintained by the two laymen of St. Paul's, Mr. Dehon, Dr. C. U. Shephard, some devoted ladies of this Church, as also Dr. Carroll who gave his services for the infirmary. The parish had a regular "Committee on St. Barnabas' Mission". In 1900 it reported building a new "large and convenient school house" called "The Shepard School", Dr. Shepard being its chief sustainer.

Mr. Glass resigned in the fall of 1902, being succeeded in charge by the Rev. J. C. Jagar. In 1903 the work was organized as a "diocesan mission" (previously "parochial") with Mr. Dehon as warden and lay reader; Mr. George Tupper, Jr., treasurer, and Dr. C. U. Shephard, secretary. The Rev. A. E. Cornish succeeded Mr. Jagar in 1907 and then followed the Rev. F. W. Ambler in 1908. In 1909 Miss Florence Ward was employed as mission worker, devoting her entire time to the work. The work went on through the years with varying fortune but always with the devoted guidance of Mr. Dehon. In 1916 it fell to the status of an "unorganized mission". It was under the charge of the Rev. A. P. Magwood for a short time in 1921 and then briefly under the Rev. A. R. Mitchell, Archdeacon. At this time it was reorganized (1922) Bishop Guerry making these appointments: W. R. Dehon, warden and lay reader; Miss Ida E. Smith, secretary; Miss Annie L. Miles, treasurer. At this time the day school under Miss Ida Smith numbered 30, the Sunday School 50 with six teachers. The mission suffered a great loss on the death of William Russell Dehon September 26, 1927. For nearly forty years he gave devoted service to this mission as warden, superintendent, and lay reader. He was the grandson of Bishop Dehon. This mission was now reduced to a considerable degree. Mr. Ambler resumed charge in 1928. Mr.

Abbott Thorndike became lay reader and later warden for a short time. Again in 1933 the mission was "unorganized", Miss Annie Miles being secretary and treasurer. In 1939 the mission became dormant. For many years the income of the St. Barnabas' Fund held by the trustees of the diocese was used to assist in the salary of Mrs. Annie Tupper as a teacher in the St. Barnabas' School. The chapel was sold in 1945. The fund now amounts to $2,700.00. The work is over, apparently, but who can tell the number that were led into "the straight and narrow way" by those unselfish laborers in the Master's vineyard.

ST. PAUL'S, SUMMERVILLE
Established 1830

In the early years of the nineteenth century Summerville was founded. It at once became, as its name indicates, a resort during the so-called sickly or summer season. This was especially true of the inhabitants of St. Paul's Parish. The Rev. Philip Gadsden had taken charge of St. Paul's, Stono, in 1826. He soon followed his members to Summerville and held services there for them in the summer. Earlier a few services had been held by the Rev. C. E. Gadsden and perhaps others. The first regular services were by the Rev. Philip Gadsden from June to December, 1829. These services were first held in a temporary building used by all denominations, then for a time simply from house to house. In February, 1829, Bishop Bowen, officiating in a building of the Congregationalists, deplored the lack of a Church building.

Very promptly a Church was built and used for the first time August 1, 1830. In the *Gospel Messenger* of July, 1830, the Church was called St. George's Chapel, plainly because it was located in "St. George's Parish, Dorchester"; elsewhere we find it called "St. Paul's Church in St. George's Parish" but the name that prevailed was St. Paul's, Summerville." A vestry was elected consisting of J. W. Brisbane and T. W. Seabrook, wardens; and T. W. Boone, C. Boyle, H. L. Alison, M.D., T. S. Gelzer, J. Miles, J. S. Peake, and J. C. Shulz, vestryman. However these men were members of St. Paul's, Stono, mostly, and we find no record of the election of vestrymen again for nearly 40 years, the Church being a chapel of ease of St. Paul's, Stono, and under its vestry. In his annual report the rector included both Churches, until the Church at Stono became dormant after the war.

The Consecration of the Church was delayed on account of Bishop Bowen's absence in Europe. He consecrated it as "St. Paul's, Summerville" June 7, 1832. This church built in 1830 was described as neat and convenient, of wood built in a plain and decent style and measures 40 feet long and 30 feet wide—in front is a beautiful portico with four Doric columns supporting an angular pediment with a plain cornice—there was a gallery for colored people. The Ladies' "Gregorie Society" supplied furniture. Mr. John Gadsden tells us in his excellent sketch that this first Church was a few feet south of the present Church. We quote from him this interesting description of the chancel which was (as now) in the west end of the Church instead of the east end: "The chancel rails came out at right angles from the western wall enclosing a space nearly square, which was entered by the minister directly from the vestry room behind it. In the centre of this space was a cumbrous reading desk with seats 'for two', and behind and above this, the inevitable tall, wine glass shaped pulpit, the stairs of which ran down from the back into the vestry room. This was thought a convenient arrangement, for when the clergyman, at the close of the Ante-Communion service, retired to exchange the surplice for the black form, he reappeared to the congregation in the pulpit." The building was very plain in its interior in 1835, "four sashes" were presented by a gentleman and the vestry hung a bell. For some years services in Summerville were only from May to November, the winter services being held at the parish church at Stono.

Although he had been promised a rectory, one was not provided and Mr. Gadsden lived in Summerville where he bought a home for $300.00 in 1835. Mr. Gadsden taught in the academy. Partly for this reason, and partly because he had to live in Summerville, and not in St. Paul's, the winter services alternated between the two churches which were sixteen miles apart. In 1841, the rector reported a congregation of about 70 and stated that at Stono there were few as the people were so scattered, the congregation drifted to Summerville. Mr. Gadsden often held services specially for the Negroes on the plantations. About 1840, the Church as a distinct body began to contribute to the rector's salary, at this time giving $100.00. During these years Mr. Gadsden often officiated in other churches, especially in St. James', Goose Creek, but also at Barnwell, Branchville, Orangeburg, etc. In 1854 St. Paul's, Charleston, gave the church a 400 lb. bell in lieu of four old Dorchester bells which had been loaned to that Church. A new Church was erected in Summerville in 1856-57. It was consecrated by Bishop Davis on June 20, 1857, being assisted by the rector, the Rev. Philip Gadsden and the Rev. Messrs. Pinckney, Porter, Marshall, Jenkins, and C. P. Gadsden, the last preaching the sermon on the text (Lev. 19:30) "Reverence my sanctuary, I am the Lord." The building, neat and commodious, if after the Grecian model with porch and collonade and cupola for the bell—there is a recessed chancel with pulpit and desk. A communion table and a Bishop's chair were given by two ladies of the congregation. Two handsome chairs for the chancel, a bell and a marble font (given later by the children) completed the furniture. The day following the Consecration of the Church, Sunday, the Rev. P. Gervais Jenkins was ordained to the priesthood in the new Church.

In 1855 the Church was incorporated as "St. Paul's Church, Summerville." However when the Church was admitted in union with the Convention in 1866, becoming at this time separated from St. Paul's, Stono, an independent parish, it was as "St. Paul's Church in St. George's Parish, Dorchester." The purpose of this was to establish a claim to the "residuary estate" of old St. George's. This consisted of a tract of land sold for $119.71 and a handsome communion service, etc. In 1870 to assist in the purchase of a rectory the vestry sold for about $200.00 two "almsdishes" and two urns—the former were consecrated and sold, one each to St. Philip's and St. Michael's. In 1875 the Convention confirmed the restoration to the Church of its old name "St. Paul's Church, Summerville." M. E. Hutchinson was the first deputy to the Convention from this Church in 1877. Rev. Philip Gadsden resigned June 23, 1864, because of age and infirmity, after 38 years of service in the joint churches. He afterwards resided in Union and Summerville. He was succeeded by the Rev. James A. Harold who served from June until December, 1866. In 1867 Mr. Gadsden reports rendering such services as he was able to render. Later he lived in Charleston, dying in 1870. The Rev. J. J. Sams became rector from June, 1867, to January, 1874. A parsonage was purchased in 1870, largely by the Ladies' "Church Aid Association". In April, 1877, the Rev. W. H. Johnson became rector (Mr. Sams going to Virginia) serving for only a short time to November. The Rev. L. F. Guerry succeeded July, 1875, serving until 1888. In 1877 under the plans and supervision of Mr. W. B. W. Howe, Jr., the church was enlarged by a 20-foot extension and a handsome stained chancel window, the gift of Mr. B. T. Rogers of New York, was installed, as well as a handsome communion table.

A parochial school was conducted in the parish about 1880. Bracket lamps were placed in the Church in 1881. In 1884 a new fence was erected around the churchyard. In 1885, Mr. Guerry established a Sunday School among the poor within two miles of the town. This was the beginning of St. Barnabas' mission, a sketch of which will be found elsewhere. Both the Church and the rectory suffered in the earthquake but were repaired chiefly by means of an appropriation of $500.00 from the Earthquake Fund in the hands of the Bishop. The Ladies' Church Aid Association was active in good works in these years. In 1888 Mr. Guerry resigned, going to Arkansas, being succeeded by the Rev. P. H. Whaley, coming from Connecticut. In 1889 a brass altar desk was given by the Sunday School in memory of the late superintendent, William A. Gammell. A brass altar cross was given about the same time by ladies of Trenton, N. J. After just two years Mr. Whaley went to Pensacola, Fla., and the Rev. J. G. Glass became rector, July, 1890. In 1892, great improvements were made in the chancel, a brass lectern given by the guild, a Bible, a new altar rail, and other furnishings. At this time a new Church was planned. St. Helena's Guild, organized in 1891, gave $100.00 and an Easter offering for the purpose amounted to $570.00. In July, 1902, Mr. Glass resigned, going to Alabama. Rev. J. C. Jagar became rector November 1, 1902. He was succeeded by the Rev. A. E. Cornish (1907-1908), who in turn was succeeded by the Rev. Francis Willis Ambler in 1908. In 1909 (July 1) the St. Barnabas' Society was organized to assist in charities about the community and especially in St. Barnabas' mission. In 1921 the Church building fund and the parish house fund was $4,500.00—and it was decided to transfer the former to the latter. The year 1924 witnessed a marked advance in the parish, the erection of a fine and attractively located parish house, in use but not completed until two years later, total cost, about $17,500.00. It was so intended and has proved most useful not only in the parish but in the community, regardless of Church lines. Mr. Ambler resigned October 1, 1940, after thirty-two years of useful service, becoming rector emeritus. About this time he received the degree of Doctor of Divinity from the University of the South. Dr. Ambler continued to live in Summerville after retirement, often assisting in the parish. The Rev. Edward M. Dart succeeded immediately as rector and he in turn was succeeded by the Rev. C. Offerall Thompson, January 1, 1946. In 1947, the fiftieth anniversary of Mrs. E. H. Hutchinson as organist was duly recognized. In 1948 a silver flagon was given by friends in the congregation as a memorial to Bishop James D.

Perry, late presiding Bishop, who died in Summerville the year before. Mr. Thompson resigned December, 1949, and was succeeded as rector by the Rev. Walter D. Roberts on July 1, 1950. In 1952 the parish house was remodeled and the organ rebuilt, also this year saw the repainting of the interior of the Church.

GOOD SHEPHERD MISSION, SUMTER
(See Archdeaconry, end this Section)

HOLY COMFORTER, SUMTER
Established 1857

The first services of the Episcopal Church in Sumter, of which we have any record, were those held by Rev. C. P. Elliott. He reports three services in Sumterville in 1844, then services in the Court House in 1851. Nothing more than the fact of these services seems to be known. Mr. Elliott's life was lost in a storm the latter part of this year, 1851. He was then the rector of St. Phillip's Bradford Springs. It was in the month of May, 1857, that the Church of the Holy Comforter had its real beginning when with the advice and consent of the Bishop, the Rev. T. F. Davis, Jr., son of the Bishop and his assistant at Grace Church, Camden, began monthly visits to Sumter. It was then a growing town of about 2,000 inhabitants, especially gaining in importance because of the coming of the Wilmington and Manchester Railroad. Mr. Davis' first service was on the last Sunday in May, 1857, held by courtesy in the Presbyterian Church; then the next month, it was in the Methodist Church. After this, services were held in a room on the third floor above Mund's Book Store. Mr. S. Mayrant assisted Mr. Davis in arranging for these services and in the efforts to build a Church.

Eight communicants now were on the ground. Steps were immediately taken toward the building of a Church. On August 24, 1857, $800.00 having been subscribed, a lot was purchased at the corner of Main and what was later Bartlett Streets, extending back to what became Harvin Street, on which later the rectory faced. Mrs. Elizabeth Buford, a devoted leader, paid for the lot, $650.00, and generously assisted in the building of the Church. In the following September, a congregation was organized, with the election of a vestry of five, with the name "The Church of the Holy Comforter". Mr. John Thompson was the secretary. The Church was incorporated by the General Assembly December 21, 1857. Bishop Davis made his first official visit to the Holy Comforter on January 24, 1858, confirming four persons. Several services were held, the

Rev. Messrs. Davis, Wagner, and A. H. Cornish assisting. After the morning service, a meeting of the vestry was held and steps taken to build a Church. At the time, about $2,700.00 had been subscribed—$1,400.00 from Sumter; $600.00, Stateburg; $300.00, St. Mark's; $150.00, Camden; Bradford Springs, $150.00; Georgetown, about $100.00. Construction was soon begun by a Mr. Long. The Rev. E. A. Wagner superintended the building of the Church and advised as to its plan.

The first service was held in the Church on the 16th of August, 1858. It was a neat Gothic Church with a recessed chancel. Dr. Kershaw in his sketch in *The Chronicles of St. Mark's Parish* tells us the Church was "the happy possessor of a 650-lb. bell, that was afterwards taken down and offered as a patriotic gift to the Confederate States of America". There seems to have been another bell that Mr. Seabrook mentions in his valuable sketch of the Church. The Holy Comforter was consecrated on Friday morning, February 18, 1859, by Bishop Davis, assisted by his son, the Rev. T. F. Davis, in charge, and Rev. Messrs. Gregg, Moore, Phillips, Roberts, Taylor, and Trapier; the last preaching. Services were continued through Sunday when the Bishop preached in the morning and confirmed four. Mr. Gregg preached at the Friday night service; Saturday forenoon, the Rev. J. W. Taylor; Saturday evening, the Rev. E. A. Wagner, who preached again Sunday evening.

The wardens elected at Easter 1858 were Samuel Mayrant and H. L. Darr; vestrymen, John Thompson, W. B. Leary, W. W. Bradford, and B. Mitchell. Mr. Thompson was a druggist, Mr. Darr an auctioneer. Beginning in March, 1859, Mr. Davis was assisted in the services by the Rev. Paul Trapier, then a professor in the seminary in Camden. A Sunday School was begun in this year, taught by Miss S. Darr. The ladies of St. Philip's Church, Charleston, gave a font and those of St. Michael's silver collection plates. Later these were matched by a similar one in memory of R. I. Manning, Jr. (1880-82). Mr. Davis was succeeded in the charge in November, 1859, by the Rev. Ezra Jones, rector at Bradford Springs, who served until the middle of 1861. There were now 23 communicants. Through the generosity of one member, a parsonage was secured in 1860. In 1862, the Rev. Albert R. Walker, a deacon, succeeded as minister-in-charge, becoming rector the next year on his ordination to the priesthood. The congregation and Sunday School were much enlarged now by refugees from the lower part of the State.

On the occasion of Potter's Raid April 9, 1865, and the battle at Dingle's Mill, Mr. Walker went from the Church at 2 o'clock after a confirmation, shouldered a musket and took part in the engagement. Bishop Davis had already left for Camden. The Church suffered at the end of the war, but not as much as others. It was used briefly as a hospital by the enemy, and many articles were stolen. Three Federal soldiers were buried in the churchyard. Dr. John Thompson, a leading member, was slain in the battle at Dingle's Mill. The rector lost much, including his horse and buggy. He left the following winter. Messrs. John Johnson and P. D. Hay, candidates for orders, then acted as lay readers. The Rev. L. F. Guerry took charge briefly in May, 1866. The Rev. Robert Wilson had charge briefly in 1867. The Rev. F. Bruce Davis, another son of the Bishop, took charge August the year following, being also rector of St. Mark's, Clarendon. Services were sometimes supplied by other ministers. January 1, 1873, the Rev. L. F. Guerry, who had previously served the Church, became its rector. After two years, he was succeeded briefly by the Rev. W. H. Johnson. The Rev. Robert F. Clute was the next rector from July, 1876, in connection with St. Mark's, Clarendon. Col. S. W. Seabrook gave an altar cross at this time. Mr. Clute ceased to officiate after August, 1878, the vestry having found it impossible to pay his salary. After a long vacancy, the Rev. Theodore A. Porter became rector January 1, 1882, having officiated for some months before. A rectory was built next to the Church in 1883 at a cost of $1,779.91. Among the contributors to the building from without the parish were St. Mark's, Clarendon, $99.00; Church in Charleston, $300.00; friends at North through Mr. Porter and his father, Dr. Porter, $675.00. The rector occupied this rectory May, 1883. The rector's salary at this time was $300.00. He also was rector of St. Mark's. Mr. Porter resigned March 1, 1885. At this time, there were 27 families connected with the parish, and 42 communicants. The deputies to the Convention of 1884 were H. L. Darr and J. F. W. DeLorme.

The Rev. John Kershaw became rector in 1885, serving also St. Mark's and Holy Cross. The Rev. J. S. Hartzell became assistant to the Rev. John Kershaw in 1892, who had added to his responsibilities St. Philip's, Bradford Springs, and St. Augustine's for colored people in St. Mark's parish. Mr. Hartzell continued until 1894 when he was succeeded by Rev. W. T. Capers. Mr. Kershaw resigned in December, 1895. During his incumbency in Sumter, he established *The Diocese*. A great event in the rectorship of Mr. Kershaw was his presention for confirmation on March 13, 1892 of Shirley Carter Hughson. Father Hughson's services to the Church reached far and wide. The Rev. S. B. Hillock of Tennessee succeeded Mr. Kershaw. In 1897, the wardens were J. F. W. DeLorme and Mark Reynolds; secretary of the vestry, Mark Reynolds; treasurer, P. P. Gaillard. The Rev. Benjamin M. Braden became the next rector in 1898, but only until March, 1899. Mr. R. I. Manning filled in a vacancy with lay reading. Mr. George Shore was superintendent of the Sunday School. The Rev. P. D. Hay next served for a brief period in 1900.

The Rev. Henry Harris Covington became deacon-in-charge in 1900, having previously held the services two summers when a candidate for orders. He became rector on ordination to the priesthood in 1901. The Church was now growing rapidly, increasing in communicants from 65 in 1900 to 303 in 1905. In contemplation of a new Church, a lot was bought ($3,300.00) at the corner of Main and Calhoun Streets in 1903. A dwelling on the corner was adapted as a new rectory, being rolled to the rear of the lot and facing Calhoun. In 1904, the old Church property at Main, Bartlett, and Harvin Streets was sold for $8,000.00. In 1905, the old Church was rolled up Main Street to the new site to serve for worship until the new Church should be built, then as a Sunday School, and later as part of a parish house. The work on the new Church began in July, 1908. The Church is in the shape of a Greek cross, with possible enlargement to the form of a Roman cross. It is built of brick with stucco finish and tile roof, completed at a cost of $17,500.00 in 1909. The next year, furniture, carpet, and heating plant were added. A Mr. Edwards was the architect and the contractor Mr. Cain. The building committee consisted of R. I. Manning, George D. Shore, Mark Reynolds, and the rector. All borrowed funds were liquidated in 1917. Governor Manning often served as lay reader. Mr. Covington, after his notable rectorship, resigned April 20, 1913. He had suffered severely in an accident the year before, which incapacitated him for several months.

The Rev. Robert T. Phillips succeeded Mr. Covington. In 1914, the wardens were R. I. Manning and Mark Reynolds; secretary, J. A. Warren; treasurer, John R. Sumter; deputies to the Convention, R. I. Manning, Mark Reynolds, Ernest Fields, and W. Percy Smith. Mr. Philips left in 1915. The Rev. J. Bentham Walker became rector January 1, 1916. The debt on the Church was soon after this entirely liquidated. The Church was consecrated by Bishop Guerry on May 13, 1917. The sermon appropriately was by the Rev. H. H. Covington, who had led in the building of the

Church. The rector and the Rev. R. T. Phillips assisted Mr. Mark Reynolds, senior warden, presented "the instruments of donation". Mr. Phillips preached at the night service. In 1919, the "Churchman's Club" of Holy Comforter was organized on motion of Mr. M. W. Seabrook, and began its influential life. Mr. Mark Reynolds was the first president. The parish house which incorporated the old Church was built in 1925-26. It was soon well equipped for its purposes, being conveniently connected with the Church. It was at this time that a new organ was installed through the generosity of Mrs. Elizabeth Wilson and her daughter, Mrs. Mary Peatross. The Rev. James McDowell Dick of the Holy Comforter was ordained by Bishop Guerry June 5, 1927. In July, 1933, another son of the parish, Thomas Sumter Tisdale, was ordained in the Church by Bishop Thomas. The Convention of the diocese met in Holy Comforter May 14-15, 1929, being the first after Bishop Thomas's Consecration. In 1940, the wardens were Mark Reynolds and W. Percy Smith; secretary, A. B. Holland, Jr.; treasurer, Mrs. Martha R. Brunner; lay reader, John Fishburne. The Rev. Mr. Walker retired in July, 1947, but continued his services to the end of this year, completing 32 years as rector, much beloved not only by his own congregation but by all citizens of Sumter. He was succeeded by the Rev. Frank V. D. Fortune January, 1948.

In 1951, the entire Church property underwent very extensive repairs and improvements costing $36,000.00. The old rectory was at this time redecorated for Church school purposes. In 1952, a set of Deagan chimes were presented in memory of his mother and sister by Mr. A. J. Ard. An entire series of nine stained glass windows have been installed in the Church depicting the life of our Lord: "Suffer the children" in memory of Elinora Norvelle, Richard Charles, and Elizabeth Sinkler Richardson; "The Resurrection" in memory of Ella Thomlinson McLeod; "The Holy Communion", tribute to the Rev. J. Bentham Walker, rector 1916-47; "The Annunciation" in memory of Elizabeth Reynolds; "The Ascension", tribute to Mark Reynolds, vestryman and warden 1890-1945; "The Nativity" in memory Henry Harris Covington, rector 1900-13; "The Boy in the Temple" in memory of T. B. M. Spann, candidate for Holy Orders; "The Baptism" in memory of Bertha Bultman Duke; "Healing of the Sick" in memory of Martha Ard and George Evans Brunner. Mr. Fortune resigned in 1955. He was succeeded February, 1956, by the Rev. W. Seddon Lee.

HOLY CROSS (CLAREMONT) STATEBURG, SUMTER
Established 1788
(See Dalcho, p. 392)

The Rev. Parker Adams was rector of Holy Cross in 1820 (since 1818). The parish was represented in the Convention of 1821 by Hon. John S. Richardson, Col. Orlando S. Rees, and Col. M. I. Keith. There were 23 families connected with the Church at this time—32 white and nine colored communicants. The parsonage, erected on land given by Thomas Waties about the time Mr. Adams took charge, was occupied by all regular rectors until the Rev. C. W. Boyd, the last to live in it. After Mr. Adams the services were held by a lay reader, a candidate for orders. In the winter of 1822 and 1823, the Rev. William Barlow officiated as visitor; in the summer of 1823, the Rev. Francis H. Rutledge officiated occasionally. He was the first Bishop of Florida. Mr. Barlow became rector in 1824. In August, 1824, a free colored man, William Ellison, was permitted to have a pew in the Church for himself and family. Hon. Thomas Waties was deputy this year. He became a leader in the Convention for many years.

In 1825, a society was formed in the parish called "The Claremont Theological Scholarship Society"; it raised $100.00 the first year for the General Theological Seminary. Mr. Barlow left November, 1826. Hon. Judge Waties served as lay reader the following months and visiting clergymen officiated. The Rev. Augustus L. Converse was minister-in-charge beginning April, 1827. Soon after he became rector. In 1829, the Church received a gift of $100.00 from the Governor of the State, Stephen D. Miller, who suggested it be used to paint the exterior of the Church. In 1831, the rector laments indifference to religion and neglect of worship of God and the ordinances of His Church. He failed in his effort to form a Bible class. Regular instruction was given to the colored people. At this time there were 24 white and 20 colored communicants. From June to December, 1833, Mr. Converse officiated also in St. Mark's at the request of the Advancement Society. In 1837, the rector sees better prospects for the Church with filling of long empty houses in the neighborhood and the establishment of Edgehill Academy and Mrs. Allston's female school. In this year, a plan of "Church Offerings" was adopted, evidencing it did not exist before. Communion was administered once in every two months. In 1840, $13.00 was given for "building of the Church at Bradford Springs, $30.00 for the General Seminary, and $95.00 for Domestic Missions in response to "extra" appeal in *Spirit of Missions*. During the time of his rectorship, Mr. Converse often would spend several months in the North. Among those who supplied were the Revs. F. B. Lee, F. H. Rutledge, and C. P. Elliott. In 1844, the deputies to the Convention were Col. John J. Moore and James N. Frierson.

Under Mr. Converse, much attention was given to work among the Negroes; in 1845, a society was organized called "The Church Society for the Advancement of Christianity among the Slaves in the parish of Claremont." He "recalled" any pledge to other missions until the object of this society was accomplished. One object was the erection of "log churches" in suitable places. In this year, he baptized nine white persons, and 34 colored. Col. J. J. Moore, a very devout churchman who acted frequently as lay reader at the Stateburg Church, built for the Negroes a Church on his plantation. It was called the "Church of Col. J. J. Moore" and had a large congregation. The Rev. C. P. Gadsden, who officiated in this Church for years, on one occasion baptized 58 Negro children. A catechist in 1846 assisted in this extensive work. In 1848, there were 41 white and 59 colored communicants. This year, the deputies were W. J. Rees, Col. John J. Moore, McKenzie Anderson, and Samuel Bradley.

In 1849 it was decided to build a new Church. The charter of the Church was amended, the name "Church of the Holy Cross" being now adopted. Some of the funds for the building came from disposal of slaves. The old Church was taken down and the new erected on the same spot. The cornerstone was laid on September 11, 1850, by the rector, the Rev. Augustus L. Converse, assisted by the Rev. C. P. Elliott, rector of St. Philip's, Bradford Springs. Bishop Gadsden, about to leave for the General Convention, could not be present but sent his greetings with the hope that "the head-stone would be brought forth with shouting." The building committee consisted of William W. Anderson, M.D., Henry L. Pinckney, Jr., and Samuel J. Bradley. Edward C. Jones of Charleston was the architect. The wardens at this time were William W. James, M.D., and Edward L. Murray; vestrymen, Marcus Reynolds, M.D., William J. Rees, Jr., and Bonneau Murray. List of articles placed in the cornerstone will be found on p. 30, Journal of the Convention, 1851. Morning Prayer was said before and an address delivered by the rector after the laying of the cornerstone. The Church was consecrated on July 14 1852, by Bishop Rutledge of Florida, assisted by the rector and the Revs. R. Henry, D.D., and P. J. Shand. Bishop Gadsden had died only about three weeks before. Further details of the Consecration will be found in Mr. Frierson's valuable sketch. He tells us the cost of the Church was $11,358.74. It was 100 feet long in the nave, 25 wide, and 56 in transepts, of Gothic design— possibly the most beautiful example of this style of architecture in the state. It is adorned with beautiful stained glass. The present organ was installed apparently at the time of the Consecration. The walls of the Church are of unusual construction, called *pise de terre,* clay tamped in forms. The handsome pulpit, appropriately on the Gospel or north side of the chancel, was installed at a cost of $500.00. The deputies to the Convention in 1852 were J. N. Frierson, Dr. M. Reynolds, and Col. J. J. Moore. Mr. Converse resigned in May, 1853; his body lies in the churchyard.

The Rev. John J. Roberts became rector November, 1853. The Rev. J. V. Welch, the Rev. T. N. Lucas, and later Mr. LeGrand Guerry (a candidate then) ministered to the colored people. It was through the generosity of this congregation and the active interest and labors of Mr. LeGrand Guerry (then a young man of St. Mark's Parish looking to the ministry) that the chapel called St. Matthew's at Providence was built. This chapel was consecrated by Bishop Davis on September 20, 1856, assisted by Messrs. Roberts, Davis, Welch (deacon), and Lucas. It was the Rev. T. N. Lucas, then rector of Bradford Springs, who ministered in this chapel until 1859. Later Mr. Roberts held the services. In 1863, the Rev. J. V. Welch was missionary to the Negroes in the parish. In this year, he baptized 195 persons of color, and Mr. Roberts 41, a total of 236; confirmed 67. The deputies to the Convention of 1864 were J. N. Frierson, W. W. Rees, W. W. Anderson, Jr., and Marcus Reynolds. In 1854-65, Mr. Lucas again assisted at St. Matthew's, Providence, and Mr. Welch was still continuing the work among the colored people. The Rev. Robert Wilson succeeded Mr. Roberts as rector in 1866. He reported in 1868 seven colored communicants; shortly before the war, Mr. Roberts reported 150. They had left *en masse.* The Rev. T. N. Lucas officiated after September, 1868, when Mr. Wilson had resigned. Mr. Lucas later became rector. In 1877, he reported holding services at St. Matthew's, Providence. The next year, he reported ten families connected with the chapel but in 1880 he was forced to "abandon" St. Matthew's. Mr. Frierson tells us the site of St. Matthew's is marked by a pile of bricks one mile south of Hillcrest School. In his last report for this parish in 1884, Mr. Lucas states that there were 29 families (two colored); communicants 52 (three colored); thus we see the large work among the Negroes had practically come to an end. Mr. Lucas was buried in the churchyard.

The Rev. John Kershaw became rector in 1885 in connection with St. Mark's, and Holy Comforter, Sumter, where he lived. He gave particular attention to renewed work among the colored people in this parish and St. Mark's, laying the foundation for the beginning of St. Augustine's below Wedgefield. The Rev. J. S. Hartzell became assistant to Mr. Kershaw in his entire field of work in 1892. He was succeeded by the Rev. W. T. Capers in July, 1894. Mr. Kershaw resigned in December, 1895. The Rev. W. H. Barnwell, coming then from Kentucky, became rector (1896) in connection with St. Mark's. In 1897, the wardens were W. W. Anderson, M.D., and J. T. Frierson; secretary of the vestry, H. L. Pinckney; treasurer, J. T. Frierson; deputies to the Convention, J. C. Pinckney, J. T. Frierson, F. M. Dwight, M.D., and W. W. Anderson, M.D. Mr. Barnwell took charge also of Ascension, Hagood. In 1903, a great misfortune came to the Church when on February 16th a storm blew down the beautiful steeple and destroyed a large part of the north wall and the roof. Repairs were soon made, but the steeple was restored only up to about 45 feet and the old cross placed on it. The old plantation chapel of the Frierson's at Cherry Vale, called St. John's, was removed and rebuilt on Route 76 called then "Bowen Church" after the Negro who moved it. It eventually was moved and rebuilt again in Sumter as the Good Shepherd. In 1915, there was only one warden, Dr. F. M. Dwight; secretary and treasurer, W. J. Rees. The deputies were Dr. Dwight, Ransom S. Richardson, Jr., W. L. Sanders, and J. L. Frierson. The Rev. H. D. Bull, native of the parish, was ordained priest in the Church June 27, 1915, by Bishop Guerry. (Others ordained in Holy Cross were the Revs. Robert Wilson, Moultrie Guerry, and Eugene West.)

The Rev. W. H. Barnwell, much beloved rector for 21 years, resigned in 1917 and was succeeded by the Rev. C. W. Boyd, noted for his fine sermons, who left in 1921 and, after a short vacancy, the Rev. William S. Stoney was rector, 1923-25; then the Rev. Moultrie Guerry, 1926-28; next the Rev. George H. Harris, 1931-1941, the Rev. J. B. Walker having supplied services in 1930. In 1928, lights were installed in the Church, beautiful iron fixtures being given by Mrs. Walter White. The rectory, not having been used as such for many years, was sold in this year. Copies of the old parish records having been made by W. P. A. copyists, the originals were now committed to the registrar of the diocese for safekeeping. In 1939, Mrs. James S. Pinckney exchanged one acre of land south of the churchyard for one acre east; the former was fenced off as an extension of the churchyard.

Mr. Harris resigned in May, 1939. The Rev. Alfred Parker Chambliss succeeded the following summer. At this time, the wardens were J. R. Sumter and W. M. Manning; secretary and treasurer, Mark Reynolds, Jr.; lay reader, W. M. Manning. Mr. Chambliss resigned September, 30, 1942. During a period now of vacancy in the rectorship, the Rev. A. G. B. Bennett of St. Timothy's, Columbia supplied services. The services in Holy Cross have often been maintained by faithful lay readers—among the more recent, Wyndam M. Manning and John L. Frierson. The Rev. Eugene West was rector 1946 for two years, when after a few months the Rev. C. M. Hobart assumed charge, November, 1948.

The 1950 members and friends of Holy Cross saw what they scarcely hoped would be accomplished in their day—the restoration of the steeple of the Church blown down in 1903. This was done through the generosity of Mrs. Walter White of Gates Mill, Ohio, formerly Virginia Saunders of this parish, in memory of her parents, Mr. and Mrs. William L. Saunders. Thus in this handsome structure restored to what Mr. John Frierson well calls its "pristine beauty." This event was commemorated at a great homecoming service on October 22, 1950, when Bishop Carruthers dedicated the new spire. Mr. John L. Frierson, senior warden, then made a valuable Historical Address; Mrs. Frierson, as for many years, presided at the organ. The Rev. W. S. Stoney, former rector, preached. The rector, the Rev. C. M. Hobart, and other former rectors assisted. Other memorials presented at this time were: a litany desk, also by Mrs. White in memory of her uncle, William Anderson; a lectern light in memory or Mrs. Julian Barnwell and the late Rev. deSaussure Parker Moore by McK. P. Moore and Mrs. William Arthur. Mr. Hobart resigned October 1, 1952, due to failing health, and retired to live at Myrtle Beach. Rev. W. S. Stoney returned to the rectorship in 1955 after an absence of thirty years much to the joy of the congregation. In the meantime a parish house was erected to the north of the Church and used for the first time on the occasion of Mr. Stoney's first service. On November 11, 1956, a very handsome bell given by the children of Mrs. W. C. (Mary Virginia) White was Dedicated by Bishop Thomas and named "Mary Virginia". The bell (cast in Holland weighing about 1,000 pounds) is given in honor of its namesake, frequent benefactress of the Church.

ALL SAINTS', VARNVILLE
Established 1817 (Extinct)

The Rev. E. E. Bellinger held services in Varnville in 1891 and 1892 in the academy and in the Methodist Church. These services were soon abandoned. When the Rev. A. R. Mitchell served as Archdeacon of the Charleston Convocation (1916-1921), he found a group of church people in Varnville, and held services for them in the Methodist Church kindly loaned. In 1917 the group was formed into a mission with Charles Kerrison as warden and E. C. Glenn, treasurer. In 1921, it was formally organized and admitted into Convention as All Saints', Varnville—warden, E. C. Glenn; secretary, Charles Kerrison; treasurer, W. W. Simmons. In 1922, the Rev. A. M. Rich, rector of St. Jude's, took charge. The Rev. Capers Satterlee was in charge for a short time, and then succeeded the Rev. Frank M. Brunton in 1924, then in 1927 the Rev. Joseph Burton. The mission was now abandoned, the people going elsewhere.

ATONEMENT MISSION, WALTERBORO
(See Archdeaconry, end this Section)

ST. BARTHOLOMEW'S PARISH, WALTERBORO
Established 1706
(See Dalcho, p. 366)

The last rector of this parish as mentioned in Dalcho was the Rev. Andrew Fowler who served the parish from 1807 to 1811. For some years longer he continued as visitor, as did also the Rev. Thomas Frost (1817), the Rev. Philip Mathews, and the Rev. David I. Campbell. Then for a time (1822) the Rev. George B. Andrews officiated followed by the Rev. Mellish I. Motte (1823). But the next regular rector was the Rev. Francis P. Delavaux (1824-1841). He was offered a salary of $1,000.00 and a "comfortable house in Walterboro". In his first report he stated that "The Church is in distress". However, "Burnt Church" (Pon Pon), a ruin for years, had been rebuilt, and there was a Sunday School thus early in Walterboro. Services in 1826 were at Pon Pon every other Sunday from November to June, at Edmundsbury (Ashepoo) on the alternate Sundays and in Walterboro June to November. These three places of worship in the parish were all chapels. St. Bartholomew's never had a parish Church. The Rev. William Edward Fripp has carefully located these chapels. Pon Pon stood on "the Parker's Ferry Road about a half mile from U. S. Highway 17, between Walterboro and Jacksonboro about three miles from the latter".

Edmundsbury or Ashepoo Chapel "stood on the west side of Ashe-poo River, between the present Highway 52 and the Atlantic Coast Line Railroad, only a few hundred yards from the highway bridge over the river." Services in Walterboro were first held in the old academy. In 1826 a chapel was built near the Church of the Atone-ment on Tracy Street. It was consecrated by Bishop Bowen in 1827. Services were held here until St. Jude's Church was built in 1855. The vestry of this Church elected at Edmundsbury Chapel April 8, 1822 was: John A. Culliatt, Thomas Boone, James Lowndes, Alfred Walters, W. M. Smith, A. Fraser, vestrymen, with Charles Webb and Jacon Warley, wardens. The rector usually attended the vestry meetings. In 1825 he was elected a member.

The seating capacity of the academy in Walterboro in 1825 prov-ing inadequate, an arrangement was made to use the Presbyterian Church for a time. However a lot was given by Dr. Burney and soon a chapel was built, $800.00 being appropriated for this pur-pose to be replaced by the sale of the "benches". The chapel was completed and benches sold the following summer. In contrast to the increasing demand for seats in Walterboro, at Pon Pon the committee reported in 1826 that they could not effect the rent of a single "bench". The members seemed to be moving from that vicinity, the number of services were reduced and after 1832 there is no record of any services at Pon Pon (the Burnt Church.) Whether this Church suffered another "burning" or simply fell into disrepair and finally into the ruin it presents today we have not ascertained. The chapel in Walterboro seems not to have been very complete; the vestry in 1827 voted to allow Mrs. William C. Pinckney to glaze the window at the back of her seat at her own cost. In 1832 Col. Lewis Morris (of Morris Town, N. Y. who built a home at Willtown) gave the Edmundsbury Chapel a stove. The parish in these times was able to make investment of excess income in stocks as endowment. There was an education society that sup-ported one pupil and a library for the parish. The rent of a so-called "bench" or pew was $10.00 a year and assessment on those owned $6.00 a year. Mr. Delevaux' rectorate came to a sudden end in 1841 after sixteen years when the vestry reduced his salary from $1,000.00 to $800.00 on the ground of the financial condition of the parish. (In 1835 the vestry had added $100.00 to his salary to enable him to travel for his health and generous sums were voted from time to time to repair the parsonage.) Mr. Delavaux resigned, charging the vestry with "want of courtesy as well as want of justice". The vestry demurred to this but later passed commendatory resolutions concerning Mr. Delavaux (who continued to live in Walterboro for some years), and then elected the Rev. James H. Fowles to be rector at a salary of $1,200.00. He resigned February, 1846, and was succeeded by the Rev. W. O. Prentiss in 1848. The following years were eventful: the Church for Negroes at Chessee was destroyed by a storm in August, 1851; the Edmundsbury Chapel was destroyed by fire in May, 1852; the new Church in Walterboro was completed and consecrated by Bishop F. H. Rutledge of Florida November 14, 1852, as St. Jude's Church, this name now being given the Church for the first time. Services continued without interruption at the Presbyterian Church near Ashepoo until the Edmundsbury Chapel was rebuilt and consecrated by Bishop Davis on April 2, 1854.

During these years great attention was given to work among the colored people, a catechist being employed for this purpose, the Atonement in Walterboro today is testimony to this. The remarkable work of the Rev. Stephen Elliott while rector in Prince Williams at Christ Church on the Combahee was within this parish. In January, 1854, the Rev. Benjamin Johnson became assistant rector to have the charge of the upper part of the parish, Mr. Prentiss continuing as rector in charge of the lower part. At Easter of 1854 Mr. Prentiss resigned the rectorship. On being called upon to hold services at Ashepoo Mr. Johnson protested and his salary was cut in half to $450.00. The Rev. Stephen Elliott became rector of the parish in February 1855, retaining charge of Christ Church for the colored people on the Combahee which he had built of his own means while rector of Prince Williams. After six months on the reduced salary Mr. Johnson resigned July, 1855. In this year St. Jude's was cut off from St. Batholomew's Parish, becoming itself a separate parish. (See the continuation of its history under St. Jude's, Walterboro.) Mr. Elliott's remark was "We divide to prosper". Ascension, Combahee, was another offspring of St. Bartholomew's (see its history in this book). In 1860, the Rev. E. J. Webb, deacon, formerly a catechist in the parish, was conducting a large missionary work among the Negroes on eight plantations, and at Chepee Church. At this time the Rev. W. O. Prentiss built a chapel on his plantation in this parish. In 1861 Mr. Elliott after serving as chaplain of the Ninth Regiment of South Carolina Volunteers at Port Royal, later removed to Camden, his services in the parish being discontinued, the people forced away by war. Mr. Webb was continuing his work among the Negroes in 1865. Mr. Elliott died in 1867. Woodwork of the Church at Edmundsbury, Ashepoo, was partially used by the enemy for a bridge over Ashepoo River during the war. In 1868 the frame was still standing. From these years St. Bartholomew's Parish became as such extinct—the old chapels at Ashepoo and Pon Pon being ruins, also Ascension later. However, the parish lives on in St. Jude's, Walterboro, as related *in loco*. In 1943 the Colonial Dames in consultation with Bishop Thomas placed a marker on Pon Pon or the Burnt Church Dedicated by the Bishop.

ST. JUDE'S, WALTERBORO
Established 1855

St. Jude's, formerly a chapel of St. Bartholomew's Parish (see above), was set off as an independent parish in 1855 and in December of that year called the Rev. Joseph B. Seabrook to be its first rector. He was succeeded by the Rev. E. Edmund Bellinger, January, 1857. Some effort was made to rebuild old "Burnt Church" at this time but it did not materialize. In 1859 Mr. Bellinger held 195 services in churches, and on plantations for the Negroes. In 1864 the Rev. W. O. Prentiss assisted in the parish. Illustrating the effects of the war, St. Jude's could pledge only $150.00 for the minister's salary —St. Bartholomew's Parish had once paid a salary of $1,200.00. During these years Mr. Bellinger did a widespread missionary work in three counties, Colleton, Beaufort, and Barnwell. In 1869 it was reported that the colored people had gradually withdrawn from the services of the Church but some remained loyal and in 1876 a Church for them was contemplated. In 1878 St. Jude's was repaired and repainted but the year following, on April 16, a cyclone completely destroyed the Church with its furniture. Mr. Bellinger living again in Walterboro happened to be home, as he was one week in the month, and witnessed the "swift destruction". The rectory nearby was rendered uninhabitable. To expedite the rebuilding the rector surrendered his salary in 1881. Services were now held in the Court House. A new Church was built "neat and well furnished" costing about $1,800.00, and was consecrated during a meeting of Convocation on January 13, 1882, by Bishop Howe, the Rev. W. O. Prentiss preaching the sermon. The Church had seats for 140 white and 20 colored persons, four pews being set aside for the latter. The Church in the diocese through the Bishop assisted largely in the building in response to a resolution passed by the diocesan Convention. At this time and for some years Mr. W. F. Bellinger was the lay reader. In 1885 the Church was the recipient of a generous donation by a member of the congregation given to be used for the improvement of the Church, and the next year new sashes and blinds were installed. Mr. W. F. Bellinger left the parish in 1887. Mr. W. E. F. Fraser then became superintendent of the Sunday School. Mr. W. C. P. Bellinger became lay reader and superintendent of the Sunday School soon after this time. In 1889 a new organ and a handsome chandelier were installed.

In 1893 Mr. Bellinger was partially relieved of the colored work when it was put in charge of the Rev. G. F. Miller. The rector was now becoming very blind and could only take the parts of the service he had memorized. The lay reader, Mr. W. C. P. Bellinger, died this year and was succeeded by Mr. G. M. O. Rivers. In 1894 the Rev. W. F. Bellinger became assistant rector. The Rev. T. T. Walsh served as assistant in the winter of 1896. Mr. Bellinger resigned as rector in 1896 becoming *rector emeritus,* after having been rector for nearly 40 years. In October of this year the Rev. Thomas Tracy Walsh became rector. In 1901, Mr. Walsh held services regularly at Hendersonville, 10 miles from Walterboro. The Rev. Albert E. Evison became rector May, 1902, serving until 1905 when he was succeeded by the Rev. L. F. Guerry for a short time and then by the Rev. Thomas P. Baker in 1906. About this time a rectory was built and in 1908 an additional room was added to it, the chancel of the Church was remodeled and a vested choir of 30 voices was installed. In 1912 a new organ was given, the rectory added to again and a new lighting plant placed in the Church. At this time the rector supplied services for the Atonement, a chapel for Negroes nearby. Mr. Baker was succeeded by the Rev. Herbert F. Schroeter in 1915, and he by the Rev. William B. Guion, February, 1918, for a short time. Rev. Alexander M. Rich became rector in 1920. The Church was vacant in 1923, then came Rev. C. Capers Satterlee, followed in 1926 by the Rev. Alvin W. Skardon who continued as rector for twenty-six years until 1952. In 1925 a handsome altar with carved raredos was placed in the sanctuary by Mrs. W. A. Roebling in memory of her parents, Walter Hamilton Witsell and Mary Ann Witsell. At this time also the interior of the Church was redecorated and an altar cross of brass added. On October 14, 1928, a beautiful Munich glass window was placed in the chancel by Mr. and Mrs. J. Mitchell Witsell in memory of their son Mitchell. In 1929 the Church was repaired and repainted by Mrs. Roebling, the Ladies' Guild added a room to the rectory, and a concrete coping was placed around the Church and rectory lot. The facilities of the Church were greatly increased by the building of a parish house in 1947. In 1950 a beautiful processional cross was given the Church in memory of Mr. and Mrs. Quentin Foster.

Mr. Skardon's twenty-fifth anniversary was celebrated with a gift from the congregation December, 1950. He retired May 1, 1951. The Rev. James O. Bodley became rector February 1, 1952. Mr. Bodley resigned October 15, 1956. During his rectorship the Church enjoyed much growth—it achieved self-support, a fine parish house was built. Mr. Bodley was succeeded December 15 by Rev. Walter D. Roberts.

ST. THOMAS AND ST. DENNIS (POMPION HILL), WANDO
Established 1706
Good Shepherd, Huger
(See Dalcho, p. 284)

When Dalcho ended his account of this parish in 1820 it had no minister, the parish Church had recently been rebuilt, smaller than the former Church, after its burning in 1815. He calls the funds "good and increasing"—these included the Berresford Bounty Fund and the Parish Fund. The Rev. C. E. Gadsden became rector in 1819 succeeded in 1821 by the Rev. John J. Tschudy. Delegates to the Convention in 1822 were Robert Smith and Alfred Huger. The Rev. Edward Rutledge was rector 1823-1826. Pompion Hill which had been "in decay" for years was repaired. The Rev. F. H. Rutledge was rector 1827-1839. He held services alternately between Church and chapel. In 1834 a rail was put around the altar at Pompion Hill. The colored people were ministered to, services often being held especially for them after the regular service. The Rev. Edward Phillips became rector Easter, 1842, and until 1852. The chapel again was neglected but once more restored by 1843. In 1847 Mr. Phillips states that his work was chiefly among the colored people, there being not sufficient room for those who wished to attend service in the parish Church. In 1851 the Rev. Andrew H. Cornish became assistant and teacher in the Berresford Bounty School, succeeded in this position the next year by the Rev. R. S. Seely. From December 1, 1853, the Rev. J. S. Hanckel was rector with Mr. Seely as assistant; the latter was succeeded in 1855 by the Rev. E. C. Logan. In this year a large school house was built at Cainhoy (also called Louisville), the rectory repaired, and a vestry room added to Pompion Hill Chapel. In 1856 there was a chapel for Negroes at Point Hope and one on the Wando. The school was flourishing at this time. In 1856 increased accommodations were provided for the colored people at the parish Church at a cost of 600 or 700 dollars. In 1859 another chapel for Negroes was built by Mr. A. C. Trenholm. In 1860 Mr. Hanckel resigned

to become professor in the diocesan seminary and was succeeded
by the Rev. Julius J. Sams from 1860 until 1865. During these years
most of the people were away as refugees, Mr. Sams officiating in
Chester often and Mr. Logan in Laurens and Newberry. The
rectory near the parish Church was burned by Federal troops; Mr.
Logan continuing as assistant until 1865, becoming rector in 1867.
The services now for a time were exclusively at the chapel in the
school house at Cainhoy. The school itself which had been discontinued on account of the war was resumed in 1871. In 1872 this
parish had a "Parochial Secretary in the Department of Women's
work Auxiliary to the Board of Missions"—a forerunner indeed! In
1863 there died Hon. Alfred Huger, for sixty years valued vestryman of this parish.

In 1876 because of the "Cainhoy Massacre" the chapel was converted into a hospital and the rectory and yard into an armed camp.
It is testified no Negro members of the Church were involved. Mr.
Logan resigned in December, 1877. The Rev. R. F. Clute became
rector in 1881, keeping the school as part of his duty. Mr. Clute
rendered a good service in printing the "Annals and Registers of
St. Thomas and St. Dennis Parish." In concluding his Annals he
remarks on the good condition of the parish Church at the time
(1883), the old vestry room in a corner of the yard still standing,
the chapel at Pompion Hill apparently in good order except the
wall cracked on the river side, some of the graves (including that
of the first rector, the Rev. Thomas Hasell) had disappeared into
the river. Only two families attend the chapel, but five are on the
Wando and these attend service in chapel in the school house at
Cainhoy. In 1886 the Rev. Edward T. Walker became rector. The
Berresford School, for years operated in conjunction with the public
school, was now separated and in partial operation. The parish
Church and chapel were in good condition at this time but services
held exclusively at the chapel at Cainhoy in 1887. Mr. Walker
states that St. Dennis Church was in bad order and hopes for its
repair thus giving testimony that this old Church was then still
standing. The work in the parish was now almost entirely supported
by the two funds—Parish and Berresford Bounty. In 1893 from
the Wando to St. Dennis besides the Berresford school, three others
for Negroes were in operation; teachers in the three schools in
1895 were John G. Schoolbred, M. L. Lucas, and Miles Collins. In
1898 the Rev. Robert J. Walker succeeded the Rev. E. T. Walker
who had resigned in 1896, serving until 1899. The Rev. Richard W.
Anderson succeeded in 1902. In 1904 the chapel at Cainhoy was

repaired and refurnished. The Rev. P. D. Hay became rector in 1906 and 1907, then the Rev. C. W. Boyd for about a year, 1909. The Rev. James W. Sparks served in 1913 and 1914. The Rev. A. S. H. Winsor was *locum tenens* in 1915. At least three Sunday Schools in the parish at this time and mission on Daniel's Island. The Rev. A. R. Mitchell as Archdeacon of the Charleston Convocation took charge of the parish in 1947 and until 1921 did an extensive missionary work until he resigned because of ill health. He conducted the mission of the Good Shepherd on Daniel's Island being assisted by Mr. J. C. Bissell as lay reader, and St. Timothy's at Huger in the upper part of the parish, holding regular services also at Wando, and at Pompion Hill Chapel. The school at Wando was suspended in 1920. Rev. Wallace Martin held services in the parish for a time, 1923-25. On November 20, 1925, this parish being now dormant under Canon V. turned over to the diocese the parish fund amounting to $6,300.00. In 1927 the Rev. W. B. Sams assumed the rectorship continuing until August, 1946. Throughout this period he held services in the chapel at Cainhoy with a few in the parish Church.

The Associate Mission formed in 1937 with headquarters at Eutawville first under the Rev. D. N. Peeples, began mission work in the Pompion Hill section of the parish. After Mr. Peeples the Rev. L. A. Taylor conducted the work centering at Huger until 1946, assisted first by Miss Magdalene Ball and then Miss Josephine Marion as mission workers. Mr. and Mrs. D. E. Combie assisted in this work acting as secretary and treasurer. The Rev. Stephen L. Skardon followed Mr. Taylor in the conduct of this work. The old school house at Cainhoy was sold in 1938.

In 1937 the parish Church having fallen into disrepair the Society of Colonial Dames inaugurated work to restore it. The undertaking was taken up by Mr. Harry F. Guggenheim who had bought much of the Church land. By his generosity the Church was completely repaired with new roof, and as well the old vestry room in the yard which had become a mere ruin was rebuilt. The Berresford Bounty Fund amounting to $37,336.21 was turned over for administration to the trustees of the diocese on February 3, 1945. In 1946, Mrs. John Gibbs turned over to the Bishop a chalice dated 1711 and a paten, 1850, belonging to this parish. Mr. Sams retired in 1946 and the Rev. L. B. Catlin assumed charge. He holds service only once a year. The mission work continues in the upper part of the parish under the Rev. Mr. Skardon in the neighborhood of Pompion Hill at Huger. The Chapel of the Good Shepherd is the center of the work (adapted from a building given by the North State Lumber Company) at Witherbee, more convenient for the people than Pompion Hill. The Rev. Harold E. Barrett succeeded Mr. Skardon in 1952.

ST. AUGUSTINE'S MISSION, WEDGEFIELD
(See Archdeaconry, end this Section)

ALL SAINTS', YEMASSEE, HAMPTON COUNTY
Established 1883

When All Saints' Church was built at Blountville near Yemassee in 1877 it was a part of Prince William's Parish and the center of its worship. This Church was organized as a separate parish in 1883. The Rev. E. E. Bellinger was rector of Prince William's in 1876 and services were held in a private house (sometimes the residence of Capt. J. M. Gregorie). Maj. John Henry Screven built this All Saints' Church at his own expense (also pledging $300.00 for salary). He was a winter resident and warden. The Church, described as "very pretty" was consecrated April 26, 1877, by Bishop Howe, the Rev. Messrs. J. H. Elliott, W. H. Hanckel, John H. Cornish and the rector assisting. In pleading for another minister for this part of the diocese the Bishop states that Mr. Bellinger, in visiting nine or ten congregations, had in a year travelled over seven thousand miles and had preached more than 350 times. In 1878 a parsonage was provided by Mr. Screven as well as a modest two-room parish house, and refreshment room for those remaining for the second service, as well as shelter for carriages and animals, and again an enclosing fence. Mr. Bellinger removed his residence from Walterboro to this parish for a time, a parsonage being prepared for him. About 1880 Mr. Bellinger held some services in Hendersonville, Colleton County, in the Methodist Church there. In 1881 the parish was represented in Convention by John W. Gregorie and Edward S. Trapier. The Church was repaired and repainted at this time. On March 4, 1883, the members of all Saints' resolved to reorganize themselves into a parish separate from Prince William's, they were so recognized by the Bishop and accepted into union with the Convention on May 11, 1883. There were 21 families in the parish. It prospered for the time.

In 1886 Mr. Bellinger reports holding services on Mr. Screven's plantation: "Here, at an expense of $1,100.00, Mrs. Screven has erected a commodious school building in which, during her sojourn in the neighborhood, she personally, and with the assistance of others employed by her, instructed all the colored children, and others of riper years, who would avail themselves of the privilege, thus offered them. Between 75 and 100 attended." By action of the trustees of the diocese, the parish benefited from the income of funds belonging to Prince William's, residents of the old parish now worshipping at All Saints' which for the time also used the communion silver belonging to the old parish. The generous warden, Maj. Stevens, painted the Church in 1887. The Church in this year was called on to bemoan the death of Captain John White Gregorie who with Maj. Screvens had been warden since the organization of the Church. Mrs. Screven's school for the Negroes continued and Mr. Bellinger ministered to them, holding many services. Mr. Bellinger we find now again holding some services in McPhersonville. In 1889 a Ladies' Guild was organized and a Sunday School opened, the latter due to a school Maj. Screven had opened in the neighborhood. Mr. James C. Rabb served as lay reader. Mr. Bellinger's eyesight began to fail at this time; one eye was lost. In 1891 he held some services in the Presbyterian Church in McPhersonville. In 1889 All Saints' was represented in the Convention by H. M. Fuller, Jr., Charles M. Rabb, Eugene Gregorie, and W. F. Colcock, Jr.

On account of his almost total blindness in 1894 Mr. Bellinger gave up most of his work among the colored people; the Rev. Mr. Miller now ministered to them. The rector was now assisted by his son, the Rev. W. F. Bellinger, but continuing his ministrations among the people of St. Jude's and of All Saints'. Mr. James C. Rabb, lay reader, also assisted the rector saying such parts of the services as he had memorized. In this year when almost totally blind he preached 165 times. He resigned the rectorship June 30, 1896. The Rev. T. Tracy Walsh became rector January 30, 1898, Mr. Bellinger now being rector emeritus. John H. Screven and W. F. Colcock were the wardens, John B. Gregorie, secretary and treasurer. The Rev. R. C. Cowling succeeded Mr. Walsh in 1902 continuing for two years. The Rev. Robert J. Walker took the charge in 1904. In 1909 Mr. Walker makes this report: "All Saints' has been closed indefinitely. The last service was held December 13, 1908." The Church was sold to the Methodists in the same year, the remaining members becoming members of the reorganized "Sheldon Church, Prince William's Parish" at McPhersonville. Thus suddenly ended the short but useful life of "All Saints', Hampton County"—just 30 years. The pews were given to St. Peter's-by-the-Sea near the Navy Yard at Charleston.

WORK AMONG COLORED PEOPLE
IN THE
DIOCESE OF SOUTH CAROLINA
(Including Archdeaconry, Convocation, and Council)

The work among the Negroes in this diocese before the War between the States was on the parish level and will be found recorded in this book as a part of the regular life of the parishes, although both Bishops Bowen and Gadsden had made efforts to broaden the scope of this work. It was the tragedy of war that brought tremendous changes. The transition cannot better be described, we think, than in the words to be found in the *Report of the Committee on the State of the Church* to the Convention of 1868. After, with "bowed and saddened hearts", reviewing the general condition of the diocese, the report turns to the colored people: "In many of our parishes (especially in the low country where this class was most numerous), the falling off of communicants is lamentable in the extreme. In some parishes where they were numbered by hundreds, there are now none. In others, the number of communicants has been reduced by one-half or one-fourth. In 1860 the whole number of communicants was 2,960 (almost equal to the number of whites, 3,166). There have been reported to us now only 291, but in the vacancy of so many Parishes these returns are but partial. In the number of attendants on the ministration of our clergy, the diminution has been equally great.

"In quite a number of our parishes, where not the Rector only, but his assistant or assistants, or a catechist, or catechists, gave weekly instruction to this class of our population—where also Sunday Schools were in successful operation, where mistresses or younger members of the family, and in some cases the master was engaged in the same good work—the answers before your committee show that in many instances no minister of our Church or any other denomination dispenses the word of life to these poor ones of our household of faith, now perishing for lack of knowledge, that in a few localities, a missionary sent out by the Methodists, is to be found. That in others, they are left to the blind guidance of ignorant, and sometimes grossly vicious preachers of their own class and color, whose only commission is a printed license to preach, issued by no authority recognized by any denomination of Christians, North or South. That in a majority of the parishes of our Diocese, there is a painful lack of instruction, religious and secular; that while some anxiety is shown for instruction, in many others there is a total indifference evinced; that while few do contribute to the support of churches and schools, the major number contribute nothing, and the means of support to their preachers is mysterious. That political and other influence combine to alienate them from their former pastors, and to deter them from attending their services. That in consequence of these and other causes now in active operation, the condition of the colored people in many parts of the diocese, physical, mental, and moral, is every day becoming worse. That in some places belief in false prophets, priests, confessors, sorcerers, and other forms of African superstition, has revived, to the ruin in body and soul of its deluded victims.

"In one parish, fourteen chapels built for their use, in another seven, in another five, in several two or three, are all deserted. One or two only being occupied occasionally for worship by the colored people with preachers of their own class. The worship thus con-ducted is compared to that of 'howling dervishes', making night hideous; at other times in dancing and other more criminal exer-cises and excitement.

"This general darkness and gloom, a darkness so intent that it may be felt, is relieved by a few rays of light and hope, which your committee gladly and gratefully hail as harbingers of what they devoutly trust and pray might prove the dawn of a better day for these benighted children of Africa, and for our Church among them."

The problem of the work of the Church among the colored peo-ple had been changed in character by the war and the abolishing of slavery. It was now to pass from the parish to the diocesan level. This was recognized very promptly at the first Convention of the diocese after the war, meeting in February, 1866 (an attempted meeting in 1865 had failed of a quorum) when a Board of Missions to Colored People and Freedmen was created with the following membership: the Revs. C. C. Pinckney, C. P. Gadsden, A. T. Porter; Messrs. E. L. Kerrison, G. A. Trenholm, and W. C. Bee. The board immediately organized. Its efforts for some time were confined to the operation of a school for colored children in the old Marine Hospital on Franklin Street in Charleston. This was done with the assistance of the Protestant Episcopal Freedman's Commission in New York. It was with the help of Major General O. O. Howard and the gift of $1,000.00 by the President of the United States that the building was secured. The school was placed under the charge of Mr. W. W. Taylor of New York, and twelve female as-sistants. Eight hundred children were enrolled. The clerical mem-bers of the board gave an hour of religious instruction each Friday. When funds from the commission were reduced, a fee was charged. For lack of funds in 1868, the work of the school was reduced and it was feared the use of the building would be lost. Also, with the aid of the Commission the other similar but smaller schools were conducted in the diocese, one in Winnsboro. In 1869 the Marine Hospital was fully paid for, chiefly by the efforts of the Rev. Mr. Porter in the North, and the continuation of the school assured. There was no immediate undertaking from a diocesan standpoint by this board beyond these schools. On January 1, 1870, the board for work among Negroes was absorbed into the board of missions of the diocese. Its work among the Negroes was very limited.

In 1871 the Bishop was encouraged by a "returning disposition" among these people. Nevertheless, he was much concerned by a lack of workers in the field, remarking, "The time must come when we must invoke the aid of colored men themselves to preach and minister the sacraments to their own race." Along this line, some beginning was made in Epiphany, Upper St. John's, under Rev. Messrs. Hay and Fuller. And not less so in St. Stephen's and Middle St. John's (Immanuel Chapel) under Rev. P. F. Stevens, laboring "with a self-denial, devotion and zeal, which are beyond all praise of man . . . sometimes keeping his appointments on foot." Mr. Bellinger, on the coast, reported encouraging work, as also did Mr. Drayton in St. Andrew's Parish. There was important work at Kaolin and a few other points in the diocese.

BEGINNING OF SEPARATELY ORGANIZED DIOCESAN WORK AMONG THE NEGROES

The year 1871 saw the beginning of an extensive work among the Negroes, centering at St. Luke's Church in Columbia. This work was begun under Bishop Howe by the Rev. B. B. Barritt, a professor at the University of South Carolina. It continued to expand, becoming an "associate mission", including in 1885 besides St. Luke's a mission in Ward One (to become St. Mary's), Lexington Mission, Littleton, and Long Run Missions, also in Fairfield County. The Rev. T. G. Harper was assistant minister but very briefly. In 1879 the Rev. Thomas B. Clarkson was appointed by the Bishop to assist the Rev. Mr. Tillinghast in lower Richland County, where, under patronage of the Clarkson family, a considerable work was conducted among the Negroes. The other principal center of the work was, of course, in Charleston at St. Mark's Church, a parish, and at Calvary, as well as in St. Andrew's Parish.

The Rev. J. V. Welch of Calvary was, in 1878, still giving instruction in religion at the school in Franklin Street. This was at the old Seaman's Hospital, which was in 1880 turned over to the St. Mark's Association. On March 28, 1877, Thaddaeus Saltus was admitted a candidate for holy orders. Having been prepared by a priest in Columbia, he was ordered deacon by Bishop Howe on February 6, 1881, and became assistant at St. Mark's—the first colored man to be ordained in South Carolina. It was on May 13, 1875, that the application of St. Mark's Church, Charleston, was communicated to the Convention. This application had been delayed some years on the advice of Bishop Howe. It was this application of this colored congregation which precipitated the bitter controversy which rent the Church in the diocese for over thirteen years. The reader will find the story written by Dr. Kershaw, an "eye witness", in the chapter on Bishop Howe's Episcopate (see *in loco*). By the year 1880, the number of colored communicants in the diocese was 545 (not many compared to the 2,960 of 1860), showing some increase in the last few years. The work was all conducted by the white priests of the diocese.

In 1881, on motion of Dr. Porter, it was resolved to refer to the Bishop and Standing Committee some effort to make "this Church effective among the colored people . . . to preach the Gospel to Africa at our door . . . to establish a ministry of their own race." The next year the committee asked for more time in view of a proposed meeting of representatives of the late slave-holding states to deal with the same matter. This important conference was held at Sewanee July 25-26, 1883. Thirteen dioceses were represented. Elaborate recommendations were adopted with great unanimity to be presented to the General Convention soon to meet, looking, in dioceses with large numbers of persons of color, to a special missionary organization; and also suggesting a change in the canon respecting qualifications for the ministry, making possible a ministry possessed of a "sound understanding and judgment, an aptitude to teach, and a large share of prudence" rather than classical attainments. While the House of Bishops agreed to practically all the recommendations, the House of Deputies refused concurrence. It contented itself with suggesting that the dioceses already had authority to establish "missionary organizations" as proposed; but also it regarded this missionary work among the Negroes a responsibility of the general Church and recommended that the general Board of Missions do all they could to assist. Thus the whole problem was thrown back on the dioceses. Bishop Howe and Dr.

Porter were principal leaders in these efforts both at Sewanee and in the General Convention.

Before any actual steps were taken to set up a separate organization of the work among the colored people, as was finally agreed upon by the Convention, Bishop Howe, in his zeal for the cause of the evangelization of these people, had already taken steps which had the effect of preparing the way for this organization. In 1889 he established an "Associate Mission of the Protestant Episcopal Church" in and about Columbia, appointing the Rev. E. N. Joyner, missionary. The work of which he assumed charge had been developed by the zeal of the Rev. B. B. Babbitt, conducting himself an "associate mission" including St. Luke's, another mission in Columbia, and one in Lexington; and by the Rev. Thomas B. Clarkson, also about Columbia and in lower Richland County. Mr. Clarkson died at this time. In his first and second reports, Archdeacon Joyner lists these centers of work: in Columbia at St. Luke's (see *in loco*), and at Green and Gates Streets to be called St. Mary's, with a day school; three chapels in Lexington County, including St. Ann's; Wateree Mission in lower Richland, Saul and St. Stephen's Chapels with a day school (Mrs. S. L. Clarkson, teacher); St. Philip's, Littleton, in Fairfield County; St. Simon's, Allston. The total communicants in these missions was 99. A paper called *The Messenger* was published by the Archdeacon in the interest of the work. The Church commissions and friends in the North aided in its support. In 1887, the Rev. John Kershaw reopened work among the Negroes in St. Mark's, Clarendon, founding St. Augustine's Mission near Wedgefield. Also under appointment of Bishop Howe, the Rev. J. H. M. Pollard at the same time was conducting another associate mission in Charleston and vicinity, being rector of St. Mark's (see *in loco*) and in charge of Calvary (see *in loco*). (The school in the old Marine Hospital on Franklin Street seems now to have been discontinued.) In connection with this center were these missions: Epiphany, Summerville; St. Andrew's Mission in St. Andrew's Parish where there was also a large day school in which the county assisted; a total of 551 communicants in this associate mission. In addition to these missions about Charleston and Columbia, there were a few others in other parts of the diocese, including All Saints' Parish and St. Stephen's Parish. The time seemed now to be ready to carry into effect the decision resulting from the long controversy to establish a separate organization for the colored people in the diocese.

ARCHDEACONRY FOR COLORED CHURCHMEN

It was on February 1, 1892, that the first overt step in this organization of the work among the Negroes was taken when Bishop Howe established an archdeaconry of the work among the colored people of the diocese by appointing the Rev. Edmund N. Joyner to be Archdeacon. Mr. Joyner spent a large part of his time in travel, at home and in the North, in the interest of the work, which had assumed large proportions by this time. We give in summary the Archdeaconry as it stood in May, 1894, including all the workers among the colored churches in the diocese, except St. Mark's, Charleston, a canonical parish, listing the workers after the name of the mission or day school: St. Andrew's, St. Andrew's Parish, the Revs. J. H. M. Pollard and E. N. Hollings, day school, A. B. Lee; St. Ann's, Lexington, the Rev. J. B. Mancebo, school, C. D. Malone; All Saints', Brook Green, the Rev. L. F. Guerry, school, S. M. A. Riley; Arthur's Plantation near Columbia, the Rev. J. B. Mancebo, Miss Hattie Parker; Atonement, Walterboro, the Rev. E. N. Hollings, school, Mrs. Jennie E. Myers; St. Augustine's, Sumter County, the Revs. John Kershaw, J. S. Hartzell; St. Barnabas', Allston, with day school, the Rev. G. E. Howell, Miss E. L. Tardif; Beech Island Mission, the Rev. J. S. Quarles, day school, A. B. Screen; Blue House, Berkeley County, with day school, Morris Collins, Jr.; Calvary, Charleston, the Rev. J. H. M. Pollard, Rev. E. N. Hollings; St. Cyprian's, the Rev. L. F. Guerry, school, Misses Belle and Sallie A. Tucker (St. Cyprian's later moved to Georgetown); Epiphany, Summerville, the Rev. E. N. Hollings; Jalapa, Newberry County; St. George's, Kaolin, with day school, the Rev. J. S. Quarles; St. Luke's, Columbia (see *in loco*), the Rev. H. T. Gregory, Prof. J. E. Wallace; St. Mark's, Willington, the Rev. O. T. Porcher; St. Mary's, Annieville, Waccamaw Neck, the Rev. L. F. Guerry; St. Philip's, Littleton, the Rev. E. N. Hollings; Quinby Plantation, Berkeley County, the Rev. E. T. Walker, with school, John G. Schoolbred; Redeemer, Pineville, in charge of a faithful churchman, Job Guess, with L. G. Harmon, lay reader; Rock Hill Mission, the Rev. Dr. G. L. Sweeney, J. H. Toole, lay reader, with school, Miss N. G. Mikel; St. Simon's, Peake, the Rev. G. E. Howell, with school (fund for chapel); Spartanburg Mission, the Rev. T. D. Bratton, the Rev. W. S. Holmes; Wateree Mission, two congregations, St. Thomas' and St. Stephen's, under Mrs. S. L. Clarkson, the Rev. Messrs. Gregory and Mancebo, visitors; Trinity Chapel, Edgefield, the Rev. W. B. Gordon, the Rev. Mr. Quarles; Wando Mission, the Rev. E. T. Walker, with school, Mrs. M. L.

Lucas. In addition, there were two hospitals; one at Brook Green, maintained chiefly by Mrs. Marinus Willett and her family, and one in Columbia, opened by Miss Mary Glenton, physician, before she went to Anvik, Alaska, and carried on by Miss Benson. The Church paper, *The Messenger*, continued.

In summary, there were at this time, 1894, 32 missions with 19 day schools (1,274 pupils). Engaged in the work there were five colored clergymen (full time) and 11 white (part time), and 28 catechists. The budget was about $14,000.00; $5,500.00 from the national Church, the balance donations and offerings. The total of colored communicants showed increase, 956 (but not the 2,956 of 1,860!). Thus do we see a positive and an earnest effort to restore the Church's work among the Negroes under the leadership of the Bishops, and in this beginning of the Archdeaconry, by the indefatigible labors of the Rev. E. N. Joyner and many other faithful workers, both men and women. Some of the 32 missions of these days ceased, but many became permanent. In 1895 the Episcopal Mission House was established in Columbia, from which the work was administered. From here much charity was dispensed. St. Anna's Memorial Chapel (formerly St. Gabriel's) in East Columbia was consecrated by Bishop Capers on December 6, 1896. It was given chiefly by Miss Coles in memory of Anna Dulles Stille. In 1903, Mrs. Stille of Philadelphia gave to the Bishop as trustee $6,000.00 to endow the chapel in memory of her daughter. The first steps toward the establishment of the Mediator Mission on Edisto was taken in 1901 when Mrs. M. C. LaRoche gave an ample lot and Trinity vestry made a contribution; the work was irregular until much later. Three new chapels were built in this year: St. Mary's, Columbia; St. Simon's, Peake, and Redeemer, Pineville. In 1903 a boarding school was begun at St. Anne's, Lexington, and conducted for some time. A mission (first called St. John's, then St. Titus') was conducted for a time in Florence, but ceased when the Rev. Harold Thomas, the founder, left the city. The Rev. J. S. Quarles, who for some years had served as deacon, was now (1904) ordained priest. On January 5, 1905, Archdeacon Joyner resigned to Bishop Capers. He had served sixteen years in the colored work, thirteen as Archdeacon. He had rendered a great service in much traveling to administer, and not least seeking means, North and South, to keep the work going. He left it so well organized that Bishop Capers, finding it practically impossible to find a successor, was enabled with the help of the Rev. J. S. Quarles in Columbia and the Rev. W. M. Jackson in Charleston to carry on the work, giving much time to it, including travels to the North where once he almost succumbed in a winter storm in Boston. In his last report, Bishop Capers expressed a judgment that the work among Negroes might well be organized into missionary jurisdictions.

COUNCIL OF COLORED CHURCHMEN

Immediately after Bishop Guerry's Consecration September 15, 1908, Bishop Capers turned over to him the colored work in the diocese. There were in the Archdeaconry four colored clergymen, (the Rev. Messrs. S. W. Grice, G. E. Howell, J. S. Quarles, J. D. Lykes) and six white co-workers (the Rev. Messrs. T. P. Baker, W. H. Barnwell, T. W. Clift, J. E. H. Galbraith, J. M. Magruder, A. R. Mitchell); 24 missions; 15 day schools with 1,408 pupils; 90 confirmations the previous year. There were in the diocese 1,127 colored communicants. The missions were as follows: Aiken, Alston, Brook Green, Columbia—St. Mary's, St. Anne's, St. Luke's; Charleston—Calvary, St. Andrew's; Eastover—St. Thomas, Emmanuel; Greenville, Kaolin, Lexington, Newberry, Pineville, Peake, Plantersville, Rock Hill, Spartanburg, Summerville, Waccamaw, Walterboro, North Augusta. Bishop Guerry zealously promoted this work to the end of his Episcopate. On May 18, 1908, he appointed the great missionary, the Rev. A. E. Cornish, to be Archdeacon. To the council of the diocese of 1909 (the "Convention" of the diocese was called "council" from 1895 to 1923), Bishop Guerry presented a memorial from the Convocation of the Archdeaconry petitioning the council to allow it under the Bishop to organize itself into a separate council with powers under the constitution of the general Convention and of the diocese. The petition was granted and immediately the Convocation was reorganized into the "Council of Colored Churchmen of the Diocese of South Carolina" with its own constitution and canons. (Printed in *The Church Herald* of June 1929.) Article II states the council is "formed to meet the peculiar needs and conditions of the colored people and to foster the spirit of self-help and self-government among them". The first meeting was held at St. Mary's Church, Columbia, September 14, 1910. This plan proved a considerable improvement over the Convocation which had no power to legislate at all. It was in 1910 that the American Church Institute for Negroes was organized. During the years 1911-12, Bishop Guerry endeavored without success to persuade the diocese to elect a Negro Suffragan Bishop. He did not really withdraw his request until after the colored people had changed their attitude on the issue in 1915, no longer desiring a Suffragan.

Mr. Cornish resigned as Archdeacon September, 1910. The position was not filled until some time later when the Rev. J. S. Quarles was appointed, who served until the appointment in 1914 of the Rev. Erasmus L. Baskervill, who had been received from the diocese of Lexington the year before and was destined to do a great work as Archdeacon. He administered the work with great wisdom, traveling usually twice a year in the North, winning a large group of friends of the work, enabling it to be maintained. *The Church Herald* was begun at this time, published in the interest of the Archdeaconry. It continued until December, 1948. The Rev. A. R. Mitchell in 1914 established St. Philip's Mission in Greenville, erecting the Church with material from the old chapel on Mrs. Eubank's place near the city. About the same time St. Paul's, Orangeburg, was begun at State College. Mr. R. S. Wilkinson, president of the college, and his wife, formerly members of St. Mark's, Charleston, were the founders. For many years he was the warden and lay reader, until his death. The Rev. George E. Howell was the first minister-in-charge. At this time also, the Church of the Good Shepherd in Sumter was founded.

The last report of the Archdeaconry before the division of the diocese (1922) showed seven clergymen and twenty-six parishes and missions—two self-supporting, St. Mark's, Charleston, and St. Luke's, Columbia. When the division was finally effected the next year, four of the clergymen (the Rev. Messrs. E. L. Baskervill, C. A. Harrison, Clyde E. Perry, and G. E. Howell) fell to the old diocese with twelve churches as follows: St. Mark's, Calvary, and St. Stephen's Charleston; Holy Cross, Brook Green; St. Andrew's, Charleston County; St. Paul's, Orangeburg; Redeemer, Pineville; Epiphany, Summerville; Good Shepherd, Sumter; Atonement, Walterboro; Holy Cross, and also Faith Memorial, Waverly Mills; St. Augustine's, Wedgefield; and six day schools. The total of communicants was 1,016. To the new diocese fell three of the seven clergymen: the Rev. Messrs. J. B. Elliott, R. N. Perry, T. N. Perry; and thirteen churches—St. Luke's, St. Anne's, St. Mary's, Columbia; St. Augustine's, Aiken; St. Thomas', Eastover; St. Philip's, Greenville; St. Luke's, Newberry; St. Anne's, Brookland; St. Simon's, Peake; St. Paul's, Rock Hill; Epiphany, Spartanburg; St. Barnabas', Jenkinsville; and eight day schools, all with 356 communicants. The old diocese the same year lost one clergyman (the

Rev. J. Clyde Perry) and the new diocese gained one (the Rev. T. T. Pollard).

The diocese of North Carolina at this time having elected a colored Suffragan Bishop, the Rt. Rev. H. B. Delany, D.D., a plan was agreed upon to have him to make visitations and hold confirmations in the Archdeaconry. This proved of great help to the Bishop of the diocese and the plan continued until the time of Bishop Guerry's death in 1928. This diocese assisted in Bishop Delany's support. The plan of a colored Suffragan was later abandoned by the diocese of North Carolina. The next step affecting the work of the Archdeaconry was the acquisition of Voorhees Normal and Industrial School by both dioceses jointly. An account of this and the history of the school will be found elsewhere (see *in loco*). By 1925 the work showed expansion. On May 25th, 1924, the new Faith Memorial Church, Waccamaw, was consecrated. This Church was built largely by the efforts of the indefatigible Archdeacon Baskervill. The American Church Building Fund assisted. Also, a church building was purchased from the Reformed Episcopal and St. Cyprian's Mission opened in Georgetown. Years before there had been a St. Cyprian's mission in Prince Frederick's. A new and modern parish house was at this time added in the rear of Calvary Church on Beaufain Street, serving as a community center for the neighborhood. A United Thank Offering worker (Mrs. Maude Callan) was secured, as a trained nurse to assist in the care of the sick at Redeemer, Pineville. This was the beginning of an extensive work through the following years in conjunction with the county physician who held clinics at Redeemer. The work on Edisto Island was reopened in 1925, the Rev. H. C. Banks in charge under the Archdeacon, a building having been erected largely through the munificence of Mrs. M. C. La Roche who had given a lot years before. The work suffered a great loss in the burning of the school house at Redeemer, Pineville, March 26, 1926. However a better one was soon erected.

Bishop Thomas in his Annual Address May, 1930, thus described the status of the work at that time: "It is a striking fact that the increase in the membership of our colored churches in the past five years has been 50 percent more rapid than among the white. We have thirteen parishes and organized missions, five active clergymen who are assisted in the work by twelve lay readers. We are now operating five parochial schools and one kindergarten in Charleston. An outstanding feature of the work is two nurses whose salaries are paid in part by the U.T.O., one at Pineville and one at Waverly Mills; the latter began her work last summer. This is a service of great value. A resident physician at Waverly Mills, Dr. Henry Norris, has during the past year on his own motion and through his own efforts established a hospital there for colored patients. Our resident nurse works in this hospital under Dr. Norris' direction. I cannot commend too highly this splendid benefaction." All this work was maintained largely through the efforts of Archdeacon Baskervill and his trips to the North. There were 1,254 colored communicants at this time. In 1931 the diocese of Pittsburgh assumed as its Advance Works Project the building of a chapel at State College in Orangeburg. Bishop Thomas presented the cause before the Convention in Pittsburgh. The depression curtailed this effort, but eventually over $2,000.00 was donated for this purpose by the Pittsburgh Woman's Auxiliary the congregation having agreed to supply the lot. During these years in the summer a Church Institute for Colored Workers was held yearly at State College. In the year 1932, all the Church property at Holy Cross, Brook Green, was sold to Mr. Huntington (who also made a generous donation to the work) and the work moved to the nearby Faith Memorial and combined with it under the name of Holy Cross and Faith Memorial. And the next year saw here the erection of a fine new schoolhouse, the Rev. W. E. Forsythe being in charge of this work for many years—from 1926 until the present. There were now five parochial schools—this with Mediator, Edisto; Redeemer, Pineville; and St. Andrew's, Charleston County; Harvin School, St. Augustine's, Pinewood—also Calvary Kindergarten, Charleston; total of pupils, 567.

The death of Archdeacon Baskervill (June 12, 1937) marked the end of twenty-three years of zealous, wise, and efficient service. Bishop Thomas said at the time of his death: "He devoted his life in season and out in an earnest and able service of the Church. A man of broad sympathies, singularly free from prejudices of any kind, his benign influence reached far and wide. In a most remarkable way he had reached and consolidated a large body of generous friends for the work he represented, these without distinction in all parts of the country. His frequent trips to various parts of the country, his often attendance upon national and provincial Conventions and committee meetings made him a nationally known and respected character. His stalwart figure, his pleasing personality, his wise counsel, will be sadly missed." The last public act of the Archdeacon was to present his son, the Rev. Louis A. Baskervill, to the Bishop for ordination to the priesthood.

Rev. C. A. Harrison, retired rector of St. Mark's Church, was appointed acting Archdeacon, serving acceptably until his death, April 8, 1942. The Archdeacon's son, who had just been ordained, was appointed executive secretary, and with this help, under the Bishop, the work went forward; Mr. Baskervill secured for a time a continuation of contributions of the large group of friends of work in the North. It was under his management that Camp Baskervill, named in memory of the Archdeacon, was established in the summer of 1939 when the first building was built and the summer camps and conferences of the Archdeaconry held there. When the Rev. L. A. Baskervill left the diocese in June, 1940, the Rev. Stephen B. Mackey was appointed executive secretary. It was at this time that the encroachment of a white housing development in the neighborhood of Calvary Church on Beaufain Street in Charleston, pre-empting the members from the neighborhood, made it necessary to move the Church (see Calvary *in loco*). In 1942 the chief resources for the work of the Archdeaconry was from the National Council $1,894.00, for U. T. O. workers $2,550.00, special fund (donations) $1,485.00, diocese of South Carolina $1,850.00, and local contributions. The counties having taken over the burden of the day schools at St. Augustine's, Sumter County, and at St. Andrew's, Charleston County and Mediator, Edisto, there were now only two parochial schools, at Holy Cross and Faith Memorial, and at Redeemer, Pineville, with two kindergartens in Charleston. At the former two points, U.T.O. nurses served the communities, at the latter place a home for the nurse which served as a "medical center" had been built. A third U.T.O. worker assisted at Calvary in Charleston. Another building had been added at Camp Baskervill where regular summer sessions were now held.

On Sunday morning, February 28, 1943, Holy Cross and Faith Memorial Church was totally destroyed by fire. There was no insurance, but by May of 1944, $1,867.55 had been accumulated looking toward rebuilding. In this year, there were eight clergymen at work in the Archdeaconry, including the Chaplain, the Rev. S. C. Usher at Voorhees; 14 churches; communicants, 1,360. The average yearly confirmations was approximately 60. A lot had been secured at State College in Orangeburg and $2,555.75 was in hand for a Church. In 1945, St. Andrew's Mission was completely renovated for $5,000.00, the national council supplying $4,000.00. The Rev. Stephen B. Mackey, who had served as executive secretary, was now appointed by Bishop Carruthers, Archdeacon. *The*

Church Herald, which had been published for about 35 years in the interest of the colored work, largely to inform Northern patrons of its progress, was discontinued December 1948. The increased diocesan and parochial support of the work made the paper less necessary. In 1950, Camp Baskervill was renovated, its facilities greatly improved generally, with a bath house; also an assembly hall was built. In the same year, St. Paul's Church, Orangeburg, was built at a cost of $25,000.00—contributions coming from the advance work fund given by the Woman's Auxiliary of the diocese of Pittsburgh some twenty years ago, from the local congregation, the diocese, and Woman's Auxiliary of South Carolina, the national council, and the United Thank Offering. The Church was consecrated on November 4, 1951, by Bishop Carruthers. In 1953 a new Church was built at Holy Cross and Faith Memorial, replacing that burned several years before. The local congregation contributed $4,000.00 toward the total cost, financial assistance coming from the diocese and the National Church. Recently, a staff house has been added to the equipment of Camp Baskervill.

In 1953, a great step forward was taken in the Archdeaconry when Bishop Carruthers was enabled to notify the National Council that henceforth no help for the colored work in this diocese would be expected. Thus it was, South Carolina after some ninety years became an "Unaided Diocese." The statistics for this Archdeaconry in 1957 were: clergymen, 6; parishes and missions, 13; baptisms, 61; confirmations, 104; communicants, 1,347.

PART TWO

DIOCESE OF UPPER SOUTH CAROLINA

SECTION I

DIOCESAN HISTORY
AUGUSTUS T. GRAYDON, ESQ.
Author of this Section

Chapter I

A NEW DIOCESE BEGINS

1922

The Diocese of Upper South Carolina was appropriately named, for its territory consists of that portion of the Palmetto State known as "The Up-Country". This section is differentiated from "The Low-Country" consisting of the tidewater area, the coastal plain and the "Pee Dee" section. South Carolina, shaped like a triangle of which its coast is the base, is divided into these two approximately equal halves. The lower or base section was formerly under the ocean many, many centuries ago, while the upper or apex half—above the "fall line"—is a Piedmont, or "foot of the mountain", area. This geographical division is not the only difference between the state's two sections. The entire lower half of the state was rather widely settled before the American Revolution, and many of the present Episcopal churches in this area predate the struggle for independence. The up-country was a wild section, sparsely settled by Scotch-Irish immigrants who for the most part came to this rolling hill country from Virginia, Pennsylvania and the north. They brought with them their own religion: protestant, simple and fundamental. Their religion was adapted to the wild, rude and primitive life which prevailed in the upper part of South Carolina.

The Established Church had spread from Charleston, Beaufort and Georgetown, as has already been recounted, to the interior as the planters took their plantations away from the coast. But the plantation, based on cotton and slave labor, was not well suited to the hilly, rolling country in the western part of the state. There smaller farms, tended by the owners themselves, were established.

A few families from the low-country emigrated to the Piedmont, and Episcopal churches were established rather early in Columbia (1812), Camden (1830) and Aiken (1844), all of which are located almost astride the line dividing the Up-Country from the Low-Country. Even in the more typical Piedmont section, parishes were established at such places as Greenville (1820), Pendleton (1820), and Edgefield (1836). Many of these parishes in their early days had a desperate and difficult struggle to keep and preserve the churches which had been established through the generosity of a few families. The overwhelming majority of the Up-Countrymen found the Baptist, Methodist and Presbyterian churches more suited to the primitive life of a developing area. The more formal and ritualistic rites of the Episcopal Church were not easily adapted to the simple life of this early frontier. Communications were difficult, communities were small and the people were poor. A Church which had largely developed in an urban atmosphere or under the plantation system during the 18th century's age of enlightenment did not appeal to the highly individual pioneers of the rugged "Up-Country".

Thus the growth of the Episcopal Church in the early years of our republic had been slow in the interior of South Carolina. As the interior of the South changed from a predominantly agricultural area in the late 19th and early 20th centuries, opportunities developed for the Church which had been transplanted to the seaports and coastal areas of the middle Atlantic and Southern colonies by Englishmen who came to America to reestablish themselves. It was this difference in history, background and economy which made the role of the Episcopal Church so different in the two sections of South Carolina. In Charleston and the older communities of the tidewater section and coastal plain, the Episcopal Church was in a real sense the Established Church—although, of course, it had no official sanction after the Revolution. The fact that all of the Up-Country churches were established after English rule had been ousted accounts in part for the difficulties which attended the development of the Episcopal Church in this "Up-Country". The Episcopal Church in the Piedmont had to struggle for growth; it could not rest on past achievement and tradition, and it had to look to the future, not the past. The grandeur and beauty of the old churches of Charleston and the fact that first families of the Low-Country were leaders in Episcopal churches there did not give life to small parishes at such places as Anderson, Laurens, Greenwood, Rock Hill and Chester.

It was this difference in outlook and background which in part caused the division of South Carolina into two dioceses. It was on May 12, 1920, at the Convention in Spartanburg that it was decided that a Bishop Coadjutor be elected as soon as practicable looking to the division of the diocese three years hence. In October of 1920, the Rev. Kirkman George Finlay, then the rector of Trinity Church, Columbia, was elected Bishop Coadjutor of the diocese of South Carolina. He was assigned the field of Piedmont, South Carolina, and on May 17, 1922, the plans for the actual division of the diocese were adopted at a meeting of the 132nd Council of the Episcopal Diocese of South Carolina in St. Philip's Church, Charleston. (See Sec. I, Chapter VI.) The council asked Bishop Guerry to take the necessary steps to have the division sanctioned and confirmed by the General Convention which met in Portland, Oregon, in September of that year. So the new diocese—rather rudely named "Upper South Carolina"—practically began its life on October 10, 1922, with its primary Convention held at Trinity Church in Columbia, from which many Episcopalians had gone out to form parishes in other parts of the Piedmont. Twenty-three clergymen, including Bishop Finlay, and seventy-one laymen from twenty-five parishes and four organized missions were in attendance. The parishes, and their ministers and deputies in attendance were as follows:

Trinity, Columbia, 1812: The Rev. Henry D. Phillips, David Gaillard Ellison, J. Nelson Frierson, Carroll H. Jones and Christie Benet.

St. Paul's, Pendleton, 1820: The Rev. George E. Zachary and Christian Hanckel.

Christ, Greenville, 1820: The Rev. Frank A. Juhan, Aug. W. Smith, Thomas Parker and J. F. Matthews.

St. John's, Winnsboro, 1827: The Rev. W. P. Peyton, G. F. Patton, F. A. DesPortes, Longstreet Gantt and J. M. Lyles.

Grace, Camden, 1830: The Rev. F. H. Harding, C. H. Yates, B. H. Boykin, J. M. Villepigue and C. J. Shannon, Jr.

Trinity, Edgefield, 1836: David Strother, R. C. Padgett and L. W. Cheatham.

St. Stephen's, Ridgeway, 1839: Mr. Peyton, R. A. Meares, Samuel Peyre Thomas, L. E. Hooten and Robert Charlton Thomas.

Trinity, Abbeville, 1842: William M. Barnwell.

St. Thaddeus', Aiken, 1844: W. W. Egerton, John Laird, W. Rothrock and L. E. Croft.

Zion, Eastover, 1846: The Rev. H. F. Shroeter, W. A. Rivers, M.D., and A. G. Clarkson.

St. Luke's, Newberry, 1846: The Rev. Thomas L. Ridout, J. F. J. Caldwell, and C. P. Weeks.

Advent, Spartanburg, 1847: The Rev. W. H. K. Pendleton, W. S. Manning, W. E. Lindsay, H. A. Ligon, Sr., and C. P. Matthews.

Epiphany, Laurens, 1847; revived 1898: Mr. Ridout, N. C. Hughes, Jr., R. W. Davis and Dr. R. E. Hughes.

Calvary, Glenn Springs, 1848: The Rev. L. W. Blackwelder, W. D. Boggs, and R. J. Smith.

Grace, Anderson, 1851: The Rev. Arthur W. Taylor, M. M. Chapman, and W. M. Webb.

Good Shepherd, York, 1855: The Rev. T. Tracy Walsh and Walter Bedford Moore.

St. Mark's, Chester, 1857: The Rev. A. Rufus Morgan, W. H. Kearseley, W. B. Coe, M.D., and T. L. Eberhardt.

St. John's, Congaree, 1858: The Rev. G. Croft Williams.

Nativity, Union, 1859: Mr. Blackwelder, W. W. Johnson, and M. A. Moore.

Our Saviour, Rock Hill, 1870: The Rev. William E. McCord, G. H. Green, and J. C. Rhea.

Good Shepherd, Columbia, 1883: Mr. Schroeter, Legrand Guerry, M.D., J. R. Roseberry, and Bryan H. Lumpkin.

Resurrection, Greenwood, 1892: The Rev. Arthur R. Price and Owen Tully.

Holy Trinity, Clemson, 1899: Mr. Zachary, W. W. Long and Paul Sloan.

St. Andrew's, Greenville, 1900: The Rev. A. R. Mitchell, Alex McBee, and E. P. Percy Long.

St. James', Greenville, 1904: The Rev. A. R. Mitchell, T. C. Stone and S. J. Taylor.

St. John's, Shandon, Columbia, 1912: Dr. Williams, Edmund Rhett Heyward, A. C. DePass and E. A. Woodruff.

Missions were represented as follows:

St. Stephen's, Willington, 1859: W. M. McIntosh.

Grace, Ridge Spring, 1873: F. T. Carwile.

Our Saviour, Trenton, 1878: J. M. Vann.

St. Luke's, Bath and Clearwater, 1852: The Rev. Edgar Van W. Edwards.

St. Paul's, Graniteville, 1885: Lawrence Richardson.

Trinity Mission, Columbia, 1901: The Rev. A. E. Evison.

In addition the following clergymen resident in the diocese were present: The Rev. Messrs. A. J. Derbyshire, T. P. Noe, John Ridout and J. H. Tillinghast.

The list is interesting because of the omissions in the same. Three facts are notable:

(1) No Negro parishes were represented at the Convention.

(2) Few missions were functioning in the industrial or mill sections of the cities.

(3) Few parishes were functioning in the developing suburban areas of the cities, where young people primarily live.

At this Primary Convention the Rev. A. R. Mitchell read a resolution of the Standing Committee of the old diocese expressing regret in the loss of valuable members to the new diocese including its president (Rev. Mr. Mitchell) and its secretary (Mr. J. Nelson Frierson). He also presented to the diocese a gavel made of wood from the pulpit of Pompion Hill Chapel, Parish of St. Thomas and St. Denis on the Cooper and Wando rivers. The new diocese, led by the Rt. Rev. Kirkman George Finlay, began work immediately. His address tells the status of the new diocese at the outset:

"In that portion of the State which has been constituted as the diocese of Upper South Carolina, there are 22 counties with a white population of 513,841 and a colored population of 394,387. In this territory we have 46 white and 14 colored churches. With all charges filled according to the present appointments we shall have 22 white and four colored clergy.

"In these white churches we have 5,945 baptized persons and 3,801 communicants. In the colored churches we have 717 baptized persons and 342 communicants.

"The money raised in this field for the year 1921 was, for self-support, $173,543.26, for church extension, $66,239.83. . . ."

And what of the future? Bishop Finlay knew the diocese of which he was now the head. He had served in Columbia as rector of Trinity Church for eighteen years. He was born in the Piedmont hills near Greenville in 1877. He had been educated at Furman University and he knew the needs of the people who had come to town to live in the mill village. He went to Clemson as a young priest.

"We may reasonably expect more or less rapid growth in our work, and therefore, we must be prepared for it. The past has taught us the importance of establishing our work at strategic points. Let me take one example from many. When that master builder of our Church, Dr. McCollough, began work in Spartanburg, he could muster but six communicants. He lived to see the Church become one of the strongest in the up-country. Today there are growing towns all over this section that in 25 or 30 years will be centers of population. We must not be left behind in establishing ourselves in them. We believe that we have a real and definite contribution to make to the Christian citizenship of these communities. It is our obligation to see that that contribution be not lacking.

"Again, the general character of our population is still rapidly changing. We have become a great manufacturing section. True, our industries are not widely diversified. But is it not reasonably certain that other forms of manufacturing will come to us in addition to the making of cotton goods? Already we have one plant for the building of automobiles. Will not others follow? We should grapple with the problem of work in industrial centers. The laboring man and his family in other parts of the country have grown indifferent, and, in many cases, hostile to the Church. So far this condition has not arisen with us. The churches in our cotton-mill communities are well attended and the people, for the most part, are connected more or less actively with some denomination. It will be the fault of the churches if this friendly and receptive attitude is ever changed. We must do all in our power to make the working man feel that he needs the Church and that the Church needs him.

"I am most desirous that as soon as possible we start one strong and adequately equipped rural Church as a practical demonstration that our Church is adapted to rural as well as city work. Which of our churches will be the first to make a beginning—a beginning which may grow to great things and be a first step towards removing the reproach that we are only a city Church."

Bishop Finlay then went on to speak of the Church Home Orphanage and the needs of a student work program at Winthrop, Clemson and the University of South Carolina. He immediately recognized the opportunity among young people at these institutions and the fact that the diocese must assume responsibility for this work. Finally, the new Bishop spoke of the work which was to be his forte—the Church's program among the Negroes:

"Let me speak now of our colored work. We have made a beginning, scarcely more. Much good has been accomplished for the moral and spiritual training of the colored people wherever work has been seriously undertaken. Our parochial schools have also done splendid work. All this is but the evidence of what our Church could do. At every turn we are crippled by lack of funds. My personal observation and the reports that I hear from other dioceses convince me that we as a Church can do much for the Negro. I think it can be demonstrated beyond a reasonable doubt that our Church has produced an outstanding type of Christian character among its membership of colored people. Our Church stands for the vital relation between religion and morality. It stands for self-respect, education, decent standards of living, parental obligations, stability of the marital relation. Are not these the things that our Negro population needs to have held continually before them?

"It is too soon for me to come before you with a definite program for our colored work. This much I can say: I want your sympathy and help in trying to carry forward our colored work with a view to building up in the diocese a strong, and, in some measure at least, self-supporting work. I hope to see the council of our Negro churches and the various organizations for work grow and advance in power and efficiency and ability to promote the work among their own people."

This was the picture which the new Bishop of a new diocese made for its future. The new diocese had few laurels to rest on as its work began. It was to require hard work in a field which so far as the Episcopal Church was concerned was largely untouched. As the Piedmont area of South Carolina emerged into a new era of industrialization and progress, a struggling new diocese was there to grapple with the challenge.

Chapter II

EPISCOPATE OF BISHOP FINLAY

1922-1938

The work of the new diocese as a separate institution began with the calendar year 1923. On January 1 of that year the meager cash balance of the two dioceses was divided and Upper South Carolina was on its own under Bishop Finlay. It was another venture in faith. A survey of the diocese's status at the time of the first Convention gives a basis for an appreciation of the work which was to be accomplished under Bishop Finlay. Quotas of $66,571.80 were set for the various parishes and missions, but only $45,747.01 was pledged. A budget of $57,800.00 was adopted out of which $13,500.00 was allocated to the National Church.

In its first year, the diocese had 6,715 church members of whom 4,558 were communicants. When the first Convention convened in May, 1923, 266 persons had already been confirmed by Bishop Finlay. Church schools of the diocesan parishes had 2,980 pupils enrolled. The worth of the churches in the diocese was estimated at $467,000.00 while the value of the parish houses was set at only $79,350.00. Including land, furniture and rectories, the total value of Church property was estimated at $1,007,200.00, against which there were mortgage indebtednesses of only $56,712.00. The proportionate smallness of the diocesan debt indicated that there had not been much "financial venturing" in the new diocese.

The new Bishop's first diocesan address, delivered at the Convention held at Christ Church, Greenville, May 8-9, 1923, emphasized the problems and challenges facing the new diocese as follows: (1) Spread of the Church's work in industrial areas; (2) Development of a program in rural sections, and, (3) Expansion of the Church's work among the Negro population. Bishop Finlay also called attention to the summer conference program and the purchase of 50 acres by the Church Home Orphanage. He urged support for the Church's own institutions, such as St. Mary's, Raleigh; Porter Military Academy, Charleston, and the University of the South at Sewanee, Tenn. He pressed for programs at the three state institutions of higher learning within the geographical area of the new diocese. Division of the diocese led to a joint support for the Church Homes for children and women, Voorhees, and Porter Military Academy. The new diocese, in the developing and expanding "up-country", was in a position to seize the initiative by laying its foundation for future growth among young people. By 1924 a development which was to affect profoundly the history and growth of the new diocese was already "being talked". The Journal for the second Convention held at Advent, Spartanburg, in January, 1924, contains the notation that "the subject of conference grounds and the proposal of Kanuga Lake as a proposed location was discussed". No action was taken at this time, although Bishop Finlay reported that two North Carolina dioceses "are, at least, interested in cooperating with us in such a plan," as well as the diocese of South Carolina.

A year later Bishop Finlay reported that a holding body had been incorporated under the laws of the State of North Carolina "with power to negotiate terms and assume possession of the property, should a sufficient number of dioceses desire to go into the project." In the following year Bishop Finlay reported further progress in the negotiations with the owner, Dr. J. S. Brown of Hendersonville. This was a brave adventure at a time when this new diocese like others in the South was having great difficulty meeting its minimum financial requirements. In 1928 conferences were held at the Kanuga center for the first time when the owners allowed the dioceses to use the property free of rent. The property, including a large hotel, numerous cottages and other buildings, had been offered the church at $87,500.00, plus interest from October 1, 1927, insurance and the cost of the campaign to raise the funds, or a total of more than $100,000.00. It was an ambitious program, and it succeeded largely through the vision and perseverance of Bishop Finlay. At the second diocesan Convention, another matter of a permanent nature was presented. The two South Carolina dioceses had been offered control of the Voorhees Institute, "an Industrial School for the Colored at Denmark, S. C., which plant is of an estimated value of $250,000.00, with about 400 acres of land, about 250 boarders and 500 day pupils, and which has been in operation about twenty years". The program at Voorhees had the support of the American Church Institute for Negroes. The new diocese pledged $2,000.00, with the old diocese in which the institution was located pledging a similar amount. In the following year, Voorhees became another "joint" diocesan institution.

But the expansion in these institutional phases of diocesan life did not mean that the diocese was making progress in its parish and mission work. In his 1928 address, the Bishop reported that the churches at Anderson, Trenton, Abbeville, Edgefield and Ridge Spring were vacant. Confirmations had declined from 269 in 1924 to 184 in 1928. In the fall of 1926 the office of general missioner and executive secretary of the diocese was created, and the Rev. A. Rufus Morgan was elected to the position created largely to take care of the churches without ministers. Mr. Morgan edited the diocesan paper, "The Piedmont Churchman", and in many other ways relieved the Bishop of executive duties. The depression in predominantly agricultural South Carolina had begun shortly after World War I; the economic situation halted the progress of the Church in a material and statistical way. St. Timothy's Church, Columbia, formed in 1923, was the only church as a regular parish to be organized in the new diocese until after World War II. The Rev. A. G. Branwell Bennett, who was to serve the diocese as secretary of the Convention and in many other capacities, became rector of the new Columbia parish in 1928. By 1928, although Wall Street was still riding high, South Carolina's economy was severely affected, and the budget for that year was set at $52,100.57. The churches within the diocese were not able to raise quotas set during the years immediately following the expansion caused by war. The financial shrinkage had meant "retrenchment here and abandonment there", Bishop Finlay reported.

In 1930 a shortage of $5,966.11 was reported on a minimum budget, and the office of general missioner and executive secretary, created to keep alive some of the diocese's smaller parishes and struggling missions, was abolished in 1931. Mr. Morgan succeeded the Rev. G. Croft Williams as rector of St. John's, Columbia, a parish established in suburban Columbia in 1914. Cuts were made in every department of the diocese's program, but Bishop Finlay always insisted first upon a cut in his own salary and allowances. He was the type of leader needed to carry a diocese through a severe depression. Bishop Finlay's keen awareness of social needs was reflected in the work of the Diocesan Department of Christian Social Service. In 1928, its chairman, Mrs. Isabelle Lindsay Cain, said the function of the department was "to seek to awaken the social consciousness of the individual church member and also of the church as a whole. . . ." The department selected for its program "the Church in its relationship here within the diocese to (a) the Inter-racial relations; (b) the Child Labor Problem, (c) the Marriage Laws. . . ."

By 1930, the department, no longer talking of social theory, was seeking ways in which to help the unemployed on an emergency basis. Under Bishop Finlay's leadership a survey of jail conditions in the state was made and the diocese recommended the establishment of a public welfare program by the state. The Bishop contributed regular articles to the Columbia newspaper on social conditions and legislation. The chairman of the diocesan department of missions reported in January, 1933, that many persons were absenting themselves from churches because of their inability to contribute. The proposed quotas for 1933 had been reduced to $40,420.82, but only $23,381.42 was pledged by the parishes and missions. Publication of "The Piedmont Churchman" had been suspended, but the diocesan paper was continued on a subscription basis through the work of the Woman's Auxiliary. With funds from endowment and other sources, the total available for the year 1933 was only $27,960.00, and the finance committee was forced to cut the budget by $13,500.00—$7,200.00 out of $12,000.00 to the National Church alone. Virtually the same budget was adopted for 1934, and the 1935 budget was set at $30,482.00 while in 1935, the amount was increased to $34,067.00. Under the New Deal of Franklin D. Roosevelt, the diocese like the nation was emerging from the depression. By the middle thirties the diocese had made some progress despite the financial crisis. An Episcopal residence had been acquired for the Bishop, and new Church buildings had been erected at Great Falls (St. Peter's), Batesburg (St. Paul's) and Greer (Good Shepherd). Seven parish houses and one new rectory were added to the physical plant, while a cottage had been built at the orphanage. Ten churches had received substantial repairs or alterations, and in two instances, at Clemson (Holy Trinity) and Ridgeway (St. Stephen's), the remodelling was so complete as almost to amount to the construction of new buildings, and five parish houses were enlarged or improved.

The diocesan capital funds had been increased from $25,000.00 when the diocese began to $57,417.00 in ten years, but the decrease in parish expenditures from $200,000.00 to $132,000.00 was a reflection of the times. A decrease in Church school enrolment also resulted from the stringent economic conditions. Among the Negroes, the communicant list had decreased from 342 to 328 by 1932, but this loss was not caused by economic conditions alone.

The status of the Negro in the Episcopal Church in Upper South Carolina was brought to the attention of the Convention in 1933 when the diocesan colored council presented a report asking that some form of representation in the diocesan council be given Negroes. In only the two South Carolina dioceses were Negroes still denied any voice in diocesan affairs. A committee appointed by Bishop Finlay to consider this matter recommended that clergy and delegates from Negro churches be allowed to vote for Bishop and to vote for deputies to be sent to the General Convention. The Constitution had to be changed, but the matter was passed over at the 1935 Convention despite a plea by Bishop Finlay that failure to pass the change would mean "a setback to the work of the Church among colored people that we of this generation will not live to see overcome."

The work among the Negroes was a favorite project of Bishop Finlay, and the Negroes of the Episcopal Church knew him as their friend and leader. But without any voice at all in the Church's government and without any prospect for achieving positions of leadership in the Episcopal Church, the Negro program was a meager effort. Negro churches in which the Negro controlled grew and progressed, while only a few Negroes remained in the Church of which so many had been members at the end of the Civil War. In 1932 Negroes within the diocese of Upper South Carolina paid only $125.99 on their pledge to the diocese and National Church, while they received $4,326.96 from these two sources. It was strictly a subsidized effort without leadership from the rank and file of the Negro population. St. Barnabas' mission at Jenkinsville, a Negro community, was reopened in 1935, and an orphanage for Negro children was opened in Cayce, a suburb of Columbia, through the efforts of Bishop Finlay and Mrs. R. S. Wilkinson. Through these practical projects, including the Voorhees school, Bishop Finlay felt that he could in some measure help the Negro in his plight. But the Negroes were to remain in an inferior status without representation in diocesan affairs until after World War II, and the program among the Negroes languished accordingly. But Bishop Finlay was one whom the Negroes respected and admired for the vigor with which he espoused their cause.

With the slow emergence from the depression, the diocese became awake. Under the leadership of the Rev. Albert R. Stuart, a new brick Church was erected in Greenwood in 1935. A record 367 persons were confirmed in 1935 when an entire congregation of

57 members from the First Congregational Church of Columbia joined the Episcopal Church. A beloved diocesan had brought the Church in Upper South Carolina through the years of the depression, and, while those years were not productive of material, financial or statistical growth, the diocese had deepened in spirit and in organization under Bishop Finlay. The work which he had so patiently and laboriously nurtured had only begun to bear fruit when he died suddenly on August 27, 1938, at Kanuga, the conference center which had been his vision. The diocese had weathered the difficult depression years under its first Bishop, and the groundwork had been laid for expansion as the economy of the state changed from a rural to an urban basis. Kanuga was a functioning success, and the diocese was organized on a basis which promised much for the future.

Chapter III

EPISCOPATE OF BISHOP GRAVATT
1939-1953

The Episcopate of Bishop John J. Gravatt began with his Consecration in Trinity Church, Columbia, on May 5, 1939. Before summer, the new Bishop had visited most of the parishes and missions in the diocese and was launched into the manifold duties of a diocesan. In June, he attended the meeting of the board of trustees of the University of the South at Sewanee, Tennessee, an institution with which he was now associated by virtue of his office. His interest in the Virginia Theological School was to continue unabated. In September, 1939, Bishop Gravatt installed the Rev. Louis C. Melcher, who had been called to Upper South Carolina from St. John's, Knoxville, as rector of Trinity Church, Columbia. Although Mr. Melcher held no official diocesan position, the fact that he and the Bishop had their offices in the same parish house made for a close relationship between them during the ensuing eight years. The first diocesan convention under Bishop Gravatt was held January 23-24, 1940, in Trinity, Columbia. The new Bishop appointed the Rev. T. P. Devlin and the Rev. Mr. Melcher as deans of the Greenville and Columbia convocations respectively.

His second Convention, changed to a spring date, was held in the Church of the Advent, Spartanburg. The Constitution and canons were at this time considerably revised—in many instances to accord with existing practices and procedures, and the committee on the state of the Church commended "the steps that have been taken to reorganize and revitalize the work among the colored people of the diocese and the appointment of the Reverend Max Whittington as Archdeacon in charge of that work." The committee called attention to the "splendid step taken by the rector and vestry of Grace Church, Anderson, in renouncing all help from the missionary funds of the diocese. It is the first time such a step has been taken by an aided parish in the diocese for many years." In a report on the work being done at St. Barnabas', Jenkinsville, Archdeacon Whittington said in part: "At the mission we have 250 acres of land and the following buildings: the

[474]

Mission House, which contains three class rooms, a library and living quarters for the minister and teachers; a three-room school building, a cannery (for the people in the community), a new church (which was built through the kindness of our friends) and a barn. In the school we have six teachers and one United Thank Offering Worker. The present enrollment of the school, which includes both the Grade and High School, is that of 165".

In 1940-41, three clergymen were called to diocesan charges: The Rev. William S. Lea, who succeeded Dr. W. H. K. Pendleton who retired from Advent, Spartanburg; the Rev. John A. Pinckney, who became rector of Holy Trinity, Clemson; and the Rev. J. Kenneth Morris, who came to St. John's, Columbia, from Japan. Equally important was the establishment of Mr. and Mrs. F. D. MacLean at the Church Home Orphanage in York. In the same period the diocese lost a loyal and active lay leader in the death of William Munro Shand, Esq., of Columbia, chancellor of the diocese since its beginning. In the year prior to the entry of the United States into World War II parish houses had been completed at Great Falls and Chester, and a Church for the Negro communicants was opened in Aiken. In 1942, John Peyre Thomas, Jr., who had served as secretary-treasurer of the Trustees of the diocese of South Carolina since 1899 and then in the same capacity for the diocese of Upper South Carolina, resigned because of his advanced years. Mr. Thomas died June 13, 1946, in his 89th year. The war inevitably affected any physical improvements in the diocese, and in 1943 three of the diocesan clergy had entered the armed forces. The Rev. J. Kenneth Morris, chairman of the Department of Christian Social Relations, noted in May, 1943, the contributions being made by Trinity, Columbia; Advent and Epiphany, Spartanburg, and Grace, Camden, in their work among members of the armed forces. Mr. Morris, long a missionary in Japan, left the diocese temporarily to serve in military intelligence.

The war presented a mixed blessing in providing a means to pay off parochial indebtedness, which by 1943 had been reduced to a mere $58,000.00, at a time when the value of the Church properties were placed at $1,554,950.00. Reporting on progress in 1943, the committee on the state of the Church said:

"The reports for the year 1943 indicate there has been progress made in the diocese, despite the fact that hundreds have been absent serving in the armed forces of the nation. A handsome and commodious Bishop's residence, costing $27,500.00 has been secured and partially paid for. St. Timothy's Church, Columbia, paid the last cent of debt on their Church and the Church was consecrated by Bishop Gravatt on January 2nd. St. Thaddeus' Church, Aiken, completed payments on a debt of $3,000.00 which they had carried for a number of years. St. John's Church, Columbia, paid several thousand dollars on the debt on the Church and within the past month bought a handsome rectory. Trinity Church, Columbia, and Christ Church, Greenville, have made substantial payments on their debts. The Church of the Good Shepherd, Columbia, has pledges to meet the last payment on the parish house in July and will be free of debt at that time. The Negro work, because of the absence of Archdeacon Max Whittington, who is serving as a chaplain in the army and of the two other Negro clergy who have left the diocese is in a critical condition. With ten churches and only one clergyman, who because of his school work at Voorhees can serve only St. Augustine's, Aiken, with the promising field at Jenkinsville, St. Anna's and St. Luke's, Columbia, as well as in several other places, it is imperative that this work receive immediate help."

An important step in improving the status of Negro parishes was taken at the 1946 convention when the Constitution of the diocese was amended to give them representation in the Convention. By the end of World War II, the diocese and its parishes were in a secure financial position and, with the return of ministers and laymen from the armed forces the Church in Upper South Carolina was ready to move forward. In September, 1945, a city missioner was obtained for the first time in the diocese; the Rev. William A. Thompson came to serve the various institutions and two churches in the Columbia area. In 1947, Christ Church, Lancaster, and Good Shepherd, Greer, were given the status of aided parishes. But in reviewing the evangelical work of the 25-year-old diocese the committee on the state of the Church said in January, 1947: "In the past 25 years only four new churches have been opened with a total communicant strength reported for 1946 of only 133 (Batesburg; Columbia; St. Matthews; Great Falls; Greer); also two churches were closed (Abbeville and Walhalla). We also report that during the past 10 years 12 churches have shown no appreciable gain in members and 13 churches have shown a loss, in other words, out of 39 churches in the diocese 25 are either static or losing ground."

In the fall of 1947, the Rev. Mr. Melcher, who had served as rector of Trinity Church since 1939, was elected Bishop Coadjutor of the missionary district of Southern Brazil. Bishop Melcher in eight years in Upper South Carolina had served the diocese in many capacities. At the Convention held at Christ Church, Greenville, in January, 1948, a diocesan committe on architecture and construction was created to make recommendations in regard to any parish construction. The committee on the state of the Church in that year reported as follows: "The growth of the Church has not kept pace with the growth of the population in the diocesan area. Parish and mission records are inaccurate and poorly kept. Every-Member Canvasses are seldom made to every member and the number of people pledging to missions is a pathetically small proportion of the number of communicants in the diocese. It is evident that too many individuals are depending on a few people to support the Church program.

"The committee recommends to the diocese a vastly increased missionary program with specific objectives and names the following as possible: 1. The establishment of chapel-missions by the larger parishes in new city areas. 2. The appointment and support of diocesan missionaries to establish new work and revive old fields. 3. For 1948, the use of any monies in excess of Budget B for the support of the first diocesan missionary to study the field and survey the needs as a part of his work; and for 1949 and 1950 respectively, two new missionaries sent into the field."

The committee on missions at the same Convention noted that: "The number of churches dying and being closed far exceeds the number of new ones being opened. For too long, we have struggled along trying merely to keep the doors of our Church open. It is felt that we must either move forward or stop, and we do not want to stop." On December 17, 1947, the diocese suffered a great loss in the death of Mrs. Helen Stevens Gravatt, wife of the Bishop. A resolution passed at the 26th diocesan Convention described her as a "true helpmate" to the Bishop and as one possessing a "gracious personality and true friendship." In the same year two lay leaders in the Church's program in Upper South Carolina had died. Major Walter B. Moore of York, who rendered invaluable service and made generous contributions to the Church Orphanage at York, died on March 12, and the Rev. Lewis N. Taylor, D.D., president of the diocese's Standing Committee for nine years and untiring parish priest, died December 3.

On May 1, 1948, Major R. E. Carwile, who had served the diocese as chancellor (legal counselor) for several years, died, and he was succeeded by R. Beverley Sloan of Columbia. A 100-acre site for a diocesan camp and conference center was given to the diocese by St. Julian Cullum of Batesburg in 1947. The tract, located south of Batesburg in the heart of the sand hill area of the state, was accessible to all parts of the diocese. The Bishop immediately began plans for buildings necessary for the development of the center. The diocesan center was designed to supplement and complement the work of the summer conference center at Kanuga, and is now known as Camp Gravatt. (See Appendix VII.) In 1949, it was recommended as a result of a diocesan survey that churches in Edgefield, Johnston and Trenton constitute one pastorate and these in Batesburg and Ridge Spring, with Camp Gravatt, constitute another. The same report recommended a pastorate for Newberry, Clinton and Laurens. Five thousand dollars was appropriated to build a new rectory in Newberry.

An important step was a recommendation for a minimum salary of $3,600.00 for married ministers and $2,400.00 for unmarried. The 1950 report of the committee on the state of the Church said in part:

". . . It is encouraging to see new fields being developed by the erection of churches and parish houses, such as Batesburg, Lancaster, Clearwater, St. Timothy's and St. John's, Columbia. New clergy into the field enables the work to go forward. The growing interest and activity of the laymen of the diocese speaks well for our future. The great advance in 'The Piedmont Churchman' enables the diocese to be more informed as to the Church's work. The interest and establishment of parochial schools in the diocese also shows a forward movement. The use of the diocesan camp last summer for the first time, and further plans for its development and usefulness to the diocese is another movement forward in the life of the diocese." On January 19, 1949, the Rev. Alexander Robert Mitchell, D.D., the founder of St. Timothy's, Columbia, St. James', St. Andrew's, and St. Philip's, Greenville, and Church of Good Shepherd, Greer, died. He had served in parishes in Piedmont, South Carolina for 63 years. He also founded several missions in the diocese of South Carolina.

In the summer of 1949, the diocese obtained for the first time exclusively for Upper South Carolina a trained worker in Christian education and youth work in Miss Mary Ravenel Burgess. Thus the importance of work among young people was receiving increased recognition. The year 1949 was also the first in which the physical layout at Camp Gravatt had permitted the holding of meetings of youths and laymen there. At the 1950 Convention Bishop Gravatt reported that the diocese had ten candidates for the ministry in theological seminaries, and during the prior year each parish in the diocese had selected a "Bishop's man" to promote and establish laymen's activities on a diocesan level. On September 15, 1950, a special diocesan Convention was called to meet at St. John's Church, Columbia, to consider the establishment of a school at Heathwood Hall in Columbia. Under the will of Francis Marion Weston, dated November 27, 1847, a fund had been left for the establishment of a school for young females in the City of Columbia. The school, after protracted discussion, was authorized by a vote of 34 to 27 upon an assurance that the diocese would not be financially responsible for the school's operation. (See Appendix VIII, I.) Since establishment this institution has abundantly grown as an ever-increasing force in its diocese for the development of Christian character. At the Convention held in Rock Hill in 1951, St. Martin's-in-the-Fields in suburban Columbia was admitted as a parish, and three organized missions were also given seats in the Convention: All Saints', Beech Island; All Saints', Clinton, and Church of the Epiphany, Spartanburg. Regular services had also been resumed at Trinity Church, Abbeville, and St. Paul's, Pendleton, had been reopened. The new hydrogen-bomb plant being developed near Aiken presented an opportunity and challenge for both dioceses. Established churches at Aiken and Clearwater were not enough; the formation of a mission at Beech Island and the organization of a Church in North Augusta were partial answers. A loan of $40,000.00 from the National Council was obtained to meet the needs of the Church in this expanding and developing area. The new mission at North Augusta, St. Bartholomew's, was admitted at the 1952 Convention. At the same time the new Church of the Redeemer, Greenville, was admitted. On recommendation of Bishop Gravatt the diocese established at this time a Foundation for lending funds to small congregations for capital improvements and for assisting in theological education. (See Appendix VIII, 3.) In addition to the churches already on the roster, St. Thomas', Eastover, and the Church of the Ascension, Seneca, were admitted as organized missions, and Holy Trinity, Clemson, was received as an aided parish in 1953.

Bishop Gravatt at the 1952 Convention had announced his plans to continue active leadership of the diocese until he reached the age of 72 when the Church's canons required retirement. He had stated that there were many projects in the diocese which he wanted to complete before ending his Episcopate, and primary among these was the development of the diocesan camp and conference center. The final Convention of Bishop Gravatt's Episcopate was held May 11 and 12, 1953, in Trinity Church, Columbia, where the second diocesan had been consecrated fourteen years earlier. Eleven candidates were nominated for the office of Bishop of the diocese, four of the nominees being priests from the diocese. Two others were from families long associated with "Upper South Carolina" and one other nominee was a former rector of one of the larger parishes. On the eleventh ballot, the Rev. Clarence Alfred Cole, rector of St. John's, Charleston, West Virginia, was elected. Because he had served in adjoining dioceses, South Carolina and North Carolina, during most of his ministry, the new Bishop was well known in Upper South Carolina. The Bishop-elect was called, immediately announced his acceptance, subject to canonical approval and visited the Convention on May 12. Reviewing the diocese's status, Bishop Gravatt said:

"We must continue to extend our missionary work in the diocese. We rejoice in what has been and is now being accomplished in this field. We hope that next month we can place another ordained man in the Northwestern area and start one or more new congregations there. In June we shall place at St. Barnabas' mission and at Newberry and Peak one of our new deacons. We are also planning to locate shortly a resident minister in Abbeville, who can also give St. Stephen's Church, Willington, a new and better chance. It has suffered from the lack of regular services for a long time, except for the ministrations of the Rev. Roddey Reid over a brief period. The Church is a substantial brick building, and should be made of real and continuing service to the people in that area. We have one or more churches in every county of the diocese. St. Stephen's Church, Willington, is the only one in McCormick County, and should be made active instead of dormant.

"We can well rejoice in our new Convocations and the way that they are functioning as areas for worship, work and fellowship. This is being carried on in the Woman's Auxiliary, the Episcopal Churchmen and the Young Churchmen of the diocese of Upper South Carolina. Because these are smaller working areas than the whole diocese, the groups and churches of a Convocation can come together more easily for joint services and meetings and can better assist each other. Making the most of our convocational opportunities will certainly strengthen the diocese.

"We are thankful for the advance that is being made in our diocese in Christian education and the various fields associated with it: our increasing number of Church schools with their increasing membership, our improved methods of education under the supervision of our Department of Christian Education and the special and valuable assistance of our consultant, Miss Winterbotham, our diocesan institutions of Christian education, our summer camps and conferences, our Canterbury Clubs for our college students, and our House of Young Churchmen in Upper South Carolina. The annual Conventions of these last two organizations were recently held very successfully at our diocesan camp and conference center. Let me urge that this camp and conference center be adequately equipped so that more persons can be accommodated at Camps and Conferences, and also that meetings can be held there any time during the year that is desirable. For instance, the pre-Lenten meeting of the clergy of the diocese has been for some years at the Bishop's house, but soon the number of that increasing body will be too large for that. If such a meeting could be held at the camp for two days, it would make the meeting more helpful, enriching and enjoyable. The same may well apply to other groups. If we make the most of our beautiful camp site, it will greatly contribute to the life, growth and fellowship in our diocese."

In 1952 a committee had been appointed to study the question of a diocesan headquarters. No action was taken in view of a proposal to make Trinity Church, Columbia, a cathedral. In 1938 the diocese expended $33,504.52; in 1952 the diocese had expended $95,492.84. Diocesan capital funds and investments had grown from $102,728.06 to $203,173.03. The value of Church properties had increased from $1,567,190.00 to $4,264,318.18. The total receipts of parishes and missions had increased from $127,463.94 to $659,666.14. The number of baptized persons in the diocese increased from 8,490 to 13,220 at the end of 1952; communicants from 6,397 to 9,245; confirmations in 1939 were 264; in 1952, 487 and the number of priests had increased from 21 to 39. The Church schools had increased from 3,444 to 4,669. This growth, as encouraging as it was, was not, however, commensurate with the development and expansion of Piedmont South Carolina. Rural South Carolina was fast deteriorating. Cotton was no longer king. With the development of a predominantly urban economy, the Episcopal Church faced a new challenge as Bishop Gravatt left the diocese to spend his retiring years in his native Virginia. His Episcopate had begun in the days in which the economy was emerging from a devastating depression which had shaken the financial, social and spiritual fibers of America. Immediately thereafter came the horror of a devastating war which was to end with the detonation of the ultimate weapon. The peace which followed was only an armed truce which erupted in the Korean "police action." South Carolina, like the rest of the nation, changed. It was visibly evident in the hydrogen bomb plant located astride the dividing line between the dioceses. The Church in Upper South Carolina faced a new challenge—more real than any, perhaps, which she had faced before.

Chapter IV

EPISCOPATE OF BISHOP COLE
1953-

Thirty-five years is not enough time in which to evaluate a new institution, but the diocese of Upper South Carolina, made up of the constituent Episcopal parishes in the Piedmont area of South Carolina, is in fact much older. When Clarence Alfred Cole became Bishop of this diocese in October, 1953, in Trinity Church, Columbia, the new Episcopal leader immediately began a survey of the area. It was not completely unfamiliar territory since he had begun his ministry in Charleston and had served as a parish priest for the most part in nearby North Carolina. Institutions and programs begun in the two prior Episcopates were to continue, but it was obvious that a severe economic depression and two wars had severely circumscribed the expansion and progress of the new diocese. A new parish had been founded in Columbia's expanding eastern section after World War Two, but the growth of the Church was not commensurate with industrial expansion and economic changes which had taken place in the diocesan area. In a little more than a quarter of a century South Carolina had changed from a predominantly rural state. By the census of 1950 the urban population comprised 36.7 per cent of the total, while in 1940 only 24.5 per cent were urban dwellers. In 1925 only 10.6 per cent had lived in urban areas, defined by the Bureau of the Census as incorporated places of more than 2,500 inhabitants.

Thus the Episcopal Church which had always developed and prospered in urban centers faced a new opportunity in Upper South Carolina's urban centers which from 1920 to 1950 had grown as follows: Columbia, 37,524 to 86,914; Greenville, 23,127 to 58,-161; Spartanburg, 22,638 to 36,795; Anderson, 10,570 to 19,770; Rock Hill, 8,809 to 24,502; Greenwood, 8,703 to 13,806. The population of the State as a whole had increased from 1,683,724 in 1920 to 2,117,027 by 1950. In May, 1954, the diocesan Convention was told that the diocesan population had increased 12% in 12 years, but the report revealed that Negro work in the diocese was "far from exemplary," and in many places "pitifully meagre and in others non-existent." New buildings and expansions had not taken place in favorable comparison with Methodist, Baptist and other denominational efforts, and diocesan boards of strategy on city, county or diocesan level were described as "non-existent or quiescent." Chaplains in the universities within the diocese reported sub-standard levels in Christian education on the part of college people coming to them from average parishes. Further the committee on the state of the Church said:

"It is noted that information as to diocesan projects, institutions and accomplishments are not well and generally disseminated. There is a disparity and paucity of knowledge on the part of the mass of our people of the needs, opportunities and many times, even the location of such places as the Church Home for Children, Voorhees, Camp Gravatt and the like.

"Salaries of Church employed people and clergy have increased but remain in some places on a subsistence level."

In 1953, the Standing Committee had authorized parishes to borrow $127,000.00 for new construction, but a coordinated diocesan expansion program, so long delayed, was not yet under way. And so in his first address as diocesan, Bishop Cole asked for approval of a survey of Upper South Carolina by the United Research and Field Study of the National Church, set up by the General Convention of 1949 with Dr. Joseph G. Moore as its executive secretary. Dr. Moore had described Upper South Carolina as "very exciting business, inasmuch as so much industry is going into that area." The survey, begun in October, 1954, was completed on November 25, 1955. Definite recommendations as to the future of the diocese were made on the basis of data gathered by the survey workers. The survey's data report said in part:

"At the end of the year 1954, the diocese was composed of 17 parishes, eight aided parishes, 31 organized missions, and two unorganized missions, for a total of 58 congregations. As compared to 1935, this indicated that the diocese had increased by four congregations in the past two decades. In 1935, there were 28 parishes or aided parishes, 20 organized missions, and six unorganized missions, for a total of 54 congregations.

"A study of the vital statistics of the entire diocese indicates healthy increases in every aspect, both as to membership and stewardship. There were 7,830 baptized members in 1935 and 14,988 at the end of 1954, for an increase of 91.4%.

"The comparative general population increase within the 22 counties of the diocese indicates that the rate of growth of the baptized members far exceeds the population increase of 25%. The approximate population in the diocesan area in 1935 was 1,005,965, and the estimated population at the end of 1954 was 1,257,068. Another indication of the growth of the Episcopal Church membership, as related to the general population, can be seen by the percentage of Episcopalians to the total population. In 1940 this percentage was .74%; .96% in 1950; and 1.65% in 1954.

"When the white membership is compared to the white portion of the population, it is seen that the Church's baptized membership in 1940 made up 1% of the white population in the diocese; 1.3% in 1950; and 2.2% of the total population in 1954."

The statistical story among the Negro members was not one of such growth and indicated a static condition in the period. But the diocese was moving forward as this financial summary shows:

"Total parochial expenditures was $110,794.00 in 1935; $126,-987.00 in 1940; $393,801.00 in 1950; and $597,527.00 in 1954, for an increase of 439.3%. At the same time, expenditures per communicant were $18.98 in 1935; $20.37 in 1940; $46.16 in 1950; and $56.28 in 1954, for an increase of 196.5%.

"While these increases seem quite startling, it must be remembered that in 1935 we were still in the depression, and people generally were in a very poor economic position. What is indicated here in the diocese of Upper South Carolina is that the membership has more than maintained the same level, as related to buying power, and since 1950 the membership has increased its pledging to the Church at a more rapid rate. The vital statistics, therefore, indicate that, in general, the diocese is moving forward, and that many parishes have excellent programs and are successfully serving new families coming into the diocese."

On the basis of detailed statistical and economic data the survey team made specific recommendations, summarized as follows:

"The major needs facing the diocese at the present time are as follows:

"A. Missionary expansion into outlying suburban areas of Columbia, Spartanburg, Greenville, and in the South Carolina section of the Augusta, Georgia, metropolitan area.

"B. Throughout the diocese, in both urban and town and country areas, there is an apparent need for renovation or enlargement of the Church facilities.

"C. A third need is one of program revision and development, so that congregations can serve wider areas of the total life of their community. Active programs of lay evangelism and visitation are needed.

"As we review the needs of the diocese, it is heartening to realize that some of the recommendations and needs expressed are in the process of being accomplished, or have been accomplished during the course of this diocesan study."

As a result of the survey, new missions have been established in Greenville, Spartanburg and Fountain Inn, and new work has been launched at Fort Mill. A diocesan capital fund campaign has been launched. Thus, at long last, the Church in Upper South Carolina was expanding beyond the coastal plain and apart from the few tidewater families which had first carried Episcopalianism into the Piedmont. In 1860, the Episcopal Church had only 60,000 Southern members, mostly in the tidewater regions in such cities as Savannah and Charleston. There were outposts of the Church in the "up-country" among planters attempting to imitate the ways of Charleston and Virginia. The frontiers had been characterized by a lack of religion in its early stages, and camp meetings and revivals fulfilled religious yearnings. The Baptist Church had the most extensive following in the up-country because it adjusted itself easily to the needs of the people. Methodism, through its schools and seminaries, also flourished. The people of the South remained religious into the twentieth century, unlike many other sections, and Piedmont South Carolina is typical of the South. As modern scientific dogma and materialistic theories gained following in the South, the question became: whether the orthodox Southern religious followers would become irreligious or whether they would follow a religious denomination capable of reconciliation with the new scientific thought.

Almost alone among churches of the South, the Episcopal Church has maintained the common-sense outlook of the eighteenth century. Its dogma and articles of faith are compatible with the theories of the atomic age, and its ritual and unified, yet democratic, organization were suited for the ways of a more sophisticated and urban population. Conversion of the orthodox Southerner with his fundamentalist beliefs, his ultra-conservative religious outlook, and static views on racial issues, will be a difficult task. Whether Southerners are to continue in some Christian denomination or, as in many other parts of the United States, are to fall victims to an irreligious urban life in a mechanistic age is the question facing the Episcopal Church in Piedmont South Carolina. Many of these orthodox Southerners will continue in or gravitate towards churches of the Baptist, Methodist and Presbyterian denominations which in urban centers are continuously copying the ways and ritual of the Episcopal Church. Into the conflict between orthodox Southern views and the atomic age, an evangelical and expanding Episcopal Church, freed of its ultra-aristocratic traditions, could perform a modern miracle in saving many who will otherwise abandon Christianity for devotion to the Sunday comics, golf courses on Sunday mornings, motion-picture palaces on Sunday afternoons, and TV's vaudeville on Sunday nights. The Episcopal Church is peculiarly and completely equipped in ritual and thought to bridge this gap.

A limited evangelical program, based in part on social prestige and class distinctions, has already accomplished some good results, but much more remains to be done. Here is an opportunity to save an entire region as a bastion of the Christian religion, and the Episcopal Church in Upper South Carolina has this opportunity to become an expanding and growing Church, rather than merely a survival of a by-gone past—a relic of an almost forgotten age. That is the challenge which faced Bishop Cole as he began his Episcopate in Upper South Carolina.

SECTION II

LIST OF PARISHES, MISSIONS, AND ARCHDEACONRY, WITH SKETCHES

DIOCESE OF UPPER SOUTH CAROLINA

Abbeville, Trinity
Aiken, St. Augustine's
    St. Thaddaeus'
Anderson, Grace
Batesburg, St. Paul's
Beech Island, All Saints'
Blacksburg, Atonement
Calhoun Falls, All Saints'
Camden, Grace
Chester, St. Mark's
Chester District, Immanuel, Landsford
Clearwater, St. John's
Clemson, Holy Trinity
Clinton, All Saints'
Columbia, Christ Church
    Good Shepherd
    Holy Comforter
    Mediator
    St. Anna's
    St. John's
    St. Luke's
    St. Martin's-in-the-Fields
    St. Mary's
    St. Matthew's
    St. Timothy's
    Trinity
Congaree, St. John's
Easley, St. Michael's
Eastover, St. Thomas'
    Zion
Edgefield, Trinity
Fountain Inn, Holy Cross
Gaffney, Incarnation
Glenn Springs, Calvary

Graniteville, St. Paul's
Great Falls, St. Peter's
Greenville, Christ Church
    Redeemer
    St. Andrew's
    St. James'
    St. Philip's
Greenwood, Resurrection
Greer, Good Shepherd
Horse Creek Valley Missions
Jenkinsville, St. Barnabas'
Johnson, St. Stephen's
Kaolin, St. George
Lancaster, Christ Church
Laurens, Epiphany
Newberry, St. Luke's
    St. Monica's
North Augusta, St. Bartholomew's
Peak, St. Simon's
Pendleton, St. Paul's
Ridge Spring, Grace
Ridgeway, St. Stephen's
Rock Hill, Our Saviour
Seneca, Ascension
Spartanburg, Advent
    Epiphany
Trenton, Our Saviour
Union, Nativity
Walhalla, St. John's
West Columbia, St. Anne's
Willington, St. Stephen's
Winnsboro, St. John's
York, Good Shepherd
Work Among Colored (Archdeaconry)

TRINITY CHURCH, ABBEVILLE
Established 1842

There is a tablet on the wall of the present beautiful Trinity Church which definitely designates Thomas Parker as "the founder of the Episcopal Church in Abbeville District." Mr. Parker abandoned the practice of law in Charleston and moved from there to Abbeville, settling on a plantation ten miles from the town. His wife was Miss Ellen Frost and he had seven sons, many of whom served on the vestry of this Church. As founder, Mr. Parker was ably assisted by Thomas Jackson from England and by Thomas Walter Thomas who had moved from St. Stephen's Parish in the low-country. The Church was organized October 16, 1842 under the name of Trinity; Rev. Edward Phillips was present. Messrs. Parker and Thomas were elected vestrymen, and Mr. Jackson, warden. Later J. F. Lee and T. H. Ashe were added as vestrymen, and James Wilson additional warden. The first services were held in the Court House, Mr. Parker being lay reader. A Church on the site of the present Church was built almost immediately. This Church was described by Bishop Gadsden as follows: "The place of worship, as to its external appearance, and its internal arrangements, must be considered very creditable to the good taste and knowledge of Church architecture and principles of those who designed it—the chief of whom (Mr. Thomas Parker) being removed by death, we humbly trust is partaker of far better satisfactions than the best temple on earth can supply. The portico (Grecian), the cupola, the door, the windows, the length, breadth and elevation, are all in good proportion and the building is an ornament to the street which it faces and interrupts. The 'Holy Table' is the object which meets the eye on entering the door. The chancel rail terminates the aisle, the desk and pulpit of the same height, are against the wall to the right and left of the chancel, a little in the rear of the communion table; a door close to each of them opens into the vestry room. They are of black walnut, and the pews have a ledge of the same wood, so peculiarly appropriate in a Church both as to its dark color and superceding the use of paint. The organ, a sweet toned one, has its gallery and the bell its proper receptacle." The Bishop consecrated this Church on November 27, 1844, being assisted by the rector, the Rev. A. H. Cornish and the Rev. Carter Page, deacon of Georgia, and the Rev. C. H. Hall, deacon of Connecticut. The Church cost $1,400.00.

Among the clergymen who first officiated in Abbeville from time to time were the Rev. Messrs. Wallace, Phillips, Potter, Pinckney and Edward Reed. The first regular rector was the Rev. A. H. Cornish of Hobart, New York, who accepted a call in October, 1843. When he was in process of moving his family south, the Church suffered a great loss in the death of Mr. Parker, which caused Mr. Cornish to hesitate, but by the Bishop's persuasion, he did not turn back. Another blow was the death of Mrs. D. L. Wardlaw who had done much to keep the Church together after Mr. Parker's death. She, though a Presbyterian, was the life of the congregation and active in supplying the Church with an organ and other needful furnishing. Mr. Cornish reports in 1846, holding 130 services, including 34 for colored congregations, 10 on plantations, and 10 other places in the district. The first persons confirmed were James Wilson and his wife Susan, Thomas Jackson, and John Taggart. On June 13, 1847, he confirmed 17 slaves on the plantation of Thomas Walter Thomas. The Church continued prosperous until 1848 when, due to lack of funds for his support, Mr. Cornish resigned, removing to Pendleton but continued to officiate occasionally as did also the Rev. Messr. Pendy as missionary, followed by the Rev. William Green, 1851-1853. The Rev. B. C. Webb became rector in 1854, but his health failed and he was succeeded by the Rev. Benjamin Johnson (1855-1857), a rectory being built the year after. In 1858 it was determined to build a new and larger Church. The cornerstone was laid by Bishop Davis on June 25, 1859 and the Church consecrated by him November 4, 1860. This Church which has always been considered one of the most beautiful in the state was built after plans by George E. Walker, architect, of Columbia, by Blease and Baxter, contractors, of Newberry. The cost including bell and organ, $15,665.00. It is described as pointed Gothic, 81 feet long and 43 feet wide apart from tower and chancel. The material of the old Church after being stored on an adjoining lot for five years was bought by the Rev. O. T. Porcher and re-erected by him at Willington. It was subsequently burnt.

The gifts and memorials in the new Trinity reveal the names of many members: The bell and cushions were given by J. Foster Marshall; the lamps by Mrs. Ellen Parker; Bible and prayer book by Mrs. James C. Calhoun; the marble font by William Henry Parker; the chairs in the chancel by the Rev. Benjamin Johnson; the pulpit Bible by Dr. Edwin Parker; the prayer book on the communion table by "a dying member of the Episcopal Church at Newberry"; the altar table with marble top by James Chalmers; the window with "Suffer the little children etc." by the children of the Sunday School; marble shelf for alms basins by Dr. Edwin

Parker in memory of his wife Eugenia; a stained glass window by friends, and also a beautiful chancel window and pipe organ; the Bishop's chair was the gift of the wife of Congressman Burt. There are many other memorial gifts in the Church and on the walls tablets to the memory of Thomas Parker; William Henry Parker and his wife; John Alfred Calhoun and his wife; Sarah M. Norwood; Charles Thompson Haskell, wife, and children; Eugene B. Gary and his brother Ernest Gary; William Campbell McGowan; Martha Calhoun Burt; William Augustus Lee; and more recently (1941) by the will of Langdon Cheves a very handsome window was erected "In memory of Sophia L. Cheves, wife of Charles Thomson Haskell, Daughter of Langdon Cheves, and her daughter Sophia Lovell Haskell, wife of Langdon Cheves." This Church contributed to the Confederate Army many soldiers and distinguished officers, and many were killed—especially great was the loss to the Church of Col. J. Foster Barnwell for many years warden, and leader in the building of the new Church, killed at Second Manassas.

The Rev. Benjamin Johnson was succeeded briefly in 1867 by the Rev. B. F. D. Perry until the Rev. William Porcher DuBose came in 1868 continuing until 1871 when he resigned to become chaplain of the University of the South, Sewanee, and dean of St. Luke's Hall, destined to be a distinguished theologian. In 1871 the wardens and vestrymen were: A. Burt, J. A. Norwood, W. A. Lee, Thomas Jackson, J. T. Robertson, W. H. Parker and Dr. E. Parker. Succeeding Mr. DuBose were Edward R. Miles, 1872; John Kershaw, 1876; S. H. S. Gallaudet, 1880; Frank Hallam, 1881; M. Stuart and Thomas F. Gadsden briefly in 1883; W. H. Hanckel, 1884; Edward McCrady, 1893; W. B. Sams, 1902; S. E. Prentiss, 1906; A. E. Cornish, 1910; S. R. Guignard, 1913; C. H. Jordan, 1916; Ambler M. Blackford, 1917; Alfred Arundel officiated in 1919; Alfred James Derbyshire, 1921; R. C. Topping, 1928-1934; Charles Holding, 1945-1948. In 1901 the senior warden and lay reader was W. H. Parker and the junior warden, secretary, and treasurer was B. S. Barnwell. On July 7, 1910, lightning struck a tree which fell on the Church tearing out two windows, one of which was stained glass. In 1915, the senior warden and secretary was J. Foster Barnwell, and the junior warden and treasurer was Lewis Perrin. Early in the century this once flourishing parish became very much reduced by deaths and removals. The Rev. Allen W. Joslin took charge of this Church in 1949. The work here now took on new life. The wardens in 1951 were William M. Barnwell and Wade

Cothran; secretary, F. E. Erskine; treasurer, Wade Cothran. In 1954, Rev. E. Cannon McCreary succeeded as priest-in-charge, until 1957.

AIKEN, ST. AUGUSTINE'S
Established 1897

(See Chapter on Work among Colored People in Diocese of S. C., and same in Diocese of Upper S. C., Part One, Sec. II; Part Two, Sec. II.)

This Church had its beginning in 1897 in the opening of a Sunday School with 26 pupils and two teachers in connection with St. Thaddeus' Church, Aiken, the Rev. T. W. Clift, rector, through his efforts and those of Mrs. H. K. Chatfield. Property for a mission was acquired in 1899. In 1902, nine communicants and 20 baptized members were reported. Mr. Clift continued in charge for 13 years, succeeded by the Rev. R. C. Jeter, who had become rector of St. Thaddeus'; later by the Rev. John Ridout. This Church from the first was included in the Archdeaconry of the diocese of South Carolina and then after the division in 1922 in that of the diocese of Upper S. C. (see *in loco*). As before at the time of the division, the rector of St. Thaddaeus' was in charge, at this time the Rev. William Johnson. In 1922 there were 35 communicants with an attendance of 65 in a day school. The Rev. Mr. Johnson continued in charge until 1937 when he was succeeded by the Rev. M. S. Whittington, who was followed by the Rev. Bruce P. Williamson in 1942, who served until 1944. In the Journal of 1947, St. Augustine's is listed as a regular "organized mission" under the charge of the Rev. S. C. Usher; treasurer, Emmanuel Johnson, who had served many years as the lay reader. The wardens in 1948 were Robert A. Brooks, and George Glover, and A. Spencer, secretary. The Rev. M. J. Kippenbrock became priest-in-charge in 1949, succeeded by the Rev. O. H. Brown, Jr., in 1951 (resident of Augusta).

ST. THADDAEUS' AIKEN
Established 1844

At Aiken, the highest spot between Charleston and Augusta, "Divine service was held for the first time, according to the ritual of the P. E. Church, by a presbyter of the same, on Trinity Sunday, June 14, the Rail-Road Company having liberally given free passage". This was in 1835. There was no immediate result. The next service was one held by the Rev. Cranmore Wallace in the summer of 1839 when Bishop Bowen had sent him on a missionary tour into the upper counties. Bishop C. E. Gadsden having been elected the following year was full of zeal for diocesan missions. Under the auspices of the Advancement Society in 1842 he sent the Rev. Edward Phillips into this region, his work centering in Aiken, Abbeville and Hamburg. Already Aiken was a health resort and it was a group of Charlestonians, visitants there, who felt the need for themselves and for the community, determined to establish the Church in Aiken. There was some opposition in the community especially perhaps because at first the vestry was a "closed corporation". However, a zealous member of the Church, Major Edward R. Laurens, obtained subscriptions sufficient for the building of a Church chiefly due to "the liberality of an individual." F. Wisner was secured as architect, and a handsome edifice erected, 'of wood, 60 by 40 feet, in the Greek style having a porch and pillars in front . . . to be supplied with large galleries for the accommodation of colored persons." An application to the Rail-Road Company for a lot had been generously granted—"a lot so spacious as to afford ample room for a cemetery, a rectory, and should it be desired a Parochial School." The cornerstone was laid on September 5, 1842, by the Rev. Edward Phillips. The Church was consecrated by Bishop Gadsden, August 9, 1843. He was assisted by the Revs. M. H. Lance, E. Phillips, P. Gadsden, A. W. Marshall, and W. J. Boone. The sermon was by the Bishop. It is interesting to note that the Rev. W. J. Boone of Walterboro, missionary to China, and later first Bishop of China, preached in the afternoon.

Now in regard to this "liberality of an individual" we quote the following from a sketch of St. Thaddaeus' by J. R. P. Smith, registrar of the diocese, written about 1880: "It may not be improper to mention here that a gentleman whom the state has crowned with its highest honors expressed to the present writer his firm belief that his mother from indications on her factor's books was the individual alluded to by her pastor, Bishop Gadsden. This statement seems to give confirmation to a tradition in the parish that the liberal contributor referred to by Bishop Gadsden was the mother of Governor Aiken. At this late day there can be no impropriety in giving names and so rendering honor where these facts so strongly indicate that it is due." The legislature issued a charter to the Church December 19, 1843, naming Edward R. Laurens, James Gadsden, William C. Courtney, Lee Allison, Benjamin Lockwood, William Gregg and James Black as vestrymen, and Jacob K. Sass, and John F. Schmidt, wardens. In 1851 the charter was amended providing for annual elections of wardens and vestrymen. This charter was finally renewed in perpetuity in 1911. The parish was admitted into union with the Convention on February 19th, 1844. The delegates were E. R. Laurens, J. K. Sass, and Col. James Gadsden. The celebrated missionary, Andrew Fowler, visited Aiken in 1844, and held services on three Sundays; he relates, "I had the gratification of meeting with a piously behaved congregation. . . . The only fault I could find with them was that they did not respond quite so loud as I could have wished." He added, "The Church at Aiken may justly be admired as the most elegant structure of the kind to be met with in any country parish in this state." The first rector of this Church was the Rev. A. E. Ford, instituted in 1845. He was suspended for heretical teaching a year later.

The roof of St. Thaddaeus' was badly damaged by the fall of a tree in the summer of 1848. Subscriptions made for an organ were diverted to the necessary repairs, a lady in Charleston having presented an organ of fine tone made by a Mr. Erben. The Rev. John H. Cornish followed Mr. Ford after an intermission when the Bishop and others supplied services. He was rector from 1847 to to 1869. On his visitation in August, 1848, Bishop Gadsden was greatly pleased to find a parochial school being conducted on the grounds of the Church. Mr. Cornish was a great missionary, holding services at many points within a few miles of Aiken, including Graniteville. This work was in 1852 put in charge of a missionary, the Rev. C. T. Bland. The Church escaped damage in the war of 1861-65. During this period the congregation was greatly increased by refugees from the coast. The Rev. Mr. Cornish resigned the rectorship in 1869, continuing to live in Aiken and do mission work. The Rev. John Grimke Drayton supplied services during a vacancy then. The Rev. E. C. Edgerton followed Mr. Cornish as rector. At this time ten new pews, a new reading desk and pulpit were installed and a fresh coat of paint was put on the exterior. In 1872-73 a parsonage was built at a cost of $4,000.00, visitors assisting. In these years the communion plate in use was the property of St. Bartholomew's parish, loaned by the Bishop although the parish had silver of its own. Half of the Church lot was exchanged for the lot on which the parsonage was built. In 1880 two memorials were added in the chancel of the Church, gifts of a lady, a stained glass window in memory of her son and an altar in memory of her husband. In 1884 extensive repairs were made to the Church, and a new organ placed in the gallery. The year following a chapel was erected in the churchyard, a memorial to the Rev. J. H. Cornish.

In 1894 a handsome marble font was installed in the Church by Mrs. McLure in memory of her daughter, Miss Julia McLure, the old font being given to the Petigrue Mission in Abbeville County. The Rev. T. W. Clift succeeded Mr. Edgerton in 1896, the latter becoming rector-emeritus; he died May 16, 1902. Mr. Clift was succeeded by the Rev. Richard C. Jeter in 1910. At this time an initial fund of $5,138.40 was raised for a new Church and $210.00 for a new organ. The Rev. John Ridout became rector in 1917. A new pipe organ was installed in 1921; the old one being given to St. Paul's, Graniteville. The Rev. William Johnson became rector at the time of the division of the diocese in 1923. The need for an enlargement of the Church culminated in 1926 when under the plans of Simons and Lapham of Charleston, at a cost of $40,000.00 the Church was elaborately enlarged—the nave lengthened, a spacious chancel and choir rooms with rector's study and sacristy were added. Also through the generosity of Mrs. George A. Heywood of Arden, N. C., a handsome marble altar was installed and the chancel redecorated. A large vested choir took part for the first time in the main service of St. Thaddaeus' when the Church was reopened. The new parts were consecrated by Bishop Finlay, January 23, 1927. The Rev. Charles M. Seymour succeeded Mr. Johnson in 1942. The rectory was entirely renovated in the fall of 1947. The Rev. Michael J. Kippenbrock became rector in 1949, continuing until 1953, and succeeded after an interval by the Rev. George H. Murphy in 1954.

A notable event in the life of St. Thaddaeus' was the organization of a chapter of the Daughters of the King (on March 13, 1955) when 60 charter members, with Mrs. Robert B. Keller as president, were enrolled. The chapter has grown rapidly—by the spring of 1956 nearly 100 members had been enrolled, and a chapter of Junior Daughters with 32 members formed. The activities of this organization were filmed and the picture shown at the General Convention. Among its activities was the establishment of a Church book store in the parish house. The executive council of the diocese recently adopted the store which is therefore now the diocesan book store.

GRACE CHURCH, ANDERSON
Established 1851

It is known that services of the Episcopal Church were held in Anderson by the Rev. W. T. Potter as early as 1840 and later by other missionaries, probably. The next report we have in the records of the diocese is in February, 1849, when the Rev. Andrew H.

Cornish, then rector of St. Paul's, Pendleton, reported holding services two days in the court house in Anderson in 1848. He had found there five families and seven communicants belonging to the Church, the nucleus he trusted of "a large and flourishing congregation." On August 20, 1849, Bishop Gadsden visited Anderson where he says he preached and administered the Holy Communion to "six females"; Mr. Cornish read Morning Prayer. The evening before, at the Bishop's request, the Rev. J. D. McCollough had held service and preached. There was, at this time, a subscription of $405.00 to build a Church. When at its meeting in 1851, the Convention of the diocese was assured not only of an amount available for the support of a minister, but also that a lot had been given for a Church, and $500.00 raised toward the building, Grace Church, Anderson, was then admitted into union with the Convention. This was on February 12, 1851. This implies that the congregation had already been duly organized. Mr. Cornish resigned St. Paul's, Pendleton, in 1850 but soon returned, keeping an eye on the group in Anderson. He reports holding four services in 1852. Mr. Cornish and those "six females" were probably the founders of the Church.

The Rev. Benjamin C. Webb held charge for some time in 1854 until his health failed. Mr. Cornish following in charge again reported 20 services for 1856. He resigned June, 1857, but reassumed charge in April, 1858. The Rev. B. Johnson followed Mr. Cornish in 1859, reporting plans for building a Church with $1,500.00 to $2,000.00 raised, and in May of the next year that the Church there was nearly finished; but there was a crisis, resources in the congregation were exhausted and a next installment of $750.00 was due. There was an earnest appeal to the Church generally in the diocese. Contributions were solicited to be sent to John V. Moore, Esq., treasurer of the vestry, the first officer of the Church to be mentioned in the records found. The Church was finally completed at a cost of $3,000.00 and consecrated by Bishop Davis on November 7, 1860. The Rev. Messrs. Johnson, Cornish and Howe assisted, the last preaching the sermon. A pipe organ was purchased from the Church in Abbeville, communion silver was borrowed from St. Helena's Church, St. Helena's Island. The Church was of Gothic design, 40 by 50 feet, with spire and bell, built mostly by the Honorable James L. Orr. The prayers and labors of an earnest band were rewarded. For the first time the Church was represented in the diocesan Convention (although admitted many years before) when it met in Abbeville, June 19-20, 1861; the deputies were

J. L. Orr, Samuel H. Owen, Elbert Rucker, John H. Marshall. So was the Church launched when the echoes of Sumter and Manassas had scarcely died away, giving place to other cannons' roar.

At this time the Church had acquired considerable property, which was subsequently sold off. The Rev. Joseph B. Seabrook officiated from May to December, 1862. He was succeeded by the Rev. John H. Elliott, January 1, 1863. At this time there were 68 communicants. The congregations were enlarged by war refugees. Mr. Elliott was assisted this year by the Rev. Messrs. Keith, Porter, Campbell and Potter. Mr. Elliott continued to 1866 when, in the fall of this year, the Rev. A. H. Cornish again took charge of the Church. Mr. Ellison Capers (afterwards Bishop) acted as lay reader. In 1870 Mr. Cornish reported 16 families and 27 communicants. He had resigned November, 1869. The Rev. E. R. Miles took charge in 1870 for two years. Convocation held its meeting in Grace Church that year, October 13-18. Among the interesting series of services was one when Mr. W. H. Campbell was ordained deacon.

The Rev. P. F. Stevens served from January 7, 1874, for two years. He found little to encourage him, but gave credit for the painting and repairing of the Church in 1875. The Rev. Mr. Stevens then was on the eve of leaving the Church for the Reformed Episcopal Church, as did also Rev. Benjamin Johnson. The Rev. H. T. Gregory followed January 1, 1876, but only for a short period; then the Rev. Thomas F. Gadsden took charge November, 1877. He stated the Church had been closed more years than open since 1860 when built. He went to work in faith, re-organizing the Church—Sunday School, choir, guild. The organ was now removed from the gallery to the body of the Church. A rectory was built at the rear of the Church in 1878, costing $1,350.00. There were now 17 families in the Church. E. M. Rucker and C. W. Webb represented the Church in the Convention. The rector also taught a private school. In 1883 improvements were made in the Church, including the addition of the tower. Lay reading by Mr. E. A. Bell was held in the absence of the rector. The Church was re-roofed in 1886. The Rev. B. B. Sams, convalescing in Anderson, preached twelve times during the summer of 1885. In 1887 a walnut communion table and a stained glass window were installed. The diocesan Convention met in this Church May 2-3, 1888. Later a credence table was given by Mrs. E. P. Morris as a memorial of this event. Now a branch of the Woman's Auxiliary was organized. In 1890 a Jardine pipe organ was installed. On December 14, 1890, the Church was seriously damaged by fire and only after two months, with temporary repairs, were services resumed in it. Plans for a new Church were made and $1,500.00 pledged. The Rev. O. T. Porcher was assistant this year. Mr. Gadsden died December 1, 1891, having given this Church fourteen years of faithful service. Mr. E. A. Bell was both warden and lay reader at this time.

In 1894 the Rev. R. P. Eubanks became rector for about two years, being succeeded by the Rev. William Theodotus Capers (afterwards Bishop of West Texas), who served until April, 1901. The Convention of the diocese met in Grace Church for the second time May 12-14, 1897. The wardens in 1899 were W. E. A. Ball and R. C. Webb; secretary, M. L. Bonham; treasurer, F. G. Brown. Plans were now developed for building a new Church to cost $8,-000.00, but it was to be some years before this was realized. The Rev. Benjamin McKenzie Anderson became rector in 1902, leaving the next year. The Rev. W. N. Meade served for a short time, going to Virginia February, 1904. It was during his time that the last service was held in the old Church on July 12, 1903. The new building, Gothic in design, of brick and granite was completed under a building committee consisting of Messrs. S. M. Orr, F. G. Brown, and R. C. Webb. The first services in the new Church were conducted by Bishop Capers on Easter Day, 1904.

The Rev. Richard Cullen Jeter became rector in July, 1904. There were 95 communicants at this time. Mr. Jeter left November, 1909, and the Rev. Sanders R. Guignard succeeded March 1, 1910. The wardens now were C. W. Webb and R. C. Webb; the secretary, J. H. Godfrey; treasurer, C. G. Sayre; T. C. Walton, lay reader. By means of a legacy of $1,000.00 and the efforts of the congregation, the debt resting on the Church since its building in 1903-4 was paid, and on Tuesday, February 6, 1912, it was consecrated by Bishop Guerry. Mr. C. W. Webb read the Request and the rector the Sentence of Consecration. It was a great occasion, services being held for several days. Those assisting the Bishop and the rector were the Rev. Messrs. Jeter, Mitchell, Pendleton, Tillinghast, and Walsh. Mr. Guignard left January 1, 1913, and the Rev. J. Haller Gibbony, Jr., became rector October 13 of that year, continuing until 1917. The Rev. Herbert F. Schroeter was rector from December, 1917 to 1919, followed by the Rev. Guy Henry Frazer, 1920-21; then the Rev. A. W. Taylor, 1922-27. The Rev. Robert Chipman Topping served from March, 1928, until 1936. At this time the old rectory was remodelled into a parish hall and a new Morris Memorial Rectory built with a legacy from Margaret Ann

Morris. Also at this time the Church was entirely renovated. The Convention met in Grace Church in January, 1933. The Rev. Henry L. Durrent, D.D., became rector in 1936, serving until 1943. The officers in 1938 were: wardens, M. L. Bonham, and W. N. Webb; L. S. Horton, secretary; R. L. Lane, treasurer; R. B. Gage, lay reader. The succeeding ministers were the Rev. Messrs. Roddey Reid, Jr. (1944-48); Lay reader Charles B. Thompson (1949-50), Samuel R. Hardman (1950), Martin I. Tilson (1951-1956).

SAINT PAUL'S, BATESBURG-LEESVILLE
Established 1908, 1930

The Rev. T. T. Walsh, then Archdeacon of the diocese, visited Batesburg-Leesville in January, 1907. On March 17 following, he returned and held the first service of the Episcopal Church in Batesburg. However, it was not until June 1, 1908, that this mission was organized by Bishop Guerry under the Rev. R. G. Shannonhouse,' minister-in-charge; warden, N. R. Bayly; secretary and treasurer, W. C. Farler. The Bishop preached that night at the Methodist Church, Mr. Shannonhouse saying the service. Monthly services were held in the Methodist Church, kindly loaned. On August 1 of this same year, a lot was purchased for $850.00. It had a building on it where a Sunday School was organized on March 18th and where lay services were held on the other Sundays, Mr. J. B. Reid, lay reader. Other names among the first members were Bailey, Craven, Carter, Cain, Baker. The arrangement of services continued until October, 1909, when the Church's building was remodeled into a chapel from which time the services were held there. Later, additional lay readers were C. E. Craven, Allen Jones, Jr., and later Dean J. Nelson Frierson of Columbia. By 1911, the chapel was completely furnished—Dr. Fox gave brasses; Good Shepherd Church, Columbia, a communion service; Mr. Reid made the altar and the lectern and also built the chancel. However, by removals the congregation had so dwindled down that at the end of 1915, the mission was disbanded and the property sold.

In 1929, the way for the reorganization of the mission was prepared at the request of Bishop Finlay by the Church Army under the direction of Capt. Sydney R. Peters (later the Rev. S. R. Peters) of Baysboro, N. Y. The mission was reorganized the year following and a Church built on Route 1 between Batesburg and Leesville, the Rev. A. G. B. Bennett, priest-in-charge. The Church was consecrated by Bishop Finlay on March 22, 1931, being assisted by the Revs. Bennett, Evison, Morgan, and Sloan. The warden then was Mark P. Hazel; secretary and treasurer, B. M. McCollough. Mrs. Hazel was the first school superintendent, then Eugene Hartley. The altar was given by St. Thaddaeus' Church, Aiken. The Rev. B. A. Williams succeeded Mr. Bennett in 1940, who continued in charge until in turn succeeded by the Rev. J. Kenneth Morris. The mission lost members and support during the war and the Church was sold in 1945 to the Methodists, the plan being to build a new Church. This was done in 1947 under Mr. Morris' leadership, with the cooperation of old and new members. Between the selling of the old Church and the building of the new, services were held in a store building and in the educational building of the Batesburg Baptist Church, Mrs. Hazel continuing the Church school. The new Church was consecrated by Bishop Gravatt. In 1951-52, a rectory was built by the joint congregations of St. Paul's, with Grace, Ridge Spring and Camp Gravatt. In 1952, the Rev. John G. Clarkson, Jr., became deacon-in-charge, under the Rev. Mr. Morris, and the next year priest-in-charge. The Church school Lenten offering of the diocese in 1955 was given to St. Paul's for a parish house ($1,-680.36).

ALL SAINTS', BEECH ISLAND
Established 1950

Perhaps as early as a century ago, services of the Episcopal Church were held from time to time at Beech Island (Cf. Horse Creek Valley missions); but the subject of this sketch, All Saints', had its origin in connection with the great influx of population in this region in view of the building of the great atomic energy plant. All Saints' Church had its birth in the mind and heart of Mrs. Paul H. Dunbar, Jr. With the help of Mrs. Leroy Simkins, a Presbyterian neighbor, and the Rev. Allen B. Clarkson, rector of the Church of the Good Shepherd in Augusta, All Saints' was unofficially organized in June, 1950, when a small group of interested Beech Island citizens met to discuss feasibility and plans. Present for this initial meeting were Mr. and Mrs. Paul H. Dunbar, Jr., Mr. and Mrs. Guy Hurlbutt, Mr. and Mrs. John B. Hill, Mrs. Chester Cromwell, Miss Elise Wilson, Mrs. John R. Hall, Sr., Mrs. William Walker, Dr. and Mrs. Linwood Morris, Mrs. Ike Jones, Mrs. William Crowson, Mrs. Leroy Simkins, Miss A. A. Dunbar, Mr. Paul H. Dunbar, Sr., the Rev. A. B. Clarkson, and the Rev. Michael J. Kippenbrock, then rector of St. Thaddeus' Church, Aiken, S. C. Only six of this group were Episcopalians, with none of the six being men. This was the first obstacle to confront the group, since the organization could not be made official until there were some men to serve as officers of the mission. It was decided to begin having services each Sunday evening, and that Mr. Kippenbrock would organize and conduct a class for instruction looking toward confirmation. This class was successful, and on January 14, 1951, Bishop John J. Gravatt, making his first visitation to the Church, confirmed Messrs. Guy Hurlbutt, Paul H. Dunbar, Jr., John B. Hill, and William Walker; and these four, together with Mr. Leroy Simkins, a Presbyterian, were constituted the first Bishop's Committee for All Saints'. Mr. Hurlbutt, a former Baptist minister, was also appointed lay reader, with permission to give addresses of his own preparation. The first officers of All Saints' reported in January, 1952, were: warden, Guy R. Hurlbutt; secretary, Paul H. Dunbar; treasurer, J. B. Hill; The Rev. M. J. Kippenbrock, priest-in-charge.

Another problem confronting the original group was a place to meet for services. This, however, was quickly solved when permission was granted the Episcopal group to use the old Beech Island Presbyterian property, which had not been in use for some years. This permission was given by the Presbytery meeting in Congaree. Leadership in the form of a pastor was not a problem. Mr. Kippenbrock and Mr. Clarkson alternated in serving the new Church until the fall of 1952 when Mr. Kippenbrock assumed sole responsibility for the evening services at All Saints'. He traveled about 40 miles round trip for each of these services, and often the service at All Saints' was his sixth for the day. Following the establishment of the Savannah River Project and the increased work at St. Thaddeus' Church in Aiken, Mr. Kippenbrock was relieved of his duties at Beech Island when Bishop Gravatt was able to secure the services of the Right Rev. Robert E. Gribbin to serve both All Saints' and St. Bartholomew's Church in North Augusta. He did this until the fall of 1953 when Bishop Gravatt was able to secure the services of the Rev. Forbes Ross de Tamble to serve All Saints' and St. Bartholomew's. Mr. de Tamble was priest-in-charge from the fall of 1953 until August, 1955. From this time until December of 1955, the Church was without a rector, the services being conducted by the lay readers of All Saints' and St. Bartholomew's, with the Rev. Charles F. Schilling of St. Paul's, Augusta, coming out each first Sunday evening for Communion. In December, 1955, the Rev. Hampton Price assumed the charge of St. Bartholomew's and All Saints', and is still serving in that capacity. All Saints' started with thirteen members and in 1956 has 21 communicants. With these, there are some ten members of other faiths who are regular worshippers, and who are quite active in the work of the Church and the Woman's Auxiliary.

The building occupied by All Saints' Church is a simple and quaint structure erected in 1836, an ideal place of worship. It formerly housed the Beech Island Presbyterian Church, which was organized in 1829. It has recently been sold to us by the Congaree Presbytery at a very nominal figure. It was in this lovely, colonial style Church that Ellen Axson, daughter of its pastor, was baptized. She later became the first Mrs. Woodrow Wilson. It is also interesting to note that Dr. Joseph Wilson, father of Woodrow Wilson, was once an elder in this old Presbyterian Church. An important arm of the Church is its Woman's Auxiliary. Similar groups throughout the State have assisted in the purchase of the cross, candlesticks, vases, communion services and other equipment for the Church.

ATONEMENT, BLACKSBURG
Established 1883

In 1883, it was reported that the great missionary of the up-country, the Rev. J. D. McCollough, had secured a lot at "Black's Station" on the Air Line Road and was already collecting material on it with which to build a Church. In 1884, he reported three communicants, public worship six times, and in 1885 that the cornerstone of the Church had been laid. In 1886, the mission was reported under the name "The Church of the Atonement, Black's Station"; the Church building was now enclosed; it was chiefly the work of the congregation. The work progressed slowly but the missionary and the little congregation persevered. In 1889, the Church was still unfinished but "an organ and a carpet, both of excellent quality" had been provided by the congregation. The minister reports good congregations through these early years. The communicants in 1894 numbered 16, the mission having begun with two. At this time, a brass cross and Bishop's chair were added, and the Church was improved, especially a masonry foundation. In 1896, the Rev. R. A. Lee assisted Mr. McCollough in the mission in what was then called not "Black's Station" but "Blacksburg." He was killed by lightning on July 16, 1896, on Rich Mountain— a most promising career ended. The Rev. R. W. Anderson became minister-in-charge in 1897 (for only a year); Mr. A. Fripp was warden, and Dr. William Anderson, secretary and treasurer. There were now only occasional services. Mr. John Beean, a candidate, acted as lay reader. The Rev. B. B. Sams held services in August and September, 1908. After this the Rev. C. W. Boyd took charge for a brief time. The Rev. G. C. Williams was appointed to the charge September, 1900, and served until November, 1904. After a period when only occasional services were held, the Rev. J. O. Babin took charge, 1907. He was succeeded by the Rev. Thomas Tracy Walsh in 1909. Mr. Walsh served the mission continuously until 1940. Dr. William Anderson was warden all these years. The Rev. Cyril N. L. Sturrup succeeded Dr. Walsh in 1940, with Dr. Victor M. Roberts, warden, B. F. Darst, treasurer, and James Whisonant, secretary. After Mr. Sturrup had served for about two years, the mission was vacant with occasional services until the Rev. William C. Cravner took charge in 1944, and until 1946; then another vacancy until the Rev. M. J. Hatchett assumed charge in 1952. This church became dormant in 1956, the members transferring to the Incarnation, Gaffney.

ALL SAINTS', CALHOUN FALLS
Established 1902 (Extinct)

At about the turn of the century, the Rev. O. T. Porcher took under his pastoral care with characteristic missionary zeal the few Church families residing at Calhoun Falls in Abbeville County, giving some services there while in charge of the Church in Greenwood. Almost immediately, a Church building was contemplated. After determined efforts and many appeals, it was begun. On the 23rd of December, 1902, when Bishop Capers made his fire visitation, he held service with Mr. Porcher, preached, and confirmed three persons. He found there a chapel nearly finished. By Mr. Porcher's zealous efforts and the final gift of $100.00 by the Church Building Fund, the work was finished, the cost a little over $500.00. The mission now in 1903 became a regular mission (unorganized) of the diocese, with the name All Saints. There were four families and eight communicants. The Church was blown down in 1903, but the following year, a new and better Church on a better lot was built. An organ was now presented to the Church. In 1909, through the generosity of the St. Michael's branch of the Woman's Auxiliary, the chancel of All Saints was greatly improved. Three families made up the major part of the congregation—the Norwoods, the Bakers, and the Calhouns. Mr. Porcher removing to Darlington in midsummer, 1912, the Rev. C. H. Jordan took charge, continuing until the Rev. W. S. Holmes came in 1917, serving until 1919. The effort to establish the Church now came to an end. In about 1919, the Church was sold to the Presbyterians in the community. The little Church (1955) is still standing.

GRACE CHURCH, CAMDEN
Established 1830
(See Dalcho, p. 393)

Since Dalcho has very little to say about the beginning of Church work in Camden, let us go back for our beginning. The town of Camden was laid out in 1760. It was then a part of St. Mark's Parish. Dalcho makes Charles Woodmason the first rector of St. Mark's. Strictly, this seems to be an error. In 1757 the Assembly created a missionary post in the upper part of St. Mark's. Charles Woodmason, who had lived in Charleston and in Prince Frederick's Parish, a merchant and also a civil officer, determined to seek orders and apply for the position. He went to England, was ordained, and licensed to South Carolina in 1766. He was duly appointed to the missionary post, and after holding services a few times at various places, including St. Mark's, he arrived at Pine Tree Hill (Camden) on September 16, 1766. For nearly six years, he did a remarkable missionary work in the whole region northward to Cheraw and the North Carolina line, from the Pee Dee to the Congaree, the work centering at Pine Tree. However, nothing of a permanent character resulted from Woodmason's labors. The next minister at Camden was the Rev. T. S. Drage, who came about 1772 from St. Luke's Church, Salisbury, N. C.

From the pen of the Rev. John Kershaw we have this interesting story of these early days. "The writer has in his possession, temporarily, a volume containing the Prayer Book of the Church of England, the Holy Scriptures of the Old and New Testaments, including the Apochrypha, and the Psalms in Metre with musical settings all bound together. It bears the date of 1636. Pinned to the fly-leaf is a statement in the handwriting of the late Dr. James A. Young of Camden whom I knew well and whose writing I am also familiar with, in which it is said that the volume was used in the Episcopal Church in Camden prior to the Revolutionary War by the Rev. Theodorus Drage, missionary of the S. P. G.; that when the British in 1780 occuppied as barracks the Church building, Miss Mary Kershaw entered the Church and carried away the volume, according to her statement to him, Dr. Young; that it remained for many years in her home, which was afterwards the rectory of Grace Church, and where, after her death, it remained also many years, and whence it came into my hands. My father more than once repeated its history to me, being perfectly familiar with it through having lived with Mary Kershaw, his aunt, and hearing the story from her. Dr. Young was a contemporary of this lady and had the story from her own lips. Of recent years, there has been recovered to Grace Church a large lot of land on which the pre-Revolutionary Church stood, surrounded by a cemetery, where, in the writer's youth, there were still remaining several family burial places. In the near vicinity are the remains of the foundations of the Presbyterian Church of a later date, with a number of graves surrounding it. In the Digest of the S. P. G. Records 1701-1892, p. 24, the name of Mr. Drage appears, with an extract from a letter of his dated February 28, 1771, in which he says he had collected the Church of England people into about forty congregations, or has as many preaching places where I meet them. His field of operations covered a territory 180 miles in length and 120 in breadth. He wrote from Rowan County, N. C., but Camden would fall easily within the territory he served. Camden was incorporated in 1760, the oldest interior incorporated town in the State, and some of its early settlers were Church of England folk. These facts, taken together, go far to establish the certainty that there was a Church of our faith in Camden prior to the Revolution. Camden suffered much during the Revolution and the British occupation, and it is not surprising that it required twenty-five or thirty years to reorganize a Church there after the War was over."

With the risk of some repetition, we next quote from a sketch by Mr. J. S. K. deLoach (Piedmont Churchman, November, 1932): "The first Church of England in Camden was on a corner lot 'near Mr. Nivon's grave' according to the Church record. As we know the minister at the time, but when Charleston was taken during the Revolution, he left for England and was never heard of again [sic]. His book and manuscript were left with Col. Kershaw and were burned with Col. Kershaw's library. It is also stated that one of his Prayer Books was saved. It is not amiss to say here that this Book of Common Prayer was owned by the Rev. John Kershaw, rector of St. Michael's Church in Charleston, and after his death it was given to Grace Church by his desire and put in the hands of the Rev. E. Harriman Harding, by the writer of this article who placed it with the other records of the Church. When Cornwallis entered Camden, the Church was torn down by the British officers and huts were built for barracks for their soldiers. The glebe land on the lower side of Broad Street was then given to the Episcopal Church, but a building was never put there. After Mr. Drage left, a Presbyterian, Mr. Logue, used the Church building until it was destroyed by the British in the manner stated above." For many years after the Revolution, the Church in Camden was dormant. (Cf. *Monthly Record*, December, 1872.)

For the next period in the history of this Church, we quote again now from a sketch by J. J. Pringle Smith, registrar of the diocese (1884-1887). "In this year (1808) the Episcopalians obtained a charter and a subscription of money, material, labor, etc. to the amount of $2,365.00. But for some unexplained reasons no collections appear to have been made. On the election in 1812 of the Rev. Theodore Dehon to the Episcopate, he turned his attention to this infant Church and made repeated visitations. The congregation being too small to support a settled rector the Bishop induced them to resort to lay-reading. This was attended with happy effect and soon after the Rev. Andrew Fowler was appointed missionary by the Protestant Episcopal Society for the Advancement of Christianity in South Carolina. In 1813 he reported the baptism of one adult and seven children—also communicants four. There was no stated place of worship (the services were held in the Court House). Partly by means of missionaries and partly by lay-reading, the services of the Church were continued during the Episcopate of Bishop Dehon. But at his death the bond of union between the small flock seems to fail and its members were dispersed. We hear again of only occasional services for some years."

"In 1827-30 a new movement was made, meetings were held of those interested and a correspondence was had with Bishop Bowen. (Such a meeting was held on January 27, 1830, in the Council Chamber presided over by Col. Jas. H. Deas, H. G. Soper, secretary. Present: Dr. W. E. Anderson, Samuel Boykin, John Cantey, James Cantey, M. I. Wheeler, David Sprook, David E. Reed.) The Bishop with his accustomed zeal drew up a subscription paper, appending his own name with a liberal donation. The Rev. Edward Phillips urged by the Bishop began in 1830 a mission, in which he was aided by the Advancement Society. He reached Camden in July, when some of the citizens were absent at the north and some at other summer residences. The Presbyterian minister who was to go northward for the summer very kindly invited Mr. Phillips to his pulpit, but as the object of the Missionary was to build up and increase his own Church, to expose his ministry to any charge or even suspicion of attempting to make proselytes, he obtained the use of the Masonic Hall. In this building divine service was held on the morning of each Lord's Day and in the afternoon in a school room in Kirkwood, a suburb of the town. The attendance was not very encouraging. But as the winter approached the numbers increased, several children were brought to baptism and the prospects brightened. On Mr. Phillip's return to Charleston he could report that a congregation had been organized, an Act of Incorporation obtained from the Legislature and that application would soon be made for admission to the Convention. It was admitted under the name of Grace Church in February, 1831. Mr. Phillips was unanimously requested to become rector. For this purpose which seemed important and had acquired great interest for him, he resigned as Domestic Missionary and the care of St. Stephen's Chapel, Charleston, and undertook the charge to which he had been thus called. The first and leading object was the erection of a Church building. A site was procured on Broad Street at a cost of about $800.00, and the subscription list (money, materials, etc.) exceeding $3,000.00, the building was begun. The cornerstone was laid by the rector, January 29, 1831. One of the papers deposited was as follows:

" 'This Corner Stone of the Protestant Episcopal Church, by name Grace Church, was laid in the town of Camden, S. C. on a lot of land purchased from Joshua Reynolds and is situated on the west side of Broad, 66 feet south of DeKalb Street. The ceremony of depositing the Corner Stone was performed by the Rev. Edward Phillips, rector, assisted in the services of Psalmody by the Handel and Haydn Society this day January 29, 1831'.

" 'At the last annual meeting of the Legislature, and Act of Assembly was passed by which John Boykin, Samuel Boykin, John Cantey, Daniel Carpenter, James Doby, Benjamin S. Elmore, Rev. Edward Phillips, Edward Anderson, and James S. Deas were incorporated under the name and title of the "Vestry and Wardens of Grace Church Camden." Samuel Freeman, principal Architect had contracted to build this Church of brick, in the Gothic style, having a square turret and belfrey in front sixty feet (60) in length, by thirty-eight (38) in breadth for the sum of two thousand ($2,000-.00) dollars, and Ralph Johnson, carpenter, contracted to furnish the woodwork necessary for the same for the sum of fifteen hundred dollars ($1,500.00). The whole building to be completed within the current year.' " (Cf. also Gospel Messenger, Vol. XIII, p. 194.)

The first service in the Church was on July 1, 1832. There were 46 pews. The women's sewing society gave an organ and a bell. Handsome donations were made by individuals of Charleston including a Bible by Mr. Bentham. The communion silver consisted of two chalices, a salver, a paten, and a baptismal bowl. The Church was consecrated by Bishop Bowen, assisted by the Rev. C. E. Gadsden, D.D. and the rector, on November 14, 1832, when sixteen persons were confirmed. The total cost of the Church with decorations was a little less than $6,000.00. Within two years the entire debt of the Church was liquidated and "the temporal and spiritual condition of the Church improving". After this the the Church lost somewhat by "emigration to the west", but there were replacements and the Church continued to grow. The Parish library numbered 350 volumes. Mr. Phillips' useful ministry ended in 1842 when he was succeeded by the Rev. Francis P. Lee, coming from Florida. There were now 40 communicants and 32 families. The Rev. Thomas F. Davis became rector in 1847. He was made Bishop of the diocese in 1853 but continued as rector until 1867. He was the first bishop to receive a regular support from the diocese. His son, the Rev. T. F. Davis, Jr., became assistant rector in 1855. His labors were not confined to this parish; he did much missionary work over the diocese. The Convention of the diocese met in this Church in 1857. The parish felt the healthful influence of the presence of the diocesan seminary in Camden during the period of its life (1857-68), the professors assisting in the services and the students doing missionary work in the environs. The Rev. T. F. Davis, Jr., died in 1865 deeply mourned.

In 1857 $5,000.00 was subscribed for a new Church and in 1860 work was begun in making of bricks, $10,000.00 having then been subscribed. The war seems to have entirely dissipated this effort until after the burning of the Church on the night of May 29, 1867. The Rev. John Johnson, having succeeded Bishop Davis, was rector at this time, having served the previous year as deacon. The Church records and most of the furniture were saved but the Church was a total loss as also the organ and the bell. All the evangelical churches offered the use of their buildings. For the following summer and winter twice a Sunday services were held in the Baptist Church except the fourth Sunday when service was held in the Methodist Church in the afternoon. In March, 1868, the Pine Grove Academy was leased and services held in it until the new Church was built. Steps were soon taken to erect the Church on a new lot more centrally located. The women and children in little more than a year contributed a thousand dollars, the children also gave books and a marble font. The contract for the Church was let in 1870, and work begun in October—a plain brick building, 300 sittings, Gothic in style. The Rev. John Johnson resigned in December of this year and was succeeded by the Rev. J. S. Kidney on April 11th following, serving only a few months in 1871. The Church was given an "English granite font" from Hagley Chapel, All Saints' Parish. The first sermon in the new Church was Bishop Davis's own last sermon, on November 19, 1871. He was assisted in the service by the Revs. John Johnson and F. Bruce Davis. His funeral was held in the Church just two weeks later on December 4th. The next rector was the Rev. B. F. Dunkin Perry. The Rev. F. Bruce Davis while never rector of Grace Church often officiated. He died January 21, 1873. The new Church was consecrated by Bishop Howe on May 7, 1873. (Cf. Description of this Church. *Monthly Record,* June, 1873.) Mr. Perry died on January 13, 1874, and the Rev. James W. Miles became rector temporarily, the Rev. Edward R. Miles following him as permanent rector, serving until 1879. Then the Rev. C. I. LaRoche (1879-81) and the Rev. William J. Alger (1881-84.)

The Rev. James M. Stoney became rector in August, 1884, continuing until his death May 19, 1897. He was not only a beloved pastor but a missionary holding services in the country at Swift Creek Chapel, built in 1888, and also in a chapel four miles east of Camden built about the same time at Malvern Hill. He later started the Church at Hagood. Then followed the Rev. William B. Gordon until he resigned May 1, 1912. The officers in 1898 were E. B. Cantey and A. D. Kennedy, wardens; W. A. Ancrum, secretary and treasurer; deputies to Convention, Edward Cantey, E. M. Boykin, A. D. Kennedy, and P. T. Villipigue. Mr. Gordon continued services at Malvern Chapel for many years. In 1905 triple windows were placed in the sanctuary in memory of Bishop Davis and his two sons, the Revs. T. F. Davis, Jr. and F. B. Davis. The first two were rectors of this Church and the last was associated with it in much service. Another window in the nave commemorates the thirteen years of service as rector of the Rev. J. M. Stoney. The children of the Sunday School about this time placed a marble tablet in the Church in memory of the lately lamented superintendent, Edgar S. Vaux. A new organ was installed in 1911. A small parish house of wood was built near the Church about this time. After his resignation Mr. Gordon became *rector-emeritus* until his death on March 28, 1921, continuing until 1917 to serve Malvern Hill Chapel and St. Philip's, Bradford Springs. The Rev. F. H. Harding was rector from the fall of 1912 until the spring of 1924. In 1913 Mr. Cantey and Mr. Kennedy were still the wardens, C. J. Shannon, Jr., secretary, and D. A. Boykin, treasurer. A splendid new rectory was built at this time. In 1915 a mission Sunday School was organized in the lower part of the city. A litany desk was given in 1916 and at this time a new heating plant was installed at a cost of $1,000.00. The Rev. I. deL. Brayshaw became rector September 1, 1924, leaving in the fall of 1928 when the Rev. Albert New supplied services for two months before the Rev. C. Gregg Richardson became rector until he retired because of ill health July, 1932. It was at this time the modernly equipped parish house was built adjoining the Church. The wardens at this time were C. H. Yates and D. A. Boykin; secretary, James de Loach, Jr.; treasurer, John M. Villipigue, lay reader, J. S. H. Clarkson. The Rev. Francis H. Craighill followed as rector, serving until 1935, then the Rev. Maurice Clarke became rector February 1, 1936. In this year choir stalls were placed in memory of the Rev. W. B. Gordon and also a memorial window was dedicated (May 10) in memory of Col. William M. Shannon and his wife, Henrietta McWillie. During the second World War the student pilots of the Southern Aviation School were often entertained by the Church. After nearly eleven years of service the rector, the Rev. Maurice Clarke, D.D., died on December 4, 1946. He had attained much distinction especially in the field of religious education. He was succeeded by the Rev. Stiles B. Lines, June, 1947.

ST. MARK'S, CHESTER
Established 1857

The first services of the Church in what was then called Chesterville are related in connection with Immanuel Church at Landsford in Chester District (see *in loco*). Its rector, Rev. R. D. Shindler, reports holding three services in the Court house in Chesterville in 1844. In 1848, the Rev. Richard S. Seely who had succeeded Mr. Shindler reports 14 services in the Court House. He resigned as rector of Immanuel in this year but was reelected in August 9, 1854, and continued work in this district until 1855. At this time Mr. Seely conducted a school in Chesterville and reports holding 37 services in his school house. Later he served in Laurens and then as assistant in St. Thomas and St. Dennis. The day before Mr. Seely's reelection Bishop Davis, making a visitation in company with the Rev. R. P. Johnson, held a service in the Court House with a large congregation. He remarked "The prospects of the Church which had almost entirely sunk, seem again to revive". In 1855, Mr. Seely makes the first separate annual report of the Church in Chesterville under the title, "St. Peter's Church, Chesterville": Communicants ten, families 13, services 24. Chester now begins to supersede the Church at Landsford in Chester District. In this same year the Rev. J. D. Gibson took charge under appointment by the Bishop.

He reports only three communicants at this time and these much discouraged. For the first time plans were now adopted to build a Church to cost about $2,000.00. On November 17, 1856, Bishop Davis visited Chester (no longer called Chesterville) and preached in the Methodist Church, finding a "fair prospect" for establishing the Church. The building of the Church was about to begin.

In February, 1857, Mr. Gibson reports the organization of a new parish in Chester with the name St. Mark's—thus the name St. Peter yielded to that of St. Peter's evangelist. St. Mark's was admitted into union with the Convention at the same time. "A handsome church" was in process of erection to cost $2,700.00—Norman Gothic, 60 x 30 feet. The Rev. A. F. Olmsted succeeded Mr. Gibson January, 1858. A year later he moved from Yorkville and became resident in Chester. At this time there were only five communicants and eight families but the average attendance was 50. This new Church was consecrated on October 7, 1860, by Bishop Davis, the Rev. J. D. McCollough preached, the rector with Rev. Messrs. Walker and Obear taking part, and at the evening service six were confirmed. The Rev. Julius J. Sams succeeded Mr. Olmsted officiating a part of the war years and was rector 1866-67. The Rev. R. P. Johnson held services for a few months in 1869. Then the Rev. A. R. Stuart succeeded (1869-71) and found strong prejudice against the Church and the building unfortunately located on the outskirts of the city. The Rev. W. H. Campbell was in charge from 1872 to 1875. Mr. Johnson returned in 1875 to serve until 1878, assisted latterly by Rev. E. C. Steele who took charge in 1878. The Rev. J. D. McCollough gave one service a month from December, 1878, a "zealous lay reader holding services every other Sunday". At this time there were ten families with 15 communicants. On March 3, 1881, the Church was completely destroyed by a cyclone. Steps were immediately taken, under the new rector, Rev. Frank Hallam (1882-84), to build a new Church. It was completed and consecrated by Bishop Howe on August 17, 1883. The Bishop was assisted in the service by the Rev. Messrs. Prentiss and Hallam, the latter read the Sentence and Mr. Judd preached. Mr. John Forest Douglas read the Request. Mr. S. H. Mellichamp was lay reader. The Rev. E. N. Joyner (1885-88) was the next rector. Mr. Joyner was assisted by the Rev. T. D. Bratton for a few months. Next in charge was the Rev. J. G. Glass (1888-90), followed by the Rev. Benj. Allston (1890-96), then the Rev. J. W. C. Johnson (1898-1902).

In September, 1899, the former Church property of the Associate Reformed Presbyterian was purchased at a cost of $1,250.00 and occupied for the first time during a meeting of Convocation. Friends throughout the diocese and Chester assisted. After improvements on April 11, 1901, in the morning was held the third Consecration of a St. Mark's Church in Chester. The Rev. J. C. Johnes and Mr. Johnson, assisted Bishop Capers in the service. In the evening the Bishop preached again to an overflowing congregation. The old Church property on Pinckney Street was sold for $1,000.00, the proceeds to be used in obtaining a rectory. After about a year Mr. Johnson was succeeded by the Rev. H. O. Judd (1903-04), then came the Rev. H. C. Mazyck (1904-05) only for a few months. He was followed for a short time by the Rev. J. C. Johnes, and then by the Rev. J. O. Babin for a portion of the year 1906. Next came the Rev. William John Webster (January 1, 1907) whose rectorate was cut short by death, July 13, 1908. At last came a minister who was to stay a while, the Rev. Thomas Tracy Walsh, ten years from 1909. This was the longest rectorship to this date in the history of St. Mark's. The mission was admitted into union with Convention in 1909. The Church as a *parish* had been dormant since 1875 and so not in union with Convention. A pipe organ was installed during Mr. Walsh's first year. He was succeeded by the Rev. A. Rufus Morgan who took up his residence in Chester May 1, 1920, serving also from here first Lancaster and Gaffney and then in place of the latter Great Falls. At this time there were 26 communicants.

This was an era of progress. The budget was largely increased, and a rectory was secured. The mission of St. Mark's was organized into a parish in 1921 and admitted into union with the Convention as such, thus renewing a status it had lost about fifty years before. Mr. Morgan extended his work beyond parish limits especially in Hi-Y and Boy Scout work. The communicant list increased to 35. Mr. Morgan resigned in 1926 but gave services a year longer when the Rev. C. B. Lucas became rector. He was ordained priest in St. Mark's but left after only a year. Services were conducted again by Mr. Morgan and by the Rev. S. R. Guignard, the Rev. C. C. Fishburne succeeding in 1931. He was ordained priest in St. Mark's continuing as rector until 1935. The rectors since have been: T. P. Devlin, 1936-40; Julian S. Ellenburg, 1940-43, and 1945-46; Gardner Dinkins Underhill, 1943-44; Harold Thomas, 1947-50; R. Hampton Price, 1952-55; Louis C. Melcher, Jr., 1956-.

IMMANUEL CHURCH
LANDSFORD, CHESTER DISTRICT
Established 1843 (Extinct)

The Rev. R. D. Shindler became missionary of the Advancement Society in Chester and York Districts in May, 1843. His labors extended to the vicinity of Landsford not far from Rock Hill, in the main through the influence of Mr. Benjamin B. Johnson who with the Hon. J. S. Sitgraves deeded six or seven acres of land to Bishop Gadsden. Mr. Shindler reports that, beginning in May, he visited from house to house holding services 45 times until he was taken ill in September. Immanuel Church was organized in December, 1843, and a Church was soon built. The neighborhood was populous but the people generally poor. Many, chiefly of Irish extraction, were drawn to the Church having been in it in the "old country". The Church was admitted into union with the Convention in February, 1844, deputies elected being J. S. Sitgraves, B. B. Johnson, William Johnson, and R. S. Seely, the last attending. Mr. Shindler was elected rector. He was an active missionary, for 1844 reporting services, Landsford School house 21; Richardson Meetinghouse three; Republican Meetinghouse 24, Chesterville in the Court House, five; Providence near Court House, 17; in all including York, 97, for Negroes 43. The Rev. L. C. Johnson at this time also officiated in this field. The first service in Immanuel Church was on the 26th Sunday after Trinity, 1845. There were then 18 families, 12 white, six colored. Mr. Shindler resigned July 6, 1846, reporting the Church ready for consecration. The Rev. R. S. Seely became rector March, 1847, and resigned July, 1848. However, later he held the services from time to time until about 1856, having been again elected rector August 9, 1854. In 1851 the Rev. J. J. Roberts reports preaching to a large congregation at Immanuel. In 1855, Mr. Seely reports holding 24 services at "St. Peter's, Chesterville" and 12 at Immanuel the previous year. On his visitation this same year the Bishop found the Church "destitute". These final ministrations of Mr. Seely apparently mark the end of the active life of this Church. The Church edifice then in more or less ruin was still standing in 1868 and shortly after this time the Rev. E. C. Steele, deacon then at Rock Hill, planned to move the building to Rock Hill but we find no record that this was ever done. In connection with the Church was a graveyard in which were buried Mr. Benjamin Johnson, his wife who was a sister of the Rev. Thomas J. Young, assistant rector of St. Michael's, and a few others.

ST. JOHN'S, CLEARWATER
Established 1947

Church work in Clearwater commenced at a much earlier date than 1947, probably first near the middle of the last century (See "Horse Creek Valley Missions"). However, it is in 1947 that we find it listed in the Journal of the diocese as a separate organized mission with the name St. John. C. L. Emmons was then warden; D. P. Linyard, Jr., secretary; Mrs. W. H. Christian, treasurer. The work at Clearwater had gone on in all those previous years in connection with the missions Kaolin, Graniteville, Langley, Bath, and other places. The year 1947 was marked especially by a Vacation Bible School held in this year in Clearwater under Mrs. Odessa Babin from Hooker School in Mexico City, and Miss Elizabeth I. Brown, who was the worker in St. John's. The school was held in the community house. The next year, 1948, the Rev. Sidney E. Heath was priest-in-charge in connection with Graniteville. This year L. R. Sisk was warden, followed the next year by Olin Murphy. The Church was consecrated by Bishop Gravatt on April 28, 1949. The Rev. Walter W. Cawthorne succeeded the Rev. Mr. Heath in 1953, then the Rev. Thom Williamson supplied from February 1955 until May 1956. The Woman's Auxiliary is active. St. John's was admitted into union with the Convention as an organized mission in 1947. In 1955 Olin Murphy was lay reader and school superintendent, Frank Kelly the warden, J. A. Taylor, secretary, and Arthur L. Gibson, treasurer.

HOLY TRINITY, CLEMSON COLLEGE
Established 1899

Services were begun by the Rev. O. T. Porcher in 1893 at Fort Hill in the Mechanical Building belonging to Clemson College, which was then being established. Mr. Porcher also held services at Clemson College at the convict stockade as long as this continued. From 1894, he held one service every month at the College on the Sunday assigned to our Church, as well as the services at Fort Hill. In his report for 1900, Mr. Porcher relates: "On May 26, 1899, the cornerstone of the Chapel of the Holy Trinity near Clemson College was laid with appropriate religious ceremonies, and on Sunday afternoon, October 15th, on the occasion of the Bishop's [Capers] visit, the first service in the Church was held, although the building was incomplete. Confirmation was administered at this our first service." Several families were at this time transferred from St. Paul's, Pendleton, to Holy Trinity. Thus was the Church at Clemson permanently established. The Church was consecrated by Bishop Capers on December 3, 1899. He was assisted by the Rev. Messrs. Porcher and McCollough. There was a large congregation—students, professors, and others. The Bishop preached and administered the Holy Communion. He referred to the Lord's Table made by Dr. McCollough, the architect of the Church, and one of his grandsons as "one of the handsomest in the diocese". The total cost, with furniture, was $1,000.00. At this time, the Ladies' Guild and the Young Ladies' Chancel Guild were active. Services were three Sunday afternoons a month beside the service in the college chapel. Misses Nora and Mary Zimmerman of Glenn Springs were large contributors to the Church. From 1893 until 1913, all the students of Clemson were required to attend morning service on Sundays in the college chapel. Mr. Porcher conducted this service once a month or provided for it until he left Pendleton.

The Rev. B. M. Anderson, having succeeded Mr. Porcher in St. Paul's, Pendleton, now (1901) took charge of this Church which now became an "organized" mission of the diocese. Col. J. S. Newham was warden, and Dr. P. E. H. Sloan, treasurer. Mr. Anderson served only one year, Rev. Kirkman G. Finlay taking charge in September, 1902. He preached in the College chapel on the third Sundays. In 1903, there were 43 communicants. In 1907, R. E. Lee was warden, and Dr. Sloan, treasurer. Soon after Mr. Finlay's coming, the rectory was built, the work becoming more independent of Pendleton. Mr. Finlay left Clemson for Trinity, Columbia, in the fall of 1907. The following winter, services were supplied by E. B. Andrews, a candidate for holy orders. The Rev. Lyttleton E. Hubard took charge in 1909, serving until the fall of 1910. The Rev. R. M. Marshall succeeded the next year and continued in charge until 1918. He introduced the vested choir. The Rev. James M. Stoney succeeded him. Mr. Stoney served as chaplain in Germany for the year commencing September, 1918, returning after a year. He removed to Alabama in the spring of 1921. He was succeeded by Rev. George E. DeWitt Zachary.

The Church became a part of the diocese of Upper South Carolina in 1922. The wardens now were C. C. Newman and Benjamin Freeman, the latter being also secretary and treasurer. After a vacancy of some months, the Rev. Capers Satterlee took charge of this work in 1926. The wardens now were F. H. H. Calhoun and W. W. Long, and treasurer, Mrs. W. W. Long. Under Mr.

Satterlee, considerable funds were raised. The National Council gave $5,000.00 from legacies, the Church Building Fund $1,000.00, and later loaned $3,000.00, then $19,000.00 was given in the State. With these means, the Bishop Finlay parish house was built, and "the Church almost made new". Prof. R. E. Lee was architect of the parish house. The Rev. Donald E. Veale succeeded Mr. Satterlee in 1935. The rectory especially was much improved under Mr. Veale. He was succeeded by the Rev. John A. Pinckney in 1941-48. The Rev. R. Emmett Gribbin followed, 1948-53; then the Rev. Robert L. Oliveros, 1954. In 1953, both the Church and the parish house underwent extensive repairs with new light fixtures. A silver chalice was given in memory of a Clemson graduate of 1902. The organizations of Holy Trinity in 1955 besides the vestry include the Woman's Auxiliary, student vestry and the Canterbury Club. The wardens at this time were Robert W. Moorman and Walter Lowry; treasurer, I. V. Trively; secretary, James P. Winter.

ALL SAINTS', CLINTON
Established 1950

The first services of this Church of which we find record were held by the Rev. W. E. Callender in 1908. He reported that he had organized a mission here, that a lot had been donated by Mr. George Ellis, and $200.00 was in hand for building a Church. There were 12 communicants reported. This "mission" did not become permanent. Mr. Callender left the field the year after. Among those who in these early days sought diligently to establish the Church here were Mrs. George Ellis and Mrs. Julia C. Baker. Three of those confirmed in Laurens in 1912 were residents of Clinton. The Rev. S. R. Guignard of Newberry and Laurens renewed the mission in 1915 when we find it first listed as an "unorganized mission" in May, 1915. There were four families and two services. There was no Church building, the services having been held in the A. R. P. Church. The next year, the Rev. C. H. Jordan had charge and reported 21 services. Then the following year, the Rev. W. S. Holmes was in charge. M. P. Hazel was the treasurer in 1919. Mr. Holmes left in 1922. He was succeeded briefly in 1923 by Rev. Thomas L. Ridout. From this time, the mission was suspended for many years. It will be noted that in these earlier years, it acquired no name. A new day came. The Rev. E. B. Clippard, the first priest-in-charge of the mission in Clinton after its rebirth, writing in the spring of 1953, tells of the new beginning: "Less than three years ago (1950), a young man with a new hope in his heart telephoned to Bishop Gravatt and said, 'Bishop, you don't know me, but my wife and I want to be confirmed and build an Episcopal Church in Clinton.' He found that already a small group of Episcopalians had met together for a baptism and prayer service held by the Rev. John Pinckney. The leaders of this group were Mr. Wallace Barnhill and Mr. and Mrs. Gordan Goodale, who have since left Clinton, much to the regret of the entire congregation. Together, they all formed the nucleus for All Saints' Church, which became an organized mission in May, 1950. The young man, Mr. R. Michael Turner, became the first warden. In September, 1951, the Rev. Edwin B. Clippard was made priest-in-charge." For this year, the other officers of All Saints' were: secretary, Kendrick Waller; treasurer and lay reader, John S. Glover. Soon after the Church was organized, it had the benefit of the guiding care and ministrations of Bishop R. E. Gribbin by which the congregation was strengthened and consolidated. Then under Mr. Clippard's able leadership, the Church prospered. In 1952, there were 24 communicants. The services of the Church for the first two years were held in the Lutheran Church.

A generous appropriation by the diocese with the gifts of the congregation made possible the purchase of the A. R. P. Church of Clinton. It was moved ten blocks to the Church lot at the corner of Calvert and South Holland Streets where it was remodelled. The lot was partly the gift of Mrs. James A. Dick of Raleigh, N. C. Brick for the new foundation of the Church was given by Miss Susan Guignard of Columbia and Mr. W. B. Ellis, Jr., of Greenville. The altar, lectern, and prayer desk are all three the work of Mr. Lester of Newberry—the first being a copy of that in Epiphany, Laurens, made by the Rev. Dr. J. D. McCollough. Thus is this great missionary of the up-country associated with another of the very many churches with which he is connected in the Piedmont. The first service was held amidst much joy at midnight on Christmas Eve, 1952, when "The love of the people of Clinton was poured out toward this new group." Mr. Clippard continued in charge until the end of the year 1953. The Rev. Clyde Lambert Ireland assumed charge in 1954.

CHRIST CHURCH, COLUMBIA
Established 1858 (Extinct)

The Church of the Mediator was promptly succeeded by Christ Church which was organized in 1858. The Rev. J. Maxwell Pringle, having resigned the Mediator, became missionary in charge, and after the admission of the Church into Convention in June, 1858, rector; its deputies to this Convention being T. B. Clarkson, G. M. Calhoun, James Steedman, L. A. Austin. The next year the deputies were R. H. Goodwyn, William Wallace, and J. H. Baldwin. On Saturday, January 15, 1859, the cornerstone of the Church was laid. The location was on the southeast corner of Blanding and Marion Streets, in the block west of the present Church of the Good Shepherd. The lot cost $4,000.00. The rector expresses his thanks for aid from Charleston, especially the Church of the Holy Communion, St. Paul's, and St. Andrew's churches. He deplores the death on August 8, 1958, of William Clarkson, a generous founder and patron of the Church. He was associated as was Mr. Pringle with the Mediator the three preceding years, so we may conclude that Christ Church was really the successor of the Mediator. The spirit and purpose of the latter lived on in the former and was yet again to be reembodied a generation later in the Good Shepherd. There were 21 families connected with this Church at this time.

The Church was consecrated by Bishop Davis on April 12, 1860. Besides the rector the following clergymen took part in the service: the Revs. C. C. Pinckney (who preached), R. W. Barnwell, C. P. Gadsden, E. E. Bellinger, W. H. Hanckel. The edifice was tasteful and appropriate, "of the Gothic order and form, with open roof; and both externally and internally, is a handsome and convenient place of worship. Beautifully situated at the corner of two of the most attractive streets of the city (Blanding and probably Marion) and shaded by those luxuriant oaks and elms for which Columbia is celebrated, it presents a most inviting appearance." The church seats 600 persons. Mr. Walker of Columbia was the architect. It was ranked with Trinity, being "two of the most beautiful places of worship to be found in the state." There were signs of outward prosperity, as well as gratifying evidences of spiritual life and energy. The contract price of the Church was $14,900.00. A notable event of the year 1861 was the second preliminary meeting of the Church in the Confederate States, held in Christ Church beginning October 16. Nine Southern Bishops and many delegates attended. The Bishops preached nightly and filled many pulpits of the city on Sunday. Bishop Davis confirmed ten persons in the Church on July 6, 1862. At this time the worshippers in the Church were greatly increased by the presence in the city of many war refugees from the lower parishes of the diocese and from without the state. In 1864, as a result of a sermon by the rector at the request of the vestry, $10,000.00 was raised and the debt on the Church paid. The war almost literally blotted out this parish. It shared the fate of the beautiful city when it was reduced to ashes by Sherman's army on February 17, 1865. It was described as "the largest and handsomest church in the diocese outside of Charleston." With organ and furnishings the loss was estimated at $30,000.00, considered by the committee of the Convention of the diocese as the heaviest blow by the war to its welfare. Mr. Pringle continued some services for a time. On August 26, 1866, he presented five for confirmation at a joint service at Trinity Church. He did missionary work about Columbia, especially in a chapel at Millwood, the old home of General Hampton, but the parish in two or three years ceased to exist. For a time in 1881 the chapel of Christ Church was used by Rev. Mr. Babbitt for some of the first services of St. Luke's Church.

CHURCH OF THE GOOD SHEPHERD, COLUMBIA
Established 1883

After the destruction of Christ Church in 1865, except St. Luke's for Negroes, there was no effort to establish another Church in Columbia until 1883. The beginning of the Good Shepherd is well described by the Rev. E. A. Penick (now Bishop of North Carolina) when he was rector: "In this year [1882] there was in the north-eastern portion of the city of Columbia, a community composed largely of worthy people of limited means, machinists, mechanics and other rail-road employees with their families. It was thought that these could best be brought to the Church through some convenient provision for Church attendance in their section of the city. Trinity Church, because of its remoteness, could not meet the conditions of the case. Local work was necessary. A scheme of Cottage Services and Lectures was devised and carried out by the Assistant Rector of Trinity Church, the Rev. Harvey Orrin Judd, a most zealous and capable worker. There being no suitable building available, these services were held at various private houses in the neighborhood. From the outset, the attendance was good and the interest manifest. A Sunday School was soon organized by a few earnest women of Trinity Church, led by Miss Kate Hampton, Miss Lucy Pride Green, and Mrs. Peter B. Glass. These devoted labors were seconded by the efficient co-operation of Col. George Russell Talcott as Superintendent. The enrollment steadily increased. The meetings were held in the Columbia Male Academy, 1883. A little later, an Industrial School for women and girls was established in the neighborhood. The workers associated with the first few years of this School's history were Mrs. John E. Bacon, Mrs. Mary Norton, Mrs. J. S. Coles, who were succeeded by Miss Lucy P. Green, Mrs. John B. Palmer, and Mrs. Southgate. Subsequently the School passed into the hands of Sister Marianna (Miss Anna Fickling) under whose management it continued until 1889. Towards the close of the year 1883 the necessity for a central church building became obvious. A lot on Barnwell Street, between Richland and Lumber (now Calhoun) Streets, was granted by a number of heirs in perpetuity of the former owner, Col. Thomas Taylor, with the stipulation that the adjacent Taylor Family Burying ground should receive the oversight and care of the church authorities. The design of the building, a wooden structure, and the supervision of its construction was under the care of Col. G. R. Talcott. The means for the erection and enclosure of the new church were contributed chiefly by the Charlotte, Columbia and Augusta Railroad Company, and by a few individuals. The cornerstone was laid in the spring of 1883 by the Rt. Rev. W. B. W. Howe, Bishop of South Carolina, assisted by the Rev. H. O. Judd. During the ensuing summer the superstructure was added."

The Rev. J. Foote had charge of the mission from November, 1884, until May, 1885, when the Church was completed and furnished. The Rev. A. R. Mitchell assumed charge October 1, 1885, having just been ordained deacon on September 20. The Church grew rapidly during the fifteen years of his ministry. The Ladies' Guild was organized early in 1886. In the spring of this year the Church became independent of the fostering care of Trinity Church, the necessary papers being signed by Rev. Peter J. Shand, rector of Trinity and Rev. H. O. Judd, assistant, and by Rev. Mr. Mitchell and laymen, George H. Talcott, Joseph H. Green, Thomas Bernard, Joseph H. Gay, R. Southgate, and Mr. Gordon. Bishop Howe thereupon approved the organization of the mission into a parish and it was recognized as such on April 16, 1886. The first vestry consisted of, wardens, George R. Talcott and Joseph H.

Green; and vestrymen, Thomas Bernard, Joseph H. Gay, R. Southgate and Mr. Gordon. After his ordination to the priesthood on the 19th of the following September the Rev. A. R. Mitchell was elected rector on a salary of $45.00 per month with $100.00 annually from the Board of Missions. The parish was admitted into union with the Convention May 3, 1888, the first deputies being G. R. Talcott, J. H. Green, Thomas Bernard, and Charles O. Brown. In 1886, a bell was donated and the next two years saw the building of a bell tower and the doubling of the seating capacity of the Church at a cost of $750.00. Also a house was built for the Industrial School. The parochial school which became an important factor in the life of the Church was organized in 1890 with Miss E. L. Blythewood as principal and Miss C. E. Thomas, assistant, with 70 pupils, and the next year a room was added to the school house. One fourth of the pupils were beneficiaries. In 1890, a guild for young women was organized called St. Agnes Guild, which became very active. A rectory lot opposite the Church was purchased ($1,500.00) in 1891 and a rectory completed in 1893 at a cost of $1,800.00. In 1891 a chapter of the Brotherhood of St. Andrew was organized.

In 1892 the rector began Church work on Arsenal Hill, resulting in St. Timothy's Church. For two years 1893-94 he also served St. Stephen's, Ridgeway. A branch of the Woman's Auxiliary was organized. In 1893 a beautiful chancel window depicting the Good Shepherd was installed, being a memorial. In 1894 a new school room was added; the school now having three teachers and 85 pupils. Quarterly parish meetings in the school house were a feature of parish life at this time. A chorister choir was instituted on Easter Day, 1894—one of the first in the diocese. The next year the chancel of the Church was remodeled and a robing room and annex added, a new organ installed on Easter Day, and a Boys Department of the Brotherhood of St. Andrew formed. In 1899 a question having arisen as to the rights of the parish to the Church lot, it was decided to move the Church and a lot was purchased on 1500 block of Blanding Street for $1,500.00. This almost synchronized with Mr. Mitchell's resignation the beginning of Lent, 1900, after fifteen years which saw the Church grow from a weak mission to a vigorous parish. The officers at this time were: C. M. Tew, C. O. Brown, wardens; Walter C. Thomas, secretary; G. M. Berry, treasurer; S. H. Mellichamp, lay reader. The Rev. William Postell Witsell, becoming rector June, 1900, immediately devoted his great energies with the congregation to the building of a new Church. The Church was built on plans by J. Hagood Sams, architect, with a building committee consisting of C. M. Tew, J. H. Sams, G. M. Berry, C. O. Brown, Edwin W. Robertson. The cornerstone was laid by Bishop Capers on St. Andrew's Day, 1900, and the first service was held in it, October 6, 1901. The Church was soon completed by the placing of many memorials and installing of a two-manual pipe organ, and the next year the parish resigned diocesan aid in its support. The diocesan council met in the Good Shepherd in 1904 and in the same year a rectory next east of the Church was acquired. The Church was consecrated on October 25, 1908. At this time the crypt of the Church was fitted up for the Sunday School. Mr. Witsell held his last service on Palm Sunday, 1909, going to Meridian, Miss., and exactly a year later he was succeeded by the Rev. Charles E. Woodson.

The year of vacancy with the development in the suburbs carried away many members, the rector himself organizing St. John's, Shandon. In June, 1914, Mr. Woodson resigned and went to Vicksburg, Miss. He was succeeded by the Rev. Edward Anderson Penick (later Bishop of North Carolina) coming in September. At this time the Every-Member Canvass was developed successfully, the Brotherhood of St. Andrew was reorganized, and the Sunday School was enlarged by the addition of an adult department. After the beginning of the war in 1916, the rector with the congregation engaged actively in work among the soldiers at Camp Jackson, the parish providing for their entertainment in the crypt of the Church. Mr. Penick resigned February 1, 1918, to become a chaplain in the army. Especially because of the urgency of the work among the soldiers, the Rev. Albert Sidney Thomas accepted the rectorship April 1, 1918, but continued only until the end of the year, being recalled to St. David's, Cheraw, immediately after the armistice of November 11. He was succeeded as rector immediately by Rev. Herbert F. Schroeter (1919-26). The Rev. Lewis N. Taylor was the next rector from 1926. September 1934 saw the completion of the parish house erected at a cost of $8,500.00. Mr. Taylor died on December 3, 1947. On December 6, 1953, a beautiful window was dedicated to the memory of this much beloved rector. It is located in the tower and visible from within the church by day and from without by night. Mr. Taylor was succeeded by the Rev. Eugene L. Nixon (1948-53), then in turn the Rev. Gale Dudley Webb (1953-54). The Rev. Ralph H. Kimball became rector December, 1954, serving until October, 1956. Walter C. Thomas retired in 1955 after

43 years treasurer, having also served for many years as warden and lay reader.

HOLY COMFORTER, COLUMBIA
(Formerly Trinity Chapel)
Established 1901

We are fortunate in having this valuable and authentic account of the beginning of this Church, being the report of the Rev. W. B. Sams, minister-in-charge, April 30, 1902: "Trinity Mission was started about June 1st, 1901, under the direction of Rev. C. Satterlee (rector of Trinity Church), assisted by the Rev. Harold Thomas [The mission was at first called St. Titus]. The Olympia Mills Company having promised $2,500.00 toward the erection of a brick chapel, on condition that the Bishop would raise $2,-500.00 more, the Bishop in conference with the rector of Trinity Church, decided at once to accept the proposition, and an appeal was soon made to the congregation to contribute to this worthy object. And, as a result, the Easter offering of Trinity Church was devoted to a Chapel Building Fund." The Rev. Churchill Satterlee, the rector of Trinity, went earnestly to work. A temporary shed was erected where the Rev. Harold Thomas held services every Sunday afternoon during the summer. The cornerstone of the chapel was laid July 21, 1901, and the first service held in it the following November 17th, when the chapel with a seating capacity of 500 was crowded. After this, services were held twice every Sunday. Mr. Thomas left the middle of the summer of 1901, and the Rev. W. B. Sams became minister-in-charge in October of this year. The Sunday School, with two sessions on Sundays, numbered 200. Deaconess A. J. Graham assisted Mr. Sams—coming to the work from Philadelphia in September. So was the work launched.

The Rev. Caleb B. Weed was now the minister. John P. Thomas, Jr., was the treasurer. A mission house was, in 1903, erected at a cost of $4,000.00. In 1904, the Rev. C. M. Niles, rector of Trinity, had taken charge. Deaconess Florence Pauline Jones had succeeded Deaconess Graham. The lay reader was Edward Andrews and treasurer Miss Jennie Gibbes. Rev. Samuel Moran became minister-in-charge in 1906. A branch mission was established at this time at Palmetto Mills. The Rev. K. G. Finlay, now rector of Trinity, succeeded Mr. Moran in charge, and so continued until Rev. Wilmer S. Poynor succeeded in 1910. The warden now was O. B. Hunter, the treasurer, Joseph E. Hare. At this time, with funds given the mission by Mrs. Satterlee and with the help of the mill, a cement walk and an iron fence were put in front of the chapel. The mission was admitted into union with the Convention in May 1912. In all these years, the mission carried on an extensive social as well as religious work under the deaconess. A large part of the support of the work came through the Mission House Board, composed of male communicants of Trinity Church. The Rev. P. J. Robottom succeeded Mr. Poyner in charge in 1916, but Mr. Finlay was again in charge the next year. In 1917, the Rev. A. W. Taylor took permanent charge. Mr. S. W. Minus was now superintendent of the Sunday School. Miss Virginia Singleton was secretary and treasurer. Under Mr. Taylor, his wife ably assisting, a very active settlement work was carried on; especially should be mentioned care for sick babies. Miss Virginia Singleton and Mrs. James R. Cain of Trinity were active assistants. The Rev. A. E. Evison succeeded Mr. Taylor in charge at the time of the division of the diocese.

Mr. Evison continued in charge of the mission until the spring of 1931, when he was succeeded by the Rev. A. Rufus Morgan. During these years, S. W. Minus was warden and H. A. Shipp was treasurer, having succeeded J. E. Hare. During these years, some of the social activities of the mission were taken over by the mill authorities. Soon after Mr. Morgan took charge, Miss Margaret Marshall, a U.T.O. worker, came to assist in the work; a Y.P.S.L. was formed, a girls' "Saturday Night Club", Boy Scouts, and other organizations. Mr. Morgan being rector of St. John's Church, Shandon, many of its members assisted in this mission, as well as members of Trinity Church, who established a useful "Loan Chest." In 1924, the congregation, for the first time, began to pay part of their minister's salary. After twelve years, Mr. Morgan was succeeded by the Rev. J. Kenneth Morris (becoming rector of St. John's) in 1941. Miss Mary A. Ramsaur, a U.T.O. worker, came to assist at this time, following Miss Marshall who went to St. Timothy's, Spartanburg. The Rev. Lewis N. Taylor succeeded Mr. Morris for about one year, 1944-45. On September 1, 1945, Rev. William A. Thompson took charge. On Sunday night, January 13, 1946, the congregation met and decided to petition the Convention for the privilege of changing its name. This was done the same month and the change authorized by the Convention, whereupon Trinity mission became the Church of the Holy Comforter, Columbia, Richland County. In 1950, Rev. Eugene L. Nixon succeeded Mr. Thompson, and after Mr. Nixon, in 1952 the Rev.

Walter W. Cawthorne assumed charge. In 1953, the warden was Paul R. McKelvey; secretary, Hamilton Young; treasurer, H. A. Shipp; Church school superintendent, James W. Player. At this time, there were 67 communicants. The Rev. Sidney E. Heath was the priest-in-charge in 1954-55. A new parish house was built in 1955, largely by a gift of the Young Peoples Advent offering.

CHURCH OF THE MEDIATOR, COLUMBIA
Established 1855 (Extinct)

It was not until 1855 that any attempt was made to establish a second Church in Columbia. Early in this year the Church of the Mediator was organized in this city, with six families, and was admitted into union with the Convention February 15, 1855. A "lecture room" was erected near the site of the proposed new Church, the Rev. J. Maxwell Pringle was called, and the first service held in the lecture room on Easter, 8th of April. The deputies to the Convention in February 1856 were W. S. Goodwyn, W. Clarkson, R. H. Goodwyn, H. P. Dougal. The Bishop visited the Church first August 12, 1855, and again on May 19 the year following when seven were confirmed. The rector reported 39 communicants in February, 1857, and services during the previous year 50 on Sundays and 52 on other days. On May 24, 1857, the Bishop visited the Church and again the following October 4, preaching at two services. The report of the rector, the Rev. J. M. Pringle, June, 1858, was for only a part of the previous year, stating he had recently accepted a call to Christ Church, Columbia. This seems to mark the end of the Mediator's short life although a resolution in the Convention, June 10, 1858, to remove the Mediator from the list of churches failed to pass, but nevertheless it then practically ceased to exist.

ST. ANNA'S, COLUMBIA
Established 1893

This work in East Columbia began under the name of St. Gabriel's in 1893. Here a very flourishing work was inaugurated under Miss Martha Parker with a day school and also a Sunday School of about one hundred each. A building was rented. In 1897, a neat chapel was given the mission principally by Miss Cole's Tuesday Missionary Bible Class in memory of Miss Anna Dulles Stille of Philadelphia, who had been a member of the class and a generous contributor to the colored work in South Carolina. In

her honor the name of the mission was changed from St. Gabriel's to St. Anna's. In 1902, Mrs. Stille of Philadelphia gave $6,-
000.00 to endow St. Anna's Chapel in memory of her daughter,
Anna Stille. At the time of the division of the diocese in 1922, this
mission was in charge of the Rev. J. B. Elliott, the Archdeacon.
In 1947 Rev. Francis G. Johnson assumed charge with Truesdell
Carr warden and Mrs. E. M. Johnson treasurer and school superintendent. In 1955 Rev. William F. O'Neal was priest-in-charge.

(See Part One, Sec. II and Part Two, Sec. II, Archdeaconries.)

ST. JOHN'S CHURCH, COLUMBIA
Established 1912

A few months after he had become rector of the Church of the
Good Shepherd in Columbia, in the fall of 1910, the Rev. Charles
E. Woodson organized a Sunday School in that section of Columbia called Shandon. Following upon this, about a year later on
October 15, 1911, he held the first service for St. John's congregation in the Knights of Pythias Hall on Devine Street. Propheti-
cally, Mr. Woodson's text was, "A great door and effectual is
opened." A meeting was held and preliminary steps were taken to
establish a Church. It was then determined to purchase a two-
thirds acre lot at the corner of Wheat and Holly Streets; also, a
Men's League was then formed with Mr. R. F. Jenkins, president.
St. John's was formally organized as a mission by Bishop Guerry
on January 21, 1912. Mr. E. R. Heyward was elected warden and
Mr. George B. Reeves, treasurer. In his first report for St. John's,
the Rev. Charles E. Woodson, minister, stated that there were 32
families with 44 communicants; Sunday School, seven teachers and
40 pupils. Steps were immediately taken toward the building of
a Church. The Church was admitted into union with the Convention May, 1912, the first deputies elected being C. B. Hipp
and J. H. Mallory, and the next year (1913) they were S. H. Mellichamp and G. B. Reeves. Mr. Woodson continued in charge until
his resignation June 1, 1914. During his last year, after October,
1913, he was assisted by the Rev. A. G. B. Bennett. The "mission"
was now organized into a "parish" and Mr. Bennett became the
first rector. The parish house was completed in this year at a
cost of $3,951.00. Until this time, the services had been held in a
second story hall. On the occasion of the first service in the parish
house, Mr. Bennett was ordained to the priesthood (October 20,

1915). He resigned in August, 1920. The communicants now numbered 142, the Church school, 80 pupils.

The Rev. Donald Miller became the second rector in March, 1921, continuing until September, 1922, when the Rev. G. Croft Williams became third rector. At this time the wardens were E. R. Heyward and J. H. Mallory; secretary, E. A. Woodruff; treasurer, H. A. Douglas; lay readers, E. R. Heyward, J. H. Mallory, S. H. Mellichamp. A beautiful stone church was built on the original lot, corner of Wheat and Holly Streets, in 1924-26. The first service was held in it on December 5, 1926. Dr. Williams continued as rector until the end of 1930. He was followed as rector by Rev. A. Rufus Morgan in February, 1931. This parish has always been blessed with groups of tireless workers, hence its continued growth. In 1930, the communicants had increased to 250. Mr. Morgan was succeeded by the Rev. J. Kenneth Morris in 1941. During Mr. Morris's absence in the service in the U. S. Army Intelligence, his place was filled for a short time by Rev. Henry C. Sartorio after December, 1943. The Rev. B. Duvall Chambers then succeeded Mr. Morris as rector for about two years. At Easter, 1945, the Church made the final payment of a mortgage for $30,000.00 which had been made in 1925. The names of the original building committee should be recorded: E. A. Woodruff, Pierre F. LaBorde, S. K. Oliver, L. A. Emmerson, and Robert Gage.

Rev. Mr. Morris (Major Morris) was recalled to the rectorship the latter part of 1945. Two workers were added to the staff of St. John's in the summer of 1947; Mrs. Wallace W. Newbrandt, Jr., became parish secretary, and Miss Gerry Ervin, director of religious education, and superintendent of youth work. In 1950, the communicants numbered 625, the Church school, 241. At this time, the wardens were Howard D. Reid and R. Hoke Robinson; the secretary, J. B. Easterling; the treasurer, R. M. Horton; lay reader, R. Hoke Robinson. An interesting event in the life of this parish was the unveiling on April 1-2, 1953, of a plaque given by the junior vestry containing the names of six members of St. John's who have gone out into all-time Church service: three priests, C. C. Fishburne, Jr., D.D., M. C. Reid, E. B. Clippard; missionary, Mrs. Eloise McKensey; and two organists, S. B. Stribling and Mrs. I. M. Mauterer. In this parish in 1955 there was set up a seminary fund by means of talent funds to assist any member of the parish studying for the ministry. The Rev. Rufus King Nightingale became assistant rector of St. John's July 1, 1955. A very complete and handsome new parish house built of granite was dedicated on July 15, 1956. It adjoins in front the old parish house called Heyward Hall and preserves this name.

ST. LUKE'S CHURCH, COLUMBIA
Established 1871

Under a commission from Bishop Howe, services which led to the establishment of this Church were begun by the Rev. Benjamin B. Babbitt, a professor at the University of South Carolina, on the first Sunday after Ascension Day, 1871, in a private house. On the following Sunday and until the October following, the services were held in the chapel formerly of Christ Church. Services were then discontinued for a time. They were resumed by Mr. Babbitt on the Fifth Sunday in Lent, 1873, and with encouraging prospects—20 families, and a growing Sunday School of 20. At this time, Trinity Church, with Dr. Shand as rector, gave formal consent to the establishment of this Church, being within the limits of Trinity parish. Dr. Shand also gave much encouragement to the work. St. Luke's was formally organized as a mission by Bishop Howe, August 5, 1873. A lot was soon purchased at the corner of Plain (now Hampton Avenue) and Marion Streets. This was afterwards disposed of. For ten years the congregation worshipped in various halls and lodges in the city. The Church was incorporated in 1876, there then being 23 families and 20 communicants. The priest-in-charge was assisted by Mr. Thaddeus Saltus, whom he was instructing as a candidate for Holy Orders. He was ordained by Bishop Howe in St. Mark's Church, Charleston, on March 3, 1882, where he became assistant to the rector, the Rev. T. A. Porter. Mr. Saltus was the first colored man to be ordained in the diocese of South Carolina. It was Bishop Howe's plan to make St. Luke's Church the center of an associate mission, as indeed it had largely become already. (See Appendix, Part One, Sec. II and Part Two, Sec. II.) A lot was acquired about 1883 at the corner of Lady and Marion Streets for $450.00, and a school building was erected upon it. Soon after, a Church was built at a cost of $2,027.85. Though not finished, worship began in it in 1884. A cabinet organ was given by St. Thomas' Church, Tomaston, Mass. Mr. Babbitt continued in charge for some 15 years until 1886, having for a time latterly been assisted by the Rev. Thomas G. Harper. He died December 20, 1888. The Rev. T. B. Clarkson next served St. Luke's from January, 1886, until his death, March 3, 1889, it being a regular parish at this time. It came, however, under the care of the Rev. E. N. Joyner as Archdeacon in 1889, as a part again of the associate mission. It is an interesting fact that on February 26, 1889, when the commission appointed for the purpose held in St. Luke's Church that notable conference with the representatives of the colored churches of the diocese relative to the settlement of the long agitation concrning the status of these churches by the organization of a Convocation of the colored churches, this Church was the only one that approved the plan. The representatives of St. Luke's were Messrs. A. M. Wallace, N. E. Lewis, and J. H. Bryant. St. Luke's had a vested choir in 1891, and at this time Prof. J. E. Wallace was the faithful lay reader conducting most of the services. For a time the Rev. H. T. Gregory had charge, then the Rev. J. B. Mancebo. The Rev. G. E. Howell assumed charge in 1908 and served for five years. It was in these years sometimes listed as a part of the Archdeaconry and sometimes as an independent parish. It was in 1911 that St. Luke's was removed from Lady Street, (this property being sold) to the new Church which had been built at 912 Hampton Avenue. This Church was consecrated by Bishop Guerry on September 13, 1913. The Rev. G. E. Howell went to Summerville soon after this event. The Rev. C. A. Harrison, afterwards rector of St. Mark's, Charleston, served the Church from 1917 to 1920, and after him the Rev. R. N. Perry until 1924, and then the Rev. Thomas D. Brown until 1928.

It was in 1926 that St. Mary's, the first mission to be established in Columbia after St. Luke's by the Rev. B. B. Babbitt, was consolidated with St. Luke's. It was located only a half-mile from the new site of St. Luke's, so it was felt that one strong congregation could better meet the needs of the community. At this time, St. Luke's was going forward; a dwelling had been rented for a parish house. The Rev. Isaac I. McDonald was rector from 1929 to 1938. The wardens in 1934 were Messrs. F. P. Paul and John Evans; vestrymen, James Bailey, I. H. Goodwin, W. A. Perry, R. H. Paul, R. S. Roberts, H. T. Marshall, and H. W. Winthrop. Mrs. Hattie Mobley was treasurer. Active organizations were: an Altar Guild, Y.P.S.L., Woman's Auxiliary, and the Men's Club. Then followed in charge the Revs. Bruce P. Williamson, 1941-42; William E. Kidd, 1942-43; George E. Harper, 1944-46. A lot was acquired at the corner of Pine and Lady Streets in 1945 and two years later the rectory was built on it. Then followed as rectors the Rev. Francis Johnson, 1946-49; Adolphus Carty, 1952-54; and next, the present rector, the Rev. Bruce P. Williamson, with Messrs.

C. D. Ingram and F. P. Paul as wardens. There are about 150 communicants. The Church building, a frame structure, proving now to be entirely inadequate, it is proposed as soon as feasible to erect a new Church on the lot adjoining the rectory at the corner of Lady and Pine Streets—a location vastly better for the present and future opportunities of the Church.

ST. MARTIN'S-IN-THE-FIELDS, COLUMBIA
Established 1950

The unique beginnings of this parish is most interestingly told in "A Journey into Faith." We abstract with permission this data from it: "In the fall of 1947, the Bishop of the Diocese, the Right Rev. John J. Gravatt, D.D., called a meeting of the Columbia clergy in the Parish House of Trinity Church. At this meeting, all of the resident clergy were present. The Bishop asked that consideration be given to the forming of a congregation in the eastern section of the Columbia area." Suggestions were made but the matter was terminated for some months. The Bishop called another meeting in his office, December 10, 1948. Studies were made in communicant location, a chart being made by Mrs. Shirley Brown. On May 14, 1949, the Bishop assembled another meeting of the clergy with some laymen. On motion of the Rev. William A. Thompson, it was resolved to secure the consent of the existing parishes in Columbia to the founding of a new parish in the eastern section of the Columbia area. This was done. In the summer of 1949, the Rev. William A. Thompson was called to be assistant rector of Trinity Church, with the understanding that he would assist personally in the formation of a new parish in the city.

On July 26, 1950, the Bishop appointed Mr. Thompson as priest-in-charge of the proposed congregation, though then non-existing. On October 6, 1950, on the call of Mr. Thompson and Mr. Theodore Jones, a meeting was held to which were invited 30 people from the several parishes. This group agreed upon another meeting held on October 23, 1950. More than 100 people from all four parishes duly met in Brennen School. Ideals for the new parish were adopted: evangelical tithing, a Church for all schools of thought in the Episcopal Church. Relative matters as to canonical conditions, site, building, financing, etc., were set forth by Mr. Thompson, Mr. Jones, and Mr. Jesse T. Reese, Jr. At this meeting, 58 signatures were secured to the application for organization, with plans to secure more, if possible 200. This "thrilling" meeting adjourned to meet again October 30. Committees were appointed relative to site (Dr. C. Tucker Weston, chairman) and a steering committee (R. Hoke Robinson, chairman). This latter committee, January 1, 1951, became with the addition of W. J. Dixon, the first vestry of the church: Theodore Jones, Jesse T. Reese, Jr., Augustus Fitch, F. C. Craft, C. T. Weston, M.D., W. F. Petty, J. G. Thomas, H. T. Stith, Jr., C. M. Scarborough, and J. S. Myers as secretary. The Church was now considered duly "organized." The priest-in-charge appointed chairmen for the following committees: Woman's Auxiliary, Church School, Youth, Men's Club, Organization of the Parish, Evangelism, Altar Guild. A third general meeting was held in St. John's Parish House on November 19, 1950, when the name of the parish, "St. Martin's-in-the-Fields", was adopted, the site now adopted being that proposed at the first by Messrs. Jones and Reese. A 4.2-acre tract was acquired at a cost of $3,000.00—Jackson Heights, Forest Acres. On December 30, a special service was held in the four Columbia churches, when those removing to the new parish were sent forth with transfers, and an offering was taken for it. The congregation was incorporated on November 30, 1950. It was planned to hold services for six weeks in Heathwood Hall, loaned by Mr. and Mrs. Burwell Manning, beginning the first Sunday in January, 1951. On the same Sunday, a Church school of 90 members assembled. Plans were soon perfected for raising funds. At a meeting of the congregation January 10, 1951, Mr. Thompson was chosen first rector.

The new congregation was admitted into union with the Convention at Rock Hill on January 23, 1951; delegates were R. H. Robinson, C. T. Weston, Jr., M.D., Jesse T. Reese, Jr., and J. S. Myers; alternates, Messrs. Jones, Fitch, Scarborough, and Thomas. Under the leadership of Mr. Thompson, this Church, which began as a fully organized parish (it was never a mission), has steadily grown. Very soon after its beginning, there was built a brick veneer chapel and parish house at a cost of $31,000.00. An extensive addition to this building was made in 1954 at a cost of $50,-000.00. By the end of the year 1952, the number of communicants had increased to 283, the Church school, 235. In the year there had been 30 baptisms and 14 confirmations. The congregation is highly organized with a high percentage of members engaged in some form of Church work. In January, 1955, the congregation decided on the construction of a church to cost approximately $130,-000.00. The plans of James Tupper, architect, have been adopted.

It is of contemporary architecture, in handsome style, with high interior beams, to seat 360, with choir accommodations for 48.

SAINT MARY'S, COLUMBIA
Established 1871

St. Mary's, located at Green and Gates Street in Ward One was one of the many missions for colored people established in and about Columbia by the Rev. B. B. Babbitt about 1871. (See Archdeaconries, Part One, Sec. II and Part Two, Sec. II.) After more than half a century of useful life in 1926, St. Mary's was consolidated with St. Luke's, the two churches being not over a half-mile apart. (Cf. St. Luke's, Columbia.)

SAINT MATTHEW'S, COLUMBIA
Established 1936 (Extinct)

This Church had a unique beginning as an Episcopal Church. It was first a Congregational Church on Huger Street in Columbia. It was ministered to by Mrs. Florence L. Squire, an ordained minister of the Congregational Church. The congregation applied to the Convention of the diocese to be admitted as an organized mission. All canonical and constitutional requirements being fulfilled, it was so admitted on January 21, 1936; the warden was Thomas T. Frick; the secretary and treasurer, John Blackwell. The worker-in-charge, Mrs. Florence L. Squires, was made a deaconess. Some 60 or more members were confirmed; the Church school numbered 125. The work was carried on under Bishop Finlay and later under the Rev. Lewis N. Taylor until the fall of 1945 when the work was placed under the Rev. William A. Thompson, who was chaplain for Episcopalians in institutions in and around Columbia. In 1950, while the Rev. W. W. Cawthorne was priest-in-charge, and Deaconess Squires had almost completely retired, and the neighborhood having changed it seemed wise to transfer the people to St. Timothy's and Good Shepherd, and the building was sold. There were very few people left at this time, and the majority of them transferred to one or the other of these parishes, and the building was sold to Park Street Baptist Church to use as a mission. This made the third group to use this building—the Congregationalists being the first. The money realized by this sale was given to the Church of the Holy Comforter, Columbia, by the department of missions and the trustees of the diocese to be added to their Parish House Building Fund. The mission was considered closed as of 1950.

SAINT TIMOTHY'S, COLUMBIA
Established 1892

This Church had its beginning in a Sunday School on Arsenal Hill, started by the Rev. A. R. Mitchell in 1892 while rector of the Church of the Good Shepherd. He gave cottage lectures, also. The mission was given the name Saint Timothy, I believe, after St. Timothy's Chapel at Porter Military Academy where Mr. Mitchell attended under Dr. Porter. The services and school were begun in a room of the home of Mr. Ben Milligan. The first superintendent of the Sunday School was Mr. Clarence N. Jordan of the Good Shepherd. A small cottage on Lincoln Street was rented, remodeled, and was used for the Sunday School, and where services were held Sunday evenings. The mission was aided by Mrs. E. M. Brayton and Mrs. T. J. Robertson. A guild was organized in 1894. Mr. E. McC. Clarkson gave a font. In 1896, a lot on Lumber Street was bought and on July 2 of this year, the cornerstone of a chapel was laid; and in a few months, it was completed. It was a memorial to Bishop Howe and cost about $1,000.00. It was soon furnished with many memorials to Bishop Howe—an altar given by St. Philip's, Charleston; book rest by Grace, Charleston; lectern by St. Michael's; altar service book by St. Helena's; brass cross by Trinity, Columbia; as well as help from Our Saviour, Trenton. Later, St. Thaddeus' gave a Bishop's chair, and there were other gifts. Messrs. A. S. Thomas, Harold Thomas, and W. J. Rice of the Good Shepherd Chapter of the Brotherhood of St. Andrew, assisted in this mission from its beginnings. The first became superintendent of the Sunday School. He was assisted by Misses Ella and Grace Gibson, Marion and Helen Brayton, and Maggie Wright. In 1898, Mr. Mitchell reported 18 families connected, with 27 communicants, Sunday School, 76. The mission had grown especially because of three months' hard work by Harold Thomas, candidate, in the winter of 1898. H. B. Chapman was treasurer.

The Rev. Harold Thomas took charge of the mission after his ordination in 1899. C. A. Calvo was treasurer. Mr. Thomas formed also another mission called St. Titus at Palmetto Mills. The work grew under Mr. Thomas. In one year, he baptized 47 infants and

10 adults. Lay readers were now W. W. Lumpkin, H. H. Lumpkin, and N. B. Mazyck. The mission became "organized" in 1900. In 1901, the chapel was enlarged at a cost of $650.00. The Rev. J. C. Jagar served for a short time after Mr. Thomas. Then, after a vacancy filled by lay reading and other occasional services, Rev. H. O. Judd became minister-in-charge 1905-07. The Rev. W. P. Witsell took charge in 1908. Mrs. C. W. Barron was treasurer. St. Timothy's was now classified as unorganized. The Rev. W. S. Poyner took charge in 1910 and the next year St. Timothy was classed as an organized mission again. The warden now was Charles W. Jacock, treasurer, John B. Rogers. The chapel now free of all debt was consecrated by Bishop Guerry on February 12, 1911. The Request was read by the warden, Mr. Jacocks, Mr. Poyner read the Sentence. The Bishop preached the sermon and confirmed a class of ten. St. Timothy's Mission was admitted into union with the Convention in May, 1912. With the intention of erecting a new Church to meet the growing needs of the Church, in the spring of this year a lot had been purchased at the southeast corner of Calhoun and Lincoln Streets. The plan was to move the chapel to this lot to be used until a new Church could be built and then and there to be converted into a parish house. The plans were changed; on the night of July 7, 1912, the chapel which had only recently been much improved was, with all its contents, totally destroyed by fire. Under Mr. Poyner's leadership, the congregation went to work on what for their limited resources seemed an impossible task—building an adequate Church. Mr. Poyner made appeals for help to the churches; only one responded, St. David's, Cheraw. Two houses on the new lot were rented, two rooms being reserved for the use of the Church. No loan could be secured for the proposed Church. However, by persistent effort the work went forward. On September 15, 1913, the cornerstone of a beautiful stone Gothic Church was laid by Bishop Guerry assisted by Rev. Messrs. Poyner, Finlay, Woodson, and Guignard. A year later, the Church was occupied and the manifold organizations of the Church in full operation. The old buildings on the lot were adapted to a parish house. On January 10, 1915, Bishop Guerry, assisted by Mr. Poyner, dedicated an altar, brass lectern, font, cross, and other vessels of the sanctuary. Ten were confirmed. During the six years of Mr. Poyner's charge, the communicants of St. Timothy's had increased from 73 to 150.

After Mr. Poyner left, there was no minister in regular residence for four or five years. The Rev. P. J. Robottom served for a year, and then Mr. Finlay, rector of Trinity, for two or three years. The Rev. Joseph R. Walker, after his ordination in June, 1918, took permanent charge. The wardens now were A. P. Brown and John McCabe, secretary and treasurer, T. C. Dixon. The old property back of the Church was now remodelled into a rectory and parish house. Under Mr. Walker's leadership, the heavy debt remaining from the building of the Church was reduced from $9,000.00 to $4,000.00, and the Church took on new life. The parish house, under a parish helper, Mrs. T. H. Yeargin, became a real community center. Miss Minna Robertson was the additional parish worker. The parish house became the busy center of many parish organizations. The Rev. Alfred J. Derbyshire was next in charge from 1923 until 1928; the wardens were O. Frank Hart and T. H. Yeargin, the secretary and treasurer, T. C. Dixon. In 1928 began the long and useful ministry in this Church of the Rev. A. G. B. Bennett. At Easter, 1932, a tablet given by the Y. P. S. L. in memory of Rev. A. J. Derbyshire, late minister, was dedicated by Mr. Bennett. There was organized in the mission now the "Men's Service Club," president, J. B. Rogers; vice-president, B. S. Milligan; secretary and treasurer, T. Robert Riley. During these years, O. Frank Hart and J. Faulk, Jr., served as lay readers. In 1943, this mission became a parish (aided). After a long and hard pull, the debt on the Church was paid off in full and it was consecrated on January 2, 1944. At the 11:15 a. m., service on Easter Day, 1944, the Rev. A. G. B. Bennett, rector, dedicated and blessed the following gifts and memorials: an alms basin, given by Mrs. Samuel Akerson; a chalice given by Mr. George V. Sumner in memory of his father, Ernest Sumner; a paten, given by Georgia Sweeney in memory of her father, Samuel L. Sweeney; a ciborium given by Mrs. R. C. Magoffin in memory of her husband, Ralph Van Deman Magoffin. These gifts have added greatly to the enrichment of the worship and service at St. Timothy's. A new parish house was built at a cost of $30,000.00 and dedicated February 5, 1950. About 1953, a lot adjoining the property of the Church was bought and paid for in cash, $2,000.00. In this year, the wardens were W. Rhett Hartin and John M. Grice; secretary, David A. Simon; treasurer, John M. Grice; Church school superintendent, John McCabe; lay reader, M. Foster Farley.

TRINITY CHURCH, COLUMBIA
Established 1812
(See Dalcho p. 394.)

The founding of this Church in the capital of the State was the first fruits of the revival of Church life which arose early in the nineteenth century in the diocese in connection with the ministries of the Rev. Nathaniel Bowen and the Rev. Theodore Dehon with the establishment in 1810 of the Society for the Advancement of Christianity in South Carolina, and the Consecration in 1812 of the latter to be our second Bishop. The Church in South Carolina had languished since the Revolution. In June, 1812, this society elected and engaged the Rev. Andrew Fowler for a period of six months to administer the "ordinances of our Church to the inhabitants of Columbia, of Camden, and the vicinity." He arrived in Columbia on July 16, 1812, and on October 5 following, reported to the society that he had gathered a considerable congregation, having held services with the consent of the Legislature in the Senate Chamber. He had baptized two adults and six infants and had administered the communion to thirteen regular communicants. In the meantime the Church was organized at a meeting held on August 8, 1812, composed of John G. and James S. Guignard, Edward Fisher, Benjamin R. Waring, Robert Stark, William Harper, Theodore Gaillard, William Branthwaite, William R. Davis, Samuel Percival, and William Marshall. A subscription, prepared by Judge Gaillard on December 27, 1913, was opened for funds to erect a Church. The society assured the vestry that it would give all possible assistance. In regard to Mr. Fowler's ministry in Columbia and Camden, Bishop Dehon remarks, "His short mission is not improbably the first link of circumstances that will extend our faith and worship throughout our upper country." The Bishop's first visitation was on May 13, 1813, when he held services in the Capitol. The congregation was incorporated by the Legislature in this year under the name, "Episcopal Church in Columbia."

Mr. Robert Moorman in his "History and Traditions" states that the more northern of the two acres of land occupied by Trinity was given by Mrs. Smythe, a widow, in 1813; and the southern acre was purchased from Col. James Gregg in 1814. Col. Gregg resided on the opposite side of Senate Street and made the sale on condition that this land be never used as a graveyard. The cornerstone of the first Trinity Church, located on the northwest corner of the northern acre was laid on March 7, 1814 and consecrated by Bishop Dehon on December 14, 1814 under the name, Trinity Church.

The Bishop's sermons were published in England and the sermon the Bishop preached on this occasion was used by direction of the Bishop of St. David's at the Consecration of a Church in Cardigan-shire, Wales. This Church was a wooden structure cruciform in shape as the permanent Trinity was to be. In assisting in the build-ing of the Church the Society for the Advancement of Christianity reports calling "to its aid the liberality of the Affluent, and the zeal of Gentlemen of Talents and Affluence, and it has particularly to acknowledge these benefactions: From several Ladies, decorations for the Altar, Pulpit and Desk, and a Folio Prayer Book and Bible. From General Hampton an Organ: From Elias Horry, Esq. a Lot of Land; and from an association of Gentlemen, a house and four acres of Land. For this Diocese, the establishment of a Church at Columbia is considered an important epoch." Bishop Dehon says that "Gen. C. C. Pinckney, Elias Horry and Peter Smith, Esqs., of Charleston endowed it with lands. Mrs. Mary Gregorie and Mrs. Sarah Russell of Charleston have likewise contributed to its endow-ment." Gen. Hampton gave more than $2,000.00 as well as the organ. There is no good evidence that the congregation availed itself of a privilege by Act of the Legislature to conduct a lottery to build the Church.

In 1813 the Legislature donated four lots (37, 38, 39, 40) to the Presbyterian and Episcopal churches in Columbia on condition that half of their value be paid by these churches to the Baptist and Methodist congregations to assist them in building houses of worship. The Presbyterians acquired all the lots by purchase from the Episcopal Church of its share and have occupied the same site to this day. Dalcho tells us that Elias Lynch Horry, Esq., of Charleston presented Trinity with a flagon, chalice, and paten. The Advancement Society on February 5, 1814, supplied the Church with a lay reader in the person of its own first candidate for Holy Orders, Maurice Harvey Lance, who was a student at the South Carolina College. On ordination, February 21, 1815, he removed to Georgetown. The first rector was the Rev. Christian Hanckel, elected on June 4, 1815, who also was appointed first a tutor, then a professor in the South Carolina College. On December 7th and 8th of this year the 28th Convention of the diocese, the first outside of Charleston, met in Trinity Church. The deputies from Trinity were: Hon. Theodore Gaillard, John Spencer Man, Edward Fisher, Mr. Guignard. These were Columbians but deputies from this Church in early Conventions were residents of Charleston who acted, it has been well suggested, as proxies. In 1819 the Church faced a crisis when the college adopted a rule prohibiting professors from holding parochial cures, thus throwing Mr. Hanckel's entire support upon the Church. The Advancement Society came to the rescue, however, with perhaps the greatest act of generosity in its whole history, appropriating $1,000.00 a year for three years to supplement his salary as rector of Trinity. However, Mr. Hanckel, receiving a call to St. Paul's, Charleston, left in January, 1821, being succeeded by the Rev. Patrick H. Folker who enjoyed most of the society's beneficence. At this time the Sunday School flourished, having 141 pupils and 13 teachers with Mrs. Sarah Joor as superintendent. The Church building was enlarged and improved in 1825 with the addition of 18 pews and an enclosing brick wall. Mr. Folker resigned in February, 1829, being succeeded in June, 1830 for only eight months by the Rev. Thomas S. W. Motte.

Now for four years, though constant effort was made by the vestry and the Bishop to secure a rector, the Church suffered from the deficiency of ministers in the diocese described by the Bishop as "melancholy", and Trinity as "unhappily destitute", dwindled away to five or six families. In the summer of 1833, with the Bishop's license, came from Charleston Mr. Peter J. Shand, a candidate for Holy Orders, to act as lay reader. He was ordained deacon January 19, 1834, and on invitation of the vestry took charge of the Church, beginning a ministry in it of over fifty years during which, through cloud and sunshine, the parish went from weakness to strength. The year 1835 saw the organization of the "Ladies Working Society" as also the redecoration of the interior of the Church and the establishment of a parish library; in 1836, the parish reciprocated the earlier generosity to itself in Charleston by contributing $1,200.00 towards the rebuilding of St. Philip's Church destroyed by fire; in 1837 a "fine-toned bell" was presented to the Church by a member; in 1838 a colored Sunday School was begun; in 1839 a handsome new organ was installed and the rector reported spiritual improvement, there now being 85 communicants. In July, 1844, a parochial school was opened for the indigent. It was about this period or earlier that a parsonage was acquired located at the southwest corner of Sumter and Senate Streets.

As early as 1841, a new Church was seriously considered as needed from many standpoints, and with a contemplated cost of $25,000.00; the congregation appealed to other parishes for help to the extent of one third of this amount, justified especially because of Columbia's vantage ground for the extension of the Church into the up-country where there were then not more than two of three

Episcopal churches. The cornerstone of the new Church was laid on November 26, 1845, by Mr. Shand in the absence of the Bishop. In the cornerstone was deposited besides the usual articles an inscription in Latin, in a sealed glass tube giving reasons for the new building with names subjoined: "Christopher Edwards Gadsden, Being Bishop of the Diocese of the Anglo American Catholic Church, Peter Johnston Shand, Rector of the Parish, Vestrymen: William Campbell Preston, John Laurence Manning, James Lewis Clark, James Madison Daniel, Gouverneur Morris Thompson, Wardens: Robert Wilson Gibbes, M.D., Maximilian La Borde, M.D., Edward Sill, Secretary and Treasurer, Edward B. White, Architect, Brown and Dillingham, Builders, William Aiken, Governor of the State." This very beautiful Church was one of the first examples of Ecclesiastic Gothic in the Southern country. The beautiful Munich windows were the gift of the Preston family. Its prototype in England is York Cathedral. The Consecration of Trinity was on February 14, 1847, by Bishop Gadsden, assisted by the rector, Revs. A. H. Cornish, R. D. Shindler, Robert Henry, D.D. A splendid description of the Church from the *Churchman* is found quoted in the *Gospel Messenger* for April, 1847, and repeated in *Our Hundred Years*. Also of Mr. White's designing may be mentioned Grace Church, Charleston; The Cross, Bluffton; and the steeple on St. Philip's, Charleston. During the years 1854-55, the Rev. Arthur Wigfall was chaplain of the Female Seminary at Barhamville near Columbia.

An enlargement of the Church was undertaken in 1860 with some misgivings as to architectual effect, but under the original architect, Mr. E. B. White, the apsidal chancel and transepts were added not only with no impairment but rather improvement. The congregation worshiped in the new chapel of the South Carolina College during the period of reconstruction until June 14, 1862, when the Church was reoccupied with great rejoicing, which, however, was not to be for long. In the burning of Columbia, February 17, 1865, Trinity Church escaped serious injury but the "picturesque parsonage" and the Sunday School building were burned, and with the latter the records of the parish. A trunk containing the communion silver and some of the rector's sermons was forcibly taken from Mr. Shand by soldiers. Some of the sermons were found later, including one of historical value, but an effort to recover the silver was fruitless except that it led to the return of some of the silver of two other churches. The loss to Trinity by the burning of Columbia was $9,000.00 or $10,000.00. Mr. Shand continued his devoted labors during the dark days following the war, the Church suffering under a heavy debt and from the loss of the Sunday School building. In 1871, a new rectory was built on the same site as the old (southwest corner of Senate and Sumter Streets), continuing in use until 1924 when the lot was sold to the State for $34,500.00. The original font in Trinity was given to the Church of the Nativity in Union. It was designed by the noted sculptor Powers through the influence of his friends, the Prestons, as was also the present font that took its place. The rector in the early seventies was assisted in the services by the Revs. C. B. Walker and B. B. Babbitt, until October, 1874, when the Rev. J. H. Stringfellow became assistant minister. At this time the Ladies' Sewing Society supported a scholarship of $300.00 for a candidate for Holy Orders at Sewanee, and a parochial school for the poor was conducted by the assistant. Mr. Stringfellow resigned March, 1878, being succeeded by the Rev. H. O. Judd in May, 1879.

At this time Grace Church, Ridge Spring, was associated with Trinity and under the care of Mr. Judd. The Church also fostered other missionary work including the Saluda mission in Lexington County for factory workers. Under Mr. Judd services were inaugurated the latter part of 1882 in the northeastern section of the city, which led to the founding of the Church of the Good Shepherd. The offering on Easter Day, 1883, was principally given for the erection of a building for the Sunday School which in due course was erected at the southeastern corner of the churchyard, supplying the place of that destroyed in the war which was on the northeastern corner. A chapter of the Woman's Auxiliary was organized in 1885, just after the South Carolina branch was established. The beloved rector, Dr. Shand, died on All Saints' Day, 1886, after fifty-four years of devoted service. He was succeeded by Mr. Judd who served until the coming of the Rev. Ellison Capers in December, 1887. In 1890 a window was placed in the chancel of the Church in memory of Dr. Shand. The organizations in the parish in 1892 included the Church Aid Society, the Woman's Auxiliary, the Church Adornment Society, the Shand Chapter of the Brotherhood of St. Andrew, the Sunday School, and the Industrial Society which conducted an industrial school on Saturday mornings. After his consecration as Bishop in 1893, the Rev. Dr. Capers was succeeded by the Rev. Dr. William E. Evans. Notable at this time was the installation of the new Jardine organ placed not in the loft over the west entrance but in the chancel, as also choir stalls, a vested choir and a choir room, also in 1898 the eagle lectern, brass and walnut litany desk and pulpit. Now was organized the Guild and the Daughters of the Holy Cross. The parish at this time sponsored St. Thomas's mission on Gates Street. Following Dr. Evans came the beloved Churchill Satterlee. His deep missionary spirit communicated to the congregation. Among the many accomplishments of his short rectorate was the establishment of Trinity Chapel at Olympia Mills, with a deaconess, and many activities. He also planned to erect a parish house but he died in 1904 and the parish house, taking the place of the old Sunday School building, was not erected until after the Rev. Charles Martin Niles, D.D., became rector. A unit of the proposed building was first used in 1907 under the name of Satterlee Hall. Under Dr. Niles the chancel of the Church was remodelled, the roof being raised and the marble altar rail installed and new choir stalls. A handsome marble reredos was also installed but it was found to hide the chancel window, memorial to Dr. Shand. A warm controversy ensued. Dr. Niles left in 1907 and the reredos was removed. The Rev. Samuel Moran assisted Dr. Niles for a time.

The Rev. Kirkman George Finlay, the next rector, served from 1907 until he was consecrated Bishop in 1920. In this period the activities of the parish greatly expanded, especially in the way of social service. As, for example, the founding of the tuberculosis camp in 1909 by the Daughters of the Holy Cross. In 1910 the right to vote was extended to all adults of the congregation, including women, and in 1913 pew rents were abolished and the Every-Member Canvass system adopted. In this year the Men's Club was organized. About this time the historic old fence about the Church was replaced by a handsome iron one, the gift of a member of the congregation. Mr. Finlay was the first rector to have a secretary. He was absent for a year on Y. M. C. A. work in France. The Rev. Messrs. G. C. Williams, H. M. Dumbell and E. A. Penick, Jr., officiated in his absence. The congregation was active in ministering to the soldiers of Camp Jackson. The Boy Scouts of Trinity were organized in 1920. And about this time the Young Peoples Service League was formed. During this rectorate contributions for missions increased from $1,500.00 to $12,500.00. Under the Rev. Henry D. Phillips (1921-1928) the membership of Trinity Church doubled to 1,200 communicants, becoming the largest Episcopal Church in South Carolina. This parish took a leading part in the organization of the new diocese of Upper South Carolina in 1922, contributing $11,500.00 for the increase of the Episcopal endowment. A new rectory at 909 Sumter Street was purchased in 1922. The handsome new parish house replacing Satterlee Hall was completed in 1926 at a cost of $122,794.00. Satterlee Hall was given to St. Peter's, Great Falls. In 1933 a new organ was installed at a cost of $14,778.37. The Daughters of the Holy Cross and the Auxiliary were reorganized in 1925. In 1934 the Men's Club was reorganized into the Men's Organization. The work of both these organizations expanded greatly as did that of religious education, especially in the Men's and Women's Bible classes and the Bible Class for University students. The parish now had a secretary for religious education. For years two members of this Church were on the National Council—Hon. R. I. Manning and by Mrs. James R. Cain. In November, 1937, the parish celebrated its 125th anniversary. In connection with this event a valuable history of the parish was published. As it had happened twice before (1893 and 1920) the parish lost its rector to the Episcopate when Dr. Phillips was consecrated Bishop of South Western Virginia, on September 27, 1938. The Rev. Louis C. Melcher became rector September, 1939. The parish continued to grow in size and influence, especially in young peoples work with a Canterbury Club and the Men's Club

There had been no assistant rectors after the Rev. J. H. Stringfellow (1874-78) and the Rev. H. O. Judd (1876-78, rector 1886-87) until 1940. Then followed the Rev. Charles M. Seymour, Jr. (1940-41), the Rev. William S. Brace (1941-45), the Rev. E. Hopkins Weston (1943-45), the Rev. Eugene L. Nixon (1945-48), and more recently, the Rev. Sandy Anderson, the Rev. William A. Thompson, the Rev. C. F. Allison, the Rev. Harold Barrett, the Rev. F. S. Sosnowski, and the Rev. Sidney Heath.

A notable event in 1946 was the celebration in November over several days of the centennial of the present Trinity's building—there were services and sermons, an historical pageant, and a great banquet with an address by Right Rev. Oliver J. Hart. Once again after ten years active service when the number of communicants increased to 1,545, Trinity lost its rector for the fourth time to the Episcopate. Mr. Melcher had been elected missionary Bishop of Brazil and was consecrated in Trinity on February 5, 1948. Mr. Melcher was succeeded by the Rev. George M. Alexander, being the twelfth rector. The Daughters of the Holy Cross after a very successful bazaar on November 17, 1954, out of the proceeds, set aside $4,000.00 as the beginning of a fund to establish "Trinity Home" for elderly people not to conflict however with the diocese home in Charleston. In the year 1955 there was added to the Church a chapel to be known as "The Seibels Memorial Chapel" on the north side of the chancel being an extension of the old baptistry. A new Möhler organ was installed in the Church in 1956. The Rev. George M. Alexander resigned the rectorship September, 1955 to accept a call to be Dean of St. Luke's, Sewanee. He was succeeded by the Rev. Gray Temple October following. He now with Rev. Messrs. Heath and Sosnowski constituted the clerical staff. Mr. Sosnowski, who was ordained priest in Trinity July 13, 1956, is assistant for young people and University students. The wardens in 1956 are Dr. W. Augustus Hart and Robert P. Kapp; deputies to the Convention, J. Willis Cantey, Robert P. Kapp, Dr. W. A. Hart, and Henry B. Thomas.

ST. JOHN'S, CONGAREE
Established 1858

This Church at Congaree in lower Richland County westward of Zion, Eastover (which was originally called Zion, Wateree), was established in 1858. This section was known as the "Adam's Settlement", also called "the Fork of Richland". Governor James Hopkins Adams was the leader in starting St. John's. The Church began with services held in the schoolhouse by the Rev. R. W. Barnwell, Jr., professor in the S. C. College. A Church was organized under the leadership of the Rev. Edward Reed of Zion Church at a meeting on May 2, 1858. Mr. Reed presided, Paul G. Chappell was secretary. Wardens and vestrymen were elected: Gov. James H. Adams, P. G. Chappell, Dr. D. W. Ray, F. Bulkley, Dr. William Weston, John P. Adams, and John D. Hopkins. In July, 1859, Mr. Reed having resigned, the Rev. William H. Hanckel became rector jointly with Zion. The next year on invitation, Mr. Hanckel resigned Zion (in July, 1860) to devote his entire time to St. John's. This arrangement continued until after the war when Mr. Hanckel reassumed charge of Zion, which arrangement continued until 1871. A contract for building a Church was made in the early part of 1859, and speedily fulfilled. The Church was consecrated by Bishop Davis, assisted by Messrs. Reed and Hanckel, on November 27, 1859. The location of the Church was the site of an old plantation. The graveyard is much older than the Church. It is enclosed with a brick wall. A comfortable parsonage was donated by a member of the Church.

These prosperous times were ended by the war. In 1868, Mr. Hanckel reports the loss of ten families. In 1859 there were 13 families and 17 communicants; the Church suffered much from the effects of the war—the Church records were lost in the burning of Columbia, having been placed there for safekeeping. The Church itself was stripped of its carpets, cushions, and books. Mr. Hanckel's resignation in November, 1871, brought to a close his twelve years of faithful service (going to St. Stephen's, Charleston). What happened in the reconstruction days is thus described: "Old families are breaking up by death and removals, and the newcomers who have purchased their lands are not of our Communion. Our young men go abroad seeking occupation, and our 'maidens are given in marriage' to outsiders." The Rev. John Huske Tillinghast became rector July, 1872, in connection with Zion Church, living at Acton. Mr. Tillinghast in addition to those in the parish churches, held services in the afternoon at Palmetto Academy. About 1880, the Church was re-roofed and re-ornamented. Mr. Tillinghast resigned March 22, 1882. The Church remained vacant for some time. Mr. James P. Adams was chairman of the vestry and lay reader.

In February, 1884, the Rev. Francis D. Lee became rector in connection again with Zion Church. The rectory, which had fallen into disrepair, was restored. Mr. Lee resigned in 1886 and Mr. Tillinghast returned to the rectorship. The deputies to the Convention in 1891 were James P. Adams, W. W. Ray, H. W. Adams, and A. Schoolbred. In those years, St. John's had only a monthly service with lay reading between. The officers in 1897 were: wardens, W. W. Weston and James A. Clarkson; secretary, James B. Weston; treasurer, F. H. Weston. In 1908, the Church was reroofed and a neat iron fence erected around it. The communicant membership which had continued during these years at about the same 20-25 in 1910 showed increase, going to 33. Mr. Tillinghast resigned in 1920, becoming rector-emeritus. The Rev. T. N. Lawrence succeeded for about a year. The Rev. G. C. Williams began his long ministry in St. John's in 1923, being also rector of St. John's, Shandon, Columbia. He held the charge for 23 years—a large part of the time being professor at the S. C. University, after he had resigned St. John's, Shandon, January 1, 1931. The officers of St. John's in 1922 were: wardens, F. H. Weston and A. G. Clarkson; secretary and treasurer, F. H. Weston. A great memorial service was held by the rector and Bishop Finlay on All Saints' Day, 1932. In 1945, Dr. Williams, much beloved by all, surrendered the rectorship to the Rev. B. Duvall Chambers. Many improvements have been made under Mr. Chambers in recent years; enlargement of the parish house, new organ, heating system, also many memorials including pulpit, Bishop's chair, prayer desk, and windows. This parish has contributed three men to the ministry of the Church:

Edward McCrady Claytor, English Hopkins Weston, and John German Clarkson. Mr. Chambers was succeeded by Rev. Sydney E. Heath (1955-56).

ST. MICHAEL'S, EASLEY
Established 1954

In 1878 the Rev. E. C. Logan, living at Welford, conducted a mission at Welford, and also held services in Easley. In 1886 the Rev. J. D. McCollough, the indefatigable missionary, reported work in Easley; a lot had been secured on which to build a Church. The Rev. Messrs. Ellison Capers and W. P. DuBose (who were both to become famous men) assisted him in this work. However, the effort was short-lived. In 1888 Mr. McCollough reported the mission discontinued, more than half the members having removed. We know of no further effort to establish the Church in Easley until 1954, when the Rev. Jack W. Cole of St. Paul's, Pendleton, with the cooperation of A. G. Clarkson, Jr., began a mission here. The first service, on November 29, 1953, was held in the chapel of a funeral home. In 1955 the mission was organized with the name "St. Michael's". It reported as its officers under the Rev. Jack W. Cole, priest-in-charge: warden, A. G. Clarkson, Jr.; secretary, Mrs. W. F. Reddall; treasurer, H. C. Milhous. Services had been held regularly every Sunday. The mission was admitted into union with the Convention on May 4, 1955, the first deputies being Dr. E. A. Jamison and L. M. McBee. A great step forward was taken on July 22, 1955, when a lot was purchased in Easley at a cost of $2,850.00—an excellent site for a proposed Church at the corner of Southway and Andrew Streets. The purchase money came chiefly from the gift of the 1953 Advent Offering of the Church schools of the diocese. Several branches of the Woman's Auxiliary also assisted generously.

During the year 1956 a period of growth began. The first confirmation of four was held December 12, 1954. The communicant strength has grown from 18 in January of 1956 to 40, 16 transfers having been received. On August 19, 1956, a building fund canvass began and pledges were received totalling $14,471.00. A building committee was appointed, composed of the following: Dr. E. A. Jamison, chairman; Messrs. A. F. McKissick, L. M. McBee, J. J. Sims, Thomas E. Myers, J. Harvey Cleveland, and Mrs. Walter L. Patton and Mrs. W. F. Reddall. To work with the building committee, a finance committee was appointed, consisting of A. G. Clarkson, Jr., H. C. Milhous, and Thomas E. Myers. On October 28, 1956, the congregation approved the plans made by these committees to build a parish house which could be used as an "all-purpose" building with the erection of a "proper" Church to come when this building is paid for. Construction began on November 9, 1956.

ST. THOMAS', EASTOVER
Established 1871

This mission for Negroes was begun through the patronage of the Clarkson family, the Rev. T. B. Clarkson and especially his wife Mrs. S. L. Clarkson and his daughter Miss Julia Clarkson. The Rev. W. N. Tillinghast having become rector of Zion Church assisted in the work. Rev. Thomas B. Clarkson had charge in 1879. His death followed soon after. It at once became a part, first of the associate mission then of the Archdeaconry. The Rev. J. B. Elliott was in charge at the time of the division of the diocese in 1922. When St. Thomas' was admitted to Convention in 1953 as an organized mission, its minister was the Rev. Adolphus Carty. Cleveland Woodward was the warden; secretary, John Woodward; treasurer, Catherine Woodward. There were 20 communicants. The Rev. Bruce P. Williamson was priest-in-charge in 1955.

(See Part One, Sec. II and Part Two, Sec. II, Archdeaconries).

ZION CHURCH, EASTOVER
Established 1846

"The origin of this Church is peculiar and deserves to be recorded as furnishing evidence of the concern felt by slaveholders in South Carolina for the spiritual improvement of the Negroes. On this subject, the world is so ill-informed that justice can never be fully done to the white people of the South. Truly the word 'slavery' as commonly understood did not correctly describe the condition of the blacks." (J. Pringle Smith, registrar.) This Church had its early beginning by the erection of a chapel (about 1820) for the use of the Negroes on his plantation in the lower part of Richland District, called Wateree, by a wealthy planter, Mr. William Clarkson. This chapel was said to have been the first one built exclusively for Negroes in South Carolina. For five years, it was the center of Church work. It enjoyed, for a time, the ministrations of the Rev. F. H. Rutledge, afterwards Bishop of Florida. On the death of Mr. Clarkson in 1825, the regular Episcopal services in this Chapel were discontinued for ten years, except that the pulpit was occasionally filled by any Christian minister willing to officiate, by Mr. Clarkson's expressed injunction. In 1835, the Rev. Napoleon B.

Screven (ordered deacon November, 1834), a very zealous clergy-man, took charge of the Church called "Wateree Chapel," minister-ing to a few whites and the colored people of the neighboring plantations for five years when he was suddenly called to his rest, greatly beloved. The Advancement Society supplied Bibles and prayer books. The Sunday School soon numbered 82, 21 white and 61 colored. A library was established. Mr. Screven had services at many points besides Wateree Chapel—the Fork, the Academy, "Watt's House," "Taylor's House," and on the plantations— about 100 times in 1837. He left 106 communicants, 97 of these Negroes.

Mr. Screven was succeeded by Rev. William Dehon, son of the Bishop, coming in 1841. It was during his short ministry that plans were made for the organization of the Church, including the build-ing of a parsonage by one member single-handed, and the giving of five acres of land deeded to the Bishop *ex-officio*. After Mr. Dehon, several clergymen officiated temporarily; Rev. William Cooley of New York held services for six months. Rev. Richard Johnson (rector of St. Matthew's Parish) officiated in the summer of 1843. He was followed by Rev. Nathaniel Hyatt and then Rev. Jedidiah Huntington, M.D., officiated the winter of 1844-45. He relates that many of the Negroes on Mr. J. Clarkson's plantation had been "taught to chant all the canticles of the Morning and Evening Prayer of the Church." In the summer of 1844, the Church was for the first time formally organized when it was decided to build another Church in the sandhills. The first vestry was now elected, consisting of William Clarkson, chairman, Hon. Dan E. Huger, Thomas B. Clarkson, Dr. John S. Murdock, John Neal, Allen Griffin, and John Clarkson. Rev. Carter Page took the charge in May, 1845, and then the new Church was built, and on February 13, 1846, was admitted to the Convention under the name Zion Church. Mr. T. B. Clarkson was the first deputy. Mr. Page began services in the new Church at the Cross Roads, continuing until the latter part of 1846. Wateree Chapel had not long before been burned. The Rev. J. Maxwell Pringle became rector in 1847. About this time, Mrs. Clarkson left a legacy of $2,000.00, the income for the support of the Church. The care of the fund was referred to the Convention of 1849. Three trustees of the fund were appointed, this trusteeship lasting until 1947.

A development of the work under Mr. Pringle was the building of a log chapel in a neglected part of the parish called Marsh. In 1851, he reported services at Zion Church, Lowe Church, and at Zion Chapel. A candidate for orders assisted in the wide work of the Church; three Sunday Schools were kept up. Zion Chapel had only the fifth Sundays and most of the people who attended were not Episcopalians. In 1855, Mr. Pringle reported (his last for Zion) 16 white communicants and 106 colored—one white and two colored had been suspended. After nearly nine years of faithful service, Mr. Pringle left, going to open the Church of the Mediator (afterwards Christ Church) in Columbia in 1855. He was succeeded for a time by the Rev. Mr. Jacocks. The Rev. R. W. Barnwell, Jr., took charge after his ordination in September, 1856. He became a professor at the S. C. College January following, and thus could give little pastoral attention to the work. The Rev. Edward Reed, who officiated in St. John's-in-the-Wilderness, Flat Rock, in the summer, assumed charge December, 1857, officiating for the winter and spring and again the following winter (1858-59). The Church had lost considerably in membership. The Rev. William H. Hanckel became rector in 1859, being succeeded by Rev. C. Bruce Walker after July, 1860. Mr. Walter Guerry, a candidate for Holy Orders, was serving as a catechist on several of the plantations in 1861. The Rev. LeGrande F. Guerry, deacon, followed Mr. Walker in 1862 and continued in charge until 1865. In June, 1867, the Rev. W. H. Hanckel reassumed charge in connection with St. John's, Congaree, serving gratuitously on Sunday afternoons. The Church was depleted to a large extent by the war, the records being lost in the fire in Columbia. The large colored membership had fallen away. There were in 1869 12 families and 21 communicants. Zion Church was repaired and painted in 1871 through the generosity of two churches of Poughkeepsie, N. Y. The long and faithful care of this Church by the Rev. William H. Hanckel ended with his resignation November 19, 1871, going to St. Stephen's, Charleston.

The Rev. John Huske Tillinghast became rector in July, 1872. He resided at Acton. He reports as part of his support "corn and forage." In 1880, a new Zion Church was built at Eastover, six miles from the site of the old "Zion Wateree." Some material from the old Church was used in the new. Mr. Tillinghast resigned March 1, 1882, when Rev. Thomas B. Clarkson, who for some time had worked among the Negroes at Wateree, took temporary charge. On April 22, 1883, the Church was much damaged by a cyclone. The Rev. Francis D. Lee became rector February, 1884. His services alternated with St. John's. He resigned in 1886 and Mr. Tillinghast was called back. In 1887, a plain chapel was erected by a lady of the congregation, Mrs. A. G. Clarkson, in the sandhills, adjourning the parsonage, for afternoon services in the summer, and for a summer Sunday School. In 1889, the Church was renovated, new pews installed, and handsome iron gates with stone posts added. The deputies to the Convention in 1891 were C. R. Clarkson, A. G. Clarkson, John A. Keith, M.D., and C. E. Eagan. Many additions and improvements were made to the Church in 1892: chancel window, new organ, silver paten, new kitchen for parsonage, and, next year, new porch to Church, hymn tablet, new communion table, and new roof and well. The wardens in 1897 were A. G. Clarkson and C. A. Eagan; secretary and treasurer, Richardson Singleton. A legacy of $500.00 was received this year, the income for the up-keep of the cemetery. In 1899, a mission for colored people called "Emmanuel Church" was established with Sunday and parochial schools; for this a chapel was built. Also, a mission for white people was begun near the site of old Zion Church, and a chapel built called the Chapel of the Cross with a Sunday School of 40. A movement to replace the Church of faulty design with a new one was begun in 1892. The rectory was enlarged in 1910.

In 1911, the new Church of brick with slate roof and concrete trimmings was completed. It was consecrated by Bishop Guerry on November 26, 1911, assisted by the rector and the Rev. H. H. Covington. The Bishop called it "one of the most churchly and beautiful buildings in the diocese." Mr. Tillinghast resigned in 1920, having been rector since 1872, except for an intermission of five years (1882-87). He now was made *rector-emeritus*. Rev. Herbert F. Schroeter then served for three years. The old Chapel of the Cross had been abandoned some years before. The officers of Zion in 1922 (the time of the division of the diocese) were: wardens, A. G. Clarkson, and J. H. Eagan; secretary and treasurer, Edwin Trumble.

The Rev. L. N. Taylor became rector in 1925 and continued so in connection with his rectorship of the Church of the Good Shepherd, Columbia, until 1940, when the Rev. A. G. B. Bennett took the charge. Zion celebrated its centennial on May 22, 1946. The Rev. A. R. Stuart, son of the parish, preached the sermon and Dr. Garden C. Stuart gave a history of the parish; a tablet was dedicated to the memory of the Rev. John Huske Tillinghast, rector for nearly half a century. Besides these there were present Mr. Bennett, Rev. L. N. Taylor, late rector, the Bishop, and many other clergymen. Mr. Bennett resigned December 31, 1954, when the Rev. Sidney E. Heath succeeded serving until March, 1956.

TRINITY, EDGEFIELD
Established 1836

Graciously for some time about 1832 Rev. Edward E. Ford of St. Paul's, Augusta, visited a group of Church members in Edgefield giving them services once a quarter. There were other occasional services. In the summer of 1833, Rev. Christian Hanckel of St. Paul's, Charleston, paid a visit to the mission, catechized the children, held service and administered Holy Communion. At his suggestion a meeting was held and the following were elected wardens and vestrymen: W. Brooks, E. B. Bacon, A. T. Wigfall, J. Terry, J. T. Jeter, T. M. Stafford, F. W. Pickens, C. Dowd, and J. Jones. The Rev. William H. Barnwell of St. Peter's, Charleston, preached on July 12th. The Bishop was informed and steps were taken to raise funds to build a Church. A member of the Church gave a lot and $1,050.00 was subscribed in the village. It was planned to erect a Church to cost about $2,000.00. Having complied with canonical requirements the Church was admitted into union with the Convention of the diocese on February 11, 1836, under the name of Trinity Church, Edgefield. E. B. Bacon took his seat as delegate at once. Probably the first service to be held in the Church was when it was still unfinished on the 13th of March, 1836; this service with Holy Communion was held by a clergyman visiting from Virginia. On this occasion he administered the communion to 13 or 14 persons and baptized one adult. The first minister of the Church was the Rev. James H. Fowles who temporarily served from May, 1836 to the end of the season. A severe storm this summer, before the Church was completed, damaged it severely, part of the roof was destroyed but repairs were made promptly. On the 19th of October, 1836, Bishop Bowen consecrated the Church: Rev. Dr. Gadsden read the Sentence of Consecration, also taking part were Dr. Shand, and Mr. Fowles, the temporary minister. The *Gospel Messenger* comments: "The *tout ensemble* of the interior of this little Church is surpassed in beauty and effect by none in the upper sections of our state, and, in fact by none of like dimensions in any portion of the Union which we have visited."

The next minister after Mr. Fowles was Rev. Arthur Wigfall for only a month, then the Rev. R. D. Shindler for a short time in 1841 to 1842. Rev. Edward Reed served in the summer of 1842 and then took charge in 1843, coming from Tennessee, beginning a long valuable ministry in the diocese. He was succeeded briefly by Revs. E. T. Walker (1844), and then Carter Page (1845). Then followed the Revs. C. Bruce Walker (1845-49), Edward Reed again (1849-

51), Richardson Graham (1851-52), E. E. Bellinger (1853-56), C. Bruce Walker, assistant (1853-56), B. E. Habersham (1857-61), E. T. Walker, 1863. In 1847 Mrs. Mary Carroll made a generous donation for the repair and improvement of the Church. She also left a legacy of $600.00 for the Church. In 1868 Mr. Walker reported considerable increase in the congregation with repairs on the Church and rectory, including reshingling the former. Many losses in the congregation, however, marked the year 1871-72, including the death of Governor F. W. Pickens who for a time chiefly himself paid the rector's salary. About this time the rector engaged in much missionary work in the surrounding country, services at the Ridge and at a chapel which Mrs. Whitfield Brooks built of brick on her plantation. She left the chapel to the Bishop and also other legacies. She, like her mother, Mrs. Carroll, was a generous lady. She was the mother of Preston H. Brooks. About this time Mr. Walker held services for colored people at his residence a few miles from Edgefield. In 1875 he reported that "We have more Church people out of Edgefield than in it." Indeed Trinity now was at a low ebb.

Mr. Walker held services monthly at Johnson Depot and at Pine House near the town. In 1876, he held services also at Port Royal. In these years the rector conducted an afternoon service for colored people. A legacy of $800.00 in 1882 made possible extensive repairs on the rectory including a new roof, and soon after a building was remodeled for a chapel for the colored people on the Church grounds. The Church was elaborately remodeled in 1883. Mr. Walker left in 1886. Trinity now became "dormant". However, in 1886 it was reorganized and Rev. A. E. Cornish was called to be rector. The Rev. J. F. Finlay was assistant in 1887 and rector the next year. The vestry at this time was: wardens, C. L. Marsh, F. A. Glover; vestrymen, J. C. Brooks, Benjamin Strother, E. S. Guerard, N. G. Evans, S. McG. Simpkins. The original portico of the Church was now removed and the tower built. Rev. A. E. Cornish resumed charge in 1889 continuing until November, 1892, when he was succeeded by the Rev. W. B. Gordon who resigned in 1897. At this time services were held for the colored people on Sunday afternoon. The Rev. Richard Wagner Anderson was the next rector (1898-1901). Rev. P. D. Hay took temporary charge in 1902. The Church at this time was so reduced that its status was changed from that of "parish" to "organized mission". Mr. F. W. P. Butler, secretary and treasurer, reports the parish depleted but with a strong man there is a "glorious opportunity". After a period of vacancy the Rev. Royal Graham Shannonhouse assumed charge in 1906. Elabo-

rate repairs were now made on the Church and it resumed its
"parish" status. The recessed chancel was built in 1907. In 1908 a
vestry room was added and the rectory was repainted and improved. In 1914 a furnace was installed in the Church and repairs
made. A beautiful stained glass window was installed in 1911 in
memory of Col. James T. Bacon who was Trinity's organist for half
a century.

Mr. Shannonhouse resigned in 1919, Rev. Louis Ashley Peatross
succeeding until 1923. The Rev. E. N. Joyner served for part of
1923 and 1924. Rev. Edward McC. Claytor then became rector.
The Church was vacant 1928 and 1929. The Rev. H. G. England
succeeded in 1930 and continued as rector until 1940. The centennial of the Church was celebrated in 1936. R. C. Padgett was warden at this time. There are tablets on the walls of the Church in
memory of Col. Whitfield Brooks, and his son, Whitfield Butler
Brooks, killed in the Mexican war. Other distinguished names of
men and women connected with Trinity are Jeter, Pickens, Wardlaw, Carroll. The Rev. Allen B. Clarkson served from 1940 to 1942
being succeeded by the Rev. William S. Brace in 1943. At this time
the Church was again classed as an "organized mission" but very
soon (1949) as an "aided parish". Mr. Brace resigned in 1948, the
Church remaining vacant until the Rev. Manney C. Reid took charge
in 1950, and until 1954. The Rev. William Arthur Beckham has
had charge since June, 1954. Trinity Church is full of memorials
recalling many distinguished men and women who were members
in years gone by.

HOLY CROSS, FOUNTAIN INN
Established 1956

Here follows the first printed notice of this new mission in the
Piedmont Churchman of May, 1956: "Twenty-two persons of the
Fountain Inn-Simpsonville area met at the Fountain Inn High
School Wednesday evening of April 4 with the purpose of securing
the ministrations of the Episcopal Church in the area. The Rev.
Clyde L. Ireland, priest-in-charge of Epiphany, Laurens, and All
Saints', Clinton, presided over the meeting at which the Rev. William Lumpkin, chairman of the diocesan Department of Missions,
and the Rev. Martin Tilson, dean of the Western Convocation,
were present." At this meeting plans were undertaken to have
regular weekly worship and to become an organized congregation of the diocese. The congregation henceforth had the temporary name of the South Greenville Episcopal Congregation.

Weekly services and Church school were conducted on Sunday afternoons at the Fountain Inn Civic Hall. An appeal was ordered for gifts or loans of altar furnishings, especially communion vessels. There were then 19 confirmed in the congregation. At a subsequent meeting, the Rev. Mr. Ireland presiding, the "Church of the Holy Cross" was chosen as the permanent name of the mission. The following officers were elected: wardens, Messrs. Stuart W. Rabb and James P. Woodside. Consideration was given to the purchase of a building site.

CHURCH OF THE INCARNATION, GAFFNEY
Established 1876

In 1876, the Rev. J. D. McCollough had begun to hold services in Gaffney, as also at Welford and at Limestone Springs, as well as at other places. He reports the congregations "large and attentive." In 1879, the services were held in the Methodist Church and at Limestone in the Female Seminary. A lot had then been given for a Church. There were but two Church families in the mission, communicants four, services 22. He said it is a "day of small things" but he had learned not to despise that. On Tuesday, April 12, 1880, the cornerstone of "The Church of the Incarnation" was laid by the missionary, the Rev. Ellison Capers delivering an address. The next year, the churchly building was enclosed but far from finished and furnished. Public worship continued regularly. This was the fourth Episcopal Church erected in Spartanburg County. In 1882, the Church was at last completed; the Greenville Convocation, Christ Church, Greenville, and others had assisted. The Church was consecrated by Bishop Howe on May 14, 1882. Dr. H. Holmes, warden, read the Request, Mr. McCollough the Sentence. Other ministers who assisted were Dr. Porter, the Revs. Benjamin Allston, T. A. Porter, and Ellison Capers, the last preaching the sermon. The Bishop called the chapel "neat and churchly . . . with a good chancel."

Dr. McCollough in 1895 surrendered the charge to the Rev. W. S. Holmes, who served about two years, then the Rev. R. W. Anderson for one year. Mr. J. C. Lipscomb was the warden and treasurer. After a vacancy of two years, the Rev. C. W. Boyd had charge in 1900, followed in 1901 by the Rev. G. Croft Williams who continued until 1904. Mr. O. E. Wilkins at this time was warden and treasurer. After another vacancy of two years, the Rev. J. O. Babin was minister-in-charge, 1907. There were now but two communicants of the Church in Gaffney. It was reported in 1910 that there had been no services since 1907. The property was in good condition. The Rev. T. T. Walsh then took charge but there were still no regular services. The mission was for years almost suspended until the Rev. S. Thorne Sparkman took charge in 1932 and resumed regular services. The warden now was John McDowell, the secretary and treasurer, J. S. Mills, the Church school superintendent, Mrs. J. C. Baker. Then followed this succession of ministers: T. T. Walsh, D.D. (1933-35), T. P. Devlin (1936-40), Gardner D. Underhill (1941-44), Vacant (1945-46), Capers Satterlee (1946-51), M. J. Hatchett (1952-). In 1940, the Rev. Mr. Devlin dedicated a font in memory of a loyal member of Incarnation, Julia Aldrick Baker. The life of this Church was greatly renewed under Mr. Hatchett. The wardens in 1953 were T. C. Callison, Jr., and George Attix, the former also treasurer and the latter also secretary. In 1956 this mission passed up to the status of an unaided parish. The wardens now were L. C. Ramset and J. T. Sims; J. C. Callison, Jr., secretary and treasurer. A handsome alms basin was presented to the Church in January, 1956.

CALVARY CHURCH, GLENN SPRINGS
Established 1848

As noted in the sketch of Advent, Spartanburg, several missionaries visited Spartanburg district during the decade following 1849 and held services—this included Glenn Springs. The Rev. J. D. McCollough, with his wife, came to Glenn Springs from Columbia in January, 1848, as a suitable place of residence while studying for Holy Orders. He immediately began lay services here and at Spartanburg on alternate Sundays. On April 29 following, a contract was made for $384.00 for "enclosing" a Church building to be called "Calvary, Glenn Springs." It was to be of wood 42 x 23 feet, chancel 10 x 12, with square bell tower. Mr. McCollough was made deacon in Trinity Church, Columbia, on June 21, 1848. Bishop Gadsden on his visitation to Calvary on August 11, 1849, said, "Since yesterday, a neat desk, and pulpit of walnut . . . had been put up, and a temporary railing made for the chancel, some of the work by the minister's own hands." On February 20, 1850, Calvary was admitted into union with the Convention. The first deputies were Dr. J. Winsmith and Dr. M. A. Moore. These were also wardens at this time, with vestrymen, Col. Whitfield Brooks, George Smitte, and Dr. A. Pratt.

The Church was consecrated on July 21, 1850, the Rev. Messrs. McCollough, Shand and A. H. Cornish assisting. On the Sunday following, Mr. McCollough was advanced to the order of priest by Bishop Gadsden in this Church, becoming rector. He was presented by the Rev. P. J. Shand, the sermon was by the Rev. J. W. Simmons. In 1848, there were two communicants; in 1860, 21. The Rev. Clement F. Jones, D.D., succeeded as rector in 1857, and continued so until 1868. Mr. McCollough resumed the rectorship January 1, 1869. During the following years, the Rev. Milnor Jones often officiated and Mr. T. B. Clarkson, Jr., acted as lay reader. In 1876, a circular window of stained glass was placed in the chancel and "new furniture for it made by the rector." At about this time, Mr. McCollough began a mission at Welford in this county. The original wooden building used by the Church of the Advent was moved there and fitted up for a Church. The Rev. E. C. Logan followed Mr. McCollough in 1798 in the care of this mission, and continued it until his death, April 30, 1896. In this period, Mr. Logan conducted missions also at Easley and Woodruff. In 1894, the Rev. W. S. Holmes assisted Mr. McCollough until January 1, 1896; the Rev. Messrs. Alston and McNeely DuBose also at times assisted him. A new Church was built in a different location and consecrated by Bishop Capers May 9, 1897. In the Church there is a memorial tablet to Dr. McCollough; also, it contains much of his own handiwork, including a reredos in memory of his wife, Harriet Bell McCollough. There are beautiful windows in memory of Mr. and Mrs. John C. Zimmerman, and Misses Mary and Nora Zimmerman; a picture to Mrs. A. E. Cates; altar cross to R. A. Cates; silver alms basins to Selma Cates; brass vases to Miss Annie Zimmerman. The old Church was torn down, but the location is retained as the cemetery. Dr. McCollough celebrated the fiftieth anniverary of his ordination in the new Church in July, 1898. He continued in charge of this Church until his death January 23, 1902, having had the charge for fifty-four years, excepting for an interval of eleven years from 1857 to 1868. The Rev. Croswell McBee succeeded February 1, 1902. He resigned March 14, 1904. The Rev. Royal G. Shannonhouse served as rector from July 1, 1904 to January 1, 1906, succeeded by the Rev. C. H. Jordan in October, 1906, who served until 1912, when, after a few months, the Rev. J. Harry Chesley took and continued charge until March 1, 1916.

On June 10, 1917, there was unveiled a beautiful mural painting, representing *"Religion"* given by Miss Nora Z. Cates to the glory of God and in memory of her parents, Robert Allen and Adrianna

Elizabeth Cates. They were among the original members of the parish. The service was by the Rev. A. R. Mitchell assisted by Mr. Blackwelder.

The Rev. L. W. Blackwelder became rector in 1916, serving until March, 1926, followed by the Rev. J. J. P. Perry, who, in turn, was succeeded by the Rev. J. Thorne Sparkman, 1929-33. Then the Rev. S. R. Guignard supplied the services for a time. The Rev. Ira C. Swanman became rector in 1935.

One of the oldest of our churches in the up-country, Calvary has continued unfailingly its witness to the Church to this day. In 1954 the number of communicants is 44. The rector is Mr. Swanman; the warden William J. Smith; the secretary Mrs. W. C. Shull; treasurer, W. F. Smith; lay reader, Julian M. Noe; Church school superintendent, E. E. Harding. We quote these words of Mr. Paul Simpson, written on an anniversary occasion in 1936: "Our expansion in these more than three-score and ten years has not been great but some of us feel Calvary Church a rich blessing in our community, and its cross, the flag of heaven, stands out against the soft blue sky, a symbol to all who pass, of the better country 'that is an heavenly', earned for us by our great High Priest who ever liveth to make intercession." The Rev. M. J. Hatchett became priest-in-charge in 1955 serving for a brief time. In the year 1956 Calvary was the recipient of a legacy from Mrs. Paul Simpson of $40,000.00 and also a building which has been used as a rectory with its lot. It is proposed to erect now a parish house, but most of the legacy will be invested and the income used for the support of the minister-in-charge. During the past two years this Church has been cared for by the rector of the Church of the Advent, Spartanburg, the Rev. C. C. Satterlee, and lay readers from there.

ST. PAUL'S, GRANITEVILLE
Established 1885

The earlier history of the work of the Church in Graniteville will be found related with the account of "The Horse Creek Valley Missions". The Rev. R. W. Barnwill had the charge in 1883. The Church was built about 1885, chiefly with funds he raised at the North. Mr. and Mrs. H. S. Williams were leaders in this work. The Church was named "St. Paul's" after St. Paul's, Baltimore, that gave a set of communion silver. This was afterwards stolen. The marble font was given by old St. Peter's Church, Charleston, having been rescued from that Church when it was burned in 1861. The Church was first listed as a regular organized mission of the diocese in 1885. Thus we begin the history of the Church in this year about the time also when the Church was built. It was at this time that the Rev. R. W. Barnwill, rector of Holy Apostles, had associated with him in this work the Rev. Andrew E. Cornish, then a deacon who took up his residence in Graniteville and labored here and in the neighboring missions in the Horse Creek Valley. He was assisted by his sister who lived with him. There were then 14 communicants in this mission. Mr. Cornish maintained services also at St. George's, Kaolin, and at Langley. On his visitation March 24, 1890, Bishop Howe records: "Rev. Mr. Cornish is doing a good work here among the factory people, and especially in his night school." A new schoolhouse for Mr. Cornish's night school was erected in 1891. The Sunday School numbered 75, the parochial school 120. During this time, Mr. Jesse Stanfield was lay reader and Miss Josephine Thorpe organist. Mr. Cornish removed to Charleston in 1894. The mission was placed in charge of the Rev. T. W. Clift in 1895. He continued in charge until 1904. During most of this time, J. E. Stanfield was warden and treasurer. The Rev. S. C. Beckwith followed Mr. Clift in charge for a year and then Mr. Clift resumed charge. Mr. J. Thorpe was treasurer at this time, but soon after Miss Josephine Thorpe became treasurer.

In 1909, the Rev. Roberts P. Johnson took charge. At this time, Deaconess Anna E. Sands came to work in the mission. This marked the beginning of a new day in Horse Creek Valley so far as the Church was concerned. New life came into the work. This was true of St. Paul's and also of missions at St. Luke's, Bath; St. Barnabas, Langley; St. John's, Clearwater; and North Augusta. In two years a parish house was built and a large Christian social work begun. Mr. Johnson left in 1911, then Mr. J. M. Stoney, a candidate, officiated for some months; after this there were occasional services by other clergymen until the Rev. John Hanckel Taylor succeeded in 1912. There were many kinds of activities for the mill people: sewing classes numbering 91; cooking classes, 113; mothers' meetings, girls' clubs, night school, etc. There were 140 in the Sunday School. The activities extended to the other neighboring missions at Bath (St. Luke's) and Langley (St. Barnabas). In 1914, the warden was David Syfrett, lay reader John H. Morgan who later was ordained. Deaconess Sands left in 1919. Some of those who had assisted her were Mrs. M. Edgerson, Virginia Gibbes, Lurline Phillips, Sara Cornish, May Brown, Deaconess Dean, and others. Mr. Taylor also left at this time, being succeeded for a time by the Revs.

T. P. Noe, Mortimer W. Glover, and A. E. Evison. At this time there were 103 communicants. The Rev. Edgar Van W. Edwards took charge in 1923. He was assisted by Miss Mary Ramsaur. Many memorials were placed in the Church by Miss Sara Cornish: altar cross, communion silver, Eucharistic lights, and processional cross. Other communion silver was also given. The Rev. William H. Folk was in charge in 1928, then a layman, Mr. C. C. Boykin. The Rev. P. E. Sloan in 1930. The wardens now were Samuel Berry and C. F. Satcher. Miss Josephine Thorpe had continued as treasurer for many years; Mr. Fred Zimmerman succeeded her in 1931. There were several memorials at this time—three-branch lights in memory of Miss Emma Knott by her brother, John T. Knott of Washington, a window to Miss Emma Wingard. Also the Church was much improved in foundation and interior finish.

Mr. Frank J. Allen succeeded Mr. Sloan in 1936, first as layman, then as a clergyman for a short time in 1938. The Rev. Chafee Croft served in 1939, then the Rev. Charles M. Seymour (1942-44), and the Rev. deSaussure P. Moore (1945-46). St. Paul's in 1947 was ranked as an aided parish, no longer merely a mission. The Rev. Sidney E. Heath served from 1948 until the Rev. W. W. Cawthorne assumed charge in 1953. A great step forward was soon taken; St. Paul's was admitted into union with the Convention in May, 1954, as a self-supporting parish. The officers of St. Paul's in 1955 were: wardens, J. B. Wingard and Walter W. Wilson, Sr.; secretary, Frank Beard; treasurer, Mrs. Ernest Perker; Church school superintendent, Samuel Berry; lay readers, Louis Togueri and Walter W. Wilson, Sr. At this time there were 148 communicants.

ST. PETER'S, GREAT FALLS
Established 1927

The Rev. A. Rufus Morgan began services at this growing industrial center on the Wateree River in 1922, having discovered eight communicants there. He with Bishop Finlay, founded this mission. A beautiful lot for a chapel was given by the company and a chapel was built on it in 1924 out of the materials of old Satterlee Hall of Trinity Church, Columbia. The diocesan children's Advent Offering assisted in the building. The first services had been held in various places—theater, schoolhouse, and home of Mrs. E. F. Pagan who was called "The Mother of the Mission." The mission was named St. Peter's. Miss Mary Ramsaur took up her residence February 1, 1925, and began nine years of notable mission work here, forming many organizations. The Rev. I. deL. Brayshaw succeeded

Mr. Morgan for a time in 1928. C. I. Pagan was now warden, and J. M. Pagan, treasurer. The Rev. C. B. Lucas was next in charge for about one year, 1929, when the mission was under the care again of Mr. Morgan who now was general missionary. The Rev. S. R. Guignard then served for a few months. The Rev. Charles C. Fishburne, Jr., served five years until 1937. St. Peter's now became an "organized mission". The Republic Mills loaned the use of a three-room cottage for a parish house. The Rev. Louis O. Thomas served in 1938 and the Rev. Frank J. Allen in 1939. After a vacancy, the Rev. Julian S. Ellenberg took charge. A splendid parish house was built in 1942, the Advent Offering of the Sunday Schools assisting again. The Rev. Joseph N. Bynum succeeded Mr. Ellenberg in 1944 for two years, the latter returning for one year in 1946. Sunday, June 2, 1946, was a red-letter day for St. Peter's. Twenty-five persons, many of whom were adults, were confirmed and several families were added. Nine had been baptized earlier in the service. The Church at this time was repainted and otherwise redecorated. The next ministers to serve St. Peter's were the Rev. William A. Thompson (1947), the Rev. Harold Thomas (1948), the Rev. Martin R. Tilson (1949-50). The officers in 1951 were: wardens, James Gladdens and C. A. Johnson; secretary, E. E. Harding; treasurer, I. E. Neely; Church school superintendent, C. T. Minors. The Rev. Daniel Stover became priest-in-charge in 1952 and until 1954. Since then the Rev. W. W. Lumpkin has been priest-in-charge. Miss Mary Ramsaur, after about twenty years of most faithful and valued service, resigned June, 1953, much beloved by young and old in the mission.

CHRIST CHURCH, GREENVILLE
Established 1820

The first ministrations of the Episcopal Church in Greenville as far as the records show were by the Rev. Patrick H. Folker who had been sent on a tour of six weeks by the Advancement Society to "the villages of Pendleton and Greenville and the parts adjacent" in March, 1820 (see account of Church in Pendleton). He was succeeded in a few weeks by the Rev. Rodolphus Dickinson (spelt also Dickerson) who succeeded by June in organizing St. Paul's, Pendleton; St. James', Greenville; and St. Peter's at the Armory of South Carolina—the site of a gun factory six miles south of Greenville. Mr. Dickinson had previously engaged in teaching in Greenville. He was a deacon coming from Massachusetts in the then Eastern diocese. It is possible that he may have held some services in Greenville before Mr. Folker's coming. His services were held in the Court House, a little wooden building "standing in the midst of Main Street." Mr. Dickinson went to New England for the summer, but on his return in December received an appointment for two years to the work in the three congregations beginning in December. All three, though not formally admitted, were represented in the Convention of the diocese in February, 1821: John Dawson for St. James's, Charles Kershaw for St. Peter's, and Col. Thomas Pinckney for St. Paul's. The Church work at the gun foundry (which was established by Adam Carruth about 1812) was discontinued in June, 1821. The Church in Greenville received its first Episcopal visitation when Bishop Bowen came in the summer of 1821. Mr. Dickinson reported to the Convention of 1822 two baptisms in St. James'. Immediately after this Convention Mr. Dickinson was ordained to the priesthood. There is no report of services in Greenville by him (or any other) for the years 1823-24, but it may be presumed that he continued services in this town where he was much beloved. This seems confirmed by an old record that "the first Episcopal Church at Greenville was built through the efforts of Mr. Dickinson and that Mr. Edward Croft, Mrs. Emily Rowland, and Mrs. Jane T. Butler rendered him valued assistance" in 1826. The cornerstone of this Church was laid with Masonic honors September 15, 1825, to be 55 by 30 feet, 18 high, to cost $3,000.00. Rodolphus Dickinson, high priest, presided. Members of the building committee were Edward Croft, Esq., Joseph P. Labruce, Dr. John Crittenden. "The site presented by Vardry McBee, Esq., Robert Wilson, Stone Mason." It was "directly in front of the present Church school chapel." Mr. Dickinson's successor, also by appointment of the Advancement Society, was the Rev. Edward Thomas. He arrived in Greenville on May 25, 1826, finding the "Church in a very unfinished state, the funds not being sufficient to complete it. [Mr. Thomas had preached in Greenville the year before, September 10, 1825.] The work being badly done, the committee compelled the contractor, Mr. Ligon, to make a deduction of about 400 dollars." Mr. Thomas officiated twice in the Court House on the 28th of the same month. Beginning the next month Mr. Thomas was assisted by the Rev. Mr. Lance for the whole period of his tenure. Mr. Lance was rector of Prince George, Georgetown. On June 18 following "having made a temporary arrangement in the Church", he and Mr. Lance held service there. This probably was the first service in the Church. Thenceforth the services were held in the Church during Mr. Thomas' period except once or twice when because "the glazing of the Church was not completed" services were at the Court House and at Mr. Rowland's house. On July 9, 1826, for the first time apparently in Greenville, Mr. Thomas celebrated the Holy Communion: those partaking were Mrs. Edward Croft, Mr. and Mrs. G. Croft, Mr. and Mrs. Draffsen, Mrs. Hunt, Mrs. Logan, Mrs. Gantt, Mrs. Butler, Mrs. Lance, Mrs. and Miss Thomas, Mrs. Alston, Mrs. Pyatt, Miss Labruce, Mrs. Pringle, Mrs. Smith. On July 16, the following vestry was elected: wardens, Henry G. Draffsen, John W. Goodlet; vestrymen, Messrs. Labruce G. Croft, C. W. Doyley, Esq. Mr. Thomas completed his mission in Greenville and left on January 25, 1827, after exactly eight months. He received for his services from the Young Men's Missionary Society in Charleston $250.00, in all $350.00. His record for the eight months is: services 37, baptisms eight, funerals two, Holy Communion three, Sunday School established with an attendance of 3.0

The Rev. T. J. Young followed Mr. Thomas in April, 1827 for a few months. He reported very good attendance but the Church building was still unfinished—a mere "shell". It was estimated that $500.00 would be needed to complete the building. The vestry after strenuous efforts found it impossible to finish the work for the time; material already purchased was sold. Bishop Bowen made an appeal for the Church at the Convention of 1828. At this Convention the Church having complied with all necessary conditions was admitted into union with the Convention by the name of "Christ Church, Greenville." Though still unfinished the Church was consecrated in 1828. The Rev. T. H. Taylor held services in the summer of this year. The Rev. P. H. Folker (the same who had begun the mission in 1820), having resigned Trinity, Columbia, became rector June, 1829, and served for four years. The first confirmation was held in 1830 when ten persons were confirmed. A gallery for colored people was added this year and a bell purchased, and later a belfry was added. Mr. Folker reported in 1833: "The Sunday School though always small, was abandoned a few months since, in consequence of my refusing to unite with the Sunday School of the Presbyterian and Baptist Churches." The next year Mr. Leverett states "The Sunday School is flourishing, though not in connection with any other denomination." The Rev. Charles E. Leverett held services in the summer of 1833 and the Rev. C. P. Elliott for a few months in 1834.

The Rev. C. C. Pinckney was rector from 1835 to 1846. He was assisted for a short time by the Rev. William Dehon and the Rev. H. M. Denison (from January to October, 1845). Mr. Pinckney reported in 1841 the erection of a parsonage adjoining the Church. This was accomplished largely by the recently organized "Ladies Working Society." At this time there were in this parish 51 white and three colored communicants, 34 families, Sunday School teachers 15, pupils 75. In 1845 $2,500.00 was subscribed for a new Church. The first vestry organized in this year consisted of the Rev. Mr. Pinckney, rector, the Rev. Mr. Denison, Edward Croft, Thomas M. Cox, Vardry McBee, A. B. Irvine, Thomas Tavell, and John Crittenden. Mr. Pinckney resigned in 1846; he was afterwards rector of Grace Church, Charleston, for nearly fifty years. The Rev. T. S. Arthur became rector in March, 1846. He was at first, as all previous ministers of the Church had been, a missionary of the Advancement Society; the contributions of the society did not cease until 1850. A most striking feature of the work of the parish at this time was the organization of the Dehon School in 1851. This parochial school operated for ten years. On April 8, 1845, it was resolved to build a new Church and a committee consisting of Edward Croft and Thomas M. Cox issued an appeal "to the friends of the Church in the lower part of the State." The cornerstone was not laid, however, until May 29, 1852. The work of taking down the old Church began April of this year. The contents of the old cornerstone not having been properly enclosed were found decayed. The bricks of the old Church were used in the foundation of the new—so the new was built upon the old in more than one sense. In the laying of the cornerstone, the rector was assisted by the Rev. Messrs. A. H. Cornish, Roberts, McCullough, and Green. The Church was reincorporated December, 1853.

The new Church was consecrated on St. Michael and All Angels Day, September 29, 1854, by Bishop Davis. He was assisted by the Rev. Messrs. Shand, Cornish, Wagner, Dehon, Shanklin, McCollough, Johnson, Webb, Prentiss, also from North Carolina, Buxton and Mason. The rector preached and read the Sentence of Consecration. A beautiful description of Christ Church is to be found in the Southern Episcopalian of January, 1856. It was designed by the noted missionary, the Rev. J. D. McCollough, who had so much to do with the building of the Church in upper South Carolina, both spiritually and materially. It is "First Point Gothic", length 112 feet, five lancet windows, western end a pentaphlet and a circle with emblem of the Holy Trinity, triplet window in chancel, glass by Wills of New York, vestry in north transept, the tower is connected with the south porch, spire rising to 130 feet, sweet-toned organ built by Jardine of New York, a fine-toned McNeely bell in the tower. Among many benefactions may be mentioned a pulpit given in 1854 by Mrs. Emily Rowland, a font by General Waddy Thompson, a loan of $2,000.00 by the Advancement Society, legacies by Edward Croft and Joel R. Poinsett. An organ loft was added later and a beautiful chandelier. The Church cost about $16,-000.00. The spacious tract of land belonging to the Church in Greenville at this time was acquired by degrees: the original Church lot was given by Vardry McBee in 1825, then over two acres sold to the Church by Edward Croft, and further increments were made in 1837 and in 1842. There was another increase in 1870, making eleven acres. At the time of the building of the Church the wardens were William B. Leary and John Crittenden, and vestrymen, Thomas Powell, Thomas M. Cox, Dr. O. B. Irvine, William Irwin, Vardry McBee, William Choice, E. P. Jones, and E. S. Irvine. In 1864 there were 59 white and five colored families, 103 communicants. Many refugees increased the congregation during the war. The rector was absent part of the time with the Army of the Potomac; among clergymen supplying were Messrs. Potter, McCollough, Campbell, Gervais, and Elliott.

On October 3, 1866, the resignation of Mr. Arthur was accepted. After his ordination to the diaconate on May 2, 1867, the Rev. Ellison Capers took charge of the Church, becoming rector after ordination to the priesthood, September 13, 1868. He resigned to go to Selma, Alabama, November 3, 1875. Mr. Capers' salary was first $600.00, increased to $800.00 the next year and in 1873 to $1,-200.00. In 1868 Mr. H. C. Markley gave $500.00 as a trust fund, the income to be used for Sunday School prizes. In 1870 Mr. Edmund Bacon was elected organist, succeeding his father, Mr. E. B. Bacon, who had served in this office gratuitously for many years. In 1875 the gallery was built. Before his departure, Mr. Capers presented the Church with a silver flagon and, also, when presented with a purse by the Parish Society, he expended the amount in a lectern, chair, and prayer book for the chancel—typical of his entire ministry. The Rev. H. Millville Jackson was the next rector, succeeding immediately but only until October. Mr. Capers being recalled resumed the rectorship November 5, 1876. During this year he organized the Ladies' Guild of Christ Church among whose many activities was the establishment in 1888 under Mr. Downman of Christ Church Hospital or Home, which operated for nearly eight years. It was described as "a comfortable haven and home for the sick and suffering of all classes of our people." The rector presided at the meetings of the Guild, Miss C. S. Dawson, secretary. Mrs.

S. A. Coxe was president of the Board of Control of the hospital; Mrs. T. B. Hayne, secretary; Miss DeChoiseul, treasurer and Mrs. Florence Rantin, matron for its entire existence. The Home had been provided by the munificence of Mrs. S. A. S. Croft. When it was discontinued in 1897, Mrs. Croft conveyed the property to the vestry unconditionally. This with the remaining funds of the Home Board enabled the vestry to reduce considerably the debt on the parish. In 1880, a chapel for Sunday School was erected largely through the efforts of the ladies, and an organ given for it. In this year, the transept was added to the Church, the chancel enlarged, a new roof put on, and a furnace installed. Mrs. S. A. Coxe in giving $3,500.00 for the transept stipulated that the seats in it be forever free. In 1880 and in 1883, improvements were made in the rectory. In 1884, Mrs. Henry Eubank built a chapel on the White Horse Road about eleven miles above Greenville; there were eight or ten families, nine communicants. Services were held irregularly. At times, the Rev. B. B. Sams held services. He assisted when the chapel was consecrated as Grace Chapel by Bishop Howe May 17, 1891. Earlier the Rev. E. C. Logan, missionary, had held services in the vicinity of Greenville as well as elsewhere in the district. Long after the Rev. Mr. Mitchell used the material in this Grace chapel to build St. Philip's chapel for colored in Greenville. In 1884 "The Little Beginners" placed a beautiful window in the Sunday School. It was later replaced by one in memory of Miss Anna R. Cox.

Mr. Capers resigned to go to Trinity, Columbia, after twenty years, December, 1887. The Rev. John Y. Downman then served for one year, followed by the Rev. Byron Holley. In 1891, improvements were made in the Church furnishings—altar rail, credence, pulpit, lectern, altar desk, choir stalls, lighting. About this time, the parish sent into the ministry two young men who afterwards became Bishops, W. T. Capers and K. G. Finlay. The salary of the rector at this time was $1,500.00, the number of communicants 366. A new organ was installed in 1893, and soon after, a vested choir was organized under Mrs. Kennedy, the organist. A great many memorials were placed in the Church at this time. Mr. Holley resigned October, 1899. He was succeeded by the Rev. Alexander R. Mitchell in February, 1900. At this time there were 307 communicants; the wardens were H. C. Markley and J. A. Finlay; secretary, S. S. Crittenden; treasurer, P. T. Hayne. In 1901, a new rectory was built. Two missions in Greenville were soon begun under Mr. Mitchell's leadership: St. Andrew's in 1902 and St. James's in 1904. This led to some loss in membership to Christ Church but this was soon regained. The organizations of the Church at this time were as follows: the Woman's Auxiliary, Senior and Junior, the Daughters of the King, and the Brotherhood of St. Andrew. In 1907, Third Sunday after Trinity, a window, the Virgin and St. Anne, was unveiled in memory of Harriet C. Mitchell, wife of the rector, presented by Mr. P. T. Hayne. In 1910, the iron and rock fence was built about the Church. Beginning in 1912, several houses were built by the vestry on spare land of the Church on E. Washington Street for endowment purposes. In 1915, a Sunday School was conducted in a mill village, and in 1914, St. Philip's was established for colored people. In this year, a beautiful memorial window in the Church was consecrated to the memory of Bishop Capers, 20 years rector. About this time the rector established a mission in Greer. Mr. Mitchell resigned in 1916, becoming Archdeacon of the Charleston Convocation. The Rev. Frank A. Juhan became rector September, 1916. In October, 1919, reports to a congregational meeting revealed that there were 608 souls in the parish, 461 communicants. Of these, less than half contributed to the support of the Church, less than 60 percent attended services, and one-third engaged in work—probably, however, better than the average of the churches in the diocese. Both the parish and the rector took a leading part in the setting up of the diocese of Upper South Carolina in 1922. During Mr. Juhan's rectorship, the population of Greenville increased rapidly. The membership of the Church nearly doubled. The Rev. R. L. Lewis assisted the rector in 1920. Mr. Juhan left to become Bishop of Florida in 1924. The Rev. Malcolm S. Taylor became rector in 1925, serving until 1932 when he resigned to become director of evangelism of the national Church. He gave himself largely to the developing of the devotional life of the parish. The parish house was enlarged at this time. The Rev. Robert T. Phillips succeeded as rector in 1933. The wardens at this time were John W. Arrington, Jr., and W. Lindsay Smith; secretary, John Bateman; treasurer, John W. Arrington; lay reader, W. F. Robertson; Church school superintendent, T. P. P. Carson. Soon after Mr. Phillips' arrival, the rectory built in 1901 was abandoned after a period of residence by Mr. Phillips on E. Washington Street, a new rectory was built. A trained leader of religious education was employed. On account of ill health, Mr. Phillips retired in 1945. He continued to live in Greenville, serving as editor of the *Piedmont Churchman.* He died in 1952.

The Rev. Oran C. Zaebst succeeded as rector in 1946. He had served for six years as chaplain in the Army. The wardens now were John H. Bateman and S. M. Beattie; secretary, Henry A. Brown; treasurer, A. W. Smith; lay reader, J. W. Arrington, Jr.; superintendent of Church school, Earle Maxwell. A new rectory was now purchased, 2401 Augusta Road. In view of the growth of the parish, it was now found desirable to have an assistant to the rector. In succession, the following clergymen served in this capacity—the Rev. Frederick Eckel, 1948-50; the Rev. Ross Baley, 1951-53; and the Rev. John Paul Jones, 1954-55. It was in this mother parish of Greenville that the movement began resulting in the establishing of the fifth Episcopal Church in Greenville, the Church of the Redeemer (see *in loco*). In 1954, the parish celebrated the one hundredth anniversary of the building of its handsome Church, which contains a large number of beautiful memorials. The parish has sent eight men into the ministry: John Gass, John F. Finlay, Kirkman George Finlay, Croswell McBee, William S. Turner, John C. Turner, Jack W. Cole, and Arthur A. Smith. Here follows a list of the organizations of the parish besides the vestry: Guild of the Christ Child, Church School, Daughters of the King, Brotherhood of St. Andrew, Young People's Fellowship, Canterbury Club, Adult Bible Class, Guild of St. Barnabas, Altar Guild, Christ Church Guild, Woman's Auxiliary, Cemetery, Choir. The rectorship of Mr. Zaebst terminated in 1955 with his resignation. The Rev. Thomas A. Roberts became rector October 1, 1956.

THE CHURCH OF THE REDEEMER, GREENVILLE
Established 1951

In February and March, 1951, a small group of Episcopalians in Greenville met to discuss the possibility of forming a new Church in the southern part of the city. There were several meetings held and in May, 1951, 55 persons signed a petition asking Bishop Gravatt's recognition of a new parish. This was granted on May 17. The first service was held at Buckhorn Fishing Camp on June 3, with Bishop Gravatt celebrating Holy Communion. A vestry was elected. It immediately got to work raising money, looking for a possible site for a building, and for a rector. Services were not held during the summer, but on September 16, 1951, just four months after obtaining parish status, a Sunday School was begun and Morning Prayer services were held. The Rev. George Farrand Taylor of Tryon, N. C., held the first of these services, the meetings were in the cafeteria of Augusta Circle School. The Woman's Auxiliary was organized in May of the same year with one chapter meeting in the morning and one in the evening. From September,

1951, until February, 1952, services were held each Sunday morning, often led by licensed lay readers from the other Episcopal churches in the city. During this time, Holy Communion was celebrated once by the Rev. J. B. Sill of Tryon, N. C., and twice by the Rev. Ross Baley, associate rector of Christ Church, Greenville. The officers of the Church reported in May, 1953, were: wardens, Henry A. Brown and George E. McDougall; secretary, Ellison C. Webster; treasurer, T. M. Marchant, Jr., lay reader, Justin E. Langille; Church school superintendent, C. F. Dawes. The first deputies to the diocesan Convention, to which the Church had been admitted on April 22, 1952, were in this year: Henry A. Brown, Justin Langille, C. B. Smith, T. M. Marchant, Jr.; alternates, G. D. Shorey, Jr., L. L. Smith, N. St. C. Smyth, R. D. Frey.

On February 3, 1952, the Rev. John T. Harrison came from Jacksonville, Florida, and conducted his first service as rector, celebrating Holy Communion. This was just one year after the group first met to discuss the possibility of forming a new parish. Land was purchased just outside the city limits of Greenville, with an option on additional ground. On May 11, 1952, ground was broken for a parish house, the first unit in the proposed plant. The actual building began early in June, with members of the parish doing a great deal of work themselves. On September 7, 1952, the first service was held in the building that is eventually to be the chapel. The ornaments and sanctuary furnishings were blessed, and then the rector celebrated Holy Communion. The parish began with 33 communicants. In February, 1955, the number had increased to about 190. At the same time, Mr. Harrison resigned as rector to accept a call to Demopolis, Alabama. The Rev. Grant O. Folmsbee became rector in 1956. This is a brief account of the beginning of the Church of the Redeemer, but it does not, and cannot, include the names of all the people who have helped to make possible the parish as it is today. Gifts of money, hymnals, prayer books, alms basins, etc., have come from various donors. The Sunday School has outgrown its present quarters, and every available room, even the kitchen, is in use at present. A nursery is open during the regular morning service, with members of the Woman's Auxiliary in charge. In 1954, a very successful Vacation Church School was held. In the winter of 1953-54, the practice of serving coffee after morning service was begun. This is also one of the services rendered by the Woman's Auxiliary. There is an active altar guild, which is responsible for the care of the altar and its preparation for all services.

SAINT ANDREW'S CHURCH, GREENVILLE
Established 1900

The first expansion of the Church in Greenville after the founding of Christ Church in 1820 took place six months after the Rev. A. R. Mitchell became rector of Christ Church in February, 1900. The town was now growing into a city. Looking to the future this great missionary priest saw an opportunity for the expansion of the Church in Greenville. Securing an "upper room" in Ferguson Hall on Pendleton Street in West Greenville, with the support of a small group, the first service was held on July 7, 1900. A Sunday School was organized with twelve children. And so began the second Church in the city with the name Saint Andrew. An industrial school was organized, meeting Saturday mornings, conducted by Mrs. Carrie Sterling, Mrs. A. R. Salas and others. A guild was organized on October 25, 1900, with the following officers and members: president, Mrs. James T. Williams; vice-president, Mrs. D. D. Friday; secretary, Miss Ada Jenkins; treasurer, Mrs. M. E. Townes; members, Mrs. E. Von Fingerlin, Mrs. John Honour, Miss Annie Logan, Miss Lizzie McBee, Mrs. Martha Dean, Mrs. A. R. Salas, Mrs. W. S. Turner, Miss Martha Logan, and Miss Sue Dease. The treasurer of the mission was John H. Honour, the lay reader, W. E. Callendar.

A fund was started for a Church building, Harriet Couturier Mitchell making the first contribution. In the fall of 1901 through the kindness of Mr. H. C. Markley, a lot was secured at the corner of Markley and Pendleton Streets for $1,500.00, nearly $900.00 of which was paid the first year. Early in 1902 the mission was organized by Bishop Capers with these officers: warden, C. H. Croskeys; treasurer, John H. Honour; secretary, John H. Hacker who, removing, was succeeded by J. B. Burgard; lay reader, E. Percy Long. The Church was now incorporated by the Secretary of State. The summer of 1904 found the lot paid for and $1,500.00 on hand for the building of a Church. The cornerstone was laid by Bishop Capers on St. Bartholomew's Day, August 24, 1904. Music was furnished by a full vested choir under Mrs. R. H. Kennedy, organist. Besides Mr. Mitchell, clergymen taking part were the Rev. Messrs. Magruder, Hodgson, Holmes, Porcher, Sams, Finlay, Jeter and Williams. The Church was completed and the first services held in it July 30, 1905. The Communion was celebrated at 7:30 A. M. when also four infants were baptized at a beautiful font given by the Rev. K. G. Finlay (later Bishop) in memory of his aunt, Miss F. W. Gunn; other services were at 11:30 A. M. and

8:30 P. M. The Church is a handsome brick Gothic building to seat 300 (70 by 30 feet) costing $5,000.00. The Good Shepherd chancel window is a memorial to the Rev. John Gass, those on either side to Mr. E. Percy Long and Mrs. A. R. Salas. The title to the property after the Church was built was turned over to the trustees of St. Andrew's by Christ Church vestry.

The Rev. W. B. Sams took charge of St. Andrew's and St. James' on August 1, 1905, succeeding the founder of both, Mr. Mitchell. Capt. J. W. Cagle, who was the contractor, himself succeeded in raising $2,600.00 in two weeks, cancelling all indebtedness and so making possible the Consecration of the Church. Mr. Sams resigned May 1, 1907, when the mission again fell into Mr. Mitchell's hands. Mr. Alexander McBee was warden. The Rev. Kershaw, Jr., took charge of the Church in the fall of 1908 but left after one month due to failure of health. The Rev. E. B. Andrews then took charge (1909-10), then the Rev. W. Norwood Tillinghast (1911-13). St. Andrew's Church was consecrated by Bishop Guerry on April 25, 1909. A handsome altar was installed in 1911 largely through the efforts of the guild, and the next year the mission received a bequest of $300.00 from Mrs. Anne Henderson with which the window in memory of Mrs. A. R. Salas was installed in the Church. After Mr. Tillinghast left, October, 1913, Mr. Mitchell again assumed charge. There were several important gifts at this time including a handsome altar book rest, a brass cross and vases. An organ also at this time was bought at a cost of $725.00 and improvements made in the Church including panelled woodwork in the chancel. Mr. Mitchell resigned the rectorship of Christ Church in 1916. St. Andrew's was then served successively by the Rev. H. B. Riley (temporarily in 1916), the Rev. R. D. Malany (1916-18) and the Rev. Robert L. Lewis (1919-20). The Rev. A. R. Mitchell, having recovered from an illness beginning while Archdeacon of Charleston Convocation, returned to the charge of St. Andrew's in February, 1921. At this time there were 27 families connected with the Church and 60 communicants with a Sunday School of 42, the wardens were Alexander McBee and J. E. Burgard; treasurer, R. J. Croskeys; lay reader, E. P. Long. St. Andrew's was admitted into the Convention of the diocese May, 1921, no longer as a "mission" but as a "parish". Its delegates were E. P. Long, C. W. Crosby, J. B. Burgard, Jr. and H. M. Needham.

This period (1922) was marked by the organization of a branch of the Woman's Auxiliary and a vested choir, also a Young People's

Service League; also by the gift of a processional cross, communion cruets, and other furnishings. About this time, after the return of Mr. Mitchell, the congregation doubled in size. In 1924 the Church received a gift of $6,000.00 from Miss Fanny Long, whereupon it was decided to build a parish house in memory of E. P. Long, her brother. The cornerstone was laid by Bishop Finlay in May, 1925, the rector and the Revs. E. N. Joyner and T. P. Noe assisting. The next year the building was completed at a cost of $14,000.00. In 1935 St. Andrew's had grown to a membership of 45 families with 125 communicants, the Church school numbering 56, including officers. The wardens at this time were J. B. Burgard and P. F. Cureton; secretary, H. Bert Mastin; treasurer, R. J. Croskeys; Church school superintendent, J. W. Slaughter; deputies to the Convention, J. R. Burgard, J. W. Slaughter, C. Guy Gunter, and Balfour Foster. Beginning in 1935 there was inaugurated a custom of commemorating the anniversary of the rector's ordination to the ministry this being the fiftieth. On the occasion of the anniversary in 1942 the *"Piedmont"* in a special article said of Dr. Mitchell, "May heaven spare him many years that he may continue to make our city and our Southland a better place in which to live." Under a canonical revision by the Convention of the diocese adopted in 1942 the status of St. Andrew's was changed from that of "Parish" to "organized mission." However, this maintained only until 1945 when this Church became an "aided parish", and then again in 1948 it was classified with the complete and unaided parishes of the diocese.

The Rev. Dr. A. R. Mitchell, founder of St. Andrew's, resigned the rectorship in 1942 after about twenty years of continuous service, apart from many previous years from time to time since 1900. The Church was now without a rector for four years, services being conducted by a lay reader. On October 7, 1945, the Rev. E. Hopkins Weston was instituted as rector by Bishop Gravatt. He also had the charge of the Good Shepherd, Greer. The wardens in 1946 were: C. H. Croskeys and J. A. Arnau; secretary Ben Roper; treasurer, Mrs. J. O. Dysart; Church school superintendent, J. W. Slaughter. Mr. Weston continued in charge until 1951. He was succeeded by the Rev. Sidney E. Heath in 1952 serving until 1954. The Rev. Carlos A. Loop became rector in 1955. During this year a new rectory was acquired on Overbrook Road and the parish house was renovated.

ST. JAMES' MEMORIAL CHURCH, GREENVILLE
Established 1904

At the turn of the century in 1900 there were 129 Episcopal families in Greenville. The city was now growing. Would the Church keep pace with this growth? It was a day of opportunity. Would it be grasped? Now, there was a man, called of God, who appeared on the scene at this time. The vestry of Christ Church then representing the Episcopal Church in the City of Greenville "builded better than they knew" when they called the Rev. Alexander Robert Mitchell to fill the vacancy in the rectorship of Christ Church. It would seem to have been providential. From his ordination he had been filled with a missionary spirit; he had as a fact just left two new growing churches in Columbia, the result of his great zeal. Dr. McCollough had indeed in this man a worthy successor as missionary to the Up-Country. While laboring hard for the development of the parish of Christ Church, characteristically Mr. Mitchell's eyes roamed beyond the limits of the parish to the developing sections of the city. Within six months after his arrival in Greenville as rector of Christ Church, a first step in the expansion of the Episcopal Church in this city took place when he held services on July 7, 1900, in an "Upper Room" in West Greenville. Five years later the congregation of St. Andrew's Church occupied its new handsome Gothic Church. Mr. Mitchell was not satisfied with the work across Reedy River; very soon his eyes turned to the northeastern section of the city. Now appears the hand of Providence again; a Baptist Church on Rutherford Street was for sale for $1,000.00. Mr. J. E. Beattie and Mr. Charles McAlister were ready to surrender to the Church the option on this property which they had secured. Mr. Mitchell, with the cooperation of friends, especially of Mr. Henry C. Markley, at once raised some funds. The Advancement Society contributed $100.00; then, with the underwriting of the balance needed by the vestry of Christ Church, the property was acquired in July, 1903. Thus a beginning was made. The Baptists continued to use the building for some months. Then it was somewhat remodeled at a cost of $100.00 and furniture was given: an altar by the Church of the Advent, Spartanburg; an organ provided by the guild; a font by the Sunday School of Christ Church, while others gave a prayer desk and a lectern.

Sunday, August 14, 1904, was a great day. Then it was that this Church, taking its name St. James' from the first Episcopal mission established in Greenville, held its first services. In the early morning the rector, Mr. Mitchell, celebrated the Holy Communion when fifty were present; in the afternoon a children's service was held and a Sunday School organized with 26 pupils, Mr. Arthur Ewbank being superintendent and Miss Eoline Richardson, treasurer. That night the first evening service was held. Mr. E. Percy Long was appointed lay reader. On Tuesday following a group of 15 women were organized into a guild. So was St. James' Church launched on its way. Leading on the roll of the founders, besides those already mentioned, were Powell, David, Kleckley, Stone, Perry, Brady, Carson, Dean, Carlisle, Watson, Bryan, and Oeland. The Rev. W. B. Sams was the first to assist Mr. Mitchell in this work. He had charge from August, 1905, until May, 1907, when Mr. Mitchell was again at the helm. Mr. Frank F. Watson was the first warden of the Church, Mr. Arthur Ewbank, treasurer, and Prof. George M. Bryan, lay reader. The Rev. John Kershaw, Jr., was in charge briefly in the fall of 1908, but his health broke, and, beginning the next summer, the Rev. Edward Bryan Andrews served for a year. The next minister was the Rev. W. Norwood Tillinghast (1911-13). These years were signalized by two important events: first, clearing off of all the indebtedness of the mission; and, second, the bequest of Miss Eliza Powell (under Mr. Mitchell's persuasion) by which St. James' received its beautiful lot at the corner of Buncomb and Lloyd Streets. Mr. Tillinghast having left in October, 1913, Mr. Mitchell again assumed charge until the coming of the Rev. Frances J. H. Coffin, June, 1914. There had been quite a succession of ministers, but the hand of the founding father was all the while ready to grasp the helm if the ship wavered.

The Church now, after ten years, reached its first turning point with the coming of Mr. Coffin. During this period up to this point, while there had been no phenomenal growth, it had been solid and steady, and prospects for the future now seemed bright, especially with the continuing growth of the city. The Church was incorporated in 1914. At this time St. James' had become an "organized mission" with a membership of 19 families and 46 communicants. The warden was Mr. John P. Oeland and the treasurer Charles A. David. In March of 1914, the Church on Rutherford Street was sold for $3,000.00, and the generous Mr. H. C. Markley gave $2,-000.00; whereupon it was decided to proceed with the building of a new Church on the lot given by Miss Eliza Powell. A contract was given for the building of a stone Church at a cost finally of approximately $9,000.00. The cornerstone was laid on St. James' Day, July 25, 1914. The architects of the Church were Martin and

Andrews, and the contractor, P. S. Butler. Mr. Coffin, with his zeal and artistic taste, was chairman of the building committee and kept a close supervision over the work. Other members of the committee were Charles A. David, Guy Foster, and Miss Ellen Perry. At this time the officers and trustees of the mission were John P. Oeland, Frank Watson, Guy Foster, R. G. Stone, E. E. Stone, Harry Cook, H. M. Perry, Charles A. David, and Dr. T. C. Stone. Officers of the guild were Mrs. B. F. Perry, president; Mrs. J. A. Cook, treasurer; Mrs. D. S. Cuttino, secretary. During the period of the building of the Church, the congregation worshipped at the residence of Mr. Eugene Stone on Earle Street. The Church, a beautiful one of pleasing design, was opened for worship on the last Sunday in January in 1915; Mr. Mitchell preached the sermon and Mr. Coffin made an address. In 1922 bronze tablets were placed on each side of the entrance to the Church—one in memory of Miss Eliza Powell who gave the lot, and one in memory of Mr. Henry C. Markley, who made the building possible. The Church itself is denominated the "Eliza Powell Memorial". We cannot now mention all the other many memorial gifts placed in the Church—the pulpit by St. James' Sunday School, the altar furnishings by Mrs. B. F. Perry, the Bishop's and rector's chairs by Mr. and Mrs. Charles Carson, cruets and bread-box by Christ Church guild, and other gifts. Changes now came in 1916 when Mr. Coffin, who had done a noble work in building up the Church both physically and spiritually, resigned and went to New York. This year also Mr. Mitchell resigned Christ Church to become Archdeacon of Charleston Convocation. When he came to Greenville in 1900, he found one Episcopal Church; when he departed in 1916, he left four: Christ Church, St. Andrew's, St. James', and St. Phillip's which he had established in 1914 for colored churchmen.

The second period in this history from 1916 to 1947 justifies the name of the *Period of Developing Strength.* Because of the rather sudden loss of leadership, indeed, this period only slowly got under way. The Rev. J. H. Gibbony of Anderson held some services, then following, the Rev. H. B. Riley had temporary charge. Next, the Rev. R. D. Malany, but for only two years, 1916-18; and then the Rev. Robert L. Lewis for about one year, 1919-20. These frequent changes were a drawback, but God had not forgotten. In February, 1921, the Rev. A. R. Mitchell, having recently undergone an illness and being completely restored to health, removed his residence from Charleston; and, under appointment of Bishop Guerry, he resumed permanent charge of St. James' and St. Andrew's missions.

At this time there were 35 families connected with St. James' and 97 communicants, with a Sunday School of 78; F. L. Watson and C. A. David were the wardens; R. G. Stone, secretary; Miss W. Hayne Perry, treasurer (an office she nobly filled for many years); and R. M. Hammond, lay reader. At the Convention held at the Church of the Holy Comforter, Sumter, in May, 1921, St. James' was admitted into union as no longer a "mission", but as a regular self-governing "parish". The following were the delegates elected to this Convention—J. C. Stone, R. G. Stone, W. P. Ligon, J. J. Boffer. At this time, Mr. Mitchell fixed himself permanently within the parish of St. James', building for himself and family a home on Atwood Street within its confines. About this time, the work of St. James' expanded to a marked degree; the congregation and the Sunday School became much enlarged, a Young People's Service League was organized, and a little later a Junior League and a chapter of the Brotherhood of St. Andrew.

In the fall of 1922, the establishment of the diocese of Upper South Carolina being confirmed by the action of the General Convention in Portland, Oregon, St. James' now became a part of this new diocese of Upper South Carolina. The year 1924 was marked by the completion of the raising of $2,600.00 to pay off all indebtedness on the new Church; whereupon the Church was consecrated by Bishop Finlay on April 27th of this year. A handsome alms basin with two collection plates were given at this time as memorials. In 1916, a great forward step was taken; a beautiful parish house was built at a cost of $5,000.00, and completely equipped for Sunday School and social purposes. In 1935 there was celebrated by St. Andrew's and St. James' the fiftieth anniversary of Dr. Mitchell's ordination to the ministry. The successive anniversaries of the rector became very happy events in the history of these parishes. On this particular occasion, the congregation of St. James' determined in commemoration of this event to install a new pipe organ. This was done and it was dedicated September, 1937. In 1935, thirty years after the founding of the Church, it numbered in membership 56 families with 160 communicants, and a Sunday School of 89, including teachers. The officers of the parish were: wardens, W. M. Perry and R. M. Hammond; secretary, E. R. Hammond; treasurer, E. A. Webster; lay reader and Church school superintendent, E. R. Thomson; deputies to the Convention, Ernest Patton, Agnew Webster, Dr. T. C. Stone, and Wales Lowery. It was in the summer of 1936 that Mr. Mitchell founded Faith Memorial Chapel at Cedar Mountain. During

Christmas week, 1937, the Church suffered a sad loss when thieves broke into the Church and carried away the set of communion silver, the processional cross, and also damaged the altar cross. There was no recovery. On April 3, 1938, a beautiful Munich glass window, representing "The Supper at Emmaus", was unveiled and dedicated to the memory of Mrs. B. F. Perry, for many years president of the guild. According to a new method of classifying the churches of the diocese according to strength, St. James' having been a "parish" for years now in 1942 became again an "organized mission", but this was only for a brief period. In 1945, it was reclassified among the twelve complete and unaided "parishes" of the diocese. On June 2, 1946, a beautiful bronze plaque was dedicated by Bishop Thomas in memory of Lieut. Robert M. Mitchell, son of the rector, who gave his life on a battlefield in Holland, September 19, 1944.

In 1946, Dr. Mitchell (his *alma mater,* the University of the South, having now conferred upon him the degree of Doctor of Divinity) celebrated his 25th anniversary as rector of St. James', and the following year he resigned at the age of 86; and, after 62 years in the ministry and less than two years later, he died January 19, 1949, and was buried in Christ Churchyard in this city. He was a stalwart churchman, indeed, free from extremes of faith and practice, devoted to the apostolic doctrines of the Church, strong in its sacramental teaching and yet full of evangelical zeal. With an unfailing love of his fellowman, he wrought mightily for his Master. St. James' Memorial Church forms the keystone of the great arch of the accomplishments in South Carolina of this servant of the Lord. In 1916, the number of communicants was 57; in 1947 there were 185, over three times as many; and the budget had gone from $423.00 to $5,400.00—over 12 times as great. The next period in the history of St. James' began with the coming to the rectorship of the Rev. John Adams Pinckney. The wardens now were Paul J. Oeland and G. W. Morrison; secretary, Mrs. L. C. Brownlie; lay reader and superintendent of the Sunday School, R. L. Phillips. The parish was fortunate in securing the services of Mr. Pinckney, still a young man, a South Carolinian with a wide experience in Church work in all parts of the State, from mountain to seaboard and a little beyond, an experience especially as a leader in the young people's movements of this day, in the Y. P. S. L. also at Clemson and at Kanuga.

Soon after Mr. Pinckney's coming, a rectory was built at a cost of $18,000.00 on property donated by Dr. T. C. Stone, always a generous supporter of this Church. Mr. Paul Oeland, Sr., drew the plans. Next after this, a large two-story building adjourning the Church, was purchased for $18,000.00 and remodeled into a modern parish house with offices and classrooms. Some five years ago, a parochial school with kindergarten and first grade was begun and continues now. Then, in this connection, was installed a new heating system for Church and parish house. Recent memorials placed in the Church were a reredos and credence shelf, cruets, hymn boards, and last but not least, thirteen stained glass windows of beautiful Munich glass. This period in the history of St. James' may rightly be called the *Period of Expansion*. There is not lacking still more evidence: four chapters of the Woman's Auxiliary, instead of one; an Acolytes Guild, with 16 boys; a Junior Choir of 15 boys and girls; the organization of the Men's Club. For 1946 St. James' reported 185 communicants; there are now 305; for 1946 the budget was $5,397.00, which has gone now to $22,000.00. Among those whose cooperation with the rector has made these accomplishments possible were: the wardens, Paul Oeland and Hext M. Perry; the choir directress, Mrs. L. R. Collins; the organist, Mrs. Carter Latimer; and many another leader in the various organizations of the parish, together with all those quiet workers whose services are also recorded in the Lamb's Book of Life. The semicentennial of the founding of St. James' was celebrated on the five Sundays in October, 1954. On October 3, Bishop Thomas celebrated the Holy Communion at 8 A. M., assisted by the rector. At 11:15, eight beautiful stained glass windows were dedicated by the rector and Bishop Thomas who preached a historical sermon "Our Heritage". On the following Sundays in the month, sermons were preached by Bishops Carruthers, Cole, Gravatt, and Phillips.

In the spring of 1956 the handsome new educational building of St. James' was dedicated and occupied. On September 7 of this year the parochial school having operated for some six or seven years was superceded by the Episcopal Day School of Greenville sponsored by all the churches in Greenville. For, the present the school is held in the St. James' educational building. A feature in the life of St. James' is the monthly meetings of the Men's Club with eminent visiting speakers.

ST. PHILIP'S, GREENVILLE
Established 1914

This mission was founded by the then rector of Christ Church, Rev. A. R. Mitchell. In 1914 he reported the building of a neat chapel. It was constructed largely of material from an old chapel on the Eubank place near the city. At the time of the division of the diocese in 1922, the Rev. St. Julian A. Simpkins was priest-in-charge and there were ten communicants. In the year St. Philip's was admitted to the Convention (1947), W. P. Calhoun was the warden; H. P. Hipscomb, secretary; Mrs. E. M. Huggins, treasurer. Dr. E. A. E. Huggins was lay reader. In 1955 Rev. Joseph N. Green was priest-in-charge. The communicants numbered 18. (See Archdeaconries—Part One, Sec. II and Part Two, Sec. II.)

CHURCH OF THE RESURRECTION, GREENWOOD
Established 1892

Believing Greenwood to be a strategic point for the Church, the Greenville Convocation on the call of the Rev. J. D. McCollough, dean, met here February 17-20, 1892. The meeting with services was held in the Presbyterian Church at the invitation of the pastor, the Rev. Mr. Matthews. Plans were adopted and Rev. Benjamin Allston held one service. Then the Rev. T. D. Bratton, rector of Advent, Spartanburg, was appointed to take charge and at once began monthly services in the armory of the Greenwood Military Company secured for the purpose by its captain, R. S. Sparkman, who with Mrs. Gibbs comprised the full membership of the Church at the time. A lot was purchased for a Church but was relinquished at considerable loss owing to the great storm on the coast bringing a prior claim on diocesan help. However, later in the year 1893, with renewed efforts a lot on Court Street, fronting on Main, was purchased for $600.00. Mr. Bratton's services were held in 1895-96 in the Methodist Church. A general appeal by the fall of 1895 brought in $200.00 and an offer of a friend to give $200.00 on condition of the raising of $300.00. The Misses Zimmerman of Glenn Springs gave this and made feasible the building of a Church. The Church was planned by Messrs. McCollough and Schad after the style of the Chapel of the Holy Comforter at Fairmont near Sewanee designed by Mr. Silas McBee, the eminent churchman. It was a plain Gothic building with the cancel marked off by a rood-screen. The American Church Building Fund gave the last $100.00 Under Mr. Bratton work was begun April 26, 1896, completed on August 29; and on Sunday, October 4, 1896, the Church was consecrated as the Chapel of the Resurrection by Bishop Capers, assisted by the Rev. Messrs. Bratton, McCollough, W. T. Capers and Edward McCrady. There were many memorial gifts— an altar given by Mr. Bratton in memory of his mother; the credence in memory of Mrs. Susan Godfrey of Cheraw; the chalice by Miss Sally Lowndes (made from family silver cups); paten by Mrs. Bratton and sisters in memory of children in Paradise; cross by Mrs. O. T. Porcher in memory of mother and sisters; processional cross by Mr. and Mrs. H. V. R. Schrader in memory of their son; later, a Bishop's chair by the Rev. Benjamin Allston and a font by Dr. Porter. In May, 1897, Mr. Bratton reported four families, 19 souls.

On August 1, 1897, the Rev. Edward McCrady, having already assisted Mr. Bratton, succeeded him in the charge of the mission. A Church school was now organized with Dr. J. R. Nichols as superintendent. The Rev. William Postell Witsell succeeded Mr. McCrady as minister September 23, 1899. A guild was formed the next month and on January 11 the mission was regularly organized by the Bishop. Major J. F. J. Caldwell was appointed warden; J. R. Nichols, treasurer, with Thomas Davis, assistant; W. M. Fisher, secretary. Mr. Witsell was the first resident minister but only for a short time, leaving June, 1900, for the Good Shepherd, Columbia. The Rev. Octavius Theodore Porcher took charge August, 1900. A rectory was now built on the grounds of the Church which was moved to make room for it. The guild was reorganized with the name of St. Agnes and continued its fine service, including paying off a large part of the debt incurred in building the rectory. In 1904 the number of communicants had increased to 34. On November 6, 1906, at a meeting of the congregation Articles of Association were adopted looking to organization of the "organized mission" into a "parish". The following were elected as a vestry: Breckenridge Lamble, B. L. Chipley, M.D., T. E. Rivers, and J. R. Nichols with T. L. Allston and H. C. Tillman, wardens. J. R. Nichols was elected secretary and treasurer. The parish was duly recognized by Bishop Capers and admitted into Convention in May, 1907, with T. L. Allston as its first delegate. H. C. Tillman and T. L. Allston were appointed lay readers. In 1909 Mr. Porcher conducted a night school at Greenwood Cotton Mill; subsequently he opened another such school.

The Church, just after being repaired and improved, was burned on November 5, 1909, but promptly rebuilt, the cornerstone being laid on All Saints' Day, 1910. The new Church was opened May 7, 1911. It was a larger Church built of brick. Citizens of the community, not all of them members, gave generously. A vested choir was organized in 1911. After twelve years Mr. Porcher resigned June 20, 1912. Then followed the Rev. C. H. Jordan (1912-16), the Rev. Ambler M. Blackford (1916-20), the Rev. Alfred W. Arundel (1920-21), the Rev. A. R. Price (1921-23), Rev. C. B. Lucas (supplied during vacancy, 1924-25), and the Rev. Justice S. Jones (1925-27). This Church was demolished and the lot and the adjacent property was sold in 1920, and a new lot with a dwelling on it was purchased on the corner of Marion and South Main Streets. The dwelling (after being moved to make room for a future Church) was converted into a chapel and parish house. Much of the furniture from the brick Church was installed. Mr. Jones held the first service in the chapel on June 7, 1925. He was ordained priest in the chapel, February 23, 1926, leaving January, 1927, for Alabama. Rev. Charles P. Holbrook was rector for a short time (1928-29). There were supply services until the Rev. Albert Rhett Stuart was ordained and took charge (1931-37). In these years the Church made much progress, especially through the organization of St. Agnes' Guild and the Auxiliary (combining), the Young People's Service League and a Layman's League. Among the leaders were Mrs. H. V. R. Schrader and Mrs. Thomas L. Alston. The parish suffered a great loss in the death in 1930 of Mr. H. V. R. Schrader with his valued services.

The cornerstone of the third Church was laid by Bishop Finlay and Mr. Stuart on All Saints' Day, 1934. The building committee was J. F. Park, Mrs. H. V. R. Schrader, Mrs. J. B. Park and Dr. H. K. Thayer. The architects were J. C. Hemphill and T. C. Cothran, and the builder was G. W. Stepp. The first service was on Sunday, November 24; taking part were the Rev. T. P. Devlin, the Rev. A. R. Mitchell, D.D. and the rector, the Rev. A. R. Stuart, who preached. The beautiful Church is modeled after the Church of the Holy Cross, Stateburg, which is thought by many to be the most beautiful Gothic building in the state. The altar and sanctuary furnishings were a memorial to Mr. Schrader; the pipe organ of Gertrude Herbert Dunn, the lectern of Thomas Lynch Alston; prayer desk of Nannie Shannon Withers; many pews are marked as memorials. The pulpit was the gift of the Young People's Service League of 1934-35, the font a gift of Christ Church, Georgetown, D. C. These gifts were all dedicated at this service. Mr. Stuart was succeeded by the Rev. Raymond E. Fuessle (1938-40). The Church was consecrated by Bishop Gravatt assisted by Mr. Fuessle on June 21, 1939. The following rectors were the Rev. Theodore Porter Ball (1941-43) who left to serve as chaplain in the Army, the Rev. Charles Holding (1945-48) and the Rev. Allen Webster Joslin (1949-). In 1943 the vestrymen were J. F. Park,

J. G. Stranch, W. W. Wilson, T. I. Hane, H. S. Pyatt, B. T. Rains-ford, J. I. Hellams and William Gambrell; the wardens, Royal S. Sanders and Randolph W. Grier. At the annual parish meeting January 26, 1956, it was resolved to build a new parish house to replace the two-story frame building back of the Church. A building committee with Dr. W. A. Simpson as chairman was authorized to employ an architect, raise funds and acquire necessary land. At a subsequent Loyalty Dinner at the Oregon Hotel, plans were shown and steps taken to raise $80,000.00 for the construction.

GOOD SHEPHERD, GREER
Established 1913

In the early summer of the year, the Rev. A. R. Mitchell, rector of Christ Church, Greenville, visited this town, and finding people desirous of the services of the Church held the first in the Presbyterian Church on June 15, 1913. After this service, a few members of the Episcopal Church met at the home of Mrs. William M. Ballenger, where Mr. Mitchell thereupon effected a tentative organization of the mission, with the name Good Shepherd. He appointed for the Bishop's approval Mr. J. C. Ferguson as warden, and Mr. Robert Pinckney as secretary and treasurer. The rector of Christ Church, with the help of lay readers, began regular services. The Rev. Mr. Mitchell's removal from Greenville in 1916 brought the mission to a state of suspension, which continued for many years.

In 1930, the Rev. A. R. Mitchell, now of St. James', Greenville, with the assistance of the Rev. M. S. Taylor of Christ Church, Greenville, reopened the work in Greer; the warden and lay reader was William Albergotti, the treasurer, Mrs. W. M. Ballinger. Services were held twice a month in a chapel loaned by Mr. John D. Wood. The trustees of the diocese gave $950.00, with which a lot was purchased. Funds were raised and with the promise of the last $1,000.00 by the Church Building Fund Commission, a Church building to cost $3,500.00 was planned. The cornerstone was laid on December 13, 1931, by Bishop Finlay, assisted by the Rev. Messrs. Mitchell, Taylor, Pendleton, and others. Much furniture was donated: Bishop's chair by Bishop Manning and the Rev. Mr. Stetson of Trinity, New York; altar and organ by Christ Church, Greenville; altar cross by family of Bishop Guerry; font once used in Good Shepherd, Columbia. The furniture is in memory of Bishop W. A. Guerry. The Church soon built is brick-veneer in Gothic style, Paul J. Oeland, architect. The first service was held in it April 10, 1932, by the Rev. A. R. Mitchell. A more formal opening of the Church was held on April 24, when Bishop Finlay preached. On the first Sunday after Easter, 1940, new pews were installed in the Church and dedicated by Dr. Mitchell in memory of Mrs. Margaret Caithness Primrose, a devoted worker in the Church. In 1940, the wardens were W. M. Albergotti and Daniel Marshall; treasurer, Daniel Marshall; Church school superintendent, Lawton Riley. Dr. Mitchell continued in active charge of this Church, being its only minister-in-charge, until 1943. After a period of vacancy, the Rev. E. Hopkins Weston took charge in 1945. This mission became an aided parish in 1946. In 1951, Mr. Weston was succeeded as rector by the Rev. Sidney E. Heath. The wardens now were P. H. Burrus and Paul Greeley; secretary, Paul Greeley; treasurer, A. S. Leckey; lay readers, P. H. Burrus and John B. Reeves. There were in this year 121 communicants; the Church school numbered 80. The Rev. Carlos A. Loop became rector in 1955; at this time a parish house was built. On October 29, 1955, it was dedicated by Bishop Cole in memory of Mrs. Margaret Wells Ballenger, charter member and faithful worker in the Good Shepherd, formerly of St. David's, Cheraw.

THE HORSE CREEK VALLEY MISSIONS
Beginning 1847

Soon after the Rev. John H. Cornish became rector in Aiken in 1847, he began missionary work in that vicinity. Several stations in the country were supplied with services. The work became too much for the rector and a special missionary, the Rev. C. T. Bland, was put in charge of it in 1852. Branchville, Graniteville, Vaucluse, Johnson's Turnout, Joice's Branch, Bath, Barnwell, and Kaolin were some of the places where services were held. At the last named place, Kaolin, services were held by Mr. Cornish on February 17, 1857, when he there and then organized St. George's Church, Kaolin. This place was twelve miles from Aiken and six from Augusta. A fine Church was built here chiefly by the Southern Porcelain Manufacturing Company. It was consecrated by Bishop Davis May 29, 1858. All this activity was slowed up by the war to almost a standstill. However, after the war when this indefatigible missionary, the Rev. J. H. Cornish, had retired from the rectorship of St. Thaddaeus', Aiken, we find him again engaged in missionary work. Among the places where he now officiated in 1870-71 were Johnson's Turnout (or Montmorency) five miles from Aiken, where a Sunday School was established. A lot for a Church was given here. He now renewed work at Kaolin and services were also held at Bath, where there was a paper mill only 1½ miles from Kaolin, at Langley's Mills 2½ miles away at Beech Island, and at other places. He went forth on foot, literally "without script or purse", often receiving no stipend whatever. His services in 1872 were at Kaolin, 11 Sundays; Langley, 9; Beech Island, 3; Montmorency, 5; "salary $100.00 from the Bishop." Other places visited in 1874-75 where services were held were Ellenton, Williston, Bromley, Elcko, and Blackville. In 1877 the work in Graniteville was reopened after some suspense by the Rev. B. B. Sams. The long and valuable missionary career of the Rev. John Hamilton Cornish came to an end by his death May 24, 1878.

After the Rev. Edward T. Walker became rector at Edgefield in 1878, he had charge of St. George's, Kaolin, and other places in Horse Creek Valley. In 1881 the Rev. E. E. Bellinger was holding services in Ellenton. The Rev. B. B. Sams officiated in Graniteville in 1879. St. George's, Kaolin, was kept in repair by the Kaolin Company which also paid $125.00 toward the minister's salary. The Church at Langley was built by the Langley Mills Company, which at this time paid $50.00 toward the minister's salary. Services were often provided for the colored people in this section in these years. A colored man looking to the ministry in 1883, studying under Dr. Smede at Raleigh, N. C., conducted a large school in the summer. In 1884, the Kaolin Company built a schoolhouse for colored children at Kaolin. The Rev. R. W. Barnwell had the charge in 1883 and subsequently. The Rev. Andrew E. Cornish succeeded Mr. Walker in Edgefield and in his missionary work in the spring of 1886. Bishop Howe thus describes this field of work at this time: "Mr. Cornish, deacon, is associated with the Rev. Mr. Barnwell [rector of Holy Apostles', Barnwell]. Together these two, the priest and the deacon, hold services at Barnwell C. H., Kaolin, Langley [St. Barnabas], Graniteville [St. Paul's], Trenton, Edgefield C. H., and Ridge Springs." Mr. Cornish resided at Granteville. This work in the Horse Creek Valley has continued to the present time. Reference to the work is made in the following sketches of one parish, St. Paul's, Graniteville; and three organized missions—St. John's, Clearwater; All Saints', Beech Island; and St. Bartholomew's, North Augusta. These last three churches are listed in 1952 as regularly "organized missions" developed from the years of missionary work in the Horse Creek Valley and the more recent influx of a large population due to the Atomic Energy plant nearby. The later history of these churches will be found elsewhere *in loco*.

ST. BARNABAS', JENKINSVILLE
Established 1889

This mission began as a part of the "associate mission" under the Rev. E. N. Joyner connected with St. Philip's, Littleton, and St. Simon's, Allston, a little before 1889, becoming a part of the Archdeaconry. Under Bishop Finlay about 1936, St. Barnabas' had become an important center of Church work. When St. Barnabas' was admitted to Convention in 1947, as an organized mission, the warden and lay reader was W. W. O'Neal. He still was lay reader in 1955 with W. E. O'Neal as warden; James Young, treasurer, and Coit Ginyard, Church school superintendent, 49 communicants.

(See Archdeaconries, Part One, Sec. II and Part Two, Sec. II.)

ST. STEPHEN'S, JOHNSTON
Established 1946

Church services were held in Johnston in the latter part of the last century, notably by the Rev. R. W. Barnwell, rector then of Holy Apostles', Barnwell, in connection with services at Ridge Spring. However, the organized life of the Church here was begun when Bishop Gravatt, in company with the Rev. W. S. Brace, visited Johnston on December 23, 1946, and held an "inspiring" service in the private home of Dr. Saye. The nearest Saint's Day was St. Stephen's, and thus did the mission receive its name. At this time, Edward R. Kleathly of Johnston and Morgan Sellers of Edgefield were confirmed. Immediately after this service, plans were made for two services a month by Mr. Brace, rector of Trinity, Edgefield. Appreciation was expressed to Mr. McQueen Quattlebaum, a Presbyterian, who gave a site for a Church. The services at first were held by courtesy in the Johnston Presbyterian Church. Largely it was through the adoption of the work as a special project by the Woman's Auxiliary that progress was made in the building of a Church before Mr. Brace left the diocese in June, 1948. During these years it was that the town of Johnston greatly increased in population through the coming of the Deering-Milliken Textile Mill. Under Bishop Gravatt's appointment, Mr. Edwin B. Clippard, then a candidate for orders, arrived on the scene the same summer and assumed active charge, holding lay reading services. He resided in the rectory at Edgefield. Mr. Clippard found the Church building a shell with a roof, work having been suspended for months. Through Bishop Gravatt, $1,900.00 was secured and work resumed under Mr. Clippard, Mr. Quattlebaum being the contractor. Changes were made in the plans and the work completed. Mr. Thomas Furman designed the arch and sanctuary. Gifts of furnishings came from many sources, among them: The altar, an old one from Trinity Church, Edgefield; communion vessels from Camp Gravatt given by Dunbar family of Beech Island (for use at the camp also); the brass cross by Mrs. Dorothy Mims of Edgefield; Eucharistic candlesticks by Mr. and Mrs. John Strother. At this time Mrs. Lon J. Courtney, Jr., was a principal leader in this work.

The first service in the Church was held in August of 1948 under direction of Mr. Clippard; the Rev. W. S. Brace was the celebrant, the Rev. Allen B. Clarkson, the preacher. An overflowing congregation made an offering of $132.00. From this time, services were held by lay readers, mostly Hoke Robinson and Theodore Jones of Columbia. In the spring of 1949, the Rev. Fred A. Pope, Jr., became priest-in-charge. We find the first report of St. Stephen's, Johnston, an organized mission, in the Journal of 1950 with Dr. W. E. Saye, warden, and John Strother, treasurer. The next year, I. Ernest Boatwright succeeded Dr. Saye as warden. The Rev. Manney C. Reid succeeded to the charge in 1951. At this time there were 11 communicants, six families, 12 children. The attendance at services greatly increased when they were changed from afternoon to a family service at 9:15 A. M. In 1953, the adjoining lot was purchased from Mr. McQueen Quattlebaum (who had given the original Church lot) with diocesan funds and local help. The Rev. William Arthur Beckham assumed charge in June, 1954. This Church became dormant in 1957.

ST. GEORGE'S, KAOLIN
Established 1857 (Extinct)

Horse Creek missions were begun in 1847 by the Rev. John H. Cornish who was succeeded by the Rev. C. T. Bland in 1852. Services were held at Branchville, Graniteville, Vauclose, Johnson's Turnout, Joice's Branch, Bath, Barnwell, and Kaolin. Mr. Cornish held services at Kaolin February 17, 1857, when he organized St. George's Church. A fine Church was built here chiefly by Southern Porcelain Manufacturing Company. It was consecrated by Bishop Davis on May 29, 1858. Work was slowed up by the war. In 1870, the Rev. J. H. Cornish, having resigned Aiken, resumed work in Horse Creek Valley, including Kaolin. (Eleven services reported there in 1872.) Mr. Cornish died May 24, 1878, succeeded by the Rev. E. T. Walker who noted that St. George's was kept in repair by the Kaolin Company. He stated that services also were provided for colored people. Mr. Walker reported in 1885 the Church in perfect order, salary $300.00. Now its chief work was among the colored people. Joseph S. Quarles, Negro candidate for deacon's orders, who was studying at St. Augustine, Raleigh, conducted at Kaolin during the summers a school for the colored people for five years. The schoolhouse was built by the Kaolin Company. The Rev. A. E. Cornish was missionary-in-charge in 1886. In 1887 he reported: families, white three, colored two; communicants, white ten, colored twelve. The Rev. J. S. Quarles was ordained deacon in 1888 and appointed minister and teacher at St. George's, Kaolin. He was assistant to Mr. Cornish. In 1889, the report was 26 colored communicants and no white. It would seem that about this time St. George's had become a Church solely for Negroes. In 1893 it was formally listed as a Church of the colored Archdeaconry. There were 18 communicants and 116 pupils in the school. This classification continued through the division of the diocese until 1924 when it closed. St. George's was sold in 1930 to the North American Clay Company and the proceeds given to St. Augustine, Aiken.

CHRIST CHURCH, LANCASTER
Established 1869

The earliest mention we have of services of the Church in Lancaster is one in 1853 conducted by the brilliant professor and for a while president of the South Carolina College, the Rev. Robert Henry, D.D. There were other occasional services through the following years until Mr. Albert R. Stuart was ordered deacon by Bishop Davis and put in charge of St. Mark's, Chester, and the congregation in Lancaster which had the fourth Sunday in the month, being organized at this time, July 30, 1869 as a mission. The next May it was reported that a lot for a Church had been given (but not used). Mr. Stuart had then visited Lancaster seven times, preaching twice on each occasion: the services, being "well received," were held in the Presbyterian Church. In 1871 about $1,-200.00 was on hand for a Church, but no more had lately been raised owing to the prevailing great depression. Mr. Stuart who was the first minister, left after about two years. Dr. McCollough states that he thinks that the $1,200.00 raised for a Church in Mr. Stuart's time was turned over to Rock Hill. Now for some ten years there were only occasional services, by various ministers including Messrs. R. P. Johnson, J. D. McCollough, and E. C. Edgerton. In September, 1875, Bishop Howe visited Lancaster with some clergymen, preaching in the Presbyterian Church. The visit involved a 24-mile buggy ride from Rock Hill. In 1881 the Rev. R. P. Johnson reports visiting Lancaster and holding some services. On November 8 of this year the Bishop made a visitation and in the Methodist Church confirmed five persons when Mr. Johnson preached. The Church again received a setback when Mr. Johnson died May 1, 1882. The comment in a report was: "The last mission work of Mr. Johnson was at Lancaster where he saw the beginning of a new parish and rejoiced in the prospect of success. May the Lord of the harvest send them a laborer like unto him whom he has called away from the field." This prayer was answered and the work went on. Mrs. Nathaniel G. B. (Rosa Clara Gregg) Chaffee was the leader now. Her. husband gave the lot on South Main Street and the Church was built. The Rev. J. D. McCollough supplied services at this time. He designed the Church himself and made the altar. The Rev. Frank Hallam was put in charge of the Church October 1, 1882. The Church was consecrated October 18, 1882, Mr. Hallam preaching. Mr. Judd preached at the night service. The Bishop commented that the Church was well and strongly built costing $1,000.00. Among the families in the Church in the early days were Chaffees, Connors, Secrests, Rivers, Erwins, and Youngs.

In 1885 Mr. Hallam went to the diocese of Indiana followed temporarily by the Revs. E. N. Joyner and John Gass. The Rev. G. A. Ottman took charge, October 1, 1885, for a short while. Then came the Rev. Theodore D. Bratton, afterwards Bishop of Mississippi, following his ordination as deacon on September 25, 1887, but only for a year, holding however some services later. The Rev. George L. Sweeney, D.D., assumed charge in 1891 for a couple of years. The Rev. Benjamin Allston succeeded in October, 1893. He makes a very gloomy report of conditions in 1895. The loss of the Chaffee family and the not-yet-coming of the McLures in part at least explains. The Rev. J. W. Cantey Johnson taking charge the next year is more hopeful of the Church's future. The Church had been painted and a bell added. A Church lot was bought in the town of Kershaw in 1897. The Rev. G. Croft Williams succeeded Mr. Johnson in 1902 and until 1904, then the Rev. R. M. Marshall from October, 1905 to 1909, followed by the Rev. C. W. Boyd from 1910 until 1914. The year 1912 was signalized by some notable improvements: the purchase of a new organ; the Church which had been about six feet below the pavement was raised and put on a brick foundation on a level with it. The Church was reshingled, painted, and electric lights installed. The Rev. F. N. Skinner assumed charge in September, 1914, and until June 1, 1919, then followed the Rev. A. Rufus Morgan from May 1, 1920 to 1927. For a year the Rev. I. deL. Brayshaw and the Rev. W. P. Peyton jointly served the Church, then Mr. Peyton assumed charge in 1929 and continued in charge for fifteen years. Then for a time the Rev. Alfred Cole supplied some services. The Rev. Alfred P. Chambliss took charge in September, 1945 until 1948 when the Rev. Martin R. Tilson succeeded first as deacon and then as priest, being the first resident rector of Christ Church. In 1946 the Church was moved from South Main Street to Chesterfield Avenue. The Church has grown rapidly in the last few years and has now become (1950) a parish. In 1948 a parish house was built with assembly room with all modern conveniences and including a rector's study. Furthermore a new organ has been installed, new communion vessels and other furnishings including a new heating system. The Sunday School has grown rapidly, the Woman's Auxiliary has a full membership, the Men's Club is awake. The vestry in 1950 was W. G. Williams, A. G. Ellison, wardens, with Keith Grady, H. R. Mathewson, J. William Medford, W. F. Covin, H. W. Boland, and Dr. R. G. Renner, vestrymen.

CHURCH OF THE EPIPHANY, LAURENS
Established 1847

The same year, 1839, in which the Rev. Cranmore Wallace held one service in Newberry, he also reports holding one service in the Court House in Laurens. We find no record of the organization of this Church, but since it was admitted to the Convention February 16, 1846, and organization was a prerequisite, it was probably organized the year previous. The Rev. Richard S. Seely was the missionary in that part of the diocese in 1846; he was probably here (as definitely he was in Newberry) the first minister and the "missionary" who reported in the summer of 1846 that a lot of land had been given by Col. James H. Irby (not a member) and $705.00 collected for a building, contributions also coming from Columbia and Charleston. Mr. Seely left the district March, 1847, going to Immanuel Church, Chester County. The cornerstone was laid in the summer of 1847 by the Rev. A. H. Cornish of Abbeville. On the occasion of his visit to the Church in July of this year, Bishop Gadsden reports the building in progress—"a neat edifice, 50 x 30, on a beautiful central site, which, including the graveyard, contains about six acres [part sold later] very suitable for a parsonage, adorned with large forest trees, truly emblematic of the quiet, and refreshment for the soul, to be had in the holy place, where especially the Lord condescendeth to meet the children of men. Amen." The Bishop was assisted on his visitation services, which lasted three days, by the Revs. M. H. Lance, A. H. Cornish, and Cranmore Wallace. Laymen we know there were to back this movement, but of their names, we know little. Dr. A. Bailey and his brother, R. S. Bailey, citizens of Laurens who had come from Edisto Island, were among these, the former being the first deputy to the Convention taking his seat at the time the Church was admitted. The Church sustained a severe blow when Dr. Bailey was thrown from his buggy and killed before the Church was finished. The Rev. T. S. Arthur was in charge briefly in 1847. The Honorable Joel R. Poinsett took an interest in the founding of this Church, contributing liberally and giving plans for the building. The Rev. L. Clements Johnson had the charge in 1847-48. He it was, probably, who reported services in the Church in the fall of 1848 where also he conducted the funeral of Mr. A. Admanson, one of the "principal friends of the Church".

The Church cost $2,230.00. A debt for a balance delayed the Consecration. Later, in July and October of 1848, the Rev. John D. McCollough, "a sort of roving missionary" (as he called himself) to the up-country, held two services. He found but "two persons connected with the Church, a substantial brick building on a lot of two acres, but no vestige of a congregation and a judgment against it in the Sheriff's Office for $1,000.00." From far and near, he raised $500.00, and with the two surviving vestrymen took the responsibility of selling half the Church lot for $500.00, and so paid the judgment. Mr. McCollough continued to hold a few services in 1849 and 1850. The Church was consecrated July 18, 1850. The Rev. Richard S. Seely, returning, became rector again in 1850. He also taught a school in Laurens at this time, but stayed only a short time, resigning November 15, 1851, having held 77 services, preached 51 sermons, and administered the Lord's Supper eight times. Church life became dormant now for several years. August 29, 1855, seemed to be the dawning of a better day. Bishop Davis, with the Rev. E. T. Walker who had taken charge in Newberry in 1853, visited the Church. They found it destitute. The Church and yard were put in order and a night service, well-attended, held when the Bishop preached. Mr. Walker now began a monthly service. A Bible and a prayer book were given by the Church of the Holy Communion, Charleston, at this time, also a beautiful font, the gift of "Dr. James Stuart and Lady" of Beaufort. Mr. Walker left after a year or two and the Church was vacant until the coming of the Rev. C. R. Hains in 1859, who officiated for a few months. In the meantime, the moving in of several families, Motte, Vernon, and Holbrook, brought more strength. In 1859, J. W. Motte and B. R. Campbell represented the Church in the Convention. At this time, through the efforts of Mr. Motte, the chancel was extended, and a plated communion service and a melodian procured. The Rev. Lucian C. Lance became rector in 1862, continuing until November, 1867, living in Laurens. For a time, he was assisted by the Rev. Edward C. Logan. The congregation was swelled during the war by refugees from the lower part of the State. In 1869, Mr. J. Ward Motte, the zealous warden, reports the Church vacant, no services since November, 1867, save two by his father, the Rev. J. W. Motte; people scattered, only three families, but the Church just put into good repair. Mr. Motte moved to Newberry, taking the Church records with him. When his home was burned, these were lost.

The Rev. E. R. Miles, deacon, took charge of Laurens and Newberry in 1870. He reported ten communicants at this time. His ministry was only to the end of 1873. For ten years from this time, the Church was dormant. Then, some faithful women succeeded in having the Church repaired and Mr. John Gass, a candidate for orders, held services in the winter of 1882-83. However, the Church was not really opened and in charge of a minister until the summer of 1885 when the Rev. E. C. Logan came and regular services began again. He reported in 1886 eight families and ten communicants, and at this time he organized a Sunday School. During the preceding year, the Church was newly ceiled and other improvements planned and later effected. The new railroad at this time had brought in new people. The life of the Church was renewed. Quite an addition to the strength of the parish at this time was the coming of Mr. Lewis Wardlaw Simkins with his family. He was for many years to give his devoted service as an officer to this Church. The Church was supplied with a bell in 1890. The Rev. Messrs. Dubose and Bratton gave additional services at this time. In 1894, Mr. Logan reports 44 services and 11 communicants. In 1895, the Church was renovated and new pews and altar installed.

Mr. Logan left this charge January, 1896, and after a time, the Rev. Wilmot S. Holmes took charge April 1, 1897. At this time, B. W. Ball and Dr. H. M. Holmes were wardens and L. W. Simkins, secretary and treasurer; the communicants had increased to 24. Soon after, Mr. Simkins became a warden in place of Dr.

Holmes, and W. W. Ball, secretary and treasurer. In 1903, the rectory which Mr. Holmes planned was completed. The Church benefited by the coming of new members in connection with the cotton mill. Mr. Holmes resigned February 15, 1902, to work in the colored Archdeaconry with the Rev. Mr. Joyner. The Rev. Edward McCrady then had charge for a short time, followed by the Rev. W. E. Callender, who held services in the fall and until the return of Mr. Holmes January 1, 1903. He stayed until March 1, 1904, when he went to Mississippi. The Rev. Henry Thomas took charge the following September. Wardens now were Dr. Rolfe E. Hughes and Robert W. Davis; secretary and treasurer, Dr. W. H. Washington. Mr. Thomas stayed just a year, going to Washington. His wife gave the credence at Easter, 1905. The Rev. W. E. Callender succeeded December 1, 1906. On a lot adjoining the Church at this time was erected a seven-room, two-story rectory. Mr. Callender held some services in Clinton. He resigned 1909. After a vacancy, then followed the Rev. A. E. Cornish (from September, 1910 to December, 1912); the Rev. Sanders R. Guignard (January 1, 1913— January 1, 1916); the Rev. W. S. Holmes (1917-22). In 1919 a new organ was installed.

The diocese of Upper South Carolina was set up October, 1922. The Rev. Thomas L. Ridout was the first rector in the new relationship, but only for a very short time. Mr. J. S. Jones, a student, supplied services the winter of 1923-24. The Rev. C. E. Clarkson had temporary charge in 1925, followed by the Rev. E. N. Joyner who served until the Rev. C. P. Holbrook's coming in 1928. He remained two years. Mr. R. E. Hughes was warden at this time, and Mrs. H. S. Blackwell, treasurer. The Rev. Albert R. Stuart became rector in 1932. An altar service book with brass rest was in this year given in memory of Judge R. C. Watts, Chief Justice, by his daughter, Mrs. Bessie Watts Royal. The next year, the furniture in the Church was renovated. Mr. Stuart went to St. Michael's, Charleston, in 1936; the wardens were M. L. Copeland and Dr. Frank Kellers; the secretary and lay reader, John Kitrell. The communicants had increased to 39. The Rev. Billert A. Williams became rector in 1939. Under a new classification of the churches in the diocese, Epiphany now ceased to be a "parish" with a rector and became an "organized mission" with a "priest-in-charge". Mr. Williams was succeeded by the Rev. E. Hopkins Weston in 1948, who in turn was succeeded by the Rev. Edwin B. Clippard in 1951, who served until January 1, 1954. The Rev. Clyde Lambert Ireland took charge June, 1954.

ST. LUKE'S, NEWBERRY
Established 1846

On April 15, 1839, the Rev. Cranmore Wallace was appointed "Missionary to Destitute Parishes and other places." Among a large number of services in the up-country, he lists one as held in the Court House in Newberry in that year. From this time, there were occasional services in the schoolhouse and in the Court House. In 1844 on Advent Sunday, the Rev. Richard S. Seely was ordained deacon and appointed as missionary to serve in "Newberry, Marion, and York." He left the field in March, 1847, going to Immanuel Church, Chester District. He reported holding 35 services in Newberry in 1846. There were only four communicants. The Rev. L. Clement Johnson was in charge in 1847-48. The Church was admitted into union with the Convention February 18, 1848, under the name St. Luke's, Newberry. On the occasion of Bishop Gadsden's visit on August 7, 1849, no place was available for a service, the Court House being considered unsafe. The Rev. Mr. McCollough, the roving missionary, held two services in the Male Academy, Sunday, December 14, 1851. However, he "saw no vestige of church or church organization"—only two churchmen. The "Mountain Convocation" met in Newberry February, 1852, with the Rev. Messrs. Arthur, Simmons, and McCollough, who held services. They persuaded Messrs. Hurd and Bailey to go on with them to the Convention in Columbia. Probably in consequence of this, the Rev. Edward T. Walker was sent as missionary to Newberry.

In November, 1852, the Church was put under the care of Mr. Walker. He started with only six Episcopalians; but nevertheless, with the large congregations which attended his services, he thought the prospects "flattering." A fine lot (75 x 200 feet), purchased and given by ten citizens of Newberry, was provided in 1852. It was located at the corner of Main and Calhoun Streets. (A lot had been offered by Gen. J. J. Caldwell as early as 1846.) A contract was made for a Church to cost $4,000.00; a large proportion was subscribed by citizens. A building to seat 300 was reported finished in February, 1855. It measured 32 x 62 feet with 19-foot walls, and had originally a tower, organ loft, and vestry room. It was built of brick, rough-cast to represent granite. The Church was consecrated by Bishop Davis, August 26, 1855, assisted by the rector and the Rev. Messrs. E. E. Bellinger and Benjamin Johnson. Seven were confirmed on this occasion, making 18 communicants. The Church building is of Gothic architecture, and handsome with self-supporting roof, stained-glass windows, and neatly furnished within. It is by a good many years the oldest Church edifice in the town; originally there was a tower at the southeast corner. The Church was built by Contractor Hamilton of Charleston, in 1854-55, from a drawing by Architect G. M. Walker of Columbia. The vestry at this time was as follows: wardens, Edward S. Bailey and Stiles Hurd; vestrymen, Norman Bronson, W. B. D'Oyley, W. C. Johnson, C. H. Kingsmore, and A. C. Garlington. We find this interesting account of the Church situation in Newberry as of October 21, 1854. It probably would apply to most of the up-country at this time. "Eighteen months ago the prospect was a gloomy one; we had no foothold in the community, our Church was thought to be Romish, and there was reason for it. You can, then, imagine what prejudice existed against us. Besides, those of us who were Episcopalians, were as one to five hundred in the community. The first service which our rector held for us, he preached to six adults in the Female Academy; but things have changed. The entire mind of this community has changed, and what has done it? Believe me, nothing but that course of conduct which sets forth peace in a community; nothing but the preaching of a sound gospel. This has done it; this has broken some prejudice; this has given the Episcopal Church a place in the affections of all who are Christians." Mr. Walker resigned in 1856 and the Church had no rector until the Rev. C. R. Hains came for a short time in 1859. The Rev. Lucien C. Lance became rector in 1862. Refugees swelled the congregation during the war. In 1864, the tower was taken down, being considered unsafe. In this year, the Rev. Edward C. Logan became assistant. He conducted a mission at Helena, railroad shops, a mile from Newberry. In 1865 from October 14, a series of services were held under charge of Bishop Davis. He was assisted by the Rev. Messrs. Lance, Logan, McCollough, and Robert Wilson. Mr. Lance left at the close of 1865 and Mr. Logan a year later. The Rev. J. Maxwell Pringle and others held occasional services. In this year, the Church was reported in a sad state near utter ruin. Bishop Davis made this statement on October 18, 1866: "After consulting with the only remaining member of the vestry, we resolved to nail up the Church to protect it from the desecrations to which it had been subjected, and wait for a better day." However, after a time with some assistance from Charleston in the way of repairing the Church, almost to the point of rebuilding, it was reopened in 1870 by the Rev. E. R. Miles. The Revs. W. P. DuBose, Ellison Capers, and E. T. Walker assisted Mr. Miles in his field of work, including Anderson and Laurens. Mr. Miles also held services in Chappell's at the home of Capt. J. N. Lipscomb. He resigned December 31, 1873.

The Rev. P. F. Stevens was in charge from January, 1874, until June, 1875, when he left to connect himself with the "Reformed Episcopal Church." For a year, there was no regular minister, but lay services were held regularly, with occasional visits of clergymen. The Rev. John Kershaw was rector from June, 1876, until May, 1879. At this time, St. Luke's had 35 communicants; the officers were: wardens, W. C. Johnson (for 24 years) and A. W. T. Simmons; vestrymen, R. H. Greneker, R. H. Clarkson, N. B. Mazyck, and J. N. Fowles. The Rev. S. H. S. Gallaudet was rector (1879-80), then the Rev. Frank Hallam (1880-82). A handsome altar was installed at this time. The next rector was the Rev. William F. Dickinson for the year 1882. He was the first resident rector. The Rev. W. H. Hanckel served from January, 1883, until his death November 1, 1892. In 1890, improvements were made in the Church. The Rev. Henry T. Gregory served for the year 1894. At this time, the chancel of the Church was enlarged and a stained-glass window installed in it; also, Dr. A. T. Porter gave candlesticks. The Rev. R. P. Eubanks served part of the year 1895, then the Church was vacant until the coming of the Rev. W. S. Holmes in 1897. The wardens this year were N. B. Mazyck and N. H. Greneker; O. McR. Holmes, secretary and treasurer. A new organ was now obtained.

Mr. Holmes opened in Newberry a mission for colored people October, 1898. He continued rector until February, 1902. It was about this time that Mr. N. B. Mazyck removed from Newberry with his large family. He had been the devoted warden and lay reader for many years, serving in the latter capacity for about a quarter-century, keeping the Church open in the absence of the rector, and during many vacancies. The Church's condition at this time was described as "dreadful." It had not had a resident rector for twenty-five years. However, Mr. Holmes returned January 1, 1903, and served his second term until March, 1904. The Rev. Henry Thomas succeeded then and served for just one year. Conditions were now greatly improved. The Rev. W. E. Callender becama rector in 1907, until 1908. A new organ was installed at this time. For the next twelve years, the ministers were as follows: Mr. C. P. Parker (then a candidate), 1910; A. E. Cornish, 1910-12; S. R. Guignard, 1913-16; W. S. Holmes (third term), 1916-22. The diocese was divided in 1922. The Rev. Thomas L. Ridout was rector 1922-23. Then, after a long vacancy filled by lay reading and services by a candidate, Justice Smith Jones, the Rev. E. N. Joyner served two years, 1926-27, followed for one year, 1928, by the Rev. Charles P. Holbrook. In 1930, the wardens were T. E. Keitt and Dr. H. G. Callison, the former also treasurer and superintendent of the Sunday School. Then followed as ministers: the Rev. A. Rufus Morgan, 1929-30; the Rev. A. G. B. Bennett, 1931-38; the Rev. Billert A. Williams, 1939-48; the Rev. W. A. Thompson, 1949-50. During these latter years lay readers, all from Columbia, often held the services, including Messrs. Gordon Thomas, W. A. Beckham, and John Fitzgibbon. In the summer of 1950, Bishop R. E. Gribbin held the services, giving lectures also during the week. In 1951, a residence on Calhoun Street was purchased and renovated for the rectory. In 1951, the Rev. Edwin B. Clippard occupied it, holding his first service in St. Luke's September, 1951. He was ordained priest in St. Luke's the year following. Mr. Clippard's ministry was marked by an awakening of Church life.

Many improvements and renovations have been made in the Church in recent years. The floor has been carpeted and the pews, organ, altar rail and balcony rail refinished, revealing the beautiful grain and mellowed texture of old pine. Stained-glass windows were placed in the southern end of the Church. A new altar and baptismal font, made of pine to harmonize with the other woodwork of the Church, were dedicated to the Glory of God, the font given in memory of Thomas Davis, son of the present senior warden, Mr. T. E. Davis. The new brass altar cross was dedicated to the memory of the late Mr. A. P. Salley, long-time senior warden of St. Luke's; and the brass altar candlesticks were dedicated to the memory of the late Prof. W. H. Gaver, former junior warden. The old Ladies' Guild of the parish, reorganized by Mrs. A. P. Salley in 1944, now affiliated as a branch of the Woman's Auxiliary, is very active with Mrs. S. D. Paysinger as president. I. B. Covington, superintendent, succeeded by Mr. L. A. Harrison, have faithfully conducted the Sunday School for many years. The Rev. Clyde L. Ireland supplied evening services beginning in July, 1954. The Rev. Gordon H. Mann assumed regular charge May 1, 1955. The rectory which had served as quarters for the Church school, bring now in demand for its proper use, Mr. T. H. Pope loaned the use of a larger building in his yard known as the Long House. In October the Church school moved to its permanent home on the newly acquired property beside the Church. The vestry for the years 1953-54 included LeRoy Anderson, R. T. Albrecht, T. H. Pope, W. F.

Rutherford, J. E. Britt, with T. E. Davis, senior warden, and I. B. Covington, junior warden. Mr. Covington also served many years as Church treasurer.

This Church, through its history, has encountered many difficulties but has remained steadfast. With laymen serving when clergymen could not be had, it has never been "dormant." For three days beginning October 16, 1955, the 100th anniversary of the building of the Church was celebrated. Three Bishops (Cole, Gravatt, and Gribbin) with many clergymen, including the rector, the Rev. Gordon H. Mann, took part in the celebration. Thomas H. Pope, Esq., presented a history of St. Luke's Church.

ST. MONICA, NEWBERRY
Established 1894

This mission admitted to Convention in 1955 as an "organized mission" under the name St. Monica was formerly known as St. Luke's mission, or St. Luke the Physician. It was under charge of the Rev. G. E. Howell when first opened in 1894. The people themselves bought a lot and built a schoolhouse where, for a time, a day school was held. The Rev. T. T. Pollard was priest-in-charge at the time of the division of the diocese in 1922. When the Rev. Edwin B. Clippard took charge of old St. Luke's Church, Newberry, in 1952, he became interested in this mission (as also St. Simon's, Peak) of the colored people then without regular services of a minister, and instituted services by himself twice a month. The Church which had fallen into serious disrepair was greatly improved and refurnished with the assistance of $987.50 contributed by the national Church. In 1955 the warden was Eugene Schumpert; Jimmie Shelton, treasurer; and John Rutherford, superintendent of the Church school; 16 communicants. (See Archdeaconries, Part One, Sec. II and Part Two, Sec. II.)

ST. BARTHOLOMEW'S, NORTH AUGUSTA, AIKEN COUNTY
Established 1951

This was not the first Episcopal mission in North Augusta. Often before services had been held in the town and efforts made to establish a permanent Church. Notably especially was this the case in 1910. On June 9 of this year, an opening service was held; this being the First Sunday of the Epiphany, the mission was called Epiphany. The Rev. Roberts P. Johnson, in charge then in Graniteville, led. R. E. Belcher was the warden and Leroy Haskins the secretary. Mrs. George Ellis and Mrs. Julia C. Baker were leaders in this movement. The work continued with irregularity. On February 28, 1912, at a meeting held in the home of Dr. Theodore Kershaw with Bishop Guerry, a building committee was appointed. However, while services were held, nothing permanent came of this work, nor of a mission for colored in North Augusta in 1908.

It was in 1951 that there occurred a great influx of population in this whole region due to the coming of the Atomic Energy Plant. This stimulated a renewal of a long-felt desire for an Episcopal Church in North Augusta. Also, Bishop Gravatt now feeling a great responsibility of the Church to meet the new condition made many visits to North Augusta, looking to organizing a Church. As the first overt step, on March 15, 1951, he sent out a letter to all Episcopalians residing in or near North Augusta. There were present at the resulting meeting some thirty to forty interested persons. The following clergymen attended: The Rev. Sidney E. Heath, St. Paul's, Graniteville; the Rev. Michael Kippenbrock, St. Thaddeus', Aiken, and the following clergy from the diocese of Georgia: the Rev. Charles Schilling, St. Paul's, Augusta; the Rev. Chaffee Croft, the Church of the Atonement, Augusta; the Rev. Allen Clarkson, Church of the Good Shepherd, and the Rev. Richard Wilkerson. The Bishop explained the conditions requisite for the organization of a mission. The next meeting was held May 14, 1951, in the lobby of the North Augusta Banking Company and was conducted by the Rev. Michael Kippenbrock, whom Bishop Gravatt had appointed priest-in-charge and the Rev. Sidney E. Heath to assist. Practically the same group was present as attended the March 26 meeting. At this time those present, being interested in and willing to support the work, voted to organize a mission. The following charter members signed the letter of application, May 14, 1951: Nancy Suman Upchurch, O. W. Belding, Annie Davis Belding, H. J. Upchurch, Ann Smith Curtis, Mary S. Ferguson, Lois Feester Brierley, James R. Brierley, Lucy P. Swearingen, Ann B. Robins, Pickens Greneker Moorer, F. Le Grande Moorer, Douglas W. Curtis, W. R. Harper and family. By a vote of the members, St. Bartholomew was selected as the name of the Church. The first officers were O. W. Belding, Sr., warden; John W. Hooten, secretary; H. J. Upchurch, treasurer; and Douglas W. Curtis, Church school superintendent. Also a Bishop's committee, headed by Mr. Belding, was appointed. A membership of 44 communicants was reported in 1952. The Masonic Lodge on Georgia Avenue was loaned for a place of meeting. After the organization, the Rev. Sidney E. Heath of Graniteville was appointed priest-in-charge, and held the first service, the Holy Communion, on Trinity Sunday morning, May 20, 1951. St. Paul's, Augusta, gave the altar used. A branch of the Woman's Auxiliary was at once organized with Mrs. Lucy Swearingen as president. The Auxiliary contributed much to the upbuilding of the mission during these early days. The congregation grew under the ministry of Mr. Heath who removed in September, being succeeded the following April by the services of Right Rev. Robert E. Gribbin, D.D. Lay readers held services in the interim. A lot having been secured in Lynhurst, a parish house was built on it under a building committee with Mr. W. R. Harper as chairman. The Rev. Forbes Ross de Tamble having been appointed priest-in-charge held the first services in this building on St. Bartholomew's Day, August 24, 1952. A Layman's League was organized, also an Altar Guild, and a Needlecraft Guild and in April, 1953, a Y. P. S. L. In December, 1953, an addition of 25 feet was added to the front of the parish house to meet the increasing demands of the work. After a most useful ministry during which the Church grew and prospered, Mr. de Tamble left the mission in August, 1955. Rev. R. Hampton Price succeeded as priest-in-charge.

ST. SIMON'S, PEAK
Established 1889

St. Simon's was one of the early missions for colored people in Fairfield County, beginning about 1889. In 1894 the Rev. G. E. Howell had charge with a day school and a Sunday School. There was a fund for a building contributed by St. Augustine's League of New York. At the turn of the century with the Rev. J. S. Quarles in charge, there were 34 communicants and about 40 in both the day and Sunday Schools. At the time of the beginning of the diocese of Upper S. C., this mission was in the charge of the Rev. T. T. Pollard. There was then a day school of 45 and 12 communicants. In 1947 and for many years to this date 1955, Mr. John Thomas was and is the faithful lay reader and treasurer. When Rev. Edwin B. Clippard became rector of St. Luke's, Newberry, in 1952, he led a movement of actual regeneration, spiritually and materially, of St. Simon's. He gave one service a month, and with the help of Church people from Newberry and Clinton, as well as the local membership, renewed the Church—floors and windows were repaired, exterior and interior repainted, new Holy Table, organ, carpet, altar cross, candlesticks, communion linen. After the Rev. Mr. Clippard left in 1954, the Rev. Joseph N. Green, first as deacon then as priest, had charge for a time. There are 14 communicants. (See Archdeaconries—Part One, Sec. II and Part Two, Sec. II.)

ST. PAUL'S, PENDLETON
Established 1820

The founding of St. Paul's Church, Pendleton, marked the first entrance of the Episcopal Church into the distinctly up-country of South Carolina. Scotch-Irish elements had held exclusive religious sway. Pendleton District at the turn of the 19th century included Anderson, Pickens, and Oconee Counties. The town of Pendleton was already a summer resort for low-country people predominantly Episcopalians and some from Virginia. The first intimation of the movement of the Episcopal Church into this region was in the Convention of 1815, when Hon. Theodore Gaillard, a deputy from Trinity Church, Columbia, moved a resolution, commending the work of the Advancement Society and appealing for its support that it might extend its work into the upper part of the state "particularly in Pendleton District". The need then was evidently felt already at this time. There were three subscribers in Pendleton to Dalcho's history, published in 1820, viz. Benjamin Dupre, Thomas Lynch Dart, John L. North; these gentlemen and their families may have been the pioneers of the Church in the up-country. It was in March, 1820 that the Advancement Society engaged the services of the Rev. Patrick H. Folker "to visit the villages of Pendleton and Greenville and the parts adjacent." His tour of six weeks was "satisfactory to the Board" and within a few weeks the Rev. Rodolphus Dickinson was appointed for a season to this field including Pendleton, Greenville and the Armory, at which places it was reported to the society that "congregations had been formed by means of Mr. Dickinson's labors" as early as June, 1820. We read in the minutes of St. Paul's the record of the actual beginning of this Church: "Pendleton C. H., June 17, 1819. At a meeting of a number of residents of Pendleton District, wishing to establish an Episcopal Church, Benjamin Dupree, Esq., was called to the chair. On motion of Major Davis an election was held for Vestrymen, and the following were chosen, viz., Benj'n Dupre, Thos. L. Dart, Laurens McGregor, Dr. Hall and Thomas Pinckney, Jr." Mr. Dickinson had previously engaged in teaching at Greenville where he had held some services. Not having been canonically accredited from his former home in the Eastern diocese, and being absent in the summer he was not permanently appointed to this work until December. In the meantime Rev. F. P. Delevaux was temporarily employed but he "was prevented from carrying the purpose into effect." The services prior to the building of a Church were held in the Court House and in the Farmer's Hall. All three of the congregations mentioned applied to the society for aid in August, 1820—the response was "They would give as much as the congregation gave to the support of a minister". The Church, though not formally admitted, was represented in the Convention of 1821 by Col. Thomas Pinckney, the two other congregations were also represented.

To this Convention Bishop Bowen reports the work of Rev. Messrs. Folker and Dickinson in the northwestern part of the state. The society had engaged Mr. Dickinson as missionary to the Churches of St. Paul's, Pendleton, and St. Peter's and St. James' in Greenville District for two years from December 1, 1820, at $500.00 per annum. At the next Convention, February, 1822, the Bishop reports the "happy occasion" of visiting for the first time "through the North Western extremity of the state." He found the society's missionary, Mr. Dickinson "faithfully performing the laborious duties of his station." In Pendleton he administered the rite of confirmation. Here measures had been taken to erect a Church, a Sunday School had been instituted, and there was found reason to hope "that the seed sown in the seemingly unfriendly soil will spring up and flourish, etc." Mr. Dickinson reported, "Public sentiment is there yielding to approbation of the pure doctrine and worship of our Zion." To this Convention was reported for St. Paul's, two baptisms and one marriage. Immediately after the Convention of 1822 Mr. Dickinson, having served to this time as a deacon, was ordained to the priesthood. At this time there was no Church of any kind within the corporate limits of Pendleton. An appeal was made, Bishop Bowen heading the list of subscribers with $100.00. In 1822 "a neat and convenient" Church (50 feet by 32) was built, due largely, Bishop Bowen states, to the generous personal exertions and sacrifices of Col. Thomas Pinckney. The lot was obtained from Mr. Samuel Cherry. Among others cooperating were Mr. B. Dupre, Dr. Hall, Mr. Talliaferro, Col. Calhoun, Col. Warren and Dr. T. Dart. The Church was consecrated by Bishop Bowen on November 23, 1823. William Morningstar was the contractor. The Advancement Society was highly pleased with the "prosperity of the Church in Pendleton, and the Bishop rejoiced that in that remote district, where there had been no friendly sentiment, now there were services having the regular attendance on them of a numerous congregation of serious worshippers, operating their influence upon the community." Mr. Dickinson in 1824 reported 27 families in the congregation, whole number of congregation (not all Episcopal) 160.

In 1829 numbers had increased, three pews, a gallery for colored persons, and a tower had been added to the Church as well as "ornamental improvements." Mr. Dickinson resigned in 1831. The Rev. F. H. Rutledge officiated from June to November, 1832. At this time the young ladies organized a Social Working Society. At their instance two silver communion cups were presented by Mrs. John L. North and other silver given the following summer. A small library was established. Lt. Gov. Charles C. Pinckney was the delegate to the Convention of 1833. The Rev. W. H. Barnwell officiated this year from May to November; the Sunday School numbered 29 white and 63 colored; five pews were added, also a vestry room and the position of the pulpit changed, improving the interior of the Church.

The Rev. William T. Potter became rector in 1834. At this time the Church was enlarged and twelve new pews added. Mr. Potter resigned in 1845, but returned for temporary service in 1847, from June until November. The Rev. A. H. Cornish served as rector from 1848 until his death May, 1875, only excepting a short interval (1850-51) when he officiated in St. Thomas' and St. Dennis'. In 1848 the ladies installed an organ at a cost of $300.00. In 1854 a parsonage was acquired at a cost of $1,100.00, again largely by the efforts of the ladies. At about this time two handsome chairs were given for the chancel and a chandelier by Mrs. R. Y. Hayne. The Church enjoyed the services of Mr. Benjamin R. Stuart of Charleston as lay reader in 1856. About this time Mr. Cornish held services also at Keowee, Windbery Chapel, and at Seneca. Mr. Cornish states that from 1820 to 1833, there was no parish register. Statistics from 1833 to 1871 are: Baptisms, white 195, colored 240; confirmed, white 100, colored 27; marriages, white 48, colored 40; burials, white 123, colored 81. In 1848 there were 13 families, and 20 communicants; in 1871 30 families and 60 communicants. Among the accomplishments of this period was the purchase of 1½ acres adjoining the graveyard and fencing the Churchyard. In these years the congregation was largely a summer group coming from the low country. On the occasion of Bishop Davis's visit in 1855 he preached four times to large congregations "and many eyes unused to weep, and hearts seldom touched, gave evidence of the emotions within." In the war years Mr. Cornish was often assisted by other ministers— C. C. Pinckney, J. H. Elliott, James Quinby and others. Col. W. A.

Hayne acted as lay reader. In 1875 Mr. Cornsh was holding services also in Seneca and Walhalla. St. Paul's lost some of its strength by transfers to these missions. Mr. Cornish died May 24, 1875. The chancel window is in his memory. The Rev. Henry T. Gregory became rector January 1, 1876, but only for less than two years, the Rev. William H. Hanckel succeeding July 21, 1878. At this time there were 54 communicants.

Mr. Hanckel was rector for nearly sixteen years to April, 1884. In July of this year Rev. Thomas F. Gadsden took charge, continuing until 1891. The altar cross is a gift in his memory. A communion table, chancel lamp, and a handsome chancel chair were added at this time. The Rev. O. T. Porcher assisted Mr. Gadsden during his last year, becoming rector himself January 1, 1891. He soon began services at Fort Hill and at Clemson, also for a time a mission service at "Old Stone Church", three miles from Pendleton, an old Presbyterian Church.   Mr. Porcher was succeeded in St. Paul's by the Rev. Benjamin MacKenzie Anderson August 26, 1900, for a year. The Rev. K. G. Finlay took charge September, 1902, in connection with Clemson College, serving until he went to Trinity, Columbia, in 1907. In 1902 Thomas Pinckney, M.D., was warden, and also Benjamin Crawford, Jr., warden, secretary and treasurer. From 1909 to 1911 the Rev. Lyttleton E. Hubard served and then from 1912 to 1916 the Rev. R. M. Marshall. The Rev. James M. Stoney became rector in 1917. The centennial of the Church was celebrated on May 2, 1920. The rector conducted the service assisted by the Rev. Guy Frazer of Anderson. The Church was beautifully decorated and a choir of forty voices (augmented from Clemson) rendered the service inspiringly. Bishop Guerry preached a great sermon on the position of the Church in Christendom. The Rev. George E. D. Zachary succeeded Mr. Stoney as rector in 1922, serving until February, 1925. The Church was vacant until the Rev. A. W. Taylor came in 1927, but only for a short time. Rev. Capers Satterlee followed in 1928. In 1932 an alms basin and a credence table were given the former by the Guild in memory of Eliza Hunter and the latter by Mr. Lucius Stevens. Mr. Satterlee was followed by Rev. Donald E. Veale in 1936, and he in 1943 by the Rev. John A. Pinckney. Then came the Rev. R. Emmet Gribbin, who in turn was succeeded by Rev. J. W. Cole in 1951. Mr. Cole was the first resident rector of St. Paul's in fifty years. On October 21, 1951, services were held celebrating the Consecration of the Church 128 years since its founding. Mr. Cole was assisted in the morning by the Rev. W. R. Baley and in the afternoon by the Rev. R. E.

Gribbin and the Rev. M. R. Tilson. At these services a large number of memorial gifts were presented. Under Rev. Mr. Cole the Church has increased from eight to 47 communicants and the budget from $120.00 to $2,600.00. The remains of many distinguished people lie in the graveyard surrounding the Church: Floride C. Calhoun, wife of John C. Calhoun, Thomas G. Clemson and wife, Generals Barnard E. Bee and Clement H. Stevens, the Rev. John Jasper Adams, founder of Hobart College, William Henry Trescott and others. Interesting details of St. Paul's will be found in a sketch by the Rev. Roland J. Whitmire, Jr. A real step forward was taken in this historic parish in 1955. In October of this year, was begun the construction of a $13,000.00 parish house which was completed in December, 1955, and opened for use in January of 1956. The parish house is of brick construction containing kitchen, four classrooms, and a parish hall. It was first used at the patronal festival for a dinner following the celebration of the Holy Communion.

GRACE CHURCH, RIDGE SPRING
Established 1873

In 1872, a group of Church people in this attractive and historic village resolved to establish the Church in their midst; so resulted Grace Church, Ridge Spring. The very first services were held in the Baptist Church by the Rev. E. T. Walker, inspired largely by Mrs. W. A. Merritt. The efforts of these and other zealous people soon resulted in the erection of a remarkably tasteful building in churchly style. The building cost between four and five thousand dollars. Considerable assistance came from the North. Messrs. Burrel T. and Sumter Boatwright gave the land for the Church, and Mr. W. A. Merritt gave an acre of land for a burial ground. A chancel window of stained glass was given by Mr. Henry E. Sharp of New York. Hangings and a font came from a lady in Philadelphia as well as financial aid. A bell was given by Prince George's, Georgetown, maybe the oldest bell in the state. It has on it 1750. On the occasion of the Bishop's first visitation, October, 1873, several services were held. The Bishop confirmed two persons. He was assisted in these services by the Rev. Messrs. C. B. Walker, J. H. Cornish, and E. C. Edgerton. The mission was committed by the Bishop to the charge of Rev. C. Bruce Walker, to give two services a month. Mrs. James Merritt was the first treasurer. She served until 1898. The chapel was consecrated by Bishop Howe on November 29, 1874. Several services were held beginning Friday afternoon and extending through Sunday evening. The clergymen assisting were, besides Mr. Walker, the Revs. J. H. Tillinghast, W. H. Campbell, E. C. Edgerton, E. T. Walker, and Kennerly of North Carolina. Dr. DuBose read the Request. The choir of Trinity, Edgefield, supplied the music.

The Rev. B. B. Sams succeeded Mr. Walker in charge October, 1876, continuing for just one year. In the summer of this year, Mrs. Moro Phillips of Philadelphia contributed $675.00, with which the Church was completed by plastering and painting. At this time, there were 11 families with 19 communicants. The Rev. William J. Alger served the mission for six months in 1878. For two years then the Rev. H. O. Judd of Trinity, Columbia, gave a monthly service, 1880-82. Then followed Rev. W. F. Dickinson of Newberry. In 1883, the Rev. R. W. Barnwell, recently ordered deacon, assumed charge in connection with the rectorship of the Holy Apostles, Barnwell. He reported 20 communicants in 1884, public worship 43 Sundays. The mission was prospering. In 1887, the Rev. A. E. Cornish succeeded Mr. Barnwell in charge with the Rev. John F. Finlay assisting for a year. Mr. Cornish continued as the minister until 1894 when the Rev. W. B. Gordon, then rector of Trinity, Edgefield, took charge. His ministrations in this Church lasted until 1897. At this time, there were 16 communicants. Mrs. James Merritt continued to serve as treasurer until 1898. After Mr. Gordon, the Rev. R. W. Anderson was in charge until 1902, when the Rev. P. D. Hay succeeded him until 1905. Miss Mary DuBose had succeeded Mrs. Merritt as treasurer, and then another faithful woman assumed the treasurership in 1903, Mrs. W. H. Stuckey, who held this office until 1950, then succeeded by Mrs. R. B. Asbill.

In 1906, the Rev. Royal Graham Shannonhouse became minister-in-charge, serving for about twelve years. Mr. Frank T. Carwile was the first warden of Grace Church, serving faithfully until 1937. Lay readers during these years were Mr. Barnabas Bryan, Mr. J. Nelson Frierson of Columbia, and Mr. Carwile. The mission became "organized" in 1908 and was admitted to the Convention. After Mr. Shannonhouse left to go to Georgia, the Rev. Louis Ashley Peatross took charge in 1920. The mission became part of the Diocese of Upper South Carolina in 1922. The Rev. E. N. Joyner, then living in North Carolina, had temporary charge until the coming of the Rev. E. M. Claytor, who continued until succeeded after a short vacancy by the Rev. H. G. England, D.D., in 1929. Dr. England retained charge for ten years. During these years, Mr. W. F. T. Carwile was warden until 1939, and Mrs. W. H. Stuckey, treasurer until 1950. The wardens, after Mr. Carwile, were W. H. Stuckey and Dr. P. A. Brunson. The succeeding ministers after Dr. England retired in 1939 were: the Rev. Allen B. Clarkson (1940-42), the Rev. William S. Brace (1943-49), the Rev. Frederick A. Pope (1950), then after two years, the Rev. John G. Clarkson, Jr. (1953). In 1954, a parish house was built adjoining the Church. It was dedicated by Bishop Cole on November 28, 1954, in memory of Mary Elizabeth Carwile, Frank T. Carwile, Mary Miller, DuBose Stuckey, Walter Hamer Stuckey, and Peter Alexander Brunson, M.D. The land on which the parish house is built was given years ago by Mrs. Sarah Barnwell Gregorie of Adam's Run, and her brother, Col. John D. Barnwell of Fernandena, Fla.

ST. STEPHEN'S, RIDGEWAY
Established 1839

As seen in the sketch of St. John's, Winnsboro, services of the Church were held occasionally in Fairfield County from 1825, the first in the vicinity of Ridgeway were services held in Aimwell Presbyterian Church, located about a mile north of Ridgeway. This was on September 25, 1839, by the Rev. Cranmore Wallace. Several persons were baptized and again the next year he held services on June 27 at the same place. A little later than this, the services were held "At the house used by the Episcopalians for the public worship of God in Edward Gendron Palmer's neighborhood." This was the beginning of the acquirement of a home by the Church people in this neighborhood. It was called the Chapel of St. John's Church (Winnsboro) at Cedar Creek. Among the first members were Palmers, Thomases, and Davises; being mostly from old St. Stephen's Church on the Santee, they named their Church St. Stephen's. The Rev. Josiah Obear after Mr. Wallace continued to minister at Ridgeway. Under his successor the Rev. John J. Roberts, St. Stephen's Church was built and consecrated by Bishop Davis on August 4, 1854, the Rev. Messrs. Johnson, Shand, Cornish, and Wigfall assisting. This building, a most attractive little Gothic Church, was designed by the Rev. J. D. McCollough, later rector. The ten acres of land on which the Church was built was given by Mrs. Catherine Ross Davis. The brick for the foundation was given by Dr. John Peyre Thomas, made at his plantation, Mt. Hope; the lumber by Mr. Edward Gendron Palmer and Colonel Henry Davis. Mr. Peay of Longtown gave $100.00 in behalf of his sister, Mrs. John Meyers. Mr. Richard Matchet of Dutchman's Creek was another early member as also some of the slaves for whom seats were provided in the rear of the Church. The communion service is the gift

of Mrs. Jane Marshall Gaillard Thomas, wife of the Rev. Edward
Thomas, brother of John Peyre and Samuel Peyre Thomas, early
members of St. Stephen's; first Church missionary to Fairfield (See
Winnsboro). In these earlier days St. Stephen's continued to be
administered practically as a part of St. John's, Winnsboro, having
the same minister. Mr. E. G. Palmer of St. Stephen's was a
deputy to the Convention of the diocese in 1858 from St. John's,
Fairfield. St. Stephen's was not admitted to Convention as a separate
Church until 1889. The deputies to the Convention this year were
John R. Thomas, J. A. Desportes, R. H. McKelvey, R. A. Meares.
The succession of ministers was therefore the same—Obear, Roberts,
Johnson, McCollough, Hutchinson, Lord, DuBose, Memminger,
then Obear again officiated until his death in 1882. He had assisted
the rector ever since his return to Winnsboro in 1855 in connection
with his school. He was greatly beloved throughout these years.
The first burial in the churchyard of St. Stephen's was that of Dr.
J. P. Thomas, January 1, 1859; the graves of two of his sons were
moved from Aimwell. The Church escaped injury when Sherman
came through, the silver being saved at Mt. Hope. In 1870 Mr.
Campbell reported both congregations as "very zealous." In 1873
St. Stephen's received the gift of "a very chaste baptismal font"
from St. Chrysostom's in New York. In this year the wardens were
Robert H. Edmunds and John Rosborough Thomas. When Mr.
Campbell left in February, 1875, Mr. Obear again took full charge.
In 1879 an organ was installed by the energies of the ladies, replac-
ing the old melodeon. In these years Major Charles E. Thomas was
treasurer and lay reader. The death of Mr. Obear in 1882 was
greatly deplored. He is commemorated on a tablet on the chancel
wall of the Church. He had been connected with the Church since
1841.

The Rev. Frank Hallam became rector in 1882. With gifts of
walnut and the help of Major C. E. Thomas he made and installed
a new altar, prayer desk, and lectern. Then followed in succession
for short periods: the Revs. John Gass, G. H. Edwards, and A. R.
Mitchell. The Rev. James G. Glass followed in 1887. The Church
was admitted into Convention in 1889. It lost its old records in the
burning of Mr. Glass's home in Winnsboro. At this time there was
a Sunday School conducted chiefly by Mr. C. E. Thomas and Miss
H. E. Thomas. The next ministers were the Revs. G. L. Sweeney,
A. R. Mitchell, S. E. Prentiss, and Edward Benedict in 1895. The
Rev. Benjamin Allston was rector from 1896 until 1899 when he
was succeeded by Rev. William Norwood Tillinghast, the first rector

serving separately from St. John's, Winnsboro, and the first to reside in Ridgeway. He resigned in 1902, being followed by the Rev. H. O. Judd (1903-1906), united with Winnsboro again, and Rev. W. J. Webster (1907-1908). There was quite a revival of life under the next rector, the Rev. Robert A. Chase (1909-1910). At this time improvements included a new altar, Bishop's chair, priest's chair, in walnut, altar desk with service book, lectern, Bible, and two crosses on the Church; then the next year a new organ. Rev. Roberts P. Johnson was rector 1910-1911. The officers at this time were: wardens, R. A. Meares, N. W. Palmer; secretary and treasurer, R. C. Thomas; lay reader, G. P. Edmunds.

The Rev. F. N. Skinner became rector in 1913. The residence of this rector in Ridgeway stimulated much increased activity in the Church, having now a flourishing Sunday School. The Church sent seven men into the first World War. Mr. Skinner resigned June 1, 1919. Then followed the Rev. W. P. Peyton (1912-1926), next, briefly the Rev. C. B. Lucas and the Rev. I. deL. Brayshaw in 1928. The Rev. S. R. Guignard assumed charge in 1929, and continued until his death May 29, 1936. On August 19, 1934, the 80th birthday of St. Stephen's was celebrated with two services: the Rev. Alexander R. Mitchell, once in charge, preached the sermon in the morning; in the afternoon, Mr. C. E. Thomas, III, presented and read a carefully prepared history of St. Stephen's and the Right Rev. Albert S. Thomas made an address.

The Rev. L. O. Thomas became rector soon after Mr. Guignard's death, followed by the Revs. Frank J. Allen (1938), Charles M. Seymour, Jr., and James L. Grant. The Rev. Harvey A. Cox died suddenly a month after beginning an auspicious ministry, May 1, 1943. In this year a mural tablet was placed in the Church in memory of those men of St. Stephen's who served the Confederacy. Also on the walls were placed scrolls with the names of those who had served in later wars inscribed. Mr. Cox was succeeded as rector by the Rev. Joseph N. Bynum, who served until 1950. On May 29, 1949, Bishop Gravatt, assisted by the rector, dedicated three windows in memory of founders of the Church: Dr. James Davis and his wife, Catherine Ross; Edward Gendron Palmer; Dr. John Peyre Thomas and his wife, Charlotte Couturier; and a tablet in memory of Richard Ashe Meares, vestryman, lay reader and warden for many years. Bishop A. S. Thomas preached the sermon. On the feast of the Circumcision, a window was dedicated in memory of Rosa Taft, wife of Robert Charlton Thomas, warden of the Church; and a credence in memory of Col. John Peyre Thomas and his wife,

Mary Caroline Gibbes made by their son, Bishop Thomas. The Rev. Richard L. Sturgis succeeded as rector in 1950. The centennial of the Consecration of the Church was celebrated on August 8, 1954. The exterior of St. Stephen's was originally of pine, painted maroon. In About 1920, a bequest of Mr. Isaac C. Thomas (last of much generosity to the Church) provided the brick veneer which now so improves the appearance of the Church. The iron fence, made possible by legacies of Mr. Robert H. McKelvey, and Miss Charlotte Anna Edmunds. A parish house has just been built adjoining the Church north of the vestry room, and dedicated by Bishop Cole, August 4, 1957, the 103rd anniversary of the consecration of St. Stephen's Church.

CHURCH OF OUR SAVIOUR, ROCK HILL
Established 1870

In 1857 a devout Episcopal family settled near Rock Hill. The Rev. J. D. Gibson, rector of the Church of the Good Shepherd, Yorkville, held services principally for them, but thereby introducing the Church to Rock Hill. Several rectors from Yorkville continued this until November 21, 1869, when Rev. Roberts P. Johnson, rector of Good Shepherd, Yorkville, began regular monthly services in Rock Hill for six or seven families of Episcopalians. He made an appeal for contributions of one dollar each throughout the diocese. The following Easter the congregation was organized into a parish and admitted into Convention May 12, 1870. There were sixteen communicants. The services were at first held in the homes. Mr. John R. London was the first delegate to the Convention in 1871. Mr. H. P. Green was lay reader. A contract was made for a Church to be built for $2,000.00; it was completed in the summer; a pleasing Gothic structure designed by Rev. J. D. McCollough. The first service in the Church was conducted by the rector July 14, 1872. It was consecrated by Bishop Howe just a month later—August 15. Mr. H. P. Green, representing the vestry, read the Request for Consecration and Mr. Johnson the Sentence; the Rev. Ellison Capers preached the sermon. The Rev. W. H. Campbell also took part in the service. There were at this time gifts of a surplice, a chalice and paten, and a memorial prayer book and Bible. The credence table was the work of the artist-clergyman, the Rev. J. A. Oertel of North Carolina, who also officiated in the Church frequently. A friend in Boston gave the font. Mr. Johnson was assisted by the Rev. E. C. Steele during 1878. In 1879 the communion silver was lost by fire but promptly replaced. In 1880 the Church was repainted and improved, a new lectern and a handsome chandelier installed. Mr. Johnson, the much-beloved rector, died in 1882. He was followed by the Rev. Augustine R. Prentiss until 1884 when the Rev. Edmund N. Joyner became rector, coming from the Diocese of North Carolina. A colored mission was organized in Rock Hill in 1885 by Mr. Joyner. He edited the *Church Messenger,* the diocesan paper, representing the Archdeaconry for Colored Churchmen. The Rev. T. D. Bratton assisted in 1887. Mr. Joyner resigned November, 1888. Mr. London now conducted a Sunday School for the parish and one at a mill.

The Rev. Gordan M. Bradley, though never canonically resident in the diocese, acted as rector 1889-90, then the Rev. G. LaVille Sweeney, D.D., 1891-95. There was no rector in the summer of 1895. A rectory was built at this time. The Rev. James Willis Cantey Johnson became rector later this year. The opening of Winthrop College at this time increased the congregation; the rector also held a monthly service at the college. The branch of the Woman's Auxiliary was reorganized. In 1897 Mr. J. R. London was warden, Mr. Philip Taylor, secretary and Mr. London, treasurer. Mr. Johnson served until 1902 when he was succeeded by Rev. John Conway Johnes. The death in 1904 of Mr. John R. London, a founder, warden, lay reader and school superintendent, was a great loss. The Rev. R. Maynard Marshall followed Mr. Johnes as rector in 1906. He organized a Bible Class for the Church girls at Winthrop, beginning a valuable service to the Episcopal students. In 1908, under Mr. Marshall, what was practically a new Church was built, the old having being enlarged by addition of transepts and choir—the whole being brick-veneered. The cost was $7,000.00. The Guild contributed pews and furniture; the altar and chancel window were given as memorials. Rev. John Kershaw, Jr., following Mr. Marshall, served the Church for a short time in 1909. The Rev. Charles W. Boyd was the next rector (1910-15). In 1910 Mrs. Alexander Long organized a Bible Class for the Winthrop girls and for nineteen years conducted it with marked success. In 1918 she gave the Church a processional cross on which was inscribed the names of the young ladies who, in her time went from the class into missionary service: Alice W. Gregg, Uto Saito, Leila Stroman, Theo Young, Chevillette Branford, Elinor Ravenel, Margaret Marshall, and Julia Gantt.

A new rectory was built under Mr. Boyd who was followed by the Rev. Nathan Matthews (1915-18). Consecrated on Christmas Day 1916 was a handsome gift of a raredos by S. R. Keesler of

Mississippi, completing his former gift of the altar. The Church school gave a brass cross for the altar. The Rev. Guy H. Frazer followed as rector (1918-20). Under the next rector, the Rev. William Edgar McCord (1920-25), the parish house was built which at once proved itself a great boon to the community as well as the Church, with its assembly hall, classrooms, kitchen, etc. The Rev. William Preston Peyton assumed charge next (1926-44). In 1935 in the parish were 117 resident communicants with a hundred at Winthrop and various organizations as follows: Auxiliary "A", and "B" later at Winthrop, Guild, Y. P. S. L., Junior and Senior, and Church school. The officers of the parish for 1935 were: wardens, T. W. Huey and W. J. Jenkins; secretary, C. N. Cole; treasurer, J. R. London; missions treasurer, A. P. McLure. The Rev. and Mrs. W. P. Peyton were the founders of the student center for Winthrop College. He engaged in much social welfare work and Mrs. Peyton was a leader in the diocesan branch of the Woman's Auxiliary, serving as president for two years. They removed to Virginia in 1944. Their valuable lives came to a tragic end February, 1947— victims of carbon monoxide poisoning. The next rector was the Rev. Alfred P. Chambliss, Jr. (1946-50), succeeded by the Rev. William Wallace Lumpkin.

ASCENSION, SENECA
Established 1876

Excepting only one year (1850-51), the Rev. Andrew H. Cornish was rector of St. Paul's Church, Pendleton, from 1848 to 1875. He was indeed a shepherd of the sheep, not alone in this town but to those scattered in the northeastern part of the diocese, especially in Oconee County. His pastoral oversight included the holding of services at many points. As early as 1854, he reports semi-monthly services at Keowee, the plantation of Ransom Calhoun. Bishop Davis tells of his visit here on August 24, 1856, holding services with Mr. Cornish here and on the plantation of Richard Porcher, where he opened a neat chapel erected for the slaves, confirming seven colored persons. The Bishop remarked, "I was happy to meet here friends of the low-country and to find them introducing the good, religious customs of their old parishes." Mr. Cornish held services also at Winberg, Rusticello, and reporting for the first time two services in Seneca in 1857, the next year fifteen. These services continued with apparent regularity until the war and then apparently with less regularity. Just before his death in 1875, Mr. Cornish reports services in Oconee at Shiloh, Seneca City, and Walhalla. The Rev. Henry T. Gregory succeeded as rector of St. Paul's, Pendleton,

January 1, 1876, and continued the work that Mr. Cornish had nurtured for so many years.

Mr. Gregory at this time (1876) transferred eleven communicants from the roll of St. Paul's, Pendleton, and organized "Seneca City Mission," there being in all five families and 13 communicants. Services were begun on fifth Sundays and some week days. Seneca City being a railroad junction, it was thought to have good prospects for growth. Mr. Gregory soon left the field. The Rev. Thomas F. Gadsden having become rector of Grace Church, Anderson, in November, 1877, now had the charge of this mission. He began regular monthly services in April, 1878, these being held in a place called the Union Building. The Rev. Frank Thompson assisted in 1879. There were now 23 communicants. In 1880, a lot for a chapel was given; however, it was not considered adequate, and another was later secured. It was contemplated that the proposed chapel be called The Cornish Memorial. The chapel was opened the first Sunday in Lent in 1882, "comfortably furnished." A walnut lectern was given by a member of St. Paul's, Pendleton. The final payment was made with the proceeds from the sale of the Church's share in the Union Building. The chapel was consecrated by Bishop Howe on May 18, 1882, Ascension Day. The chapel was named "Chapel of the Ascension." Very soon, additional "benches" had to be installed to accommodate the congregation. In 1887, the Church was repainted inside and outside by the efforts of the ladies; soon after, blinds on the outside and lamps on the inside were installed. The Rev. O. T. Porcher began assisting January 1, 1891, giving one additional service each month. He soon had entire charge, Mr. Gadsden dying December 1, 1891. Rev. J. D. McCollough took charge in 1892. He reported in 1895 six communicants, 12 public services. The Rev. W. T. Capers followed Dr. McCollough in 1896. Mr. W. B. Cherry was the warden in 1897. The Rev. B. M. Anderson succeeded Mr. Capers in 1901 for one year, then came the Rev. K. G. Finlay, in September, 1902, giving one Sunday and one week-day service per month. Mr. H. P. Boggs became the lay reader in 1906, Dr. E. A. Hines, treasurer. The next year, Henry P. Boozer was lay reader. Mr. Finlay left December 1, 1907, being succeeded by the Rev. L. E. Hubard, who served until the fall of 1910. The Rev. W. N. Tillinghast took charge the next year, serving until October, 1913. The Rev. R. M. Marshall followed in the charge until 1918. The Rev. H. F. Schroeter served then for a short time, followed by the Rev. G. H. Frazer in 1921. Mrs. E. A. Hines was treasurer at this time. It was she who was the principal force in keeping this Church together for many years. The Rev. G. E. D. Zachary next had the charge. In 1923, the wardens were Warren R. Davis, Jr. (also treasurer), and John Eldridge Hines. The Rev. Capers Satterlee assumed charge in 1926. He was succeeded by Rev. Donald E. Veale in 1935, serving until 1941. The Rev. John A. Pinckney had charge from 1944 to 1948, then the Rev. R. E. Gribbin from 1948 until 1951, succeeded then by Rev. Jack W. Cole who took charge in connection with St. Paul's, Pendleton, in the summer of 1951. The Church in Seneca had grown, and on May 11, 1953, it was admitted into Convention as an organized mission—the warden was J. A. Gallimore; secretary, John McDavid; treasurer, R. W. Kaff. The Rev. Philip G. Clarke took charge July 1, 1953, Ascension's first resident minister. The Church now has a bright future. A parish house was erected in 1955. It was dedicated on May 19 of this year, the 72nd Anniversary of the Consecration of the Church on Ascension Day, 1882, by Bishop Howe. The parish house is named the "Mary Hines' Parish House" in honor of Mrs. E. A. Hines, devoted sustainer of the Church for over 50 years.

ADVENT, SPARTANBURG
Established 1847

This section of the state was visited by missionaries of the Church under the auspices of the Advancement Society, beginning about 1839. The Rev. Cranmore Wallace was probably the first. For a decade, occasional services were held at Limestone Springs, Glenn Springs, and in Spartanburg. Among these ministers were, after Wallace, Revs. C. C. Pinckney (who in 1840 probably held the first Episcopal service in Spartanburg), C. P. Elliott, Edward Reed, R. D. Shindler, W. T. Potter, L. C. Johnson, and M. H. Lance. Mr. Elliott, who labored in the field for four months, reported in 1843 that the best prospect for establishing a Church was at Limestone Springs (near the present Gaffney). It was then a popular resort. He organized a congregation with a vestry there; and at about the same time, although there was only one Episcopal family in the town (Kennedy), did likewise at Spartanburg. The vestry here consisted of Col. H. H. Thompson, Charles Wear, G. W. H. Legg, L. H. Kennedy, Dr. L. C. Kennedy, A. S. Camp, and W. L. Rowland. There was so much prejudice against the Episcopal Church here that he regarded the prospect as "gloomy."

In 1845, the Convention of the diocese received an application from the "Episcopal Church in Spartanburg District" for admission to the Convention. The application was rejected on the ground that the state of organization contemplated by the canons as required did not exist—the applicants consisted of two district vestries, one at Spartanburg Court House and one at Limestone Springs; there was no Church building at either place, though in expectation of one at the latter place, and that a minister would have to be paid by missionary funds. Soon, the importance of Limestone ended as the company that had organized it as a health resort had failed. In 1847, the Rev. L. C. Johnson reported "service on Sunday at Spartanburg Court House and in Presbyterian Church—eleven communicants and ten Episcopal families in the district, including Glenn Springs." These all combined and organized a congregation which was admitted into the Convention in February, 1848, as "The Church of the Advent, Spartanburg." Previously the mission had been called St. Timothy's. In January, 1848, Mr. John DeWitt McCollough, a candidate for Holy Orders, took up residence in Glenn Springs. He immediately began services on alternate Sundays here and in Spartanburg, acting as lay reader. Thus began this great churchman's long connection with the Advent. He was made deacon on June 21, 1848, in Trinity, Columbia. The services in Spartanburg were held in "the female academy" and in the "male academy" near the S. and U. Depot. There were eleven communicants, four non-communicants, and seven children. In 1851, fourteen were confirmed.

Early in 1850, a contract was entered into to erect a Church building of brick. The cornerstone was laid on a lot given by Major J. E. Henry on June 23, 1850, by Bishop Gadsden, assisted by the Rev. Messrs. McCollough, Shand, J. W. Simmons, and A. H. Cornish, who made the address. Mr. McCollough now became first rector of the Advent, being made priest on June 28, 1850, at Glenn Springs. The contractor abandoned the work on the Church when the walls were only four feet above ground. After standing thus for two years, Mr. McCollough had these walls torn down and made a new contract for a building of the same dimensions, but of stone. Meantime, in 1851, a small wooden building had been erected on the lot for temporary use by the worshippers; this served that purpose for several years. It was later used as a parochial schoolhouse. This chapel was subsequently moved to Welford. "The walls of the Church were progressing, when unfortunately, a controversy arose as to the use of the lot for burial. The donor of the lot had died without executing a title and the heirs were minors. Hence, the work was again suspended and services were held in the chapel of St. John's School, kept by the Rev. Mr. McCollough. Just at this time, the necessary removal of this gentleman from the parish caused a cessation of the work. Soon after, a tender was made of the lot on which the Church had been begun, which was accepted by the vestry, and during two or three years following, services were held again in the little schoolhouse" (J. R. P. Smith). Mr. McCollough was assisted by the Rev. J. W. Simmons (1852-53) and the Rev. E. A. Wagner (1855-56). In 1857, he was succeeded by the Rev. C. F. Jones, D.D., for two years. He returned July, 1859.

Preparations for building the Church for a time were paralyzed by the war. So many refugees came at this time that services were held at the Court House. However, this influx of refugees so stimulated the plans to build the Church that it was finished during the war. By a process, in part, of barter (e. g., yarn was traded for planks, etc.), the work was done, and on May 10, 1864 the Church was consecrated by Bishop Davis. The Diocesan Convention met in it the next day. This building of stone at this time measured: nave 60 x 28 feet, chancel 16 x 18, vestry 9 x 12, porch 6 x 10. The walls are two feet thick. A part of the lot is used for burial. Besides this, there were 12 acres originally intended for an orphanage. The completion of the Church was greatly facilitated by the generosity of Mr. and Mrs. Jason H. Carson. The rector was the architect. The communion service at this time consisted of two chalices and two patens, plated, one of each being used at Glenn Springs. The font was presented by the Church of the Holy Communion, Charleston, and there was a fine bell.

During the war and later, Mr. McCollough was assisted by the Revs. Paul Trapier and J. S. Hanckel, professors of the diocesan seminary which had been removed from Camden to Spartanburg; also by the Rev. T. F. Gadsden and the students of the seminary. The deputies to the Convention in 1863 were William Irwin, J. H. Carson, H. Thomlinson, and Charles Kerrison. In 1867 and for some years, a parochial school was conducted in the old chapel by the ladies of the congregation. In 1870, a tower for a bell was added to the Church and the next year a cabinet organ was given by the Sewing Society. Mr. McCollough continued in charge of the Church until July 1, 1875, when his resignation was accepted with great regret. The Rev. Nathaniel B. Fuller took charge November 1st of this year, serving until March 1, 1878, when the Revs. Milnor Jones (deacon), E. C. Logan and Mr. McCollough supplied until Mr. Jones took charge in 1879. At this time, two white and one mission Sunday Schools were conducted in the suburbs, as also a parochial school in the parish. A new organ was installed at this time at a cost of $600.00. Mr. Jones resigned in the spring of 1880 to devote himself to missionary work in the vicinity.

He was followed by the Rev. S. H. S. Gallaudet July 1, 1880. A rectory was built this year by subscription, and the sale of lots. About this time the Sunday School doubled in number, and the congregations were much increased. Mr. Gallaudet was succeeded as rector by the Rev. F. A. Meade in 1886, who stayed only about two years. The Rev. Theodore D. Bratton (later Bishop of Mississippi) became rector in 1889. In addition to his duties as rector, he did a large amount of missionary work in the diocese, especially at Greenwood, and taught in Converse College. In 1893, he started a mission for Negroes in the city, called Epiphany. In 1897, the Church was rebuilt at a cost of $12,000.00, transepts and choir were added to the building; in fact, it was practically a new Church, only some of the old walls were utilized and Mr. McCollough's style of architecture was preserved. At this time the wardens were Dr. T. S. Means and W. S. Manning; secretary, Joseph M. Elford; treasurer, A. Irwin. After a fruitful ministry of eleven years, Mr. Bratton was succeeded by the Rev. J. M. Magruder in 1900. During his ministry the membership of the Church was doubled. On Easter, 1901, a beautiful Carrara marble font was consecrated by Bishop Capers. In 1905, an adjoining lot to the north was purchased, chiefly for protection of the Church property. In 1907 many improvements were made: the interior of the Church was redecorated, its grounds were adorned, cement walks laid about the Church and to the rectory, and electric lights installed. The Rev. W. H. K. Pendleton became rector May 6, 1909. St. Timothy's Chapel at Arkwright Mills was erected in 1912, and the next year All Souls at Spartan Mills built by the mill. Deaconess Eva Crump assisted the rector at these missions, and later Miss Marion H. Perkins. The cornerstone of a modern parish house, built of stone conforming to the Church in architecture, was laid July 22, 1912, and opened April 13, 1913. The building committee consisted of Dr. H. A. Ligon, W. S. Manning, Dr. J. F. Cleveland, and Aug. W. Smith.

In 1915, the tower of the Church was built, given by Mr. John B. Cleveland in memory of his wife. The parish house and the tower were designed by A. H. Elwood and Sons of Elkhart, Indiana. In World War I, the Church rendered much service to the soldiers stationed at Camp Wordsworth by conducting the Tri Color Tea Room for nearly two years—the parish house being converted into a soldiers' club. Misses Edith Main and Mary Schirmer were the workers at the mill missions in 1917. In 1922, the wardens were W. S. Manning and M. G. Stone; secretary, E. M. Mathewes; and treasurer, C. M. Lindsay. The rector was a leader in the setting up of the Diocese of Upper South Carolina in 1922, and the Church of the Advent was one of the three churches which had to bear much of the responsibility, which it did very generously. The income of a legacy of $5,000.00 by Mrs. Nancy A. Attleton in 1923 was, in 1927, devoted to the salaries of the workers at the mill chapels. In 1928, the rector, in ill health, was off duty for eight months; Rev. Messrs. Ira C. Swanman, S. T. Sparkman, and C. G. Richardson supplied. The chimes consisting of ten bells were given in 1926 by Mr. Jesse F. Cleveland in memory of his wife and his daughter. In 1929, the Church was redecorated and a new lighting system installed by the family of the long-time warden of the Church, Mr. W. S. Manning, in his memory.

Mr. Pendleton resigned his rectorship of thirty-one years May, 1939. After some months, Rev. William S. Lea served until October, 1944; the next month the Rev. C. Capers Satterlee succeeded. A list of reports at the annual parish meeting in 1947 will reveal the scope of the activities of this parish under Mr. Satterlee: These were (besides those of the rector and vestry) Chuch school, nursery school, acolytes, Young Peoples Service League, Canterbury Club, Men's and Women's Bible Classes, Altar Guild. At this meeting, Mr. C. M. Lindsay, refusing re-election as warden, Messrs. T. W. Crews and James Zimmerman were elected. At this time the wardens were T. W. Crews and J. M. Zimmerman; secretary, F. F. Kay; treasurer, Thomas Evans. The deputies to Convention were T. W. Crews, H. A. Ligon, C. M. Lindsay, and Dr. E. M. Gwathmey.

In 1954 the Church had increased to a communicant membership of 704. The new and very handsome parish house of the Advent was erected and occupied in 1953. The construction is of stone to harmonize with the Church, with which in due season, it is proposed to be connected by cloisters. Generous provision is made in modern style for the Church school and other needs of the parish.

As of May, 1955 the Rev. William Miller Davis became assistant rector of this parish, the first regular assistant of the Advent.

EPIPHANY, SPARTANBURG
Established 1894

The mission was opened in 1894 by the Rev. T. D. Bratton, then rector of the Church of the Advent (afterwards Bishop of Mississippi) assisted by the Rev. W. S. Holmes. It was begun in faith with two communicants. Its history is included in that of the Archdeaconry. At the time of the division of the diocese (1922) it was in the charge of the Rev. St. Julian A. Simpkins with 36 communicants. Epiphany was admitted to the Convention as an organized mission in 1951 being then under the charge of the Rev. Bruce P. Williamson, having 35 communicants, Dr. G. T. Mansel, lay reader. At this time (1956) Rev. Joseph N. Green is in charge, E. L. Collins, lay reader, 38 communicants. (See Archdeaconries—Part One, Sec. II and Part Two, Sec. II.)

OUR SAVIOUR, TRENTON
Established 1878

It was the Rev. Edward T. Walker who had just become rector of Trinity, Edgefield, and in charge of St. George's, Kaolin, who held apparently the first services of the Church in Trenton in 1878. There were then eight communicants. The next year he reported "a beautiful lot" and $500.00 raised for a Church. The Church was completed October, 1881. It was said to have been built at a cost of $1,200.00 by "two young ladies." The Bishop's first visit was on March 5, 1882, when he preached and confirmed four persons and celebrated the Holy Communion in the Church now called Our Saviour. He was assisted by Mr. Walker. The Church was finished and consecrated by Bishop Howe on June 30, 1882. Dr. Teague read the Request, Mr. Walker the Sentence, the Rev. H. O. Judd preached. The Rev. Messrs. Pinckney, Edgerton, and Prentiss also took part. A fine bell was installed at this time. Mr. Walker continued in charge of Our Saviour until in 1886 when the Rev. A. E. Cornish succeeded him as rector of Trinity, Edgefield, then taking charge of this Church, being assisted by Rev. John F. Finlay for a short time. It was in 1893 that a handsome black walnut altar rail was installed. The Rev. W. B. Gordon was then in charge and until 1898, next Rev. Richard Warren Anderson until 1902, then the Rev. P. D. Hay until 1905, next the Rev. Royal Graham Shannonhouse (1906-19). Among the laymen who served as officers of Our Saviour during these years should be named: Messrs. S. T. Hughes, P. D. Day, D. R. Day, and Julius Vann. The Rev. A. E. Evison took charge for a year in 1921, then followed the Rev. L. A. Peatross for two years. The Rev. Edmund Noah Joyner, then of western North Carolina, served as *locum tenens* until the Rev. E. M. Claytor became minister in charge in 1926, serving for two years. After a year's vacancy, the Rev. H. G. England, D.D., was in charge until

1939. Mr. J. D. Mathis was warden and Mr. D. R. Day, warden and treasurer during these years. The Rev. Allen B. Clarkson was the next minister (1940-42). Mr. Clarkson was ordained to the priesthood by Bishop Gravatt in the Church of Our Saviour on June 28, 1940. The Rev. William S. Brace then served until 1948. Rev. F. A. Pope officiated in 1950, then the Rev. Manny C. Reid, 1952 to 1954, when the Rev. W. A. Beckham assumed charge.

CHURCH OF THE NATIVITY, UNION
Established 1859

The first service of this Church in Union, apparently, was held by the Rev. R. S. Seely in 1844. He had a good congregation but found only one Episcopal family. Later the same year services were held by the Rev. L. C. Johnson. He found the outlook "discouraging" but saw two other places besides Union as possible locations for work—Fish Dam Fork and Dawkin's store. On July 29, 1850, Bishop Gadsden in company with the Revs. P. J. Shand and J. D. McCollough held service in the Methodist Church in Union. In 1852, the Rev. Henry Elwell, under the Advancement Society, was sent to "York, Union and Laurens." He held some services finding two members, Mrs. T. N. Dawkins and her sister, Miss Charlotte Poulton. In January, 1855, Bishop Davis appointed the Rev. C. T. Bland missionary to Union and Spartanburg to assist the Rev. Mr. McCollough in his school and in services in both places. Thus were regular services begun in February, 1855, twice each month in the Presbyterian Church. There were now four communicants—Mrs. J. W. McLure, Mrs. T. N. Dawkins, Miss Charlotte Poulton (all sisters), and Mrs. J. Flanigan. Mrs. Douglas was a temporary resident. A desirable lot was secured and steps taken to build a Church. The cornerstone was laid with all appropriate ceremony on May 1, 1855 (St. Philip and St. James' Day); the procession came from the nearby Academy. The Rev. J. D. McCollough assisted by the Revs. A. H. Cornish, C. T. Bland, E. A. Wagner and T. S. Arthur conducted the service, the last preaching the sermon. The customary deposits were made in the stone. Because of their untiring efforts, Judge and Mrs. T. N. Dawkins are to be reckoned among the chief founders of this Church. It is related that Judge Dawkins' teams hauled the stone.

The erection of the Church was begun just a year later. In the meantime, stone was quarried and other preparations made. The Church of granite, beautiful in its simplicity, was an exact copy of the Isleworth Chapel about ten miles from London on the family estate of the Poultons called "The Shrubs." Mrs. Dawkins secured the plans from London (in part extant, in Union). The chapel of the Bishop of Fredericton, Nova Scotia, is similar. Judge Dawkins and Mr. C. Wilson furnished the principal part of the cost of $15,-000.00. The Church is of stone, 52 feet by 23 feet (inside) with two porches, north and south; the bell gable rose above the roof. The building was not completed until after the war. Mr. McCollough, having been made principal of the Female Academy, removed to Union in 1858. The Church of the Nativity was organized in 1859 with the Rev. J. D. McCollough as rector; wardens were David Johnson and Dr. T. L. Chase; vestrymen, T. N. Dawkins, J. W. McLure, J. L. Young, and William Rice. It was admitted into Convention in May of the same year. The Church was consecrated by Bishop Davis on September 2, 1859; besides the Bishop and the rector eight clergymen took part in the service. Mr. McCollough continued in charge until 1869, except for a short time in 1857-58 when in Winnsboro and 1861-62 when chaplain of the Holcomb Legion. The Revs. Philip Gadsden and E. A. Wagner assisted during the war when there were many refugees in the congregation. The Rev. Paul Trapier, D.D., succeeded Mr. McCollough as rector on May 30, 1869. Though he stayed only until September, 1870, he won the hearts of the people. At this time stained glass windows were placed in the Church on both sides, given by Mrs. Dawkins; and an improved heating plant given by friends in Charleston was installed. Rev. M. E. Wilson served for a few months and then the Rev. A. R. Stuart for four months in 1871. In 1872 a pipe organ was installed. The Rev. Mr. Wilson prepared the specifications and superintended the purchase. Mr. McCollough was now again on duty, assisted by lay readers among whom was Mr. Robert Shand. The year 1873 was marked by a sad event—Rev. F. B. Davis, son of the Bishop, had been called to the rectorship; accepting and giving promise of valuable service, he had been in residence only two or three weeks when, in January, he was thrown from his horse and killed. Mr. McCollough resumed charge from Advent, 1873.

The font by the celebrated sculptor Powers came from Trinity, Columbia, given by Col. J. S. Preston, who replaced it at Trinity with another by Powers; the altar is of native granite; the communion plate was given by Mrs. Breuster and others; the chancel windows by the vestry in memory of two rectors, Trapier and Davis; and a memorial window to children of Dr. McCollough. The chancel furniture was given by Dr. McCollough, his own carving. In 1877 occasional services were given by the Rev. H. O. Judd, supplementing the rector's services and lay reading. In 1885 Mr. Mc-Collough was assisted by Rev. McNeely DuBose, who became rector in December, 1885. At this time the parish had grown to 18 families and 52 communicants. Mr. DuBose continued rector until he went to North Carolina in 1889. The Rev. Benjamin Allston became rector in 1890. Among Mr. Allston's devoted labors were constant services at the county almshouse and services at the villages of Carlisle and Lockhart. He resigned in 1896, going to Fairfield. The wardens at this time were J. W. McLure and B. F. Arthur; secretary and treasurer, M. A. Moore, Jr. Rev. Sanders Richardson Guignard became rector in 1898. During his tenure he began a mission at the cotton factory. After some intermission Rev. Crosswell McBee became rector July 1, 1901. He resigned March 24, 1904. Then in July following Rev. Royal Graham Shannonhouse took charge, serving for a little over one year, when Rev. Clarence H. Jordan succeeded in September of the following year, 1906. An organization of young women called "Nativity Mission" about this time gave Eucharistic candlesticks and a Bible in memory of an early member, Miss Charlotte Poulton. The Rev. J. Harry Chesley became rector in 1913. A pipe organ was installed in the Church in 1915 serving until recent years. The Rev. L. W. Blackwelder was rector from 1917 to 1926. The parish house was built during this rectorship, also a heating plant was installed, and the choir stalls brought to the level of the floor. Next the Rev. J. J. P. Perry served for two years followed by the Rev. S. Thorne Sparkman (1929-32). After a vacancy of two years the Rev. T. P. Devlin became rector (1934-40). He was succeeded by the Rev. Gardner D. Underhill (1941-44), then came the Rev. Billert A. Williams (1946-51) and next the Rev. R. Hampton Price. The Nativity now, with 85 communicants, is in a flourishing condition.

ST. JOHN'S, WALHALLA
Established 1875

In connection with the account of the Church of the Ascension, Seneca, mention will be found of the earliest services of the Church in Walhalla in 1875. The Rev. Thomas F. Gadsden, rector of Grace Church, Anderson, in 1884 reports holding five services in Walhalla. The next year, he reports increased interest with seven communicants. On his visit October 16, 1885, Bishop Howe confirmed five persons. The services were held in the Methodist Church. In 1887, Mr. Gadsden reported a lot had been purchased an $600.00 on hand for the erection of a chapel. The chapel was built in 1889, and used immediately, the congregation becoming a regular mission of the diocese in 1890. The chapel was consecrated by Bishop Howe with the name of St. John's Church on September 17 of this year. Mr. Martin, the lay reader, read the Request for Consecration, the Rev. Mr. Gadsden the Sentence, with the following clergy assisting: the Rev. Messrs. McCollough, Logan, Holley, and Bratton. The Greenville Convocation was holding its meeting here at this time. On January 1, 1891, the Rev. O. T. Porcher, then deacon, was appointed to assist in this field, giving one Sunday service to Pendleton, Anderson, Seneca, and Walhalla. Mr. Gadsden's death on December 1, 1891, ended this plan and the Rev. J. D. McCollough, D.D., took charge January 1, 1892. He reported in 1895, 20 communicants and 78 public services. The officers of St. John's in 1898 were D. B. Darby, M.D., warden; secretary and treasurer, V. F. Martin. At this time, Dr. McCollough also held services in a schoolhouse four miles in the country. Continuing in charge, Dr. McCollough reported in 1900 many losses in membership by removal; the next year, he reported 22 communicants. Dr. McCollough died in Walhalla on January 26, 1902, this distinguished priest having served St. John's for ten years.

The Rev. K. G. Finlay followed Dr. McCollough in charge from September, 1902, until December 1, 1907. The Rev. L. E. Hubard succeeded in 1909, leaving in the fall of 1910. The Rev. W. N. Tillinghast took charge the next year, continuing until October, 1913. The Rev. R. M. Marshall now assumed charge in connection with his work at Pendleton and Clemson, also now having Seneca, continuing until 1918. The Rev. H. F. Schroeter then served for a short time, followed by the Rev. G. H. Frazer in 1921. Mrs. G. M. Ancel was treasurer at this time. The Rev. George E. D. Zachary took charge in 1922, followed by the Rev. A. W. Taylor. The Rev. Capers Satterlee assumed charge in 1926, then the Rev. Donald E. Veale in 1935 until 1941. During the latter part of Mr. Veale's charge, the Church was abandoned—doors locked, windows boarded, the people being advised to worship in Seneca. The Rev. Jack W. Cole, then deacon, assumed charge of St. Paul's, Pendleton, on August 1, 1951. He promptly visited Walhalla, and gathering up about six Church members began services in the Presbyterian Chapter House in October. The old Church had fallen into a dreadful state of disrepair—the building even sagging on one side. Funds were raised and the Church completely repaired with restored foundations and a new roof. Mr. Cole had been ordained priest on April 2, 1952. The Church was reopened on September 28, 1952, by Mr. Cole; the Rev. Capers Satterlee preached, Bishop Gravatt presided. St. John's, never having been officially abandoned, now resumed its position as an organized mission of the diocese, Garlon Kelly, warden; Charles Collins, secretary; and Jack Light, treasurer. Delegates to the Convention were elected. Mr. Cole continued in charge until July 1, 1953, when the Rev. Philip G. Clarke, Jr., newly ordained deacon, took over the charge in connection with Ascension, Seneca, serving under Mr. Cole until he was ordained priest in May, 1954. So was St. John's completely revived.

ST. ANNE'S, WEST COLUMBIA
(Formerly St. Ann's)
Established about 1875

This mission developed from the associate mission conducted by the Rev. B. B. Babbitt in and about Columbia beginning in 1871. At one time, Mr. Babbitt conducted four missions in Lexington County. This one passed under the care of Archdeacon Joyner's associate mission in 1889 and then the Archdeaconry in 1892. It was first located on the lands of Mr. Alex Guignard in Lexington near Columbia. It was during these years and until 1922 known as St. Ann's. In 1891, the mission was relocated about four miles from Columbia. In connection with it there was for a time operated a reform school.

At the time of the division of the diocese, it was located in what was known as New Brookland (now West Columbia) and called St. Anne's. At this time it was under the charge of the Rev. J. B. Elliott, Archdeacon. In 1947 it was under the charge of the Rev. Francis G. Johnson with John Earl as warden, Mrs. Leola Blakely treasurer and school superintendent. In 1955 the Rev. Bruce P. Williamson was priest-in-charge with the same officers. (See Archdeaconries—Part One, Sec. II and Part Two, Sec. II.)

SAINT STEPHEN'S, WILLINGTON
Established 1859

About the middle of the last century, Octavis Theodore Porcher of Pineville in St. Stephen's Parish came to Willington to take charge of the community school, at one time the famous school of the celebrated Dr. Moses Waddell. After conducting this school for a time, Mr. Porcher established one of his own, a Church school for boys. He continued this except for a brief period during the war until his death in 1873. Other members of the Church moved into the neighborhood. In 1859, Mr. Porcher bought the materials from the old Church in Abbeville (when the present Trinity, Abbeville, was built) and rebuilt near Willington on a lot given by the Pettigrew family. This Church was consecrated by Bishop Davis on June 25, 1861. Mr. Porcher entered the ministry as a deacon in 1868, and was the first regular minister of his own Church. This first St. Stephen's Church was burned down in 1870, the year Rev. Mr. Porcher became priest. Plans were made for a new Church at once, however after money had been raised and materials gathered, the bank which held this money failed, the money was lost, and the work thus stopped. A building near Mr. Porcher's residence was fitted up as a chapel and here services were held for many years. Mr. Porcher died in 1873. Services were supplied then successively by the Revs. P. F. Stevens, John Kershaw, S. H. S. Galludet, Frank Hallum, and W. H. Hanckel, but there was a falling off of the congregation after Mr. Porcher's death.

With some funds rescued by Mr. William Henry Parker of Abbeville from the bank, and the sale of bricks and shingles accumulated for a Church soon after the first was burned, it now (1885) became possible to build a Church. A lot in a more desirable location than the original site was given by Mrs. Louisa C. Link, and plans by Dr. McCollough, and a Church was built. The new site was in Willington, a station on the newly built railroad. This new and attractive Church was about one and a half miles from the site of the first. It was consecrated by Bishop Howe on September 27, 1887, the Rev. Ellison Capers preaching the sermon. Mr. O. T. Porcher, Jr., assisted Mr. Hanckel in the services while a candidate for orders. A new organ was installed in 1890. The Rev. W. H. Hanckel continued in charge until 1891 when he was assisted by the Rev. O. T. Porcher, son of the founder of this Church, who after this time took charge of the Church and so remained until he went to Darlington, except for about two years when the Rev. S. E. Prentiss had charge (1907-08). Mr. Porcher was ordained deacon in this Church (December 17, 1890) and also priest (November 11, 1891). Dr. DuBose preached on the former occasion and Dr. McCollough on the latter. This little Church contributed another priest to the Church, the Rev. E. B. Andrews. The Rev. W. P. Witsell assisted Mr. Porcher in 1900. There were then 43 communicants. Mr. James Drinkard was warden for many years, and Thomas A. Andrews, secretary. The mission was admitted into Convention in 1902. Brass vases and a re-table were added to the Church furnishings. At this time, there was a Sunday School and a day school in operation. Also connected with St. Stephen's was St. Mark's, not far, where services were held for colored people and where also was conducted a Sunday School and a day school; Miss M. V. Stevenson was teacher of both. Mr. Porcher also held services at Pettigru eight or nine miles below Willington where a chapel was built in 1893 called the Good Shepherd.

After Mr. Prentiss resigned St. Stephen's, Mr. Porcher returned to the charge October, 1908. Mr. Archibald Bryan Andrews was now warden and Guildford W. Cade, treasurer. Mr. Porcher severed his long connection with this Church in 1912, going to Darlington. He had conducted a mission also at Ninety Six from 1908 until 1912. He was succeeded by the Rev. C. H. Jordan. Some of the communicants of this Church lived in Georgia. They were not included after 1915. The Rev. W. S. Holmes took charge in December, 1916, continuing until succeeded by the Rev. A. J. Derbyshire in 1921 to 1923. Mr. T. F. Walsh held the services for a time (1923-24). The ministers following with often intervening vacancies were: the Revs. J. S. Jones (1926), Charles P. Holbrook (1928), R. C. Topping (1929), and A. R. Stuart (1932-36). Then after a long vacancy, the Rev. Roddey Reid (1947-48) reopened St. Stephen's with regular services for a time. The Church was renovated and reopened for services by Rev. E. Cannon McCreary of Abbeville in 1954. However, the Church was struck by lightning in June of the same year and the Church is now dormant, the members having removed to Trinity, Abbeville. The Rev. O. T. Porcher, sometime in charge and son of the founder, has given this list of early families and members of St. Stephen's: Cades, McIntoshes, Andrews, DuBoses, Porchers, Mitchells, Alstons, Pettigrews, Hesters, Bowens, Burdette, Ford, Tubbs, Robinson, Bouchillon, Murphys, Burt, Stoneys, and Drinkards.

ST. JOHN'S, FAIRFIELD, WINNSBORO
Established 1827

The early settlers of Fairfield District were mostly Scotch-Irish Presbyterians but there were some Church people. The earliest record we have of the Church in Fairfield is that in the Journal of 1825, "Rev. Edward Thomas, Missionary to Fairfield District." He was a descendant of Samuel Thomas, the first S. P. G. Missionary to South Carolina, and similarly himself one of the first missionaries to upper South Carolina. The significance of the above record is explained in the annual report of the Advancement Society January 6, 1826, where it is stated that the "Mission to Fairfield" was not successful. Mr. Thomas had been sent to Fairfield in 1825. He found a Mr. Clark and a Mr. Pearson each willing to contribute $300.00 toward the building of a Church, the former also offering to give a lot. However, there were so few disposed to "our Communion" that Mr. Thomas was transferred to Greenville where he organized a Church. The editor of Miss Katharine Theus Obear's "Old Winnsboro" 1940 (Dr. C. J. Milling) recalls that Mills, in his *Statistics,* states that in 1826 there was one small Episcopal Church in Winnsborough. This is not likely. When the Rev. W. H. Mitchell visited Winnsboro in 1827, he held services in the Court House. At this time a congregation was organized and "measures taken for erecting a Church." This did not materialize but in following years services were held at different times. Winnsboro was visited by the Rev. W. H. Barnwell in 1833. He found that some members had left and some had united with other communions. He held two services with good congregations in the Court House, but finding only three Church members. These were ready to do their utmost to build; but it was thought inexpedient to take any overt steps at this time. However in the following years numbers of Church families moved from the low country to Fairfield. Especially did they come from St. John's and St. Stephen's parishes. Among the early Church families, mostly from the low country, were these: DuBose, Gaillard, Porcher, Couturier, Aiken, Egleston, Bratton, Thomas, and Palmer. The Rev. P. J. Shand, rector of Trinity, Columbia, visited Winnsboro and held a service in the Court House December 17, 1837. He found $1,100.00 subscribed for a Church. Rev. Cranmore Wallace came as a missionary to Fairfield in 1839, now with more prospects of success. He reports holding services 24 times in Winnsboro, once at Aimwell Presbyterian Church near Ridgeway, and eight times at DuBose settlement a few miles north of Winnsboro where a congregation was organized and $450.00 subscribed for the support of a minister, and pledges made for building a Church. This was the more distinct beginning of the Church taking at this time the name, St. John's, Winnsboro. The next year he reports services again in Winnsboro and at Dubose settlement. The Church in Winnsboro, being composed of so many members from St. John's Parish in Berkeley, received as its name, St. John's.

In 1841 Rev. Josiah Obear, coming from Vermont, became the first "Rector of St. John's Church, Fairfield, and Missionary to Winnsboro." being a missionary of the Advancement Society. He entered upon his duties May 26, 1841. He had served a short time on James Island and at Wilton. Up to this time the services in

Winnsboro had been held in the Court House, those at DuBose settlement in the Baptist Church, and those in the Ridgeway neighborhood in the building fitted up for the purpose in Edward Gendron Palmer's neighborhood. Now a lot was purchased in Winnsboro, paid for, and $2,400.00 subscribed and a Church built. This was the third Episcopal Church to be built in the state above Columbia—only Pendleton and Greenville were earlier. Land for this first Church was given by Mr. David Evans enlarged by a strip given by Mr. David Aiken. The Church was opened for worship July 24, 1842, and consecrated the 28th of the September following. St. John's was admitted to Convention February 8, 1843. Mr. Obear also conducted a private school. He left for lack of sufficient maintenance, returning to Vermont, January 1, 1850. He had been compelled to give up his school because of impaired health. A communion service was given by ladies of Charleston in 1843. In 1844 St. Paul's Church, Charleston, presented the Church with a bell which was found "quite useful" after the vestry had it recast; it was originally one of the bells of old St. George's, Dorchester. The Rev. John J. Roberts took charge in 1850 continuing until November 1, 1853. After the Rev. R. P. Johnson had served for a while, then the Rev. J. D. McCollough succeeded in 1856. In the meantime Mr. Obear had returned to Winnsboro (1855) and though in impaired health had rendered some service and was again in charge of a school for young ladies. Mr. McCollough resigned in the summer of 1859 and on the following January, 1860, the Rev. James T. Hutcheson took charge. He reported 19 families, and 33 white and 10 colored communicants. The Rev. W. W. Lord took charge July, 1864. The parish suffered severely in Sherman's raid. The Church was wantonly burned. The organ, furniture, books, all perished including the old St. George's, Dorchester, bell. The loss was about $5,000.00. The Rev. William Porcher DuBose returning from his chaplaincy in the Confederate Army became rector in the fall of 1865, coming to his home. He was the son of Theodore DuBose of Roseland Plantation, north of Winnsboro. He was ordained to the priesthood by Bishop Davis on September 9, 1866. Mr. DuBose was succeeded by the Rev. R. W. Memminger in 1868. The services just after the war were held in the Court House and also in the Methodist Church. The Church was rebuilt 1868-69, not on the same spot, however, but near the heart of the town. This was the first Church to be built in the diocese after the war. It was described as "a neat and elegant structure, made of wood, after the Gothic Style of Architecture." The Rev. W. H.

Campbell following Mr. Memminger served as rector from 1870 to 1875, when Mr. Obear took charge with Ridgeway. He had constantly held services supplementing those of the rector in previous years, and now again on appointment by the Bishop he assumed full charge. He reports at this time 16 families with 35 communicants—two colored. He became full rector in 1880, serving until his death, February 25, 1882, beloved by his people.

The Rev. Frank Hallam became rector October 1, 1882, continuing until December, 1884. The Rev. John Gass followed for one year. The Rev. Mr. Edwards held service for a short time from January, 1887. The Rev. James G. Glass came next, October, 1887, until July, 1890. On March 1, 1888, the Church was again totally destroyed by fire. Undaunted, the congregation with some outside help immediately rebuilt the Church at a cost of $4,300.00, involving a debt of $750.00. The architect was Schuyler, the contractor George W. Waring of Columbia. The cornerstone was laid on November 2, 1888, and the first service held in it on March 19, 1889. The Church is of pleasing Gothic design—St. John's third Church. Mr. Glass resigned July, 1890, followed for about two years by the Rev. G. L. Sweeney, D.D. Bishop Capers held his first confirmation after his Consecration in this Church on August 6, 1893. The Rev. S. E. Prentiss became rector in 1894 for a short time, then the Rev. Edward Benedict in 1895. The Rev. Benjamin Allston became rector the following year. At this time the wardens were C. S. Dwight and Henry A. Gaillard, secretary and treasurer, L. Gantt. Mr. C. W. Boyd supplied services the winter of 1897–98, Mr. Allston being in ill-health, and resigning the next year. Rev. Harold Thomas, missionary, had charge then for a short time. The Rev. H. O. Judd then took charge (1903-1906) followed by the Rev. W. J. Webster (1907-1908). Electric lights were installed in 1905. Mr. L. T. Baker was lay reader. Rev. Robert A. Chase of Chicago took charge in 1909, first for six months, then permanently. Improvements at this time were a handsome copper cross on the church tower and an altar book rest; then the next year: organization of a vested choir and the gift of two memorial windows. Mr. Chase resigned in 1910 then Rev. Roberts P. Johnson served for a year, and the Rev. C. W. Boyd followed from 1912 to 1915, and then the Rev. S. Nathan Matthews (1916-1918), Guy Henry Frazer (1919-1920), W. P. Peyton (1921-1926), C. B. Lucas (1927-1928). The Church was vacant until 1932 when the Rev. Charles C. Fishburne, Jr., took charge until 1935. He was succeeded by the Rev. L. O. Thomas who had just been ordained deacon at Kanuga, 1936, then the Rev. Frank J. Allen for a year 1938. He was followed by the Revs. Charles M. Seymour, Jr., 1940, and James L. Grant, 1942. In 1941 a fine organ was given the Church by Mr. Edward Sloan of Greenville in memory of his father, Mr. E. D. Sloan of this parish. On May 1 began the promising ministry of the Rev. Harvey A. Cox. He died after one month, succeeded by the Rev. Jos. N. Bynum (1944-1950), then the Rev. Richard L. Sturgis, since which time a splendid Parish House has been built.

CHURCH OF THE GOOD SHEPHERD, YORK
Established 1855

Bishop Gadsden visited Yorkville August 28, 1849, and held service in the Presbyterian Church. This seems to have been the first service of the Episcopal Church in this town. The Bishop states that he was "brought on by the carriage of Rev. Mr. McCollough," who was not, however, with the Bishop because he himself states that he first "visited Yorkville in 1852" and was then told that only one service had previously been "held in the village." His visit was at the request of William B. Wilson (son of a clergyman whom Mr. McCollough had known in college days) who desired him to baptize his "first-born." He held service in the Presbyterian Church with a large congregation. He later returned and on one of his three subsequent visits baptized three adults and ten infants. A subscription of $1,500.00 was obtained in one day in the community for a Church. This was not immediately followed up. Mr. McCollough made an appeal for help in maintaining services to the Advancement Society with the result that Rev. Henry Elwell was sent as a missionary to York, Union and Lancaster. He arrived August, 1852, finding in York two male and four female communicants. Mr. Elwell was successful in commending the Church to the community; there were additions in membership at once, and $1,200.00 was now subscribed for a Church. Mr. Elwell died in June of the following year. Bishop Davis visited Yorkville Saturday, August 12, 1854, holding service in the Methodist Church assisted by the Rev. Roberts P. Johnson; services being held the next day also. The Church was now in process of erection. Services were sometimes held in the Court House. The Church was organized at a meeting at Rose's Hotel on May 25, 1855 by the election of the following as vestrymen: Col. W. B. Wilson, Micah Jenkins, Asbury Coward, Dr. J. M. Lowry, W. H. Hackett and W. E. Rose; a constitution was adopted and a name selected— "The Church of the Good Shepherd" (previously called Christ Church) and the Rev. James D. Gibson elected rector.

The Church was built of brick at a cost of $5,000.00 on a lot given by Mrs. Louisa Avery Lowry. The Consecration of the Church was a great occasion. Yorkville by this time was a thriving town of 1,500 inhabitants. The many services in connection began on Friday night and lasted until Tuesday night, the Consecration being on Sunday morning, November 18, 1855. Bishop Davis was assisted by the rector, Mr. Gibson, and the Rev. Messrs. Roberts, Cornish, Wagner, Gadsden, Hewitt (N. C.). The architecture of the Church is plain Gothic with a pretty tower, the interior very chaste. On the wall over the pulpit is a tablet in memory of Rev. Henry Elwell, whose labors assured the building, with the inscription "Cruix Christi, Nostra Corona." There was still a debt which, however, was soon paid off. (At that time there was no canon law prohibiting Consecration with a debt.) The ladies of the congregation gave a fine-toned bell. The Church was admitted to Convention February, 1856. In this year a by-law of the Church was changed whereby the senior warden was made chairman of the vestry.

Mr. Gibson resigned in July, 1857, being succeeded by the Rev. A. F. Olmsted, January, 1858, who moved to Chester in January, 1859, where he taught school but continued in charge in York until the Rev. James Stoney became rector in April, 1861 continuing until he returned to his old parish of St. Luke's, Bluffton, in 1866. In 1923 the descendants of Mr. Stoney donated a marble altar in memory of him and his wife. Mr. Stoney had held services also at "Ebernezerville" near York. A notable incident occurred in this Church in May, 1860, when seven ladies pledged $100.00 a year for ten years for the diocesan seminary recently established. These were Mrs. B. L. Wheeler, Mrs. W. A. Latta, Mrs. W. B. Wilson, Mrs. J. M. Lowry, Mrs. G. B. Meacham, Mrs. M. Jenkins, and Mrs. A. Coward. Mr. Stoney was succeeded by the Rev. Julius J. Sams. Mr. Sams conducted a school for poor children in the parish. He went to Summerville in 1867. The Rev. Roberts P. Johnson became rector November, 1868. In this year an organ costing $200-.00 was installed and the rector was given a "black gown." The Rev. E. C. Steele assisted in 1878. Mr. Johnson for quite a time held services at Black's Station in York County. After a long and faithful ministry he died May 1, 1882. His last words to Bishop Davis were, "The dear Lord give me patience in my sickness and resignation to His blessed will." His memory is perpetuated by a tablet in the Church and a beautiful memorial window. The Rev. Augustine Prentiss served then (1882) for about a year, succeeded by the Rev. E. N. Joyner. In 1886 the Rev. G. A. Ottman was briefly in charge, Mr. Joyner returning the next year. The Rev. T. D. Bratton assisted him in 1888. After Mr. Joyner left and then Mr. Bratton there followed a period of vacancy after which the Rev. K. S. Nelson served for two years. After he left Mr. G. W. S. Hart as lay reader kept the services going regularly. From December 1, 1893, until March 6, 1894, the Rev. W. A. Guerry (then chaplain at Sewanee) officiated. On January 15 he presented twelve for confirmation.

The Rev. Robert A. Lee (Mr. Lee and W. S. Holmes, candidates, had supplied services the winter before) assumed charge in 1895. A stroke of lightning on Rich Mountain in August, 1896, brought his promising career to a sudden end. There is a tablet in the Church to his memory and several other memorials, also Major W. B. Moore gave to the parish a home on Wright Avenue known as Lee Memorial House (now the rectory). The Rev. R. W. Anderson was the next rector until the coming of the Rev. John Conway Johnes, who served temporarily at first, becoming rector September 1, 1898, and continuing for six years, followed by the Rev. J. O. Babin from 1905 until 1908. The Rev. T. T. Walsh (lately Archdeacon of the diocese) became rector and chaplain of the Church Home for Children which was at this time (May 13, 1909) removed from Charleston to York. Wherever Mr. Walsh went he stimulated interest in Church music and so in York in 1910 a new pipe organ was installed in the Church. In the same year a marble font was acquired. At this time the wardens were G. W. S. Hart (also treasurer) and M. C. Willis; secretary, R. C. Allein. Mr. Hart served this parish for many years as its lay reader; many were the days he kept the Church doors open when no minister was available. The Church school was greatly enlarged by the coming of the Children's Home to York. Dr. Walsh was rector and chaplain of the Home until his retirement in 1935 when he returned to his old home in Walterboro where he died January 8, 1937. His writings on the Church were of great value, as were his services in a long ministry in South Carolina. After Mr. Walsh's retirement the Rev. T. P. Noe, superintendent of the Home, served as rector until the coming of the Rev. Andrew D. Milstead, who left after one year 1938. After Mr. Noe served another year there came as rector the Rev. Cyril N. L. Sturrup for two years. The Rev. William C. Cravner succeeded (1943-46), then the Rev. C. Earle B. Robinson (1947-50) and next, after a year, the Rev. E. Hopkins Weston (1952-57). Since the coming of Mr. Weston many improvements have been made in the equipment of the parish. The centennial of the Consecration of the Church was celebrated on November 18, 1955, when the Rt. Rev. Oliver J. Hart, D.D., Bishop of Pennsylvania, a native of York, preached the sermon. Bishop Cole, the rector and other clergymen took part. Mr. Joseph E. Hart, Jr. presented a valuable *"Centennial History, 1855-1955"* at this time.

CHURCH WORK FOR COLORED PEOPLE
(Archdeaconry and Council Missions 1922-46)

From the time of the division of the diocese (1922) this work under the deep conviction held by Bishop Finlay of its great importance was prosecuted with vigor during his Episcopate. The plan of the organization of the work was that which had maintained in the undivided diocese with an Archdeacon and an annual council. The primary council was held in St. Mary's Church, Columbia, July 8-10, 1923. The ordination of the Rev. Theophilus T. Pollard to the priesthood by Bishop Finlay was held at the opening service. Clergymen present and taking part in the "laying-on of hands" were the Right Rev. Henry B. Delany, D.D., Suffragan of North Carolina, an assistant to the Bishop in this work, the Ven. J. B. Elliott, Archdeacon, the Ven. E. L. Baskervill, Archdeacon of the diocese of South Carolina, the Rev. R. N. Perry, and the Rev. St. Julian A. Simpkins took part in the service. The Constitution of the colored council of the mother diocese was tentatively adopted, a committee being appointed to suggest revisions at the next meeting. A branch of the Woman's Auxiliary was organized in a separate session. The composition of this colored work at its beginning in 1922 was, under Bishop Finlay, the Rt. Rev. H. B. Delaney, D.D., visitor; the Ven. J. B. Elliott, Archdeacon; (in charge of St. Anne's, New Brookland, St. Anna's, Columbia, St. Thomas', Eastover); the Rev. R. N. Perry (St. Luke's, Columbia); the Rev. T. T. Pollard (St. Mary's Columbia, St. Simon's, Peak, St. Luke's, Newberry); the Rev. St. J. A. Simpkins (Epiphany, Spartanburg, St. Philip's, Greenville). White clergymen assisting: the Rev. William Johnson, St. Augustine's, Aiken; the Rev. William E. McCord, St. Paul's, Rock Hill; lay readers: Walter O'Neil, St. Barnabas', Jenkinsville; H. B. Bailey, St. George's, Bath; N. C. Lewis, St. Luke's, Columbia. Mrs. T. T. Pollard became president of the Woman's Auxiliary; Mrs. St. Julian A. Simpkins, vice-president, Greenville Convocation; Miss Estelle Weston, vice-president, Columbia Convocation; Mrs. Hattie Dinkins, secretary; Mrs. H. H. Mobley, treasurer.

Churches:

Parish:	*Baptized*	*Communicants*
St. Luke's, Columbia	128	98

Missions:

	Baptized	*Communicants*
Aiken, St. Augustine's	75	34
Bath, St. George's	10	4
Columbia, St. Anna's	25	13
Columbia, St. Mary's	92	50
Eastover, St. Thomas'	213	32
Greenville, St. Philip's	20	16
Newberry, St. Luke's	27	17
New Brookland, St. Anne's	50	40
Peak, St. Simon's	81	12
Rock Hill, St. Paul's	8	2
Spartanburg, Epiphany	53	36
Jenkinsville, St. Barnabas'	2	2
Total	778	356

In his address to the first annual Convention of the diocese, the Bishop had this to say concerning this work: "Wherever I go I find a group of interested and loyal worshipers, and almost without exception dilapidated buildings for Church and school. It is my policy and purpose to urge the people to make every effort toward self-support, but their means are very small, for the most part, and for a long time to come, the work must be carried in part by the white people." He urged the interest and help of neighboring white congregations. "I have a strong and growing conviction that our Church is capable of developing a superior type of character, and a more practical conception of religion among the Negroes than is generally found. The Negro is naturally religious but his religion needs to be made more intelligent and to be linked more closely with his everyday life. This our Church can do. I ask your interest and practical cooperation in carrying on and expanding our religious and educational work for our colored people. We have made a beginning, but scarcely more than a beginning." The Constitutions and Canons were revised at the second Annual Council of Colored Churchmen, held in the Church of the Epiphany, Spartanburg, July 13-15, 1924. The next Council was held at St. Anne's, New Brookland, July 17-19, 1925. At this time, James B. Brown was ordered deacon. Soon after, the Convention of the diocese resolved "that every moral and personal influence should be brought to bear about fair and just treatment of the Negro." In 1927, St. Luke's Church and St. Mary's, Columbia, hardly half a mile apart, were combined—a building being secured for a parish house. Pursuing his policy of parallel development of Church work in all lines with the white work, the Bishop's Crusade (1927) services were held in St. Luke's while being conducted also at Trinity Church. Young People's Service Leagues were organized at St. Luke's, Columbia, and St. Thomas', Eastover.

The Archdeaconry lost the assisting services of the Rt. Rev. H. D. Delany, D.D., by his death in April, 1928. The statistical report for 1930 showed: nine churches, 19 baptisms, 15 confirmations, 114 families, 313 communicants, 22 Church school teachers, Church school pupils 318, day school four, teachers seven, pupils 284, total receipts $3,764.06, appropriation by the diocese $1,500.00; clergymen, the Revs. J. B. Elliott, James B. Brown, Isaac I. McDonald, William Johnson White, assisting, Aiken; lay readers, Emmanuel Johnson, Aiken, N. C. Lewis, Columbia, W. W. O'Neal, Peak. It will be seen that some of the day schools had been closed— four remaining—due to the provision of improved educational facilities being supplied in some communities. At the seventh annual Council, held November 28-30, in St. Philip's, Greenville, a very distinctive series of ten resolutions were adopted determining advance work in the Archdeaconry. In 1931, a mission was opened in Greer by the Rev. James B. Brown. The eighth Annual Council of Colored Churchmen meeting in St. Luke's Mission, Newberry, August 28-30, 1931, adopted a memorial to the Convention of the diocese as follows: "Resolved, That in view of the needs of the colored work and its unsatisfactory present status, we desire to request earnestly that some form of representation in the diocesan Council be given to our group." It was referred by the Convention of 1932 to a committee to report the following year. The questions proposing the admission of colored delegates as to the Convention were considered through four successive Conventions and finally lost by a failure of concurrence of the orders voting on an amendment to Article III, Sec. 1 of the Constitution on January 22, 1935.

In 1931 the Rev. James B. Brown held services in Greer. The work now suffered much from the great financial depression of this time, especially in regard to upkeep, many buildings of the Archdeaconry being in "deplorable" condition. During all these years, the Woman's Auxiliary of the Archdeaconry held its annual meeting in connection with that of the Council of Colored Churchmen. In 1934 great interest was manifested in connection with the organization of an Advancement Society. This was effected at the Council held October, 1935, at St. Barnabas', Jenkinsville, but never amounted to much. In 1934 the work of the Church at St. Barnabas', Jenkinsville, was revived under the charge of the Rev. M. S.

Whittington, whose recent ordination added strength to the work of the Archdeaconry. The Bishop established here under Mr. Whittington a center for conferences and missionary work. It is quite satisfactory to note that in what was to be his last annual address in January, 1938, Bishop Finlay found cause for encouragement in this colored work: in its better organization—three of the regular departments of Church work had been set up, Religious Education, Missions, and Finance; Young People's Conferences were held at Jenkinsville; plans were being formed to rebuild St. Luke's Mission, Newberry; $3,000.00 on hand to build new St. Augustine's, Aiken; five delegates of Woman's Auxiliary attended the Triennial in Cincinnati; the day school at Jenkinsville crowded to capacity. He then said to the Convention "We should always remember that our special missionary challenge in this section of the country is work amongst the colored people." In his death on August 27, 1938, this work lost a friend indeed. A year later, the retirement of Archdeacon Elliott, after some 17 years of service, inaugurated another distinct change. One of Bishop Gravatt's first acts was to appoint the Rev. Max S. Whittington as his successor. Bishop Gravatt presided for his first time at the 16th Annual Council at Jenkinsville, October 20-22, 1939. He noted the expansion of the work at Jenkinsville with the erection of a chapel.

In 1940, in the Archdeaconry there were ten churches, 406 communicants, Church school teachers 23, pupils 213. The clergy were the Ven. M. S. Whittington, Archdeacon and in charge St. Barnabas' and center at Jenkinsville, St. Augustine's, Aiken; the Rev. J. B. Brown, Epiphany, Spartanburg and St. Philip's, Greenville; the Ven. J. B. Elliott, D.D., retired; the Rev. S. C. Usher, chaplain, Voorhees School; the Rev. Bruce Williamson, Holy Cross, Fairwold. The Ven. J. B. Elliott died December, 1940. In 1942 the officers of the colored council were invited to meet with the executive council of the diocese. In 1944 there was only one colored clergyman in service; the Rev. M. S. Whittington had gone into the Army as a chaplain, the Revs. Williamson and Jackson had accepted calls, only the Rev. S. C. Usher was left, chaplain at Voorhees and serving St. Augustine's, Aiken. Many lay readers stepped in to help. It was at this Convention that the question of Negro representation after nine years again came up for consideration in view of the Bishop's remarks in his address. It was resolved in 1945 as a preliminary action that the words "of the white race" be removed from Articles III and VII of the Constitution, thus permitting such representation. The resolution received final adoption in January,

1946. Throughout the life of the Archdeaconry, its support was an annual appropriation from the national Church of varying amounts (averaging $5,000.00); from the diocese also varying amounts (averaging $300.00 to $4,000.00) and from the churches about $1,-500.00.

Subsequent to the action of the convention of the diocese in 1946 admitting the churches of the colored members into union with the Convention, the function of the Council of Colored Churchmen with the Archdeaconry organization assumed a somewhat new function. The churches of the Archdeaconry with their reports were now listed with the other churches of the diocese and included with them in practically all respects. However, the colored Council has continued in its character as a Convocation meeting annually in the interest of the work among the Negroes of the diocese. Bishop Gravatt's farewell to the colored Council was said at its 30th annual meeting held at St. Luke's Church, Columbia, September 27, 1953. Resolutions were adopted expressing the warm appreciation of the Bishop's constant care for the work and wise leadership. At the Council held in St. Philip's, Greenville, October 29, 1955, as usual, in connection with the annual meeting of the Negro branch of the Woman's Auxiliary, Bishop Cole remarked with satisfaction on the increase in the number of communicants and the physical improvement in Church property.

APPENDICES TO PART ONE
DIOCESE OF SOUTH CAROLINA
I-V

Appendix I—*Lists*

I. LIST OF CLERGYMEN, 1820-1957
Diocese of South Carolina
(With Period of Canonical Residence)
(See Dalcho, p. 432)

(Abbreviations: O—ordained; R—received; T—transferred; D—died; Dep.—deposed)

R	1825	John Jasper Adams	T 1826, R 1829, T 1838
R	1818	Parker Adams	T 1822
R	1881	William J. Alger	T 1884
R	1947	C. Raymond Allington	———
O	1877	Benjamin Allston	D 1900
R	1908	Francis Willis Ambler	D 1955
O	1900	Benjamin McKenzie Anderson	Dep. 1903
R	1897	R. W. Anderson	T 1904
O	1861	Zenophon Y. Anderson	D 1876
O	1909	Edward Bryan Andrews	T 1910
R	1822	George B. Andrews	T 1822
R	1821	Henry Anthon	T 1821
O	1846	Thomas J. Arthur	T 1872
R	1920	Alfred W. Arundel	D 1936
R	1871	Benjamin B. Babbitt	D 1888
R	1844	Pierre Teller Babbitt	T 1848
R	1906	J. O. Babin	T 1909
R	1909	Robert Bagwell	T 1918
R	1949	Robert C. Baird	———
R	1895	Thomas P. Baker	T 1900, R 1907, T 1918
O	1938	Theodore Porter Ball	T 1940
R	1924	Herbert C. Banks	T 1926
R	1824	William Barlow	T 1826
O	1856	Robert W. Barnwell	D 1863
O	1883	Robert W. Barnwell	T 1887, R 1894, T 1901, R 1911, D 1952
O	1833	William H. Barnwell	D 1863
O	1876	William H. Barnwell	T 1885, R 1896, D 1928
R	1954	John M. Barr	———
O	1952	Harold E. Barrett	T 1955
R	1916	C. H. Bascom	T 1917
R	1913	Erasmus Lafayette Baskervill	D 1937
O	1936	Lewis Austin Baskervill	T 1939
R	1948	John Q. Beckwith	———
R	1904	Stanley Cary Beckwith	D 1939
R	1895	Allen E. Beeman	T 1896
O	1900	John Beean	T 1900
O	1852	Edward Edmund Bellinger	D 1907
R	1894	W. F. Bellinger	D 1894
O	1953	William States Belser	———

R 1895   Edward Benedict . . . . .T 1896
O 1913   Albert G. Branwell Bennett. . . . . .T 1922
O 1947   Gordon Durand Bennett. . . . . .T 1951
O 1897   Isaac Franklin Abraham Bennett. . . . . .T 1900
R 1884   H. C. Bishop. . . . . .T 1886
R 1912   Ambler M. Blackford. . . . . .T 1920
R 1919   Randolph F. Blackford. . . . . .T 1926
R 1917   L. W. Blackwelder. . . . . .T 1922
O 1848   Charles Theodore Bland. . . . . .T 1856
R 1952   James O. Bodley. . . . .   _____
R 1802   Nathaniel Bowen (Bishop). . . . . T 1809, R 1819, D 1839
O 1836   William J. Boone (Bishop of China). . . . . .T 1844
R 1904   W. H. Bowers. . . . . .D 1913
O 1899   Charles William Boyd. . . . . .D 1926
R 1898   Benjamin M. Bradin. . . . . .T 1900
O 1887   Theodore DuBose Bratton (Bishop of Miss.). . . . . .T 1903
R 1923   Ilbert DeLacy Brayshaw. . . . . .T 1924
R 1921   William Brayshaw . . . . .T 1923
R 1885   H. J. Broadwell. . . . . .T 1887
R 1880   H. K. Brouse. . . . . .T 1886
O 1898   John Henry Brown. . . . . .T 1903
R 1862   R. T. Brown. . . . . .T 1866
R 1924   William Henry Brown. . . . . .T 1930
R 1924   F. M. Brunton. . . . . .T 1926
O 1914   Henry DeSaussure Bull. . . . . T 1923, R 1925, D 1957
R 1926   Roger E. Bunn. . . . . .T 1926
R 1838   John Burke . . . . .T 1841
R 1928   Edgar C. Burnz. . . . . .T 1933
R 1926   Joseph Burton. . . . . .T 1929
R 1949   Joseph N. Bynum. . . . . .T 1952
R 1956   Maurice John Bywater. . . . .   _____
R 1905   Charles Eugene Cabaniss. . . . . .D 1907
R 1924   Howard Cady. . . . . .T 1926
O 1903   William E. Callender. . . . . .T 1909
R 1909   Dwight Cameron . . . . .T 1910
R 1928   George F. Cameron. . . . . .T 1930
R 1942   Colin Reid Campbell. . . . . .T 1944
O 1819   David Irving Campbell. . . . . .D 1840
R 1840   John Barnwell Campbell. . . . . .T 1868
O 1870   William H. Campbell. . . . . .D 1901
O 1867   Ellison Capers (Bishop). . . . . T 1875, R 1876, D 1908
O 1895   William Theodotus Capers (Bishop of West Texas). . . . . . . .T 1901
R 1909   Wallace Carnahan . . . . .D 1926
R 1944   Thomas Neely Carruthers (Bishop). . . . .   _____
R 1947   Llewellyn Catlin. . . . .   _____
O 1940   Alfred Parker Chambliss, Jr. . . . . .T 1942
O 1819   John White Chanler. . . . . .D 1852
R 1913   J. Harry Chesley. . . . . .T 1917
O 1879   Thomas Boston Clarkson. . . . . .D 1889

R 1957 Sidney Grayson Clary.................................. ——
R 1951 Edward M. Claytor.................................... ——
R 1954 Edwin B. Clippard.................................... ——
R 1896 Theodore Wood Clift ....D 1913
R 1876 Robert F. Clute ....T 1884
O 1833 Daniel Cobia ....D 1837
R 1926 C. R. Cody..D 1939
O 1931 Edmund Gwynn Coe.................................... ——
O 1913 Francis J. H. Coffin..............................T 1916
R 1936 Clarence Alfred Cole (Bishop of Upper S. C.)............T 1938
R 1830 Augustus L. Converse............................Dep. 1855
R 1834 Thomas A. Cook....................................T 1837
R 1926 Albert S. Cooper..................................T 1928
O 1885 Andrew Ernest Cornish.................T 1913, R 1916, D 1920
R 1843 Andrew Hiram Cornish..............................D 1875
O 1842 John Hamilton Cornish.............................D 1878
R 1907 Joseph J. Cornish.................................T 1908
O 1911 Arthur Temple Cornwell............................T 1915
O 1900 Henry Harris Covington ....T 1913
O 1954 Ralph E. Cousins, Jr. .... ——
R 1901 Rozier Cleon Cowling..............................T 1903
O 1951 G. Milton Crum, Jr. .... ——
O 1951 Thomas L. Crum....................................T 1956
O 1940 John Quantock Crumbly.............................T 1951
R 1847 M. A. Curtiss.....................................T 1856
O 1814 Frederick Dalcho, M.D. ....D 1836
R 1940 Edward M. Dart....................................T 1945
R 1953 A. Nelson Daunt.................................... ——
O 1868 F. Bruce Davis....................................D 1873
R 1846 Thomas F. Davis (Bishop).........................D 1871
R 1855 Thomas F. Davis, Jr..............................D 1866
R 1892 G. F. Degen.......................................T 1893
R 1809 Theodore Dehon (Bishop)..........................D 1817
O 1841 William Dehon.....................................D 1862
O 1818 Francis Podmore Delavaux.........................D 1854
R 1857 Henry M. Denison..................................D 1858
O 1920 Alfred James Derbyshire...........................T 1922
R 1913 Frederick Ancrum deRosset........................D 1915
O 1926 James McDowell Dick...............................T 1928
O 1821 Rodolphus Dickinson............................Dep. 1844
R 1882 William F. Dickinson, M.D. ....T 1887
R 1957 Joseph A. diRaddo.................................. ——
O 1953 Kenneth Donald ....T 1956
O 1845 Elijah H. Downing.................................T 1847
R 1887 J. Y. Downman.....................................T 1889
O 1851 J. Grimke Drayton.................................D 1891
O 1884 McNeely DuBose....................................T 1890
O 1863 William Porcher DuBose............................D 1918
O 1922 Paul Duè..T 1924
R 1923 Norvin C. Duncan..................................T 1926
O 1836 Thomas C. Dupont..................................D 1848

R 1891 Phineas Duryea ....D 1898
O 1868 Everett C. Edgerton.................................D 1902
R 1920 Edgar Van W. Edwards..............................T 1922
O 1824 Charles Pinckney Elliott.............T 1828, R 1831, D 1850
O 1849 James Habersham Elliott.............T 1866, R 1870, D 1877
O 1910 John Brown Elliott..................................T 1922
O 1861 John H. Elliott.....................................T 1868
O 1835 Stephen Elliott, Sr. ....D 1866
O 1835 Stephen Elliott, Jr. (Bishop of Georgia)..................T 1841
O 1835 William Elliott...............................Dep. 1837
R 1844 Henry Elwell..T 1853
R 1893 William E. Evans....................................T 1900
R 1902 Albert Edward Evison................................T 1922
R 1893 R. Percy Eubanks....................................T 1895
O 1844 John Richard Fell...................................D 1869
O 1827 John S. Field.......................................T 1831
O 1886 John Frederick Finlay...............................D 1889
O 1902 Kirkman G. Finlay (Bishop Coadjutor)
        (Bishop of Upper S. C.)............................T 1922
O 1957 John M. Flanigen, Jr. ....——
O 1823 Benjamin Huger Fleming..............................D 1823
O 1819 Patrick Hinds Folker...........................Dep. 1842
R 1845 Alfred E. Ford ....T 1846
O 1926 William E. Forsythe.................................——
R 1948 Frank Van Dusen Fortune.............................T 1956
R 1853 John Foster ....T 1855
R 1807 Andrew Fowler ....D 1850
O 1835 James H. Fowles.....................................T 1845
R 1793 Hugh Fraser...D 1838
R 1919 Guy Henry Frazer....................................T 1921
O 1899 Francis LeJau Frost, Jr. ....T 1901
O 1870 Nathanial B. Fuller ....T 1878
O 1807 Christopher Edwards Gadsden (Bishop)................D 1852
O 1847 Christopher Philip Gadsden..........................D 1871
O 1825 Philip Gadsden ....D 1871
O 1866 Thomas Fisher Gadsden...............................D 1891
R 1908 J. E. H. Galbraith..................................T 1936
R 1879 S. H. S. Gallaudet..................................T 1882
R 1913 Frederick A. Garret............................Dep. 1916
R 1957 Karl C. Garrison, Jr. ....——
O 1882 John Gass.............T 1883, R 1885, T 1887, R 1890, T 1894
R 1790 Thomas Gates..D 1833
R 1919 Willis P. Gerhart...................................T 1920
R 1892 R. H. Gernand.......................................T 1892
O 1807 Paul Trapier Gervais................................D 1856
O 1817 Allston Gibbes................................Dep. 1847
R 1818 Henry Gibbes..D 1833
R 1914 J. Haller Gibbony, Jr. ....T 1917
R 1855 J. D. Gibson..T 1858
R 1819 Joseph Morgan Gilbert...............................D 1824

R 1854   T. J. Girardeau................................Dep. 1862
R 1898   William Louis Githens.......................D 1911
O 1887   James G. Glass..............................T 1902
O 1832   Alexander Glennie..........................D 1880
O 1920   Mortimer Worth Glover......................T 1925
R 1929   Conrad H. Goodwyn..........................T 1937
R 1897   Edward Louis Goodwyn.......................T 1900
R 1893   William Baker Gordon.......................D 1921
R 1848   Richardson Graham ....T 1859
O 1955   Henry Lacy Grant...........................———
O 1857   J. Mercier Green ....D 1891
R 1852   William Green ....T 1853
O 1846   Alexander Gregg (Bishop of Texas)..........T 1859
R 1876   Henry T. Gregory...........................T 1896
R 1900   J. Wilmer Gresham..........................T 1902
O 1912   Robert Emmet Gribbin (Bishop, West. N. C.)...T 1915
R 1893   John Drayton Grimke........................D 1895
O 1905   Samuel W. Grice............................T 1931
O 1932   Edward Brailsford Guerry............T 1935, R 1946, ———
O 1860   LeGrand Felder Guerry...........T 1888, R 1892, D 1908
O 1925   Moultrie Guerry ....T 1928
O 1921   Sumner Guerry.................T 1921, R 1933, T 1944
O 1888   William Alexander Guerry (Bishop)..........D 1928
O 1867   Walter C. Guerry...........................D 1867
O 1897   Sanders Richardson Guignard................T 1921
R 1918   W. B. Guion................................T 1920
R 1847   B. E. Habersham............................T 1866
R 1859   Claudius R. Hains ....T 1860
R 1849   Charles H. Hall ....T 1857
O 1868   F. M. Hall.................................D 1869
R 1906   Joseph C. Hall.............................Dep. 1908
R 1880   Frank Hallam ....T 1884
O 1813   Christian Hanckel ....D 1870
O 1838   James Stuart Hanckel...........T 1852, R 1853 T 1869, D 1892
O 1846   William Henry Hanckel......................D 1892
O 1943   William Henry Hanckel......................T 1945
R 1909   F. Harriman Harding........................T 1922
O 1941   Floyd Romain Harding.......................D 1954
R 1952   John W. Hardy..............................———
R 1949   William L. Hargrave........................T 1953
R 1884   Thomas G. Harper...........................T 1885
R 1930   George Hazelhurst Harris...................T 1949
R 1918   Charles Alonzo Harrison....................D 1942
R 1865   James A. Harrold...........................T 1866
O 1916   Oliver James Hart (Bishop of Pa.)..........T 1921
R 1892   Jacob S. Hartzell..........................D 1943
R 1947   Louis A. Haskell...........................T 1953
R 1957   Marion J. Hatchett.........................———
O 1824   George W. Hathaway.........................T 1829
O 1866   Perroneau Dawes Hay........................D 1930

O 1949   George Edward Haynsworth..........................T 1953
O 1938   Waties Rees Haynsworth..............................——
R 1837   Raymond A. Henderson..............................T 1839
O 1840   Robert Henry......................................D 1855
R 1896   S. B. Hillock.....................................T 1897
R 1927   Claude M. Hobart.................................D 1956
O 1936   Duncan Monroe Hobart.............................T 1940
R 1949   Roderick James Hobart.............................——
R 1889   Byron Holley.....................................T 1900
O 1888   E. N. Hollings...................................T 1906
O 1893   Wilmer S. Holmes................T 1904, R 1907, T 1921
R 1925   Homer L. Hoover..................................——
R 1955   Joseph Robert Horn III...........................
O 1838   Robert T. Howard.................................T 1866
O 1847   William Bell White Howe (Bishop).................D 1894
R 1896   George E. Howell.................................D 1929
R 1908   Lyttleton E. Hubard..............................T 1911
R 1842   F. M. Hubbard....................................T 1842
R 1936   Kenneth de Poullain Hughes.......................T 1940
O 1896   Shirley Carter Hugeson...........................T 1896
R 1848   Joseph Hunter....................................   1866
R 1844   Jedediah Huntington, M.D.......................Dep. 1849
R 1860   J. T. Hutcheson..................................T 1865
O 1844   Nathaniel Hyatt..................................   1866
O 1902   John Carl Jagar..................................T 1907
R 1875   H. M. Jackson....................................T 1876
R 1878   J. E. Jackson....................................T 1880
O 1924   Roderick Humes Jackson (Mis. Japan, 1928-33)......T 1940
R 1902   William M. Jackson...............................D 1928
R 1893   Herbert Munson Jarvis............................D 1905
R 1946   L. Stanley Jeffery...............................T 1949
R 1857   Paul Gervais Jenkins, M.D.............T 1865, R 1882, D 1911
R 1904   Richard Cullen Jeter.............................D 1916
R 1898   John C. Johnes...................................T 1905
R 1847   Benjamin Johnson.................................T 1866
O 1868   John Johnson.....................................D 1907
O 1895   J. W. Cantey Johnson.............................T 1902
O 1844   Laurence Clement Johnson.......................Dep. 1851
R 1834   Richard Johnson..................................T 1845
R 1852   Roberts Poinsett Johnson.............T 1857, R 1859, D 1882
O 1909   Roberts Poinsett Johnson.........................T 1911
R 1857   William Johnson..................................T 1870
R 1834   William Johnson..................................T 1835
O 1872   William H. Johnson...............................T 1875
R 1898   George Harbaugh Johnston.........................D 1918
R 1857   Clement Frederick Jones..........................D 1877
R 1885   Custis P. Jones..................................T 1887
R 1860   Ezra Jones.......................................T 1861
O 1908   Jacob R. Jones...................................D 1921
O 1876   Milnor Jones.....................................T 1882

R	1904	Clarence H. Jordan	T 1916
R	1945	Allen Webster Joslin	T 1948
R	1884	Edmund N. Joyner	T 1905
O	1899	James Joyner	T 1913
R	1877	Harvey Orrin Judd	T 1888, R 1903, D 1906
R	1917	Frank A. Juhan (Bishop of Florida)	T 1922
R	1836	Abraham Kaufman	D 1839
R	1881	James W. Keeble	T 1882
O	1825	Paul Trapier Keith	D 1868
R	1841	Ezra B. Kellogg	T 1842
O	1875	John Kershaw	T 1884, R 1885, D 1921
O	1905	John Kershaw, Jr.	D 1916
R	1857	John Steinfort Kidney	T 1866, R 1871, T 1872
O	1956	George LaBruce	——
O	1855	Lucien C. Lance	T 1868
O	1815	Maurice Harvey Lance	D 1870
O	1879	Christopher Innis LaRoche	T 1881, R 1913 T 1918
R	1883	James H. LaRoche	T 1885
R	1920	Thomas N. Lawrence	T 1921
O	1839	Francis Beckman Lee	T 1845
R	1884	Francis D. Lee	D 1891
R	1842	Francis Prioleau Lee	T 1847
R	1873	Henry T. Lee	T 1879
O	1894	Robert Alexander Lee	D 1896
R	1956	William Seddon Lee	——
R	1944	Emmanuel A. LeMoine	——
O	1832	Charles Edward Leverette	D 1869
R	1947	Frank L. Levy	T 1948
R	1929	Harrell J. Lewis	D 1930
R	1943	John Randolph Lewis	D 1947
R	1916	John Smith Lightbourn	D 1924
O	1957	Richard B. Lindner	——
R	1944	Malcolm W. Lockhart	D 1946
O	1848	Edward C. Logan	D 1896
R	1916	Mercer P. Logan	D 1928
R	1915	John London	D 1928
R	1865	W. W. Lord	T 1870
R	1851	Thomas N. Lucas	D 1886
O	1907	Hope Henry Lumpkin	T 1914
O	1936	William Wallace Lumpkin	T 1948
O	1907	Jesse David Lykes	D 1912
R	1930	Robert Nelson MacCallum	T 1934
O	1934	Stephen B. McF. Mackey	——
O	1952	Lynwood Cresse Magee	——
R	1898	James Mitchell Magruder	T 1908
O	1918	Andrew P. Magwood	D 1937
O	1917	Rollin D. Malany	T 1919
O	1893	J. B. Mancebo	T 1905
O	1953	Gordon Hossley Mann	T 1955
O	1828	Alexander W. Marshall	D 1876

O 1903　R. Maynard Marshall.................T 1916, R 1919, D 1957
O 1957　Franklin Martin...................... ———
O 1942　Richard Beamon Martin..................T 1944
O 1945　William Livingston Martin.............T 1947
R 1922　Wallace Martin......................D 1946
O 1796　Edmund Matthews.....................T 1809
R 1916　Nathan Matthews.....................T 1918
R 1804　Philip Mathews ....D 1828
R 1923　William Herbert Mayers...............T 1928
O 1904　Henry C. Mazyck.....................T 1920
O 1900　Croswell McBee ....T 1904
O 1848　John Dewitt McCollough...............D 1902
R 1921　William E. McCord...................T 1922
O 1892　Edward McCrady, Jr...................T 1892
R 1890　A. A. McDonough.....................D 1896
R 1892　H. S. McDuffey......................T 1892
O 1831　David McElheran.....................D 1875
R 1836　James A. McKenny....................T 1837
R 1931　Osmond Jonathan McLeod...............D 1950
O 1950　Moultrie H. McIntosh................T 1956
R 1887　Stewart McQueen.....................T 1892
R 1885　Frank A. Meade......................T 1888
R 1903　William N. Meade....................T 1904
O 1955　Loren B. Mead....................... ———
R 1947　Ralph S. Meadowcroft................. ———
O 1842　Stiles Mellichamp...................D 1872
O 1867　Robert Withers Memminger...........T 1873, R 1879, D 1901
O 1906　Willis Wilkinson Memminger..........T 1910
R 1918　Richard L. Merryman.................T 1922
O 1898　Henry Judah Mikell (Bishop of Atlanta).................T 1908
O 1869　Edward R. Miles.....................D 1885
O 1841　James Worley Miles..................T 1845, R 1848, D 1875
R 1920　Donald Millar......................T 1922
O 1891　G. F. Miller........................T 1894
R 1786　Thomas Mills........................D 1830
O 1885　Alexander Robert Mitchell............T 1922
R 1930　Charles Baird Mitchell..............D 1938
R 1908　Walter Mitchell (Bishop of Ariz.)....T 1924
O 1821　William H. Mitchell.................T 1831
O 1852　Augustus Moore......................D 1876
R 1947　deSaussure P. Moore.................T 1948
R 1926　H. Randolph Moore...................T 1928
O 1940　William Moultrie Moore, Jr...........T 1942
O 1953　John M. Moncrief....................D 1955
R 1905　Samuel Moran........................T 1908
R 1917　A. Rufus Morgan....................T 1917
O 1925　John H. Morgan.....................T 1927, R 1930, T 1931
O 1926　William M. Morgan...................D 1930
T 1955　John Burnett Morris................. ———
R 1948　Turner W. Morris....................T 1951

O 1867	John Ward Motte	D 1919
O 1823	Mellish Irving Motte	Dep. 1826
O 1830	Thomas S. W. Motte	T 1831
O 1817	Albert Arney Muller	T 1823
R 1890	K. S. Nelson	T 1893
O 1824	Edward Neufvilla	T 1827
R 1879	Charles W. Newman	T 1879
R 1904	Charles Martin Niles	T 1907
R 1919	Thomas Pasteur Noe	T 1922
R 1910	Walter R. Noe	T 1911
R 1841	Josiah Obear	T 1850, R 1857, D 1882
O 1943	John Legare O'Hear	T 1945
O 1949	Robert L. Oliveros	T 1954
R 1857	A. F. Olmsted	T 1866
R 1823	Thomas Osborne	D 1826
R 1885	G. A. Ottman	T 1886
R 1845	Carter Page	T 1846
R 1952	Earle Cornelius Page	T 1954, R 1956, ——
R 1927	Richard E. Page	T 1929
R 1889	W. J. Page	T 1890
O 1903	Halbert Noble Palmer	T 1903, R 1906, Dep. 1908
O 1956	Luther W. Parker	T 1957
R 1910	H. A. St. A. Parris	T 1914
R 1939	Richard C. Patton	T 1949, R 1954, T 1957
O 1862	W. W. Patrick	T 1867
R 1920	Louis Ashley Peatross	T 1922
O 1934	David Nathaniel Peeples	T 1938
O 1912	Edwin Anderson Penick (Bishop of N. C.)	T 1919
R 1909	W. H. K. Pendleton	T 1922
R 1871	B. F. D. Perry	D 1874
R 1948	DeWolf Perry	——
O 1916	Julian Clyde Perry	T 1922
O 1875	J. B. Perry	T 1876
R 1835	M. A. Perry	T 1835
R 1920	Robert Nathaniel Perry	T 1922
R 1920	William Preston Peyton	T 1922
R 1886	H. H. Phelps	T 1890
O 1822	Edward Phillips	D 1855
R 1922	Henry D. Phillips (Bishop of S. W. Va.)	T 1922
O 1856	Henry L. Phillips	T 1868
R 1915	Robert T. Phillips	T 1915
O 1835	Charles C. Pinckney	D 1898
O 1931	John Adams Pinckney	T 1941
O 1848	G. L. Platt	T 1850
R 1887	J. H. M. Pollard	T 1898
O 1868	Octavius Theodore Porcher	D 1873
O 1890	Octavius Theodore Porcher, Jr.	D 1941
O 1957	Philip G. Porcher	——
O 1854	Anthony Toomer Porter	D 1902
O 1879	Theodore Atkinson Porter	D 1917

R 1834 William T. Potter...................................D 1879
R 1909 Wilmer S. Poynor........T 1916, R 1918, T 1946, R 1948, ————
R 1947 Henry Powers.....................................T 1954
O 1882 Augustine Prentiss.................................T 1884
O 1908 Paul Trapier Prentiss..............................T 1909
R 1893 Stephen E. Prentiss...............................T 1909
O 1846 William Otis Prentiss..............................D 1897
R 1922 Arthur R. Price...................................T 1922
R 1949 Quentin E. Primo.................................T 1956
O 1847 James Maxwell Pringle.............T 1869, R 1895, D 1905
O 1953 Malcolm H. Prouty................................ ————
R 1910 John J. Pusey....................................D 1912
O 1887 Joseph S. Quarles.................................D 1913
O 1856 James Hamilton Quinby.............................T 1866
R 1895 Scott Bogie Rathbun..............................T 1899
R 1924 Gordon M. Reese..................................T 1925
R 1839 Edward Reed.....................T 1839, R 1842, D 1862
R 1954 Manney C. Reid.................................. ————
R 1920 Alexander M. Rich................................T 1945
R 1920 C. Gregg Richardson..............................T 1922
R 1917 John Ridout......................................T 1922
O 1922 John Ridout, Jr...................................T 1923
O 1922 Thomas L. Ridout.................................T 1922
R 1943 Lawton Riley.....................................T 1952
O 1956 John Rivers...................................... ————
R 1943 Alexander M. Roberts............................. ————
R 1851 John J. Roberts...................................T 1867
R 1951 Walter D. Roberts................................ ————
R 1911 Percy J. Robottom................................T 1917
R 1953 Waddell F. Robey.................................T 1957
R 1822 Edward Rutledge..................................T 1826
O 1823 Francis Huger Rutledge (Bishop of Fla.)..............T 1845
O 1909 Henry Cook Salmond...............................T 1913
O 1881 Thaddeus Salters.................................D 1884
O 1857 Barnwell Bonum Sams..............................D 1903
R 1854 Julius J. Sams....................................T 1873
O 1901 William Bee Sams...................T 1902, R 1921, D 1952
O 1923 Charles Capers Satterlee...........................T 1925
R 1901 Churchill Satterlee...............................D 1904
O 1841 Robert D. Shindler................................T 1849
R 1916 Herbert F. Schroeter..............................T 1922
R 1880 F. S. Scott.......................................T 1885
O 1834 Napoleon B. Screven..............................D 1840
O 1848 Joseph B. Seabrook...............................D 1877
R 1931 John Creighton Seagle.............................D 1947
R 1917 Charles S. Sedgewick..............................T 1918
O 1844 Richard S. Seely..................................T 1860
R 1853 John Selwood ....T 1856
O 1856 James R. W. Selwood..............................T 1856
O 1834 Peter J. Shand...................................D 1886

R 1854	J. A. Shanklin..D	1856
R 1904	Royal Graham Shannonhouse.........................T	1919
R 1956	Levering Bartine Sherman............................T	1957
O 1848	J. Ward Simmons......................................D	1855
R 1912	John S. Simmons.......................................T	1913
R 1893	James Simonds ....T	1893
O 1915	St. Julian Aaron Simpkins................T 1922, R 1931, ——
O 1941	St. Julian Aaron Simpkins, Jr........................T	1945
R 1821	Samuel Sitgreaves....................................T	1821
R 1926	Alvin W. Skardon.................................. ——
O 1946	Stephen Lee Skardon.................................T	1951
R 1913	Frederick Nash Skinner..............................D	1927
R 1948	Edward T. Small......................................T	1956
R 1922	Carl S. Smith...D	1946
R 1906	Charles Irvin Smith...........................Dep.	1909
R 1849	J. H. Smith...T	1850
R 1810	Charles Blair Snowden...............................D	1825
O 1955	Frederick Skinner Sosnowski.........................T	1957
R 1907	James W. Sparks......................................D	1916
R 1835	William Wallace Spear...............................T	1855
O 1944	Victor Bland Stanley, Jr............................ ——
R 1916	Homer Worthington Starr, Ph.D......................D	1936
O 1938	Homer Pilgrim Starr..................................T	1940
O 1877	Edwin C. Steele......................................D	1885
O 1861	P. Fayssoux Stevens...............................Dep.	1875
R 1874	George Waldo Stickney...............................D	1888
R 1874	J. H. Stringfellow...................................T	1878
R 1852	James Stoney, M.D....................................T	1868
R 1950	James Stoney..T	1952
R 1884	James Moss Stoney....................................D	1897
O 1913	James Moss Stoney (Bishop of N. Mex.)....T 1915, R 1917, T 1921
O 1922	William S. Stoney........................T 1925, R 1955, ——
O 1869	A. R. Stuart..T	1872
R 1936	Albert Rhett Stuart (Bishop of Ga.).................T	1947
O 1857	Junius W. Stuart.....................................T	1857
R 1844	Isaac Swart...T	1851
R 1891	George Laville Sweeney................T 1896, R 1898, D 1900
R 1818	Robert S. Symmes.....................................D	1825
R 1917	Arthur W. Taylor......................................T	1922
O 1849	B. F. Taylor...T	1850
O 1822	Thomas House Taylor ....T	1834
O 1857	J. W. Taylor...D	1861
O 1911	John Hanckel Taylor ....T	1917
R 1936	Lincoln A. Taylor.................................. ——
O 1900	Albert Sidney Thomas (Bishop)...................... ——
O 1825	Edward Thomas..D	1840
O 1899	Harold Thomas..........T 1905, R 1905, T 1947, R 1951, ——
O 1922	Josiah Johnson Thomas...............................T	1924
R 1904	Henry Thomas ....T	1905
R 1946	C. O'Ferrall Thompson...............................T	1950

R 1872   John Huske Tillinghast............................T 1922
R 1843   N. P. Tillinghast.................................T 1848
O 1897   William Norwood Tillinghast............T 1901, R 1911, T 1913
O 1933   Thomas Sumter Tisdale............................ ——
R 1950   Robert Tomlinson .... ——
O 1829   Paul Trapier.....................................D 1872
R 1857   Richard Shubrick Trapier.........................D 1895
R 1942   Marshall E. Travers.............................. ——
R 1807   John Jacob Tschudy...............................D 1834
R 1948   A. Campbell Tucker...............................T 1950
O 1937   William Davis Turner.............................T 1939
R 1904   Basil Benjamin Tyler..........................Dep. 1908
R 1822   Peter Van Pelt...................................T 1827
O 1850   Edwin Adolphus Wagner.............T 1860, R 1869, T 1871
O 1862   A. R. Walker.....................................T 1867
R 1845   Charles Bruce Walker.............................D 1875
R 1873   Edward T. Walker.................................D 1896
O 1900   J. Bentham Walker.....................T 1902, R 1916, ——
R 1822   Joseph R. Walker.................................D 1879
O 1918   Joseph R. Walker.................................T 1921
R 1898   Robert Jefferson Walker..........................D 1910
R 1853   Henry Wall.......................................T 1853
O 1836   Cranmore Wallace.................................D 1860
O 1895   Thomas Tracy Walsh...............................T 1922
R 1918   William M. Walton................................T 1921
O 1898   James Cash Waring.............................Dep. 1907
O 1953   Hallie D. Warren.................................T 1956
R 1901   William Way .... ——
R 1836   Benjamin C. Webb.................................D 1855
O 1860   Edward J. Webb...................................T 1865
R 1906   William John Webster.............................D 1908
O 1855   Jacob V. Welch...................................D 1890
O 1945   Eugene Jagar West.....................T 1953, R 1955, ——
R 1888   Percival H. Whaley.................T 1890, R 1908, D 1915
R 1836   Ulysses W. Wheeler...............................D 1841
R 1841   Arthur Wigfall...................................D 1866
R 1914   Edward F. Willett................................T 1919
O 1900   George Croft Williams.............T 1904, R 1916, T 1922
O 1867   Gilbert F. Williams..............................T 1867
R 1889   Joseph Bentham Williams..........................T 1898
R 1935   Merritt H. Francis Williams......................T 1941
R 1887   G. T. Wilmer.....................................T 1892
O 1864   Robert Wilson......................T 1869, R 1885, D 1924
R 1829   William Stanyarne Wilson.........................D 1834
R 1948   Robert E. Withers, Jr............................T 1948
O 1899   William Postell Witsell..........................T 1908
R 1902   Louis George Wood...............................D 1934
R 1910   Charles E. Woodson...............................T 1914
O 1840   Alsop Woodward ....Dep. 1858
R 1912   James Herbert Woodward...........................D 1928

R 1941   S. Alston Wragg...................................D 1953
O 1827   Thomas J. Young..................................D 1853
R 1922   George E. DeWitt Zachary.........................T 1922

2. CONVENTIONS OF THE CHURCH IN THE DIOCESE OF SOUTH CAROLINA
(With Place of Meeting and Date)

Preliminary Meeting......................Charleston, February 8, 1785
1st Convention.................State House, Charleston, May 12, 1785
2nd Convention..............................Charleston, July 12, 1785
3rd Convention............................Charleston, April 26, 1786
4th Convention..........................Charleston, May 29-31, 1786
5th Convention.....................Charleston, February 20-22, 1787
6th Convention.........................Charleston, October 18, 1787
7th Convention.............................Charleston, May 6-8, 1789
8th Convention...............St. Philip's, Charleston, October 19, 1790
9th Convention..........St. Michael's, Charleston, October 18, 20, 1791
10th Convention..............St. Michael's, Charleston, October 18, 1792
11th Convention..............St. Michael's, Charleston, October 16, 1794
12th Convention.......................Charleston, February 10, 1795
13th Convention............St. Michael's, Charleston, February 16, 1796
14th Convention......................Charleston, October 20-21, 1796
15th Convention.........................Charleston, October 19, 1797
16th Convention.................... Charleston, October 18, 23, 1798
(No Conventions October 23, 1798 to February 20, 1804.)
17th Convention..........St. Michael's, Charleston, February 20-21, 1804
18th Convention............St. Michael's, Charleston, February 18, 1805
19th Convention..........St. Michael's, Charleston, February 17-20, 1806
20th Convention..........St. Michael's, Charleston, February 16-18, 1807
21st Convention..........St. Michael's, Charleston, February 15-16, 1808
22nd Convention..........St. Michael's, Charleston, February 20-21, 1809
23rd Convention..........St. Michael's, Charleston, February 20-21, 1810
24th Convention..........St. Michael's, Charleston, February 18-22, 1812
25th Convention..........St. Michael's, Charleston, February 16-19, 1813
26th Convention..........St. Michael's, Charleston, February 15-17, 1814
27th Convention..........St. Michael's, Charleston, February 21-22, 1815
28th Convention..................Trinity, Columbia, December 7-8, 1815
29th Convention..........St. Michael's, Charleston, February 18-20, 1817
30th Convention..........St. Michael's, Charleston, February 17-20, 1818
31st Convention..........St. Michael's, Charleston, February 16-19, 1819
32nd Convention..........St. Michael's, Charleston, February 15-21, 1820
33rd Convention..........St. Michael's, Charleston, February 14-17, 1821
34th Convention..........St. Michael's, Charleston, February 13-16, 1822
35th Convention..........St. Michael's, Charleston, February 19-21, 1823
36th Convention..........St. Michael's, Charleston, February 18-21, 1824
37th Convention..........St. Michael's, Charleston, February 16-18, 1825
38th Convention..........St. Michael's, Charleston, January 25-26, 1826
39th Convention..........St. Michael's, Charleston, February 14-16, 1827

40th Convention..........St. Michael's, Charleston, February 13-15, 1828
41st Convention...........St. Michael's, Charleston, February 18, 1829
42nd Convention..........St. Michael's, Charleston, February 17-19, 1830
43rd Convention...........St. Michael's, Charleston, February 9-10, 1831
44th Convention..........St. Michael's, Charleston, February 15-17, 1832
45th Convention..........St. Michael's, Charleston, February 13-14, 1833
46th Convention...........St. Michael's, Charleston, February 5-6, 1834
47th Convention..........St. Michael's, Charleston, February 25-27, 1835
47th Convention..........St. Michael's, Charleston, February 10-12, 1836
48th Convention...................Trinity, Columbia, May 3-4, 1837
49th Convention..........St. Michael's, Charleston, February 15-16, 1838
50th Convention..........St. Michael's, Charleston, February 6-8, 1839
51st Convention..........St. Michael's, Charleston, February 12-15, 1840
52nd Convention..........St. Michael's, Charleston, February 10-15, 1841
53rd Convention..........St. Michael's, Charleston, February 16-19, 1842
54th Convention..........St. Michael's, Charleston, February 8-11, 1843
55th Convention..........St. Michael's, Charleston, February 17-20, 1844
56th Convention..........St. Michael's, Charleston, February 13-15, 1845
57th Convention..........St. Michael's, Charleston, February 12-16, 1846
58th Convention..........St. Michael's, Charleston, February 4-8, 1847
59th Convention..........St. Michael's, Charleston, February 9-11, 1848
60th Convention..........St. Michael's, Charleston, February, 14-15, 1849
61st Convention..........St. Michael's, Charleston, February 20-22, 1850
62nd Convention..........St. Michael's, Charleston, February 12-13, 1851
63rd Convention..............Trinity, Columbia, February 11-12, 1852
64th Convention..............St. Michael's, Charleston, May 4-7, 1853
65th Convention...........St. Philip's, Charleston, February 8-10, 1854
66th Convention..........St. Philip's, Charleston, February 15-16, 1855
67th Convention..........St. Philip's, Charleston, February 13-15, 1856
68th Convention.....................Grace, Camden, May 6-8, 1857
69th Convention.............Christ, Greenville, June 9-11, 1858
70th Convention.............St. Peter's, Charleston, May 11-14, 1859
71st Convention.............St. Philip's, Charleston, May 16-18, 1860
72nd Convention ....Trinity, Abbeville, June 19-20, 1861
73rd Convention............Grace, Charleston, February 12-14, 1862
74th Convention..........St. Philip's, Charleston, February 11-12, 1863
75th Convention.............Advent, Spartanburg, May 11-12, 1864
76th Convention...........Grace, Camden (no quorum), May 24, 1865
77th Convention..................Grace, Charleston, May 8-10, 1867
78th Convention...........St. Philip's, Charleston, May 13-16, 1868
79th Convention.............St. Philip's, Charleston, May 12-14, 1869
80th Convention..................Trinity, Abbeville, May 12-14, 1870
81st Convention.............St. Philip's, Charleston, May 11-15, 1871
82nd Convention................St. Philip's, Charleston, May 9-11, 1872
83rd Convention.....................Grace, Camden, May 8-10, 1873
84th Convention.............St. Paul's, Charleston, May 13-16, 1874
85th Convention.............St. Philip's, Charleston, May 13-15, 1875
86th Convention.................Trinity, Columbia, May 10-13, 1876
87th Convention.............St. Philip's, Charleston, May 10-12, 1877
88th Convention.............St. Philip's, Charleston, May 8-11, 1878

89th Convention.................... Christ, Greenville, May 14-16, 1879
90th Convention............... St. Philip's, Charleston, May 12-15, 1880
91st Convention............... St. Philip's, Charleston, May 11-13, 1881
92nd Convention................. Advent, Spartanburg, May 10-12, 1882
93rd Convention................ St. Philip's, Charleston, May 9-12, 1883
94th Convention................ St. Philip's, Charleston, May 15-17, 1884
95th Convention.................. Trinity, Columbia, May 13-16, 1885
96th Convention............... St. Luke's, Charleston, May 12-15, 1886
97th Convention............... St. Philip's, Charleston, May 12-14, 1887
98th Convention.................... Grace, Anderson, May 2-3, 1888
99th Convention................ St. Thaddaeus', Aiken, May 8-10, 1889
100th Convention........... Holy Communion, Charleston, May 7-9, 1890
101st Convention.................. Christ, Greenville, May 13-15, 1891
102nd Convention.............. Holy Comforter, Sumter, May 11-13, 1892
103rd Convention...................... Grace, Charleston, May 3-5, 1893
104th Convention.................. Trinity, Columbia, May 9-11, 1894
105th Council...................... Grace, Camden, May 8-10, 1895
106th Council.............. St. Philip's, Charleston, May 6-8, 1896
107th Council...................... Grace, Anderson, May 12-14, 1897
108th Council............. Holy Communion, Charleston, May 11-14, 1898
109th Council.................... St. David's, Cheraw, May 3-5, 1899
110th Council.................. St. Thaddaeus', Aiken, May 9-11, 1900
111th Council...................... Christ, Greenville, May 7-9, 1901
112th Council.............. Prince George, Georgetown, May 14-16, 1902
113th Council................. Good Shepherd, Columbia, May 5-7, 1903
114th Council..................... St. John's, Florence, May 3-5, 1904
115th Council...................... Grace, Camden, May 2-4, 1905
116th Council...................... Grace, Anderson, May 8-9, 1906
117th Council.................... Trinity, Columbia, May 14-16, 1907
118th Council................ St. Philip's, Charleston, May 12-14, 1908
119th Council.................. Advent, Spartanburg, May 11-13, 1909
120th Council.................. Holy Comforter, Sumter, May 3-5, 1910
121st Council................. Good Shepherd, Yorkville, May 2-4, 1911
122nd Council..................... St. Helena's, Beaufort, May 7-9, 1912
123rd Convention...................... Grace, Charleston, May 6-8, 1913
124th Convention.................... Christ, Greenville, May 12-14, 1914
125th Convention................... St. John's, Florence, May 11-13, 1915
126th Convention.................. Trinity, Columbia, May 16-18, 1916
127th Convention................... St. David's, Cheraw, May 8-9, 1917
128th Convention............... St. Thaddaeus', Aiken, May 14-16, 1918
129th Convention........... Prince George, Georgetown, May 13-15, 1919
130th Convention.............. Advent, Spartanburg, May 11-13, 1920
            Special Council............... Trinity, Columbia, October 12, 1920
131st Convention............... Holy Comforter, Sumter, May 17-19, 1921
132nd Convention.............. St. Philip's, Charleston, May 16-17, 1922
            Adjourned Session.............. Grace, Charleston, October 17, 1922
133rd Convention.................. St. John's, Florence, May 15-16, 1923
134th Convention................ Redeemer, Orangeburg, May 7-8, 1924
135th Convention.............. St. Paul's, Charleston, January 27-28, 1925
136th Convention............... St. Helena's, Beaufort, February 2-3, 1926

137th Convention............St. Michael's, Charleston, January 25-26, 1927
138th Convention.........Prince George, Georgetown, January 25-26, 1928
    Special Convention.........St. John's, Florence, September 18, 1928
139th Convention..............Holy Comforter, Sumter, May 14-15, 1929
140th Convention.................St. Philip's, Charleston, May 6-7, 1930
141st Convention..............St. Paul's, Summerville, April 21-22, 1931
142nd Convention.................St. David's, Cheraw, April 26-27, 1932
143rd Convention............St. Andrew's, Mt. Pleasant, April 25-26, 1933
144th Convention.........Holy Communion, Charleston, April 24-25, 1934
145th Convention....................St. John's, Florence, May 7-8, 1935
146th Convention..............St. Luke's, Charleston, April 28-29, 1936
147th Convention.............Holy Comforter, Sumter, April 27-28, 1937
148th Convention.............Redeemer, Orangeburg, May 11-12, 1938
149th Convention............Prince George, Georgetown, May 3-4, 1939
150th Convention.............St. Michael's, Charleston, April 16-17, 1940
151st Convention.................St. David's, Cheraw, May 13-14, 1941
152nd Convention.........Holy Communion, Charleston, April 28-29, 1942
153rd Convention..................St. John's, Florence, May 11-12, 1943
    Special Convention............St. John's, Florence, January 18, 1944
154th Convention...............Holy Comforter, Sumter, May 9-10, 1944
155th Convention..............St. Peter's, Charleston, April 24-25, 1945
156th Convention..............Redeemer, Orangeburg, May 14-15, 1946
157th Convention ....St. Paul's, Summerville, April 15-16, 1947
158th Convention...............St. Helena's, Beaufort, April 13-14, 1948
159th Convention....................Grace, Charleston, May 3-4, 1949
160th Convention...........Prince George, Georgetown, April 25-26, 1950
161st Convention..............St. Philip's, Charleston, April 10-11, 1951
162nd Convention...........St. Michael's, Charleston April 29-30, 1952
163rd Convention.................St. David's, Cheraw, April 21-22, 1953
164th Convention........St. Luke and St. Paul, Charleston, May 4-5, 1954
165th Convention..............St. John's, Florence, April 26-27, 1955
166th Convention.........Holy Communion, Charleston, April 17-18, 1956

3. OFFICERS OF THE DIOCESE

President of the Standing Committee:

Rev. Edward Jenkins (earliest recorded).......................1806-08
Rev. William Percy 1809-18
Rev. Christopher E. Gadsden.................................1819-40
Rev. Paul T. Gervais..1841
Rev. Christian Hanckel......................................1842-69
Rev. Charles C. Pinckney, D.D. 1870-97
Rev. A. Toomer Porter, D.D. 1898-1900
Rev. John Johnson, D.D. 1901-06
Rev. William B. Gordon.....................................1907-15
Rev. John Kershaw 1916-20
Rev. Alexander R. Mitchell..................................1921-22
Rev. Albert S. Thomas......................................1923-28
Rev. S. C. Beckwith...1929-35

Rev. Homer W. Starr, Ph.D. 1936
Rev. Frank W. Ambler..1937-43
Rev. Henry D. Bull, D.D. 1944-57

Secretary of the Standing Committee:

Rev. Frederick Dalcho, M.D. 1822
Rev. Allston Gibbes.......................................1823-33

* * * * *

Rev. Paul Trapier Keith.....................................1853-62
Rev. Christopher P. Gadsden.................................1863-66
Rev. Charles C. Pinckney......................................1867
W. Alston Pringle, Esq. 1868-80
Henry P. Archer, Esq. 1888-96: 1903-05
F. L. Frost, M.D. 1897-1902
William C. Bissell, Esq. 1906-17
J. Nelson Frierson, Esq. 1918-22
C. Willoughby Middleton, Esq. 1923-28
R. W. Sharkey, Esq. 1929-39; 1941-44; 1947
Sam J. Royal, Esq. 1940
J. Ross Hanahan, Esq. 1945-46
W. Allston Moore, Esq. ....1948-__

Secretary of the Convention:

Records of early Conventions are incomplete (William Hasell Gibbes acted as secretary in 1786, George Reid in 1804, David Alexander in 1805). Until 1861, the secretary was also treasurer.

Rev. Nathaniel Bowen.......................................1805-09
Rev. James D. Simons...1810
Rev. Charles B. Snowden....................................1812-13
Rev. John J. Tschudy.......................................1814-19
Rev. Frederick Dalcho, M.D. 1820-35
Rev. William W. Spear......................................1836-40
Rev. Cranmore Wallace 1841-49
Rev. Paul T. Keith...1850-59
Gen. W. E. Martin..1860-61
Rev. W. B. W. Howe...1862-63
Rev. John D. McCollough....................................1864-96
Rev. James G. Glass.......................................1897-1902
Rev. Albert S. Thomas.......................................1903-22
Rev. William B. Sams..1923-48
Rev. Waties R. Haynsworth...................................1949-__

Treasurer of the Convention:

In the first years of the Convention, the office of treasurer of the Convention was combined with that of secretary (See Secretary of the Convention). Gen. W. E. Martin (1860-61) was the last secretary to hold both positions. In 1861, following the action of the

General Convention, the Diocesan Convention made the treasurership a separate office when C. E. B. Flagg was elected as the first
treasurer under this rule.

C. E. B. Flagg..1861
F. P. Elford...1862-70
E. H. Frost..1871-74
F. A. Mitchell...1875-1908
William Godfrey...1909-28
Frank K. Myers..1929-38
Isaac M. Bryan..1939-50
Louis D. Simonds..1951-___

Secretary and Treasurer of the Trustees:

Bishop and Standing Committee (1880-99)
W. Alston Pringle
A. Markley Lee

Trustees (Organized 1899)
John P. Thomas, Jr., Esq....................................1899-1931
William Egleston, M.D. 1932-33
B. Allston Moore, Esq. ....1933-___

Chancellor:

(Office established by Constitution, 1891)
Robert W. Shand, Esq..1891-1914
F. R. Frost, Esq. 1915-32
Nathaniel B. Barnwell, Esq. 1933-50
Jack Wright, Esq. ....1951-___

Registrar:

(Office created 1873 by Canon, later by Constitution)
Rev. John Johnson...1873-83
Rev. T. A. Porter, D.D. 1890-94
Rev. A. R. Mitchell...1894-98
Mr. Joseph I. Waring.......................................1898-1926
Rev.Percival H. Whaley, Assistant...........................1909-15
Rev. William Way, D.D. 1926-31
William H. Johnson, M.D. 1931-34
Mrs. Henry P. Jervey..1935-45
Rt. Rev. Albert S. Thomas...................................1945-___

Historiographer:

(Office created by Constitution, 1915)
Rev. Percival H. Whaley.....................................1915
Rev. John Kershaw 1916-21
Rev. Albert S. Thomas.......................................1921-___

Diocesan Headquarters Secretary:

Miss Henrietta Jervey 1922-33
Miss Harriett E. Coffin.....................................1933-45
Miss Ida Dwight ....1945-___

Appendix II—*Societies*

1. THE PROTESTANT EPISCOPAL SOCIETY FOR THE ADVANCEMENT OF CHRISTIANITY IN SOUTH CAROLINA

BEING NOW
THE CHURCH FOUNDATION
Founded 1810

The Protestant Episcopal Society for the Advancement of Christianity in South Carolina was the first organization in the Episcopal Church in the United States for the extension of the gospel, being the first of several similar societies established in America in the early years of the nineteenth century, and modeled after the venerable Society for the Propagation of the Gospel in Foreign Parts (the S. P. G.), which had contributed so largely to the establishment of the Anglican Church in this country. To appreciate the zeal and the motives of the founders of this society, two things especially should be borne in mind: first, that, in South Carolina at the time, the diocese (as was the case more or less everywhere in America) was a very incompletely organized body. There was, indeed, a Standing Committee, but not much more. Such a thing as a Department or Board of Missions, not to say an Executive Council or Board of Trustees, was unheard of; there was no systematic provision for the prosecution of any missionary or educational work. The activities of the Church were almost entirely parochial. The situation in the dioceses in America was not exactly like, but not dissimilar from that which existed in England when the awakening there a hundred years before had led to the founding, first, of the Society for Promoting Christian Knowledge (the S. P. C. K.) in 1699, and then, two years later, the S. P. G.

Then, again, the founders of the society were moved by the deplorable condition into which the Church in South Carolina had fallen. When the Declaration of Independence was signed, there were twenty clergymen and twenty-two parishes in the state, most of these quite flourishing, and all having become so strong as to have relieved entirely the S. P. G. of its nurturing care of the previous seventy-five years. The venerable society had sent fifty-four ministers to South Carolina during that time, beginning with Samuel Thomas in 1702, who was the third sent to America—next only to Keith and Gordon. The Church had become strong. But the Revolution delivered a crushing blow to the Church in South Carolina. No other state was so completely overrun by the invader from mountain to seaboard; in no other state were the citizens so divided upon the issues, and in no other did they so generally participate personally in the struggle. With the war came disestablishment (1778) and loss of all ministerial supply, followed by disintegration, and destruction. After the war, there were only a very few churches outside the city of Charleston which were not practically in ruins, either burned, dilapidated or abandoned, and mostly without clergymen. After Bishop Smith's death in 1801, and one futile effort to secure a successor to him, the situation seemed almost hopeless—there was no Standing Committee, and no diocesan Convention had been held for five years. The Church, as it had been in its halcyon days, was confined to the seaboard, but now the up-country was growing rapidly, and no effort was being made to extend the Church into that section. Not a single new parish had been established since the war, although several chapels had been erected in existing parishes. It was under the urgency of this situation that the idea of a society was conceived. At the critical juncture, God raised up men of faith and vision to lead the "remnant" to a better day.

It was the vision, courage, and faith of two men, Nathaniel Bowen and Theodore Dehon, which contributed most to the revival of the Church in South Carolina in the early part of the nineteenth century. And, closely connected with this as cause and effect, these two were the chief founders of this society. Although the youngest minister in the diocese at this time, it was due to the activity of Nathaniel Bowen that the diocesan Conventions were renewed in 1804 after a lapse of five years. He became secretary of the Convention and also secretary of the Standing Committee. Previous to the arrival of Dehon in 1810, Bowen "had suggested to several of the clergy and laity the expediency of instituting a Society to collect a theological library for the use of the members and others—with which other purposes useful to the Church might be connected." So we find Bowen, not only suggesting an organization, but actually tarrying in Charleston, after his acceptance of a call to Grace Church, New York, and after Dehon had been installed as his successor in St. Michael's, "to set the institution on foot in April 1810, a meeting for the purpose and the first on the subject that was held, May 8th, by him at the house of the Rev. J. D. Simons."

The Rev. James D. Simons was the rector of St. Philip's Church in Charleston at the time.

Immediately after the inception of the plan and the one meeting held, Bowen left the diocese, and Theodore Dehon assumed the leadership. So was it, as Bishop Gadsden sums up: "Dr. Bowen and Dr. Dehon having communicated to each other their respective views, it was concluded to form a society 'for the advancement of Christianity,' which of course would embrace several objects, subsidiary to the great one named in its title." On June 10, 1810, the next and first definite step was taken looking to the organization of a society for the advancement of Christianity in South Carolina; a group of churchmen met under the leadership of Dr. Dehon, formulated a constitution, and issued an address to the Church in South Carolina. Dehon was the author of both documents. In the proposed constitution the objects of the society were set forth: "The promotion of Christian Knowledge, learning, and piety in the state," and its name was given as "The Protestant Episcopal Society for the Advancement of Christianity in South Carolina." The address was characterized by both the literary style and force which made the writings of Dehon outstanding, not only in America but in England, as we shall see. He said in part, "The pure faith and undefiled religion of the gospel is the most valuable gift, which the Almighty has bestowed upon the inhabitants of the earth—this religion Episcopalians enjoy in all its perfection; and they cannot be too thankful to its adorable author, for the sound faith, the useful, and happily combined, orders of ministry, and the rational, decent, holy forms of worship, with which their Church is distinguished."

His strong appeal found a ready response. The Spirit of God was brooding over the almost prostrate Church. Just four weeks later, on July 2, 1810, such members of the Church as had become interested met at St. Michael's Church, where the Constitution as proposed was adopted, and officers were elected as follows: The Rev. Dr. Theodore Dehon, president; Keating Simons, Esq., vice-president; Thos. Higham, corresponding secretary; David Alexander, recording secretary; and trustees, Robt. Dewar, Robt. Hazelhurst, the Rev. C. E. Gadsden, Wm. Doughty, Charles Kershaw, the Rev. P. T. Gervais, Robt. J. Trumbull, Jno. Dawson, Jr., Theodore Gaillard, the Rev. Jas. D. Simons, John Ball, Henry Deas. This was the birthday of the society.

Another meeting was held on July 17th, when the decision was made (and it has been maintained ever since) to divide the funds of the society into two parts—the Permanent Fund, for capital investment to afford a regular income, and the Common Fund, to meet the current needs of the society. The regular annual membership fee was set as five dollars, and life membership, $50.00. The society was incorporated on December 19, 1810, by act of the legislature of the state. It was provided that the annual meeting should be held on the feast of the Epiphany. In order to the drawing closer of the ties of friendship and social intercourse, a feature of the annual meeting in the early days was a dining together of the members. The first annual meeting convened at St. Michael's Church on January 6, 1811. The officers and trustees just mentioned were re-elected for the year, with Charles Kershaw as treasurer. Prompt efforts were made through circular letters and agents to make known the existence and purposes of the society in all parts of the diocese. The trustees, at the time of the first annual meeting, were able to report that already there were 234 regular members of the society, with ten life members. From the beginning the special objects of the society were defined as threefold: "The distribution of the Sacred Scriptures, the Book of Common Prayer, and other Religious Works of approved reputation; The Education of Young Men of Genius and Piety for the Ministry of the Church; and The sending forth of Missionaries into various parts of this State, where there is reason to believe their labors will be useful."

Thus it is seen that the society took up itself, more or less, the duties of the executive council of the diocese as of today. Nor did the young society sleep upon its oars. Already in the first report of the trustees, Epiphany, 1811, it is modestly stated "that though the shortness of time and the infancy of the institution have not allowed them to accomplish more . . . yet the work of the Society has been auspiciously begun": 140 copies of the Book of Common Prayer had been secured for distribution; they had caused to be published for the society a cheap edition of Bishop Porteous' Christian Evidences, and 300 copies of Nelson's Christian Sacrifice; also, though the funds of the society did not yet justify undertaking the payment of tuition for candidates for the ministry, a set of books recommended by the House of Bishops for theological students had been ordered. An annual offering for the work of the society had been begun in the diocese, the first year yielding $669.80, and the Permanent Fund had grown to $2,050.00. In 1811, a seal was adopted, with an attractive device, symbolic of the objects of the society, executed by Robert Mills, Esq., the noted architect. The handsome emblem is still in use.

By resolution of the society, correspondence was begun at an early date with sister societies in both England and America. In the report of 1814, the society felicitates itself not alone upon the happy consequences of its labors which have been manifested in this diocese, but upon the fact that its laudable example has been followed by the diocese of Pennsylvania. Corespondence with the S. P. G. in England had led to the constant exchange of literature between the two societies. In 1816, a plan was adopted to inaugurate, as auxiliary to its permanent fund, a building fund for the purpose both of restoring old churches and building new ones. This fund developed very slowly and after a few years its its accumulations and functions were taken over by the permanent fund of the society. Some years later, a Church Building Fund was organized in the diocese independent of the society, which functioned usefully for many years. The society from the first recognized building as included in its objects; indeed, for over a century there were not many Church buildings erected in the diocese that did not receive help from the society, and this still continues to be true. The society acquired a new character as a board of trustees of other Church funds than its own at an early date. In 1818, immediately after Bishop Dehon's death, the convention of the diocese established a Bishop's Permanent Fund, with a view of relieving in time the Bishop of the diocese of duty as rector of a parish. The society was requested to act as trustee of this fund. The trust was accepted. The legislature of the state now granted the society an expansion of its legal powers. It was stipulated that when the income of this Bishop's fund should amount to $4,000.00 yearly, the Bishop would receive this amount as his salary and he should "immediately cease to be rector of any particular Church." This goal was not reached for many years, though the fund did supply an expense account for the Bishop. It was not until 1854, the year following the Consecration of Bishop Thomas F. Davis, that the proposed goal was almost if not quite reached. The fund had received a comparatively large increment, through a legacy of Mrs. Frederick Kohne, amounting to nearly $10,000.00. At the Convention of that year, the allowance of $1,200.00 for the Bishop's expenses, which had maintained from the time of Bishop Bowen (1818-39), was changed to a salary of $3,500.00, and increased the next year permanently to $4,000.00; and then at last the diocese assumed the support of its Bishop. The society continued as trustee of the Bishop's Permanent Fund until 1913, when the fund was transferred to the trustees of the diocese.

We must now return to the beginning and briefly see with what success the institution fulfilled its original threefold purpose to distribute literature, to assist in the education of candidates for Holy Orders, and to do missionary work. The first of these objects received foremost attention in the beginning, due especially to the fact that its labors at the first in both the field of education and of diocesan missions was limited by the lack of candidates for Holy Orders and of clergymen, as well as by scarceness of funds. More attention consequently was given at first to the distribution of sacred literature. But this work had also for a time its limitations due to the War of 1812, cutting off supplies from across the sea and making communication with the North difficult, through curtailment of transportation by boat. But, as we have noted, this work had a good beginning during the society's first year. Many of the Bibles and prayer books were given to the recently established Sunday School Institute. The organization in 1827 of the "Episcopal Bible, Prayer Book, and Tract Society" took over part of the work of the society in this field, functioning for nearly one hundred years. Its funds left to the Bishop are still at work.

Connected with this work of distributing literature, the formation of a permanent diocesan library was almost immediately begun with the securing, as noted above, of the books recommended by the House of Bishops for theological students. In 1880, Dr. A. T. Porter gives an estimate of $6,000.00 as having been spent on the books up to that time, but the larger part of what became an extensive library were books given to the society. This library has a history of its own. It was moved from place to place in Charleston in the early days. For a time it was in the home of our great diocesan historian, Dr. Frederick Dalcho, assistant in St. Michael's Church, who was the first librarian. For a time it was in the north vestibule of St. Michael's. In 1823, the library was located at No. 80 Queen Street, E. Thayer, Jr., librarian. In 1833, the society itself erected a library building on Chalmers St., at a cost of over $4,000.00. This continued to be the home of the library until the War between the States, when this property was sold. In 1860, the library was loaned to the diocesan seminary which had been established in Camden, South Carolina. Here the larger part of the books fell victim to the war, many being lost in a fire in Camden. The remnant was moved to the Church school in Spartanburg, thence back to Charleston, first over Fogarty's book store at 181 King Street, later being housed in the building in the rear of St. Stephen's Church on Anson Street. The few remains of this old library are today in the gallery of St. Stephen's Church. The Rev. Dr. Robert Wilson was the last regular librarian.

After Bishop Dehon's death in 1817, the society gained permission to publish for distribution some of his writings, including his discourses on Confirmation, on Baptism, and his sermon on the Death of Children. In 1819, with the widow's consent, the Bishop's sermons were published in Charleston in two volumes. The very high regard in which these sermons were held was not only local. The sermons were republished in England and went through at least three editions, the agreement being that this society should share in the profits. In 1833, the society had actually received nearly $2,000.00 from this source. Always, from the first, the society recognized as one of its fundamental purposes "the Education of Young men of Genius and Piety for the Ministry of the Church"; or, as Bishop Dehon expressed it, "to bring youthful genius forward from languishing in obscurity, and under the invigorating influences of a benign patronage to train it up for the service of the temple and the altar." The prosecution of this purpose was slow in getting underway, for the reasons already suggested. This phase of the society's work has continued to this day, annual appropriations for theological education being regularly made.

The educational work of the society was further advanced by its trusteeship of theological scholarships. Soon after Bishop Dehon's death in 1817, the women of the diocese established such a scholarship in his memory, and entrusted its care and administration to the society. Later, but during his lifetime, a similar scholarship was established by the Convention of the diocese in honor of Bishop Bowen and put in care of the society. Again later, in 1833, the Rev. Dr. Thomas Gates left to the society $2,000.00, establishing the Gates scholarship for a student from the diocese at the General Theological Seminary. All three of these scholarships are intact today, the two former having been allocated to the diocese of Upper South Carolina after that diocese was set apart in 1922. More recently the society has received an additional endowment for theological education from a member of St. Michael's Church. Although lack of funds and lack of available missionaries retarded what was to be the society's greatest work—the encouragement and support of diocesan missions—an important beginning was made as early as June 17, 1812, when the Rev. Andrew Fowler, one of the greatest missionaries of that century in the American Church, was "elected and engaged by the Society for six months to administer the ordinances of our Church to the inhabitants of Columbia, and vicinity." He was to receive $500.00 for his services. The missionary was well received, especially so in Columbia, and here he inaugurated a permanent and important work, as also in Camden.

This missionary objective, which became the society's chief and most valuable work, was conducted with great system: there were carefully prepared "Rules for the Regulation of Missionaries," requiring regular reports, and all accounts were scrupulously kept and regularly audited. The next strictly advance work after Fowler's was that of the society's missionaries, the Rev. Messrs. Patrick H. Folker, Edward Thomas and Rodolphus Dickinson, in the first planting of the Church in the Piedmont section of the State in Pendleton and Greenville. In the meantime, other missionaries, under employment by the society, were busy in the work of bringing back into life many of the old parishes. Among these earlier workers should be mentioned the Rev. Albert A. Muller, followed by the Rev. Messrs. Francis P. Delavaux, David I. Campbell, John W. Chandler; and again the indefatigable Andrew Fowler in Cheraw. The missionary activity of the society went on through the years, much the larger part of the work of the Church in the diocese at this time being that of missions and aided parishes, including, up and down the diocese, as many as forty-five chapels for Negroes. Let us here listen to some contemporary testimony. In 1845, Bishop Gadsden has this to say of the society: "It has contributed more than any other human means to the revival of our Church, which has for its date the election, after a long suspension of Episcopal services, of our second Bishop." And, for a later testimony, we quote from the address of the Rev. Charles Cotesworth Pinckney on the occasion of the jubilee celebration of the society in 1860: "Thus working her way against prejudice and misconception, our Church has gradually extended itself through the middle and upper regions of our State. The two Churches in Columbia, the Church in Camden, Cheraw, Fairfield, Yorkville, Spartanburg, Greenville, Pendleton, Abbevile, Edgefield, Newberry, Laurens, Aiken, Barnwell, have all been founded by the labors of this Society; and in fifteen other localities we have congregations gathered, some with Churches built, some in progress, and some as yet the nucleus of a future Episcopal Church. Out of the seventy Parishes in our State, thirty-six have been established by this agency, and every Church in the middle and upper country established in the last fifty years is the off-spring of this Society. Nor is it an unnatural mother. It watches over the young, and aids them in their infancy, and encourages them until able to stand alone."

It was indeed in this jubilee year of the society that it reached its climax in the extent of its activities. The grim spectre of war, however, was now raising its head again. As in the beginning the work of the organization was largely the overcoming of the effects of one war, now another, with its destructive power both to the spiritual and material welfare of the Church, altered the trend of its work. At the beginning of the War between the States, the appropriations of the society for missionary work were upwards of $7,000.00; in 1869, they had fallen to $2,650.00. The society's own losses were crippling—$56,000.00 of its permanent fund; and of the other vested funds of the diocese held in trust by the society, $184,-000.00. However, the society did not lose courage. Resolving even to use capital funds if necessary, it sought to meet the pressing needs as it was able. "Jacob shall arise and the Gospel in our diocese will have free course and be glorified." Symptomatic of the time, the annual membership fee was changed in 1868 from $5.00 to $2.00. The first step toward a board of missions for the diocese was taken in 1868 when, by recommendation of a joint committee of the Convention of the diocese and the society, the latter itself was requested to act as a board of missions; in reality, it had been acting in this capacity all along, only now its appeal to the Church was stronger. It was not until 1877 that the diocesan Convention adopted a canon establishing a Board of Missions. So after some sixty-seven years the society was relieved of its responsibility for diocesan missions in South Carolina. Henceforth the missionaries would no longer make their reports to the society, but to the Bishop and the board, and henceforth their missionary stipends would be from the latter.

Since 1877, however, the society has continued its work, making appropriations not to individual missionaries usually, but voting amounts in bulk to the board, and especially in after years giving its income to more distinctly advancement causes in the diocese. From 1830 to 1881, the society expended $187,956.08. In 1881, the permanent fund of the society amounted to $30,032.43. This fund, though always scrupulously conserved, had suffered large losses on two occasions, first, when the U. S. Bank failed in 1836, and again, as we have seen, through the loss in Confederate States' securities. In view of the fact that the funds of the society had all been given with the implied trust that they were for the benefit of he Episcopal Church in the entire State, it was determined by the society, soon after the division of the diocese, to divide its funds equally as far as possible between the two dioceses, a similar society being organized to hold the funds in the new diocese. After the pasage of an Act of the General Assembly, approved March 23, 1926, and by a decree of the Court of Common Pleas for Charleston, this was done by a Committee consisting of Frank R. Frost, W. M. Shand, and John P. Thomas, Jr. To the diocese of Upper South Carolina was assigned one-half of the Common Fund $18,-500.00; the Dehon Scholarship Fund $2,600.00; and the Bowen Scholarship Fund $1,400.00; a total of $22,500.00. The old society was allocated of the Common Fund $18,500.00 and the Gates' Scholarship Fund of $3,300.00; total $21,800.00. The permanent fund of the society now (1951) amounts approximately to $25,-000.00, including the Gates' scholarship.

So much for what this society has done in the past, and in no small measure still is doing. But there is another word to add concerning its future. At the 1951 Convention of the diocese on April 10, the recent establishment, with the endorsement of the general Convention, of a national Episcopal Church Foundation to receive gifts for religious, educational, and charitable purposes was brought before the Convention, with the suggestion that a similar foundation to receive gifts for the extension of the work of the Church in the diocese is very desirable; and with the further suggestion that this society is, in accordance with the purposes of its incorporation, ready to serve just this purpose. Thereupon the following resolutions were adopted:

Whereas, The Church realized its life chiefly in its advance work in fulfillment of the great commission imposed upon it in the beginning by our Lord in the words, "Go ye into all the world"; and,

Whereas, There are great responsibilities and opportunities to further the work of the Church in the diocese, evangelically especially in the establishment of new churches, educationally in schools, and conferences, and in other ways; and,

Whereas, The diocese must look to the good will and generosity of its present members to supply the means by which this great challenge is to be met; and,

Whereas, It is desirable that there be an official organization or foundation duly incorporated by the laws of the State to receive, conserve, and dispense, according to the respective trusts imposed, any gifts or legacies which our people may feel disposed to devote to the aforesaid cause of Church extension; and,

Whereas, The Protestant Episcopal Society for the Advancement of Christianity according to its charter and its declared purposes already in existence and fully incorporated with a carefully prepared constitution, stands ready to serve the objects here set forth; therefore, be it

Resolved (1) That the Convention of the diocese of South Carolina hereby heartily endorses the P. E. Society for the Advancement of Christianity in South Carolina in its purpose to collect and receive funds by gift, devise and bequest, and administer the same for evangelical, educational and charitable purposes in the diocese apart from the appeal of existing institutions, and recommends to the people of the diocese, when they are able, the making of such gifts to the society for the Extension of the work of the Church in the diocese.

Resolved (2) That this endorsement is condititioned on an agreement with the society by which a majority of its board of managers shall be elected by the society on nomination of the Convention of the diocese.

Resolved (3) That the editor of *"The Diocese"* be and is hereby requested to carry each month a notice of the society embodying briefly a statement of its purpose as indicated in these resolutions, inviting donations and legacies.

It is greatly to be hoped that the Advancement Society, with such an honorable past, will now, in keeping with present conditions, renew its life, and that the Church will again be advanced on a larger scale by its activity. The treasurers of this society from the beginning have been as follows: Charles Kershaw, 1810-22; the Rev. Frederick Dalcho (also librarian), 1822-24; Daniel Ravenel, 1824-28; Thomas Gadsden, 1828-44; James R. Pringle, 1844-49; T. G. Simmons, 1849-51; John Hanckel, 1851-67; Evan Edwards, 1867-91; W. H. Prioleau, M.D., 1891-1921; John P. Thomas, Jr., 1921-27; G. W. Duvall, 1927-30; G. W. Sharkey, 1930-44; Bishop A. S. Thomas, 1944-55; W. C. Coleman, 1955; J. W. Coleman, Jr., 1955- .

2. THE SOCIETY FOR THE RELIEF OF THE WIDOWS AND ORPHANS OF THE CLERGY

Organized 1762

Dr. Kershaw traces the beginning of this society as follows:

"It was the custom of Commissary Garden to summon the Clergy of the Province to an annual meeting in Charleston, at which, in obedience to the Canon Law of the Church of England, they exhibited their letters of orders and licenses to perform the ministerial office in this Province. Prior to 1749, since the year 1731, these gatherings were called 'visitations', but on Dr. Garden's resignation as Commissary in 1749, they were known as 'Annual Meetings'."

"The death rate in the Province generally was high, and none the less so among the clergy. This fact, coupled with the distresses to which the families of many of the clergy were exposed in consequence of their decease, called forth the active sympathies of the survivors, and in 1762, a Society was formed by the clergy for the relief of widows and orphans of their deceased brethren. That year, says Dalcho (p. 189), was a memorable one in the annals of the clergy in South Carolina. At their fourteenth annual meeting it was, that the Society was organized April 21, 1762. The preamble was as follows: "We, Alexander Garden, James Harrison, Robert Baron, Winwood Sergeant, Robert Smith, Robert Cooper, John Tonge, Abraham Imer, Joseph Dacie Wilton, Joseph Stokes, and Offspring Pearce, having taken into consideration the distressed condition in which the widows and orphans of our deceased brethren of the Clergy of the Church of England in the Province of South Carolina are frequently left, and being moved with compassion, as well as with a due sense of religion, and of the obligation all men are under to exercise Christian charity, have agreed to enter into a Society to be hereafter called The Society for the Relief of the Widows and Children of the Clergy of the Church of England in the Province of South Carolina: and for the better furthering the end and design of this Society, have agreed upon and signed a certain set of Rules and Orders.' "

It was the first regularly organized society of the kind in the Church in America, though some steps had been taken in this line in Virginia in 1754 and later societies were organized in Pennsylvania, New York, and New Jersey in 1767. The Rev. Dr. Robert Smith, who took great interest in the welfare of his fellow clergymen and who was its treasurer for 30 years, is thought to have been the principal founder of the society. The organization went rather slowly on with its work when, with the admission of laymen (David Deas was the first), more prosperous times arrived. The funds in 1763 amounted to $168.72, in 1818 to $45,461.11. At the opening of this period, the society was in a flourishing condition. It was incorporated in 1786. After 1795, annually in October a sermon was preached and a collection taken for the society in the city churches. In 1820, Dr. William Read was president of the society; James R. Pringle, vice-president; and, John Bay, treasurer. The society lost nearly $17,000.00 of its capital in stock of the U. S.

Bank when it failed in 1841. One of the largest donations received by this society was a legacy of $20,000.00 from the estate of Francis Withers, 1847. The purpose, however, was directed for aged and infirm clergy. He also gave $5,000.00 for the objects of this society.

In 1860 the funds of the society had reached the sum of $126,-000.00, and at that time there were 170 lay members and 54 of the clergy. Ten years later, after the great diaster, the funds had fallen to $71,000.00 (and only part bearing interest), lay members 115, clergy 34; the income of less than $7,000.00 being expended for the relief of 20 families (including 15 widows and 28 children). The funds of the society have been always administered with great care and the objects of the society fulfilled to the extent of its means. In 1900, the officers of the society (with that for Relief of Clergy) were: president, H. E. Young; secretary, Casper A. Chisolm; treasurer, F. A. Mitchell. At the time of the adoption of the Church Pension Fund, the society, apart from special appropriations, gave its income to the diocese to assist in the payments of the pension assessments on the clergy of the diocese. In 1943, the president was J. P. Frost; vice-president, Arthur Young; secretary, I. M. Read; treasurer, Miss M. C. Bull. At this time, the capital of the society was reported as $135,000.00. The officers in 1955 are: president, D. E. Huger, Jr.; vice-president, Stephen Shackelford; secretary, K. L. Simons, treasurer, Miss M. C. Bull. For many years, the business of this society has been administered in conjunction with that of the Association for the Relief of Aged and Infirm Clergy (see following).

ASSOCIATION FOR THE RELIEF OF AGED AND INFIRM CLERGY
Established 1843

This association was a development from the Society for the Relief of the Widows and Orphans of the Clergy, with which it has always been closely associated as now the two organizations are under the same control. It was at the 76th anniversary of the older society in 1838 that it resolved to petition the legislature to so amend its charter to authorize it to act as trustee for any sums that might be given for the relief of superannuated and infirm clergymen. It was reported the next year that the fund for this purpose was slowly increasing. It was on February 19, 1842, that the following resolution was adopted in the Convention, being the next step toward effecting this organization: On motion of Mr. James H. Ladson, it was "Resolved, That a committee of five, consisting of two Clergymen and three Laymen, be appointed to take into consideration the propriety and best method of making some provision for the relief of aged and infirm Clergymen, who have ministered in this Diocese." Those appointed were the Rev. Paul Trapier, the Rev. Cranmore Wallace, J. H. Ladson, G. W. Egleston, and Edward R. Laurens, Esq. The committee reported at length to the next Convention, February 9, 1843, favorable to action, recommending an annual offering for the purpose on Thanksgiving Day but that no permanent fund be created; three lay trustees with the Bishop to conduct the work, one of whom shall be elected treasurer and secretary of the board of the "Trustees of the Fund for Aged and Infirm Clergymen." The Bishop appointed as trustees with himself: N. R. Middleton, G. W. Egleston, and J. R. Pringle. The last was elected treasurer. On February 17, 1844, he reported collections amounting to $332.59. The next year, he reported $601.49, and the first appropriation of the trustees, $200.00 to the Rev. Andrew Fowler—how appropriate! Already at this time he had served in the diocese for 38 years, one of the greatest missionaries in the history of the diocese! The society was launched. The report of 1847 shows the beginning of a permanent fund—$500.00 invested in railroad bonds at 7%. This society has been, for many years, merged for administration with the Society for the Relief of Widows and Orphans. (Cf. preceding sketch.)

3. THE EPISCOPAL BIBLE, PRAYER BOOK AND TRACT SOCIETY OF SOUTH CAROLINA
Established 1827

This society was organized in Whitsuntide-week June 8, 1827, Bishop Gadsden being present and giving his consent. Thus was removed from "the charitable females of our communion . . . the opinion which might otherwise have been entertained that they were not suitably impressed with the importance of a third great means of advancing Christianity by the dissemination of approved books" (the other means, missionary work and the ministry). At the anniversary meeting of the society at St. Stephen's Chapel on May 27, 1828, Whitsun Tuesday, it then consisted of 11 life members and 111 annual subscribers; books and tracts distributed 79 Bibles, 84 books of common prayer, 1,446 tracts of 38 kinds, comprising 34,980 pages, of which 192 were sold. The following ladies were elected officers and managers for the ensuing year: Mrs. J. W. Mitchell, directress; Mrs. Ann Hanckel, assistant directress; Miss C. Hart, secretary and treasurer; Managers, Mrs. W. Aiken, Mrs.

E. C. Ball, Mrs. Dehon, Miss E. Grimke, Miss M. Harris, Miss S. A. Marshall, Miss M. A. Miller, Miss E. Seabrook, Mrs. E. E. Thayer, Miss H. L. Thayer, Mrs. Jennings Waring, and Mrs. H. Wilson. Whitsun Tuesday was the regular time for the annual meeting.

In 1830, the society resolved to give monthly to each family of the Church in Charleston, willing to receive it, one of its tracts. In the first three years of its existence the society distributed: 235 Bibles, 283 prayer books, and 6,342 tracts. The membership in 1831 was 26 life and 175 annual. The treasurer reported $226.37½, balance in hand $4.62½. About this time 800 copies of a tract, "The Old Paths" were distributed at the expense of a "philanthropic lady." In 1837, the distribution of tracts without the city is interesting: Whiteville, 80; Edgefield, 80; Walterboro, 48; Pendleton, 130; Cheraw, 100; John's Island, 74; Alabama, 300. The distribution of the tracts in the city was usually to visitors by hand. In 1858, 9,133 tracts and 30 copies of the sailors' manual were distributed. Mrs. Eliza Ball was treasurer at this time. After the war, the work of the society lessened. But in 1870 the society was reorganized and the work renewed. At this time the membership was 100; in 1861 it had been 325. In 1872, Mrs. Thomas J. Young was directress; Mrs. M. T. Girardeau, assistant directress; Mrs. M. E. Toomer, secretary and treasurer; Mrs. W. M. Fitch, librarian. Total number books and tracts distributed this year, 980. At about the turn of the century, the directress was Mrs. C. C. Pinckney, and Mrs. J. A. Finger, secretary and treasurer. After 1911, the only officer of the society was the latter. Mrs. Finger continued in charge of the work of the organization until 1922, when it was decided to suspend the society. It was then decided to turn over the capital to the Bishop of the diocese, who would in the future use the income in keeping with the original purposes. In 1922, Bishop Guerry reported receiving to his trusteeship from the society a total amount of $4,130.75. Thus through the agency of the Bishop of the diocese, the original purposes of the society continue on. The corpus of the fund now is $1,900.00.

4. THE CHURCH BUILDING SOCIETY
Established 1857

The life of this society was short but its service most valuable for the time. It seems to have originated chiefly as the result of two things: first the earnest and reiterated appeals of Bishop Davis in behalf of houses of worship and residences for the clergy, which he considered "the most pressing necessity we have which money can remove," especially in the upper part of the diocese. Then, secondly, the services of Mr. John Bryan who was designated as the originator of the society—his energy and zeal it was that brought the organization into life whereby it took its place among the important institutions of the diocese. The organization was effected at a meeting of a large number of the clergy and laity at the Episcopal Library, Chalmers Street, Charleston, on January 13, 1857. A constitution based on that of the Advancement Society submitted by the Rev. C. P. Gadsden was adopted. The officers chosen were: president (*ex officio*), Bishop Davis; vice-president the Rev. C. Hanckel, D.D.; secretary, the Rev. A. T. Porter; trustees, the Revs. A. W. Marshall, D.D., C. C. Pinckney, Paul Trapier, C. Wallace, J. H. Elliott; Messrs. J. K. Sass, E. L. Kerrison, F. P. Elford, J. F. Blacklock, C. Edmonstone, Sr., G. A. Trenholm. The trustees elected Mr. John Bryan treasurer. It was reported that there were fourteen churches in the diocese in process of erection, the majority of which would need aid, and many parsonages were needed. The society met with great favor in the diocese and its work went forward. Its object was specifically stated to be "to aid in building Churches, Chapels, and Parsonages in this Diocese." The aid granted was limited to one-fourth of the amount already secured for the erection of the building; also a fee simple must be had to the lot before any gift was made. The money appropriated was not to be considered a debt to the society but a record would be kept in hope the Church, when able, would assist in the work of the society. Life membership was fixed at $100.00; annual dues, $5.00.

At the annual meeting of the society in May, 1860, it was reported that $2,300.00 had been appropriated during the preceding year to churches in the diocese, mostly in the up-country. Since the beginning of the society, gifts amounting to $4,075.00 had been made as follows: Holy Apostles, Barnwell, $500.00; St. Mark's, Chester, $500.00; Holy Comforter, Sumter, $500.00; Redeemer, Orangeburg, $275.00; Christ, Columbia, $500.00; Holy Communion, Charleston, $500.00; St. John's, Richland, $300.00; Trinity, Abbeville, $500.00; Nativity, Unionville, $500.00. By this time a permanent fund had been established amounting to $1,572.80. Its income was not to be used until it amounted to $10,000.00. At the annual meeting at the Convention of the diocese held in Abbeville May 1861, the death of Mr. John Bryan was announced. The Rev. A. T. Porter was secretary. Resolutions were adopted commemorating Mr. Bryan as the "founder and zealous promoter" of the society. Mr. Edwin Heriot was elected to succeed him as treasurer. Both of these gentlemen were among the most devoted laymen of the period. Already now the interruption of war was very apparent; there had been but one application for aid, and the board had only appropriated $200.00 for Grace Church, Anderson. This noble work it would appear was now practically coming to an end; such is war's destruction. Interestingly we learn that at this meeting in Abbeville, Mrs. A. R. Young became a life member ($100.00) as a thank-offering for the "bloodless" victory of Sumter. It was at another Convention of the diocese in Abbeville nine years later that we find the Rev. A. T. Porter, one of the founders and originally secretary of the society, when its very existence seems almost to have been forgotten, introducing this resolution: "That this Convention recommend the revival of the Church Building Society, and suggest, for the present, that the annual subscription be one dollar a year and life membership fifty dollars," (originally $5.00 and $100.00). Mr. Porter stated that at the last meeting during the war he had been made treasurer of the society and that the capital at this time amounted to $1,500.00 invested in City stock, S. C. Railroad stock, and Charleston City Railway stock. The resolution was adopted. However, there seems never to have been any actual revival, nor have we discovered what disposition was made of the $1,500.00.

5. THE DALCHO HISTORICAL SOCIETY
Established 1945

On the 23rd of April, 1945, a group of interested persons met in the library of St. Philip's Church Home, Charleston, and organized *The Dalcho Historical Society of the Diocese of South Carolina* for the "study and preservation of the history of the Diocese of South Carolina, its origin and development, and the stimulation of interest in the same". The Rev. H. D. Bull, D.D., suggested the organization and, therefore, should be called the founder of the society. The following officers were elected: president, the Rev. H. D. Bull, then of Georgetown; vice-president, Bishop Thomas; secretary-treasurer, Miss Marie Heyward of Charleston. The executive committee consisted of the above officers with Bishop Carruthers and Mr. C. Richard Banks of St. Matthews. In 1952 Mr. George W. Williams succeeded Mr. Bull as president, and Mr. Banks followed as secretary-treasurer. The membership and annual fee is one dollar, (later $2.00) contributing membership five dollars. The society holds only

one meeting a year, usually in winter, with a special speaker. The
society, under the leadership of Mr. Williams, has published many
important articles on diocesan history. (Cf. Bibliography at end of
this volume.)

Appendix III—*Organizations*

1. THE SOUTH CAROLINA BRANCH OF THE WOMAN'S AUXILIARY

At the General Convention meeting in Baltimore in 1871, the Woman's Auxiliary to the Board of Missions was organized with Miss Mary Emery as secretary to have charge of organization and direction. She was soon succeeded by her sister, Miss Julia C. Emery, who served with such devotion for forty years that at the end of this time, there was a branch in every diocese and missionary district. It was in 1885 that the South Carolina branch was organized. In "Fifty Years of Service" of which this sketch is largely a condensation, the first fifty years are divided into three periods.

I. *Beginnings, 1885-1900.* A meeting was held in Grace Church Sunday School, Charleston, presided over by the Rev. Dr. C. C. Pinckney. After Miss Julia C. Emery had given an account of the auxiliary, it was unanimously decided to organize a branch in this diocese. At a second meeting on May 20, a constitution drawn up by Miss Emery was, with a few alterations, adopted. On nomination by a committee with one lady from St. Philip's, St. Michael's, St. Luke's, and Holy Communion, the following officers of the executive board were appointed: president, Mrs. Robert Wilson; vice-presidents, Mrs. H. P. Archer, Charleston, Miss Hampton, Columbia, Mrs. William Beattie, Greenville; corresponding secretary, Miss Pinckney; recording secretary and treasurer, Miss A. P. Jervey. Mrs. Wilson, in twenty-one years, laid the foundations of the South Carolina branch. In 1908, in grateful recognition of her services, the auxiliary undertook the support of a school in Hankow and named it the Nanna Shand Wilson School. Again in 1924, after the great earthquake in Japan, a beautiful silver chalice and paten was given to the True Light Church in Tokyo. By the first annual meeting, 17 branches had been formed in South Carolina and money and boxes given to the value of $1,300.00. The first annual meeting away from Charleston was in Greenville in 1891, when the diocesan representation was much more general. Two years later began the custom of having a preparatory service of the Holy Communion and an all-day session. The annual meetings were now held alternately in each Convocation. By 1900, there were 47 branches on the roll. Eight of these were junior branches, a junior auxiliary having been organized in 1888. This junior work expanding, Miss Katie Lee of the Holy Communion, Charleston, was appointed to the charge of this work. The first baby branch was formed in Darlington in 1900. In the early days, the work of the auxiliary was mostly confined to diocesan projects, then one branch decided to devote $20.00 to the education of a Chinese girl—then began the command to be heard, "Go ye into all the world." Secretaries from headquarters and missionaries came into the diocese and proclaimed the missionary motive and described the field. This diocese did not participate in the first United Thank-Offering in 1889, but in 1892, $269.00 was sent, and in 1904 the amount had increased to $1,100.00.

II. *Growth and Development, 1900-20.* During this period, the development was along two lines, educational work and the Offering of Life. The branches at first had four business meetings a year when information was given as to "the box", and missions assisted. Soon, however, programs of mission study were inaugurated, "mission study classes" were formed. Materials were sent out more and more from headquarters for this purpose. In 1912, the office of "Diocesan Educational Secretary" was created. The first educational institute was held in Sumter and summer conferences were becoming common. Coeval with this educational movement was another, linked with the United Thank-Offering, the Offering of Life. Miss Sarah Thurston, the first woman missionary from the diocese, went to Cuba, followed a year later by Miss Eliza H. McCollough, going to Porto Rico. In 1911, the office of United Thank-Offering custodian was created with, a year later, the added duty of chairman of the committee on the "Offering of Life". Miss Virginia Taylor Singleton was the first to offer through the auxiliary, but owing to failure of health never went to foreign fields, but she had been trained and did much work at home. Alice Gregg of Mars Bluff went to China; Uto Saito, the Japanese girl trained at Winthrop, went to Japan; then Irene Muriel Moore and Mary Trapier Gadsden to Porto Rico. During this period, the plan of "summer volunteers" was begun under Mrs. Alexander Long, chairman on Offering of Life. This limited service has sometimes led to life service.

III. *Widening Fields of Service, 1920-35.* It was doubtless the prayers of the women of the Church in no small measure which led to the great Nation-wide Campaign in the Church, beginning in the spring of 1919. Consideration afresh of the mission of the Church led the General Convention in Detroit in 1919 to some great changes in the organization of the Church. The National Council was now set up and the Woman's Auxiliary instead of being auxiliary to the Board of Missions became auxiliary to the National Council in its five departments of work. Under the leadership of its president at the time, Mrs. William P. Cornell, the new organization was adapted gradually to the diocesan branch and to the chapters in the various churches. The work of the Auxiliary had become much widened in scope. Important changes were made now in other ways. The junior work was transferred to the Department of Religious Education, being implemented by the Y.P.S.L. and the Church schools. The Church Service League, to cover practically all activities of the diocese, was formed, but continued only for a couple of years, not being found necessary. The disbursements for 1939 were $3,687.00. The last annual Convention of the auxiliary before the division of the diocese was held in Columbia in May, 1922. The ideals of the organization were here re-emphasized and the separation accepted with sadness, indeed, but with confidence in it as a step forward.

To bring the chapters into closer touch for cooperative work, in 1925 the auxiliary in the diocese was divided into six districts: Beaufort, Charleston, Orangeburg, Florence, Georgetown, and Sumter. Semi-annual meetings were held in each district. This led to the creation of many new offices with the distribution of responsibilities. In this same year, the first year book was issued, compiled by Mrs. W. S. Poynor, who was then president. It has formed the model for all subsequent year books. Mrs. L. D. Simonds, who was president from 1928 to 1931, was a pioneer in interesting and training younger women in the work of the Women's Auxiliary, and many officers and leaders have come from this group due to her untiring effort through the years. The United Thank-Offering continued to increase until paralyzed by the world-wide depression. In 1922, just before the division, it had risen to $8,192.00. After the division in 1925, it was $6,644.00. In the depression, the offering sank to $2,110.45 in 1937. In 1944, it amounted to $11,255.78. The offering in 1952 was $23,385.22.

IV. *Expansion, 1936.* The number of branches in the diocese in 1936 had grown to 68—48 parishes and missions represented. At this time, under Mrs. Rembert as president, the auxiliary rallied to the help of the Society for the Advancement of Christianity in S. C., and has continued this help regularly since, enlisting memberships. Also at this time, the practice began to send the president and the educational secretary to Kanuga, as well as to supply one or two scholarships there for other women. Educational institutes were now regularly held. In 1938, under Mrs. Grimball, the president, the six districts were changed to seven by dividing Charleston into East and West Charleston. In this year, a committee was appointed consisting of Miss M. H. Heyward and Mrs. L. D. Simonds, with the president to act in an advisory capacity with the colored branch. At this time, several of the parishes were reorganized under the central plan. At this time also it became the custom of the president, on response to an invitation, to make an annual report of the work of the auxiliary to the diocesan Convention. The annual disbursements in 1942 were $5,164.86. The president now had become *ex officio* a member of the Board of Trustees of the Voorhees School. Mrs. Grimball was the first to attend a meeting. The president also was made a member of the Board of Managers of Kanuga.

In 1941, Mrs. Skardon, the president, reported the beginning of the holding of "Quiet Days" for the auxiliary. Kanuga had become very popular with the auxiliary—in 1941, forty-three members attended the Conference. The budget of the auxiliary for 1940 was: Christian Education, $300.00; Missions, $850.00; Negro work, $255-.00; Provincial Gift, $100.00; Supply Department, $750.00; Delegate Fund, $200.00; Clergy House—Saluda, $25.00; Bishop's Discretionary Fund, $150.00; Expense, $190.00; Contingent, $300.00. Total, $3,120.00. In 1941 at a meeting of the auxiliary of this province in Charleston, a medal for past presidents was proposed by Mrs. W. H. Grimball of this diocese. The plan was adopted and Mrs. H. D. Bull was commissioned to design the medal. Owing to the scarcity of materials during the war, it was not until 1950 that her beautiful design of a silver cross imposed on the seal of the Province of Sewance was executed. At the convention of the auxiliary of this diocese in the fall of 1949, the "cross' was presented to the eight living past presidents. Since then all past presidents have received the cross.

In order to coordinate the work of the diocesan branch with that of the national and provincial organizations, in 1942 the Constitution was revised. It was in this year that the time of meeting of the annual Convention was changed from January to the fall, meeting this year at the Church of the Holy Communion, Charleston, November 12, 1942. Consequently, upon this change the districts gave up their fall meetings, meeting henceforth only once a year in the spring. In the summer of 1943, under Mrs. McLeod as president, an adult conference was held at Poinsett Park. This became a custom. It was called the Pilgrims' Conference. The auxiliary in 1943 adopted as a diocesan project the erection of a hall at the conference center of the diocese in honor of Bishop Thomas. The branch's United Thank-Offering presented in Cleveland in 1943 amounted to $11,255.78. (Total presented was $1,119,255.78.) Always, the annual Conventions of the auxiliary have a report of its president, an address by the Bishop, usually a visiting speaker, and a banquet in the evening. At the meeting in December, 1946, Mrs. Bull being president, the Constitution and by-laws were revised again. A chief change was an executive committee, composed of the president and two members of the executive board to be appointed by the Bishop to act in cases of emergency. At this time all reports of officers and department chairmen were printed and given to each delegate to take home to share with her parish branch. This custom has continued to the present time. In 1948, it was decided to have six days of prayer in different parts of the diocese instead of one or two, and at this time "workshops" for the training of officers and department chairmen were first introduced. In 1951, under Mrs. C. E. Perry as president, the Constitution was revised to require that officers shall be communicants of the Church. The by-law was also changed to make the fiscal year from April 1 to March 31; the district meetings were now changed back to the fall. A large accomplishment of the West Charleston District in 1952 was the raising of $6,027.40 to remodel Pinckney Cottage at the Home in York.

The United Thank-Offering presented at the general Convention at Boston in 1952 was two and a half million dollars, of this, South Carolina gave $23,385.22. At the seventieth Convention held in Orangeburg, May 11-12, 1954, it being the tenth anniversary year of Bishop Carruthers' Episcopate, he was presented with a dime for each member of the auxiliary, and the hostess branch presidents (Redeemer and St. Matthew's) presented an anniversary cake to the Bishop. In 1954, a committee consisting of the past presidents having been appointed to "create" a book of remembrance, reported the gift of the book by the grand and great-granddaughters of Nanna Shand Wilson, the first president of the auxiliary in the diocese. It is beautifully illuminated by Miss May Ball, one of the granddaughters.

PRESIDENTS OF THE WOMAN'S AUXILIARY
SOUTH CAROLINA BRANCH

1. Mrs. Robert Wilson 1885-1906
2. Mrs. Albert Heyward 1906-12
3. Mrs. William Haskell 1912-14

 4. Mrs. Alexander Long 1914-15
 5. Miss Katie Lee 1915-18
 6. Mrs. William P. Cornell 1918-22
 7. Mrs. Thomas Hazelhurst 1922-24
 8. Mrs. W. S. Poynor 1924-28
 9. Mrs. Louis D. Simonds 1928-31
10. Miss Caroline P. Cain 1931-34
11. Mrs. Edward E. Rembert 1934-37
12. Mrs. William H. Grimball 1937-40
13. Mrs. Alvin W. Skardon 1940-43
14. Mrs. Frank McLeod 1943-44
15. Miss Fannie B. Duvall 1944-46
16. Mrs. Henry D. Bull 1946-50
17. Mrs. Charles E. Perry, Jr. 1950-53
18. Mrs. Everette Hall 1953-56

2. THE YOUNG PEOPLE'S SERVICE LEAGUE AND YOUTH MOVEMENT

The young people's movement in the general Church and in the province of Sewanee was already under way when the young people of this diocese gathered for their first joint summer outing at Camp Capers at Etowah, N. C., with the diocese of Upper South Carolina. This was in 1924. Already, too, a parochial league had been formed in the Church of the Holy Communion, the Rev. H. W. Starr, rector, in October, 1921, and the number in the diocese had grown to eleven by this summer. Then arose among the 100 campers a strong feeling that there should be formed a diocesan organization of the Y.P.S.L. So it was that a call went out and at once under the leadership of the Rev. I. deL. Brayshaw and the Rev. M. W. Glover an organization was effected at 2 p. m. July 24, 1924", when a constitution was adopted and officers elected as follows: president, Margaret Prentiss, Charleston; vice-president, Stanyarne Burrows, Bradford Springs; secretary, Dorothy Wragg, Blackville; treasurer, H. P. Duvall, Jr., Cheraw. Miss Dorothy Alston was elected delegate to the provincial convention at Sewanee. The Rev. M. W. Glover was elected executive secretary in the fall, by the executive committee, presided over by the Rev. H. W. Starr, Ph.D., under whom as chairman of the Department of Religious Education the League found its official connection with the diocese, its constitution having been approved by Bishop Guerry. It was decided with the consent of the editor to publish annually a "Young People's Number" of *The Diocese*. Oliver Wallace edited the first number, April, 1925, and Miss L. O. Roberts the second, May, 1926. By the activity of Miss Prentiss, and the other leaders, the League had so grown that by the time of the first Annual Convention in Florence, May 16-18, 1925, there were 21 Leagues in the diocese, and 18 represented in the Convention by 145 delegates. The usual order of the conventions from the first was a banquet the first (Friday) night, followed by a social period and then a service of preparation for the Corporate Communion early Saturday. Then later came the business session, the president's message, and addresses. Then in the afternoon an outing and on Sunday the annual sermon with the installation of officers. The Bishop's test was a feature of League life from the first. Bishop Guerry called the first Convention "one of the happiest occasions of my ministry". It was an epoch-making event in the history of the diocese. Dr. Starr and the Rev. Mr. Glover were the leading spirits among the clergy during the first years. So the League with its five ideals, Prayer, Worship, Service, Fellowship, and Gifts, and an "Eleven Point Standard", was launched in the diocese. The first two summer camps were held at Etowah, the next two at Transylvania Camp near Brevard with the diocese of Upper S. C., under Bishop Finlay, and then in 1928 and permanently at Kanuga.

The second annual Convention in Charleston was so large (about 300) it was decided to restrict representation of Leagues to officers and two delegates. The annual dues were 35¢. At the fifth annual Convention, in 1929, Bishop Thomas having succeeded Bishop Guerry after his tragic death, made an address on "The Challenge of the Living Christ to the Youth of the Day". The year following the League presented Dr. Starr with a beautiful linen surplice, token of appreciation of his leadership. In 1928 the first year book was issued by the League under editorship of Jane Mae Fishburne, who was then president, Herbert Haynsworth, and Caroline Gillespie. Caroline Gillespie, after serving as president, 1929, was assisted later by the League in her preparation in New York for mission work. In 1929 the five ideals were reduced to four as at present by combination, and soon after this the Eleven Point Standard was changed to Twelve by the addition of "Definite Place for the Observance of the Five Rules." At this time great enthusiasm developed in the League by the inauguration of district meetings. Just after the tenth annual Convention in St. David's, Cheraw, 1934, the Rev. J. A. Pinckney, who then became executive secretary, made two important contributions to the League by issuing a new mimeographed handbook and by beginning the publication of a monthly bulletin. The triennial Y.P.S.L. Thank-Offering of the province of Sewanee, begun in 1928, amounted to $615.19. Miss

Sarah Louise Starr was a leader in establishing the Thank-Offering in this diocese. At the eleventh annual Convention of the League, held in Charleston, in 1935, the League presented to Bishop Thomas a handsome set of Episcopal robes. A sad event for the League was the death in 1936 of Dr. Starr, the director and guiding spirit of the League from its birth in 1924.

The annual Convention of 1939 was cancelled because of polio-myelitis but a Leadership Training Conference for the League was held at St. Christopher's on Seabrook Island under the direction of the Rev. T. S. Tisdale. At this time the Young Churchmen Movement was considered and a Rule of Life suggested for it: 1. Worship, 2. Prayer, 3. Work, 4. Gifts conforming to the League ideal. At this meeting officers for the year were elected. The meeting closed with the installation of the officers just elected and a service of rededication conducted by Bishop Thomas in the new Chapel. The year 1940 was notable in the appointment of Miss Alice Hartley as the first field worker for the Young People of the diocese to build up Leagues and to inaugurate in the diocese the "Young Churchmen Movement" In 1941 Miss Caroline Hines was this student worker at Winthrop College. In 1943 Miss Gertrude Bull became the first full-time Youth Worker to serve in this diocese and in the upper diocese. She continued in this service until 1946. In the fall of this year Miss Mary Harper became director of Young Peoples' work for this diocese alone. At the Convention in 1944 in Marion, Bishop Carruthers made his first address to the Convention. At this time too Bishop Thomas was presented a farewell gift by the League—a beautiful silver coffee pot. At this Convention, the Twelve Point Standard was changed to the present Ten Point Standard.

In the meantime, a change was taking place in the youth work of the diocese under the leadership of the Department of Christian Education. In an effort to broaden the scope of this work throughout the Church, the committee on youth organizations of the national Church had set up the United Movement of the Church's Youth (UMCY). Under the influence of this movement and with a realization that the Y.P.S.L. did not include all of the work among young people, a youth commission of the diocese was organized in the fall of 1943, first temporary and then permanent. It was following this that on November 13, 1943, a joint meeting of the movement in the two dioceses was held at Trinity Church, Columbia. Under the chairmanships of the Rev. Colin R. Campbell for this diocese, and the Rev. John A. Pinckney for the diocese of Upper S. C., and with Miss Gertrude Bull as worker for both dioceses, the "movement" was launched. Its first emphasis was a "Rule of Life" for all young people. Although all youth organizations of the diocese had been invited to the annual Convention of the League as early as 1941, it was in 1946 that the Convention became the "All Youth Convention of the Diocese." Many youth organizations in addition to the Y.P.S.L. are represented at these annual gatherings of the young people of the diocese, the whole movement being under the permanent youth commission of the diocese. The activities under this commission of the diocese, in conjunction often with the Y.P.S.L. since Miss Harper became diocesan youth worker, are almost too numerous to detail here: paper called *Youth's Message,* training conferences, youth library, weekly study programs, vacation schools, work camps, retreats, corporate communions, etc., etc., besides more material accomplishments—the greatest, the building of the fine chapel at Camp St. Christopher at a cost of $10,000.00.

PRESIDENTS OF YOUNG PEOPLE'S SERVICE LEAGUE

1924-26	Margaret Prentiss
1926-28	Evans Canon
1928-29	Whitney Tharin
1929-30	Caroline Gillespie
1930-31	Mendel Rivers
1931-33	Hamilton Warren
1933-35	Mary Lou Thompson
1935-36	Elizabeth Bowie
1936-38	Alice Hartley
1938-39	Alex Grimsley
1939-41	Elizabeth Van Keuren
1941-42	LeRoy Wooten
1942-43	William E. Little
1943-44	Sarah F. Bull
1944-45	Faith Crawford
1945-47	Allan Hass
1947-48	Sidney Jones, Jr.
1948-49	Sarah Bailey Hood
1949-50	Julia Gervais
1951-52	Charles Duvall
1953-54	Sarah Williamson
1954-55	LeRoy Attaway
1955-56	John Porcher
1956-57	Eugene Meyer

EXECUTIVE SECRETARIES

1924-26	The Rev. M. W. Glover
1926-29	The Rev. Moultrie Guerry
1929-33	The Rev. Edgar C. Burnz
1933-34	The Rev. R. H. Jackson
1934-37	The Rev. J. A. Pinckney
1937-39	The Rev. C. Alfred Cole
1939-41	The Rev. T. S. Tisdale
1941-43	The Rev. Edward M. Dart
1943-44	The Rev. Colin R. Campbell
1944-46	The Rev. M. E. Travers
1946-47	The Rev. C. O'F. Thompson
1947-48	The Rev. F. V. D. Fortune
1948-51	The Rev. M. E. Travers
1951-53	The Rev. E. B. Guerry
1953-54	The Rev. H. L. Oliveros
1954-55	The Rev. R. C. Baird
1955-56	The Rev. T. L. Crum
1956-57	The Rev. Malcolm Prouty

CHAIRMEN OF DIOCESAN YOUTH COMMISSION

1946-48	Ralph Hendricks
1948-49	Mimi Wannamaker
1949-50	Charles Rosson
1951-52	Julia Gervais
1952-53	Koga Porcher
1953-54	Charles Duvall
1954-55	Martha Duvall
1955-56	Bette Lee
1956-57	Edwin Williamson

3. CAMPS AND CONFERENCES (S. C.)

(1) KANUGA (See Appendix XII.)

(2) ST. CHRISTOPHER

(3) BASKERVILL

We trace the origin of the movement for Camps and Conferences within this diocese of S. C. to the summer of 1935 when the Rev. D. N. Peeples in charge of Epiphany, Eutawville, St. Mark's, Clarendon and St. Matthias', Summerton, assisted by William Moultrie Moore, a postulant, had a very successful outing for twenty-five boys of his parishes at Bluffton in the month of July.

ST. CHRISTOPHER

The movement this inaugurated was continued the following summer, by the associate mission whose work was centered at Eutawville and extended over St. John's, Berkeley, into St. Stephen's Parish around Pompion Hill Chapel, and into Clarendon County. The associates, Rev. D. N. Peeples, L. A. Taylor, and D. M. Hobart held this second camp at Edisto Beach in August, 1936. Twenty-six boys attended. The next year they again conducted a camp in July at the same place. Miss Florence Lucas was the matron for the boys and Mrs. W. T. Palmer for the girls.

Before another year passed interest in the camp spread in the diocese. At this time the Rev. A. R. Stuart held conferences with Mr. Victor Morawetz who had become owner of Seabrook Island. This generous layman was interested and gave the diocese a ten-year lease on six acres on Seabrook Beach. A committee consisting of the Revs. A. R. Stuart, M. F. Williams, L. A. Taylor, and W. W. Lumpkin met with Bishop Thomas on the beach April 18, 1938, to survey the ground and determine a site under the lease. This being done, steps were taken immediately by the Bishop to erect necessary buildings. Two small buildings, on the site chosen near the mouth of the North Edisto River were repaired and two other new buildings erected—a central building for general purposes including dining room and kitchen, and a girl's dormitory. The funds amounting to $2,310.10 for this first construction, including water works came from two generous persons in the diocese, a lady and a gentleman, from two Christmas offerings of St. Michael's Church, and from the Bishop's discretionary fund. The associate mission held the first (third in all) conference at the new location in 1938.

In 1939 another building, a boy's dormitory, was erected largely through the efforts of the Rev. L. A. Taylor. There were no conferences during the summer of 1939 due to an epidemic of poliomyelitis. Progress was made however by the addition in the late summer of a chapel, quite the most finished building at this time, of pleasing appearance in Gothic style. On the peak of the roof was an imposing cross which could be seen quite a distance out to sea. It was adequately furnished for the service of the Church, the brass cross on the altar was one that had been used in a chapel in East Florence. Later Mrs. Henry Jervey of St. Michael's Church gave a pair of candlesticks in memory of her husband, Gen. Henry Jervey. The chapel was dedicated on the 4th of November, 1939, when the officers of the Y.P.S.L. for the year were installed and a large group of young people took part in a service of rededication. A training conference was held also this fall, the Rev. W. R. Haynsworth assisting Mr. Taylor who was very active in the camps at this time. During the summer of 1940 regular conferences were held,

but were interrupted on August 11th in the morning. While the Rev.
Mr. Taylor was holding a service in the chapel, word came of the
near approach of a great hurricane. The warning was very brief,
but by the skillful management of Mr. Taylor with the assistance
of Mr. Jean Walpole and Mr. Simons Waring and others, all sixty
children were evacuated to the safe and kindly home of Mr. Andell,
being marooned there for thirty-six hours. The damage to the buildings on the beach was not serious, and the next year (1941) regular
conferences were held except that the last conference was cancelled
because of continuous rain and deterioration of the road. Camp
St. Christopher was for a time under the direction of the Rev. A. R.
Stuart, then managed by a committee on camps and conferences
with the Rev. W. W. Lumpkin as chairman. It was placed later
under the charge of the Department of Religious Education with
the Rev. M. F. Williams, chairman.

After the beginning of the war in the fall of 1941, owing to the
exposed position of Seabrook's Beach, it was thought unwise to
have gatherings there. The conferences were continued however
at Burnt Gin in Sumter County, the directors for 1942 being the
Revs. A. R. Stuart, T. S. Tisdale, and W. M. Moore. The conferences
were held for five years at Burnt Gin, and then at State Park near
Cheraw (Camp Juniper) for two years. During the war the Coast
Guard occupied the buildings at Seabrook Beach, later paying the
diocese $1,500.00 for this use. During this period the chapel was
destroyed by wind and wave. In 1942 Messrs. Percy R. Porcher and
Richard Dwight Porcher gave a site for a conference center for the
diocese on Lake Marion near Bonneau. It was thought for a time that
this would be a more desirable place than Seabrook Beach. Steps
were taken toward erecting a building here by the purchase of some
dismembered huts from a Santee-Cooper construction Company.
The Woman's Auxiliary of the diocese began work on a fund for
the erection of a central building at the conference center to be
in honor of Bishop Thomas. However after the war with a renewed
interest and a desire to develop the conference center it was resolved in 1949 to return St. Christopher to Seabrook Beach, especially since Mrs. Victor Morawetz gave assurance of a further and
larger grant for the camp on the beach, soon promising to leave the
entire island to the diocese in fee simple at her death.

In 1948-1949 under the leadership of Bishop Carruthers com-
mittees were appointed and steps taken for the development of
St. Christopher's as the conference center of the diocese at Seabrook
Beach. Steps were taken to overcome the early difficulties of bad

roads and inadequate water supply. Under Rev. Edward Guerry as chairman of a building committee contracts were let for the building of a new dining hall and for other improvements. Beginning with the year 1949, regular conferences have been held each summer at the center. The summer of 1951 saw the completion of two new buildings, the Clergy Cottage given chiefly by Mrs. A. F. Storm and Dr. J. P. Cain, and the Wilmer Poynor Cottage, given by the Woman's Auxiliary of St. John's Church, Florence. On June 24th of this year at a large gathering of Church members, Mrs. Victor Morawetz made a formal presentation of the entire beach property to the diocese in memory of her husband, Mr. Victor Morawetz and Mr. Benedict Nott, her nephew. The gift was received by the Bishop. On this occasion Bishop Carruthers held a Service of Dedication of the entire camp site and especially of the dining hall presented by Mrs. Charles Perry, president, on behalf chiefly of the Woman's Auxiliary of the diocese in honor of and to be called "Bishop Thomas Hall" and the cottage in honor of and to be called "The Wilmer Poynor Cottage." Other buildings have since been built including notably the new chapel in 1952 given through the efforts of the young people themselves, consecrated on June 24, 1953. In 1957 a splendid activities building was added to the plant.

CAMP BASKERVILL

Coeval with the camp at Seabrook's Beach, Bishop Thomas planned to develop a similar center for colored churchmen. This was immediately possible by the fact that a suitable site was at hand on the grounds of Holy Cross and Faith Memorial School House near Pawley's Island. In the summer of 1939 a building for this purpose was erected at this place under the supervision of the Rev. Lewis A. Baskervill, executive secretary of the Archdeaconry for colored churchmen, son of the late Archdeacon. He did much of the work with his own hands. The name selected "Camp Baskervill" as in memory of the late able and devoted Archdeacon, E. L. Baskervill. The first use of this building was in 1939 for a camp of Boy Scouts from Calvary Church, Charleston. However the epidemic of poliomyelitis prevented other gatherings that summer. The building, primarily designed for a dining room for the Camp was used by Holy Cross and Faith Memorial school term as an overflow schoolroom and also a lunch room for the school. In 1941 another building for a dormitory was added to the plant, the Rev. Stephen B. Mackey being appointed director, the Rev. L. A. Baskervill having left the diocese. The staff included, the Revs. St. J. A.

Simpkins, W. E. Forsythe, and R. B. Martin. The Rev. St. J. A. Simpkins, Jr., also assisted. The first regular conference was one for boys in 1942. The next summer a period for girls was added. The use of this camp has since continued under the direction of the Ven. Stephen B. Mackey, Archdeacon.

Appendix IV—*Various*

1. THE THEOLOGICAL SEMINARY

The first step toward this institution was taken on February 14, 1856, when the Rev. J. B. Campbell, rector of St. Philip's Church, offered resolutions in the Convention that it was expedient to establish a diocesan Theological Seminary and that a committee be appointed to report on the best method of carrying this resolution into effect. A committee was appointed to study the whole question and report to the next Convention. The report was made but final consideration was postponed. This carried the question over until the Convention of 1858. The committee in charge reported then that it was painfully true that no adequate mode existed for the training of clergymen for the Diocese—none that brought the candidates into contact with the minds of the Bishop and clergy, no fellowship with the sympathies and wants of the diocese. It was not thought that such establishment would tend to the injury of the University of the South being planned at this time, or any other institution without the diocese. The sentiment in the diocese, in marked contrast with the intense devotion of this diocese to the General Theological Seminary in earlier days, indicated a change of view. The committee recommended that the beginning be upon a modest scale. It was then decided to establish a seminary to be under the control of the Bishop and a board of trustees elected annually by the Convention, that for the present the seminary be located in Camden, and that plans be made to raise the necessary funds. The professors were to be appointed by the trustees on nomination of the Bishop. The first trustees elected were the Revs. C. P. Gadsden, P. J. Shand, J. J. Roberts, and Messrs. H. D. Lesesne, J. B. Kershaw, and W. E. Martin.

Immediately after this Convention, the trustees convened in Camden and laid the foundations of the seminary. A building had been rented near the Bishop's residence. This was used only for a few months. The seminary was relieved of this expense by the vestry of Grace Church, which supplied an appropriate two-story brick building free of rent. This was occupied January 1, 1860. The title of the institution adopted was "The Theological Seminary of the Protestant Episcopal Church in the Diocese of

South Carolina." Col. J. B. Kershaw was elected secretary of the board of trustees, and H. D. Lesesne, treasurer. The exercises of the seminary began on the 17th of January, 1859, with a strong faculty, larger than the student body of three! The Bishop gave occasional lectures in Ecclesiastical Polity; the Rev. Edward Reed was Professor of Systematic Divinity, the Rev. T. F. Davis, Jr., instructed the students in Hebrew and Greek Literature and Biblical Learning, and the Rev. Paul Trapier was Professor of Ecclesiastical History, including Scriptural Exegesis and the Evidences of Christianity. The diocese was very proud of the seminary. In connection with an appeal for books, we find these words: "Quietly without sound of hammer and axe has this valuable institution been set on foot." A warm laudation in the *Southern Episcopalian* included this: "We were struck at the Convention with the desire expressed in many quarters, for catechists and teachers for our Negroes. The want of suitable persons to engage in this great and necessary work is much felt."

Life, growth, and promise were reported for the second year of the seminary. A constitution had been adopted. The student body had increased to seven. Mr. Reed's health failing, the Rev. J. S. Hanckel was now enlisted on the faculty. The library of the Advancement Society was loaned to the seminary and removed from Charleston to Camden. Mr. Trapier's salary was increased to $1,500.00, Mr. Davis' to $500.00. The next year, the students were increased to ten, all salaries were paid, and an endowment fund commenced ($1,141.78). This fund the next year was increased to $1,953.00. But, alas, all this was on the verge of crisis. The very next year at the Convention, it was reported the seminary had closed as of June 30, 1862. The sixth Annual Report (1864) while the institution was closed, all salaries were paid as also all arrears from the previous year and an increase in the endowment fund to $39,450.50! For our next item, we quote Bishop Davis's words to the Convention of May 1865 at Grace Church, Camden, which did not have a quorum: "Soon after the passage of Sherman's Army through the country, our Seminary buildings in this place were entirely destroyed by the act of an incendiary. At least two-thirds of the books contained in it were burnt up. This is greatly to be lamented. To it must be added, I fear, the funds of the Seminary. Still it is very much desired that this institution shall commence its labors as soon as possible; let me commend it to your prayers and sympathies, and entreat for it your best efforts." The entire endowment was lost, being in Confederate securities.

The seminary continued dormant only until October, 1866, when it was reopened in Spartanburg in a building of pleasing architecture presented to the diocese for the purpose by a layman of Charleston; put in order at an expenditure of $2,750.00. This new beginning of the seminary was made possible largely by this generous gift, the funds raised by the Rev. A. T. Porter at the north—over $5,000.00, and the good response to the Bishop's appeal to the diocese. Rev. Messrs. Trapier and Hanckel were now the only professors, the Bishop's health now permitted lecturing only for a time. The Rev. Prof. Lester of Wofford College instructed the students in Hebrew. There were now seven students. The remnants of the library of the Advancement Society, removed from Camden with other books, made some 2,000 volumes. There were donations to the library from England. The diocese planned $4,000.00 yearly for current expenses. There seemed to be a good hope for the future. It did not last long; by the time of the Convention of May, 1868, the report confesses that never was its condition so precarious, its prospects never so dark. The South's impoverishment was apparent—no funds and no students. On May 16, 1868, the Convention resolved to close the seminary. The buildings were placed in the charge of the trustees. Salaries were paid up in full and the Rev. J. D. McCollough was requested to reside at the buildings. Parts were rented. A building in Orangeburg, which had been given by Hon. G. A. Trenholm, was sold. The assets left, apart from the buildings, amounted to $3,663.39 at this time. In October, 1872, the Rev. J. D. McCollough opened a school for girls in the buildings of the seminary called St. John's Hall. However, for lack of support it continued for only about three years. The property was subsequently sold to Converse College. The proceeds, with accumulations, survives now, in the care of the trustees of the diocese constituting "the Theological Fund", the income used for candidates for the ministry. Thus does the old seminary of the diocese, so much cherished during its short and tragic career, survive in this support of candidates for the ministry.

2. THE SEAL OF THE DIOCESE

There was no diocesan seal in the early days of the diocese. There was a personal seal used by Bishop Bowen early in the nineteenth century. The motto on the present seal came from this. No step was taken to adopt a diocesan seal with arms until

1908 when the Standing Committee appointed a committee to suggest an appropriate seal. It reported to the Convention of the diocese recommending a seal designed by the Rev. Robert Wilson described as follows:

Arms of the Diocese of South Carolina

Blazon

Ar. a palmetto tree, ppr. (for the State). On a Chief Az. a Cross Exaltie between two altar lights burning, or,

Cr. A mitre ppr.

Motto:

The motto on the seal will be accompanied with the words, "Seal of the diocese of South Carolina."

The report was signed by John Kershaw, Richard I. Manning, and C. S. Gadsden. It is printed in the *Journal* of the Convention for 1908 and appears on the cover of the *Journal* for that year. The report however was not adopted and we find no further use or reference to a seal for the diocese until the Convention of 1911, when Dr. Kershaw reported for the committee after long delay, suggesting another design similar to that in use today except: there was no motto and had altar lights in both first and second quarters and palmetto trees in both third and fourth quarters; above the shield was, as now, a mitre between a Key and a Crosier in satire. This seal was then adopted and continued in use for years. In 1928, Bishop Guerry suggested to the Convention that it had been discovered that the seal of the diocese was heraldically incorrect, therefore a committee was appointed to revise the seal as necessary to its correction. The next year a committee consisting of Bishop Thomas, the Rev. S. C. Beckwith and Mr. Walter Hazard made a report which was adopted. It was provided, "That the seal of the diocese be changed that in the First Quarter of the change be a candlestick, signifying Christ, the Light of the World. In the Second Quarter, the change be a Pelican, in her piety, signifying the Gospel brought to this country. The Third Quarter, the change to be a symbol of the Church of England and the Diocese of London, signifying the relation to the Mother Church [the Swords of St. Paul from the seal of the diocese of London]. The Fourth Quarter, the change to be a Palmetto Tree, signifying the present State." The following year, 1930, the committee made some further modifications in its final report which was then received and the committee's action confirmed: "Change (in Seal of 1911) the words, 'Seal of the Diocese of South Carolina' to 'Diocese of South Carolina', with this motto added in the original Greek 'Let no man despise thee' (Titus II:15). This motto being taken from an old seal used in the Diocese as early as 1818.

The Quarters of the Seal Changed as follows:

First, gu. a candlestick or holding a candle arg. flamed of the first.

Second, az. a pelican-in-her-piety, arg.

Third, az. a palmetto tree, arg.

Fourth, gu. 2 swords in saltire arg. histed or."

The two swords in saltire are from the seal of the diocese of London, used with the Bishop's expressed consent—the swords of St. Paul—thus is signified the original connection of this diocese with the Church of England and especially the diocese of London of which in Colonial days it was a part. A resolution also thanked Mrs. Walter White, Barrough House, Stateburg, for her valuable assistance in the development of the seal.

3. PERIODICALS OF THE DIOCESE

The Sunday Visitant was the first Church paper or magazine published in the diocese and thought to have been oldest in the U. S. It was a private enterprise of the great missionary, Andrew Fowler, A. M. He was both editor and proprietor. It was issued every Saturday afternoon and was chiefly devoted to instruction in Church life, history, and biography, containing little local church news. Subscription price was $2.50 a year (later $3.00). It continued from January 5, 1818, until December 25, 1819—fifty-two numbers. "T. B. Stevens, Printer, 8 Tradd Street, opposite Carolina Coffee House, 4 pp." The paper had agents in Wilmington, Fayetteville, and Georgetown. (File in diocesan Archives.) The next publication of a much more ambitious character was "*The Gospel Messenger and Southern Christian Register.*" It was published (like the *Visitant*) not officially by the diocese but by "A society of gentlemen, members of the Protestant Episcopal Church." It was inclusive in character containing diocesan and general Church news with editorials and articles pertaining to theology and the Church. It was fully endorsed by the Bishop (who had desired such a paper) and was his organ and that of the diocese. The editors kept their names out of print but these were chiefly Rev. Frederick Dalcho and the Rev. C. E. Gadsden (later Bishop). It was the first work of the kind published in the Southern states and supplied a great need. The publisher was C. C. Sebring, Charleston, S. C. It continued from January, 1824, until 1853.

The *Gospel Messenger* was succeeded by '*The Southern Episcopalian*." At first it came out twice a month in newspaper form, being dated from Charleston and Savannah June, 1853, until March, 1854. It was called "a religious family newspaper." Published by Walker and James, 3 Broad Street, Charleston. Agents were Bryan and Carter, Columbia; J. M. Cooper and Co., Savannah; George H. Oates, Augusta; the Rev. J. A. Shanklin, Macon; Z. J. DeHay, Camden. *The Southern Episcopalian* assumed a new (magazine) form and began a new Volume I, April, 1854, and continued its valuable existence until stopped by the war. It was edited by the Rev. C. P. Gadsden and the Rev. J. H. Elliott and was printed and published by A. E. Miller, No. 3 State Street, Charleston, S. C. The last issue we have found is for August, 1863, Messrs. Gadsden and Elliott were still editing. In this issue is a form of service set forth by Bishop Davis for Friday, August 21, as a day of "Fasting, Humiliation, and Prayer."

The next diocesan publication was first called "*The Record of the Diocese of South Carolina.*" Its first issue was in June, 1870. The name was changed the following March to "*The Monthly Record.*" It was founded by the Rev. W. P. DuBose, then of Abbeville, and Rev. J. D. McCollough of Spartanburg. It served more strictly diocesan purposes than its two more ambitious predecessors. The file contains a great many sketches of parishes. It was published by Walker, Evans, and Cogswell, Charleston, except during the first year, when it seems to have been published in the up-country. It continued until July, 1880. It carried as its motto, "Truth and Peace." The next periodical of a diocesan character was "*The Church Herald*" established August, 1880. Thus this paper followed almost immediately after the demise of "*The Monthly Record.*" It was first edited and published jointly by the the Rev. J. D. McCollough in Spartanburg and the Rev. Ellison Capers, then of Greenville. Later the paper was removed to Winnsboro where it was edited and published by the Rev. Frank Hallam. It carried at its head as a motto, "The Unity of the Spirit, in the Bond of Peace." We have been unable to ascertain how long after January, 1884, this paper continued—this is the date of the last issue in our very incomplete file. Mr. Hallam left the diocese December, 1884. In 1891, the Rev. John Kershaw edited and published from Sumter, when he was rector the *Diocesan Intelligencer*. It continued for about two years.

Following the *Diocesan Intelligencer* came our present diocesan paper, "*The Diocese*." It was established by the Rev. John Kershaw, then rector of the Church of the Holy Comforter, Sumter, and was published in that city. The first issue was that of November, 1893. At the head of the first page was the motto, "In essentials, unity; in non-essentials, liberty; in all things, charity." It continued along the lines of *The Herald* and *The Monthly Record*, but later was much expanded and at one time was a forum or a medium for the exchange of ideas in the diocese by editorials, correspondence, and articles. It was adopted as the official organ of the Bishop and the diocese. At first the subscription price was 60¢ a year, later 50¢, then $1.00. *The Diocese* was later moved to Columbia and published by Capt. J. P. K. Neatherry under Bishop Capers, who edited it for a time. The Rev. T. D. Bratton was the next editor, the paper being published in Spartanburg (1899). Then after a year or so it was published in Columbia with the Rev. W. S. Holmes as editor until 1903 when the following succeeded: the Rev. W. P. Witsell (1903-9); the Rev. H. H. Covington (1909-13); the Rev. A. S. Thomas (1913-28); the Rev. H. D. Bull (1928-45). *The Diocese* served the new diocese in 1922 and 1923 until *The Piedmont Churchman* was established as the paper of Upper South Carolina. Since 1945 *The Diocese* has been published by Bishop Carruthers from headquarters. The place of publication was usually in either Sumter or Columbia and laterly Charleston. Since 1945 the paper has been sent free to every family in the diocese.

Two other papers were published in the diocese in the interest of the Archdeaconry of South Carolina for work among colored people. First, *The Church Messenger* (not to be confused with *The Gospel Messenger*, see above) established by Archdeacon Joyner in 1891. This paper continued in publication until the resignation of Mr. Joyner in January, 1905. Next, the *Church Herald* (again not to be confused with the diocesan paper of the same name, see above). This paper was published by Archdeacon Baskervill beginning in 1914. It had a large circulation both in the diocese and at the North where it gave information to the many contributors to the work in the Archdeaconry. It was finally discontinued in 1948, the appeal to the North having discontinued and sufficient reports of the work being printed in *The Diocese*. The last editor was the Rev. Stephen B. Mackey.

4. SCHOLARSHIPS

(1) *Dehon*—Established by the women of the diocese soon after Bishop Dehon's death in 1817 in his honor.

(2) *Bowen*—In the Bishop's honor, established by the Convention in his lifetime. These two scholarships fell to the diocese of Upper S. C. at the time of the division in 1922.

(3) *Gates*—Given by the Rev. Dr. Thomas Gates in 1733 for a student from this diocese at the General Theological Seminary. (*Cf. Episcopate of Bishop Bowen and Appendix II. 1.*)

(4) *St. Andrew's*—At Sewanee for student of theology from S. C., given in 1877 by Mrs. C. M. Manigault (who also gave St. Luke's Hall). Originally two scholarships—one now assigned diocese Upper S. C.

(5) *Hobart College*—"James and Marie Antionette Evans Fund" given in honor of his parents by Powell Evans, originally of Florence, S. C., South Carolina student to have priority claim on it.

5. THE CHURCH OF THE REDEEMER AND THE HARRIOTT PINCKNEY HOME FOR SEAMEN
Established 1915

WITH PORT SOCIETY ORGANIZED 1823

This institution is an evolution from early efforts in behalf of seamen in the Port of Charleston. The first organized effort was by the Marine Bible Society April 14, 1818. The next year, the Female Domestic Missionary Society of the Circular Church instituted services for seamen in Cleafort's Sail Loft on Lathrop's (Accommodation) Wharf; then in a larger loft of McNellage on Duncan's (South Atlantic) Wharf. The Carolina Coffee House on Tradd Street was the scene of a meeting on December 22, 1820, when a committee was appointed which soon collected $3,000.00 for a Mariners' Church. They bought from the Baptists a church edifice on Church Street near Stoll's Alley. This was the Mariners' Church of Charleston for several generations. In this church was a unique pulpit in the form of the prow of a boat and around the font in letters of gold: "He taught them out of a ship." It was estimated by Chaplain Chichester in 1885 that up to that time, 50,000 sailors had listened to the preaching of the Gospel from this pulpit. It is now in the Church of the Redeemer. The Charleston Port Society was organized on January 4, 1823. This venerable society continues to fulfill its original purpose as

we shall see to this day. Among the faithful ministers who car-
ried on this work during the succeeding years were the following:
Chaplains, Joseph Brown (1823-32), W. B. Yates (1836-72), and
C. E. Chichester.

In 1826, The Ladies' Seamen's Friend Society opened a temperance boarding house for seamen, probably the first boarding
house for seamen in the world; three years later something of
the kind was started in London. In 1840, through the efforts of
distinguished citizens, especially Richard Yeadon, Esq., and Col.
Wade Hampton, a new building on Market Street at State was
bought by the Port Society and converted into a sailors' home,
just a block from the present home. In 1853, Miss Harriott Pinckney, the second daughter of Gen. Charles Cotesworth Pinckney, donated the corner of her garden to be held in trust until there should
accrue from the rental a fund sufficient to finance the erection of
a Church for the free use of seamen frequenting the Port of
Charleston. The lot ran 140 feet on Market Street and 95 feet
on East Bay. The deed given was to a body of trustees headed
by Rev. Charles C. Pinckney "in trust to erect or cause to be
erected upon the said premises a church building for the worship
of Almighty God, according to the Liturgy of the Protestant Episcopal Church in the United States of America, the seats in which
said church shall be appropriated to the free use of seamen frequenting the Port of Charleston, and in further trust that the
said Trustees or a majority of them for the time being shall from
time to time appoint for the ministry of the said Church such
Minister as they may select from among the Clergy of the said
Protestant Episcopal Church, in good standing therein, and the
said Trustees or a majority of them for the time being shall have
authority from time to time to remove or displace any Minister
whom they may appoint and another to appoint in his place—
Provided, The person appointed shall always be a Minister officiating according to the Liturgy of the said Protestant Episcopal
Church." (Register of Mesne Conveyance for Charleston County
at page 38 *et seq.* of Book P. 13). Other provisions of the trust
follow: property to be leased until funds be accumulated sufficient to build Church, how trustees to be continued, charter of
incorporation to be obtained, etc. The charter was obtained by
Act of the General Assembly, November 27, 1877. The Rev.
Charles C. Pinckney, D.D., was the president of the trustees from
the first until his death August 12, 1898. The books and papers of
the trustees were lost in the burning of a house in Camden where

they had been placed for safekeeping on the approach of the enemy. At the end of the war, the treasurer of the trustees, Mr. William C. Bee, recovered possession of the lot from the U. S. Authorities and rented the place again. Soon after in accord with the original deed was elected a board of managers which was incorporated as the "Church of the Redeemer." The old trustees turned over to this corporation the lot at the corner of East Bay and Market Streets and personal property amounting to about $28,000.00, all having accrued from the original lot. Dr. Pinckney was likewise president of this board of managers until his death in 1898. He was succeeded by his brother, Captain Thomas Pinckney, continuing until his death November 15, 1915.

In 1915, the Church of the Redeemer and the Charleston Port Society combined their resources. Under the agreement, the minister in charge was always to be an Episcopalian. The Bishop is chairman of the joint executive committee, consisting of three members from each of the bodies. At the time of this combining of forces, the funds of the corporation of the Church of the Redeemer amounted to $55,000.00. Some $35,000.00 of this amount was used for the building in 1915 of the Church and the Home; the balance of about $20,000.00 was to be used for the upkeep of the institution. On April 3, 1916, Bishop Guerry consecrated the Church of the Redeemer. The Bishop preached. He paid tribute to many who had contributed to the consummation achieved, and gave a story of the work. All the clergy of the city were present and participating. The Rev. Alexander Sprunt of the First Presbyterian Church spoke for the other churches of the city and for the Port Society. The same night at the Home, addresses were made by the mayor of the city and others. The handsome chapel and home are an ornament to that part of the city. The chapel is completely furnished with fumed oak pews and chancel furniture. This includes the unique pulpit from the old Mariners' Church in the form of the prow of a ship. A few months later, a third building to the north was purchased, enlarging the facilities of the Home. The new combined institution was called "The Church of the Redeemer and the Harriott Pinckney Home for Seamen." Soon after its establishment, Rev. A. E. Cornish took charge as rector and chaplain. In May, 1917, he reported 52 Sunday services and 100 other days, and 575 seamen had been guests of the Home. Mr. Cornish also served St. James', James Island. He continued in this charge until his death October 12, 1920.

In 1921, the Rev. Wallace Martin, coming from Montrose, Pa., succeeded Mr. Cornish, becoming superintendent and chaplain. For twenty-five years, until his sudden death on Good Friday, 1946, he carried on this important work, often in the face of great discouragement due to failure of support. His chief helper and efficient manager of the Home was Mr. C. F. Carter, who is continuing his invaluable services to the present time (1955). In these years activities of the Seamen's Home, which led up to the services on Sunday evenings in the Church of the Redeemer, consisted in the following: supplying reading room, finding employment for seamen, furnishing lodgings (these have been up to 7,000 a year) paid and unpaid, receiving and holding mail, checking baggage, safekeeping of funds, canteen supplies, distribution of literature, relief department (meals, etc.), and entertainment. Especially should be mentioned free dinners on Thanksgiving and at Christmas. Mr. Martin constantly visited ships in the harbor contacting the seamen. Bishop Guerry thus describes his visit to the Home April 22, 1823. "At six o'clock . . . I preached in the Church of the Redeemer adjoining the Seamen's Home, and with Mrs. Guerry and other visitors sat down to a bountiful supper served to the seamen who were present by the ladies of the Episcopal and Presbyterian Churches of James Island."

This work has always lacked proper support, beyond the incomes of the Home and the Port Society. About 1935, the national Council abolished its "Seamen's Church Institute of America", and in consequence, this Home lost $500.00 annually; the diocese had never appropriated anything for the Home until 1936, when it gave $500.00 annually. The institution lost a source of income when the Port rules for employment of seamen, which had been handled by the Home, were changed. At one time, the Community Chest assisted, but later this was withdrawn. The buildings were badly damaged by the tornado of September, 1939. A government loan assisted in some repairs. About this time, Mr. Edward Hughes made a legacy of $10,000.00 to the Port Society. This was a great help. Mr. Martin and Mr. Carter often were forced to the necessity of "making bricks without straw." It should be mentioned that often city churches, notably St. Michael's, came to the help of the Home, especially in the endeavor to keep the institution in repair. Since Mr. Martin's death in 1946, the chaplains have been the Rev. E. A. LeMoine (1950) and the Rev. Edward M. Claytor from 1951. Quite recently the entire plant has been splendidly renovated.

6. PERMANENT FUNDS

(1) Held by Trustees

THEOLOGICAL EDUCATIONAL FUND—$5,050.00

This sum was realized from the sale of Church School property in Spartanburg, S. C. (see Journal 1898, pp. 74, 75) for $10,000.00. On division of the diocese the principal amount plus interest accretion was divided equally. The income of $700.00 formerly and originally earned was given. $500.00 to Sewanee and $200.00 for candidates for Holy Orders. Later all income for candidates. The entire income on this fund is now paid to the Bishop for theological education.

BISHOP'S PERMANENT FUND—$53,825.62

This fund, before the division of the diocese, amounted to $80,-000.00 and on division, by agreement $55,000.00 went to the diocese of South Carolina and $25,000.00 to the upper diocese. The income was and still is applied on the salary for the Bishop.

CITY MISSIONARY FUND—$1,000.00

This fund was given in 1900, donor unknown, for Charleston city missionary work. The income is paid to the Bishop to be used for city missionary work.

PRINGLE FROST MEMORIAL FUND—$1,800.00

This fund originated on 31 March, 1892 by a gift of Dr. Francis L. Frost and his wife, Rebecca P. Frost, in memory of William Pringle Frost and with interest accretion it was divided equally between the two South Carolina dioceses on their separation in 1922. The income is devoted to candidates for Holy Orders and is paid over to the Bishop for that purpose.

BERRESFORD BOUNTY—$37,336.21

This sum was received in 1945 from St. Thomas and St. Dennis School Fund, the income of which, under the will of Richard Berresford, to be used for the support, maintenance, tuition and education of the children of the poor of the Parish of St. Thomas in Berkeley County.

ST. THOMAS AND ST. DENNIS—$6,300.00

This trust was received in November, 1925 and represents funds of a dormant parish.

SCHULER FUND—$1,150.00

On August 19, 1914 the trustees received from the estate of D. Weston Schuler $2,035.75 and it was decided that the income was to be used for the upkeep, repair and preservation of Church property in the diocese. When the diocese was divided the sum was split between the two.

ST. BARNABAS', SUMMERVILLE—$2,700.00

This sum was received in May, 1923, being originally $2,000.00 for mission work, and the income was used for the support of the school at Summerville. It probably originated as a gift from Dr. Chas. N. Shepard, who owned a tea farm near Summerville.

MISSION AT McBEE—$505.56

The Rev. A. S. Thomas conducted a mission for a few years at McBee, S. C. when he was rector at St. David's, Cheraw. When the mission was discontinued the Ladies Guild turned over its assets of $100.00 to Mr. Thomas, who later turned this sum over to the trustees with its increment, to be used for a Church at McBee. The trustees also hold deeds to certain town lots in the town of Mc-Bee, County of Chesterfield.

CHURCH OF THE MESSIAH, NORTH SANTEE—$476.34

The origin of this fund was a suit at law resulting in the trustees receiving $975.37 in February, 1921 from this parish, which had become dormant. In the suit the trustees received a beach lot which was sold and the corpus was increased to $2,074.98 in 1929, which has built up over the years of interest accretion. The vestry of Prince George, Winyah, undertook to take care of the building. The property has been given to the new Church of the Messiah, Maryville and the Church moved there.

ADDIE THOMPSON MEMORIAL FUND—$1,824.72

The *Journal* of 1945, page 58, recites that in May, 1923, this fund was established for "upkeep and furnishing" of St. Alban's, Blackville. If the Church discontinued, the income was to be used for candidates for Holy Orders in the diocese.

SOPHIE P. CARROLL MISSIONARY FUND—$500.00

The will of Sophie P. Carroll established a fund of $1,000.00 for diocesan missions. See *Journal* 1924, page 73. At the division of the diocese the fund was divided equally. The entire income is paid annually to the Bishop.

O. J. HART TRUST FUND—$500.00

In April, 1932 the Rev. Oliver J. Hart, now Bishop of Pennsylvania, gave $75.00 to the trustees, the income to be used for St.

John's, John's Island, when the principal sum reached $500.00; later Bishop Hart completed the fund to $500.00.

MARY R. ALLSTON TRUST FUND—$2,820.56

This trust was set up by the will of Mary R. Allston, the income to be used for the upkeep of the graveyard at All Saints, Waccamaw and payments of income are made to the Churchyard Committee of that parish.

ST. MARK'S CHURCH, PINEWOOD—$1,045.44

In May 1944, the trustees were notified by St. Mark's Cemetery Committee that St. Mark's Church, Pinewood, Sumter County, had raised an endowment fund for the upkeep of St. Mark's Cemetery amounting to $610.00 and requested the trustees to administer the fund, which has increased during the years by interest accumulation and by additions in principal.

PRINCE WILLIAM PARISH FUND—$930.89

This parish includes old Sheldon at McPhersonville. In 1946 the trustees received from the Rev. R. M. Marshall the sum of $930.89 to establish this fund, the income to be used as requested in the parish.

ST. PETER'S, GEORGETOWN—$1,260.00

About 1882 a Mrs. Richardson deeded one acre of land to the trustees of the diocese and on this acre the Rev. Benjamin Allston built a Church. This fund is the result of a settlement in 1945 out of a suit in Federal Court, with the U. S. Government for use of the St. Peter's property during World War II as part of the Myrtle Beach bombing range. The income on this account has been accumulating.

PERCY HUGER FUND—$7,456.00

The Percy Huger Memorial Fund was set up in 1951 by Mr. James H. Lynah of Savannah, Georgia for the benefit of the Church of the Cross, Bluffton, by an initial gift of $2,000.00 for the purchase of General Motors stock at the market, the income to be used for the maintenance, both exterior and interior, of the Church building by the Governing Body of the Church of the Cross, the principal to be delivered to the Church of the Cross when it is admitted as a parish of the diocese. The trustees, therefore, are simply the custodians of the fund until the Church acquires full parochial status. In 1952 Mr. Lynah increased the memorial by giving 88 additional shares of General Motors stock, thus increasing the principal to $7,456.00.

DR. WILLIAM EGLESTON TRUST—$2,000.00

Income to apply on the salary of the rector of St. Bartholomew's Church, Hartsville.

ST. STEPHEN'S, ST. STEPHEN'S—$150.00

(2) HELD BY TRUST COMPANY IN BOSTON

WILLIAM H. SCHAEFER FUND—$275,000.00

Given by will of Mrs. Lena Warren Schaefer—the income to be used for the cause of the Church in the diocese of South Carolina.

(3) HELD BY THE BISHOP

K. M. HAVEN LEGACY FUND

For "the benefit of gentlefolk who are in reduced circumstances through no fault of their own".

CHURCH OF THE HEAVENLY REST FUND

Elizabeth Martin Legacy	$ 244.02
Augustus B. Jones Memorial	6,000.00
Bessie Evans Martin Cozart Memorial	2,000.00
Total	$8,244.02

Given for the support of the Church of the Heavenly Rest in Hampton County (Cf. *Journal* 1945, p. 56). Also by the will of Eliza M. Jones, 50 acres of land adjoining the Church.

ELIZABETH LaBORDE FUND

Given by Miss LaBorde for "diocesan missions. Originally the corpus was $500.00. One-half went to upper S. C. and one-half to this diocese. This amount suffered depletion in bank failure. At this time, it is $171.83.

PROTESTANT EPISCOPAL PRAYER BOOK AND TRACT SOCIETY—$1,900.00

The income to be expended by the Bishop in furtherence of the purposes of the society (see sketch of this society in Appendix II).

CLAUDIA S. RHETT FUND—$4,800.00

Given by Pauline S. Thomson in memory of Claudia S. Rhett, the income to be used for the Episcopal Church Home for old ladies.

BASKERVILL FUND—$504.45

Founded by Archdeacon Baskervill for the extension of Church work among the colored people of the diocese.

JULIA L. GAILLARD, CAMP ST. CHRISTOPHER
SCHOLARSHIP FUND—$1,500.00

OSCAR L. MITCHELL FUND

For educational purposes of St. Augustine's Church, Sumter County. Corpus held by American Security and Trust Company of Washington, D. C.

7. STATISTICS, DIOCESE OF SOUTH CAROLINA
(As Far as Available)

Year	Clergymen	Communicants		Expenditures
		Total	Colored	
1820	23	1,500	400	$........
1830	34	2,011	521	....
1840	46	3,269	689	....
1850	71	4,916	2,247	....
1860	69	6,126	2,960	50,209.69
1870	53	2,991	358	46,119.43
1880	47	4,549	617	66,239.84
1890	47	4,844	661	66,485.40
1900	62	6,743	699	82,348.21
1910	62	9,124	1,119	117,670.99
1920	69	11,117	1,264	208,940.19

Diocese Divided 1922—

1930	37	8,621	1,254	166,733.81
1940	39	10,053	1,487	154,870.04
1950	53	11,330	1,465	437,682.22
1956	61	12,774	1,347	768,485.73

Appendix V

BIOGRAPHICAL SKETCHES OF THE BISHOPS OF
SOUTH CAROLINA

Sketches of the first and second Bishops of South Carolina are found in Dalcho's history and, therefore, are not given here further than these notes:

First Bishop, the Rt. Rev. Robert Smith, D.D., born August 25, 1732; died October 28, 1801; Consecrated September 13, 1795. (Cf. also sketch in *Historical Magazine of the Protestant Episcopal Church* by this author, March, 1946.)

Second Bishop, the Rt. Rev. Theodore Dehon, D.D., born December 8, 1776; died August 6, 1817; Consecrated October 15, 1812. (Cf. *The Diocese*, April, 1934; also *Life* by Bishop Gadsden, Charleston, 1833.)

Third Bishop, the Rt. Rev. Nathaniel Bowen, D.D., born June 27, 1779; died August 25, 1839; Consecrated October 18, 1818. (The following sketch is from *The Diocese*, March, 1834.)

Like his distinguished predecessor, Bishop Dehon, the subject of this brief sketch, was born in New England. His father, the Rev. Penuel Bowen, was a native of Connecticut, a graduate of Harvard, and a Congregational minister who in 1787 took orders in the Episcopal Church and came to South Carolina. He was the son of Penuel, son of Isaac, son of Henry, son of Griffith, the immigrant. He was born at Woodstock, June 28, 1742. He became rector of St. John's Church, Colleton, but died shortly afterwards, October, 1787. Nathaniel Bowen, the second son, was born in Boston, June 29, 1779. The fatherless boy attracted the attention of the Rev. Dr. Robert Smith, then rector of St. Philip's Church and later first Bishop of South Carolina: he took him into his home and later entered him in Charleston College of which Dr. Smith was at one time the head. Young Bowen finished college with an A.B. degree at the age of fifteen.

He commenced the private study of theology, at the same time teaching for a livelihood, first in Maryland, then in Virginia, and finally at Newport, Rhode Island: at the latter place he was associated with the Rev. Theodore Dehon, later second Bishop of South Carolina. He was made deacon in Trinity Church, Boston,

June 3, 1800, by Bishop Bass of Massachusetts, soon thereafter taking temporary charge of St. John's Church, Providence, R. I. On his return to South Carolina in December, 1800, he became chaplain of the Charleston Orphan House with the promise that he should have "charge of a congregation, occupying a chapel to be built in Vanderhorst Street, back of the Orphan House." Having been ordained priest he became in 1802 assistant rector of St. Michael's Church, and shortly thereafter rector. In 1809 he accepted a call to become rector of Grace Church, New York, at that time a new parish. Here he remained until the death of his friend, Bishop Dehon in 1817, when he was called back to South Carolina to succeed him both as Bishop of the diocese and as rector of St. Michael's Church. He accepted the call and was consecrated Bishop in Philadelphia October 8, 1818, by Bishop White, Hobart, Croes, and Kemp.

Bishop Bowen was assiduous in his duties, being especially active in extending the influence of the Church in the upper part of the state and visiting and administering confirmation in Georgia: he was deeply interested in Sunday Schools and in the development of Church colleges and preparatory schools, also in the religious training of Negroes. A number of new churches were erected during his Episcopate.

* * *

About this time, an epidemic of revivals swept over the state: the Bishop wrote at great length concerning them: he had grave doubts as to their edification; he disapproved of "eccentric enthusiasm" and preferred that "our congregations be more grounded and settled in the sober, Scriptural, practical Christianity of our Church." In 1831 his health being badly impaired, a visit to Europe was prescribed by his physician. He traveled in Ireland and England, being hospitably received by the Church authorities in the latter place, especially by Archbishop Howley and the then Bishop of London. He attended a meeting of the Society for the Propagation of the Gospel in Foreign Parts, and speaks of a bust of Bishop Dehon, executed by Mr. Cogdel, received by them and in their keeping. After long ill-health he passed away in Charleston on Sunday morning, August 25, 1839; his body was interred under the chancel of St. Michael's Church. He was survived by his widow, the former Miss Margaret Blake, and several children. (Cf. Discourse on Bishop Bowen by Bishop Gadsden, Charleston, 1840.)

Fourth Bishop, The Right Rev. Christopher Edwards Gadsden, D.D.; born November 25, 1785, died June 24, 1852; Consecrated June 21, 1840. (The following sketch is from *The Diocese*, April, 1934. Cf. also Historical Mag. of P. E. Church, Sept., 1951— Sketch by this author.)

The subject of this sketch was the eldest son of Philip Gadsden and his wife, Catherine Edwards, and the grandson of the revolutionary patriot, General Christopher Gadsden. He was born in Charleston November 25, 1785, and as a boy attended a private school of the city known as the "Associated Academy." In 1802 he, with his brother John, went to Yale College where he entered the Junior class. At Yale he was the classmate of John C. Calhoun; these two men were congenial spirits and became lifelong friends. He graduated high in the class of 1804 and was elected a member of Phi Beta Kappa. On his return to South Carolina he entered upon the study of theology and was ordained deacon on July 25, 1807, in New York by Bishop Benjamin Moore in St. Paul's Chapel. His first charge was St. John's, Berkeley. He became assistant at St. Philip's February, 1810. On April 14, 1810, he was ordained priest by Bishop Madison of Virginia. Bishop Smith of South Carolina was long dead and no successor had been elected so the candidate was compelled to go to Williamsburg, Virginia, the home of Bishop Madison. The latter was President of William and Mary College. The local rector was absent, and the only other priest to be found was one in the country who had abandoned the ministry and taken up farming. He was with some difficulty persuaded to resume for the moment his sacred calling, the Bishop even having to supply the vestments. Mr. Gadsden preached his own ordination sermon.

He became rector of St. Philip's Church in 1814 and continued in that office to the end of his life. On the death of Bishop Bowen, he was elected fourth Bishop of South Carolina and was consecrated in Boston in June, 1840. He held his first confirmation in St. Michael's Church, Sept. 9, 1840, when 126 persons were confirmed, 20 or 30 of them being colored people. This last fact is significant of a lifelong interest in the spiritual welfare of the Negro. In 1841 he confirmed 316 people of whom more than 200 were colored; and in the three-year period ending 1850 he confirmed 939 persons of whom 558 were colored. On serveral occasions he visited Georgia and Florida in the interest of the Church, in 1843 going to St. Augustine where his grandfather, General Christopher Gadsden, had been imprisoned in a dungeon during the Revolution. And in October, 1851, he presided at the Consecration of the Rev. Francis H. Rutledge to be Bishop of Florida.

At the General Convention of 1844 two of his clergy were elected missionary bishops: Dr. Wm. J. Boone to China, and the Rev. Alexander Glennie of Waccamaw to Western Africa (the latter declined election). In the spring of 1850 he conducted at St. Philip's Church the funeral service of his friend, the great statesman, John C. Calhoun. Bishop Gadsden was Bishop at the time that has come to be thought of as the golden age of South Carolina; the period of the development of great estates by the cotton and rice planters, of wealth, of the culture and refinement that went with that wealth, of powerful political influence in the Union. In a measure the Church in South Carolina shared that prosperity and was influenced for good by that civilization. How much that civilization was influenced by the Church is another question. He married first Miss Elizabeth Bowman who died without issue, and second, Miss Jane Dewees who, with three daughters and two sons, survived him. He died June 24, 1852, and was buried in the chancel of St. Philip's Church. A contemporary says of him: "Without any thing imposing in his person, in size small, in habit of body meager, careless of his person and dress, often abrupt in speech, he yet exercised an influence for good which few men are able to obtain. Moving in the most refined and polished circles among the old aristocracy of perhaps the most refined and aristocratic state in the Union, though little regardful of its conventionalities, he was everywhere received with respect, his motives and acts generally appreciated. Among those who knew him better, who could make allowances for the peculiarities of a man without vanity, negligent of self, and wholly intent upon one great object in life, he was greatly beloved." (Cf. sketch in *Historical Magazine of the Protestant Episcopal Church,* September 1951, by this author.)

Fifth Bishop, The Rt. Rev. Thomas Frederick Davis, D.D.; born February 8, 1804; died December 2, 1871; Consecrated October 17, 1853. (The following sketch, taken from *The Diocese* of June 1934, was written mostly by the Bishop's granddaughter, Miss Eleanor Gaillard Porcher, of Texas.)

Thomas Frederick Davis was born near Wilmington, N. C., February 8th, 1804. His ancestors were rice planters on the Cape Fear River, but later removed to Wilmington. He was educated at Chapel Hill, entering a preparatory and boarding school at the age of ten. Four years at the school and four more at the University of North Carolina completed his education. After his graduation, he studied law at Wilmington where he was admitted to the bar and practiced with success for six years. During that time, he married his first wife, Elizabeth Fleming, by whom he had one son, Thomas Frederick Davis, Jr., who was first honor man at the University of North Carolina and later entered the ministry. The early death of his young wife turned Mr. Davis to the Church and the ministry. He was ordained a deacon at St. James' Church, Wilmington, by Bishop Ives. The following year he was ordained to the priesthood in the town of Pittsboro and in the Church of St. Bartholomew on the 16th day of December, 1832. The ministry of his diaconate and the first year of his priesthood was spent in hard, fatiguing missionary work. He then removed to Wilmington where he was rector of St. James' Church for three years. His health broke down and he had to rest for a year when he moved to Salisbury where he was rector of St. Luke's Church for ten years. His views on Churchmanship differed so greatly from that of his Bishop, that rather than continually oppose him, he left the diocese of North Carolina, accepting a call to Grace Church, Camden, S. C., in 1846, whither he went with his wife and his family of six children. Here he served as rector for six years, when he was elected Bishop of the diocese of South Carolina, May 1853.

He was consecrated, together with Bishop Atkinson of North Carolina in New York, October 17th, 1853. He took his seat for the first time as Bishop of the Diocesan Convention in January 1855, on his fiftieth birthday. Severe nervous debility from which he had suffered all his life was the cause of his blindness, which in spite of the best medical and surgical care at home and abroad became total about 1862. In spite of his blindness and frail health he fulfilled all the duties of his high and difficult office, traveling continuously over the diocese accompanied by one or the other of his two daughters. He never murmured because of his affliction, and he declared repeatedly that if it were God's will to restore his eyesight, he himself would hardly consent to give up in exchange those spiritual blessings which in his blindness had been given him.

He established the theological seminary in Camden, with ten students, one of whom was the distinguished Dr. William Porcher Dubose of Sewanee. He had two sons in the ministry, the Rev. T. F., Jr., and the Rev. F. Bruce Davis. The burden of restoring the diocese after the devastation of the Civil War, and the loss of twenty of his clergy, told greatly on his frail body and weary mind. In 1870, he asked for an assistant Bishop. Nearly two years later, he died suddenly at his home in Camden on December 2nd, 1871. In the cemetery of Camden is a marble shaft with the words, "Stablished, strengthened, settled by his wide administration, the Diocese of South Carolina erects this monument to him in grateful memory." (End of Miss Porcher's account.)

Bishop Davis entered up his Episcopate at a time of growth and prosperity in his diocese, but even then war clouds were gathering and soon the storm burst in full force. He was in full sympathy with the movement for secession and entered whole-heartedly upon the task of organizing the Church in the Con-federacy. He attended the preliminary Convention in Columbia October 16, 1861, and also the first and only General Council of the Church in Augusta, Georgia, November, 1862. When at last the South was overwhelmed he was reluctant to give up the plan of an autonomous Southern Church; he writes in February, 1866: "I had hoped that it might be the will of our God that we should have an independent, united, self-sustaining Southern Church. To such hope my sympathies and affections strongly clung; I thought I could see, too, a purer atmosphere for faith." Yet he was ready to frankly and bravely face the facts of the situation; he writes— "God has otherwise determined; we will follow the divine deter-mination. I advise the immediate return of the diocese into union with the Church in the United States." In his old age and blind-ness his diocese was devastated and impoverished, but his gentle, saintly spirit never wavered; in adversity, as in prosperity, he was a true and faithful apostle of Jesus Christ.

Sixth Bishop, the Right Rev. William Bell White Howe, D.D., born March 23, 1823, died November 25, 1894, Consecrated October 8, 1871.

(The following sketch is a condensation of that in the volume of his sermons published in New York, 1897.)

William Bell White Howe, the sixth Bishop of the diocese of South Carolina, was a native of New Hampshire. He was born in Claremont, N. H., March 23, 1823, and graduated from the University of Vermont at Burlington in 1843. Carefully reared in the nurture of the Lord, it is not surprising that he should have contemplated the holy ministry. He was not physically strong, however, and in the judgment of his father, the climate of his native State was too severe in winter for his delicate lungs. At the General Convention of 1844, the Rev. Mr. Howe brought his son to the attention of Bishop Gadsden, and expressed a wish to have him prosecute his studies in the milder climate of the South. Arriving in South Carolina, he was assigned by Bishop Gadsden as a postulant to the care and instruction of the Rev. Cranmore Wallace, rector of St. John's, Berkeley. He was admitted a candidate for Holy Orders on the 12th of February, 1845, and, while prosecuting his studies, assisted Mr. Wallace as lay reader and catechist in the old churches on the west branch of the Cooper River, Biggin and Strawberry Chapel. As catechist, his work was chiefly among the Negro slaves on the plantations. Mr. Howe was ordered deacon by Bishop Gadsden in St. Philip's Church, Charleston, on Friday, the 9th of April, 1847, his beloved instructor and friend, Mr. Wallace, preaching the sermon and presenting the candidate. His ordination to the priesthood took place in St. Stephen's Church, Charleston, on June 3, 1849, Mr. Wallace again presenting him to the Bishop.

The first twelve years of his ministry were spent in the parish of St. John's, Berkeley, first as assistant minister and then as rector of the parish. They were golden years in the Bishop's life. It was then that he gave himself to reading, to study, and to the preparation of sermons. After twelve years he accepted the invitation to be assistant in St. Philip's, and until some time after being called and consecrated to the Episcopate, Rev. Mr. Howe was rector of this parish. After the great debate between the North and the South drew to an angry close, and the war burst in its fury upon Charleston, it found the rector of St. Philip's in the faithful discharge of his holy office, in fullest sympathy with the cares and anxieties of his flock, a warm friend of their cause. Bursting shells drove the congregations of St. Philip's, St. Michael's, and Grace away from their churches, and they united on Advent Sunday, 1863, for holy worship in the spacious church of St. Paul's, which was beyond the reach of the bombardment. Here Mr. Howe, in connection with the Rev. Mr. Keith and the Rev. Mr. Elliott, minister and assistant minister of St. Michael's, ministered the consolations of the gospel to a large flock until all came to an end on the first Sunday in Lent, March 5, 1865.

He was consecrated to the office of a Bishop in the Church of God in St. Paul's Church, Baltimore, during the sitting of the General Convention, October 8, 1871, the Bishop of Lichfield, England, preaching the sermon, the presiding Bishop, with the Bishops of South Carolina, North Carolina, Maryland, Texas, and

Lichfield, being his consecrators. Bishop Howe took up the pastoral staff, determined, as he declared in Convention, to know nothing among us but his supreme obligations to our crucified and glorified Lord. And he made good his promise. His task was a most difficult one, but he rose to the height of his responsibility and did his duty as he saw it in the light of the law, in the fear of God, in love of man. His active Episcopate, covering a term of nearly twenty-one years, was marked by a decided revival of Church life and Church growth, notwithstanding its stormy nature (See Chapter 4). There are forty-four ordinations recorded in his journal, and the admission to the communion of the Church by confirmation of 6,700 souls.

While visiting the congregation of St. Paul's, Summerville, at Easter, April 17, 1892, Bishop Howe suffered a slight stroke of paralysis, which increased in seriousness and incapacitated him for further work. In response to the resolutions of the Standing Committee, the good Bishop yielded himself up to rest, and went to his mountain home at Saluda, N. C. But he was fatally stricken, and on the 25th of November, 1894, he entered into rest at his home in Charleston. He was buried in the cemetery of St. Philip's, in the place he had selected, by the side of his beloved wife and near the chancel where he had ministered for so many years. He was a divine of great learning and deep piety.

Seventh Bishop, the Right Rev. Ellison Capers, D.D., born October 14, 1837, died April 22, 1908; Consecrated July 20, 1893.

The Capers family settled on the coast of South Carolina in 1689, coming from England, probably of Huguenot descent. The father of Ellison Capers was William Capers, a Bishop of the Methodist Church. Bishop Ellison Capers was born in Charleston on Calhoun Street a few doors east of Pitt. He entered the Arsenal Academy in Columbia in 1854, and was graduated from The Citadel (the South Carolina Military Academy) in 1858. At once he became an instructor. When the war began, he immediately entered into military service, rendering important service to the end when he became a Brigadair General. In 1859 he married Charlotte Rebecca Palmer. He was blessed in his life with a wife who was not only one to strengthen but to advise with great wisdom. He had five sons—Frank F., banker of Greenville; John G., lawyer; William Theodotus, Bishop of West Texas; Ellison, pharmacist; Walter B., priest; and two daughters— Mary S. M., who married Capt. C. B. Satterlee; and Lottie P., who married William H. Johnston, M.D. Bishop Capers died on April 22, 1908, and was buried in Trinity Churchyard in Columbia.

That which follows of this sketch was written soon after Bishop Capers' death by the author.

On Wednesday, the 22nd day of April, 1908, the soul of Ellison Capers was translated from the Church Militant to the Church Expectant after nearly a year of suffering; his strong, handsome, kindly, genial, and saintly face which always seemed to carry with it a benediction to those on whom he looked was to be seen no more. It is seldom given to men to complete such a full and rounded career as that of Bishop Capers. The influence of his personality extended far and wide, beloved by all within the Episcopal Church and without—Confederate General, beloved citizen, and Churchman. First as assistant Professor at the South Carolina Military Academy (The Citadel), he helped to mold the characters of many of the youths of the State. In 1861, when the call to arms was sounded, at once he stepped to the front, and in the front he stayed until the end of the war four years later when he had become probably the youngest Brigadier General in the Confederate service. Then he served his native state in civil capacity, being elected in 1866 to the office of Secrtary of State, though he was at this time a candidate for the ministry. He was ordained in 1867 by Bishop Davis and at once went to Christ Church, Greenville, where he soon became rector and continued so except for one year at St. Paul's, Selma, Ala. (1875-76) until 1887 when he became rector of Trinity Church, Columbia. After a happy ministry of six years at Trinity, he was elected on the first ballot Bishop Coadjutor on May 4, 1893, and on June 20, the month following, he was consecrated in Trinity Church, Columbia, this being the first Consecration of a Bishop in South Carolina. The Rt. Rev. T. B. Lyman, D.D., presided, and the Rt. Rev. H. M. Jackson, D.D. (assistant Bishop of Alabama) preached on Rom. X:14. Other Bishops taking part were Weed and Watson. The coadjutor became Bishop the following year on the death of Bishop Howe. The most conspicuous trait of this noble life was the predominance of love as the sanction of all his words and actions. Love was seen in the beignity of his countenance, it was expressed in the gentleness of his gesture, it was revealed in the tones of his voice. Here we have the key to an understanding of his greatest service to the diocese. When he became Bishop of the diocese, it was sorely rent by the long agitation over the status of the colored churches in the diocese. The wounds were far from healed. It was through his gentle and Christlike guiding that the ministers and churches that had drawn out from the Convention (or Council as it was then called) came back one by one and the wounds of the body were finally healed. His broad spirit of charity also had the effect of lessening the spirit of prejudice against the Church in the State. His catholicity of mind and heart marked him for all as a true follower of Jesus Christ. Another feature of this character was its growth. He was a greater man when the paralysis claimed him than he had ever been before—greater as a Churchman and greather as a man of positive and decided views. He was chosen over many Bishops to be Chancellor of the University of the South which position he held from 1904 until his death. His friends had expected, if the reaper had not come, to make him chairman of the House of Bishops.

Eighth Bishop, the Right Rev. William Alexander Guerry, D.D., born July 7, 1861, Consecrated September 15, 1907, died June 9, 1928.

Bishop Guerry was born at the old home of his maternal grandfather, Pine Grove in Sumter County. He was the son of Rev. LeGrand Felder Guerry and Margaret Serena Brailsford. His father was for many years a prominent clergymen of this diocese. He was a direct descendant of Pierre Guerri, a Huguenot immigrant to South Carolina. His wife was a direct descendant of General William Moultrie. His family has supplied many other honored names in the history of this State. The Bishop was a student of the Porter Military Academy from 1876 to 1881 and of the University of the South from 1881 to 1888, receiving successively the degrees of A.B. and M.A., and later, after his Consecration, that of Doctor of Divinity from his Alma Mater. He was ordained deacon by Bishop Howe in 1888 and priest by him the year following. Upon ordination, he took charge of his first and only parochial charge, St. John's Church, Florence, together with the churches at Mar's Bluff, Marion and Darlington. Under his leadership in 1893 a handsome stone Church was built in Florence.

On November 27, 1889, at St. Luke's Church at Lincolnton, N. C., he was married to Miss Anne McBee, daughter of Vardry Alexander McBee and Mary Sumner McBee. They had five children, all of whom survived him: William Alexander, Jr., who became vice-chancellor of the University of the South; three other sons who entered the ministry—Sumner, Moultrie, and Edward Brailsford—the last first practiced law briefly. The daughter, Anne, married James Young Perry.

In 1893 Mr. Guerry became chaplain and professor of Homiletics and Pastoral Theology in the University of the South. Here he wielded a wide influence, not only upon a large number of young men preparing for the ministry at St. Luke's Hall, but upon all the students in the University. While serving as chaplain, he laid the foundation and began the construction of the present great All Saints' Chapel. During the entire period of Bishop Guerry's Episcopate, he kept up a close connection with Sewanee, maintaining a summer home there. He was elected Bishop Coadjutor of this diocese on May 15, 1907, becoming Bishop nine months later on the death of Bishop Capers. He had in the meantime taken up his residence in Charleston and begun his active career as Bishop, an activity that extended beyond the diocese. In 1917, he was elected president of the Province of Sewanee. During the first World War, Bishop Guerry served overseas under the auspices of the Y.M.C.A. from August, 1918, to March, 1919. He was special preacher and lecturer and served in England, Scotland, and France. He attended the Lambeth Conference of 1920. The outstanding event of his Episcopate perhaps was the division of the diocese in 1922 and its reorganization under the plan of an Executive Council in 1921. The leading questions to which Bishop Guerry gave much attention were the problems connected with the Church's work among colored people, the question of marriage and divorce on which subject he was a leader in the General Convention, being a member of the Commission on Marriage and Divorce. He was an advocate of no exception to the Church's traditional rule of no divorce for any cause. Another matter to which he gave much attention was the great question of the unity of Christendom. While a strict Churchman, he had hopes of a great reunion, and just before his death was undertaking the formation of a League for Unity. He was a strong supporter of the institutions of the diocese: the Seaman's Home, the Church Home, and especially the Porter Military Academy. It was largely due to his influence that Voorhees was espoused by the diocese.

As one has well said of him, "Few were so deeply versed in the history and sacred tradition of the Church in which he was a shepherd and overseer, nor more deeply conscious of the Apostolic character of the succession he held. . . . An accomplished theologian, a student of Church polity, a man of strong convictions and determined purpose, he left his mark upon the Church in South Carolina and America." His tragic death is related in the story of his Episcopate (Chapter VI). His remains lie in the western section of the churchyard of St. Philip's, the mother parish of the diocese.

Ninth Bishop, the Right Rev. Albert Sidney Thomas, LL.D., D.D., S.T.D., born February 6, 1873, Consecrated November 30, 1928, retired officially December 31, 1943—served until May 4, 1944.

Albert Sidney Thomas was born February 6, 1873, in Columbia, South Carolina, the son of Col. John Peyre Thomas and Mary Caroline Gibbes. He was a descendant of the Rev. Samuel Thomas, the first missionary of the S.P.G. to Carolina. [Also descended from another S.P.G. missionary, the Rev. Thomas Hasell, for 35 years rector of St. Thomas' and St. Denis' Parish.] He was baptized in Trinity Church, Columbia, and was educated in the public schools of Charleston and Columbia. On October 1, 1888, he entered The Citadel, and was graduated with the degree of Bachelor of Science in July, 1892. Following his graduation he was assistant principal of the Laurel Street school in Columbia, for three years, advancing in 1895 to principal. While teaching in Columbia he attended lectures in physics and chemistry at the South Carolina College and in the summer studied theology at the University of the South. He was received as a postulant by Bishop Capers of South Carolina, February 4, 1895, and subsequently as candidate for Holy Orders. In September, 1897, he entered the General Theological Seminary in New York, was graduated there and received the degree of B.D. From 1893 to 1900 he was superintendent of the Sunday School and lay reader at the Church of the Good Shepherd, Columbia, where he was confirmed by Bishop Lyman of North Carolina. In Trinity Church, Columbia, he was ordained deacon by Bishop Capers, July 22, 1900, and priest, March 3, 1901. Following his ordination he was appointed rector and missionary in charge of St. Matthew's, Darlington; Advent, Marion; and Trinity Church, Society Hill, remaining in this extended charge until September 1, 1908. During this period a new Church was built at Darlington and missions were established in Hartsville and Mullins.

From there Mr. Thomas removed to the rectorship of old St. David's, Cheraw, assuming charge also of St. Paul's, Bennettsville. In 1910 he resigned the latter and shortly thereafter again took charge of Trinity Church, Society Hill. During his rectorship in Cheraw, Mr. Thomas designed and built a handsome new Church in the center of town, the new St. David's, the old Colonial Church being inconveniently located for the congregation. The new tower is "a faint copy of that at the General Theological Seminary." As in Darlington, again in Cheraw, Mr. Thomas instituted the vested choir. During his Cheraw ministry he held services once a month in the Presbyterian Church at McBee, which was made available by that congregation. [All that remains of this mission work is a fund in the hands of the trustees of the diocese and a lot in McBee.] He remained in that charge until 1921, serving for one year, 1918, as rector of the Church of the Good Shepherd, in Columbia. While in Cheraw, he married Emily Jordan Carrison of Camden, S. C. They have three children: Henry, Professor of Chemistry in Yale University [now at the University of N. C.], Albert, Jr., architect of Columbia, and Emily [who married Gerald Watts Scurry, M.D.]. From early in his ministry he was active in diocesan work, serving as secretary of the Convention from 1902 to 1922, deputy to the General Convention, triennially from 1907 to 1928, member of the Standing Committee from 1908 to 1928, for many years secretary, treasurer, and chairman of the Department of Missions, editor of *The Diocese,* 1913 to 1928, examining chaplain, and dean of the School of Prophets of the Kanuga Conferences from 1933.

From St. David's, Mr. Thomas accepted the call to St. Michael's and began to officiate here October 1, 1921. During his period of service the parish house was enlarged, the Young People's Service League was organized, and the change from a quartet to a vested choir was effected. Both Morning and Evening Prayer were said every Sunday and the Holy Communion was offered on all Sundays and Holy Days. In addition to his work at St. Michael's, from 1922 to 1926, Mr. Thomas had charge of St. Andrew's Mission, King Street. He was also president of the Charleston Bible Society. Mr. Thomas continued in St. Michael's until St. Andrew's Day, 1928, when he was consecrated ninth Bishop of the diocese of South Carolina. His episcopal ring and robes were presented him by St. Michael's. Bishop Thomas was awarded the honorary degree of Doctor of Divinity by the University of the South, Doctor of Sacred Theology by the General Theological Seminary in 1930, and Doctor of Laws by The Citadel in 1931. Bishop Thomas continued in service as the Bishop of the diocese for fifteen and a half years, retiring in 1944. Since then he has had occasional charge of several churches for varying periods: Grace Church, St. Michael's, Charleston; St. John's, John's Island, with St. James', James Island, and St. Paul's, Meggett, having designed the new Church of that parish [also St. Luke and St. Paul in 1955]. His interest and his duties as Registrar and Historiographer of the diocese have engaged him in research in the history of the diocese for many years. He is vice-president of the Dalcho Society. He is the author of articles in the *Historical Magazine* of the Episcopal Church: "History of the Curch in South Carolina;" "Robert Smith, the First Bishop of South Carolina;" and "Christopher Gadsden." [also an article on "Samuel Thomas, also this *Account*. For some years (1914) he was chaplain general of the Sons of Confederate Veterans; and many years he has been chaplain of the Huguenot Society of South Carolina, chaplain of the Society of Colonial Wars of South Carolina, and also for a time chaplain general of the National Society.] Bishop Thomas now lives in active retirement in Rockville, Wadmalaw Island.

(The above sketch is a reprint from *St. Michael's, Charleston, 1751-1951*, by George W. Williams, M.A., University of South Carolina Press, Columbia, 1951. Used by permission of the Press, and the vestry of St. Michael's Church.)

Tenth Bishop, the Right Rev. Thomas Neely Carruthers, born June 10, 1900, Consecrated May 4, 1944.

Thomas Neely Carruthers, the son of Thomas Neely and Linnie Louise (Hunter) Carruthers, was born in Collierville, Tennessee. His father was a captain in the Tennessee Cavalry of the Confederate Army. His grandfather, Thomas Neely Carruthers, moved from the York District of South Carolina in the 1820's and settled in West Tennessee. He attended the public schools of his native town, graduating in 1918, being a member of St. Andrew's mission in which he was baptized and confirmed. He entered the University of the South in 1918, receiving the Bachelor of Arts degree *optime merens* in 1921, having studied also in the summer in Vanderbilt University. At Sewanee he was on the track team, winner of several medals, member of Kappa Sigma fraternity. From 1921 to 1923, he taught school in Baltimore, Md., and in Swarthmore, Pa. Attending the graduate school of Princeton University, 1923-24, he received the Master of Arts degree June, 1924. He now became a postulant in the diocese of Tennessee. He returned to Sewanee and finished the course in St. Luke's Hall, being ordained deacon June, 1925, by Bishop Maxon, and priest the next year in St. John's Church, Ashwood, by Bishop Gailor, on the occasion of the annual pilgrimage to this ancient shrine. Having served the Church as a lay reader from time to time for several years, in 1925 as deacon he took charge of the Church of the Messiah, Pulaski and Holy Cross mission, Mt. Pleasant, in Tennessee. As priest in 1926, he became rector of St. Peter's in Columbia, Tenn., with charge still of Holy Cross mission. At this time he was chaplain of the Columbia Institute and Junior College for girls, an Episcopal school, and teacher in the school. In the summer of 1927, he toured Europe, visiting France, Switzerland, Italy, and England. On December 27, 1927, he married Ellen Douglas Everett of Columbia, Tennessee, a recent graduate of Smith College. They have two sons, Thomas Neely, Jr., now practicing law in Birmingham, Ala., and Ewing Everett, now in the college at Sewanee. In 1929 he received (in course) the degree of B.D. at the University of the South, and in 1944 the degree of Doctor of Divinity. In these years in Tennessee, the Rev. Mr. Carruthers served as chairman of the Department of Christian Social Service.

He became rector of Trinity Church, Houston, Texas, in 1931 serving for eight years, being on the diocesan executive board and the Standing Committee and deputy to two general conventions. During these eight years, Trinity Church expanded in membership to 2,100—one of the 12 largest parishes in the United States. Rev. Mr. Carruthers accepted a call to Christ Church, Nashville, in February, 1939. During his period of service at Christ Church, he held leading positions in the diocese, being twice deputy to the General Convention, in 1940 and 1943. He served on several commissions of the General Convention. In his different places of residence, he has been a member of the Rotary Club and also the Exchange Club. Since his Consecration as Bishop of South Carolina in 1944, he has served in several positions of importance in the national Church in addition to his duties as Bishop of this diocese (See Chapter VIII): Commission on Holy Matrimony; chairman of program of the great Anglican Conference in 1954 in Minneapolis, involving some three years work; attended Lambeth Conference of 1948 and World Council at Amsterdam. He has been much in demand as a Lenten preacher. Bishop Carruthers conducted the Adult Conference at Kanuga from 1949 to 1953. He was president of the Synod of the Fourth Province from 1953 to 1956. He served for some years on the board of regents of the University of the South and in 1956 was elected Chancellor of the University. Bishop Carruthers is the author of the book "Sparks of Fire".

APPENDICES, PART TWO
DIOCESE OF UPPER S. C.

Appendix VI—*Lists*

1. LIST OF CLERGYMEN
Upper South Carolina
(With Period of Canonical Residence)
1922-56

(Abbreviations: O—ordained; R—received; T—transferred; D—Died; Dep—deposed)

R 1949	George M. Alexander		
O 1937	Frank J. Allen	Dep.	1951
O 1952	Christopher FitzSimons Allison		
R 1952	Sandy Anderson	T	1954
R 1952	William Ross Baley	T	1953
R 1941	Theodore Porter Ball	T	1947
R 1954	Harold E. Barrett	T	1955
O 1954	William Arthur Beckham		
R 1928	A. G. Branwell Bennett		
R 1922	Locke W. Blackwelder	T	1926
R 1942	William Shannon Brace	T	1948
R 1925	Ilbert de L. Brayshaw	T	1928
O 1957	Gaston DeFoix Bright		
O 1925	James B. Brown		
R 1927	Thomas D. Brown	T	1928
R 1942	Joseph N. Bynum	T	1948
R 1953	Adolphus Carty	T	1954
O 1951	Walter W. Cawthorne		
R 1945	B. Duvall Chambers		
R 1946	Alfred P. Chambliss	T	1951
R 1936	Maurice Clark	D	1946
O 1953	Philip Griffen Clarke, Jr.	T	1956
O 1939	Allen B. Clarkson	T	1942
O 1952	John Gorman Clarkson	T	1956
O 1924	Edward M. Claytor	T	1927
O 1951	Edwin B. Clippard	T	1954
R 1954	Clarence Alfred Cole (Bishop)		
O 1951	Jack Wallace Cole		
R 1943	Harvey A. Cox	D	1943
R 1933	Francis H. Craighill, Jr.	T	1935
R 1943	William C. Cravner	T	1947
O 1938	N. Chafee Croft	T	1939
R 1952	Forbes Ross de Tamble	T	1955
R 1955	William Miller Davis		
R 1922	Alfred James Derbyshire	T	1927
O 1934	Theodore P. Devlin	T	1940
R 1937	Henry Lester Durrant	D	1948
R 1948	Frederick L. Eckel	T	1950
R 1922	Edward Van W. Edwards	T	1927

O 1940   Julian Sproles Ellenberg.............................. ———
R 1923   John B. Elliott..D 1940
R 1929   Howard G. England, D.D. ....D 1944
R 1922   Albert Edward Evison.............................D 1932
O 1931   Charles C. Fishburne.............................T 1935
O 1927   William Hayne Folk...............................T 1928
R 1956   Grant O. Folmsbee.............................. ———
R 1938   Raymond E. Fuessle.............................T 1940
R 1956   William Lawrence Gatling...................... ———
O 1957   James Hardin George, Jr. .... ———
R 1942   James L. Grant...................................T 1943
R 1939   John J. Gravatt (Retired Bishop)............... ———
O 1953   Joseph Nathaniel Green, Jr. .... ———
R 1948   Robert Emmet Gribbin, Jr. ....T 1954
R 1930   Sanders R. Guignard.............................D 1936
R 1922   Frank Harriman Harding........................T 1924
R 1949   Samuel R. Hardman.............................T 1954
R 1945   George E. Harper.................................T 1945
O 1957   Rogers Sanders Harris........................... ———
R 1952   John Townsend Harrison........................T 1955
O 1951   Marion J. Hatchett..............................T 1957
R 1947   Sidney Ernest Heath............................. ———
R 1945   Charles Holding..................................D 1950
R 1928   Charles P. Holbrook.............................T 1929
R 1955   Frank K. Hughes.................................T 1956
O 1954   Clyde Lambert Ireland.......................... ———
O 1942   Ellsworth Bertram Jackson.....................T 1944
O 1957   Marshall Orr James.............................. ———
O 1932   Innis L. Jenkins.................................T 1932
R 1949   Francis Goodwin Johnson.......................T 1949
R 1922   William Johnson.................................T 1944
R 1954   John Paul Jones.................................T 1955
O 1925   Justice Smith Johns.............................T 1926
R 1948   Allen Webster Joslin........................... ———
R 1925   Edmund N. Joyner...............................T 1928
R 1922   Frank A. Juhan (Bishop of Fla.)...............T 1924
O 1953   Herman McGolrick Kennickell, Jr. .... ———
R 1942   William E. Kidd.................................T 1945
R 1954   Ralph Herbert Kimball..........................T 1956
R 1950   Michael J. Kippenbrock.........................T 1953
R 1941   William S. Lea..................................T 1944
O 1957   Giles Floyd Lewis.............................. ———
R 1947   Stiles B. Lines................................. ———
R 1954   Carlos A. Loop.................................T 1956
O 1928   Champe B. Lucas................................T 1929
O 1934   William Wallace Lumpkin ....T 1935, R 1951
R 1955   Gordon Hossley Mann............................T 1956
R 1922   William E. McCord..............................T 1925
O 1953   Ernest Cannon McCreary........................ ———
R 1930   Isaac I. McDonald...............................T 1938

R 1940 Louis Chester Melcher (Bishop of Brazil)...............T 1948
O 1954 Louis Chester Melcher, Jr. .... ———
R 1937 Andrew D. Milstead.......................................T 1938
R 1922 Alexander Robert Mitchell..........................D 1949
R 1957 Turner W. Morris... ———
R 1945 deSaussure P. Moore....................................T 1946
R 1922 A Rufus Morgan...T 1940
O 1925 John H. Morgan..T 1925
R 1942 J. Kenneth Morris... ———
R 1957 Turner Wesley Morris..................................... ———
R 1954 George H. Murphy... ———
R 1955 Rufus K. Nightingale...................................... ———
R 1946 Eugene L. Nixon..T 1954
R 1922 Thomas P. Noe...T 1941
R 1954 Robert L. Oliveros.. ———
O 1954 William Fletcher O'Neal.................................. ———
R 1957 Richard C. Patton... ———
R 1922 W. H. K. Pendleton.......................................D 1956
R 1927 John James Patrick Perry................................D 1928
R 1923 Robert Nathaniel Perry..................................T 1924
R 1922 William Preston Peyton..................................T 1944
R 1922 Henry D. Phillips (Bishop of S. W. Va.)...................T 1939
R 1933 Robert Theodore Phillips................................D 1952
R 1941 John Adams Pinckney...................................... ———
R 1923 Theophilus T. Pollard...................................T 1927
O 1949 Frederick A. Pope..T 1951
R 1922 Arthur R. Price...T 1924
R 1952 R. Hampton Price... ———
O 1951 Manney C. Reid...T 1954
O 1944 Roddey Reid..T 1948
R 1930 C. Gregg Richardson.....................................T 1934
R 1922 John Ridout...T 1923
R 1922 Thomas Leadbeater Ridout...............................T 1923
R 1956 Thomas Adams Roberts.................................... ———
O 1957 Charles A. Robinson, III.................................. ———
R 1947 C. Earle B. Robinson.....................................T 1950
R 1927 C. Capers Satterlee....................T 1935, R 1944, ———
R 1922 Herbert F. Schroeter.....................................T 1925
R 1941 Charles M. Seymour, Jr. ....T 1950
R 1923 St. Julian A. Simpkins...................................T 1928
O 1929 Paul Earle Sloan...T 1934
O 1929 S. Thorne Sparkman......................................T 1932
R 1955 Homer Pilgrim Starr...................................... ———
R 1952 J. Daniel Stover...T 1953
O 1931 Albert Rhett Stuart (Bishop of Ga.).....................T 1937
R 1951 Richard L. Sturgis .... ———
O 1939 Cyril N. Sturrup...T 1941
R 1935 Ira C. Swanman... ———
R 1922 Arthur W. Taylor...T 1927
R 1948 George Farrand Taylor .... ———

R 1926   Lewis Nathaniel Taylor..............................D 1947
R 1926   Malcolm S. Taylor..................................T 1935
R 1955   Gray Temple ....———
R 1947   Harold Thomas.....................................T 1950
O 1936   Lewis O'Vander Thomas.............................T 1938
R 1945   William A. Thompson...............................———
O 1948   Martin Robert Tilson..............................T 1956
R 1922   John Huske Tillinghast.............................D 1933
R 1929   R. Chipman Topping................................T 1936
R 1941   Gardner D. Underhill..............................T 1944
O 1932   Samuel Cleveland Usher............................T 1947
R 1936   Donald E. Veale...................................T 1941
O 1925   Tracy F. Walsh....................................T 1926
R 1922   Thomas Tracy Walsh................................D 1937
R 1954   Gale D. Webbe.....................................T 1954
O 1943   E. Hopkins Weston.................................T 1957
O 1934   Maxwell S. Whittington............................———
R 1940   Billert A. Williams................................T 1951
R 1922   George Croft Williams.............................———
R 1954   William L. Williams...............................———
R 1940   Bruce P. Williamson...............................———
R 1922   George E. DeWitt Zachary..........................T 1925
R 1946   Oran C. Zaebst....................................T 1957
R 1957   Henry Albert Zinser...............................T 1957

2. CONVENTIONS OF THE CHURCH IN THE DIOCESE OF UPPER SOUTH CAROLINA
(With Place of Meeting and Date)

Primary Convention...............Trinity, Columbia, October 10-11, 1922
1st Convention......................Christ, Greenville, May 8-9, 1923
2nd Convention...............Advent, Spartanburg, January 15-16, 1924
3rd Convention...........Good Shepherd, Columbia, January 20-21, 1925
4th Convention.......................Nativity, Union, January 26, 1926
5th Convention...............Good Shepherd, York, January 25-26, 1927
6th Convention...............St. John's, Columbia, January 24-25, 1928
7th Convention...................Christ, Greenville, January 22-23, 1929
8th Convention...............Advent, Spartanburg, January 21-22, 1930
9th Convention...........Good Shepherd, Columbia, January 20-21, 1931
10th Convention.............St. Thaddeus', Aiken, January 19-20, 1932
11th Convention..................Grace, Anderson, January 17-18, 1933
12th Convention..........Good Shepherd, Columbia, January 23-24, 1934
13th Convention....................Grace, Camden, January 22-23, 1935
14th Convention.............St. John's, Columbia, January 21-22, 1936
15th Convention..........Ressurrection, Greenwood, January 19-20, 1937
16th Convention.............Our Saviour, Rock Hill, January 18-19, 1938
Special Convention..................Trinity, Columbia, January 10, 1939
17th Convention.................Christ, Greenville, January 24-25, 1939
18th Convention.................Trinity, Columbia, January 23-24, 1940

19th Convention.....................Advent, Spartanburg, May 6-7, 1941
20th Convention.............Good Shepherd, Columbia, May 12-13, 1942
21st Convention.................St. Thaddeus', Aiken, May 11-12, 1943
22nd Convention..................... Trinity, Columbia, May 4-5, 1944
23rd Convention...................Trinity, Columbia, May 15-16, 1945
24th Convention..............Advent, Spartanburg, January 22-23, 1946
25th Convention................Trinity, Columbia, January 21-22, 1947
26th Convention.................Christ, Greenville, January 20-21, 1948
27th Convention..............St. Thaddeus', Aiken, January 18-19, 1949
28th Convention..........Good Shepherd, Columbia, January 24-25, 1950
Special Convention..............St. John's, Columbia, September 15, 1950
29th Convention.............Our Saviour, Rock Hill, January 23-24, 1951
30th Convention.................Advent, Spartanburg, April 22-23, 1952
31st Convention.....................Trinity, Columbia, May 11-12, 1953
32nd Convention.........................Grace, Camden, May 4-5, 1954
33rd Convention...................Advent, Spartanburg, May 3-4, 1955
34th Convention...................St. Thaddeus', Aiken, May 1-2, 1956

3. OFFICERS, DIOCESE OF UPPER SOUTH CAROLINA

President of the Standing Committee:

The Rev. Alexander R. Mitchell, D.D. 1922-35
The Rev. Henry D. Phillips, D.D. 1935-39
The Rev. Louis N. Taylor, D.D. 1939-48
The Rev. A. G. Branwell Bennett............................1948-52
The Rev. C. Capers Satterlee, D.D. ....1952-___

Secretary of the Standing Committee:

J. Nelson Frierson..1922-44
Carroll H. Jones..1944-50
R. Hoke Robinson 1950-52
Henry A. Brown...1952-53
The Rev. John A. Pinckney.................................1953-54
The Rev. Martin R. Tilson.................................1954-56

Secretary of the Convention:

The Rev. F. H. Harding....................................1922-23
The Rev. A. Rufus Morgan..................................1923-34
The Rev. A. G. B. Bennett.................................1934-53
The Rev. J. A. Pinckney...................................1953-___

Treasurer of the Convention:

William Anderson Clarkson.................................1922-25
Bryan H. Lumpkin..1926-28
E. R. Heyward...1928-47
D. Jennings Lucas...1947-___

Secretary and Treasurer of the Trustees:

John Peyre Thomas, Jr. 1922-42
Kirkman G. Finlay...1942-46
Dorothy V. Crawford.......................................1946-___

Chancellor:

William M. Shand, Esq. 1922-41
R. E. Carwile, Esq. 1941-49
R. Beverly Sloan, Esq. 1949-51
W. Croft Jennings, Esq. ....1951-___

Registrar and Historiographer:

The Rev. A. E. Evison.....................................1923-33
The Rev. A. R. Mitchell...................................1933-45
Dr. Archibald Rutledge....................................1945-48
The Rev. Robert T. Phillips...............................1948-51
James R. Cain, Esq. 1951-57
Commander Charles E. Thomas..............................1957-___

Headquarters Secretary:

Mrs. William P. Cornell...................................1922-26
Mrs. H. L. Forbes...1926-37
Miss Dorothy V. Crawford..................................1937-___

Appendix VII—*Organizations*

1. CHURCH WOMEN'S WORK IN THE DIOCESE OF UPPER SOUTH CAROLINA

THE WOMAN'S AUXILIARY

The primary Convention of the diocese of Upper South Carolina was held in Trinity Church, Columbia, on October 10, 1922. It was just one week later, October 17, that a great meeting of the women of the new diocese was held in Grace Church, Anderson, to make plans for their own organized work. After services with a quiet hour conducted by Bishop Finlay, who also made an address, a steering committee of twelve with Mrs. J. R. Cain as chairman was appointed. This committee later made a report, which was adopted, recommending that branches of the following organizations be organized in the diocese of Upper South Carolina: the Church Service League, the Woman's Auxiliary to the National Council, the Girls' Friendly Society of America, the Church Periodical Club, and the Daughters of the King. The Church Service League had been organized two or three years before in the undivided diocese in response to the national movement to combine in one organization all the lay forces of the Church, including men's clubs. This was a part of the general plan of reorganizing the work of the Church which took place about this time in connection with the setting up of the national Council. Mrs. James R. Cain, president, and Miss Leora Rivers, secretary were elected to represent the women in the Church Service League in this diocese. This organization, however, did not prove practicable and never functioned in the new diocese.

In a separate meeting on the same day, presided over by Mrs. M. D. Chase as chairman and Miss Sarah Cornish as secretary, the Girls' Friendly Society in the diocese was reorganized. The by-laws in force in the old diocese were adopted. The following officers were then elected: Mrs. Marianna P. Ford, president; Mrs. T. P. Noe and Mrs. Mary E. Wylie, vice-presidents; Mrs. M. D. Chase, secretary and treasurer. At this time there were seven branches in the diocese. This society continued to function in this diocese until 1935. The last diocesan officer was Miss Emilie Carter of Aiken. It was planned that the Daughters of the King would organize a diocesan chapter under direction of Mrs. George L. Dial, provincial vice-president for South Carolina. This was done and the chapter continued its life under its two rules of prayer and service, similar to the Brotherhood of St. Andrew, until 1932. The last diocesan officers were Mrs. J. E. McDaniel and Mrs. James L. Reid of Columbia. The Bishop was requested to appoint a correspondent for the Church Periodical Club. The club functioned separately but as a part of the Woman's Auxiliary.

At this same meeting in Anderson on October 17, 1922, a branch of the Woman's Auxiliary to the National Council in the diocese of Upper South Carolina was organized. It was resolved that the Constitution of the branch of the undivided diocese be adopted, provision being made for certain necessary changes. It was decided that the annual Convention should be held in January of each year (but omitting 1923) and that the convocational meetings be held in the spring. A budget was adopted for 1923. Officers were elected as follows: Mrs. W. P. Cornell, president; Mrs. F. N. Challen, vice-president of Greenville Convocation, and Mrs. P. M. Feltham of Columbia Convocation; secretary, Mrs. Robert Childs; treasurer, Mrs. W. W. Long; Mrs. James R. Cain, chairman of the executive committee. Miss Virginia T. Singleton was appointed United Thank-Offering Custodian. The Auxiliary was organized into departments along the lines of the national and diocesan Councils adopted generally by all units of Church work at this time. The work of the branch was planned and conducted through the agency of an executive committee, later called Executive Board, consisting of the diocesan officers, department chairmen, district directors, and three members at large. Before the first convention adjourned, it adopted this slogan: "A Branch of the Woman's Auxiliary in Every Parish and Mission of the Diocese", since then practically realized. It is not possible to here recount in detail the great work accomplished by this splendid organization in the past quarter century. We shall here give a summary of the report of the treasurer, Mrs. W. W. Long, for the year 1924, showing the extent of the work even in the earlier years. The receipts, including apportionments and specials, amounted to $4,636.84. Among the expenditures were the Bishop Tuttle Memorial, $222.39; Bishop Rowe Scholarship, $100.00; Ramsaur Memorials, $606.87; work at Graniteville, $133.00; summer volunteers, $215.00; Uta Saito work in Japan, $50.00; Liberia, $52.25; Japanese reconstruction, $114.00; chapel at Great Falls, $50.00; St. Andrew's, Wuchang, China, $25.00; Nanna Shand Wilson Memorial, $132.05; DuBose Memorial School, $100.00;

Church program, $200.00. These were all "specials" and apart from the regular appropriations through the departments as follows: Christian Social Service, $1,163.10; Supply, $540.00; Publicity, $234-.65; Finance, $9.10; Headquarters, $425.98.

A comparison of these figures of 1924 with those presented to the last annual meeting in January, 1956, will reveal the wonderful expansion of the work of the branch in this period. We cannot give the details, but the total in 1924 of receipts and expenditures amounting to $4,636.84 had increased fourfold to $19,519.21! This figure represents manifold appropriations to good causes both within and without the diocese, and this, too, being apart from the great United Thank-Offering presented every three years. The Offering of Life has ever been emphasized. Aside from a large number who have offered for homeland work, we should name, going to the extra-continental field, Eunice Haddon to Honolulu and Theodore Young to China. Evidence of the development of this great work may be summarized as follows: 1. The development of the district plan; 2. The adoption of prayer partners; 3. The establishment of the Bishop's discretionary fund; 4. The adoption of missionary objectives in the domestic and foreign fields; 5. The national mission project; 6. The Bene Dial loan and scholarship fund; 7. The establishment of a diocesan institute to train officers; 8. The issuing of the Auxiliary handbook; 9. Participation in camps and conferences; 10. Cooperation with diocesan convocations; 11. Securing representation on diocesan departments of the executive council of the diocese; 12. Increasing emphasis on retreats and quiet days.

Although this is the youngest and one of the smallest auxiliaries in the province, it has furnished three provincial presidents—Mrs. Joseph E. Hart, Mrs. James R. Cain, and Mrs. B. Duvall Chambers. Also, one member elected to the national executive board who was also one of the first four women placed on the National Council, Mrs. J. R. Cain. Another important contribution of this diocese to the general Church was Mrs. D. D. (Augusta Jones) Taber, a field worker for the national Church from 1923 to 1928, visiting with an effective message nearly every diocese in the United States, working especially in cooperation with the Auxiliary.

LIST OF PRESIDENTS

Mrs. William P. Cornell	1922-24
Mrs. James Ravenel Cain	1924-26
Mrs. Joseph E. Hart	1926-29
Mrs. James Ravenel Cain	1929-30
Mrs. Ben W. Aiken	1930-33

Mrs. A. C. Hammett 1933-36
Mrs. R. Beverly Sloan..1936-39
Mrs. J. E. Boatwright..1939-42
Mrs. W. Preston Peyton.......................................1942-44
Mrs. William Fewell 1944-46
Mrs. G. Richard Shafto.......................................1946-47
Mrs. B. Duvall Chambers......................................1947-50
Mrs. Robert B. Olney...1950-53
Mrs. C. Frederic McCullough..................................1953-56
Mrs. James A. Vaughan ....1956-___

2. THE Y. P. S. L. AND THE YOUTH MOVEMENT IN THE DIOCESE OF UPPER SOUTH CAROLINA

Immediately upon the organization of the diocese of Upper South Carolina in October, 1922, attention was given to the work of the Church among the young people of the new diocese. A forward movement was at once inaugurated under the Department of Religious Education of the Executive Council of the diocese, of which Rev. W. H. K. Pendleton was chairman and Rev. F. A. Juhan, associate chairman. A Young People's department was organized by Mr. Juhan. Under his leadership and with the active help of Mrs. F. N. Challen. field worker of the diocese, as executive secretary, it was reported at the Convention of the diocese in January, 1924, that 15 Young People's Service Leagues had been formed in the diocese—largely the result of a training camp held the summer before.

The first Convention of the young people of the diocese was held in the Church of the Advent, Spartanburg, May 2-3, 1924. An Easter offering of $4,500.00 was then presented, indicating the interest and activity of the young people. It was at this Convention that the Y. P. S. L. of the diocese was formally organized. The following summer, separate camps for boys and for girls were held at Bowman's Bluff near Etowah. The annual Conventions were held for some years in conjunction with the Church school conventions. The rapid growth of the league in the diocese was enhanced especially by the annual Conventions and by the summer camps. After 1924 these camps were held for three years at Camp Transylvania, Brevard, N. C. (a private camp site for boys) and called Camp Capers. It was still called Camp Capers when after 1927 it was located at Kanuga; but, later it merged into the Kanuga Young People's Conference. (See Sketch of Kanuga, Part One, Appendix III, 3.) The success of the youth movement in the diocese may be said to have been due primarily to the devoted leadership of Bishop Finlay;

especially his great interest in camps and conferences. This is illustrated by this quotation from his annual address of 1931 to his Convention concerning Kanuga:

"Last summer I think marked the highest point reached in our conferences and camps. The Y. P. S. L. group—age 14 to the early 20's, was not as large as the year before, owing to the fact that East Carolina had a conference of their own. We had, however, about 200 young people from South Carolina, Western North Carolina and this diocese. The spirit and quality of work done was the best in our history. The Adult conference was the largest and most satisfactory that we have ever held. The most disappointing factor was the attendance of the clergy. As to this I have certain plans for the coming year which I think will bring marked improvement. The Junior camps, 14 and younger, enrolled close to 300. The camp of 180 girls was carried out most successfully, due primarily to the wonderful group of women counselors we were able to secure. The boys' camp of some 90 was somewhat undermanned in counselors and the discipline was not as good as in former years. This must be remedied the coming summer. Our summer program is now entirely self-supporting."

The Y. P. S. L. for years after its founding proved a great force for the strengthening of the Church in the diocese. Its members were challenged by the opportunity it offered for personal development, as indicated by its accepted four ideals which included worship, service, fellowship, and study. Its motto, *Non sibi; sed allis*, was remembered as its work was developed in the five fields of service. The Young People's Thank Offering was an important element of its work. In 1940, in response to an idea that a young people's organization of a more inclusive character than the Y. P. S. L., to embrace it and also other young people's organizations, was needed in the Church, there was launched on a national scale "The United Movement of the Church's Youth." The Bishop took steps to further the "movement" in this diocese on May 12, 1943, by appointing a Youth Commission of the diocese with the Rev. John A. Pinckney as chairman. Miss Averill Boatwright was appointed to act as president of the diocesan Young People's Convention until the meeting in the fall. This was held in Spartanburg, November 4-5, 1943. It was on November 13 following in Trinity Church, Columbia, that a joint meeting of the youth of the two dioceses was held. The Rev. John A. Pinckney was chairman for Upper South Carolina and the Rev. Colin R. Campbell for South Carolina. The purpose of the joint meeting was not only to outline the purposes of the "movement" but to coordinate the work of the two dioceses, since it was to be under a joint worker for the two dioceses. This was Miss Gertrude C. Bull, who began her services September 1, 1943.

One of the chief matters of business before the Convention was the reforming of the diocesan Youth Commission. In addition to the eight young people from the four interested groups, a young person was elected by the Convention to serve as vice-chairman. This person was MacGregor Boyle of Trinity Church, Columbia. Jeanne Crawford, Trinity, Columbia, was chosen to serve on the inter-diocesan staff of "co-workers" and to serve on the Youth Commission. Also on the Commission as chairman of the Youth Offering and promotion of Youth Sunday was Olivia Conyers. The four interested groups referred to were: (1) Acolytes and Junior Brotherhood of St. Andrew; (2) Y. P. S. L.: (3) Girls' Friendly, Junior Choir and Junior Altar Guild; (4) Church School, Senior Department. The Y. P. S. L. on the diocesan level gave way about 1947 to the general youth movement which officially is named "The House of Young Churchmen of the Diocese of Upper South Carolina." An annual All-Youth Convention is held each year when it elects the diocesan Youth Commission. These meetings since 1949 have been held at Camp Gravatt. The Y. P. S. L. has continued on the parochial level.

It was in October of 1949 at the diocesan Youth Convention, held at Camp Gravatt and under the direction of Mary Ravenel Burgess, our diocesan Youth Director, that a reorganization of youth work was undertaken. Following the *"Plan"* of the United Movement of the Church's Youth (UMCY), sponsored at the National Council, all young people in our diocese elected the Council of Young Churchmen. This included the diocesan officers and officers of the four districts within the diocese, with representatives of six interested groups: *i. e.*, Junior High, Y. P. S. L., Young Adults, Junior Choirs, Canterbury Club, and unorganized youth. At the Youth Convention of 1950, held in April of that year at Camp Gravatt, the name House of Young Churchmen was first applied to all the youth, organized and unorganized, within the parishes. Also at this Convention a Youth Commission was elected by the House of Young Churchmen. In 1952, the older groups (that is, Canterbury Club and Young Adults) having withdrawn, the membership of the House of Young Churchmen was set as consisting of all young people between the ages of twelve and eighteen who are interested in the youth work of the Episcopal Church.

This Commission consists of the Bishop of the diocese, the director of the youth work, lay and clerical advisors from each Convocation, the president, first and second vice-presidents, secretary-treasurer, convocational president, diocesan delegate to the provincial Youth Convention, and the diocesan member of the provincial Youth Commission.

PRESIDENTS OF THE YOUNG PEOPLE'S SERVICE LEAGUE

Valeria Prioleau 1927
William C. Cantey 1928
Arthur Dehon 1929
Daysie Lee Powell 1929
Arthur Dehon 1930
Joseph H. Faulk 1931-32
Ellen Sayle Pelham 1933
William Overton 1935
Isabella Alston 1936-37
Connie Riddick 1938
Margaret Ray Overton 1939-40
Jack Faulk 1941
Hasell Thomas LaBorde 1942
Averill Boatwright 1943
Allison Fitz Simons 1943
Harriot Barnwell 1944
Donald Campbell 1945
Pat Shaddock 1946

3. CAMPS AND CONFERENCES

(1) KANUGA (See Appendix VII)

(2) CAMP GRAVATT

(3) JENKINSVILLE

For several years without success, Bishop Gravatt and others, with some urging from the young people, began looking for a site for a diocesan camp. It was to the Convention of 1947 that Bishop Gravatt announced to the diocese the gift of such a site by Mr. St. Julian Cullum. It is located near Batesburg, consisting of 100 acres of land, including a beautiful lake of 15 acres. The gift had been accepted by action of the executive council. Though the gift was a thank-offering for the life of his beloved wife, it was not his wish that the camp should bear his family name. However, Bishop Gravatt gave the promise that the central meeting hall, when built, would be named "Cullum Hall" in memory of his wife, Gertrude Perkins Cullum. Before her death, she had planned a Church school on the same spot. The planning committee thereupon gave the

Camp the name "Camp Gravatt". The Bishop strongly recommended the development of the camp as soon as possible. Both North Carolina and South Carolina had already established diocesan camps. The next year, plans were made to raise $3,700.00 for the development; quotas were assigned the congregations of the diocese, payable in three years. The first use of the site was for a picnic in the fall of 1947 by the Y. P. S. L. of the Church of the Good Shepherd, Columbia, when twenty members attended under the direction of their rector, Rev. Lewis N. Taylor, D.D. The spring of the following year saw the first diocesan use of the site when was held a Church School rally for a service of presentation of the Lenten Mite Box offering. Bishop Gravatt, assisted by the Rev. E. Hopkins Weston and the Rev. Roddey Reid, conducted the service.

In the spring of 1949, the Rev. Charles Seymour, then rector of St. Thaddeus', Aiken, secured for $100.00 an old building at the Aiken Army Air Base. This was removed to the camp and fitted up as a kitchen, dining, and recreation hall, and chapel; for five and a half years it served these purposes. Also at this time, through proceeds of the quotas assigned the congregations with some gifts, the initial buildings were completed—a boys' bath and dormitory, a girls' bath and dormitory, and a girls' staff cabin. Thus it was made possible now to hold conferences at Camp Gravatt. The first was the Junior Conference, which was opened on June 13, 1949, under the direction of the Rev. Alfred P. Chambliss. Eleven girls and seven boys attended. Bishop Gravatt presented each one of these campers with a certificate making that person a "Pioneer of Camp Gravatt". Later in this same summer, other conferences were held by the Girls' Friendly Society and by the Acolytes of St. John's, Columbia. Thus was the great work to be at Camp Gravatt launched on its way. The Rev. John A. Pinckney was appointed the first chairman of the Camp Gravatt Commission of the diocese, which managed its affairs.

It was not long before a much-needed additional building was secured through the activity of the Rev. B. Duvall Chambers, when a pavilion was built to serve the purpose of chapel, recreation hall, classroom, and picnic shelter. By the year 1953, the old original building falling into ruin, steps were taken to build a new dining hall and kitchen. Under a committee composed of R. T. Neblett, J. B. Boatwright, and T. E. Davis, and with a very large help of the Woman's Auxiliary, this building was completed and equipped in July, 1954. The need for more sleeping quarters in 1955 was met by the borrowing of tents from the State Parks Division of the S. C.

Forestry Commission. Substantial floors were built for these tents with the view of use in the erection of shacks on them. This was duly accomplished, especially with the help of the Men's Club of St. Martin's-in-the-Fields, whose men themselves did part of the work. Messrs. Leek and Moxley led in this project. Mr. R. F. Niedhardt, with a group of the men of St. John's, Columbia, and contributions by those of Trinity Church, Columbia, erected two more shacks. After the Convention of 1954 had authorized loans for the purpose of building the long proposed Cullum Hall in memory of the wife of the donor of the camp site, plans made by Gilmer Petroff of Trinity Church were adopted and construction begun under Mr. R. T. Neblett, chairman of the building committee, in cooperation with Bishop Cole. W. W. Clamp of Batesburg was the builder. The hall was used first on July 14, 1956. The generous donor of the site of Camp Gravatt lived only long enough to see the work begun on Cullum Hall.

Since 1949, this conference center of the diocese has been in constant use not only for conferences in the summer, but throughout the year for many sorts of meetings. Here are held the Conventions of the House of Young Churchmen, meetings of the Episcopal Laymen, training institutes of the Woman's Auxiliary, clergy conferences, under the Bishop, and various other gatherings, both diocesan and parochial. There were also five sessions of the Young People's Conference in the summer of 1956 under the leadership of the Rev. Messrs. A. W. Joslin, Hampton Price, W. A. Beckham, L. C. Melcher, Jr., and C. L. Ireland. The Rev. John A. Pinckney, the first chairman of the Camp Gravatt Commission, was succeeded in 1953 by the Rev. O. C. Zaebst, who resigned in the spring of 1955, being succeeded by Mr. R. Michael Turner of Clinton, who served until May, 1956, when the camp commission was dissolved by the Diocesan Convention and the administration of the camp was made a function of the Department of Christian Education. (This sketch largely from data kindly supplied by the Rev. John G. Clarkson, Jr.)

3. See also Conference Center at Jenkinsville in Chapter on Archdeaconry of Colored Churchmen.

Appendix VIII—*Various*

The seal of the Diocese of Upper South Carolina was adopted at the Convention of 1930, designed by Dr. A. H. Noll of Sewanee.

1. HEATHWOOD HALL

Heathwood Hall Episcopal School was established in 1951 under the terms of the will of Frances Marion Weston in 1847. The legacy was for the establishment of a school for "young females" in Columbia in the event his only son died without issue. He also made provision for a school for Negroes. The son died childless in 1867, and $7,000.00 came to the Bishop of South Carolina for the school in Columbia. The history of this fund is remarkable. While it apparently suffered some loss at an early date, its increase has been great. In 1910 the total amount of the fund was reported as $6,126.92. After the division of the diocese in 1922, since the legacy naturally belonged to upper South Carolina, Bishop Guerry turned over to Bishop Finlay the entire corpus of the fund, with interest, amounting to $12,673.08. But the rate of increase was yet to become greater —at the time of the establishment of this school, the fund had grown to $42,608.27. In the meantime, some part of the income of the fund had been used for scholarships at St. Mary's Junior College, of which the diocese is a joint owner. The first overt step to the founding of this school was the calling of a special Convention of the diocese (September 15, 1950) by Bishop Gravatt, who had conceived the idea of establishing the school, "to consider the election of trustees of the Weston School which may be established at Heathwood Hall, Columbia". It was decided by the Convention to establish the school as proposed by Mr. Weston's will for "young females", that the diocese and churches, as such, would not incur financial responsibility and the following were elected trustees according to the will, four clergymen and four laymen: the Rev. Messrs. Michael J. Kippenbrock, Oran C. Zaebst, George M. Alexander, and J. Kenneth Morris; and Messrs. Louis S. Horton, Wyndham M. Manning, Hoke Robinson, and Mrs. W. Bedford Moore. Also, the Bishop was authorized to add associate trustees without the right to vote.

The trustees found that it would not be practicable to begin a school with the restriction to "young females", and thereupon secured a court order that since "the only feasible way to accom-

plish the primary intent of the donor" was "to admit boys on the
same term as girls." The trustees next purchased a splendid property for the school, Heathwood Hall, in the developing eastern section of the city, with its 4.78 acres. The site had before 1862 belonged to Mr. Ellison S. Keitt when it came into the possession of
the Roman Catholic Church and here was established "The Ursuline
Convent of the Immaculate Conception," called Valle Crucis. Mr.
M. C. Heath acquired the property in 1911. The site was beautified
and a very handsome mansion erected upon it by Mr. Heath at a
cost of over $100,000.00. "Of white solid brick construction with
broad porches and 14 large Corinthian columns in front, it was
designed by Edwards and Sayward, Atlanta architects." Later the
building was extensively redecorated and the site landscaped by
Harlan P. Kelsey of Salem, Massachusetts. The purchase of the
property was made possible by the generous offer of its owners, the
two daughters of Mr. and Mrs. M. C. Heath, Mrs. Burwell Deas
Manning and Mrs. Elizabeth Heath Coleman, at a purchase price
of $58,000.00, far below the market value. They also made a re-
duction of $2,500.00 on a first payment. It was decided that the
school would be called Heathwood Hall in appreciation of the
generous deed of these ladies. Repairs and alterations to adapt the
building to the requirements of the school were made in the
summer of 1951. The spacious hall on the upper floor was converted
into an attractive chapel. During this summer, the Church of the
Good Shepherd decided to discontinue its parochial school and the
principal and several of the teachers agreed to accept similar positions at Heathwood Hall for 1951-52.

On Monday, September 10, 1951, the school was formally opened
with exercises in the chapel conducted by Bishop Gravatt, under
whose leadership this great day had been reached. Classes began
on Tuesday, September 11th. Mrs. Susan Gibbes Woodward was
the principal, with the following faculty: Miss Mary Lide, Mrs.
C. M. Lide. Mrs. Robert P. Searson, Mrs. Margaret Buckley, Mrs.
Alexander M. Sanders, Mrs. J. S. Farr, Jr., Miss Peggy Belser, Miss
Nell V. Mellichamp (music), Professor Maurice Stephan (French).
The first student body numbered 98. It was planned to add the
fifth and sixth grades the next two years. Under the inspiring leadership of Mr. R. Hoke Robinson, chairman of the board of trustees,
the school was a success from the very beginning. The 1952 session
opened with a student body of 152. Now was added a pre-kinder-
garten class for four-year-olds, under Mrs. Albert Gilpin, and a
fifth grade under Miss Belle Dunbar. Mrs. G. Dwight Cathcart,

in the spring of 1953, succeeded Miss Peggy Belser, being elected by the trustees the Religious Education director for the school. Mrs. Thomas Glazebrook was appointed assistant director. In 1954, the enrollment was 200 when a sixth grade was added under Mrs. R. B. Cunningham. In the spring of 1955, the splendid leadership of Mrs. Susan G. Woodward (now Mrs. David W. Robinson) came to an end with her resignation. She was succeeded by Mrs. Dick Anderson.

It should be noted that the success of Heathwood Hall has been not a little due to the cooperation of the Columbia churches. Nor should we fail to mention how much the school owes to the zealous and able leadership of Mr. R. Hoke Robinson and to the devoted and efficient treasurer from the beginning, Mr. Harold E. Jervey. As Mrs. Cathcart has beautifully expressed it, "Who can say to what lengths the influence of such a school as Heathwood Hall may go, or how much the whole diocese and the nation may profit from this newest venture in faith?" May we not hope that there, in the Church Expectant, Francis Marion Weston today rejoices in the fruition, after more than a century, of his noble benefaction.

2. THE SOCIETY FOR THE ADVANCEMENT OF CHRISTIANITY IN THE DIOCESE OF UPPER SOUTH CAROLINA

As its name indicates, this society is a branch of the old society of this name, founded in the diocese of South Carolina in 1810 (See Part One, Appendix II). In view of the fact that the funds of the society had all been given with the implied trust that they were for the benefit of the Episcopal Church in the entire State, it was determined by the society, soon after the division of the diocese, to divide its funds equally as far as possible between the two dioceses, a similar society being organized to hold the funds in the new diocese. After the passage of an Act of the General Assembly, approved March 23, 1926, and by a decree of the Court of Common Pleas for Charleston, this was done by a committee consisting of Frank R. Frost, W. M. Shand, and John P. Thomas, Jr. To the diocese of Upper South Carolina was assigned one-half of the Common Fund, $18,500.00; the Dehon Scholarship Fund, $2,600.00; and the Bowen Scholarship Fund, $1,400.00; a total of $22,500.00. The old society was allocated of the Common Fund $18,500.00 and the Gates' Scholarship Fund of $3,300.00; total $21,800.00 John P. Thomas, Jr., Esq., who had been secretary of the old society since 1921, continued as secretary of this society until 1942. In that year, F. J. Dana became temporary secretary, acting until W. Bedford

Moore, Jr., was made secretary in 1945, continuing until his death in 1952 when Mr. John N. LeMaster, Jr., the present secretary (1956) succeeded to the treasurership.

About 1930, Bishop Finlay stimulated a great interest in the society, resulting in membership dues amounting to nearly $1,000.00 a year for a time, enabling the society to make large appropriations for diocesan missions. In 1935 the society suffered a loss of a mortgage of about $1.400.00 of the Common Fund mostly soon regained by reinvestment. In 1941 a loss in mill stock reduced the capital of the Bowen Scholarship from $1,400.00 to $850.00. In 1945 the president and treasurer of the society were made trustees of a special fund of $10,000.00 for advance work in the diocese in their discretion. This fund was later turned over to the Foundation and administered by it. About 1944 the Common Fund suffered a loss of $675.00. The total of permanent securities of the society in 1954 amounted to $16,033.08. In 1954, through reinvestment, the Common Fund of the society was increased to $51,743.15, making the total permanent funds of the society in all $56,895.21. The Common Fund obligations of the society are discharged by appropriations to the treasurer of the diocese for diocesan work and the scholarship income through the Bishop.

3. THE CHURCH FOUNDATION IN THE DIOCESE OF UPPER SOUTH CAROLINA

In his address to the Convention in April, 1952, Bishop Gravatt recommended very strongly the formation in the diocese of a Foundation, especially to meet the needs of parishes and missions desiring to build churches or parish houses, to assist candidates for Holy Orders, and to underwrite loans impossible to be obtained otherwise. The Bishop's recommendation was adopted and a new canon (Canon XXI) set up controlling the organization and work of the Foundation. The canon required the consideration in a certain time of the advisability of merging the Foundation with the trustees of the diocese and the Advancement Society. The first officers elected by the executive council were, besides the Bishop *ex officio* President: first vice-president, Wyndam M. Manning; second vice-president, the Rev. C. Capers Satterlee; secretary, Albert R. Simonds; treasurer, Ernest Patton. In addition, the trustees of the diocese and the treasurer of the Advancement Society were declared members of the Foundation. In addition to these, the canon provided that two clergymen and two laymen should be elected by the Convention. The next year the canon of the Foundation was revised changing the officers to be as follows (with the names of those elected at this Convention): Chairman of the Board, the Bishop ex officio; president, a layman (Mr. W. M. Manning); a senior priest of the diocese (the Rev. C. Capers Satterlee); secretary (Mr. Albert R. Simonds); treasurer (Ernest Patton); members, the Revs. W. W. Lumpkin and O. C. Zaebst, Messrs. D. S. DuBose and Walter Montgomery, also, Mr. J. N. LeMaster, Jr., as treasurer of the Advancement Society, and the trustees of the diocese. Ten thousand dollars given by Major Walter B. Moore for advancement work in the diocese, which had been held by the Advancement Society, was turned over to the Foundation. The Foundation in 1954 made its first gift of $2,500.00 to Trinity Church for a parish house, together with a loan for the same through the underwriting of the executive council, this amount being later refunded to the Foundation. Mr. David G. Ellison, Jr., succeeded Mr. Manning as president.

4. PERMANENT FUNDS

HELD BY TRUSTEES OF THE DIOCESE

Bishop's Permanent	$ 55,567.08
Theological Education	5,050.00
Pringle Frost Memorial (Theo. Education)	1,800.00
Shuler	1,150.00
St. John's, Congaree	4,700.00
Elizabeth La Borde (Diocesan Missions)	250.00
Julia R. Backman (Home in Columbia)	14,000.00
Baker (Work among Negroes)	5,020.50
Sophie P. Carroll (Missionary)	500.00
Richard I. Manning (Missionary)	10,000.00
Mountain Work	558.62
Atonement, Blacksburg	350.00
St. Paul's, Graniteville	15,074.14
Sub-Total	$114,021.23
Reserve—Gain from Sales	56,981.39
Total	$171,002.62

HELD BY THE BISHOP

Prayer Book and Tract Society	$ 8,850.00
Anna Stille (St. Anna's, Columbia)	3,427.00
Nora Zimmerman	604.62
Mary Zimmerman	604.62
Carrie Zimmerman	862.22
Honoria Z. Cates	2,039.49

Annie F. Cates 707.24
Hart Fund 2,316.98
Sulzbacker 927.83

Total ....$ 20,340.00

STATISTICS, DIOCESE OF UPPER SOUTH CAROLINA

Year	Clergymen	Communicants	Total Expenditures
1922	27	4,598	$119,677.22
1930	25	5,321	151,247.31
1940	32	6,469	127,109.44
1950	32	8,310	442,367.49
1956	50	10,655	812,899.18

Appendix IX

BIOGRAPHICAL SKETCHES OF THE BISHOPS OF THE DIOCESE OF UPPER SOUTH CAROLINA

BY AUGUSTUS T. GRAYDON, ESQ.

First Bishop, The Right Rev. Kirkman George Finlay, D.D., born October 1, 1877, consecrated, January 20, 1921, died August 27, 1938.

This sketch of the life of Bishop Finlay contains only the bare facts—as his career is the story of the diocese of Upper South Carolina in its first 17 years.

Kirkman George Finlay was born near Greenville in the heart of Piedmont, South Carolina. His father, James A. Finlay, had been sent in order to repair his health from his native Scotland to Canada. In this new land he met the daughter of an Irish officer in the British army, who had moved to Canada. The Bishop's father and Marian Ponsonby Gun were married and moved to Rice Lake, Canada, where eight of their children were born. Because of Mrs. Finlay's health, the family moved to a farm near Greenville, but the move presaged tragedy, for five of their children died soon thereafter of diphtheria. The arrival of Kirkman George in 1877 somewhat assuaged the family's grief. The youngest Finlay received his education at Professor Von Fingerlin's private school in Greenville, and he then studied at Furman University from which he received his Bachelor of Literature degree in 1899. While there he organized a Sunday School among employees of the mills recently erected in the Greenville area. Shortly after his graduation from Furman, Mr. Finlay entered the Theological Seminary of the University of the South at Sewanee, Tennessee. Here again his missionary spirit was shown when he organized a mission among the mountain folk living around the University. Even more important than this mission was an event in the summer of 1901, when he first met Miss Lucy Reed at Sewanee.

After his graduation from seminary, Mr. Finlay went to Clemson College as chaplain, and he also served charges at Pendleton, Seneca and Walhalla. In April, 1903, the romance begun at Sewanee was culminated by the marriage of Mr. Finlay and Miss Reed; the young couple, taking up their residence in the hotel at Clemson, soon became a part of campus life. In 1907, the young priest's abilities and talents were recognized when he was called to be

[742]

rector of Trinity Church, Columbia. Under his guidance, the system of rented pews was abolished in this parish and the Every-Member Canvass was instituted as the financial basis for parish support. Under his leadership a Men's Club was organized at Trinity with a resultant increased interest in the Church Home Orphanage. Under his leadership a chapter of the Woman's Auxiliary, the Daughters' of the Holy Cross, assisted in the maintenance of the tuberculosis sanitarium at Ridgewood Camp. This institution now operated by Richland County had been established by John P. Thomas, Jr., in 1914. In addition to these parochial activities, Bishop Finlay took an active leadership in civic affairs. During his rectorship at Trinity, the four Finlay children were born—Kirkman, Jr., Edward Reed, Elinor, now Mrs. Leighton Collins, and Marian, all of whom live in Columbia, except for Mrs. Collins, who resides in New York.

The abilities which made Kirkman Finlay such a success as a parish priest and community organizer were demonstrated again when the United States entered World War One. Although Trinity Parish began immediately to succor the spiritual and social needs of the soldiers at nearby Camp Jackson, the rector did not feel that this was enough. He asked the vestry for a year's leave of absence to go to France with the Y. M. C. A. of the American Expeditionary Forces. At the war's end, he returned to his parish and entered again into the life of his Church, community, state, and nation. Although he respected and followed the American constitutional precept of division of church and state, Kirkman Finlay made numerous appearances before civic and legislative groups to advocate measures which he believed promoted social justice or to oppose proposals which he felt were inimical to any group's welfare. When the decision to divide the diocese was made in 1920, it was only logical that the first diocesan of Upper South Carolina should have been this son of the Piedmont who had been so successful in a ministry of more than a quarter of a century, all within the red hills of the diocesan area which he was now to serve. His services as Bishop-Coadjutor of South Carolina began in January, 1921, and in October, 1922, he became Bishop of the new diocese. In summarizing the work of Bishop Finlay in the diocese, Bishop Albert S. Thomas of the diocese of South Carolina said in a memorial address delivered before the Diocesan Convention on January 24, 1939:

"The organization of a new diocese with the establishment of its ideals, including not merely the methods, but the spirit of its life, is no small task. It requires long and patient labor to make a diocese.

The chief responsibility must rest upon the Bishop. In the pioneer years Bishop Finlay had the assistance of able and consecrated clergymen and laymen, but upon him necessarily rested the main burden, and bravely and right well did he bear it. Both laymen and laywomen, in the momentous days in the beginning, rallied behind the Bishop; and the new diocese went forward with its work with self-sacrificing enthusiasm. The immediately succeeding years after establishment witnessed a marked expansion in the work and membership of the diocesan branch of the Woman's Auxiliary. It saw also the rise of newly organized activities among the Church schools of the diocese with the development of the Young Peoples Service League, summer camps and conferences. I need not say that the Bishop was, if not in every case the leader, yet the chief inspiration of these movements. Especially is this true in his sympathetic efforts in behalf of the Negro race, the Church's work among them in the diocese, and in his unflagging interest in behalf of Voorhees Normal and Industrial School at Denmark. We should not fail to mention that under Bishop Finlay's leadership the record of this diocese in its support of foreign and domestic missions as well as all its diocesan or joint diocesan institutions is one of which you may be justly proud."

His work among the Negroes of the diocese and his leadership in establishing and developing the summer conference center on Kanuga Lake near Hendersonville have been detailed in the chapter on his Episcopate. It was at his beloved Kanuga on August 27, 1938, that he died of a heart attack after an illness of only a few hours. From Kanuga, his body was taken to Columbia for interment in Trinity Churchyard. Thus Bishop Finlay died at the place which is today an active and living memorial to his ministry and he is buried in the yard of the Mother Church of the diocese which he formed and moulded. Between Kanuga and Trinity lies the Piedmont of South Carolina where Kirkman Finlay was born, educated, served as priest and finally as Bishop of a new diocese. This man was "Upper South Carolina".

Second Bishop, the Right Rev. John James Gravatt, D.D., born October 31, 1881, consecrated, May 5, 1939, retired, October 3, 1953.

Bishop Gravatt was born in Hampton, Virginia, the son of the Rev. John James Gravatt, D.D., rector of St. John's Church there, and the former India Wray Jones. He spent his early boyhood in this tidewater city near the mouth of Chesapeake Bay. At the age of 12 he entered McGuire's School in Richmond to which city his family had moved. He next entered the University of Virginia at Charlottesville where he received his A.B. degree in 1903. The future Bishop returned to McGuire's to teach for two years; and in the fall of 1905, he entered the Virginia Theological Seminary at Alexandria. In 1908, the young Virginian was ordained a deacon in the Seminary Chapel by Bishop Peterkin, acting for Bishop Gibson, and in the following year he became a priest in a ceremony conducted by Bishop Gibson. In his year as a deacon, he served as assistant secretary of the Church Student Missionary Association and from 1909 to 1911 as student secretary of the Board of Missions of the Episcopal Church. His parochial ministry began in 1911 when he became rector of Slaughter Parish at Rapidan in Culpepper County, in the central section of Virginia. Two years later, he became rector of the Church of the Ascension at Frankfort, Kentucky, where he served until 1918. During World War One he entered the Chaplain's Training School in Louisville and served overseas after the Armistice.

Upon his return to the United States, Mr. Gravatt became the rector of Trinity Church at Staunton, Virginia, where he was to remain until he was consecrated Bishop in 1939. On April 19, 1922, he married Miss Helen Stevens of Richmond, Virginia; Mrs. Gravatt died on December 12, 1947, in Columbia. The Gravatts had two children, Helen Stevens Gravatt, now Mrs. William J. Watt, and George Stevens Gravatt who died in infancy. In 1932 Virginia Theological Seminary conferred the honorary degree of Doctor of Divinity on him, and the same degree was conferred by the University of the South in 1939 after his election to the bishopric. On August 27, 1938, Bishop Finlay died at Kanuga and the convention to elect a new Bishop for the Diocese of Upper South Carolina met at Trinity Church, Columbia, January 10, 1939. Fourteen clergymen were nominated, and on the fourth ballot Dr. Gravatt was elected Bishop of the 17-year-old diocese.

Save for five years in Kentucky and a year in the army, Bishop Gravatt had lived entirely in Virginia—first in tidewater, then in Richmond and the foothills and finally in the mountains. But for fifteen years he was to devote his life and ministry to the Piedmont area of South Carolina. The Bishop-elect attended his first diocesan Convention on January 24, 1939, at Christ Church, Greenville, as a special guest. On May 5, 1939, in Trinity Church, John J. Gravatt was consecrated as second Bishop of the diocese of Upper South Carolina. The master of ceremonies for the Consecration was the Rev. A. Rufus Morgan of Columbia, and the presiding Bishop, the

Rt. Rev. Henry St. G. Tucker, was the Consecrator. The new Bishop's uncle, Bishop William Loyall Gravatt, retired, of West Virginia, and Bishop Robert C. Jett of Southwestern Virginia, were co-consecrators. The sermon was preached by Bishop Robert E. L. Strider of West Virginia. The Coadjutor of Virginia, Bishop Frederick D. Goodwin, and Bishop Middleton S. Barnwell of Georgia read the Epistle and the Gospel. Bishop Henry D. Phillips read the Litany, and the consent of the Bishops was read by Bishop William Brown of Southern Virginia. The Rt. Rev. Thomas C. Darst of East Carolina and the Rt. Rev. Albert S. Thomas of South Carolina were the presentors. The new Bishop and Mrs. Gravatt and their daughter had moved to Columbia to make their home. His offices were in Trinity Parish House.

As the Bishop he became president of the trustees of the Protestant Episcopal Church in Upper South Carolina, president of the Society for Advancement of Christianity in Upper South Carolina, vice-president and later president of the Church Home Orphanage at York; president of the diocesan convention, and later president of the Voorhees School and a trustee of the University of the South at Sewanee, Tennessee. Bishop Gravatt attended his first Convention as Bishop January 23-24, 1940, in Trinity Church, Columbia. The diocesan work of Bishop Gravatt is covered in the textual account of his Episcopate. At the Convention held in Spartanburg, April 22-23, 1952, Bishop Gravatt announced that he would retire in accordance with the canon on October 3, 1953, his 72nd birthday. He presided over the Convention which elected his successor at Trinity Church, Columbia, May 11-12, 1953, and shortly after his retirement, he and his daughter moved to the Bishop's farm and county seat near Natural Bridge, Virginia. He has visited the diocese frequently since that time.

Third Bishop, the Right Rev. Clarence Alfred Cole, D.D., born June 15, 1909, consecrated October 20, 1953.

Clarence Alfred Cole was born in Washington, D. C., the son of Carl Adams Cole and Blanche Margaret Mack Cole. The future Bishop was educated in the public schools of the District of Columbia and was graduated in 1930 from Benjamin Franklin University there with the degree of Bachelor of Commercial Science. He then entered Duke University at Durham, North Carolina, from which he obtained his Bachelor of Arts degree three years later. The postulant of Bishop Freeman of Washington became a candidate for the priesthood when he enrolled in the School of Theology of the University of the South at Sewanee, Tennessee, in the fall of 1933. He received his Bachelor of Divinity degree from Sewanee in June, 1936. He was first assigned to the diocese of South Carolina as assistant rector of Grace Church, Charleston, under Dr. William Way, D.D. He was ordained priest by Bishop Thomas in Grace Church. During his last year in Charleston (1938), he taught at Porter Military Academy for a semester. On June 1, 1938, Mr. Cole married Miss Catharine Tate Powe of Durham, North Carolina. They have six children: Clarence Alfred, Jr., Ellerbe Powe, Catharine Powe, Carl Adams, Laura Markham and Elizabeth Mack.

From 1938 until 1941, he was rector of St. Stephen's Church, Oxford, North Carolina, and priest-in-charge of St. Peter's Church, Stovall; Holy Trinity Church, Townsville and St. Mark's Church, Roxboro. In 1941, he became rector of St. Martin's Church, Charlotte, where he did most of his work as a parish priest and spiritual leader of a growing congregation. He remained in Charlotte until 1952 when he accepted a call to become rector of St. John's Church, Charleston, West Virginia. He was elected Bishop of Upper South Carolina on March 11, 1953, only a little more than a year after he became rector of West Virginia's largest parish. His Consecration as Bishop took place in Trinity Church, Columbia, on October 20, 1953, with Bishop Edwin A. Penick of North Carolina as Consecrator and Bishop Gravatt, retired diocesan of Upper South Carolina, and Bishop Carruthers of South Carolina as co-consecrators. Bishop Robert Edward Lee Strider of West Virginia was preacher, and Bishop Thomas Henry Wright of Eastern Carolina was the litanist. The Epistle was read by Bishop Matthew George Henry of Western North Carolina and Bishop Middleton Stuart Barnwell of Georgia read the Gospel. Since coming to Upper South Carolina, Bishop Cole and his family have lived in the Bishop's official residence on Heathwood Circle in Columbia. He maintained his offices at first in Trinity Parish House where the Bishop's office had been located since 1925, but in 1955, he moved the diocesan headquarters to the Security Federal Building, 1231 Washington Street, in the heart of downtown Columbia.

Appendix X-XII—*Joint Ownership and Control*

Appendix X—*The Church Homes*

1. FOR WOMEN, CHARLESTON AND FOR CHILDREN, YORK

It was over one hundred years ago that devout souls in the diocese, being then the State of South Carolina, conceived the idea of an institution which would find its life in the doing of that duty which our Blessed Lord admonished concerning "one of the least of these". In Bishop Gadsden's Journal there is an entry that on April 15, 1850, being Tuesday in Holy Week, he took part in the exercises connected with the opening of the Church Home in Charleston. It was a great day. A large congregation had assembled in St. Stephen's Chapel on Anson Street to take part in the special services set forth by the Bishop. Morning Prayer was read by Rev. Edwin A. Wagner, deacon, minister of the Church of the Holy Communion, the Ante-Communion was said by Rev. Cranmore Wallace, minister of St. Stephen's Chapel, and chaplain of the Home, and an address was delivered by Rev. Thomas John Young, assistant at St. Michael's and vice-president of the council of the Home, and leader in the founding of the Home. He begain his address with these words, "It has pleased God to reveal Himself to us as 'a Father of the fatherless, a Judge of the widows' and a 'Deliverer of the poor and needy': and our blessed Lord has so identified Himself with the destitute and afflicted of His mystical Body, the Church, that he has declared that the most trifling kindness shown to them, to be a favor conferred upon Himself. 'Inasmuch as ye have done it unto one of the least of these my brethren ye have done it unto me.'" He saw in the occasion "the dawning of a brighter day—the beginning of a good work which, growing and spreading from day to day and from year to year would make the Church, in her every branch, what she was in the beginning—the home of the destitute, the comforter of the poor and the afflicted. 'There ariseth a little cloud out of the sea, like a man's hand.'" He saw in the little cloud the good hope of the success of the work. Mr. Young's prophetic words under God's blessing are fulfilled, as today we see the little cloud grown large and, after one hundred

[748]

years, the Home fulfilling its mission in two institutions, one for children and one for adults. After the exercises in the chapel, the company adjourned to the handsome old mansion at 55 Laurens Street which had been acquired for the residence of the Home. As they entered the house, the choir chanted the angelic anthem "Glory to God in the Highest and on earth peace, good will to men". The Bishop then said "Peace be to this house and to all that dwell in it". The first words as they entered were these words of adoration, confession, thanksgiving, and supplication for the Divine favor for this and like institutions. After these devotions, Rev. Cranmore Wallace, the chief founder of the Home, made an address. So was the work launched on its way as distinctly a religious institution and this character it has maintained for all these years.

While this was the beginning of the Home. in actuality, some five years before, it had been conceived in the mind of that devoted missionary, Rev. Thomas C. Dupont who was then minister-in-charge of St. Stephen's Chapel. The care of four helpless little ones had been thrust upon him, and this it was which brought to him the conviction that the Church had too long neglected a solemn duty. He was assisted in his efforts by some faithful women, notably Mrs. Benjamin D. Roper. However, he passed to his reward, and Mrs. Roper, too, without seeing any tangible fruit of their efforts, but a beginning had been made and a small sum, which he had collected for the purpose of founding a Home, was left bearing a silent witness. It was from the shoulders of Thomas C. DuPont then that the mantle fell upon Cranmore Wallace. However, had it not been for the support of Mr. Young, assistant of St. Michael's, by whose efforts chiefly the necessary funds were supplied, the Home could never have been started. Let us then divide the honors—DuPont, Wallace, Young—these were the founders of the Home. It is worthy of note that of the first seven laymen on the council six were from St. Michael's Church. These men had always the sympathy and encouragement of that great man of God, our fourth Bishop, Christopher Edwards Gadsden, being president *ex officio*. This was doubtless needed; Mr. Wallace testifies that the work was begun not without opposition, sometimes "contemptuous and bitter." It was at first planned to rent a house for the Home near St. Stephen's Chapel but a legacy of $2,000.00 from Mr. Boisseau of New York, with the prospects of other large gifts determined the decision to buy the handsome residence of James Jervey, Esq., in Laurens Street. This was done for $11,000.00. which with $1,000.00 for repairs made the cost $12,000.00. All except $4,000.00 was soon paid, the balance secured by mortgage. In the carefully prepared "fundamental rules" it was stated that the objects of the Home were threefold—to provide a retreat for deserving females, called "beneficiaries" who would find work to do, and care for the younger members of the household; second, to provide a support for orphan girls and to train them and provide for them secular and religious education; and thirdly, to provide a corps of visitors for the sick and poor. These last were called "associates". This feature of the Home seems not to have proven successful. All inmates of the Home thus were to be females. The experience of the early days as stated by Mr. Wallace in his first annual report was that also of later years, it is difficult to maintain adults and children in the same home. But it was done for a time.

The Home was governed by a council consisting of a president (the Bishop ex-officio), a vice-president and twelve trustees. There was to be a secretary and a treasurer, a chaplain who was superintendent also, and a lady superintendent. There were to be patrons at $500.00, life members at $50.00, and subscribers at $10.00 per year. On the opening day there were received into the Home eleven children, two adult beneficiaries, two resident associates, and a lady superintendent—sixteen in all. The resident associates paid $75.00 per year and seven of the girls had the same amount paid for them. The lady superintendent required only that her expenses be paid. Thus there were no salaries to be paid. It was estimated at first that it took $1,200.00 to operate the Home for a year. Mrs. M. C. Hentz was the first lady superintendent. She was succeeded after a few months by Miss Sarah Brailsford and, in 1853, Mrs. Anna Wilson became the third lady superintendent. There were morning and evening devotions in the Home and all inmates attended daily service at St. Stephen's. The children attended a school connected with this chapel. At the third anniversary celebration (these by rule being held on St. Barnabas' Day) the deaths of both the president, Bishop Gadsden, and the vice-president, Mr. Young, were reported with sorrow. The Rev. Dr. Christian Hanckel filled out Mr. Young's term as vice-president. The Rev. P. T. Keith then succeeded. In 1853 a charter was obtained for the Home from the Legislature. The Rev. Thomas F. Davis, D.D., Bishop-elect, preached the sermon on the third anniversary ending with these words: "Who shall say, that this institution shall not yet, furnish a rich harvest of souls, and future daughters of the Church rise up to call us blessed? To bless, is God's. It is ours to *work*. With Him, be the issue. With us the prayers, the duty and the faithfulness". Here is a voice from the past to us today.

In 1854 a dairy was added and a partial heating system installed in the Home. In 1855 the remaining debt on the Home through the generosity of friends was paid in full. In this year the title "chaplain" was changed to "rector". Mention should be made of the pyhsician who gave his services freely for many years, Dr. Francis Peyre Porcher (and others too as consultants) as well as the druggists, Drs. Stoney and Wiltburger who furnished medicines free, to say nothing of the solicitors like B. D. Roper, Jr., Esq., who gave their services without charge. In 1858 the total number of inmates of the Home was 38 as compared with 16 at the beginning, and the annual expenses about $4,000.00 as compared with $1,200.00 at first. During these years there was always a struggle for funds. After fiftten years the Home reached the first turning point in its history. After the war in 1865 in the demoralization of the day the children in the Home were all transferred to the Orphan House in Charleston and then for nearly thirty years the building on Laurens Street was filled with elderly ladies only. These were rather uneventful years. During the latter part of this time Rev. Dr. Robert Wilson of St. Luke's Church was rector. He resigned in 1893 and was succeeded by Rev. A. E. Cornish. We reach here the second turning point in our history.

In the meantime, there had arisen in Charleston another institution of Christian kindness, the work of faithful women of the Church. It was called the House of Rest, and was founded by Miss Emma Jane Wayne, and Miss Celia Campbell, who "gave generously of their fortunes as also their time, and even their lives to this charity." Dr. A. T. Porter was the chaplain and chief patron. Miss Mary E. Sass, writing to Rev. T. T. Walsh says, "It was a temporary resting place for women, who discharged from the City Hospital and still not fit to work, could be cared for there until strong, and there must have been hundreds, who under that roof, were blessed with this tender care". Latterly there were more children under this friendly roof than adults. The House of Rest occupied the building on the southwest corner of Spring Street and Ashley Avenue, later occupied by the Home. In 1894, just twenty years after its begininng, the faithful matron, Miss Wayne, had worn herself out in service, and then too the Rev. Dr. A. T. Porter who had always been the chaplain of the House of Rest, retired in favor of the Rev. A. E. Cornish. So Mr. Cornish, suddenly as were, found both the Home and the House of Rest, institutions with similar purposes, on his hands. Fortunate it was that the responsibilities were his. Mr. Cornish ranks as one of the great missionaries of the Church in South Carolina. We must put him in the class of those men who contributed most to the building up of the Church in this state, like Andrew Fowler, in the earlier days, John D. McCollough in the up-country, Alexander R. Mitchell, all over the state, and some others perhaps just as great. The second turning point in the history of the Home was marked by the merging of these two institutions in 1896 under Mr. Cornish, with the name of "The Church Home and Orphanage". The building of the House of Rest at the corner of Ashley Avenue and Spring Street became its dwelling place, the Home paying a small remaining mortgage on this property. It was conveyed by the House of Rest to the Home in 1897. The old house at 55 Laurens Street was still for a time occupied by a few ladies. It was under the care of Miss Dismukes. The building was sold soon after 1901 for $2,500.00, and the ladies were settled at 67 Anson Street. This new beginning was on St. James' Day, 1896, when Dr. Porter and Mr. Cornish held a celebration of the Holy Communion in the chapel of the Church Home and Orphanage. Miss Sophie LaBorde of Columbia, who had been matron of the House of Rest, assumed charge under Mr. Cornish, with forty-five children and a very few adults, if any. Thus at this second turning point the emphasis returned to work among children; under the new régime boys were cared for as well as girls. Mr. A. F. deJersey was treasurer as well as a great friend of the Home at this time. It was at this time that the practice of giving the Thanksgiving Offering to the Home was adopted throughout the diocese. Through the efforts of the Ascension Guild of St. Michael's Church a day school was conducted for the children of the Home at this time.

This change in the life of the Home was generally coeval with a change in the Episcopate in the diocese. Bishop Howe died in 1894, Bishop Capers having been elected in July, 1893. Bishop Capers from the first took a loving interest in the Home in Charleston and he it was who engineered the merger of the Church Home and the House of Rest. At the annual Convention held in the Church of the Holy Communion in 1898, in his address, we find him exhorting the members of that body in behalf of the board of managers and the matron to "visit and inspect this most worthy Church Charity" located only a few steps from the Church. He said, "Your Bishop, brethren, feels a deep interest in its success, and must look to the parishes and missions to aid him in building up an institution than which no other institution of the diocese pleads so tenderly with us in behalf of the little ones whom God in his providence has entrusted to our care." He constantly urged the formation of orphanage associations over the diocese which was largely done. The general interest in the Home in the diocese is shown in a single report in 1898 which showed help from "the Mizpah Circle", the Cheraw "Sunbeams", "the pupils of Miss Sass's Class", the "Ascension Guild", Cake, Mrs. John Kershaw, "The Union Branch of the Orphanage Associations" the "Florence Sewing Society". We see that though not yet legally or canonically a diocesan institution the Home had practically become so. Important additions were made to the Home in 1903—an infirmary, and two large rooms, but the quarters were cramped with 50 children. The beloved Miss Sophie LaBorde retired as matron after eight years of faithful service. She found forty-five when she took charge and left fifty-five when she retired in 1904. She was succeeded by Miss M. A. DeLorme who served for two years. Mr. Cornish resigned as chaplain in 1905 and was succeeded by the Rev. A. E. Evison. The year 1906 was notable because it was then that Miss Mary Trapier Gadsden, at this time preparing for the mission field in the New York Training School for Deaconesses, was called to fill the position of deaconess-in-charge of the Orphanage. On Mr. Evison's resignation in 1908 she became superintendent. Two rectors of the Church of the Holy Communion succeeded as chaplains, the Rev. H. J. Mikell, afterwards Bishop of Atlanta, and the Rev. F. H. Harding who served until the orphanage department was removed from Charleston. In 1908 also, Deaconess Evelyn Wile, another graduate of the New York Training School, came as House Mother and served as Deaconess Gadsden's assistant for years. Thus the Orphanage was in the capable hands of trained workers. Miss Dismukes continued as matron of the Ladies' Department. In the Diocesan Convention of 1906, a committee appointed the year before with Rev. W. P. Witsell, rector of the Church of the Good Shepherd, Columbia, as chairman, recommended that the diocese take over and assume entire responsibility for the Church Home Orphanage. Later a canon was adopted providing for the election of twelve trustees with the Bishop as *Ex-officio* chairman for the government of the Home— eight for the Church Home Orphanage, and four for the corporation of the "Home". The first trustees for the diocese were: The Rev. Messrs. O. T. Porcher, A. S. Thomas, W. P. Witsell, and

Messrs. A. M. Lee, Thomas Pinckney, H. P. Duvall, R. I. Mannning, and P. T. Hayne.

By 1908, it began to be realized very keenly that the quarters of the Home on Ashley Avenue were too cramped and realized also that adults and children could not well be cared for in the same building, so consideration became serious concerning the removal of the Orphanage department. Some time before this a ten-acre lot south of Hampton Park had been purchased for the purpose but now ideas of greater changes arose, and a committee was appointed to consider the question. At the Convention of this year it was decided in accordance with the action of the trustees and on the strong recommendation of Bishop Guerry who had now succeeded Bishop Capers after the latter's deplored death, that the principal building at the proposed new Home be a memorial to Bishop Capers. The movement came to a climax on November 20, 1908, and so we now arrive at the third great turning point in our history. A committee consisting Hon. R. I. Manning and the Rev. O. T. Porcher, after visiting many towns that had given invitations and made offers, reported to the trustees in favor of the City of Yorkville with its offer of the old King's Mountain Military Academy and 11 acres of land. In addition that noble and generous hearted churchman of Yorkville, Mr. W. B. Moore, agreed to donate $4,000.00 for endowment; which afterwards proved to be just a beginning for him. The City Council offered free lights, water, and sewerage; physicians also offering free services and there was the possibility of acquiring 25 or 30 additional acres of land at a moderate price. The report of the committee was accepted. The additional land was immediately purchased and the children were moved to their new Home arriving May 13, 1909. After getting in some degree settled in the new Home, Deaconess Gadsden wrote "It is all so beautiful. We feel we ought to sing, more than ever, heartfelt praises to the Heavenly Father, who has given us so many blessings." She said Mr. Moore had accomplished wonders—plumbing almost completed, larder filled. Indeed, Major Moore was a man sent by God, as he proved more and more. He became treasurer of the Orphanage immediately after the move. Capt. M. C. Willis supervised the farm, Rev. T. T. Walsh, rector of the Good Shepherd, was chaplain. In making its report to the Convention the trustees were careful to state that full care for the continuation of a Home in Charleston would be taken. They stated, "It is the desire of the trustees to make the Home for the old ladies of the Church as attractive and well-conducted as the Orphanage department of the Institution".

On November 23, 1909, a meeting of a special committee to take charge of the Ladies' Home was held in St. Michael's Parish House to make plans for the care of the Home in Charleston. The old ladies were moved from 67 Anson Street to the Ashley Avenue Home. For the present only lodging was to be furnished; there was a common sitting room but no common dining room. Mr. R. I. Manning resigned from the committee and Mrs. James Conner, widow of General Conner, was elected in the place leaving the committee with the Bishop to consist of Messrs. Thomas Pinckney, A. M. Lee, and Mrs. Conner. Miss Helen Lee was added as secretary. By action of the Convention, Good Friday was established as the day for a stated offering for the Old Ladies' Home This was changed to Mother's Day a few years ago. In 1910 the Convention took steps to raise $10,000.00 for a memorial to Bishop Capers to take the form of a double cottage at the Home in Yorkville. Just a year later, the day before the meeting of the diocesan Convention in the Good Shepherd, Yorkville, the cornerstone of the Bishop Capers Cottage was laid by Bishop Guerry. In 1912 Mrs. Augustus S. Jones gave to the Orphanage the cottage in memory of her mother—called the Elizabeth Evans Martin Memorial Cottage. It was finished and dedicated December 19, 1911. It was the babies' cottage and was finished before the Capers' Cottage. With the latter there are now seven cottages— two Caper's Memorial Homes (Bishop Capers and General Capers), the Martin Home, the Gadsden, Pinckney, Heyward, and Moore Homes. On June 13, 1913, there were 100 children in the Homes. It was in this year that a printery was established with first Mr. C. H. Prince, then Mr. J. P. Booker in charge. Mr. W. B. Moore, Jr., and the chaplain, Rev. T. T. Walsh, assisted with the printery. A brick building was built for the printery. It published both the *Diocese* and the *Reminder* for a while but soon discontinued printing the former. The latter began publication June 20, 1914. Mrs. W. B. Moore with Mrs. R. T. Allison, as chairman of a committee of Yorkville ladies, beautified the grounds. It would be impossible to name the benfactors of the Home in these days, but perhaps I should mention the Men's Orphanage Associations of Spartanburg and Greenville, and the Twelve Times a Year Circle of St. Michael's, Charleston. Frequently, however, the deaconess found her larder almost empty and bills to pay as witnessed by her urgent appeal of September, 1914. We should not fail to mention the devoted and free medical services of Dr. R. A. Bratton and Dr. A. Y. Cartwright as dentist as well as other doctors. Deaconess Evelyn Wile after long and faithful service departed from the Home in February, 1913.

Bishop Guerry was very earnest in his efforts to make the diocese realize its equal responsibility for the Home in Charleston, constantly emphasizing the Good Friday Offering. Mrs. James Conner, chairman of the Board of Managers in Charleston, deplored the lack of interest in this Home ouside of Charleson. In 1911 the building on Ashley Avenue was legally made over to the Home for Ladies as the equivalent of the McBurney legacy which belonged to the Ladies' Home. It was improved by the churches in Charleston. Most of the rooms in the Home had been renovated. By this time a common dining room had been inaugurated. The matrons in these days were first Mrs. McLure, then Mrs. Brown. The house was badly damaged by the storm of August, 1911. There were 11 inmates in 1912. It was reported at this time that this Home was largely supported by St. Michael's, Grace, and St. Luke's churches. Maj. Walter Bedford Moore, who might well be called the second founder of the Orphanage, resigned as treasurer in 1917 and was succeeded by Capt. M. C. Willis. Maj. Moore, however, retained the treasureship of the permanent funds. the deaconess said about this time "What the Home now is W. B. Moore has by his energy and generous devotion made it. . . . He has been its inspiration and untiring benefactor". Deaconess Gadsden after twelve years of consecrated and successful service resigned the next year, 1918. She took charge of 31 children in their contracted quarters in Charleston in 1906 and left a total population of about 125 persons in York twelve years later. Capt. M. C. Willis was elected manager and treasurer in 1919. He continued until the coming of one in 1920 who was for years to come to dedicate himself unreservedly to the work of superintendent of this Institution, the Rev. Thomas P. Noe. He was also chaplain. For years the work centered about him and his life centered about it, in love for the children committed to his care. His name became a household word in both dioceses. In the year 1922 the Orphanage received a notable legacy of $10,000.00 to endow two scholarships for the Elizabeth Evans Martin Cottage by the donor of that cottage, Mrs. Elizabeth Martin Jones. It was about this time also Maj. Moore gave the rectory, known as the Moore Cottage. This released the Pinckney Cottage for children, increasing the Orphanage's capacity to 125 children.

In 1917 Miss E. H. Dunkin became the treasurer of the Church Home in Charleston, serving until 1922 when she was succeeded by Miss Clare Jervey who in turn was succeded by Miss Emma McCabe. In 1923 Miss Clara A. Fishburne became matron of this Home. Mrs. James Conner was chairman of the local board from the departure of the Orphanage in 1909 until 1928 when after the many years of noble service she departed this life. She was succeeded by Mrs. Joseph Maybank. Early in 1928, the Ladies Home was the recipient of a princely gift for a new Home—the handsome building at the corner of Ashley Avenue and Bee Street, known as the old Mercy Hospital, by William King McDowell. The old Home was sold, the proceeds being used mostly for the remodelling of the new Home where the ladies were soon settled in comfort. The Home in Charleston while under the common trustees was governed by a local board of managers with a chairman together with an executive committee, all elected by the trustees. In the death of Bishop Guerry in 1928 both Homes lost a true, able, and constant friend. In 1928 Right Rev. K. G. Finlay, who had been vice-president of the Home since he became Bishop of the diocese of Upper South Carolina in 1922, became president and Rt. Rev. A. S. Thomas of the diocese of South Carolina, vice-president. The Gadsden Home is on property acquired in 1923. The house was remodeled and made into a cottage for boys in memory of the deaconess. In 1926 the Orphanage for the first time began to share in the munificent foundation of Mr. J. B. Duke of North Carolina. The yearly contributions from this fund have been of very great assistance in the maintenance of this institution and is greatly appreciated. The farm from the first, especially the dairy department, has been a great source of well-being at this Home. That splendid and self-sacrificing friend, Capt. M. C. Willis, helped greatly here as in many other ways. It is impossible to give anything like a complete list of the agencies that have helped the Homes— first the Dioceses of course, then the Church schools, the Y.P.S.L., the guilds, the associations, and, to an incalculable extent, the Woman's Auxiliary of the two dioceses.

In 1938 the Home was called to mourn the loss by death of one of its greatest officers, the Rt. Rev. Kirkman George Finlay. He was the friend of everyone in the Home from the smallest child to every worker, taking always a deep and loving interest in the cause. Bishop Thomas succeeded at this time as president and Bishop John J. Gravatt, vice-president. It was in this year that a

gift of funds from Rev. O. T. Porcher and family for the erection
of a chapel, to be called the Good Shepherd, was received. It was
consecrated on April 3, 1940, by Bishops Gravatt and Thomas,
assisted by Mr. Noe. Thus was supplied a supreme need of the
Home. At the same time Bishop Thomas consecrated the memorial
windows in it: Triple windows of the chancel to Governor R. I.
Manning by Mrs. Manning; single windows to Mr. and Mrs.
Charles Stevens by Col. and Mrs. Wyndham M. Manning; Mrs.
Carl H. Hart by Mr. Hart; Miss Caroline Louisa Price by Rev.
and Mrs. T. P. Noe; R. B. Heyward by Mrs. B. H. Heyward;
Frank T. Carwile by Mr. W. E. Carwile; Mrs. J. J. Pringle by
Holy Cross Chapter, Trinity, Columbia; Miss Virginia Taylor
Singleton, by Mrs. Alex E. King; Robert Augustus Hart by Mrs.
Nellie Hart French; and also windows in appreciation of Deaconess
Gadsden and the Rev. Octavius Theodore Porcher by the Home.
After the services under the Gadsden Oak on Pilgrimage Day on
May 18, 1941, a beautiful altar, given by the Woman's Auxiliary
of the Diocese of Upper South Carolina, and dedicated to the
honor of the Rev. Thomas P. Noe, was consecrated in the chapel.

After ten years of faithful service as matron of the Home in
Charleston, Miss. Clara A. Fishburne retired in 1933, being succeeded most acceptably by Miss Mae Brown until 1943. Mrs.
Munn then served for a brief period. In 1943 the trustees were
fortunate in securing the services of Mrs. Ruth A. Carpenter who
continued most acceptably as matron until 1948. Then for a
short time followed Mrs. Ruddoch, and later Mrs. Celia Semkin.
Life at the Home during these years has been rather uneventful
except for those recurring sad experiences when the elderly ladies
have passed to their better Home. Certainly it is a good work for
the Church to supply a comfortable dwelling place for the latter
days of those who else would be more or less wanderers in this
world. Miss Marie Heyward was chairman of the local board from
Mrs. Maybank's death in 1935 until 1943 when she was followed
by the present incumbent, Mrs. Thomas P. Stoney. Miss McCabe's
retirement as treasurer in 1942 involved not only the loss of an
efficient financier but one who personally watched over the Home
with loving care. She was succeeded by the present treasurer, Mr.
J. E. Stelling. The Rev. Harold Thomas continued as chaplain of
this Home holding regular services and acting as pastor for some
twenty-five years until he left Charleston for Chester in 1947. About
1945 a complete modern fire alarm system was installed, and, in
1947, the cottage in the rear of the main building of the Home was

completely renovated for an infirmary, and while it was found not practical to use it for this purpose, this work materially increased the capacity of the Home. Also the heating plant was completely overhauled at this time and the building weatherstripped. A practical nurse is now employed in the Home giving most needed service and one of the residents, Mrs. Etta Hamilton performs the duties of secretary. This Home received in 1946 $1,500.00 from the reconstruction fund of each of the two dioceses. Mrs. Carpenter resumed as matron in 1952. In 1957 the trustees began steps for the erection of a chapel where the *porte cochere* now stands, an initial gift of $1,000.00 was given as a memorial to Miss Eleanor Bellinger Taft and her brother, Lewis Spring Taft.

The Consecration of the chapel at the Home in York in 1940 was soon followed by Mr. Noe's resignation after serving twenty years. During these years he baptized 187 children and presented 255 for confirmation. The children loved him as a father. Among his manifold, and one of his best services, was that he kept the Home out of debt during the hard years of the depression when income was reduced, and left it possible to have a forward movement later. It was on October 4, 1940, that Mr. F. D. MacLean was elected superintendent with Mrs. MacLean as assistant superintendent. I need not dwell now on the fine work of Mr. and Mrs. MacLean. I need only say, *circumspice*. Mr. Moore resigned as treasurer of the permanent funds in 1944 and was succeeded by Mr. Carl H. Hart who had been his assistant, for some years. Mr. Hart retired in favor of Mr. W. Bedford Moore, Jr., who had from the time of the founding of the printery been one of the Home's constant helpers. In 1941 a great campaign for funds to repair, modernize, and improve all the properties which had much depreciated during the years of depression was inaugurated by authority of the two Conventions. While not completely successful this campaign led by Rev. R. T. Phillips and Col. W. M. Manning resulted in the raising of $40,000.00. We can only list what Mr. MacLean was enabled to do largely with this money—new farm cottage, new barns, new farm equipment, new milk room with equipment, new laundry equipment, new furnaces in all cottages except Gadsden, new refrigerators and electric stoves in all cottages, many ceilings repaired, new cannery. I should mention also the later complete remodelling of Heyward Cottage by the Men's Club of Trinity Church, Columbia, and also the complete repair of Moore Hall, the main building, by Mrs. Joseph E. Hart and W. Bedford Moore, Jr., and last but not least the successful work of the 4-H Club plan. Since the first, the domain of the Home here has ben increased from 11 acres to 87 and nine-tenths acres. The rectory or Moore Cottage was destroyed by fire about New Year's, 1942. It was soon rebuilt with insurance and help of Miss Susan Guignard and Rhett Hartin. The Rev. S. C. Y. Sturrup, W. C. Cravner, and C. E. Robinson have been the chaplains since the coming of a layman as superintendent. The chaplain at present is Mr. Robinson. In 1944, the permanent funds of this Home were placed in the trust department of the South Carolina National Bank.

We come now to relate the sad event of the death of Maj. Walter Bedford Moore and his beloved wife. His occurred on March 12, 1947, and hers shortly after on Easter Day, April 6, so in death they were not divided. I cannot now even list the benefactions to this Home of these noble servants of the Lord. The beauty of Maj. Moore's benefactions was that they were never merely of his bank account but of his heart—he loved, he served, he gave. May light perpetual shine upon both of these who now are numbered with the saints in life everlasting. There has often been some confusion as to the correct name of the institution whose history we have related. This is rather natural in view of the deliberate adoption of changes from time to time. Until the merging with the House of Rest, it was called simply "The Home", and then it was called "The Church Home and Orphanage". When the institution was taken over by the diocese in 1906, it was renamed "The Church Home Orphanage". Until recently this was the correct name as the canon showed, however in practice the title had varied as *e.g.* in Charleston, the home there was called "The Diocesan Home" and here the "Orphanage" or simply "The Church Home". Let me now conclude this history by merely stating another change in name and this brings us to the fourth and last turning point in the history of the united homes for children and for ladies. In 1948 by canonical action of each of the two dioceses, the Homes were separated in their trustees and government and given each a new name; one "The Episcopal Church Home for Children", and the other "The Episcopal Church Home for Women". This degree of separation was logically in keeping with the judgment of Rev. Cranmore Wallace expressed in 1852, and according to the experience of after years. It would seem not necessary to undertake to even mention the many improvements in the Home in more recent years under the superintendent, Mr. F. D. MacLean with the valuable assistance of his wife. These are evident before our eyes. Mr. MacLean resigned, much to the regret of all the friends of the Home, in 1957. Recent large accomplishments at the Home in York were the renovation of Pinckney Cottage by the West Charleston District of the Auxiliary of the diocese of South Carolina and the building of a fine new Gadsden Cottage for boys. "The Christmas Tree Club," inaugurated by W. E. Duvall of Cheraw, has raised large supplemental funds for the Church Home. Joseph E. Hart, Jr., has headed the club in recent years.

2. CLERGY HOUSE, SALUDA, N. C.

"The Clergy House Association was formed to provide a restful vacation home in a healthful, beautiful village with a high, cool climate for those of the Clergy of the Church and their families who need the change from work and climate." This inter-diocesan association "came into being as a result of sundry gatherings of Church people at Saluda during the summer of 1893. On September 26, 1893, the first steps were taken and the organization begun by the election of Dr. Frank L. Frost, Charleston, S. C., as president; Hon. R. I. Manning, Sumter, S. C., vice-president; the Rev. William Stanley Barrows of Asheville, N. C., as treasurer; and Dr. E. B. Goelet of Saluda, N. C., as secretary. At a later meeting, the Rev. E. N. Joyner was made vice-president. These four were authorized and instructed to draw up the proper papers and to act as the incorporators." On November 16, 1893, a meeting was held and the Articles of Agreement accepted and the charter applied for. On March 26, 1894, the incorporators ratified the charter, which is a part of the minutes of the association. The Woman's Auxiliary Board was formed at the first meeting, with Miss Hattie E. Howe of Charleston, S. C., Miss S. P. Carroll of Columbia, S. C., Mrs. Thomas W. Patton of Asheville, and Miss C. D. Dawson of Greenville, S. C., as members.

"Six and three-fourths acres of land, lying between Louisiana Avenue and Laurel Run Road, on the eastern boundary of Saluda, were purchased. This land has been laid off into eleven lots with a board avenue through the center. . . . The association stands ready to donate any lot to the diocese, parish, or clergyman who will, within twelve months after such donation, erect thereon a building not to cost less than $750.00, and to be approved by the building committee of the association, to be used only in accordance with the regulations of the association." (Extracts from Handbook of the association published in 1910 where will be found the by-laws of the association and of the trustees. Copy in Archives of diocese of S. C.)

In 1898, the association entertained a clergyman in a rented cottage. It then, in 1901, erected a building and from then on had guests regularly. In 1908, the diocese of South Carolina erected a clergy cottage, which since that time has been occupied generally by clergymen in the summer, usually for a month. In 1910, the diocese of Georgia purchased the building erected by the Association and has used it since. The Woman's Auxiliary of the association has always been of great value in this work. In 1911, the president was the Rev. E. N. Joyner; vice-president, Hon. R. I. Manning; treasurer, Miss Hattie E. Howe, Charleston, S. C.; secretary, Mr. J. Frank Wilkes, Charlotte, N. C. Honorary trustees were the Bishops of the province, and 40 trustees, representatives of the associated dioceses. The Woman's Auxiliary members in 1910 were: Mrs. Henry H. McKee, Miss Hattie E. Howe, Mrs. Frank Doremus, and Mrs. R. Lockwood Jones, who was succeeded as secretary by Mrs. H. P. Locke of Saluda, who for many years literally took care of this enterprise. The association has always been closely associated with the Church of the Transfiguration in Saluda; many of its guests have officiated *locum-tenens* for the Church. The officers of the association in 1922 were the Rev. Alfred R. Berkeley, president; the Rev. Matthew Brewster, vice-president; Rev. Mr. White of Florida, treasurer; and Dr. Smith of Spartanburg, secretary. After the division of the diocese of South Carolina, the two Bishops cooperated in the assignment of guests for the South Carolina House—the requests for use came mostly from clergy of the old diocese. The Woman's Auxiliary of this diocese for many years has made an appropriation for the upkeep of the House. About 1940, a new roof was put on the House, chiefly with funds appropriated by the Advancement Society of the diocese of South Carolina under Bishop Thomas. The association continues its beneficent work.

Appendix XI—*Schools*

1. PORTER MILITARY ACADEMY

The first step toward this famous institution, it may be said, was taken when in 1856 the Rev. A. T. Porter, who had taken charge of the Church of the Holy Communion when he was ordered deacon on May 16, 1854, purchased a lot adjoining the Church, giving his personal bond for $1,400.00. In three years, with the help of the Sewing Society of the Holy Communion, the lot was paid for and in June, 1859, a contract to build a schoolhouse for $6,400.00 was made with Walter Cade. Mrs. G. A. Trenholm gave $1,000.00, and $5,000.00 was borrowed. During the war period, the rector was absent on duty in the Army from time to time. On October 25, 1864, Mr. T. D. Wagner gave Dr. Porter a check, paying all indebtedness on the schoolhouse as well as on the Church. After the war, Dr. Porter, at the request of Bishop Davis, went North and raised considerable funds for the Diocesan Seminary and the Freedman's School at the old Marine Hospital on Franklin Street.

The wonderful story of the Porter Military Academy is to be found in vivid detail, especially the remarkable spiritual background, in Dr. Porter's own book *Led On Step by Step*. We can only give here an outline beginning with this incident as related by Bishop Guerry: "On October 25, 1867, at two o'clock in the afternoon, to quote the language of his autobiography, he had gone up to Magnolia Cemetery, to visit the grave of his oldest son, John Toomer, who had died of yellow fever in 1864. Arrived at the grave, he knelt and prayed for submission to the Divine Will. While in this attitude of prayer, with his face in his hands, he tells us that he suddenly heard a voice in distinct and articulate tones saying 'Stop grieving for the dead and do something for the living.' 'What can I do for the living?', was his answer. And then the second time the voice, speaking with authority, said, 'Your child is enjoying what you are only hoping for; but see his young companions who are mostly orphans, are without churches or schools, take them and educate them.' Whether this conversation was a purely subjective experience or not, matters little, the effect was the same. After four hours of what he believed was a true spiritual communion with God, he came away from the child's grave with the conviction which never afterwards left him and the school which he was sent to found was the result of a direct command of God. . . . Thus the Porter Military Academy was born in faith, nurtured in prayer, sustained by a spirit of consecration, worthy of the best ideals and traditions of the South." Dr. Porter states that the object of the school was "to save for the Church and the country at large the representative families of the South" who had lost everything by the war, and to give education to deserving boys who otherwise would have been deprived of an education.

Mr. Porter was "not disobedient to the Heavenly vision." He gave notice to tenants of his house on Ashley Avenue. Mr. John Gadsden fortunately accepted the principalship. Mrs. John Bryan was matron the first year, then Miss Septima Seabrook for a long time. The large day school was opened on December 9, 1867. Mr. Porter reports, May, 1868, that it "consists of 300 children and 3 male and 7 female teachers." The boarding department opened March 21, 1868, with 33 boarders. These were chiefly sons of fellow citizens reduced by the war from wealth to poverty. The two departments of the institution were maintained at $800.00 per month, contributed chiefly by friends in Baltimore. The name of the school was *The Holy Communion Church Institute*. In 1869, there were 74 boys in the boarding department and 250 residing in the city in attendance, and at this time for $5,100.00 a house adjoining the Church was purchased for the Home. From May, 1869, to May, 1870, Mr. Porter raised $20,810.75 for the school— $13,502.00 was collected in Newark, New York, Philadelphia, Baltimore, and Washington, with $6,709.03 from South Carolina tuition fees and donations. Over $15,000.00 of this went for current expenses and $5,000.00 for the Home, also part payment on four boys sent to Trinity College, Hartford—one of these a candidate.

In 1873, a gift of $10,000.00 was received from J. O. Hoadley of Lawrence, Massachusetts, for the endowment fund. Mr. Porter reports $16,000.00 collected abroad for the school in the summer of 1873. There were 60 boys in the school for whom not a cent was paid, $200.00 being the largest amount paid by any. Mr. Porter had a serious breakdown in health, lasting from May to Advent 1874. There were six graduates now (1874) in preparation for the ministry. Mr. Gadsden reported in May, 1878, $2,000.00 due for board and tuition, of which only $1,000.00 possibly would be collected. Expenses for the year $15,472.75, receipts $12,889.70, a deficiency, allowing $1,000.00 on collections, of $1,585.05. In the eleven years there was upwards of $12,000.00 due in unredeemed promises and pledges. There were at this time 100 boarders and 150 day pupils. Mr. Porter went to England in the spring of 1879, seeking help. He returned with $8,000.00 for the school. A most remarkable story is told that led to the establishment of the school at the old U. S. Arsenal, where it now is (see *Led On Step by Step*): the help of a Federal soldier (Lieutenant John A. McQueen) during the burning of Columbia, great deeds of kindness in return to this soldier by Mr. Porter, including giving him a letter, which later maybe saved his life, the removal of the U. S. troops from the Arsenal, Mr. Porter's trip to Washington, contact with General Sherman, the cooperation of Senators Hampton and Butler, the Act of Congress transferring the Arsenal property to Mr. Porter at first for 99 years and later indefinitely, but on condition it be used for educational purposes.

There is a dramatic sequel to this story which, as it is not so well known, we give in full as related by Dr. Kershaw: "When the city of Chicago some years later erected a monument to the deceased Confederates who, as prisoners of war, had died there, the authorities secured General Hampton to deliver the address on the occasion of the unveiling. He said that as he thought about the speech that he was asked to deliver, and what would be appreciated, he recalled the circumstances that have been related in regard to Dr. Porter's school, and remembered that Lt. McQueen was from Illinois. He determined to make the story the *piece de resistance* of his speech. There was an immense crowd present, and apparently deeply interested in his story. Among other things, he went on to say that Lt. McQueen must have been a noble fellow, that he would like to know him and even after the lapse of so many years to tell him how his chivalrous behavior to Dr. Porter and his friends during that night of terror had been remembered and so on. He said that he observed a movement in the crowd near the platform, but paid no attention to it and continued his speech until suddenly he was confronted by a large man with a big, black beard, with his hand in the breast pocket of his coat, who said 'General Hampton, I have never had the opportunity of meeting you or of presenting the letter that Dr. Porter gave me, and addressed to you, but (drawing the letter from his pocket) here is the letter! I cannot deliver it to you, however, for it is one of my most cherished possessions.' The General added that he had never seen such an effect produced upon any crowd as this incident gave rise to. They cheered themselves hoarse while the tears ran down their cheeks and hand clasped hand in spontaneous outburst of comradeship."

The Arsenal property was transferred on December 19, 1879, and on January 8, 1880, Dr. Porter and the trustees took formal possession. It was a notable occasion, as described by Mr. J. S. Plowden in the *Greenville Observer* in August, 1843: "A short service was held in the church and then at five o'clock the large procession, headed by St. Patrick's Helicon Band, with the Washington Light Infantry, whose captain was G. D. Bryan, the Charleston Riflemen, with Captain R. J. Magill, the bishop and clergymen in vestments marched around the arsenal and through the grounds to the building in which twenty-six years before Dr. Porter had held his first religious service." There were speeches by Hon. W. D. Porter, William A. Courtenay, mayor of the city, S. Y. Tuper, president of the Chamber of Commerce. Bishop Howe made the closing address of thanksgiving for God's blessing on the work. On February 2, 1880, Mr. Gadsden, Miss Seabrook, the faculty and the boys moved into their new quarters. Bishop Guerry was one of those boys. Later, Dr. Porter moved into the grounds with his family. It cost $10,000.00 to adapt the buildings to the needs of the Institute. By 1882, the endowment fund of $16,000.00 had been accumulated, there were then 276 pupils—166 being boarders and 100 did not pay anything—13 sons of clergymen paid nothing. During the summer of this year a four-story building, with dining room to seat 350 and dormitory for 120, was erected at a cost of $12,500.00, and also St. Timothy's Chapel at a cost of $6,500.00. In 1886, the Board of Trustees, meeting in the absence of the rector, changed the name of the school from the "Holy Communion Church Institute" to the "Porter Military Academy". A great addition was made now to the equipment of the school in the building of the handsome library, the gift of Rev. Dr. Charles Hoffman of New York. The cornerstone was laid October 19, 1893, and the library opened January 26, 1894. Dr. Porter gives this summary of his work in 1897: "I have been permitted to carry on this great school for thirty years, and have given a more or less finished education to over three thousand boys, fully twenty-five hundred of these fully gratuitously or for a mere pittance; have sent over 200 boys to college, and have educated 150 sons of clergy gratuitously; have furnished twenty-two men to the ministry, with several candidates for Holy Orders at this moment preparing for the ministry; have acquired a whole block of property from the United States Government; have erected seven houses on the grounds, . . . have raised and expended in Christian Education nearly one million of dollars; have labored and suffered, had disappointments and sorrows, met with ingratitude, and with the warmest love and gratitude of others, and close up after thirty years with a deficiency of five thousand dollars staring me in the face. But blessed be God, though perplexed, yet not in despair, for I believe there are loving hearts beating in some breast which shall be moved to see me through." (*Led On*, p. 429.)

In November, 1900, Bishop Capers was called to Charleston to find Dr. Porter so ill that he could not carry on longer as head of the Academy. The trustees were called together and immediately took over the responsibility for the conduct of the Academy. Dr. Porter died on March 30, 1902. Bishop Capers said of the school: "The strong will and active mind, and tireless energy that controlled it, and provided for its support, and on whom the institution depended for guidance and direction are now no more. Dr. Porter is at rest, and his work is done." He presented the problem now for the Church—the splendid property, the fine school, the operation cost $15,000.00 a year with regular income of only about $6,500.00. The school had essentially belonged to Dr. Porter, now it belonged essentially to the Church. Mr. C. J. Colcock of the faculty acted as rector from April, 1902, to January, 1904. Mr. Colcock had for many years been Dr. Porter's unfaltering assistant. Captain David G. Dwight, a Citadel graduate, then served in this capacity in 1904 and 1905 with the Rev. H. J. Mikell, rector of the Church of the Holy Communion as chaplain. Then Mr. Mikell (later Bishop of Atlanta) served as rector of the Academy during 1906-07. The school opened in 1907 with 110 boarders besides day scholars.

The Rev. Walter Mitchell became rector on July 30, 1908, coming from Fairmount School for Girls, Monteagle, Tennessee. Thus was the headmastership of the school definitely separated from the rectorship of the Church of the Holy Communion. Bishop Guerry succeeded Bishop Capers in the spring of 1908 as Bishop of the diocese and chairman of the Board of Trustees. He pronounced Porter's "the most valuable, the most important and the most far-reaching in its influence of any institution connected with the Church in this Diocese". Being himself a graduate of the school, he became its indefatigible head until his death. Many improvements were made in the next few years under Mr. Mitchell— heating plant, renovated mess hall, 160 new desks, bathrooms, etc. Attendance began to climb as so did the scholastic standard. In 1912, the statement is made concerning Mr. Mitchell's work:

"He has increased the enrollment from less than 100 to 212 this year. The school has been thoroughly reorganized, its curriculum enlarged and improved, considerable money spent on physical and educational improvement of the school, and the standing of the institution raised to one of the leading preparatory schools of the South." The tuition fee in 1915 had increased to $300.00 from the $200.00 of the days of Dr. Porter. The year 1918-19, with an enrollment of 347, has been called the most successful year in the history of the Academy. It was at this time that the day boys were first required to drill. Bishop Guerry stated in his semicentennial sermon that from 1908 to that year, 1917, $30,000.00 had been given away in scholarships. Dr. Mitchell became Bishop of Arizona.

During these years, an ambitious effort to supplement the income of the school by conducting a truck farm on land rented from St. Andrew's Church in St. Andrew's Parish was made. This proved a losing proposition. Indeed, the tide of prosperity now in 1923 began to turn (whether for boll-weevil depression, competition, or whatnot), the income fell disastrously below cost and the repeated hard times of the schol was on again. The diocese maintained a scholarship fund at this time. Other scholarship funds had been set up by friends of the school as follows: Carwile, Elizabeth A. Coxe, Iva S. Hemphill, Pinckney, and Morgan (Cf. Minutes Trustees May 25, 1955). In 1923, an extensive campaign for $200,000.00 was launched to pay the debts of the school and to set up an endowment. It met with only partial success. However, adjustments were made with the many creditors of the school and the work went forward. The Rev. S. Cary Beckwith, rector of St. Philip's Church, acted as administrative head of the Academy during 1924 until the Rev. Gordon M. Reese became rector, serving only for a short time, when Major Isaac B. Brown, long a valued member of the faculty and friend of the school took charge, serving until 1927 when Mr. William S. Gaud became rector.

The coming of Mr. Gaud, an experienced educator, marked a change in the administration of the school. The idea was now to put more emphasis on scholarship. Buildings were renovated and the military feature of the school was discontinued. The experiment proved a failure, the attendance of boarders fell from 100 to 20. Confronted with large indebtedness and another deficit, the trustees decided to lease the school to Major P. M. Thrasher and Major Raines. After a time, by agreement, Major Raines withdrew. The lease was on definite financial conditions, including the maintenance of the scholarships as well as the continuance of the

Church character of the school, religious instruction should be continued, and an Episcopal chaplain engaged. Bishop Guerry stated that "while the Church has lost temporarily the control of the Institution, it remains to all intents and purposes a school of the Protestant Episcopal Church in the U. S. A." Each of the associated dioceses was to be represented on an advisory board to Major Thrasher. The school resumed its former military feature. Major Thrasher continued the successful operation of the school all through the depression period until his death August 31, 1947; the enrollment 1946-47 was 137 boarders and 157 day pupils. The military features of the school were emphasized. A Reserve Officers' Training Corps was established with the assignment to the school of Army officers. The Board of Trustees, with Bishop Thomas as chairman and Mr. J. E. Jenkins as secretary and treasurer, continued to meet. Its function under the lease was in part nominal. However, the vested interests of the school were managed, including the care and payment of bonds with dividends of the school. It should be mentioned that with assistance of Federal funds a large work of renovation and repair was accomplished under the trustees and Col. Thrasher, 1936-38. Soon after this time, the school was presented by the city with an unexpected bill for paving—over $25,000.00. The city agreed to a compromise of about one-half, and this by installments has been paid. The Rev. W. W. Lumpkin was chaplain in these years.

After Col. Thrasher's death, the trustees resumed the operation of the Academy. Col. Robert T. Ellett of Col. Thrasher's staff, was made president of the school. The attendance began to fall and deficits recurred. Efforts were made without success to borrow money to refinance the school. It was felt that extensive renovation of the buildings was essential. To accomplish this, the trustees succeeded in securing from the Federal Government an unconditional fee-simple title to the property. The validity of the title has been confirmed by the Supreme Court of South Carolina. Efforts to finance the school continued to be very difficult, a considerable deficit had to be faced. Plans were perfected in 1951 for a campaign to raise a development fund. At this time the school was drawn into closer relationship to the Church by a revision of the Constitution, whereby the trustees are elected only on nomination of the Conventions of the dioceses of South Carolina and Upper South Carolina, with the election of one trustee to represent the city of Charleston and one nominated by the alumni. The development campaign produced finally about $140,000.00.

Col. Ellett resigned in 1951 and was succeeded for a year by the Rev. W. L. Hargrave, who operated the school successfully for a year, when Mr. Roger A. Walke, Jr., was made president. He likewise served for one year. In the meantime, under a plan of development, suggested by a committee of the trustees, and with the advice of a Boston firm of architects, as a first step, the trustees succeeded by means of a loan to build the first unit in the plan—a new dormitory, named for a distinguished alumnus, Gen. C. P. Summerall. However, for the present, the pursuit of this plan is arrested. Mr. Walke resigned after one year, when the trustees, to meet the financial crises, decided to discontinue the Upper School and appointed Commander Charles E. Owens (1953) to the charge of the school. Later he became president. Commander Owens, with Lieutenant Commander Warren L. Willis as business manager has restored the enrollment of the school to capacity and also accomplished with the aid of the trustees and friends of the school a remarkable renovation of its physical condition—including the chapel, library, Gadsden Hall, and other schoolrooms, and the dining room. The school, now animated by good prospects, is facing a bright future. Commander Willis succeeded Commander Owens as president. In 1957 a ninth grade was added—a first step toward the restoration of the high school.

2. VOORHEES SCHOOL AND JUNIOR COLLEGE, DENMARK

Elizabeth Evelyn Wright, a graduate of Tuskegee, with one teacher and fourteen pupils in two rooms over an old store in Denmark, S. C., began this school on April 14, 1897. She had previously made a futile attempt to establish a school in Hampton County. The late Senator S. G. Mayfield encouraged the founder in her heroic efforts and was in many respects responsible for the location at Denmark. He later became a trustee. After three years, the school was moved to a tract of 280 acres just outside the town. It was now named Voorhees Industrial School in honor of Mr. and Mrs. Ralph Voorhees of Clinton, N. J., who gave money to buy the land and put up a number of buildings. The institution was incorporated in 1902. In 1905 Mrs. Voorhees gave 100 additional acres of land. Miss Wright labored for ten years building an institution which is a monument to her memory. She left her work in charge of Mr. M. A. Menafee, who had been for some years the treasurer of the school. For some years it had a hard time to exist, being a private institution. In 1924, meeting was held under the leadership of Rev. Robert W. Patton, D.D., representing the American Church Institute for Negroes, Bishop Guerry of the diocese of South Carolina, Bishop K. G. Finlay of the diocese of Upper South Carolina, Dr. George Peabody, Mr. Menafee, and others. Steps were taken to affiliate the school with the Institute. Both dioceses finally agreed to assume charge of the operation of the school with the assistance of the Institute, and a Board of Trustees was organized, the charter of the school being duly amended. Bishop Guerry became chairman of the board, and Bishop Finlay vice-chairman. Dr. J. E. Blanton was principal.

At the time the Church took over, a supposedly permanent endowment of the school had, through difficult years, been reduced from some $80,000.00 to $36,000.00. It had then about 400 acres of land and about $200,000.00 in buildings. For support at this time, in addition to fees and some little income from endowment, the school was pledged $6,000.00 by the American Church Institute for Negroes, and each diocese agreed to endeavor to raise $2,000.00; also, the General Education Board agreed to continue a contribution of $5,000.00. It was understood that any debts the school might incur would not legally rest on the controlling dioceses. At this time there were 200 boarding pupils and between 400 and 500 day pupils. The two dioceses were perpetually to have a majority of the Board of Trustees (each nine)—some also were from Denmark and some from the North. In 1928 Mr. W. B. Moore of York gave $5,000.00 towards a chapel for the school. At this time a regular chaplain was appointed, the Rev. H. R. Moore. In 1929 a junior college was added and the name of the institution changed to the Voorhees School and Junior College. At this time a new building program was launched in cooperation with the American Church Institute for Negroes under the leadership of the Rev. Dr. R. W. Patton, its executive secretary. This soon resulted in the erection of the Massachusetts Hall ($79,000.00), an academic building with a large auditorium, and St. James' Building, the gift of St. James' Church, Wilmington, N. C. ($14,-000.00). Then soon followed the girls' dormitory ($42,000.00). In 1935-36, the chapel was built, made possible by the gifts of $5,000.00 by Mr. W. B. Moore of York, and $10,000.00 by the United Thank-Offering of the women of the Church. The dioceses at this time held annual pilgrimages to the school. It was on the occasion of one of these on October 9, 1936, that the chapel, now completed, was consecrated as St. Philip's Chapel by Bishops Finlay and Thomas.

The school had financial struggles during the period of the great depression, but largely by the generous help of the American Church Institute for Negroes, the school was kept out of debt; the amount of $2,000.00 pledged by the dioceses had been paid by the diocese of Upper South Carolina but only in part by South Carolina, though an amount of $1,000.00 toward this purpose had been put in the regular budget of the diocese in 1930. In 1938, through the death of Bishop Finley, who had been president of the trustees since Bishop Guerry's death in 1928, the school lost a staunch friend. He was succeeded as president by Bishop Thomas. In 1940 there were 746 pupils; the budget was $35,000.00. The appointment at this time by the trustees of two committees: a budget committee (functioning under the efficient treasurer, Mr. W. L. Glover of Orangeburg), and the academic committee, added much to the efficient conduct of the institution. The Rev. S. C. Usher served as chaplain and teacher from 1933 to 1947. The Rev. Matthew A. Jones served as chaplain until 1951. Opportunities for worship and the development of Christian character are outstanding features of the program of this school.

Voorhees public school work with elementary school children of Bamberg County was relinquished in 1952. It still continues under agreements with the District Board of Education to provide high school instruction for Negroes of School District No. 2 of Bamberg County. Professor J. E. Blanton, having served as principal from 1922 until 1947, was succeeded by Mr. Earl H. McClenney, president from 1947-50, then Mr. Cecil D. Halliburton (1950-53). Professor T. H. Moore acted as president 1953-54, then the present incumbent, Professor John F. Potts, became president. Right Rev. Thomas N. Carruthers, D.D., is now (1956) president of the Board of Trustees; Rt. Rev. C. A. Cole, D.D., vice-president; Mr. J. C. Horne of Denmark is treasurer.

(3) THE UNIVERSITY OF THE SOUTH AND ST. MARY'S JUNIOR COLLEGE

We cannot within this volume supply full sketches of these two great seats of learning which belong in part to the two dioceses of South Carolina. However, it is desirable to make brief statements:

The University of the South at Sewanee, Tennessee, finds its beginning in the call for a meeting of Southern Bishops July 1, 1856, to consider the establishment of a great Church University in the South. This call had its culmination in a great meeting at Lookout Mountain, July 4, 1857; after imposing ceremonies, a declaration of principles was adopted and steps taken to further the project. A "princely domain" of 10,000 acres was secured, a half-million endowment raised, and a cornerstone laid (October 10, 1860). Then came the war when all was lost. The last ante-bellum meeting of the trustees was held in Columbia, October 14, 1861. After the war, efforts were resumed. A school was actually opened on September 18, 1869, culminating in the great University of today. South Carolina has always been associated very closely with the life of the school as these names, among others, attest—DuBose, Wiggins, Guerry, Capers, Finney, Porcher, McCrady, Elliott, Kershaw, Gregg, as well as the many students from South Carolina.

St. Mary's Junior College, Raleigh. This famous school for girls was founded by the Rev. Albert Smedes, D.D., May 12, 1842. The school from the first met with great success. After Dr. Smedes' death April 25, 1877, the school passed to the care of his son, the Rev. Bennett Smedes. In 1897, it was turned over to the Church, and with a new charter was taken over by the dioceses in North and South Carolina. On May 4, 1899, it was that the Convention of South Carolina adopted a resolution: "To adopt St. Mary's School, Raleigh, as the diocesan school for girls for the diocese of South Carolina, and as such commend it to the patronage and support of the people of South Carolina". South Carolina had been a patron of the school from its early days and has greatly benefited from its Christian culture. Many of its officers have been South Carolinians—the Rev. Theodore DuBose Bratton (later Bishop of Mississippi), who succeeded Dr. Bennett Smedes until 1903; then the Rev. McNeely DuBose, who served as rector four years; Miss Eleanor Walter Thomas of Columbia was teacher and lady principal from 1900 until 1917. (See further Education in South Carolina.)

4. RELIGIOUS EDUCATION IN THE DIOCESE

By Rev. John Kershaw, D.D.

(Written in 1920)

When in 1701 the Society for the Propagation of the Gospel in Foreign Parts was incorporated in England, it was especially charged with the religious instruction of the colonies in America and the West Indies. At that time it was estimated that there were in this province about 5500 persons beside Indians and Negroes. There was but one clergyman of the Church of England settled out of Charles Town, the Rev. William Corbin, officiating among the settlements on Goose Creek. The colony sorely needed the services of additional clergymen and of schoolmasters. It was to supply these that, in large part, Archbishop Tennison labored for the formation of the S. P. G. The society issued instructions to its missionaries, catechists and schoolmasters, extracts from which are to be found in Dalcho, pp. 43-50, covering their duties not only to the colonists but also the Indians and Negroes. Analyzing these instructions it may be said that "they contain the substance of the Christian religion," that "the end of education is, not only to fit the young for the business of life but to make them moral and religious beings, disposing children to believe and live as Christians"; that to this end the children must be taught to read the Holy Scriptures and other pious and useful books; thoroughly instructed in the Church catechism, obliged to attend the services of the Church, and publicly catechised, taught to abhor lying and falsehood and to avoid all manner of evil speaking; to love truth and honesty, to be modest, gentle, well-behaved, just and affable, and courteous to all their companions; respectful to their superiors, particularly towards all who minister in holy things, and especially to the minister of their own parish; "and all this from a sense and fear of Almighty God". It is doubtful if this could even now be improved upon as a scheme for the religious and moral instruction of youth, but in these days when children know nothing of "superiors" or "betters" as the Church catechism calls them, the scheme is rendered difficult of application. However, these extracts indicate what the S. P. G. had in mind in sending missionaries and teachers to the province. The Rev. Samuel Thomas was their first appointee. He was instructed to attempt the conversion of the Yemassee Indians who surrounded the settlements, but the Governor, Sir Nathaniel Johnson, deeming it imprudent for him then to go among the Indians, appointed him to the cure of the settlers on Cooper River, his residence to be at Goose Creek [He lived with Gov. Nathaniel Johnson at Silk Hope on the Cooper River]. The Governor and Council, in a letter to the society, expressed their gratitude for the society's intentions toward "our poor infant Church in this Province", and their pleasure at the arrival of Mr. Thomas. His ministry, though blest, was brief. He died in 1706 soon after a visit to England. He brought back with him as missionaries of the S. P. G. the Rev. Thomas Hasell and the Rev. Francis Le Jau, the latter becoming the rector of St. James', Goose Creek.

He frequently represented to the society the need of schools in the province both for religious and secular instruction and earnestly recommended their establishment. In particular he urged the sending of a schoolmaster to his parish, and in 1710 the society sent out the Rev. Benjamin Dennis. A good school was soon collected and the number of scholars was increasing, when the Indian war of 1715 dispersed the school and drove most of the inhabitants to Charles Town for protection. No further mention of this school is made by Dalcho, but that Dr. LeJau's interest in schools did not abate is evident from the fact that his name appears in the list of commissioners appointed under the Act of Assembly of 1710 for the founding and erecting of a free school in the province. After his death in 1717, the Rev. Richard Ludlam came out as the society's missionary and in 1723 was elected rector of the parish. He evinced great interest in education, and when he died in 1728, it was found that he had left all his estate real and personal to the society, in trust, "for erecting and maintaining a school for the instruction of the poor children of the parish". This legacy, somewhat diminished by the changes and chances of nearly two hundred years, is still in existence, the interest being used for education, although the parish being now "dormant", the beneficiaries of the fund are not always chosen from the residents thereof, but from such families as the trustees may designate, according to the spirit and intent of the founder's will. To return—the subject of education having now greatly engaged the attention of the colonists. letters from missionaries and many others to the society urged that it should make provision for the establishment of schools, declaring that "the spiritual as well as temporal interests of the people were at stake, as an ignorant, uneducated community was but a small remove from the habits and feelings of savage life". Feeling the force of the appeal, the society in 1711 established a school in Charles Town and placed it under the care of the Rev. William Guy, whom also they appointed as assistant to the rector of St. Philip's. Mr. Guy was then in deacon's orders, an Englishman born and receiving ordination at the hands of Dr. Compton, Bishop of London. Two schools were thus established in the province in 1711. Of this school in Charleston, McCrady says, "It was at this school that the S. P. G. first assisted in the education of the children of the colonists, charging its teachers to take special care of the manners of the children both in and out of school", etc. The Rev. Mr. Guy remained but a short time in charge of the school, having removed to Beaufort as minister of St. Helena's Parish. He was succeeded by the Rev. Thomas Morritt, who remained in charge until 1728 when he became rector of Prince George's (Winyah) Parish. The school continued until broken up by the Revolution of 1776. In March, 1721, Richard Beresford, by his will, bequeathed to the vestry of St. Thomas' Parish a considerable sum of money for the support, maintenance and education of the poor of that parish. This fund, considerably impaired by losses, is still in existence, and two schools are now (1918) in part, maintained by the income from it. Among the rules agreed upon by the vestry, to be observed by the master and pupils of the Beresford Bounty, are these: "III. The master shall bring the children to church every Lord's Day when there is public worship, and shall teach them to behave themselves with all reverence while they are in the House of God, and to join in the public service of the Church, for which purpose they are to be furnished with Bibles and Common Prayer Books as soon as they can use them. IV. The master shall use prayers morning and evening in the school, and teach the children to pray, and to use Grace before and after meals."

TRACING RELIGIOUS EDUCATION AMONG THE WHITES

While it is true that these and other schools which were thus early provided for by the colonists, either individually, or by legislative action, were not strictly speaking, schools in which religious education was primarily sought to be given, yet as McCrady says, (Vol. 14, p. 15, Coll. S. C. Hist. Soc.)—"It will thus be observed that the education of the lower part of the state was carried on by legislative aid and authority, *in connection with the Church of England.* In the upper part of the state which was settled by the Scotch-Irish Presbyterians, churches and schoolhouses were built together by the ministers of that church which has always been foremost in education in this country". Dr. Howe in his History of the Presbyterian Church in South Carolina (Vol. 2, p. 20) says, "Education was deemed a part of the religious duties of the clergy, whether Presbyterian, Covenanter or Churchman." McCrady has shown in the paper referred to that there were, prior to the Revolution, "not only five free schools in the colony, but many others maintained by charitable societies and churches." Even during that struggle, the work of establishing schools went on. The Mount Zion Society, organized in 1777, founded a school in Winnsboro; in 1778, another such society was incorporated for the purpose of founding, endowing and supporting a public school in the district of Camden; in the same year, an Act was passed incorporating in the parish of St. David, a society for the same purpose. But it is beyond the scope of this undertaking to trace more at length the development of education in general in South Carolina. That has been well done by abler men to whose utterances, full and free access is to be had by all concerned, and we must confine ourselves to the work of our Church in this direction. It was in 1836 that we find notice of a classical school founded by the rector of St. Phillip's, Charleston, the Rev. Christopher Edwards Gadsden, and his assistant, the Rev. Daniel Cobia. Bishop Bowen in his Convention address of that year refers to it as "a nursery of sound religious character in the rising generation of our Church". Two years later, following the appointment of a committee for that purpose, a report was presented advocating the establishment of an Episcopal school, in which the principle is laid down that "religious principles for proper application to future life, should be interwoven with the whole structure of education, moral and scholastic."

The Bishop in his annual address commented on the objection that had been raised "by our people and by them almost alone, to what is called sectarian education," contrasting this with the attitude of other Christian bodies in regard to denominational schools. It may be observed in passing that to this day the same objection is sometimes heard. It is assumed by the objectors that such an attitude is evidence of a board and liberal spirit. It may be so, but is also evidence of such a failure to grasp the full meaning of education as it should be, as to arouse our pity and excite the suspicion that such as make the objection, have, in reality, no great concern for either education or religion. In consequence of the agitation referred to, the proposed school was opened in Charleston, Nov. 1, 1841, with thirteen pupils in attendance. This number increased to thirty the next year and fell to twenty-two in 1844, varying in numbers in the years that followed until 1849 when the exercises of the school were suspended by reason of failure to support it. It is evident that religious education was a subject very near to the heart of Bishop Gadsden. He speaks with earnestness of it in each of his annual addresses at this period. He alludes with satisfaction in 1850 to the fact that following the suspension of the "Conventional School" as it was termed, the St. Philip's Parish School for Boys had been revived, and states that several of the clergy have commenced or desire to commence similar schools, the support of which he urges. These parochial schools evidently failed of support, and after dragging out a more or less brief and precarious existence, finally died. It was during this period that the Rev. John D. Mc-Collough established at Glenn Springs, Spartanburg County, St. John's School for Boys, which the year following was removed to the town of Spartanburg, and the Rev. Peter J. Shand, rector of

Trinity Church, Columbia, reports a parochial school in operation, under the control and management of the women of the congregation, "by whom the school was originated and is sustained." This, and other like schools were intended chiefly for the benefit of the "poor whites" of their respective communities, but they were not patronized by the well-to-do at any time. Private schools met the educational needs of the latter. The War between the States came on, resulting in the disruption of our entire industrial system and the consequent impoverishment of our people. The Church suffered with the State, and the chief consideration exercising the minds of all was to procure the bare necessities of life. The people of our coast country, in particular, were in dire straits. Not only were their former slaves set free, but many of them had lost their homes, their plantations had, perforce, been abandoned, and were in a condition approaching ruin; many churches had likewise been destroyed, and in cases where they were not, there were no clergy to open them, while schools were simply non-existent, thus imperiling an entire civilization by exposing to the perils of ignorance and the lack of organized and regular religious influences, the rising generation of that day.

It was at this juncture that the Rev. Anthony Toomer Porter, rector of the Church of the Holy Communion, Charleston, was led to essay the opening of a school for boys and girls which might in some measure furnish the means of education to the sons and daughters of those who otherwise would have no school advantages. [This great undertaking is described elsewhere.]

St. John's, Spartanburg
Porcher's, Willington

The Rev. John D. McCollough, one of the Church's foremost missionaries in the up-country, about 1851 or 1852, after having conducted a Church school for several years at Glenn Springs, in Spartanburg County, decided to establish a similar school for girls at the county seat. Largely, if not wholly, with his own means, he erected a building having a central part flanked by two wings. The wings were completed and used but the center was not finished until the property was acquired by the trustees of Converse College. Here, a school for girls was opened and continued for some years. It was a private enterprise, and after experiencing various vicissitudes, it was closed, owing to the lack of support, and hence of means of carrying it on. Mr. McCollough was a firm believer in Christian education, both in itself, and as a means of promoting the spread of the Church, and he showed his faith by his works, in that he impoverished himself in the effort to establish a Church school in a part of the diocese where it seemed most to be needed. The property, as related elsewhere, was purchased by Mr. James T. Welsman of Charleston, and presented by him to the diocese as a site for the diocesan seminary. After the destruction in 1865 of the seminary buildings in Camden, St. John's was occupied for a year or two as a seminary, but the support needed was not forthcoming and it was closed. Mr. McCollugh again opened it as a Church school for girls, but as before, it failed of the necessary support, and after a feeble existence of possibly three years, he was compelled to close it. Its fate is only another instance of the inexplicable indifference of our Church people to Church schools, whereas, other denominational schools are warmly fostered and supported by their respective adherents. Perhaps, we may find in this one explanation of their growth and of our failure to grow as we should.

The Rev. O. T. Porcher a graduate of the South Carolina College, about 1849 or 1850, accepted the position of teacher in the school at Willington, in Abbeville County, formerly conducted by the famous Moses Waddell, where had been educated many of the most prominent men in the State and elsewhere. After teaching in the school for a year or two, Mr. Porcher established a school of his own. He received a limited number of boarders, and boys from the vicinity also attended. It was emphatically a Church school. The boys were instructed in the principles of the Christian religion "as this Church hath received the same", and the daily services of the Church were maintained with regularity. The course of instruction was based upon that employed in the great English preparatory schools. Latin and Greek were especially emphasized. The personality of Mr. Porcher impressed itself profoundly upon his pupils and the fruits and effects of his teaching are still evident in that vicinity, and among the survivors of the student body. The school was maintained until 1864, when boys from 16 to 18 were called into service. Mr. Porcher then closed the school and himself entered the service until the end of the war. As soon after as practicable the school was reopened and continued until a few weeks before his death, Dec. 30, 1873. Mr. Porcher was always deeply interested in Sewanee and a number of his pupils entered the University after the completion of their course in his school. With him, the school died. It never had been what is termed a paying proposition, but it marked a gallant attempt on the part of a devoted churchman to give to the youth of the State an ideal education in which sound Christian instruction should go hand-in-hand with the classics. [There have been many parochial schools in the diocese notably that of Church of Good Shepherd, Columbia.]

RELIGIOUS EDUCATION OF NEGROES

In 1712, the Legislature of the Colony passed "an Act for the better ordering and governing of negroes and slaves", in which, after reciting that "since charity and the Christian religion which we profess, obliges us to wish well to the souls of all men, and that religion may not be made a pretence to alter any man's property and right, and that no person may neglect to baptize their negroes, or suffer them to be baptized for fear that thereby they should be manumitted and set free", it was enacted that the legal and civil status of any Negro or Indian slave should not be altered by the fact of their being baptized. It was not until 1742 that actual provision was made for the instruction of Negro slaves, though the subject had long engaged the feelings and the attention of the clergy and conscientious laymen. In that year, through the influence and exertions of Commissary Garden, a schoolhouse was built in Charles Town, by private subscription, and a school opened. The commissary purchased at the expense of the society (the S. P. G.) two intelligent Negro boys, with the intention of having them prepared in this school for teaching others of their race, chiefly "to enable them to read the scriptures and to understand the nature of Redemption". Dalcho says the two boys received the baptismal names of Henry and Andrew; that they continued in the school, and that there were in 1819 colored persons then living who had been taught by them to read. The commissary thought it probable that if the experiment thus began, succeeded in town, it would be extended to country parishes, where the services of these youths would prove of signal benefit, since he believed that the Negroes would receive instruction more readily and willingly from persons of their own color than from white teachers. This school continued for more than twenty years, but evidently the experiment was not taken up as it had been hoped it would be. Dalcho (p. 193) says that Andrew, one of the teachers, died, and the other, Henry, turned out a profligate. As there were no other black or colored persons competent to take charge of the school, it was discontinued in 1764.

However, we find in the Digest of S. P. G. Records, 1701-1892, further reference made to the subject of instructing slaves. It met with considerable opposition from their owners, we are told, but there were many who were zealous in encouraging the instruction of their slaves so far back as 1713. Their example was followed in later years by many others, so that it became rather the rule than the exception to accord to slaves elementary religious instruction, and the time came when many of the clergy habitually catechised and taught the Negroes as part of their parochial duty, and masters and mistresses were diligent in preparing them for the visits of the clergy, as the journals of Convention testify. Indeed the journals of the period, 1835-1860, are full of references to the concern of the clergy and laity in the spiritual welfare of the slaves. In many instances, chapels were built wherein they gathered for worship, conducted by the rectors of the parishes within whose bounds they were built, or by the catechists employed and paid by the owners of the slaves. These catechists went regularly from one plantation to another. The Negroes at the appointed times, were assembled in the chapel or in the parish church, and elementary religious instruction given, while at other times the clergy conducted service and preached to them as regularly as to the whites under their charge. Sunday Schools for them, conducted chiefly by ladies, were common, especially in the low country. So great was the interest shown in this work that in 1857 Bishop Davis in his Convention address, reported forty-five chapels and other places of worship for slaves, with a force of one hundred and fifty laymen and women engaged in giving catechetical instruction to an equal number of Negro congregations. The results of this work were manifest when in 1860 an abstract of the parochial reports showed that out of 6,126 communicants, 2,960 were Negroes, and of the 389 confirmed, 175 were also Negroes. During the war period, 1861-1865, the good work continued as best it could, although it was much demoralized by the removal into the interior of many families from the coast and the sea islands, with their slaves, and the scarcity of clergy who were compelled to flee with their flocks to safer places. It is noteworthy that when in May, 1865, sixteen clergy and lay representatives of six parishes assembled in Convention in Camden, the duty of the Church towards the Negroes was not forgotten. The Reverend P. F. Stevens, then in charge of Trinity Church, Black Oak, referring to Potter's Raid and its disturbing influence on the Negroes, said he had been rather encouraged than discouraged by their conduct. "Firmly convinced that while there have been instances of disorder and some Negroes have left because of the offer of freedom to them, it has been alone the restraining influence of the Gospel in its effects on both masters and slaves which has so absolutely prevented outrage and kept the great body of Negroes quiet". (Journal, 1865.)

In 1866 the matter was referred to again in the Bishop's address and a committee appointed to report upon it. In its report, the committee after reviewing the work done among colored people from the earliest days of South Carolina's settlement, to the end of the recent war, declares that "although released from the duties of ownership, yet as partakers with them of a common redemption, and as fellow-members of the same household of faith, we cheerfully acknowledge ourselves as debtors to bond and free, wise and unwise, being all one in Christ Jesus." The committee recalls "their faithful services, and how, with rare exceptions, they resisted all instigations to revolt and insurrection, and remained true to their former owners and their families throughout the war." It considers it as not surprising that they were carried away by their freedom and the vague and extravagant expectations they had been led to indulge in, attributing the fact that they had not run to greater excesses to the preaching of the Gospel among them in former years, and saying that unless this evangelizing process could be continued, a relapse into flagrant heathenism must ensue. The committee goes on to say that as those whose destiny is most closely identified with them, we have the deepest interest in their moral and spiritual elevation, and as long as associated with them and best understanding them, we must undertake this work or they will be left to the invidious instruction of others or to their own ignorant and blind guides. "Duty, interest, religion, humanity, all urge us to keep or reclaim them to the wholesome teaching of the Church." As a step in this direction, the committee refers to the offer of "material aid which we may gladly avail ourselves of" extended by the Freedmen's Aid Commission of our General Convention, "especially as the Diocese of South Carolina has never in time past received any aid from the Domestic Missionary Society" of the Church, and recommends the formation of a Board of Missions for this work, the duties of which should be to revive and sustain the missions among the colored people existing before freedom; to establish parochial schools with industrial features engrafted, wherever practicable; to search out and take by the hand such colored men as they find desirous of entering the ministry, and to provide for their training and education, with the Bishop's sanction and approval; to secure for Church and school purposes such Church property as is no longer used or needed by the whites;

to appoint a missionary agent to visit the colored people and ascertain their general condition, needs and wishes; to collect all information pertaining to the work, and to solicit aid within and beyond the diocese.

Reporting two years later, the Board of Missions for this work said that a school had been opened in Charleston with twelve teachers and six hundred pupils, supported by the Freedmen's Commission of the Church; that encouraging reports had been received from many clergy ministering to colored people; that the prejudices of the last few years were melting away beneath the kind and Christian sympathy of their former owners, and advocating the training up of teachers of the colored race as one of the best means of retaining influence over them, and incorporating them more thoroughly into the "Body of Christ". Notwithstanding such efforts and endeavors, some of them quite successful, the great majority of the Negroes formerly in the communion of the Church, withdrew, and associated themselves with other religious bodies, chiefly Methodists and Baptists, of their own color. In some instances in which a part of the parish Church had been reserved for them, the Negroes, with few exceptions, failed to attend, preferring to go to themselves, and with the assistance of their white friends, places of worship were erected and services held by the parish clergyman. It must be remembered that in the period of which we are now speaking, the antagonisms of the Reconstruction era were developing under the demagogical teaching of political adventurers seeking to alienate the races and enkindle in the Negroes the fear of a return to slavery, should the whites regain control of the State government. Incendiary appeals to race pride based upon race hatred were common in those dark days, and it required great moral courage, such as could hardly be expected of them, and an unusual degree of intelligence also on the part of the Negroes, to associate even in worship with the whites, and to stand in with them, even religiously, as being their best and truest friends. No greater political crime was ever committed and no greater political blunder ever perpetrated than that of which the dominant party of that day was guilty, when it fomented discord between the races in the South, sowed the seeds of distrust and suspicion of the whites in the hearts of the Negroes, enkindled in them wild dreams of an impossible social equality, and evoked race hatred where before had been good feeling and some degree of mutual confidence. But the Church did not relax its efforts to minister in spiritual things to the Negroes or to give them what advantages it could in the way of education that would fit them for the duties of Christian citizenship.

When in 1889, the work of the Church in this diocese was reorganized on the basis of a separation of the races, giving to the Negroes under the Bishop, a Convocation of their own, it was felt that a great cause of friction had been removed and that the work would go forward in a more satisfactory manner. This hope has been realized. Archdeacon Baskervill, himself a colored man, in his annual report for the year 1918, states that the missionaries and teachers are making real sacrifices in the work, laboring untiringly and uncomplainingly in this important field; that "our Church people as a whole are showing a remarkable spirit of self-help"; that "many of our white people are giving of their means, and several, of their services, for the advancement of the work"; that "we are trying in our fifteen schools, located in different parts of this state, to give the masses an opportunity, and train them to become useful citizens. In all our work we are stressing thrift, economy, honesty, and race integrity." Eleven colored and two white clergymen serve twenty-eight parishes and missions, having 1,225 communicants. There are eighteen lay readers. Several of the day schools have waiting lists while 1,600 children are actually enrolled. The schools are graded to correspond with the grading of the public schools while the course of instruction is equivalent to that given in the public schools grade for grade. More might have been done, but what has been done is sufficient to show that the Church in South Carolina is not unmindful of its duty to the colored race, a subject that has engaged its interest ever since the venerable S. P. G. more than two centuries ago sent its missionaries over to minister to the slaves and the Indians. (See also Archdeaconry for Colored Churchmen.)

Appendix XII

KANUGA

Probably no institution of the Church in the Carolinas in the past quarter-century has had more influence on its life than Kanuga. The main building at this mountain retreat in North Carolina was built originally for a clubhouse; after several years the club was disbanded and the building was used as a summer hotel. Five miles outside of Hendersonville, it was inaccessible to the public at large but failed in this second venture. In 1928 the area was offered to the five dioceses of the Carolinas—North Carolina, Eastern Carolina, Western North Carolina, South Carolina, and Upper South Carolina—to be tried as a demonstration project. It was a loan for one year. A temporary board of managers was organized. Bishop Finlay was made president of the summer conferences which were planned. The Rev. A. Rufus Morgan, executive secretary of the diocese of Upper South Carolina and its general missionary, was made treasurer and business manager. It was an ambitious program these officers undertook. How successful it was may be judged by the fact that after one year's operation by the Church it declared a profit of a gratifying sum. The year following, the profit was found to have increased. The first Y. P. S. L. camp at Kanuga in 1928 was called Camp Ellison Capers.

Kanuga was the logical step following the camps that had already been held at Etowah and at Brevard for several years. It was the Right Rev. Kirkman G. Finlay, catching a vision of the institution that was to be, who became the leading spirit of the enterprise and by whose efforts chiefly it could be announced at a conference held in Columbia in the winter of 1929 that $87,000.00 of the requisite of $100,000.00 was in sight. Those who attended this historic meeting were Bishop Finlay with the Rev. A. R. Morgan, representing Upper South Carolina; the Rev. J. W. C. Johnson, Western North Carolina; the Rev. H. W. Starr, South Carolina; the Rev. I. deL. Brayshaw, East Carolina. Soon the property, including four hundred acres of surrounding land, the large inn, and thirty-nine attractive cottages bordering the lake and running back into the pine-crested hillsides, became the property of the Episcopal Church as represented by the aforementioned dioceses, except that North Carolina declined to become one of the joint owners for some years.

A board of trustees was formed with one representative from each of the four associated dioceses to hold the property for the use of the Church. The dioceses did not as such incur any financial responsibility. A board of managers was also organized to operate the institution. The dam that holds the beautiful lake was destroyed by a storm in September 1928, involving a loss of about $1,500.00. It was restored with the lake by the summer of 1929. From the beginning there were four regular conferences or camps. These, with the first directors, were: the Junior Camp and the Young People's Camp, Director Bishop Finlay himself; the Adult Conference, the Rev. J. W. C. Johnson, director, succeeded in 1930 by the Rev. J. L. Jackson; and the Clergy Conference or School of the Prophets, with the Righ Rev. T. D. Bratton of Mississippi, a native of South Carolina, director. The Rev. H. W. Starr was dean of the faculties. In addition to the regular Summer Conference, many other Church meetings were held from time to time at Kanuga. These conferences, as well as that at Sewanee, had now large enrollments from many of the associated dioceses; the currculum covered the entire field of Church life. In October, 1929, an organization meeting was held in Columbia where by-laws were adopted; the board of managers was to consist of, from each diocese, a clerical and a lay representative of the Woman's Auxiliary, and one from the Y. P. S. L.

In 1933, Bishop Thomas succeeded Bishop Bratton as director of the Clergy Conference. Through the following years from the first, worship held a prominent part in the life of the Conferences— the Communions in the rotunda, the twilight services with special preachers by the lakeside, the services in the Leafy Chapel. For many years the Rev. W. H. K. Pendleton, as chaplain, had charge of worship. For a sample of a summer program in 1937 there was a retreat for women June 7th; the Midget Camp with Miss Alice Boney as director; the Junior Conference, Bishop Finlay, director; the Young People's Conference under the Rev. John A. Pinckney; the Adult Conference, the Rev. J. L. Jackson, director; the College Conference, Bishop Thomas C. Darst, director; the Clergy School, Bishop Thomas, director. There was a camp for boys under Mr. James Y. Perry, director, and a guest period beginning the latter part of July when the conferences were over. Nor should the lighter side of the life at Kanuga be overlooked—swimming, boating, hikes, entertainments in the evening, and notable banquets to close the various Conferences. Another important feature of Kanuga life was the annual Laymen's Conference held in the summer.

There had been very slight warning of any weakness and so it was when Bishop Finlay suddenly passed to the higher life at his cottage at Kanuga on August 27, 1938, it came as a shock to the Church in all the associated dioceses. Kanuga had been built largely around his personality and therefore there were now many adjustments to be made. The Rev. A. Rufus Morgan now became superintendent and business manager with individual leaders for the different Conferences. The Rev. H. A. Donovan had charge of the guest period as guest chaplain for a couple of years. Funds had been accumulating for years for the building of a chapel at Kanuga. Before Bishop Finlay's death the site had been chosen and soon after it was determined that it would be a memorial of him. It was consecrated on July 19, 1942, as the Chapel of the Transfiguration to "The Glory of God and in memory of Kirkman George Finlay." The service was conducted by the Right Rev. Robert E. Gribbin, who at this time was president of Kanuga Conferences. Bishop Darst preached the sermon on Isaiah 13:2 "Lift ye up a banner upon the high mountain." Others taking part in the service were Bishop John L. Jackson, for years director of the Adult Conference, Bishop A. S. Thomas, director of the Clergy School, the Rev. A. Rufus Morgan, superintendent, the Rev. W. H. K. Pendleton, chaplain of the Adult Conference, the Rev. B. Duvall Chambers, the Rev. Louis C. Melcher, and the Rev. John A. Pinckney, director of the Young People's Conference. The music on this occasion was in charge of William G. Robertson. Many other clergymen were in procession, including Bishops Gravatt, Dandridge, and Wing. There are many memorials in the chapel dedicated to the memory of friends and workers at Kanuga. Mr. Robertson and his wife for many years added much to the life of the Conferences by their musical and other talents. Whether the occasion was "lively or severe," their contribution was always fitting. Rev. B. Duvall Chambers succeeded Bishop Thomas as director of the Clergy School.

For some time before his death, Bishop Finlay, realizing that someone should be in prospect to take over control after him, had selected Rev. John A. Pinckney as such an "understudy," so it was natural that in due time, in 1944, he was appointed after Mr. Morgan to be superintendent of Kanuga Conferences. He continued in control under the trustees for six years of devoted service. A finance and business committee was organized at this time to assist in the management. The first members of this committee were F. D. MacLean, Ernest Patton, and W. L. Mauney, the first being

treasurer. After Bishop Gribbin, Bishop Gravatt was president of
the trustees until 1948 when Right Rev. George Henry succeeded
him. In 1950, Mr. W. P. Verduin succeeded Mr. Pinckney, becoming
also business manager. The diocese of North Carolina became one
of the joint owners of Kanuga in 1948, thus it is now owned by the
five Carolina dioceses. Bishop Jackson's long tenure as director of
the Adult Conference ended only with his death in 1948. He was
affectionately known as the "Big Wheel". He was succeeded by Rev.
Henry Johnson in 1948. Then the Right Rev. T. N. Carruthers held
this position from 1949 to 1953; followed by the Rev. William S.
Lea, 1954; the Right Rev. T. H. Wright, 1955; and Right Rev. R. H.
Baker, 1956. Four new buildings have lately been added to Kanuga;
one for the clergy conferences, Pendleton Hall, in honor of Dr.
Pendleton who served for many years as chaplain; also a counsellor
cabin; a director's cabin; and an office cabin. Also, there has been
an extensive reroofing of the buildings and among other improvements, an extensive new sewerage system. The Right Rev. M.
George Henry succeeded Bishop Gravatt as president of Kanuga
Conferences in 1948. A portrait of Bishop Finlay has been presented
to Kanuga by the Woman's Auxiliary of Upper South Carolina,
painted by Miss Grace Annette DuPre of Spartanburg. Mrs. C.
Frederic McCullough, president of the auxiliary, made the presentation in the presence of Mrs. Finlay and her children and
grandchildren.

Appendix XIII

FOREIGN AND EXTRA-CONTINENTAL MISSIONARIES FROM THIS STATE

The Right Rev. William J. Boone, First Bishop of China, 1844. Called "The first bishop consecrated for strictly foreign missionary service, within the Anglican Communion." (Manross, *History of the American Episcopal Church*, p. 263.) (The diocese contributed the following continental missionary Bishops, the first in their respective fields: Stephen Elliott, Georgia; Frances Huger Rutledge, Florida; Alexander Gregg, Texas. Bishop Samuel David Ferguson of Liberia was a native of South Carolina.) ,

The Rev. James Warley Miles, Mesopotamia, 1843.

Sarah C. Thurston, Cuba, 1907.

Eliza Herron McCollough, Porto Rico, 1908.

The Rev. Hope Henry Lumpkin, Alaska, 1914.

Alice W. Gregg, China, 1916-52.

Uto Saito, Japan, 1917.

Mary Trapier Gadsden, Porto Rico, 1920.

Irene Muriel Moore, Porto Rico, 1920.

Eunice Haddon, Honolulu, 1920-28.

The Rev. Sumner Guerry, China, 1921-26.

Marion Kirk, Liberia, 1923-28.

Maria J. Ravenel, China, 1923-27.

Leila Stroman, China, 1924-30.

Mary Theo Young, China, 1925-31.

James B. Moore, Cuba, 1927-28.

The Rev. Roderick H. Jackson, 1927-33.

Chevillette Branford, Philippines, 1928-32.

Hawkins K. Jenkins, M.D., Philippines, 1930-35.

The Rev. Lincoln A. Taylor, O.H.C., Liberia, 1952-55.

The Rev. Paul Washington, Liberia, 1947-54.

Marion I. Webb, Alaska, 1945-55.

Charlotte Hutchinson, China, 1947-49.

The Rev. Moultrie McIntosh, Nicaragua, 1950-53.

Right Rev. Louis C. Melcher, Bishop of Central Brazil, 1948—.

PLATES

1. BISHOP SMITH (1795-1801)   2. BISHOP DEHON (1812-1817)

3. BISHOP BOWEN (1818-1839)   4. BISHOP GADSDEN (1840-1852)

5. BISHOP DAVIS (1853-1871)

6. BISHOP HOWE (1871-1894)

7. BISHOP CAPERS (1893-1908)

8. BISHOP GUERRY (1907-1928)

Diocese of South Carolina

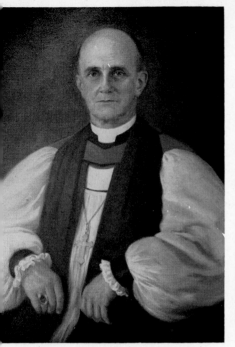

9. Bishop Thomas (1928-1944)   10. Bishop Carruthers (1944-——)

11.   Diocesan Headquarters, 138 Wentworth Street, Charleston

[795]

Diocese of Upper South Carolina

12. BISHOP FINLAY (1921-1938)

13. BISHOP GRAVATT (1939-1953)

14. BISHOP COLE (1953-——)

15.   TRINITY, Columbia

16.

17.

St. Michael's, Charleston

18.

ST. HELENA'S, Beaufort

19.

St. Thaddeus', Aiken

20.   S<small>T</small>. J<small>OHN</small>'s, Johns Islan•

St. Luke's and St. Paul's, Charleston

22. ST. MARK'S, Charleston

23.   PRINCE GEORGE, Winyah, Georgetown

24.   TRINITY, Edgefield

25.

26.   HOLY CROSS, Stateburg

27.

28.

Trinity, Abbeville

29.

30.

NATIVITY, Union

31.

RESURRECTION, Greenwood

32.

33.

GOOD SHEPHERD, York

34.

35.

St. Matthew's, Darlington

36.

St. Paul's, Pendleton

37.

HOLY APOSTLES, Barnwell

38.

THE CROSS, Bluffton

39.

ST. STEPHEN'S, Ridgeway

40.

41.

42.

ST. MATTHEW'S Fort Motte

Notes on Plates

1. Portrait of the Rt. Rev. Robert Smith: artist, James Earle, Charleston, 1894-96. Owned by J. J. Pringle Smith, Esq., Charleston. A similar portrait by the same artist owned by the Misses Alice R. Huger Smith and Caroline R. Huger Smith, Charleston.

2. Portrait of the Rt. Rev. Theodore Dehon: artist, John Stevens Cogdell, of St. Michael's, Charleston, 1819, "a labor of memory." Owned by deSaussure P. Dehon, Esq., Summerville.

3. Portrait of the Rt. Rev. Nathaniel Bowen: copy of the Samuel F. B. Morse portrait, painted in Charleston, 1818-20. Owned by Grace Church, New York. This smaller copy in brown tones done before 1841, owned by St. Michael's, Charleston. Copyist unknown.

4. Portrait of the Rt. Rev. Christopher Edwards Gadsden: artist unknown. Owned by St. Philip's, Charleston.

5. Portrait of the Rt. Rev. Thomas Frederick Davis: From engraving by John Sartain of portrait by Louis Lang, Europe, 1858. Owned by Mrs. Henry W. Davis, Atlanta.

6. Portrait of the Rt. Rev. William Bell White Howe: artist, Poindexter Page Carter, Charleston, 1893. Owned by St. Philip's, Charleston.

7. The Rt. Rev. Ellison Capers: photographer, W. A. Reckling, Columbia, circa 1900. A portrait from this photograph was painted by Grace Annette DuPre, Spartanburg, 1950. Owned by the University of the South, Sewanee.

8. The Rt. Rev. William Alexander Guerry: photographer, Russell, Chicago, circa 1927. A portrait from this photograph is owned by Mrs. Alexander Guerry, Chattanooga.

9. Portrait of the Rt. Rev. Albert Sidney Thomas: artist, Haskell Coffin, Charleston, 1935. Painted for the Diocese of South Carolina. Photograph by R. G. Sargent.

10. The Rt. Rev. Thomas Neely Carruthers: photographer, Charles Richard Banks at St. Philip's, Charleston, 1957.

11. Photograph of Diocesan Headquarters by Charles Richard Banks.

12. The Rt. Rev. Kirkman George Finlay: photographer, Miss Bayard Wooten, Kanuga, 1938. Portrait by Grace Annette DuPre of Bishop Finlay presented Kanuga by Woman's Auxiliary of Upper South Carolina.

13. The Rt. Rev. John James Gravatt: photographer, Foster Studios, Richmond, 1939.

14. The Rt. Rev. Clarence Alfred Cole: photographer, Charles Old Studio, Columbia, 1953.

All photographs by Charles Ricard Banks, unless otherwise indicated.

Research on portraits of the Bishops by Charles E. Thomas.

The frontispiece (St. Philip's, Charleston, "The Mother Parish of the Church in South Carolina"), and the other 28 photographs of South Carolina churches were made especially for this book by Charles Richard Banks, St. Matthews, S. C. It was not possible to photograph every church; many others of rare architectural and historical interest are not included. These are but a small but we hope representative group from each section of South Carolina. Information about the buildings can be found in the parish sketches.

Addenda

AUTHORITIES

Journals of the Conventions.

Diocesan Periodicals: *The Sunday Visitant, The Gospel Messenger and Southern Episcopal Register, The Southern Episcopalian, The Monthly Record, The Diocese, The Piedmont Churchman, The Church Herald.*

Archives of the diocese, generally, including parish registers and vestry books, parish histories, pamphlets, clippings, etc.

South Carolina Historical Magazine.

Historical Magazine of the Protestant Episcopal Church. Compare also following Bibliography.

BIBLIOGRAPHY

An Historical Account of the Protestant Episcopal Church in South Carolina. Frederick Dalcho, Charleston, 1820.

Memorial of Special Services at St. Philip's Church with Parish Records. Charleston, 1876.

Pictorial History of the Diocese. Marie H. Heyward, 1938.

A Short History of the Diocese of S. C. Members Dalcho Society, Edited by George W. Williams, 1953.

Protestant Episcopal Society for the Advancement of Christianity. Anniversary Address, Rev. A. T. Porter, D.D., 1881. History, A. S. Thomas, S.T.D., 1952.

Life of the Right Rev. Theodore Dehon, D.D. C. E. Gadsden, 1833.

Discourse on the Right Rev. Nathaniel Bowen, D.D. C. E. Gadsden, 1840.

The Soldier-Bishop, Ellison Capers. The Rev. Walter B. Capers, 1912.

Kirkman George Finlay. Mary Hardy Phifer, 1949.

PARISH HISTORIES AND RECORDS

St. Philip's, Edward McCrady, Charleston City Year Book, 1896. Also records Edited by A. S. Salley.

St. Thomas' and St. Dennis', Annals and Registers, Robert F. Clute, D.D., 1884.

St. James', Goose Creek, J. I. Waring, 1897.

St. Helena's, Beaufort, Minutes of Vestry, 1726-1812, Edited by A. S. Salley.

Prince Frederick's Register, 1916.

St. James', James Island, Capt. E. L. Rivers, 1894.

St. John's, Colleton, John's Island, the Rev. Robert N. MacCallum and Sophia Seabrook Jenkins, 1934.

St. Michael's, History, George S. Holmes, Charleston City Year Book, 1886; History, John Kershaw, D.D., 1918; History, 1951, George W. Williams; Vestry Book, 1758-1797.

St. Mark's, History, James M. Burgess, M.D., 1888.

All Saints', Waccamaw. H. D. Bull, D.D., 1948.

St. Matthew's Parish, Minutes, 1767-1838, Edited by A. S. Salley.

St. David's, Cheraw, History, W. R. Godfrey, 1916; History, Woman's Auxiliary, 1947.

Trinity, Edisto, History to 1850, Seabrook. History, A. S. Thomas, S.T.D., 1953.

Holy Cross, Stateburg, Thomas Sumter, 1934; History, John L. Frierson, (Mss.) 1950.

St. Paul's, Radcliffboro, History, Com. of Vestry, 1878.

Trinity Church, Columbia, Anniversary, 1937.

Christ Church, Greenville, S. S. Crittenden, 1901.

Church of the Advent, Spartanburg, 1948.

Grace, Charleston, The Rev. William Way, D.D., 1948.

St. Luke's, Newberry, T. H. Pope, 1955.

Good Shepherd, York, Joseph E. Hart, Jr., 1955.

Marion Churches, Victor Blue Stanley, Jr., 1938.

St. Stephen's, Ridgeway, Charles E. Thomas, 1934.

Port Society, Charleston City Year Book, 1884.

Archives of the Diocese, including files of Diocesan periodicals, vestry books, parish registers, annual reports of the Society for the Advancement of Christianity in S. C., and collections of pamphlets, etc.

The Historical Magazine of the Protestant Episcopal Church. 5 Paterson Street, New Brunswick, New Jersey (Generally and Especially as Follows):
> Thomas Gates, Vol. 1V.
> Church in S. C., A. S. Thomas, Vol. XV.
> List of Colonial Clergymen, 1745-81. Lamb, Vol. XIII.
> Bishop Robert Smith, A. S. Thomas, Vol. XV.
> List of Colonial Clergy, 1696-1716. Clement, Vol. XVI.
> Church in Confederate States, Pennington, Vol. XVII.
> List Colonial Clergy, Clement, 1710-44, Vol. XVII.
> Bishop Christopher Gadsden, Thomas, Vol. XX.
> Clergy in S. C. in 1785, Thomas, Vol. XX.
> The Rev. Alex Gordon, Keen, Vol. XX.
> The Society for Advancement of Christianity in S. C., Thomas, Vol. XXI, 4.
> The Rev. Samuel Thomas, Vol. XXIII, Thomas.

Publications of the Dalcho Society:
1. The Episcopal Church on Edisto Island and the First Confirmation in the Diocese. Albert S. Thomas, S.T.D., 1953.
2. A Short History of the Diocese of S. C. 1953, Edited by George W. Williams.
3. The Pre-Revival of the Church in S. C. William H. Patterson, 1953.
4. The Rev. James Worley Miles. George W. Williams, 1954.

5. *Colonial Church Architecture in S. C.* Samuel Gaillard Stoney, 1954.
6. *The Rev. John Jacob Tschudy.* Edgar Legare Pennington, S.T.D., 1954.
7. *Autobiography of the Rev. Paul Trapier.* Edited by George W. Williams, 1954.
8. *St. Peter's Church, Charleston.* Albert Sidney Thomas, 1955.
9. *The Library of the Rev. J. W. Miles.* 1956, Edited by George Walton Williams.
10. *Charleston Hymnal of 1792,* 1956.

The South Carolina Historical Magazine, Vols. I-LVII (1900-1956). Wealth of material, Reprints of parish registers, vestry books, and much other material pertaining directly and indirectly to the history of the Episcopal Church in South Carolina.

Digest of the Records of the Society for the Propagation of the Gospel in Foreign Parts. London.

Transcripts of S. P. G. Records in Library of Congress.

History of the Old Cheraws, Right Rev. Alexander Gregg, D.D., 1867. Reprint with Addenda, John J. Dargan, 1905.

The Church in the Confederate States, Bishop J. B. Cheshire, 1912.

Presbyterian Church, The Rev. George Howe, D.D., 1870.

Carolina Backcountry on the Eve of the Revolution, Charles Woodmason. Edited by R. J. Hooker, Chapel Hill, 1953.

Rambles in the Pee Dee, Harvey Cook.

The Historical Background of Religion in S. C. David Duncan Wallace, Ph.D., 1916 (pamphlet).

Histories of South Carolina, especially Rivers, Logan, Ramsay, McCrady, and Wallace.

Histories of the Church in U. S.: Perry, McConnell, Tiffany, Manross.

Men and Movements in the Church. The Rev. E. C. Chorley, D.D., 1946.

Frank J. Klingberg: *An Account of the Negro in Colonial South Carolina; Carolina Chronicle* (Commissary Johnston); *Chronicle of Dr. Francis LeJau.*

GENERAL INDEX

(Index of Names, see Page 841)

INDEX OF NAMES

(*See* General Index, Page 831; Complete Clergy Lists:
Diocese of S. C., Page 637; Upper S. C., Page 721)

(Indices Compiled by Commander Charles Edward Thomas)

SUBSCRIBERS

The Rt. Rev. John J. Gravatt, D.D., *Bishop of Upper South Carolina, Retired*
The Rt. Rev. Thomas N. Carruthers, D.D., *Bishop of South Carolina,* and
    Mrs. Carruthers
The Rt. Rev. C. Alfred Cole, D.D., *Bishop of Upper South Carolina*

Diocese of South Carolina

Christ Church, Adam's Run:
Mr. and Mrs. Theodore Baumeister
Carroll (M. C.) Boineau
Helen Smith Boineau
John H. Boineau
Mr. and Mrs. William Douglas Gregorie
Mrs. T. G. Legare, Sr.
Woman's Auxiliary

Holy Communion, Allendale:
Dr. and Mrs. Richard E. Boyles
Rev. Milton Crum, Jr.
Mr. and Mrs. Charles H. Farmer
Mr. and Mrs. Francis Ewing Gibson, Jr.
Mr. and Mrs. Thomas Oregon Lawton, Jr.
Mr. and Mrs. J. C. Dunbar Oswald
Mrs. Antionette A. Parks, Ann Parks and
    John Parks
Henry Allen White

St. Luke's, Andrews:
Miss Mary Harper
Samuel Paul Harper
Mr. and Mrs. C. A. Milhous

Holy Apostles, Barnwell:
Dr. William T. Ashby
B. P. Davies
Dr. Luther M. Mace
W. L. Molair
W. Guy Suter
Woman's Auxiliary

St. Helena's, Beaufort:
Mrs. John C. Calhoun
Capt. and Mrs. Walter E. Campbell
Mrs. Derrill de Treville
Ellis de Treville
Dr. Robert de Treville
Marie Louise de Treville
Mrs. John S. Foster
Mr. and Mrs. L. R. Gregorie
Ruth de T. Richter

St. Paul's, Bennettsville:
Mr. and Mrs. Henry E. Avent
Mr. and Mrs. J. J. Avent
Rev. and Mrs. Robert C. Baird
Mr. and Mrs. J. J. Baldwin
Mr. and Mrs. L. Kistler Breeden

Dr. and Mrs. Randolph C. Charles
Frank Harllee Covington
Mr. and Mrs. Walter W. Gregg
Henry Baker Gregorie
Henry Baker Gregorie, Jr.
Lynda Louise Heriot
Mr. and Mrs. John M. Jackson, Jr.
Charles E. Lynch
Judge and Mrs. Walter M. Newton
Mrs. H. W. Palmer
Mary Caroline Rogers
Mrs. Fred A. Rogers
William A. Rogers
St. Mary's and St. Anne's Auxiliaries
Mr. and Mrs. S. S. Tison
R. W. Walker, Jr.

St. Alban's, Blackville:
Mrs. Hammond Salley

The Cross, Bluffton:
Mrs. W. F. Burley
Mrs. Alfred Fripp
Mrs. H. R. Gilbert
William C. Hahn
D. H. Heyward, Jr.
Gaillard S. Heyward
Mr. and Mrs. H. E. McCracken
Alexander H. Morris
Mr. and Mrs. Charles M. Parrish
Miss Mamie Verdier
Woman's Auxiliary
Hannah McCord Wright

St. Philip's, Bradford Springs:
Mrs. DuBose Fraser
Calvary, Charleston:
Gabriel W. Bonaparte
Mr. and Mrs. John W. Bonaparte
Howard Brennen
Mr. and Mrs. E. L. Frasier
Mr. and Mrs. Wm. L. Gailliard
Mrs. Emily M. Hutchinson
Rev. Stephen B. Mackey

Grace, Charleston:
Col. R. M. Byrd
Mr. and Mrs. George P. deSaussure
Rees Ford Fraser
Mrs. Richard Gadsden
Grace Church

J. Ross Hanahan
Mrs. Howard W. Houghton, Jr.
Mr. and Mrs. Julian W. King
Mr. and Mrs. Charles L. Lyon
G. Simms McDowell
Mrs. Herbert McNulta
Mrs. Julia C. Simmons
Mr. and Mrs. Bachman Smith
Thomas E. Thornhill
T. Wilbur Thornhill
Mrs. I. Ripon Wilson, Jr.

Holy Communion, Charleston:

Mrs. Frances Moore Burgess
Mrs. Adela Burns
Church of The Holy Communion
Rev. Edwin B. Clippard
Sophie Wallace Clippard
Mrs. Eleanor Ball Combé
E. Louise Fischer
Mrs. H. W. Pearce
R. Buford Sanders
James Edward and Shirley Thompson
   Seegers
Mrs. Charles J. Shuler
Elizabeth Dearing Simons and Eleanor
   Ball Simons
Miss Ann E. Thomas
Louisa Edmondston Gaillard Thornton
Mrs. Howard Knight and Mrs. O. H.
   Wieters

St. John's, Charleston:

James W. Almeida
Egbert C. Burris
Jack P. Grooms
Rev. and Mrs. Waties R. Haynsworth
Mrs. Lewis L. Hollis
Edward P. Malone
Rev. Franklin Martin
Michael P. Ollic, Jr.
Marion A. Todd
Bessie M. Webber

St. Luke's and St. Paul's, Charleston:

Mr. and Mrs. Wilfred H. Adams
Mr. and Mrs. William C. Bailey
Letha Bell Benton
Mary Elizabeth Thomas Buist
C. Lester Cannon
Mr. and Mrs. George M. Caulfield, Jr.
Katherine G. Crocker
Mrs. James F. Eisenmann
Mr. and Mrs. Francis S. Glover
Mrs. Thomas Craig Hunley
Library of St. Luke's and St. Paul's
Miss Emma C. McCabe
Charles T. Nagle
Rev. Earle C. Page
Mrs. Philip G. Porcher, Sr.
Mrs. René Ravenel
Y. W. Scarborough, Jr.
Cordelia R. Schroder
Marie Walker Shingler

Miss Katherine D. Simons
Rev. Harold Thomas
Mr. and Mrs. Harold Thomas, Jr.
Miss Ola C. Verdier
Mrs. Arthur D. Wall
Mrs. J. C. Wieters

St. Michael's, Charleston:

Mr. and Mrs. Grover L. Anderson
Edna Scott Andrews
Mrs. Frank Herndon Bailey
Mr. and Mrs. John B. Bailey
John Coming Ball, Jr.
Nathaniel I. Ball
Mrs. W. C. P. Bellinger
Mr. and Mrs. Harry Grey Blaising
The Misses Bull
Miss Ida Moore Colson
Caroline Conner
Mr. and Mrs. Richard K. Donovan
Mr. and Mrs. C. Stuart Dawson
Mrs. Sidney Lanier Eason
Mr. and Mrs. J. Nelson Frierson
Mrs. William S. Gaud
Berkeley Grimball
Panchita Heyward Grimball
Mrs. Thomas M. Hanckel
Mrs. Samuel Mortimer Hasell
Mrs. G. Lee Holmes
Mrs. O. K. Horton
Joseph E. Jenkins
Mrs. Henry Jervey
Mrs. Bohun B. Kinloch
Samuel B. King
Mrs. John C. Koster
Mr. and Mrs. Samuel Lapham
Mildred Weston Lewis
Capt. and Mrs. George C. Logan
Mrs. J. Heyward Lynah
Mrs. Alexander Martin
Hulda Witte Mazyck
Mr. and Mrs. George Abbott Middleton
Charles F. Middleton
B. Allston Moore
Mr. and Mrs. Benjamin Allston Moore, Jr.
Maj. and Mrs. McKenzie P. Moore
Miss Ellen Parker
Dr. and Mrs. McKenzie Parker Moore, Jr.
Francis LeJau Parker, II
Louis T. Parker
Rev. and Mrs. DeWolf Perry
Miss Anne A. Porcher
Robert R. Pregnall
William H. Prioleau
Mrs. J. Clifton Quattlebaum, Jr.
Julia R. Raoul
Beatrice Ravenel
Mr. and Mrs. Thomas L. Read
Harry V. Salmons
Albert Simons
Miss Henrietta Simons
Mrs. James Gaillard Snowden, Sr.
Mrs. Carl Otto Sparkman

Miss Mary A. Sparkman
Mrs. J. Manly Stallworth
Mr. and Mrs. Arthur Jervey Stoney
Mrs. Robert Burbidge Taft
Mrs. E. S. Van Benschoten
Mrs. Hettie B. Walsh
Miss Elizabeth S. Williams
George W. Williams
Harriott Cheves Williams

St. Philip's, Charleston:
Charles L. Anger
Mr. and Mrs. I. G. Ball
Constance F. Burden
Mrs. Gabriel Cannon
Miss Jeannie T. Cason
Rev. S. Grayson Clary
Thomas Benjamin Curtis III
Mrs. E. Roy Daniell
Charles Shepard de Forest
Charles H. Drayton
Miss Lena Lucas
Coming B. Gibbs
Malcolm D. Haven
Mrs. Christopher G. Howe
S. Edward Izard, M.D.
Ellen Heyward Jervey
Mrs. Lottie Capers Johnson
Henry J. Mann
Miss Ethel Mazyck
Leila Barnwell Pringle
Harold S. Reeves
Martha L. Rivers
Anna Wells Rutledge
St. Philip's Church
Mr. and Mrs. Donald D. Sams
Mr. and Mrs. Huger Sinkler
Mrs. B. Burgh Smith, Jr.
Mrs. William C. Smith
William Mason Smith
Mr. and Mrs. Richard G. White
Mrs. Arthur R. Young

St. Peter's-by-the-Sea, Charleston Heights (Navy Yard):
Rev. E. M. Claytor
Gerald Francis McGregor, MA3

Old St. Andrew's, Charleston County:
Mr. and Mrs. Helge C. Andersson
Mr. and Mrs. E. Leo Blitch, Jr.
J. Hagood Chaplin
C. Norwood Hastie, Jr.
Mrs. Oscar L. Long
Rev. and Mrs. Lynwood C. Magee
Mr. and Mrs. J. B. Mauldin
Mr. and Mrs. James F. McGowan
Samuel A. Meeker
Mr. and Mrs. J. C. Rourk

Holy Trinity, Windermere, Charleston County:
Mrs. Francis Marion Dwight
Rev. and Mrs. Marshall E. Travers

St. David's, Cheraw:
Rev. John M. Barr
Ernest H. Duvall
Miss Fannie B. Duvall
Hal Duvall
H. E. Duvall
W. E. Duvall
Miss Cora Page Godfrey
Mrs. G. F. Goodwyn
Mr. and Mrs. J. Lewis Hill
William A. Hill
Mrs. F. D. Hyatt
Col. William Millice
John D. Nock
James E. Powe
Mrs. Thomas H. Sutton
William H. Thrower
Mrs. R. W. Timmerman
Caroline Coker Tucker

St. Paul's, Conway:
Mrs. A. M. Burroughs
F. G. Burroughs
Mr. and Mrs. Ervin Dargan
Miss Florence Theodora Epps
Lucile Godfrey
Mr. and Mrs. E. Martin Meadows
Mrs. Perry C. Quattlebaum
L. S. Redick, Jr.
Mr. and Mrs. George C. Rogers
Dr. and Mrs. R. C. Smith

St. Matthew's, Darlington:
T. C. Coxe, Jr.
W. E. Dargan
Jack Frierson
John L. Frierson, Sr.
Mrs. Melvin Hyman
Mrs. Cornelius Kollock
Jacob Sherman Ramsey
Mrs. Pierce A. Riley
Mrs. Frank E. Rogers, Jr.
Mr. and Mrs. Thomas Ogier Simons
Mr. and Mrs. Hugh S. Thompson
T. Evans Wilson
Woman's Auxiliary

Christ Church, Denmark:
Gaston Gee
Campbell C. Freeman, M.D.
Mr. and Mrs. Byron A. Palmer
Mr. and Mrs. Chester D. Palmer

St. Barnabas', Dillon:
Mrs. C. E. Bethea
Mr. and Mrs. Don Bracy
Woman's Auxiliary

Trinity, Edisto Island:
Arthur W. Bailey, Sr.
Mrs. W. C. Bailey
Mr. and Mrs. Thomas H. Burns
Mrs. A. L. Glen
McGowan Holmes

Mrs. Edward John Jenkins
Stephen Elliott Puckette
J. L. Seabrook
Mrs. Irvin C. Tavel
Mr. and Mrs. Marion H. Whaley
Percival H. Whaley

Epiphany, Eutawville:

Church School Library
J. Rutledge Connor
Mrs. Rose Taylor Connor
Mr. and Mrs. Elias F. Couturier
Mrs. Peter C. Gaillard, Sr.
Dr. and Mrs. Peter C. Gaillard
Mr. and Mrs. William S. Gaillard
Mr. and Mrs. Richard K. Gaillard
Mrs. Henrietta G. Miles
Mr. and Mrs. H. E. Padgett
Mr. and Mrs. Thomas A. Pigott
Mr. and Mrs. F. K. Simons, Jr.
Miss Josephine Simons
Wade Waddill
Mr. and Mrs. George D. Wetherford

St. John's, Florence:

Mr. and Mrs. Vernone H. Allen
Miss Jessie Ashby
Mr. and Mrs. Frank H. Barnwell
Mrs. William A. Beaty
Mrs. Charles F. Bowie
R. Vaughan Clarke
Mrs. Norwood Mullins Ellerbe
Mrs. Frank R. Gadsden
Mrs. Charles Gardiner
Mrs. John Eli Gregg
Walter Moore Hart, M.D.
Mrs. Harry Howell Heard
Miss Mary Clyde Hodges
Francis Bonneau Johnson
E. H. Lucas
Mrs. H. Ravenel Lucas
Mrs. Simons R. Lucas
Dr. and Mrs. Walter R. Mead
Mrs. Caroline Ravenel Lucas Miller
Mrs. Thomas V. Moore
John M. O'Dowd
Emily Dixon Patterson
Rev. Wilmer S. Poynor
R. W. Sharkey
James Robert Spruill
Miss Anne Gaillard Stacker
Mrs. Phil Stephenson
Miss Edith B. Tobin
Dr. and Mrs. George S. Tyson
Mr. and Mrs. Walter Gregg Wallace
Mr. and Mrs. Hugh L. Willcox
Jack J. Wright

St. Matthew's, Fort Motte:

Mrs. Kate Early Banks and C. R. Banks
Mr. and Mrs. W. Peter Buyck
Mr. and Mrs. Daniel M. Cox
Elizabeth McLure Darby
Mr. and Mrs. J. Keitt Hane, III

Mr. and Mrs. John Keitt Hane, **IV**
Mr. and Mrs. J. Tennant Hane
Mr. and Mrs. Porcher Hane
Mr. and Mrs. W. C. Hane
Mrs. Robert B. Hartzog
Mr. and Mrs. R. G. Keefe
Mrs. J. M. McCabe
Mr. and Mrs. J. Montieth McCabe, **Jr.**
Mr. and Mrs. Robert F. Nickells
Mr. and Mrs. W. T. Oliver and
    W. T. Oliver, Jr.
Mrs. J. T. Pearlstine
Mrs. Alfred H. Pitts
Rev. Philip G. Porcher, Jr.
Mrs. Nell Peterkin Reid
St. Matthew's Parish
Mr. and Mrs. Dan Savitz and
    Miss Charlotte Savitz
Mr. and Mrs. William Thomson **Taber**
Mr. and Mrs. Julian D. Wiles
Mrs. Oredia A. Wiles

Prince George, Georgetown:

Mrs. Bessie F. Betancourt
Mrs. H. D. Bull
Miss Aileen T. Donaldson
Miss Helen Butler Freeman
Lewis F. Freeman
Miss Elizabeth A. Gaillard
Mrs. Eugene Fitz Simons La Bruce
J. B. Morrison
Mr. and Mrs. Louis Overton
Miss Harriet Oliver Plowden
Mrs. Charlotte Plowden Wylie
William C. Young

Holy Trinity, Grahamville:

Mr. and Mrs. N. B. Bass
Mrs. Charles E. Perry

Ascension, Hagood:

Mary Kirk Brown
James Lafayette Haynsworth
Mrs. I'Ans M. Jackson
Mrs. Charles W. Sanders
Rev. and Mrs. Wm. S. Stoney

All Saints', Hampton:

All Saints' Church
Martha Bee and Allen E. Anderson
Dr. and Mrs. James A. Hayne
Mrs. W. C. Mauldin
Mr. and Mrs. Wilder H. Mauldin
Mr. and Mrs. Frank A. McClure, Sr.
Mrs. Elizabeth Miller Rentz
Rev. and Mrs. John Rivers
Miss Rachel Sauls
Woman's Auxiliary

St. Bartholomew's, Hartsville:

Lawrence K. Anthony
Mrs. Myrtle C. Chaley
Blanding DeSaussure Clarkson
Mr. and Mrs. Dan H. Coker

James Earl Copenhaver
Mr. and Mrs. F. E. Fitchett
Rev. Carl Garrison
Rev. H. L. Hoover
Mr. and Mrs. Richard W. Turnage

St. James', James Island:

Mr. and Mrs. Alston Calhoun Badger
Mr. and Mrs. Benjamin Mood Badger
Pinckney and William R. Bailey
Mr. and Mrs. Edmonds Tennent Brown
Mr. and Mrs. Edmund Allan Burns
Mrs. V. R. Caldwell and Family
Mrs. Francis W. Clement, Sr.
Mr. and Mrs. Francis W. Clement
Mr. and Mrs. James King Davis
Floyd Isaac Dovell, Jr.
Dr. and Mrs. Daniel W. Ellis
Mr. and Mrs. Francis M. Harleston
Dr. and Mrs. James Grant Hayden,
  George Hayden
Mr. and Mrs. Jack Warford Henley
Mrs. John R. Jefferies
Mr. and Mrs. John Micah Jenkins
John and Daphne Keith
Mrs. William Herbert Langford
William E. McLeod
Mr. and Mrs. W. Gresham Meggett
Mrs. W. H. Mikell, Sr.
Mr. and Mrs. E. Clark Morrison
Edward P. Porcher
Arthur Ravenel
Mr. and Mrs. John Thomas Robinson
Francis S. Rodgers
Mr. and Mrs. E. Marshall Shingler
William Henry and Elizabeth W.
  Simmons
Virginia and Silas B. Welch
Miss Virginia F. Welch
Mr. and Mrs. Bonum Sams Wilson

St. John's, Johns Island:

Donald McKay and Mary Fitz Simons
  Allston
Caroline S. Alston
Constantine Bailey and Elizabeth
  Grimball Stevens
Dr. and Mrs. E. H. Barnwell
Cosmo and Marguerite Puckett
  Brockington
John and Dorothy Cunningham Bryan
Richard Roper Bryan
Edmund L. Bull
J. Lewis and Mary Hart Gervais
John Lewis, Jr., and Dorothy Sams
  Gervais
Philip Emanuel and Julia Leland Gervais
Ethel M. Glover
Harold L. and Evelyn Seegars Glover
Harold and Lillian Legare Grimball
Thomas P. and Anna G. Grimball
Rev. Edward B. and Ella H. Guerry
Joseph Seabrook Hart

William LaRoche and Anne LaRoche
  Hart
John J. III and Jeanette MacLeod Horres
Benjamin R. and Eleanor McElveen
  Jenkins
Mr. and Mrs. D. Frank Jenkins
Julian Beverly and Jessie Wilson Jenkins
Melvin W. and Leize Wilson Jenkins
Sophia Seabrook Jenkins and
  William H. Jenkins
Mrs. Pauline Grimball King
Robert S. and Alma Jenkins LaRoche
Martin and Rose Meyer
Mr. and Mrs. Stanley F. Morse
John Owen and Allie Mae Hart Murray
James Lynah and Patricia Bourne Palmer
Mr. and Mrs. Thomas W. Perry
Thomas Ansel Price and Leila Hart Price
Mr. and Mrs. David Bruce Reed
Henry F. and Evelyn Hart Rivers
Nancy M. and Joseph L. Rivers
Oliver M. and Frances G. Rutledge
Fred and Ann Glover Schaffer
Grace S. Seabrook
Julia Bryan Seabrook
Margaret and Oliver Seabrook
Mary Sosnowski Seabrook
John F. and Eliza F. Sosnowski
Dr. John Richard and Elizabeth Tyson
  Sosnowski
Agnes L. Stevens
Mrs. Mark Tolbert
Alvin R. Veronee, Jr.
H. Benj. and Adelaide Hill Walpole
Ephriam Clark and Cornelia Jenkins
  Whaley
Merle Batson Whaley
John S. and Mary Townsend Whaley
William and Marian Wilkinson Whaley
Fannie Sams Wilson
Martha Mary Wilson
Mr. and Mrs. W. E. Wilson
Mrs. A. C. Wingo
Mr. and Mrs. N. F. Zittrauer and Gloria

St. Alban's, Kingstree:

J. B. Alsbrook, Jr.
Jack Arrowsmith
J. O. Arrowsmith
Mrs. M. L. Few
Rev. John Flanigen, Jr.
Mrs. Cornelia Gourdin Gamble
Mrs. Myers E. Hanna
John Allen Hauenstein
Julia Pledger Hodges Hauenstein
Mrs. Margaret Hodges Hauenstein
Philip Kellogg Hauenstein
Mrs. Jane T. James
Mrs. Eleanor G. McMaster
Mrs. Mary P. Mishoe
Miss Marie L. Nelson
John E. Rogers
St. Alban's Church
Mr. and Mrs. Pel Seignious

Mrs. Annie B. Swails
Mrs. Louise Alsbrook Switzenburg
Mrs. Bradley Wilkins

Advent, Marion:

Miss Addie W. Bethea
Miss Eloise Bethea
Mary MacLeod Bethea
Mr. and Mrs. C. A. Bianchi, Jr.
Mrs. Samuel O. Cantey, Jr.
Isabelle Hopkins Chamblis
Mrs. William Lee Hewitt, Sr.
Julise McIntyre Johnson
Mrs. Howard S. McCandlish
Elizabeth Mullins McIntyre
Mr. and Mrs. William G. Moore
Mr. and Mrs. Ernest Lelon Oulla, Jr.
Mrs. T. F. Salmon
Mrs. H. L. Tilghman, Sr.
Bishop Thomas Chapter, Woman's
   Auxiliary

St. James', McClellanville:

St. James', Santee Church
Beulah and Jay Greenleaf
Mrs. John T. Liles
Mrs. John Marion Lofton
Mr. and Mrs. Alexander Hume Lucas
Thomas Cordes Lucas
Mr. and Mrs. Harrington W. Morrison
Mrs. Paul Trapier Prentiss
Dr. and Mrs. Archibald Rutledge
Mr. and Mrs. Paul Hamilton Seabrook
Mrs. Charles A. von Ohsen

Sheldon, McPhersonville:

Alex F. Gregorie

St. Paul's, Meggett:

Edda P. Ackerman
Elizabeth B. Bunch
Mrs. H. H. Butler
Mrs. John W. Geraty, Jr.
Mr. and Mrs. Peter K. Murray
Dr. and Mrs. R. R. Prentiss
Edward C. Sanders
Mrs. W. B. Searson, Sr.
Daniel A. Stevens
Mr. and Mrs. Stanyarne Y. Stevens
Frank J. Towles
Mrs. Natalie Searson Towles
William James Whaley
Woman's Auxiliary

Christ Church, Mount Pleasant:

I. Dennis Auld
Mrs. Isaac Auld
J. Seabrook Auld
Anna King Gregorie
Mrs. Ferdinand Gregorie
Miss Harriet Hamlin
Mr. and Mrs. H. C. Heyward, Jr.
Mr. and Mrs. LeGrand H. King
Julia Blakely McConnell

Miss Catherine Cordes Porcher
Francis Peyre Porcher
Koga Weldon Porcher
Sedgwick L. Simons
Francis A. Wayne, Jr.
Mary K. Wayne

St. Andrew's, Mount Pleasant:

Mrs. Thomas Stanley Barnhill
Edward Stanley Bullock
Andrew H. DuPre
Mr. and Mrs. J. Wyman Frampton
J. Everett Guerry, Sr.
Mr. and Mrs. Osgood A. Hamlin
Anne Lee Hill
Charles deSaussure Jett
Mrs. John Edward Jussely
Mrs. James H. Kidder
Mr. and Mrs. D. S. Lesesne, Jr.
Alexander Lucas Lofton
Mrs. Thomas Gadsden McCants
St. Andrew's Church
Allan P. Sloan
Mr. and Mrs. Donald M. White, Jr.

Christ, Mullins:

Mr. and Mrs. William D. Atkinson

Redeemer, Orangeburg:

Mr. and Mrs. Frank B. Best
Church of the Redeemer Library
Miss Susan V. Dibble
Mr. and Mrs. William W. Dukes, Jr.
Mrs. L. B. Fersner, Jr.
Mrs. Salley Fuller and
   Mrs. L. S. C. Barton
W. L. Glover
Mrs. Edgar King LaCoste
Mrs. Charles A. Mobley
Mrs. William Manning Richardson, Sr.
Mrs. Sarah S. McCoy
Mrs. George Reynolds
Mr. and Mrs. Richard Rhame
Susan S. Sheriff
Mr. and Mrs. Sidney S. Stokes
Mrs. Claudia M. Summers
Rev. Thomas Sumter Tisdale
Miss Mary Moore Wannamaker
Mrs. N. W. Wannamaker, Jr.
Mrs. T. Elliott Wannamaker

All Saints', Pawley's Island:

Rev. A. Nelson Daunt
Mr. and Mrs. R. S. Dingle
R. S. Ennis
Mrs. D. W. Green
Mrs. Frederick LeFayette Green
Mr. and Mrs. A. H. Lachicotte
Mrs. Philip R. Lachicotte
Mrs. E. C. McGregor
Capt. and Mrs. J. J. Ward

St. Mark's, Pinewood:

Mrs. N. L. Broughton
Mr. and Mrs. F. Marion Dwight, Jr.

Mr. and Mrs. Mark Reynolds, Jr.
James A. Richardson
Mrs. John S. Richardson
Louise Simons Richardson
Robert H. Salley

Trinity, Pinopolis:

Joseph F. Heyward
Rev. Loren B. Mead
Mrs. Dwight Porcher
A. E. Power
Mrs. Sarah Owens Schumann
Mrs. Harriet Vardell
J. Russell Williams, Jr.

Prince Frederick's, Plantersville:

Carrie C. Ard
William Arthur Cooper
Mickle Howell

St. Stephen's, St. Stephen:

Mrs. Margaret Marion Breland
Mrs. Eljule Gourdin Everett
Mrs. John K. Gourdin, Sr.
Mr. and Mrs. John K. Gourdin, Jr.
T. B. Harper, M.D.
Mrs. Matt Marion Kemp
Charles Gourdin Marion
Mrs. Edward St. J. Marion
Miss Josephine F. Marion
Robert Marion
Mrs. Bertha Gladden Neighbors
Samuel O. Schumann, M.D.

Holy Cross, Sullivans Island:

Rev. Maurice John Bywater
Robert Elliott Magwood, Jr.
Charles H. Schroder, III

St. Matthias', Summerton:

Mr. and Mrs. L. E. Brailsford
Mr. and Mrs. H. E. Davis
Mr. and Mrs. J. W. Sconyers
Mrs. W. G. Simms

St. Paul's, Summerville:

Mrs. Herbert L. Bailey
Mr. and Mrs. William A. Boyle
de Saussure Parker Dehon
Mrs. E. H. Hutchinson
Mrs. Ethel F. Jones
T. S. Long
Miss Rebecca Cordis Low
Miss Joanna Ward Manigault
J. W. Miles, Jr.
Mrs. Mary Ambler Mitchell
Robert E. O'Neal
Mr. and Mrs. Cannon F. Prettyman
Miss Bertha Richards
Mrs. Elise Gadsden Robertson
Harold M. Sebring
Jaquelin Ambler Simons
Mrs. Susie Hutchinson Smith

Mrs. George Tupper, Sr.
Rev. Eugene J. West

Holy Comforter, Sumter:

Mr. and Mrs. Albert S. Alderman
Mr. and Mrs. Charles S. Alston
Mrs. Charles Saxby Anderson
Mrs. Caroline Richardson Bowman
Mr. and Mrs. J. L. Brogdon, Jr.
Miss Glenn V. Brown
Dr. and Mrs. C. B. Burns
Mrs. Stanyarne Burrows
Mr. and Mrs. Julian Buxton
Dr. and Mrs. Fred F. Converse, Jr.
Mr. and Mrs. John H. Dawson
Miss Ida Dick
Dr. Tyler B. Dunlap
Mrs. R. L. Edmunds
Raymond S. Fowler, Sr.
Mrs. C. P. Gable
Mr. and Mrs. John Gable
Mr. and Mrs. John W. Godbey
Mrs. Benjamin Deland Hodges
Mr. and Mrs. Ralph Holland
Mrs. J. Craig Hurst
John D. Lee
Mr. and Mrs. Ross McKenzie
Mr. and Mrs. Frank A. McLeod
Mr. and Mrs. Frank A. McLeod, Jr.
Mr. and Mrs. Richard Kirk McLeod
Mrs. Augustus L. Middleton
Mr. and Mrs. Fenwick H. Murray
Mr. and Mrs. J. Herman Myers
Mr. and Mrs. Joseph Palmer
Mr. and Mrs. Robert D. Palmer
Mrs. Honor L. Phillips
Mrs. Lyman Quincy
Porcher Rembert
Miss Julia Rees Reynolds
Miss Anne Sinkler Richardson
Miss Eleanora S. Richardson
S. S. and J. S. Richardson
Mr. and Mrs. Colclough E. Sanders
Mrs. Marion W. Seabrook
Mr. and Mrs. Thomas H. Siddall, Jr.
Mr. and Mrs. Warren E. Sipple
Mrs. Ida Vernon Dick Verdades
Rev. J. Bentham Walker
Miss Mary Walker
Dr. and Mrs. R. Murdoch Walker
Mr. and Mrs. Arthur Harrison Wilder

Holy Cross, Claremont, Stateburg:

Anne Peyre Moore Arthur
Mrs. Margaret Gillespie Ecker
Mrs. Sam. W. Gillespie
L. E. Leavell, Jr.
Mr. and Mrs. S. Oliver Plowden
James Gaillard Simons
Mrs. Walter C. White
Mrs. John Frank Williams
W. Blackburn Wilson
Mrs. William Wilson

St. Jude's, Walterboro:

Miss Lucile Buckner
Miss Katharine Doar
Mrs. I. M. Fishburne
Lucius Gaston Fishburne
Mr. and Mrs. H. Quintin Foster
Mrs. H. C. Fripp
William E. Fripp
Mrs. B. H. Guy, Jr.
Mr. and Mrs. Thomas M. Howell, Jr.
Mrs. P. J. Lucas, Jr.
Mrs. Poyas Marvin
Mrs. Annie Lesesne Murray
Rev. and Mrs. Walter D. Roberts
Mrs. E. Berrien Sanders

Mr. and Mrs. S. H. Searson
James Warren Skardon
Mr. and Mrs. C. A. Witsell
Mrs. J. M. Witsell

St. Thomas' and St. Dennis', Wando:

Mrs. Marie Ball Dingle
J. Lockwood Murphy

St. Augustine's, Wedgefield:

Mr. and Mrs. Isham L. Mitchell
Joseph Mitchell
Mrs. Susan Pleasent
David V. Ragins
Richard R. Ragins
Mrs. Viola Ragins

DIOCESE OF UPPER SOUTH CAROLINA

Trinity, Abbeville:

Mr. and Mrs. Benjamin S. Barnwell
Hume M. Fraser
Percy James Leach
Mrs. John L. LeRoy
Raymond L. Phillips

St. Thaddaeus', Aiken:

F. Wheeler Caney
Marianna Porcher Ford
Mary M. and Frank E. Kinard
Mrs. B. Courtney McLean
Mrs. Wilhelmina Hutto Moody
Miss Anne S. Rothrock
Mrs. Clio R. Stewart
Miss Nancy DuBose Sudlow
Mrs. R. G. Tarrant

Grace, Anderson:

Dr. and Mrs. Allen C. Bradham
Dr. and Mrs. H. Grady Callison
Charles G. Carothers
John D. Clark
Chaplain (Lt. Col.) Julian S. Ellenberg
Mrs. J. E. Fennell
Mr. and Mrs. Arthur E. Holman, Jr.
Dr. and Mrs. Preston B. Jones
Mrs. Baylis C. Maxwell
Mr. and Mrs. Henry Campbell Miller
Robert O. Muller
Mr. and Mrs. Deas Manning Richardson
Mr. and Mrs. Kenneth D. Saylors
Mr. and Mrs. Cordes G. Seabrook. Jr.

St. Paul's, Batesburg:

Mr. and Mrs. Charles B. Bostick
Rev. and Mrs. Rogers S. Harris
Mrs. Emory C. Mitchell
Mr. and Mrs. Robert T. Neblett
Mr. and Mrs. Roy Bradford Whitney

Grace, Camden:

Dr. and Mrs. J. W. Brunson
Moultrie B. Burns

Henry G. Carrison
Mrs. Maurice Clarke
John K. de Loach
Horace and Elizabeth Greenfield
Mrs. James L. Guy
Ralph F. Johnson
George Pitt Lachicotte
Rev. Stiles B. Lines
Mr. and Mrs. E. N. McDowell
Selma P. and A. Clifton McKain
Mrs. Harriett Shannon Steedman
Herman W. Woods
Elizabeth C. Waite

St. Mark's, Chester:

J. Edward Davis
James H. Fanning, Jr.
Mrs. W. M. Fewell

Holy Trinity, Clemson:

F. H. H. Calhoun
Holy Trinity Library
Mrs. Tracy H. Jackson, Sr.
Mrs. Frank J. Jervey
Rev. Robert L. Oliveros
Dr. M. A. Owings
Mr. and Mrs. James H. Sams
Hoke Sloan
Fred Taylor
I. A. Trively
Mr. and Mrs. Robert E. Ware

All Saints', Clinton:

Mrs. Lillian Blake Brown Hart
Dr. Newton B. Jones
Rev. Giles F. Lewis, Jr.
Dr. James Macdonald

Good Shepherd, Columbia:

Miss Ferebe Babcock
Mrs. Ethland Foster C. Brock
Mrs. Frank Norman Ehrlich
Mrs. Maye M. Hane

Miss Edith S. Goodale and
  Mrs. Nell G. Hook
Mrs. Caldwell Jones
Mr. and Mrs. Hasell Thomas LaBorde
D. J. Lucas
Bryan H. Lumpkin
M. H. Maner
Mrs. George F. Murphy
Hoyett G. Parker
John W. Riley Sons
Edward A. Rouffy
Mr. and Mrs. Arthur St. J. Simons
Mrs. Annie Jennie Smith
Mrs. Sidney C. Snelgrove
Mr. and Mrs. Joseph E. Sprott
Miss Catherine Thomas
Miss Cornelia Lee Thomas
Walter Couturier Thomas
Jack W. Tompkins, Jr.
Woman's Auxiliary

St. John's, Columbia:

Miss Ellen Iredell Butler
Samuel Rice Capers
Mrs. W. D. Drew
Mrs. J. B. Easterling
Mrs. W. O. Galletly
Mrs. E. R. Heyward
Charles E. Huntley
Charles West Jacocks, Jr.
Harriet Virginia LaBorde
Mrs. Irene Thomas LaBorde
Mrs. E. R. Lipscomb
Mrs. Thomas F. Mauldin
Mrs. Robert D. McClure
Lewie G. Merritt, Jr.
Mr. and Mrs. W. C. Mikell
Mrs. Edward M. Moore
Miss Allie Rhett Murray
Mr. and Mrs. Claude H. Neuffer
Mr. and Mrs. John H. Overton and
  Family
Mrs. Gerald D. Ryan
Caroline Schiffley
Mrs. Elizabeth Nelson Sullivan
Mr. and Mrs. W. R. Turbeville
John R. Turnbull
Miss Catherine Thomas Ulmer
Mrs. Harriet Thomas Ulmer
Charles H. Waterfall
Mrs. Amarinthia Lowndes Webb
Mrs. William Cozby White

*St. Michael's and All Angels' Mission,
  Columbia:*

Rev. and Mrs. Clyde L. Ireland
Mr. and Mrs. Daniel Praete

St. Martin's-in-the-Fields, Columbia:

Mr. and Mrs. Eugene Middleton Baker
Betty Brooks
Daniel H. Burns
Buford S. Chappell, M.D.
Mr. and Mrs. Dean H. Davis

Caldwell Robertson Dial
Mr. and Mrs. T. Clarence Dixon
Mr. and Mrs. Willoughby J. Dixon
Mrs. Guy H. Elder, Jr.
Mrs. Irma S. Graham
Mr. and Mrs. J. Sheppard Jones
Mr. and Mrs. Daniel De Saussure Lang
J. B. Leek
Sarah Graydon McCrory
Mr. and Mrs. Maurice M. Moxley
Mr. and Mrs. H. C. Nuckols
Walter F. Petty
Thomas Hart and Margaret Fletcher Price
Mr. and Mrs. Robert Hoke Robinson
St. Martin's-in-the-Fields
Mr. and Mrs. Frederick M. Schiffley
Mr. and Mrs. H. Talcott Stith, Jr.
Dr. and Mrs. Tucker Weston
Mr. and Mrs. John E. Yochum

St. Timothy's, Columbia:

Rev. A. G. Branwell Bennett
Mrs. L. F. Bolin
Mrs. Carl L. Cannon
Mrs. A. A. Cassanova
Ernest L. Gaillard, Jr.
William H. Patterson
James Moore Rhett

Trinity, Columbia:

Mr. and Mrs. Charles L. Adams
Mr. and Mrs. Robert Adams, Jr.
Miss Roberta Aldrich
Mrs. J. Richard Allison
Richard K. Ambrose
Mrs. Sadie M. Jenkins Battle
Mr. and Mrs. W. K. Beckham
Mr. and Mrs. John Dupont Bell, Jr.
Mr. and Mrs. Joseph M. Bell
Mrs. Caroline McKissick Belser
Edwin H. Betsill
Mr. and Mrs. Edward W. Boineau
Mrs. Calvin Michael Bruton
W. M. Bryan, Jr., M.D.
Mrs. Clara H. Buchanan
James F. Byrnes
Mrs. Pinckney L. Cain
J. Willis Cantey
Mrs. C. Dwight Cathcart
John A. Chase
Mrs. Rufus R. Clarke
Mrs. A. Crawford Clarkson, Jr.
Mrs. John Coker
Mrs. C. Alfred Cole
Miss Dorothy Vernon Crawford
Mrs. Geddings Hardy Crawford
Mrs. W. Hall Crawford
Wallace Elliott Crum
Frank J. Dana
Miss Louise C. DeBruhl
Mrs. R. S. DesPortes
Dr. and Mrs. Thomas D. Dotterer
David S. DuBose
Mr. and Mrs. John B. DuBose

Miss Martha P. Dwight
Mrs. Henry Harman Edens
Mr. and Mrs. David G. Ellison
David G. Ellison, Jr.
Mrs. Willis C. Evans
J. Henry Fair
Mr. and Mrs. James Wilks Fant
Mrs. Kirkman G. Finlay
Kirkman Finlay
Mary T. Fitch
Mrs. Henry L. Forbes
Mr. and Mrs. Levin Wilson Foster
Mrs. William M. Gibbes
Mr. and Mrs. Augustus T. Graydon
Mrs. Clint Graydon
Mrs. Marian H. Griffin
Edward Percy Guerard
Ambrose G. Hampton
Dr. and Mrs. George C. Hart
Dr. and Mrs. John R. Harvin
Mrs. R. Beverley Herbert
Albert R. Heyward
Albert R. Heyward, II
Miss Mary B. Heyward
Mr. and Mrs. E. L. Hipp
James G. Holmes, Jr.
Dr. Theodore Jervey Hopkins
Mr. and Mrs. Herbert M. Hucks, Jr.,
   and Dorothy M. Hucks
Mr. and Mrs. J. L. M. Irby
Mr. and Mrs. H. M. James
John W. and Florence Jennings
Dr and Mrs. Richard B. Josey
Mrs. George E. Lafaye
Thomas W. Lane
Arthur F. Langley
Mrs. Claudia Seabrook Langley
Claudia and Arthur Langley
Miss Gladys Boykin Lawton
Mr. and Mrs. Thomas C. R. Legaré
John N. LeMaster, Jr.
Mrs. Charlotte Brown Lide
Mrs. Alva M. Lumpkin
Mr. and Mrs. Alva M. Lumpkin, Jr.
John Adger Manning
W. M. Manning
Mrs. Foster Marshall
J. Q. Marshall
Admiral Charles Franklin Martin and
   Susie Gaillard Martin
Dr. and Mrs. George T. McCutchen
Mr. and Mrs. W. T. Mikell
Henry W. Moore, M.D
Mrs. W. Bedford Moore, Jr.
Charles Henry Moorefield
Mr. and Mrs. W. S. Moye, Jr.
Mr. and Mrs. Allan C. Mustard
Thomas E. Myers
P. H. Nelson
Mr. and Mrs. P. H. Nelson
Mrs. William L. Otis
Mr. and Mrs. Henry H. Plowden, Jr.
John W. R. Pope
Robert Vaux Read

Mrs. Reed Stoney Salley
Mr. and Mrs. Alexander M. Sanders
Mrs. Annie Gribbin Sanders
Joe H. Sanders, Jr.
Mrs. Clarence E. Saunders
Mrs. George Saussy
Mrs. Irene Adger Scott
Mrs. Frances H. Sparkman
Dr. and Mrs. Gerald W. (Emily
   Thomas) Scurry
Mr. and Mrs. Grenville Seibels, II
Julian B. Shand
Mr. and Mrs. C. Gregg Shockley
Alice L. Simmons
Richard Simons
Mr. and Mrs. Joel A. Smith, Jr.
Mrs. Stephen Taber
Mrs. James Alan Taylor
Capt. and Mrs. Albert S. (Mary
   Watson) Thomas, Jr.
Albert Sidney Thomas, III
Mr. and Mrs. Graham McRee Thomas
Mrs. J. Waties Thomas
Joseph Watson Thomas
Miss Mary Watson Thomas
Gov. and Mrs. George Bell Timmerman, Jr.
Mr. and Mrs. James A. Vaughan
Major Clark D. Waring
Eugenia Childs Westmoreland
Mr. and Mrs. Boyce Wideman
Mr. and Mrs. Berkeley A. Woodruff
Miss Susan Woodward
Simpson Zimmerman, Jr.

St. John's, Congaree:
Mrs. Isaac Hayne
Mrs. Catherine Palmer Hopkins
James Hopkins
Laura J. Hopkins
Mrs. Sarah C. Hopkins
Mrs. Hunter R. Lang
Rev. Richard C. Patton

St. Michael's, Easley:
A. G. Clarkson, Jr.
Dr. and Mrs. E. A. Jamison
Luther M. McBee, Jr.
Mr. and Mrs. Henry C. Milhous
St. Michael's Church
J. J. Sims

Zion, Eastover:
Thomas S. Armour
William Howard Faver, Sr.
Miss Leora Rivers
Miss Julie Palmer Wieking

Trinity, Edgefield:
Dr. J. F. Byrd
Miss Sarah Rainsford Collett
R. H. Norris
Mrs. Charles E. Stark

St. Paul's, Graniteville:
Frank Beard
J. B. Wingard, Jr.